D0075497

THE CONSERVATIVE PRESS IN TWENTIETH-CENTURY AMERICA

Recent Titles in
Historical Guides to the World's Periodicals and Newspapers

This series provides historically focused narrative and analytical profiles of periodicals and newspapers with accompanying bibliographical data.

American Mass-Market Magazines
Alan Nourie and Barbara Nourie, editors

Military Periodicals: United States and Selected International Journals and Newspapers
Michael E. Unsworth

Regional Interest Magazines of the United States
Sam G. Riley and Gary W. Selnow, editors

Business Journals of the United States
William Fisher, editor

Corporate Magazines of the United States
Sam G. Riley, editor

American Literary Magazines: The Twentieth Century
Edward E. Chielens, editor

Consumer Magazines of the British Isles
Sam G. Riley, editor

Trade, Industrial, and Professional Periodicals of the United States
Kathleen L. Endres, editor

Popular Religious Magazines of the United States
Mark P. Fackler and Charles H. Lippy, editors

Women's Periodicals in the United States: Consumer Magazines
Kathleen L. Endres and Therese L. Lueck, editors

Women's Periodicals in the United States: Social and Political Issues
Kathleen L. Endres and Therese L. Lueck, editors

The Conservative Press in Eighteenth- and Nineteenth-Century America
Ronald Lora and William Henry Longton, editors

THE CONSERVATIVE PRESS IN TWENTIETH-CENTURY AMERICA

Edited by

Ronald Lora
and William Henry Longton

SANTA FE COMMUNITY COLLEGE
LIBRARY
3000 N. W. 83 STREET
GAINESVILLE, FL 32606

Historical Guides to the World's Periodicals and Newspapers

Greenwood Press
Westport, Connecticut • London

Library of Congress Cataloging-in-Publication Data

The Conservative press in twentieth-century America / edited by Ronald
  Lora and William Henry Longton.
      p.   cm.—(Historical guides to the world's periodicals and
  newspapers, ISSN 0742–5538)
    Includes bibliographical references and index.
    ISBN 0–313–21390–9 (alk. paper)
    1. Conservatism in the press—United States.   2. American
  periodicals—History—20th century.   I. Lora, Ronald.   II. Longton,
  William Henry, 1937–   .   III. Title: Conservative press in 20th-
  century America.   IV. Series.
  PN4888.C598C664   1999
  070.4′4932052′09730904—dc21   98–51891

British Library Cataloguing in Publication Data is available.

Copyright © 1999 by Ronald Lora and William Henry Longton

All rights reserved. No portion of this book may be
reproduced, by any process or technique, without the
express written consent of the publisher.

Library of Congress Catalog Card Number: 98–51891
ISBN: 0–313–21390–9
ISSN: 0742–5538

First published in 1999

Greenwood Press, 88 Post Road West, Westport, CT 06881
An imprint of Greenwood Publishing Group, Inc.
www.greenwood.com

Printed in the United States of America

The paper used in this book complies with the
Permanent Paper Standard issued by the National
Information Standards Organization (Z39.48–1984).

10 9 8 7 6 5 4 3 2 1

Contents

For
Alice Chumbley Lora
and
Maria Longton

Preface

The sixty-five journals examined in this book are a representative sample of conservative periodicals published in the United States during the twentieth century, with several beginning earlier amid the rise of industrial capitalism when laissez-faire conservatives sang hymns to bountiful America. Addressing a wide variety of topics from conservative points of view, the journals provide a focused survey of the history of American conservative thought from the late nineteenth century to the end of the cold war. Testifying to the persistent vigor and importance of conservatism during the twentieth century, they make clear that the implications to be derived from fundamental principles common to conservatism have been varied and even contradictory. While this goes far to account for the comprehensiveness and richness of the conservative periodical press in America, in a work of this sort it poses difficult problems of precise definition and requires judgmental determinations of what to include and how to organize what is included.

Leaving aside for now the question of definition, which we address in the Introduction, the most painful of the editorial problems was to determine which journals to include. On occasion, difficulty in securing a contributor well-informed about a particular journal's tradition proved decisive. On others, journals such as *National Interest* and *Inquiry*, for example, were omitted for reasons of space, not substance. Finally, having elected to address what have been for the most part *responsible* conservative publications, we determined, as a general rule, to include monthlies and quarterlies and to exclude both weeklies and the daily press. Usually we were able to do this, although in practice we were not willing to exclude all weekly publications. Partly this was because of the fluctuating periodicity of some journals. The *Gospel Advocate*, for example, began as a monthly; then, for over a hundred years, it was a weekly; it became a semimonthly in 1978, but ten years later, in 1988, it was made a monthly again. Journals that began as weeklies or biweeklies sometimes became monthlies, as with *Christian Economics*. It was impossible to exclude weeklies for the reason too that some of them were simply too significant to ignore—J. Sterling Morton's *Conservative*, and Albert Jay Nock's *Freeman*, for instance.

Even with the considerable pruning these measures occasioned, the problem of organization remained. Each essay is a scholarly study that explores the conservative themes of its subject journal, and these have varied according to circumstance and authorial temperament. The conservative press has scarcely spoken with a single voice, whether the topics the journals treat or even the times they inhabit are different or the same. Still, all these periodicals, save for several that are more idiosyncratic and extreme, are connected by their nearer or farther association with core values of conservatism, and among themselves, as variant strains of a recognizable tradition. The organization of this work reflects our reading of these connections.

We have followed a broad chronological sequence when possible and have developed several parts according to such external organizational guides as political or denominational affiliation. Thus the first, fifth, eighth, and tenth parts discuss matters of politics, individualism, isolationism, anticommunism, the New Right, neoconservatism, and public policy. The second and third parts bring together, respectively, orthodox Protestant and Catholic periodicals that examine issues within the context of religious conservatism. In the fourth part our classification turns on an internal feature of the periodicals. It concerns twentieth-century journals (two that began in the previous century) united by their major focus on literary topics and their cultural connections. The remaining parts—six, seven, and nine—examine libertarianism, traditionalist perspectives, and the extreme right-wing frame of reference.

In developing these classifications we were compelled to make several tough decisions. Space was made for "anticommunist publications." Should the same have been done for periodicals whose fundamental viewpoint often appeared to be "antiliberalism"? Should the *New Guard* be included with libertarian or New Right publications? Might the periodicals included under "Extreme Rightist Publications" be properly identified as "conservative"? We think not; however, that part is included because popular usage often holds otherwise and, more significant, because the articles highlight conservative prudential politics and respect for law by demonstrating their great distance from that tradition. Occasionally the emphasis given by our contributors settled similar questions, but in disposing of them we have generally been governed by the belief that the most distinguishing feature of the periodical's conservatism ought to control its placement. The Contents indicates our resolution of these multiple perplexities.

Each essay contains an "Information Sources" and "Publication History" section. The former is designed to be useful as an aid to further research. In it are references to indexing sources and reprint editions of the journal wherein we have made use of abbreviations, explained in the following notes.

A NOTE ON INDEX SOURCES

Following are the abbreviations used for the indexes cited in the Information Sources section accompanying each essay in this work, the sources to which they refer, and the years they cover.

General Indexes

Poole	*Poole's Index to Periodical Literature.* 6 vols., 1802–1907.
ALI	*Annual Literary Index*, 13 vols., 1892–1904.
19th Cent RG	*Nineteenth Century Readers' Guide to Periodical Literature*, 2 vols., 1890–1899.
RG	*Readers' Guide to Periodical Literature*, vols. 1–current, 1900–present.
RG Supp	*Readers' Guide to Periodical Literature Supplement*, 2 vols., 1907–1919; superseded by:
II	*International Index to Periodicals*, vols. 3–18, 1920–1965; superseded by:
SSHI	*Social Sciences and Humanities Index*, vols. 19–25, 1965–1974; superseded by:
Soc Sci Ind	*Social Science Index*, vols. 1–current, 1974–present; and:
Hum Ind	*Humanities Index*, vols. 1–current, 1974–present.
Access	*Access: The Supplementary Index to Periodicals*, vols. 1–current, 1974–present.
AHI	*American Humanities Index*, vols. 1–current, 1975– present.
AHCI	*Arts and Humanities Citation Index*, 1975–present.
Art Index	*Art Index*, vols. 1–current, 1929–present.
Bio Ind	*Biography Index*, vols. 1–current, 1946–present.
CMC	*Current Magazine Contents*, 2 vols., 1928–1929.
Curr Cont: A & H	*Current Contents: Arts & Humanities*, vols. 1– current; 1979–present.
FLI	*Film Literature Index*, vols. 1–current, 1973–present.
Mag Ind	*Magazine Index*, 1977–present.
PAIS	*Public Affairs Information Service Bulletin*, vols. 1– current, 1915–present.
PPI	*Popular Periodical Index*, nos. 1–current, 1973– present.
SSCI	*Social Sciences Citation Index*, 1966–present.

History, Political Science, and Sociology Indexes

ABC Pol Sci	*ABC Pol Sci: Advance Bibliography of Contents: Political Science and Government*, vols. 1–current, 1969–present.
Amer Hist & Life	*America: History and Life: A Guide to Periodical Literature*, vols. 1–current, 1964–present.
Comb Ret Ind JPS	*Combined Retrospective Index to Journals in Political Science*, 8 vols., 1886–1974.
Hist Abst	*Historical Abstracts*, vols. 1–current, 1955–present.
URS	*Universal Reference System: Political Science, Government, and Public Policy Series*, 10 vols., to 1966, with annual supplements, 1967–1979; name changed to:
Pol Sci Abst	*Political Science Abstracts*, 1980–present.
Sage Urb Stud Abst	*Sage Urban Studies Abstracts*, vols. 1–current, 1973–present.
Soc Abst	*Sociological Abstracts*, vols. 1–current, 1955 present.
Urb Aff Abst	*Urban Affairs Abstracts*, vols. 1–current, 1971 present.

Writings Amer Hist	*Writings in American History*, 1902–present.

Literature Indexes

Articles Amer Lit	*Articles in American Literature, 1900–1950*. Lewis Leary, comp.
	Articles in American Literature, 1950–1967. Lewis Leary, comp.
	Articles in American Literature, 1968–1975. Lewis Leary and John Auchard, comp.
MLA Abstract	MLA Abstracts of *Articles in Scholarly Journals*, 1970–1975.
MLA Amer Bib	*MLA American Bibliography of Books and Articles on the Modern Languages and Literatures*, 1921–1955; superseded by:
MLA Intl Bib	*MLA International Bibliography of Books and Articles on the Modern Languages and Literatures*, 1956–present.

Religion and Philosophy Indexes

Ind Rel Per Lit	*Index to Religious Periodical Literature*, vols. 1–12, 1949–1976; superseded by:
Rel Ind One	*Religion Index One: Periodicals*, vols. 13–current, 1977–present.
NTA	*New Testament Abstracts*, vols. 1–current, 1956–present.
OTA	*Old Testament Abstracts*, vols. 1–current, 1978–present.

Law Indexes

Jones	*Index to Legal Periodical Literature*, 6 vols., 1790–1937. [Cited by the name of its first editor, Leonard Jones.]
ILP	*Index to Legal Periodicals*, vols. 1–current, 1926–present.

Business Indexes

Bus Ind	*Business Index*, vols. 1–current, 1979–present.
BPI	*Business Periodicals Index*, vols. 1–current, 1958–present.
BPIA	*Business Periodicals Index and Abstracts*, 1983–1985.
IAI	*Industrial Arts Index*, vols. 1–45, 1913–1957.

Book Review Indexes

BRD	*Book Review Digest*, vols. 1–current, 1925–present.
BRI	*Book Review Index*, vols. 1–current, 1965–present.
Comb Ret Ind Bk Revs Sch J	*Combined Retrospective Index to Book Reviews in Scholarly Journals*, 15 vols., 1886–1974.
Comb Ret Ind Bk Revs Hum	*Combined Retrospective Index to Book Reviews in Humanities Journals*, 10 vols., 1802–1974.
Curr Bk Rev Cit	*Current Book Review Citations*, 1976–1982.
Ind Bk Revs Hum	*An Index to Book Reviews in the Humanities*, vols. 1–current, 1960–present.

A NOTE ON REPRINT EDITIONS

The following abbreviations are used for publishers of the reprint editions cited in the Information Sources section accompanying each essay.

AN	Ayer Publishing Company
ATLA	American Theological Library Association Preservation Board
BLH	Bell and Howell

DA	Datamics, Inc.
ISI	Institute for Scientific Information Press
KIP	Kraus International Publications
KTO	Kraus Reprints and Periodicals
LC	Library of Congress
MCA	Microforming Corporation of America
MIM	Microforms International, Inc.
PMC	Princeton Microfilm Corporation
UMI	University Microfilm International

ACKNOWLEDGMENTS

We thank The University of Toledo for supporting this project in various ways, including two summer grants and a sabbatical leave, and members of the interlibrary loan staff of the Carlson Library for securing needed material. The Horace Rackham School of Graduate Studies, the University of Michigan, earned our gratitude by providing visiting scholar privileges and opening to us the magnificent collections in the university libraries. Julie Herrada, Assistant Curator of the Labadie Collection, assisted us in several inquiries. Several periodicals not carried by many libraries were provided us by staff members of the main branch of the Toledo–Lucas County Public Library. Thanks are due our graduate students, especially Steven Fitch, Leslie Heaphy, Kenneth Bindas, Jeff Irvin, and Jason Hribal, who assisted us in this project over the years. We acknowledge too the pleasure of our conversations with colleagues Theodore Natsoulas, Michael Kay, Alfred Cave, Michael Jakobson, and William Hoover, for insights into ideologies, ranging far beyond our focus on conservatism. Alice Chumbley Lora, whose arcane computer skills compensated for our own primitive capabilities, graciously and competently bore the brunt of preparing the manuscript for the publisher. We are deeply grateful for the commitment and patience that Cynthia Harris, our editor at Greenwood Press, displayed though the years. Never losing faith in the project's value, she provided deeply valued support; her advice and suggestions have improved the book in numerous ways. Finally, we are indebted to David Palmer, of Greenwood, who guided the book efficiently through the production process and helped to smooth the process of final revision.

American Conservatism in the Twentieth Century

What is conservatism? Is it not adherence to the old and tried, against the new and untried?

—Abraham Lincoln

[Conservatism prefers] the familiar to the unknown...the tried to the untried...fact to mystery, the actual to the possible, the limited to the unbounded, the near to the distant.

—Michael Oakeshott

LATE NINETEENTH-CENTURY SOCIAL DARWINISM

Among conservatives, finding agreement on the principles of their faith is made difficult because many of its representatives have not considered it their business to state a fully fashioned philosophy. Nevertheless, during the first half-century of the American Republic, certain themes recurred in conservative works. Religious veneration and faith in a providential plan that governs society, defense of property rights, and a desire for a natural aristocracy based on education, talent, and an ethical code to rule and model standards of conduct figured prominently among conservatives from John Adams to Orestes Brownson. To these were joined other themes, among them a distrust of universal suffrage, a preference for indirect elections, and a sense of the fallibility of man strong enough to insist on states rights and checks on majority rule. Law, order, and obedience were virtues so obvious as to constitute a folk wisdom only barely in need of philosophical justification. American conservatives, with many exceptions, attempted to carry on a set of ideals that had developed over centuries: honor, loyalty, self-discipline, and conviction that the standards of right conduct lay in religion and history. Citizens were to enjoy ordered liberty in which the blessings of family and community were equal to those of the individual person.

American society and thought underwent a profound change during the decades following the Civil War. Not only had the constitutional and proslavery arguments of Southern political intellectuals been discredited, but rapid advances in science and technology created a crisis in the old order and foretold a shift in intellectual orientation. There appeared in many quarters a serious search for underlying laws that explained the workings of human behavior and of society. In biology, philosophy, psychology, and elsewhere, older texts came under heavy criticism in the universities. The earliest conceptual breakthroughs came in social philosophy and in biology, the most significant of which was the *Origin of Species*, published by Charles Darwin in 1859. Its evolutionary view of life and nature forced a reconsideration of societal development. In what must have been seen as merely fortuitous by those not alert to the sociology of knowledge, the new method of science fit easily, if controversially, with the origins of the new industrial state. The English social philosopher Herbert Spencer, a proponent of "survival of the fittest" notions before the *Origin*, aggressively embraced Darwin's biological theories, and in short order found widespread support in American intellectual circles. Because the social order ran by laws analogous to those in nature, he argued, prudent philosophers would let it alone. Avoid public health measures that would help the unfit; do nothing that would prolong the errors of the misguided and unfortunate. Spencer's evolutionary doctrine was meant to support genuine progress, yet it embraced a degree of social violence and bitter failure that contradicted the religious culture's message of love and compassion.

Other leading intellectuals concurred. Two years after Darwin published his revolutionary work, Charles Eliot Norton, shortly to become a Harvard professor and editor of the *North American Review*, acknowledged the wastefulness and suffering of the Darwinian synthesis but concluded that in the long run the unsettling elements promoted health and social betterment. It was common to portray the new evolutionary hypothesis as a necessary component of a broader politico-economic philosophy that rationalized and undergirded Spencer's "nightwatchman" theory of the state. What appeared cruel at first glance was actually best in the long run: if the state resisted social intervention, not only would individual freedom flourish, but society would purify itself of good-for-nothings and move to higher levels of prosperity and culture. The foremost American proponent of this philosophy, soon to be known as Social Darwinism, was William Graham Sumner. Educated first as a clergyman, he studied Darwin and the English classical tradition of political economy. For the Yale professor the religious hypothesis soon lost its meaning, and he took comfort in the advantages that free markets and limited government offered to society. Individual and social advance depended on hard work and self-denial; those who accumulated capital were the modern heroes. Such were the conservative implications of Darwinian science and English classical political theory.

Defenders of the status quo after the Civil War did not need Darwin to exalt individualism. During the Jacksonian era, Alexis de Tocqueville had written that democratic Americans "owe nothing to any man, they expect nothing from any man....Not only does democracy make every man forget his ancestors, but it hides his descendants and separates his contemporaries from him; it throws him back forever upon himself alone and threatens in the end to confine him entirely within the solitude of his own heart." In the minds of many intellectuals, however, Social Darwinism justified the distribution of economic power that characterized post-Civil War America. If natural selection had tested the survival value of human folkways and customs, who was to declare them wrong? Though many arose to do just that—among them Richard T. Ely, Lester Frank Ward, Edward Bellamy, Josiah Royce, and Thorstein Veblen—the doctrine of laissez faire nevertheless provided Americans with an ideological rationale for unchecked capitalism and opposition to reform. Perhaps no other conservative movement in American history took stronger hold among the people, both the educated and the wider populace steeped in the Protestant ethic. It was also the strangest variety of conservatism ever to engage the public mind. Its individualism bordered on anarchy and stood in opposition to central authority, carrying little loving attachment to the traditions and saving graces that had characterized traditional conservative thought. The normal religious orientation of conservatism yielded to a rationalist, secular outlook that encouraged atomistic rather than organic connections with life and culture. Although its proponents were often able to indulge a taste for symbols and emotive appeals such as flags and patriotic celebrations, the new theory itself had no place for them.

To note these historical inconsistencies, however, is to pay tribute to the serious attempt of the first Darwinian generation to bring society under the explanatory power of natural law theory. Sumner, for his part, led other late nineteenth-century intellectuals in founding the discipline of sociology, which would interpret human affairs in terms of the new science of biology and physics. That was accomplished at the very moment industrial capitalism was revolutionizing society with a rugged dynamic unequaled in American history. Together with the relative absence of a feudal past, that transformation helps to explain the ambiguities in the meaning of "liberalism" and "conservatism" in American history. The defenders of a politico-economic philosophy that opposed all manner of social reform were not merely advocates of the wealthy. Many also favored free trade and Jeffersonian democracy, and, like Sumner and J. Sterling Morton, they condemned American imperialism during the 1890s. Later generations would see that their economic philosophy resulted in the widespread destruction of the very institutions and customs that were the special province of conservatism to preserve. The resolute defense of private property, free trade, and decentralized government helped eventually to bring a degree of prosperity that only utopian visionaries dreamed of, but the price was heavy in terms of the communal relationships once celebrated in conservative thought.

Although Social Darwinism won the day for at least three decades of our national life, several conservative spokesmen for a more humane and ethical strategy appeared. When Mark Hopkins, then president of Williams College, taught the sanctity of private property, he also insisted that individualism had its limits. The obligations of stewardship meant that one ought not to turn away from the fallen and lesser privileged. Charitable responses to hardship would at once provide avenues for moral action and obviate the need for social reform. Steel magnate Andrew Carnegie understood that the concentration of economic power had created a dependent class that lived in perpetual uncertainty and insecurity. The natural laws of economic growth remained in place, but the victors in the competitive struggle, he wrote, should look on their wealth as a trust to be used for the public good.

LIBERTARIANS, FUNDAMENTALISTS, AND TRADITIONALISTS

As the nineteenth century yielded to the twentieth, American conservatism was grounded in private property and in opposition to the enlarged role for government envisioned by populists, progressives, and proponents of the Social Gospel. Three expressions gained dominance: laissez-faire conservatism, a variety of Social Darwinism shading off to libertarianism; religious evangelicalism, which soon would slough off a fundamentalist variant as the nation experienced profound social and economic dislocation in the first third of the century; and traditionalism, which stressed maintenance of the educational and cultural values of order, hierarchy, and social harmony.

Among the laissez-faire conservatives several themes predominated. The first was the preference for market capitalism. To many it seemed to sum up the wisdom of the industrial age. Nicholas Murray Butler asserted that "capitalism is the only economic system compatible with liberty." Allowing for nuanced interpretation, the National Association of Manufacturers, the Chamber of Commerce, all U.S. presidents between Lincoln and the second Roosevelt, and a majority of clergymen in the country would have agreed. For conservatives, little had changed in economic thought from the day when Justice Stephen F. Field, in his 1872 dissent in the *Slaughterhouse* cases, remarked that economic freedom superseded all other forms of freedom. A generation of exciting advances in the social sciences, of Thorstein Veblen's and Simon Patten's critiques of the American economy, of John Dewey's instrumentalist philosophy and of the pragmatic "revolt against formalism," had not shaken Butler's conviction that the nation's industrial and financial leaders continued to operate "in full accord with the public interest." Though never unchallenged, most social commentators understood capitalism as the economic expression of what Adam Smith called the "system of natural liberty," in which individuals are best left to pursue their own interest in ways of their own choosing. In the previous century, classical liberals had made much of this doctrine. Individuals seeking their private good appear to act selfishly; in actual practice, however, their work is transvalued into the essential good of all. In Smith's formulation, "it is not from the benevolence of the butcher, the brewer, or the baker, that we expect our dinner, but from their regard to their own interest." Whether understood through the writings of Butler, a college president, Elihu Root, a politician, or Billy Sunday, an evangelist, it differed from Social Darwinism primarily in the sense that none of these individuals grounded their assent in a naturalistic theory of human nature and of social change. That was significant for American thought; nevertheless, at that moment in history it constituted a stern doctrine for millions of working men and women.

A second and third principle of laissez-faire conservatism flowed logically though not necessarily from the doctrine of free economics. There was always in early twentieth-century conservatism a distaste for the widening river of democracy. Whether examining the thought of Nicholas Murray Butler, or of Paul Elmer More, Irving Babbitt, H. L. Mencken, Albert Jay Nock, and Elihu Root, one encounters the fear that progressive politics downgraded democracy, linked as it was to public opinion, in their view a vaporous compound of weakness, prejudice, and folly. Demagogues and class-obsessed politicians flourished amid such conditions— hence, the recurring emphasis on rule by a nonhereditary elite, a principle that laissez-faire conservatives shared with traditionalists and libertarians.

Ridicule of democracy and wish for an aristocracy of talent found its liveliest expression in the analyses of H. L. Mencken and Albert J. Nock, two influential editors and essayists who combined the self-reliance of Emerson and Sumner with the cultural pessimism of the literary naturalists to produce some of the most full-blooded libertarianism that has appeared in American thought. Both argued that democracy was destructive of high culture and that "surface reforms" such as extending the franchise would not improve it. Both assailed reformers for failing to understand that planning for freedom was a contradiction in terms. Mencken described himself as "a libertarian," one who believed in liberty "in its widest imaginable sense—liberty up to the extreme limits of the feasible and tolerable." He was "against forbidding anybody to do anything, or say anything, or think anything so long as it was at all possible to imagine a habitable world." Tensions were inevitable when holding this view even in one of the world's most open democracies. Mencken scorned liberalism but tolerated minority ethnic groups, defended free speech to the utmost but writhed under the consequences, opposed economic and social planning but held in contempt the finer products of laissez-faire economics, and advocated individualism to the point of anarchy but admired authoritarian periods of history. Critics thought his conception of liberty inverted. It meant not the right of the majority to legislate its will but the right of the strong and talented to dictate to the common folk. Through this Nietzschean idea Mencken revealed his wish for an aristocracy of talent that would produce such blessings as civilized society is capable of enjoying, correct the enthusiasms of the populace, protect the eccentricities of the upper orders, and by so doing free America for the life of the mind.

Albert J. Nock concurred with much of his friend's social and political criticism. He too was irreverent, irreligious, and unpatriotic in the popular usage of the term. He shared Mencken's contempt for politicians and distrust of reformist passion. A libertarian by inclination, Nock pushed individualism the full way to philosophical anarchism. Nock's reputation was made when he joined with friends in 1920 to found the *Freeman*, often judged to have been the finest magazine in the country during the early years of the decade. It was a "radical paper," said Nock, the purpose of which was to popularize "fundamental economics" (his phrase for the single tax plan of Henry George) and to examine the cultural inadequacies of American democracy. The *Freeman* consistently stood in opposition to legalists and authoritarians of all varieties, and hammered away on the theme that laws that existed in order to satisfy someone's economic interests were in fact an expression of privilege bereft of moral justification. Anarchic freedom was the right to live without the received moral codes, if one so chose. In an environment free of the demands of conformity and of state-supported privileges, solitary individuals could develop their talents and strengthen their moral fiber.

During the Great Depression and numerous New Deal programs to end it, Nock, for reasons that are not wholly clear, became increasingly pessimistic and threw overboard all prudential considerations. The epigraph to *Our Enemy: The State*, his most extended discussion of centralized government, included quotations from Spencer, Mencken, and José Ortega y Gasset, all of whom testified that the sovereignty of the state is a baroque excrescence from centuries past during which it brought order out of feudal breakdown and at times stood between the people and an avaricious nobility. In the twentieth century, however, the state is hostile to industrious and decent citizens. It taxes them and marches them off to war. It grants favors to the wealthy, and by reflecting so closely the interests of the business world serves to perpetuate the belief that the good life is the life of activity, exploitation, and the well-paying job. So argued Nock, who then declared his freedom by refusing responsibility for society. That was the apolitical but creative task he offered to the intellectual elite, yet for Nock as for Henry Adams, cultural criticism often degenerated into peevish discourse without a program.

While Mencken and Nock developed their libertarian expression of laissez-faire conservatism, a different conservatism emerged, grounded in a religious worldview that preferred traditional modes of understanding reality. Perhaps it should have been expected, considering the enormous economic and demographic changes that the United States underwent from the 1880s to the end of World War I. Millions of immigrants entered the United States in those years, the majority from Poland, Italy, Greece, and other southern and eastern European countries that had not figured significantly in earlier migrations to America. Few spoke English, and many were Catholic. Their numbers, swelled by Americans leaving the farm, produced the great cities in all their haphazard form and pluralistic excitement. The new religious and linguistic addition to the melting pot was highlighted by American participation in what began as Europe's war and from which President Wilson avoided direct military engagement for more than two and a half years. The war experience revealed that the melting pot had not worked as its proponents had promised, that nationalist connections with European homelands remained significant in shaping both individual and government decisions for war and peace. Once the war ended and peace negotiations commenced, fear and division characterized the social fabric. The right-wing reaction was the re-emergence of nativism at levels not seen for half a century. It deprived radicals and hyphenate Americans of civil rights; a small number were killed. Its most popular manifestation was the renaissance of the Ku Klux Klan, an anxiety-ridden organization whose platform of "Christian America" reflected a yearning for the establishment of white Protestant dominance. It battled to purge American life of alien influences, becoming so popular that for several years its members could march openly in major cities, even down Pennsylvania Avenue in the nation's capital.

Many Protestants within the mainline churches joined the antiradical and anti-immigrant movement. In addition to demographic and economic changes, they found troublesome the theology of the Social Gospel, Darwin's theory of natural selection, and the handling of basic religious texts by proponents of the Higher Criticism. These trends lay at the heart of modernism, conceived as the compromising adaptation of religious beliefs to secular culture. The new scientific and ideological ways of understanding human society, often overlaid with Marxian, Freudian, and naturalistic assumptions, provoked a response on behalf of *The Fundamentals*—twelve books edited by Reuben Torrey and A.C. Dixon, and published just before World War I that defined the preferred orthodoxy and defended the authority of Scripture. They offered Christians a five-point creed: (1) the inerrancy of Scripture, (2) the virgin birth of Jesus, (3) his substitutionary atonement, (4) his bodily resurrection from the grave, and (5) his imminent second coming. Not until the twentieth century did fundamentalism, as distinct from evangelicalism, arise within mainline Protestantism, and not until 1920 was "fundamentalist" used to identify the premillennial wing of conservative denominations that subscribed to the five-point creed and undertook spirited if haphazard sorties into politics.

The most striking distinction of fundamentalism was dispensationalism, the division of history into eras (dispensations) involving a "tribulation" period followed by Christ's return and his thousand-year reign on earth. In each dispensation (the number ranged from three to ten), God interacted differently with the world and his people. Dispensationalism was pessimistic in its underlying implications, for the allied doctrine of premillennialism held that history would end in worldwide war and suffering, a conflagration from which born-again Christians would be spared. Meanwhile, it could be argued that political activity amounted to wasted effort, as alert Christians looked for signs as foretold in prophecy of just when the end time would arrive. It is a measure of how deeply troubling was the modernization of American society that fundamentalists nevertheless donned evangelical trappings and moved into the political arena to nourish the spread of Christian doctrine.

This worldview—and it was that—lay behind the evolution controversy of the 1920s. Fundamentalists defended a literal reading of the Genesis account of creation, and for it suffered the calumny of the liberal intellectuals. Yet initially fundamentalists appeared to enjoy successes. John T. Scopes was convicted for teaching evolution in school; moreover, in the battle against demon rum, conservative Protestants had enjoyed the support not only of liberal Protestants but of middle-class reformers alarmed at the damage liquor inflicted on the lower orders. Textbooks routinely note that fundamentalism was a last-ditch effort to hold back the forces of modernism in education, the arts, and religion. Too often overlooked is the substantial intellectual tradition that lay behind it, including the work of J. Gresham Machen, of Princeton Theological Seminary. The New Testament scholar understood that religious systems and the particularities of faith expression give meaning to life, that in the context of disrupting societal change many people seek psychological security in a set of rules that define righteous behavior. It cannot escape notice that fundamentalists, who drew on the Bible for their worldview, had much in common with traditionalist conservatives such as the Humanists, Agrarians, and New Conservatives of the 1950s, who drew on the arguments and sensibility of Edmund Burke to defend an organic view of society, impervious to the corrosive culture of modernism. Russell Kirk, Richard Weaver, John Hallowell, Frederick Wilhelmsen, and M. E. Bradford would have understood J. Gresham Machen and B. B. Warfield, both of whom had been fully aware of a crisis in culture and Christianity, had defended the intellectual foundations of conservative Presbyterianism as important to the Lord's work, and were confident that the truths of the gospel would prevail in the end time.

When politicizing their religious convictions resulted in failure (though later defenders of orthodoxy could take heart when for the rest of the century nearly half of all Americans continued to reject evolutionary theory), fundamentalists suffered such ridicule that they retreated from the political fray to nurse their embarrassment. If it is too much to say that American Protestant fundamentalism went underground, it remains true nevertheless that between the Scopes Trial and the establishment of the Moral Majority half a century later, no leader arose—not Billy James Hargis or the Reverend Carl McIntire or (by choice) Billy Graham— to convert fundamentalist views into a coherent political force.

To the delight of a dwindling band of advocates, traditionalist conservatism (the third major conservative formulation) found itself restated in the twentieth century when the erudite literary critics Irving Babbitt and Paul Elmer More declared war on the dominant assumptions of modernism. They had grown uneasy over the type of culture emerging out of industrial capitalism and progressive democracy, brooded over declining standards and taste, and scorned literary innovation. Against the cultural themes of positivism, naturalism, materialism, liberalism, and romanticism, they posed older ideals: virtue, order, hierarchy, authority, and discipline. Moral and social norms, they argued, were rooted in a transcendent order beyond appearance. From his first book, *Literature and the American College* (1908), to *Rousseau and Romanticism* (1919) and *Democracy and Leadership* (1924), Babbitt stood firm against the contention that, in Mencken's words, "the critic is first and last simply trying to express himself." If so, what would "guarantee adherence to standards and how would one find the permanent amidst the flux of existence?" More argued that the artist "should fix his imagination on what is best in man and attempt to build models of character." Modern literature, combining new techniques and the modern sensibility, was philosophically barren and joyless. John Dos Passos's *Manhattan Transfer* (1925), with its "spattered filth," reminded More of "an explosion in a cesspool."

The origins of the Humanists' disenchantment with the present lay in their understanding of romanticism. Babbitt's works in particular summed up the conservative case against the romantic temptation personified by Jean Jacques Rousseau. The French philosopher, Babbitt asserted, symbolized the impulsive and uncontrolled man, the sentimental humanitarian, the scorner of all prescriptive institutions. Like most other traditionalist conservatives, the New Humanists were uneasy with the Rousseauistic emphasis on rights. Duty, work, discipline, and deference provided better grounds for an ordered liberty. Against the disordered flux of the phenomenal world, the Humanist intellectual posed a "higher law" above the sway of individual impulse, stressed awareness of human frailty, and the consequent need for authority, order, and virtue. They could be inculcated best by a return to a classical education that would instill in students the ideal of moderation in all things. In a person's deepest awareness lay an ethical center that when energized could bring order to the evanescent multiplicity of raw human experience.

The Humanists enjoyed a small and devoted following among literary and cultural conservatives, but elsewhere came under heavy fire. Liberal critics such as Malcolm Cowley saw in their philosophy little more than a collection of snobbish, dogmatic, and puritanical beliefs that could never humanize culture. Others took exception to the dualistic concept of body and mind that Humanists defended, insisting that the nature of the universe as revealed by modern science made unacceptable an absolute rendering of human values. Nor did critics detect in the traditionalist conservatism the vibrant, hopeful curiosity about life and nature that had animated Renaissance humanism. Even though disintegration of the New Humanism as a movement came with a Great Depression–induced social consciousness, the insistent Humanist voice that individuals of character must conserve cultural and ethical values would appeal to later generations.

A second flowering of traditionalism attempted to remedy the lack of connection with the country that characterized so many genteel figures during and after the Gilded Age. It developed in the 1920s at Vanderbilt University, where young intellectuals such as John Crowe Ransom, Allen Tate, Robert Penn Warren, and Donald Davidson gathered to study poetry and literature. The Nashville "Fugitive Poets," as they came to be known, had a rural background in the years concurrent with the early phases of industrialization south of the Mason-Dixon line. They saw at first hand that industrialization was a tough process, that in company towns "freedom" took on new and inverted meanings, and that the Southern tradition of individualism worked effectively in giving mill owners a free hand in employer-employee relations. In reviews and essays they attacked the babbittry and boosterism of the New South. Donald Davidson remembered bitterly that in his boyhood years "industrial commercialism was rampant....Old and historic communities were crawling on their bellies to persuade some petty manufacturer of pants or socks to take up his tax-exempt status in their midst."

Although the Agrarians deplored this development and wrote lyrically of the pleasures of subsistence agriculture, their major interests were aesthetic and cultural. In his reconstruction of the Agrarian movement, Davidson wrote that all were disgusted with "the spiritual disorder of modern life—its destruction of human integrity and lack of purpose." They saw a war of culture developing in the United States, with the "northern" spirit of abstraction, science, materialism, and centralized government pitted against "southern" tradition, religion, community, and states rights. A rapid succession of events after World War I had placed the South on the defensive. There was Mencken's savage portrayal of cultural sterility in the "Sahara of the Bozart," the sensational press reports on Georgian chain gangs, and the

Scottsboro case. Most important of all was the controversy over the Scopes Trial, which like a firebell in the night interrupted the purely literary pursuits of the Fugitives. Determined to alert Southerners to the importance of their distinctive heritage, the twelve Agrarians in 1930 published a manifesto that smote liberal philosophy hip and thigh. The essays in *I'll Take My Stand* argued that the utopian dreams, faith in human progress, and the "soulless worship of science" characteristic of laissez-faire doctrine, as well as mainstream liberalism, were shallow and dangerous. Better to substitute respect for the past, religious sensibility, and a rural way of life for a greedy ethos of entrepreneurial freedom and an illusory quest for equality.

The Great Depression, which had driven the New Humanism into eclipse, encouraged the Agrarians to undertake social and political analysis. In the pages of the *American Review* and elsewhere they produced a spate of articles designed to clarify the conditions for a better society. In an article entitled "Happy Farmers," Ransom declared that "the apostasy of American farmers from primary subsistence farming is the greatest disaster our country has yet suffered." Borrowing from English distributists, Frank Owsley suggested that giant corporations be divided into smaller units and that the federal government pursue policies designed to create a society in which small agricultural market towns dominated social and economic life. Several Agrarians also contributed to *Who Owns America?* (1936), edited by Allen Tate and Herbert Agar. Following the earlier distributists G. K. Chesterton and Hilaire Belloc, they underscored in one last joint effort their belief that "monopoly capitalism is evil and destructive" and that a stable society required the widespread ownership of property, the majority of it held in land.

These occasional pieces of programmatic reform drew a predictable response, as the condescending titles of several reviews suggest: "So Did King Canute," "Young Confederates," and "Look Away Dixie." Yet the Southern Agrarians represented an impressive home-grown critique of American development and liberalism, all the while reminding their generation that not all thoughtful conservatives admired the ways of industrialism and that devotion to either a steady stream of consumer goods or a self-seeking dream of personal liberation is not the only way to measure the success of a society. If the agrarian mode of living virtually passed from view, it nevertheless remained true that the texture of modern life could be improved by a renewed sense of place, grounded in organic social relations that flow from families, churches, and human-scale communities. That humane call continued to resonate for decades to follow.

CONSERVATIVE RENEWAL IN COLD WAR AMERICA

The state of the world that emerged out of the chaos unleashed in World War II served to produce a political and intellectual climate of anxiety. Nearly 50 million humans had died in the carnage. Powerful weapons, not least the atomic bombs that destroyed Hiroshima and Nagasaki, forecast a new age of terror should the great powers prove unable to resolve their political and ideological differences. Uneasy amid the darkening shape of the future, many intellectuals turned inward in search of essences that transcended the evanescent fads of the moment. Domestically it entailed more attention to traditional customs and structures than had characterized the experimental style of the New Deal era. Seeking reasons for the crisis in Western civilization, conservative intellectuals rejected relativism on a number of fronts and lamented a decline in manners and morals, echoing earlier complaints of the New Humanists. A renewed appreciation of absolutes emerged from the Nuremberg war trials, which concluded that there are values beyond those of a particular culture to which all humans are responsible. Philosophers spoke of a return to fundamental law.

As during the first half of the twentieth century, the conservative response was not monolithic in character. Even in the traditionalist camp, again one of three dominant conservative formulations after World War II, theological conservatism shared attention with natural law theorists and Burkean proponents of tradition. Many of the former were Catholics, who called for a reassertion of religious orthodoxy to challenge growing secularism. Thomas Molnar, Frederick Wilhelmsen, and John Courtney Murray produced an impressive body of literature critical of rationalist ways of knowing. Grounded less in religious tradition, the Natural Law proponents emphasized the classical heritage of the West as a bulwark against modern rationalism. The seminal scholars Eric Voegelin and Leo Strauss, following the written word as opposed to biography and socioeconomic background, focused on the moral, philosophizing nature of an ideal world, its high standards the measure of human behavior. Others such as Willmoore Kendall and Eliseo Vivas promoted a majority rule version of conservatism that entitled a political majority to legislate its value system into a public orthodoxy, however tenuous and inimical it was to supposed personal rights.

A third version of the traditionalist school placed at its center the claims of community and the Burkean notion of organic society. No one did more in this connection than Russell Kirk, whose *The Conservative Mind* (1953), wrote William F. Buckley, "inaugurated the modern conservative intellectual movement." There emerged in Kirk's conservatism of permanence and preservation a sense of communal feeling seldom matched save in traditionalist societies and the legends of old socialism. In this Kirk enjoyed substantial support from a lengthy list of scholars, including Richard Weaver, Anthony Harrigan, John Hallowell, Peter Stanlis, Francis Wilson, and Robert Nisbet. Each cherished the deep roots of community that suffered from undernourishment in a mass society.

Generous in his praise of Kirk's contributions, Buckley was unequaled in resuscitating modern American conservatism and bringing a diverse array of individuals into the movement. His buoyant spirit and intellectual energy lay behind the remarkable success of *National Review*, one of the most influential journals of the cold war era. In it he linked traditionalist themes with a second postwar expression of the American Right, which followed closely the tradition of Sumner, Butler, Coolidge, and iconoclastic writers such as Nock, and was known popularly as libertarianism. It originated long before World War II and strictly speaking was not conservatism. It gained impetus, however, as reaction set in against the legacy of Franklin D. Roosevelt. Potential New Deal expansion in education, housing, national health insurance, and full-employment legislation was blocked as Republicans won congressional majorities in 1946 and again in 1952. Though hostile to the growth of statism and skeptical of the rationale for mounting defense expenditures, libertarians on occasion made common cause with conservatives in an attempt to roll back New Deal programs. Once called classical liberals, the postwar libertarians stressed the autonomy of the individual, whose rights took precedence over all other values, in the noneconomic as well as the economic sphere. Religion, morality, conscience—all lay beyond the reach of government.

When we examine William F. Buckley's founding of the *National Review* in 1955, we come into the presence of conservatives who, even as they insisted otherwise, understood that disposition was not enough. To be effective, one must act. The editors of *National Review*, in the journal's first number, listed several articles of faith: the functions of government should be cut and limited to the protection of the citizen's life, liberty, and property; other government activities diminish freedom and hamper progress; free economic competition "is indispensable to liberty and material progress"; and the greatest crisis of the era is the conflict between the social engineers who seek to manipulate people into conformity with scientific utopias and the disciples of truth who defend an "organic moral order."

This creedal statement defined mainstream conservative doctrine for the remainder of the century. It is a rights-based conservatism, grounded in the assumption that the individual exists prior to his country and community. If a modest definition of ideology refers to "a body of ideas reflecting the social needs and aspirations of an individual group, class, or culture," postwar conservatism had become an ideology. Even a more energetic definition—for example, "a rational structure of ideas energizing men and women in their quest for a better world"—fits the creedal statement.

The early cold war years generated a third major expression of conservative thought and politics. Nothing united cold war conservative intellectuals more solidly than the conviction that communism was a moral enormity, behaviorally wrong and ethically evil. Herbert Hoover, who occupied the center of the conservative spectrum, represented conservative thought on this issue. In June 1941, several days after Nazi Germany attacked the Soviet Union, he described the communist power as "one of the bloodiest tyrannies and terrors ever erected in history...a militant destroyer of the worship of God." The United States should stand aside and allow the two nations to destroy each other. Other conservatives agreed. Clare Booth Luce, an important link between conservative intellectuals and Republican politicians, wrote shortly after the collapse of the Chinese Nationalists that the communist doctrine of man held simply that he was "an animal without a soul." In the communist view, one was "born to live and die like a pig; you root, and rut, and rot." On the conservative Left, the poet-historian Peter Viereck characterized the Soviet Union as "the extremist plutocracy in history. The most savage and relentless enemy of all workmen all over the globe is Russia's rich ruling class. The Soviet Union is the highest fulfillment of the selfish ideals of unlimited monopoly capitalism." And following the death of Senator Joe McCarthy (R, Wisconsin), William S. Schlamm, then an editor of *National Review*, pronounced the conventional conservative judgment on McCarthyism: "At the heart of what McCarthy said and did was the very essence of Western Civilization." McCarthy "saw the central truth of his age: that his country, his faith, his civilization was at war with communism." He had seen "the gargoyles of the Anti-Christ staring and sneering at him from everywhere, and innocently he reached out to crush them...and it killed him." This philosophical-religious vision enabled conservative intellectuals to invest "the crisis of our times" with both historical and metaphysical meaning. Such a vision, in turn, appeared to preclude negotiation, for believers could hardly compromise with issues so fervidly defined as evil. In matters of good and evil, Whittaker Chambers wrote his son, "evil can only be fought." Such absolutist thought poisoned the political climate following World War II and furnished the link that united the efforts of conservatives to establish a moral and intellectual conscience in American society with James Burnham's advocacy of preventive war against the Soviet Union.

THE WIDENING RIVER OF AMERICAN CONSERVATISM

It was as a tripartite movement, then, that Old Right conservatism entered the 1960s, a decade that for many came to represent moral decay in cultural, religious, and sexual behavior. Courts had imposed restrictions on school prayer yet took them away on abortion. New Deal liberalism, identified with labor unions, blue-collar politics and middle-class reform, had metamorphosed into "gnosticism," the "divinization of society and government." Too many incursions of the Left had produced social schemes that ignored human realities and imposed new regulations on middle Americans. For those who saw themselves as Truman (cold war liberal) Democrats, the high tide of political irresponsibility came in 1972 when the Democratic party nominated as its presidential standard bearer South Dakota senator George McGovern. A dove on the war in Vietnam and a proponent of egalitarian policies, his candidacy made many old-style liberals newly receptive to conservative politics.

The cultural polarization of the 1960s spawned additional expressions of conservatism. Among them were talented wordsmiths who came to be called the neoconservatives. In Irving Kristol's formulation, they were "liberals who had been mugged by reality." Perhaps few other movements have had so many visible intellectual leaders relative to their small public following. Settled in the universities and the media, their names dotted the pages of the intellectual journals: Irving Kristol and Gertrude Himmelfarb, Norman Podhoretz and Midge Decter, Nathan Glazer, Daniel Patrick Moynihan, Richard Pipes, and Jeane Kirkpatrick. They founded the *Public Interest* as one of their flagship publications and redirected *Commentary*, founded as a pro-Israeli, anti-Soviet periodical in the early years of the cold war, into the leading neoconservative publication. Read in the White House and discussed by foreign heads of government, the public policy intellectuals defended the welfare state but opposed the Great Society version of it. Whereas the Old Right had opposed New Deal programs such as social security and the Tennessee Valley Authority, neoconservative contributors to *Commentary* and

Public Interest focused their wrath on the Office of Economic Opportunity, affirmative action, and employment quotas.

The neoconservatives insisted that excessive government programs, made worse by a redistributive bias, had resulted in bureaucratic overload, attenuating the conditions of freedom. "Wherever possible," wrote Kristol, "people should be allowed to keep their own money—rather than having it transferred (via taxes) to the state—on condition that they put it to certain defined uses." Aid to Families with Dependent Children, for example, can become a narcotic, whereas tax deductions for private pensions and insurance programs effectively combine government encouragement and market decisions. As former liberal Democrats, with a newly acquired sense of the limits to political promises and social expectations, neoconservatives understood that the answer to many problems is not no regulation but more intelligent regulation: limited government, yes; unlimited absence of government, no. Above all, what must be avoided is utopianism— meaning, in Jeane Kirkpatrick's words, "excessive faith in reason, equality, democracy, social engineering, [and] moral idealism." A "new class" of social engineers had arisen to manipulate society as if one could create "a world without poverty," "a world without hate," and "a world without war." Kirkpatrick's attack coincided with the views of fellow neoconservative Irving Kristol, who argued that poverty can never be abolished by economic redistribution because "there is never enough to redistribute." Moreover, words like *poor* and *handicapped* often mislead. They rightly suggest obligation to those in difficult circumstances, but should not be understood as conferring "rights" to the property of others. Equality of opportunity in a free society would not create equality of conditions, nor should affirmative action policies run interference toward that end. The essential answer, Kristol concluded, lay in market-driven economic growth, as economic conservatives and classical liberals before him had insisted.

In foreign affairs lay a second factor crucial to the emergence of neoconservatism. Originally a part of the anticommunist coalition that dominated American liberalism since the late 1940s, a number of Democrats grew uneasy during the early 1970s as the McGovern wing of the Democratic party gained strength and, still later, Americans elected Jimmy Carter to the presidency. Podhoretz, Kirkpatrick, Decter, Moynihan, Glazer, and Ben Wattenberg feared that Carter had cast traditional balance of power politics aside in the belief that communist expansion and Third World revolution no longer posed major threats to American security. Particular concern arose over Middle Eastern policy. Because many of the neoconservative intellectuals were Jewish, they viewed with alarm President Carter's efforts to negotiate with Arab leaders. Might not his administration force Israel to trade land for empty promises of peace? Carter's pursuit of a Middle East settlement that included a homeland for Palestinian refugees did not sever traditional Democratic ties with the American Jewish community, but it did lead to a break with the neoconservative vanguard. Several who had once scorned the "paranoid" style of Goldwaterism, in the 1980s turned to Ronald Reagan, who, like the Arizona senator, stressed the need for economic growth and limited government and opposed the progressive income tax as socialistic and interest group politics as disruptive, one step from class warfare. Both spoke of a "moral crisis" in America, and in foreign relations occasionally hinted of nuclear war with the Soviets. Though small in number, the neoconservatives not only contributed a number of its own to serve in the Reagan administration, but provided an important new base in the public forum of ideas.

Concurrent with the neoconservative revolt there developed a more broadly based conservatism that political analyst Kevin Phillips called the New Right. The movement took wing on an acute sense that the 1960s had inaugurated moral decay in society. It remembered that Senator Barry Goldwater had led the conservative Right against the policies of the Kennedy and Johnson administrations, though not always with gratitude. The new populist Right's political program included issues that had never won the senator's support. The Old Right funded government programs lavishly to contain communism abroad but was penurious on domestic programs. The Old Right had focused almost entirely on economic issues; the New Right would stress domestic social issues and was prepared to mobilize government on their behalf. Analysts found it remarkable that the populist Right coalesced around a host of frustrations from within its traditional base of support, among them President Nixon's policy of détente and penchant for expedient politics, the crimes of Watergate, and the naming of liberal Republican Nelson Rockefeller as vice-president. During the same decade the New Right opposed the equal rights amendment, abortion on demand, gay action groups, federal social action programs, busing, SALT II, and the Panama Canal Treaty. Its leaders put a positive gloss on the new opposition, seeking a human life amendment, the protection of school prayer, the teaching of "scientific creationism," and increased defense spending— the last a costly and symbolic response to the unhappy conclusion of the war in Vietnam. The Old Right had been ready enough to spend billions in its anticommunist crusade; the New Right agreed and incorporated that into a more nationalistic stance on all foreign issues.

Combining themes of economic libertarianism, social traditionalism, and militant anticommunism, the New Right's "newness" reflected both its timing (to defend against the perceived victory of Great Society liberalism and the threat Watergate posed to conservatism's future) and its emphasis on social issues, anti-elite rhetoric, and populist inclinations. Its core leaders included Richard Viguerie, a direct-mail fundraiser; Howard Phillips, head of Conservative Caucus; Paul Weyrich, head of the Committee for the Survival of a Free Congress; John Terry Dolan, head of the National Conservative Political Action Committee; and Jesse Helms, head of the Congressional Club. Others closely linked with the core leaders were Phyllis Schlafly, who organized against the equal rights amendment; Pat Buchanan, political columnist and Nixon operative; and religious figures, including Pat Robertson and Jerry Falwell. By the end of the 1970s they comprised a political network of research institutes, newsletters, direct-mail fundraising, action committees, and television stations that effectively mobilized new constituencies in both local and national elections.

The New Right affirmed both God and capitalism, a linkage most clearly apparent in George Gilder's popular success, *Wealth and Poverty* (1981). With this book, Gilder emerged during the early years of the Reagan administration as the chief theologian of supply-side economics. From its pages appeared capitalists dressed not as profit maximizers and robber barons but as workers in God's vineyard. The "function of the rich," in Gilder's formulation, lay in "fostering opportunities for the classes below them in the continuous drama of creation of wealth and progress." What sounded like the trickle-down theory of Sumner and Hoover became, in the hands of Gilder, a theological justification of triumphant capitalism. Productivity and wealth and the sacredness of entrepreneurial activity were joined with profamily social issues, work, family, and faith. In a revision of traditional conservative philosophy, individualism became community: the free market would teach Americans "the brotherhood of man and the fatherhood of God."

The tenor of Gilder's analysis reflected the rise in the late 1970s of a related branch of the conservative movement called the religious Right. Convinced that secular society had grown increasingly hostile to religious practice, and energized by Supreme Court decisions on school prayer, abortion, and pornography, the resurgence of religious fundamentalism vastly strengthened the conservative movement. Emergent organizations such as the Moral Majority, the Christian Voice, the Religious Roundtable, and Christian Coalition for Legislative Action, together with energetic leaders such as Ed McAteer and Pat Robertson and Jerry Falwell, constituted a profamily movement that understood freedom less in economic terms than in the right to think for themselves and raise families free of obtrusive government. Its heart and soul could be found among white evangelical and fundamentalist Christians, who saw the promise of American life as being undercut by social and spiritual decay: high divorce rates, broken homes, promiscuity, abortion, and the rise of feminist politics. These were the social issues of the 1970s, taken up by evangelicals and fundamentalists who, while opposed to any theory of political salvation, nevertheless once again turned political to do what metaphysics once did to bring "virtue" and unity to American society. It was they who built the superchurches and electronic ministries that connected independent fundamentalist churches nationwide.

The election in 1976 of Jimmy Carter, a Baptist Sunday school teacher and born-again Christian, heightened the self-esteem of religious conservatives. By 1980, however, the New Right, then the most powerful political movement in the nation, had grown disenchanted with the president's lack of assertiveness and had reverted to their decade-and-a-half revolt against the Democrats, largely because of civil rights. A substantial majority of its members joined the neoconservatives and the traditional pro-business, antidistributive, and tax-cutting Republican party base to make up the Reagan coalition.

In a few short years the coalition achieved part of what it sought. Federal tax rates were lowered and the federal government reduced its oversight role in business activity. The inflationary spiral of the 1970s was broken, and domestic programs for the nonworking poor were reduced. Little was done on social issues, however. Illegitimacy, divorce, and family patterns remained much as they had been, in part because mainstream conservatives were uneasy with religious fundamentalists' seeming obsession with school prayer, creationism, and below-the-belt social issues.

"We are speaking the language of Charles Grandison Finney," said Ralph Reed, executive director of the Christian Coalition. "But the larger society suspects that they hear the sneering voices of Hiram Wesley Evans and George Wallace." With the exception of the abortion issue, however, conservative Christians in the past quarter-century have not entered politics for theological reasons. Relatively few have problems with Catholics and Jews of similar moral persuasion. Rather, they wish to challenge the prevalence of pornography and sexual licentiousness in ways that courts and the media are reluctant to do. The wider culture moved in on them before they moved outward to it.

In other areas activist government continued without a hitch, especially in foreign policy. It seemed fitting that the most astonishing event of the 1980s—the collapse of communism in Eastern Europe and the breakup of the Soviet Union—came with an authentic conservative in the White House. Few had spoken out more clearly against communist power abroad or more eloquently about freedom at home than had Ronald Reagan. Although more was involved in the communist crack-up, conservatives could claim that their expensive hard-line policies had at least hastened the demise of their oldest and greatest foreign enemy.

A BACKWARD GLANCE

A backward glance at the wayward course of American history reveals that as liberalism in the twentieth century adopted a positive role for government, in hopes of sheltering workers from the harsh winds of chaotic capitalism, conservatives in large numbers moved toward a laissez-faire position. They traded positions much in the manner of the two drunks who, as Abraham Lincoln told it, "engaged in a fight with their greatcoats on, which fight, after a long and rather harmless contest, ended in each having fought himself out of his own coat and into that of the other." In theory at least, if not always in practice, mainstream American conservatism has had much in common with the Manchester liberalism of the nineteenth century, when even William Graham Sumner, resolutely opposed to government intervention in the economy, might with reason have called himself a liberal. Prior to his day, it was the "liberal" Jeffersonians who thought that government best which governed least and the "conservative" Hamilton who stood for the active state. Whatever the crisis of the age or the vagaries of the moment, the basic differences between liberals and conservatives during the twentieth century have lain in their class commitments, feelings about change, and attitude toward government. Believing that the market system is an impartial, self-equilibrating mechanism, conservatives trust it instead of liberal reformers to define the procedures of economic activity and to allocate rewards efficiently. Conservatives have long insisted that liberals embody "the morale of an army on the march," to adopt an observation that Michel Chevalier, a nineteenth-century French visitor to the United States, once made of the American people. They argue that liberals, rationalistic in method, relativistic in standards, and permissive in morals, seek always to define new rights, prepare new laws, and prescribe initiatives to prevent new oppressions from harming people.

How ironic when there emerged within the ranks of conservatism a populist

Right, pursuing an activist government strategy to ensure a moral consensus rooted in Christian piety. It produced an unstable coalition, based on a contradiction. Mainstream Republicans defend the free market, free trade, and the global economy, at the same time posing as advocates of community and family values. The traditionalist wing of the conservative movement, however, insists that nothing else has wreaked such havoc on traditional values and institutions as has individualistic capitalism. Small towns, small businesses, family farms, craftsmanship, a powerful sense of community-rootedness, and more have been battered by the gospel of efficiency and profit. The "creative destruction" of capitalism, in Joseph Schumpeter's phrase, produced vastly higher living standards, but the cost was heavy.

That internal contradiction has not been resolved. The religious Right reflects a disposition more than a doctrine; their preference for the familiar belief, the tried program, and the orthodox understanding of God and morality drove them into politics. The traditional base of conservatism in politics, however, has responded more readily to doctrine, the crucial component of which is private property. Although American liberals too have appreciated private property and the market system, conservatives have sanctified both. For Old Right members of the conservative coalition, property provides a main avenue for incentive, risk taking, and freedom. Traditionalist conservatives understand private property as guaranteeing liberty, since its existence limits the economic power of the state and in addition provides incentives for the less virtuous aspects of human nature. Although a resolution of those differences is no nearer than it was forty years ago, when "fusionism" was all the rage in conservative circles, in the contending branches of conservatism one sees an instructive front-page story on the untidy politics of American democracy at work and of an unsettled, pluralist society still in formation.

Ronald Lora and William Henry Longton

Part One

LAISSEZ-FAIRE AND PRO-BUSINESS JOURNALS

Conservatism of place, reverence for traditional ways, and affection for the proliferating variety of classes and institutions encountered an environment more challenging in the United States than anywhere else in the industrial world. During the century following the birth of the Republic, the forces of democracy and industrialization swept so powerfully through society that the conservatism of John Adams, John C. Calhoun, and Orestes Brownson was pushed toward the corners of political and intellectual life. Conservative journals at the turn of the twentieth century reflected that change as they drew ever more heavily on the American idea of freedom and individualism. Throughout the previous two centuries, however, freedom had not meant one particular thing. During the colonial era, Puritan ministers located freedom in submission to God as revealed in the Scriptures, especially as they interpreted them. One could perceive freedom while remaining a slave of right conduct. In a later formulation offered by the Jeffersonians, freedom meant throwing off restraining institutions (such as a monarchy, established church, and standing army) or injurious masters (such as one's baser self, religious prejudices, and ignorance). The individual was not yet master, for the cultural milieu and deferential politics of the age invested freedom with a public character that it would not later possess.

Other understandings competed, but as the republican experiment matured, Jacksonian philosophy promoted federal laissez faire, leaving the people to free enterprise. Moreover, the westward movement of thousands, then millions, of settlers pressed forward the question as to how individuals could best protect freedom. The answer more often than not centered on property. Its protection under the Fourteenth Amendment, reaffirmed by judicial review, became the dominant form of freedom talk. Once it moved to the center of political discourse, and the first reading of the new biology defended competition as a way of life, the related doctrine of laissez faire emerged triumphant. It held that the natural course of events, if undisturbed by regulatory policies, would work toward the maximum well-being of the individual and, by extension, society. Derived from the French Physiocrats of the eighteenth century and the work of Adam Smith, Jeremy Bentham, and John Stuart Mill, the principle of state noninterference—in rhetoric, if not practice—assumed the status of natural law. A generation of laissez-faire conservatives that overlooked the Scottish philosopher's endorsement of trade unions and public works could with little difficulty maneuver the conservative aspects of his thought to such a conclusion.

Contributors to the journals represented in Part One defended a concept they termed "individualism." It meant the primacy of personal choice and self-determination. If for Alexis de Tocqueville, individualism raised alarms about diminished civic responsibility, a majority of Americans responded more favorably to Ralph Waldo Emerson's celebration of self-reliance. Among the educated, individualism possessed economic and political components, both associated with John Locke's theory of property and the doctrine of unalienable rights. In endless editorials and sermons of the post-Civil War era, however, economic and political interests merged in the individual. Intertwined, they prospered under the prevailing conditions of laissez-faire political economy, as conservatives and classical liberals, many of whom were one and the same, argued that the possession of property enlarged a person's scope for free activity.

The two periodicals in this part whose origins lay in the nineteenth century placed their doctrine of freedom vigorously against America's imperialist outburst during the 1890s. Writers in both the *Conservative* and the *Conservative Review* relied heavily on constitutional arguments. Expansion into contiguous areas, from ocean to ocean, was one thing, having enjoyed the support even of strict constructionist Thomas Jefferson. Aggression in noncontiguous territory was quite another matter. Imperialism meant governing other peoples in ways that were inconsistent with the political principle of freedom, a point that William Graham Sumner also made repeatedly. Other reasons surfaced. Given their non-Western customs, their different color and historical experience, and the supposed problems of race mixing, Filipinos were "unassimilable." In an era when Anglo-Saxon Christians were thought to enjoy the special favor of Providence, it was a common argument. On balance, however, conservatives stated their anti-imperialist case in terms of political philosophy: if republican government rests on the consent of the governed, its denial would convert the United States into an empire, inhospitable to liberty under law.

By the testimony of these pages, at the beginning of the twentieth century the United States was securely in the grip of free-market ideology, watered down by little save business advocacy of high tariffs and opposition to the labor movement. The *Conservative*, the *Exponent, American Industries*, and *Constitutional Review* carried in their pages a deep hostility to unions as inimical to economic progress and coercive in that they bolstered the constituency supportive of "class legislation." As the value of competition yielded in importance to that of profit and individual initiative, the principle of individualism served to promote monopoly. One wing of the progressives—and a larger wing of New Dealers—would conclude with

John Dewey that "there is a perversion of the whole ideal of individualism to conform to the practices of a pecuniary culture." Individual decisionmaking too often protected neither the investors nor the environment, and it saw little profit in extending electricity to American farms. In 1900, however, all that lay in the future.

The dynamic agents of social change in the United States at the turn of the century primarily came from the business and managerial classes. The life of Henry Ford represents as well as any other the dichotomy of conservative inclination and uprooting social change. In habits and opinions the inventor of the mass-produced automobile was deeply conservative, much enamored of agricultural routines and the old houses of early America and elsewhere. Yet he was second to none in forcing a people to adopt a change in values and mobility and economic growth that closed the door to the cultural traditions of his youth. His story highlights the dilemma genuine conservatives have faced in the United States, indeed in modern history.

Seven decades after Ford's application of the moving assembly line to the automobile industry, Robert Bellah, co-author of *Habits of the Heart* (1985), an examination of the ideas of individualism and commitment published when Ronald Reagan occupied the White House, worried that "individualism may have grown cancerous" and harmful to freedom itself. But conditions then differed significantly from those that existed in 1900, when the nation was still primarily rural, its citizens rooted in the routines of smalltown life, and so much of its business conducted by a handshake. In that world, individual freedom evaded the load of isolation and escape from responsibility that Tocqueville had assigned it. When J. Sterling Morton, editor of the *Conservative*, printed as "conservatisms" such statements as "imposed obligations are slavery" and "no man is responsible for the acts of another unless he assumes the obligation," he did not believe that he was asocial, or irresponsible, or subversive of Christian obligation to others. Rather, he understood individualism to mean the opportunity to so improve or enrich oneself that society itself would benefit, in definite and assignable ways. Moreover, individualist theory fit well the views not only of Social Darwinists, but of those who championed the gospel of wealth: do whatever you can to increase your competence, but share it before death comes. Such a theory could—and did—rationalize the hard work of a great many entrepreneurs of the late nineteenth century. It also provided a powerful thread of continuity in American history.

Conservative
1898–1902

The burgeoning urban populations, the giant corporations, and the rise of numerous movements protesting traditional economic and political assumptions in late nineteenth-century America tried the patience of political and intellectual leaders who had long called themselves Jeffersonians. One such person was J. Sterling Morton, the distinguished Nebraska statesman who served the territory as editor, boomer, and political leader and later the state and nation as conservationist, U.S. secretary of agriculture, and once again as editor of a journal of discussion, the *Conservative*. Rooted in rural, smalltown America, Morton placed the *Conservative*, which he edited and published on the west bank of the Missouri River from 1898 until his death in April 1902, at the service of Jeffersonianism as it was generally understood before political philosophers of the twentieth century harnessed the great Virginian to their dreams of social democracy. In the last eloquent effort of his life, Morton hoped "to do a large missionary work among the economic savages of the Western country."[1]

Born in New York in 1832 and raised in Michigan, Sterling Morton on the October day of his wedding in 1854 set out with his bride to make his fortune in the Nebraska Territory. Traveling to Chicago and then south to St. Louis by rail, the Mortons took a steamer to St. Joseph, arrived at Council Bluffs by stage, and settled in Bellevue during the first winter. Shortly after arriving in Nebraska, Morton bought a quarter-section of land west of Nebraska City for $200 from the man who had preempted it from the government. Living in a small log house, he supervised the construction of a four-room frame house. Several remodelings through the decades produced Arbor Lodge, the stately mansion that stands today on that same parcel of land on the subhumid prairie, a monument to one of our most devoted conservationists.

In 1854, however, Nebraska was not yet a white man's land. Herds of buffalo still roamed the lower Platte, and the footsteps of Indians sounded in the near distance. Although few whites, save for trappers, hunters, and settlers who could go no farther, lived in the territory, there was much activity. The Platte Valley was a major highway to the West. Gold seekers and Mormons, missionaries and migrants filled the overland trails before the Civil War. As the land yielded to permanent settlement, young Morton saw with his own eyes the process of civilization of which Frederick Jackson Turner was to write so eloquently. Nebraska City, Morton's adopted town, was a favored location in prairie country. It became a shipping center, supplying the settlers who passed through and the military outposts established in part to protect them. There, at 933 feet altitude, the undulating land is rich, the water good. The silty loess soils are fertile and deep, yielding easily to the plow. Nebraska City was hot in summer and cold in winter, but enjoyed fairly dependable rainfall. Beyond Kearney, however, just 180 miles west and 2,100 feet above sea level, and on out to Scottsbluff, where at 3,900 feet the annual rainfall averaged sixteen inches, the land was far more resistant to settlers' dreams.

Five months after entering Nebraska, Morton agreed to edit the *Nebraska City News*, the only newspaper both published and printed in Nebraska at the time. That decision marked the beginning of his rise to eminence, for frontier editors wielded considerable power. Their newspapers educated citizens and molded opinion. Other than letters from home and the welcome conversation of travelers, they often were the sole source of news and link to a larger world. Battles for political power and economic development were fought in the newspapers as well as in the sometimes raucous legislatures. Not surprisingly, an impressive number of early political leaders emerged from the ranks of journalism. In this motley world where rancorous debate flourished, life was often at risk, and versatility conferred fitness in the struggle for existence, young Morton made his way with an eye to the main chance.[2]

His literary and forensic talents soon brought him into politics. President Buchanan appointed him secretary of the Territory of Nebraska, during which time he served a brief stint as acting governor. In succeeding years he sought office repeatedly, usually to be turned aside. Meanwhile, the young editor from Otoe County used his position in newspapering and politics to spread his agricultural and tree planting convictions across the Territory. It was his resolution that in 1872 established Arbor Day in Nebraska. Years later, when the holiday was recognized throughout the country, his birthday, 22 April, would become the official date of recognition. Morton's work in agriculture, arboriculture, and horticulture, together with his hard money views, made him a worthy candidate to head the young U.S. Department of Agriculture. He served at President Cleveland's request from 1893 to 1897, the first person from west of the Missouri River to hold a cabinet position. Some believed that the secretary of agriculture, whose courage and moral integrity were not in doubt, would have made an excellent president, but he was in fact too independent and contemptuous of the crowd and popular vagaries to have been an effective candidate.[3]

When William McKinley defeated William Jennings Bryan in their first encounter, Secretary Morton at sixty-four was not ready to retire. Casting about for a creative outlet to harness his energies, he found his four sons, already successful and desirous of keeping their father occupied near home, ready to help. Together they raised capital, incorporated the Morton Printing Company, and the former agriculture secretary again became an editor, this time of a new weekly, called the *Conservative*. The statement of purpose printed in the first number on 14 July, 1898, informed readers that the *Conservative* would publish "in the interest of the conservation of all that is deemed desirable in the social, industrial and political life of the United States." It would defend the rights of individuals and the rights of labor as well as respect the rights of capital. The gold standard would with all vigor be extolled as the measure of honesty and justice in political economy. Because all are "laborers," no attempts to divide Americans into classes could be recognized. Frugality at all levels of government deserved support, as did the civil service merit system. Finally, the *Conservative* hoped to become "useful as a truth-teller, and influential as a militant exponent of everything...which the experience of one hundred and twenty-two years of national independence has proved to be worth conserving." As the nation was entering the progressive era, Morton wrote to a correspondent that he hoped in his years as editor to protect individuals against the group by preaching the message of economic freedom to "the free silver sinners of this country."[4]

Morton's journal of discussion appeared every Thursday. Its typography was extremely neat. In approximately sixteen pages, with three columns per page, the *Conservative* covered a wide range of topics, including trusts, sound money, politics, trees and conservation, railroads, and William Jennings Bryan, whose activities appeared under the heading "Bryanarchy."[5] The arguments against overseas expansion were thoroughly aired. The editor wrote much for his own weekly, but solicited articles from persons he thought would make competent contributors and frequently reprinted articles and speeches that interested him.[6] William Graham Sumner appeared, with the first number carrying an extract from "What the Social Classes Owe to Each Other." So did Edward Atkinson, advocate of hard currency and one of the founders of the *Nation*, whose western counterpart the *Conservative* hoped to become. Other contributors included Carl Schurz, Chicago professor J. Lawrence Laughlin, Dr. George L. Miller, editor of the *Omaha Daily and Weekly Herald* and old friend, and Professor Arthur Latham Perry of Williams College, author of *Elements of Political Economy*. The majority of contributors, however, were lesser-known persons—local leaders, businessmen, Western history enthusiasts. All were treated equally, regardless of reputation; no contributor received payment for his thoughts.

Occasionally entire numbers were devoted to single themes, or to symposiums on education and the chances for success of young men in the United States. "American Miscellany" sections appeared regularly, as did "Scientific Miscellany," "Current Comment," and peppery comments on politics. Contributors at times submitted apothegms that appeared in a column of "Conservatisms"—for example—

- Imposed obligations are slavery.
- Conservatism is the acme of intelligent self-preservation, individual or national.
- There is nothing higher or nobler than intelligent self-control.

- No man is responsible for the acts of another unless he assumes the obligation.
- Wars inaugurated for any other purpose than national preservation are usurpation of power by the government.
- The true conservative thinks. The true conservative reads. The true conservative thinks again.[7]

Although Morton involved himself in the business affairs of the *Conservative*, day-to-day responsibility fell to John Nordhouse, who doubled as private secretary, a position he held while the editor had been U.S. secretary of agriculture. Subscribers received the weekly for the modest charge of $1.50 per year, payable in advance. When important events loomed in the near future, such as the presidential election of 1900, readers were offered a three-month subscription for thirty-three cents.[8] Advertisements became an increasingly important source of revenue, filling three pages per issue at first and growing to nine or ten during the last year of publication. A thousand dollars bought a full-page advertisement for a year. Wanting desperately for the operation to pay for itself, Morton conducted a voluminous correspondence to drum up support from all manner of businesses, the railroads, and local banks.[9] The subscription list varied from 5,000 to 15,000, with a middle number the normal printing. Special issues, however, called for larger printings, up to 18,000, a good number a century ago.[10] The *Conservative* was in competent hands in both an editorial and business way, but was so integrally connected with Morton's political and intellectual interests that with the editor's death, it ceased publication.

In assessing the intellectual thrust of the *Conservative*, it is important to note that the editor took pride in being a Jeffersonian. Morton venerated the Sage of Monticello, whose works he owned, and Monticello loomed in the background as he remodeled Arbor Lodge. By Jeffersonian, Morton meant a believer in limited government, the strict construction of the Constitution, religious toleration, the love of liberty, and the practice of individual freedoms. Especially did he insist with William Graham Sumner that the federal government not direct the economic life of society, pass protective tariffs, grant subsidies to special interest groups, or perform tasks normally undertaken by families. He held to the primacy of the individual over the government in time and in moral authority. The government protected life, liberty, and property; all else was oppression.[11] This seems clear enough, yet contradictions remained. When thinking of the vast social and economic transformations that attended the industrial process, the intellectual writing privately remembered another Jefferson who held that intelligent citizens of a republic could through a process of reasoning better determine the nature of appropriate government actions than by slavishly following tradition: "Each man must do his own thinking and each age determines its own social and political problems for itself. The Past can not prescribe with accuracy for the Present."[12]

In Morton's estimate, however, the powerful currents of political and economic protest that swirled about in the 1890s, calling for a more just America, forced this Jeffersonian principle to yield to others with more dogmatic import. Again and again, the themes of self-reliance and self-denial echoed from the *Conservative* as the keys to individual success or failure. As he had staked all on the future of the West, so might other risk takers find success in the twentieth century. Morton's faith in golden America found support in a symposium published on the young man's chances for success under existing economic conditions. The fifteen participants were self-made men, representing the legal, railroad, educational, ministerial, and journalistic fields. A pronounced optimism that the road to success had never been more easily traveled suffused the symposium columns. Diligent work was required, and loyalty and fidelity, too, but effort would be noticed and in time rewarded. "To say that the young man who has the greatest talent or natural aptitude for the work will get to the top, is to state a truism that applies to every...profession," wrote the editor of the *Chicago Record-Herald*.[13]

Men in the full swing of their careers cannot be expected to appear as detached intellectuals, but few other symposiums have been so lacking in detachment and objectivity. The Horatio Alger stories popular at the time often displayed greater realism. Contributors recognized, as Alger did not, that success under modern conditions required technological skill and organizational know-how. Unlike the popular writer of boys' stories, however, none assigned a role to luck. Chance meant opportunity, not good fortune. The symposium closed with lines that defined the stance of the symposium participants:

> There's little in life but labor;
> And tomorrow may find that a dream;
> Success is the bride of endeavor,
> And luck but a meteor's gleam.

The Alger hero succeeded in life, to be sure, but not merely because he mixed work with ability. He willingly accepted help from friends as he kept watch for fortune to smile. Symposium contributors, on the other hand, argued that the successful created their opportunities. Gone were the humility, benevolence, and sense of creaturehood in a circle of friends that readers found endearing in Alger.

Several readers complained that contributors, "selected from the hirelings of plutocracy," saw success on a one-dimensional and morally hazardous plane of money and material accumulation. The charge was just. Only one had expressed doubts about the morality of those who owned and operated society. The president of small Defiance College (Ohio) had warned against the young men who in the "hurry up" age of turn-of-the-century America neglected their education in pursuit of the Big Money: "The mercenary spirit of our age is...the greatest foe of education and religion. In our hurry to get rich we have scarcely time to become either learned or pious." The celebration of America found a large audience, however, as demand exceeded the week's printing of 17,500. Other newspapers reprinted portions of the "Young Man's Chances," and Morton did likewise in the following month.[14]

What the *Conservative* feared above all else from its vantage point in the West was the decline of individuality in the face of a coming collectivism. Herbert Spencer's dictum that no government can be better than the people who staff it and

George Washington's warning sounded in his Farewell Address, that men beware of "that love of power and proneness to abuse it, which predominate in the human heart," were common themes. The "polishing processes of modern civilization seem to grind away all of the sharp corners of individuality," wrote one contributor; concentrated urban centers "grind away and erase independence." The once-proud individual melts into the crowd, and civilization itself weakens before the onslaught of deracinating massness and concentration. In the presence of the clamor that "government shall run railroads, telegraphs, farms, and warehouses, or confronted by combined and arrogant avarice, commanding that taxes shall be laid upon *all* to make incomes for a *few*," only educated citizens, themselves rededicated to defend the limited powers doctrine in the American constitutional tradition, could effectively conserve the Republic.[15]

Morton's administration of the Department of Agriculture faithfully reflected his views on government. He had proved himself a forceful taskmaster, establishing the civil service system and repeatedly insisting that department personnel practice efficiency and frugality in the use of public funds. Not long after assuming office, he wrote to the chief of the Weather Bureau complaining of "luxurious extravagance" and recommending cutbacks and job terminations. To the superintendent of the Veterinary Experiment Station in Washington, D.C., the new secretary bluntly declared his seriousness of purpose: "I wish it distinctly understood that wherever there is an opportunity to economize, it should be embraced with alacrity, and that if you do not economize someone will be put in your place who will." No money would be spent to eradicate weeds, sell seeds, advertise for farm groups, subsidize starch plants, push for tariff support, or inspect meat. Indeed, he vigorously opposed the passage of pure food laws. What good would food investigations do? Citizens concerned for their own health will check food themselves. There was little doubt that President Cleveland had found a serious follower of the Jeffersonian gospel on government. During his tenure in office, the Department of Agriculture returned to the Treasury a little more than $2 million, about 18.5 percent of what had been appropriated.[16]

Among the creative achievements for which Morton is best known, insofar as he is known at all beyond the plains country, was his crusade to plant trees. Nothing expressed better his forward-looking self. There is a quiet drama in seeing the conservative take a grand risk, leaving settled society for a largely treeless section of the old Louisiana Purchase with few signs of successful settlement, preparing to improve the environment for future generations. Having played in the Michigan woods as a child, the pioneer settler stood aghast at the barrenness of the prairies. Although he came to love the expanse of the western horizon, there were moments in the early years when it was touch-and-go whether the psychological and aesthetic losses occasioned by the wind-swept landscape would drive him to heed his father's advice and return home. From the beginning, he had trees sent to him from the East, not only shade and forest trees but several varieties of fruit trees. Together he and his young wife made plans for an orchard. Meanwhile, he championed the planting and preservation of trees to all who read the *Nebraska City News*, and he promoted the cause in his political work. There were many in the prairie states who cared deeply about trees and forests, and territorial legislatures added their encouragement, but it was Morton's resolution the Nebraska legislature accepted, establishing that one day each year be devoted to tree planting. On that first Arbor Day in April 1872, a splendid moment in American conservation history, Nebraskans planted a million trees.[17] On the occasion of the first tree planting celebration in Nebraska, Morton wrote, in the *Omaha Daily Herald:*

Trees grow in time. The poorest landowner...has just as large a fortune, of time, secured to him, as has the richest. And the rain and sunshine and seasons will be his partners, just as genially and gently as they will be those of any millionaire, and will make the trees planted by the poor man grow just as grandly and beautifully as those planted by the opulent....There is a true triumph in the unswerving integrity and genuine democracy of trees, for they refuse to be influenced by money or social position and thus tower morally, as well as physically, high above Congressmen and many other patriots of this dollaring age.[18]

Behind the poetry, the founder of Arbor Day had a solid grip on the economic and political necessity of trees. From the Dakotas to Texas, wood and water were scarce, an unfortunate fact that provoked bitter complaints from the overlanders and early settlers. This more than pioneer hardships and hostile Indians kept settlers from the prairie plains before the Civil War. Wood was needed for fuel, construction, fencing, and, some believed, even to bring rain.[19] With a vigorous tree planting campaign, barren Nebraska in its competition with other states could place its claim on the future: timber would lure settlers, and settlers would bring the railroads, statehood, and economic prosperity. His several positions as acting territorial governor and legislator, newspaper editor, and railroad agent provided Morton with an ideal base from which to promote trees, ever mindful of what the publicity would do for Nebraska as a center of environmental improvement.

It was predictable that the *Conservative* would become one more vehicle for Morton's crusade. Nearly every number of the *Conservative* carried word of forestry, conservation, and horticulture. A special *Arbor Day* edition, opening with the admonition to "Plant Trees," reminded readers of other uses of trees. They provided railroad ties and telegraph and telephone poles; they provided shade, sheltered wildlife, and protected against winter blasts; retained water and soil and protected river banks; provided wood for wagons, implements, and furniture. The aesthetic dimension of finely planted groves enhanced the spirit against the bleakness of winter.[20] City dwellers learned that trees and parks would benefit them by tempering the heat reflected from brick and asphalt and by helping to purify the air of noxious fumes. Articles pertaining to woodland management on farms were more common, however. Several called for planning on a large scale. Unless inducements in the form of reduced taxes were offered, private capital would not flow into forest management. Private forests (95 percent of the woodlands in the United States) would vanish. Sounding a more sentimental theme, various writers proffered farm beautification as one means of keeping sons and daughters at home, a plea that resonated less and less in an urbanizing society. Create a farm home environment that is "rich in cultivating influences, a live inspiration, a perennial joy to the farmer, his wife and children," so that if children head for the city "they will never fully rest till they come back to the old farmstead."   In a triumph of hope over reality, E. Benjamin Andrews of the University of Nebraska told the National Farmers' Congress at Sioux Falls, South Dakota: "You can have this so if you will."[21]

There is a poignancy in this awareness in agrarian America that husbands and fathers must somehow surmount their cash-poor status so as to enrich and lighten the burdens shouldered by their wives and daughters: "the dreary sameness of their experience, rare breaks or pauses in work that can never end, the treadmill, the plodding, the ever-abiding shadow."[22]   For too many, the years of toil and hardship had smothered the sweet affirmations of womanhood.

As Morton entered the evening of his life, nothing save the loss of a family member caused him such bereavement as the destruction of fruit or forest that he would never see replaced in size and character. He was quite prepared to write obituaries to trees downed by a storm.[23] This sentimental identity with nature's bounty colored too his views of Christmas, which he shared with readers of the *New York World* in December 1901. As the seasonal pomp and display of worldly wealth ill fits the teachings of the man from Nazareth, so "cutting down symmetrical and beautiful young conifers to hang toys upon is rank treason to posterity, whose lumber and timber are thus wantonly wasted. Christmas trees...are the destruction of a necessity for coming generations, to merely please the children of this generation. The Christmas tree ought to be abolished."[24]

More central to the political objectives of the *Conservative* was its campaign for sound money. Nearly every issue carried at least a short plea for the virtues of the gold standard. Quotations abounded from Jefferson, Paine, Adams, and Webster, all against the issuing of paper money. The conservative Nebraska Democrat had given much thought to money and had not trimmed on the matter when it would have been politically expedient to do so. He refused to truck with farmers of the South and West who had long protested the unprofitableness of their vocation. Nor would he recognize that the Populist search for a cheaper currency grew not out of agrarian radicalism but out of the farm depressions of the late nineteenth century. With silver readily available, Populists asked, why not enter it into the national currency to increase its volume and presumably stir new economic activity? Substantial amounts would almost certainly have had an inflating effect, precisely what farmers wanted. It was on this issue that Nebraska villagers and farmers split as they struggled for political power. Morton, a long-settled pioneer who had never been a dirt farmer, was the leading Gold Democrat in Nebraska to stand against the silver tide. Coin must have intrinsic value, he argued. Silver dollars minted at a sixteen-to-one ratio with gold would cheapen the dollar since sixteen ounces of silver would not, in a free market, buy an ounce of gold. Why subsidize the silver miners while robbing workers of part of their earnings? Sooner or later his countrymen must reckon with the truth that individual welfare rested not on easy money, but on exertion and frugality.[25] Whatever the shortcomings of Populist economic theory, Morton had evaded rather than solved the problem of the nation's serious money shortage.

The money issue lay behind a related theme that brought an incandescent glow to the pages of the *Conservative*: Morton's campaign against William Jennings Bryan. The vitriol poured on "The Commoner" suggests that a personal element was at work, for Bryan had replaced Morton as Mr. Democrat in Nebraska. Although Morton had long carried the flag for the Democracy, he had also demonstrated a notable talent for losing elections. His campaign for Congress in 1860 brought defeat. Nominated for the governorship in 1866, he lost, and then lost again in that year's congressional race. Three subsequent races for the governorship brought no change. Although Nebraska was a Republican state after the Civil War, as were most in the North for the remainder of the century, Morton undermined his various candidacies by his outspoken honesty and known sympathy for large corporations.

Bryan's willingness to cooperate with Populists and to accept the silver issue as his own made a break between the two Democrats inevitable. How difficult Morton found it to read references to the "peerless" leader, the "matchless orator," the "friend of the masses," and "the great commoner." Readers of the *Conservative* prior to the 1900 election were schooled in "Bryanarchy," which Morton eagerly defined: "The difference between anarchy and Bryanarchy is that the former believes in *no* government at all, and the latter believes in no government *without* Bryan. No government is bad enough, and why any sane citizen should yearn for anything worse, is beyond comprehension." Bryan was not unlike Populist demagogues "who turn furrows with their tongues and raise crops by resolutions." All were scamps, out to "farm the farmers."[26]

By election time, Morton had had more than enough and committed the *Conservative* to the victory of McKinley, the lesser of two evils. McKinley would approve an equitable arrangement for the Filipinos, or if not, at least could be depended on "to preserve the present financial fabric." In a postelection analysis, the *Conservative* editor told his readers to rejoice in the triumph of American citizenship over "anarchistic tendencies" and "demagogic appeals to class prejudices." Meanwhile, his correspondence brimmed with admonition for the Democrats to eliminate Bryanarchy or adjourn *sine die*.[27]

Doubting the will of the Democracy to cleanse itself of its free silver heresies, yet unwilling to commit to the imperialistic policies of the Republicans, the conservative Gold Democrat renewed efforts to organize a new national organization to be called the Conservative party. He had pursued this intermittently since 1896, hoping that the best elements of the existing parties, especially conservative Democrats and Republicans at odds with their president over Cuba and the Philippines, could gather in Philadelphia's Independence Hall to support sound money and a tariff for revenue only and to propose an alternative to the imperialistic venturings of President McKinley. His extensive correspondence and frequent appeals in the *Conservative* won attention but moved no one to undertake the needed organizational chores. Most doubted that success would come. Approaching seventy years of age and unwilling to leave Arbor Lodge for extended periods, the editor had tried to accomplish with his pen what only foot soldiers could do, and he had to acknowledge defeat.[28]

Sound money, individualism and self-reliance, limited government, conservation, arboriculture, opposition to Bryanism at home and imperialism abroad—these were salient themes of the *Conservative*, leaving one to be added. The *Conservative* occasionally read as if it were printed in Railroad, USA. No one should have been surprised. When the railroads built westward in the 1860s and 1870s, they enjoyed close relations with the territorial and state governments. The settlers, too, coveted railroads for their communities and as enticements voted bonds for their construction. To isolated communities, the whistle of the locomotive promised markets and prosperity, and brought softer whispers of a place in the national community. Once the railroads were built, a task that had furnished jobs for the local populations and had required food and provisioning, questions arose over their operation. High freight and passenger rates, in the context of drought, insufficient markets, and falling agricultural prices produced some of the most critical battles of the era.

The editor of the *Conservative*, however, never wavered in his conviction that the West required railroads to prosper. An energetic booster of Nebraska while editor of the *Nebraska City News*, Morton had worked assiduously to entice railroads to the territory. Competition among them to obtain settlers was stiff, and when Morton sold his newspaper in 1870, the Chicago, Burlington & Quincy Railroad hired the gifted editor to speak and write on its behalf to promote the sale of its bonds in Iowa and Nebraska, and to serve as a lobbyist in Washington, D. C.[29] He was handsomely rewarded. The Burlington paid him $5,000 per year, plus expenses. Some years saw his income swell to double that figure—and at a time when a factory worker might earn $300 for a year's work. In 1875 Morton wrote to George Pullman, offering his services to the Pullman Corporation, again for $5,000 per year. For a Nebraskan with political ambitions, it was ill-advised to hire out his talents to railroad corporations even as they were coming under popular attack. The question is not one of integrity, for Morton saw little hope for the western economy without a well-developed transportation system. Nevertheless, it would be accurate to describe Arbor Lodge as the house the railroads built.[30]

Years later, wanting to place the *Conservative* on a firm financial base, Morton found it natural to turn to old friends such as Charles Perkins, once the land commissioner and later the president of the Burlington and Missouri. Additional letters went out to the president or general manager of the Union Pacific, the Atchison, Topeka & Santa Fe Railroad System, the Chicago & Northwestern, and the Illinois Central Railroad Company, asking them to take from five hundred to a thousand subscriptions at the regular rate of $1.50 per year.[31]

His message was blunt: the railroads must pay for an articulate voice on their behalf. "In this way," wrote Morton, "a public sentiment may be founded on right premises. The American people are going to be educated either to a regard for the rights of property, or to a communism. The teachers of the latter seem to be far more active than the instructors in the former." It helped that three of his sons at one time or another had worked for the railroads, with Paul then serving as vice-president of the Atchison, Topeka & Santa Fe. In a letter to Kidder-Peabody & Company, Morton appealed to nonrailroad corporations as well: the *Conservative* "must be sustained...by conservative citizens who think it important that the American people continue steadfast to the gold standard. Therefore, I look for advertising patronage from banks, insurance, manufacturing and railroad companies all over the country."[32]

The railroads responded generously, providing the financial base Morton coveted. Each railroad enclosed with its order a list of persons along its lines who were to receive the weekly without cost. Later Morton would suggest that the need to counter Bryan's paper, the *Commoner*, should be sufficient to open the coffers on behalf of his journal. He harbored some hope of pushing circulation to 100,000, in part by getting the *Conservative* into all the rural barbershops in Nebraska, Iowa, and Kansas.[33]

Not surprisingly, the *Conservative* published studies on the benefits railroads brought to the western states—the positive impact on land values, travel, and geographical mobility. Nor did it fail to demonstrate that freight charges on agricultural commodities had declined significantly over the years.[34] He was able to score points with the data published, but in the public mind he was linked forever to the interests of the wealthy and powerful.

How frustrating it was to find one's self-image so at odds with reality. He deemed himself an apostle of Thomas Jefferson. But which Jefferson? In an age of reform, the question mattered. The third president has been claimed by the faithful among antistatists, states-righters, agrarians, rationalists, civil libertarians, constitutional democrats, and isolationists—seven Jeffersons.[35] A case can be made that J. Sterling Morton, when it suited him, found comfort in each of these houses. Both Jefferson and Morton harbored a deep faith that free individuals could better themselves and society without government help. Freedom meant the warding off of public control, not the harnessing of collective intelligence to effect social change. Both believed that men of the soil were the chosen people of God, that large cities were dens of iniquity. One can easily imagine Jefferson sharing Morton's tolerance of Mormons and dislike of the prohibition movement.

Yet important differences existed, too. Jefferson believed that good government was founded on public opinion; Morton believed it was based on sound money and credit. Jefferson, whose passion was liberty, feared oppression; Morton, a self-made man, feared attacks on property. Jefferson exhibited a serene confidence that men when not oppressed would exercise good sense; Morton feared that prejudice and passion often accompanied the casting of a ballot.[36] We cannot know whether Jefferson would have been a progressive in the mode of Senator La Follette and President Wilson. It is conceivable, however, that the president who concluded the Louisiana Purchase, imposed a hurtful embargo, and fought a small war against the Barbary pirates would in the twentieth century have advised with Herbert Croly the occasional use of Hamiltonian means to achieve the promise of American life. Morton's Jefferson, the agrarian, antistatist, states-righter, and isolationist, was one Jefferson. In the social and economic matrix of the late nineteenth century, this Jeffersonianism buttressed the conservative defense of privilege. Morton's enemies had an equally valid claim on the rationalist Jefferson, the civil libertarian, constitutional democrat, and Revolutionary leader who took his stand with the men of good hope.

At first glance it is curious that a community builder who worked so diligently to bring civilization to his corner of the world saw so little that could be done to shape the larger national society. Part of the reason lies in the age of rapid western expansion and industrial development in which Morton lived. The new manufacturing, transportation, and communication technologies pulled the semi-autonomous island communities into a national market and polity that together constitute the most profound transformation in American history. In Morton's early years the land could be tamed and communities built under traditional forms of social and economic life. The new urban-industrial order, however, would require professionalism, bureaucratic decision-making, and large-scale organization to rationalize the tumultuous process of social and economic change.[37]

Having won success in frontier America, Morton saw little need to square his inherited moral standards and ideology with the economic factors that gave rise to numerous protest movements. The spirit of reform we associate with Progressivism that arose at the time he founded the *Conservative* held few charms for the conservative Democrat from Otoe County. Having opposed the land-based Populist movement, Morton could hardly be expected to support a reform movement stemming largely from the urban middle class, particularly one that found the solution to overweening corporate power and human suffering in the expansion of governmental authority. Even when reform meant new rules of the game rather than the enlargement of government power, Morton held firm. The initiative and referendum that brought voters more fully into the political process were "absolutely against all the principles of representative government," wrote Morton. "We delegate the power to make laws to legislative bodies. A referendum is an assault upon this system."[38] Like many others of his time, Morton took the Jefferson who responded to historical conditions and froze his responses into absolutes. A strong central government had been a danger—and Jefferson feared it. Government had been by the rich—and Jefferson opposed it. Morton, doing likewise a century later, made the *Conservative* a spokesman for laissez-faire conservatism.

Notes

1. [An earlier version of this essay appeared in Roy Wortman, et al., eds., *For the General Welfare* (New York, 1989), pp. 131–59.] J. Sterling Morton to John J. Valentine, 31 May 1899, J. Sterling Morton Papers, Roll 67, Nebraska State Historical Society, Lincoln, Nebraska.

2. Everett Dick's *The Sod-House Frontier* (Lincoln, Nebraska, 1954) provides an arresting portrait of frontier newspapers and county politics. See especially pp. 417–34 and 459–79.

3. Charles Dabney, "The Presidency and Secretary Morton," *Atlantic Monthly* 77 (March 1896): 388–94.

4. *Conservative* 1 (14 July 1898): 1; Morton to H. H. Porter, 29 August 1898, Morton Papers, Roll 66.

5. "Bryanarchy," *Conservative* 2 (31 August 1899): 2–3; (7 September 1899): 5; (28 September 1899): 8.

6. Morton to George L. Miller, 20 July 1898; to John DeVitt Warner, 21 July 1898; to Gov. R. W. Furnas, 22 July 1898; to Edward Atkinson, 29 July 1898; Morton Papers, Roll 66.

7. *Conservative* 2 (12 September 1899): 11; (5 October 1899): 11; *Conservative* 4 (10 October 1901): 5.

8. *Conservative* 3 (13 September 1900): 15.

9. Typical of the companies advertising in the *Conservative* were The Morton Printing Co.; Deere & Co. (Illinois); Jay Morton & Co. (Illinois); Merchants National Bank (Nebraska); Union Pacific Railroad; Springfield Fire and Marine Insurance Co. (Massachusetts); National Starch Co. (Nebraska); and the Atchison, Topeka & Santa Fe Railway Co.

10. After a year of publication, circulation figures for the *Conservative* amounted to approximately 7,000. Morton to Henry G. Smith, 5 October 1899, Morton Papers, Roll 67.

11. Morton to John W. Lewis, 17 October 1898, Morton Papers, Roll 66; Morton to Douglas I. Hobbs, 22 June 1901, Morton Papers, Roll 69.

12. Morton to A. S. Phelps, 15 July 1901, Morton Papers, Roll 69.

13. "What Are the Young Man's Chances?—A Symposium," *Conservative* 4 (15 August 1901): 2.

14. *Conservative* 4 (15 August 1901): 9; (19 September 1901); *Charlotte (N.C.) Observer*, 26 August 1901, reprinted in the *Conservative* 4 (5 September 1901): 2–3.

15. *Conservative* 4 (26 September 1901): 1–2.

16. Morton to Mark Harrington, 16 May 1893; to F. L. Kibourne, 20 May 1893; to A. J. Wedderburn, 26 June 1893; Morton Papers, Roll 51; James C. Olson, *J. Sterling Morton* (Lincoln, Nebraska, 1942), p. 362.

17. James C. Olson, "Arbor Day—A Pioneer Expression of Concern for Environment," *Nebraska History* 53 (Spring 1972): 10.

18. Quoted in Olson, *J. Sterling Morton*, p. 165.

19. Edward Everett Dale, "Wood and Water: Twin Problems of the Prairie Plains," *Nebraska History* 29 (June 1948): 87–104.

20. *Conservative* 3 (11 April 1901).

21. Louis Windmuller, "A Plea for Trees and Parks in Cities," *Conservative* 2 (10 May 1900): 8–9; C. A. Schenck, "The Capitalist and Forestry," *Conservative* 2 (18 January 1900): 10–11; E. Benjamin Andrews, "The Farmstead Beautiful," *Conservative* 4 (17 October 1901): 6–7.

22. Andrews, "The Farmstead Beautiful," p. 7; for Morton, anything was better than living in cities. He told readers of the *Conservative* that "it is better, much better, to live in a small and healthful town in the West, than in one of the great, rancid, furious, smothering, diseased masses, crawling with deformed and unnatural human animals, that we call world-cities. Boys may grow up to be good men in those surroundings, but there are terrible chances against them. And we do not believe it is wholly infection or example that causes the harm. There can be no normal life in a city; the existence is unnatural." *Conservative* 4 (10 October 1901): 5.

23. *Conservative* 1 (14 July 1898): 8.

24. "For *N.Y. World*," Morton Papers, Roll 69.

25. *Conservative* 1 (14 July 1898): 4; (28 July 1898): 1–2; (4 August 1898): 2–3; and (13 April 1899): 4–5. Edward Atkinson, "Force Bills on the Money Question," *Conservative* 1 (15 September 1898): 6–9; and Hon. J. M. Carey, "The Gold Standard from the Standpoint of the Western States," *Conservative* 1 (13 October 1898): 10–13. Morton to James A. Cherry, 18 May 1895, Morton Papers, Roll 47. In 1857, Morton became a vice-president of the National Sound Money League and was elected president the following year. Republican victories diminished the threat of the silver crusade, and the group disbanded in 1900.

26. Morton to Paul Morton, 21 September 1899, Morton Papers, Roll 67; Morton to Edward Campbell, Jr., 8 November 1900, Morton Papers, Roll 68. *Conservative* 2 (21 September 1899): 8–9; (3 May 1900): 2; *Conservative* 3 (19 July 1900): 2–3; (6 September

1900): 6–11; (1 November 1900): 1–2; William Allen White, "W. J. Bryan," *Conservative* 3 (12 July 1900): 8–9.

27. *Conservative* 3 (25 October 1900): 4; (15 November 1900): 1–2. Morton to S. B. Evans, 24 November 1900, Morton Papers, Roll 68.

28. *Conservative* 1 (10 November 1898): 2; (28 November 1898): 11; (6 April 1899): 1. Morton to John W. Lewis, 17 November 1898, Morton Papers, Roll 66; Morton to A. J. Sawyer, 10 November 1900, Morton Papers, Roll 68.

29. John D. Unruh, Jr., is the author of two fine articles that demonstrate the effective role railroads played in the settling of the Great Plains: "The Burlington and Missouri River Railroad Brings the Mennonites to Nebraska, 1873–1878," parts I and II, both published in *Nebraska History* 45 (March 1964): 3–30, and (June 1964): 177–206. J. Sterling Morton served as a commissioner for the railroad in the 1870s.

30. Rolls 5, 6, and 71 of the Morton Papers are useful in documenting Sterling Morton's work for the Burlington railroad. For an example of money received for services, see Roll 71, frame 078965 (1875). Morton to George M. Pullman, 24 June 1875, Morton Papers, Roll 47.

31. See, for example, the following letters in the Morton Papers, Roll 66: Morton to R. R. Cable, 30 June 1898; to Paul Morton, 3 July 1898; and to J. C. Stubbs, 18 July 1898; in Roll 67, to E. P. Ripley, 10 June 1899; to T. P. Shonts, 11 August 1899; and Stuyvesant Fish, 19 August 1899. Stuyvesant Fish to Morton, 10 August 1900, Roll 44.

32. Morton to H. H. Porter, 30 August 1898, Morton Papers, Roll 66; to C. W. H. Strongman, 16 August 1898.

33. Morton to Stuyvesant Fish, 17 December 1900; to Horace C. Burt, 17 December 1900, Morton Papers, Roll 68.

34. H. T. Newcomb, "Railroad Rates and Competition," *Conservative* 1 (8 September 1898): 5; "Passenger and Freight Rates on American Railways,"*Conservative 1* (18 August 1898): 5–7; "Railroads and Politics," *Conservative* 4 (30 January 1902): 6–8.

35. Seven Jeffersons is an arbitrary number. See Clinton Rossiter, "Which Jefferson Do You Quote?" *Reporter* 13 (15 December 1955): 33–36.

36. Morton to John M. Carson, 27 October 1900, Morton Papers, Roll 68.

37. Cf. Robert H. Wiebe, *The Search for Order, 1877–1920* (New York, 1967).

38. Morton to S. B. Evans, 17 December 1900, Morton Papers, Roll 68.

Information Sources

BIBLIOGRAPHY:
Olson, James C. *J. Sterling Morton*. Lincoln, Nebraska, 1942.
INDEXES: None.
REPRINT EDITIONS: Microform: Nebraska State Historical Society.
LOCATION SOURCES: Complete runs: Nebraska State Historical Society; Newberry Library, Chicago; Michigan State Library Services, Lansing; University of Missouri.

Publication History

TITLE AND TITLE CHANGES: *The Conservative: A Journal Devoted to the Discussion of Political, Economic and Sociological Questions.*
VOLUME AND ISSUE DATA: Numbers 1–47, volumes 1–47, 14 July 1898–29 May 1902.
FREQUENCY OF PUBLICATION: Weekly.
PUBLISHER: The Morton Printing Company, Nebraska City, Nebraska.
EDITOR: J. Sterling Morton.
CIRCULATION: Varied from approximately 5,000 in 1898 to approximately 14,000 in 1902.

Ronald Lora

Conservative Review
1899–1901

In February 1899, the Neale Publishing Company of Washington, D.C., issued the first number of a journal named the *Conservative Review: A Quarterly*. After seven numbers had been more or less evenly issued, in October 1900 its first editor, William Lyne Wilson, died, and Walter Neale, the publisher, took his place, whereupon the review itself soon died, ending abruptly with its tenth number, out of season, in September 1901.[1]

In its brief existence inexact in its attention to quarterly periodicity, the *Conservative Review* was similarly irregular in its conservatism. In the main, it spoke for the sound money element in the Southern wing of the Democratic party. Both its editors and most of its writers were Southerners, by either birth or residence, and a number of them had been connected with the administrations of Grover Cleveland as supporters or appointees. The West Virginian, Wilson, for instance, had served as postmaster general for two years in Cleveland's second term. Markedly hostile to radical agrarianism, whether of the Populist or Bryanesque variety, the review was also fervently anti-imperialist, with three long essays in the first number denouncing American aggrandizement overseas, suggesting that this exigent cause was one of the principal reasons for its coming into being in the first place. Thus it hoped to appeal to conservative Republicans even as it represented conservative Democrats, taking these to be, as a rare editorial comment remarked in November 1899, "equally opposed to McKinleyism and Bryanism."[2] But in uniting these two groups, it admitted to its pages writers and opinions not easily consonant with a deeper conservative consensus, and as a result the journal bore a singularly eclectic appearance. Its contributors included, for example, several Confederate veterans and, in Franklin Benjamin Sanborn, a former radical abolitionist, one of John Brown's "Secret Six"; Dora Murdoch, who favored women's suffrage, and Philip Alexander Bruce, who did not; Edward Abram Uffington Valentine, a struggling young author perhaps even at that time of his association with the *Conservative Review* groping toward the plot and characterizations of his first novel, *Hecla Sandwith*; and the Midwesterner Hamlin Garland.

Still, the dominant thrust of the journal was a coherent and eminently conservative political outlook, which centered on the question of American annexation of the Philippine Islands. The critical point of that question was in two senses constitutional, involving issues of both fundamental law and the nature of the Republic, and it opened with a crucial distinction that writers in the review made between a legitimately constitutional power of the United States to acquire nearby territory by "expansion" and an unconstitutional wresting of foreign lands through "imperialism." "Expansion," William Henry Fleming, a member of Congress from Georgia and a distant relation of Thomas Jefferson, explained, "means the enlarging of the same thing," while imperialism meant "the taking on of a different thing."[3] Earlier American territorial acquisitions had been, with one exception, normally peaceful movements into contiguous and often unoccupied lands (the exception, Alaska, "though not coterminous, was in a certain sense contiguous"), and had led to the assimilation of new states into the Union as republics fully equal to the older ones, sharing the same "institutions, laws, manners, sentiments, and ideals" as they, in a process contemplated and wholly approved in the Constitution.[4]

Annexation of the Philippines was far different. Not only were those distant islands not contiguous to the United States in any serious sense, but they had been seized by a blatant act of aggression accompanied latterly by a morally indefensible war "undertaken to subjugate a foreign people and to impose upon them a government against their will." Although they might be brought into the Union and the Filipinos given all the "civil rights, privileges, and liabilities" of citizenship, "irrespective of race, color or previous condition" (in which case an inferior "Asiatic element" would "share the task of governing us with the African, which now holds the balance of power"), it was more likely that they would become the first of many exotic colonies of the United States, peopled with "barbarous and semi-barbarous inhabitants...incapable of assimilation with us," and governed, in the absence of constitutional sanctions, by absolute, arbitrary executive force.[5]

Seen in that way, wrote Isaac Lobe Straus, a Baltimore, Maryland, attorney who in 1907 became his state's attorney general, empire represented "a radical and revolutionary departure from the fundamental theories of the Government."[6] Allowing the government to assume powers not within its competence under the Constitution on the outrageous ground that it derived them immediately from the sovereignty of the United States was to repose ultimate power in government, and not in the people. This, he objected, was "the principle of absolutism," and the fear was that, as William Baird wrote, given "the nature of power to cling closely to what it holds, and to use it as a means to further aggrandizement," the absolute and arbitrary power the American government wielded in possessions overseas would be transferred to the domestic sphere as well.[7] If the American people adopted imperialism and abandoned the limitations the Constitution imposed on government in one place, they surrendered the security and liberty it guaranteed them in all. Imperialism, as Fleming said, like "a foreign fungus," would "sap the life of the Republic"; it would prove to be, Straus remarked, its "ultimate doom."[8]

That was really the point of the alarm. Imperialism, these anti-imperialists believed, was fatal to republican government, that is, self-government in the traditional Jeffersonian sense: individuals entrusted with the conduct of their own affairs without the interference of the state. As Franklin Smith explained it, in an argument that set down fundamental premises of the *Conservative Review*, self-government also involved the corollary that the exercise of individual freedom benefited society by generating a diversity necessary for political liberty and for maximum economic opportunity. The process by which this occurred, being neither forced nor contrived, suggested an organic and evolutionary character to republican society. The fact that individual liberty, or private enterprise, promoted social harmony and developed public prosperity testified to a "force" binding "every useful member of society" together in an organic unit, and the fact that this force tended to an "inevitable integration of society," that is, to "a multiplication and perfection of parts, and a more complete dependence of each part upon the others," declared what he called "the miracle of evolution." Social evolution, however, required conditions of peace and security, and it was to acquire these that, after "countless ages of violence," "human beings first came together" and "formed the first state." No natural organism itself, but merely an artificial "association of the inhabitants of a given territory for the protection of life and property" "against enemies at home and abroad," the state was to be strictly confined to that fundamental work for which it was made, so much so that "laws not in protection of person and property," Smith wrote, were "an attack upon both" and led certainly to despotism.[9]

Signs of just such a "centralized despotism" had already begun to appear in the United States in tariffs, which Smith held were no more than government grants to producers to exact tribute from consumers (the Dingley Tariff, then in place, he regarded as "the grossest violation of freedom, the most effective implement of plunder, and the heaviest drag upon commerce ever inflicted upon the American people"), and, on the other side of the coin, government regulation of the private sector, a euphemistic expression for the forced submission of business to "the vicious control of legislators." Similarly despotic were state control of the postal system, which created inefficiency and tended to "kill" competition; state involvement in education, which, having "failed to turn children into angels," had led to yet more state interference in private life in "curfew laws...enacted from the Atlantic to the Pacific" and prisons erected "for training truants"; and state funding for libraries, parks, and institutions for the care of "lunatics and consumptives," all of which were robberies of every taxpayer unable to use them.[10]

These aggressions by the state affected all the values and ethical standards of society, exciting a false esteem of place and power and money, provoking blatant acts of plunder, and creating "social divisions based on artificial distinctions" unrelated either to excellence of character or native ability.[11] Encouraged by the egregious example of government, individual initiative in the private sector had resulted in such things as corporate monopolies and national labor unions, which

Smith regarded as perversions of liberty that jeopardized republican government as much as the state did. His strict antistatism forbade recommending governmental intervention as a remedy, but they remained offensive to his immaculate laissez-faire individualism.   Philip Alexander Robinson, on the other hand, a young economist who, like Smith, advocated self-government and private enterprise, distinguished between them as Smith did not. Monopolies he defended as natural products of "the organic complex of matter and force," which in the course of social evolution had conferred benefits on society far in advance of those provided by inefficient competition. They did not, he thought, negate individual liberty; they fulfilled it. Aside from approving "such measures of state supervision as circumstances may from time to time indicate," he was as opposed as Smith was to regulation of them, either to restore competition or to place them under public control.   State ownership he dismissed as outright socialism and its proponents generally as belonging to "races of socialistic tendency," and he objected to breaking up monopolies as a "reactionary" regression to an "ultra-primitive ideal" of equal competitors, equally small. Best to trust monopolies to regulate themselves, on the understanding that their "enlightened self-interest" was probably the surest guarantee against abuse and because that was "in accordance with the most fundamental interests of self-government."[12]

Labor unions were different. Because they restricted freedom in the marketplace and enforced obedience to their will by organized mob violence, they reversed the republican tradition of individual liberty and violated the republican principle of social benefit. Serving the interests of a single class, they perverted the Republic itself, for as Robinson wrote: "A nation ruled by one class or order is no longer a true republic, whether that class be millionaires or wage-earners, farmers or miners, aristocrats or thugs." If it was "called by the name of democracy" and represented the majority of the whole population, then, by enforcing "mediocrity and...conformity to conventional standards," the real enemy of republican liberty was not corporate monopolies but precisely this "juggernaut of the great cult of modern democracy."[13]

Based on the notion that all men were fundamentally equal and naturally good, democracy was unsound at its heart. All men were not naturally good, averred William Hand Browne, professor of English at Johns Hopkins; some were naturally and ineradicably evil, and between the "kingdom of Satan" and "God's kingdom there could be neither peace nor truce."[14] Nor were all men equal. Some might be distinguished by excellence, but others were competent neither "to act conscientiously nor rationally."[15] The "people," en masse, were not endowed with supernal virtue in which universal equality might be esteemed worthy. Far from it, asserted Edward Farquhar, a professor of history at Columbia University; the advances that mankind had made had never arisen from the undifferentiated democratic masses but from "the really better class," the "choicer men," the gentlemen. Jesus of Nazareth, for example, together with his apostles, had been "distinctively of the gentleman class."[16] An "aristocracy," in some form or another, Robinson wrote, was "inevitable." To try to alter the "gradations" among men that sprang from "difference of personal capacity" to try to impose an "unattainable and undesirable" equality was to lay an axe to "the biological roots of society," destroy the fruits of human liberty, and thwart the forward course of social evolution.[17]

Not liberty but order appeared most seriously threatened by democratic egalitarianism to George Hibbard, a Harvard graduate practicing law in Buffalo, New York, for whereas liberty, he observed, already received "inordinate consideration" "in this land of the rather too free," too little attention was paid to the critical need for social order. Believing, as he did, that a struggle would soon engage the nations of the world and that only the "most complete and manageable national organism" was going to emerge as the survivor, he was convinced of the necessity for a social organization in which every individual subordinated himself to the community through a "willingness to reverentially suffer direction, either the direction of some compelling ideal or some trusted leadership." By instilling a feeling of reverence for the naturally hierarchical way things are, those unable to rise above the lowest ranks would, he thought, understand and accept their lot in life without any accompanying sense of "humiliating subjection."[18] In this his views largely coincided with Robinson's, which denounced labor unions as unambiguous expressions of the craving of the masses for an unnatural equality (and a jealous desire to punish superiority), and hence as "retrograde and reactionary growths" unhealthy in republican society. "Men do what they are best fitted for," observed the libertarian, Franklin Smith, with like intent; "they receive what merit and effort, the true test of worth, entitle them to." "That," Farquhar affirmed, was "the conclusion of the whole matter. When every individual is conceived as having his own place and duty in the world, as better fitted for that than for other things," then the evolution of society could proceed toward "free and peaceful self-government," uncorrupted by democratic and egalitarian impurities.[19]

Thus pressing the case that self-government was vital for liberty and for social evolution took some writers in the review into extreme libertarianism and others into an organicism equally extreme in its stress on control. But most, if not all, of the journal's contributors agreed that natural inequalities meant that the capacity for self-government itself, that is, not simply the power to act but "self control and deference for the rights of others" too, varied among different people.[20] Sometimes they associated this incapacity with merely individual character, sometimes with age or sex, and sometimes with ethnicity or nationality. Most often they associated it with race. William Hand Browne seems to have had race in mind when he observed that some men were not able to acquire the practical arts of self-government because they were endowed with an "animal nature" that governed them.[21] Opinion on specifics was far from unanimous. William Baird, the anti-imperialist, thought that Filipinos were able to govern themselves, but Champ Clark, the future speaker of the House of Representatives and also an anti-imperialist, disagreed, dismissing Filipinos as "a horde of Cannibals" utterly unfit for self-government. American Indians he held to be incapable of civilization and he agreed, "reluctantly," he said, with the sentiment that "'there is no good Indian but a dead Indian.'"[22] On the other hand, Charles W. Super, the president of Ohio University in Athens, Ohio, was sure that Indians were in fact becoming civilized.

Charles William Sommerville, a Hampden-Sydney divinity graduate, believed the history of Liberia "demonstrated the capacity of the negro for self-government, if given the proper environment," but Samuel Phillips Verner, an American missionary in Africa, contended that "the African race" was "not endowed with the qualities of the Anglo-Saxon and may never reach the height of his attainments."[23] Similarly, Josiah Patterson of North Carolina, although acknowledging that blacks were "only beginning to tread the paths of civilization," insisted that they were "wholly unfit for the exercise of the elective franchise."[24] Philip Alexander Bruce, of the University of Virginia, was convinced that blacks in the South since the Civil War had exhibited so little self-control that they could not sustain liberty. Nor was their situation likely to improve because, as Bruce explained, with segregation all but ending illegal miscegenation in the South, there was "a fast increasing tendency in the black race to revert physically to the original type," an intellectually inferior "pure negro."[25] For the Virginia historian James Curtis Ballagh, blacks, mulattos, and Indians were all inferior to whites.

Racism, protestations of fealty to republican principles, and bitter criticisms of statism all reflected the *Conservative Review*'s identification with themes traditionally associated with the South, a connection confirmed throughout the journal's career in both the background of its contributors and the many essays it printed in praise of men and events in Southern history. For example, in the first number of volume 1, Randolph Barton, a veteran of the Stonewall Brigade who had been wounded five times during the Civil War, contributed an essay on his old commander, "Stonewall" Jackson; Kate Mason Rowland, a Richmond, Virginia, member of the United Daughters of the Confederacy and author of a two-volume biography of George Mason and another of Charles Carroll of Carrollton, defended the reputation of the early Virginia colonist Captain John Smith; and Bernard C. Steiner, librarian at the Enoch Pratt Free Library in Baltimore, provided a sketch of the Georgia author Richard Malcolm Johnston, which served to introduce a serial publication of Johnston's autobiography, run in the review in 1900 and 1901. The *Conservative Review* also published Peirce Bruns's appreciation of the South Carolina poet Henry Timrod; Glen Levin Swiggett's of the Georgia poet Sidney Lanier; and Janey Hope Marr's of her father, an obscure Virginia poet named James Barron Hope. There were notices of James Madison by Gaillard Hunt and of Patrick Henry by Susan Bullitt Dixon; reminiscences of the Virginia Secession Convention of 1861 and of the Confederate Congress by John Goode, who had been a member of both; and recollections of Confederate service on land by a chaplain in a Georgia outfit and at sea by a former lieutenant in the Confederate navy. In the last number of the final volume, Martha Hunter appeared with a memoir of her father, the Virginia politician Robert Mercer Taliaferro Hunter.

Aside from the tone of filial respect for the South and its past in these articles, several substantive points appeared that were pertinent to the review's conservatism. To begin with, it was held that no moral responsibility attached to the introduction of slavery into the South; it had developed out of evolutionary forces and simply expressed natural inequalities. Once established, slavery had produced among Southern whites men and women of character and honor whose course before the

Civil War had not been motivated by a defense of slavery but of constitutional rights and who had neither seceded from the Union nor fought for independence on account of slavery but, again, in defense of those same rights to republican liberty. Their historical struggle against the despotic tendencies of governmental consolidation had not ended with military defeat. Forty years after secession, it continued in the protest against imperialism. Aggression in the Philippines, in the opinion of writers in the *Conservative Review,* was the modern form of the South's ancient enemy, and in opposing it, the journal stood squarely in the current of an important Southern tradition.

Appropriately it was a Confederate veteran who warned that the two great dangers facing the country as the twentieth century began were precisely those the South had feared in 1861: "centralization, which would place the governing powers in the hands of the few and thus...rob the people of their liberties," and "corruption, bribery and fraud" among public officials.[26] These were also the results that William Baird foresaw rising from the militarism and bureaucracy that he believed were the inevitable "concomitants" of imperialism: armies stationed abroad to defend conquered territories, others, for their "re-enforcement and relief," ominously stationed at home, both prepared to enforce the will of a single executive authority; and a large civil service ostensibly appointed to handle colonial administration, but in reality a loyal cadre functioning to support government policy, controlled by executive patronage, sinecures, and bribes.[27] Perhaps with equal appropriateness, against these dangers all the *Conservative Review* had to offer were the South's old, familiar responses: the defense against consolidation was states rights, guaranteed in the Constitution, according to which state governments were supposed to possess "inherent powers of sovereignty—all such inherent powers not prohibited," while the national government had "no inherent sovereignty, but only the sovereign powers expressly granted to it, and those implied in or incidental to the grants."[28] As for corruption, what availed against it was virtue, which depended for its free exercise on the limited, republican system of government that, once again, the Constitution guaranteed.

There was more in these animadversions on the "despotism" and "corruption" that government policies were said to be threatening or already to have occasioned than a mere fastidious constitutionalism. There was a real sense of urgency reflecting a distinctively late nineteenth-century Southern understanding of just how tenuous constitutional guarantees were and how precarious was the preservation of individual liberty. Moreover, in the desperate and reiterated insistence that unless imperialist aggression were brought to an immediate halt, states really would be reduced to the status of "dependent corporations" of the federal government, serving simply as administrative agents of its "virtually absolute central authority," and that, under this tyranny, "the debased morals inherent in war and politics" would continue to "penetrate to the furthest corner of the national fabric and poison all social, intellectual, industrial and professional life," urgency blended into pessimism.[29] The South, after all, had lost its struggle; the nation might well lose now.

Without any advance notice, the *Conservative Review* ceased publication with the September 1901 number. In a way, it was fitting that it ended then. Begun when there was still some hope of defeating the Treaty of Paris in the Senate, its first number appearing simultaneously with the outbreak of the Filipino insurrection, it ran through the re-election of President William McKinley in November 1900, the capture of the insurgent leader Emilio Aguinaldo in March 1901, and the establishment by the Taft Commission of civil government in the Philippines that July. In September the rebellion in the islands entered its final phase and, like it, the journal's cause was lost.

Notes

1. Frank Luther Mott, *A History of American Magazines*, vol. 4, *1885–1905* (Cambridge, Mass., 1957), p. 73.

2. Editorial note, *Conservative Review* 2 (November 1899): 211 (hereinafter cited as *CR*).

3. William Henry Fleming, "A Question of National Honor," *CR* 1 (May 1899): 207.

4. William Baird, "Imperialism," *CR* 4 (September 1900): 139.

5. James B. Eustis, "Dreyfus and the Jewish Question in France," *CR* 2 (August 1899): 21 ("undertaken"); Felix Branigan, "A Legal Aspect of the Philippine Question," *CR* 3 (March 1900): 35 ("civil rights"; "irrespective"); Baird, "Imperialism," p. 141 ("Asiatic element"; "share the risk"); A. Leo Knott, "The Treaty with Spain," *CR* 1 (February 1899): 168 ("barbarous").

6. Isaac Lobe Straus, "The Constitution or Absolutism?" *CR* 1 (February 1899): 6.

7. Ibid., p. 39 ("principle"); Baird, "Imperialism," p. 155 ("the nature of power").

8. Fleming, "A Question of National Honor," p. 207; Straus, "The Constitution or Absolutism?" p. 39.

9. Franklin Smith, "A Fiction of Political Metaphysics," *CR* 5 (March 1901): 88, 93 ("laws...attack"); Franklin Smith, "Signs of Decadence in the United States," *CR* 5 (September 1901): 193 ("a multiplication").

10. Smith, "A Fiction of Political Metaphysics," pp. 94 ("kill"; "lunatics"), 96 ("vicious"); Smith, "Signs of Decadence in the United States," pp. 196 ("centralized"; "grossest"), 197 ("failed...curfew...truants").

11. Smith, "Signs of Decadence in the United States," p. 202.

12. Philip Alexander Robinson, "Economic Consolidation and Monopoly," *CR* 4 (September 1900): 35 ("organic"), 54 ("races"), 61 ("enlightened"), 68 ("in accordance"), 71 ("such measures"), 87 ("reactionary"), 92 ("ultra-primitive").

13. Philip Alexander Robinson, "The Labor Trusts," *CR* 5 (March 1901): 23; Robinson, "Economic Consolidation and Monopoly," pp. 93–94.

14. William Hand Browne, "A Scholar's Mistakes," *CR* 5 (March 1901): 100.

15. Smith, "A Fiction of Political Metaphysics," p. 91.

16. Edward Farquhar, "Whence Comes Our Help?" *CR* 5 (March 1901): 58 ("distinctively"), 60 ("really"), 61 ("choicer").

17. Robinson, "Economic Consolidation and Monopoly," pp. 74 ("biological"), 93 ("aristocracy...inevitable...unattainable"); Robinson, "The Labor Trusts," p. 12 ("gradations").

18. George Hibbard, "The Value of Reverence," *CR* 5 (September 1901): 269.

19. Robinson, "The Labor Trusts," p. 12; Smith, "Signs of Decadence in the United States," p. 194; Farquhar, "Whence Comes Our Help?" pp. 59 ("free"), 75 ("conclusion").

20. Smith, "Signs of Decadence in the United States," p. 194.

21. Browne, "A Scholar's Mistakes," p. 103.

22. Champ Clark, "American Policy of Expansion," *CR* 1 (February 1899): 88 ("there is"), 100 ("horde").

23. Charles William Sommerville, "Robert Goodloe Harper," *CR* 1 (May 1899): 404; Samuel Phillips Verner, "The Cape to Cairo Railway," *CR* 1 (May 1899): 252.

24. Josiah Patterson, "Sound Money Democracy in the South," *CR* 2 (November 1899): 213.

25. Philip Alexander Bruce, "The Negro Population in the South," *CR* 2 (November 1899): 276, 277.

26. William T. Fitch, "Personal Recollections of the Civil War, from 1861 to 1865," *CR* 5 (September 1901): 262.

27. Baird, "Imperialism," pp. 155 ("re-enforcement"), 157 ("concomitants").

28. Straus, "The Constitution or Absolutism?" p. 8.

29. Baird, "Imperialism," p. 156 ("dependent corporations"; "virtually absolute"); Smith, "Signs of Decadence in the United States," p. 211.

Information Sources

BIBLIOGRAPHY: None.
INDEXES: Each volume indexed; *Poole*.
REPRINT EDITIONS: Microform: DA; LC.
LOCATION SOURCES: Widely available.

Publication History

TITLE AND TITLE CHANGES: *The Conservative Review. A Quarterly*.
VOLUME AND ISSUE DATA: Volumes 1–5, February 1899–September 1901.
FREQUENCY OF PUBLICATION: Quarterly.
PUBLISHER: Neale Company, Washington, D. C.
EDITORS: William Lyne Wilson, February 1899–September 1900; Walter Neale, December 1900 September 1901.
CIRCULATION: Unknown.

William Henry Longton

World's Work
1900–1932

A great American periodical debuted in November 1900. Called *World's Work: A History of Our Time*, it came from the newly organized firm of Doubleday, Page & Company of New York City, and a seasoned journalist, Walter Hines Page, quickly established the magazine's course.

Much of the thirty-two-year history of *World's Work* is the story of Walter Hines Page. Unlike some other periodical heads, Page exercised enormous control over his publication's content and permanently shaped its personality. Born in North Carolina in 1855 and educated at Trinity College (Duke University), Randolph-Macon College, and the Johns Hopkins University, the brilliant and hard-driving future chief of *World's Work* launched his distinguished career in journalism in 1880 when he joined the *St. Joseph* (Missouri) *Gazette* as a reporter. Later his work took him to his native North Carolina and then to New York City. After stints with two magazines, the *Forum* and the *Atlantic Monthly*, Page became a partner in 1899 in Doubleday, Page & Company, and the next year he started his labor of love, *World's Work*, for which he served as editor until 1913. His aggressive and competent leadership prompted a rival journalist to comment: "He had a genius for making friendships that yielded literary by-products; he made a friend of almost every contributor and a contributor of almost every friend."[1] In politics Page enthusiastically embraced the ideas and values of Jeffersonian democracy; he never fully accepted the reform notions of the western (or William Jennings Bryan) wing of the Democratic party and certainly not those that challenged the concept of states rights. Like so many of his fellow countrymen, Page had a hopeful bent. He believed that the promise of American life would soon be realized by all diligent, honest folk. Both this conservatism and optimism became immediate hallmarks of the new Page publication.

No one who read *World's Work* with regularity ever thought it an inferior product. For one thing, it was physically attractive. Each of the early issues had 116 pages that were usually well illustrated and nicely printed with large type. The casual reader surely must have found the frequent pictorial essays, some of which after 1916 contained color prints, a delight. The quality of the illustrations used in J. M. Bowles's November 1904 piece, "Business Buildings Made Beautiful," was without equal in contemporary mass circulation magazines. The standards for writing, moreover, were unusually high. Page himself wrote a remarkably fresh column, "The March of Events," in which he commented on both national and international happenings. His pellucid prose captivated tens of thousands of faithful followers. And the magazine employed able and fussy copyeditors. The price of twenty-five cents seemed reasonable indeed.

World's Work, though, had a decidedly conservative flavor in an age of liberalism. Although few reform-minded progressives found fault with Page's paeans of praise for the New South, or his enthusiasm for scientific agriculture, or even his dedication to internationalism, they generally objected to his abiding belief in the greatness and essential honesty of the American business community and its leaders. At a time when muckrakers were blowing the whistle on a plethora of shortcomings, Page and *World's Work* usually overlooked such matters. When journalists discovered that exposé articles on life insurance evils were as well received as earlier ones had been on railroads and oil companies, the Page publication failed to join the long list of magazines that devoted considerable space to this consumer concern. Only when these stories triggered a sensational explosion of life insurance reform that commenced with the New York State Armstrong investigation during the summer of 1905 did Page begin to pay attention. *World's Work* first worried that the probe would give "an impetus...to what we loosely call socialism."[2] Later, as policyholders became incensed about the industry's abuse and arrogance, the magazine suggested that the solution rested merely with new business blood taking over the enterprise. And after New York lawmakers enacted a multitude of tough reforms, *World's Work* only reluctantly accepted them. It then proceeded to underscore the belief that since a major housecleaning had occurred, the companies should now enjoy a life free of governmental meddling.

Advanced progressives likely found a number of feature articles appalling. The magazine regularly published short biographical sketches of business leaders, who were viewed universally as industrial statesmen. The February 1908 issue told the tale of "General William J. Palmer, A Builder of the West."[3] Palmer, Civil War hero, railroad magnate, and metals king, had a keen sense of civic responsibility: he gave generously to widows and orphans, community projects, and higher education. Nothing, however, was mentioned about the general's questionable business dealings or his shabby treatment of workers. In the same manner, Walter Hines Page enlisted prominent business executives to explain their worldview to the general reader. One such series began in November 1909 when Great Northern Railway president James J. Hill, backer of the ill-fated Northern Securities Companies and avid opponent of federal regulation, introduced his "Highways of Progress" essays. The "Empire Builder" boosted the service territory of his railroad, encouraged expansion of the Asiatic trade, and blasted government interference in the operations of corporations. Hill unmistakably reinforced Page's own view when he wrote that "the principle of consolidation in business...is a permanent addition to the forward moving forces of the world."[4] Page had, after all, long thought the well-to-do business class to be a principal factor in the socioeconomic progress of all humankind. And, too, the true liberal of the progressive era objected to the decidedly racist and xenophobic content of *World's Work*. The publication held out little hope for assimilation of the nation's blacks, and it worried about the massive influx of immigrants, particularly those from eastern and southern Europe. Likewise, the magazine's stance on labor matters troubled uplifters. *World's Work* published William English Walling's "Can Labor Unions Be Destroyed?" which argued that "union domination in the shops...means union men, union rules, and an increased cost of production."[5]

Walter Hines Page and *World's Work* occasionally showed some willingness to endorse positive change. But this tended to be along lines that glorified order and efficiency rather than social justice. A good illustration is Arthur Wallace Dunn's "How a Business Man Would Run the Government." This 1911 multipart work argued that the taxpayer would benefit if politicians would end their logrolling and pork barrel antics. Dedicated managers should control the federal bureaucracy. This series smacked of the "googooism" that had characterized the genteel civil service crusade of the 1870s and early 1880s. In the same vein, the magazine showed an interest in protecting the nation's natural resources, even as it argued for their full exploitation, albeit in a logical and practical fashion. John Muir and fellow "ascetics" did not appreciate this "utilitarian" position.

World's Work consistently boomed the advantages of an intelligent, well-managed business structure. As early as March 1904, the magazine carried Hrolf Wisby's carefully reasoned essay, "The Modern Industrial Manager," which argued that "industrial management has become a science." He believed that the fundamental principle in operating a modern industrial establishment was "to get the men in love with their work, their surroundings," and their supervisors.[6] Naturally Page accepted a piece by Frank Park Stockbridge for the April 1911 number on the University of Cincinnati's pioneering cooperative engineering program. Students not only took traditional academic subjects but learned first-hand the "real world" skills of track ballasting, ironmolding, and machine tending. The University of Cincinnati graduates would then join that new breed of highly trained managers, who were making American industry the most progressive and enlightened in the world.

When Walter Hines Page left the helm of *World's Work* in 1913 to accept President Woodrow Wilson's offer of the ambassadorship to the Court of Saint James in London, the magazine retained its historically conservative stance. It continued to emphasize the greatness of American business, especially its technological triumphs. For instance, the automobile and aircraft industries received extensive coverage, just as the electric interurban railway, steamship, and telephone enterprises had been spotlighted earlier. Then, shortly after World War I, *World's Work* began to decline; the quality of production and writing slipped. The mid-1920s saw an overall improvement in each area, but the catastrophic stock market crash of 1929 severely hurt the magazine's financial position; both circulation and advertising revenues dropped markedly. The end came in 1932 when Doubleday, Doran & Company, successor to Doubleday, Page & Company, sold *World's Work* to its long-time rival, *Review of Reviews*.

During the final decade, *World's Work* held true to earlier traditions. Its continuing conservatism reflected the dominant nonprogressive character of the 1920s. It was a publication that would please a Calvin Coolidge or a John W. Davis. *World's Work* showed a deep interest in trends in science, business, and foreign affairs. For example, the November 1923 number contained Edwin Slosson's optimistic piece, "The Story of Insulin"; the May 1926 number featured Harvard University professor of business William Z. Ripley's widely quoted "On with Railway Consolidation!"; and the number for April 1929 carried Henry Kittredge Norton's "Leaders of the New Germany," which told of the transformation of that nation from an absolute monarchy into a democracy. In line with the temper of the postwar decade, many readers must have enjoyed Gino Speranza's six-part series, "The Immigration Peril," which ran between November 1923 and April 1924. These articles told of the "menace to American ideals" from, especially, the Greeks, Italians, and Slavs: "Their mass aggressiveness in demanding that America shall accept foreign ideals" threatened to create "a mongrelized civilization."[7] An equally vicious article appeared in February 1930. Titled "What's Wrong with Textiles?" its author, William R. Bassett, blamed foreign immigration for disruptive strikes within this basic industry. The piece once again reflected *World's Work*'s xenophobia and dislike for organized labor.

Appropriately, *World's Work* printed its final number on the eve of the New Deal. Its coverage varied little from the maiden issue: news of world events, several essays on the untapped potential of Latin America's economy, and an examination of the domestic wood products industry. Unquestionably the advent of a federally centered reform era would have troubled the editors and staff; presumably they found solace by reading the *American Review*, *American Mercury*, or *Time* during the age of Franklin Roosevelt.

Notes

1. *The Outlook* 149 (27 June 1928): 356.
2. "The March of Events," *World's Work* 10 (August 1905): 6558 (hereinafter cited as *WW*).
3. *WW* 15 (February 1908): 9899–9903.
4. *WW* 19 (March 1910): 12,738.
5. *WW* 8 (May 1904): 4757.
6. *WW* 7 (March 1904): 4531, 4535.
7. *WW* 47 (November 1923): 57.

Information Sources

BIBLIOGRAPHY:

Cooper, Jr., Milton. *Walter Hines Page: The Southerner as American, 1865–1918*. Chapel Hill, North Carolina, 1977.
Mott, Frank Luther. *A History of American Magazines,* vol. 4, *1885–1905*. Cambridge, Massachusetts, 1957.
Rusnack, Robert J. *Walter Hines Page and World's Work: 1900–1913*. Lanham, Maryland, 1982.

INDEXES: Each volume indexed; *ALI*; *CMC*; *PAIS*; *Poole*; *RG*; *Writings Amer Hist*.
REPRINT EDITIONS: Microform: UMI; PMC.
LOCATION SOURCES: Widely available.

Publication History

TITLE AND TITLE CHANGES: *World's Work*, November 1900–June 1929; *World's Work: A History of Our Time*, July 1929–July 1932.
VOLUME AND ISSUE DATA: Volumes 1–61, November 1900–July 1932.
FREQUENCY OF PUBLICATION: Monthly.
PUBLISHER: 1900–1926: Doubleday, Page & Company; 1927–1932: Doubleday, Doran & Company. Both in New York.
EDITORS: Walter Hines Page, 1900–1913; Arthur Wilson Page, 1913–1926; Carl G. Dickey, 1927–1928; Barton Currie, 1928–1929; Russell Doubleday, 1929–1931; Allan C. Collins, 1931–1932.
CIRCULATION: 100,000–140,000.

H. Roger Grant

American Industries
1902–1931

American Industries first appeared in August 1902. Unprepossessing in appearance and style (it was published in newspaper format) and issued bimonthly, the new publication was successor to *American Trade* (1897–1902). *American Industries* became the official publication of the National Association of Manufacturers (NAM) in 1904 but was closely linked with it from the beginning. The new publication from the outset carried much material, including lead editorial articles, penned by NAM leaders, and the journal's publisher and editor, Marshall Cushing, continued as editor for several years after the NAM became the publisher in 1904.

The "American Danger," the political and economic machinations of organized workers, editorially preoccupied *American Industries* almost entirely in its first years. In Congress, as *American Industries* saw it, an antilabor injunction measure and an eight-hour bill were being propelled forward by a strong "labor lobby." In the plants and mines, boycotts and strikes (the great anthracite coal strike was under way in the fall of 1902) were being organized by a "world-wide conspiracy" of unionists. American manufacturers would go the way of Britain's, so enmeshed in social and union restrictions as to be incapable of economic progress, if countermeasures failed. The great countermeasure was organization— "one great, central organization of the manufacturers of the United States."

The "American Danger" consistently and continually held the central place in *American Industries*'s editorial concerns until World War I. After 1915, the journal softened its anti-union rhetoric, but until then, its pages presented an uninterrupted stream of antilabor abuse. Its vision of the future, if the union danger were not turned, was unrelievedly cataclysmic. Economic downturns, blamed on labor agitation, foreshadowed the industrial future if union activities went unchecked. "Organized labor," wrote *American Industries*'s editor in 1911, "is ready and willing to bring our national structure to the verge of collapse, and beyond if necessary, to gain its own ends."[1]

Scarcely an issue of *American Industries* failed to furnish a detailed account of labor atrocities somewhere in America. These tales of labor's misdeeds often contained as their resolution the defeat of the union at the hands of a stalwart defender of the law. In form these accounts are news stories, but their melodramatic quality nearly makes them qualify as a fictional genre, the "labor horror story." Notable examples were the 1903 account of William Travers Jerome's struggle against corruption in the New York City building trades and "Cleveland's Shame," the story of union persecution of a courageous worker who opposed the 1911 garment strike.[2]

The intention of this uninterrupted stream of exposé and outrage was to put unionism beyond the pale of acceptability. At no other time was this clearer than during the great furor over the dynamiting of the *Los Angeles Times*. Samuel Gompers, head of the American Federation of Labor, had supported and helped arrange for the trial defense of the accused, the McNamara brothers. When their dramatic confession in court occurred, *American Industries* pronounced Gompers guilty of complicity, as he must have known of their guilt all along. The AFL therefore was an accomplice in dynamiting. "If labor cannot organize and behave with decency," fumed the NAM's president, John Kirby, Jr., in a lengthy 1912 article, "then...I say it has no business to be organized, and the rest of the people...should put an end to it."[3]

American Industries portrayed the NAM as effectively combating the labor threat. The winter of 1902–1903 was seen as a watershed. Thanks to NAM alertness, businessmen were awakening to the dangers of pending labor legislation in Congress and the threat of militant union organization and strike activities, as seen especially in the anthracite coal strike. The NAM's activities blocked the immediate proposals of the "labor lobby" in Washington, and in 1903 called into existence the Citizens Industrial Association of America (CIAA), a league of local, state, and industry employer associations. Together the NAM and the CIAA went on to form, in 1907, the National Council for Industrial Defense (NCID). James A. Emery, famed already as the effective and tough legal adviser of the San Francisco Manufacturers Association, became the NCID's counsel and later would be nationally known as the NAM's chief counsel. The NCID specialized in defeating prolabor legislation at both state and national levels. Emery's periodic reports of his latest success in defeating all legislative attempts to soften the use of injunctions in labor disputes, or otherwise improve the position of unions or workers through legislation, now frequently graced *American Industries*'s pages.

By 1905 *American Industries* apparently felt the labor union danger was well enough in hand to warrant attention to other concerns. That year the journal first took note of the progressive movement, which, it noted, President Theodore Roosevelt and journalistic elements such as the Hearst press were popularizing. One phase of progressivism was the exposure of abusive and overbearing behavior by businessmen. Because a major part of this criticism was aimed at the utilities and finance, or at the largest manufacturing combinations, and because NAM members came mainly from independent manufacturing concerns, *American Industries* could safely take note of it and even support it, though with the hope that self-correction would be the outcome, lest legislative reforms go too far.

But *American Industries* drew far more attention to another phase of progressivism: its belief in the application of "scientific method" for the sake of "national efficiency." The national problems *American Industries* emphasized—tariff, immigration, labor, commercial expansion, conservation, education—all were, it argued, amenable to solution by a proper understanding of facts and application of scientific method. *American Industries's* notion of reform was, in other words, patently elitist. "The manufacturing interests of the country," the journal's editor modestly intoned in 1905, "want nothing but what the country wants, provided the country wants what is best for it."[4] The outstanding issues were, *American Industries* said, "business questions." They all related to "the Great Business Issue," which was "to discover in a business way what is the greatest good for the greatest number."[5]

Of these issues, tariff reform was the one continually discussed in the pages of *American Industries* throughout the whole prewar period, especially during 1907–1908 and 1912–1913, when President Woodrow Wilson forced through the Underwood Tariff, the first significant reduction in duties since before the Civil War. The theme was to take the tariff "out of politics" by relegating tariff modification to a commission of experts entrusted to provide a rational and consistent protection.

American Industries's conception of progressive reform involved a tariff commission, conservation of "human resources" through strengthened industrial education, and a more active immigrant assimilation policy. Politically, the journal became more and more openly wedded to traditional Republicans and antagonistic to Democrats. Criticism of the Democratic party began in 1911 when, capitalizing on the congressional victory of 1910, it passed tariff reform bills, though the still-incumbent Republican president, William Howard Taft, vetoed them. During the celebrated three-way presidential contest of 1912, *American Industries* solidly backed Taft and attacked the Bull Moose third-party candidate, Theodore Roosevelt, because of the labor and political reforms his platform proposed. *American Industries* reserved its most bitter criticism for the Democrats, with their "virtual free trade policy" and friendliness toward the goals of organized labor.[6]

Woodrow Wilson, elected in 1912 with a Democratic majority in Congress, did little to please *American Industries*, which detected "hostility to business" in many of the Democratic reform moves of 1913–1914. The overwhelmingly rural nature of the Democrats, as *American Industries* saw it, made them incompetent to govern an industrial country, and their tariff revision, "destructive regulation" of business, antitrust prosecution of valuable corporations, and supporting attitude toward organized labor, even if largely symbolic, made their rule dangerous and threatened the economy with disaster.

With the outbreak of war in Europe, a new ideological departure for the NAM appeared in *American Industries* and developed apace during 1915 and 1916. A new editor, Frederic W. Keough, took over the journal in January 1914, shortly after the first NAM presidency of George M. Pope began. Pope's addresses in 1914 struck a new tone, echoed editorially by *American Industries*. First a softening of anti-union rhetoric appeared and an ideal of employer-employee cooperation was held out. Soon this was joined with the theme of national opportunity for economic expansion as war engulfed European manufacturers, opening markets worldwide to Americans. Finally, a fully new ideological line appeared, which persisted through the war years. Business, through educational campaigns, would persuade the nation to follow its leadership in meeting the challenge, once the war was over, of world economic preeminence. "Education" would mold public opinion to rebuke anyone who would "humiliate, harass or embarrass patriotic American businessmen." It would persuade labor to cooperate. In 1916 and 1917, somewhat earlier than anticipated, the NAM launched a major propaganda effort with the slogan "Industrial Preparedness" setting the tone.[7]

American Industries's effort after 1914 to tie together the themes of progressivism as efficiency with the concept of national integration and expansion under business leadership brought the journal's message into the mainstream of the business community's ideological development. But the effort at ideological modernization of 1914–1918 (which continued during the years of Pope's presidency) never really took hold. After the war *American Industries* never returned to the obsolete labor baiting of the 1902–1913 era, but neither did it ever manage to present a cohesive, persuasive, and modern corporatist vision to its readers. During the critical postwar period, *American Industries* seemed curiously restrained, almost adrift. The years 1919 and 1920 were ones of critical strikes and labor unrest and of public fear of radical agitation. *American Industries* continued to call for labor-management cooperation and failed to return to the old-style denunciations. Even when identifying the coal strike of 1919 as the "crisis" of the Republic, the journal editorially maintained a moderate tone.[8] "The Platform of American Industry," adopted by the NAM and promoted by *American Industries* in 1920 to influence the party platforms at the upcoming conventions, was merely a tepid variant of the business Republicanism of the day. *American Industries* virtually ignored the Red Scare of 1919–1920, a fact worth noting. To its credit, the journal's editorial line never had, and did not now attempt (as so many conservative and antilabor effusions did), to link unionism and socialism. Traditionally, *American Industries* had tended to dismiss the socialist threat, and even now largely ignored it.

A fresh attempt began in September 1920 to upgrade *American Industries*, this time not ideologically but stylistically. A new editor, D. M. Edwards, from the editorial staff of the *New York Herald-Sun*, took command and immediately set out to modernize the magazine's format and broaden its appeal in what appears an effort to compete with *Nation's Business*, the U.S. Chamber of Commerce periodical. *American Industries* had always filled its pages with reprints of speeches by NAM figures, reports of NAM committees and technical articles penned by engineers. The prose was dreary and the layout amateurish. Now Edwards tried to make his magazine the businessman's window on the world, with many more of the articles written by professionals, and with a much broader range of topics.

Edwards's new departure failed. A greatly expanded circulation would have been required to sustain the magazine's ambitious new design. *American Industries*'s circulation had always been tied closely to NAM membership, which in 1918 stood at approximately 3,500. With the first number of volume 27, in August 1926, *American Industries* changed its title to *Pocket Bulletin: Official Publication of the National Association of Manufacturers.* Harsh cost cutting failed to save the journal, however. In April 1928 it regained its traditional title, but continued with the same modest format and scope. It ceased publication in December 1931, an early victim of the depression, which was already causing a downturn in NAM membership.

In its last five years *American Industries* became more than ever before merely the NAM house organ. The tone of articles and reports, penned entirely by NAM officers and members, became almost unrelievedly negative. A regular report from a newly established NAM Women's Bureau was designed to demonstrate how well manufacturers were treating female and child labor in order to counteract "sentimental demands" reformers were making of state legislators for protective legislation. Reports on strikes, NAM proposals for tax, and, above all, tariff revision appeared regularly. Preservation of the open shop and prevention of restrictions on the use of labor injunctions were the main goals of NAM propaganda on the labor question. A tone of pompous self-importance appeared. In 1928, a presidential election year, *American Industries* detailed the stages in the drafting of the NAM's "Platform of American Industry" as though the whole country were awaiting it with anticipation. When the party platforms were adopted and compared with the NAM's, the Democrats' was found unacceptably soft on the labor injunction issue.

On the whole, *American Industries* reflected the stultifying, old-fashioned conservatism that drastically limited the NAM's appeal in the later 1920s. It was a conservatism that could have served equally well in 1910 as in 1929, except that it lacked the spirit and rhetorical interest of the earlier period. The NAM, and its journal, simply defended the status quo. In only one circumstance did *American Industries* key into liberal corporatist thinking, into the heady atmosphere of economic planning and welfare capitalism that the luminaries of the business world were touting in the late 1920s. In what might have been a rather promising series of articles, NAM members reported on their successes with "employee representation" schemes. But it soon became clear that these were nothing more than co-optation plans, a forum in which managers could "explain to their fellow workers" management's decisions.[9]

The *American Industries*'s brand of conservatism was a typical, old-line business conservatism consisting largely of a defense of businessmen's prerogatives in running the economy with a certain amount of support and stimulation by the national government. When the depression came in 1929, *American Industries* was thus consistent in backing Herbert Hoover's leadership. There was no difficulty in supporting Hoover's White House conferences or his requests for business cooperation in maintaining wage rates and employment levels. But it was not the prospect of business-government cooperation in managing the economy that mainly held *American Industries*'s editorial interest as the depression gathered momentum in 1930. It was, rather, the danger the depression presented to the existing state of business-labor relations. *American Industries* realized that the economic conditions of 1930 were rapidly strengthening the supporters of labor legislation. In its last months the journal was less interested in Hoover's recovery program than in alerting its readers to the implications of two threatening legislative proposals. These were Senator Robert F. Wagner's bill for a national employment system and the measure that would, during the next year, become the Norris-LaGuardia Anti-Injunction Act. It was fitting that, as its history ended, *American Industries* should recognize in these measures a new spirit that would fundamentally alter the relative power and the autonomy of businessmen in the nation's economy.

Notes

1. John Kirby, Jr., "The Menace to Business," *American Industries* 12 (September 1911): 8 (hereinafter cited as *AI*).

2. "Larceny, Blackmail, Extortion: Every-Day Crimes of Walking Delegates," *AI* 1 (15 June 1903): 1–2; "Cleveland's Shame," *AI* 12 (August 1911): 7–8.

3. John Kirby, Jr., "The Relation of Industrial Abuses to Our Foreign and Domestic Trade," *AI* 12 (January 1912): 15.

4. "Wanted: The Scientific Method," *AI* 3 (1 August 1905): 8.

5. "Statesmanship and Business," *AI* 4 (1 January 1906): 8.

6. "Why Radical Political Policies and Parties Are Unsafe," *AI* 13 (October 1912): 15.

7. George Pope, "A Campaign to Stabilize American Business," *AI* 16 (April 1916): 7.

8. Stephen C. Mason, "The Government and the Coal Strike Issue," *AI* 20 (December 1919): 7.

9. Charles Cheney, "Employee-Management Cooperation," *Pocket Bulletin: Official Publication of the National Association of Manufacturers* 27 (March 1927): 10.

Information Sources

BIBLIOGRAPHY: None.
INDEXES: *IAI*; *PAIS*.
REPRINT EDITIONS: None.
LOCATION SOURCES: Complete runs: New York Public Library; Library of Congress.

Publication History

TITLE AND TITLE CHANGES: *American Industries*, August 1902–January 1926; *American Industries Pocket Bulletin*, February 1926–March 1926; *Pocket Bulletin of American Industries*, April 1926–March 1928; *American Industries*, April 1928–December 1931.

VOLUME AND ISSUE DATA: Volumes 1–31, August 1902–December 1931. No numbers issued December 1930–November 1931.

FREQUENCY OF PUBLICATION: Bimonthly, August 1902–August 1909; monthly thereafter.

PUBLISHER: National Association of Manufacturers, New York.

EDITORS: Marshall Cushing, 1902–1906; Henry Harrison Lewis, 1906–1913; Frederic W. Keough, 1914–1920; D. M. Edwards, 1920–1930.

CIRCULATION: In 1926, 3,761.

Robert F. Himmelberg

Exponent
1904–1911

At the dawn of the twentieth century organized labor in the United States enjoyed unparalleled growth. Membership in the nation's premier workers' association, the American Federation of Labor (AFL), stood at a modest 278,000 in 1898, but within seven years had soared to 1,676,000. Although the rate of expansion subsequently slowed, the AFL claimed more than two million followers by 1914. Moreover, another half-million workers belonged to unions unaffiliated with the federation. Although organized labor generally lacked truly radical features, businessmen often perceived it as troublesome and, sometimes, even a threat to capitalism itself.

One place that experienced major business-labor conflict was St. Louis, Missouri. By the end of the nineteenth century this bustling metropolis of 575,238 had changed from being a sleepy yet strategic fur trading post to a city with a mixed industrial base producing household goods, boots and shoes, and transportation equipment. Labor disputes affected most of these concerns during the late nineteenth and early twentieth centuries; the most spectacular disruption, a bitter streetcar strike, occurred in the spring of 1900. When the St. Louis Transit Company, the local surface railway monopoly, slashed wages, hundreds of employees left their posts. A combination of factors in the traction firm provoked this dispute, including bad management, the negative impact of the 1893–1897 depression, and continuing financial woes. The company, however, still sought to keep its cars rolling. So when protestors demanded a "living income," they were replaced by "scabs," many of whom were nonresidents. Heightened tension quickly erupted into almost daily acts of violence between the two groups, both frequently armed with guns and clubs. In time, though, the transit firm won, and an uneasy peace returned to the city.

The legacy of the St. Louis streetcar strike of 1900 was varied. For one thing, it triggered a concerted drive on the part of trade unionists, concerned consumers, and some politicians for municipal ownership of all local public service corporations.

It also provoked a conservative backlash among the community's upper-income group, most notably formation of a vigorous pressure group, the Citizens' Industrial Association (CIA).

The guiding force behind the new organization was businessman James Wallace Van Cleave (1849–1910). Born in Marion County, Kentucky, of pioneer stock, Van Cleave served in the Confederate army before migrating to Louisville at the close of the Civil War. Soon he joined the stove manufacturing firm of J. S. Lithgrow & Company and remained with it until 1888. In that year he moved to St. Louis as an official of the thriving Buck's Stove & Range Company. With hard work, considerable skill, and good luck, Van Cleave in time emerged as the firm's president.

James W. Van Cleave's actions consistently revealed a strongly conservative worldview. Although a states rights Democrat until the "heresy" of William Jennings Bryan and the free silver campaign of 1896, he became a loyal member of the McKinley wing of the Republican party. Van Cleave's burning interest was not the currency or even tariff matters, however, but control of growing labor power, especially in the wake of the riotous transit strike of 1900. His anti-union passion is revealed clearly in this utterance: "Let conservative, law-abiding people everywhere, who out-number the labor-union agitators, the demagogues, and the social disturbers many times to one, unite."[1]

The CIA, having as its major objective advancement of the so-called open shop, became James W. Van Cleave's vehicle for promoting "law and order." Van Cleave and his associates sought through moral suasion and legal avenues to guarantee a place of employment where the worker could opt not to be a union member. As the organization put it: "The Open Shop spells Freedom: For the laborer, it means his right to work, to prove his worth, to do as to him seems best for the interests of himself and of those who are dependent on him. For the employer it means that new and improved methods of production will not be opposed by an organized resistance and that he will remain unhampered in conduct of his business."[2] Soon this St. Louis-based movement formed an affiliation with the National Association of Manufacturers (NAM) and worked directly with its National Council for Industrial Defense after its creation in 1907. This is understandable not only because of shared values but because Van Cleave himself had been an NAM founder in 1896.

To provide a forum to inform the membership of the CIA and to promote the organization within the community and the nation, a monthly magazine was begun in 1904, located in the downtown St. Louis Chemical Building. For nearly two years the publication was known as the *Citizens' Industrial Exponent,* reflecting its parent group's name. The title was shortened to simply the *Exponent,* although it sported the same lengthy subtitle: "A Journal of Law and Order Devoted to the Welfare of the People."

Backers of the *Exponent* never left readers in doubt about their publication's principles. In fact, these consistently held notions were duly proclaimed in an early issue:

1. No restrictions as to the use of tools, machinery, or materials
2. No closed shop
3. No limitation of output
4. No restrictions on the number of helpers and apprentices
5. No boycotts
6. No sympathetic strikes
7. No sacrifice of the individual to the union
8. No compulsory use of the union label.[3]

Although cast in a negative fashion, the list contains a positive thrust. Personal liberties meant much to members of the CIA. They strongly believed that the nation's emergence as an industrial giant related directly to an environment where union activities had not heretofore unduly interfered with the work of capitalists. But the milieu of the new century seemed to suggest the rise of a powerful, even dangerous laboring class. Of course, if workmen wished to strike, they could quit their jobs. "But when they have once left their tasks, let them not assault with bricks and clubs and iron bars the men who take their places."[4]

Throughout its seven-year life, the *Exponent* maintained a consistent format. Logically, the magazine kept readers posted on the affairs of the CIA and related organizations. But most of the twenty-four to forty-eight pages contained news items on strikes, judicial and legislative actions, and special features on such topics as "Co-operation and Profit-Sharing in the Labor Field" and "Improved Homes and Recreation for Workmen." After May 1906 the *Exponent* ran illustrated pieces of general appeal, for example, travel stories and homemakers' tips.

Occasionally the publication included original poems, sketches, and short stories. A typical work of fiction, "The Reward of Independence," by William Edgar Johnson, appeared in the issues of September and October 1906. This piece told the tale of a strike against a small midwestern print shop. Two workers, however, refused to "go out." Guilloz, the handsome foreman, and Miss Gibson, a lovely compositor, while compassionate souls, felt that the stoppage was unnecessary and interfered with their right of free choice. Yet in the end they found a union that they could truly support. Explained Guilloz, "I have in mind a Matrimonial Union!" The two then quickly entered the state of marital bliss.[5] "The Reward of Independence" served two purposes: it had an obvious political message, and it catered to the popular taste for late Victorian sentimentality.

Likely more meaningful than a tale of the open shop leading to true love was another periodic feature, a list of union-boycotted businesses. In one labor dispute with the liverymen of St. Louis, the *Exponent* noted eighty-four establishments that were being boycotted and urged readers "to show your sympathy in a practical way by patronizing them."

The details of editorial and financial matters of the *Exponent* are obscure. The masthead never listed an editorial staff but only officers of the CIA. The price of the publication was reasonable: ten cents a single copy or one dollar annually. Membership in the CIA was available for two dollars per year, and it included a subscription to the *Exponent*. By 1909 the CIA boasted 8,000 members, so at least that many copies were printed, and a minimum of several thousand dollars generated in that year. A portion of the magazine's cost came from faithful advertisers, mostly local businesses and regional railroads. Undoubtedly Van Cleave, wealthy and dedicated to the sponsoring organization and its activities, underwrote some of the expense.

The reasons for the *Exponent*'s eventual demise are not necessarily related to its overall financial picture. Van Cleave retired from the Citizens' Industrial Association in April 1909 and died within a year. Since the *Exponent* was so closely associated with him, its last issue, appearing in January 1911, may well have occurred because Van Cleave was no longer present. Furthermore, the structure of the CIA changed. It gave way to the National Association of Manufacturers' National Council for Industrial Defense and the newly created Missouri Manufacturers' Association. These organizations possessed their own forums and thus lessened the need for the *Exponent*. Finally, the course of the open shop movement itself changed appreciably. Initially the crusade succeeded in checking the growth of unionism, but because of the rise of political progressivism during the 1910s, the campaign weakened. Antilabor agitation flared again after World War I but with neither James Wallace Van Cleave nor the *Exponent* to serve the cause. Yet the conservative legacy would continue in St. Louis. The local business community remained well organized and determined to minimize what it considered to be the negative dimensions of organized labor. And trade unionists nationally experienced difficult days until Franklin D. Roosevelt and the New Dealers became powerful, helpful allies.

Notes

1. *Exponent* 5 (April 1908): 1.
2. *Exponent* 3 (March 1906): 8.
3. *Exponent* 2 (September 1905): 10.
4. *Exponent* 3 (March 1906): 9.
5. *Exponent* 3 (October 1906): 19.

Information Sources

BIBLIOGRAPHY: None.
INDEXES: None.
REPRINT EDITIONS: None.
LOCATION SOURCES: Partial runs: New York Public Library; Missouri Historical Society, St. Louis; St. Louis Public Library; State Historical Society of Missouri, Columbia; University of Michigan.

Publication History

TITLE AND TITLE CHANGES: *Citizens' Industrial Exponent: A Journal of Law and Order Devoted to the Welfare of the People*, 1904–1905; *The Exponent: A Journal of Law and Order Devoted to the Welfare of the People*, 1905–1911.
VOLUME AND ISSUE DATA: Volumes 1–8, 1904–1911.
FREQUENCY OF PUBLICATION: Monthly.
PUBLISHER: Citizens' Industrial Association, St. Louis, Missouri.
EDITOR: None listed.
CIRCULATION: Probably 8,000–9,000 by 1907.

H. Roger Grant

Nation's Business
1912–

Nation's Business first appeared in September 1912 as the organ of the Chamber of Commerce of the United States, which had itself been formed only a few weeks previously. In structure the chamber was a federation of local and state chambers of commerce, trade associations, and other business organizations. The first editor of *Nation's Business*, G. Grosvenor Dawe, looked on the leaders of these constituent bodies, and newspaper editors generally, as his intended readership. Accordingly, the monthly issues of *Nation's Business* at first appeared unattractively in newspaper format. Not until April 1913 did a shift to a magazine format and a conception of *Nation's Business* as a large-circulation, general membership periodical occur.

After enduring two changes of editors in as many years, the Chamber of Commerce in 1916 secured a new editor for its journal, an experienced professional well known in trade paper as well as journalism education circles. In July of that year, Merle Thorpe moved from the chairmanship of the journalism department at the University of Kansas to Washington, D.C. (where chamber headquarters are located and where *Nation's Business* has always been published) and immediately placed his stamp on the journal. He remained at the helm for twenty-eight years, energetically shaping the editorial perspective of *Nation's Business*, as well as its scope and appearance.

With Thope's advent, the progress made under previous editors toward adoption of an attractive style now culminated as Thorpe modeled *Nation's Business* on the layout and design of contemporary mass circulation magazines. Thorpe's aim was to acquire a truly large circulation and make *Nation's Business* the contemporary businessman's magazine of news and opinion, seeking not merely the leaders of the Chamber of Commerce as readers, but the general membership as well. The role as mouthpiece for the chamber continued but was muted in favor of a new professionally journalistic air. By the early 1920s Thorpe's stewardship raised circulation of *Nation's Business*, below 25,000 when he became editor, to 150,000.

By 1929, it rose beyond a quarter of a million.

Thorpe's modernized *Nation's Business*, with its contemporary format, attracted high-quality journalists to write news, features, and informational pieces. The journal became and has remained, in appearance and content, much more than the house organ for the Chamber of Commerce. But Thorpe introduced no major change, except in sophistication of expression, in the message or the ideological outlook that the journal had, from the beginning, sought to convey. This, the first issue of *Nation's Business* had declared, was to preach correct principles, especially "commercial patriotism," the thesis that business was "the foundation of our national life," and the proposition that "the interests of each are the interests of all," that is, that conflict among economic classes or groups was unproductive and unnecessary.

These theses represented an outlook that in current academic parlance is called "liberal corporatism." Since business is the "foundation of...national life," mechanisms of business-government cooperation should arise to foster and stimulate business. And since "the interests of each are the interests of all," government evidently should refrain from promoting or abetting challenges to business from farmers or workers.

Nation's Business's early years coincided with the return to power of the Democrats, who sought to enact a broad agenda of reform. Confronted by major reform initiatives ranging from tariff revision to a more severe antitrust policy, *Nation's Business* advanced its own version of the Democratic proposals, seeking to shape and direct, rather than combat, the coming of new economic policies. During the tariff reform debate of 1913, the journal argued for "scientific" revision through a commission of experts, rather than ad hoc "political" revision. It endorsed agrarian Democrat demand for rural credits legislation on the theory that rural prosperity would stimulate business and, more important would tend to "the preservation of the conservative element," the farmers, who gave "balance and judgement to the thought of the nation." Much more editorial concern, however, was addressed to the question of antitrust law revision, as *Nation's Business* elaborated the conception of a new, cooperative business-government nexus. The proper function of the new trade commission President Wilson was proposing would be not to harass but to advise businessmen what they legally could do under the antitrust laws. But the greatest editorial preoccupation of these early years of *Nation's Business* was attaining "World Pre-Eminence in Exports" through government support and by repeal of antitrust restrictions on export cartels.

These inherited themes Thorpe elaborated and expanded during the next twenty years, making *Nation's Business* the leading journalistic exponent of liberal corporatism. Thorpe's last decade as editor saw a major shift, however, as his journal moved from advocacy of government-business cooperation into opposition to the New Deal. Thenceforth *Nation's Business*'s conservative message evolved in a new direction as Thorpe and his successors elaborated arguments for limited government and a large scope of independence for business.

As America entered the war in 1917, *Nation's Business* seized the opportunity to chronicle the magnitude, which it never underestimated, of the effort of American industry. Eschewing criticism of wartime tax policies, *Nation's Business* instead emphasized the need for a major business-government cooperative effort to contain inflation and prevent production bottlenecks. This cooperation in fact did materialize, in the form of the War Industries Board and other mobilization agencies. Editorially, the efforts of the dollar-a-year men, of the willing acceptance by the corporate leaders of wartime regulation, Thorpe portrayed as "radical"—a marvelous self-subordination of business to the needs of the nation. Recent historical analysis, however, has pointed out that the real aims of business leaders were not quite so altruistic. The aim rather was to avoid the imposition, otherwise inevitable, of a heavy-handed bureaucratic wartime regulation and thus to guide business unscathed through the dangers of a war economy. Another aim was to popularize the thesis that the great success of wartime cooperation among businessmen proved the value of expanded license for cooperation in peacetime as well.

Never before, or after, did the pages of *Nations's Business* express as much confident self-assertion as in the months following the armistice. The postwar plans and demands of chamber leaders, made at the so-called Reconstruction Congress of the chamber in December 1918, were broadcast enthusiastically during the early months of 1919. The most discussed proposal was for a revision of antitrust restrictions on cooperation in business and for continuation of the governmentally sponsored cartelism of the war years. Thorpe unfolded a vision of a business-led American future, a new prosperity created by business cooperation in place of competition, aggressive capture of world markets, and government-business cooperation to enhance industrial efficiency through a partnership approach to industrial and vocational education.

This confident spirit of 1919, this vision of a new era in process of accomplishment, *Nation's Business* would maintain for the next decade. Even when the social and political climate turned unfavorable or even hostile, its spirit of confidence and optimism continued. When economic conditions turned sour later in 1919–1921, first as inflationary pressures rose and then gave way to postwar depression, social dissension and conflict broke out. Prospects of the chamber's accomplishing its postwar agenda disappeared as many political voices, including some of those in the Wilson government, now blamed instead of praised business. Unable to advance the business program, Thorpe might have directed his columns to the antiradical, antilabor propaganda battle that many newspapers undertook during the confused months of radical alarms and labor-capital conflict. But *Nation's Business* participated in the Red Scare and the antilabor propaganda very little and then in a very low key.

This is not to say that *Nation's Business* was so confident in the ultimate triumph of its vision of a liberal corporate state that in the years after the war, it gave no voice to the more traditional conservative concerns of businessmen in America. *Nation's Business* never neglected to condemn "The Blight of Government in Business," when inviting targets arose. When Robert M. La Follette's (R, Wisconsin) candidacy in 1924 seemed to threaten the stability of the Republican coalition that had elected Warren G. Harding and now was needed to keep Calvin Coolidge in the White House, Thorpe's editorializing fell in with the thesis that La

Folletteism meant the coming of "bloc government" to America. It threatened the two-party system and the very survival of the democratic tradition in America. Aside from what was seen as a potential crisis in 1924, however, *Nation's Business*, while sometimes bitterly hostile toward farm bloc leaders, often preferred to belittle them rather than confront them seriously. Indeed, a mocking and patronizing tone toward politicians and politics (other than the Republican administration) was a hallmark of Thorpe's editorial line during the 1920s.

In the pages of *Nation's Business*, however, the 1920s unfold mainly as the history of the advance of sanity in government policy and the progress of positive interaction between government and business. Early in the 1920s, an overzealous Justice Department and Federal Trade Commission, together with threatening decisions from the Supreme Court, had seemed to endanger the development of trade associations, which *Nation's Business* regarded as the primary instrument of business cooperation and planning. By 1925, with the aid of Coolidge and Commerce Secretary Herbert Hoover, business (spearheaded by the Chamber of Commerce) had obviated this threat and enjoyed a friendly and supporting administration of the antitrust laws, and all manner of organizational assistance from the Commerce Department. "A peaceful revolution as dramatic as the industrial revolution of 1800 is under way," Thorpe rhapsodized in 1927. "The great new force is group endeavor." But business was triumphing also in the struggle for intellectual and spiritual leadership. Businessmen, Thorpe wrote, had triumphed over the "Babbitt-baiters," the "demagogues and parlor pinks." Business was practically the entire source of American living standards and well-being, he continued, and it now was clear to all that "business intelligence" was vastly superior to "political intelligence."[1]

In his contemptuous attitude toward reformers and the intellectuals, this claim to a special and singular capacity of the business community for productive leadership, should one suspect the beginning of an antidemocratic outlook, of a disposition to seek a special status, relatively immune from popular influence, for business leadership? Such a thesis is lent a certain plausibility by the chamber's revival, in the closing years of the 1920s, of former demands for drastic changes in the antitrust laws. Many articles and editorials of *Nation's Business* demanded more freedom for businessmen to exercise "self-regulation" over industrial behavior. These attitudes are at least faintly akin to the critique of the liberal state that was in vogue in Europe during the 1920s. Indeed, *Nation's Business* discussed Benito Mussolini and his supposed economic achievements more than once, though with no propensity to endorse fascist ideology. Julius Barnes, the chamber's president in 1927 and its most influential leader for several years afterward, in a very interesting feature article appearing late in that year, acknowledged Mussolini's economic successes but explicitly rejected his politics. These might be suitable for Italy, he wrote, but not for America, where superior results could be expected to flow, as always, from the traditions of freedom and self-government. That Barnes, speaking, as it were, as the ideologist of the chamber, should put the case for liberal constitutionalism on the pragmatic ground of superior material success is perhaps unsettling. But it is nonetheless true that the brand of corporatism *Nation's Business* preached during the 1920s, though it claimed a special capacity for businessmen to lead American development, demanded freedom from political interference and legal restrictions on industrial planning and cooperation, contemptuously disdained business's critics, and never offered fundamental criticism of the American constitutional or political system. During only one political episode, La Follette's crusade in 1924, did *Nation's Business* undertake sustained political analysis, and in this instance the anti-La Follette rhetoric and argumentation were drawn from the classic repertoire of American conservative constitutionalism. And this, rather than appeals to exotic antidemocratic ideology, would be the journal's recourse when New Deal reformism in the next decade would again cast it and the chamber onto the defensive.

But it would be some time before the outlook of *Nation's Business* grew defensive. The confidence and assertiveness of the business mind survived the crash in 1929. During the Hoover years, and even the first stage of the Roosevelt epoch, the assumption that the chamber's corporatistic economic proposals had a presumptive claim to political acceptance, continued to reign. For the first two years of the depression, the chamber and its organ were content to follow the lead of Herbert Hoover. The champion during the 1920s of the trade association movement and business-government cooperation, Hoover asserted leadership in 1929–1930 with his White House Conferences, through which he argued his fundamental proposals for limiting the depression and stimulating recovery. If through the organized cooperation of the business community wages, payrolls, and investment schedules were maintained, recovery would be prompt.

Until mid-1931 *Nation's Business* loyally reflected the chamber's active support for Hoover's strategy. But then Hoover's evident failure and the sharply worsening conditions opened a breach between the chamber and the president, which Thorpe's editorial policy reflected during 1932. The breach arose because although Hoover held fast to his policies and convictions, the chamber moved toward an assertion of greater independence for business and insistence on narrower limits for government. The chamber's shift was clearly a response to rapidly worsening economic conditions, the mounting federal deficit, and widespread political demands for government initiatives, often predicated on the grounds that the business system had failed.

Nation's Business gave its readers a thorough exposure during 1932 to the chamber's vision of a cartelized and planned business system. It also, even more enthusiastically, began to accuse the federal government of causing the continuing depression. Although couched in generalized language and aimed against proposed as well as existing policies, *Nation's Business*'s editorial line became, during 1932, by direct implication a harsh and bitter criticism of the administration and, at a short step removed, Hoover himself. Thorpe's editorials above all assailed Democratic spending proposals, the bonus, and unemployment relief. But they also bitterly criticized the cost of established policies and programs that the Republican administrations of the preceding twelve years had all accepted. Severe budget cutting, especially by terminating all government services that competed with or overlapped with business activities, Thorpe now saw as the major contribution Hoover could make to recovery.

Thus arose the paradox that *Nation's Business* saw out the Hoover era with sour criticism and welcomed Franklin Delano Roosevelt's economy moves in March and April 1933. In May 1933, Thorpe applauded "an administration that acts" and "bids fair to do in a dozen weeks what other administrations spent a dozen years in discussing, in promising and planning."[2] Then came Roosevelt's endorsement of a recovery proposal, the National Industrial Recovery bill, which seemed fully to embody the antitrust relaxation the chamber had been demanding for years. In June 1933 *Nation's Business* acclaimed Roosevelt's appearance at the May Chamber of Commerce convention, reading his speech as an invitation to "partnership" and "self-regulation" on precisely the terms the chamber had long sought.

For several months more, whether because it seemed a useful fiction or because of euphoria, Thorpe maintained the line that a new era in business-government relations had begun. But by December 1933, the mounting evidence that Roosevelt included groups other than business in the new political economy and that business's views would not dominate the New Deal was too strong to ignore. After editorially reviewing the new securities act, the effects of section 7(a) of the National Industrial Recovery Act, the threat posed by the Tennessee Valley Authority, the housing projects, and even the factories being built by Harry Hopkins's Federal Emergency Relief Administration, Thorpe concluded that "partnership of government and business...has become confused with compulsion." By the spring of 1934, unease gave way to distress, and by summer the anti-New Deal position had been adopted that would be the central editorial theme of *Nation's Business* for years to come. "Free Us from Fear," Thorpe demanded in June 1934. If the intention was not to "supplement private business" with socialism, then the New Deal government should "disclose the whole scope of its program and fix clearly its limits."[3]

For the remainder of the decade this would be *Nation's Business*'s editorial thesis and preoccupation: that the New Deal's policies inevitably, whether intentional or not, would lead to "socialism" or "collectivism." The corporate liberal philosophy disappeared, never to reappear. Not until 1937 did Thorpe guide his journal into a less implacably hostile stance. As the New Deal continued to falter in terms of political and economic success, Thorpe detected an upswing in public opinion of regard for the business system and now portrayed the business community as the "loyal opposition" that could, through "education," check collectivistic excess and even bring about revision of the taxation and regulatory policies that prevented business from creating jobs. But cooperation and partnership, Thorpe editorialized, were out of the question, because the New Dealers, though checked, still harbored collectivistic objectives.

Not even the coming of the war or the war mobilization experience itself revived the corporate liberal position in the pages of *Nation's Business*. The contrast with the journal's editorial strategy in 1915–1917 is remarkable. Then the strategy was to take the lead in preparedness and endeavor to take command of the economy during the coming war. Clearly the traumatizing wounds the New Deal inflicted on business confidence were deep and severe, and had not healed. As war grew closer in 1939 to 1941 and the administration enlarged arms production under the rubrics of preparedness and all aid short of war to the victims of aggression, *Nation's Business* (and the official chamber positions it reported), while never directly opposing the president's basic policies, continually ventilated reservations, doubts, and distrust.

One of the major attacks on business prestige during the 1930s had come from the vastly popular conclusion of the Nye committee that big business had, for profit, dragged the nation into World War I. Fearful of revival of such charges, Thorpe frequently denied that business wanted war, and, though gingerly, alluded to the issues that the partisans of America First were raising about the president's intentions and the consequences of entering the European conflict. Was it really the administration's intention to avoid war through aid to the Allies, Thorpe asked? Could business swallow the "tragic paradox" that though the administration acted out of expressed hatred of totalitarianism, its policies were the same as had led to totalitarian regimes in Germany and Italy?

When war came, Thorpe immediately pronounced a litany of unity, calling for full cooperation of business with the administration and an end to recrimination. But *Nation's Business*, though fully devoted to the war effort, never during the war diminished its ideological struggle with the New Deal. Every month in his editorials, Thorpe found cause in the administration's wartime policies for unease about the postwar future. Labor's strength was growing, and its demands (for example, those of the United Auto Workers for a share in management) were "akin to what our country is fighting against." By early 1944, when Thorpe relinquished the editorship, the ideological themes he presented in the journal had come full circle. His last major editorial piece, in January 1944, rejected New Deal overtures (expressed through the Natural Resources Planning Board) for a revival of "partnership." The board's proposal sounded, Thorpe said, like what the Germans "accepted from Mr. Hitler." The only hope for America was in positive revival of the "pioneer heritage," of a political climate encouraging the "risk-taking spirit."

A *Nation's Business* era ended in February 1944, when Merle Thorpe's last editorial appeared. In March Lawrence F. Hurley assumed the editorial role. For many months the journal's editorial viewpoint simply drifted. Not until February 1946 did Hurley provide a replacement for Thorpe's featured commentaries and begin to fashion a coherent editorial point of view for *Nation's Business*. The new editorialist was Felix Morley, a former college president with a background in political philosophy. The essential message Morley delivered over the next two decades differed from Thorpe's conservatism not so much in substance as in expression and the mode of argumentation. The same central thesis, that expansion of government activities threatened enterprise, the increase of national wealth, and political liberty, he clothed in more sophisticated garments, drawing on traditions stemming from the ideas of Tocqueville and Burke. Political circumstances had of course changed. The forces of the Roosevelt political coalition now were contained by Republican recovery in the Congress and, in the 1950s, by Dwight D. Eisenhower's presidency. In the relative prosperity of the postwar era, the reputation of the business community rebounded, and self-confidence returned. *Nation's Business* responded to the new environment by voicing a more reflective conservatism, which tacitly accepted the fundamental New Deal reforms but promoted a philosophy of governmental restraint in the name of higher values.

The editorial line of *Nation's Business* in the postwar period thus had much in common with the well-known conservative intellectual currents of the age. It echoed the conservative thought of Robert A. Taft (R, Ohio) (though perhaps more moderately than he in coming to terms with the New Deal's programs) in the 1940s; in the 1950s, it had much in common with both "modern Republicanism" and the "new conservatism."

Morley's monthly lectures set the editorial tone for *Nation's Business*. Part political philosophy, part comment on the political scene, they recycled endlessly a few central ideas. To preserve its "form" and thus its historic greatness, America must preserve its characteristics of "self-reliance," "classless cooperation," and "limitation of power."[4] The tendency for special interest groups (especially labor) to violate these canons made imperative the appearance of selfless leaders who could rise above class limitations. The "natural leaders" were the businessmen, who should strive to assume the role they deserved by reason of their capacity for selfless guidance and the relative importance of their contribution to national life. American uniqueness was historically expressed also in the design of the "federal republic," that is, by "Constitutional government," which limited the exercise of power and left much authority and decision making in the hands of such traditional institutions as home, church, school, and business.

In political commentary, Morley, his associated feature writer, Edward T. Folliard, and others reflected a relatively hard conservative line in criticizing Roosevelt's wartime diplomacy and its results in the years after 1945. The Truman policies in the cold war were vaguely supported, but always in the context of criticizing Roosevelt's wartime decisions as the source of postwar diplomatic problems and defeats. *Nation's Business* in 1951 was sympathetic to General Douglas MacArthur as a symbol who exposed the Europe-centeredness of American policy at the expense of the Far East, but it stopped short of supporting his challenge to President Truman.

Despite its formally partisan policy, *Nation's Business* developed a remarkably close identification with the Republican administration during the 1950s. But editorial impatience arose when Eisenhower Republicans failed to check the rise of spending and even led to a sharp attack on the administration's 1957 budget. In the great national debate over economic issues in the late 1950s (the slowing growth rate, incipient inflation, unemployment) *Nation's Business*, led by Morley, fought strenuously for tax cutting and budget limitation, and against the popular view that higher spending would promote employment and growth. Only investment from funds freed by tax reduction could stimulate economic growth. Little or nothing was conceded to the Keynesian viewpoint.

Few changes appear in the format, editorial preoccupations, or article topics of *Nation's Business* in the passage from the 1950s to the 1960s. Alden Syphen, who had replaced Hurley as editor early in the 1950s, in turn gave way to Jack Wooldridge in 1965. Syphen then joined Morley as feature editorialist. These two shaped the editorial response of *Nation's Business* to the Great Society reforms under President

Lyndon Johnson, to the Vietnam War, and to the increasing turbulence in the nation's social scene. They functioned somewhat as a team—Morley measured, reflective, and philosophical, Syphen punchy, hard-hitting, and sarcastic.

It is clear that *Nation's Business* and its editorialists realized by 1966 that the Great Society reforms, projected above all as a war on poverty and inequality, had captured too much popularity and conveyed too much hope that the promise of American life could be fulfilled, to be treated and countered as though merely an extension of New Deal spending and social supervision. The aims and hopes of the Great Society programs *Nation's Business* writers therefore endorsed, but the implementations they at first sadly, then bitterly and sarcastically, mocked as wasteful, inefficient, and unsuccessful. It condemned other major Johnson-era interventions with even greater scorn. Price guidelines were too often enforced by threats and amounted to "government by fear." The flood of consumerist regulation would stall economic progress. The Johnson fiscal policies would lead to disastrous inflation.

But increasingly in 1967 and noticeably in 1968 and 1969, *Nation's Business* drew back from mere criticism of the Great Society reforms and even tempered its attacks on Naderism. The apparent reason was the conviction that negative responses were futile or counterproductive. Evidence for this observation comes from the remarkable volume of comment, in both editorial features and news stories, about the crisis of values afflicting the nation, especially the college population. The business system was on trial, readers were told, and stories defending the system multiplied. The traditional defense, the system's historical success, appeared, but more frequently a new defense was added, one portraying businessmen as the true social reformers. They were pictured as tearing down racial barriers and providing work for the "hard-core unemployed." Morley refocused and renewed his pleadings with businessmen to assert their right of leadership, arguing that only they could steer a middle course and enable the nation to fulfill its ideal goals without falling into disastrous pitfalls.

Late in 1969 *Nation's Business* underwent considerable revamping. Format, which had scarcely changed since Thorpe's day, was modernized. The magazine became more pictorial, and print layout, even the writing style, quickly came to resemble more closely the current practice of the leading news magazines. More significant, Morley and Syphen abruptly disappeared in favor of a new first-page feature, "Panorama of the Nation's Business," devoted to showing how business could solve social problems. "How U.S. Steel Takes on the Housing Shortage," and "How A.T.&T. Tackles Urban Problems," are typical titles in this feature. Series were launched devoted to glorifying the great figures and accomplishments of the business system. Topical articles now stressed not the managerial skills they had emphasized since the late 1940s but the personal and psychological needs of the businessman. "Do You Drive Your Secretary up the Wall?" or "Should There Be a Business Day?" (analogous to Labor Day), *Nation's Business* asked its readers.[5] Articles treating political affairs adopted a subdued and informative rather than ideological tone, arguing the technical merits of reform proposals rather than the philosophy of limited government. Thus, in the early 1970s, *Nation's Business,* and presumably its readers, were beset by the same anxieties afflicting most of the other traditionally self-assured and influential entities of American life. Anxious lest the business system and its operators be seen as reactionary and unattractive in the eyes of mainstream young Americans, *Nation's Business* hastened, like President Richard M. Nixon, whose flexibility and "middle course" economic policies the journal praised, to stress the ability and willingness of businessmen to accommodate to an age of social reform and of uncharted stagflationist economic difficulties.

By 1974, however, a more conservative political-social climate encouraged *Nation's Business* to revive its ideological traditions. A hard-hitting feature editorial on the magazine's lead page returned in January 1974. These features, penned by James J. Kilpatrick, subjected the legacy of the 1960s to harsh scrutiny, in the tradition of Thorpe, Morley, and Syphen. *Nation's Business* now forthrightly condemned excessive spending and taxation, as well as overzealous consumerist regulation, as the cause of the stagflationist economy and boasted of the Chamber of Commerce's lobbying efforts to secure correctives.

Nation's Business greeted Ronald Reagan's election with relief and enthusiasm, acclaiming his announced policies of tax cuts, budgetary control, and toning down of federal regulation. Forty-five years after the New Deal had launched the great debate over how to obtain stable economic expansion (promoting demand through deficits versus promoting investment through tax cuts), *Nation's Business* could have boasted of the consistency over time of its original position. Consistent too was its position on the harmfulness of federal consumerist regulation. The adjustment made ideologically in the late 1960s, however, to allow the legitimacy of shared government-private efforts to promote racial and social equality, was a major and lasting change from which *Nation's Business* showed no sign of retreating as it neared the end of the century.

Notes

1. Merle Thorpe, "Business, the Soul of America?" *Nation's Business* 15 (March 1927): 11 (hereinafter cited as *NB*); Merle Thorpe, "The Business Revolution of 1927–1937," *NB* 15 (March 1927): 27–28.

2. Merle Thorpe, "Government Expenses Cut," *NB* 21 (May 1933): 27.

3. Merle Thorpe, "Free Us from Fear," *NB* 22 (June 1934): 13.

4. Felix Morley, "The State of the Nation," *NB* 33 (March 1946): 15.

5. *NB* 58 (December 1970): 23, 50–53.

Information Sources

BIBLIOGRAPHY: None.
INDEXES: *Bio Ind*; *Bus Ind*; *BPI*; *BPIA*; *CMC*; *IAI*; *Mag Ind*; *PAIS*; *Pol Sci Abst*; *RG*; *URS*; *Urb Aff Abst*; *Writings Amer Hist*.
REPRINT EDITIONS: Microform: UMI; BLH. Bound edition: UMI.
LOCATION SOURCES: Widely available.

Publication History

TITLE AND TITLE CHANGES: *Nation's Business*.
VOLUME AND ISSUE DATA: Volumes 1–current, September 1912–present.

FREQUENCY OF PUBLICATION: Monthly.

PUBLISHER: Chamber of Commerce of the United States, Washington, D. C.

EDITORS: G. Grosvenor Dawe, 1912–1914; Basil Miles, 1914–1915; Louis E. Van Norman, 1915–1916; Merle Thorpe, 1916–1944; Lawrence F. Hurley, 1944–1953; Alden H. Syphen, 1953–1964; Jack Wooldridge, 1964–1975; Kenneth W. Medley, 1975–1979; Wilburt Martin, 1980; Peter Janssen, 1980; Grover Heiman, 1980–1982; Robert T. Gray, 1982–1995; Mary Y. McElveen, 1995–.

CIRCULATION: 1915: 25,000; 1923: 100,000; 1947: 574,000; 1954: 750,000; 1997: 865,000.

Robert F. Himmelberg

Constitutional Review
1917–1929

The eclectic journal *Constitutional Review* was published during the eventful years from World War I to the stock market crash of 1929. Begun in response to sixteen years of "progressivism" in the states and bolshevism abroad, the journal represented a "strict constructionist" perspective on constitutionalism and posed a conservative intellectual challenge to the universal spread of radical ideologies. The *Review* first appeared in April 1917 as the educational and propaganda organ of the newly formed National Association for Constitutional Government and projected the organization's defense of representative political institutions and its apprehensiveness of populism and political centralization of power. Ironically, its lifetime spanned a period of conservative restoration and was doctrinally compatible with the policy orientation of the Harding and Coolidge administrations throughout the 1920s. It ceased publication without warning in 1929, among other factors a casualty of increasing costs and declining membership aggravated by the onset of the depression.

The National Association for Constitutional Government, an ostensibly nonpartisan patriotic society, was formed in 1914 by Henry Campbell Black and the statesman David Jayne Hill, former president of Bucknell College and former ambassador of the United States to Germany. Black, the driving force behind both the association and later the *Review*, was a well-published constitutional scholar and lawyer in Washington, D.C., home of the organization. While publishing many books and articles in prestigious journals, he achieved greatest prominence as the author of the classic *Black's Law Dictionary*.

The year 1913 was marked by a rising tide of radicalism in political thought in the United States such as had not been known since the establishment of the federal Constitution. The politically discontented were the targets of the major parties in the 1912 presidential campaign, which had been one marked by the promise of a new democracy. Novel uses of this concept, such as the initiative, referendum, and recall, all designed to allow for the popular veto of traditional institutional decisions, gained popularity in the states and to many conservatives appeared to threaten the very fabric of the federal system. Even more alarming to constitutionalists was the clamor to recall judicial decisions and clamp restraints on the review power of the courts, especially the Supreme Court. Populists had long regarded the Court as the final line of defense against attempts to uproot and destroy the privileged sanctuary of private property, characterizing the Constitution, according to Hill, as "an outgrown conception" and structurally "fit to be relegated to the scrap heap."[1]

It was this headlong rush to change and the uninformed readiness of the public to sanction radical constitutional surgery that caused legal scholars to pause and regroup. Under the initial impact of a widely circulated article that appeared in a 1913 number of the *North American Review*, entitled "The Crisis of Constitutionalism," Black, Hill, and a group of lawyers and statesmen, including such luminaries as Colonel Archibald Hopkins, John Jay Edson, and Charles Ray Dean, met to discuss a plan of action. Discussions centered on the need to establish a voluntary organization of an educational character that would explain and defend the principles of constitutional government as they had developed in the United States.

Final impetus for the founding of the association came about as a result of the formation of a "League" committed to promote the passage of what was then called the "Gateway Amendment" to the Constitution. If adopted, this amendment would have permitted the complete change of any provision of the Constitution by a majority vote secured solely through the initiative and referendum. The initiative would allow for amendments to be placed on the ballot and, if approved, added to the Constitution. The referendum would call for the removal of provisions already in the Constitution. This method would bypass the traditional two-thirds requirement in Congress to initiate an amendment, and the three-fourths requirement in the states to ratify it, thus leaving the terms of the Constitution subject to outright majoritarian control. Black and his associates viewed this as the determinative step toward the ultimate destruction of the American political system and one that had to be countered with an aggressive educational strategy. Their mission was not only to alert the public to the dangers of the Gateway Amendment but to rekindle the latent spirit of "Americanism" in political life. The charter for the National Association for Constitutional Government was adopted 6 May 1914, and the organization went into operation.

In its initial three years, the association carried on its educational mission chiefly through the preparation and circulation of folders and pamphlets designed to explain the fundamentals of constitutional government. In addition, pocket editions of the Constitution were distributed to interested civic groups, libraries, and schools throughout the country. It was evident, however, that as the war drew to a close and the calls for postwar revolutionary change rose, a more substantial vehicle for the dissemination of information would be needed. So it was that in April 1917 the first issue of the journal appeared under the title of *Constitutional Review: A Quarterly Magazine Advocating the Maintenance of Constitutional Government and Recording Its Progress at Home and Abroad.* Under Black's editorial direction, the purposes of the association and the policy of the journal were intertwined.

The *Review* was published quarterly and featured lead articles solicited from a broad range of experts, mostly persons in government, legal scholars, attorneys, and judges. Those contributing articles included such notables as Charles C. Dawes, vice-president of the United States and author of the Dawes Plan for postwar reparations; James M. Beck, former assistant attorney general and congressman from Pennsylvania; Andrew Mellon, secretary of the treasury; and former president William Howard Taft. James Beck was to play an important role on the executive committee of the association, and in the final years he sat on the editorial board of the journal.

In addition to the feature articles, each issue contained an extensive editorial section, book reviews, and critical commentary on contemporary works of a political nature appearing in the popular media. Editorial policy was Black's preserve and through the years it reflected his intransigence toward "radicalism," whether of the bolshevik, socialist, or progressive variety (distinctions never made clear in his writings), and his outspoken opposition to tampering with the institutional foundations of the U.S. and state constitutions. Black's political theory, which dominated the journal, was most succinctly presented in his text *The Relation of the Executive Power to Legislation*, published in 1919, two years after the journal commenced publication. The thesis, briefly stated, identified four dangerous trends in modern political systems: the centralization of power at the national level, the domination of that power by the executive, the use of governmental power to "balance social accounts," and the headlong attack on the judiciary, which in the United States was the one institution standing in the path of social and economic change.[2] These were the themes hammered on by the journal over its thirteen years of publication. In addition, Black, like Hill and Beck, authored over 12 of the 219 major articles that appeared in the journal.

In the course of publication, the *Review* critically examined many landmark political works, including Edwin Corwin, *Doctrine of Judicial Review*; Max Farrand, *The Making of the Constitution*; Ernst Freund, *Standards of American Legislation*; and Charles Warren, *Congress, the Constitution, and the Court*, all classics in the literature of constitutional law and American government. Revealing of the texture of these reviews and the editorial preoccupation with the socialist specter was its treatment of Charles Beard's famous and controversial work, *An Economic Interpretation of the Constitution*. Beard argued that the overwhelming majority of the framers of the Constitution were immediately and personally involved in the outcome of their labors at Philadelphia and were to a greater or lesser extent economic beneficiaries of the Constitution. The journal acknowledged that the work was carried out with perfect sincerity, scholarly care, and thoroughness, with no prejudice, pet theory, or other motive than to make a significant contribution to history. Not to end it there, however, the critique went on:

But it unfortunately happens sometimes that the fruits of a pure and abstract scholarship can be seized upon and perverted to an unimagined use, by those who lack both scholarship and the ability to see more than one side of a question. And thus we may find an eminent authority acclaimed (to his discomfort, one may surmise) as the high priest of a cult to which he has no leaning and the preacher of a gospel in which he does not believe. In this way Professor Beard has played into the hands of the socialists.[3]

The journal went on to point out that on the authority of the Beard book, a prominent member of the Socialist party had written a text entitled *Our Dishonest Constitution*, describing members of the Constitutional Convention as "good gamblers" and a "group of grafters." This tendency to diverge from a strictly detached critique was characteristic of the journal and demonstrated an interest less in the inherent merits of the work in question than its impact in the realm of partisan politics.

The constituency of the journal was never very large. Initially distributed among members of the association as the communications vehicle for the exposition and dissemination of matters pertaining to constitutional developments in the states and abroad, the journal maintained a continued scrutiny of all proposed amendments to the federal Constitution and state constitutions. It was at first procured by large urban libraries, and by 1927 the ten volumes published to date were in the major private and public universities throughout the country. The thirteen volumes that constitute the full publication record can now routinely be found in all law school libraries as well.

It is difficult to estimate how large and widespread the National Association became, but to provide some insight into its scope, a treasurer's report issued at the annual association meeting in 1926 showed the following membership pattern: honorary members, 3 (these were President Calvin Coolidge, Chief Justice Taft, and Elihu Root); life members, 83 (those paying $100 in one sum); sustaining members, 305 (this was the membership that by advanced subscription kept the journal afloat); contributing members, 54; and annual members, 884. The annual receipts for the association that year totalled $14,597.52 and expenditures were $13,104.51. The *Constitutional Review* that year grossed $1,078.81; at $1.00 per subscription this suggests a nonassociation circulation of approximately 1,100, a circulation inordinately low given the quality and credentials of the contributors.[4] Substantial financing for the journal necessarily came out of the reserve fund of the association. Although its appeal was essentially to the Right, particularly in its outspoken defense of laissez-faire economics, it was the intellectual conservative and not the corporate conservative whom the editors finally reached. There was a continued lament at the annual meetings over the inability of the association to attract large financial supporters for its various causes, especially the journal. Both the permanent membership and the circulation slowly eroded due to death and attrition, which would indicate that the original membership reflected an older clientele and that the association failed to capture the allegiance of younger conservatives.

On 19 March 1927, Black died, taking much of the heart out of both the association and the *Review*. At the annual meeting that year, it was determined that the *Review* should go forward with essentially the same mission but with a substantially altered editorial structure. Moving from the single dominant framework Black fostered, the *Review* established an editorial structure of four, including a managing editor. The board members included Beck and Hill, the two remaining lifelong members of the association, joined by the prestigious constitutional scholar Charles Warren, former assistant attorney general of the United States and author of the Pulitzer Prize-winning three-volume history, *The Supreme Court in the United States*. The managing editor, of equal stature in the field, was Herbert F. Wright, prolific author, and political science professor in the School of Foreign Services at Georgetown University. Considering the legacy of Black and the enormous prestige of the four-member panel, the *Constitutional Review* certainly must be categorized as one of the best journals of its kind then in print.[5]

In the two years following Black's death, a clear change occurred in the level of rhetoric in the editorials and in the complexion of the feature articles. Fewer diatribes against radicalism appeared. Articles took a notable turn toward historic analysis of the growth of the Constitution and reflected a more balanced distribution of features relating to contemporary political developments. Although polemical essays did still appear, attention shifted to the structural treatment of individual provisions of the Constitution, those dealing, for example, with the commerce clause, due process, and separation of powers. Then, in 1929, with no forewarning evident in the annual meeting that year, the journal ceased publication.

What happened may be conjectured. Presumably the unanticipated burden placed on the editorial board coupled with declining membership in the face of a widespread depression caused the association to seek affiliation with some other publication.

At this time the George Washington Law School was interested in introducing a law review of its own, and discussions were held with the association over a possible merger. According to Hugh Bernard, librarian emeritus of the George Washington University Law Library and currently commissioned to write a history of the law school, trustee minutes of the law school indicate that some discussions were held in 1931–1932 over the advantages of merger to ease the financial burdens of both groups. But because the *Constitutional Review* was considered to have been an "ultra right-wing conservative" journal, nothing came out of the merger talks.[6] It is, however, interesting to note that in the masthead of the first issue of the *George Washington Law Review*, the following statement appears in the editor's notes:

A short time ago this University took over from the National Association for Constitutional Government a periodical known as the *Constitutional Review*. This review has been combined with and will be published as an integral part of *The George Washington Law Review*. As the Federal Constitution is the primary source of our federal governmental law, we shall continue the purpose of the earlier publication by our presentation of the developing principles of constitutional law.[7]

This is the last known reference to the journal and certainly indicates at least some aspect of an accommodation. As far as can be ascertained, the *George*

Washington Law Review was finally modeled on the *Harvard Law Review* as a traditional law school journal with no distinctively ideological caste, certainly not that of the conservatism of the *Constitutional Review*.

Synthesizing the ideological posture of the *Review* poses a problem not only of volume but of scope: the journal contained 210 feature articles and over 300 editorials spanning the economic, political, and social spectrum. Overall policy, however, stemmed from and remained in complete accord with the purposes of the association: to propagate knowledge of the Constitution, to foster respect for the organic law of the land, and to preserve the judicial system as a check on legislative power especially as it affects the fundamental rights of life, liberty, and property. This policy was to be carried out in an intellectual, nonpartisan, and educative fashion, a goal that was to suffer a congenital weakness—almost a schizophrenic ailment—from the outset. A report at the Second Annual Conference stressed the educative philosophy of the *Review* but could utter in the same breath "that a chief aim is to carry on the propaganda of the association by the presentation of well reasoned articles by writers of recognized ability and authority...not so much to instruct the members of the association as to furnish them with ammunition by means of which they, personally and individually, may help to spread the doctrines for which the association stands and combat the rising tide of untempered radicalism."[8]

This ambiguity of mission between presenting "well-reasoned articles" to inform and dispensing "propaganda" for "ammunition" purposes is an unmistakable trait manifest through the life of the journal, varying only in intensity according to the issue. Thus when the volatile question of woman's suffrage was proposed on 14 June 1919, and declared law on 26 August 1920, the *Review* stood mute, publishing not a single feature either in support of or in opposition to the constitutional suitability of the Nineteenth Amendment. Instead, the association unabashedly lobbied the newly emerging women's groups, especially those on the Right, such as the Daughters of the American Revolution, offering propaganda materials and editorial space in support of such selective feminist goals as preserving the American family life, opposing pacifism and paternalism, and supporting a major defense buildup.[9]

Despite its apparently contradictory purposes, the *Review* usually approached the efficacy of constitutional systems at three clearly discernible if not interrelated levels: at the ideological level, it maintained a steady barrage against all forms of "radicalism" from the violent Bolsheviks at one end of the scale to the pacifists at the other; at the institutional level it railed against the majoritarianism of the populists and attacks on the Constitution and the political institutions that grew out of it; and at the policy level—the end product of radical theory and progressive institutional reform—it lamented the inevitability of "class legislation" and the attendant subsidization of social goals and regulation of corporate enterprise. Underlying this threefold mosaic was the special concern for safeguarding the prerogatives of the judiciary. For it was the courts, and the Supreme Court in particular, that must ultimately use the Constitution to preserve liberty from the radicals, institutional integrity from the progressives, and the economic system from the reformers.[10]

The menace posed by the transplantation of alien ideologies to the United States in the wake of the violent imposition of bolshevism in Russia and socialism in Europe engrossed the *Review*. For Henry Campbell Black, bolshevism was less a theory than a form of behavior, "not so much a school of political philosophy as a career in crime deriving its strength from the criminal class which infests the underworld of every civilized community ready to break into plunder and murder when the last vestiges of law are swept away."[11] Tragically, American intellectuals in alarming numbers were being duped into blindly carrying forth the communist message. Such was the case of John Reed, the revolutionary socialist who so vehemently argued the Red cause in the United States. Bemoaned the *Review*, "Men such as he find their immunity only in the amazing carelessness and incurable optimism of the American people." Bolshevism was nothing new; it reached back into bloody history, and if these reactionary tendencies of so-called modern revolutionary doctrines could be exposed, the American people would return to their traditional roots, to evolution and not revolution.

As John Reed and bolshevism drew editorial fire, so did Republican Senator Robert La Follette of Wisconsin and the progressives. An article attributed to Black reveals the depth of the writer's feeling:

There are radicals in America who want to govern without a written constitution. There are still more superradicals who want to govern without any written law. In Russia they have originated a government without either constitution or written laws, and they are now reaping their harvest of bitter regret. Let every man in America who wants the unlimited rule of the majority—the worst tyranny that God has ever permitted on the surface of the earth— proceed to sympathize with the Senator from Wisconsin.[12]

Characteristically, little distinction was drawn between the destructive totalitarianism of bolshevism and the seductive majoritarianism of the progressives. The welfare state, paternalism, and liberalism all equally paved the way for the ultimate destruction of constitutionalism.

Paralleling this ideological engagement, the *Review* gave considerable attention to three issues that dominated the rhetoric of the 1920s: education, immigration, and criminal sedition. Each in its own way reflected the journal's preoccupation with loyalty and "Americanism." The process of education was considered pivotal in altering the nation's consciousness. Education was viewed not so much as a means of exploring new ideas but as a way to fulfill the goal of bringing to the public the fundamentals of the American way of life. To indoctrinate on the one hand, while exposing the reactionary underpinnings of modern radical movements on the other, was the educational mission supported by the *Review*. Because colleges and universities were fast becoming the seedbed of dangerous ideologies, vulnerable to the Left, they were continually under editorial attack. "Parlor Bolsheviki," as intellectuals were endearingly called, seemed everywhere to oppose the cherished notion sponsored by the association that "children and college students should be taught patriotism, concrete citizenship, and one-hundred percent Americanism." This philosophy was characterized by the Left "as the most terrible menace to American schools and colleges and to free liberal thought in the lifetime of the nation."[13] This perception of the academic Left was to last until Black's death in 1927; thereafter the diatribe against the intelligentsia subsided.

Among the problems of the 1920s, the most significant was formulation of a new immigrant policy. The journal supported the terms of the Johnson Immigration Act of 1924, which fixed quotas at 2 percent of the foreign born of each nationality according to the census of 1890, thus reducing the annual number of immigrants from 350,000 to 164,000 and discriminating against southern and eastern Europeans. To compound this, the *Review* supported the tightening of regulations of naturalization, including strict language requirements and commitments on the part of applicants to abandon their cultural heritage. An article written in 1925 by R. E. Saner, chairman of a citizens' naturalization lobby group, reveals the extremes to which the *Review* could deteriorate:

It is fashionable to call this country the "melting pot." There was a time when races of northern Europe constituted our chief immigration, the Nordic races, carrying in their veins the same blood as ours, insensibly and in the second generation melting into our national life. But with the influx of the debased races of southern and southeastern Europe, there is no longer a melting pot in America.[14]

This borderline racist treatment reflected a prevalent attitude on the Right that the inroads made by radicals was attributable to newly arrived ethnic groups. Coming from politically unstable regions, uneducated, clustering in ethnic ghettoes, having no lasting devotion or experience with constitutional government, they were particularly susceptible to the socialist contagion. Stemming this tide was critical to suppressing the disease.

The disruption and insecurity caused by the war, and the crippling apprehensiveness of violence associated with the growth of Communist party cells in the United States, gave rise to alarmingly restrictive laws governing national security, political expression, and voluntary association. The federal government enacted sedition laws punishing as a criminal conspiracy even the expression of actions that might in some ill-defined way lead to threats to the Selective Service System and the conduct of military operations. In the early 1920s, the states began widespread experimentation with criminal anarchist and syndicalist laws to restrain the growth of radical organizations and punish those individuals, usually communists or "Wobblies," who might be inclined to preach violence to achieve their political objectives. Writers in the *Review* uniformly supported such legislation and were particularly outspoken in favor of the role again played by the Supreme Court in reviewing these laws.[15]

In a spate of famous rulings in the early 1920s, the Supreme Court emasculated the speech and association provisions of the First Amendment under the Holmes doctrine of "clear and present danger." According to these decisions, whether or not the government could prove a serious plot to overthrow the system, the mere membership in organizations theoretically committed to do so, and the mere utterance of revolutionary philosophy could result in fine and imprisonment.[16] The *Review* supported the ruling in *Gitlow* v. *New York* (1925), wherein it was held that the government had the right "to suppress even a spark if it was capable of leading to the conflagration."[17] Article upon article argued the need to emphasize national security more than freedom of speech, and loyalty to the system more than the right to entertain unpopular political beliefs. When the *Review* spoke of preserving "liberty," it did not have in mind liberty of thought.

At the institutional level, a continued debate raged throughout the history of the *Review* over the controversial choice posed by the Left between democracy in its pure form and the representative system that evolved in America. The *Review* in a number of articles took the position that the framers, fearing majorities, never intended to create a democracy but a republic. Federalism, separation of powers, limited law-making authority, and tight restrictions contained in a Bill of Rights, all guaranteed by a rigid, written constitution and protected by a neutral and politically insulated judiciary, were the legacy of the framers. The very institutions and practices that matured under this framework were to be fatally undermined by the propagation of the virus of majority democracy: initiatives, referendums and recalls, direct primaries, simplified amending process, circumscribing the appellate jurisdiction of the Supreme Court, and eliminating judicial review.[18]

Foremost among the association's concerns was that the process of amending or revising constitutions, federal or state, should be made as difficult as possible. Writers persistently took the position that complex procedures forced deliberation, that "operative surgery of the vitals should not be committed to hasty tempers or rash hands."[19] Changing the fundamental law of the land by arbitrary majoritarian procedures would destroy the restraints so carefully built into the system by the framers and ultimately place power in the hands of demagogues, as was happening throughout the world. Time and again, the *Review* pointed to developments in Europe, especially Spain, Italy, Germany, and Russia, whose constitutions were disintegrating, cautioning that only adherence to the strict principles of law could prevent a similar fate here. Legitimate social, economic, and political change must be implemented slowly through balanced judicial interpretation and not mass emotional response. This function left for the legal system a crucial responsibility, and the *Review* challenged all attempts to tamper with judicial prerogatives. In one significant challenge, the *Review* conducted a protracted campaign against the La Follette amendment that would have subjected Supreme Court decisions affecting the constitutionality of legislation to congressional veto. Such legislation would have effectively eliminated the judicial branch as a check on power. The fundamental constitutional question of federalism—the relationship between the national government and the states, and the relationship among the three branches of the central government—was at the center of controversy sparked by the events of the war and prohibition. Although writers in the journal covered different facets of each problem, they emphasized the alarming acceleration these events gave to expanding national power generally, and executive power especially. One result of the centralization of power was the widespread delegation of executive authority to commissions and agencies and the inevitable growth of bureaucratic control. Fears were continually expressed that once this apparatus was set in place, it would remain of its own inertia to stifle peacetime industrial recovery and dampen the essential elements of laissez-faire economics. The problem of national power was compounded by the Volstead Act, which placed enormous regulatory power in the hands of federal liquor control agencies and further cut into the essential police powers of the states.[20]

Much has already been written concerning the attitude of the journal to such devices as initiatives, referendums, and the like. The journal's central theme held that if the structure of representative government, painstakingly fashioned over the years by sound constitutional doctrines, was to be undermined by a mass-based majoritarian system, these would be the fatal instruments. Elected officials, facing such overwhelming pressures, would inevitably capitulate to the fashionable. As one writer said: "Democracy is probably the only thing in the world that gets admittedly bad when it gets pure."[21]

For the association and all those who labored over the *Review*, the dreaded consequence of socialist ideology and majoritarian institutions would be the welfare state and its insidious offspring: class legislation and the destruction of individual and property rights. Throughout the journal, an endless flow of articles assailed all forms of social legislation: minimum wage laws, child welfare laws, collective bargaining, and regulatory law, especially as embodied in the Federal Trade Act and the commission brought about to enforce it. Writers expressed little sympathy with "the poor who after slaving all day go home at night to have nothing to eat but food and nothing to wear but clothing."[22]

Federal attempts to regulate minimum wages and the conditions of employment for selected professions illustrate the position of the journal as it matured in later years. The *Review* not only vehemently opposed all such legislation but lauded the critical role the Supreme Court played in settling the matter. Nothing is more revealing of the relationship between property and constitutional doctrine than the Court's handling of two extraordinary cases. In *Hammer* v. *Dagenhart* (1918), the Court impeded congressional attempts to use the commerce clause as a basis for regulating wages and hours of children, broadly construing the Tenth Amendment reserved power clause in favor of the states against federal intrusion. In *Lochner* v. *New York*, settled in 1905, the Court articulated perhaps the most lavish defense of property ever to find shelter under the law, using the Fourteenth Amendment due process clause not to defend human rights as intended by its framers in 1868 but to prohibit the states from passing legislation having the effect of altering property rights. This doctrine of substantive due process, as it came to be called, prevailed in the courts into the Great Depression, climaxing in the famous Holmes ruling in *Nebbia* v. *New York* (1934), which ended by judicial doctrine the Court's veto over social legislation.[23]

In retrospect, the *Constitutional Review* epitomized the conventional conservative platform of the 1920s. It was a final gasping attack on the growth and social obligation of government at once to subsidize and regulate the economy, spread the largess, unleash the powerful labor movement, and remove the obstacles to greater political participation. In defending constitutionalism, it was really defending the judiciary. Liberty meant liberty of property. It is ironic that in the end, the very Supreme Court the *Review* looked on as the last defender of constitutionalism should have, with the shifting of one justice in the 1937 *Jones & Laughlin Steel* case, finally opened the floodgates to the nationalization of the economy.[24] With the addition of Hugo Black and William Douglas and the aggrandizement of the judicial role under the Warren Court, strict constructionists today have abandoned the judiciary and look once again to preserving legislative prerogatives. It is also ironic that the instruments of direct democracy and progressivism, which so haunted the journal, have been used often by conservatives to impede the growth of government power by redistributing tax obligations and restricting government spending. To the editors and supporters behind the *Constitutional Review* such a glimpse into the future would have been numbing.

Notes

1. David Jayne Hill, "In Memoriam: Doctor Henry Campbell Black," *Constitutional Review* 11 (April 1927): 67–76 (hereinafter cited as *CR*).

2. Henry Campbell Black, *The Relation of the Executive Power to Legislation* (Princeton, 1919).

3. "An Economic Interpretation of the Constitution," *CR* 1 (April 1917): 121.

4. Report: Annual Meeting of National Association of Constitutional Government (hereinafter cited as NACG), *CR* 10 (July 1926): 168–71.

5. "The Future Conduct of the Review," *CR* 11 (July 1927): 131–33.

6. Interview with Professor Hugh Bernard, librarian emeritus, George Washington University Law Library, 18 May 1983.

7. *George Washington Law Review* 1 (November 1932): 92.

8. Report: Annual Meeting of NACG, *CR* 2 (April 1918): 119.

9. "Women's Political Study Clubs," *CR* 5 (October 1921): 248–50.

10. Gaillard Hunt, "The Bolshevist Idea and the American Idea," *CR* 6 (January 1922): 36–42; Henry Campbell Black, "In Defense of the Judiciary," *CR* 1 (April 1917): 23–34; Edward P. Buford, "Federal Encroachments upon State Sovereignty," *CR* 8 (January 1924): 23–40.

11. Black, "The Enemy Within Our Gates; Bolshevism's Assault Upon American Government," *CR* 3 (April 1919): 67.

12. "Assault Upon the Courts," *CR* 6 (October 1922): 231.

13. "Radicalism in Schools and Colleges," *CR* 6 (April 1922): 124.

14. R. E. L. Saner, "American Citizenship," *CR* 7 (July 1923): 178.

15. "Sedition, Its Definition and Punishment," *CR* 2 (October 1918): 242–47; Charles S. Thomas, "Judicial Power a Defense against Tyranny and Anarchy," *CR* 8 (October 1924): 204–12.

16. *Shenck* v. *United States*, 249 U.S. 47 (1919); *Gitlow* v. *New York*, 268 U.S. 652 (1925).

17. "Free Speech and Criminal Anarchy," *CR* 9 (October 1925): 239–46.

18. Charles S. Thomas, "Federal Encroachments," *CR* 4 (October 1920): 206–16; Leslie M. Shaw, "A Republic, Not a Democracy," *CR* 9 (July 1925): 140–43; Black, "The Discredit of the Direct Primary," *CR* 10 (October 1926): 211–24.

19. Report: Annual Meeting of NACG, *CR* 1 (April 1917): 35.

20. Ira Jewell Williams, "Wartime Property Rights under the Constitution," *CR* 2 (October 1918): 212–19; Linton Satterthwaite, "The Real Menace of the Eighteenth Amendment," *CR* 3 (October 1919): 217–21.

21. Martin W. Littleton, "Mob Rule and the Canonized Majority," *CR* 7 (April 1923): 86–90.

22. Floyd E. Thompson, "Some Dangerous Tendencies in Government," *CR* 7 (July 1923): 170.

23. *Hammer* v. *Dagenhart*, 247 U.S. 251 (1918); *Lochner* v. *New York* 198 U.S. 45 (1905); *Nebbia* v. *New York*, 291 U.S. 502 (1934).

24. *NLRB* v. *Jones and Laughlin Steel Corp*, 301 U.S. 1 (1937).

Information Sources

BIBLIOGRAPHY:

Black, Henry Campbell. *The Relation of the Executive Power to Legislation*. Princeton, New Jersey, 1919.

INDEXES: Each volume indexed; *Jones*; *ILP*; *PAIS*; *Writings Amer Hist.*

REPRINT EDITIONS: Microform: PMC.

LOCATION SOURCES: Widely available.

Publication History

TITLE AND TITLE CHANGES: *The Constitutional Review*.

VOLUME AND ISSUE DATA: Volumes 1–13, April 1917–October/December 1929.

FREQUENCY OF PUBLICATION: Quarterly.

PUBLISHER: National Association for Constitutional Government, Washington, D.C.

EDITORS: Henry Campbell Black, 1919–1927; Editorial Board: David Jayne Hill, James M. Beck, Charles Warren, and Herbert F. Wright, 1927–1929.

CIRCULATION: Approximately 1,100.

Winfield S. Bollinger

Part Two

RELIGIOUS PERIODICALS—
FUNDAMENTALIST
TO EVANGELICAL

When William Jennings Bryan went forth to help prosecute a young biology teacher in the mountain town of Dayton, Tennessee, for advancing the theory of evolution, the old champion of free silver could not have known that the Scopes trial would come to represent religious fundamentalism as opposition to cultural diversity, intellectual freedom, and religious tolerance. What had been a respectable religious tradition with a lively intellectual life became an object of derision. Bryan was ill equipped to play the role he had chosen for himself. He was not a genuine fundamentalist and had not practiced law for nearly three decades. However, as a rural politician who had once attracted a populist following, he understood that great changes were afoot in society. In short order the nation had become more urban, with large-scale industry and occupational diversity dotting once-remote corners of the land. Whether the talk was of Fords, flappers, sports, or Florida land sales, it was clear that the culture yielded new secular and cosmopolitan elements, not yet dominant, but clearly growing. Religious fundamentalism was one important means by which people made vulnerable by such changes could fend off the new by holding onto the old.

Although its roots reach back to the revivalist movement of the early nineteenth century, fundamentalism gathered steam among evangelical Christians only after the Civil War, in response to pivotal developments in the disciplines of science, philosophy, and history, particularly the Higher Criticism of Scripture, which viewed the Bible as an ancient literary document. Some believers took as atheism the contextual considerations deemed indispensable in such works as David Friedrich Strauss, *The Life of Jesus* (1835–36), and Albert Schweitzer, *The Quest of the Historical Jesus* (1906). The continual discovery of layered meaning in old doctrines was mischievous, perhaps even a trick of Satan to test their faith. Conservative Christians adamantly believed in an anthropomorphic God who sent his son to redeem the world, who in turn was crucified, buried, and arose from the grave on the third day. In God's own time, Christ would return to rescue the faithful remnant from earth's torments. The old-time religion offered this comforting assurance: though the economic and cultural world may be confusing, demanding endless adjustments and causing anxiety, in one's belief system certainty was possible.

The nineteenth-century positivist view of religion as superstition makes little sense today, when it is commonly understood that science and religion are different approaches to reality and that the traditional ways of proving and disproving God's existence no longer carry explanatory power. When nineteenth-century legatees of the Enlightenment expected that religion would soon reach the end of its intellectual tether, they relied on their faith in science and the power of reason to discern the shape of the future. Like the state in Marxist theory, religion would wither away. Neither prediction proved correct. Instead the state grew in power, religion remained at the core of American conservatism, and the consequences of science and reason—which together were to solve most human problems—became ambiguous. Linking science ever more closely to technology, humans gained enormous power over nature, yet the twentieth century became one of the more destructive periods in human history.

Second in accounting for the burgeoning strength of fundamentalism was the manner in which modern science appeared to undercut traditional belief in divine creation. Orthodox Christians were reluctant, as are fundamentalists today, to distinguish between biology as science and "creationism" as religious doctrine. In numerous pulpits, urban and rural pastors preached that the Higher Criticism of Scripture, when linked with the theory of natural selection, meant that modern man faced nothing better, as Bertrand Russell put it, than "extinction in the vast death of the solar system." So threatened were Christian fundamentalists that they mobilized forces to pound away at "demon modernism" in all its forms—modern science and evolutionary biology, to be sure, but also a variety of liberating and secularizing trends, including women's fashions and women's smoking. When fundamentalist ministers regularly portrayed Roman Catholicism as counterfeit Christianity, their theistically oriented followers pursued overt political goals. Militant faith in "the one right way" fed movements against the teaching of evolution and the production and sale of alcohol, favored immigration restriction and legislation to purge American life of "urban" vices such as gambling, pornography, and prostitution, and helped to swell the numbers of the Ku Klux Klan.

The dispute over evolution brought contumely on fundamentalist Christians, and in most theological schools their champions suffered a loss of influence. Yet the conventional wisdom that they lost the public debate was overly optimistic: opinion polls in the last years of the twentieth century continued to document that a near-majority of the American people reject human evolution as a fact. On a broader front, in the years following the fundamentalist-modernist controversy of the 1920s other politically oriented ministers such as Billy James Hargis, Carl McIntire, Gerald L. K. Smith, Dr. Frederick C. Schwarz, and Major Edgar Bundy (an Air Force Intelligence officer when ordained in the ministry by the Southern Baptist Convention, who later headed the extremist Church League of America) emerged to translate religious fervor into radical rightist politics. Still later, the Moral Majority would enter the sandbox of politics to oppose the equal rights amendment, abortion on demand, pornography, and the removal of Bible reading and prayer from public schools. Then as in the 1920s, the fundamentalist vision was not pluralist, but rather was grounded in the position that its adherents, alone granted access to a higher truth, should determine public policy.

It bears repeating, however, that at the center of Christian fundamentalism lies a distinctive religious viewpoint. It subscribes to a premillennialist view of history, holding that social justice and the triumph of the righteous cannot come before Christ returns to earth. Most fundamentalists have understood this to mean that efforts to usher in the good society through thoroughgoing political reform are useless. Better to "save souls" than to "polish the brass rails of the sinking social ship," it was said. Only at such times as their freedoms were thought to be endangered have they entered the public square aggressively. During the 1920s the enemy was modernism; in recent years it has been secular humanism.

The fundamentalist periodicals in this section sided with premillennialist doctrine, defended the five-point creed as propounded by fundamentalist fathers early in this century: the inerrancy of Scripture, the divinity of Jesus, the virgin birth, the substitutionary atonement, and the Second Coming of Jesus; and they opposed evolutionary theory, modernism, and the Higher Criticism of sacred texts. *Bibliotheca Sacra*, with a fascinating history of mergers and absorption of other periodicals (including *Bible Champion*), is the oldest and the longest-running journal appearing in these pages. Influential in the nineteenth century, often carrying opposing views not only in theology but on labor, big business, and ethical issues, the quarterly (published by Dallas Theological Seminary since the 1930s) retreated in the twentieth century to a more rigid presentation of fundamentalist and premillennialist dogma. *King's Business* impressed readers with its ability to know what John on the Isle of Patmos meant when writing of "red" horses, and its ability to detect that the invading army of Gog, as prophesied in Ezekiel 36, is Russia. With his roots deep in the radical Right, the Reverend Carl McIntire at times enjoyed over one hundred thousand subscribers to the *Christian Beacon*, which he edited, but millions more knew him as the radio voice of the Twentieth-Century Reformation Hour. The *Sword of the Lord*, similar though not identical to McIntire's publication, provides an example of a conservatism that prefers small government but nevertheless asks it to provide a massive defense establishment and to legislate morality, abolish abortion, and end Sunday shopping.

Although fundamentalist by any standard, *Moody Monthly* moved to a more moderate position after the war against fascism, supporting a "new evangelicalism" and providing favorable coverage of the Reverend Billy Graham, who emerged from the Youth for Christ movement in hopes of shedding the restrictive fundamentalist label. The young itinerant evangelist had conducted popular crusades in Los Angeles and in England, tapping public anxiety over the cold war abroad and McCarthyism at home. His criticism of labor unions and the United Nations, and his expressed alarm over "betrayal" at Yalta and "immorality" in high places, found a ready audience. Asking of his listeners only that they prepare themselves for the "latter days" by making a decision for Christ, Graham found himself at the center of a "return to religion" that together with the consumer ethic and troubling arms race profoundly shaped the public mood. His vision led to the founding of the fortnightly *Christianity Today*, destined to become the dominant voice of evangelical Christianity. Edited by Carl F. H. Henry, a learned and highly regarded theologian at Fuller Theological Seminary (the flagship educational institution of postwar evangelicalism), and heavily subsidized by Sun Oil millionaire J. Howard Pew, who supported many rightist organizations, *Christianity Today* at first opposed political involvement, fearing it would deflect attention from its redemptive message. However, new directions in Protestant thought and the tumultuous events of the 1960s drew the journal into discussions of politics and conscience. How could religious conservatives work in the world without compromising their primary obligation: to focus on the gospel, witness to the need for human inner transformation, and relate personal piety to social issues? Orthodox in theology, conservative in politics, and pious in habit, midcentury evangelicals brought renewed vigor to the cause of worldwide missions. This outlook dominated the chief pillars of its institutional base, which included Gordon-Conwell Theological Seminary, Fuller Seminary, and Wheaton College (Illinois). It was for them and millions of like-minded religious conservatives that *Christianity Today* spoke.

Two midcentury periodicals that applied conservative religious themes to economic analysis were *Christian Economics* and *Faith and Freedom*. Neither took inflexible positions on theological issues, but Eckard Toy has found that fundamentalists and evangelicals constituted the larger portion of their readers. The former was published by Christian Freedom Foundation, a procapitalist venture supported by wealthy industrialists, including J. Howard Pew, who contributed more than a million dollars to the organization in the late 1950s and early 1960s. While it found reason to question the extent to which Christians could support laissez-faire doctrine, *Faith and Freedom* also published many of libertarianism's leading lights, among them Frank Chodorov, Murray Rothbard, and Ludwig von Mises. The uneasy blend of libertarian and religious principles perplexed some readers, however, and contributed to the publications' eventual demise.

Bibliotheca Sacra
1843–

In 1843 *Bibliotheca Sacra*, the "sacred library," was founded in New York by Edward Robinson (1794–1863), professor of biblical literature at Union Theological Seminary. Less than a year later, after issuing only three numbers of the journal, he transferred it to his friend and former student, Bela Bates Edwards (1802–1852), professor of Hebrew at Andover Theological Seminary in Massachusetts.

This was not the first time Robinson had started a journal, then turned it over to B. B. Edwards. In 1831, while teaching at Andover, he had begun the *Biblical Repository*, giving it to Edwards, then editor of the *American Quarterly Observer*, at the end of 1834. Edwards had combined these two journals in 1835 as the *Biblical Repository and Quarterly Observer*, which, after he stepped down as editor in 1837, was moved to New York and renamed the *American Biblical Repository*. (Subsequently it absorbed the *Quarterly Christian Spectator*—a continuation of the *Christian Spectator*, a Congregationalist monthly begun in 1819—and in 1845 it began to appear under the title *Biblical Repository and Classical Review*.) Meanwhile, the *Bibliotheca Sacra*, which Edwards took over from Robinson in 1843, recruiting his Andover colleague, Edwards Amasa Park (1808–1900), as coeditor, had appeared in 1844, as *Bibliotheca Sacra and Theological Review*. Seven years later, in 1851, it absorbed the *Biblical Repository and Classical Review*; the new journal was named *Bibliotheca Sacra and American Biblical Repository*, a title shortened in 1858 to *Bibliotheca Sacra and Biblical Repository*.[1]

Thus was born, amid a bewildering array of periodicals connected to the *Bibliotheca Sacra* first by editorial responsibility and later by merger, a journal that has survived for more than one and a half centuries. When it celebrated its centennial in 1943, its associate editor proclaimed it "the oldest theological quarterly in America (it may be, in the world)."[2]

From its beginning the *Bibliotheca Sacra* unmistakably reflected the character of its inveterate editors and through them the spirit of Andover Theological Seminary.

Chief among Congregational seminaries in the nineteenth century, Andover, itself a product of the reaction of old-line Congregationalists to the loss of Harvard Divinity School to the Unitarians in 1805, stood as the citadel of the New England Theology. Founded in the eighteenth century in the valley of the Connecticut River with the preaching of Jonathan Edwards at Northampton, Massachusetts, nurtured on Andover hill by Moses Stuart and Leonard Woods in the early nineteenth century, and given systematic exposition at its pinnacle in the 1870s by Edwards A. Park, that theological descendant of Calvinism continued to assert the sovereignty of God, accommodated a conception of man as having the capacity to choose good or evil, promised eternal punishment for those who chose evil, gave way only slightly to the winds of rationalism released in the years after Darwin, and through all rested on an imperturbable faith in the divine inspiration of the Scriptures. This theology was embodied in the Andover Creed, a statement that faculty members signed and were expected to profess.[3]

Robinson's preliminary volume admirably fulfilled his intention expressed in the preface that the *Bibliotheca Sacra* would "exhibit a full and thorough discussion of the various topics which may at any time be taken up, so as to be of permanent value as a work of reference."[4] In addition to lengthy, erudite articles on biblical geography by Robinson and others, it contained pieces on the Greek New Testament manuscripts and other subjects by his mentor, the distinguished scholar Moses Stuart (1780–1852), professor of biblical literature at Andover. Under Robinson's successors, the journal continued to present the most serious subjects and treat them with lengthy, authoritative, exhaustive analyses. Its scholarship was impeccable. It contained original contributions from the principal theologians of New England and elsewhere, and it offered translations of European scholarship. Its heavy, well-indexed tomes contained the works of philologists, historians, philosophers, and classicists. It reviewed books both religious and secular. Its editors encouraged discussions of controversial issues, chiefly those touching on church polity, the definition of Calvinism, and the defense of orthodoxy against Unitarianism, Universalism, and rationalism. It allowed the opposition to state its case, gave respectful hearing to writers whose positions were at odds with the editors', and steadfastly refused to allow discussion to descend to namecalling.

In 1852, both Moses Stuart, for many years an associate editor of the *Bibliotheca Sacra*, and B. B. Edwards, who had succeeded Stuart as Andover's professor of biblical literature in 1848, died, leaving Edwards A. Park the principal editor of the journal. Park had been graduated from Andover in 1831. In 1836, after serving as a minister and instructor at Amherst College, he returned to Andover, where he taught for forty-six years, first as professor of sacred rhetoric and after 1847, systematic theology. Having already served as coeditor for eight years, Park would command the *Bibliotheca Sacra* for the next thirty-one years and would make it possibly the most influential conservative theological periodical in the United States.

The *Bibliotheca Sacra*'s stature in the middle of the nineteenth century resulted in part from Park's determination to open the journal to mature discussions of the challenges from science that began to confront American churches during the period of his editorship. Park reflected the conservatives' discomfort with some of the implications of modern science, especially its seeming denial of God's participation in the course of human history, but he was confident that their traditional faith would survive the new scientific doctrines.

In the decade before Charles Darwin, Park had published articles by such renowned naturalists as Edward Hitchcock of Amherst, who would forever deny Darwinian evolution, and James Dwight Dana of Yale, who would finally allow it. After the appearance of Darwin's *Origin of Species* in 1859, Park published notices of the work of Harvard geologist Louis Agassiz, Darwin's most effective scientific opponent in America in the 1860s, but he also communicated the work of Asa Gray, Harvard botanist and Darwin's most effective American ally. Determined to "elucidate the agreement between Science and Religion," Park made his journal one of the first theological periodicals in America to notice Darwin and to attempt to give balanced treatment to the English naturalist's work.[5]

The 1860s and 1870s saw two more mergers and some changes in Park's editorial staff. First, at the end of 1863, the *Bibliotheca Sacra* absorbed the *Christian Review*, a Baptist quarterly begun in 1836; the first issue of 1864 carried the abbreviated title of *Bibliotheca Sacra*. Late in 1871, it took over the *Theological Eclectic*, edited by George Edward Day (1815–1905), professor in Yale Seminary. Since 1852, when B. B. Edwards had died and Park had taken on Samuel Harvey Taylor (1807–1871), principal of Phillips Academy, as his coeditor, Day's name had been listed as an associate editor of the *Bibliotheca Sacra*. Now, with Taylor's death in January 1871, Day became his replacement, and for a few years the quarterly was called the *Bibliotheca Sacra and Theological Eclectic*. In 1876 it reverted to its original title, *Bibliotheca Sacra*. The following year, in 1877, Archibald Duff, Jr. (1845–1934), of McGill College (Canada), then United College (England), joined Park and Day as a coeditor. In 1880, however, for the first time since its beginning, only one editor's name appeared on the quarterly's masthead—that of Edwards A. Park.

Now in his seventy-second year, Park had guided the *Bibliotheca Sacra* for nearly four decades. In keeping with an early pledge "to cherish a catholic spirit among the conflicting schools of evangelical divines," he had opened its pages to contributors from "different Schools and different Sects," even publishing articles that he and his coeditors did "not, in all respects, endorse."[6] At the same time, Park became Andover's staunchest spokesman for the New England theology, which he and his predecessors, Leonard Woods, Moses Stuart, and others had taught at the seminary since its beginning. But times had changed. By the 1880s some Andover professors, sympathetic to the doctrine of "future probation" and the Higher Criticism of the Scriptures, were finding it difficult to profess allegiance to the Andover Creed. In the face of what he called a new departure on the part of these Andover liberals, Park retired from teaching in 1881 to devote his time to preparing a systematic theology for publication and to deploy the *Bibliotheca Sacra* to safeguard his seminary from further liberal contamination.[7]

Although Park lived nine more years, he succeeded at neither task. Fearing that liberals would try to assume control of the *Bibliotheca Sacra*, he began to transfer editorial responsibility to another editor—and another seminary: Oberlin

Theological Seminary in Ohio. In some ways more liberal, though not more learned, than Andover, Oberlin was a western hub of Congregationalism; it put great store in the freedom of the will and the necessity for benevolent action. Progressive religious, social, and scientific causes seldom lacked support there. George Frederick Wright (1838–1921), the man to whom Park turned to succeed him as editor, was a graduate of Oberlin College (1859) and its seminary (1862). A contributor to the *Bibliotheca Sacra* in the 1870s, most notably as a defender of theistic evolution, his accommodationist stance placed him in the company of theologians and naturalists considered heterodox by their antievolutionist opponents. Taken under the wing of Dartmouth geologist Charles H. Hitchcock and, especially, Asa Gray, he earned a reputation as an effective spokesman for theistic evolution. (It was Wright who persuaded Gray to publish *Darwiniana* in 1876.) In 1881 Wright accepted a professorship at Oberlin, where he taught for nearly three decades, in 1892 becoming professor of the harmony of science and revelation. He studied glacial phenomena in the United States, Alaska, Greenland, Europe, and Asia, and was the author of sixteen books and nearly six hundred articles.[8]

Yet as he began his editorship of the *Bibliotheca Sacra*, his career began a gradual change in the direction of a more conservative theology, a shift discernible as early as January 1884, when he reviewed George Trumbell Ladd's *Doctrine of Sacred Scripture* (1883), a detailed and sympathetic summary of the Higher Criticism. It argued that the creation account in Genesis was mythical, the story of Jonah and the fish was allegory, the book of Isaiah had more than one author, and Moses did not write the Pentateuch. While the book received predictable praise from the new *Andover Review*, the journal founded by the Andover liberals, Wright portrayed it as flawed—a misguided rationalist attack on the orthodox conviction that the Bible was the divinely inspired word of God.[9]

Thereafter, Wright continually moved the *Bibliotheca Sacra* away from a flexible, progressive theology. Seldom after 1900 did the quarterly carry contributions from major theologians. Instead, in the early twentieth century, it would champion a conservatism that equated Higher Criticism with atheism. Wright, whose Christian Darwinism had once made him a rising leader among progressives, had become a scientist-theologian whose investigations supported belief in biblical infallibility. A charter member of the board of directors of the American Bible League, founded in 1903, Wright served as an associate editor of the league's organ, the *Bible Student and Teacher* (which in 1913 became the *Bible Champion*). Early in the second decade of the twentieth century he wrote three of the essays in *The Fundamentals*, a series of twelve booklets that marked the increasing rigidity of the conservative Protestant position and presaged a more militant fundamentalist movement a few years later.[10]

Wright was never short of advisers who feared for the safety of the *Bibliotheca Sacra*. His first coeditor, Judson Smith (1837–1906), an Oberlin church historian, served less than a year before moving to Boston to become foreign secretary of the American Board of Commissioners for Foreign Missions. For years thereafter Smith pleaded with Wright to keep the journal true to its orthodox heritage. An adviser of a different sort was Frank Hugh Foster (1851–1935), who replaced Smith on both the Oberlin faculty and Wright's editorial board in 1884. Foster served as coeditor until 1892, when he left Oberlin for California's Pacific Theological Seminary. Foster was listed as an associate editor until 1912, when, unable to tolerate what he saw as Wright's outdated theology, he resigned.[11] William Gay Ballantine (1848–1937), professor of Old Testament language and literature at Oberlin, served as coeditor from 1884 until he became president of Oberlin in 1891.

Beginning in the 1890s Wright gave social issues more prominence in the *Bibliotheca Sacra* than ever before. Although he was personally acquainted with such advocates of the Social Gospel as Washington Gladden and Josiah Strong and had published Gladden's work in his quarterly, his own views were more conservative. When the *Bibliotheca Sacra* was struggling to meets its expenses in 1894, Wright secured financial assistance with the help of Zephaniah Swift Holbrook (1848–1901), a "practical, hardheaded" Chicago businessman and sometimes lecturer on "Christian Sociology," and purchased the quarterly from E. J. Goodrich, its Oberlin publisher. Wright made Holbrook, who did not share Gladden's sympathy for the condition of the worker, coeditor that year and in 1895 added a subtitle to the journal: *A Religious and Sociological Quarterly.* Thereafter, the *Bibliotheca Sacra* devoted even more space to topics such as labor organizations and violence, ethical issues surrounding big business, and pacifism. Holbrook served as coeditor until 1899 and thereafter as associate editor until his death.[12]

Wright retired from his Oberlin professorship in 1907, but continued to edit the *Bibliotheca Sacra* until he died in April 1921 at the age of eighty-three, after service as principal editor longer than that of any other editor of the journal. His family put the quarterly up for sale when he died, and after missing a number that year, it reappeared in January 1922 in a new home, Xenia Theological Seminary, in St. Louis, Missouri.[13]

The man who succeeded Wright as editor was Melvin Grove Kyle (1858–1933), Xenia's new president. Kyle had served as an associate editor of the *Bibliotheca Sacra* since 1910 and had contributed a number of articles on his specialty, biblical archaeology. In St. Louis Kyle added an "editorial comment" section that concerned itself with world affairs and domestic politics in addition to religious news. Kyle promised "the same adherence to the Word of God, the same earnest seeking after truth, and the same charitable permission of discussion—reverent, reasonable, believing discussion—of Biblical subjects in which each contributor signs his name and is responsible for his own views."[14] Within a short time, however, the quarterly's notices of scientific matters were less scholarly than before, and its coverage of the evolution question was pitched in an adversarial tone. If under Wright's moderate hand at Oberlin the *Bibliotheca Sacra* contended for an enlightened conservatism, under Kyle it grew narrower and more strident.

At the end of the decade Xenia closed its doors in St. Louis and merged with Pittsburgh Seminary, an institution of the Reformed Presbyterian church, as Pittsburgh-Xenia Theological Seminary. In 1930, the *Bibliotheca Sacra*'s place of publication changed from St. Louis to Pittsburgh, and Kyle, who retired as president and professor, moved to Pittsburgh to continue to oversee the quarterly. He took on as coeditor John Hunter Webster (1862–1933), professor of New Testament language and literature at Pittsburgh-Xenia and instrumental in bringing the quarterly to St. Louis.[15]

The deaths of both Kyle and Webster in May 1933 brought an end to the *Bibliotheca Sacra*'s brief stay in Pittsburgh. Announcing that it was "too burdened" to continue its publication, the seminary offered the quarterly "to a number of theological institutions assuring acceptance to the first which would meet our terms."[16]

In 1934 the *Bibliotheca Sacra* went west again, this time to Dallas, Texas, and a ten-year-old seminary founded by Lewis Sperry Chafer (1871–1952). Ordained to the Congregationalist ministry in 1900, Chafer joined the Presbyterian church in 1903.[17] In 1919 he participated in the calling of a fundamentalist conference attended by six thousand of the faithful in Philadelphia, Pennsylvania. An outgrowth of that gathering was the formation of the World's Christian Fundamentals Association (WCFA), an organization led principally by premillennialists who defended biblical inerrancy and attacked the teaching of evolution. At a meeting in Fort Worth, Texas, in 1923, that fundamentalist group expressed its desire for "a great evangelical premillennial seminary."[18] With the encouragement and support of like-minded associates, Chafer founded his Evangelical Theological College the next year in Dallas and became its first president. In 1936 the institution changed its name to Dallas Theological Seminary. Although it had no connection with the WCFA, it was clear that Chafer intended that the seminary would fulfill the hope of the WCFA to counter what it saw as apostasy in many denominational schools.

For some time, the institution had considered starting its own journal to help disseminate its doctrinal position. Its leaders were acquainted with Kyle, who had occasionally taught courses on biblical archaeology at Dallas after his retirement from Xenia, and they jumped at the chance to acquire the venerable *Bibliotheca Sacra*.[19] No longer under the wing of Edwardsean Calvinism or its direct theological descendants, the *Bibliotheca Sacra* abruptly abandoned its traditional latitudinarianism and became an agency of the seminary's distinctive theology. Henceforth it would not tolerate deviation.

The young seminary and its old quarterly proudly embodied the spirit of former Dallas pastor Cyrus I. Schofield (1843–1921), the major American popularizer of premillennialist dispensationalism. Schofield, influenced by the English theologian, John Nelson Darby (1800–1882), taught that God had divided history into seven distinct periods, or dispensations. Christ will usher in the final dispensation— including the millennium and eternity—with the Second Coming. Hence, because mankind was now in the sixth period, these dispensationalists often referred to their eschatological doctrine as premillennialism, the emphasis being on readiness for events that would signal the millennium. Chafer, who knew Schofield "intimately for twenty-two years as a son may know a father and as those are related who are associated in work," became pastor of the Schofield Memorial Church in Dallas and determined to make his seminary the instrument of his mentor's theology.[20]

The *Bibliotheca Sacra*'s new editor was Rollin Thomas Chafer (1869–1940), professor of hermeneutics and apologetics and brother of L. S. Chafer. R. T. Chafer announced that at Dallas the journal would voice an editorial policy that "demands loyalty to the doctrinal position of the College." He divided every issue among several "departments," each corresponding to a distinct segment of the seminary's curriculum and headed by the appropriate Dallas faculty member. Since 1934 a high percentage of the articles appearing in the *Bibliotheca Sacra* have been written by Dallas professors and students. The quarterly clearly became a mouthpiece for premillennialism.[21]

Thus editor R. T. Chafer and seminary founder and president L. S. Chafer transformed the *Bibliotheca Sacra* into a major vehicle of fundamentalism. L. S. Chafer's lead article in their first issue (January 1934) advanced Dallas's distinctive position and set the journal's tone for the next half-century. Soon R. T. Chafer, eager to combat "the false philosophers of our time," was deriding "modernist" denominations and their seminaries. "The modernist tail has become so powerful that it wags the conservative body," he charged. Chafer opened the quarterly to antievolutionists and regularly condemned "liberals," "modernists," and social gospelers.[22] Its conversion to militant fundamentalism gave the staid old *Bibliotheca Sacra* a new lease on life. The number of its subscribers apparently doubled within its first year at Dallas.[23]

Another signal of the *Bibliotheca Sacra*'s new militancy was its absorption of *Christian Faith and Life* in 1939.[24] During its first three decades the journal had taken over several periodicals and their antecedents, but nearly seventy years had passed since the old *Theological Eclectic*, the last of that generation, had come under its control. *Christian Faith and Life*, last edited by Frank J. Boyer in Reading, Pennsylvania, was the descendant of various late nineteenth and early twentieth-century conservative religious periodicals such as *Religious Outlook*, *Sermonizer*, and the *Whitened Field*. Most notable of the ancestors of *Christian Faith and Life* was the *Bible Champion*, organ of the Bible League of North America (formerly, the American Bible League) from 1904 until 1930. This family of magazines provided an outlet for the combative fundamentalism of many of the movement's most prominent spokesmen, including such luminaries as William Bell Riley, founder of the WCFA; J. Oliver Buswell, president of Wheaton College; and the aggressive antievolutionist George McCready Price. The friendship that G. Frederick Wright's *Bibliotheca Sacra* had begun thirty-five years before with the WCFA monthly became a marriage with the blessing of the Chafers.

At the death of R. T. Chafer in April 1940, the editorial responsibilities fell to his brother. A sign of how closely the *Bibliotheca Sacra* was tied to Dallas was the fact that L. S. Chafer became acting editor and then was named editor "by action of the faculty of Dallas Theological Seminary and Graduate School of Theology," publishers of the quarterly.[25] Author of an eight-volume *Systematic Theology* (1948) in defense of premillennialism, Chafer at the outset of his editorship heralded the *Bibliotheca Sacra* as "the voice of the conservative Biblical doctrine of the Dallas Theological Seminary" and vowed that it would "remain unchanged." By the time of his death in 1952 the *Bibliotheca Sacra* had become little more than "an instructive agent" for that theology.[26]

By action of the Dallas board of regents that year, L. S. Chafer was succeeded as president of the seminary, professor of systematic theology, and editor of the *Bibliotheca Sacra* by Dallas alumnus John Flipse Walvoord (b. 1910), who had served on its faculty since 1936 and had been a frequent writer for the quarterly. For over thirty years Walvoord, who proclaimed that current events were fulfilling biblical prophecy, maintained the *Bibliotheca Sacra* as a bulwark against the inroads of modernism, including evolution. Between 1959 and 1972 he published ten antievolution articles by Henry M. Morris, a civil engineering professor first at Rice Institute and then Virginia Polytechnic Institute, and coauthor of *The Genesis Flood* (1961), prior to his establishment of the Institute for Creation Research at Christian Heritage College in San Diego, California. Walvoord, whose views understandably reflected those of the Dallas Theological Seminary, discontinued the *Bibliotheca Sacra*'s editorial section and its departmental arrangement, but under his leadership and that of his associate editor and successor Roy B. Zuck, the Dallas message has been spread. Typically as much as half of each number of the journal is reserved for articles by faculty members; articles by alumni of the seminary also regularly appear.[27]

Having passed its sesquicentennial, the *Bibliotheca Sacra* is, according to Zuck, who became editor in 1986 upon Walvoord's retirement, "the oldest continuously published theological journal in the western hemisphere."[28] While it has always had a seminary professor as its editor in chief—it has had only nine principal editors since 1843—it has never been more closely attached to a seminary than at its present home in Dallas. Once latitudinarian, even progressive, the *Bibliotheca Sacra* in the twentieth century has grown more and more conservative. By the mid-1930s it had become a fundamentalist quarterly inhospitable to contributions from writers considered nonconformist by its editors. One more characteristic has bedeviled the *Bibliotheca Sacra* throughout much of its long life: what historian Frank Luther Mott called "its reputation for dullness—even for deadness." The often stuffy *Bibliotheca Sacra* has earned Mark Twain's 1888 appellation—"that literary museum."[29]

Notes

1. Information on the complex family of periodicals surrounding the *Bibliotheca Sacra* (hereinafter cited as *Bib Sac*, a term of affection used by its editors virtually since its beginning), unless otherwise indicated, is from Frank Luther Mott, *A History of American Magazines*, 5 vols. (New York; Cambridge, Massachusetts, 1930–1968); Arnold D. Ehlert, "Genealogical History of Bibliotheca Sacra," *Bib Sac* 100 (January 1943): 31–52; Ehlert, "Further Genealogical Notes," *Bib Sac* 100 (October 1943): 476–78; the *Union List of Serials in Libraries of the United States and Canada*, 3rd ed., 5 vols. (New York, 1965); and the periodicals themselves.

2. John Henry Bennetch, "The Biography of Bibliotheca Sacra," *Bib Sac* 100 (January 1943): 8.

3. Frank Hugh Foster, *A Genetic History of the New England Theology* (New York, 1907), and Henry K. Rowe, *History of Andover Theological Seminary* (Newton, Massachusetts, 1933).

4. *Bib Sac* [1] First Series (November 1843): iii. See also Philip J. King, "Edward Robinson: Biblical Scholar," *Biblical Archaeologist* 46 (December 1983): 231.

5. For Hitchcock, see "The Relations and Consequent Mutual Duties between the

Philosopher and the Theologian," *Bib Sac* 10 (January 1853): 166–94; "Special Divine Interpositions in Nature," *Bib Sac* 11 (October 1854): 776–800; and "The Law of Nature's Constancy Subordinate to the Higher Law of Change," *Bib Sac* 20 (July 1863): 489–561. For Dana, see "Science and the Bible," *Bib Sac* 13 (January 1856): 80–129; "Science and the Bible: Number II," *Bib Sac* 13 (July 1856): 631–56; "Science and the Bible: Number III," *Bib Sac* 14 (April 1857): 388–413; "Science and the Bible: No. III (Concluded)," *Bib Sac* 14 (July 1857): 461–524; and "Thoughts on Species," *Bib Sac* 14 (October 1857): 854–74. For Agassiz, see Joseph P. Thompson, "Quatrefages and Godron in Reply to Agassiz on the Origin and Distribution of Mankind," *Bib Sac* 19 (July 1862): 607–32; Hitchcock, "Law of Nature's Constancy Subordinate to the Higher Law of Change," pp. 526–27; and review of Agassiz, *The Structure of Animal Life*, in *Bib Sac* 23 (October 1866): 698. For Gray, see Thompson, "Quatrefages and Godron in Reply to Agassiz," pp. 607–8. Park's statement is quoted in Bennetch, "Biography of Bibliotheca Sacra," p. 20. For other notices of Darwin, see J. M. Manning, "The Denial of the Supernatural," *Bib Sac* 20 (April 1863): 264–67; P. A. Chadbourne, "Final Cause of Varieties," *Bib Sac* 21 (April 1864): 359–61; Andrew P. Peabody, "The Bearing of Modern Scientific Theories on the Fundamental Truths of Religion," *Bib Sac* 21 (October 1864): 710–24; and Frederic Gardiner, "Darwinism," *Bib Sac* 29 (April 1872): 240–89.

6. [Park], "Note to the Subscribers of the Bibliotheca Sacra," *Bib Sac* 14 (April 1857): 460, and Park's 1862 "Prospectus," quoted in Bennetch, "Biography of Bibliotheca Sacra," pp. 20–22.

7. Foster, *Genetic History of New England Theology*, and Daniel Day Williams, *The Andover Liberals: A Study in American Theology* (Morningside Heights, New York, 1941).

8. Information on the transfer of the *Bib Sac* to Oberlin, and on Wright's editorship, is from the G. Frederick Wright Papers, Oberlin College Archives, Oberlin, Ohio. See William J. Morison, "George Frederick Wright: In Defense of Darwinism and Fundamentalism, 1838–1921," Ph.D. dissertation, Vanderbilt University, 1971, and Ronald L. Numbers, "George Frederick Wright: From Christian Darwinist to Fundamentalist," *Isis* 70 (December 1988): 624–45. See also G. Frederick Wright, *Story of My Life and Work* (Oberlin, Ohio, 1916), pp. 392–406; John D. Hannah, "*Bibliotheca Sacra* and Darwinism: An Analysis of the Nineteenth-Century Conflict between Science and Theology," *Grace Theological Journal* 4 (Spring 1983): 37–58; and James R. Moore, *The Post-Darwinian Controversies: A Study of the Protestant Struggle to Come to Terms with Darwin in Great Britain and America, 1870–1900* (Cambridge, England, 1979), chaps. 11 and 12.

9. George Harris, "The Doctrine of Sacred Scripture," *Andover Review* 1 (January 1884): 46–61; [Wright], review of Ladd, *Doctrine of Sacred Scripture*, *Bib Sac* 41 (January 1884): 197–202; [Wright], "Dr. Ladd on Alleged Discrepancies and Errors of the Bible," *Bib Sac* 41 (April 1884): 389–98. For other examples of *Bib Sac*'s response to modernism, see Frank Hugh Foster, *The Modern Movement in American Theology: Sketches in the History of American Protestant Thought from the Civil War to the World War* (New York, 1939), and William R. Hutchison, *The Modernist Impulse in American Protestantism* (Cambridge, Massachusetts, 1976).

10. On *The Fundamentals* in particular and fundamentalism in general, see George M. Marsden, *Fundamentalism and American Culture: The Shaping of Twentieth-Century Evangelicalism, 1870–1925* (New York, 1980); Ernest R. Sandeen, *The Roots of Fundamentalism: British and American Millenarianism, 1800–1930* (Chicago, 1970); and Ferenc Morton Szasz, *The Divided Mind of Protestant America, 1880–1930* (University, Alabama, 1982).

11. The publication in 1907 of Foster's book, *A Genetic History of the New England Theology*, confirmed his placement squarely in the liberal camp by those who refused to

acknowledge the collapse of the New England theology.

12. Wright, *Story of My Life and Work*, p. 395, and John Barnard, *From Evangelicalism to Progressivism at Oberlin College, 1866–1917* (Columbus, Ohio, 1969).

13. G[eorge] B. M[cCreary], "A Final Word," *Bib Sac* 90 (October 1933): 389.

14. [Kyle], "Editorial," *Bib Sac* 79 (January 1922): 3.

15. "John Hunter Webster, D.D.," *Bib Sac* 90 (July 1933): 265–66, and *Who Was Who in America*, (Chicago, 1942–1981), 1: 1314.

16. M[cCreary], "A Final Word," p. 389.

17. On L. S. Chafer, see C. F. Lincoln, "Lewis Sperry Chafer," *Bib Sac* 109 (October 1952): 332–37, and George G. Houghton, "Lewis Sperry Chafer, 1871–1952," *Bib Sac* 128 (October 1971): 297.

18. John A. Witmer, "'What Hath God Wrought'—Fifty Years of Dallas Theological Seminary, Part I: God's Man and His Dream," *Bib Sac* 130 (October 1973): 295; see also Marsden, *Fundamentalism and American Culture*, p. 152, and Sandeen, *Roots of Fundamentalism*, pp. 243–47.

19. Witmer, "God's Man and His Dream," p. 301, and John D. Hannah, "The History of *Bibliotheca Sacra*," *Bib Sac* 133 (July 1976): 238–39.

20. L. S. Chafer, "Editorials," *Bib Sac* 100 (January 1943): 5.

21. [Chafer], "Brief Statement by the New Owners of Bibliotheca Sacra," *Bib Sac* 90 (October 1933): 390; Hannah, "History of *Bibliotheca Sacra*," pp. 239–40.

22. L. S. Chafer, "Unabridged Systematic Theology," *Bib Sac* 91 (January 1934): 8–23; R. T. Chafer, "Editorials," *Bib Sac* 91 (July 1934): 260. On dispensationalism, see L. S. Chafer, "Evils Resulting from an Abridged Systematic Theology," *Bib Sac* 91 (April 1934): 143–46.

23. Bennetch, "Biography of Bibliotheca Sacra," p. 29.

24. R. T. Chafer, "Editorials," *Bib Sac* 96 (July 1939): 257–58.

25. *Bib Sac* 98 (April 1941): 132.

26. L. S. Chafer, "Editorials," *Bib Sac* 97 (April 1940): 129, and "Editorials," *Bib Sac* 99 (April 1942): 129.

27. Ronald L. Numbers, "Creationism in 20th-Century America," *Science* 218 (5 November 1982): 541–44; Witmer, "'What Hath God Wrought'—Fifty Years of Dallas Theological Seminary, Part II: Building upon the Foundation," *Bib Sac* 131 (January 1974): 3–13.

28. John F. Walvoord and Roy B. Zuck, eds., *The Bib Sac Reader: Commemorating Fifty Years of Publication by Dallas Theological Seminary, 1934–1983* (Chicago, 1983), back cover. See also Roy B. Zuck, "Bibliotheca Sacra's Sequicentennial Anniversary," *Bib Sac* 150 (January–March 1993): 3.

29. Mott, *History of American Magazines*, vol. 1, *1741–1850*, p. 740.

Information Sources

BIBLIOGRAPHY:

Bennetch, John Henry. "The Biography of Bibliotheca Sacra." *Bibliotheca Sacra* 100 (January 1943): 8–30.

Ehlert, Arnold D. "Genealogical History of Bibliotheca Sacra." *Bibliotheca Sacra* 100 (January 1943): 31–52.

Hannah, John D. "The History of *Bibliotheca Sacra*." *Bibliotheca Sacra* 133 (July 1976): 229–42.

Morison, William J. "George Frederick Wright: In Defense of Darwinism and Fundamentalism, 1838–1921." Ph.D. dissertation, Vanderbilt University, 1971.

Mott, Frank Luther. *A History of American Magazines*, vol. 1, *1741–1850*. New York, 1930.

INDEXES: Each volume indexed except 78. Four cumulative indexes have been published: 1–13 (1844–1856); 1–30 (1844–1873); 91–127 (1934–1970); 128–137 (1971–1980). Also: *Poole*; *RG*; *Rel Ind One*; *SSHI*.

REPRINT EDITIONS: Microform: American Periodical Series (UMI), reel 379 (1843 only).

LOCATION SOURCES: Widely available.

Publication History

TITLE AND TITLE CHANGES: *Bibliotheca Sacra: or, Tracts and Essays on Topics Connected with Biblical Literature and Theology*, 1843; *Bibliotheca Sacra and Theological Review*, February 1844–January 1851; *Bibliotheca Sacra and American Biblical Repository*, April 1851–January 1858; *Bibliotheca Sacra and Biblical Repository*, April 1858–1863; *The Bibliotheca Sacra*, 1864–1870; *The Bibliotheca Sacra and Theological Eclectic*, 1871–1875; *The Bibliotheca Sacra*, 1876–1894; *The Bibliotheca Sacra: A Religious and Sociological Quarterly*, 1895–1912; *Bibliotheca Sacra: A Religious and Sociological Quarterly*, 1913–1929; *Bibliotheca Sacra*, 1930–present.

VOLUME AND ISSUE DATA: Numbers 1–3, 1843; volumes 1–current, 1844–present. Combined number issued for July–October 1921.

FREQUENCY OF PUBLICATION: Quarterly.

PUBLISHERS: 1843: Wiley and Putnam, New York; 1844–1846: Allen, Morrill, and Wardwell, Andover, Massachusetts; 1847–1849: William H. Wardwell, Andover; 1850–1883: Warren F. Draper, Andover; 1884–1894: E. J. Goodrich, Oberlin, Ohio; 1895–1921: Bibliotheca Sacra Company, Oberlin; 1922–1930: Bibliotheca Sacra Company, St. Louis, Missouri; 1930–1933: Pittsburgh–Xenia Theological Seminary, Pittsburgh, Pennsylvania; 1934–present: Dallas Theological Seminary (until 1936 called Evangelical Theological College), Dallas, Texas.

EDITORS: Edward Robinson, 1843; Bela B. Edwards and Edwards A. Park, 1844–1852; Edwards A. Park, 1852–1883; Samuel H. Taylor, 1852–1871; George E. Day, 1871–1879; Archibald Duff, Jr., 1877–1879; G. Frederick Wright, 1884–1921; Judson Smith, 1884; William G. Ballantine, 1884–1891; Frank H. Foster, 1884–1892; Z. Swift Holbrook, 1894–1899; Melvin G. Kyle, 1922–1933; John H. Webster, 1930–1933; Rollin T. Chafer, 1934–1940; Lewis S. Chafer, 1940–1952; John F. Walvoord, 1952–1985; Roy B. Zuck, 1986–present.

CIRCULATION: Approximately 9,000.

William J. Morison

Moody Monthly
1900–

Since its beginning in 1900, the *Moody Monthly*, published by the Moody Bible Institute of Chicago, has championed the concerns of a unique variety of American conservatism, the fundamentalist movement. The *Monthly* has enjoyed a widespread constituency of pastors, evangelists, missionaries, and lay people, thanks to the prestige of the Moody Bible Institute, founded in 1886 by Dwight L. Moody, who was then America's leading evangelist. It has made no claims to erudition but always has been popular in style. The *Monthly*'s readers affiliate with scores of different denominations, but they tend to be conservative Baptists, Presbyterians, and independent "Bible church" people, the typical constituents of American fundamentalism. This magazine, called the *Institute Tie* at first, renamed the *Christian Workers Magazine* in 1910 and the *Moody Bible Institute Monthly* in 1920, evolved from a largely in-house alumni news and promotional effort to a general-purpose religious journal with national circulation and a strong editorial line. It has played a mediating role in fundamentalism by maintaining lines of communication and essential unity of purpose between the combative, separatist wing of the movement and its more moderate counterpart, now called conservative evangelicals.

The heart of the *Monthly*'s conservatism has been religious. Many Protestants have accommodated Christian doctrine to the naturalistic trends of twentieth-century thought, but the *Monthly* has defended the supernatural origins and character of Christianity, including the verbal inspiration and inerrancy of the Bible, the deity of Jesus, his virgin birth, his miraculous ministry, the redemptive power of his blood shed for sinners, his bodily resurrection, and his future personal return to defeat Satan's forces and reign on earth. While liberal Protestants have stressed social and political reform as the means for advancing Christ's kingdom, the *Monthly* has insisted that evangelism and spiritual nurture are Christians' foremost priorities. Its conservative instincts in public affairs have been prompted by a premillennialist pessimism about social and political reforms. Culture can be improved only as individuals' hearts are changed. Even this kind of renewal is temporary, since satanic forces and human depravity will thwart genuine progress until Jesus returns to defeat evil and establish his millennial kingdom. Thus the *Monthly* has challenged the assumptions behind progressive-liberal programs while claiming to stand for the "individualism which forms the warp and woof of the Bible."[1] The *Monthly*'s preoccupation with personal evangelism and the Second Coming, however, has prevented it from articulating a comprehensive conservative ideology. Public affairs have served more as object lessons of either the inevitable downgrade of civilization before the Second Coming or of the need for a spiritual revival.

The *Institute Tie* first appeared in November 1891, but ceased publication in 1893. It was revived in 1900 by A. P. Fitt, an administrator at the institute. It was to inform alumni, donors, and friends about the institute's activities and provide practical suggestions and Bible study outlines to use in ministry. Although Fitt had no plans of making the *Institute Tie* into a general religious magazine, it grew in circulation and scope, since its restriction to those in some way "associated with Mr. Moody's enterprises" in fact included thousands of people across the continent, in the British Isles, and on scattered missions throughout the world.[2]

Moody's successors promoted other interests as well. Reuben A. Torrey, the first dean of the institute, was a widely acclaimed Bible teacher and revivalist. When Torrey resigned the deanship in 1904 to return to evangelistic work, he was succeeded by James M. Gray, a Reformed Episcopalian pastor from Boston who also was a respected Bible teacher. Named the *Institute Tie*'s coeditors in 1907, with Torrey "at large" and Gray at the institute, these men began to enlarge its scope by soliciting material from a broad network of evangelicals and commenting editorially on current events. The *Institute Tie* soon became an omnibus religious magazine with a question-and-answer column, serialized Bible study outlines, assorted materials "For Sermon and Scrapbook," religion in the news, reports on missions and evangelism, reader-contributed notes, and book notices. The editorial work soon fell to Gray as Torrey became head of the Bible Institute of Los Angeles. Under Gray's control, the Moody Bible Institute and its magazine became major components of the emerging fundamentalist movement.

The *Moody Monthly*'s development from Gray's tenure to the present reveals both the trials and the continued vitality of fundamentalism in the twentieth century. Like the movement, the *Monthly* has been able to communicate the old-time faith in contemporary accents, but never has been able to resolve a tension between cultural stewardship and premillennial alienation. Throughout its career, the *Monthly* has struggled with living responsibly in an ultimately doomed civilization.

This dilemma appeared immediately as Gray took over the *Institute Tie* during the peak years of the progressive movement. One might have expected a premillennial cultural pessimist to attack progressivism head on, but Gray praised the growing spirit of reform. Christians had a duty, he said, to purge dangers from society. If one saw a banana peel on the sidewalk, one would remove it; hence one should fight against saloons, gambling, prostitution, and political graft. But the reformers mistakenly expected to conquer the world in the present age. The more he saw of social problems, Gray admitted, "the more we are convinced that their solution is beyond human ken."[3]

Things were getting worse, not better, he thought. Prayer was being forced out of many public schools, suffragettes attacked women's divinely ordained place, and while idealists dreamed of peace palaces and world tribunals, the nations armed for war. Worst of all, Protestant liberals such as President William Rainey Harper of the University of Chicago called for a "new type of Christianity" which would replace biblical doctrine and evangelism with ethical ideals and social service. Gray and his contributors hammered at liberals for their departure from evangelicalism, rationalistic criticism of the Bible, and faith in evolutionary progress. These high-minded, well-intentioned men were repeating the Tower of Babel fiasco by presuming to reach the heavens through their own efforts.[4]

World War I brought the liberals and conservatives into open conflict. The war came as no surprise to Gray; it confirmed his belief that liberals' faith in progress was naive. Angered liberals responded with accusations against premillennialists, which they aimed, accurately enough, at the Moody Bible Institute. Premillennialism, they charged, was an inhibitor of missionary zeal, pacifistic, and financed by German agents to breed disloyalty. That last charge rankled premillennialists the most, since it was clear to them that the liberals' "new type of Christianity" was based on the implications of German biblical criticism. Liberals also embraced evolution, which in Prussian hands had become a rationale for aggression. If these trends were not stopped, conservatives insisted, American civilization would fall prey to infidelity and militarism also. Gray and others called for an alliance to combat error and to uphold the fundamentals of the faith.

As a voice of that alliance, Gray's journal, then called the *Christian Workers Magazine*, was retitled the *Moody Bible Institute Monthly*. The institute, Gray said, was trusted in these "dark days of apostasy" by thousands who sought its "advice, instruction and comfort," so its mouthpiece should bear its name.[5] The magazine enhanced its image by changing from pocket size to the larger format used by such respected journals as the *New Era* and the *Literary Digest*.

During the fundamentalist-modernist conflicts of the 1920s, Gray devoted the *Monthly* to critiques of modernist spokesmen and clarifications of the fundamentalist position. One of the more surprising positions Gray took in these years concerned the controversy over the teaching of evolution in the public schools. The *Monthly* regularly featured special creationists' critiques of evolutionary theory and warnings that evolutionism was an insidious social philosophy. Yet during 1925 and 1926, when the public debate intensified, the *Monthly* scarcely mentioned the Scopes Trial, other than in tributes to William Jennings Bryan after his death. In an editorial the following spring, Gray expressed his support for those who fought evolution, but urged them to appeal to "reason...calm logic and...statements of fact," and confessed that he thought it was wrong to forbid the discussion of evolutionary theory in the classroom. He had no use for legally enforced obscurantism, and regretted the vulgar level to which the whole discussion had descended.[6]

Unfortunately, Gray could not resist the urge to smite the enemy with an occasional cheap shot. Alongside fairly responsible critiques and exposés, he printed articles asserting, for example, that belief in evolution and modernism would lead to the sins of Sodom and that perhaps modernist Harry Emerson Fosdick was demonically inspired. The *Monthly* also fell prey to the general spirit of reaction in the 1920s. Gray gave the Ku Klux Klan mixed reviews, upheld the conviction of Sacco and Vanzetti, supported immigration restriction, warned against Roman Catholic threats to liberty in Al Smith's candidacy, and suggested that when Henry Ford apologized for anti-Semitic remarks he had made, it was because of Jewish financial pressure. While the *Monthly* urged fundamentalists to contend for the faith with decency and restraint, it was not immune to the excesses that observers took for the movement's death throes.

By decade's end, fundamentalism may have lost its appeal to "the best brains and good sense of the modern community," as Walter Lippmann put it, but the movement lost none of its vitality on the popular level.[7] As old-line denominations succumbed in varying degrees to the forces of modernism, fundamentalists turned in large numbers to organizations such as the Moody Bible Institute, and it responded by instituting a new pastoral training course, increasing enrollment in Moody correspondence courses, stepping up its publishing, founding radio station WMBI, and sending more recruits into the missionary ranks. The institute was becoming the national giant among fundamentalist organizations, a denominational surrogate that eclipsed traditional Protestant churches to such an extent that by the early 1940s one confused reader of the *Moody Monthly* asked: "Why don't you publish something on the other denominations once in a while?"[8]

The *Moody Monthly* itself, its circulation expanding from about 27,000 in 1928 to over 70,000 by the mid-1940s, reflected the increasing vigor of fundamentalism in these years. Its basic message did not change. It continued to castigate theological liberalism and the secularization of American life, and to prescribe traditional formulas: domestic and foreign evangelization, popular Bible instruction, and the cultivation of spirituality. But at the same time its outlook turned grimly pessimistic. The *Monthly* had reported many developments in the past that seemed to confirm premillennialist prophecy, but these earlier speculations paled before the upheavals of the 1930s. Communism, with its godless creed and stated goal of world revolution, seemed to be the red dragon of the Book of Revelation. Mussolini seemed to emulate the Antichrist by calling for the resurrection of the Roman Empire, as did Hitler, with his plans of world conquest and persecution of the Jews. Gray feared that even America was drifting toward dictatorship, as the people surrendered their liberties in exchange for economic security. Yet these grim signs should not lead to despair, Gray reminded his readers in 1935: "The darkest hour, beloved brethren, is just before the dawn." They should take heart and "look for the Morning Star," their returning Lord Jesus.[9] Gray himself soon entered the dawning, and the editorship of the *Monthly* fell to a distinguished Baptist preacher, Will H. Houghton, the new president of the institute.

Will Houghton's leadership at Moody would bring institutional growth and a slightly changed outlook. Like Gray, he warned about the prophetic sweep of events and lashed at national sins. He blamed World War II on materialistic ideologies. He flayed liberal theologians as well: "You have denied the blood of the Cross," he accused, "and as a result you have shed the blood of a million."[10]

Yet Houghton hoped for a temporary detour from the road to Armageddon. Throughout his tenure at the *Monthly*, he voiced the hope that a great national revival might turn the nation around, and he called on fundamentalists and other evangelicals to unite in an effort to begin the work. To this end, he launched evangelistic chain broadcasts called "Let's Go Back to the Bible" over WMBI and eleven major Mutual Network stations in 1938 and 1939. In 1940, he began a transcribed weekly program, which by 1942 was sent to 197 stations in forty-three states.

The mid-1940s brought cause for both hope and dismay. After actively encouraging the founding of the National Association of Evangelicals (NAE), a broad coalition initiated in 1942 by some of his fundamentalist colleagues, Houghton found himself unable to endorse the association editorially because of radical separatists' attacks on the NAE's inclusive posture. The *Monthly*, he felt, could not afford to take sides among its constituents. During the war and immediately following it, Houghton continued to call for revival, even as he deplored new symptoms of national decadence and impending doom. He died in 1947, just as signs of a new religious stirring appeared.

Houghton's successor at the institute was William Culbertson, a Reformed Episcopal pastor and bishop who had been dean of education. Culbertson's tenure, like Houghton's, would bring continued curricular and institutional development, but he would not put so deep a stamp on the *Monthly* as had his predecessors. As Culbertson's administrative and public relations tasks grew, professional journalists took on more responsibility for the *Monthly*. Their influence brought a new look to the magazine. Its editorial pages shrank and its religious news section grew; photographs increased, while type became larger and articles somewhat shorter. Thus the *Monthly* began to look more like its popular contemporaries, *Life* and the *Saturday Evening Post*.

During the 1940s, the *Moody Monthly* dealt with several new trends in fundamentalism. First, there was a sense that revival was within reach, if not already breaking. Billy Graham, a young fundamentalist evangelist, had achieved national renown and had become the major figure of a surging evangelical coalition. Propelled by Youth for Christ revivals, record numbers of young people crowded into Bible schools and colleges, and thousands of them volunteered for missionary service. While rigid fundamentalists assaulted this movement's lack of ecclesiastical separation and doctrinal exactitude, the *Moody Monthly* gave it glowing coverage.

This new evangelistic thrust prompted moderate fundamentalists to restore the movement's public image. If they were to reach the world, they needed to win respect, to show that they were responsible people with a timely message. They criticized some of their colleagues for being old-fashioned, censorious, and unscholarly. While the *Monthly* published some of these perspectives, editor Culbertson disclaimed any sympathy with "smart, harsh or wholesale criticism" of fundamentalism's founding fathers. At the Moody Bible Institute, they were revered as "part of our sacred heritage."[11] Again, the *Monthly* refused to take sides and so retained its broad support among fundamentalists.

The cultural climate of the 1950s and early 1960s was more congenial to fundamentalists and evangelicals than any other they had experienced in several decades. Church membership soared. Billy Graham counseled national leaders, and presidents and congressmen denounced godless communism, attended prayer breakfasts, inscribed "In God We Trust" on coins, and added "Under God" to the national pledge of allegiance. In this atmosphere, fundamentalists and evangelicals felt needed, and they contributed to the cold war struggle with evangelistic crusades and global missionary expansion. This activist thrust would lead the *Monthly* to support U.S. involvement in Vietnam until the bitter end and to call repeatedly for national repentance and revival. In this age of crisis, America could not afford to "go soft," to wallow in its material plenty while militant, disciplined atheism advanced.[12]

In these years, the *Monthly* displayed conservative evangelicals' accommodating spirit toward postwar America. Reflecting the new concern for the family, articles by "Christian psychologists" dealt with child rearing, marriage relations, and emotional stress. While fundamentalists had once disparaged psychology, now the trend was to urge Christians to recognize the reality and complexity of personal problems. While rejecting the permissive implications of Benjamin Spock's and Alfred Kinsey's writings, evangelical family counselors strove to reconcile biblical norms and psychological theories by stressing the therapeutic value of personal faith.

Other articles struggled with the consumer habits of the middle class, such as installment buying, life insurance, the movies, and television. How relevant were older injunctions against indebtedness, concern for the future, and worldly entertainment when these things seemed so normal, respectable, and affordable? The *Monthly* offered only one clear proscription: movies were still off-limits. On other things, readers should ask only if the practices honored God or whether they hindered one's witness for him. The basic question for these comfortable years, as one writer put it, was, "How different shall we be?"[13] "Not very," seemed to be the answer. Fundamentalists claimed to be a separate and "peculiar" people, but they were conforming to the prevailing standard of the good life.

This easy-going relationship to the culture was severely shaken as the 1960s wore on, and the revival of public religiosity cooled off. The first major tremor was the Supreme Court's decisions in 1962 and 1963 against established school prayer and Bible reading. Commented the *Monthly*, this decision nullified the United States's claim to be a God-fearing nation and signified to young people that faith does not matter and that the Bible is no longer recognized as a moral authority. From then on, it all seemed to go downhill. When America set aside the Bible, said the *Monthly* in 1967, it lost its "ability to produce people of self-restraint and moral strength," and turned instead to a new morality and self-indulgent ethics. The result was an increase in crime, divorce, racial violence, draft card burnings, hippie love-ins, and the disintegration of the political process. Yet the *Monthly* implored its readers not to isolate themselves from a world that needed their witness. Indeed, it noted that a new spiritual vitality was emerging from, of all places, secular university campuses.[14]

Conservative evangelicals now were devoting a great deal of energy to reaching young people. Youth for Christ rallies had sprung up in hundreds of cities in 1944–1945, and out of that movement came many postwar leaders, most notably Billy Graham. Responding to the rapid growth of higher education in the 1950s and 1960s, evangelicals fostered campus Christian movements for fellowship and evangelism. Inter-Varsity Christian Fellowship, a British import, spread to scores of campuses and attracted thousands of collegians to its triennial missionary conferences at Urbana, Illinois. The Navigators, a personal evangelism and Bible study movement, rapidly reproduced their cell groups on campuses. The most aggressively evangelistic group was Campus Crusade for Christ, founded in southern California in 1951 by businessman Bill Bright. Brandishing tracts called "The Four Spiritual Laws," Campus Crusaders energetically witnessed to their peers. They and the other student groups ranged from Berkeley, California, to the Florida beaches with their message of born-again Christianity.[15]

From this burgeoning movement came new concerns as well as converts. Christian students felt the need for a gospel that spoke to the intellectual and moral ferment of the campuses, and a wing of the student Christian movement, influenced by countercultural perspectives, began to voice its discontent. At Inter-Varsity's Urbana Convention of 1970, the *Monthly* reported, some of the students sported long hair and beards and denounced the gospel's capture by white, middle-class American culture. Yet they were excited by the transcultural gospel they heard from Third World speakers. Evangelical students were stimulated also by Francis Schaeffer, an American evangelist to Europe's young intellectuals. He presented a Christian worldview as the answer to modern despair and called for action on social problems.[16]

As William Culbertson retired from the presidency of the Moody Bible Institute in 1971 and handed over his work to George Sweeting, then pastor of the Moody Memorial Church, the *Moody Monthly* was again changing its format. In an effort to update its image, it now featured lavish color layouts, still shorter articles, human interest stories, and interviews. Throughout the 1970s, more articles appeared by freelance writers who reduced complex subjects to simple levels of comprehension. The *Monthly* now resembled the slick-paper magazines of the drugstore and supermarket racks, which no doubt was the price for holding the attention of television-jaded readers. At any rate, the *Monthly*'s staff knew its business well; for the magazine's circulation grew to more than a quarter of a million by 1980.

The new look at the *Monthly* involved more than style. It reflected a renewed evangelical engagement in public affairs. Alongside mutterings about America's moral rottenness appeared the first calls for Christian social action as fundamentalist evangelicals responded to the upheavals of the late sixties and early seventies. Congressman John B. Anderson (I, Illinois) urged pastors to tell their congregations that social action was their Christian duty, while journalist Wesley Pippert charged that evangelicals had lost their prophetic voice by identifying so uncritically with the Nixon White House.[17]

Pleas for public responsibility increased in the following years as evangelicals became emboldened by media exposure, a new sense of their collective strength, and by the examples of Christians engaged in public life. But despite openness to a few evangelical liberals such as Senator Mark Hatfield (R, Oregon) and some interest in world hunger and new roles for women, the *Monthly* reflected the overwhelming conservatism of its constituents. There was an alien, threatening America that was secularizing the public schools, trying to abolish traditional sexual roles and morality, aborting millions of fetuses and making concessions to the communists in foreign policy. Articles criticizing the SALT II treaty, evolution, and secular humanism in the schools, the equal rights amendment, the Supreme Court's proabortion decisions, and recognition of the People's Republic of China filled the pages of the *Monthly* in the 1970s and 1980s. However, as the presidential election drew near in 1980, a guest editorial warned against turning politics into a new Christian crusade. Earlier drives, said the writer, had lured conservative evangelicals into extremism, produced internal discord, and discredited their witness. So once again the *Monthly* sang the old refrain: the church should stay out of politics; its business is soul saving.[18] *Moody Magazine*, which followed the *Monthly* in 1991, continues in that vein.

The fundamentalist movement's decades-long struggle with being in the world but not of it was still unresolved. As the *Moody Monthly* faithfully reflected, its instincts have been conservative, but it has proved surprisingly adaptive. Yet this very flexibility, together with the new prominence of the fundamentalist evangelicals, has increased fundamentalist evangelical uncertainty. Desirous of doing good but distracted by millenarian visions and narrowly evangelistic priorities, they seem to drift on the cultural tide from issue to issue. Fundamentalism provides spiritually hungry people with a vital personal faith, but its ambivalent sense of calling limits its ability to sustain a social vision.

Notes

1. "Human Interests," *Moody Bible Institute Monthly* 35 (August 1935): 553 (hereinafter cited as *MM*); George M. Marsden, *Fundamentalism and American Culture: The Shaping of Twentieth-Century Evangelicalism, 1870–1925* (New York, 1980), pp. 62–71, 80–93, 206–11.

2. "Editorial," *Institute Tie* 1 (September 1900): 26–27 (hereinafter cited as *IT*).

3. "The Second Coming of Christ and Reform Movements," *IT* 10 (July 1910): 856; "Social Problems," *Christian Workers Magazine* 12 (May 1912): 588 (hereinafter cited as *CWM*).

4. "A New Type of Christianity," *CWM* 11 (September 1910): 11–13; "Bishop Hoss and Church Union," *CWM* 12 (January 1912): 331; "Another Milestone on Our Way," *CWM* 20 (July 1920): 851.

5. "Another Milestone on Our Way," *CWM* 20.

6. "The Fight against Evolution," *MM* 26 (April 1926): 364.

7. *A Preface to Morals* (New York, 1929), p. 31. Joel Carpenter, "Fundamentalist Institutions and the Rise of Evangelical Protestantism, 1929–1942," *Church History* 49 (March 1980): 62–75, documents the movement's vitality in these years.

8. "A Magazine for All," *MM* 40 (February 1942): 249.

9. "Nearing the Crisis?" *MM* 36 (December 1935): 165.

10. "Unbelief and Its Fruit," *MM* 42 (September 1941): 4.

11. "Faith of Our Fathers," *MM* 59 (July 1959): 7.

12. "America's Soft Streak," *MM* 60 (March 1960): 9

13. Wallis A. Turner, "How Different Shall We Be?" *MM* 56 (July 1956): 15–16.

14. "Terror in the City," *MM* 68 (September 1967): 21 (quote); "The Supreme Court's Crucial Choice," *MM* 63 (September 1963): 16; "Is The Supreme Court Right?" *MM* 63 (July–August 1963): 16; "A Nation in Social Upheaval," *MM* 65 (February 1965): 19–21; "The Widening Gulf," *MM* 67 (June 1967): 14; "Petting the Bears," and "A Time of Opportunity," *MM* 68 (October 1967): 21.

15. Ted Seelye, "Beachhead at Fort Lauderdale," *MM* 63 (April 1963): 76–77; Fritz Ridenour, "The Spiritual Climate on the College Campus," *MM* 65 (September 1964): 20–22, 40–42; Phil Landrum, "The Letter Two Million Have Read," *MM* 66 (September 1965): 20–23; Bob Flood, "A Revolution on the Campus?" *MM* 67 (September 1966): 22–25, 42–43; "Crusade for Christ at Berkeley," *MM* 67 (March 1967): 12, 14; Robert Flood, "Impact at Urbana," *MM* 68 (March 1968): 28–30.

16. "Christians and Ecology," *MM* 71 (September 1970): 8; Francis A. Schaeffer, "Our Generation's Awesome Choice—God or Nobody Home in the Universe," *MM* 71 (January 1971): 23, 48–51; Kay Oliver, "Urbana and the Rising Generation," *MM* 71 (March 1971): 28–29, 74–77.

17. "Can We Reclaim the American Dream? An Interview with John B. Anderson," *MM* 68 (July–August 1968): 21–23; Wesley G. Pippert, "Perspective from Washington," *MM* 71 (April 1971): 13.

18. Ted Miller, "Shall We Join the New 'Christian Crusade'?" *MM* 81 (September 1980): 20, 22.

Information Sources

BIBLIOGRAPHY:

Fowler, Robert Booth. *A New Engagement: Evangelical Political Thought, 1966–1976.* Grand Rapids, Michigan, 1982.

Getz, Gene A. *MBI: The Story of Moody Bible Institute.* Chicago, 1969.

Marsden, George M. *Fundamentalism and American Culture: The Shaping of Twentieth-Century Evangelicalism, 1870–1925.* New York, 1980.

INDEXES: None .

REPRINT EDITIONS: Microform: UMI.

LOCATION SOURCES: Complete runs: Moody Bible Institute Library; Andover-Harvard Theological Library; Texas State Library and Historical Commission; Library of Congress; University of Michigan; University of Illinois; Free Library of Philadelphia.

Publication History

TITLE AND TITLE CHANGES: *Institute Tie*, September 1900–September 1910; *Christian Workers Magazine*, October 1910–August 1920; *Moody Bible Institute Monthly*, September 1920–January 1938; *Moody Monthly,* February 1938–June 1991; *Moody Magazine*, July/August 1991–present.

VOLUME AND ISSUE DATA: Volumes 1–current, September 1900–present.

FREQUENCY OF PUBLICATION: Monthly, 1900– June 1991; bimonthly, July/August 1991–present.

PUBLISHER: Moody Bible Institute, Chicago, Illinois.

EDITORS: A. P. Fitt, 1900–1907; James M. Gray and Reuben A. Torrey, 1907–1908; James M. Gray, 1908–1935; Will H. Houghton, 1935–1947; William Culbertson, 1947–1971; George Sweeting, 1971–1987; Joseph M. Stowell, 1987–1989; Jerry B. Jenkins, 1989–1993; Andrew Scheer (Managing Editor) 1990–present.

CIRCULATION: 1982: 300,000; 1999: 120,000.

Joel A. Carpenter

Bible Champion
1900–1939

Bible Champion (1913–1930) was the longest-lived and probably most-recognized title in a string of related magazines that began in 1900 as *Bible Student* (1900–1903), continued as *Bible Student and Teacher* (1904–1913), and ended in 1939 when its successor, *Christian Faith and Life* (1931–1939) was absorbed by *Bibliotheca Sacra* (1843–present). Known principally as the organ of a conservative Protestant organization, the Bible League of North America (earlier named the American Bible League), the *Bible Champion* family provided a platform for many of the principal American Protestant fundamentalists in the first four decades of the twentieth century.[1]

In January 1900, William Marcellus McPheeters (1854–1935), professor of Old Testament literature at Columbia Theological Seminary, Columbia, South Carolina, issued the first number of the monthly *Bible Student*. Associated with McPheeters were coeditors Benjamin B. Warfield (1851–1921), George T. Purves (1852–1901), and John D. Davis (1854–1926), of Princeton Theological Seminary, and Samuel M. Smith (1851–1910) and Daniel J. Brimm (1862–1948), of Columbia. A typical issue contained several pages of "Editorial Notes" written by the editors; a half-dozen or more signed articles underscoring the reliability of the Old and New Testaments; the "Current Biblical Thought" section, consisting of brief comments, some signed, on religious issues such as biblical criticism; and a book review section. Intended for an audience of pastors, professors, and seminary students, the articles for the most part were serious and substantive. In addition to the editors, the writers included such well-known conservative biblical scholars as Archibald T. Robertson, Melvin G. Kyle, William G. Moorehead, and William B. Greene, Jr.[2]

In a sense *Bible Student* was indicative of a transitional period in American Protestant conservatism, one preliminary to the more militant fundamentalism of the 1920s. Although the journal was dominated by Presbyterians (both northern and southern), it published the work of Baptists, Methodists, Congregationalists, and others, somewhat in the spirit of the so-called Bible conference movement of the late nineteenth century. Magazines like the *Bible Student* and gatherings like the Bible conferences brought together conservatives across denominational lines, but these efforts were largely sporadic and lacked the characteristics of permanent organization. What they did have, though, was a deep faith in traditional biblical doctrines, an aversion to arguments of the new Higher Criticism, a fear that theological seminaries were becoming infiltrated by "rationalists," and a determination to speak out and reassure their followers that the faith of their fathers was unshaken.

The formation of the American Bible League (ABL) was the culmination of ten years' work principally by Daniel Seelye Gregory (1832–1915), editor of *Homiletic Review* and former president of Lake Forest University, Illinois. In 1894 Gregory had written "The Twentieth Century's Call to Christendom," which, he reported, he sent to as many as eighty thousand ministers and other "Christian readers" to convey "a Providential Call to a Great Awakening in the Churches and Christendom." Similar papers followed, some written by New York businessman William Phillips Hall (1864–1937). Within a few years, Gregory, a Presbyterian, and Hall, a Methodist, had formed the Twentieth Century Gospel Campaign Committee to inspire the "Evangelical Denominations" to join in a "great Evangelistic Movement" against "loss of faith in the Bible as the Word of God." Additional meetings led to the formal establishment of the ABL in New York City in July 1903, with Hall as president and Gregory as general secretary.[3]

When the ABL began to consider publishing a magazine, McPheeters, a member both of the inner circle of those who founded the ABL and of its first board of directors, proposed that his *Bible Student* be transferred from South Carolina to become the league's official organ. The league accepted his proposal, renamed the magazine *Bible Student and Teacher*, placed it under the purview of an education committee, and installed Gregory as editor. Although McPheeters continued as associate editor and a member of the league's education committee, with Gregory as editor it was clear that the periodical was going to be different from its predecessor, one designed to rally American Protestants to the conservative banner of the ABL.[4]

Issued as volume 1, number 1, in January 1904, *Bible Student and Teacher* was both more popular and more militant than *Bible Student*. Gregory, who was confident of signing up ten thousand subscribers "at once," quickly stamped the periodical with his relentless sense of mission. Early numbers were filled with plans for enlisting the public in a great crusade by means of the formation of "Branch Leagues" across the country, within which were to be "League Circles" for Bible study, and throughout, a "League of Students for Bible Mastery" that would "reach every Christian school, college and seminary" in the land. The ABL, Gregory wrote in 1906, was "the only organized movement in this country in opposition to the unsound and unscientific radical criticism." Two years later, in 1908, *Bible Student and Teacher* announced that the ABL was changing its name to the Bible League of North America (BLNA) to emphasize its aspirations to organize in Canada and Mexico too. Asserting that the church was "in the midst of one of the most appalling crises in the history of Christendom," Gregory pushed the BLNA's "proposed campaign" to "organize the conservative evangelical forces in the churches...to counteract completely the current false teachings, and to bring right-thinking men back to a reasonable and settled faith in the Bible as God's revelation of salvation."[5]

Gregory's single-minded determination to make the BLNA and its journal the chief force in American Christendom proved to be his ruin. In 1910, when a well-financed and supremely ambitious project to publish *The Fundamentals* threatened to divert dollars and manpower from the BLNA and in an instant overshadow and undermine his life's work, Gregory bitterly accused it of pirating materials from *Bible Student and Teacher*. This drew such an effective response that he was forced to apologize publicly for his "overstatements," but it was a mistake from which he never recovered, and it signaled a period of decline for his journal. Borrowing money for it over his own signature and driving himself to exhaustion, Gregory broke down completely early in 1911. In the two years after April 1911, only seven numbers of *Bible Student and Teacher* appeared, and those only because of the aid of volunteers. Although Gregory resurfaced long enough to make a last-ditch appeal for support, in April 1913 he acknowledged the BLNA's "comparative failure" in an issue of *Bible Student and Teacher* that was destined to be the last. The BLNA, however, "rallied from the misfortunes caused by the long illness and breakdown" of the editor, and later that same year it issued a new journal, now under a new, more militant title, and guided by a new editor.[6]

Jay Benson Hamilton (1847–1920), former president of Walden University in Nashville, Tennessee, and pastor of Trinity Methodist Episcopal Church in Harlem, New York, was alarmed by what he saw as a "systematic and aggressive...movement to destroy the faith of men in the genuineness, authenticity and authority of the Bible as the Word of God," and when he accepted the BLNA's offer to become general secretary and editor of its journal in the midsummer of 1913, it was to enlist an "army" of "ministers and laymen" against "the assaults of false scholarship upon the authority of the Word of God," creating "an interdenominational movement...[of] all loyal Christians of all evangelical denominations to repel...this modern form of unbelief." Pledged to this "new departure," the journal, renamed *Bible Champion*, made its first appearance in August 1913.[7]

It lived up to its new name. Defending "the old faith and the old Book," it featured attacks on "false scholarship" from the beginning: with World War I, Hamilton associated at least some of that scholarship with the enemy, accusing "German infidelity" of seeking the Bible's "utter and complete overthrow" and assailing all the Higher Criticism as the "Hun plot against the Bible." But there were other enemies too, and in a section of the journal he added when he took over as editor, called "The Arena"—"where bouts were fast and frequent"—Hamilton met them all, leaving no imagined challenge unanswered. He was especially fond of defending the faith against evolution, which he termed "Devilution." One notable series of antievolution articles, by Luther T. Townsend (1838–1922), professor emeritus of the Boston University School of Theology and the "last of the clerical anti-Darwinists in America," went on for seven years, from 1913 to 1919, coming to an end not long before their octogenarian author himself died.[8]

Aggressive as it was, *Bible Champion* did not prosper under Hamilton's editorship. Although Hamilton had hoped, in the summer of 1913, to reach a circulation of 100,000 "before the snow flies!" solvency and success eluded the journal. Hard-pressed to pay its printer, it was always making pitiful pleas for money. Hamilton frequently mentioned that he served as editor without compensation in offices provided by his church. In the summer of 1915 "overwork" nearly led to his "nervous breakdown." In 1917, the year Hamilton was transferred to Brooklyn's First Methodist Episcopal Church, *Bible Champion* had to change to a bimonthly as a "war-measure" to keep from raising prices.[9]

In 1918, with its magazine at the point of collapse, the BLNA took the only road open to it to continue publication. Unable to generate more subscribers or donors, it accepted the offer of a veteran publisher of religious periodicals, Frank J. Boyer, to take over the magazine. Boyer, based in Reading, Pennsylvania, combined *Bible Champion* with his *Sermonizer* and changed it back to a monthly. After Hamilton died in January 1920, Boyer succeeded him both as editor of *Bible Champion* and as secretary of the BLNA.[10]

Under Boyer's direction, *Bible Champion* devoted still more of its pages to attacks on modernism and evolution. Antievolutionism in particular became a constant theme of the *Bible Champion* throughout the 1920s, expressed in articles by such fundamentalist luminaries as William Jennings Bryan (1860–1925), whose final crusade was against evolution; Amzi C. Dixon (1854–1925), first editor of *The Fundamentals* (1925); Leander S. Keyser (1856–1937), a Lutheran and professor at Hamma Divinity School in Springfield, Ohio, and Boyer's "right hand man" after Hamilton's death; George McCready Price (1870–1963), self-taught geologist and defender of a highly literalistic interpretation of the biblical account of creation; and William Bell Riley (1861–1947), founder of the World's Christian Fundamentals Association and "one of the chief architects of fundamentalism."[11]

In early 1930, Boyer absorbed a missionary magazine entitled *Christian Field*, edited by Canadian-born Thomas S. Nelson, for many years president of the American Bible School in Indianapolis, Indiana, who now became an associate editor of *Bible Champion*. Then, at the close of 1930, Boyer announced that he was merging *Bible Champion* with the *Essentialist*, whose editor, Harold Paul Sloan (1881–1961), was to become editor of the new magazine, to be named *Christian Faith and Life*. Sloan, an influential Methodist conservative, had earlier been listed as an associate editor of *Bible Champion*. As for the BLNA, *Christian Faith and Life* henceforth mentioned that organization only in the past tense.

In 1933, ill health forced Sloan to reduce his activities, and Boyer, who had been acting as the journal's publisher, now resumed its editorial responsibilities. At the same time, he announced another merger, this time with the *Methodist*, a fundamentalist periodical edited by Leander W. Munhall (1845–1934), a long-time veteran of many evangelistic campaigns. He was taken on as an associate editor, one of a staff of associates that in the 1930s included, among others, Horace M. DuBose (1856–1956), long-time associate editor of *Bibliotheca Sacra*; the creationist Harry Rimmer (1890–1952), a "Presbyterian minister and self-styled 'research scientist'"; and J. Oliver Buswell, Jr. (1895–1977), president of Wheaton College. It was partly due to the energy of these men that *Christian Faith and Life* was able to continue as long as it did during the 1930s, because, its various mergers notwithstanding, its financial position was not sound. As early as the summer of 1933, Boyer gloomily, though prematurely, announced the demise of his beloved journal, and in fact no numbers were issued in August and September that year. But in October it reappeared as a quarterly, and in that form it managed to continue in existence for a few, final years.[12]

In those last years of its publication, *Christian Faith and Life* became yet more reactionary than before, especially during 1937–1939, when Riley, Buswell, and Rimmer were doing much of the writing. Having theretofore kept premillennialism at arm's length, *Bible Champion* now embraced it. A periodical that had always taken pains to appeal to mainline Protestant denominations, it now allowed William Bell Riley to use it to denounce the Federal Council of Churches as "mainly the organization of modernists designed expressly to be a medium of propaganda for their new theological conceptions commonly known as the *social gospel*." And George McCready Price, a Seventh-Day Adventist who had earlier been put in charge of the "Current Scientific Discoveries" department, continued to push his theory of "flood geology," the argument that the earth's geological formations, including the fossil record, were caused by a universal Noachian deluge, an idea Price believed was the most effective weapon for creationists to use against evolutionists.[13]

Despite its aggressive brand of fundamentalism and the energetic work of its contributors and associate editors, the journal was unable to survive the death of its editor, Frank Boyer. With his passing in 1939, the magazine ceased, the quarterly number issued in July that year being the last. It was an unceremonious end for the *Bible Champion* line, a family of magazines that had exacted life-consuming labor of editors Daniel S. Gregory, J. Benson Hamilton, and Frank J. Boyer. When it was over, it was as if there was no one left to mourn its passing, so many of its friends had gone before it. In accordance with an arrangement with the Boyer estate, *Christian Faith and Life* was absorbed by the venerable *Bibliotheca Sacra*, which filled the remaining obligations to its subscribers.[14]

Notes

1. Information on this family of magazines, unless otherwise indicated, is from Arnold D. Ehlert, "Genealogical History of Bibliotheca Sacra," *Bibliotheca Sacra* 100 (January 1943): 31–52; Ehlert, "Further Genealogical Notes," *Bibliotheca Sacra* 100 (October 1943): 476–78; the *Union List of Serials in Libraries of the United States and Canada*, 3d ed., 5 vols. (New York, 1965); and, principally, from the periodicals themselves.

2. *Bible Student* identified itself as a "new series" in continuation of the monthly *Bible Student and Religious Outlook* (1899), edited by McPheeters in Columbia, which in turn was volume 3 in continuation of volumes 1 and 2 of the monthly *Religious Outlook* (1897–1898), also published in Columbia, and edited by McPheeters and Brimm. In 1898 Columbia colleague Samuel C. Byrd (1868–1951) joined them as managing editor.

3. *The Bible Student and Teacher* (hereinafter cited as *BST*) and *The Bible Champion* (hereinafter cited as *BC*) are the best sources of information about the league's activities.

See, for example, Gregory, "The Aims and Methods of the American Bible League," *BST* 4 (June 1906): 440–52, and "What Is the Bible League of North America?" *BST* 9 (November 1908): 347–48.

4. [Gregory], "Editorial Notes and Points," *BST* 1 (January 1904): 65–66, and McPheeters, "An Editorial Notice," *Bible Student* 8 (December 1903): 301. The early leadership of the ABL included conservative Protestants from many denominations and seminaries across the United States. Charter members of the education committee, in addition to Gregory and McPheeters, were Willis J. Beecher, David James Burrell, Henry A. Buttz, Robert Mackenzie, Howard Osgood, J. P. Sheraton, Edmund J. Wolf, and G. Frederick Wright.

5. [Gregory], "Editorial Notes and Points," p. 66; [Gregory], "The Present Need and Opportunity," *BST* 5 (July 1906): 82; [Gregory], "Change of Name, and What It Means," *BST* 8 (April 1908): 326; and [Gregory], "Proposed Campaign of the Bible League of North America," *BST* 12 (January 1910): 79–82.

6. [Gregory], "Grounds of the Appeal of the Bible League for Christian Support," *BST* 13 (August–September 1910): 149–50; [Gregory], "Correction of Overstatements Concerning 'The Fundamentals'," *BST* 13 (November 1910): 262; "A Break-Down with Months of Disablement," *BST* 14 (April 1911): 212; "Reasons for the Late and Irregular Issue of the Magazine," *BST* 14 (April 1911): 249; [Gregory], "Program and Progress of the Campaign for Making the League Efficient," *BST* 15 (May–June 1912): 65–66; [Gregory], "League Notes and Points," *BST* 15 (November–April 1912–1913): 225–28; Hall, "The Bible League of North America," *BC* 16 (August 1913): 35; and Hall, "President Hall's Appeal," *BC* 18 (August 1914): 33. See also Hall, "In Memoriam: Daniel Seelye Gregory," *BC* 19 (May 1915): 195. On the publication of *The Fundamentals*, see George M. Marsden, *Fundamentalism and American Culture: The Shaping of Twentieth-Century Evangelicalism, 1870–1925* (New York, 1980), pp. 118–23.

7. Hall and Hamilton, "To All Christian Ministers," *BC* 16 (November 1913): 170; Hall, "An Appeal to Our Friends," *BC* 17 (June 1914): 273; and [Hamilton], "The New Aim and Name," *BC* 16 (August 1913): 30.

8. Hall and Hamilton, "To All Christian Ministers," p. 170; Hamilton, "To the Bible Leaguers," *BC* 24 (July 1918): 284; [Hamilton], "The Hun Plot against the Bible," *BC* 25 (September 1919): 395–96; Ehlert, "Genealogical History of Bibliotheca Sacra," p. 48; [Hamilton], "Evolution—Devilution," *BC* 24 (March–April 1918): 86. On Townsend, see James R. Moore, *The Post-Darwinian Controversies: A Study of the Protestant Struggle to Come to Terms with Darwin in Great Britain and America, 1870–1900* (Cambridge, England, 1979), pp. 198–99.

9. Hamilton, "Memoranda," *BC* 16 (August 1913): 41; [Hamilton], "To the Readers of the Bible Champion," *BC* 20 (November 1915): 183–84; [Hamilton], "The Holy City," *BC* 23 (July–August 1917): 225; [Hamilton], "What Hath God Wrought!" *BC* 20 (December 1915): 230; [Hamilton], "The Outlook for 1916," *BC* 21 (January 1916): 37; and "A Message from the Associate Editors," *BC* 23 (November–December 1917): 328.

10. Although Boyer continued *Bible Champion* under its old name, editor, and issue numbers, its pagination apparently followed the *Sermonizer*'s. While Hamilton and Boyer used the word *consolidation* to describe the new arrangement, in a sense it was the *Sermonizer* that took over *Bible Champion* instead of the reverse. Boyer had begun the *Sermonizer* in 1910. It probably was related to earlier Boyer magazines beginning with *Preacher's Assistant* in 1889. See Hamilton and Boyer, "The Sermonizer and the Bible Champion Consolidated," *BC* 24 (July 1918): 241; Boyer, "The Champion and the Essentialist Merge," *BC* 37 (December 1930): 625; and Ehlert, "Genealogical History of Bibliotheca Sacra," pp. 32, 42–45, 48–49.

11. Boyer, "Our Parting Salutation," *Christian Faith and Life* 39 (July 1933): 314 (hereinafter cited as *CFL*). The characterization of Riley is from Marsden, *Fundamentalism and American Culture*, p. 127.

12. Munhall had edited *Eastern Methodist* from 1916 until 1925, when its name changed to the *Methodist*. See Ehlert, "Genealogical History of Bibliotheca Sacra," pp. 39–42. Boyer, "Our Parting Salutation," pp. 313–14, and Boyer, "Our Magazine to Be Continued," *CFL* 39 (October 1933): 365–67. On Rimmer, see Ronald L. Numbers, "The Dilemma of Evangelical Scientists," in George M. Marsden, ed., *Evangelicalism and Modern America* (Grand Rapids, Michigan, 1984), p. 151.

13. [Hamilton], "Pre and Postmilleniansm," *BC* 26 (January 1920): 21–22; Busell, "A Premillennial Argument," *CFL* 43 (October 1937): 249–53; Riley, "The World's Christian Fundamentals Association," *CFL* 45 (July 1939): 203–204; and Price, "Watchman, What of the Night?" *CFL* 44 (April 1938): 151–53. Several premillennialists had been active in the BLNA, but in nondispensationalist roles. See Marsden, *Fundamentalism and American Culture*, p. 118. For Price, see, for example, "The Fallacy about the Time-Values of the Fossils," *CFL* 40 (April 1934): 134–38. On flood geology, see Numbers, "The Dilemma of Evangelical Scientists," pp. 151–52.

14. "Merger with 'Christian Faith and Life'," *Bibliotheca Sacra* 96 (July 1939): 257–58; R. T. Chafer, "Merger with 'Christian Faith and Life'," *Bibliotheca Sacra* 96 (October 1939): 389.

Information Sources

BIBLIOGRAPHY:

Ehlert, Arnold D. "Genealogical History of Bibliotheca Sacra."*Bibliotheca Sacra* 100 (January 1943): 31–52
————"Further Genealogical Notes." *Bibliotheca Sacra* 100 (October 1943): 476–78.
INDEXES: Irregularly indexed.
REPRINT EDITIONS: None.
LOCATION SOURCES: The Presbyterian Historical Society, Presbyterian Church (U.S.A.), Montreat, North Carolina has a complete run; partial runs widely available.

Publication History

TITLE AND TITLE CHANGES: *The Bible Student*, 1900–1903; *The Bible Student and Teacher*, 1904–1913; *The Bible Champion*, 1913–1930; *Christian Faith and Life*, 1931–1939.
VOLUME AND ISSUE DATA: Volumes 1–45, January 1904–July 1939.
FREQUENCY OF PUBLICATION: Monthly, 1904–1917; bimonthly, 1917–1918; monthly, 1918–1933; quarterly, 1933–1939. Publication frequently irregular.
PUBLISHERS: 1900–1903: William M. McPheeters, Columbia, South Carolina; 1904–1918: American Bible League (name changed to Bible League of North America in 1908), New York; 1918–1939: Frank J. Boyer, Reading, Pennsylvania.
EDITORS: William M. McPheeters, 1900–1903; Benjamin B. Warfield, 1900–1903; George T. Purves, 1900–1901; Samuel M. Smith, 1900–1903; Daniel J. Brimm, 1900–1901; John D. Davis, 1900–1903; Daniel S. Gregory, 1904–1913; Jay Benson Hamilton, 1913–1920; Frank J. Boyer, 1920–1930; Harold Paul Sloan, 1931–1932; Frank J. Boyer, 1933–1939.
CIRCULATION: In 1908, about 6,000; by 1917, fewer than 2,300.

William J. Morison

King's Business
1910–1970

King's Business, begun in January 1910, was a monthly periodical published by the Bible Institute of Los Angeles (BIOLA), a fundamentalist Bible school. It represented the views of moderate Protestant fundamentalists, who more recently have been known as the New Evangelicals. On a religious and political continuum, it may be placed somewhere between Carl McIntire's *Christian Beacon* and Carl F. H. Henry's *Christianity Today*.

In understanding the theological and political orientation of this publication, it is helpful to remember that the editors over the decades from the 1920s to 1970 assumed that God is in history, working, giving signs, guiding, guarding, loving, and reproaching his people. Moreover, fact and faith are one. The facts of history have to be interpreted to confirm the faith or the teachings that one receives through the proper and "obvious" interpretation of God's word, the Bible. It was fundamentally an a priori approach that assumed that absolutes of God's word would always be confirmed by the experiences of history. Ironically, it was basically a system identical to the Thomistic synthesis, devoid of traditional church teaching and a papacy. Editors of this publication, much like their Protestant forefathers, merely substituted the Bible for the institutional church and its tradition. The conclusions of nonbelievers, scholars, ministers, laypersons, or churches outside their orientation that did not concur with their perception of God's message were dismissed as misguided opinion at best and vainglorious egotism at worst. The wisdom of this world was often foolishness to God.[1]

In light of the above characterization, the editors and writers of *King's Business* were observers, watching events of the world and interpreting the cosmic significance of those events in light of their reading of the Bible. The Allied victory in Africa in 1942, for example, was "one of the most remarkable triumphs in the history of warfare" because from it came the preservation of ancient archaeological sites that confirmed "Biblical Truths." "One can imagine," says the writer, "the

Satanic glee with which the anti-God masters of the Nazi regime contemplated the disruption of the excavations which are unearthing so much new evidence of the truth of the Old Testament."[2]

What might be considered of greater cosmic significance than the preservation of archaeological sites was articulated a few years later when the editor asserted that God's wrath was visited on nations that failed to acknowledge that "He is Lord of Lords, the King of Kings, and the Prince of the judges of the earth."[3] It was for this reason that *King's Business* (the "king" in the title refers to God) declared in 1947 that the British empire was in trouble: one-third of its population, the magazine reported, did not believe in God, and only a small percentage of it attended a house of worship on the Lord's Day. (It did not help matters that the British had shamefully renounced the Balfour Declaration, which promised a national homeland for the world's Jews.)[4] Even as God used nations as instruments of his wrath in Old Testament times to punish nations, so he used the United States as his punishing agent in World War II. But Germany's fate could befall the United States too, should it fall into apostasy. While "historians" were alleged to have discovered that it was the influence of the Bible that had been most important in making the United States the mightiest industrial nation ever, *King's Business* warned that "history is strewn with nations that once enjoyed God's gifts and then forgot the Giver. Let us solemnly consider and be warned," wrote the editor.[5]

History also demonstrated that God could and did perform miracles as of old. In 1950 a regular contributor to *King's Business*, Louis S. Bauman, cited a sermon he had preached fifty years earlier, "The Doomed Turk." At the time he delivered the sermon, he wrote, there were many who were skeptical of scriptural prophecy. How could God ever give the Jews their homeland back when Muslims had occupied the land for 400 years? Indeed, 300 million Turks would rise in a holy war should anyone try to expel them for the Jews. Yet "General Allenby marched into Jerusalem, and delivered the city from the grasp of the Turk, without firing a shot. At his very presence the Turks ran like scared rabbits. Our God can still perform miracles."[6]

History fulfilled prophecy, and because this was true, prophecy was both a key to understanding history and a map to the present and future. In the ancient world of Scripture lay the whole world of modern life. To demonstrate this, Bauman cited John on the Isle of Patmos, who wrote: "And another horse came forth, a red horse, and to him that sat thereon it was given to take peace from the earth, and that they should slay one another, and there was given unto him a great sword."[7] This passage Bauman found fulfilled in the twentieth century as indicated by the following newspaper headlines:

> "U. S. Soldiers Battle Jap *Reds*."
> "U. S. Won't Use Veto to Block *Red* China."
> "Russians [Reds] in Shanghai Estimated at 3000."
> "Soviet [Reds] Offers West Europe Gain."
> "Communists Display Serious Show of What *Reds* Can Do."
> "400 Planes Sent to Chinese *Reds*."

The conclusion to Bauman was obvious: "Newspaperdom is literally covered with items concerning 'Reds', i.e. Russians or Moscow Satellites. Need anyone have to guess who the rider of the 'red horse' may be?"[8]

This kind of approach to world events controlled the magazine's view on major global and domestic issues throughout its career. Of particular importance was the contemporary Jewish question, central to its understanding of the direction and development of history itself. Fascinated for decades by the "number one wanderer in the world," *King's Business* turned an especially bedazzled attention to the question in the years 1947–1950, when it printed several articles and editorials about it, all of them pervaded with a sense of anticipation. Just as ancient prophets no doubt foretold events because of their shrewd ability to analyze their current situation, so the editors of and contributors to *King's Business*, sensing that something of significance was about to occur in Palestine, announced prophetically that God was preparing to return the Jew to his homeland. Ezekiel, chapter 37, prophesied that the Dry Bones (signifying the whole house of Israel after centuries of weariness and scattering) would come together and be covered with flesh and skin. This prophecy had been approaching fulfillment since the founding in 1896 of the Zionist movement, that worldwide organization God used to restore Palestine to the Jews. It was furthered in 1917 in the Balfour Declaration, when God, using Great Britain for his purpose, provided what Louis Talbot in 1947 called one of many significant signs that Israel would again see the Messiah, "perhaps very soon."[9] The Jew was at last coming into his rights; the day of his exile was soon to end. With the creation of the Jewish state in 1948, editors and writers of *King's Business* were awestruck. Wrote Talbot, "My friends, it is thrilling to be living in a day when this prophecy of the restoration of Israel is taking place as God has spoken it."[10] The editor of *King's Business* declared: "Bible students should ponder the tremendous prophetic implications of the re-emergence of Israel as a nation. The Jew has always been God's time clock which although silent for nineteen centuries, has once more begun to tick loudly enough for everyone to hear. Many of God's wisest saints feel that the hour of the return of Christ will strike soon."[11]

According to Ezekiel, chapter 38, however, before the drama could unfold completely, additional conditions and events had to occur. There must be many Jews living in Palestine; there had to be unwalled villages there, existing without fear of invasion or plunder; there had to be attention to commercial agriculture and religious pursuits rather than to military preparedness; and there had to be guaranteed protection of national and territorial integrity by a noncommunist international force.[12] And, in spite of security arrangements, there had to be an invasion: Palestine was to be invaded by a northern confederacy (Russia and Germany)—the armies of Gog, as prophesied in Ezekiel—descending like a storm (modern mechanized warfare, as described by Ezekiel 3,000 years ago), and covering the land like a cloud (air war and paratroopers). The motive of the attack would be to exterminate the Jews, for since Jews "have gotten cattle and goods," they will have become the possessors of valuable lands, the envy of the Russians who will seek to seize them. [13] The international force will protest the invasion verbally only, which "reminds us somewhat of the impotency of the protests lodged by the nations of the world in the anxious months before the outbreak of [World War II]," and Gog will conquer Palestine.[14]

But Gog will be destroyed in its turn, perhaps by a combination of natural disasters and the noncommunist international police force, and "every man's sword shall be against his brother." The invading army of Gog will be virtually annihilated (an enemy army of twenty million will lose five-sixths of its soldiers, which "does not seem the least fantastic since the atom bomb was developed"), Israel will be preserved, and God will be glorified.[15] God will then destroy the land of Gog (Russia), making it defenseless against its enemies. Observing such miraculous power, the Jews will convert to Christ.

These successes of creating a homeland for the Jews and subsequently annihilating Gog will set the stage for the final confrontation at Armageddon. The noncommunist alliance, already being forged by the United Nations, will establish a world state with the goal of attaining power over all nations, and its leader will be the Antichrist. This army of unregenerate nations will fight against Christ at Armageddon. "The Lord will go forth and fight against those nations. Hallelujah! By the marvelous grace of God I expect to be in that army!" exclaimed Louis Bauman. "The enemies of God will be in the gizzards of the buzzards (Rev. 19:21) and the peace of mankind will cover the earth as the waters cover the sea."[16]

There was a curious paradox in this analysis, for even as *King's Business* saw the Jewish people as the crucial element in the unfolding of God's purposes in history, it tended to look on Jews with a degree of disgust it only managed to overcome by a peculiar process wherein Jews stopped being Jews. Bauman cautioned readers of *King's Business* in 1950 to "keep your eye on the Jew. No trustworthy sign has been given and will not be given, unless the Jew is in the picture.... However towering human events may be, if they have any real prophetic meaning, you will find the Jew lurking in the shadows somewhere."[17] That last phrase insinuates an anti-Semitism that the magazine's conviction that Jews will ultimately convert to Christianity merely underlines. "There is coming a day," Talbot wrote in 1948, "when the hearts of unsaved, commercial, grasping Jews will be changed by the love of God."[18] But the conversion of Jews that *King's Business* contemplated involved more than this. While Talbot noted in early 1948 that "all the world hates Jews because they are more clever and aggressive than Gentiles," a few months later the editor of the magazine remarked that "the Jews [in victory] were too tough, too smart and too vigorous for the divided and debilitated Arab world to conquer," and he went on to imply that this was true because "the race seemingly is running to the large-boned, blue-eyed, blond athletic type of Jew. Disappearing, apparently, are the short stocky Jews typical of the Middle Ages."[19] God's chosen people, the restorers of Israel, were coming to look like white Anglo-Saxon Protestants. They were coming to act like them too: Bauman commented with satisfaction in 1950 that even with an influx of 100,000 immigrants from Iraq alone that year, there was no unemployment in Israel; and while 5,000 factories were running full blast there, "over the line in Old Jerusalem the turbaned (Esau) Arab sits on the ground amidst squalid surroundings, working only with his ancient stick for a plow, jealous and despising his brother Jacob."[20] God's chosen people were on the way to Western-style prosperity, and it was all prophesied to be so.

This interpretation of biblical prophecy, regardless of its idiosyncratic details, is distinctly premillennal in orientation: world conditions will inevitably worsen until the Second Coming of Christ and the victory at Armageddon. In this view, any human attempt to meliorate the conditions of human life is futile. The inexorable course of prophetic history all but ruled out the feasibility of any efforts designed to alleviate human suffering. But *King's Business* did not rebuke social activism on premillennial grounds alone, for it was convinced that social programs were, in the main, part of the international movement that would ultimately be directed by Antichrist. "The World Government movement," the journal reported, "gets the vote of the vast proletarian masses of the world's greatest democracies by promising them practically everything, housing, insurance, hospitalization, education, pensions under the guise of social welfare."[21] This was all wrong. What was needed, the periodical advised its readers, was to accept Christ. "There is only one way to deal with the sinful heart," it held, "and that is to regenerate it through the means which God Himself has provided in the sacrifice of His Son."[22] One must be ready to be removed from this scene (the Rapture) before the end comes, and must keep "unspotted from the world, ardently devoted to Jesus Christ and faithful in telling others of these coming events, and pray for a supernatural revival of the Church of Jesus Christ and for the ingathering of souls before the Lord catches away his church."[23] Yet even as it advised this, *King's Business* insisted that world conversion was not possible, not even to be desired, because the fulfillment of prophecy required that it should not occur. Criticizing a "well known denominational leader who was advocating that America be Christianized first and then evangelize the world," the periodical declared that "prophecy tells us that God's plan is for everyone in the world to have the opportunity to hear the Gospel and receive the Saviour''; but that was all.[24]

King's Business thus found itself in the odd (though not unusual) position of declaring that prophecy must be fulfilled, even though many of those involved in that work were evil, and that while those same people must be given the opportunity to receive Christ, prophecy required that many of them must not accept him. This paradox runs consistently through the history of the journal, and nowhere more clearly than in its topical commentaries on the United States and its relations with the rest of the world, for, in its view, the United States was under the special care of God, and while doom was the ineluctable fate of this nation along with the rest of the unregenerate world, *King's Business* was proudly, incurably nationalistic.

Its understanding of the Constitution and the federal system tended to be traditional. In a 1936 essay, Dan Gilbert asserted that the Constitution did not create human rights; it merely spelled out rights already given by God, affirming and enforcing the moral law as it has been revealed to us. It operated to keep Caesar within his legitimate sphere; it created a government by and for the people, through majoritarian democracy. However, the majority could not violate the Constitution in the mistaken belief that the people as a whole more than people individually were above the law. Gilbert rejected as an unequivocal evil the modern doctrine of the "divine right of the majority" not only because it was a frightening threat to the rights guaranteed in the Constitution and the moral law of God, but because it was "the basest form of paganism." Pagan governments, Gilbert held, were founded on the belief that individual rights are the gift of government and its citizens, and what government gives it can take away. But the government of the United States was founded on the Christian principle that individual rights are the gift of God, and that what God gives, government may not take away. Hence, the majority, whether a two-thirds or a nine-tenths majority, "has no right to infringe...the God given right of the individual." Applying this argument specifically to the question of religious liberty, Gilbert wrote that even if 99 percent of the American people favored denying religious liberty to a small group, and Congress, as the voice of that majority, were to enact legislation to deny religious liberty to even a single person, then the Supreme Court, as the interpreter of the God-given law, would have the duty of upholding the God-given rights of the individual against the wishes of the 99 percent.[25]

The Court, not the democratic masses represented in Congress, was the final arbiter of constitutionality. To argue otherwise would be "equivalent to saying that Congress should be almighty above the Constitution." It was not, and when it enacted laws clearly in violation of the Constitution, the legislation was really no law at all. According to Gilbert, New Deal legislation fit in this category, because "for a legislative act to be *law* it must be fair and just to all its citizens. *Congress may not steal*. The court has said that to take property from one class and to give it to another is...robbery."[26] Gilbert's obvious indignation brought him perilously close to usurping the very function of declaring on the constitutionality of laws he had just attributed through close argument to the Supreme Court alone.

But others at *King's Business* found the New Deal, and the events of the 1930s in general, distressing for reasons that had little to do with Gilbert's legalities. Bauman agreed that the Congress was doing things all wrong. He lamented that the richest, most favored nation in the world, "after an unprecedented spending spree in which we have filched billions upon billions from the pockets of our children yet unborn, in an effort to create employment and restore prosperity, 20 millions—a larger number than ever before—are still fed on the dole," and he agreed that "the best brains or the worst brains that ever directed our old ship of state candidly admit that the only way out that they know, is through methods that the Supreme Court denounces as but little better than pillage." But he saw darker forces at work than mere wrongheadedness and robbery. "Our enthroned leaders," he wrote, "are utterly confused, confounded, befuddled."[27] They no longer provided a government for the whole nation but instead only one for the have-nots, bringing into America for the first time the class spirit of the rest of the world.

Nor was this the end of it, for this class spirit came into America through a foreign conspiracy that promoted labor unrest. Among the foreigners accused of mischief was the Englishman, John Brophy, "a communistic candidate for the United Mine Workers and the first American trade unionist delegate to Russia." Another villain was known by *King's Business* only as "Germer," born in Weslan, Germany, and formerly a national secretary of the Socialist party. Finally, there was Leo

Krzychi, "a communistic charter member of the Socialist Party in Milwaukee. He now spends his time trotting from one strike to another....These men of foreign breed are here instilling the old world class hatreds into the bosoms of the American workingman, and are paralyzing this great industrial city [Akron, Ohio] of a quarter of a million souls. And this—in America! What must the rest of the world be like?"[28]

It was one thing to have class hatreds imported to the United States by foreigners, but quite another that Americans, and especially Christian liberals, fell for this conspiratorial activity. Some of the sharpest words written in *King's Business* were reserved for Christian liberals who were "fructifying supposedly in the spirit of brotherly love, good will, peace, and civic and moral righteousness," but whose gullibility made them loathsome. "The vile serpents of human hate glide forth as never before from their filthy dens, and entwine themselves about the bodies and souls of men." The particular "vile serpents" singled out by *King's Business* for peddling this "sweetness and light" were socialists, altruists, utopians, ethical culturists, humanists, Oxford Groupists, behaviorists, nudists, "and every other sort of an *amicus humani generis* that can be classified under the term modernist."[29]

Little wonder that *King's Business* was more than irritated when at a dinner attended by Eleanor Roosevelt, Florence Jackson Stoddard, an alleged direct descendant of Andrew Jackson, recited the "Ballad of the Nine Old Men." The occasion was doubly irritating because Mrs. Roosevelt did not complain or protest this "insult on the Supreme Court." The incident revealed to *King's Business* editors how little difference there was between Mrs. Roosevelt and the "Bolshevistic hoodlums who...hung in effigy along a public highway the six justices of the Supreme Court who held the AAA unconstitutional....Mrs. Roosevelt should have resented the insult to the Supreme Court."[30]

But all of these expressions of irritation, indignation, and disgust seem to be directly contradictory to the conviction of the writers for *King's Business* that the emergence of class conflict and discourtesy to sacred institutions was evidence that the coming of the Lord was near, since his coming was to be immediately preceded by great strife between employer and employee, rich and poor, capitalist and proletarian. So declared prophecy; so it must be. *King's Business* consequently fell back to its premillennial message. Humanitarian agencies had not learned that they could not substitute the Golden Rule for the fact of man's sin. These "Fatherhood-of-Godists and Brotherhood-of-Manists," Bauman wrote, "are trying to veneer the old man—polishing up on the outside while ignoring the deceitful, wicked heart that beats in the breast of Cain."[31] What the nation sorely needed was a leader "in this dark and solemn hour who would call the nation back to God."[32]

Still, after World War II and during the 1950s and 1960s, the idea of a foreign-inspired, conspiratorial enemy that ought to be combated was never far from the minds of the writers for *King's Business*, ineffectual though the combat against it might be. The journal identified communists as the conspirators who were infiltrating American life and whose insidious influence was suspected in the liberal National Council of Churches, public and private schools, the State Department, and all the other branches of government too. Evidence that *King's Business* cited of this conspiratorial meddling included the Social Gospel, the push for school desegregation, and sex education in schools. All this, and in fact any domestic programming that smacked of the New Deal, Fair Deal, or the Great Society, was at once useless and at the same time misguided, the work of dupes of the communist conspiracy.

Similarly useless and misguided was the Marshall Plan, of which the journal editorialized in 1947: "Of course the $9,000,000,000 for the Marshall Plan over a three year period would be a good investment if it ensured peace. But, we know from the Word of God that the expenditure of $9,000,000,000 or $90,000,000,000 will not bring peace to the world in the grip of a fallen nature and under the domination of the arch-enemy of God, that old serpent, the devil."[33] Two years later, however, in 1949, *King's Business* conceded that the Marshall Plan was a fine act of generosity for which the United States was blessed. "Hearts and purses have opened," it exclaimed. "Do not think for a moment that God is unacquainted with this!" Indeed, America in a sense had already been repaid by God for its charity by the overwhelming harvest of its acres "during the past 8 or 10 years."[34] But neither the Marshall Plan nor the North Atlantic Treaty Organization promised ultimate peace, and neither did the United Nations, which *King's Business* warned against: "Already," it declared in 1950, "Old Glory is battling to maintain its preeminence above the [U.N.] flag."[35] House-to-house preaching was what *King's Business* recommended, but even that could not avert the impending doom imposed by God's plan.

When *King's Business* ceased publication in 1970, a new emphasis within fundamentalism was articulated by the so-called New Evangelicals, who advocated an increased social involvement in the affairs of the world, an emphasis contrary to that represented by *King's Business*. It is possible that this subtle but perceptible change of emphasis within fundamentalism had an effect on the demise of *King's Business*. The reason for the end of this publication was purported to be economic—that subscriptions were dropping, or at least not increasing, while costs were rising. Additionally, there was an apparent restlessness among the readership because of an alleged lack of central purpose. Was it to be a family publication, a publication emphasizing the Sunday school, or one that educates in world and national affairs? Also, the editorial staff and writers for the publication had been entrenched for years, resistant to change, at a time when the New Evangelical movement appeared to be making some moves toward advocating a social application of the gospel.[36] To solve these problems BIOLA ended the publication.

This profile of circumstances serves to give insight into the nature of *King's Business*, a moderate fundamentalist publication within the broader New Evangelical movement, which is noted for its willingness to engage in meaningful dialogue with other Christian orientations. It would appear, however, that New Evangelicalism left *King's Business* behind. The broader movement has been able to change and grow. *King's Business* was not so agile.

Perhaps it was difficult to maintain its various tensions within reasonable control: its belief that the dispensations of God rendered social action for melioration feckless, and its belief that the "conspirators" needed to be openly and actively resisted; its belief that conversion to Christianity was the best means of combating the forces of evil in the world, and its belief that until the supernatural intervention of Christ, this could never be wholly successful; its belief that all the world was doomed, but that doomed America was an object of God's particular love. Still, while these apparently mutually inconsistent views could be managed before New Evangelicalism gained force, *King's Business* provided, again in a paradox, a message at once of pessimism and comfort. Although the terrifying nuclear era had exploded into human consciousness in the summer of 1945, and although the signs multiplied that Armageddon was at hand, *King's Business* consoled its readers with soothing reassurance: "At this very moment [of fear] the spirit of God seemed to whisper concerning the safety of the position of the children of God. First, we are in the hand of God's Son to whom is given all power both in Heaven and earth. Then we have the added protection of being in the hand of the Father, the creator and sustainer of all things. Surely this brings peace and quiet to the troubled heart."[37]

Notes

1. 1 Cor. 1:20.

2. Dan Gilbert, "God's Hand in the African Victory," *King's Business* 34 (August 1943): 284 (hereinafter cited as *KB*).

3. "Editorially Speaking" (hereinafter cited as "E.S."), *KB* 36 (September 1945): 327.

4. "R. S.," *KB* 38 (November 1947): 4.

5. "E.S.," *KB* 38 (October 1947): 4; *KB* 40 (November 1949): 6.

6. Louis S. Bauman, "Israel Lives Again," *KB* 41 (October 1950): 9.

7. Rev. 6:4.

8. Bauman, "The Russian Bear Growls Forth," *KB* 41 (August 1950): 12.

9. Talbot, "Palestine, Russia and Ezekiel 36," *KB* 38 (November 1947): 8, 9.

10. Talbot, "Palestine, Russia and Ezekiel 36, " *KB* 39 (July 1948): 10.

11. "E.S.," *KB* 39 (December 1948): 4.

12. Talbot, "Palestine, Russia and Ezekiel 36," *KB* 39 (February 1948): 13.

13. Ibid.

14. Talbot, "Palestine, Russia and Ezekiel 36," *KB* 39 (March 1948): 13.

15. Talbot, "Palestine, Russia and Ezekiel 36," *KB* 39 (April 1948): 14; (March 1948), p. 9.

16. Bauman, "The Nations Marshalling for Armageddon," *KB* 41 (December 1950): 30.

17. Bauman, "Israel Lives Again!" *KB* 41 (September 1950): 7.

18. Talbot, "Palestine, Russia and Ezekiel 36" [February 1948], p. 13.

19. "E. S., " *KB* 39 (October 1948): 4.

20. Bauman, "Israel Lives Again!" *KB* 41 (October 1950): 9.

21. Bauman, "1935—A Prophetic Review," *KB* 27 (April 1936): 129.

22. "E.S.," *KB* 40 (February 1949): 4.

23. "E.S.," *KB* 27 (February 1936): 51. The Rapture will occur before the final battle of Armageddon whereby the Lord will take away his church with him, literally sweeping people away through the air who are saved. The concern for the salvation for as many souls as possible, therefore, was not for the purpose of changing society, but to allow for as many people as possible to be taken with the Lord.

24. "E.S.," *KB* 37 (December 1946): 3.

25. Gilbert, "God and the Constitution," *KB* 26 (July 1936): 254 .

26. Ibid., pp. 255, 271.

27. Bauman, "1935—A Prophetic Review," *KB* 27 (March 1936): 91.

28. Bauman, "1935—A Prophetic Review," (April 1936): 129.

29. Ibid., p. 128.

30. "E.S.," *KB* 27 (March 1936): 91.

31. Bauman, "1935—A Prophetic Review" (April 1936): 129

32. "E.S.," *KB* 27 (February 1936): 112.

33. "E.S." (October 1947): 3.

34. "E.S.," *KB* 40 (August 1949): 4.

35. Bauman, "The Nations Marshalling for Armageddon," p. 30.

36. Telephone interview with Professor Gerald Goodin of BIOLA Library, 20 May 1983.

37. "E.S.," *KB* 36 (September 1945): 327; Bauman, "Does the Hydrogen Bomb Mean the End?" *KB* 41 (June 1950): 238.

Information Sources

BIBLIOGRAPHY:

Vinz, Warren L. *Pulpit Politics: Faces of American Protestant Nationalism in the Twentieth Century.* Albany, New York, 1997.

INDEXES: None.

REPRINT EDITIONS: None.

LOCATION SOURCES: Complete runs: Bible Institute of Los Angeles Library; Moody Bible Institute, Chicago; Library of Congress; Garrett Theological Seminary, Evanston, Illinois.

Publication History

TITLE AND TITLE CHANGES: *King's Business*.

VOLUME AND ISSUE DATA: Volumes 1–61, January 1910–December 1970.

FREQUENCY OF PUBLICATION: Monthly.

PUBLISHER: The Bible Institute of Los Angeles, Los Angeles.

EDITORS: J. H. Sammis, November 1911–September 1912; R. A. Torrey, October 1912–December 1918; T. C. Horton, January 1919–December 1926; John Murdoch MacInnis, January 1927–January 1929; William P. White, July 1929–February 1933; John C. Page, April–August 1933; Paul W. Wood, November 1935–October 1938; Louis T. Talbot, November 1938–March 1953; Samuel H. Southerland, April 1953–December 1970.

CIRCULATION: 30,000.

Warren L. Vinz

Sword of the Lord
1934–

The *Sword of the Lord* was begun on 28 September 1934, by a colorful, fire-eating, hell-fire and damnation fundamentalist preacher-evangelist, John R. Rice. Rice was the founder and editor of the *Sword* for forty-six years until his death in 1980, dominating and overshadowing all contributors to the periodical.

He was Southern Baptist and trained for the ministry, but soon left the Southern Baptist Convention because "he could not serve Christ and denominational bosses—and he would not!"[1] Such a parting is not surprising since throughout his career he was outspoken, spectacular, sensational, and, according to his followers, scriptural. Some of his sermon topics give an indication of his style that made even Southern Baptist Convention leaders nervous. A sampling of his homiletical renditions include: "The Man Who Went to Heaven Without Baptism, Without Joining a Church, Without a Mourner's Bench, Without Even Living a Good Life"; "Wild Oats in Dallas—How Dallas People Sow Them and How They Are Reaped"; "The Dance-Child of the Brothel, Sister of Gambling and Drunkenness, Mother of Lust—Road to Hell!"; "Company for Supper—And Not a Rite in the House"; "Filling Stations on the Highway to Hell."[2]

While serving an independent fundamentalist Baptist church in Dallas, Texas, Rice decided to extend his ministry by publishing the *Sword of the Lord and of John R. Rice,* the title being based on Judges 7:20: "and they cried, the sword of the Lord, and of Gideon." Soon after its beginning, the periodical was called only the *Sword of the Lord*; it continues with that title to this day.

Consistent with Rice's independent ways, the *Sword* is independent of any institutional support, relying on subscriptions and underwritten by contributions from fundamentalist churches and individuals. A list of writing contributors to the *Sword* is a who's who in extreme fundamentalism, including Dr. Bob Jones, Sr., and Dr. Bob Jones, Jr., founder and president of Bob Jones University, respectively; Dr. Curtis Hutson, who succeeded Rice as editor of the *Sword* in 1980; Dr. Carl

McIntire, founder of the fundamentalist American Council of Christian Churches; and the Reverend Jerry Falwell, leader of the Moral Majority. For a time Dr. Billy Graham served on the Sword of the Lord Cooperating Board, and Dr. Rice on the board of trustees of Northwestern Schools, of which Dr. Graham was president. Graham's revival messages were printed in the *Sword* along with the revival statistics of the Graham evangelistic campaigns. However, when Graham endorsed the Revised Standard Version of the Bible, the relationship cooled, with Rice asking his subscribers to pray for Billy. When Billy actually cooperated in revival ventures with affiliate churches to the National Council of Churches and refused to accept a New York City crusade under sponsorship of only evangelical, fundamental churches, "and refused to be classified as a fundamentalist—opting for the terminology 'Conservative-Liberal' or 'Constructionist'—John Rice took his stand against a brother he loved in the Lord so that he himself might walk in the way of 'thus saith the Lord.'"[3]

Rice's writing and editing was not limited to publishing the *Sword*, but by the time of his death included over 200 titles of books and pamphlets with a combined circulation exceeding 60 million copies. Added to this prolific record is the circulation of the *Sword* of 150,000 subscriptions, which included readers in every state in the union, 100 foreign countries, and 40,000 preachers, evangelists, and missionaries. The influence of Rice and the *Sword* is obviously formidable.

The statement of purpose heading each issue of the *Sword* reads: "An Independent Christian Bi-Weekly Standing for the Verbal Inspiration of the Bible, the Deity of Christ, His Blood Atonement, Salvation by Faith, New Testament Soul Winning, and the Premillennial Return of Christ. Opposes Modernism, Worldliness, and Formalism."

In addition to the *Sword*'s fundamentalist position, the periodical insisted on the practice (nearly elevated to a doctrine) of separation from the unsaved.[4] According to Rice, there are only two plans for salvation. The first is salvation by human works, believed and practiced by Catholics, liberal Protestants, Hindus, and Mohammedans. "It is all one thing" with these religions. The second plan is salvation by the blood of Christ subscribed to by all Bible-believing fundamentalists. According to the *Sword*, "you are not to have those two kinds of seeds in the same field."[5] One qualification to this precept is that it refers only to "hitching them [believers with nonbelievers] up for the Lord's business." That is forbidden. But the practice of separation does not apply to riding on the same bus with the unsaved, trading at the same supermarket with them (unless the market sells beer), riding on a train with a conductor who is not a Christian, or working in a company in which some employees are unsaved. "The ox and the donkey may be in the same pasture, they may drink out of the same pond, they may even walk around together."[6] But they must not join together to do the Lord's work.

What appears to be a contradiction to this rigid call for separation is not only the *Sword*'s immersion in political issues, using literal interpretations of Scripture to justify their political affinity, but also its support of politicians whose religious affiliations represent communions historically and bitterly anathematized by Protestant fundamentalists in general and the *Sword of the Lord* in particular.

One such religion historically hated by the *Sword* was Roman Catholicism. Typical of the *Sword*'s traditional view of this major communion was an editorial that graphically described the dangers of the Roman Catholic system to the safety of the United States. "Romanists Still Claim the Right to Burn Heretics," declared the editorial title. Quoting a Father Gallagher, chaplain of St. Anthony's Boys Home in Albuquerque, New Mexico, the editorial continued: "If one of its members [the Roman Catholic church] goes wrong it has the right to cut him off, to excommunicate him, and if need be *burn him at the stake*....The Church has the innate and proper right independent of human authority to punish her guilty subjects with both spiritual and temporal penalties."[7] The editorial went on to warn that New Mexico was not only the state where Roman Catholics were behind senatorial vote frauds, but also the state where the "Romanists" were plotting to extract special privileges at the expense of the Protestant majority. Worse still, it was the state that, to prevent nuns from teaching in the public schools, had to take court action. In other editorials and articles throughout its lifetime, the *Sword* has accused the Roman Catholic church of being idolatrous, blasphemous, hostile to the Bible, and full of shame, bigotry, and intolerance.[8] The alleged goal in such Romanist activity was to take over the governments of the state and nation through Catholic officials.[9]

However, fear of the Roman Catholic church miraculously vanished with the rise of Roman Catholic senator Joseph McCarthy (R, Wisconsin) and his anticommunism crusade of the 1950s. Editor Rice wrote in 1954: "We are for the fine work Senator McCarthy is doing in exposing Communists infiltrating our government. We agree with the fine commendation of Mr. J. Edgar Hoover, so long head of the F.B.I. He says: 'I've come to know Senator McCarthy well, officially and personally. I view him as a friend and I believe he so views me. Certainly he is a controversial man. He is earnest and he is honest. He has enemies. Whenever you attack subversives of any kind...you are going to be the victim of the most extremely vicious criticism that can be made. I know. But sometimes a knock is a boast.'"[10]

The danger of popery emerged again in traditional fashion with the potential presidential election of John F. Kennedy. In this case, declared Walter Hanford, assistant editor of the *Sword*: "Politics is not the issue." Rather: "The issue is a religious one....What is actually at stake in this current campaign is our whole basic idea of liberty and freedom of worship. We believe it is impossible for a man to be a thorough going Roman Catholic and to follow the dictates of his religious leaders, as good Catholics are expected to do, and still be faithful to the obligations of the President of the United States."[11]

Curiously, however, religious liberty and freedom of worship was not an issue in the 1964 election since the *Sword* supported Senator Barry Goldwater (R, Arizona) and his Roman Catholic running mate, William Miller (R, New York). Lest one conclude that Miller's Roman Catholicism was not an issue since he was only a vice-presidential candidate, one need only point to the *Sword*'s reasons for rejecting the Johnson-Humphrey ticket of 1968. Rice opposed Hubert Humphrey's place on the Democratic ticket because "a man who is elected Vice President has a thirty percent chance of becoming President according to past records." The 30 percent chance that Miller would have had of becoming president did not seem to bother Rice.[12] Whereas if Humphrey, with his alleged socialist persuasion, became president, a litany of disaster would ensue. Humphrey's election would include a turning loose of the liberals, "the friends of Russia, the friends of Red China, those who want to make peace with Castro, those who want to disarm America, who want to give the United Nations power over our country, who want to increase federal power over the states, increase public spending and public debt. Humphrey is a dangerous left wing liberal."[13]

A left-wing liberal was perceived to be more dangerous than a right-wing Roman Catholic. The *Sword* was always consistent on the dangers of the political Left, if not consistent on the dangers of Roman Catholicism. During the 1950s, Adlai Stevenson was "Unitarian, Socialist and pro-Truman, and hence should be rejected in favor of Eisenhower." In fact, "Christians everywhere ought to vote for the Republican nominee, ought to send Republicans to Congress and so free America from the hateful, immoral, unchristian New Deal which threatens to throttle private enterprise."[14] The *Sword*, in a typical display of invective, asserted that the New Deal administration gave East Germany to Russia, welcomed the communists to Japan, and

sold the Christian president Chiang Kai-shek down the river and insisted that he allow Communists to come in and take a controlling part in his government. Roosevelt, Truman and Acheson, with the help of Democratic leaders, turned China over to the Communists, did it willingly and gladly. They suppressed the facts from the American people because they were personally favorable to Socialism which is the guiding principle of the Communists. Christians should remember that the New Deal administration kept Alger Hiss high in the federal government when he was a traitor....Remember that it was Senator Nixon, the present Republican vice presidential nominee, who led in exposing Hiss, though he was endorsed by Truman, by Dean Acheson, and by Adlai Stevenson....Remember how Truman fired America's greatest general, MacArthur, even as he now derides General Eisenhower.[15]

Hence, the *Sword* was not only immersed in the politics of the nation in spite of its attitude of separation, but the religious affiliation of public officials, even if Roman Catholic, clearly took a secondary importance to their political philosophy.

If the *Sword* demonstrated some curious inconsistencies in its strict separationist position, it sanctified every political, social, or economic position that it took with copious references to Scripture. The *Sword* demonstrated biblical presentism in the ultimate since the Bible was considered the source of all knowledge for present-day living, complete with instructions. Therefore, since the subject of abortion was a present-day issue, there must be relevant biblical instruction on that issue, however implicit it might be. Dipping into the biblical well, John B. Ashbrook, a fundamentalist minister writing for the *Sword*, drew out Jeremiah 1:5 for the situation. "Before I formed thee in the belly I knew thee; and before thou camest forth out of the womb I sanctified thee, and I ordained thee a prophet unto the nations." Ashbrook then expounded: "Do you get the point? God considered Jeremiah a person and ordained him a prophet while he was still what we would medically call a fetus. Is the fetus a person? You just read the answer from the

Bible." "Add to this, continued Ashbrook, "the Sixth Commandment, Exodus 20:13 'Thou shalt not kill,'" and you have the biblical answer on the abortion issue.[16]

The application of this alleged biblically based position was a condemnation of the National Council of Churches, and especially the General Conference of United Methodists and the United Presbyterian General Assembly, all of which supported a move to take abortion procedures out of the criminal code by placing them in the medical practices regulations. "In other words," declared Ashbrook, "these clergymen recommend that abortions be considered like tonsillectomies and appendectomies."[17]

Biblical presentism was more easily demonstrated through the *Sword*'s featuring of Old Testament wars on behalf of God to justify modern-day and potential wars at the perceived behest of God. The God who thundered the call to slay the human-sacrificing Canaanites was the same God thundering for the annihilation of human-sacrificing communists.[18] Moreover, on a near equal to Scripture for Rice was D. L. Moody, who "was not a pacifist either."[19] Not even the emergence of atomic power could change the position of the *Sword* in the slightest. Right is right after all, with situational ethics out of the question.

Not surprisingly, this kind of biblicalism called for and justified a belligerent course of action for the U.S. government in its foreign policy. Armed with Scripture, the *Sword* called the Iranian seizure of the American embassy "America's most degrading, devastating disaster" in which "a pigmy holds a prince hostage."[20] Abram of old rescued his brother Lot from Dan, smote his captors, and returned safely with his brother, all their goods and their women.[21] The Israelis in 1976 made a successful raid in Entebbe, Uganda, and brought their citizens home in triumph. The West Germans successfully raided Mogadishu, Somalia, in 1977, freeing their hostages. Although President Jimmy Carter thought his mission would succeed, "America had no David to face the giant of the godless Philistine host."[22] What went wrong? The Bible supplied a ready answer: "For which of you intending to build a tower, sitteth not down first and counteth the cost, whether he has sufficient to finish it?"[23] The answer was simple: President Carter had scaled down the operation for humanitarian reasons. But humanitarianism did not convince the Ayatollah Khomeini, reasoned the *Sword*. The failure of the mission rested in the fact that the president was "unwilling to use force in the conduct of foreign affairs."[24] In this lesson was the call for a strong military to smite the heathen.

Among other reasons for America's failure was that it turned its back on such friends as Taiwan, "our only friend in the Far East," and instead directed its solicitude to the socialist republic of China. The United States allegedly had done what God judged Israel for doing long ago. America was "as a wife that committed adultery, which taketh strangers instead of her husband.... Thou givest gifts to all thy lovers, and hirest them, that they may come unto thee on every side for thy whoredom."[25] In effect, America had prostituted itself in foreign policy by hiring lovers.[26]

The most curious use of biblical presentism to judge American foreign policy was the *Sword*'s attitude toward the Panama Canal treaties of 1979. With the Eighth Commandment ("thou shalt not steal") the *Sword*'s basis for rejecting the treaties, one is hard pressed not to remember the boast of President Theodore Roosevelt—"I took Panama"—and marvel at the wondrous use of God's word for direction in specific present-day issues. Without debating who pilfered what, the *Sword* identified the thieves as the Panamanians and the U.S. Senate, the latter of which "by 68 to 32...voted to give away the canal and associated property in spite of many, many public opinion polls which showed the great majority of the U. S. public strongly against doing so. This is stealing. The Canal and Zone belong to the people of the U.S.—paid for and developed with U. S. tax dollars."[27] As for the Panamanians, they were "not satisfied with just stealing the canal." They demanded the buildings and facilities adjacent to the canal, restored and in usable condition, with all moveable equipment thereon becoming the property of Panama. Moreover, they demanded retroactive jurisdiction over businesses and individuals in the zone since 1971 for tax purposes. "Unfortunately the U. S. State Department has not challenged these claims....The treaties are immoral."[28]

The *Sword* also applied biblical presentism to justify American capitalism in general, often condemning the New Deal in particular. According to Rice, the Bible clearly taught that the profit motive was good. While not overlooking the centuries of church history during which a social, cultural, and economic climate of opinion rejected the profit motive, Rice simply treated them as the dark ages of the church when God's word was not followed. The biblical justification of American capitalism was the Ten Commandments, which Rice believed taught a free economic order declaring a man's right to own property. The Eighth Commandment meant that a man had the right to use his property to make a profit. The "profit motive is not a sin."[29] Moreover, it was the profit motive that had made America great. More specifically, Rice was tireless in excoriating the New Deal, with its "soak the rich" schemes that denied the fruits of labor to the productive members of society, as the antithesis of the profit motive.

If every issue the *Sword* covered did not have a specific proof text and exegetical rendition, it certainly revealed at all times an unambiguous position. "Right was Right, and Wrong was nobodies' right." The *Sword* fits Harry and Bonaro Overstreet's observation perfectly: that extremists of any persuasion, Left or Right, demonstrate an inability to deal with ambiguity.[30] Put positively, the *Sword* knew that it expressed the truth of God as revealed in the Bible. The publication did not have the slightest tendency to agonize over controversial issues in a pluralistic American society.

Consider the question of the status of American public schools, the nature of their strengths, their ills, their regional differences, and the various proposed solutions for a better educational system, all agonized over by honest, intelligent, and knowledgeable people for well over a decade. To Don Boys, an educator writing for the *Sword*, however, no such agonizing ever occurred since the issue was quite simple. The public schools of America were seen as "poisoned pots," and the poison was humanism. School boards need only to get rid of humanistic teachers, humanistic textbooks, and humanistic administrators, and then, putting God and discipline in the classroom, the problem would be solved. Even identifying the poison was simple since humanism was seen as a creed without variations.

Moreover, it was taught by all public schools, from Alaska to Florida, Maine to California, Texas to North Dakota. To demonstrate such a sweeping generalization, let the *Sword* (through Boys) speak for itself:

The humanist has made it clear where he stands. He says in his statement of belief: "I believe in no God and in no hereafter. It is immoral to indoctrinate children with such beliefs. Schools have no right to do so, nor indeed have parents. I believe that religious education and prayers in schools should be eliminated. I believe that denominational schools should be abolished. I believe that children should be taught religion as a matter of historical interest, but should be taught about all religions including humanism, Marxism, Maoism, Communism, and other attitudes of life. They must also be taught the objections to religions. I believe in a non-religious, social morality. Unborn babies are not people. I am yet unsure whether the grossly handicapped are people in the real sense. I believe that there is no such thing as sin to be forgiven and no life beyond the grave with everlasting death." That is the heart of humanism.... This is the heresy that students are getting in *all* public schools, and in some Christian schools.[31]

An example of humanism in English textbooks, representative presumably of all English textbooks used by all public school departments of English in the United States, was a text entitled *Mixed Bag*. Wrote Boys:

In *Mixed Bag*, a high school English text, some examples of poetry are offered. "Roses are red, violets are black, you'd look better with a knife in your back!" That seems to encourage violence. Well how about the following cultural offering for high level thinking? "Boys are made of greasy grimy, gopher guts, marinated monkey meat, French fried parakeet, all that vomit rolling down a country street. Wish I had a spoon." Such humanism is degrading our schools and destroying our society. The religion of secular humanism is being taught in all the public schools, even though it is unconstitutional to teach religion in tax-supported schools and the U.S. Supreme Court has ruled on two occasions in 1964 and 1969 that humanism is religion.[32]

In a more magnanimous mood, Boys declared that texts "in most public schools are riddled with sex, vulgarity and violence. They are anti-American, anti-enterprise, and antiparents."[33] The reader who accepts the word of the *Sword* is left with no doubt about the nature of humanism, and its place in American public schools.

The complex was made simple yet again by the *Sword* in its consideration of the relationship between socialism and communism. Ambiguity was not in the *Sword*'s vocabulary on this subject because it saw no real difference between the two. Franklin D. Roosevelt, while not a communist, gave communism an entree by creating the socialist New Deal.[34] Socialism, according to Rice, was defined as a democratically controlled economy that went by such various names or phrases as: "economic democracy," "a more Christian economic order," "social justice," "economic brotherhood," and the "social gospel."[35] Since Russia claimed to have all of the above features in its society, they were obviously communistic features, and therefore inappropriate in American society. When the *Daily Worker* took a position on an issue, one must take the opposite view or be considered soft on communism. When the World Council of Churches (WCC) condemned the use of atomic power and encouraged disarmament, the *Sword* condemned WCC members as "naive do-gooders, who are un-American, unpatriotic, short sighted and irresponsible, following the line of the *Daily Worker*, a Red paper."[36] Again, nothing was ambiguous; issues and people could be easily identified as either good or bad, realistic or naive.

The *Sword*'s absolutist style did not mean that it was always consistent in its political and social philosophy. Opposed to big government on the one hand, it advocated government legislation of morality on the other hand. Government, it argued, must keep its hands off the churches and should not display any semblance of planning the economy or implementing social reforms. It should not tax big cars since that would "hurt our missionaries [who] do God's Work," or force school busing for integration since that wastes gas. But government should clamp down on television profanity, smash pornography, harass homosexuals, abolish abortion, outlaw smoking in restaurants and airplanes, close shopping areas on Sunday ("to save gas"), and continue to view the possession of marijuana as a criminal act.[37] Government involvement in these and other areas should be on all levels, including the federal. The *Sword* even called on all of its readers to write to President Carter requesting his support in these moral issues.[38] No question about the *Sword*'s unambiguous position on right and wrong, even if it was not consistent on the appropriateness of big government in American society.

But consistency in itself was not an issue of concern to the *Sword*, especially if such inconsistencies were to be cited by the heathen. What mattered to the *Sword* was whether the Lord's will, as the periodical perceived it, was being accomplished through the efforts of his faithful. Hence, inconsistency in political and social philosophy, in separationism, in attitudes toward the dangers of Roman Catholics to American life, or in the practice of biblical presentism were all merely examples of the Lord's anointed doing battle with the "wisdom of this world." "For the wisdom of this world is folly with God."[39] If the God of Israel could make the sun stand still or part the waters of the Red Sea, it was certainly no startling or incongruous feat for God to use an anathematized Roman Catholic or two for his purposes in the twentieth century. Hence, the *Sword* was impervious to the views of all, both in and out of the Christian tradition, who did not share in its view of what God was saying to his people through his word.

The *Sword* must be viewed as a major leading publication for the ultrafundamentalist position, and is comparable to the *Christian Beacon*, the voice of the American Council of Christian Churches and of Carl McIntire. Both publications feature each other's articles: Rice is published in *Christian Beacon* and McIntire in the *Sword*. Moreover, both treat the same political and social issues of the day and posit similar conclusions. They are both far to the right of the New Evangelicals, in the sense of rejecting any cooperation with moderate or liberal churches or denominations, and in the sense of steadfastly adhering to a premillennial theology.

Together they constitute an influential force not only among thousands of independent evangelical fundamentalist churches across America, but within denominational churches as well. The *Sword* is subscribed to by thousands of church members who belong to mainline churches and who, through the influence of the *Sword*, sometimes represent what might be described as a fundamentalist fifth column within churches and denominations. This kind of influence affects not only monetary contributions to denominational churches adversely, but is undoubtedly influential in pushing those churches that happen to have a substantial number of members under the influence of the *Sword*, to a more conservative theological, social, political, and economic stance.

Notes

1. Fred M. Barlow, *Dr. John R. Rice, Giant of Evangelism* (Murfreesboro, Tennessee, 1983), p. 9.

2. Ibid., p. 7

3. Ibid., p. 24.

4. Deuteronomy 22: 9–11 is the basis of the *Sword*'s practice of separation.

5. John R. Rice, "No Mixed Seed, Mixed Teams, Mixed Mates, Mixed Garments," *The Sword of the Lord* (21 October 1977): 10 (hereinafter cited as *SL*).

6. Ibid.

7. John R. Rice, "Romanists Still Claim Right to Burn Heretics," *SL* 18 (June 1954): 5.

8. Ibid.

9. Warren L. Vinz, "The Politics of Protestant Fundamentalism in the 1950s and 1960s," *Journal of Church and State* 14 (Spring 1972): 248.

10. Ibid., p. 249.

11. Ibid., p. 250.

12. Ibid., p. 251.

13. Ibid.

14. Ibid., p. 247.

15. Ibid.

16. John B. Ashbrook, "The Bible and Abortion," *SL* (1 November 1974): 8.

17. Ibid., p. 1.

18. Vinz, "The Politics of Protestant Fundamentalism," p. 244.

19. Ibid.

20. Kenny McComas, "America's Most Degrading Disaster," *SL* (17 October 1980): 13.

21. Genesis 14:12–16.

22. McComas, "America's Most Degrading Disaster," p. 13.

23. Luke 14:28–32.

24. McComas, "America's Most Degrading Disaster," p. 13.

25. Ezekiel 16:32–37.

26. McComas, "America's Most Degrading Disaster," p. 13.

27. G. Russell Evans, "Panama Canal," *SL* (17 August 1979): 1.

28. Ibid., p. 16.

29. Vinz, "The Politics of Protestant Fundamentalism," pp. 242, 243.

30. Harry and Bonaro Overstreet, *The Strange Tactics of Extremism* (New York, 1964).

31. Don Boys, "Public Education a Poisoned Pot," *SL* (27 February 1981): 4. (emphasis added).

32. Ibid.

33. Ibid.

34. Vinz, "The Politics of Protestant Fundamentalism," p. 242.

35. Ibid., p. 243.

36. Ibid., p. 244.

37. Hugh Pyle, "Let's Start an Avalanche," *SL* (1 July 1977): 1.
38. Ibid.
39. 1 Corinthians 3:19.

Information Sources

BIBLIOGRAPHY:

Barlow, Fred M. Dr. *John R. Rice, Giant of Evangelism*. Murphreesboro, Tennessee, 1983.

Vinz, Warren L. *Pulpit Politics: Faces of American Protestant Nationalism in the Twentieth Century*. Albany, New York, 1997.

INDEXES: Each volume indexed.

REPRINT EDITIONS: Microform: Right Wing Collection, University of Iowa (MCA), partial run, 1953–1976 (reels 123–126); ATLA.

LOCATION SOURCES: Complete runs: *The Sword of the Lord*, Murphreesboro, Tennessee; Moody Bible Institute, Chicago.

Publication History

TITLE AND TITLE CHANGES: *The Sword of the Lord and John R. Rice*, 1934–1935; *The Sword of the Lord*, 1935–present.

VOLUME AND ISSUE DATA: Volumes 1–current, 28 September 1934–present.

FREQUENCY OF PUBLICATION: Biweekly.

PUBLISHER: *The Sword of the Lord*, Murphreesboro, Tennessee.

EDITORS: John R. Rice, 1934–1980; Curtis Hutson, January 1980–March 1995; Shelton Smith, April 1995—present.

CIRCULATION: 100,000.

Warren L. Vinz

Christian Beacon
1936–

The *Christian Beacon*, an eight-page religious tabloid, has been published weekly since 1936 by its founder and only editor, Carl McIntire. Instituted to combat a major decline in conservative thought and action, the *Christian Beacon* grew out of a split that had been brewing for years between liberals and conservatives in the Presbyterian church. McIntire, born into a Presbyterian minister's family in 1905, was raised in "true Scottish Presbyterian tradition" in Durant, Oklahoma. He graduated in 1927 from Park College, Parkville, Missouri (a Presbyterian school from which his parents had graduated), and entered his father's alma mater, Princeton. When Princeton Seminary was reorganized in 1929 by liberal Presbyterians, several professors left to form the conservative Westminster Theological Seminary in Philadelphia. McIntire, then a second-year student in the Princeton Seminary, joined other students and followed these professors. McIntire graduated from Westminster in 1931, was ordained in the Presbyterian Church U.S.A., which became the United Presbyterian church, and after a merger in the 1980s was named Presbyterian Church (U.S.A.), and served for two years as pastor of the Chelsea Presbyterian Church, Atlantic City, New Jersey. In 1933 he became the minister of the Collingswood Presbyterian Church, the largest Presbyterian church in New Jersey, and a strict adherent to the conservative fundamentals of the faith.

Throughout the early 1930s McIntire retained close ties with J. Gresham Machen, his former mentor who had helped found Westminster Theological Seminary, but he opposed Machen on the issue of personal ethics (gambling, movies, dancing, "cocktails and smoking") as well as on the necessity of belief in premillennialism. This would lead to yet another split, and in 1937 McIntire withdrew his support from Westminster Theological Seminary and formed the conservative Faith Theological Seminary in Philadelphia.[1]

Alarmed that liberal missionaries had been sent to foreign mission fields by the modernist Presbyterian Board of Foreign Missions, McIntire and Machen formed a new Presbyterian missionary agency in 1934, the Independent Board of Presbyterian Foreign Missions, and published the magazine, *Biblical Missions*. The United Presbyterian church retaliated by bringing them to trial for establishing a competing mission board. At the conclusion of the trial in 1936, both were defrocked as Presbyterian ministers. Not accepting the defrocking, McIntire and his Collingswood Presbyterian Church withdrew from the United Presbyterian church and formed a new denomination, the Bible Presbyterian church, to be a "defender of militant Christianity patterned after the original Presbyterians."[2]

As the emerging leader of the newly formed Bible Presbyterian church denomination, McIntire, then twenty-six, founded the *Christian Beacon* to reach beyond his pulpit to explain the reasons behind the great fundamentalist-modernist conflict and to promote his explanation for the founding of a new Presbyterian denomination and seminary.[3] The readers of the *Christian Beacon* in the 1930s and 1940s were the faculty, students, and pastors who had left the Presbyterian Church U.S.A. for the Bible Presbyterian church; ministers McIntire urged to leave the Presbyterian church; and the pastors and congregations of any denominations who subscribed to the fundamentals of the traditional conservative theology. At that time the great majority of readers lived in the Northeast, primarily New Jersey and Pennsylvania; in the 1950s readership became nationwide.

Early issues covered such topics as: "How to Become a Christian, Accept Christ as Savior," and why "Fundamentalists Adopt Pre-Mil View." He compared the fate of Christians under ecumenical liberalism in America to the suffering of Jews in Germany, the Nazi plan to absorb Christianity, and the "Red Terror" in the Soviet Union. He warned that communism is satanic, robbing one of liberty of conscience and freedom of worship. The repression of churches by Nazis and communists, McIntire said, was "the same tyranny and lawlessness which characterized Christians in the Presbyterian Church in the U.S.A." If not stopped it would "mean the abandonment of liberty and democracy in America."[4]

The *Beacon*'s format included editorials and articles on religious events, political events, and other events important to McIntire; sermons; Sunday school lessons; and (particularly significant) photographically reproduced articles, speeches, and letters by friend and foe. This last feature, McIntire felt, demonstrated the *Beacon*'s objectivity by allowing the reader to judge for himself, as the *Beacon* carried news based on "facts" which the liberal press refused to print. McIntire asserts that no single paper in the Christian world has done so much to report true Christian American beliefs, successes of God's work through McIntire and his followers, and to expose the apostasy and communism of the World Council of Churches (WCC), the National Council of Churches (NCC), the Revised Standard Version of the Bible, the international conspiracy of communist Russia, China, Korea, and Vietnam, the United Presbyterian church, Billy Graham, and all liberal-inspired and supported departures from the Christian faith.[5]

In 1941 McIntire formed the American Council of Christian Churches (ACCC) as a fundamentalist alternative to the liberal Federal Council of Churches (now NCC). After World War II, in an attempt to expand his fundamentalist reformation worldwide, McIntire organized the International Council of Christian Churches (ICCC) to combat the liberal attacks the WCC had made on American capitalism and the WCC's association with other liberal denominations such as the Russian Orthodox church, a church McIntire claims "is controlled by Communist Russia and used to infiltrate churches worldwide but particularly in America." To highlight this apostasy, McIntire's ICCC held annual meetings at the same time and location as those of the WCC and NCC. He has remained president of the ICCC since 1948.

All of McIntire's organizations are affiliated with and sponsored by the Christian Beacon Press: the ICCC, the Bible Presbyterian church, the Twentieth-Century Reformation Hour (radio), Faith Seminary, Shelton College, Faith Christian High School, a home for the aged, and summer Bible conferences at Cape May, New Jersey, and Cape Canaveral, Florida. At the end of the 1980s, McIntire was president, chancellor, chairman of the board, and/or managing editor of all the above organizations. The Christian Beacon Press and McIntire's office are in a red brick former public school building at 756 Haddon Avenue, Collingswood, New Jersey.[6]

The *Christian Beacon*–sponsored ACCC and ICCC continued to hold their annual conventions at the same time and place as the NCC and WCC to gain maximum press and radio coverage, a technique that succeeded in drawing national attention to McIntire and the *Christian Beacon*. Portrayed by the national press as David attempting to slay Goliath, McIntire attacked the NCC and WCC for creating a worldwide superchurch that would be neither Christian nor capitalist, hence not American, but dominated by Russia and Satan. His militant attacks coincided with conservative American fears in the 1940s and 1950s that the United Nations would create a one-world government.

A larger national audience came to the *Beacon* as Senator Joseph McCarthy (R, Wisconsin) and the House Un-American Activities Committee (HUAC) reported communist infiltration of American churches. McIntire encouraged and assisted McCarthy and HUAC in their investigations of McIntire's charge, "How Red Is the Federal Council of Churches?" He sustained an attack on the NCC by initiating an investigation into the affiliations of Bishop G. Bromley Oxnam, a leading Methodist bishop and also an NCC leader. He published books and pamphlets; put on national rallies carrying the theme "Marx or Christ," "Bible vs. Communism," "Investigate Communist Clergy," and "Put Oxnam under Oath"; and continually challenged Oxnam to a debate on the issues of the times and to appear before HUAC to explain his associations with communists. Bishop Oxnam did appear before HUAC on 21 July 1953, to clear his name of the charges made by McIntire and HUAC. These charges were identical, as McIntire had supplied HUAC with much of its information. Although HUAC issued a statement that no evidence had been found linking Oxnam with the Communist party, McIntire continued to proclaim that Oxnam had "aided and comforted the Communist movement."[7]

Many of those whom McIntire asked to help in his crusade later became prominent New Right religious leaders. Major Edgar C. Bundy, one of the most influential, joined McIntire's staff as a part-time research and intelligence expert in 1949. Bundy made national news in 1949 when, testifying for Senator Kenneth McKellar (D, Tennessee), he warned that if the United States allowed China to go communist, then Japan, Korea, Malaysia, Burma, the Dutch East Indies, and India would fall as well. He also predicted that North Korea would invade South Korea. In 1956 Bundy became executive director of the Church League of America and severed his official relationship with McIntire, although he continued to speak at *Beacon*-sponsored conferences. He described the *Beacon* as the best paper on socialism and communism in religion and urged that all students who want to know the truth about communism read the *Christian Beacon*. Years later, in 1982, Bundy included McIntire among distinguished religious leaders, a man who was, he said, "In the tradition of great men of God such as St. Paul, St. Peter, John Calvin, Zwingli, Huss, Martin Luther, John Knox, Charles Haddon Spurgeon, Dwight L. Moody,...and Aleksandr Solzhenitsyn."[8]

Another far Right fundamentalist preacher, Billy James Hargis of Tulsa, Oklahoma, was hired by McIntire in 1953 to be a member of his staff and to supervise an ACCC-ICCC project using balloons to fly King James versions of the Bible into iron curtain countries. This project continued for five years and gained McIntire national press coverage, associating him with conservative America's desire to Christianize the peoples of communist countries and free them from communist rule. Hargis left McIntire in the late 1950s and formed his own Christian Crusade. In that same decade McIntire, on an ICCC trip to Australia, recruited Frederick Charles Schwarz because of his reputed knowledge of communism and his evangelistic fervor as a speaker. Schwarz spoke at ACCC-sponsored anticommunist rallies across the United States. Schwarz remained with McIntire a short while and then broke away to form the Christian Anti-Communism Crusade based in Waterloo, Iowa.[9]

In the 1960s McIntire increased his activities, focusing on the fundamentalist concern that the ecumenical movement, which he said was now backed by President Kennedy and Pope John XXIII, would unite the Roman Catholic church and the WCC. The *Beacon* headlined: "Communists Win Greatest Victory in the WCC"; "Paris Meeting Unanimously Received Communist-Controlled Churches." International communism, according to McIntire, was supported by President Kennedy. McIntire quoted Kennedy's speech at the American University in Washington, D.C., in which he stated, "If we cannot end now our differences at least we can make the world safe for diversity." McIntire wrote in the *Beacon*: "so the United States of America can make the world safe for Communism." To McIntire, this speech confirmed the no-win policy of the Kennedy administration. As evidence of communist approval of this policy, McIntire said, Kennedy's speech was reproduced in full in *Pravda* and *Izvestia*, the official newspapers of the Communist party and the communist government of Russia.[10]

To McIntire, these events were signs of the times that a one-world government led by an Antichrist would soon be formed. Another sign was the Supreme Court's ruling that to read the Bible and say the Lord's Prayer in public schools was unconstitutional and a violation of the First Amendment. McIntire warned that if atheist and liberal organizations such as the American Civil Liberties Union, NCC, and WCC had their way, the Pledge of Allegiance ("under God") and the Star-Spangled Banner ("In God is our trust") would be banned, and "In God We Trust" would be removed from our coins. America would then be "a Godless nation."[11]

Under the *Beacon* headline "Kennedy Administration Cracks Down on Fundamentalist Churches," Kennedy, called the "Czar in Washington," was accused of harassing Bible-believing churches by having the Internal Revenue Service withdraw tax-exempt status from all independent churches that were not affiliated with the NCC. Alarmed at losing tax-exempt status for "fundamental, independent, separated churches not connected" with the NCC, McIntire and the *Beacon* urged that Christians nationwide immediately begin working for a "Liberty Amendment" to the Constitution to repeal the Sixteenth Amendment instituting income taxes. Why, the *Beacon* asked, should Christians be taxed "to maintain pagan and atheistic public school institutions?"[12] But the most important reason to abolish the income tax, McIntire maintained, was that "almost all of the Fabian, Keynesian, Neo-Marxist and communist growth can directly or indirectly be traced to the financial support" from the personal income tax.[13]

To mobilize public opinion behind the liberty amendment McIntire launched a nationwide freedom rally from Constitution Hall, Washington, D.C. The *Beacon* presented any tax laws that made local churches conform to government standards as a violation of church and state separation. McIntire worked with the National Committee for Economic Freedom to pass the liberty amendment, and the *Beacon* gave McIntire credit for influencing the legislatures of Wyoming, Texas, Nevada, Louisiana, Georgia, and South Carolina to support the amendment. McIntire has continued to decry government attempts to "harass" churches through denial of tax exemption, supporting the Reverend Robert Schuller and his Crystal Cathedral in Schuller's 1983 tax dispute with the state of California.[14]

Another reason communist influence grew in the 1960s, according to the *Beacon*, was increased sales of communist "slave labor"–produced merchandise in America. American money used to purchase such merchandise enabled the communists to finance their "conspiracy to rule the world," McIntire charged. Businessmen, more concerned with making money than with principles, and the State Department, whose policies approved of trade with communist countries, were partners with the communists in this conspiracy. In 1982 the *Beacon* published a chart compiled by a Florida commission to warn of the arrival of communist merchandise on the local scene, to help readers identify products commonly imported from Soviet bloc countries and the People's Republic of China.[15] McIntire always viewed liberal criticism of his movement as proof that his assertions were true. For example, in 1962 Fred J. Cook wrote in the *Nation* that the Church League of America, the Christian Crusade, and the Twentieth-Century Reformation Hour were the most active hate clubs on the air. Cook identified McIntire, then speaking over 546 radio stations daily, as the "number one spokesman of the radical right." This attack, McIntire said, was to be expected as Cook had been naive about communists since his support of Alger Hiss, and the *Nation*'s editor, Carey McWilliams, had supported "Communist activities for more than twenty years."

Cook's article was sent to the chairman of the National Democratic Committee, who sent a letter to every radio station on which McIntire broadcast, notifying them that those broadcasts were in violation of the Federal Communications Commission's fairness doctrine. McIntire and Bundy then launched a national campaign "to expose" the Democratic National Committee for its attacks on "ordained ministers preaching the Holy Scriptures and proclaiming righteousness in the land." A *Beacon* cartoon showed the Democratic National Committee using its power in an election year to silence the *Twentieth-Century Reformation Hour.*[16]

In the early 1960s John A. Stormer, chairman of the Missouri Federation of Young Republicans and a member of the Republican State Committee of Missouri, became a frequent speaker and writer for the *Christian Beacon*. McIntire considered Stormer's "careful compilation of facts," published in 1964 as *None Dare Call It Treason*, a triumphant call to action. He applauded Stormer for exhorting conservative Christian Americans to get into politics "properly trained, organized, and directed," and to vote for Christian candidates. The *Beacon* followed this theme for the next two decades, and by the 1980s McIntire claimed to have distributed 9 million copies of Stormer's book.[17]

During the Vietnam War and its aftermath, McIntire's movement achieved its greatest strength by calling the attention of *Christian Beacon* readers (circulation at its maximum, 145,000) and Twentieth-Century Reformation Hour listeners (maximum 610 stations) to his repeated statements for twenty years that Christians should fight communism. He applied to the Vietnam War the theme that communism is an attack upon God, the work of the devil, and a system that enslaves one totally, offering a socialist world kingdom prohibiting the accomplishment of the Great Commission. America's failure to defeat communism, McIntire said, would lead to the loss of Southeast Asia to the communists. He repeatedly warned his readers not to accept appeasement as had occurred when Truman lost China, Eisenhower lost North Korea, Kennedy granted Russia a test ban, and Nixon and Carter negotiated nuclear disarmament treaties with the Russians. Détente with the Soviet Union under Nixon, Ford, and Carter, the *Beacon* said, would lead to the victory of communism, for "slavery and freedom cannot co-exist." McIntire exhorted his readers to demand victory over communism in Vietnam, and the *Beacon* sponsored numerous anti-communist, provictory rallies in Washington, D.C., two of which drew between 100,000 and 150,000 people.[18]

Although McIntire protests the "use by a political leader of a religious body to advance his cause," he does believe that freedom is the "church's business." He has appealed to many politicians to have their speeches reproduced in the *Beacon* and to speak at the Christian Admiral Congress Hall Bible Conference and Freedom Center in Cape May, New Jersey. For example, Senator Strom Thurmond (R, South Carolina), speaking on "America, 1970," echoed a common charge of McIntire that only at the Freedom Center could one hear the truth. Government and secular universities, Thurmond said, "might not have allowed me to speak to you tonight." Thurmond lamented that the United States was not seeking victory over communism in Vietnam, and that far too many young people were "unknowingly...cannon fodder for a revolution." No one should underestimate the American people. The average American "has the old-fashioned virtues of independence, initiative, industry, respect for law and order, and faith in God." Georgia governor Lester Maddox, in another *Beacon*-sponsored rally, said he was happy to be speaking to "God-fearing, flag-waving Americans." Others whose reproduced speeches, letters, and activities have appeared in the *Beacon* include the Reverend Ian Paisley, Major General Edwin A. Walker, Senators Jesse Helms (D, North Carolina), and Harrison A. Williams (D, New Jersey), Congressmen John Schmitz (R, California) and Francis E. Walter. (D, Pennsylvania), and Phyllis Schlafly.[19]

One religious evangelical whom McIntire has long distrusted is the Reverend Billy Graham. Much of his enmity arose when the young Graham refused to join the ACCC, but McIntire always felt that the evangelist was too quick to compromise with modernists in an "unscriptural yoke with unbelievers." McIntire's greatest criticism followed Graham's trips to the Soviet Union in 1982 and 1984. *Beacon* headlines exclaimed "Graham's Moscow Speech Reveals His Betrayal of Christianity and His Union with Buddhists, Muslims, Hindus, Jews, Pagan Religions." Graham's denial of Reagan's assertion that Russia was a "focus of evil" brought more denunciations. Issue after issue of the *Beacon* attacked Graham, including a lengthy article by Major Bundy.[20]

Even Jerry Falwell is not spared criticism by the *Beacon* and its contributors. Fundamentalists were urged to understand the view of Bob Jones, Jr., and Bob Jones III of Bob Jones University that Falwell is scorned not for his political activities but for "his alliances with Mormons, Roman Catholics, and Liberals." Readers were reminded that fundamentalists had always seen it as their Christian duty to be political. The Joneses claimed that evangelists Billy Sunday and Bob Jones, Sr., were "largely responsible" for passage of the Eighteenth Amendment and the defeat of Al Smith for president. Readers were reminded that Bob Jones University would never be open to "dishonest Liberals like Ted Kennedy, but welcomed distinguished secular speakers and conservative politicians."[21]

McIntire saw little value in seeking impeachment of liberal justices of the Supreme Court because a liberal president would appoint more liberal judges. He would, however, oppose confirmation of liberal judges, as he did with Judge Sandra Day O'Connor's nomination for the Supreme Court. Though not a liberal, Judge O'Connor's opposition to First Amendment rights for radio broadcasting was sufficient cause. McIntire thought the best remedy would be to elect a conservative president who would appoint conservative members of the Supreme Court whose terms would last twenty to fifty years.[22]

The *Beacon* counseled that political support should never be given to politicians who cooperate with communists or liberals. Earlier presidents Lyndon Johnson and Richard Nixon, McIntire said, compromised with the Soviets with no-win policies in Vietnam. Although Jimmy Carter was a born-again Christian, he supported the liberal *Christian Century*. Carter's letter congratulating *Christian Century* on its hundredth anniversary was reproduced in the *Beacon* so readers could draw their own conclusions. Democratic candidates Walter Mondale and Geraldine Ferraro, said the *Beacon*, were extensions of the liberal New Deal, and

Ferraro was the worst. "She is a Roman Catholic," was the verdict—a prominent Roman Catholic whose views approached Marxist liberation theology. McIntire reminded *Beacon* readers that the great Protestant Reformers had identified the Roman Catholic church as the "scarlet woman" of Revelation 17 and 18.[23]

Reagan was the *Beacon*'s choice for the conservative, fundamentalist, born-again vote in 1980 and again in 1984. McIntire supported Reagan because he believed Reagan held the same doctrinal views as fundamentalists. He believed Reagan agreed with his opinion of the WCC and stated in a *Beacon* headline, "Reagan Recognized WCC's Radical Ideas." The *Beacon* reproduced a column written by Reagan, "Radical Ideology of the WCC." Reagan wrote that the WCC had become "radically-minded" and "an indiscriminate supporter of Marxist terrorists." More important, the WCC had "distorted the teachings of Christ." Don't allow your church funds to go to the WCC, wrote Reagan, where money may "end up as a bullet in a terrorist's gun." "Mr. Reagan does understand" what the *Beacon* had warned of for three decades, McIntire exclaimed. He ought to appreciate the work of the ICCC, the *Beacon* said, adding "and perhaps he does."[24]

A *Beacon* banner headline in 1984, "The Consequences of Religion in U.S. Election," headed an editorial on the victorious merging of religion and politics. The faith of the people carried into voting, and "Almighty God bestowed" renewed love of freedom on the nation. Cries of liberals that religion was being imposed on others, McIntire admonished, made those who feared God more determined that America should become a "Christian nation where God as the Author of Liberty" would guarantee the free exercise and equal protection of belief.[25]

At ninety, McIntire remained a strong, committed reformer, fighting evil and apostasy where he saw it and working for a Christian America. Never missing a week's publication, he and the *Beacon* have never changed theological positions "one iota" from Princeton to the present. Never has his message departed from Bible Presbyterian fundamentalism: the virgin birth, crucifixion, resurrection, inspiration of the Bible, premillennial return of Christ, and Armageddon.

Remembering his mother's admonition to him as a boy to be willing to "die for Christ" and country, he dreamed of building a great, free Christian nation. To accomplish these goals he and the *Beacon* built a complete subculture of elementary, high school, college, and seminary institutions; established research institutes with files of liberals' names and activities from every corner of the nation and much of the world; published pamphlets, books; and sponsored *Christian Beacon* conferences, protest rallies, satellite TV—all reported in the *Christian Beacon*.

Yet he worried, in 1984, about reversing what he believed was a downward trend that began in America shortly after the publication of Karl Marx's *Communist Manifesto* and deepened with John Dewey's progressive education, evolution in the schools, and the banning of religious instruction, prayer, the Bible, Christmas carols, and the Ten Commandments from the schools during the 1960s and 1970s. Always on guard, the *Beacon* warned against the NCC, WCC, neoevangelicals, and new liberal organizations such as George McGovern's National Coalition for Common Sense and Norman Lear's People for the American Way.[26]

At no time did McIntire and the *Beacon* gain the respect of intellectuals that

Machen received, nor his institutions the respect that either Princeton or Westminster enjoyed. From 1946 on, the *Beacon* never transcended its narrow position but did on several occasions expand its audience by riding the wave of national issues. By 1990 Carl McIntire was largely ignored in the mass media, subscriptions to the *Christian Beacon* had declined, and the outreach of the Bible Presbyterian church seemed limited to the faithful elderly and young who shared his beliefs and fears of a complex and changed liberal world. Nevertheless, McIntire often exulted in the *Beacon* that a reformation lay ahead: converts to be added to the fundamentalist fold, leaders to be trained, schools to be built—and all would need the *Christian Beacon*.[27]

Notes

1. Margaret C. Harden, comp., *A Brief History of the Bible Presbyterian Church* (Collingswood, New Jersey, n.d.), pp. 7–24; *Carl McIntire's Fifty-Year Ministry in the Bible Presbyterian Church* (Collingswood, New Jersey, 1983); Carl McIntire, interviews with author, Chicago, Illinois, 28 December 1962, and Collingswood, New Jersey, 16 April 1984; *Christian Beacon* (11 February 1937): 1–2 (hereinafter cited as *CB*); *CB* (24 March 1980): 1, 8; *CB* (22 September 1983): 1–8 (an issue that celebrates the fiftieth anniversary of McIntire's pastorate of the Collingswood Presbyterian Church).

2. *CB* (14 May 1981): 1, 3–6; Earle R. White, interview with author, Philadelphia, 18 April 1984. Dr. White is a long-time colleague of McIntire and the fourth general secretary of *Biblical Missions*.

3. The *CB* has never been under the auspices of the Bible Presbyterian church, but was incorporated by Carl McIntire and published by his Christian Beacon Press. Hence, the *CB* was controlled by McIntire and could not be taken from him by any church organization as had occurred in the Princeton-Westminster split and in the seizure of the Collingswood Presbyterian Church building by the United Presbyterian church.

4. *CB* (31 January 1937): 3; *CB* (15 April 1937): 1; *CB* (22 April 1937): 1; *CB* (24 June 1937): 4; *CB* (16 September 1937): 1; *CB* (5 February 1976): 1, 8; *CB* (20 October 1977): 1, 8. Carl McIntire, interview with author, Los Angeles, California, 2 February 1984. In this interview McIntire said his position had not changed in his entire ministry. All "varieties of communism, socialism, and liberalism" are satanic.

5. Carl McIntire, interview with author, Chicago, 28 December 1962; *CB* (24 January 1963): 1; *CB* (5 February 1981): 1, 8; *CB* (11 June 1981): 1–2; *CB* (5 April 1984): 1, 2; *CB* (6 December 1984): 1–2.

6. Carl McIntire, interview with author, Collingswood, New Jersey, 18 April 1984. Ralph Lord Roy, *Communism and the Churches* (New York, 1960), p. 228. Roy describes McIntire's association with these organizations as follows: "He created the...groups, has held their important offices, uses his personal periodical, the *Christian Beacon*, as their mouthpiece, coins their catch phrases, and writes most of their resolutions." Lynn Gray Gordon, interview with author, Philadelphia, 4 April 1983. Gordon, president of the Independent Board for Presbyterian Missions, referred to McIntire as a "tireless leader" in the crusade against communism and apostasy and made continual references to the *Beacon*, citing it as a source of accurate information.

7. Roy, *Communism and the Churches*, pp. 254–60; Carl McIntire, *Bishop Oxnam, Prophet of Marx* (Collingswood, New Jersey, n. d.); *CB* (23 February 1950): 1; *CB* (5 October 1950): 1, 8; *CB* (14 December 1950): 4; *CB* (21 February 1952): 1, 8; *CB* (21 May 1953): 1, 8.

8. Edgar Bundy, in *News and Views* (July/August 1981): 1, 2. This forty-seven-page issue contains photocopied articles critical of "Billy Graham's Moscow Performance"; it

was distributed by the Christian Beacon Press.

9. *CB* (11 October 1962): 1, 7. Louis Cassels, "The Rightist Crisis in Our Churches," *Look* (24 April 1962): 46: "The big wheels of the religious Right are Carl McIntire, Edgar Bundy, and Billy James Hargis."

10. *CB* (19 July 1962): 1; *CB* (11 October 1962): 1; *CB* (27 June 1963): 1, 2; *CB* (23 August 1963): 1, 8; *CB* (31 October 1963): 1, 2.

11. *CB* (18 April 1963): 1; *CB* (20 June 1963): 1, 8; *CB* (26 September 1963): 1; *CB* (6 February 1969): 1; *CB* (6 March 1969): 1, 5; *CB* (30 July 1970): 1, 8.

12. *CB* (19 July 1962): 1; *CB* (27 June 1963): 1–3.

13. *CB* (19 July 1962): 1, 3, 8; *CB* (8 November 1962): 1, 2, 5–8.

14. *CB* (8 November 1962): 1–8; "Rev. Schuller—Taxing Situation," *Los Angeles Times* (7 May 1983): II:4.

15. *CB* (2 August 1962): 1, 2, 4; *CB* (6 December 1962): 2, 8. McIntire urged the distribution at supermarkets of cards which announced: "Always buy your COMMUNIST FOODS at FOODFAIR," and on the reverse: "Hams from Poland...inspected for your table by COMMUNISTS." "TCTWOTAOCMOTLBS," [The Committee to Warn of the Arrival of Communist Merchandise on the Local Business Scene] *Newsweek* (3 December 1962): 93–94. *Soviet Slave Trade: How the Soviet Government Has Sold Russian Christian Girls into White Slavery* (n. p., 1972); *CB* (1 August 1982): 1–8.

16. *CB* (2 July 1962): 1, 4, 5, 8. Fred J. Cook, "The Ultras," *Nation* (30 June 1962): 565–66.

17. *CB* (8 December 1966): 3, 4, 8; John A. Stormer, *None Dare Call It Treason* (Florissant, Missouri, [1964]), pp. 230–34.

18. *CB* (23 May 1963): 1, 5, 8; *CB* (15 June 1967): 1, 2; *CB* (16 April 1970): 1, 3; *CB* (25 June 1970): 1, 2, 5; *CB* (6 August 1970): 1; *CB* (22 October 1970): 1, 5; *CB* (25 February 1972): 1; *CB* (17 January 1983): 1, 8.

19. *CB* (23 October 1963): 1; *CB* (10 April 1964): 1; *CB* (25 June 1970): 1, 5, 7; *CB* (6 August 1970): 1, 8.

20. *CB* (17 November 1966): 1, 8; *CB* (29 December 1977): 1, 8; *CB* (8 January 1981): 1, 8; *CB* (24 June 1982): 1, 2, 8; *CB* (19 April 1984): 1, 2; *CB* (7 June 1984): 1, 2; *CB* (17 September 1984): 1, 2; *CB* (20 September 1984): 1, 5; *CB* (21 February 1985): 1, 2, 7.

21. *CB* (30 October 1980): 1, 7; *CB* (12 April 1984): 1, 4; *CB* (22 November 1984): 1, 7.

22. *CB* (30 July 1981): 1, 7; *CB* (20 August 1981): 1, 7.

23. *CB* (19 July 1984): 1, 5, 7.

24. Carl McIntire, "'Born-Again' Politics," sermon delivered in the Collingswood Presbyterian Church, *CB* (14 September 1980): 3–20; *CB* (29 January 1981): 1; *CB* (5 February 1981): 1, 8; *CB* (14 May 1981): 1, 2; *CB* (10 March 1983): 1; *CB* (25 October 1984): 1, 7, 8; *CB* (8 November 1984): 1, 3.

25. *CB* (8 November 1984): 1, 3.

26. *CB* (30 October 1980): 1, 7; *CB* (15 December 1980): 1, 8; *CB* (18 October 1984): 3; *CB* (24 October 1984): 1–7.

27. E. Morgan, telephone conversation with author, 19 March 1985. Morgan said that circulation had declined due to cancellation of complimentary copies. Also there were many conservative newspapers available to readers in the 1980s.

Information Sources

BIBLIOGRAPHY:
Ferris, Thomas John. "The Religious Right: A Study in American Religious Fundamentalism." Master's thesis, North Texas State University, 1963.
Gasper, Louis. *The Fundamentalist Movement, 1930–1956.* Grand Rapids, Michigan, 1963.

Handy, Robert T. *The Protestant Quest for a Christian America, 1830–1930.* Philadelphia, 1967.

Marsden, George M. *Fundamentalism and American Culture.* Oxford, England, 1980.

McIntire, Carl. *Author of Liberty.* Collingswood, New Jersey, 1946.

INDEXES: None.

REPRINT EDITIONS: None.

LOCATION SOURCES: Complete run: Christian Beacon Press, Collingswood, New Jersey.

Publication History

TITLE AND TITLE CHANGES: *Christian Beacon*, 1936–1961; *Christian Beacon, sponsoring Twentieth-Century Reformation Hour*, 1961–present.

VOLUME AND ISSUE DATA: Volumes 1–current, 1936–present.

FREQUENCY OF PUBLICATION: Weekly.

PUBLISHER: Christian Beacon, Collingswood, New Jersey.

EDITOR: Carl McIntire.

CIRCULATION: 1936: 10,000; 1963: 37,000; 1973: 145,000; 1987: 20,000, 1996: 20,000.

Thomas J. Ferris

Faith and Freedom
1949–1960

The brief history of *Faith and Freedom* illustrates clearly the intellectual ferment and the contradictory trends of the conservative movement of the 1950s. From the first issue in December 1949 until it ceased publication a decade later, *Faith and Freedom* reflected the religious issues and the political turmoil of the Truman and Eisenhower years. Spiritual Mobilization, which had its roots in the reactionary conservatism of the depression era, established this monthly magazine as a forum for opponents of the welfare state and to unite ministers and laymen against the ecumenical movement and the Social Gospel. But the pages of *Faith and Freedom* also provided nurture and a lively forum for "the intellectual libertarian underground" that emerged after World War II.[1]

The depression-era reaction against Franklin D. Roosevelt and the New Deal had taken many forms, and Spiritual Mobilization had the institutional vitality and found the issues that ensured its survival into the postwar period. When Donald J. Cowling, president of Carleton College, and William Hocking of Harvard University joined the Reverend James W. Fifield, Jr., as the founders of the Mobilization for Spiritual Ideals in the spring of 1935, their goal was "to arouse the ministers of all denominations in America to check the trends toward pagan stateism [*sic*]."[2] Fifield, who served as president of Spiritual Mobilization for nearly twenty years and then as chairman of the board until his resignation in October 1959, explained that their greatest challenge "was to find some vehicle through which the will of God and the teachings of Jesus could be made more effective in behalf of Freedom Under God against the then-rising tides of collectivism, including communism."[3] Under his leadership, Spiritual Mobilization found its principal constituency among ministers and laymen of the Congregational, Presbyterian, and Episcopal churches.

The organization grew slowly and avoided political confrontations. Although it was overshadowed initially by the more radical challenges to the New Deal by Huey Long, Father Charles E. Coughlin, and the Townsendites, Spiritual

Mobilization survived while they did not. Its advisory committee resembled a who's who of the corporate and educational elite of the 1930s and 1940s, but Fifield was the central figure. He was the principal spokesman and set the ideological tone. Shortly after founding Spiritual Mobilization, he resigned from his pulpit in Grand Rapids, Michigan, to become pastor of the First Congregational Church of Los Angeles. Fifield arrived in California in 1935 and found fertile ground for his ideas in the sprawling metropolis. Although he was neither a fundamentalist nor a Calvinist, Fifield effectively combined popular religion with pleas for economic orthodoxy.[4] Fifield was distinguished in appearance and deliberate in speech, and though he was described by one friendly writer as "the apostle to millionaires," he attracted a large congregation to his church and a large local audience for his radio and television programs.

Spiritual Mobilization's strength ebbed and flowed with the tide of conservative attacks against the New Deal and liberalism before 1945, but the partisan politics of the cold war period provided a new stability. With the promise of rapid expansion nationally, Fifield sought help to administer the growing programs of his organization. As Fifield reduced his administrative activities, James C. Ingebretsen assumed a significant role behind the scenes. He had impeccable credentials. A cum laude graduate of Stanford Law School, Ingebretsen was a prominent attorney in Los Angeles and a former chief counsel of the U.S. Chamber of Commerce. As legal counsel and successively vice-president and president of Spiritual Mobilization, Ingebretsen brought new contacts and a revitalized ideological impulse to the organization.

Ingebretsen and William Johnson, who served as editor for eight years, created *Faith and Freedom* and pushed the magazine into the forefront of Spiritual Mobilization's activities. Johnson's contributions were important. He was a veteran journalist, an accomplished editorial technician, and the principal contact with many of the conservative and libertarian authors. In addition, he wrote monthly editorials and numerous articles for the magazine.

As *Faith and Freedom* evolved into the principal voice of Spiritual Mobilization, the magazine and its parent were increasingly bound together in a mutually dependent relationship that provided ideological sustenance and eventually produced a similar fate for each. Faced with increasing competition from other conservative and libertarian organizations, Spiritual Mobilization shelved its ambitious plans for national expansion early in the 1950s. Ingebretsen and Johnson explored new directions for *Faith and Freedom*, but they could not escape fully the image of conservative reaction and militant anticommunism that Fifield represented. Moving toward a libertarian position, yet uncertain how to define the word, Ingebretsen and Johnson never achieved the delicate balance between a conventional religious magazine and a journal of opinion. Although *Faith and Freedom* had a potentially large audience among Protestant ministers and laymen in the Midwest and on the Pacific coast, it would eventually succumb to the financial reverses and the ideological disputes that simultaneously crippled Spiritual Mobilization.

Even though it survived only one decade, *Faith and Freedom* was more than an interesting journalistic experiment. Neither as politically liberal as *Christian Century* nor as theologically conservative as *Christianity Today*, *Faith and Freedom* differed even more from *Christian Economics*, which began publication in May 1950 as the organ of the Christian Freedom Foundation. Its blending of religious themes with libertarian dialogue set *Faith and Freedom* apart from the latter's strict economic and social orthodoxy. "Spiritual Mobilization," Ingebretsen explained, "became decidedly 'libertarian' under my direction, while the Christian Freedom Foundation," under the leadership of Howard E. Kershner, "was decidedly conservative." Ingebretsen rejected Kershner's more traditional focus on political economy, emphasizing instead the psychological and spiritual dimensions of "a personal fusion of inner freedom and outer liberty."[5]

Faith and Freedom differed from its principal competitors in another significant way. Spiritual Mobilization had maintained its headquarters in Los Angeles for nearly fifteen years. Although *Faith and Freedom* continued to depend on writers and financial contributors from the East and the Midwest, Los Angeles provided a stimulating ideological environment and allowed it to combine newer with older sources of funding. World War II and the cold war introduced economic and demographic changes for California that were revolutionary in their impact. This westward tilt rapidly transformed California into a national influence and the virtual arbiter of the politics and culture of the Sun Belt.

Ingebretsen exploited these advantages and reinforced the connections between Spiritual Mobilization and its magazine. He carefully supervised its progress and content, and he ensured continuity by creating an advisory board that was virtually identical with that of Spiritual Mobilization. The list included corporation executives, prominent clergy, and college presidents. Roger W. Babson, Ely Culbertson, the Reverend Norman Vincent Peale, and Leonard E. Read were on the board, and Robert A. Millikan, president of the California Institute of Technology, Robert Gordon Sproul, president of the University of California, and Rufus B. Kleinsmid, president of the University of Southern California, also served.

The first issue of *Faith and Freedom* confirmed its emphasis on continuity and change. Johnson described the magazine as a "journal of opinion...intended for the ordained clergy" and interested laymen. "There are countless questions unanswered about individual liberty," Johnson explained, "and we believe that many of the answers are to be found in the spiritual area," and "many hinge upon the answer to a sincere question: 'What is the nature and destiny of man?'" *Faith and Freedom* was intended as "a magazine which will serve the ministers who will shape the answers to these questions, a magazine which will stimulate them, a magazine which will challenge them, a magazine which will earn a place in their busy schedules."[6]

Published monthly, except for a July and August hiatus, *Faith and Freedom* maintained a simple format, each issue averaging between fourteen and twenty-four pages with few photographs and only occasional cartoons or other illustrations. If the magazine was conventional in appearance, it grew less predictable in content as Johnson experimented with new themes and new authors. He invited contributions from the clergy and published sermons from contests sponsored by

Spiritual Mobilization. The magazine also featured original articles and included reprints from other publications or speeches by prominent political, business, and religious figures. Johnson contributed editorials, and Ingebretsen provided an occasional essay.

In addition to its staff members and a small group of clergy who were regular contributors, *Faith and Freedom* provided an outlet for a growing network of conservative and libertarian writers. Frank Chodorov, Felix Morley, Murray Rothbard, Leonard Liggio, Leonard E. Read, Rose Wilder Lane, Henry Grady Weaver, F. A. Harper, Henry Hazlitt, Karl Hess, William Henry Chamberlin, Ricr C. Cornuelle, the Reverend Edmund A. Opitz, and Ludwig von Mises published in *Faith and Freedom*. Chodorov and Rothbard, among the most prolific and iconoclastic of the libertarian authors, each wrote a political column for several years.

As the editor searched for a more consistent style, the appearance and content of *Faith and Freedom* changed accordingly. Johnson revised the format in March 1953, expanding the magazine to twenty-four pages and adding monthly columns, "Along Pennsylvania Avenue" by Frank Chodorov and "With the Opinion Makers." Opitz, who joined the staff of Spiritual Mobilization in 1951, became book review editor of *Faith and Freedom* in 1953, and Rothbard, writing under the pseudonym of Aubrey Herbert, took over Chodorov's column in 1954. Johnson confirmed the magazine's new emphasis by adding "libertarian" to the masthead statement in December 1953.

If its direction seemed ensured, success was far from guaranteed. Ingebretsen never found a satisfactory way to finance *Faith and Freedom*. The magazine did not carry advertising and did not charge for subscriptions. Initially distributed to 20,000 clergymen, the magazine reluctantly instituted a voluntary subscription rate of one dollar. That annual rate was well below cost, and voluntary contributions recovered only a portion of the expense of publication and distribution. The magazine became a costly burden for Spiritual Mobilization. Attempting to reduce the financial drain, *Faith and Freedom* doubled the subscription rate to two dollars in 1954. When few of the ministers renewed their subscriptions, Ingebretsen abandoned the decision in January 1956, again eliminating any charge for the magazine.

Financial problems were only one reason for the failure of *Faith and Freedom*. The first issues of the magazine confirmed the antistatist and anticommunist legacy of Fifield, merging neatly with the political themes of the McCarthy period. Contributors consistently condemned the lack of spiritual content in the policies of the Truman Fair Deal, balancing these political themes with criticism of the collectivist impulses of the National Council of Churches and denominational social action programs. During the Korean War and other periods of international crisis, conservative and revisionist critics of American foreign policy found in *Faith and Freedom* a ready outlet for their views. Despite its low subscription cost and potentially large readership, however, the journal never found a marketable message for its target audience.

The quality of the articles was as varied as their range of topics was narrow.

Some articles were silly or simplistic. George S. Benson, the president of Harding College in Searcy, Arkansas, contributed a tale about the seagulls that died when the "handouts" they had become dependent on were no longer available. "The moral," Benson wrote: "A welfare state for gull or man, always first destroys the priceless attribute of self-reliance." Some articles were simply irritating. In "Federalized Race Prejudice," a critique of the Fair Employment Practices Commission of the Truman period, Frank Chodorov concluded that "the only thing to be done with the irrationality of prejudice is to ignore it," thus avoiding inflaming prejudice through government intervention. Other articles were noteworthy. The exchange between Edmund A. Opitz and John C. Bennett of Union Theological Seminary about the role of government in modern society, and the spirited debate about international intervention with Murray Rothbard contesting William Henry Chamberlin a William Schlamm, revealed the potential for a magazine like *Faith and Freedom*.[7] Although seldom achieved, this potential was demonstrated most clearly in the book reviews. Unlike many fundamentalist and evangelical publications, *Faith and Freedom* introduced its readers to a variety of current and influential books from secular and religious publishers. If the reviews were generally predictable in their criticism of liberal or internationalist themes, the range of the books covered and the quality of the reviews were generally superior to that of the articles.

Although *Faith and Freedom* provided Fifield with the "Director's Page" column, Ingebretsen increasingly guided Spiritual Mobilization and the magazine away from the legacy of the founder. After assuming the presidency of Spiritual Mobilization in 1954, Ingebretsen became initiator as well as administrator. He was instrumental in gaining financial contributions for the magazine, and he shifted its emphasis from economic and political themes toward an exploration of the psychological and moral content of libertarianism. These changes, which became most apparent after 1955, coincided with new competition for conservative readers from *National Review* and *Christianity Today*.

These external challenges coincided with significant changes in Ingebretsen's personal life. Facing new responsibilities, he reduced his legal practice. Simultaneously, the tragic death of a daughter contributed to a traumatic conversion experience that drew him toward psychological experiments and the study of Eastern religions and philosophy. Under the sponsorship of his own Foundation for Social Research, he began probing these new ideas with author and lecturer Gerald Heard and a small group of friends in an association they named the Wayfarers. The members of this group were predominantly urban, upper-middle-class members of Protestant churches. Dissatisfied with conventional religious practices, the Wayfarers resembled the Oxford Group in their social background, psychological emphasis, and spiritual activities.[8] In a series of conferences and retreats, the Wayfarers explored the "Growing Edge" of psychological experiences with the charismatic Heard.[9]

As Ingebretsen moved toward this more experiential emphasis, Fifield reduced his activities with Spiritual Mobilization. *Faith and Freedom* increasingly became the focal point for the organization, but Ingebretsen and Johnson still struggled to establish its identity. They dropped "libertarian" from the masthead statement in December 1955, referring to *Faith and Freedom* as "a journal of opinion." This constant search for a journalistic hook may have confused readers, and many ministers canceled their subscriptions. Although Spiritual Mobilization and its magazine would survive for several years, the erosion in support was costly. As they searched for an audience, Ingebretsen and Johnson changed the description of the magazine again and again. In March 1956 they identified *Faith and Freedom* as "a monthly magazine for individual liberty," and in September of that year the statement read: "*Faith and Freedom* is published by Spiritual Mobilization, a national, nonprofit, nonpartisan, nonsectarian organization founded in 1935."[10]

These shifting emphases were only the beginning of a lengthy period of uncertainty and decline for *Faith and Freedom*. By 1957 Spiritual Mobilization faced numerous problems. Fifield's interest had waned even further, and he would soon turn toward a more militant brand of political reaction with the John Birch Society. The "Eisenhower recession" and competition from the accelerated activities of the radical Right would reduce contributions and siphon off support. In addition, some of Spiritual Mobilization's major donors objected to Ingebretsen's plan to reduce expenses by moving Spiritual Mobilization's headquarters from Los Angeles to a ranch in the desert near San Jacinto, California. Ingebretsen hoped that the new headquarters at Campbell House would also become a spiritual and recreational oasis where "the future will see some of our friends in weekend or vacation homes clustered around our headquarters, all using the spiritual atmosphere and seclusion for the religious growth of themselves and their families."[11]

Ingebretsen's hopes would soon be shattered. The financial crisis nearly overwhelmed Spiritual Mobilization, and in the late spring of 1957 he expressed doubt about continuing the publication of *Faith and Freedom*.[12] Johnson resigned as editor, and the magazine ceased publication for the remainder of 1957. But *Faith and Freedom* would survive for two more difficult years. Ingebretsen momentarily stemmed the financial losses, partly by cutting back the number of issues published and also by pushing Spiritual Mobilization and *Faith and Freedom* into the 1958 campaign in California for a right-to-work law. The Reverend Edward W. Greenfield replaced Johnson as editor in 1958. A Presbyterian clergyman who had been active in right-to-work campaigns in Indiana, Greenfield brought a renewed spiritual emphasis to the job. He introduced "a new cover with a new concept" and a new title, *New Perspectives in Faith and Freedom*. A cross was now displayed prominently on the cover, and Greenfield explained that it was a universal symbol of "eternal verities of conserved and conserving principles." In a new column, "Perspective on Faith and Freedom," Ingebretsen introduced Greenfield and explained that the changes reinforced the heritage: "The basic philosophy that governs *Faith and Freedom* remains as it has been."[13]

But change was more apparent than continuity. By 1959, Gerald Heard had moved toward more open experimentation with LSD, and pressures from within and outside Spiritual Mobilization forced Ingebretsen to alter his relationship with him. The split was amicable, and it freed Ingebretsen to concentrate on reorganizing Spiritual Mobilization. Despite a mounting loss of support among the clergy, he had retained the loyalty of a small group of wealthy donors. Ingebretsen hoped that a new declaration of principles would blunt the criticism and reverse the decline of Spiritual Mobilization. But Ingebretsen had no answer for the competition from the newly organized John Birch Society and the increasing influence among fundamentalists and militant anticommunists of the Reverend Billy James Hargis, the Reverend Carl McIntire, Dr. Fred C. Schwarz, and Major Edgar Bundy. Fifield even sponsored Robert Welch's early efforts to organize the Birch Society in California.

As *Faith and Freedom* entered its tenth year of publication and Spiritual Mobilization approached its twenty-fifth anniversary, Fifield resigned as director of the organization. His departure, though expected, came at a critical time and deprived Spiritual Mobilization of its most recognizable leader. *Faith and Freedom* carried Fifield's "Farewell" in the first issue of volume 10, and in "A Reaffirmation of Faith and Purpose," Greenfield pledged adherence to "the central core of beliefs which brought both the organization and the magazine into existence." Quoting from the new statement of principles he had drafted with Ingebretsen, Greenfield warned "that the conscience of both church and community must be informed and aroused against every coercive or seductive force in government or elsewhere." If the new principles reaffirmed the legacy of Fifield, there was also evidence of Gerald Heard's continuing influence on Ingebretsen. The statement emphasized that in "working within the historical framework of Christianity, new insights and understanding need to be absorbed from the growing-edge discoveries in the social, psychological, and biological sciences."[14]

Neither approach succeeded. *Faith and Freedom* ceased publication early in 1960, and Spiritual Mobilization survived barely a year longer. Opitz confided that Spiritual Mobilization had achieved so little since the spring of 1957 that many of its old friends were finally abandoning it. *Faith and Freedom* and Spiritual Mobilization had drifted into what Opitz uncharitably described as a "vague spirituality." He was convinced that Spiritual Mobilization's contributions to the libertarian cause were "far less than the potential it displayed in the years 1950–1955."[15] Opitz was correct in his assertion and in his judgment about the timing of the change, but he overlooked economic and political factors that neither Fifield nor Ingebretsen could control. Spiritual Mobilization had never been a comfortable home for many conservatives and libertarians. *Faith and Freedom*'s constantly shifting perspective revealed the difficulty in attempting to blend spiritual themes with traditional libertarianism. Fifield's departure was simply the final blow. Spiritual Mobilization could no longer compete in the accelerated drive for Christianity, militant anticommunism, and money.

Similar judgments might be made about *Faith and Freedom*. Journalistic vitality could not compensate for lack of money. Without advertising revenue and with only limited income from subscriptions, *Faith and Freedom* depended on the success of its parent organization. But the content of the magazine was also a problem. Was it conservative or libertarian? Ingebretsen searched for a workable definition of libertarian until the very end. *Faith and Freedom* never established a consistently large and loyal following. Its readers were confused by inconsistencies and often put off by the shrill tone of many of the articles. Although the journal failed, California of the 1960s still provided many opportunities for religious and philosophical seekers of all ages. Greenfield moved on to work as a minister and counselor for Knott's Berry Farm, and Ingebretsen intensified his personal quest for the "growing edge" of knowledge and experience.

Notes

1. George H. Nash, *The Conservative Intellectual Movement in America: Since 1945* (New York, 1976), pp. 18, 28.

2. Quoted in Ralph Lord Roy, *Apostles of Discord: A Study of Organized Bigotry and Disruption on the Fringes of Protestantism* (Boston, 1953), p. 286.

3. James W. Fifield, Jr., "Dr. Fifield's Farewell after 24 Years with Spiritual Mobilization," *New Perspectives in Faith and Freedom* 9 (December 1959): 2.

4. His master's thesis for the School of Divinity of the University of Chicago, "A Study of Fundamentalism in the Presbyterian Church since 1900" (1925), was critical of fundamentalism. See also Fifield, "The Director's Page," *Faith and Freedom* 1 (January 1950): 3.

5. James C. Ingebretsen, conversation with author, 9 April 1981; John V. Cody, "Some Spiritual Dimensions in Modern Libertarianism: The *Faith and Freedom* Circle" (paper delivered at the Midwest Libertarian Scholars Conference, Chicago, 13 April 1984), p. 7.

6. "Masthead," *Faith and Freedom* 1 (December 1949): 2; "The Editor Comments," *Faith and Freedom* 1 (December 1949): 1.

7. George S. Benson, "The Conch Island Disaster," *Faith and Freedom* 1 (June 1950): 4; Frank Chodorov, "Federalized Race Prejudice," *Faith and Freedom* 1 (May 1950): 5; Nash, *Conservative Intellectual Movement in America*, p. 28.

8. See Eckard V. Toy, Jr., "Spiritual Mobilization: The Failure of an Ultraconservative Ideal in the 1950s," *Pacific Northwest Quarterly* 61 (April 1970): 77–86; Ingebretsen, conversation with Stephen A. Hoeller, 8 March 1979, James C. Ingebretsen Papers, Special Collections, University of Oregon.

9. See Eckard V. Toy,"The Conservative Connection: The Chairman of the Board Took LSD before Timothy Leary," *American Studies* 21 (Fall 1980): 65–77.

10. *Faith and Freedom* 7 (December 1955, March and June 1956): 2; *Faith and Freedom* 8 (September 1956): 2.

11. *Spiritual Mobilization's New Headquarters* (n.p., n.d.), James W. Clise Papers, Special Collections, University of Oregon.

12. Toy, "Spiritual Mobilization," p. 83.

13. Ingebretsen, "Perspective on Faith and Freedom," *Faith and Freedom* 9 (September 1958): 2, 3–5.

14. Fifield, "Dr. Fifield's Farewell," *Faith and Freedom* 10 (December 1959): 2, 3, 6. [Spiritual Mobilization], *The Liberating Spirit of Spiritual Mobilization* (San Jacinto, California, n.d.), p. 3, James W. Clise Papers, Special Collections, University of Oregon.

15. Edmund A. Opitz, "The Remnant: A Summary of Activities, 1 July 1959–1 July 1960," Memorandum, p. 5, and Opitz to James W. Clise, 23 November 1960, both in James W. Clise Papers, Special Collections, University of Oregon.

Information Sources

BIBLIOGRAPHY:
Roy, Ralph Lord. *Apostles of Discord: A Study of Organized Bigotry and Disruption on the Fringes of Protestantism*. Boston, 1953.

Toy, Jr., Eckard V. "Spiritual Mobilization: The Failure of an Ultraconservative Ideal in the 1950s." *Pacific Northwest Quarterly* 61 (April 1970): 77–86.

INDEXES: None.

REPRINT EDITIONS: Microform: UMI.

LOCATION SOURCES: Complete runs: New York Public Library; Yale Divinity School; Arizona State University; UCLA; Pacific School of Religion, Berkeley, California; University of Southern California; Garrett Theological Seminary, Evanston, Illinois.

Publication History

TITLE AND TITLE CHANGES: *Faith and Freedom: The Monthly Journal of Spiritual Mobilization*, December 1949–May 1957; *New Perspectives in Faith and Freedom*, 1958–1960.

VOLUME AND ISSUE DATA: Volumes 1–10, December 1949–1960.

FREQUENCY OF PUBLICATION: Irregular.

PUBLISHER: Spiritual Mobilization, Los Angeles (1949–1957) and San Jacinto (1958–1960), California.

EDITORS: William Johnson, 1949–1957; Edward W. Greenfield, 1958–1960.

CIRCULATION: Perhaps 40,000–50,000.

Eckard V. Toy

Christian Economics
1950–1972

The Christian Freedom Foundation (CFF), which links the Old Right of the 1930s with the New Right of the 1970s, published *Christian Economics* from May 1950 through December 1972. Distributed without cost to Protestant clergy, it reached more than 200,000 ministers at its peak circulation in the 1960s. But as a platform for the economic arguments and theological perspectives of Howard E. Kershner, its editor, and J. Howard Pew, its principal financial contributor, it found its most receptive audience among evangelicals and fundamentalists.

The CFF was the offspring of Kershner and a few other organizers, among them the Reverend Norman Vincent Peale, who planned its establishment in a series of meetings held in 1949 and early 1950.[1] When, on 3 May 1950, New York State granted a corporate charter to the CFF, it was described as a nonprofit educational foundation that would "engage in and promote the dissemination of information by the printed word, the spoken word, through radio, motion pictures and television on subjects of religion and education, in the fields of education, economics, religion, sociology, and public welfare."[2] The incorporators and some ministerial allies met in New York City later that month and elected officers and a board of directors. With the exception of Kershner, who was elected president, all of the officers and directors of CFF were Protestant clergymen, an overwhelming majority from mainline denominations in New York and the mid-Atlantic states. The South and Southwest had the fewest representatives.

Kershner, born in 1891, grew up in rural Kansas and Missouri, where he acquired the traits and values of the Middle Border. After being graduated from Friends University in Wichita, Kansas, he worked briefly as a journalist before serving with the newspaper section of the War Industries Board during World War I. During the two decades between the wars, Kershner enjoyed modest success in various manufacturing and publishing enterprises. Like his fellow Quaker Herbert Hoover, Kershner's religious beliefs and business success reinforced his political attitudes.

He reacted against contemporary trends, publishing a harshly critical assessment of Franklin D. Roosevelt's New Deal in 1936. In *The Menace of Roosevelt and His Policies*, Kershner equated the New Deal with the collectivistic tendencies of socialism and charged that "Mr. Roosevelt has endangered our entire heritage of political and economic freedom."[3]

Partly because of his alienation from American politics, Kershner retired from business in 1939 and devoted the next decade to humanitarian work with refugees. He served from 1939 to 1942 as director of relief in Europe for the American Friends Service Committee and successively after that with Herbert Hoover on the National Committee on Food for the Small Democracies, the International Commission for Child Refugees, Save the Children Foundation, the United Nations International Children's Fund, and CARE.[4]

Kershner's principal ally with *Christian Economics*, J. Howard Pew, came from a very different background. He was a member of an established and wealthy Philadelphia family whose fortune came from the Sun Oil and Sun Shipbuilding interests. An unyielding ideologue, he was a prominent member of the American Liberty League during the 1930s. He also served nearly forty years as chairman of the United Presbyterian Foundation, devoting much time and energy resisting the social action movements within his denomination and in the National Council of Churches.[5] Pew, who never served in any official capacity in CFF but nevertheless ensured its financial viability, intended to use *Christian Economics* as the primary weapon in his ideological struggles, and he shared with Kershner the role of ideological guardian of the journal. But he was also instrumental in establishing and financing *Christianity Today* as another weapon for his fight.

Where Pew preferred to work in obscurity, Kershner thrived on publicity. Yet their personal relationship resembled the mutual dependency between CFF and *Christian Economics*. Just as CFF provided an institutional base and tax-exempt status for *Christian Economics,* which incurred most of the costs and also provided most of the organization's visibility, so Pew contributed money while Kershner contributed his journalistic experience. Through CFF, Kershner made contacts with numerous other conservative organizations, and he gave them access to the pages of *Christian Economics*. This organizational cross-fertilization exposed a large number of clergy to the appeals of ultraconservatism during the 1950s and 1960s. Willis E. Stone of the American Progress Foundation, Fred Schwarz of the Christian Anti-Communism Crusade, and T. Coleman Andrews, a former third-party presidential candidate and a founder of the John Birch Society, found a positive reception in the pages of *Christian Economics*. Kershner, in turn, received awards from the Freedoms Foundation and lectured at Freedom Forums sponsored by the National Economic Program at Harding College and Pepperdine University.

Christian Economics was the principal medium for delivering CFF's message, and Kershner was the principal spokesman and architect of the publication. He followed a well-established pattern in developing its circulation. The American Economic Foundation loaned him a mailing list of businessmen and professionals, and he solicited denominational lists of ministers and lists of faculty and students in religious seminaries. After producing seven trial issues of *Christian Economics* during the spring and summer of 1950, testing the publication with a limited distribution to several thousand clergymen, CFF began regular fortnightly publication in September. In a simple and inexpensive four-page newsprint format, the periodical usually featured an editorial by Kershner, a column on economics by Percy L. Greaves, several original articles, including contributions by economist V. Orval Watts, former congressman Samuel B. Pettengill, and Frank C. Hanighen, publisher of *Human Events*, unsigned reprints, some news items, and Bible verses. Although *Christian Economics* dropped Greaves after a few years, the basic format survived for two decades.

Christian Economics increased its circulation to 90,000 subscribers within a year of its appearance. As circulation continued to rise, costs of publication increased proportionately. Kershner estimated that the cost for printing and mailing each issue was approximately $5,000.[6] But income was low. Its tax-exempt status meant that *Christian Economics* could not solicit advertising, and there were seldom more than 1,000 subscribers who paid the voluntary rate of one dollar annually. Yet while the publication never achieved financial independence, it had a stable source of income. During its first year of operation, for example, CFF received contributions and loans of more than $430,000, most of them in cash donations and stock transfers from Pew family trusts.[7] These contributions from the Pew family averaged more than $300,000 annually for nearly twenty-five years.[8] *Christian Economics* was the primary beneficiary, but the money also paid for distribution of "Sermonettes" to nearly 1,500 churches and for the production of newspaper columns and *Howard Kershner's Commentary on the News*, a fifteen-minute program carried by more than 150 radio stations.

The editorial board had little control over the content and policies of *Christian Economics*, and Kershner seldom shared major decisions with his associate editors George H. Cless, Jr., and the Reverend Irving E. Howard. Kershner did not have complete editorial autonomy, for Pew, who sometimes disagreed with him about ethical issues involved in capitalism, monitored the publication closely, commenting regularly over the telephone or by memo and meeting periodically to discuss controversial issues with Kershner. But it was Kershner who set the tone and shaped *Christian Economics* into a publication midway between a religious periodical and a journal of opinion. He rejected as inaccurate a description of *Christian Economics* as a "bimonthly newspaper of fundamental Protestantism." It was much more than that, he explained. "We do treat of the relationship among religious faiths, free government, sound economics and prosperity, but our main drive is to set forth the errors of Socialism and to show the soundness of free market economics." Kershner estimated "that economic analysis makes up about 50% of the content of our paper, and the relationship of that science to moral principles the other half," adding, as an afterthought: "Some attention is paid to anti-Communism...and the need for limiting government to the purposes outlined in the Constitution."[9]

Kershner was a prolific writer whose style may be described as pedestrian and polemical, though his message was brief. As *Christian Economics* proclaimed it on its masthead: "We stand for free enterprise—the economic system with the least amount of government and the greatest amount of Christianity." Critics questioned the implications of that statement and the name of the publication. Robert McAfee Brown of Union Theological Seminary asked rhetorically, in an article with the same title, "Is It 'Christian Economics'?" Kershner's persistent reply to his critics was a simple economic message cloaked in spirituality. "The laws of economics," he argued, "are part of the laws of God."[10] "The cold truth," he editorialized, "is that Socialism—Welfare Statism—is a reversal of God's plan for man." Yet while he opposed regulation of the economy, he argued against totally laissez-faire economics, insisting that one must make distinctions between moral economic activities and immoral ones. What was moral, in this sense, was what was beneficial. "This makes a vast difference," he explained to a fellow Quaker, "between laissez faire economics and Christian economics."[11] In *Christian Economics* he assured his readers that "Free market capitalism permeated by Christian ideals" was "Christian capitalism," which he described as "the best form of society that the minds and hearts of men have been able to devise."[12]

Kershner thrived on controversy and periodically endangered CFF's tax-exempt status by addressing controversial social and political issues. These took on a distinctly ideological tinge in the pages of *Christian Economics*. Regarding the world as a battleground between the forces of good and evil, in which socialism was evil and liberalism was, in general, no different from socialism, Kershner predictably condemned "atheistic communism" and praised Senator Joseph R. McCarthy (R, Wisconsin) and the John Birch Society. He denounced social action movements within the churches as "essentially Marxist" and revealed his increasing alienation from his own denomination by labeling it the "Socialist Society of Friends."[13] He also wrote critically of the civil rights movement and defended the racial policies of Rhodesia and South Africa. Privately he favored racial segregation and believed in the innate racial and cultural inferiority of blacks. "The best authorities agree," he told a correspondent, "that the Negro race is some 300,000 to 400,000 years behind the white race in its evolutionary development."[14] Yet publicly he advocated "voluntary" compliance with civil rights laws.

Reactions to *Christian Economics* were seldom neutral. Many clergy simply discarded it, while thousands of others wrote letters supporting or repudiating its views. Interviews conducted by Opinion Research Corporation with 311 Protestant ministers in Philadelphia, Cincinnati, and Atlanta in 1953 indicated that 15 percent of the respondents relied "heavily" on *Christian Economics* for information about social, political, and economic issues. Eighty-eight percent of the ministers receiving *Christian Economics* said they read it regularly or occasionally, with a high percentage disagreeing with its positions.[15]

By the mid-1960s, *Christian Economics* was increasingly out of step with the times and isolated from its early sources of support within the mainline churches. An aging J. Howard Pew began to lose interest in *Christian Economics* and encouraged Kershner to seek other sources of funding. Northwood Institute made a tentative offer to acquire CFF, but Kershner moved to California, where the Reverend James W. Fifield, Jr., of the First Congregational Church of Los Angeles, and former head of Spiritual Mobilization, secured an appointment for him in his church as minister of applied Christianity.[16] In the spring of 1967 Kershner moved the editorial office of *Christian Economics* to Los Angeles and found renewal in the conservative environment of Fifield's church.

Despite these favorable circumstances, *Christian Economics* survived only a few years longer. After J. Howard Pew's death in the early 1970s, Kershner stepped down as editor of the journal and left CFF to become visiting professor of current economic problems with Northwood Institute and edit a new monthly publication, *Answers to Economic Problems*. The Pew family trusts continued to support CFF, but the organization itself was beginning to turn away from ministers in search of a more youthful audience. Early in 1971 it commenced publication of *For Real*, described as a Christian "underground paper" aimed at high school and college students, and claiming a circulation of more than 100,000.[17] In these circumstances, the new editor of *Christian Economics*, Edward Rowe, phased the periodical out at the end of 1972, changing its name to the original subtitle, *Applied Christianity*. It survived only briefly.

The demise of *Christian Economics* symbolized a significant change in the content and character of conservatism after the 1960s. Although CFF lost its original leaders and its connection with the Old Right, the political and religious ferment of the 1970s placed CFF in the forefront of the New Right. Richard M. DeVos of Amway Corporation and a group of fellow conservatives acquired control of CFF in 1975, and Ed McAteer, formerly a district sales manager for Colgate-Palmolive Company, became a field representative and seminar organizer for CFF the following year. McAteer went on to work for Howard Phillips of the Conservative Caucus and became a catalyst for organizing the New Right among evangelicals and fundamentalists. Later he was instrumental in bringing Phillips together with fund raiser Richard Viguerie and evangelist Jerry Falwell to found the Moral Majority. McAteer followed that by establishing the Religious Roundtable in 1979.[18]

Although *Christian Economics* faded into relative obscurity, it had played a significant role in preserving the conservative legacy of the cold war period and, through CFF, projected that legacy into the 1980s. *Christian Economics* was not a great journalistic achievement, but many of the religious and ideological issues of two crucial decades of the twentieth century are revealed in its pages.

Notes

1. CFF had no connection with William Dudley Pelley's Foundation for Christian Economics (1932–1933), which he incorporated in Asheville, North Carolina, shortly before founding the Silver Shirts in 1933. Kershner claimed that he "planned this organization and its publication *Christian Economics* before it was my privilege to know Mr. Pew." He explained that "Dr. Norman Vincent Peale was the first man to join with me in planning for this Foundation" and "my close friend and chief backer in this operation...has been and is Mr. J. Howard Pew." See Howard E. Kershner to Dr. Thomas Law Coyle, 10 January 1950; the Reverend Dallas L. Browning, 7 December 1962; and Art Linkletter, 7 February 1968, Howard E. Kershner Papers, Special Collections, University of Oregon (hereinafter cited as HEK Papers). Kershner and the other founders extended an "invitation" to twenty-seven clergymen to join them at a meeting in New York City to organize CFF. Kershner, the

Reverend Norman Vincent Peale, and others to Dr. Harold Paul Sloan, 25 January 1950, HEK Papers.

2. "Certificate of Incorporation of Christian Freedom Foundation, Inc.," State of New York, 3 May 1950, HEK Papers.

3. Quoted in George Younger, "Protestant Piety and the Right Wing," *Social Action* 17 (15 May 1951): 35.

4. Kershner's book, *Quaker Service in Modern War: Spain and France, 1939–1940* (Englewood Cliffs, New Jersey, 1950) outlines the contributions of the AFS and other Quaker organizations.

5. See E. V. Toy, Jr., "The National Lay Committee and the National Council of Churches: A Case Study of Protestants in Conflict," *American Quarterly* 21 (Summer 1969): 190–209.

6. Kershner to Clarence Manion, 27 May 1960, HEK Papers.

7. CFF financial statement for 1951, HEK Papers.

8. Budgets and letters of transfer, HEK Papers.

9. Kershner to Carol D. Bauman, 19 February 1968, HEK Papers.

10. Quoted in Ralph Lord Roy, "God, Free Enterprise, and Anarchy," *The Christian Register* 132 (April 1953): 10.

11. Kershner to B. A. Rogge, 20 December 1965, HEK Papers.

12. Robert McAfee Brown, "Is It 'Christian Economics'?" *Christianity and Crisis* 10 (27 November 1950): 155–58, and Howard E. Kershner, "Voice of the Editor," *Christian Economics* 9 (8 January 1957): 1–2.

13. Kershner to Mrs. James E. Rose, 18 June 1963, HEK Papers.

14. Kershner to Charles Wolfe, 16 August 1963, HEK Papers.

15. "Clergymen Appraise 'Christian Economics,'" by Opinion Research Corporation, April 1953, HEK Papers.

16. After lengthy and detailed negotiations, Kershner accepted a position at the Texas branch campus of Northwood Institute, a private college founded in 1959 in Midland, Michigan. See Kershner to Arthur E. Turner, 22 November 1967, and Turner to Kershner, 20 August 1969, HEK Papers.

17. Edward Rowe to Mrs. V. Weger, 1 August 1972; David J. Juroe to the Reverend Matthew J. Welde, 4 October 1972, HEK Papers.

18. John S. Saloma III, *Ominous Politics: The New Conservative Labyrinth* (New York, 1984), pp. 53–54.

Information Sources

BIBLIOGRAPHY:

Bruce, Steve. *The Rise and Fall of the New Christian Right: Conservative Protestant Politics in America, 1978–1988.* New York, 1989.

Crawford, Alan. *Thunder on the Right: The "New Right" and the Politics of Resentment.* New York, 1980.

LaHaye, Tim. *The Battle for the Mind.* Old Tappan, New Jersey, 1980.

Liebman, Robert C., and Robert Wuthnow, eds. *The New Christian Right: Mobilization and Legitimation.* New York, 1983.

Peele, Gillian. *Revival and Reaction: The Right in Contemporary America.* New York, 1984.

Roy, Ralph Lord. *Apostles of Discord: A Study of Organized Bigotry and Disruption on the Fringes of Protestantism.* Boston, 1953.

Younger, George. "Protestant Piety and the Right Wing." *Social Action* 17 (15 May 1951): 5–31.

INDEXES: *PAIS*.

REPRINT EDITIONS: None.

LOCATION SOURCES: Complete run: San Francisco Theological Seminary.

Publication History

TITLE AND TITLE CHANGES: *Christian Economics*.
VOLUME AND ISSUE DATA: Volumes 1–24, May 1950–December 1972.
FREQUENCY OF PUBLICATION: Seven numbers issued May–August 1950; biweekly
(except July and August) to April 1970; monthly, May 1970–December 1972.
PUBLISHER: Christian Freedom Foundation, New York and Buena Park, California.
EDITORS: Howard E. Kershner, 1950–1971; Edward Rowe, 1971–1972.
CIRCULATION: 1962: 200,000 claimed; 1972: 49,000.

Eckard V. Toy

Christianity Today
1956–

In 1979 the Gallup poll organization found that *Christianity Today* was the most widely read religious periodical among clergy in the United States.[1] Two years later, in 1981, a year that marked the twenty-fifth anniversary of the magazine's founding, the bimonthly journal recorded a circulation of nearly 200,000. Through the years it became a primary voice for conservative evangelical Christianity, a movement Gallup estimated in 1979 as numbering over 30 million persons in the United States and an ever widening population around the world. Its conservative expression, however, underwent various twists and turns, which may be followed by studying the circumstances of its founding and examining the development of certain critical themes within its pages.

Originally *Christianity Today* reflected the vision of Billy Graham, who in the mid-1950s was coming to the forefront of Christian evangelism. In late 1953 Graham conceived the idea of an alternative to the *Christian Century*, a magazine boasting a circulation of nearly 40,000 and respected as the only Protestant magazine quoted in the secular press.[2] Graham wanted a less liberal voice that would speak to evangelical clergy and intelligent laypeople, many of whom were in fundamentalist and denominational churches supporting his crusades. He saw such a publication as a forum for posing various sides of an issue, ultimately providing a rallying point for those of orthodox Christian belief. Graham believed that by avoiding extremes of right and left in Christianity, he could effectively underscore the pertinence of long-established Christian beliefs in the rapidly changing modern world. He vowed to send a free copy to all clergy for a two-year period in order to demonstrate the worth of its contents.

To begin the magazine, Graham persuaded several key individuals to commit themselves to the project. His first enthusiastic supporter was his father-in-law, Dr. L. Nelson Bell. Although a busy surgeon, Bell was the founder of the *Presbyterian Journal* and a prolific writer for all kinds of magazines. Bell helped by interviewing prospective staff, setting up the magazine's offices in Washington, D.C., and, as publisher, by soliciting funds. Of possible financial backers, Bell and Graham persuaded J. Howard Pew, chairman of the board of Sun Oil Company, and W. Maxey Jarman, chairman of the board of the General Shoe Company, the world's largest apparel conglomerate, to join the enterprise. To head his board of trustees, he enlisted Harold Ockenga, then emerging as an evangelical pastor. Ockenga could create cooperative alliances among clergy and theological educators. Finally, on the recommendation of Harold Lindsell, a professor at Fuller Theological Seminary in Pasadena, California, and later the second editor of the magazine, Graham chose Carl F. H. Henry as editor. A Baptist and a forty-nine-year-old professor at Fuller, Henry agreed to take the job for a year in order to "get things moving in the right direction."

Henry was a well-educated, forceful Christian scholar. Raised as an Episcopalian, he had edited a weekly newspaper in Smithtown, New York, at the age of twenty. At that point he experienced what he called "a dynamic Pauline" conversion that led him to obtain a divinity degree from Chicago's Northern Baptist Theological Seminary and a Ph.D. in philosophy from Boston University. By the time he became editor, Henry had already written several books. Most of them addressed ways in which biblical faith could have a contemporary focus. For example, in his *Uneasy Conscience of Modern Fundamentalism* (1947), Henry declared that fundamentalism had lost Christianity's impetus for social reform and had become absorbed in personal sins such as drunkenness, dancing, and smoking.[3] Conservative churches, he insisted, ought to broaden their platforms and address a wide range of temporal concerns. It was a theme that would be reiterated in *Christianity Today*, and when, with the able assistance of Dr. Bell, who had given up his full-time surgical practice, Henry launched the magazine in October 1956, he sought to establish not only high standards for the publication but a wide-ranging program for it as well. In the words of the first editorial: "*Christianity Today* will apply the Biblical revelation to the contemporary crisis, by presenting the implications of the total Gospel message for every area of life. This Fundamentalism has often failed to do."[4] By addressing issues directly and offering alternative Christian perspectives, Henry and the others hoped to avoid the one-sided anti-intellectualism found in other fundamentalist approaches.

Henry and Bell dominated the magazine's editorial slant for the next twelve years, until 1968. But throughout its existence, the editors of *Christianity Today* have addressed many areas of life with a vigorous and generally conservative perspective. As their highest priority the editors began by focusing on such traditional doctrines as Christ's redeeming grace and the authority of the Bible. They maintained that the ancient creeds and the Bible could preserve believers from the manifold intellectual, ethical, and spiritual crises that faced modern, secular man. They advertised and reviewed the explosion of postwar biblical translations, paraphrases, and studies. They printed excerpts of devotional and biblical monographs on virtually any topic, and they pressed theologians in the best churches and educational outposts for pieces on current issues. These articles often attacked preeminent liberal and neoorthodox theologians such as DeWolf, Tillich, Barth, and Bultmann. The section on current religious news soon became the best in religious reporting. And the reporters frequently covered the terrain of a burgeoning evangelical church in both America and abroad. Commentators often harked back to the Protestant leaders of the past for examples of piety and robust, biblically grounded preaching. Though perhaps not always attractive in an increasingly secular and highly pluralistic world, the traditional Christian message won an ever growing number of adherents. By 1962 the circulation of *CT*, as it came to be known, had reached 140,000.

Clearly the magazine provided a popular, well-articulated, authoritative stance from which to address a bewildering number of liberal theological ideas. It ridiculed the Death of God theological movement and other "nihilistic" and intellectual attacks on the foundations of the Judeo-Christian tradition. Perhaps most characteristic in the doctrinal controversies was the battle over biblical authority. It was Harold Lindsell, the magazine's second editor, from 1968 to 1978, who brought this battle to the forefront.

For a century critics had attacked the normative authority of the Old and New Testament for human life. Neoorthodox theologians contended that the word of God was contained in the written Scriptures but that portions of the Bible contained human errors. These same theologians taught that interpreting God's meaning was fraught with difficulties because of those errors and highly subjective interpretation. Mandates that seemed to be situational or culturally limited led to a reduction of universal truths. The more liberal views held that the meaning of biblical texts was tied so closely to its originating culture that understanding the same meaning in a later culture would be impossible. Normative truth from God would never be possible to discern from the biblical text.

While Lindsdell presented views contrary to his own, he and writers of his persuasion rejected the liberal and skeptical positions. Instead they argued for an inerrant authority buttressed by fundamental doctrines such as Christ's deity, the virgin birth, and Christ's atoning crucifixion and bodily resurrection. Primarily they sought to stake out proper theological and hermeneutic principles of biblical interpretation. Application of those principles, as in arguments over the origin of the earth or man or how to live a Christian life, had to take second place. The principles they endeavored to establish included such traditional ones as the unity of the authority of Christ with the authority of Scripture. In their view Christians should accept the position they claimed Christ took, which was to criticize common interpretations but not to question the truth of the text itself. Scripture itself should be considered God's word in human language, much as Christ had become God incarnate. As conservatives argued it, God in the person of the Holy Spirit would enable believers to appropriate God's truth and then set it forth in their lives and published statements. The Holy Spirit was the agent of proper hermeneutics. Thus by elaborate argument, the editors and writers in *Christianity Today* reasserted old principles of biblical authority. They aimed to fend off increasing intellectual challenges to the notion that supernatural guidance existed for man. For those who substituted an organization or a charismatic leader for that supernatural authority, *Christianity Today* offered in response the authority of the Bible.

But the magazine discussed these matters of fundamental, orthodox doctrine only occasionally. The bulk of its feature and editorial columns, reflecting the original concern of its founders, aimed to apply biblical revelation to every aspect of life. In doing this, it departed widely from the view of twentieth-century liberal Christians and presented instead distinctly conservative political, economic, and social values.

Articles on politics generally advocated individual rather than corporate action. While it was acceptable for the church or the magazine to condemn political corruption or racism, it was for individuals, and not the church as a corporate body, to enter politics. This outlook was familiar in traditional Protestant circles. It reflected the two-kingdom theory set forth by Protestant reformers, wherein the political and religious spheres overlapped for some purposes, such as showing compassion for the afflicted, but in which the kingdoms of this world were definitely limited in their power and connection to the sacred world. The main political obligation of the Christian was to support the constituted civil authority. Such a position often led logically to support America, right or wrong. A heightened sense of patriotism and the image of a Christian America appeared in editorials. For example, in 1963 Lieutenant General William K. Harrison maintained that if another nation attacked the United States, then nuclear retaliation would be morally justified. The pages of *Christianity Today* carried the following unchallenged assertion by General Harrison: "The massive destruction caused by nuclear weapons is not an ethical bar against their use in a war justifiable on other moral considerations."[5] Although such statements later would be challenged by the editors, and even Graham himself, support of civil authority could quickly shift to pride in nation. For many years conservative sectors in American politics legitimately saw *Christianity Today* as supporting their anticommunist, militaristic positions.[6]

From 1963 through 1968 the magazine carried more than a dozen articles and editorials that criticized liberal churchmen for mixing in political affairs without scriptural mandates.[7] In a 1966 piece, for example, Howard Kershner argued that Jesus had commanded Christians to go into the world and preach the gospel, but that that did not mean involvement in the Peace Corps or civil disobedience. Years before, founding fathers of the journal J. Howard Pew and L. Nelson Bell had made general statements against political involvement. By taking political stands, Bell declared, the church moved "away from its devotion to God's Word."[8] The fairly consistent position of Billy Graham and his associates was to avoid specific political issues for fear such commentary would confuse people about the essence of the gospel.

But such a position of noninvolvement was in tension with the purpose of *Christianity Today* to speak out on issues. Indeed, Graham befriended and advised every president from Eisenhower to Reagan. He located the magazine in Washington so that it would carry "an unusual authority." The publishers also wanted the editor to "mingle with congressmen, senators, and government leaders so he could speak with first-hand knowledge on issues of the day."[9] After a few years, perhaps a period of maturation, Graham and other evangelical leaders encouraged Christians to participate in politics and selectively addressed moral issues, such as racism and nuclear arms control, that had political implications.

When they became forthright, the political positions espoused by *Christianity Today* editors usually reflected conservative adherence to constituted order. Perhaps the journal's reaction to the Watergate episode shows this most vividly. Billy Graham and *Christianity Today* had shown strong support for Richard Nixon in the election of 1968 and through his administration into 1972. When the news on Watergate became darker and darker for the Republican administration, both Graham and *Christianity Today*'s editor, Harold Lindsell, continued to uphold that administration, to their later embarrassment. At first, the magazine seemed to accept Nixon's plea of innocence, but it did urge him to act promptly and punish the guilty.[10] As demands for Nixon's resignation increased, Lindsell argued that the president could be removed from office for "high crimes and misdemeanors" only, and not for slight moral indiscretions. Because resignation would leave many questions about Nixon's guilt or innocence unanswered, the magazine favored using the constitutional process of having the Senate act as a high court. If guilt was proved, only then ought the president to resign.[11] Upon Nixon's resignation the editorials applauded President Ford's handling of the situation and urged support for the new Republican president.

But a thorough reading of the magazine, particularly as the evangelical movement developed by the mid-1970s, will show more variety of viewpoints than conservative stereotypes might allow. Especially under Kenneth Kantzer (editor, 1978–1982) themes have appeared on political justice, antimaterialism, and the threat of nuclear warfare. More reports have come on political stands taken by Christian groups that have criticized established political values. Features on such political matters were still secondary to other pietistic and pastoral concerns, but the editors have moderated or broadened their principal political concerns. No longer do the goals seem to be simply the presentation of narrowly conceived constitutional freedoms or the defense of the existing American political order.

A similar development of *Christianity Today*'s conservatism can be followed in economic matters. Unlike ultraconservatives, the editorial and feature writers for *Christianity Today* have not advocated the destruction of America's monetary system, social security, the Federal Trade Commission, or other regulatory agencies of the established economic institutions of America. But they have consistently sided with conservative economic theory. One finds favorable references to the neo-Austrian economic school of Friedrich Hayek and to American popularizers such as Henry Hazlitt and Milton Friedman, but none to John Maynard Keynes, John Kenneth Galbraith, or other critics of the conservative camp.[12] A brief review will illustrate the magazine's support of traditional positions.

Writers for the magazine have used various arguments to link Christianity and the free market system. In a 1958 piece, "Christian Approach to Economics," Irving Howard of the Christian Freedom Foundation advanced several Christian rationales for capitalism. One is that inequality in wealth is part of God's providence or plan, another that God gave man free choice in the Garden of Eden. With these "facts" of providence and creation serving as the criteria for assessing all economic systems, it followed that restricting freedom or demanding equality would be contrary to God's principles for the world and thus immoral. So, according to Howard, the biblical approach would "insist upon voluntarism and limit government to a police function."[13] A classic conservative corollary of this position followed by other writers in *CT* is that government constitutes a continual threat to freedom. Government by nature is coercive, and its forms of taxation, prohibitions, and regulations limit the range of free choice. As L. Nelson Bell noted in 1968, enlisting the power of the federal government leads "straight to the concept of a socialistic state, despite the ever-increasing evidence of the failure of socialism wherever practiced." Howard's fear, sounded frequently among conservatives, was that "a government which controls the economic life of its citizens today will control their thoughts and souls tomorrow."[14]

Still another corollary of the free market idea was that labor unions are incompatible with or detrimental to the Christian economic system. According to editorials in *CT*, labor forces illegitimate restrictions on capital and gets its way through government coercion. Its legislative demands and electoral pressure become exploitative, and mandatory membership in unions limits freedom of individuals. *CT* editorials have spoken out also against the collectivist if not socialist (read: Marxist) mentality of labor leaders. According to editorials, attempts to control the economy or to expand atheistic notions should be stopped. Other articles have criticized the labor movement for racketeering and violence. An editorial in 1958, for example, cited "pay-offs, threats, black-mail, violence and disruption" as major characteristics of the labor movement.[15] But *Christianity Today* has written little or nothing to expose abuses within the ranks of management.

Other conservative economic proposals have called for the replacement of "welfare-statism" with voluntary church welfare and philanthropy.[16] An editorial in 1960 claimed that welfare programs were "inherently anti-Christian." Through the 1960s and 1970s, attacks on liberal Democratic programs were clearly in evidence. In 1974 a member of the editorial board wrote that "the welfare state saps individual initiative, increases the size and cost of sustaining bureaucracy" and "at last assures some form of totalitarian control that spells the death of democracy." To replace such dependency, Carl Henry and others suggested programs headed by the church and voluntary agencies. Compassion should be the work of the church, not government; the proper sphere of government was in providing retributive justice, not charity.

In these areas of economics *Christianity Today* has clearly taken classically conservative stands. Further exploration of areas such as balanced budgets and anti-inflation would produce the same conclusion. But as with politics, the journal has shown a moderating position over the years. It has come to avoid and even to make fun of "proof-texting" Bible passages for support of certain conservative positions. And by evaluating principles found in the Sermon on the Mount and attempting to apply scriptural commands to love one's neighbor, editors have begun to put limits on the overriding instrumental value of freedom. It is even possible to find places where there is not a totally skeptical or negative view of economic intervention by government. Perhaps in response to arguments in the *Sojourners* and the *Other Side*, journals of a biblically based protest movement, *Christianity*

Today moved in the late 1980s to include critical perspectives on the economic system. Articles now include ideas from the Anabaptist-Mennonite tradition that stress the simple lifestyle as a demonstration of independency of the system. Protests against the Vietnam War, the concentration of wealth in America, and the wasting of resources have appeared in the statements of feature writers and editorials.

In the areas of politics and economics, new perspectives have manifested themselves slowly in *Christianity Today*. But for years the journal had little to offer in the area of social thought, at least in comparison with evangelical efforts in the nineteenth century.[17] Then evangelicals led in movements expressing social concern, and working against such evils as slavery, greed, and poverty. After America's industrialization in the 1870s and 1880s, the philanthropic works of churches rarely made much progress against the enormous problems of poverty, unemployment, disease, crime, and substandard housing. And evangelicals reacted negatively to reform forces such as Marxism and Christian liberalism that emerged in America during the first part of the twentieth century.

Despite the good intentions of Carl Henry when the magazine began in 1956, *Christianity Today* has continued to reflect conservative Protestant interest in assailing personal sin rather than corporate social misdoing. Its concern for personal morality appeared in one of its earliest editorials. As from a pulpit, the cry came forth: "Raise in a church council a question on Christian race relations and an almost unanimous response is assured. Raise the question of moral conduct, and often there is little effective reaction."[18] One does read calls for social renewal, but this comes with the warning not to replace the full gospel with a social gospel. Articles often refer to social evils such as violent crime, juvenile delinquency, and prostitution as personal sins.[19] So before redeeming changes can take place in society, the task of evangelicals is to bring individual men and women into a saving relationship with Christ. Being born again is primary; after that, personal conversion will produce an increased social concern. This primary emphasis on personal evangelism comes through clearly in featured writings by Billy Graham and those connected with the National Association of Evangelicals. *Christianity Today* did move away from fundamentalists who argued that the church's only mandate was evangelism. But the train moved slowly and not very far from the station.

The moderating position of *Christianity Today* can be seen in several ways. During the first year, only four articles dealt with individualist issues such as sex, cheating, or alcohol abuse, while more than a dozen articles concerned matters that could be labeled as "social." No randomly selected year over the next two decades provided issues in which personal themes had a higher than one-to-five ratio as compared with social concerns.[20] Less clear is whether there was a systematic social ethic operating in the selection of articles or treatment of themes. Generally the magazine's approach to issues such as poverty, hunger, civil rights, and labor seemed to be consistent with its political conservatism. That meant a rejection of governmental attempts to aid such causes and little support of movements working for social causes.

Treatment of social concerns began to evolve by 1970. In 1974 Henry began to see the overcoming of social alienation as "a necessary aspect" of the evangel.[21] Third World evangelicals and neoevangelicals began to argue that the gospel included a call for social justice as well as personal conversion. In an entire issue devoted to the Social Gospel, Ron Sider in 1976 led the charge of neoevangelicals in calling for an inseparable gospel of evangelism and social concern.[22] It remains to be seen if *Christianity Today's* appreciation of indispensable social implications of the Christian gospel will continue to have a prominent place.

The future direction of *Christianity Today* when charted in any of the aforementioned areas is likely to remain conservative. Its vocal constituency is still quite conservative. Disapproving letters pour in when the magazine publishes material that smacks of a well-recognized liberal position. The governing board long remained an inbred conservative group. And its fourth editor, V. Gilbert Beers, touched all the traditional ground: Northern Baptist Seminary, Wheaton College, and a term as editor in a publishing house that is one of fifteen businesses that have long advertised in *Christianity Today*.[23] Shortly after, Beers used his background in developing Christian education materials for publication in producing feature articles for the periodical. The 1979 Gallup poll showed that evangelicals possessed a high degree of traditional morality, but that a shamefully high percentage of them also professed ignorance about the Bible and traditional Christian doctrines.[24] Despite forty years of struggling with tough spiritual and intellectual issues, *Christianity Today* has seemingly had little effect beyond its target group of well-educated ministers and laity. With such ignorance among the larger Christian public, the urgent need for revival of personal and corporate piety in many sectors, and strong threats of advancing secular trends opposed to Christianity, the magazine continued to stress themes of yesteryear—personal Bible studies, evangelism, personal morality. Traditional pietistic views remain in the vogue. Reliance on such themes in *Christianity Today* may prevent it from reaching its goal of dealing seriously enough with social issues to challenge the minds of its elite.

Notes

1. The Gallup Organization, Inc., and the Princeton Religion Research Center, "Evangelical Christianity in the United States: National Parallel Surveys of General Public and Clergy," conducted for *Christianity Today*, 1979, p. 247 (hereinafter cited as *CT*). The report showed a 30 percent readership among all clergy for *CT*, followed by *Christian Century* with a 12 percent readership. *CT* has a 46 percent readership among evangelical clergy, followed by *Moody Monthly* at 22 percent. For circulation and press run statistics, see *CT* papers in the archives of the Billy Graham Center, Wheaton College, Wheaton, Illinois, especially Box 4, folder 1.

2. "In the Beginning...Billy Graham Recounts the Origins of *Christianity Today*," *CT* 25 (17 July 1981): 26.

3. Carl F. H. Henry, *The Uneasy Conscience of Modern Fundamentalism* (Grand Rapids, Michigan, 1947), p. 20.

4. "Why Christianity Today," *CT* 1 (15 October 1956): 20.

5. William K. Harrison, "A Christian General's View: Is Nuclear War Justifiable?" *CT* 7 (21 June 1963): 5.

6. Richard V. Pierard, *The Unequal Yoke: Evangelical Christianity and Political Conservatism* (Philadelphia, 1970), chaps. 4, 5.

7. Dennis P. Hollinger, "American Individualism and Evangelical Social Ethics: A Study of *Christianity Today*, 1956–1976" (Ph.D. dissertation, Drew University, 1981), p. 138.

8. Ibid., p. 139.

9. "In the Beginning," p. 27.

10. Harold Lindsell, "The Watergate Wrangle," *CT* 17 (13 April 1973): 30; Lindsell, "Political Espionage," *CT* 17 (25 May 1973): 33.

11. Lindsell, "The Appeal to Resign," *CT* 18 (23 November 1973): 41; "Should Nixon Resign?" *CT* 18 (17 June 1974): 28–29. See also E. W. Lutzer, "Watergate Ethics," *CT* 18 (13 September 1974): 26–27.

12. Hollinger, "American Individualism and Evangelical Social Ethics," p. 197.

13. Irving Howard, "Christian Approach to Economics," *CT* 2 (18 August 1958): 8.

14. Hollinger, "American Individualism and Evangelical Social Ethics," p. 202.

15. Ibid., pp. 209ff.

16. Ibid., pp. 204ff.

17. John Woodbridge, Mark Noll, and Nathan Hatch, *The Gospel in America* (Grand Rapids, Michigan, 1979), passim.

18. "Is the Church Too Silent about Personal Morality?" *CT* 1 (12 November 1956): 23.

19. Irving Howard, "Christ and the Libertarians," *CT* 2 (17 March 1958): 10.

20. Hollinger, "American Individualism and Social Ethics," pp. 122ff.

21. Carl Henry, "Gospel and Society," *CT* 18 (13 September 1974): 67.

22. Ronald Sider, "Evangelism or Social Justice: The Options," *CT* 21 (8 October 1976): 29.

23. "Introducing CT's Fourth Editor," *CT* 26 (22 October 1982): 15.

24. "The Christianity Today-Gallup Poll: An Overview," *CT* 23 (21 December 1979): 12–15; James Repsome, "Religious Values: Reflection of Age and Education," *CT* 24 (2 May 1980): 23–25. When *Christianity Today*'s publisher, Harold Myra, started a new journal, *Leadership*, that addressed pastoral concerns and personal piety, it rapidly acquired a circulation of 50,000.

Information Sources

BIBLIOGRAPHY:

Christianity Today Archives, Billy Graham Center, Wheaton College, Wheaton, Illinois.

Ezell, Macel. "The Evangelical Protestant Defense of Americanism, 1945–1960." Ph.D. dissertation, Texas Christian University, 1969.

Fowler, Robert B. *The New Engagement: Evangelical Political Thought, 1966–1976.* Grand Rapids, Michigan, 1982.

Hollinger, Dennis. "American Individualism and Social Ethics: A Study of *Christianity Today*, 1956–1976. Ph.D. dissertation, Drew University, 1981.

Pierard, Richard. *The Unequal Yoke: Evangelical Christianity and Political Conservatism.* Philadelphia, 1970.

INDEXES: Each volume indexed; *Bio Ind*; *Curr Bk Rev Cit*; *FLI*; *Ind Rel Per Lit*; *Mag Ind*; *NTA*; *OTA*; *RG*; *Rel Ind One*.

REPRINT EDITIONS: Microform: UMI; BLH. Bound edition: UMI.

LOCATION SOURCES: Widely available.

Publication History

TITLE AND TITLE CHANGES: *Christianity Today*.

VOLUME AND ISSUE DATA: Volumes 1–current, 1956–present.

FREQUENCY OF PUBLICATION: 1956–1978, semimonthly; June 1978–December 1980, semimonthly, but monthly in July and August; December 1980–June 1982, semimonthly, but monthly in July, August, and December; June 1982–June 1983, semimonthly, but monthly in June, July, August, and December; June 1983–present, semimonthly, but monthly in January, May, June, July, August, and December.

PUBLISHERS: 15 October 1956–1 April 1957: Today's Publications, Inc.; 15 April 1957–21 December 1962: Christianity Today, Inc.; 4 January 1963–2 January 1970: Wilbur D. Benedict; 16 January 1970–8 October 1971: David R. Rehymeyer; 22 October 1971–20 June 1975: Harold Lindsell; 4 July 1975–4 April 1986: Harold Myra; 18 April 1986–present: Christianity Today, Inc. Through 8 July 1977, Washington, D. C.; from 29 July 1977, Carol Stream, Illinois.

EDITORS: Carl F. H. Henry, 15 October 1956–5 July 1968; L. Nelson Bell, 19 July–13 September 1968; Harold Lindsell, 27 September 1968–24 March 1978; Kenneth Kantzer, 7 April 1978–22 October 1982; V. Gilbert Beers, 12 November 1982–5 April 1985; Harold Myra, 19 April 1985–7 February 1986; Terry C. Muck and George K. Brushaber, 21 February 1986–22 July 1991; George K. Brushaber, 19 August 1991–present.

CIRCULATION: In 1987, 185,000.; in 1998, 187,555.

Kenneth W. Shipps

Part Three

CATHOLIC AND EPISCOPAL JOURNALS

Among the institutions that hold society together, religion is one of the most powerful. In the midst of social change, theological and religious conservatives attempt to maintain an orthodoxy. Catholicism, its church the nation's largest religious denomination since the middle of the nineteenth century and at the close of the twentieth able to claim a quarter of the population, has long been an important basis for conservatism in America. It possesses an especially rich history of attempting to validate the relevance of traditional values, though in an influential essay for the Jesuit journal *Thought* ("American Catholics and the Intellectual Life," Autumn 1955), Monsignor John Tracy Ellis could with reason claim that Catholicism had until then contributed relatively little to the life of the mind in the United States.

Throughout the nineteenth century suspicion of the "universal" Roman Catholic church was such that a significant amount of the church's energies were devoted to establishing its American credentials. Especially as immigrant numbers increased did one question grow more insistent: How could Catholics express full loyalty to both their religion and their adopted country? Traditionalists within the church contested with newer immigrants as to the appropriate model (American or European) of the church, and whether English or Latin should be the language of prayer. One of the most brilliant of nineteenth-century intellectuals, Orestes Brownson, in 1854 had argued for a full assimilationist position. Three and a half decades later, with Civil War passions subsiding and with immigrants arriving in staggering numbers—many of whom worshipped in Catholic churches and Jewish synagogues—the issue of Americanization surfaced again over the question of language and culture. Anxiety declined somewhat when the Vatican refused to support a petition from American priests calling for nationality rights and privileges for Catholics equal to those enjoyed by English-speaking churches and pastors, but the matter would not die. At the time of World War I, herculean efforts were made through fund-raising rallies, loyalty banquets, promotion of military recruitment, and Episcopal statements of patriotism to demonstrate Catholic loyalty to the American Republic. For more than a century, that had been a major goal of the Catholic hierarchy; hence, it appeared as a recurring theme in many Catholic periodicals.

The journals in Part Three represent the traditionalist school of conservatism that survives with much difficulty in the United States. It finds enduring principles in history, natural law, or religion, all affirming a higher law existing above individual whim and the fashions of a particular generation. More than other schools, it holds to an organic view of society, believing that society is not "built," as is a machine, but "grows" in biological fashion, slowly and with purpose, while providing continuity to past, present, and future generations. Organic societies comprise many groups—families, localities, professions, churches, races—each with a life of its own, yet interpenetrated by the others and integral to the whole. Individuals remain important, yet their claims must yield to those of society. The eccentric and even anti-American *Triumph* excepted, the journals that follow served to counter the intellectual poverty lamented by Catholic historian Ellis and played an important role in affirming the existence of certain absolutes that stand in opposition to the prevailing winds of liberal theological doctrine.

The preference for growth over mechanical change does not necessitate the avoidance of politics, however. Catholic responses to the pressing issues of the day range, and change (as they do with Protestant fundamentalists), from political abstention to intense involvement. Theological and cultural conservatives in *Thought* and in *Catholic Mind*, staunchly traditionalist on moral issues and suspicious of the individualistic, even atomizing, aspects of a mechanical, little-regulated market system, were keenly alive to political and economic issues. Here is a conservatism that finds its significance outside the ethos of economic commercialism and supply-side theory of the late twentieth century. Wishing to alleviate harsh economic distress, its proponents have supported workers' rights, labor unions, and social security. The *New Oxford Review*, begun as an organ of conservative Episcopalians edited by laypeople who progressively moved to an avowedly Roman Catholic point of view, has been especially notable in this regard. Whether waging war on theological liberalism or defending orthodox Christianity and a conservative moral and social order, it feared what church historians termed (for an earlier era) "the Babbittonian captivity of the church." It remained deeply skeptical of Reaganomics and capitalist pieties in general. Its editor has defended a version of Christian socialism as a bulwark against the disruptive innovations so characteristic of a barely checked profit system. In his estimation, the defense of traditional family life and the pursuit of social justice demanded that religious conservatives become innovative in public policy. More than a century earlier, the *New York Review*, edited by Episcopal minister Caleb Sprague Henry, had also criticized unchecked democracy, democratic individualism, and excessive appetites for material possessions, all of which were to flourish during the development of a new industrial order.

It was after World War II that the greatest change came to American Catholics.

To the bitter disappointment of contributors to *Triumph*, who feared the foundations of their world had given way, the reforms brought by Pope John XXIII and the Second Vatican Council (1962–1965) with respect to religious liberty and church policy on the liturgy and on ecumenism dealt Catholic separateness a decisive blow.   In the turbulence that followed, nothing in belief or practice was left untouched.   As reforms took hold, discipline was relaxed: priests assumed leadership roles in the movement against the war in Vietnam, bishops faced criticism from priests over public policy, and the laity in increasing numbers ignored church teachings on such matters as birth control and abortion. The twentieth century had opened with many Americans anxious over the growing number of Catholics in the nation's cities and with conservative Catholics suspicious that American values would undermine the religious faith of the laity.   It ended with Catholics fully acculturated, in general holding the same values as did their Protestant counterparts.

Catholic Mind
1903–1982

When *Catholic Mind* began publication in 1903, it set as its "humble task" the presentation of the "living Catholic mind." Working for nearly the next eighty years with the aid of the America Press, the journal's Jesuit editors accomplished this by collecting and printing the best in Catholic thought from newspapers and periodicals around the world. They also included all of the major pastoral letters of Catholic bishops and the encyclicals of all the popes from Leo XIII to John Paul II.[1] In the process, the scope and complexity of the living Catholic mind clearly emerged. Catholic men and women, clergy and laity alike, were shown in their attempts to retain the traditions of their faith and to apply them to the difficult problems of the twentieth century. By so doing, they created the vision of a new civilization where men and nations would respect the dignity of the individual, the sacredness of life, and the basic brotherhood of all. On the basis of this vision, contributors to *Catholic Mind* advocated traditional conservative religious and moral beliefs, while at the same time calling for the most liberal social and political reforms.

In its opening decades, *Catholic Mind* faced a world that was intellectually hostile to the church. Many intellectuals considered the Catholic religion the expression of a more superstitious age, now superseded by the wisdom and methods of science. When the "great cataclysm" of World War I occurred, they hoped that Catholicism would go the way of other autocratic governments.[2] Critics also charged that the church's beliefs were as outdated as its government. Man was the product of evolution, and his humanity rested in his brain, not in some ghostly object Catholics had long called the soul. Law and morality rested in custom, and not in man's nature, as Catholics had taught for centuries. Nature itself was not the preordained creation of God but the chance result of material evolution. Life everywhere was competitive. Just as animals were set against animals, so men were set against each other for their very survival. But while competition was cruel, it opened the way for human progress. Man in the twentieth century was advanced precisely because he had rejected much of the past, including the Catholic church.

Contributors to *Catholic Mind* could not accept such views. They could not see the progress of the twentieth century as a rebellion against all which preceded it. They denied that the Catholic church was the last surviving autocracy, or any autocracy at all. Autocratic power was "self derived," while the power of the church was derived from Jesus, "her Divine founder."[3] Catholics explained that the authority of the church rested on Jesus's statement, "Thou art Peter and on this rock I will build my church." Peter was the first apostle to understand that Jesus was both the Messiah and the son of God, and all the papal successors of Peter have stood witness to the enduring Catholic belief in the incarnation, from which the traditions and the authority of the church are derived. Authors in *Catholic Mind* also denied that the church was antidemocratic. From the beginning of its history, Catholicism had opened its doors to all peoples and nations on an equal footing. As the Roman empire crumbled, only the Catholic church survived, to form the heart of Western civilization. It slowly molded the many barbarian tribes into the nations of Europe and united them in their common Christendom. In the process, the church gave much to the world, including law, government, education, science, philosophy, theology, agriculture, drama, literature, music, and architecture.[4] Protestants might look back with longing to the biblical patriarchs and rationalists might mourn the passing of the ancient republics, but modern civilization rested on the work of the Catholic church.

Contributors to *Catholic Mind* saw the present as the outgrowth of the past, but they did not accept the present uncritically. While they believed that many of the best qualities of modern times could be attributed to Catholicism, they also attributed the worst evils to the rebellion against the church. First uncontrolled capitalism, then excessive nationalism, and finally atheistic communism had upset the delicate balance between the individual and society, which the church had long struggled to achieve. Catholics believed individuals and the wider society were so closely bound to one another that they could hardly be separated. Each individual came into the world with certain God-given qualities that must be developed for the good of both the individual and society. Individuals could not exist without society, and society could not exist without individuals. The unity of all men and women was so fundamental that it would continue after death when all will be one with Christ in the perfection of his mystical body. With these traditional beliefs in mind, contributors to *Catholic Mind* offered a new vision of human society balanced between the extremes of "restrictive capitalism" and "compulsory collectivism." In restrictive capitalism, a few men owned most of the wealth, while in compulsory collectivism, the state forced communal ownership of the means of production and exchange. Both were equally unjust. Catholic authors advocated "distributive ownership" in which the best aspects of both systems would be combined. Individuals in agrarian communities would be allowed to own land, and individuals in industrial communities would be allowed to organize, strike, participate in management, and own stock.[5]

Catholics did more than simply advocate a new social theory. They applied this theory, at once traditional and modern, to various problems in the early twentieth century. On the most general level, it led them to reject the pervasive belief in Social Darwinism. The theory of evolution might well be true and the church did not fear it, for the truth of science and the truth of religion could never conflict. But the theory of Social Darwinism was condemned as a foul and despicable doctrine that set man against man. In the face of such intellectually enshrined competitiveness, Catholic spokesmen vowed to protect the unprotected, especially workingmen and workingwomen. As Father J. C. Harrington explained in 1926, "The Church today, as in all ages past is on the side of the under dog, on the side of oppressed labor."[6] Contributors to *Catholic Mind* called for the right to organize and strike, workmen's compensation, unemployment insurance, social security, labor participation in management, cooperative stores, better housing, the abolition of child labor, and equal pay for men and women.[7] When the Great Depression struck, Catholic authors pointed to the greedy and immoral practices of big business as the culprit. They generally supported the New Deal in its attempts to transform business from "an activity regulated by a technical observance of the law to an activity guided by the demands of practical morality."[8] In international politics before World War II, contributors to *Catholic Mind* favored the League of Nations and all efforts toward mutual disarmament. Despite the defects of the league and the many prewar peace conferences, international cooperation was always preferable to war, they said.

In their attempts to analyze and solve twentieth-century problems, Catholics thus developed a philosophy of history that served well as World War II approached. The church in its early days had stood firm against the hordes of barbarians in order to protect civilization. In more recent times, Catholicism withstood the equally barbaric tides of unchecked capitalism, communism, atheism, Social Darwinism, and racism. As fascism unleashed itself in the very heart of Europe, the church promised not to give up its two-thousand-year-old tradition. To the church, there were no superior or inferior races. All men and nations were equal in the eyes of God. In Christ, there was no Jew and no Gentile. Beginning in the early 1930s, *Catholic Mind* warned that Hitler was out to destroy this tradition and civilization itself. The journal published all pastoral letters of the German bishops, all sermons of German clergymen denouncing nazism, as well as Pius XI's dramatic 1937 encyclical *Mit brennender Sorge*, urging the German people to guard their children and remain faithful to Christ in the face of persecution.[9] German authors told of priests and nuns exiled, schools closed, and clergymen silenced by the Gestapo. According to the many European and American contributors to *Catholic Mind*, the situation was nothing less than desperate. The newly elected pope, Pius XII, understood the situation well when in 1939 he urged Catholics to cling to their faith as the world passed into the "hour of darkness."[10]

Although most contributors to *Catholic Mind* considered America's entrance into the war both necessary and inevitable, they generally hoped that once the war was over, a new civilization could be built on Christian principles. The internationally renowned scholar Christopher Dawson best described this hope in a series of articles published immediately after the war. Dawson fully grasped what Catholics from around the world had been saying for most of the twentieth century. He traced the disintegration of organic Christian civilization to the Protestant Reformation. At that time, man as a believer became totally disengaged from the world at large. Christianity was no longer the center of civilization and was eventually little more than a Sunday morning duty. This splintering of man's oneness with his God and his civilization was intensified by the atomistic individualism of nineteenth-century utilitarianism. Since then, all important cultural matters have been decided by a mere counting of heads. Dawson feared that the disintegration of civilization would be made even worse by the two new extremes of technology and Barthian theology. Only an understanding of the roots, development, and future of Christianity could solve this. By creating an educational system with spiritual principles at its center, an organic Christian civilization could be reconstructed. A true Christian culture where human life was sacred and where men worked together for the common good could rebuild the world nearly destroyed by Hitler.[11]

Despite their hope for the reconstruction of civilization through education—a hope shared by many secular, cultural conservatives—it soon became obvious that this was not to be in the postwar world. The ideal of a renewed Christian culture went down in the face of the cold war conflict between the United States and the Soviet Union. Interestingly enough, although no other group objected more strongly to the atheistic communism of Russia than did many contributors to *Catholic Mind*, they consistently refused to be part of the New Right. Throughout the darkest days of the cold war, authors reminded readers that the "Left" was an honored term in the American labor movement. Any Catholic who considered himself an "Ultra-Conservative" was ignorant of church doctrine in the twentieth century. Any Catholic who came to the defense of uncontrolled capitalism or the "economic dictatorship" of big business was openly criticized.[12] Thus, during the conservative tide of the late 1940s and 1950s, writers in *Catholic Mind* continued to call for liberal social and political reforms, including full civil rights for black Americans, national health insurance, and increased foreign aid. As they had done throughout the journal's history, they did so now on the grounds that these reforms were the true expression of traditional Catholic beliefs.

While it was one thing to stand within the bulwark of Catholicism and call for change in the world according to traditional principles, it might well be quite another matter when the church itself decided to change. Early in the 1960s, Pope John XXIII declared that the church stood in an improper relation to the modern world. In the fortress it had built around itself since the Reformation, the church looked down on contemporary problems, calling for changes here and changes there. But now it was time for the church to open its doors to the modern world and change as well. Authors published in *Catholic Mind* took the reforms of the Second Vatican Council in stride. As lay author Gerard E. Sherry explained in 1961, Catholics must not be afraid of the new vitality in the church for "the divine truths which we espouse, and which we must constantly propagate, are unchanging." The true issue at hand was how to bring the gospel to life for modern men and women.[13] According to the many contributors to *Catholic Mind*, the Second Vatican Council represented exactly what they had strived for throughout the twentieth century. Eternal truth must be discovered in and applied to each successive age, and it could be employed to justify social and political reform. In the same spirit, most contributors favored the changes instituted by the Second Vatican Council, including the vernacular mass, greater participation of laity, and increased cooperation between Catholics and non-Catholics.

While the traditions of Catholicism led to the call for liberal reforms in the world and the church, this cannot be said of moral issues. For nearly eighty years, clerical and lay contributors to *Catholic Mind* argued against divorce, artificial birth control, sterilization, abortion, and artificial insemination. For Catholics, man and God were so intimately bound together that human life was itself sacred. Each life came from God, and each life returned to God. Existence was always better than nonexistence. Authors published in *Catholic Mind* claimed that bringing children into the world, educating them, and allowing them to participate in the sacramental life of the church was an unchanging part of the Catholic tradition. As Jesuit Father John Danihy wrote in 1920, "The right of the child to life, forever disposes of the parents' right to destroy that life." During the 1930s and 1940s, Catholics connected this stand with their opposition to Hitler. If Hitler's policies were followed throughout the world, "marriage would not differ from cattle breeding." To the Catholic church, there was no greater treasure than the life of children. This respect for life reached its fullest expression in Pope Paul VI's 1968 encyclical *Humanae Vitae*.[14] From the standpoint of sixty-five years of *Catholic Mind*, it was the logical outcome of the church's long defense of the child's right to life. According to *Catholic Mind*, no one needed more protection in this brutal century than children.

Despite their conservative stand on moral issues, contributors to *Catholic Mind* supported various liberal social and political reforms during the 1970s. At heart, the need for reform rested on the need for a greater respect for human life. In the United States, disrespect for life was most obvious in the legalization of abortion. It was also apparent in the continued mistreatment of blacks, Indians, and Mexican-Americans. It was present in the escalating arms race and the unending war in Vietnam. By the early 1970s, the American Catholic hierarchy openly opposed the war in Southeast Asia. At this time, *Catholic Mind* published all pastoral letters dealing with the church's opposition to the war. As the American bishops stated in 1971, "Whatever good we hope to achieve through continued involvement in this war is now outweighed by the destruction of human life and of moral values which it inflicts."[15] In subsequent pastoral letters, American bishops called for racial and economic justice, full employment for men and women, decent working and housing conditions, as well as education and health care for all. Government must be responsible for the welfare of its citizens, and business must share its profits with the workers who helped create them. In international affairs, developed nations were told to share their wealth with the Third World. They were also urged to "promote genuine development in poor societies, not mere consumerism and materialism."[16]

Although *Catholic Mind* ceased publication in 1982 because of rising costs and declining circulation, the journal's final editor, Father Joseph O'Hare, believed that other Catholic periodicals would now carry on the work of *Catholic Mind*.[17] The work was worth carrying on, for the church still had much to offer the world. Father Pedro Aruppe, superior general of the Society of Jesus, stated in the late 1970s that the church pointed the way to both "the world's transformation and man's liberation." Unlike the many modern pessimists who turned away from all human effort and responsibility, the Christian was the first to seek "a world more just and more human." In the face of hardship, oppression, and even death, the Christian "never gives up hope."[18] But unlike secular reformers who also seek a better world and a better man, the Christian knows that both can come only through the grace of God. The best thing that the Christian can do is to possess this grace and live as a witness to it. Even in a supposedly post-Christian age, men are still seeking such grace in which to anchor their lives and their hopes. In the words of Pope John Paul II, "Man is the being who seeks God."[19] For nearly eighty years, *Catholic Mind* stood as a testament to this belief.

Notes

1. "The Fortieth Anniversary," *The Catholic Mind* 41 (January 1943): 1–2 (hereinafter cited as *CM*).

2. John P. Carroll, "World Democracy and the Church," *CM* 17 (8 May 1919): 193.

3. Ibid., pp. 193–95.

4. Ernest R. Hull, "The Church and Civilization," *CM* 14 (22 January 1916): 25.

5. Joseph Husslein, "Three Social Systems," *CM* 25 (15 June 1927): 221, 237.

6. J. C. Harrington, "The Church and Labor," *CM* 24 (22 June 1926): 228–29.

7. Carroll, "World Democracy and the Church," p. 202.

8. Wilfrid Parsons, "What Caused the Depression?" *CM* 30 (8 April 1932): 165–68; Johannes Mattern, "Thoughts on the New Deal," *CM* 32 (8 October 1934): 374.

9. "Pastoral of the German Bishops, January 3, 1937," *CM* 35 (8 February 1937): 57–59; Pius XI, "*Mit brennender Sorge*," *CM* 35 (8 May 1937): 185–204.

10. Pius XII, "*Summi Pontificatus*," *CM* 37 (8 November 1939): 915.

11. Christopher Dawson, "Education and the Crisis of Christian Culture," *CM* 45 (May 1947): 266–77.

12. John C. Cort, "The Left and the Right," *CM* 45 (January 1947): 19–21; Ralph Gorman, "The Ultra-Conservative Catholic," *CM* 53 (September 1955): 654–55; Carl P. Hensler, "Does the Catholic Church Approve the American Economic System?" *CM* 46 (May 1948): 304–13.

13. Gerard E. Sherry, "Liberal and Conservative: Two Approaches to Reality," *CM* 59 (January–February 1961): 14–17.

14. John Danihy, "Birth Control and the Natural Law," *CM* 18 (8 June 1920): 221; Peter Aruppe, "Eugenics: The Suicide of a Nordic Race," *CM* 36 (22 June 1938): 235; Paul VI, "*Humanae Vitae*," *CM* 66 (September 1968): 35–47.

15. "American Bishops' Resolution on Southeast Asia," *CM* 70 (February 1972): 55.

16. National Conference of Catholic Bishops, "A Pastoral Letter on Racism," *CM* 78 (March 1980): 62–63.

17. Joseph A. O'Hare, "Editor's Note," *CM* 80 (April 1982): i.

18. Pedro Aruppe, "Is the Church Still the Bearer of Men's Hopes?" *CM* 76 (February 1978): 26–27.

19. John Paul II, "The One Who Seeks," *CM* 77 (March 1979): 44.

Information Sources

BIBLIOGRAPHY: None.

INDEXES: Each volume indexed; *CPI*; *CPLI*.

REPRINT EDITIONS: Microform: Volumes 1–50, PMC; UMI; BLH.

LOCATION SOURCES: Complete runs: Library of Congress; University of Pennsylvania; Fordham University; Michigan State University; University of Detroit; College of the Holy Cross; Cleveland Public Library.

Publication History

TITLE AND TITLE CHANGES: *The Catholic Mind*, January 1903–January–February 1957; *Catholic Mind*, March–April 1957–April 1982.

VOLUME AND ISSUE DATA: Numbers 1–1,362, volumes 1–80, January 1903–April 1982.

FREQUENCY OF PUBLICATION: Monthly.

PUBLISHER: America Press, New York.

EDITORS: No individual editors listed, 1903–1943; journal under the direction of the editors of the Catholic monthly journal *The Messenger*, 1903–1909, then under the editorship of the America Press, 1909–1943; individual editors thereafter: John LaFarge, S.J., 1944–1948; Robert C. Hartnett, 1949–1955; Thurston N. Davis, S. J., 1955–1968; Donald R. Campion, S.J., 1968–1975; Joseph A. O'Hare, S. J., 1975–1982.

CIRCULATION: In the final years, about 5,000.

Mary Stockwell

Thought
1926–1992

Late in the spring of 1926, Jesuit scholars in New York City founded *Thought*. Published under the auspices of the America Press, the journal was to offer "a liberal education at once humanistic, cosmopolitan and Christian." It would present articles by Catholic and non-Catholic authors from the United States and abroad on topics in philosophy, theology, literature, the arts, history, the social sciences, and philosophical aspects of the physical sciences. Certain they could appeal to the specialist and the general reader alike, the editors of *Thought* also "intended to supply a need of the times." By discussing "questions of permanent value and contemporaneous interest in every field of learning and culture," they hoped to preserve "the values of the past for the needs of the present."[1] Despite the many changes in the world and the Catholic church since the inception of *Thought,* the journal remained true to its original intentions.

From the beginning, the editors of *Thought* were well aware that many contemporary scholars might consider such a task hopelessly out of date. We supposedly live in a world where truth is relative, where man is the unfortunate product of mindless evolution, and where human existence is confused at best, hopeless at worst. In the face of such views, the many contributors to *Thought* have maintained a profound and unshakable belief in the dignity of man. That dignity arises out of the relation of man to his creator. Man is made in the image and likeness of God. His intellect is capable of grasping eternal truth, which does exist, for God exists. Man's life in this world and the next must be based on a proper relationship to this truth. But while truth is eternal, this does not mean that those who seek it live removed from the world. Rather they are better able to solve the many problems of modern life precisely because they understand man's true nature and destiny. While the Catholic intellectual remains faithful to the truth, he likewise does his best to help others in the world. In the words of the French Thomist Jacques Maritain, the Catholic lives the "painful paradox" of "fidelity to the eternal" on the one hand and "compassion for the tribulations of our time" on the other.[2]

The first major issue scholars faced in this context was the relationship of the Catholic church to the United States. Among the charges that had long been leveled at the church was that a Catholic's loyalty to the pope superseded his loyalty to the Constitution. Similarly, it was alleged that the Catholic belief in unchanging truths stood in the way of progress, and since America and progress were synonymous, Catholics were "un-American." Meeting these charges, scholars writing in *Thought* from the inception of the journal well through the 1950s insisted that Catholicism favors both progress and the United States. In the first article published in *Thought*, Peter Guilday of the Catholic University of America affirmed that "as the one permanent institution in civilization, the Catholic Church can never be considered as a thing apart and passive in the history of modern progress." It was Catholics who first brought freedom of religion to America in the colony of Maryland. It was Catholics who in modern times advocated the rights of the workingman in the rising labor movement. According to Guilday and many other scholars in *Thought*, "there is nowhere visible on the horizon of the past any institution which has so steadfastly and so eminently advanced the best interests of the country as the Catholic Church."[3]

In further defense of their religion and their patriotism, authors argued that Catholic thought could be of great service to the United States. More specifically, Thomism could act as the best philosophical foundation for the American political system. Although most authors admitted that Thomas was a man of his time and so did not believe in democracy, they nevertheless asserted that his understanding of the relationship between the individual and society was still valuable. According to Thomas, man is a political animal, naturally gregarious, and naturally invested with individual rights, which society must protect. In contrast to this balanced view, America now found itself caught between two political extremes. On the one hand, individualism had been so glorified that countless people suffered in the name of free enterprise, but on the other, and in reaction to the excesses of capitalism run wild, communism offered a collectivism in which the individual was to be sacrificed for the welfare of the people. To remedy this situation of "individual absolutism" battling it out for supremacy with "state absolutism," Catholicism proposed a political philosophy in which the rights of the individual and the society were balanced for the good of both. It was hoped that Americans would choose a society based on "the intrinsic equality of men cooperating under a government that operates in the service of the common good of its citizens."[4]

As America stumbled through the Great Depression and fascism marched across Europe, scholars writing in *Thought* claimed that the world was in trouble precisely because it had turned away from such a humane and balanced philosophy. Since the Protestant rebellion against Catholicism, Western man had lost faith in God and in himself. Luther and Calvin had preached that man was hopelessly depraved, that mankind and society were past saving, and that only a few elect would ever be rescued. In contrast to traditional Catholic thought, such Protestant philosophers as Thomas Hobbes reasoned that it was not natural for man to live in society, and that he had joined with his fellows only to protect himself and his property from the cruelty and viciousness of some original state of nature. Man was nothing but an animal driven by brutal instincts who must be controlled by equally brutal social pressures; society, instead of being natural, was an unnatural compromise of the last resort. Modern thinkers such as Hegel, Darwin, and James had completed this self-destructive picture by describing man as a collection of historical, material, and psychological forces. In such an atmosphere, democracy itself had been reduced to the lowest and most brutal passions of mass opinion. As Jesuit Father Moorhouse F. X. Millar explained in a 1942 essay, the troubles of the modern world were but "the product of the antecedent Protestant vilification of human nature and of the consequent Pragmatic assumption of the essential irrationality of man." For the authors in *Thought,* the line from Luther to Hitler was clear.[5]

Just as the war in Europe broke out in 1939, the Jesuit editors of *Thought* decided that their journal—as a "vehicle of learning and culture"—called for a university setting, and in March 1940, the ownership, editorship, and administration of *Thought* was transferred to Fordham University.[6] But while *Thought* had now found a better atmosphere in which to publish scholarly articles on art and literature, the times seemed to demand an extraordinary response. Under the editorship of Father Gerald Walsh, *Thought* began each issue during the 1940s with a series of editorials. More important, for the first and only time in its history, *Thought* openly supported a contemporary political figure. In the opinion of *Thought*'s editors, Franklin D. Roosevelt practiced the political philosophy they had long advocated. In the chaos of a depression caused by uncontrolled capitalism, Roosevelt had stepped in knowing "something had to be done to save the country." Facing problems on a day-to-day basis, he did whatever seemed necessary to help both individuals and the wider society. As fascism threatened, he prepared for war but hoped a new world was coming into being, a world where men recognized their unity as children of the same divine father. According to the editors of *Thought*, Roosevelt rightly understood that the individual could not be trampled on in the name of profit and that nations must join together for the good of all.[7]

Throughout the war years, the contributors to *Thought* were optimistic that America and the rest of the world were on the road to a more just and humane society. They hoped that Western man had come to see just where his supposedly "modern" philosophy had taken him. If there is no truth, no God, and no perfection toward which we are tending, then what does it matter if a man like Hitler rules the world? As Henry Bamford Parkes of New York University wrote, "Why should one fight Nazism if it is merely an inevitable expression of social forces? And why should one sacrifice oneself for an ideal if good and evil are meaningless words?"[8] If evil must be stopped, then good must truly exist, and we must build a new society with that good in mind for all. Even as the harsh reality of the cold war set in, the contributors to *Thought* refused to give up hope. They refused to join with those who blamed all our woes on the New Deal and all foreign woes on Yalta. They considered this seeking after villains in the past simply a "neurosis of the post-war age." With the future yet to be won, it was "absurd" to be preoccupied with "the relatively few shameful moments" of our past.[9]

With this acceptance of the past and faith in the future, *Thought* faced postwar America. Its authors believed that Catholics had at last proved themselves as Americans and as modern men who squarely faced the problems of the world today. As contributors looked back over the previous decades, they saw much progress. They agreed that tensions between Protestants and Catholics had lessened. Catholics realized that Protestants did not want to be converted, and Protestants realized that Catholics did not want to give up their religious identity in order to be certified as true Americans.[10]

Despite such obvious progress, contributors to *Thought* during the 1950s were no less willing to defend the Catholic faith. This is especially apparent in the many articles written on education during the decade. Whereas Catholics believed they had somehow proved their Americanism in World War II, they now felt it necessary to defend their educational system against its many "progressive" critics. Authors argued that the progressive approach to education was really a new secular religion.[11] According to several contributors, the constitutional separation between Church and State was being subverted in the name of secularism. Instead of all schools receiving aid from the state, only those schools avowing progressive secularism would be given help. No other issue more stirred the authors in *Thought* during the late 1950s and early 1960s than the need to win federal aid for Catholic schools. No other action came as more of a shock than the refusal of the Kennedy administration to countenance giving public aid to parochial schools. Yet even with this shock, contributors to *Thought* never blamed the president. They blamed Secretary of Health, Education and Welfare Abraham Ribicoff instead.

Despite their concern for aid to education as well as such other pressing social issues as civil rights, the authors in *Thought* became less interested in political problems as the 1960s progressed. Developments within the Catholic church were of far greater interest to them. The new openness brought about by the Second Vatican Council in the mid-1960s is quite apparent in the pages of *Thought*. There is a greater willingness to listen to positions not specifically Catholic, and not to present them merely to dismantle them in the face of the sounder Catholic approach. This is not to say that the authors of *Thought* renounced any belief in the truth or in man's ability to discover and explain it. But now they are a bit quieter about their own beliefs. They seem suddenly overcome with the awareness that truth can present itself anywhere and not simply in the Catholic tradition. They go out searching for the truth about human life with the understanding that it does not necessarily have to be expressed with reference to Thomistic philosophy. In fact, it is nothing less than revolutionary how quickly scholasticism disappears from the church in general and the pages of *Thought* in particular. In the winter 1967 issue, the great Thomistic scholar Anton Pegis complained that no one read Aquinas anymore. He blamed the loss on scholars who had tried to make a modern philosopher out of a medieval theologian, using him as a sword to fight modern battles that contemporary scholars were too unwilling or too uncreative to fight for themselves. But for Pegis, all was not lost. He hoped that in the new atmosphere where dialogue had replaced disputation, we would listen to Thomas and not simply use him.[12]

If scholars were no longer willing to listen to Thomas, they seemed to listen to everyone else with obvious eagerness. Before the Second Vatican Council, phenomenologists and existentialists had generally been dismissed as too subjective. Their approach to philosophy could never go beyond private experience. The search for the ground of being or existence led only to Heidegger's Being or Sartre's existence.[13] But now contemporary thinkers were respected for their attempts to explain our often anguished experience in this most difficult of centuries. Authors with pessimistic outlooks such as Albert Camus and Tennessee Williams were studied precisely because they expressed the misery in contemporary life so well. Even Luther—once vilified as the precursor of Hitler—was now seen as a true seeker, a catalyst who set off much needed reform in the Catholic church. Contemporary Protestant thinkers such as Barth, Niebuhr, and Tillich were also examined. But despite this new openness, the secularism of the more radical Protestant theologians was not accepted wholeheartedly. From the Catholic viewpoint as expressed in *Thought*, the current angst in American Protestant theology seemed strangely behind the times. Catholic intellectuals had left the horrors of World War II behind, but Protestant thinkers remained trapped in the world of Bonhoeffer's death camps. To Catholics, the "death of God" theologians embraced a world that no longer existed.[14]

Far more exciting developments were under way in Catholic theology, and during its final decades, *Thought* followed every major trend in Catholic religious writing at home and abroad. The broad and basic tenets of Catholic theology that had long seemed beyond debate or discussion were all subjected to review. Nothing seemed certain; everything remained to be discovered. Many articles were published on the French paleontologist Pierre Teilhard de Chardin, who seemed to express the same optimism and faith in man that *Thought*'s contributors had long claimed was the heart of Catholicism. Scholars also followed developments in biblical and ecumenical studies. They described the new understanding of the Genesis account of creation and studied in depth the Zen path to enlightenment.[15] Despite the changes in the church in the 1960s and 1970s, however, the editors and authors of *Thought* retained their faith in the existence of God and in man's ability to discover him, even though we may not know him or ourselves quite as well as we once thought we did.

If much changed in the pages of *Thought*, much remained the same. Although the attitude became one of listening and trying to understand rather than defending and trying to explain, certain basic beliefs continued. Man was still a being created in the image of a God who loves him and who has destined him for perfection. Truth might be difficult to attain, but men can gain some kind of perspective on it and live in accordance with it by moving ever closer to it. It is this unchanging, basic belief in the God-given dignity of man that underlay the journal's opposition to segregation in the early 1960s, its support of the papal encyclical *Humanae Vitae* in the late 1960s, and its call for greater understanding of the theology of the Third World in the 1970s.[16] In the opening decades of *Thought,* authors had argued that we are more than a haphazard collection of physical and psychological drives. Later, they argued that we are more than the color of our skin, more than our sexuality, more than our economic status. While the language of Thomas disappeared, the spirit remained. We are still seekers after truth, though we must go looking for it in places we never looked before. We live in the faith that ultimately we will find it for this is the true end of human existence. According to the authors of *Thought,* this is the permanent quest we are on through all the vicissitudes of time and history.

Notes

1. Joseph E. O'Neill, "The Fortieth Anniversary of *Thought*," *Thought* 41 (Spring 1966): 5.

2. Jacques Maritain, "Catholic Thought and Its Mission," *Thought* 4 (March 1930): 547.

3. Peter Guilday, "The Catholic Church in the United States: A Sesquicentennial Essay," *Thought* 1 (June 1926): 4, 19–20.

4. Helen M. McCadden, "Bewildered America," *Thought* 6 (March 1932): 548.

5. Moorhouse F. X. Millar, "The Dehumanization of Man," *Thought* 17 (March 1942): 68.

6. O'Neill, "Fortieth Anniversary of Thought," p. 5.

7. Francis X. Talbot, "Roosevelt and Revolution," *Thought* 14 (September 1939): 351–52; Wilfrid Parsons, "The Pope, the President and Peace," *Thought* 15 (March 1940): 5–8.

8. H. B. Parkes, "Origins and Background of the War," *Thought* 8 (Spring 1943): 397.

9. "Editorial," *Thought* 26 (Spring 1951): 6.

10. Gustave Weigel, "Catholic and Protestant: End of a War?" *Thought* 33 (Autumn 1958): 382–97.

11. Charles Donahue, "Freedom and Education, the Sacral Problem," *Thought* 28 (Summer 1953): 219.

12. Anton Pegis, "Who Reads Aquinas?" *Thought* 42 (Winter 1967): 488–504.

13. Quentin Lauer, "Four Phenomenologists," *Thought* 33 (Summer 1958): 204.

14. E. L. Mascall, "Reflections on the 'Honest to God' Debate," *Thought* 41 (Summer 1966): 196–97.

15. Christopher F. Mooney, "Teilhard de Chardin and Christian Spirituality," *Thought* 42 (Autumn 1967): 383–402; Donald P. Gray, "Teilhard de Chardin's Vision of Love," *Thought* 42 (Winter 1967): 519–42; Donald F. X. Connolly, "Genesis 1," *Thought* 37 (Summer 1962): 211–25; James Albertson, "Genesis 1 and the Babylonian Creation Myth," *Thought* 37 (Summer 1962): 226–44; William Johnston, "The Zen Enlightenment," *Thought* 42 (Winter 1967): 165–84.

16. Robert W. Gleason, "The Immorality of Segregation," *Thought* 35 (Autumn 1960): 349–64; Joseph V. Dolan, "*Humanae Vitae* and Nature," *Thought* 44 (Autumn 1969): 358–76; Julius Hejja, "A Theology of Liberation," *Thought* 48 (Winter 1973): 474–77.

Information Sources

BIBLIOGRAPHY: None.

INDEXES: *Amer Hist & Life; AHCI; Bio Ind; BRI; CPI; CPLI; Comb Ret Ind Bk Revs Hum; Curr Bk Rev Cit; Curr Cont: A & H; Hist Abst; Hum Ind; Ind Bk Revs Hum; MLA Abst; MLA Amer Bib; MLA Intl Bib; NTA; OTA; PAIS; SSHI; URS; Writings Amer Hist.*

REPRINT EDITIONS: Microform: DA; UMI.

LOCATION SOURCES: Complete runs: Fordham University; Andover-Harvard Theological Library; Princeton Theological Seminary.

Publication History

TITLE AND TITLE CHANGES: *Thought: A Review of Culture and Ideas.*
VOLUME AND ISSUE DATA: Volumes 1–67, June 1926–December 1992.
FREQUENCY OF PUBLICATION: Quarterly.
PUBLISHERS: 1926–1940: America Press; 1940–1992: Fordham University Press.
EDITORS: Wilfrid Parsons, S.J., 1926–1936; Francis Talbot, S.J., 1936–1939; Gerald G.
    Walsh, S.J., 1940–1950; William F. Lynch, S.J., 1950–1956; Joseph E. O'Neill,
    S.J., 1956–1976; Joseph E. Grennen, 1976–1978; G. Richard Dimmler, S.J., 1978–
    1992.
CIRCULATION: About 2,000.

Mary Stockwell

Triumph
1966–1976

L. Brent Bozell founded *Triumph* in 1966 as a magazine for American Catholic conservatives. In the late 1960s it claimed nearly 30,000 subscribers, but its circulation dwindled rapidly after 1973 when the editors, believing they were forced to choose between loyalty to the Catholic church and loyalty to the American nation over the question of abortion, chose the church and made a virtual declaration of war against America. From beginning to end *Triumph* was beset by an awkward dilemma: it saw its role as the preservation of traditional Catholicism just when the church was transforming itself. The editors and contributors were temperamentally and intellectually disposed in favor of the familiar customs of Catholic life; they idealized Catholic Spain. Their obedience to Rome, however, obliged them to defend many of the reforms of their church in the years following the Second Vatican Council (Vatican II, 1962–1965), about which they had personal misgivings. They disliked some Catholic intellectuals' willingness to criticize the church, and they feared that the "openness" promoted in the spirit of Vatican II was really, as one of them said, "a spiritual loss of nerve, a religious exhaustion, which reaches into the souls of men who accept with enthusiasm every criticism leveled against their faith by its ancient enemies."[1]

Bozell came from Omaha, Nebraska, but served in the merchant marine during World War II. As a Yale undergraduate at the end of the 1940s, he was a political liberal and world federalist. A gifted public speaker, he and William F. Buckley, Jr., led a successful Yale debating team; soon after graduating, Bozell married Buckley's sister, Patricia. He also converted to Catholicism and adopted increasingly conservative political views, to buttress his anticommunism. He and his brother-in-law co-authored *McCarthy and His Enemies* (1954), in defense of the Wisconsin senator, and Bozell went on to become McCarthy's chief speechwriter. He also ghost-wrote Barry Goldwater's best-seller *The Conscience of a Conservative* (1960), contributing to the Goldwater presidential candidacy of 1964. Bozell's only personal bid for political office was unsuccessful; he ran in 1964 against an incumbent congressional Republican, Charles Mathias, in Montgomery County, Maryland, and baffled suburban voters with references to the gnostic heresy, and the arcana of Spanish legitimism.[2]

Bozell was a member of the editorial board of *National Review* from its inception in 1955. He belonged to the most ardently anticommunist faction among the editors and opposed Buckley's decision, in 1961, to criticize the John Birch Society's conspiratorial vision of world history. Many of the staff of *National Review* were Catholics, but they showed what Bozell considered insufficient respect for Pope John XXIII's encyclical letters on economics and world peace, *Mater et Magistra* (1961) and *Pacem in Terris* (1963). These differences prompted Bozell's resignation from the editorial board in 1963. In the following years he wrote *The Warren Revolution* (1966), which dissected the major Supreme Court decisions of the preceding twelve years. Bozell believed that Chief Justice Earl Warren had violated the Constitution, abandoned a venerable tradition of judicial restraint, and ushered in a social revolution whose price was contempt for the rule of law.[3]

Bozell was dissatisfied with the direction of American intellectual conservatism in the mid-1960s. For example, growing concern about overpopulation led Buckley, Garry Wills, and other conservatives at *National Review* to discuss the possibility of reforms in the American abortion laws. Bozell was dismayed at their apparent neglect of the Catholic teaching against abortion, and he wrote angry protests to his former colleagues. Shortly thereafter, he assembled the first issue of *Triumph* and began publication of this new lay Catholic monthly in September 1966. With Bozell on the editorial board sat Michael Lawrence (whom he had met during the 1964 congressional campaign), Frederick Wilhelmsen, and, for a time, Jeffrey Hart and John Wisner. They, and most of the other contributors to *Triumph*, were *National Review* writers, and many of this staff continued to write for both journals. Among them were Russell Kirk and Gary Potter (both Catholic converts), Charles Rice, Thomas Molnar, and John Lukacs. At first, *National Review* praised *Triumph* as a fine manifestation of the "church militant" at a time when much American religion had been debased by the worship of false idols. Later, the strident activism of *Triumph*'s editors led to an estrangement between the two journals.[4]

Triumph's Catholic conservatism always took priority over its political conservatism, and it took the truth of the Catholic faith as axiomatic. Spurning religious or cultural relativism, *Triumph* writers insisted that their church had preserved a unique deposit of faith through the ages and that it was incumbent upon them to bring this truth to the people among whom they lived. As they rose to the defense of Catholicism as uniquely true, however, the church itself deemphasized this teaching; the religious liberty declaration of Vatican II, *Dignitatis Humanae*, ended the era in which Rome said, "Error has no rights." Many American Catholics welcomed religious pluralism, but *Triumph* lamented it. Bozell argued that the refusal to seek the conversion of American Jews to Catholicism was a form of contempt rather than respect, a new variety of anti-Semitism: "By abandoning their most valuable possession...Christians would deny to Jews the fulfillment of the promises made to Israel and awaited anxiously throughout the centuries."[5]

Other Catholic reforms also distressed *Triumph*. It carried elegies to the Latin mass, now displaced by Vatican II's turn to the vernacular. Latin was the lingua franca of Christendom, said *Triumph*, and to abandon Latin was to abandon, symbolically, the unity of the Christian West. Above all, writers in the journal disliked the eagerness of some American Catholic priests to embroil themselves in the political and social disputes of the moment. As one of them wrote, "In secular matters the Church is, and can be, no more than a shamefaced neophyte, like an immigrant, no longer able to speak its own tongue, Latin: and unable to speak English without exciting the derision of the natives." Whenever the Vatican spoke definitively, *Triumph* submitted. So long as debate over ecclesiastical and liturgical reforms was permitted, however, it spoke out against intemperate change. Disliking the new missal when it was published in 1969, *Triumph* reserved the right to criticize until it was formally installed. One writer declared, "The Pope has not commanded Catholics to fall silent about their misgivings. Therefore, Catholics should not suspend their critical faculties. At least until Advent 1971 or until there is some relief from the present agony, the faithful are free and obliged to submit their own judgments to the Holy Father in a respectful manner." Their complaints were unable to forestall a succession of new teachings in the late 1960s and early 1970s.[6]

The founders of *Triumph* hoped that the church could maintain its internal integrity and serve as the foundation for a Christian politics. More enamoured of Franco's Spain than of Richard Nixon's America, they admired Franco's preservation of the Catholic church and his zealous anticommunism. Bozell and his family lived in Spain in the early 1960s, and between 1960 and 1967 Frederick Wilhelmsen worked as a professor of philosophy at the University of Navarre in Pamplona. Each summer, *Triumph* and its Society for a Christian Commonwealth held Castilian summer schools in the shadow of the Escorial. Wilhelmsen argued that of all the Western nations, Spain held a unique place because "there is only one nation in history that has bested at arms both Islam and Marxism and that nation is Spain.... The crescent and the hammer and sickle: ultimately they have but one common enemy, the cross of Christ, and the civilization that took root and flourished from the wood of Golgotha." Wilhelmsen was at heart a monarchist rather than a Francoist, but he accepted Franco provisionally as the best substitute for a legitimist restoration.[7]

Wilhelmsen, a philosopher, was one of a handful of authors who gave *Triumph* an intellectual gravity, whatever the strangeness of its political nostrums. He adapted the Thomist philosophical tradition and natural law theory to such contemporary phenomena as television and made a searching critique of the epistemological basis of science. The dominant scientific mind in contemporary America, Wilhelmsen argued, commits a fallacy of misplaced concreteness by taking the abstractions of scientific language to embody knowledge of things as they are. By contrast, he asserted, "scientific truth over a thing is had in proportion to the *failure* to know the thing as it is." The scientific claim to objectivity, he said, is the entering wedge of totalitarianism; he warned historians and social scientists to turn their backs on the entire scientific project, writing: "Not only is such objectivity impossible theoretically, but it is not even an ideal to be desired if ever it were reached. The achievement of historical objectivity would destroy man's participation in existence because it would require man to empty himself of the substance of his being." In place of scientific language, Wilhelmsen looked for ways to reintroduce intelligent subjectivity, intuition, loyalty, imagination, and faith. His prolific writings on these themes, both inside and beyond the pages of *Triumph*, represented an attempt to vindicate Thomism and condemn the philosophical descendants of Descartes.[8]

An age devoted to science had, of course, spurned the seemingly irrational principles of monarchy. But to Wilhelmsen hereditary monarchy was the ideal form of government because it adapted the reality of blood loyalty to the political exigencies of society. The monarchy he envisioned, however, would be consonant with Christian principles and the natural law, whereas the absolute monarchs of early modern Europe had violated these principles. He hoped that revulsion in the face of totalitarianism and two world wars would induce mankind to abandon mechanical models of government and rationalist political science. Totalitarianism, he argued, is at war with the fundamental unit of society, the family. The totalitarian state breaks down all the natural intermediate institutions that stand between the individual and the state, until it is left with isolated individuals, who can then be manipulated according to criteria of efficiency and state power. Liberal democracy, far from offering a sure counterweight to totalitarianism, is implicated in the logic of "scientific politics" and the individualist fallacy. In voicing these themes, Wilhelmsen joined a critique of positivist thought made by Left and Right in recent years, though few social critics were so sweeping as Wilhelmsen in condemning secular rationalism *tout court*.[9]

Jeffrey Hart, another contributor to *Triumph*, converted to Catholicism in 1968, only to find that the church he had admired from without seemed to be dissolving from within. Hart, a professor of English at Dartmouth College, was also an editor of *National Review*. He argued in articles for *Triumph* that many of the great literary figures of the twentieth century, including W. B. Yeats, T. S. Eliot, Ezra Pound, Ernest Hemingway, and Evelyn Waugh, had found intellectual nourishment only in Christian values, rejecting the pieties of liberalism as inadequate. Hart denigrated authors (notably Edmund Wilson) who resisted the truths of religion and exalted those who had finally welcomed the embrace of the church, writing, "The fact that Hemingway actually became a Catholic has not been much noted by his biographers and critics [but in fact] as a writer he was deeply a part of his civilization, and the values he celebrated, themselves ancient ones, represent much that is best in the traditions of the West."[10]

Triumph did not confine itself to articles on religious, philosophical, and cultural matters, because it saw its mission as the nurturing of a conservative Christian polity. The editors had hard words for secular American conservatism. Historically, they noted, capitalism developed earliest in the non-Catholic nations of Europe and North America, and a tradition of papal encyclicals, beginning with Leo XIII's *Rerum Novarum* (1891), made strictures against the characteristics and consequences of capitalism. For most American conservatives, by contrast, the defense of capitalism was the sine qua non of the conservative faith; in *God and*

Man at Yale (1951) William Buckley had made the case for Christianity and capitalism as the twin pillars of American prosperity and freedom. Although *Triumph* distanced itself from capitalism, it had no interest in the alternative of socialism, against which there was also a century of papal opposition. Bozell later said that only the "distributism" of G. K. Chesterton came close to the economic views of *Triumph*. Its antagonism toward all prevailing economic practices contributed to the quixotic character of the journal when it addressed economic questions.[11]

On foreign policy questions, *Triumph* blended an ardent anticommunism with an almost finicky attention to methods. It supported the principle of America's war effort in Vietnam but not the practice, which appeared to violate Catholic "just war" theory. Just war theory had been developed in the Middle Ages in an attempt to mitigate the worst excesses of war between Christian nations, and it included the principle that war must be conducted between sovereign entities after formal declaration of hostilities. In Bozell's judgment, the Tonkin Gulf Resolution of 1964 did not constitute such a declaration, and the assassination of President Ngo Dinh Diem in 1963 (apparently with the sanction of the United States government) had violently removed the Catholic leader of South Vietnam. The first issue of *Triumph*, which set the tone of its reporting about Vietnam, declared: "Yes, we are patriots, but we are Christians first. We support the war, provided it is a war worthy of a Christian's sacrifice. It is not such a war if our soldiers are asked to die merely to help install a South East Asian branch of H.E.W." Removal of the Catholic Ngo family soured *Triumph* on the war, and the editors were further dismayed by rumors of American use of chemical weapons: "There can be no equivocation: the use of chemical and biological warfare is absolutely forbidden a nation that wants to consider itself limited to morally just means of warfare." Repudiating pacifism as sentimental utopianism, they nevertheless insisted that "Christians today can and should fight for the good but only with weapons and battle plans that seem pleasing to God."[12] One principle of just war theory is the proportionality doctrine—that the good realized by a war must outweigh the damage inflicted on the enemy. This principle and the noncombatant immunity principle were the basis of *Triumph*'s opposition to nuclear deterrence. Anticipating by fifteen years the American Catholic bishops' pastoral letter of the early 1980s, *Triumph* believed that the use of, and the threat to use, nuclear weapons was incompatible with the Catholic faith and should be abandoned. One contributor described America's deterrence posture, particularly its plan to make second strikes against Soviet cities, as "a Pact with Hell."[13]

During the 1950s and early 1960s, most American Catholics, conservative and liberal alike, favored a vigorous anticommunist foreign policy. Cardinal Spellman, the American primate in those years, echoed and amplified the passionate anticommunism of Pope Pius XII. Indeed, declarations of anticommunism and conspicuous nationalism were two of the ways in which American Catholics refuted the persistent imputation of *dis*loyalty that had long dogged Catholics in America. Few Catholic conservatives could find *Triumph* congenial for long when it attacked the verities of American capitalism and nuclear anticommunism.[14]

Sex was the issue to which *Triumph* devoted its greatest energy. In a 1966 statement Pope Paul VI affirmed the traditional teaching against artificial birth control. Many American Catholics had expected that this long-awaited statement would permit them to use effective contraceptives such as the anovulent pill, as a papal commission had recommended. The pope, however, argued that the natural integrity of each act of conjugal intercourse required that it be open to the transmission of life. *Triumph* was in a minority among American Catholic publications in greeting this statement enthusiastically; *America*, the *National Catholic Reporter*, and *Commonweal* described it as "a wretched piece of intransigence." *Triumph* answered: "This 'wretched piece of intransigence' is the key to the mighty mystery of sex, which unlocks the door to the even more awesome mystery of life, which in turn reveals the reality of the supernatural. If the Church does not own this key it does not own any keys at all." The trend of the sexual revolution of the 1950s and 1960s had been to treat procreation as only one of the possible uses of human sexuality; many American Catholics now favored a more expressive marital sexuality. The pope denied the validity of this development and reaffirmed the traditional teaching in the encyclical letter *Humanae Vitae* (1968), which *Triumph* applauded. In practice, many American Catholics did avail themselves of artificial contraceptives in the following years, and by 1980 were using them with the same frequency as members of the general population.[15]

The possibility of abortion law reform was even more dismaying to *Triumph* than the contraception controversy. Catholic teaching about pregnancy had changed over the centuries, but advances in embryological knowledge had led the church to declare early in the twentieth century that the fetus was a person from the moment of conception, that it was ensouled, and that its termination would represent the killing of a person. The combined concerns of feminists, population theorists, and doctors, however, led to revision of many states' abortion laws after 1967, and this was the issue that finally drove *Triumph* to begin its stark denunciation of America as an enemy of the Catholic faith. In 1970 Bozell and his son Christopher led a group of protestors to the George Washington University Clinic in one of the nation's first antiabortion protests. Calling themselves the Sons of Thunder and wearing the red beret of the Spanish Carlist movement, they chanted *Viva Cristo Rey* (Long live Christ the King) and other pious Spanish slogans, and were arrested after scuffling with police and breaking windows. So long as America had been guided in some measure by Christian principles, said the editors, it had been possible to live here peacefully while working to construct a Christian social order. But once the killing of the unborn was permitted by law, a Catholic's dissent had to be absolute. According to *Triumph*, "If she is to protect herself and if she is to abide by her divine mandate to teach all peoples, the Catholic Church in America must break the articles of peace, she must forthrightly acknowledge that a state of war exists between herself and the American political order."[16]

Worse was to follow. When the Supreme Court handed down its decision in *Roe* v. *Wade* (1973), granting women a right to first-trimester abortions at their own discretion, *Triumph* published its next issue with an all-black cover and every page edged in black, in funereal acknowledgment of the unborn who would be killed as a result of this decision. *Triumph* was an early leader in antiabortion journalism, discussing constitutional amendments, and the ethical and political ramifications of *Roe* v. *Wade*. By now many of its most gifted writers had forsaken *Triumph*; Jeffrey Hart observed that his own sympathy with the initial objectives of the journal was lost when it began to treat the United States as a force of evil of comparable magnitude to the Soviet Union. The journal shrank from its twenty-four-page glossy format into a newsletter in 1975 and ceased publication completely with the farewell edition of January 1976, in which the editors reprinted many of the most notable articles from the journal's earlier days.[17]

In the later 1970s and the 1980s, *Triumph*'s antiabortion work was carried on in the pages of the *Human Life Review* while other Catholic conservative voices could be found in the pages of *Catholicism and Crisis*, the *New Oxford Review* and, as before, in *National Review*. None of these journals found it necessary to denounce the United States or to apotheosize Franquist Spain or monarchism, and they had a correspondingly more certain grip on the loyalties of American Catholic readers than the *Triumph* group ever achieved.

Notes

1. Frederick Wilhelmsen, "Catholicism is Right, So Why Change it?" *Saturday Evening Post* (15 July 1967): 10.

2. Biographical details based on author's telephone interview with L. Brent Bozell, 4 January 1989, and from John Judis, *William F. Buckley, Jr.: Patron Saint of the Conservatives* (New York, 1988), pp. 55–57 (Yale), p. 111 (McCarthyism), p. 221 (Goldwater), p. 318 (congressional campaign). L. Brent Bozell and W. F. Buckley, Jr., *McCarthy and His Enemies* (Chicago, 1954). Barry Goldwater, *The Conscience of a Conservative* (New York, 1960).

3. On Bozell's estrangement from *National Review*: George Nash, *The Conservative Intellectual Movement in America: Since 1945* (New York, 1976), pp. 310–13, and L. Brent Bozell, *The Warren Revolution* (New Rochelle, New York, 1966).

4. On *National Review* (hereafter, *NR*) and abortion: Garry Wills, "Catholics and Population," *NR* 17 (27 July 1965): 643; L. Brent Bozell "Mater, Si, Magistra, Si!" *NR* 17 (7 September 1965): 772; and welcome to *Triumph*: "At Last: A Conservative Catholic Magazine," *NR* 18 (16 September 1966): 870; and subsequent criticism: "Abortion," *NR* 22 (30 June 1970): 658–59.

5. "Anti-Semitism in the Vatican?" *Triumph* 5 (February 1970): 42.

6. On Latin: Dietrich von Hildebrand, "The Case for the Latin Mass," *Triumph* 1 (October 1966): 10, and Lawrence R. Brown, "The Language of the West," *Triumph* 1 (December 1966): 14; on "shamefaced neophyte": *Triumph* 1 (December 1966): 10; on the new missal: "The Pope and the Mass," *Triumph* 5 (April 1970): 8.

7. Frederick Wilhelmsen, "The Future of Catholic Spain," *Triumph* 10 (June 1975): 11.

8. On television: F. Wilhelmsen and Jane Bret, *The War in Man: Media and Machines* (Athens, Georgia, 1972), and Wilhelmsen and Bret, *Telepolitics* (Montreal, 1972); on science: Wilhelmsen, "Technics and Totalitarianism," *Commonweal* 60 (23 April 1954): 58–61; on historical objectivity: review of Eric Voegelin, *Israel and Revelation*, *Modern Age* 3 (Spring 1959): 182–89.

9. F. Wilhelmsen, *Christianity and Political Philosophy* (Athens, Georgia, 1978), pp. 111–38. On monarchy: "Royalist Revival in Central Europe," *National Review* 5 (18 January 1958): 61–63; "Charlie and Legitimacy," *Triumph* 9 (July 1974): 20.

10. Jeffrey Hart, "War and Refuge," *Triumph* 5 (April 1970): 28.

11. L. Brent Bozell, "Letter to Yourselves," *Triumph* 4 (March 1969): 11; personal interview, January 1989.

12. "The War," *Triumph* 1 (September 1966): 37; "Stop CBW," *Triumph* 4 (March 1969): 7; "Wars, Right, Left and Christian," *Triumph* 5 (January 1970): 40.

13. Gary R. Potter, "Counter-Value: America's Pact with Hell," *Triumph* 4 (July 1969): 11.

14. On Spellman and Catholic anticommunism in the 1950s see John Cooney, *The American Pope: The Life and Times of Francis Cardinal Spellman* (New York, 1984).

15. "Birth Control: The Pope Has Spoken," *Triumph* 1 (December 1966): 37.

16. "Sons of Thunder," *Triumph* 5 (July 1970): 7; M. Lawrence, "The Trial," *Triumph* 5 (October 1970): 11. On declaring war against America see "The Silent Church," *Triumph* 5 (January 1970): 42.

17. Author's interview wlth Jeffrey Hart, Hanover, New Hampshire, 29 February 1988.

Information Sources

BIBLIOGRAPHY: None.
INDEXES: *CPLI.*
REPRINT EDITIONS: Microform: UMI (1970–1976 only).
LOCATION SOURCES: Widely available.

Publication History

TITLE AND TITLE CHANGES: *Triumph.*
VOLUME AND ISSUE DATA: Volumes 1–11, September 1966–January 1976.
FREQUENCY OF PUBLICATION: Monthly.
PUBLISHER: 1966–1972: Triumph Magazine, Inc., Washington, D.C.; 1972–1976: Society for the Christian Commonwealth, Warrenton, Virginia.
EDITORS: L. Brent Bozell, Michael Lawrence, Frederick Wilhelmsen, Gary Potter, and John Wisner, concurrently, 1966–1976.
CIRCULATION: In 1969, 28,000; in 1975, 5,000.

Patrick Allitt

New Oxford Review
1977–

In February 1977 the American Church Union, an organization of conservative Episcopalians with headquarters in Oakland, California, launched the *New Oxford Review*, a monthly journal of religious, social, and cultural commentary.[1] The new magazine replaced the *American Church News,* which since the early 1940s had devoted itself to two causes: publicizing Anglo-Catholicism and waging war on theological liberalism within the Episcopal church. The *New Oxford Review* sought a broader audience among people "who may *not* be fascinated by the internal politics of the Episcopal Church." Invoking both the name and spirit of the English Oxford movement of the 1830s and 1840s, the promoters of the magazine announced a twofold mission: to defend "the Apostolic ministry and the authentic Catholicity of the Anglican experience" and to combat "secularism, Gnosticism...[and] the Spirit of the Times."[2]

The young editor of the *New Oxford Review*, Dale Vree, brought an unusual background to his defense of Christian orthodoxy.[3] While a student at the University of California at Berkeley in the early 1960s, he had plunged into the tumultuous politics of the Free Speech movement. The Berkeley radicals had not been radical enough for Vree; he saw in them nothing more than spoiled children of affluence playing at revolution and indulging in "bourgeois frivolity." Vree's search for a serious commitment to revolution led him to join the Maoist-inspired Progressive Labor party. Afire with a vision of communist purity, he left the United States in disgust in 1966, seeking through expatriation to East Berlin an escape from the decadence and hedonism of the West. Once settled in East Berlin Vree quickly suffered disenchantment. Rather than the "New Man" promised by Marxism, he found communists who were as obsessed with material comfort as the Germans on the other side of the wall. To his surprise he discovered something else, though: among East Berlin's Protestants, a despised minority of devout Christians, he observed the transforming power of the gospel. Here lay the love, the brotherhood, the selflessness that he had sought in vain in political radicalism. Dale Vree became a Christian.

Returning to the United States, Vree entered graduate school at Berkeley, took a doctorate in political science in 1972, and then taught briefly at Earlham College in Indiana. While back in Berkeley in 1976 on a Rockefeller fellowship, he joined the staff of the *American Church News*. That same year he published *On Synthesizing Marxism and Christianity*, an illuminating analysis of how Christianity inevitably forfeits its integrity when it covets the approbation of Marxists.

In assuming the editorship of the *New Oxford Review* Vree sought to realize his vision of a journal that would voice the opinions and concerns of *all* "traditional Catholics," whether Anglican, Roman Catholic, or Eastern Orthodox. "It is my expectation," he said to the executive council of the American Church Union in November 1977, "that when people want to know what traditional Catholics are thinking, increasingly they will turn automatically to the pages of the *New Oxford Review*."[4] The exigencies of the moment, however, precluded such catholicity; it would not be as easy as Vree hoped to escape the ghetto of Episcopalian "internal politics."

The inception of the *New Oxford Review* coincided with the culmination of a crisis that had been building within the Episcopal church for several decades. By 1977 conservatives had had enough of what the Reverend Francis W. Read, associate editor of the *Review*, called "a studied and deliberate change in ecclesiastical direction from Godward to manward."[5] Two issues especially incensed the conservatives: at the General Convention held in Minneapolis in 1976 the liberals had succeeded in winning approval for the ordination of women; concurrently the drive to revise the Prayer Book of 1928 had pushed on toward success. In response to these innovations nearly two thousand dissident Episcopalians and Anglicans from the United States and Canada gathered in St. Louis, Missouri, in September 1977 to voice their discontent. Out of this meeting came the "Affirmation of St. Louis," which reasserted the beliefs and practices of historic Anglicanism. "We continue to be what we are," the document read in part. "We do nothing new. We form no body, but continue as Anglicans and Episcopalians."[6] Despite this disclaimer the participants at the St. Louis gathering did anticipate a new "body," an anticipation that took flesh in January 1978 with the consecration of four bishops in the newly formed Anglican church in North America.

This upheaval drove the *New Oxford Review* into a preoccupation with exclusively Episcopal affairs; prayer books and "priestesses" dominated the *Review*'s pages in its first year of publication. Yet Vree and his colleagues never lost sight of the broader significance of the controversy that swirled through their church; the stakes, they realized, were much higher than the future of Episcopalianism. "The Episcopal crisis," wrote Father George W. Rutler, president of the American Church Union and a contributing editor of the *Review*, "is part of the Realignment of Christendom, no longer between Catholic and Protestant, but between Orthodox and Modernist."[7] This perception saved the *New Oxford Review* from parochialism and impelled it into a broader arena that encompassed the full range of religious, cultural, and social issues that bestirred America and the West in the last quarter of the twentieth century.

As part of Rutler's "Realignment of Christendom," the *New Oxford Review* sought readers and writers among theologically conservative Protestants. In moving into these circles, the *Review* forged its strongest links with Protestants of what might be called the "Wheaton connection," a form of evangelical Protestantism whose axis lies in the western suburbs of Chicago where one finds such institutions as Wheaton College, the Inter-Varsity Fellowship, and Tyndale House publishers. The Wheaton connection prides itself on combining theological conservatism, piety, and evangelical fervor with an intellectual acuity and cultural sophistication that disdain the crabbed defensiveness of old-fashioned fundamentalism. Early in 1978 Dale Vree persuaded Carl F. H. Henry, founding editor of *Christianity Today* and then the Wheaton connection's favorite contemporary theologian, to join the *Review*'s board of contributors. Robert Webber, professor of theology at Wheaton College, early began writing for the magazine and in 1981 joined Henry as a contributing editor. Webber in particular espoused the type of evangelicalism that appealed to the *New Oxford Review*, for he played an important role in formulating the "Chicago call" of 1977 in which forty evangelicals urged their fellow believers to explore such "Catholic" aspects of the faith as sacramentalism, creedalism, tradition, church authority, and Christian unity.[8] Significantly, a half-dozen of the signers of the "Chicago call" either had written for the *New Oxford Review* or would soon do so.

Although the Chicago callers were eager to discuss historically divisive points of theology, most evangelicals were not; for them, any meeting of the minds between Catholics and Protestants must be founded on something other than theology. The greatest agreement between traditional Catholics and evangelical Protestants lay in an area Rutler singled out in his address to the St. Louis Congress in September 1977: "We are waging here nothing less than the battle between Christianity and secular humanism."[9] Detailing the deleterious effects of secular humanism became a prominent feature of the *New Oxford Review*. The *Review* devoted much attention to the inroads this foe of Christian orthodoxy had made in such areas as education and psychology. More important, the magazine's writers frequently linked secular humanism to the breakdown of Christian morality and the attendant confusion over sexuality and sex roles. In assailing feminists, advocates of abortion, homosexual activists, and pornographers, the *New Oxford Review* established a basis on which Protestants and Catholics could unite to defend conservative and Christian moral standards. To some observers the *Review*'s vehemence in this area identified the magazine as a combatant in the conservative counterrevolution that had thrust Jerry Falwell into the newspapers and Ronald Reagan into the White House. As *Newsweek* commented in January 1981, the *New Oxford Review* often echoed the older and better-known *National Review*.[10]

It must have amused Dale Vree to be lumped with William F. Buckley, Jr., for although Vree had repudiated Marxism when he converted to Christianity, he had remained a socialist and had no intention of allowing the *New Oxford Review* to fall "into the right-wing rut."[11] The most crucial matters to Vree were theological and moral, not political, a point he emphasized in an early issue of the magazine:

"There is no political orthodoxy for Christians because there is no single political outlook that necessarily follows from the fundamentals of Christian faith. It is possible for a Christian to be a conservative—or a liberal, a socialist, a reactionary, or even nonpolitical—and still be a faithful Christian."[12] In keeping with this outlook, politics and economics did not figure prominently in the early numbers of the magazine; when such issues did arise, they were tackled by writers as ideologically disparate as Paul Seabury, a Berkeley political scientist and social democrat, and John P. East, a professor at East Carolina University and later to become a U.S. senator and a leader of the New Right.

The *New Oxford Review* did not join the conservative chorus that hailed Ronald Reagan's election to the presidency in 1980 as a victory for moral decency and Christian rectitude. Vree viewed Reagan's triumph with apprehension, fearing that the new administration would cater to corporate capitalism at home and unleash the jingoes abroad. Early in the Reagan administration Vree steered the *Review* toward a greater concern with politics, economics, and foreign policy, and, at least in the opinion of some of his critics, he moved the *Review* into a leftist orbit. The addition in April 1981 of Robert Coles as a contributing editor lent substance to this contention, for the Harvard psychiatrist had long been a prominent figure on the American Left. Despite the fears of some conservatives, the *New Oxford Review* had not betrayed its earlier principles, for it continued to promote conservatism in religion, morals, and social issues. But the *Review*'s increasingly obvious divergence from conservative canons in other areas distressed some readers. "The whole g—d—[sic] world is suffering from one form or another of idiot socialism," wrote an irate reader, "yet the *New Oxford Review* seems entirely innocent of this fact."[13]

The extent to which Dale Vree disagreed with his conservative allies did not become fully apparent until 1983 when he published his six-part series, "Christianity, Communism, and Sexual Revolution." Vree endeavored in these articles to establish a full-scale justification for what the *New York Times Magazine* called a "curious mix": conservatism in religion and morality combined with leftism in politics and economics.[14] Vree chided conservatives for defending capitalism, a disruptive, innovative, and amoral (if not immoral) system that sought profits wherever they could be made; capitalism had, for example, promoted the very sexual revolution that conservatives so angrily deplored. Those most likely to support capitalism—the rich and affluent who reap its benefits—were the same people, Vree contended, who generally scorned traditional morality; the working classes, by contrast, energetically defended what the upper classes derided as old-fashioned. "There is, then," Vree wrote, "a clear and significant tendency for cultural libertinism to increase as one goes up the occupational, income, and educational ladders, so much so that one may speak of a cultural/moral form of class struggle between the upper-middle class and the common people."[15]

To rectify this sorry state of affairs Vree advocated the establishment of a socialism rooted in Christian orthodoxy: a union of religion and economics best exemplified in the philosophy of work and worship promulgated by Pope John Paul II in such documents as the encyclical *Laborem Exercens*. For Vree, the Christian family—an institution grounded in love, cooperation, and self-sacrifice—

served as a model for the good society; with this ideal in mind, Christians should strive to establish (so far as possible in a fallen world) a social order cleansed of economic exploitation and moral decay. The cultural revolution born in the 1960s could be suppressed, or at least retarded, if men of decency on both the Left and Right would trace the consequences of their ideologies. "The time is ripe," Vree wrote, "for the Left to face the fact that its support of the cultural revolution actually reinforces the capitalist ethos it loathes, and the Right to admit that its support for the capitalist ethos fuels the liberationist program it deplores."[16]

That Vree should have singled out Pope John Paul II for special praise was no accident; since the beginning of his pontificate in 1978, the charismatic Polish pope had captivated Vree and many of the writers, both Catholic and non-Catholic, who appeared in the *New Oxford Review*. Even without John Paul, however, the *Review* would have paid close attention to Roman Catholicism; after all, Anglo-Catholics are Catholics, doctrinally separated from their Roman brethren by little more than the matter of papal supremacy. Since the rise of the Oxford movement in the nineteenth century, the lure of Rome—the temptation to rejoin the Mother Church—has tugged at Anglo-Catholics, and many have succumbed, most notably John Henry Newman and Ronald Knox. In the first issue of the *New Oxford Review* Vree noted this problem and remarked that "the Oxford Movement suffered from a certain inordinate attraction to Rome. Let it be clear that we intend to remain Anglicans, that we Anglo-Catholics are not going to fragment."[17]

The "inordinate attraction" proved stronger than Vree's promise of continuing loyalty to Canterbury. Rutler abandoned the Anglo-Catholic communion for Roman Catholicism in the fall of 1979; two years later the *Review*'s poetry editor, Sheldon Vanauken, followed Rutler to Rome. Vree himself looked favorably on the Roman church, writing, for example, in March 1980 that "whatever one's feelings about the doctrine of papal infallibility, there can be no doubt that the Vatican…is the spiritual center of the world."[18] Toward this center the *Review* gravitated, a movement noted with dismay by some of the magazine's supporters. "The contents have almost entirely come to be dominated by *Roman* Catholic authors writing articles of particularly *Roman* interest," a reader complained in September 1982.[19] Having become in effect a Roman Catholic magazine, the *New Oxford Review* severed its ties to the American Church Union in July 1983. Three months later Vree announced that he and his wife, Elena, managing editor of the *Review*, had been received into the Roman Catholic church.[20]

Despite this new departure, Dale Vree foresaw no drastic changes in the *New Oxford Review*; in a long editorial in the April 1984 issue, he sought to reassure his readers of this continuity. Although the magazine would be avowedly Roman Catholic, it would not be "exclusivist, triumphalist, inquisitorial, or truculent"; rather, the *Review* would continue to serve as "a meeting ground for Christians of various church allegiances." Vree hoped to make of the *New Oxford Review* a magazine that would meet the standards once set forth by Hilaire Belloc in an essay entitled "The Faith through the Press." Such a magazine, Vree wrote (quoting liberally from Belloc's essay), "would not concentrate on ecclesiastical affairs, but…would discuss 'any subject of the day.' Such a periodical…would be 'an arena for controversy,' be read not only by Roman Catholics, and the effect of its Catholicsim would be 'felt without direct intention.' And on social and economic questions, it 'would not prefer tranquility to justice.'"[21] By early 1984, in its eighth year of publication, the *New Oxford Review* had already moved far toward meeting Belloc's criteria and fulfilling Vree's hopes.

Notes

[Editorial note: Because this essay was completed in the late 1980s, several of the views expressed in it may be dated.]

1. The American Church Union, founded in 1937 and for many years headed by the Reverend Canon Albert J. duBois, defined itself as "a missionary activity for the teaching and defense of the historic Catholic and Apostolic Faith of the Church. It is part of the world-wide Church Union Movement dedicated to upholding the Doctrine, Disciple and Worship of the Episcopal Church as a true part of the historic Holy Catholic Church of Christ." This statement appears on the inside of the back cover of each issue of the *American Church Quarterly*, a theological journal published briefly in the 1960s by the American Church Union.

2. Dale Vree, "Why the *New Oxford Review*?" *New Oxford Review* 44 (February 1977): 2, 3. Italics in original. Because the *Review* (hereinafter cited as *NOR*) viewed itself as a continuation of the *American Church News* it began with volume 44 instead of volume 1.

3. Biographical information on Vree comes from two articles he wrote: "From Berkeley to East Berlin and Back," *NOR* 50 (January–February 1983): 12–23, and "God's Beloved East Germany," *NOR* 50 (March 1983): 10–22.

4. Dale Vree, "The Executive Editor's Report to the ACU Council," *NOR* 44 (December 1977): 4.

5. Francis W. Read, "The St. Louis Congress: What Is at Issue," *NOR* 44 (September 1977): 4

6. "The Affirmation of St. Louis," *NOR* 44 (October 1977): 7.

7. George W. Rutler, "The Realignment of Christianity," *NOR* 45 (February 1978): 4.

8. The May 1979 issue of *NOR* printed the text of "The Chicago Call" and a symposium on the document.

9. George W. Rutler, "Our Theological Imperative," *NOR* 44 (October 1977): 9.

10. "Today's Oxford Movement," *Newsweek* 97 (12 January 1981): 80.

11. Dale Vree in a reply to letter to the editor, *NOR* 47 (May 1980): 7.

12. Dale Vree, "Traditionalists and Other Conservatives," *NOR* 44 (June 1977): 22. This is a review of George H. Nash, *The Conservative Intellectual Movement in America: Since 1945*.

13. Letter to the Editor, *NOR* 48 (April 1981): 5.

14. Fran Schumer, "A Return to Religion," *The New York Times Magazine* 133 (15 April 1984): 94.

15. Dale Vree, "Cultural Imperialism and Women's Lib," *NOR* 50 (June 1983): 15. This essay is part V of "Christianity, Communism, and Sexual Revolution."

16. Dale Vree, "Sex in the Service of Capitalism," *NOR* 50 (May 1983): 23. This essay is part IV of "Christianity, Communism, and Sexual Revolution."

17. Vree, "Why the *New Oxford Review*?" p. 2.

18. Dale Vree, "We Stand with the Pope," *NOR* 47 (May 1980): 3

19. Letter to the Editor, *NOR* 49 (September 1982): 10. Italics in the original.

20. "Agreed Statement on the Separation of the *New Oxford Review* from the American Church Union," *NOR* 50 (September 1983): 2; Dale Vree, "On Becoming Roman Catholic,"

NOR 50 (October 1983): 2.

    21. Dale Vree, "Speaking Heart to Heart," *NOR* 51 (April 1984): 2, 4.

Information Sources

BIBLIOGRAPHY: None.

INDEXES: None.

REPRINT EDITIONS: Microform: UMI. Bound edition: UMI.

LOCATION SOURCES: Complete runs: *New Oxford Review*, Berkeley, California; Emory University Candler School of Theology; Boston College; University of Michigan; Princeton University; Southern Illinois University.

Publication History

TITLE AND TITLE CHANGES: *New Oxford Review*.

VOLUME AND ISSUE DATA: Volumes 44–current, February 1977–present.

FREQUENCY OF PUBLICATION: Monthly; combined numbers July–August and, beginning in 1979, combined numbers in January–February.

PUBLISHERS: 1977–1983: American Church Union, Oakland, California; September 1983–present: New Oxford Review, Berkeley, California.

EDITOR: Dale Vree.

CIRCULATION: 1987: 5,500; 1998, 15, 531.

James J. Thompson, Jr.

Part Four

LITERARY REVIEWS

Cultural conservatives are men and women whose philosophical principles are those of the Right and who believe that life, liberty, and the pursuit of happiness are attainable, whatever a nation's political handiwork. They are skeptical of the "open" society that purports to operate without automatic regulators of human conduct, and believe that the increasing tendency of modern society to function in a plebiscitary manner is unfortunate. Harboring doubts about human capabilities, they invariably believe that a past age was more congenial than the present to the development of talent and character. These negatives imply positives. Cultural conservatism embodies values of its own, such as duty, order, discipline, deference to elders and superiors, reverence for authority, and a "natural" order of things. Its adherents respect high aesthetic standards—the tradition of centuries of poetry, perhaps, or the conventions of religion, the treasures of art—and any heritage of an artistic form that nourishes the soul and confers meaning to life. The literary conservatives seek affirmation in the abiding mysteries of life.

Nowhere is this sensibility more fully expressed than in literary quarterlies, said by Allen Tate to be "necessary to the welfare of American intellectual life." Literary magazines serve to create small intellectual communities of poets, novelists, and men of letters, who, though separated by distance, share common traits and wish to engage literature in a serious way. In addition, they authenticate originality and create networks of influence, thereby establishing new centers of power within the culture. Unlike academic quarterlies, literary magazines publish some fiction and poetry but prefer the long, unfootnoted critical essay or review. Literary theory holds precedence over creative work, though it should be emphasized that a quarterly such as *Kenyon Review*, when edited by John Crowe Ransom, published the leading poets of the early postwar period, including W. H. Auden, James Dickey, Robert Graves, Dylan Thomas, and Robert Lowell. Other than the *American Mercury*, the periodicals in this section depended less on the financial bottom line than did the more popular magazines. With a small circulation (often between one thousand and five thousand paid subscriptions), they required subsidies, whether by a university, foundation, or wealthy individual, because leading writers could not be attracted without payment. Free to uphold high standards and to print contributions that commercial magazines would not consider, it followed that the literary quarterlies appealed not to the common reader but to the highbrow whose standards the public found to be ivory towered, even uninteresting. Moreover, they enjoyed another freedom that reviews with large circulation numbers such as the *New York Times Book Review*, the *New York Review of Books*, and, earlier, the *Saturday Review of Literature* did not: they were under no obligation to discuss new books, a signal advantage for those who, regardless of the current cultural situation, wished to reflect on the best that is known and thought.

Close personal and critical bonds linked three quarterlies in this section, especially when edited by southern literati who had earlier collaborated as Nashville Fugitives and again in preparing the 1930 Agrarian manifesto, *I'll Take My Stand*. *Kenyon* was the intellectual heir of the *Southern Review* (which ceased publication in 1942, as Louisiana State University, like most other colleges and universities, underwent extreme belt tightening due to World War II) and became perhaps the most influential of all the quarterlies during the succeeding decade and a half. The *Sewanee Review*, much the oldest of the three and published by the University of the South, had flirted with the Humanist movement of the late 1920s and early 1930s and at one time refused to print contributors who also appeared in the pages of the *Southern* and *Kenyon* reviews. In the 1940s, however, former Agrarians Andrew Lytle and Allen Tate, in successive editorial stints, reconstructed the quarterly, connecting it with the formalist critical position of the other two. The New Criticism, as it was also called, used the method of *explication de texte*, a structural analysis concerned with a text's supreme control of itself. It attempted to demonstrate how the aesthetic imagination, operating through works of art and creative writing, might provide a way to truth (or an understanding of the mysteries) that science had not superseded. The presumptuous application of scientific criteria to all human activities reflected a truncated reason that in the hands of the positivists cut persons off from the just-as-real world of cultural myths and religious symbols. We should not be surprised that in staking out claims for the stark opposition between poetry and science, excessive claims for the critical imagination at times were made at the expense of the empirical sciences.

The *American Mercury* stands at some distance from the quarterlies in this section. During its early years under H. L. Mencken, before degenerating during the 1950s into racist and anti-Semitic bigotry, the *American Mercury* exercised considerable influence over American literature. Its interests were broader than that, however. The opinionated journal with green covers surveyed American culture more than literature, its editor unable to resist the journalistic impulse to laugh at fools and poke fun at the idiocies of American life. Mencken thought it funny that the mass of Americans acted like greyhounds who race frantically around the track in pursuit of a mechanical rabbit they will never catch; the New Humanists and Southern Agrarians thought it deplorable. Though scorned by other conservatives in the literary quarterlies for his Nietzchean celebration of literary naturalism and libertarian sentiments that conflicted with the conservative's yearning for an organic, structured society, Mencken joined the Humanists and Agrarians in their attack on numerical democracy, arguing that anything so destructive of high culture constituted a poor national religion. Furthermore, artists were under no obligation to conform to political and cultural convention, or, as Mencken characteristically put it, to the moral and patriotic theories of university pedagogues. America's salvation lay instead in the resurrection of an aristocracy of talent.

It is remarkable the number of cultural conservatives who became dominant in Western civilization in the twentieth century, many of them named in the following pages. They produced a disproportionate number of the finest literary works and labored unceasingly to preserve the best of the past. Defending a more complex conception of reality than did the legatees of the Enlightenment, their own could hardly be expected to win dominance on Main Street, U.S.A. Reservations about the growing sway of plebiscitary democracy, the strengthening of big business capitalism (as recorded, for example, in the pages of the *American Review*), and the powerful theme of intense individualism in the American experience enjoyed some resonance among the populace but remained a minority point of view. It is important to reiterate the contempt for science that so many of the literary conservatives felt, for it somewhat constricted their own understanding of human nature. Accordingly, contributors to the literary quarterlies found the going rough as the century wore on and society appeared to immerse itself ever more deeply in the values of objectivity, science, scholarship, and facts. Yet such a statement does not do justice to the openness of the traditionalists to opposing views in literature that often were fresh and valuable for a better understanding of the human drama— not a small contribution in a century that witnessed the Holocaust, the gulag, and perhaps a hundred million dead in war.

The Sewanee Review
1895–

As the journal announces on its masthead and on its stationery, the *Sewanee Review* is the "Oldest Literary Quarterly" published in America, its first number having appeared in November 1892. Its first editor, William Peterfield Trent, the author of the controversial but influential biography of William Gilmore Simms, described in its first issue the kind of journal he wished to produce—a southern equivalent of the *North American Review*. Although he intended to concentrate on the humanities, he published essays and literature as well as studies of history, philosophy, religion, politics, and reconstruction economics. For the eight years (1893–1990) of Trent's editorship, before he left Sewanee to go to Columbia, the *Sewanee Review* was a journal of general culture, resembling closely the modern versions of the *American Scholar*, the *Virginia Quarterly Review*, and the *Yale Review*. A breakdown of the subjects covered during Trent's tenure will demonstrate fairly accurately the nature of the journal during his editorship: five essays on the requisites for a humanistic education (one written by the editor); twelve essays on the plight of blacks in the South (although the essays express widely different points of view, ranging from the ultraconservative to the ultraliberal, they tend to argue the New South philosophy of Walter Hines Page and Henry W. Grady more often than they do that of the archconservatives Thomas Nelson Page and John Esten Cooke); biographical articles on Robert E. Lee (three), Stonewall Jackson, Nathan Bedford Forrest, Wade Hampton, Sam Houston, J. P. Benjamin, Joseph Glover Baldwin, and W. M. Baskerville (a former chairman at Vanderbilt who along with Trent argued forcefully for American literature as an academic subject); fifteen essays on the Greek classics, thirteen on Latin language and literature, three on Sanskrit, five on Hebrew, particularly the Bible; twenty-one on English prose, three on American, and three on southern; forty-five on English verse, twenty-five on American, and six on southern. There were also five essays on American literature, including southern, as a separate discipline and a half-dozen on southern education.

Although there were three editors with long tenure—John Bell Henneman

(1900–1908), John M. McBryde, Jr. (1910–1919), and George Herbert Clarke (1920–1925)—the journal changed little until William S. Knickerbocker, a student of Trent at Columbia, assumed the editorship in 1927 and remained in that post until 1942. Knickerbocker used his position to editorialize, more than his predecessors had, with the possible exception of Trent. He expressed his views on a number of subjects, ranging from politics and economics to religion and literature. Soon after he became editor he wrote a long review of John Crowe Ransom's *God Without Thunder* (1930) and entitled it "Theological Homebrew," calling the book the second phase of the fundamentalist campaign, the first being the Scopes Trial in Dayton, Tennessee, which concentrated on the biological theory of evolution. "Ransom's book," Knickerbocker wrote, "is one of the most challenging books of the moment because it poses a question everyone must answer not only with the head but with the heart." In short Ransom is presenting the "most vital of all theories: the inscrutable mystery of God."[1]

Although Knickerbocker accepted articles from the Agrarians in which they advanced their arguments against aggressive materialism—he published Ransom's "Reconstructed but Unregenerate," though he changed the title to "The South— Old or New?" because, Ransom said, he had found the old title "too stiff" and had provided a new one "with an antebellum tone"—he called *I'll Take My Stand* the "most audacious book ever written by Southerners" and "the most challenging book published in the United States since George's *Progress and Poverty*."[2] Later he engaged both Ransom and Donald Davidson in public debates on issues raised in the book. In his debate with Ransom in New Orleans and the one with Davidson in Columbia, Tennessee, his arguments were about the same—ideas and attitudes he had expressed in the pages of the *Review*: if the South is to maintain its rightful position in regard to the other sections of the country, it must develop a "diverse economy combining a carefully regulated combination of industry, commerce, and agriculture." In a letter to Donald Davidson in which he agreed to debate him at Columbia, Knickerbocker gratuitously admitted that Ransom had defeated him in New Orleans. Ransom's "plea for the farmers," he wrote, "who were little more than robots as mill workers screwing on bolt no. 47 day after day, won the audience for agrarianism."[3]

As editor Knickerbocker published more essays on English and American literature than Trent had—in addition to his editorial duties he was also head of the English department—and fewer on classical language and literature. He published poetry, as his predecessor, Tudor Seymour Long, had, but no fiction. Although he published essays on both sides of the Agrarian controversy, he carried fewer articles on other economic and political issues. A large percentage of the space of the journal was devoted to literature, but since the contributors were not paid, most of them were associated with some academic institution because, as Tate argues, the professional writer felt he must be paid for his work. The *Review* was provided a firmer financial basis than it had had because the University of the South undertook to furnish regular support for the publication; therefore it did not have to depend on the editor to raise most of what he had to have to get along. Too, there seemed to be a closer relation between the University of the South and the *Review* than ever before, with many members of the faculty, even the vice chancellor, submitting essays and other materials to it regularly.

When Knickerbocker suffered a nervous breakdown in 1942, Andrew Lytle, a member of the history department, was persuaded, under the title of managing editor, to edit the *Review* until a permanent editor could be found. Under Lytle's management, the journal entered a new era. With considerable assistance from Allen Tate, who was an advisory editor, Lytle in a period of two years (1942–1944) introduced several significant changes, the most important of which was initiating the practice of publishing fiction. When he published Robert Penn Warren's "Statement of Ashby Wyndham," a 20,000-word segment of the unpublished novel *At Heaven's Gate*, Lytle used this event, with Tate's enthusiastic assistance, to increase circulation. Again aided by Tate's indefatigable efforts, Lytle attracted more important contributors: in poetry, Tate, Wallace Stevens, Robert Lowell, John Berryman, William Meredith, and Randall Jarrell, and in criticism, he published Tate, Richard Weaver, Jarrell, and R. P. Blackmur. When Lytle left after Tate was appointed editor in the summer of 1944, the journal was well on its way toward becoming an international literary review.

Because Allen Tate for many years depended on the earnings from his pen for his livelihood, he knew the *Sewanee Review* could never attract work from many of the best writers if the journal did not pay its contributors. As a consequence of this conviction, he would not accept the position of editor until the administration and trustees at the University of the South agreed to pay contributors to the *Review* on a scale that would be competitive with the *Partisan Review* and the *Kenyon Review*. During the two years of his editorship (1944–1946), Tate built on the excellent foundation that Lytle had laid and made the *Review* a literary journal known and read internationally. He placed it in many leading bookstores throughout the United States, including Brentano's in New York. He tripled the paid circulation, and the new policy of payment for contributions attracted, as he expected, work of many writers who had never contributed to the journal before.[4]

By the standards he himself set for the literary quarterly, however, his editorship was at best only a qualified success. He wrote in "The Function of the Critical Quarterly" (1936):

If the task of the quarterly is to impose an intelligible order upon a scattering experience that the monthly and the weekly may hope only to report, the task of the editor may be one of difficulty and responsibility.... There can be little doubt that the success of the *Criterion* [under the editorship of T. S. Eliot]...has been due to concentrated editorship functioning through a small group of regular contributors.... By group I mean a number of writers who agree that certain fundamental issues exist and who consent, under direction of the editor, to discuss them with a certain emphasis.[5]

Since Tate resigned from the *Review* in the summer of 1946 to accept a position with Henry Holt in New York, succeeding editors of the journal—John E. Palmer (1946–1952), Monroe K. Spears (1952–1961), Andrew Lytle (1961–1973), George Core (1974–)—have pretty much followed the course he set. There have been some deviations, of course. Under John Palmer, perhaps the reader was provided more essays by the authors we now call the New Critics and more attention was given to the creative writers of the high modern period. But although essays by the historical critics and offerings from critics of any other persuasion have never been barred from the journal, its most popular subjects for the past forty years have been Modernism and the New Criticism. Palmer also initiated the practice of special issues—the most popular of which, perhaps, was devoted to John Crowe Ransom (summer 1948). Seldom does the most distinguished literary quarterly in the country devote an entire number to assessing the works of a living writer. Some of the best critics in America contributed. Donald Stauffer wrote: "A cartoonist, making a little critical map of the United States, would undoubtedly draw the suave, white haired, self-contained figure of Mr. Ransom sitting on his hill at Kenyon."[6] Such a representation would be an appropriate suggestion of Ransom's contribution to American poetry and criticism. Other important critics offered essays to indicate their approval of Stauffer's assessment: Cleanth Brooks, F. O. Matthiessen, Wallace Stevens, Randall Jarrell, and others.

Monroe K. Spears continued the tradition of publishing outstanding fiction, including that by such well-known writers as Andrew Lytle and Madison Jones, and of carrying on the tradition of honoring individual writers by devoting a special issue to allow interested critics to comment on the several aspects of their artistic careers. The fall 1959 issue of the *Sewanee Review* was devoted to a celebration of Allen Tate's sixtieth birthday, with tributes by R. P. Blackmur, Malcolm Cowley, John Crowe Ransom, Donald Davidson, Robert Lowell, Katherine Anne Porter, and Herbert Read, among others. The issue also included a French translation by Jacques and Raïssa Maritain of "Ode to the Confederate Dead." Although, as has been the case of all the editors of the *Review* since Tate—whose "wide acquaintance in the world of letters, both at home and abroad…and his ability to solicit the authors," Andrew Lytle has written, "set the tone and quality which his successors have followed"—Spears made an obvious attempt to mix poetry and fiction with a group of essays that moved broadly over a wide range of English, American, and Western European literature, his greatest emphasis was on that which was written since World War I.[7]

Lytle's *Craft and Vision: The Best Fiction from the Sewanee Review* (1971), gives a list of the contributors since 1935, and one would be hard pressed not to find the name of a significant poet, critic, and writer of fiction operating at the time in America, England, and much of Western Europe Perhaps the most important issue of the quarterly was that edited by Allen Tate in 1966 in memory of T. S. Eliot. Its contributors included I. A. Richards, Herbert Read, Stephen Spender, Bonamy Dobrée, Ezra Pound, Frank Morley, C. Day Lewis, E. Martin Browne, Helen Gardner, Robert Speaight, Conrad Aiken, Leonard Unger, Frank Kermode, Robert Richman, G. Wilson Knight, Mario Praz, Austin Warren, Wallace Fowlie, Cleanth Brooks, Janet Adam Smith, Robert Giroux, Francis Noel Lees, H. S. Davies, B. Rajan, and Neville Braybrooke. The list of authors included in Lytle's collection of fiction from the *Review* is almost as impressive: Harry Crews, William Faulkner, Caroline Gordon, Madison Jones, Andrew Lytle, Flannery O'Connor, Peter Taylor, Robert Penn Warren, Eudora Welty, and others.

There are several differences immediately obvious in the *Review* edited since 1974 by George Core. One is a successful effort to get contributors from outside the South, in a conscientious attempt to make the *Review* an accurate voice of all of America and, to the extent possible, of the Western world. Core's most popular special issue, and he has had several, was that devoted to Irish writers (winter 1976). The one most significant to his readers, however, was that devoted to commonwealth literature, but the writers included or evaluated in that issue are so little known by American readers of the *Review* that some time will probably have to pass before its true value is known.

There are definitely two different versions of the *Sewanee Review*—the general culture review published from 1892 to midsummer of 1942 and the literary review that has appeared since. Despite the fact that its circulation has seldom been above 4,000, its influence has been much greater than this figure would seem to indicate. Many of its subscribers are libraries, and several readers see each copy; these readers—consisting chiefly of writers, critics, college teachers, and students—are in a position to influence a wider segment of society than they represent. Although its purpose was quite different for its first half-century of existence and its quality much more impressive since the editorship of Tate in the mid-1940s, no other literary quarterly in America can match its length of service to the arts and few others can equal the quality of its contribution. Even fewer have fulfilled as completely the responsibility of maintaining literature as a unifying center for American culture.

Since the *Review* is a literary quarterly rather than one with its primary emphasis on political, social, or economic issues, its degree of conservatism must be determined by the kind of literary criticism, poetry, and fiction it publishes. It has published little Marxist criticism and less of that known as postmodern. Nearly all of the poetry and fiction reflect the close attention to form and structure associated with the writers whose best work was done in the high modern period: Eliot, Stevens, Pound, Faulkner, Hemingway, and Fitzgerald.

Notes

1. *Sewanee Review* 39 (January–March 1931): 103–11 (hereinafter cited as *SR*).

2. Thomas Daniel Young, *Gentleman in a Dustcoat: A Biography of John Crowe Ransom* (Baton Rouge, Louisiana, 1976), p. 204.

3. Ibid., p. 224.

4. Some of them were T. S. Eliot, Jacques Maritain, St. John Perse, R. P. Blackmur, Robert Penn Warren, Cleanth Brooks, Robert B. Heilman, Randall Jarrell, Robert Lowell, Wallace Stevens, Dylan Thomas, Louis Aragon, Herbert Read, John Peale Bishop, Marshall McLuhan, Austin Warren, Delmore Schwartz, Peter Taylor, Jean Stafford, and, of course, Tate himself.

5. Allen Tate, *Essays of Four Decades* (Chicago, 1968), pp. 54–55.

6. Donald A. Stauffer, "Portrait of the Critic-Poet as Equilibrist," *SR* 56 (Summer 1948): 426.

7. Andrew Lytle, Foreword to *Craft and Vision: The Best Fiction from the Sewanee Review* (New York, 1971), p. ix.

Information Sources

BIBLIOGRAPHY:

Core, George. "The *Sewanee Review* and the Editorial Performance." In *The Yearbook of English Studies*. Vol. 10. Edited by G. K. Hunter and C. J. Rawson. London, 1980.
————Foreword to *The Sewanee Review: A Forty Year Index: 1943–1982*. Edited by Mary Lucia Snyder Cornelius and Elizabeth Moore Engsberg. Medford, New Jersey, 1983.

Janssens, G. A. M. *The American Literary Review: A Critical History, 1920–1950*. The Hague, 1968.

Lytle, Andrew, ed. *Craft and Vision: The Best Fiction from the Sewanee Review*. New York, 1971.

Mott, Frank Luther. *A History of American Magazines*, vol. 4, *1885–1905*. Cambridge, Massachusetts, 1957.

Spears, Monroe K. "The Present Function of the Literary Quarterlies." *Texas Quarterly* 3 (Spring 1960): 33–50.

Tate, Allen. "The Function of the Critical Quarterly." In *Essays of Four Decades*. Chicago, 1968.

INDEXES: Each volume indexed; cumulative index, vols. 1–10; 40–year index, 1943–1982; *AHI; ALI; AHCI; Bio Ind; BRI; Curr Bk Rev Cit; Curr Cont: A&H; Hum Ind; Ind Bk Revs Hum; II; MLA Amer Bib; MLA Intl Bib; 19th Cent RG*; PAIS; *Poole; RG Supp; SSHI; Writings Amer Hist.*

REPRINT EDITIONS: Microform: UMI; PMC; KIP; Brookhaven Press. Bound editions: UMI; Kraus Reprint Company.

LOCATION SOURCES: Widely available.

Publication History

TITLE AND TITLE CHANGES: *The Sewanee Review*.

VOLUME AND ISSUE DATA: Volumes l–current, November 1892–present.

FREQUENCY OF PUBLICATION: Quarterly.

PUBLISHER: University of the South, Sewanee, Tennessee.

EDITORS: Telfair Hodgson, 1892–1893; William Peterfield Trent, 1893–1900; John Bell Henneman, 1900–1908; various faculty members, 1909; John M. McBryde, Jr., 1910–1919; George Herbert Clarke, 1920–1925; Tudor Seymour Long and William Skinkle Knickerbocker, 1926; William Skinkle Knickerbocker, 1927–1942; Andrew Lytle, 1942–1944; Allen Tate, 1944–1946; John E. Palmer, 1946–1952; Monroe K. Spears, 1952–1961; Andrew Lytle, 1961–1973; George Core, 1974–present.

CIRCULATION: Before 1944, under 1,000; 1946–1965, about 3,000; since 1965, about 4,000.

Thomas Daniel Young

Bookman
1895–1933

When Seward Collins bought ownership of the *Bookman* in 1927 the venerable literary journal had passed its glory years. But this young Princeton graduate and man of independent fortune gained for the faltering publication a new notoriety. An enthusiastic convert to the New Humanist movement led by Irving Babbitt and Paul Elmer More, Collins opened the pages of the *Bookman* to the younger disciples of Humanism and he himself seized the editorial columns of the publication to trumpet the cause.

The *Bookman* had made its debut in 1895. It was founded by Frank Howard Dodd, president of Dodd, Mead, and Co. of New York City, and edited for twenty-two years by Harry Thurston Peck, professor of Latin language and literature at Columbia University. The *Bookman* aspired throughout its career to be a window to the events of the publishing world, and with reviews, essays, best-seller lists, and animated literary portraits of writers familiar and new, it succeeded to a position of great prestige as an arbiter of refined taste in American and European letters. It was rather popular besides, attaining a respectable circulation of about 40,000 by 1907, probably the highest in its half-century of life.[1] Through later editorships, the *Bookman* managed for the most part to stand above the vociferous critical debates of the 1920s, giving an open hearing to all partisans. But Collins was not one who could be disinterested in such matters, and the *Bookman* prepared for a new departure under his editorship.

The New Humanism that Collins espoused had made its way very slowly over three decades to a sudden burst of popularity at the end of the 1920s. Irving Babbitt, professor of romantic literature at Harvard University, had been leading an assault on the baneful influences of romanticism and naturalism in Western culture and called for a counterattack on the pervasive moral relativism that he perceived as the dangerous by-products of these cultural forces. Babbitt's extensive writings on human nature outlined a philosophy of dualism that stressed man's capacity for evil and the need for self-discipline. The ethical imagination became the key to Babbitt's program, for it functioned as the critical capacity of human beings to transcend their expansive and egoistic "lower selves" and discipline them through a life governed by the perceived universal moral truths of a higher human nature. Babbitt was supported in this effort by Paul Elmer More, editor until 1914 of the *Nation* and then professor of classical literature at Princeton University. Their common stance led the two to a neoclassical literary standard, a program for a humanistic recovery in American higher education, and an antisocialist, neo-Burkean conservatism in their political opinions. By the end of the 1920s, amid the waning tide of literary rebellion, the traditionalist appeal of Babbitt and More gained a host of new followers, and Collins as one of them was ready to take a stand.[2]

First, Collins had to do some purging. His editor, Burton Rascoe, proved to be no friend of Humanism and gave too cozy a reception, for Collins's taste, to the likes of Theodore Dreiser, James Branch Cabell, and e. e. cummings. Collins himself seized the editorial reins and with the March 1929 issue placed himself fully in charge.[3] The next year Collins restored an old *Bookman* trademark, the "Chronicle and Comment" section, and used that forum to defend the journal's new literary stance. The United States, Collins said, had undergone in the last decade what Europe had endured some thirty years before—"a virulent attack in every walk of life of the 'insurrectionist' tendencies" that had corrupted traditional values. But in the end, he added, the new energy yielded only "blind, monotonous revolt and sterile innovation."[4] Collins also went after those literary critics who had been midwives to the literary rebellion: Van Wyck Brooks, whom he dismissed as a Tolstoyan humanitarian, and H. L. Mencken, who embraced the wretched refuse, "the backgroundless, the disinherited, the pathological; first-generation immigrants, unhappy college-boys, paranoiac newspaper reporters, intellectual bohemians." So when Babbitt, More, and the younger Humanists issued their manifesto of 1930, *Humanism and America,* it was the occasion for an official welcome by the *Bookman* and for a call by Collins for rebellion against rebellion, with Babbitt and More as models.[5]

Both Babbitt and More, who died in 1933 and 1937 respectively, did some of their last writing for the *Bookman.* The magazine therefore served to introduce the New Humanism to a number of people who probably had not pursued the subject in works such as Babbitt's *Rousseau and Romanticism* and *Democracy and Leadership.* Collins solicited from Babbitt several essays that summarized his literary philosophy and allowed him to renew his long-standing grievances with the early romantics, like Wordsworth, and more recent, diseased expressions of the genre, such as those of James Joyce. In "The Primitivism of Wordsworth," Babbitt contrasted the lethargic revery of indulgent romantics with the more genuine spiritual meditation of the religious models from Christianity and Buddhism.[6] Babbitt, who had spent a lifetime debunking "geniuses," now rejected Rebecca West's application of that label to James Joyce. Joyce's *Ulysses,* he asserted, "marks a more advanced stage of psychic disintegration than anything that has come down to us from classical antiquity."[7] But Babbitt was more restrained in his essay "On

Being Creative," urging the distinction between genuine creative insight and mere spontaneity of expression.[8] Babbitt's contributions to the *Bookman* generally reinforced the Humanistic plea that what the modern world needed above all was a check on enthusiasm and a measure of self-discipline in all things.

An able and prolific disciple of Babbitt was Norman Foerster, who expanded the offerings of the major Humanists to the *Bookman*. Foerster mounted the charge against naturalism in modern culture, romanticism's twin among the modern menaces. The Humanists had been making their case against the inroads of Darwinism in literary criticism, especially in the fashion of viewing literary works as products of biological and environmental determinism, the effects of culture, race, and climate on the human imagination. Under the influence of the "literary historians," Foerster complained, critics sought out the "vital forces" that made literature a unique expression of a particular historical period or the genesis of a special race or national culture. The result was an aesthetic relativism as dangerous as that forged by romantic subjectivism. Foerster pleaded for the Humanists a return to standards of judgment that measured literature according to its unique depiction of the universal human spirit, its capacity to express and transcend the relative conditions of time and place. Referring to Henry Seidel Canby of the *Saturday Review of Literature*, Foerster lamented that too much literary criticism was merely journalistic reporting of literary events. In short, critics had become passively tolerant; their faculties of judgment had atrophied.[9]

But there were younger Humanist critics ready to put on armor, and the *Bookman* found one of its useful roles in providing them a forum. Thus Alan Reynolds Thompson, in bidding "Farewell to Achilles," decried the influence of naturalism in depriving modern literature of genuine qualities of tragedy. Naturalism had obliterated Emerson's law for man and law for thing, and a truly humanist sense of an inner war of good and evil in the human breast had been lost to the modern literary vision.[10] G. R. Elliott, perhaps the best among the younger Humanist critics, recovered older models, John Donne among them, and judged them favorably against the modern poets.[11] But unlike Babbitt and More, the younger Humanists were not indisposed to taking on the contemporary scene directly, and the *Bookman* partly answered the charge of Humanism's critics that it had not promoted the cause of a single living author. Gorham Munson, however, had high praise for F. Scott Fitzgerald and lauded the poetry of Robert Frost.[12]

Literature remained the nearly exclusive focus of the *Bookman* in the Collins years, but one foray outside that field brought it to the subject of American higher education. It was in the college and university that Humanism was most prepared to stand its ground against all the inroads of modernism. In a lengthy series on this issue, Robert Shafer advanced the cause of humanistic education as the sole business of the colleges and the underlying support of the universities and professional schools as well. Shafer here echoed what had been Babbitt's jeremiad even from his undergraduate days at Harvard: the invasion of the campus by new academic specialties in proliferation, the advancement of the public service ideal in education, and the general dissolution of the life of the mind by the life of the world. Higher education, the Humanists believed, had succumbed to every external pressure and had lost its sense of identity. And the legacy of Charles William Eliot's elective system had fragmented the viable core of traditional collegiate studies. "The attempt to become all things to all students," Shafer wrote, "is, in fact, an act of desperation." Homer and Shakespeare had lost out to business English, and the college had ceased to be a vehicle of civilization.[13]

Although the *Bookman* tried to make its appeal as a New Humanist voice, it merged with and fostered other conservative sentiments in the late 1920s and 1930s. It attracted writers who chose not to be identified as Humanists and sometimes voiced criticisms of certain aspects of the Humanist credo. But the *Bookman* did appeal to antimodernist sentiments of all kinds. It echoed the views of an increasing number of intellectuals skeptical of democratic culture and mass tastes, of materialism and the values of a business society, and of the leveling principle in all segments of American life. The *Bookman* therefore brought together three cultural strains that were otherwise noticeably differentiated: the libertarian, elitist, and thoroughly antimaterialist opinions of A. J. Nock;[14] the religious conservatism and aesthetic traditionalism of T. S. Eliot and G. K. Chesterton;[15] and the anticapitalism and regional provincialism of the Southern Agrarians.[16]   In fact, the critical perspectives of these individuals were somewhat muted in the *Bookman*'s pages, but their presence was significant. Collins seems gradually to have recognized that he could join the literary perspectives of these individuals with their social, political, and economic views to forge a thoroughgoing conservatism that was both antidemocratic and anticapitalist. Seizing that opportunity, he would later abandon the *Bookman* and inaugurate the *American Review*.

But to the end the *Bookman* looked mostly at the contemporary arena of belles-lettres. What the *Bookman* essayists found perhaps most troublesome and threatening in this arena was the lure of the irrational as reflected by modern culture in its literature. Whether as disciples of Babbitt or otherwise, the *Bookman* critics trembled before all the disorderly forces of modern life; their preferences were for control, discipline, and beauty as the countervailing forces of modern primitivism. The *Bookman* never answered to the call that literature reflect "real life." Its gentility accepted literature even as a veneer for a sordid world, and many of its spokesmen never abandoned hope that art might also redeem the world. So when Dreiser and others reported the external chaos of a disintegrating society and when D.H. Lawrence and William Faulkner depicted tumultuous passions driving their characters, *Bookman* reviewers recoiled and refused to admit that literature in this guise reflected the norms of human nature. They chastised the modern writers for "a love of violence for its own sake," for a new kind of Gothic cult of the grotesque. One reviewer of Faulkner's *Light in August* analogized the book to an epileptic fit,[17] and Alan Reynolds Thompson dismissed the "subliminal uprushes" of Lawrence's characters as "the phantasies of a romantic dreamer," their psychotic author.[18] Responding to these horrors, Douglas Bush offered his essay, "The Victorians, God Bless Them!" For all their faults, he contended, the Victorians rooted their literature more solidly in "normal human experience" than did their successors. In the literary world of the moderns, a little puritanism was not out of order.[19] Ruth Frisbie Moore believed as much, and in "The Right to Be Decent" absolved moral critics from charges that they were crucifying the human spirit by their censures. Judging by the popular books and movies, she concluded that the "market value of a wanton aunt exceeds that of a sainted grandmother." What, she asked, has become of the well adjusted?[20] And Thompson spoke for most of the *Bookman* people in asserting that however much modern writers and readers may thrill to "the crude visceral sensation," we at least in honesty ought not to confuse its literary manifestations with art.[21]

In these and other ways the *Bookman* made its points. Yet it must be said that ultimately its editorial bark was worse than its contributors' bite—or at least blunter and more dogmatic. In the first place, the *Bookman* did keep its eye out for fresh new fiction and openly welcomed some of it. One of its contributors called attention to new directions in black literature and hailed the "renascence" of Negro writing from the South to Harlem.[22] Florence Kiper Frank, in "The Presentment of the Jew in American Fiction," acknowledged a progression from stereotype to "authentic creation" in recent works.[23] The *Bookman* also looked for new writers on the scene. Dayton Kohler, for example, hailed the work of Glenway Wescott, finding amid a Proustean outpouring a noble human quest. "His family history becomes a Midland saga," Kohler wrote of Wescott, "a humble ethic of endless striving in circumstances removed from the mere heroic."[24] The *Bookman* here echoed the sentiments of the liberal and democratic humanist Stuart P. Sherman, who had called for American writers to tap the emotions and aspirations of America's ordinary people and make of American literature a new religion of democracy. Had the *Bookman* heeded that call more consciously, it might not have suffered from a reputation for coldness of heart.

Second, the *Bookman* did not shun controversy, and it welcomed opposing views. Many of its essays were wholly remote from Humanism and did not reflect the Humanist influence in any way. Partisans of other literary perspectives shared the *Bookman*'s platform. V. F. Calverton, a Marxist critic, was a contributor, as was C. Hartley Grattan, leader of the anti-Humanist movement and editor in 1930 of *The Critique of Humanism*. *Bookman* readers also received varied viewpoints on contemporary writers; William Faulkner, for example, was the subject of several essays that counterbalanced negative assessments. Most dramatic of these family quarrels was the celebrated letter of resignation from Rebecca West, who for years had been the *Bookman*'s European correspondent, offering lively and informative reports on the literary life abroad. But Collins's editorship had been taking the journal every year further in a direction she deplored. She wanted nothing to do with the New Humanism. "I think it likely to exercise a stultifying influence on the next few years," she wrote, "and I wish to take none of the blame." This was her "Last London Letter."[25]

The *Bookman* could be stultifying to free literary spirits, but in its own way it was a useful reminder that the life of letters was a higher calling. There should be qualities of elegance and taste about it. The *Bookman* typically reflected its character in 1931, for example, when it introduced a new section on "Typography, Art, and Design," one worthy of the true book lover.[26] Furthermore, the *Bookman* loved fine photography, and Collins continued to embellish its pages with it. "The

Literature under the Lens" section in 1929 offered excellent character portraits of noted literary figures and accompanied these with brief descriptions. That of H. L. Mencken's portrait was apt: "The eyes of this militant paleface lack nothing of defiance though the whoop of his enemies resounds across the pra-i-ree and ten thousand tomahawks flash in the bright sunshine." Later issues contained some superb studies in black and white: Joseph Hergesheimer, Waldo Frank, Esther Forbes, Carl Van Vechten, John Galsworthy, William Faulkner, Edith Wharton, Ernest Hemingway, John Dos Passos, Booth Tarkington, and many others.[27]

The *Bookman* died in 1933, to be reborn as the *American Review*. It had lived in a fragile world, and now amid the depression that world was crumbling—so it seemed, at least, to Collins. Culture alone could not save it, and Collins was convinced that the real crisis was economic in nature. A useful journal must address that question. But even for Collins the economic question remained a matter of first principles. In literature, education, politics, even religion, the democratic and individualistic credos had become corrosive. The world faced a crisis of authority, he believed, and its drift could not be set aright even by the high taste and moral correctness of the *Bookman*. Collins saw the *Bookman*'s circulation decline to 12,000, published its last issue in March, and followed it immediately with the *American Review*.[28] In the realm of politics and economics, he thought, America should consider the advantages of fascism.

Notes

1. Frank Luther Mott, *A History of American Magazines*, vol. 4, *1885–1905* (Cambridge, Massachusetts, 1957), pp. 432–36.

2. J. David Hoeveler, Jr., *The New Humanism: A Critique of Modern America, 1900–1940* (Charlottesville, Virginia, 1977), chaps. 1, 2.

3. Mott, *A History of American Magazines*, vol. 4, *1885–1905*, p. 440.

4. "Chronicle and Comment," *Bookman* 70 (January 1930): 529–30.

5. "Criticism in America: The Origins of a Myth," *Bookman* 71 (June 1930): 256; "Chronicle and Comment," pp. 543–44.

6. *Bookman* 74 (September 1931): 7.

7. "Coleridge and the Moderns," *Bookman* 70 (October 1929): 124.

8. *Bookman* 73 (April 1931): 113–22.

9. "The Literary Prophets," *Bookman* 72 (September 1930): 41; "The Literary Historians," *Bookman* 71 (July 1930): 370.

10. "Farewell to Achilles," *Bookman* 70 (January 1930): 470.

11. "John Donne: The Middle Phase," *Bookman* 73 (June 1931): 337–46.

12. "Our Post–War Novel," *Bookman* 74 (October 1931): 141–43; "Robert Frost and the Humanistic Temper," *Bookman* 71 (July 1930): 419–22.

13. "University and College: Dr. Flexner and the Modern University," *Bookman* 73 (May 1931): 225–40; "University and College: Is Liberal Education Wanted?" *Bookman* 73 (June 1931): 387–400; "University and College: A New College in the Modern University," *Bookman* 73 (July 1931): 503–21.

14. For example, Albert J. Nock, "The Absurdity of Teaching English," *Bookman* 69 (April 1929): 113–19.

15. For example, T. S. Eliot, "Experiment in Criticism," *Bookman* 70 (October 1929): 225–33; T. S. Eliot, "Poetry and Propaganda," *Bookman* 70 (February 1930): 595–602; and G. K. Chesterton, "The Spirit of the Age in Literature," *Bookman* 72 (October 1930): 97–103.

16. For example, Donald Davidson, "Criticism Outside New York," *Bookman* 73 (May 1931): 247–56.

17. Archer Winsten, *Bookman* 75 (September 1932): 736. The preceding quotation is also by Winsten.

18. "D. H. Lawrence: Apostle of the Dark God," *Bookman* 73 (July 1931): 498.

19. *Bookman* 74 (March 1932): 594–96.

20. *Bookman* 75 (May 1932): 114, 118 (the quotation).

21. "The Cult of Cruelty," *Bookman* 74 (January and February 1932): 487.

22. John Chamberlain, "The Negro as Writer," *Bookman* 70 (February 1930): 603–11.

23. *Bookman* 71 (June 1930): 270–75.

24. "Glenway Wescott: Legend–Maker," *Bookman* 73 (April 1931): 144.

25. *Bookman* 71 (July 1930): 513–22.

26. *Bookman* 74 (October 1931): xii–xiii.

27. *Bookman* 69 (August 1929): 625–40; *Bookman* 72 (October 1930): 129–44; *Bookman* 75 (December 1932): 775–90.

28. *Newsweek* 1 (15 April 1933): 29–30.

Information Sources

BIBLIOGRAPHY:

Hoeveler, J. David, Jr. *The New Humanism: A Critique of Modern America, 1900–1940*. Charlottesville, Virginia, 1977.

Mott, Frank Luther. *A History of American Magazines*, vol. 4, *1885–1905*. Cambridge, Massachusetts, 1957.

INDEXES: Each volume indexed; *ALI*; *Articles Amer Lit*; *BRD*; *Comb Ret Ind Bk Revs Hum*; *19th Cent RG*; *PAIS*; *Poole*; *RG*; *Writings Amer Hist*.

REPRINT EDITIONS: Microform: UMI; PMC; DA.

LOCATION SOURCES: Widely available.

Publication History

TITLE AND TITLE CHANGES: *The Bookman. An Illustrated Literary Journal*, February 1895–February 1901; *The Bookman. An Illustrated Literary Magazine,* March–August 1901; *The Bookman. An Illustrated Magazine of Literature and Life*, September 1901–February 1918; *The Bookman. A Review of Books and Life*, March 1918–August 1927; *The Bookman. A Revue of Life and Letters*, September 1927–August 1928; *The Bookman*, September 1928–March 1933.

VOLUME AND ISSUE DATA: Volumes 1–76, February 1895–March 1933.

FREQUENCY OF PUBLICATION: Monthly.

PUBLISHER: 1895–1918: Dodd, Mead, and Co.; 1918–1927: George H. Doran Co.; 1927–1933: Bookman Publishing Co. All in New York.

EDITORS: Harry Thurston Peck and James McArthur, 1895–1899; Harry Thurston Peck and Arthur Bartlett Maurice, 1899–1907; Arthur Bartlett Maurice and Frank Moore Colby, 1907–1910; Arthur Bartlett Maurice, 1910–1917; G. G. Wyant, 1917–1918; Robert Cortes Holliday, 1918–1920; Henry Litchfield West, 1920–1921; John Chipman Farrar, 1921–1927; Burton Rascoe, 1927–1928; Seward Collins, 1928–1933.

CIRCULATION: 12,000–14,000.

J. David Hoeveler, Jr.

American Review
1933–1937

Creation of the *American Review* in 1933 was the work of Seward B. Collins. Independently wealthy, a product of the Hill School and Princeton University, Collins had tried without success to revitalize a prestigious but faltering literary journal, the *Bookman*, and decided finally to enter vigorously into the day's controversial discussions of politics and economics. He never abandoned literary, religious, and philosophical matters, but integrated them into the wider issues of fascism, communism, and capitalism. Collins, and most of the contributors to the *American Review*, perceived a mounting crisis in Western civilization. As they addressed it, they made of the *American Review* a surprisingly fresh, curiously perverse, and highly provocative journal of the Right.

Collins made clear his intentions for the monthly publication at the very outset. His editorial comments in the first volume gave a welcome to all critics who judged the world from "a traditional basis." But Collins had in mind particular groups: the American New Humanists, led by Irving Babbitt and Paul Elmer More; the Southern Agrarians, who would contribute in great numbers to the review; the English Distributists, who furnished most of Collins's economic preferences; and the partisans of neo-Thomist philosophy in Europe and the United States, who in fact played a relatively small role as the journal progressed.[1] This assemblage could not, of course, ensure a consistent conservatism. Humanists and Agrarians, in fact, had fought each other on occasion before. But Collins did succeed in producing a journal with a clear common denominator: an articulate antimodernism marked in particular by a trenchant opposition to industrial capitalism. With this spirit, the review attracted a great variety of writers, among them some notable names: Herbert Agar, Irving Babbitt, Cleanth Brooks, Ralph Adams Cram, Donald Davidson, Norman Foerster, Paul Elmer More, John Crowe Ransom, Allen Tate, Austin Warren, and Robert Penn Warren. And from abroad: Hilaire Belloc, Nicholas Berdyaev, G. K. Chesterton, Christopher Dawson, and José Ortega y Gasset.

Most references to the *American Review* cite and highlight its profascist slant.[2] The review certainly did embrace fascism editorially, but neither Mussolini nor any European political movement was the *American Review*'s raison d'être. It would be more accurate to say that for many of the review's contributors, fascism was only a possible answer to the contemporary crisis in the Western world. Its perception of that crisis was what gave the *American Review* its traditionalist conservative character. Its writers often surveyed the wreckage of a once cohesive Christian culture, an organic society that provided individuals a sense of place, and a political arrangement based on privileged but benevolent elite leadership. But the Western world had now become a mass society of uprooted souls, bereft of any sense of belonging, alienated, and directionless. Modernism had produced a culture of ugly utilitarianism in architecture, a solipsistic, antitraditionalist cult of individuality in literature and art, and a nihilistic skepticism in philosophical pursuits. To this extent the *American Review* offered familiar conservative laments, more indigenous perhaps to Europe than America, but not strange to followers of the New Humanists, and later of neoconservatives like Peter Viereck and Russell Kirk. But what gave the *American Review*ers a special brand of criticism was their insistence that the roots of decay, of the destructive and corrosive individualism in the West, lay in the conquests of industrial capitalism, and in the corollary phenomenon of mass democracy and the servile state. Ralph Adams Cram made the point: "The factory, the joint-stock limited liability company, the banking system and usury, money-capitalism and technological mechanization soon did away with intimate personal relationship and the sense of duty, loyalty, and individual obligation."[3]

Seward Collins labeled capitalism the ethics of "greed."[4] Its single standard of measurement was materialism, cloaked deceptively in the secular gospel of progress and embraced even by the modern liberal Protestant churches. Redemption from this godlessness required a genuine religious recovery, and *American Review* essayists gave much attention to this possibility. Some, like the Agrarians, were sympathetic to an old-fashioned Protestantism with a Calvinistic ethic of sin and damnation, but most writers more enthusiastically embraced a high church Catholicism as the best hope for a recovery of traditional Western norms. Christopher Dawson, one of the favorites of this journal's reviewers, urged that "it is still not too late to restore the integrity of European culture on the basis of a comprehensive and Catholic order."[5] Clearly needed was a greater sense of supernaturalism in modern religion. Liberal Protestantism, Cleanth Brooks believed, concentrated too much on the brotherhood of man and too little on the fatherhood of God. Socialism became a by-product of this worldly humanitarianism.[6] Mason Wade, in reviewing Dawson's *Religion and the Modern State*, endorsed his contention that the socialistic atheism of communism derived simply from the secularization of older Christian ideals.[7] But the nemesis of materialism produced other corruptions, such as individualistic capitalism. Paul Elmer More excoriated the egocentric ethics of Adam Smith's worldly philosophy and its by-product, the cruel edifice of Manchesterian capitalism. The church, More insisted, has a duty to combat "the egotism of the natural man." It must urge self-control on the rich, while fighting "sentimental socialism."[8]

Not only the churches, but American colleges and universities had gone the way of directionless materialism. Here the *American Review* mostly echoed the charges made over the previous three decades by New Humanist critics that higher education had betrayed its major purposes. Beginning in the later nineteenth century with Harvard's Charles W. Eliot, curricular reform had deprived the college of a common focus and students of a common educational heritage. Norman Foerster charged that Eliot's cult of "power and service" handed the collegiate enterprise over to a utilitarian standard that promised students only an easier path to a comfortable existence.[9] Once again, Edd Winfield Parks found, the strongest proponents of both industrial capitalism and materialistic communism are allied.[10] Sacrificed in this process was everything that had once made the college the bearer of a traditional culture of classical and Christian learning. The proliferation of courses, the decay of the required curriculum, and the mechanical and utilitarian ethos had all conspired to produce the antitraditionalist college. Students, Foerster insisted, have a right to be given a world to live in, not a cultural chaos.[11] And it was almost with a note of nostalgia that Austin Warren offered an appreciative essay on Harvard's renowned classicist and "gentleman," Charles Eliot Norton.[12]

The recovery of a humane and organic society, however, was more than a matter of institutional reform or cultural reorientation. Eric Gill, recapitulating an argument that Agrarians had often proffered, contended that industrial life is spiritually alienating and deprives the human soul of its aesthetic inclinations. Industrial society consequently had divorced art from work and use from beauty.[13] But alienation applies also in people's relations to each other. Herbert Agar, in considering "The Task for Conservatism," urged that true traditionalists must be alert to the dangers of their close affiliation with a plundering, rapacious capitalism. Agar wrote with a force that did not exaggerate the *American Review*'s disdain for the prevailing economic order in the United States. "The obvious task for Conservatives is to redefine the historic purpose of America, to scotch forever the association of this purpose with the obscenities of Big Business." Competitive capitalism has untied the protective bonds of human relationships and created a public of citizens defined only by their relations to an impersonal cash nexus and an anomalous corporate structure.[14]

The *American Review* exercised a less clear attitude toward democracy. For some, like W. E. D. Allen, democracy was simply the political coefficient of industrial capitalism and the vehicle of control for the bourgeoisie.[15] Ralph Adams Cram considered the problem in greater depth. The social product of capitalism, he believed, was the undiscriminating, tasteless mass society that flourished in the modern industrial countries. Democracy had become an amalgamation of uprooted souls; it offered only a fictitious liberty. But capitalism, Cram believed, further divided this society into two warring factions—the organized proletariat and the interlocking financial, industrial, and commercial powers. Each faction, motivated only by "pure greed," had lost all social and communal values. The titanic struggle between these factions took all society with it, and Cram spoke with sympathy for the "forgotten classes" who might otherwise be the solid foundation of a stable democracy. In this group Cram included farmers, small shop-keepers, craftsmen and artisans, literary people and intellectuals, clergy, clerks, and the mass of ununionized laborers. "This is the class whose interests call for recognition," Cram believed. But he was not optimistic. The saddest spectacle in America was the spiritual debilitation of this group by the technological parapher-nalia of industrialism—the automobile, the radio, the telephone, and the mail-or-der catalogue. A class so debilitated by commercialism could never be the hope of a rejuvenated democracy.[16]

Concern for this matter naturally drew the *American Review*'s attention to the South and its economic situation. The Agrarian theme in the review conveyed both an anti-industrial interest and a strong note of concern for the condition of the South's small landholders and tenant farmers. Donald Davidson and other Agrar-ians believed that agrarianism furnished the only realistic hope for a truly organic society, one in which work is a natural part of the whole life process and integrated with religion and art. Commercial farming had brought the mores of industrial capitalism to the South, however, and farming for profit became an end in itself; the agrarian labor force of tenants and hired day hands became indistinguishable in kind from assembly line workers.[17] William Terry Couch called these Southern-ers "the most neglected and hopeless peasantry in the Western world."[18] The Agrar-ians offered solutions. Some welcomed the reform program of the English Distributists and called on the American government to intervene in a thorough program to destroy absentee ownership, re-create small farms by land distribution, and supply new owners with sufficient material stock to make them permanent managers.[19] John Crowe Ransom urged an extreme course, calling for a return from commercial farming to farming for home consumption and proposing that farmers utilize "literal horse-power, mule-power."[20]

The Agrarian theme in the *American Review* reflects another of its interests, an encouragement of regionalism in American life. The *Review* represented a kind of conservatism that is provincial, enamored of folkways, and greatly respectful of the pluralistic strands in American life. It liked small town virtues, strong commu-nal values, and traditional ways generally. This emphasis put the *Review* only slightly at cross-purposes with its appreciation of classical and Christian values derived from the whole Western experience. Both parts of its program should be seen as cures for the alienating, deracinating effects of industrial capitalism. Both represented the *Review*'s quests for the humanization of modern life.

Cosmopolitan influences in modern life the *American Review* regularly dis-dained. Ransom, in "The Aesthetic of Regionalism," warned that wealth produces a plutocracy with indiscriminate cosmopolitan tastes that threaten organic culture. That threat, Davidson said, came mostly from New York City and the metropolitan East. He examined classroom texts used around the country and found that these New York publications showed considerable ignorance of history and culture west of the Hudson River. Academic sociologists, caught in a web of statistical mea-surements, had lost sight of the wisdom and folklore of America's provincial en-claves.[21] To John Gould Fletcher, New York City had become excessively interna-tionalist, aping Parisian styles in art and fashion, and holding them up for emulation to the rest of the nation.[22] Davidson took up this issue in its literary aspects. He directly attacked Granville Hicks's book *The Great Tradition* (1935) for its renunciation of a literature of localism and its call for a more relevant confrontation with the great public issues of the day. Davidson perceived the Marxist concerns of Hicks and replied that nationalism and regionalism are variants of the American experience and that American literature has flourished only through its regionalist expressions. That fact is a measure of our difference from Europe, he believed. "The domestic problem is, not how shall we achieve a unity that may be spurious and deceptive, but how shall we secure the artistic and cultural equilibrium that will give free play to our diverse regional geniuses."[23]

The *American Review* recognized that it shared with leftist writers a contempt for industrial capitalism. Why then was the *Review* so belligerently anticommunist? Those contributors who addressed this question contended that in fact capitalism and communism were essentially two sides of the same coin, industrialism. Geoffrey Stone, in a lengthy review of Stephen Spender's *Forward from Liberalism*, replied to that author's urging that unless we opt now for communism, we will prepare the way for fascism. Stone replied that historically fascism arises as a response to communism, that is itself the natural product of capitalist decay. Fascism furthermore endeavors to restore those traditional values, which capitalism has already eroded but that communism would destroy forever.[24] Collins's interpretation was similar. The Soviet Union enjoyed a better press in America than fascist Italy because it emulated all the worst in our own society: science, humanitarianism, feminism, "modern" education, the decay of family, and materialism. Communism, then, was just another aspect of modernism.[25]

Fascism attracted *American Review* writers for a number of reasons. Some admired Mussolini. Collins called him "the most constructive Statesman of our age."[26] Allen waxed even more enthusiastic. Mussolini, he wrote, is "that occasional phenomenon of the ages which embodies a synthesis of the 'man of action' and the serene philosopher."[27] Ross J. S. Hoffman called the Italian leader "a man of tradition with whom Aristotle or St. Thomas or Machiavelli might…feel at ease."[28] And whereas capitalism and communism were antinationalist, fascism, according to Allen, "respects the old primal values and holds in honor the continuing traditions of the nation." For this reason especially, fascism and the corporate state could restore better than any alternative the cohesive communal bonds destroyed by competitive individualism.[29] Harold Goad emphasized that "the first principle of fascist theory is that all citizens are in the State and no individual can be outside it or against it."[30] And to others there was something about the drama and flare of the rightist movements in Europe that captured their imaginations. Hoffman Nickerson viewed fascism romantically. It promised to rejuvenate with a new martial spirit the effete and decadent society fashioned by modern materialism. "In a restored social order," he wrote, "Fascism may beget a new aristocracy of gentlemen-at-arms."[31]

Romanticism combined with nostalgia in the neomedievalist ethos of the *American Review*. Many of its contributors called explicitly for a return to the culture and society of the Middle Ages. Medievalism represented to the *American Review* a Christian society—one that was hierarchical, monarchical, and aristocratic in leadership, but protective of the lower classes too. It suggested also a qualitatively superior society, the more so as it contrasted to modernity's surfeit of materialism. "We instinctively feel," wrote Christopher Dawson, "that there is something honourable about a king, a noble, or a knight which the banker, the stockbroker or the democratic politician does not possess."[32] The *American Review* also had in Ralph Adams Cram the leading architect and theorist of the late nineteenth- and twentieth-century Gothic revival in American architecture. The review published several autobiographical chapters by Cram, and they narrated his discovery of high church Catholic culture in Europe, his conversion to Anglicanism, and his own commitment to a medieval recovery in the United States. His own career in architecture began, he wrote, against the background of the "sterile and vapid productions of my own country" after the democratic revolution wrought by Andrew Jackson effectively terminated the great neoclassic period of the old aristocratic republic.[33] Cram, Nickerson, and Collins stated strong preferences for monarchism on the medieval model.

Toward the end of its brief life, the *American Review* allied its conservative philosophy with the Francoist side in the Spanish Civil War. Douglas Jerrold tried valiantly to dress Franco in progressive colors—"He is an ardent Christian and he is fighting for social justice"—but his defense was a whitewash of the rightist atrocities in Spain.[34] As Mussolini faded in glory and lost his credibility, Franco seemed to be a possible alternative hope. But it did not really matter. The *American Review* was also fading. It missed an issue in the spring of 1937, and Collins promised his readers an extension of their subscriptions. But the next issue was the last. The *Review* died unceremoniously after the summer offering that year.

The *American Review* was a unique journalistic expression in America. Its lack of success cannot be surprising. It spoke against too much that had become ingrained in the American psyche: individualism, competition, democracy, egalitarianism. With its mystique of monarchy and aristocracy, Gothic churches and armored knights, it was almost an Old World voice in a New World environment. But it labored hard to ingratiate itself with that environment, to blend its conservatism with American ideals. So it took up the cause of the victims of industrialism, called attention to the needs of poor farmers, and celebrated local communities, folkish ways, and pluralistic styles in America. It reminded its readers that the founders themselves had based democracy on wide ownership of property among the people. Against the milder reforms of the New Deal and its safe and pragmatic course, the *American Review*'s program seemed radical to many and irrelevant to others. But to those who sensed that something had been lost in America's headlong rush into twentieth-century "progress," who believed with regret that modern life had become materialistic and impersonal, the *American Review* could speak with sympathy.

Notes

1. Seward Collins, "Editorial Notes," *American Review* 1 (April 1933): 122–25 (hereinafter cited as *AR*).

2. See for example Albert E. Stone, Jr., "Seward Collins and the *American Review*: Experiment in Pro-Fascism, 1933–37," *American Quarterly* 12 (Spring 1960): 3–19.

3. "The Return to Feudalism," *AR* 8 (January 1937): 340.

4. "The Revival of Monarchy," *AR* 1 (May 1933): 244.

5. "The Significance of Bolshevism," *AR* 1 (April 1933): 49.

6. "The Christianity of Modernism," *AR* 6 (February 1936): 436–37, 441.

7. "A New Faith for the New State," *AR* 6 (January 1936): 348–49.

8. "Church and Politics," *AR* 3 (September 1934): 428, 419.

9. "The College, the Individual, and Society," *AR* 4 (December 1934): 130–31, 138.

10. "On Banishing Nonsense," *AR* 1 (October 1933): 560–64.

11. "Chicago and General Education," *AR* 5 (September 1933): 418–19.

12. "Mr. Norton of Shady Hill," *AR* 8 (November 1936): 86–114.

13. "Art in Relation to Industrialism," *AR* 6 (January 1936): 328–30.

14. *AR* 3 (April 1934): 10, 16.

15. "The Fascist Idea in Britain," *AR* 2 (January 1934): 343–44.

16. "The Forgotten Class, I," *AR* 7 (April 1936): 32, 40–41; "The Forgotten Class, II," *AR* 7 (May 1936): 180.

17. Donald Davidson, "I'll Take My Stand: A History," *AR* 5 (Summer 1935): 309–11; Andrew Nelson Lytle, "The Backwoods Progression," *AR* 1 (September 1933): 409–14.

18. "An Agrarian Programme for the South," *AR* 3 (June 1934): 319.

19. Ibid., 322–23; Frank L. Owsley, "The Pillars of Agrarianism," *AR* 4 (February 1935): 529–47.

20. "Happy Farmers," *AR* 1 (October 1933): 529.

21. "The Aesthetics of Regionalism," *AR* 2 (January 1934): 290–310; "Regionalism and Education," *AR* 4 (January 1935): 315; "Still Rebels, Still Yankees," *AR* 2 (November 1933): 59. See also Robert Penn Warren, "Some Don'ts for Literary Regionalists," *AR* 8 (December 1936): 142–56.

22. "The Stieglitz Spoof," *AR* 4 (February 1935): 588–602.

23. "Regionalism and Nationalism in American Literature," *AR* 5 (April 1935): 49, 53–58.

24. "Excelsior," *AR* 9 (Summer 1937): 299–300.

25. "Revival of Monarchy," p. 253.

26. Ibid.

27. "Fascist Idea in Britain," p. 328.

28. "The Totalitarian Regimes," *AR* 9 (September 1937): 336.

29. "Fascist Idea in Britain," p. 331.

30. "The Principles of the Corporate State," *AR* 1 (April 1933): 86.

31. "Gentlemen Wanted," *AR* 7 (Summer 1936): 440.

32. "Significance of Bolshevism," p. 45.

33. "Many Adventures," *AR* 6 (November 1935): 56, 58; "Tradition Plus Modernism: The Relation of Architecture to Society," *AR* 6 (December 1935): 157.

34. "The Issues in Spain," *AR* 9 (April 1937): 20, 23.

Information Sources

BIBLIOGRAPHY:

Stone, Albert E., Jr. "Seward Collins and the *American Review*: Experiment in Pro-Fascism, 1933–37," *American Quarterly* 12 (Spring 1960): 3–19.

INDEXES: Each volume indexed except 9; *BRD*; *RG*; *Writings Amer Hist*.

REPRINT EDITIONS: Microform: PMC. Bound edition: Kraus Reprint Company.

LOCATION SOURCES: Widely available.

Publication History

TITLE AND TITLE CHANGES: *American Review*.

VOLUME AND ISSUE DATA: Volumes 1–9, April 1933–October 1937. No numbers
  issued for May, June, July, and August 1937 except one "Summer" number.

FREQUENCY OF PUBLICATION: Monthly.

PUBLISHER: Bookman Publishing Company, New York.

EDITOR: Seward B. Collins.

CIRCULATION: Unknown.

J. David Hoeveler, Jr.

American Mercury
1924–1980

Wishing to associate his publishing house with a periodical, young Alfred A. Knopf in early 1923 approached the coeditors of the *Smart Set*, H. L. Mencken and George Jean Nathan. Under their aegis since 1914, the *Smart Set* had flourished essentially as a review of the arts. Now, however, it was suffering from financial difficulties as well as from a desire on Mencken's part to provide more articles dealing with politics and economics. After some deliberation, Knopf decided not to purchase *Smart Set* but instead to back an entirely new venture that would be coedited by Mencken and Nathan, and called, at Nathan's suggestion, the *American Mercury*. Within a few years after its initial January 1924 issue, the *Mercury* would prove the most popular new magazine of the decade and one of the most influential magazines then in existence in the United States.

The editors of the *Mercury* promised in the first issue to provide "civilized entertainment," to "lay chief stress at all times upon American ideas, American problems, and American personalities," and to "attempt a realistic presentation of the whole gaudy, gorgeous, American scene." They also hastened to assure readers that they viewed the nation's system of capitalism "if not exactly amorously, then at all events politely."[1] Less than two months after that initial issue and its harmonious overtones, Nathan resigned as coeditor. Much more concerned with questions of aesthetics than his partner, he wished their new enterprise to focus more sharply on literary themes. Mencken, wishing it to become more inclusive in its interests, insisted to Knopf that continued coediting of the journal would be impossible. Since Knopf originally did not want Nathan as a coeditor in any case, the problem was quickly and rather amicably resolved. Nathan continued to contribute theater reviews and various essays until 1930, but the *Mercury* henceforth was to bear the cachet only of Mencken, who, according to Walter Lippmann, became "the most powerful personal influence on this whole generation of educated people."[2]

Even before the *Mercury* appeared in print Mencken noted, "To one side the Liberals must chase butterflies; to the other side the Otto Kahns, Henry Morgenthaus and other such great patriots sob and moan for endangered capital. Certainly there must be room in the middle for an educated Toryism—the true Disraelian brand. It exists everywhere, but in the United States it has no voice."[3] It was his intent to reach an audience of cultivated, sensible, middle-class readers by avoiding and denouncing political and socioeconomic extremes. Yet this middle-of-the-road conservatism frequently found observance more in the breach than in reality since Mencken—in his personal views and editorial policies—gave strong and often simultaneous enunciation to libertarian and reactionary points of view. A tenacious commitment to individual liberty clashed persistently with a generally low opinion of humans and a corresponding distrust of democracy.

As a libertarian, Mencken generously contributed to the intellectual discontent of the 1920s by opening the pages of the *Mercury* to individuals and groups generally unpopular with rank-and-file Americans eager to return to normalcy in the postwar period. With verve, humor, satire, and invective, Mencken affirmed the right to dissent. Liberals and radicals alike benefited from his deep-seated belief in the freedom of expression. In part this tolerance of the Left stemmed from a mutually shared animus against traditional religion, an animus that contradicted his dominant conservative values. (This indulgence, it should be noted, applied more to left-wing politics than to culture. Increasingly the *Mercury* eschewed the culturally experimental in favor of the traditional.) As a libertarian, Mencken encouraged and published other overlooked or despised writers. Various black contributors, such as George S. Schuyler (later to become a staunch conservative), Countee Cullen, Langston Hughes, W. E. B. Du Bois, and James Weldon Johnson, appeared in the *Mercury*, as did an occasional inmate serving a prison term. In a similar vein, he printed the works of others who shared his aversion to intolerance. Typical examples were Gerald W. Johnson's "The Ku-Kluxer" in the February 1924 issue and Harry Elmer Barnes's "Hunting Bolsheviks" in the September 1924 issue.

Taking up the cudgels on behalf of freedom of expression nearly led to Mencken's own incarceration. The April 1926 issue of the *Mercury* contained Herbert Asbury's "Hatrack," an account of a small-time prostitute. The Watch and Ward Society of Boston, in good Comstockian fashion, announced plans to suppress sales of the issue. At the suggestion of Arthur Garfield Hays, the noted defense attorney, Mencken journeyed to Boston, sold a copy of the issue in question, and was promptly arrested. Happily for him, the judge decided against the Watch and Ward Society. Other censorship attempts also failed, but as Mencken wrote to Upton Sinclair apropos of one such attempt by the post office: "It tried to ruin my business, and failed by only an inch."[4]

As editor of the *Mercury*, Mencken paraded his libertarianism by espousing religious freethinking along lines set down by his boyhood hero, Thomas Huxley. Mencken did not flail religion qua religion. Indeed, he usually adopted a muted tone toward Roman Catholicism and once described himself as a sort of Christian socialist.[5] Protestantism, on the other hand, incurred his wrath. Enumerating the most salient examples of intolerance in the United States during the 1920s—

fundamentalism, prohibition, nativism, the Klan—he found Protestant leadership at the root of the problem. In an early issue of the *Mercury* he excoriated both Baptist and Methodist ministers as "responsible for the Anti-Saloon League and its swineries, and they are responsible no less for the Klan....Hordes of poor creatures have followed these appalling rogues and vagabonds....The result, in immense areas, is the conversion of Christianity into a machine for making civilized living impossible. It is wholly corrupt, rotten, and abominable. It deserves no more respect than a pile of garbage."[6] A few months later Mencken journeyed to Dayton, Tennessee, for the Scopes Trial and found further occasion to malign the fundamentalists, their "pope," William Jennings Bryan, and their attempts to impose their beliefs and values on other Americans.

Juxtaposed to libertarianism in Mencken was a decided strain of the reactionary. As he proudly noted, "A progressive is one who believes that the common people are both intelligent and honest; a reactionary is one who knows better."[7] Probably not surprising for one who used the tenets of Darwinism to explain the natural world, he preached a version of Social Darwinism, particularly as it had been promulgated by William Graham Sumner. Mencken's hero in certain ways resembled the nineteenth-century sociologist's "forgotten man," the good citizen who minded his business and asked for no special favors. For Mencken, however, the "forgotten man" was not necessarily an economically successful figure but one who was artistically and intellectually free from cant, smugness, and the philistinism of the "booboisie." Mencken's Social Darwinism, resonating with healthy individualism, also embraced a certain racism. While condemning the atrocities of the Klan and writing warmly to black writers, he could still announce in the *Mercury* that the "vast majority of the people of their race are but two or three inches removed from the gorillas."[8]

Neither Mencken's libertarian nor his reactionary views were ipso facto responsible for the *Mercury*'s meteoric rise in circulation to its zenith of some 84,000 in early 1928.[9] Nor was the success of the journal mainly attributable to the galaxy of noteworthy contributors that include Zachariah Chafee, Jr., Paul de Kruif, Henry F. Pringle, Joseph Wood Krutch, Margaret Mead, Albert J. Guerard, Edgar Lee Masters, William Faulkner, James T. Farrell, F. Scott Fitzgerald, Sherwood Anderson, Lewis Mumford, Carl Van Vechten, and Bernard De Voto, to name several. Rather, it was Mencken's irreverent humor and engaging style that drew readers to his witty editorials and his reviews ("The Library"), and to his collection of national oddities and foibles ("Americana"). Whether it was the debunking obituary for Bryan published in the *Mercury*'s October 1925 issue or the incessant jibes at Calvin Coolidge, southerners, and farmers, the Mencken wit quickly won an audience of largely urban, educated, middle-class Americans, many of whom were attending colleges throughout the nation. It has been estimated that fully one-third of the *Mercury*'s contents between its inception and 1929 was satirical in nature.[10] To the question, "If you find so much to complain of in the United States, then why do you live here," Mencken replied, "Why do men go to zoos?"[11]

Not all Americans were amused by the antics of the *Mercury* and its editor. Particularly distressed were those whose politics or cultural tastes occupied the further ranges of the Left and the Right. The Left applauded the antireligious bias of the *Mercury*, as well as Mencken's castigation of puritanism, rural values, intolerance, and the traditional politics of both parties. Yet the radical Left, exemplified by Michael Gold, deplored Mencken's confirmed disbelief in revolution or even political reform. They remembered Mencken's scornful warning in the *Mercury*'s first issue that the radical proposal to destroy capitalism is "as full of folly as the Liberal proposals to denaturize it by arousing its better nature." American politics, he lamented, was quixotically utopian.[12] Socialists, labor agitators, economic reformers—all were objects of Mencken's scorn. The artistic Left, in turn, never forgave him for the *Mercury*'s early denunciation of Greenwich Village bohemianism, avant-gardism, or the expatriatism of American artists and writers, and wrote off the Sage of Baltimore as hopelessly middle class and conservative in both his antitheoretical cast of mind and dislike for abstractions.

No less vocal than the *Mercury*'s left-wing critics were its right-wing ones. Some objected to the magazine's attacks on religion, prohibition, and nativistic fervor; others complained of assaults on President Coolidge as well as other assorted political figures and institutions. More reasoned criticism emanated from New Humanists like Irving Babbitt, Paul Elmer More, and Stuart Sherman. For Babbitt, the Harvard professor, Mencken penned "intellectual vaudeville" rather than "serious criticism."[13] The latter retorted by labeling the New Humanism the "natural and inevitable refuge of all timorous and third-rate men—of all weaklings for whom the struggle with hard facts is unendurable—of all the nay-sayers of Nietzsche's immortal scorn."[14]

Having reached the height of its popularity in early 1928, the *Mercury*'s circulation then began an inexorable decline, thanks originally to the accelerating bombardment from the Left and the Right, and then to the vicissitudes of the Great Depression. Although it had introduced a section on financial investment in its pages in 1928, the *Mercury*, remarkably, featured few articles and little editorial advice pertaining to the depression until after the election of Franklin D. Roosevelt. Like a number of his countrymen, Mencken had simply concluded that prosperity was just around the corner; his belief in capitalism never wavered. During the 1920s he had applauded various American businessmen, such as Henry Ford, and, to the amusement or consternation of many, he reappraised Coolidge in the April 1933 issue of the *Mercury* as having been not as poor a president as he had earlier opined. As he noted, "There were no thrills while he reigned but neither were there any headaches. He had no ideas, and he was not a nuisance."[15] At the same time he stressed that Americans needed to be less spendthrift in their ways and should not go begging to the government for greater spending.[16] By 1934 he was vehemently denouncing Roosevelt and the New Deal for fomenting class antagonisms, concluding that democracy and capitalism were antipathetic, with the former responsible for the current ills of the nation.[17] By January 1934, however, Mencken had resigned from the *Mercury*. Concerns for personal finance (he was receiving no salary) and for his ailing wife, a desire to concentrate on writing books, and perhaps the galling sting of the loss of popularity, his own as well as that of the magazine, convinced him to quit.

Mencken handpicked as his successor Henry Hazlitt, who had been serving as an editor of the *Nation*, one of the country's most stalwart liberal periodicals. The association was misleading. Hazlitt had begun his career as a writer for the *Wall Street Journal* and had retained a conservative position on economic questions. Indeed, in the December 1933 issue of the *Mercury*, the last one edited by Mencken, appeared Hazlitt's anti–New Deal piece, "The Fallacies of the N.R.A." It took only a few months on the job, however, to convince both Hazlitt and Knopf that the new position presented too many difficulties. In August 1934 Charles Angoff replaced Hazlitt.

A young Harvard graduate, Angoff had accepted Mencken's invitation in 1925 to assume the duties that George Jean Nathan was relinquishing. Soon he became managing editor. By the time he became editor, Angoff, unlike Hazlitt, knew the intricacies of the periodical's workings. Also, unlike Hazlitt, he was a convinced liberal—Mencken said he became a communist once he assumed the editorship[18]—who gave promise of a *démarche* in the political position of the *Mercury*. Upset with Angoff's political leanings, as well as with the continued decline in the magazine's circulation, publisher Knopf in 1935 peremptorily sold the *Mercury* to Paul Palmer.

A long-time friend and former associate of Mencken, Palmer assumed for himself the task of editing the *Mercury*, while turning over the position of publisher to another Harvard graduate, Lawrence E. Spivak. The latter had been with the magazine as business manager since 1933 and now successfully used his experience and acumen to revise its format and price, both of which helped to halt the decline in circulation. Palmer, for his part, halted the magazine's brief flirtation with liberalism and steered it back to its conservative moorings. He also continued the *Mercury*'s practice of printing the essays of prominent man of letters Albert Jay Nock, the communitarian architect Ralph Adams Cram, the Catholic Agnes Repplier, and the philosopher George Santayana. Under Palmer's tutelage the magazine also readopted a strong anti–New Deal, anti-Roosevelt posture.

In 1939 Palmer sold the *Mercury* to Spivak, who, after personally serving as editor for one issue, appointed Russian-born Eugene Lyons to that post. Lyons had been a UP correspondent to the Soviet Union and had been sympathetic to bolshevism. In 1934, however, the Soviets ejected him from the country, and Lyons subsequently became staunchly anticommunist. Still regarded as basically liberal in his politics, he surprised not a few by clinging to a middle-of-the-road position rather than extending a more cordial welcome to the policies of the New Deal. Less than pleased with the nation's wartime friendship with the Soviets, the *Mercury* remained anti-Stalinist both at home and abroad. When Lyons retired in 1944, Spivak again accepted the dual responsibility of editor and publisher, and turned the magazine in a more liberal direction. He even brought back Angoff, who was to serve first as literary editor and then as managing editor. Under Spivak's leadership the *Mercury* reached a monthly circulation of roughly 80,000 by the end of World War II.[19] Though in 1946 the *Mercury* absorbed *Common Sense*, a strongly anticommunist magazine, continued financial difficulties induced Spivak four years later to sell.

The new purchaser of the *Mercury* was Clendenin J. Ryan, an erstwhile reformer who was a prominent financier and the son of an even more prominent financier, Thomas Fortune Ryan. Ryan turned over the actual running of the magazine to the writer William Bradford Huie. As editor, Huie was determined to place less emphasis on political matters. Yet he was also a confirmed conservative. In 1952, for example, he worked assiduously through the pages of the *Mercury* to convince readers that Dwight D. Eisenhower must secure the Republican presidential nomination, defeat his Democratic opponent, and then work in tandem with Senator Robert A. Taft (R, Ohio) to guide the nation back to a conservative, anti–New Deal, anti–Fair Deal pathway.[20] Huie accepted articles from younger as well as established conservatives. In July 1952, by way of illustration, the *Mercury* printed "Second Thoughts: The Rich and the Poor," by a youthful William F. Buckley, Jr., whose *God and Man at Yale*, published the previous year, achieved a *succès d'estime* among conservatives. Addressing antistatists, Buckley argued in his article that "perhaps the most melancholy effect of the redistributionist program is the transfer of power from the individual to the State, and all that implies."[21]

Buckley's warning against statism did not represent the proverbial voice crying in the wilderness. During the postwar years the *Mercury* vigorously defended free enterprise by consistently opening its pages to those who extolled the merits of capitalism and eulogized defenders, both past and present, of individual liberties. Mortimer Smith, for example, in 1950 lauded one of Mencken's great nineteenth-century heroes, William Graham Sumner, the advocate of classical economics: "In a period when collectivism is on the march, when the historical idea of the omniscience of the State is again being advanced and compulsory cooperation finds its mystical advocates, perhaps nothing could be more salutary than the reemergence of the massive figure of this great libertarian."[22]

While praising capitalism and its defenders, the *Mercury* articles of this period also attacked the shortcomings of organized labor and its leaders, fearing that both imperiled the nation's freedom and well-being. A. H. Raskin warned workers that John L. Lewis possessed no confidence in the masses or their abilities. A victim of frustrated childhood resentments, the leader of the coal miners had to be restrained, Raskin argued, until psychiatry permitted us to understand him more completely.[23] Ralph de Toledano, on the other hand, eschewed psychoanalytical judgments of the powerful leader of the auto workers, Walter Reuther, whom he found "complex and fascinating." Still, according to de Toledano, "as a demagogue, Reuther bows to no man, with the possible exception of Harry S Truman."[24]

The year 1952 witnessed yet another sale of the *Mercury*, this time to J. Russell Maguire, who had derived his considerable wealth from oil and munitions manufacturing. At this juncture the political position of the magazine moved from conservative to radical Right. Convinced that communism threatened the United States as fully at home as overseas, Maguire gave full support to Senator Joseph McCarthy (R, Wisconsin) and his campaign to uncover and extirpate domestic subversives. Frequently he wrote editorials expressing alarm over the communist menace. A typical one, written in 1956, found Maguire praising Father Charles Coughlin while denouncing FDR, General George Marshall, and Justice Felix

Frankfurter, who, in his opinion, had shielded both Alger Hiss and Dean Acheson.[25] A number of the *Mercury*'s contributors during these years were passionate cold warriors—John T. Flynn, Harold Lord Varney, James Burnham, William Henry Chamberlin, Ralph de Toledano, Louis Budenz, Eugene Lyons, and J. B. Matthews, to name a few—some of whom earlier had embraced or at least had been more sympathetic to the Soviet experiment. As the decade progressed, the *Mercury* seemed convinced of a ubiquitous communism which had infected, among other victims, the United Nations, American churches, and the nation of Israel.[26]

More startling was its espousal of racism. In the year Maguire purchased it, the *Mercury* was continuing Mencken's tradition of publicizing the works of minority writers. The August 1952 issue, for example, contained James Baldwin's "Exodus: A Story"; two months later appeared William Barrett's favorable review of Ralph Ellison's *The Invisible Man*. Shortly, however, the *Mercury* adopted an anti-Semitic stance, equating Zionism with communism.

After Maguire sold the *Mercury* in 1961, it passed under the control of various right-wing groups. Changes in ownership and editorship, however, failed to deflect the *Mercury* from the course charted in the 1950s. Anti-Semitism, for example, remained a consistent theme. The title of the editorial for the fall 1970 issue asked, "Shall We Die for Israel?" and concluded that only Israel and the Soviet Union were victors in World War II.[27] The 1973 summer and winter issues featured Frank A. Capell's two-part "International Bankers and the Communist Conspiracy," a thinly veiled attack on Jewish financiers in the aggregate and the Rothschilds in particular. Not surprisingly, the *Mercury* was also persistently antiblack during the 1960s and 1970s. While one article in the mid-1960s equated cowardly calls for negotiations in Vietnam with attempts to impose racial integration on Mississippi, another in 1980 suggested that blacks return to Africa.[28] Gerald S. Pope, who edited the magazine in 1961, seems to have given form to future *Mercury* sentiments as well as his own when he declared: "Enlightened Americans are not intimidated by propaganda that says discrimination in any form is wrong. They know that such philosophy is the work of the enemies of freedom who seek to destroy individualism and to create in its place a collectivism that treats man as a faceless member of society."[29]

During the 1960s and 1970s the *Mercury* gave voice to other frustrations and attacked *bêtes noires* that troubled many Americans but particularly those of a right-wing persuasion: the failure to win a military victory in Vietnam, communist China, the Internal Revenue Service, and fluoridation. On occasion, as if to underscore that it had ceased to be an essentially conservative enterprise and instead espoused the radical Right, the magazine asserted that the Nobel prizes were "little more than a tool in the service of International Communism," denounced William F. Buckley, Jr., for his failure to support the presidential aspirations of George Wallace in 1968, and pondered whether Henry Kissinger might not actually be a communist.[30] Perhaps most illustrative of its apostasy from traditional conservatism was the *Mercury*'s decision to print an article which praised national socialism for its defense of the concepts of folk and race.[31]

The *Mercury* as it developed in the 1960s and 1970s diverged sharply from the

Mercury of H. L. Mencken. Yet it continued to claim ties of strong kinship with its predecessor. Mencken was extolled not only as the founding editor but as the mentor whose ideas and attitudes continued to serve as a guiding spirit. On the occasion of Mencken's centennial in 1980, the *Mercury* editorialized that his America had been a vastly different one and that he had departed "before America really began to fall apart—before the Negro race riots in the cities, protests on college campuses by unwashed bearded youths, and wholesale debauchment of the nation's money via the printing press."[32] Six years earlier, in commemorating the fiftieth anniversary of its founding, the *Mercury* had lavishly praised the Sage of Baltimore for his wisdom and achievements. Although duly noting his religious skepticism and irreverence, it still contended that he would approve of the magazine's current values and positions because he was not a liberal in today's sense, one contaminated by Anglomania or "Judeolatry."[33] Whatever claims to affinity with Mencken the modern *Mercury* might put forth, the old *Mercury* differed markedly. Witty, urbane, more catholic in taste, the magazine under Mencken, for all its prejudices and limitations, was an extraordinary achievement, providing a rich fare of intellectual provocation and genuine amusement. In its last years, however, obsessed with racial views and experiencing a decline in circulation, *American Mercury* ceased publication in the spring of 1980.

Notes

1. Editorial, *American Mercury* 1 (January 1924): 28, 30 (hereinafter cited as *AM*).

2. Walter Lippmann, "H. L. Mencken," *Saturday Review of Literature* 3 (11 December 1926): 414.

3. Henry Louis Mencken (hereinafter cited as HLM) to James Branch Cabell, 16 August 1923, in Henry L. Mencken, *The New Mencken Letters*, ed. Carl Bode (New York, 1977), pp. 173–74.

4. Quoted in M. K. Singleton, *H. L. Mencken and the* American Mercury *Adventure* (Durham, North Carolina, 1962), pp. 180–81.

5. HLM to the Right Reverend James Cannon, Jr., 29 June 1934, in Bode, ed., *Mencken Letters*, p. 312.

6. Editorial, *AM* 3 (November 1924): 291–92.

7. Quoted in Douglas C. Stenerson, *H. L. Mencken: Iconoclast from Baltimore* (Chicago, 1971), p. 172.

8. HLM, "The New Aframerican: New Style," *AM* 7 (February 1926): 255.

9. Singleton, *Mencken*, p. 256.

10. Ibid., p. 65.

11. HLM, "Clinical Notes," *AM* 3 (September 1924): 63.

12. Editorial [January 1924], p. 28.

13. Quoted in Charles A. Fecher, *Mencken: A Study of His Thought* (New York, 1978), pp. 199–201.

14. HLM, "Pedagogues A–Flutter," *AM* 20 (May 1930): 127.

15. HLM, "What Is Going On in the World," *AM* 28 (April 1933): 390.

16. Ibid., p. 387.

17. HLM to the Right Reverend James Cannon, Jr., 29 June 1934, and to Lee Hartman, 11 October 1934, in Bode, ed., *Mencken Letters*, pp. 312–13, 324.

18. HLM to H. W. Seaman, Esq., 26 February 1935, ibid., p. 347.

19. Frank Luther Mott, *A History of American Magazines*, vol. 5, *Sketches of 21*

Magazines, 1905–1930 (Cambridge, Massachusetts, 1968), p. 23.

20. See, for example, "In the Mercury's Opinion," *AM* 74 (May 1952): 3–9. See also James Burnham, "The Case against Adlai Stevenson," *AM* 76 (October 1952): 11–19.

21. William F. Buckley, Jr., "Second Thoughts: The Rich and the Poor," *AM* 75 (July 1952): 125.

22. Mortimer Smith, "William Graham Sumner: The Forgotten Man," *AM* 71 (September 1950): 366.

23. A. H. Raskin, "John L. Lewis: God of Coal," *AM* 70 (May 1950): 532–33.

24. Ralph de Toledano, "The Walter Reuther Story," *AM* 76 (May 1953): 3, 12.

25. Russell Maguire, "In the Mercury's Opinion," *AM* (December 1956): 97–98.

26. Representative articles by J. B. Matthews are "Communism and the Colleges," *AM* 76 (May 1953): 111–14; "Communists in the White House," *AM* 76 (February 1953): 8–16; "Reds and Our Churches," *AM* 77 (July 1953): 3–13; and "Red Infiltration of Theological Seminaries," *AM* 77 (November 1953): 31–36. See also Martin Berkeley, "Reds in Your Living Room," *AM* 77 (August 1953): 55–62; Chet Schwarzkopf, "Rid Us of Reds," *AM* 78 (January 1954): 123–27; Stella Andrassy, "Communist Voices in America," *AM* 81 (July 1955): 131–36; and Paul Harvey, "UNESCO—Communism's Trap," *AM* 87 (July 1958): 81–86. The *Mercury* advertised the sale of the reprints "Reds in Our Churches" and "Communism in Israel" on the back pages of the September and December 1958 issues, respectively.

27. "In the Mercury's Opinion," *AM* 106 (Fall 1970): 3–4.

28. Edward A. Walker, "Vietnam—Vietnam—Vietnam—Mississippi—Mississippi—Mississippi," *AM* 101 (March 1965): 36; Samson Prime, "Censorship in Graven Stone," *AM* 116 (Spring 1980): 31–33.

29. Gerald S. Pope, "Discrimination...Vice or Virtue?" *AM* 92 (June 1961): 90.

30. Hilary Grey, "Nobel Prizes and International Communism," *AM* 92 (January 1961): 8–15; "The Rise and Fall of Bill Buckley," *AM* 104 (Summer 1968): 4–5; Frank A. Capell, "Is Kissinger a Soviet Agent?" *AM* 110 (Summer 1974): 48–51.

31. Colin Jordan, "National Socialism: A Philosophical Appraisal," *AM* 113 (Spring 1977): 20–22.

32. "In the Mercury's Opinion," *AM* 116 (Spring 1980): 3.

33. "In the Mercury's Opinion," *AM* 110 (Spring 1974): 3–4.

Information Sources

BIBLIOGRAPHY:
Mencken, Henry L. *The New Mencken Letters*. Edited by Carl Bode. New York, 1977.
Nolte, William H. *H. L. Mencken: Literary Critic*. Middletown, Connecticut, 1966.
Singleton, M. K. *H. L. Mencken and the* American Mercury *Adventure*. Durham, North Carolina, 1962.
INDEXES: Each volume indexed; *Articles Amer Lit; Bio Ind; Comb Ret Ind Bk Revs Hum; CMC; RG; Writings Amer Hist.*
REPRINT EDITIONS: Microform: UMI (1924–1980).
LOCATION SOURCES: Widely available.

Publication History

TITLE AND TITLE CHANGES: *American Mercury*, January 1924–November 1950; *New American Mercury*, December 1950–February 1951; *American Mercury*, March 1951–Spring 1980.
VOLUME AND ISSUE DATA: Volume 1, number 1–volume 116, number 536, January 1924–Spring 1980.

FREQUENCY OF PUBLICATION: Monthly, January 1924–March 1963; quarterly, issued irregularly, April 1963–Spring 1980.

PUBLISHERS: 1924–1950: American Mercury, Inc., New York; 1950–1961: American Mercury Magazine, Inc., New York; 1961–1962: Defenders of the Christian Faith, Oklahoma City, Oklahoma; 1962; 1963–1980: Legion for the Survival of Freedom, Inc., Torrance, California; Spring 1980, Houston, Texas.

EDITORS: H. L. Mencken, 1924–1933; Henry Hazlitt, 1934; Charles Angoff, 1934; Paul Palmer, 1935–1939; Lawrence E. Spivak, 1939; Eugene Lyons, 1939–1944; Lawrence E. Spivak, 1944–1950; William Bradford Huie, 1950–1952; J. Russell Maguire, 1952–1961; Gerald S. Pope, 1961–1962; Marcia C. J. Matthews, 1963; 1963–1965: Jason Matthews; 1965–1966: Edwin A. Walker; 1965–1966: La Vonne Doden Furr, 1966–1980.

CIRCULATION: Selected average annual figures: 1928: 77,000; 1934: 31,000; 1945: 80,000; 1980: 8,000.

Robert Muccigrosso

Southern Review
1935–1942

The *Southern Review* (1935–1942) was the robust product of literary vision, academic ambition, and regional ferment. Its base was Louisiana State University (LSU) in Baton Rouge during a time of intellectual excitement and academic reform.[1] Indeed, LSU President James Monroe Smith, an appointee of Huey Long, had high ambitions for the university that included the founding of a literary quarterly. *Southern Review*'s editorial board was composed of Dean of the Graduate School Charles Pipkin, a liberal political scientist; two moderate and rather apolitical literary men, Robert Penn Warren and Cleanth Brooks, both graduates of Vanderbilt, both former Rhodes scholars (as was Pipkin), and both teachers of English at LSU; and Albert Erskine, the first business manager and later an editor at Random House, who was succeeded by John Palmer, later editor of both *Sewanee Review* and *Yale Review*.

As the story goes, one Sunday afternoon in February 1935, Smith picked up Warren and his wife, along with Erskine, and took them for a ride in his large black Cadillac. When he deposited them later in the day, *Southern Review* had been conceived. The first issue appeared in July of that same year with assurances from President Smith of financial support and an editorial free hand. By all accounts the latter promise was faithfully observed. The quarterly lost around $7,000 per year, while its subscriptions approximated 1,500 and were augmented by library sales. *Southern Review* did have the advantage of paying its writers a decent sum (one and a half cents per word of prose; thirty-five cents a line for poetry) during its existence. With the onset of World War II the university no longer felt it could afford to keep *Southern Review* alive and it ceased publication in 1942.[2]

The *Southern Review* was the first literary quarterly to come under the direction of former Vanderbilt Agrarians and their sympathizers. It was followed in 1939 by the founding of *Kenyon Review* by poet and critic John Crowe Ransom and the assumption of the editorship of *Sewanee Review* by Andrew Lytle in 1942. These two quarterlies, along with the leftist *Partisan Review*, were to dominate the literary scene in America after the end of World War II. Thus in a broad sense the founding of the *Southern Review* in 1935 lay the foundation for what Randall Jarrell later called the "age of criticism."

A typical issue of *Southern Review* ran around 200 pages. Near the end of its existence entire issues were devoted to critical assessments of Thomas Hardy (Summer 1940) and W. B. Yeats (Winter 1942). But normally an issue opened with several general essays on political, historical, or broadly literary topics. After the lead essays came several pages of poetry, more often than not from newer poets such as Jarrell or John Berryman, and two or three pieces of short fiction. Early and frequent contributors were Katherine Anne Porter, later wife of Albert Erskine, and Eudora Welty. Then followed several more literary essays of a more focused and technical nature and at times omnibus poetry or fiction reviews. In general, *Southern Review* tended to devote more space to literary matters than to public affairs, to be more attentive to poetry than to fiction.

A retrospective look at *Southern Review* reveals a rich mix of perspectives and contributors. To be sure, ten of the original twelve Vanderbilt Agrarians contributed at various times. Authentic southern liberals, more at home in Chapel Hill than Baton Rouge, were also included. Here names such as Broadus Mitchell, Will Alexander, W. T. Couch, James McBride Dabbs, Virginius Dabney, Rupert Vance, and C. Vann Woodward might be mentioned. According to Cleanth Brooks, a rough count taken sometime well into the life of *Southern Review* revealed that approximately half of the contributors were from the South.[3] Indeed a prospectus for the quarterly spoke of the goal of "presenting and interpreting Southern problems to a national audience and...relating national issues to the Southern scene."[4]

There were numerous articles from non-southerners and nonconservatives, however. Leftist critics such as Kenneth Burke, Malcolm Cowley, and F. O. Matthiessen and publicists such as Max Lerner, I. F. Stone, and Frederick Schuman appeared, as did the core of what came to be known as the New York intellectuals. Sidney Hook wrote several essays on leftist controversies and Marxist disputes, while Delmore Schwartz contributed several long pieces on poetry and fiction. Mary McCarthy published various stories; Lionel Trilling did a piece on the Victorians; and Philip Rahv, coeditor of *Partisan Review*, contributed a strong critique of proletarian literature. All in all, *Southern Review* displayed a kind of literary and intellectual cosmopolitanism largely unknown in the South up to that time.

All that having been said, *Southern Review* was informed by a relatively coherent literary vision and purpose. (This is, however, less true of its political intentions.) Indeed as Allen Tate pointed out in "The Function of the Literary Quarterly," only by shaping rather than merely reflecting taste and values could a literary quarterly be said to be fulfilling its most crucial function.[5] Although this did not automatically make *Southern Review* a conservative publication, the magazine did in fact serve as the mouthpiece for what Louis Simpson has called the vision of the "traditionalist moderns."[6] To emphasize literary studies and downplay politics in such a highly politicized period was to be conservative in an oblique way. At its best the conservatism of *Southern Review* was a way of understanding and acting, primarily through literature and critical discourse, so as to preserve a complex view of human nature and society the editors felt to be radically at odds with the conventional literary-political views of their contemporaries.

The sphere of influence that *Southern Review* most successfully carved out as its own was literary criticism. Within that its main objectives were twofold: to reassess and rewrite the Anglo-American literary canon and to develop and apply what came to be known as the New Criticism. Central here was Cleanth Brooks. In the several chapters of his *Modern Poetry and the Tradition* (1939) that first appeared in *Southern Review*, Brooks linked modernist poets, especially Eliot, Yeats, Tate, and Ransom, with the metaphysical poets of the seventeenth century. Common to both poetic movements were wit, metaphor, irony, and the deployment of intellectual as well as emotional energies. In addition, Brooks contended that the literary value of a piece was a function of the skill of poetic rendering, not of the inherent poetic qualities or truth value of the materials used by the poet. The critic (or reader) should be concerned more with *how* a poem meant than *what* it meant. Brooks wanted to distance literary works from didactic, political, or religious intentions. In an early issue John Crowe Ransom added another dimension to the emerging practice and theory of New Criticism when he suggested a dichotomy between prose and poetry, science and literature, future and past. The poems "we cherish as perfect creations…are dramatizing the past."[7] Thus the New Criticism was both a technique of reading and a vision of the ideal society and polity.

Allen Tate contributed an early attack on Kenneth Burke for judging literature by its political content and commitment of its author rather than by its intrinsic worth. For Tate, literature had a cognitive as well as purely emotional function; indeed it furnished "the only complete, and thus the most responsible, versions of our experience."[8] In making this claim for the cognitive superiority of literature over science, Tate was turning the tables on the logical positivist claim, then being voiced, that literature, ethics, and aesthetics were emotive utterances with no scientific and philosophical standing. (His claim was no more convincing than that of the positivists.) Moreover, by designating literature a "form of knowledge," Tate was also denying that it was the residue of historical or social forces or the vehicle for communicating ideological truths. Clearly Tate was attacking left-wing and positivistic claims about literature, its origins and purposes, in the name of what purported to be a nonideological form of critical analysis.

Finally, the method of critical reading advocated by representative critics in *Southern Review* called for close reading and analysis of texts, primarily poetic ones. The reader should isolate and then analyze the internal, formal workings of the text, while de-emphasizing the intentions of the poet, the poem's context of appearance, and the effect of the poem on the audience. Literary history, the dominant way of approaching literature at that time, was to be replaced by literary criticism, context de-emphasized in favor of the text, the message devalued in favor of an examination of the means of execution.[9] By implication, the lack of a strong political or social concern in modernist literature was not a moral failing, as Edmund Wilson had suggested in *Axel's Castle*, but a point of pride. Literature should be composed and studied for its own sake. But further, the ideal poem was an organic unity of formal tensions. As such it suggested the kind of society and culture that had regrettably disappeared with the onset of modernity.

Another way of understanding the critical tendency represented by *Southern Review* is to say that history was replaced by tradition as the larger concern of critical inquiry. The description of historical settings and development was replaced by a normative account of writers, texts, and formal qualities, all making up a kind of transhistorical tradition. The poem and the poet of quality were set over and against history. They were located in a tradition of forms and values that was antiscientific, antiprogressive, antimaterialist, and antimodern. Thus, on this new critical account of literary tradition, modernists and metaphysical poets had more in common than modernists and their nineteenth-century predecessors. In the pages of *Southern Review* the traditionalist moderns received the critical defense appropriate to the kind of literature they produced.

To work out the actual political and ideological implications of this critical stance was another matter. Most of the essays in *Southern Review* that dealt with national or international politics were of a middle-of-the-road, descriptive nature. Clearly, sympathies lay with the Allies, and not the National Socialists or fascists. Although European politics received a fair amount of attention, the Spanish Civil War was scarcely mentioned.

Yet there was one serious engagement in the ideological battles of the 1930s, and it had to do with the Soviet Union and the Moscow trials. In 1936 *Southern Review* published a piece by Frederick Schuman ("Liberalism and Communism Reconsidered") that called for a new appreciation of the achievements of the Soviet Union and claimed that the world struggle was about the conflict between democracy and privilege, not capitalism and communism. Liberals and communists, declared Schuman, must unite forces.[10] The summer 1937 issue carried another essay by Schuman, "Leon Trotsky: Martyr or Renegade." While allowing that neither Stalin nor Trotsky was a figure of conventional virtue, Schuman did brand Trotsky a "renegade who failed" and went on to urge that "the democratic West...dry its tears for fallen heroes and accept Moscow's hand."[11]

Not unexpectedly this combination of realpolitik and Popular Front special pleading prompted Sidney Hook to respond. In the following issue Hook deployed his formidable polemical skills against Schuman and ended by claiming that the Moscow Trials and the Stalinist polemics against Trotsky masked the essential failure of socialism in the Soviet Union. Hook went on to publish several other pieces in *Southern Review* that attacked the Stalinist betrayal of socialism and defended the value of Marxism as such.[12] The larger irony here is that *Southern Review*, ostensibly a journal of conservative sensibilities, first published two pro-Soviet pieces and then had to get one of its newly found allies on the Left in New York to counter the claims made in those articles. It is no wonder that *Southern Review* steered clear of such matters thereafter.

Aside from this rather strange episode, the main source of political and polemical energies was the South. Here the combative, fire-eating wing of the Agrarians stepped in to do its duty. Along with distributists such as Herbert Agar and Hilaire

Belloc, Frank Owsley, Donald Davidson, and Andrew Lytle called for resistance to the growing power of finance and industrial capitalism, supported the strengthening of small-scale agriculture, and wrote in favor of a decentralized, constitutional federal republic. Historian Owsley stressed the economic depredations of northern plutocracy before, during, and after the Civil War, the illegitimacy of the Fourteenth and Fifteenth amendments, and the contemporary threat from communists, neoabolitionists, and capitalists. Other enemies who drew fire from these erstwhile Agrarians were New South industrialists and publicists, home-grown defamers of the region such as Erskine Caldwell and W. J. Cash, and Yankee sociologists such as John Dollard, who confirmed every suspicion about the pernicious use of social science to encourage things like race-mixing.[13] Room was made in *Southern Review* for southern liberals to suggest that agricultural reform was possibly more pressing a matter than cultural polemics and that the South's colonial status could be traced to southern as well as northern causes.[14]

Surprisingly, though Brooks, Warren, and Tate all later championed the career of William Faulkner, the only piece on Faulkner in *Southern Review* was a patchy and ambivalent essay by Delmore Schwartz. One of the early issues had carried a rather lukewarm discussion of Thomas Wolfe by John Donald Wade.[15] But overall, *Southern Review*'s specific contribution to the development of southern letters lay in its willingness to publish new poetry and fiction from younger southern writers such as Jarrell, Porter, Welty, and Peter Taylor.

As the representative journal of the Agrarian-New Critical position, *Southern Review* embodied three central tensions: (1) between political and social analysis and literary criticism; (2) between a kind of Jeffersonian agrarianism and a more literary dream of an aristocratic, hierarchical culture; and (3) between the work of art in isolation from the world and the work of art as an internally complex, organic unity. The political and social vision gradually gave way to the literary critical concern. The New Criticism in turn was domesticated and became a deflection and sublimation of politics. In short it became a technique. With that accomplished, the New Critical approach comported quite well with an essentially liberal understanding of the relationship of literature and society. In avoiding any confusion between literature and society, the implication was that the two realms had little, if anything, to do with one another. Finally, then, *Southern Review* established the essential framework for what Allen Tate called the "republic of letters which is the only kind of republic I believe in, a kind of republic that can't exist in a political republic)."[16] Such a republic of letters could, however, coexist with a liberal capitalist order. In that sense *Southern Review* was conservative, but by default.

Notes

1. Robert Heilman, "Baton Rouge and LSU Forty Years After," *Sewanee Review* 88 (January–March 1980): 126–43.

2. This account is taken from Cleanth Brooks and Robert Penn Warren, Introduction to *An Anthology of Stories from the Southern Review* (Baton Rouge, Louisiana, 1953), pp. xi–xvi. It is reprinted in *The Southern Review, Original Series, 1935–1942: A Commemoration* (Baton Rouge, Louisiana, 1980), pp. 1–8.

3. Ibid., p. 5.

4. Quoted in A. J. Montesi, "The *Southern Review* (1935–42)," *Chicago Review* 16 (1964): 203.

5. Allen Tate, "The Function of the Critical Quarterly," *Southern Review* 1 (Winter 1936): 551–59 (hereinafter cited as *SR*).

6. Lewis P. Simpson, "The *Southern Review* and Post–Southern American Letters," *Triquarterly* 43 (Fall 1978): 93.

7. Cleanth Brooks, "Metaphor and the Tradition," *SR* 1 (Summer 1935): 151–63; "Wit and High Seriousness," *SR* 1 (Autumn 1935): 328–38; "Metaphysical Poetry and the Ivory Tower," *SR* 1 (Winter 1936): 568–83; "The Waste Land: An Analysis," *SR* 3 (Summer 1937): 106–36; "The Vision of William Butler Yeats," *SR* 4 (Summer 1938): 116–42; John Crowe Ransom, "The Tense of Poetry," *SR* 1 (Autumn 1935): 230.

8. Allen Tate, "Mr. Burke and the Historical Environment," *SR* 2 (Autumn 1936): 363–72; "The Present Function of Criticism,"*SR* 6 (Autumn 1940): 236.

9. Much of *SR* 6 (Autumn 1940) was devoted to a discussion of "Literature and the Professors." This project, undertaken jointly with *Kenyon Review*, was an attack on the dominance of literature history in American universities and a bid to replace it with literary criticism.

10. Frederick Schuman, "Liberalism and Communism Reconsidered," *SR* 2 (Autumn 1936): 326–38.

11. Frederick Schuman, "Leon Trotsky: Martyr or Renegade," *SR* 3 (Summer 1937): 51–74.

12. Sidney Hook, "Liberalism and the Case of Leon Trotsky," *SR* 3 (Autumn 1937): 267–82; "Reflections on the Russian Revolution," *SR* 4 (Winter 1939): 429–62; "What Is Living and What Is Dead in Marxism," *SR* 6 (Autumn 1940): 293–316.

13. See, for instance, John Donald Wade, "Sweet Are the Uses of Degeneracy," *SR* 1 (Winter 1936): 449–63; Donald Davidson, "Expedients vs. Principles—Cross-Purposes in the Society," *SR* 2 (Spring 1937): 647–69; Frank Owsley, "The Foundations of Democracy," *SR* 1 (Spring 1936): 708–20; and "A Key to Southern Liberalism," *SR* 3 (Summer 1937): 28–38.

14. Rupert Vance, "Is Agrarianism for Farmers?" *SR* 1 (Summer 1935): 42–57; C. Vann Woodward, "Hillbilly Realism," *SR* 4 (Spring 1939): 676–81.

15. Delmore Schwartz, "The Fiction of William Faulkner," *SR* 7 (Summer 1941): 145–60; John Donald Wade, "Prodigal," *SR* 1 (Summer 1935): 192–98.

16. Allen Tate to John Peale Bishop, 23 December 1933, in Thomas Daniel Young and John J. Hindle, eds., *The Republic of Letters in America: The Correspondence of John Peale Bishop and Allen Tate* (Lexington, Kentucky, 1981), p. 94.

Information Sources

BIBLIOGRAPHY:

Brooks, Cleanth. *Modern Poetry and the Tradition*. Chapel Hill, 1939.

Cutrer, Thomas W. *Parnassus on the Mississippi: The* Southern Review *and the Baton Rouge Literary Community, 1935–1942*. Baton Rouge, 1984.

Simpson, Lewis. *The Possibilities of Order: Cleanth Brooks and His Work*. Baton Rouge, 1976.

Stewart, John L. *The Burden of Time*. Princeton, New Jersey, 1965.

Webster, Grant. *The Republic of Letters*. Baltimore, 1979.

INDEXES: Each volume indexed; *Comb Ret Ind Bk Revs Hum*; *II*; *PAIS*; *Writings Amer Hist*.

REPRINT EDITIONS: Microform: UMI. Bound edition: Kraus Reprint Company.

LOCATION SOURCES: Widely available.

Publication History

TITLE AND TITLE CHANGES: *The Southern Review*.

VOLUME AND ISSUE DATA: Volumes 1–7, July 1935–Spring 1942.

FREQUENCY OF PUBLICATION: Quarterly.

PUBLISHER: The Louisiana State University Press, Baton Rouge, Louisiana.

EDITORS: Charles Pipkin, editor, 1935–1941; Cleanth Brooks and Robert Penn Warren, managing editors, 1935–1941 and editors, 1941–1942; John Palmer, managing editor, 1940–1942.

CIRCULATION: 1,500 plus library subscriptions.

Richard H. King

Kenyon Review
1939–

The eminent poet and literary critic John Crowe Ransom founded the *Kenyon Review* at Kenyon College in Gambier, Ohio, in the winter of 1938–1939, shortly after he had left Vanderbilt University to accept a teaching position at Kenyon. During the subsequent twenty-one years of Ransom's editorial leadership the *Kenyon Review* became one of the most influential literary journals in the world, a "quarterly of a quality seldom equaled anywhere in this country," a quality apparent in the established authors whom it published and in the new writers it helped to introduce.[1] During the 1940s and 1950s the *Review* was preeminent in spreading the principles of the New Criticism and was probably unsurpassed among American journals in its contribution to the critical study of literature.

Ransom established the *Kenyon Review* as a quarterly devoted to arts and letters. Although each issue usually contained one or more articles on music, architecture, or the visual arts, the *Review* focused primarily on literary criticism and, secondarily, on the presentation of new poetry and fiction, with greater attention given to poetry. In the first issue of the *Review*, Ransom announced that we live in an "Age of Criticism....We shall have other ages in which the criticism relaxes, and poetry spontaneously increases, but now our age is critical."[2] The *Kenyon Review* published both theoretical and practical contributions to the cause of literary criticism. Led by Ransom's own articles arguing for analytical or formal criticism, the *Review* presented numerous essays on the theory of literary criticism along with other articles that applied critical principles to particular authors and works.

Ransom described the *Review* as "a semi-philosophical as well as a critical journal."[3] Philip Blair Rice, the associate editor of the *Review* with whom Ransom worked closely for almost two decades, was a professor of philosophy, and both men shared a deep interest in broad philosophical, cultural, and religious questions. The *Kenyon Review*, Ransom announced several years after its founding, sought to address "such questions as, how much can be preserved from the Christian and other religious traditions? Must we resign ourselves to a primarily scientific and technical culture? Is a new humanism possible and desirable?"[4] The possible grounds and sources of such a humanism, the nature of poetic as against scientific understanding, man's contrasting needs for form and tradition, but also for innovation and change, man's relation to and capacity for understanding nature— such were the broad concerns of some of Ransom's own essays in the *Review* and the focus of some of the articles he published, particularly those contained in symposia on "Naturalism" and on "The American Culture." But with the exception of a few articles by students in philosophy such as Rice, Walter Kaufmann, and Ernst Nagel, the *Review* approached these broad questions through the presentation of literary works and essays on literary criticism.

Ransom's deliberate preference for literature as the medium for understanding the human condition, a preference that guided his editorship of the *Review*, was rooted in his understanding of the nature of poetry and of literature more generally. He argued that poetry has an essentially dual aspect, a logical argument, which can be stated in prose, and a "tissue of meaning," which is rendered in the language of rhythm, metaphor, and sentiment. A poem, and literature in general, should not be irretrievably obscure, an abstract manipulation of poetic devices, or simply an appeal to sentiment. But as it should not be devoid of argument, neither should it be reducible to argument. Since the time of Plato, Ransom declared, philosophic reason has sought understanding through the grasping of unembodied, abstract universals, a quest that culminated in modern science's efforts to control and manipulate natural objects for practical use rather than to understand and value them for their own sake, as poetry seeks to do. Poetry can "restore the balance between reason and sensibility," the major human faculties that have become dissociated in modern times under the influence of the scientific outlook and the romantic reaction to it.[5] Poetry celebrates the rich, multifaceted, contingent, elusive particularity of objects, of what Ransom called "the world's body." Poetry is above all an ontological or metaphysical act. It enables us to know the truths most important to our well-being in the only way we as human beings can know them, as "concrete universal[s]." Poetry and other forms of literature render the "moral universal which is abstract and conceptual, concrete and perceptual," and thereby accessible to us.[6]

Confronted by what he perceived as widespread uncertainty and purposelessness resulting from the waning authority of tradition and religion, Ransom concluded that literature was the one "universally reputable" authority that might provide a "rule of action which is positive and lifegiving." But literature is "cryptic" and its "rule of life" is hidden: the best literary works have "one content that is visible and another content which is not so visible." Dependent as we are, in the absence of other authorities, on the aesthetic truths grasped through literature, we more than earlier ages need the "critic who must teach us to find the thing truly authoritative but hidden."[7] The *Kenyon Review* was to serve under Ransom's direction as a forum and promoter of literary critics who could elucidate the hidden truth found in literature.

Ransom recognized that the insights found in quality literature could not become publicly or politically authoritative, for the attention of a scientific and commercial culture was diverted elsewhere, and these insights were, in any case, inaccessible to most readers, even with the aid of criticism. The followers of a particular author might "constitute a community of letters" based on the insights of that author, but what would be the source of the life-giving rules needed by the broader society within which these smaller literary societies flourished?[8] Ransom provides no clear answer. He was quite clear, however, that the audience for the *Kenyon Review* would be "a few choicer spirits here and there who can respond to an order of fiction advanced either in its boldness or in its subtlety."[9] By providing an outlet for the best literature and criticism, the *Kenyon Review* would spread appreciation and understanding of the creative arts among the sensitive and discerning, thereby benefiting them and raising the standard of accomplishment of those who wrote for this more discerning audience.

To attain these ambitious goals, the *Kenyon Review* published the works of many of the more eminent authors and critics in Europe and America during the 1940s, 1950s and early 1960s: Jacques Maritain, Scott Fitzgerald, Robert Penn Warren, Irving Howe, W. H. Auden, T. S. Eliot, Ford Madox Ford, Allen Tate, Lionel Trilling, William Carlos Williams, Peter Viereck, Philip Rahv, Delmore Schwartz, Wallace Stevens, William Barrett, Jacques Barzun, Erwin Panofsky, T. W. Adorno, André Gide, Herbert Read, George Steiner, Paul Goodman, and Harold Rosenberg. The *Review* helped to establish a number of younger poets and writers too, including Thomas Pynchon, Robert Lowell, John Ciardi, Howard Nemerov, Karl Shapiro, Eric Bentley, and Richard Chase. Most critical essays published in the *Review* focused on nineteenth- and twentieth-century authors such as Yeats, Wordsworth, Wolfe, Kafka, Mann, Huxley, Faulkner, or Waugh. Under Ransom's editorship, the *Review* presented symposia on "Literature and the Professors," Henry James, Gerard Manley Hopkins, Dante, and different approaches to literary criticism. A typical issue of the *Review* contained a number of reviews of recent books, previously unpublished or untranslated poetry and fiction, and, most important, critical essays, which were usually the focus of the issue.

The editors Ransom and Rice were assisted for many years by three distinguished advisory editors: Lionel Trilling, Cleanth Brooks, and Robert Penn Warren. (Brooks and Warren became advisory editors in 1943 upon the demise of the *Southern Review*, which they had edited.) In 1947, Eric Bentley was also named an advisory editor. Philip Rice died in 1956 and Ransom carried on as editor for three more years, relinquishing his post to Robie Macauley in 1959. Under Macauley's editorship, the *Review* stressed fiction over poetry or criticism, particularly fiction by young authors, among whom were Nadine Gordimer and Herbert Gold. During his seven years as editor, Macauley increased subscriptions from 2,500 to over 3,000, but the eminence of the *Review*'s contributors and the general quality of its articles declined. These trends accelerated under the editorial direction of George Lanning, who succeeded Macauley in 1966. (A year later Lanning became coeditor with Ellington White.) Confronted with an operating deficit of some $80,000 caused largely by increased costs of publication, the trustees of Kenyon College voted in January 1970 to terminate publication of the *Review*.

This decision was preceded by the appointment of an evaluation committee which concluded that the *Review* lacked a clear focus and was out of touch with many of the significant literary figures and developments of its time.

Eight years after its demise, the *Kenyon Review* was revived, under the editorship of Ronald Sharp and Frederick Turner, as an "international journal of literature, culture, arts and ideas." The new *Review* was to celebrate the "whole life of culture" by facilitating the gathering together "of diverse voices, a sort of Olympic Games." Literature would continue to be the primary focus of the *Review*, but the new editors announced that they would adopt a very broad view of what constituted literature. "We want," they noted, "to question the current conception of literature as a narrow specialization or expertise and broaden the definition to include many types of writing not usually thought of as literature."[10] Thus essays on scientific subjects, science-fiction, translations, interviews, and essays on anthropology, politics, and history were all to find a place in the new *Review*.

Ronald Sharp left the *Review* in the fall of 1982, and Turner resigned six months later in favor of an editorial committee composed of William Klein, Galbraith Crump, Philip Church, and, for several months prior to his retirement, Robert Daniel. The new editors, reverting to a more traditional view of literature, sought to publish the best available literary and critical work by recognized and emerging authors, giving equal weight in their pages to fiction, poetry, and criticism.

Measured against the predominantly leftist orientation of literary journals of his day, the *Partisan Review*, for example, Ransom's *Kenyon Review* appeared conservative. It did not promote avant-garde literature or art nor did it take up the cause of modernism. As a prominent academic journal it appeared too academic and stuffy to most progressives and radicals. But if the *Review* was not a left-wing journal, neither was it a forum for promoting conservative causes or a bastion of traditionalism. In his literary views Ransom was an innovator, and he sought to publish, as he wrote to Allen Tate, "new kinds of writing, that is critical writing; the less standard and conventional in shape and tone the better. We ought to make a little racket every time we appear."[11] Some of the *Review*'s contributors, men such as Goodman, Howe, Adorno, or Read, were left, not right, of center. Still, in the world of literary journals, the *Review* had a deserved reputation for being conservative.

From 1927 to 1936 Ransom was a leading member of the Southern Agrarians, among whom were several other writers who were later featured prominently in the *Kenyon Review*: Tate, Warren, and Brooks. The Agrarians marched under the banner of conservatism and openly rejected the views of those they considered liberal, progressive, or forward looking. Their sense of the natural differences in human capacities led them to oppose the Left's glorification of the workingman. Some were fitted by their courage and intelligence to be owners, while there were others, Ransom argued, "whose natural quality fits them to work for hire." The Left's quest to bring about a "propertyless state" by destroying the freedom of owners would lead, moreover, to a society "in which nobody is to be free."[12] The Agrarians were equally critical, however, of big business, which they feared would destroy the widespread ownership of small, owner-managed businesses. But the major thrust of their criticism was directed at the baneful effect of industrialism and its helpmate, scientific technology. Perpetually grasping, devoid of higher purpose, frenetically mobile, antitraditional, the "insidious industrial system" was the enemy of family life, of political and social stability, and of human excellence and happiness. Industrialism, Ransom asserted, "is a program under which men, using the latest scientific paraphernalia, sacrifice comfort, leisure, and the enjoyment of life to win Pyrrhic victories from nature."[13] In its unending quest to conquer nature, scientific industrialism subjects us to an unremitting toil that deprives us of the leisure required to cultivate our higher faculties.

An agrarian society, in contrast, in which agriculture is the leading vocation, seeks a more modest prosperity conducive to a more reflective, aesthetic, and thus more fully human life. An agrarian society seeks to live in harmony with rather than to conquer nature. Living on the land humbles men by giving them a sense of their "precarious position in the universe" without which there is no "deep sense of beauty, no heroism of conduct, and no sublimity of religion."[14] Finally, an agrarian society derives stability from a social and cultural establishment supported by a respect for tradition, for popular myths and forms, and for a religion centering on an inscrutable god.

As he tried to work out in detail the economic foundation of this agrarian society, Ransom came to see its impossibility. Under modern circumstances the whole nation was becoming irretrievably industrial; a different way of life was not open to the South. Thus by 1936 Ransom had abandoned the economic and politically conservative views associated with Agrarianism and had become a supporter of the New Deal. One of the reasons he left Vanderbilt in 1939 and went to Kenyon was to separate himself from the waning agrarian movement centered in Nashville. In 1945 he wrote an epitaph in the *Review* for his association with the agrarian "nostalgia," observing that a return to an agrarian economy would be a "heavy punishment."[15]

The broad economic, political, and cultural concerns at the root of the agrarian movement were discussed from time to time in the *Review*, but they were addressed from a variety of perspectives and were not central to the *Review*'s interests. From its inception, the *Review*'s articles reflected Ransom's initial decision, which ran contrary to President Gordon Keith Chalmers's preference for a more general quarterly, to confine the *Kenyon Review* to literature and the arts. Ransom's position was stated clearly in a letter to Allen Tate written in December 1939: "I would not like to see the *Review* pinned to any economic or political program…it seems to me that our clue would be to stick to literature entirely. There's no consistent, decent group writing politics."[16] Under Ransom, the *Review* did not concern itself, except tangentially, with the political, economic, or social conservatism associated with Southern agrarianism. Still, it seemed the *Review* could not escape at least indirect association with the aristocratic conservatism of the Agrarians as long as its prominent editor, two of its advisory editors, and several of its leading contributors were widely known to have been leading advocates of Agrarianism during the 1920s and 1930s. But if the *Review* cannot be tied to conservatism through the Agrarians, it can more properly be connected with a certain kind of conservatism through its close association with the New Criticism.

As advocated by Ransom and its other supporters in the *Kenyon Review*, the New Criticism, or, more precisely, formalist criticism, stood for the primacy of the text: the literary critic was to derive his insights from an intensive study of the text itself, from its constitution and structure as revealed in the form and literary techniques employed by the author. Formalist criticism was intensely analytical and objective in the sense that it focused on the artistic object itself rather than on its author, its place in literary history, its subject, or its reader. The formalist critics assumed that an author was interested in his work for its own sake, and they sought his intention only as it was revealed in the work itself. In their view the proper study of literature was critical rather than historical, ethical, biographical, or psychological. None of these other approaches, Cleanth Brooks argued, should "be confused with an account of the work. Such studies describe the process of composition, not the structure of the thing composed."[17] The critic should consider the literary work apart from the forces that may have affected its composition. Ransom suggested that many of those who look first to the political or economical motivation of an author or to the moral or social message of a literary work were ideologues, enthusiasts, or reformers rather than serious critics or authors. Ultimately a literary work was to be read for the truth, particularly the moral truth, it might reveal, but this truth was accessible only through formal analysis of the text.

From the perspective of the Left, the *Review* appeared so academic, formalistic, and indifferent to immediate moral and political issues that it necessarily defended the status quo and was therefore conservative, if not reactionary. In a literal sense, the *Review* was conservative in that Ransom saw it as an instrument for keeping alive or sustaining the best literary works of the past by means of the serious, critical study of those works. But even here Ransom advocated a "positive traditionalism" that was both open to change and concerned that its innovations made use of, and were assimilated to, the traditional.[18] The *Review* might also be said to have been conservative in its stress on the importance of form and structure in literature, and although this was more a theme of Ransom's own writings than of other articles in the *Review*, of form and manners in sustaining civilized life by restraining elemental natural desires. But at the same time that the mature Ransom was convinced of the importance of form and structure, he was not wedded to any particular forms. On the contrary, he stressed that forms must change and believed that he was living through a time of change whose task was to generate new ways to organize its literature and culture.

Despite the different emphasis they gave to poetry, fiction, criticism, and other kinds of essays in the *Review*, the editors who followed Ransom continued to stress, if often only implicitly in their selection of work to be published, the importance of both literary form and focusing on the text itself. They also continued to keep the *Review* above the dominant political concerns of the day. The new *Review*, in particular, stood apart from the enthusiasms and skepticism of the political Left in the name of those enduring values that are discernible through literature. Rejecting what they viewed as the "exhaustion and aimlessness" of the late 1960s, editors

Sharp and Turner viewed the new *Review* as a vehicle for cultivating the "golden apples" that still could be found in fields ravaged by relativism and skepticism.[19] Thus whatever the surface differences, there was a deeper continuity of outlook between the old *Kenyon Review* and the new.

Was the old *Kenyon Review* conservative because the formalist criticism that it promoted assumed artistic autonomy to the extent that a literary work could be understood independent of the internal and external forces playing on the artist? Was it conservative because many of its writers, led by Ransom, had a somewhat detached, ironical view of human affairs derived from their sense of the limitations of our earthly existence? Was it conservative because its leading writers were more interested in understanding than in changing human affairs, and therefore did not rank political and social concerns of first importance? Was it conservative, that is, because many of its contributors would have agreed with Ransom's observations that "politics is the means and not the end of life"[20] and that although "politics does indeed touch wide and vital surfaces of life," it "scarcely reaches to the heart"?[21] In part, the answer is yes, but the fact that we might be content simply to label it conservative rather than moderate may tell us as much about our own inflated aspirations for the reform of human affairs as about the true ideological orientation of the *Kenyon Review*.

Notes

1. Thomas Daniel Young, *Gentleman in a Dustcoat: A Biography of John Crowe Ransom* (Baton Rouge, 1976), p. 343.

2. John Crowe Ransom, "Editorial Notes: The Teaching of Poetry," *Kenyon Review*, 1 (Winter 1939): 81–82 (hereinafter cited as *KR*).

3. Quoted in Young, *Ransom*, p. 341.

4. John Crowe Ransom, "Editorial Notes: A Word about Naturalism," *KR* 4 (Winter 1942): 87.

5. Young, *Ransom*, p. 83.

6. Thomas Daniel Young, "The Evolution of Ransom's Critical Theory: Image and Idea," in Thomas Daniel Young, ed., *The New Criticism and After* (Charlottesville, 1976), pp. 34–35.

7. John Crowe Ransom, ed., *The Kenyon Critics: Studies in Modern Literature from the Kenyon Review* (Cleveland, 1951), p. ix.

8. Louis D. Rubin, Jr., "A Critic Almost Anonymous: John Crowe Ransom Goes North," in Young, *The New Criticism and After*, p. 19.

9. Quoted in ibid., p. ix.

10. Ronald Sharp and Frederick Turner, "The Apples of Olympia: Editorial," *KR* n.s., 1 (Winter 1979): 1–2.

11. Quoted in Young, *Ransom*, p. 300.

12. John Crowe Ransom, "What Does the South Want?" in Herbert Agar and Allen Tate, eds., *Who Owns America? A New Declaration of Independence* (New York, 1936), p. 190.

13. John Crowe Ransom, "Reconstructed But Unregenerate," in Twelve Southerners, *I'll Take My Stand: The South and the Agrarian Tradition* (1930; reprint ed., Gloucester, Massachusetts, 1951), pp. 25,15.

14. Ibid., p. 10.

15. John Crowe Ransom, "Art and the Human Economy," *KR* 7 (Fall 1945): 687.

16. Quoted in Young, *Ransom*, pp. 298–99.

17. Cleanth Brooks, "The Formalist Critics," *KR* 13 (Winter 1951): 74. See also John Crowe Ransom, *The World's Body* (New York, 1938), pp. 335–43.

18. Young, *Ransom*, p. 262.

19. Sharp and Turner, "The Apples of Olympia: Editorial," pp. 1–2.

20. John Crowe Ransom, review of Eudora Welty, *Delta Wedding, KR* 8 (Summer 1946): 507.

21. John Crowe Ransom, "Editorial Notes: E. M. Forster," *KR* 5 (Fall 1943): 619.

Information Sources

BIBLIOGRAPHY: None.

INDEXES : *Amer Hist & Life*; *AHI*; *AHCI*; *Bio Ind*; *BRI*; *Comb Ret Ind Revs Hum*; *Curr Cont: A&H*; *Hist Abst*; *H Ind*; *Ind Bk Revs Hum*; *II*; *MLA Amer Bib*; *MLA Intl Bib*; *SSHI*; *Writings Amer Hist.*

REPRINT EDITIONS: Microform: UMI. Bound editions: AMS Press (1939–1970); UMI.

LOCATION SOURCES: Widely available.

Publication History

TITLE AND TITLE CHANGES: *The Kenyon Review.*

VOLUME AND ISSUE DATA: Volumes 1–32, 1939–1970; n.s. volume 1–current, 1979–present.

FREQUENCY OF PUBLICATION: Quarterly.

PUBLISHER: Kenyon College, Gambier, Ohio.

EDITORS: John Crowe Ransom, 1939–1959; Robie Macauley, 1960–1966; George Lanning and Ellington White, 1967–1970; Ronald Sharp and Frederick Turner, Winter 1979–Summer 1982; Frederick Turner, Fall 1982–Spring 1983; Philip D. Church, Galbraith M. Crump, William F. Klein, and Robert W. Daniel, Summer 1983; Philip D. Church, Galbraith M. Crump, and William F. Klein, Fall 1983–Sumer 1984; Philip D. Church and Galbraith M. Crump, Fall 1984–Summer 1988; T.R. Hummer, Fall 1988–Summer 1989; David H. Lynn, Fall 1989–Fall 1990; Marilyn Hacker, Fall 1990–Fall 1994; David H. Lynn, Winter 1995–present.

CIRCULATION: 500–3,000, original series; 4,000–6,000, new series.

Kirk R. Emmert

Part Five

OLD RIGHT ISOLATIONIST PERIODICALS

Isolationism names the policy of pursuing a nation's interests without engaging in diplomatic and military entanglements with other nations. In his Farewell Address (1796), George Washington counseled his successors to "steer clear of permanent Alliances," having with foreign nations "as little political connection as possible." Thomas Jefferson aligned his new political party with that understanding, calling in his First Inaugural Address (1801) for "peace, commerce, and honest friendship with all nations, entangling alliances with none." Two decades later President James Monroe echoed those realistic admonitions, laying out what later became known as the Monroe Doctrine: the United States henceforth would consider European colonialism in the Western Hemisphere as objectionable and would itself refrain from interfering in Europe: "It is only when our rights are invaded, or seriously menaced that we resent injuries or make preparations for our defense." For more than a century, even though it precipitated the Spanish-American War and joined World War I (but as an "Associate," not an "Allied" power), the United States retained political isolationism as a major motif of its foreign policy and avoided formal alliances and binding multinational arrangements.

Several factors entered into play encouraging the United States to practice isolationism. Eighteenth- and nineteenth-century geopolitical considerations made such a policy realistic. The new republic was not only geographically separate, but economically and militarily weak. Involvement in the quarrels of other peoples would have risked its independence, undermined concentration on internal development, and disrupted the more pressing need to develop a sense of national unity. It was a luxurious moment in time. Protected by the Atlantic Ocean and the European balance of power, the United States could live without allies, building democracy at home and creating a worldwide commercial empire.

Nevertheless, the United States was not a hermit nation. In commerce and in culture, Americans interchanged freely with other peoples and saw no contradiction in extending their sway over lands lying in the West and, later, in the Caribbean and the Pacific. After the United States chose intervention in World War I, however, political isolationism reasserted itself, forcing an abandonment of Woodrow Wilson's dream for a new world order. The U.S. Senate rejected both the Treaty of Versailles and U.S. membership in the League of Nations. During the 1930s the isolationist cause attracted support from both of the major political parties, counting among its partisans such old progressives as Senators William Borah (R, Idaho), Hiram Johnson (R, California), Burton K. Wheeler (D, Montana), and George Norris (R, Nebraska). Liberals and conservatives alike lined up behind the neutrality legislation of 1935–1937. As the Great Depression lingered, however, and as President Franklin D. Roosevelt moved to support Great Britain in its war with Nazi Germany, conservative isolationists moved to the forefront. Men of wealth (especially in the Republican party), fearing that entanglement in European conflicts would further weaken the American free enterprise system, came to dominate the America First Committee, the most powerful pressure group working against political and military involvement abroad. Most were virulent opponents of the New Deal also, believing that Roosevelt's domestic program meant class warfare and socialism. With their preferred world of limited government and economic individualism under attack by social reformers at home and fascist dictators abroad, conservatives and isolationists joined in affirming American uniqueness and pursuing policies designed to preserve its economic and social institutions against revolutionary change.

Between the two world wars the term *isolationist* was often ambiguous. Diversity abounded among those so labeled. All isolationists, including pacifists such as journalist Oswald Garrison Villard, former editor of the *Nation*, favored international trade, but nearly all opposed involvement in alliances and collective security commitments. However, some believed that *unilateralist* was a better defining term, permitting interventionism in Latin America, though not elsewhere; to others *independents*, *neutralists*, and even *nationalists* seemed more appropriate. Justus Doenecke, a leading scholar of isolationism and the author of the articles in this part, includes among the old isolationists such congressmen and senators as John Rankin (D, Mississippi) and Robert A. Taft (R, Ohio), writers, intellectuals, and publishers such as Lawrence Dennis, Garet Garrett, Harry Elmer Barnes, Felix Morley, William Henry Chamberlin, Frank Hanighen, Frank Chodorov, John T. Flynn, and Colonel Robert R. McCormick, as well as an assortment of individuals that included Colonel Charles A. Lindbergh, and pro-Nazi spokesmen Gerald L. K. Smith and Gerald Winrod. Denying that Hitler sought the conquest of Europe, they supported appeasement policies during the 1930s in hopes of avoiding war, blamed profiteering international bankers for intensifying if not creating conflict among nations, criticized British colonialism, and opposed American aid to Russia. At home they spoke on behalf of "Fortress America": the United States could guarantee its security by protecting its ocean borders.

Among the more interesting and controversial of the isolationists was Lawrence Dennis. This Harvard-educated intellectual, who underwent a fascinating journey before ending up on the American Right, and who edited both the *Weekly Foreign*

Letter and the *Appeal to Reason*, differed from other isolationists in his sweeping views of historical processes that stressed the inadequacy of democracy and capitalism. In a series of hard-headed analyses, Dennis broke through the hypocrisies of liberalism and conservatism, defended a corporate state that differed from traditionalist conservative visions of an organic society, and was as certain as any determinist that because of the economic contradictions of capitalism, some variety of socialism (which he labeled fascism) was coming to America. His abstract cast of mind was fertile, and he lectured all who would listen that World War II could be avoided only through the rational creation of an "expansive totalitarian collectivism directed by a non-hereditary functional elite." Such arguments, following his earlier announcement that the U.S. Constitution was politically dysfunctional and no longer served the national good, frightened liberals and angered conservatives, winning for Dennis the tag of "intellectual fascist." Like many other isolationists, Dennis suffered from a measure of moral blindness on the Nazis, apparently believing that their expansionism differed little from British and French imperialism. Doenecke makes important distinctions in discussing Dennis's "fascism," however. To argue that Dennis was cut from the same cloth as George Sylvester Viereck, a German agent, and William Dudley Pelley, head of the Silver Shirts, or that he was a conspirator and a seditionist, was a measure of how seriously the wartime U.S. Justice Department misread its intellectual enemy. The prosecution of Dennis may more accurately be described as a failed government attempt to silence a right-wing critic of Roosevelt's war policies.

When World War II ended, Dennis absorbed as did few others the economic weakness of the Soviet Union. At home he developed greater sympathy for capitalism, even though he understood that the market system was inadequate to protect the public interest, including the preservation of private property. Earlier than most liberals, Dennis recognized that in two world wars lay not only the growth of the state but of the war powers of the president. With this combination of insights to guide him, he became an early and vigorous critic of postwar foreign policy. Winston Churchill's speech at Fulton, Missouri, was too confrontational, especially as Dennis could detect no serious Soviet threat to Western Europe. He opposed the holy war thrust of the Truman Doctrine as statist in its economic implications and risky as foreign interventionism. In varying details, he insisted, much the same was true of the Marshall Plan, the North Atlantic Treaty Organization, and U.S. intervention in Korea. With an energy and passion matched by few fellow critics of containment policy, Dennis warned readers that even as it voiced and defended democratic ideals, the United States was in the throes of creating a new empire, a Pax Americana. A decade and a half later, in the midst of an unsuccessful anticommunist war in Vietnam, liberal intellectuals and politicians arrived at similar views, especially on the dangers of growing executive power. On that score, at least, Dennis could claim to have sounded an early alarm.

Scribner's Commentator
1939–1942

During the debate over intervention in the years just prior to Pearl Harbor, opponents of President Roosevelt's foreign policy felt themselves under siege. With initiatives increasingly in the hands of the administration and with the influential media endorsing such measures as "cash-and-carry" and conscription, anti-interventionists were ever anxious to secure new outlets for their message. True, the *Reader's Digest* opened its pages to both sides of the debate, and it would carry a condensation of such books as Anne Morrow Lindbergh's *The Wave of the Future* (1940). So too did *Harper's Magazine* and the *Atlantic Monthly*. The editorials of the *Saturday Evening Post,* written by Garet Garrett, also attacked the foreign policy of Franklin D. Roosevelt. However, anti-interventionists still hoped to have a journal devoted entirely to their cause, one able to reach a mass public.

Early in 1940, they had their break, for *Scribner's Commentator* became militantly anti-interventionist. The journal was the product of a merger between *Scribner's* and the *Commentator*. *Scribner's* was a monthly owned until January 1938 by the prominent publisher Charles Scribner's Sons. In the course of its fifty-year history, it was primarily known for its literary excellence. Among the authors featured were such luminaries as Rudyard Kipling, Henry James, Thomas Wolfe, and Ernest Hemingway. Lacking working capital, in May 1939 *Scribner's* suspended publication.

The *Commentator,* a pocket-sized journal, had first appeared in January 1937. Served by Lowell Thomas as editor and H. V. Kaltenborn as managing editor, it specialized in carrying original articles by radio commentators. Financier and lawyer Charles S. Payson, president of Payson Publishing Company, owned the journal. Then in his mid-forties, Payson was a graduate of Yale and husband of Joan Whitney of the prominent Whitney fortune. In May 1939, Payson bought the title and subscription list of *Scribner's* and within four months merged the two journals under the name *Scribner's Commentator*. In the course of its relatively brief history,

Payson invested over $300,000 in the new magazine; by the fall of 1941 it was losing $6,000 a month.[1]

In November 1939, the new journal appeared. Francis Rufus Bellamy, long a prominent magazine editor, was its first editor, with Lowell Thomas relegated to advisory editor. Its first few issues resembled the *American Mercury* under the editorship of Lawrence E. Spivak. Singer Kate Smith and comedian Fred Allen vied with such political writers as Blair Bolles, Carl Crow, and Maurice Hindus.

March 1940 marked the big turning. The publishing firm reorganized itself as P. and S. Publishing, Inc., with Payson as president and Douglas M. Stewart as vice-president. Stewart, a Harvard graduate and naval veteran, was a conservative Wall Street economist who strongly opposed the New Deal. At the same time, the journal took on a new digest-size format. By the middle of 1940, Bellamy and Thomas had gone, and George T. Eggleston had become editor.[2] Eggleston had first become involved in journalism at the University of California, where he had edited a humor magazine. After graduation, he first worked for *College Humor,* then edited the humor weekly *Life*. When, in 1936, Henry R. Luce bought out *Life* and turned it into a picture weekly, Eggleston joined Luce's staff, after which he was employed by Condé Nast publications.

Scribner's Commentator first appeared on newsstands at a quarter a copy. In September 1941, the journal was sold only by subscription, as the editors accused newsdealers of sabotaging over-the-counter sales. One year cost three dollars. In July 1941, editorial offices moved from Madison Avenue, New York, to Lake Geneva, Wisconsin, where the staff worked in a remodeled two-story blacksmith shop. Once it moved to Wisconsin, *Scribner's Commentator* also published a strident anti-interventionist weekly, the *Herald*.

The format of *Scribner's Commentator* seldom varied. It contained about twenty digest-type articles, and about half of these were devoted to nature stories and human interest features. There was no mistaking, however, the fundamental focus of the journal, which was to present the case against involvement in World War II in as many ways as possible. The picture of a prominent foe of intervention adorned the cover, with a laudatory biographical sketch or an article written by the individual frequently featured inside.[3] Inside covers often contained aphorisms from the founders. Cartoons, drawn by Eggleston himself, attacked Roosevelt's foreign policy. Several pages of introductory material, entitled "Cabbages and Kings," took a similar position, as did various picture sections. A "listener's digest" offered speeches from a variety of anti-interventionists, including such liberals as the prominent radio preacher Harry Emerson Fosdick and President Robert Maynard Hutchins of the University of Chicago. Don Herald, a movie reviewer who had written for the old *Scribner's,* attacked such films as *A Yank in the R. A. F.* Albert J. Nock, a right-wing anarchist elitist, contributed hostile reviews of such books as Douglas Miller's *You Can't Do Business with Hitler* (1941). Brief one-act plays reviled the Episcopal clergy, which the journal accused of fostering intervention, and mocked as well Clarence Streit's *Union Now,* a movement designed to promote federation with Great Britain. "Who Said It?" a monthly quiz, juxtaposed embarrassing quotations of interventionist spokesmen with prophetic warnings of their opponents. In August 1941, a $1,500 essay contest centered on the theme "George Washington's Foreign Policy Today," which, in the words of the editors, was "being conducted as a result of this magazine's campaign for a rebirth of continental Americanism." To aid people who entered its contest, *Scribner's Commentator* offered a bibliography composed solely of anti-interventionist authors, including John T. Flynn, Charles A. Beard, and Boake Carter.

Although the tone of *Scribner's Commentator* was decidedly rightist, it seldom attacked Roosevelt's domestic policies head-on. At one point, it declared that during the past decade every executive and legislative act "has been destructive of free enterprise, and productive of regimentation."[4] At other times, it opposed government spending and a high national debt.[5] However, it published a radio speech by James B. Carey, general secretary of the Congress of Industrial Organizations, defending labor's position in current defense strikes.[6] More important, it seldom, if ever, singled out particular New Deal programs and agencies for attack. Obviously it wanted to gain the broadest possible support for its foreign policy, and with such labor leaders as John L. Lewis becoming outspoken foes of intervention, it undoubtedly saw silence on domestic issues the better part of wisdom.

Nevertheless, *Scribner's Commentator* represented the ultraconservative wing of the isolationist movement, something that can be seen most clearly by looking at the various cultural themes found within the journal. While some themes could strike a ready chord among liberal as well as conservative anti-interventionists, others would be welcomed primarily by the American Right.

One motif centered on the American tradition. Isolationist warnings of the founders were quoted often, and one issue featured the cry of John Adams: "America has been the sport of European wars and politics long enough."[7] Furthermore, it cited figures as disparate as Mark Twain, Theodore Roosevelt, and Will Rogers, all of whom offered fearful prophesies of future conflict or endorsed a strident nationalism.

If harkening back to a more traditional America might create a consensus among anti-interventionists, a second theme might create dissent. *Scribner's Commentator* stressed the supposed dichotomy between the "authentic" America of the internal heartland and the "artificiality" of the eastern seaboard. For example, one article claimed that Manhattan, the center of the nation's publishing and journalism, was "about as far from traditional America as a social cuisine could get."[8] Conversely, an editorial referred to "the great Mississippi basin" as a "storehouse of sanity."[9] Refugees in particular were given unfavorable treatment, with Jews often singled out as a special category. Here the journal was showing its rightist and nativist bent, for such liberal anti-interventionists as Norman Thomas were asking the Roosevelt administration to admit more refugees.[10]

When *Scribner's Commentator* attacked the media, it undoubtedly expressed the beliefs of a wide variety of isolationists, both liberal and conservative. In its pages, John T. Flynn found radio "intervention's trump"; even jazz bands, quartets, and radio vaudeville shows, said the prominent journalist, contained "dramatic plugs for the good old war."[11] Hollywood too was highly suspect. As one writer commented, "If you seek escape in a movie theatre there is a good chance that an added attraction will present a spy with a thick German accent stealing our latest bombing sights or planting T.N.T. along the locks of the Panama Canal."[12] According to another contributor, friends of the interventionist actor Douglas Fairbanks, Jr., used to boast that whenever a cricket bat hit Fairbanks on the nose, out trickled "not blood but the thin red lines of Empire."[13] Actress Lillian Gish repented for having made propaganda films during World War I.[14] Even comic strips were not immune. Senator Gerald P. Nye's secretary wrote of strips portraying American marines in active combat somewhere south of the U.S. border, secret underground hangars constructed by German-sounding enemies, and sinister characters with distinctly oriental leers.[15]

In other ways as well, this anti-interventionist monthly continually warned of war propaganda. Correspondent Frazier Hunt denied that German planes had strafed refugees in Belgium and France.[16] Mrs. Bennett C. Clark, wife of Missouri's isolationist senator and herself a leader of the America First Committee in Washington, D.C., referred contemptuously to "Government by Gallup." She also accused *Life* magazine of gross exaggeration by emphasizing interventionist sentiment within a small Missouri town.[17]

Tied to such suspicions was strong opposition to Britain. Here *Scribner's Commentator* took a far more rigid stand than most other isolationists. For example, nearly all the leaders of the America First Committee voiced sympathy with the British war effort, and many of them declared that Britain's defeat would be a loss to the world.[18] To *Scribner's Commentator*, however, Britain was always an object of suspicion, and to show Albion's perfidy, it went so far as to reproduce anti-American cartoons from *Punch* originally printed in the nineteenth century.[19] Dr. Samuel Johnson's denigration of Americans as "a race of convicts" and *Blackwood Magazine*'s attack on the "devilish" Emancipation Proclamation supposedly represented the longstanding and widespread hostility of the British toward their American offspring.[20]

Winston Churchill met with the journal's particular scorn. Former senator Rush D. Holt portrayed the British prime minister as a bloodthirsty youth who murdered Egyptians on the Sudan and Indians on the northwest frontier, endorsed concentration camps for Boers, and joined the Spanish army to fight Americans in Cuba.[21] William Griffin, publisher of the *New York Enquirer*, asserted that in August 1936 Churchill had personally told him that the United States should have stayed out of World War I; its participation led only to continuation of the conflict, which led to the rise of totalitarian dictatorships.[22]

Other prominent Englishmen were also attacked with vehemence. Handsome Anthony Eden, appointed Britain's secretary of war in May 1940, emerged as "Beau Saboteur," a man whose dreams of collective security merely played into the hands of the Russians.[23] Former progressive Amos Pinchot accused the prominent socialist intellectual Harold Laski of plotting with Roosevelt to seize private property within both Britain and America.[24] Cecil Rhodes, long perceived by isolationists to be a Machiavelli, did not escape attention, for his schemes were not limited to British rule over the United States but went so far as to include domination of the world itself.[25]

Given this general orientation, it is hardly surprising to find so much focus on British colonialism. One contributor ironically called Gandhi's imprisonment "British democracy."[26] Reviewer Nock found in Nehru's internment renewed evidence that "anyone who trusts them [the British] may be expected to be sold down the river at a moment's notice."[27]

When contributors turned their attention to France, they showed a strong rightist bent. Liberals among the isolationists would deny that Léon Blum's Popular Front government bore any responsibility for French defeat, and they usually had little use for Vichy's leaders.[28] *Scribner's Commentator*, however, hailed France's new ruler, Marshall Philippe Pétain, and the Count de Chambrun, a Vichy emissary to the United States, with cover stories.[29] Contrasted to such eulogies were attacks on various Third Republic leaders. For example, a pictorial essay listed Léon Blum, Pierre Cot, Paul Reynaud, and Maurice Thorez as significant contributors to France's defeat.[30] Under the premiership of Léon Blum, so two contributors argued, "a red flag flew over Paris City Hall and a general strike paralysed the nation."[31] To one writer, the Vichy government's outlawing of Freemasonry was justified, for—so the author claimed—continental masonry had been engaged in anti-Christ activities from the time of the French Revolution.[32]

The monthly commented on other countries as well, revealing similar rightist sentiments. One contributor not only opposed American aid to Russia, but found Stalin's regime so oppressive that a popular revolt was in the offing.[33] Another contributor praised Portugal's ruler, António de Oliveira Salazar: "The Portuguese dictatorship is on the ancient Roman order, a courageous remedy imposed in a state of crisis and calling for sacrifices for the welfare of the country."[34] A veteran of the Abraham Lincoln Brigade pointed to Russian manipulation of Spain's Loyalist cause. "All the people of Europe," he wrote, "are not anxious to be saved by Americans."[35] At one point the journal accused the Loyalists of having "applied the torch to Christian Spain," hardly language that would be used by such Loyalist sympathizers among the isolationists as Oswald Garrison Villard, Norman Thomas, or the *Progressive*.[36]

Turning to the Pacific, former State Department official Ralph Townsend referred to Japan as "our commercial prize." As the United States sold more to Japan than to all other countries of Asia combined, it was foolish, claimed Townsend, "to jeopardize our own peace on behalf of the Chinese."[37] Another contributor claimed that the Chinese had "made war upon each other for centuries and have often cruelly tortured the vanquished."[38] The fact that most anti-interventionists expressed strong sympathies for China's cause showed that *Scribner's Commentator* was taking an extreme position within isolationist ranks.[39]

When Charles A. Lindbergh claimed that the Jews, the British, and the Roosevelt administration were "agitating for war," *Scribner's Commentator* said that the prominent aviator had identified "the trinity of ugly forces which would plunge our people into foreign war."[40] To some contributors, "international bankers" were at the root of America's evil. In a highly publicized article, Henry Ford wrote of "greedy financial groups" who were "seeking to extend their domination over people and lustful for power in every branch of human endeavor." Not only did these "mysterious conspirators" plot strikes and inflation, but even used Hitler and Mussolini as their puppets.[41] Similarly, Senator D. Worth Clark (D, Idaho) and former senator Holt found Wall Street behind American intervention.[42]

Yet to *Scribner's Commentator,* it was not only "international bankers" who were at fault. Its series, The Interventionist Hall of Fame, accused prominent Roosevelt backers of harboring communist sympathies. Poet Archibald MacLeish was identified as "former chair-man of the Stalin-directed Second American Writers' Congress." Kansas editor William Allen White had strived "for U.S. recognition of Soviet Russia and has always rushed to aid all movements towards a closer understanding with that country." Columbia Teachers College professor Harold Rugg wrote a series of "pink" textbooks, in which he claimed that the Soviet Union had made greater advances than had England, France, or the United States. Rabbi Stephen S. Wise had praised the Jewish people for having contributed so much to the Russian Revolution.[43]

The journal presented a gloomy picture of the consequences of war, and here at times liberals were featured. A radio broadcast of Robert Maynard Hutchins pointed to pressing national needs in housing, education, and general welfare; a radio sermon of pacifist Harry Emerson Fosdick voiced the fear that the United States would itself become totalitarian in any war against totalitarianism.[44] A black newsman, looking at Jim Crow practices at home, pointed to "the recrimination and the abuse heaped upon the souls and bodies of black folk by a liberty-loving people."[45]

Economic self-sufficiency was often stressed. Wheeler McMillin, editor of *Farm Journal* and a strong protectionist, claimed that Americans exported relatively little of their goods, and hence were not dependent upon foreign markets. Frank Chodorov, director of the Henry George School of Social Science and a free-trader, claimed that American purchases of German goods would give the United States leverage in any transaction. "Let us buy in order that we may influence, even dictate, Germany's political policies," Chodorov wrote.[46] To John T. Flynn, Germany contained the seeds of its own decay, for the more it regulated its economy, the less profit it could accumulate.[47] Several contributors stressed the need for increased trade with Latin America and in the process pleaded for admitting more Latin American products.[48] One author endorsed Herbert Hoover's plan to feed occupied Europe.[49]

The defense policy of *Scribner's Commentator* can be summed up in one sentence: the United States can stand alone. General Johnson Hagood stressed the difficulties of invading Japan, as did Colonel Robert R. McCormick, publisher of the *Chicago Tribune,* concerning Europe.[50] Colonel George Chase Lewis and Major Al Williams, equating airpower with survival, called for huge increases in the number of antiaircraft guns, planes, and tanks.[51]

Once the Japanese attacked Pearl Harbor, *Scribner's Commentator* folded. The last issue, dated January 1942, featured General MacArthur on the cover and called for "the complete victory of our armed forces over those of our enemies all over the world."[52] In November 1941, two executives of the magazine had been subpoenaed by a special grand jury in Washington on the grounds that its extensive mailing list would somehow be used, in the words of a government prosecutor, "for a serious and sinister purpose."[53] Although charges were temporarily dropped, as late as October 1946 the journal was under federal investigation. The Department of Justice accused *Scribner's Commentator* of receiving a total of $39,000, in four different installments, from the German embassy in 1941. Vice-president Stewart claimed that he had gotten the money from rich American industrialists who wanted to remain anonymous. In March 1947 the grand jury of a federal district court in Washington absolved Stewart of all charges.[54]

If one could tie *Scribner's Commentator* to any particular form of anti-interventionism, it would be to that of Charles A. Lindbergh, whose views it often featured and to whom the editors were personally close.[55] While the journal would occasionally reprint radio addresses by such liberals as Hutchins, articles written especially for the journal tended to be by authors opposed to all of Roosevelt's major programs, foreign and domestic. It was also far more vocal in its opposition to Great Britain than were many other anti-interventionists, and it warned against war with Japan far more frequently. Its editor, George T. Eggleston, later said that both he and publisher Payson believed in May 1940 that "since France was about to drop out of the war, England could negotiate an honorable peace with Germany and let Hitler and Stalin fight it out to a point of exhaustion that would eventually bring the downfall of both dictators."[56] Because *Scribner's Commentator* was so well publicized, and because of the administration attacks on it, historians have occasionally thought that it epitomized the anti-interventionist case. However, as a variety of scholars have recently pointed out, the anti-interventionist cause was quite a diverse one, and *Scribner's Commentator* was a vigorous spokesman for its most extreme right wing.

Notes

1. *New York Times*, 5 May, 20 September 1939. For the memoirs of its editor, see George T. Eggleston, *Roosevelt, Churchill, and the World War II Opposition: A Revisionist Autobiography* (Old Greenwich, Connecticut, 1979), pp. 71–73, 141–43.

2. In November 1940, P. and S. Publishing reorganized itself, with Eggleston as president and Stewart as vice-president. Stewart's cousin, Jeremiah Milbank, banker and formerly eastern treasurer of the Republican party, backed the firm financially. In September 1941, Payson was listed as president and Stewart vice-president.

3. Among the prominent isolationists on the cover were Charles A. Lindbergh, Gerald P. Nye, Robert A. Taft, Hiram Johnson, Eddie Rickenbacker, Henry Ford, Fulton J. Sheen, Frank Lloyd Wright, and Lillian Gish. Europeans so featured included Marshal Philippe Pétain, Marshal Carl Mannerheim, and Captain René de Chambrun, a prominent French officer and son-in-law of Pierre Laval.

4. "Cabbages and Kings," *Scribner's Commentator* 10 (August 1941): 6 (hereinafter cited as *SC*).

5. See, for example, Daniel A. Reed, "Fiscal Foolishness and Defense," *SC* 8 (July 1940): 6–9; "Cabbages and Kings," *SC* 10 (May 1940): 6.

6. James B. Carey, "Labor and Defense Strikes," *SC* 9 (January 1941): 83–87.

7. *SC* 9 (March 1941): inside cover.

8. Freeman Tilden, "The New York Influence—America's Journalistic Poison," *SC* 9 (December 1940): 9.

9. "Cabbages and Kings," *SC* 10 (July 1941): 4.

10. See, for example, Jane Ellsworth, "Backwash from the Wave of the Future," *SC* 10 (June 1941): 7–12; Albert Hall, "Reviewing the Refugee Problem," *SC* 10 (September 1941): 45–51: Howard M. Yates, "Bolivia's Refugees—A Warning," *SC* 10 (October 1941): 47–50; Abbott Hamilton, "Refugee Scholars and American Education," *SC* 11 (December 1941): 87–92. For a contrasting attitude of a prominent anti-interventionist toward refugees, see Norman Thomas to Franklin D. Roosevelt, 11 June 1940, Norman Thomas Papers, New York Public Library.

11. John T. Flynn, "Radio—Interventionism's Trump," *SC* 9 (April 1941): 45–49.

12. Kenneth Monroe, "British Propaganda: 1940 Version," *SC* 9 (November 1940): 55.

13. John Selfridge, "Hollywood Crown Colony," *SC* 9 (January 1941): 45.

14. Lillian Gish, "I Made War Propaganda," *SC* 11 (November 1941): 7–11.

15. Gerald W. Movius, "Comic Strip Propaganda," *SC* 11 (November 1941): 17.

16. Frazier Hunt, "A Lesson in Propaganda," *SC* 8 (October 1940): 85.

17. Miriam Marsh Clark, "Government by Gallup," *SC* 10 (September 1941): 31–36.

18. Wayne S. Cole, *America First: The Battle Against Intervention, 1940–1941* (Madison, Wisconsin, 1953), p. 37. See also Manfred Jonas, "Pro–Axis Sentiment and American Isolationism," *Historian* 29 (February 1967): 221–37.

19. "Ribbing 'Uncle Shylock,'" *SC* 10 (September 1941): 69–76.

20. Harvey Weston, "Anglo–American Relations," *SC* 10 (September 1941): 68, 79.

21. Rush D. Holt, "Is Churchill Good Enough for Roosevelt?" *SC* 10 (July 1941): 34–36.

22. William Griffin. "When Churchill Said Keep Out!" *SC* 9 (February 1941): 25–28. Griffin claimed that he sued Churchill three years later, when Churchill denied having made such statements.

23. Lois and Donaldson Thorburn, "Beau Saboteur," *SC* 8 (June 1940): 64–71.

24. Amos Pinchot, "The Roosevelt-Laski Scheme," *SC* 10 (October 1941): 69–76.

25. Albert Hall, "Cecil Rhodes: Father of 'Union Now,'" *SC* 10 (June 1941): 77–82.

26. Robert Carroll, "Is This My War?" *SC* 10 (July 1941): 61.

27. Albert Jay Nock, review of Jawaharlal Nehru, *Toward Freedom*, *SC* 10 (August 1941): 91.

28. See, for example, Frank C. Hanighen, "Were the Social Reforms of the Popular Front Responsible for the French Defeat?" *Uncensored*, no. 41 (13 July 1940): special supplement, pp. 1–4.

29. Stanton B. Leeds, "The Real Pétain," *SC* 10 (July 1941): 13–18; Stanton B. Leeds, "Chambrun—Soldier of France," *SC* 9 (January 1941): 11–12, 21–23.

30. "These Rule France," *SC* 9 (January 1941): 13–20.

31. Lois and Donaldson Thorburn, "Dear Elmer," *SC* 8 (August 1940): 42. Also eulogized was King Leopold III of Belgium, whom one author hailed for holding the line to permit the British a safe retreat. J. Perry Carmer, "Leopold and Dunkerque," *SC* 11 (December 1941): 65–68.

32. Kenneth Monroe, "Freemasonry—A Study in Contrasts," *SC* 10 (June 1941): 63–68.

33. Boris Brasol, "Aid to Stalin? Incredible," *SC* 11 (November 1941): 21–26.

34. Paul R. Sanders, "Europe's Mildest Dictator," *SC* 11 (November 1941): 33.

35. William G. Ryan, "I Fought in Spain," *SC* 11 (December 1941): 7–12.

36. Remarks on Spain included in sketch of Marshall Field III, "Internationalist Hall of Fame," *SC* 9 (December 1940): 20. For a general study of American opinionmakers and the Spanish Civil War, see Allen Guttmann, *The Wound in the Heart: America and the Spanish Civil War* (Glencoe, Illinois, 1962).

37. Ralph Townsend, "Japan—Our Commercial Prize," *SC* 9 (November 1940): 46.

38. John J. Whiteford, "The Paradoxical Chinese," *SC* 9 (February 1941): 24.

39. See Jonas, "Pro-Axis Sentiment and American Isolationism," pp. 221–37.

40. "Cabbages and Kings: Flight of the Twilight Patriots," *SC* 11 (December 1941): 3.

41. Henry Ford, "An American Foreign Policy," *SC* 9 (December 1940): 3–6.

42. D. Worth Clark, "The Men behind Our War Scare," *SC* 8 (September 1940): 107–09; Rush D. Holt, "Patriotism in Rearmament," *SC* 9 (November 1940): 7–10.

43. MacLeish and White in "Internationalist Hall of Fame," *SC* 9 (December 1940): 16, 19; Rugg and Wise in ibid., *SC* 9 (November 1940): 16, 20.

44. Robert Maynard Hutchins, "The Proposition Is Peace," *SC* 10 (July 1941): 93–98; Harry Emerson Fosdick, "Are We Fit for Democracy?" *SC* 9 (January 1941): 89–92.

45. Ernest E. Johnson, "Shall Negroes Save Democracy?" *SC* 11 (November 1941): 61.

46. Wheeler McMillan and Frank Chodorov, "Hitler—Economic Threat?" *SC* 9 (March 1941): 29–34 (Chodorov quotation: 33).

47. John T. Flynn, "Nazi Economy—A Threat?" *SC* 10 (August 1941): 19–25.

48. Roger Wylie, "Latin America—Economic Pawn," *SC* 10 (May 1941): 45–50; Owen Baldwin, "Latin American Markets," *SC* 11 (November 1941): 12–16; Paul Arden, "Pan American Relations," *SC* 11 (December 1941): 58–64.

49. William Hague, "Should We Feed Europe?" *SC* 9 (January 1941): 29–34.

50. Johnson Hagood, "When We Invade Japan," *SC* 7 (June 1940): 3–5; Robert R. McCormick, "Can America Fight in Europe?" *SC* 9 (February 1941): 88–90.

51. George Chase Lewis, "The Truth about Our Air Defenses," *SC* 10 (July 1940): 3–5; Al Williams, "Real Air Power for Americans," *SC* 8 (August 1940): 104–08.

52. "Cabbages and Kings," *SC* 11 (January 1942): 3.

53. "The Strangers," *Time* 38 (17 November 1941): 74–75; *New York Times*, 6 November 1941. Prosecutor quoted in Eggleston, *Roosevelt, Churchill, and the World War II Opposition*, p. 37.

54. *New York Times*, 27 October; 20, 27, 28 November 1946; 12, 13, 14, 19, 26 March 1947. For the original charges, see government prosecutor O. John Rogge, *The Official German Report* (New York, 1961), pp. 300–03. Eggleston presents his rebuttal in *Roosevelt, Churchill, and the World War II Opposition*, pp. 191–203.

55. Articles praising Lindbergh include C. B. Allen, "Lindbergh Today," *SC* 8 (September 1940): 11–26; Paul Palmer, "Col. Lindbergh's Mail—An American Phenomenon," *SC* 8 (October 1940): 43–52; Al Williams, "I Rebuke Seversky," *SC* 10 (July 1941): 7–12. Lindbergh's own articles include "Impregnable America," *SC* 9 (January 1941): 3–6; "Lindbergh for the Record, *SC* 10 (August 1941): 7–13; and "Time Lies with Us," *SC* 11 (November 1941): 88–93. In 1940, the journal printed a pamphlet containing five of Lindbergh's speeches. *The Wartime Journals of Charles A. Lindbergh* (New York, 1970) is replete with Lindbergh's contacts with Eggleston and Stewart.

56. Eggleston, *Roosevelt, Churchill, and the World War II Opposition*, p. 72.

Information Sources

BIBLIOGRAPHY:
Eggleston, George T. *Roosevelt, Churchill, and World War II Opposition: A Revisionist Autobiography.* Old Greenwich, Connecticut, 1979.
INDEXES: *PAIS*; *RG*.
REPRINT EDITIONS: None.
LOCATION SOURCES: Widely available.

Publication History

TITLE AND TITLE CHANGES: *Scribner's Commentator*.
VOLUME AND ISSUE DATA: Volumes 7–11, November 1939–January 1942.
FREQUENCY OF PUBLICATION: Monthly.

PUBLISHERS: November 1939–March 1940: Payson Publishing Company; March l940–
    January 1942: P. and S. Publishing, Inc., both in New York until July 1941; thereafter,
    Lake Geneva, Wisconsin.
EDITORS: Francis Rufus Bellamy, 1939–1940; George T. Eggleston, 1940–1942.
CIRCULATION: 30,000.

Justus D. Doenecke

Weekly Foreign Letter
1938–1942

From 30 June 1938, until 9 July 1942, the *Weekly Foreign Letter* commented on economic and political trends. A mimeographed weekly, it was first edited by A. I. Nazaroff, a nationalized White Russian who had reviewed books on Russian life and history in the 1920s and early 1930s for the *New York Times*. On 21 July 1938, V. D. Gravenhoff, another naturalized White Russian, became coeditor; he was responsible for the business affairs of the journal.

On 17 February 1939, political writer Lawrence Dennis became coeditor, and Nazaroff, disappointed by the lack of income, severed his ties. Henceforth, Dennis wrote most—if not all—copy, while Gravenhoff continued to supervise printing, distribution, and subscriptions. On 14 March 1940, Dennis became sole editor. For $290, Gravenhoff, who was embarrassed by Dennis's views, sold his interest in the journal. In the public mind, the *Weekly Foreign Letter* was always associated with Dennis's views.[1]

Before its demise, 206 issues had been published. The newsletter was strictly a one-man performance, as Dennis often lacked secretarial help. Within its three to seven mimeographed pages, one found racy headlines ("SITZ VERSUS BLITZ. BLITZ LOSES"), followed by Dennis's extensive commentary. Sometimes whole paragraphs were printed in capital letters. Although the newsletter never reached a mass audience, it was read by a number of leading isolationists, some of whom Dennis knew personally.[2] Dennis's comments were pithy and frequently sardonic. But beneath what was often biting sarcasm, he drew on a host of sources and often on British ones.[3] Many of the ideas he espoused were given a wider audience in his various books.

To most historians, and to much of the general public as well, the name of Lawrence Dennis has long been linked to American "fascism."[4] Beginning in the 1960s, some commentators started to refer to Dennis in slightly more appreciative terms.[5] However, the uncompromising nature of Dennis's arguments enabled

Secretary of the Interior Harold L. Ickes in 1941 to find him one of the "Quislings who, in pretended patriotism, would cravenly spike our guns and ground our airplanes in order that Hitlerism might more easily overcome us." Dennis's rationale also allowed columnist Dorothy Thompson to label him the "braintruster extraordinary to the forces of democratic defeat," and exposé writer Avedis Derounian, whose pen name was "John Roy Carlson," to call him "Liberty's chief hangman."[6]

Dennis began his career on the lower rungs of the American establishment. He was born in Atlanta in 1893, and received his formal education at Phillips Exeter Academy and Harvard. During World War I, he served overseas as an infantry officer. Then came several years in the foreign service, followed by employment abroad with J. & W. Seligman and the National City Bank of New York. In 1930, Dennis began to attack the overseas activities of American investment banking, publishing his broadsides in such liberal journals as the *Nation* and the *New Republic*.[7]

Soon Dennis began to offer sweeping solutions for the Great Depression, solutions that increasingly centered on a corporate state. Like F. A. Hayek and Joseph Schumpeter, he saw the coming world as a collectivist one; unlike them, he welcomed this world vigorously. His world was always much closer to that of George Soule or Stuart Chase than to that of Ludwig von Mises. In 1934, as associate editor of a right-wing tabloid, the *Awakener*, he attacked the "half-way" measures of the New Deal and called for more centralized economic controls. His "fascist" reputation, however, was rooted in his book *The Coming American Fascism* (1936), as well as in a series of articles written in the mid- and late 1930s for such journals as the *American Mercury*, *Social Frontier*, and the *Annals of the American Academy of Political and Social Science*.

The industrial countries, he said, faced inevitable collectivization. Fascism, communism, even the American New Deal were all parts of a historical process so mechanistic that individual rulers counted for little. Capitalism—once nourished by extensive geographical frontiers and rich world markets—was no longer workable; the New Deal, a mere step on the collectivist road, had little to offer but deficit spending and make-work projects. Given the need for a thoroughly collectivized society, Dennis found America facing the choice of fascism or communism. Of the two, he claimed that fascism was preferable. Unlike the Soviet system it offered class unity, used the market mechanism, and retained skilled managerial elites.[8]

Dennis, in fact, claimed to be describing "a desirable fascism." He used the example of Huey Long as "our nearest approach to a national fascist leader" and spoke of how fascism would initially gain power through control of varied state governments. A militarized party organization would then compete in national elections. Assuming power legally, the new ruling elite would call private enterprise to "the colors as conscripts in war." In addition, it would reorganize the Congress on vocational lines and replace the two-party system with a single party, one "holding a mandate from the people." Specific economic measures included nationalization of banks and major monopolies, redistribution of wealth and income through progressive taxation, and subsidization of small enterprises and farming. In the new society, all institutions—press, radio, cinema, schools, and churches—would have to foster the "national plan" designed to coordinate the entire economy.[9] The organic society of Lawrence Dennis had little in common with that of Burkean conservatives. Rather, it was rooted in the technocratic dream of rule by a managerial elite.

The question of whether Dennis was a proponent of "fascism" depends on how the term is defined. Dennis would use the noun interchangeably. At times he meant any kind of centralized economy that was not communist. At other times he was referring solely to the political and economic systems of Germany and Italy. At still other times he was outlining his utopian vision for America. Dennis long denied that he was ever a fascist, declaring that he had never joined a fascist movement or backed a fascist cause. Rather, he was a neutral observer, trying to analyze events without ideological bias.[10]

If, by fascism, one means a state in which one-party rule is combined with strident nationalism, continental autarchy, and centralized economic controls that mold private ownership to public will—in short, a truly corporatist and organic society transcending localized interests—then Dennis's system might legitimately be call fascistic. If, however, one defines fascism as involving the clear-cut *Führer prinzip*, terror system, and permanent purge so often associated with Nazi Germany, then Dennis was not a fascist. He adhered to the racism of neither an Alfred Rosenberg or a Vidkun Quisling; rather, his politics centered on the twin poles of economic corporatism and rigid isolationism.[11]

Dennis's isolationism developed naturally from his corporatism. He argued that a self-sufficient and disciplined United States would not have to venture outside the hemisphere. In contrast to the fascist powers of Europe, the United States could sustain full employment without the need for additional markets and territory overseas. Dennis was far from being a pacifist, and in 1936 his foreign policy included control of the Panama Canal, "naval parity with the greatest power, a professional army of at least four hundred thousand men, fully equipped, and universal compulsory military service." The United States, by maintaining a strong war potential, could "rope off a large section of the globe within this hemisphere as territory in which outsiders may not come and fight." Far better, Dennis believed, to construct a Fortress America than to fight "another holy war," one that could only result in "world revolution and chaos."[12]

Despite the unconventional nature of some tenets, Dennis did not always have a bad press. Several reviews of *The Coming American Fascism* were quite respectful, with the *Times Literary Supplement* of London claiming that the book had "substantial value as a fresh and penetrating analysis of the present situation." Such critics as Ernest Sutherland Bates and Dwight Macdonald denied that Dennis was advocating a European form of fascism. What Dennis meant by fascism, said Macdonald, appeared to be "a kind of Technocracy and not at all what Hitler and Mussolini meant." As late as June 1940, the *New York Times* covered his addresses before foreign policy groups, always referring to him as a "banker," "economist," or "former member of the diplomatic service"—never as a "Fascist."[13]

Even in 1940 and 1941 Dennis was not entirely excluded from mainstream political forums. True, Harper and Brothers, finding Dennis "too hot" a property, dropped sponsorship of a Dennis volume that they had intended to publish, and Dennis had to publish *The Dynamics of War and Revolution* himself. However, Dennis addressed the prestigious Institute of Public Affairs of the University of Virginia in 1940. The next year the *Nation* featured a debate between Dennis, political scientist Frederick L. Schuman, and journalist Max Lerner, and *Fortune* magazine welcomed his participation in a roundtable forum on the world economy.[14]

It was only after the fall of France that Dennis was opposed by the very groups that had once tolerated, and at times welcomed, his views, and it is doubtful whether any isolationist except Colonel Charles A. Lindbergh so aroused the interventionists' ire. Such opposition might have been inevitable, for as Germany, Italy, and Japan began to assault the Versailles system, Dennis devoted increasing attention to foreign policy. In *The Dynamics of War and Revolution* (1940) and in a privately circulated bulletin entitled the *Weekly Foreign Letter* (1938–1942), Dennis propounded the doctrine that wars of conquest were inevitable. The British empire, now a status quo power, had been founded by "pirates, slavetraders and fighting men"; the United States had stolen its territory from the Indians. As aggression was rooted in human nature and in the world's unequal distribution of goods, it was folly to think in Wilsonian terms of a "war to end wars."[15]

Even before the outbreak of World War II, Dennis had placed himself squarely on the side of the so-called have-not nations. The breakdown of world capitalism, he said, forced the "socialist" nations—Germany, Russia, Italy, and Japan—to develop economic spheres totally independent of traditional trade and financial networks. He therefore found the Munich Pact an act of rationality, a "realistic" attempt to secure peaceful change. If, in the process, the agreement made Germany master of all Europe, it avoided a general war and the accompanying triumph of communism.

By the same token, England's guarantee to Poland, made in late March 1939, was sheer stupidity. The British, having just given Hitler the keys to Eastern Europe, were suddenly forbidding him to use them. To Dennis, it was the height of folly to fight Germany, the world's greatest military power, without an alliance with the Soviet Union. Furthermore, Britain's action delivered the small Baltic nations over to "the tender mercies of Moscow."[16]

As early as March 1939, Dennis predicted German moves against Memel, Danzig, and Rumania. Yet to the very eve of World War II, he thought Britain and France would capitulate to Hitler. He also forecast that Germany would not attack the Western front because any strike against the Maginot Line would prove fatal. More accurate predictions included the Soviet attack on Finland and British activity in Norway.[17]

Once hostilities started, the *Weekly Foreign Letter* gave several reasons that it believed Germany was bound to win. First, it claimed that Germany, in contrast to the democracies, possessed dynamic leadership. In its eyes, Roosevelt was "a semiparalyzed country squire" who lacked the toughness necessary to lead a major war effort. Such policymakers as Secretary of State Cordell Hull, Secretary of the

Navy Frank Knox, and Secretary of War Henry L. Stimson were superannuated and confused. America's military and naval heads were "mostly goldbraided senior Civil Service clerks." It found Winston Churchill as incompetent as Roosevelt, "a senile alcoholic who [had] never been a success at anything except writing alibis for his failures"; most of England's parliamentary leaders were equally inept.[18]

The *Weekly Foreign Letter* saw Hitler, however, as a man of "genius." Rather than vying to be "the darling of American women's groups," the German leader dismembered Czechoslovakia, isolated Russia, and secured food from Eastern Europe for his "eighty million German bellies." Later evidence of Hitler's brilliant leadership, it commented, could be seen in his ability to unite the "have-nots" against "the capitalistic plutodemocracies."[19]

Second, Dennis's newsletter asserted that only the totalitarian nations possessed the élan vital necessary for victory. The British and the French, unlike the Germans, lacked "the willingness to die by the tens of thousands." True, Germany's armed manpower, industrial mobilization, and geographical location contributed to its superiority, but it saw more as well. While the American laborer would go on strike to secure benefits, the Nazi worker—knowing that the industrialists were being (according to Dennis) equally disciplined—willingly accepted long hours and low wages.[20]

Third, the *Weekly Foreign Letter* asserted that the totalitarian states had more attainable war aims. Dennis always denied that Hitler sought world conquest; rather, Germany merely wanted additional *Lebensraum* in eastern Europe. By integrating the agricultural Balkan states with an industrialized Reich, a prosperous continent could remain independent of an Anglo-American commercial system. Such German domination of Europe, Dennis frequently maintained, preserved rather than threatened the world balance of power. Fragmented continents, packed with small sovereign states, were economically unworkable; world prosperity of necessity depended on continental blocs. Here Dennis envisioned an expanded Russian zone, an Asia dominated by Japan, a somewhat reduced British empire, a Western Hemisphere controlled by the United States, and a Europe run by Germany.[21] The Americas were in no danger, he often said, for German or Japanese efforts to extend their domain overseas would be far too costly.

By contrast, the *Weekly Foreign Letter* claimed that Allied war aims were both Carthaginian and messianic. Britain, anxious to preserve world hegemony, offered Germany only perpetual foreign domination. Sometimes the *Weekly Foreign Letter* would portray America as an unwitting underwriter for England's bankrupt system. Sometimes it would claim that the United States hoped to inherit Britain's naval supremacy. Sometimes it would assert that the United States sought a closed door at home and an open door abroad. Accusing Roosevelt's "knights of the round table" of attempting to internationalize New Deal relief through a series of overseas credits, it tersely remarked, "The Germans are fighting for groceries; if we fight it will be for the right to give away groceries." The United States, it declared, was foolishly hoping to restore Anglo-American supremacy based on the gold standard, international capitalism, and a monopoly of raw materials.[22]

To the *Weekly Foreign Letter*, the utopian rhetoric of the Allies was even more infuriating. Establishing the Four Freedoms everywhere, it said, was "about the craziest enterprise any nation ever embarked upon in modern history." Dennis often argued that America's own racial hypocrisy and the British suppression of India's nationalism revealed the real aim of the interventionists: to supplant the Nazi "Heerenrasse" with a world system in which Anglo-Saxon "Heerschaft" is implicit.[23] Dennis was particularly acid concerning the treatment of American blacks. The United States, he charged, had expedientially "soft-pedaled" its blatant discrimination since the nation was founded in 1776. Yet once racial equality became part of the nation's propaganda arsenal, American blacks—like the inhabitants of India—would rebel against all "broken promises."[24]

Since, according to Dennis, the totalitarian nations possessed the advantage of dynamic leadership, superb organization and morale, and feasible war aims, it was hardly surprising that their military strategy was superior.[25]

The United States, so the *Weekly Foreign Letter* said, could actually benefit from a Hitler victory and a quick peace. While America developed its own self-sufficiency, it could conduct a prosperous trade with Axis Europe. Furthermore, the nation could come to the rescue of the vanquished British ("a grand people," Dennis mused), first by admitting some 20 million immigrants, second by taking over both Canada and Australia. True, England would have to surrender all decision making to the United States, but it could help form a viable Anglo-Saxon bloc. ("The royal family," it remarked, "might be kept as a tourist attraction like the quintuplets in Canada.") Such an America could also serve as a refuge for persecuted Jews, though Dennis later noted that his countrymen preferred "a Hitler lynching party."[26]

Dennis contributed ten dollars to the America First Committee, but he found most isolationists unreceptive to his ideas. America First, he said, was foolish even to advocate limited aid to Britain or to attempt to hold Roosevelt to his peace pledges. Far better, he frequently remarked, to recognize realities, which meant acknowledging that the United States was already in the conflict. The isolationists were minimizing their appeal and hence playing into the hands of their opponents. Only by combining a program of absolute nonparticipation with promises of either a welfare state or the annexation of the entire continent could they ever secure a mass base.[27]

Roosevelt's alternative, the *Weekly Foreign Letter* commented in March 1941, was staggering. The very phrase "all-aid-short-of-war" was self-contradictory, for the United States could not afford both guns and butter. America's living standards were bound to decline. Big business and labor might flourish, but the middle classes and farmers faced ruin.[28]

By fighting totalitarianism overseas, the *Weekly Foreign Letter* predicted that America would succumb to it at home. The nation would experience the "wrong kind" of fascism, one imposed without debate or direction. In fact, the House Committee on Un-American Activities, which had released a white book on German operations in the United States in 1940, inadvertently revealed the direction the country was headed. Since the Dies Committee lacked evidence that it could support legal conviction, Dennis accused it of serving as a true "People's Court."[29]

Yet as the nation drew increasingly closer to actual fighting, the *Weekly Foreign Letter* found it woefully unprepared. The United States lacked the strategy needed to conquer Europe. Moreover, it was barely ahead of backward Italy in technology and could never raise the needed 10 million men. American convoys only prolonged England's agony without seriously harming Germany. In the two years necessary for the United States to raise a competent army, Hitler would have conquered all Russia, the Mediterranean, and the Near East.[30]

The *Weekly Foreign Letter* found America's opposition to Japan equally foolish. As Japan's natural expansion was blocked by Western trade and immigration barriers, it was forced to follow an imperialist course. Roosevelt was aiding China's "military gangsters," and thereby had revealed that he was out to ruin the island kingdom. Dennis predicted that the Chinese would eventually force Japan out of their land. A sudden Japanese withdrawal, however, would simply throw some 2 million demobilized soldiers into a country whose trade prospects were already poor. Given such a bleak outlook, the Japanese were driven into an alliance with Germany and forced to seek territory in southeast Asia.[31]

To the *Weekly Foreign Letter*, Roosevelt's last-minute diplomacy was particularly irresponsible. Knowing that a Pacific war would make interventionism popular, the president—so Dennis's newsletter claimed—refused to allow a face-saving truce. In addition, after presenting the Japanese with unacceptable terms, Roosevelt allowed his navy to be "caught napping" at Pearl Harbor. Such activity could only hasten America's day of reckoning: communism would inevitably triumph in Asia, for the open door was "a sucker's game at which we cannot possibly win."[32]

Events soon forced Dennis's weekly to modify some of its analysis. On 22 June 1941, German armies invaded Russia. During the 1930s, Dennis had opposed Soviet Popular Front efforts. Russia, he said, was unrelentingly plotting war and global revolution against the capitalist powers. When war broke out in 1939, he warned that conflict within Western Europe was suicidal and served only to bring the world closer to bolshevism. He made no secret of preferring "a new order in Europe with Hitler and without a second A. E. F. to any adventure involving a second A. E. F."[33]

Germany and Russia, the *Weekly Foreign Letter* frequently repeated in 1940 and early 1941, were in "permanent partnership." Just twelve days before Germany struck, it claimed that the Reich had stationed Wehrmacht troops on the Rumanian border simply to divide the spoils with the Soviets. But when Hitler moved, it found the German attack additional evidence of the führer's "decision, daring, surprise, and speed." Nazi armies, it predicted, would certainly reach Leningrad and Moscow by the end of the summer.[34]

Only when Hitler's troops became bogged down in the Russian snows did the *Weekly Foreign Letter* call the German ruler a "fanatic," one "who would die for his dragon-slaying act." Hitler had been victimized by his anti-Semitic and anticommunist ideologies, and had thereby betrayed his nation's interest.[35]

Dennis soon filled his bulletin with tributes to Russia's leader. Stalin, head of "the Russia First Committee," was the only leader on the world scene who was fighting for concrete, not messianic, aims. Indeed, because Stalin's forces were engaged in the bulk of the fighting, Dennis nominated him as head of an Allied war council; the Soviet dictator could serve as "generalisimo of the United Nations' military forces." Since the war was creating a revolutionary situation throughout the world, Dennis commented that the United States was fortunate in having a major ally whose ideology could cope with it.[36]

With America now in the war, Dennis was totally shunned. In July 1942 he discontinued his weekly bulletin. He denied that the administration had made overt moves to suppress the *Weekly Foreign Letter*, but claimed that in wartime his patriotism was bound to be questioned. He was soon investigated by the Federal Bureau of Investigation as a suspected German agent and threatened with removal from the Eastern Military Area.[37] In 1944, Dennis was indicted for sedition, an event that made national news, but after close to eight months, charges were dropped.[38]

During the cold war, Dennis resumed his isolationist newsletter, giving it the title *Appeal to Reason*. In it he strongly opposed America's cold war militancy, harkening in vain for the nation's withdrawal to the American continent.

Some historians now support several of Dennis's specific arguments. A newer generation of cold war revisionists have argued that America's World War II involvement was rooted in a desire to sustain global capitalist expansion amid the closed economic blocs of the totalitarian powers. Japanese expansion, in particular, has recently been explained in terms of Western strangulation. Other claims made by the *Weekly Foreign Letter* receive support from some members of the academy: the intransigency of American negotiations with Japan, the folly of Allied military strategy and likelihood of Britain's eventual defeat, and U.S. indifference to the fate of Europe's Jews.

Yet many people could not be at ease with Dennis's writing. He was so loose with his definitions, and so vague about his own "fascist" notion, that it is often difficult to grasp just what his ideology was.

On a deeper level, Dennis never separated his espousals from his supposed objectivity. Sometimes he claimed that national survival depended on keeping ethical principles analytically distinct from unbiased assessments of national interest. Hitler's racism, he said, was less of a "sin" than an "error," a blunder interfering with efforts to organize a genuine anticapitalist coalition. At other times he would feign indifference. He declared that he cared little, for example, whether the United States entered the war, whether Germany or Russia emerged triumphant in Europe, or even whether Reich emissaries were treated fairly in American courts. He was simply an observer, one who called "a spade a spade" and believed that "it is better to face facts than to shut one's eyes to them."[39] At still other times, he was avowedly partisan. Once he compared himself to an early Christian who, peering out of the catacombs, exulted in the realization that his ideas "were among the most active agents of the rampant disintegration about him."[40]

All in all, however, Dennis and his *Weekly Foreign Letter* remain provocative. Writing in terse, elliptical prose, Dennis saw himself cutting through conventional rhetoric in order to pierce prevailing illusions. Like George Fitzhugh a century earlier, he posed inescapable dilemmas, and then claimed to show the path of escape. Not only was he one of the most extreme anti-interventionists the United States ever produced, he couched his arguments with a logic that would do justice to a Niccoló Machiavelli and a style that would do credit to a Thomas Hobbes.

Notes

1. O. John Rogge, *The Official German Report* (New York, 1961), p. 181.

2. See, for example, *The Wartime Journals of Charles A. Lindbergh* (New York, 1970), p. 391; Lawrence Dennis to Robert E. Wood, 10 October 1941 (copy), Harry Elmer Barnes Papers, University of Wyoming Library; Robert E. Wood to Robert E. Wood, Jr., 5 May 1941, and Robert E. Wood to J. Edgar Hoover, 30 January 1943, Robert E. Wood Papers, Herbert Hoover Presidential Library, West Branch, Iowa; Lawrence Dennis to Harry Elmer Barnes, 29 September 1941, Barnes Papers; Sterling Morton to Robert E. Wood, Sterling Morton Papers, Chicago Historical Society; John Foster Dulles to Lawrence Dennis, 18 November 1940, Lawrence Dennis Papers, Hoover Institution on War, Revolution and Peace, Stanford University; John Cudahy to Lawrence Dennis, 18 November 1941, Dennis Papers; Alfred Bingham to Lawrence Dennis, 31 March 1941, Dennis Papers.

3. Among the British journals cited were the *Times* (London), *Economist, Nineteenth Century, Contemporary Review, Round Table, Economic Journal* (London), *National Review, Tribune, Daily Herald* (London), *New Statesman and Nation, Fortnightly Review,* and *Political Quarterly.*

4. Arthur S. Link, *American Epoch: A History of the United States since the 1890s,* 2nd ed. rev. (New York, 1963), p. 448; Charles C. Alexander, *Nationalism in American Thought, 1930–1945* (Chicago, 1969), p. 12. For Dennis's general political philosophy, see Alan Pendleton Grimes, *American Political Thought* (New York, 1955), pp. 415–28, and David Spitz, *Patterns of Anti-Democratic Thought* (New York, 1949), pp. 59–92.

5. Arthur M. Schlesinger, Jr., *The Politics of Upheaval* (Boston, 1960), p. 78; Frederick L. Schuman, "Reflections of a Pragmatist," *Nation* 209 (8 December 1969): 641; Justus D. Doenecke, "Lawrence Dennis: Revisionist of the Cold War," *Wisconsin Magazine of History* 55 (Summer 1972): 275–86; Ronald Radosh, *Prophets on the Right: Profiles of Conservative Critics of American Globalism* (New York, 1975), p. 332.

6. Ickes, quoted in *New York Times,* 26 February 1941, p. 13; Thompson, quoted in *Life* 10 (20 January 1941): 27; John Roy Carlson [pseud. Avedis Derounian], *Under-Cover* (New York, 1943), p. 499.

7. "Lawrence Dennis," in Maxine Block, ed., *Current Biography* (New York, 1941), pp. 218–20.

8. Dennis, mimeographed memorandum on "Peace Aims," 14–16 February 1941, 8th Fortune Round Table, Princeton, New Jersey; Dennis, *The Coming American Fascism* (New York, 1936), pp. 169–73.

9. Dennis, "Portrait of American Fascism," *American Mercury* 36 (December 1935): 407–08; Dennis, *The Coming American Fascism,* esp. pp. viii, 137, 198–99, 211–12.

10. For Dennis's varied use of the term *fascism,* see Leo Ribuffo, "Progressive Manqué: Lawrence Dennis" (unpublished manuscript), p. 20, and *The Coming American Fascism.* For Dennis's denial that he was ever a fascist, see *New York Times,* 19 December 1940, p. 22; Dennis to *Harvard Crimson,* 26 March 1956, copy in Harry Elmer Barnes Papers, University of Wyoming; Dennis to Robert J. Alexander, 8 December 1954, Dennis Papers, Hoover Institution.

11. Dennis declared that race was no disqualification for citizenship, but at the same time he insisted that no religious, racial, or cultural minority could "inculcate doctrines or

impart social attitudes violently inconsistent with social order." Dennis, *The Coming American Fascism*, pp. 109–11, 119.

12. Ibid., pp. 287, 282, 277, 296.

13. *Times Literary Supplement* (London), 28 March 1936; Ernest Sutherland Bates, *Books* (periodical), 12 January 1936, p. 3; Macdonald, *Common Sense* 5 (February 1936): 26–27. For sample stories from the *New York Times*, see 11 April 1938, p. 24; 5 April 1939, p. 10; 18 June 1904, p. 23.

14. For the initial Harper commitment to publish Dennis's *Dynamics of War and Revolution*, see *Weekly Foreign Letter*, supplement to no. 97, 6 June 1940 (hereinafter cited as *WFL*). See also Dennis to Ordway Tead, 30 April 1940, Lawrence Dennis Papers, Hoover Institution. For the Institute of Public Affairs, see *New York Times*, 18 June 1940, p. 23. For *Nation* debate, see "Who Owns the Future?" *Nation* 152 (11 January 1941): 39–41; (25 January 1941): 111. Dennis's participation in the *Fortune* forum is found in his "Peace Aims."

15. *WFL*, no. 166 (2 October 1941); *WFL*, no. 159 (14 August 1941); *WFL*, no. 98 (13 June 1940).

16. *WFL*, no. 117 (24 October 1940); *WFL*, no. 85 (14 March 1940).

17. *WFL*, no. 33 (16 March 1939); *WFL*, no. 57 (31 June 1939); *WFL*, no. 65 (26 October 1939); *WFL*, no. 73 (21 December 1939).

18. *WFL*, no. 106 (8 August 1940); *WFL*, no. 149 (5 June 1941); *WFL*, no. 157 (31 July 1941); *WFL*, no. 115 (10 October 1940); *WFL*, no. 92 (2 May 1940). Dennis did apologize for his remark concerning Roosevelt's disability, declaring that he admired the president for overcoming his paralysis. At the same time, he repeated his claim that "cripples" could not sustain a wartime pace. *WFL*, no. 107 (15 August 1940).

19. "After the Peace of Munich," pp. 115–16; *WFL*, no. 103 (18 July 1940).

20. *WFL*, no. 86 (21 March 1940); *WFL*, no. 93 (9 May 1940); *WFL*, no. 107 (15 August 1940).

21. *WFL*, no. 136 (6 March 1941); Dennis, *The Dynamics of War and Revolution* (New York, 1940), p. 210.

22. *WFL*, no. 168 (16 October 1941).

23. *WFL*, no. 166 (2 October 1941).

24. *WFL*, no. 194 (16 April 1942).

25. Dennis did not have the same enthusiasm for Italian and Japanese "dynamism" that he did for Germany's. In 1936, he had praised Mussolini's regime for offering a "dynamic social system" that subordinated private ownership to public desires. "What Is Mussolini?" *American Mercury* 37 (March 1936): 372–75. Yet once Italian forces in North Africa began to be routed, Dennis claimed that the Italian ruler was far too influenced by the Vatican, the monarchy, and the feudal landlords to sustain a revolution or to adopt an innovative war strategy. See *WFL*, no. 123 (5 December 1940); *WFL*, no. 140 (3 April 1941). Japan, dominated by traditionalist naval officers and industrialists, would eventually be led by its generals into national socialism. It could never defeat China and would eventually be forced to yield to a Russian-backed revolutionary regime. *WFL*, no. 115 (10 October 1940); *WFL*, no. 146 (15 May 1941); *WFL*, no. 134 (20 February 1941).

26. *WFL*, no. 118 (31 October 1940); *WFL*, no. 101 (3 July 1940); Dennis, *Dynamics of War and Revolution*, p. 159; *WFL*, no. 108 (24 August 1940); *WFL*, no. 131 (3 February 1941); Lawrence Dennis to Norman Thomas, 27 February 1944 (copy), National Council for the Prevention of War Papers, Swarthmore College Peace Collection.

27. For Dennis's critique of the isolationist mainstream, see *WFL*, no. 127 (2 January 1941); *WFL*, no. 132 (6 February 1941). The John T. Flynn Papers at the University of Oregon contain a master list of contributors to the America First Committee.

28. *WFL*, no. 119 (7 November 1940).

29. *WFL*, no. 121 (20 November 1940); *WFL*, no. 191 (26 March 1942); *WFL*, no. 117 (24 October 1940); *WFL*, no. 122 (28 November 1940).

30. *WFL*, no. 140 (25 July 1940); *WFL*, no. 185 (12 February 1942); *WFL*, no. 106 (8 August 1940).

31. *WFL*, no. 31 (2 March 1939); *WFL*, no. 155 (17 July 1941); *WFL*, no. 115 (10 October 1940); *WFL*, no. 173 (19 November 1941); *WFL*, no. 113 (25 September 1940).

32. *WFL*, no. 174 (27 November 1941); *WFL*, no. 179 (2 January 1942); *WFL*, no. 103 (18 July 1940).

33. *WFL*, no. 46 (15 June 1939); *WFL*, no. 136 (6 March 1941).

34. *WFL*, no. 150 (12 June 1941); *WFL*, no. 152 (26 June 1941); *WFL*, no. 151 (17 June 1941).

35. *WFL*, no. 200 (28 May 1942); *WFL*, no. 178 (24 December 1941).

36. *WFL*, no. 187 (28 February 1942); *WFL*, no. 195 (23 April 1942).

37. *WFL*, no. 188 (5 March 1942); Robert E. Wood to Lawrence Dennis, 9 January 1943; Major David Tiger to Lawrence Dennis (copy), 18 January 1943; Robert E. Wood to J. Edgar Hoover, 30 January 1943, all in Robert E. Wood Papers, Herbert Hoover Presidential Library.

38. Before war broke out in Europe, Dennis had written for a German-financed publication, *Today's Challenge*, and had spoken before the German-sponsored American Fellowship Forum. Even after the European conflict began, he received small sums from the German embassy. The matter of German money channeled to Dennis can be found in Alton Frye, *Nazi Germany and the Western Hemisphere, 1933–1941* (New Haven, Connecticut, 1967), pp. 145–46, and in Klaus Kipphan, *Deutsche Propaganda in den Vereinigten Statten, 1933–1941* (Heidelberg, 1971), pp. 174–75. The sedition charges against him, however, were quite different ones: violating the Smith Act of 1940 by being part of a worldwide Nazi conspiracy that, amid more cosmic aims, plotted insubordination in America's armed forces. The prosecution, unable to show that the twenty-eight defendants acted in concert, spent much time drawing parallels between their propaganda motifs and those of the Nazis. The sole evidence presented against Dennis consisted of six items reprinted in the weekly of the German-American Bund, *Deutscher Weckruf und Beobachter*. These items included strong attacks on the British and the Dies Committee, but contained nothing to link Dennis to any conspiracy. Two of these selections were the *Weekly Foreign Letter*.

39. *WFL*, no. 188 (5 March 1942).

40. Lawrence Dennis to Dorothy Thompson, 9 October 1940, Lawrence Dennis Papers, Hoover Institution.

Information Sources

BIBLIOGRAPHY:

Doenecke, Justus D. "The Isolationist as Collectivist: Lawrence Dennis and the Coming of World War II." *Journal of Libertarian Studies: An Interdisciplinary Review* 3 (January 1979): 191–207.

Radosh, Ronald. *Prophets on the Right: Profiles of Conservative Critics of American Globalism*. New York, 1975.

INDEXES: None.

REPRINT EDITIONS: None.

LOCATION SOURCES: Complete runs: Hoover Institution; New York Public Library.

Publication History

TITLE AND TITLE CHANGES: *Weekly Foreign Letter.*

VOLUME AND ISSUE DATA: Numbers 1–206, 30 June 1938–9 July 1942.

FREQUENCY OF PUBLICATION: Weekly.

PUBLISHERS: June 1938–February 1939: A. I. Nazaroff; July 1938–March 1940: V. D. Gravenhoff; February 1939–July 1942: Lawrence Dennis.

EDITORS: A. I. Nazaroff, 30 June 1938–17 February 1939; V. D. Gravenhoff, 21 July 1938–14 March 1940; Lawrence Dennis, 17 February 1939–9 July 1942.

CIRCULATION: Probably 700–1,000.

Justus D. Doenecke

Appeal to Reason
1946–1972

The Japanese attack on Pearl Harbor did not mark the end of American isolationism. Despite the fact that Senator Arthur H. Vandenberg (R, Michigan) became a much-publicized convert to interventionism, a good many opponents of American entry into World War II still opposed political and military commitments overseas. True, such anti-interventionists often had notable lapses, as when they endorsed the proposals of General Douglas MacArthur for victory in Asia and called for total victory over Russia through the use of airpower. However, one isolationist remained absolutely consistent, calling for complete neutrality in all cold war controversies.

This was commentator Lawrence Dennis, who publicized his views in a weekly newsletter, *Appeal to Reason*. Dennis's analysis was trenchant enough for one historian to call him the nation's "earliest and most consistent critic of the Cold War."[1] Like its predecessor, the *Weekly Foreign Letter*, *Appeal to Reason* was usually three to five pages long and usually mimeographed. It was first published at Dennis's farm in Becket, Massachusetts, but after a decade it was moved to Northampton, Massachusetts, and then Northfield. Until Dennis's divorce in 1956, his wife, Eleanor, did all of the typing and mailing.[2] With an annual subscription rate of twenty-four dollars a year, its circulation remained confined to several hundred subscribers, usually from the nation's more conservative business and political elite.[3]

Dennis started *Appeal to Reason* on 30 March 1946, a time when Russian diplomat Andrei Gromyko walked out of the U.N. Security Council and Winston Churchill had just given his Iron Curtain speech in Fulton, Missouri. In the first issue, *Appeal to Reason* called for "a return to the principles of international law and neutrality as preached by the founding fathers of this Republic....Through their abandonment we are moving swiftly towards international disaster."[4] In its twenty years of active life, the message never changed.[5]

As with the *Weekly Foreign Letter*, Dennis combined pungent headlines

("ATLANTIC PACT COPY OF HITLER'S ANTI-COMINTERN, EQUALLY IRRATIONAL") with a terse, pungent style. British sources were often used.[6] Dennis was not above sarcasm, as revealed by his reaction to Eisenhower and MacArthur's commands early in 1951: "Mac fix China; Ike fix Russia. Heap big chiefs."[7] By 1960, however, Dennis had lost some of his bite. He seldom commented on personalities, devoting most of his attention to abstract issues of inflation, unemployment, and the arms race. Much of the material first written in *Appeal to Reason* in the 1960s found its way into his book, *Operational Thinking about Survival* (1969).

Appeal to Reason resembled the *Weekly Foreign Letter* in another respect: its immediate influence was limited. Nevertheless, Dennis's bulletin sometimes found its way into the radio commentary of liberal J. Raymond Walsh, a column of World War II interventionist Dorothy Thompson, a history by revisionist Charles C. Tansill, a pamphlet by industrialist Sterling Morton, a speech by Congressman Howard Buffett of Nebraska, and a brief note in the *Nation*. On occasion, his financial backers expressed reservations. Chicago industrialist Sterling Morton claimed to agree "with a substantial amount of what he [Dennis] says," but Morton had the impression that "he is a good deal of a wild man."[8] Dennis referred to another backer, General Robert E. Wood, as seeing him as "a poor devil needing relief or assistance," not as one whose anti-intervention could still save the United States.[9]

In short, Dennis was basically a loner. Beginning in 1941, Dennis was cut off from the mass audience he had sometimes enjoyed in the 1930s, when he had occasionally written for the *American Mercury*, the *Nation*, and the *New Republic*. But being free from advertising and editorial pressures, he could damn a Harry Truman and a Douglas MacArthur with equal passion.

In one way, however, the *Appeal* differed from the *Weekly Foreign Letter*. Having been burned in the 1930s by his advocacy of a corporate state, Dennis never again offered a full-scale vision of the good society. One historian claims that Dennis's ideology was one of "persistent laissez-fairism," but such a comment is a bit off the mark.[10] True, in July 1949 Dennis did warn that "we are wrecking capitalism by pegged farm prices, pegged wage rates, pegged selling prices of big business monopolies and high taxes which means a world war every few years." However, when journalist John T. Flynn issued his broadside against "creeping socialism," *The Road Ahead* (1949), Dennis denied that American collectivism was rooted either in fabian conspirators or American fellow travelers. Rather he saw economic regimentation as the inevitable result of two world wars. "America's present foreign policy," he wrote in October 1949, "calls for a totalitarian state....To say that the state should undertake to enforce world peace and meddle all over the world but should not go so far at present in the pursuit of domestic welfare is unworthy of respect."[11]

If Dennis had one prognosis for the American economy, it was inflation. From the spring of 1948 on, Dennis predicted permanent inflation, a phenomenon that he viewed without alarm. Inflation, said Dennis, created the buying power needed for continued prosperity. While seldom invoking the name of John Maynard Keynes, Dennis claimed that so long as America's productive capacity remained strong, there were no limits to the inflationary deficit spending. Dennis even went so far as to assert that had Sewell Avery, board chairman of Montgomery Ward, acted on the *Appeal*'s prediction of continuous inflation and expanded his company, his firm would have experienced the economic boom of his rival, Sears, Roebuck. Conversely, to Dennis, the economic alternatives advanced by American conservatives—deflation, balanced budgets, and sound money—could only lead to "another Hoover depression."[12] As with most of his other writing, Dennis claimed to have no economic prediction of any sort. He was simply a neutral observer.

The significance of the *Appeal* does not lie in its influence. Rather, it lies in the rigor of Dennis's analysis and the consistence of his logic. At every turn, Dennis challenged defenders of cold war policy to reconsider fundamental assumptions. He repeatedly asked critics of particular American involvements, usually focusing on Europe, to oppose intervention in Asia and the Middle East as well.

To Dennis, the cold war was a mere replay of World War II. "Everything said against Hitler," he wrote, "can be repeated against Stalin and Russia."[13] America, he often stressed, should have learned its lesson rather than search continually for new commitments. Continued intervention could only spread world communism. Furthermore, containment was bound to speed up the very domestic "statism" and "intensification of class warfare" that interventionist conservatives most feared. America and Britain, said *Appeal to Reason*, could have controlled all of Europe only by negotiating peace with Germany in 1943, "while German armies were still deep in the heart of Europe." In 1946, it "made no sense to denounce Russia for pursuing self-interest and taking advantage of our imbecilities."[14]

In the immediate future, both communism and revolution were bound to triumph. "We have to ride it out, not stop it," the *Appeal* kept stressing. Later "we shall have opportunity to encourage and aid genuinely popular local resistance movements." In the meantime, showdowns were insane, for the scenario was bound to be frightening: within a few weeks, Russian armies would overrun Europe. America's airpower could destroy major cities, but its troops could never hold 9 million square miles of Eurasian soil. In fact, victory would leave the United States worse off than ever. "Once Western Europe had been destroyed by our bombers, communism and the Asiatic hordes would be residuary legatees."[15]

Yet the *Appeal* argued that the Soviet Union could be contained. In Western Europe, a variety of factors were at work: Catholicism, regionalism, traditionalism, nationalism, and high living standards. A Franco-British alliance could create an effective buffer zone between the Russian and American superpowers. In the Near East, Islamic culture offered strong resistance; in the Far East the Russians faced "nearly a billion people who could never be made puppets of the Slavs, even though they all turn communist."[16]

From the very start, the *Appeal* found little to admire in Truman's foreign policy. Claiming that the varied loans to Great Britain were grounded in expediency, it said: "We need a contented Britain to help us fight World War III." It also found America's continual demands for convertibility of sterling and the lifting of commonwealth tariffs "utterly immoral—as well as being impossible of realization without continual disaster."[17] U.S. opposition to Russian control of the Dardanelles was equally hypocritical: Soviet penetration was "as logical and inevitable...as our military control of Panama or Britain's of Gibraltar and Suez."[18]

To Dennis, the Truman Doctrine of 1947 was particularly infuriating. He found it designed in part to protect Standard Oil interests in the Middle East, in part to ensure Truman's re-election in 1948. The result? "A new holy war on communist sin all over the world,...a messianic crusade all over the planet." Most important of all, it was an effort to continue the heavy exports seen necessary to American prosperity. "We shall," said the *Appeal*, "have a limitless market for American farm products, manufactures, and cannon fodder." The Truman Doctrine served as a substitute for the large-scale foreign loans that underpinned much of Wall Street in the 1920s.[19] Once Secretary of State George Marshall outlined his recovery plan at that famous Harvard commencement on 5 June 1947, Dennis wrote: "We are deliberately giving away money to foreigners to keep up war inflation to prevent postwar deflation, depression, and unemployment."[20] And in 1949 the *Appeal* asserted: "It is no mere coincidence that the theatrical smash hit of the year in New York is the DEATH OF A SALESMAN."[21] The United States should not be inaugurating plans that simply postpone the eventual communist control of Europe. Rather, in words that appealed more to the Left than to the Right, it should be financing huge domestic welfare projects, such as slum clearance, highway construction, and care for the aged.[22]

To the *Appeal*, Belgrade's break from Moscow in 1949 seemed proof of Dennis's strictures: "Give them time. Give them plenty of rope. No nation can ever dominate the world, no matter how much or how fast it may, for a time, expand....Russia and communism have more to fear from their nationalism and heresies than from our billions and bombs."[23] America, unfortunately, stubbornly ignored such trends, and the North Atlantic Treaty Organization, established in 1949, was merely saving "the Reds from their own mistakes and follies." Indeed, NATO was a foolish imitation of the Anti-Comintern Pact of 1936: "We fought Hitler, now to ape him." Russia would be forced into permanent partnership with the non-Western world; the United States would be saddled with the futile task of preserving Western imperialism.[24] Truman's accompanying demand, a military assistance program, was tantamount to a "declaration of war" against Russia.[25]

The *Appeal* was scathing toward administration China policy. In May 1946, it said that American involvement could only backfire. Neither the Chinese communists nor the Kuomintang wanted a powerful Chinese state encroached on by Americans. "If the Communist nationalists win out in China, they are bound to be anti-Moscow," commented Dennis in 1949.[26] The mediation efforts of General Marshall were bound to fail; U.S. aid simply hastened the communist triumph. After China fell to Mao's forces in 1949, Dennis found only one lesson: "The more Americans and westerners supply arms and know-how to the colored world, the sooner the latter will use them against the west."[27]

When, early in 1950, conservative Republicans demanded that the U.S. navy interpose itself between Taiwan and the Chinese mainland, Dennis wrote: "The right is confused. It doesn't read *The Appeal to Reason* and it can't think for itself." Rather than continue the futile bombing and blockading of the China coast, he said: "We should write off China and try to save America." The *Appeal* was soon calling for recognition of communist China.[28]

Appeal to Reason adamantly opposed America's participation in the Korean War. The United States, it wrote, was again committed to a "corrupt, incompetent and locally unpopular regime." Its war conduct was barbarous, its planes "committing mass murder" and "turning large areas into scorched earth."[29] Indeed, the whole venture was the height of folly, as it created an artificial alliance between Russia and China. Even victory would be disastrous: the peninsula was a "permanent liability," with occupation costs alone staggering. (And, in a prescient warning when Truman announced aid to French forces in Southeast Asia in June 1950, Dennis wrote: "Indo-China is now beckoning thousands of Americans to fresh-dug graves.") Within a month of Truman's intervention, Dennis called for withdrawal from Korea: "To quit is the only sensible course ever in respect to a holy war."[30]

Unlike so many other conservative isolationists, the *Appeal* held no reverence for MacArthur. Even before communist China sent troops into Korea, Dennis's newsletter blamed the flamboyant general for "pushing red China into war with us." "Would America," it said, "bow to the fiat of a European bloc, calling itself the UN, and stay out of Mexico while a European nation dominated Mexico and approached our border with a large armed force?" To Dennis, MacArthur's removal in 1951 was the best news he had heard since the Crash of 1929. The general's proposals for meeting the new Chinese threat would lead to more "mass murder of millions of innocent, non-combatant Chinese, à la Hiroshima or Dresden." Any invasion of China would be "at limitless cost" to American taxpayers; it would also necessitate "a limitless supply of American cannon-fodder."[31]

In 1952 the *Appeal* endorsed the presidential candidacy of Senator Robert A. Taft, as it saw the Ohio Republican as the contender least enticed by overseas crusades. "The case for him," it said, "is not so much what he would do as what he probably would not do."[32] Eisenhower's election was received with the following headline: "IKE VOTE WAS FOR A HERO, RELIGIOUS WAR IDEAS—NOT ECONOMIC SELF-INTEREST." When John Foster Dulles, who had been stressing the "liberation" of Eastern Europe, was appointed secretary of state, the *Appeal* commented, "Nothing short of total global victory over red sin will satisfy Dulles." It endorsed Eisenhower's Korean truce as fulfillment of his long-desired "quitter's peace," but was appalled by Dulles's pronouncement of "massive retaliation." Secretary Dulles, it said in January 1954, could involve the nation in atomic war "when and wherever sin starts popping."[33]

As far back as 1950, Dennis feared the consequences of intervention in Vietnam. He warned: "Washington is committed to fighting another Korea in French Indo-China and can't make a face-saving run-out on its Korean commitment as yet. Apparently, Washington wants to keep its perpetual wars for perpetual peace limited to not more than two or three at a time." When, in the spring of 1954, talk of full-scale military action in Indochina resumed, Dennis commented that in any skirmish with the "colored world," "We can't pick a winner, for the winner will not pick us." The fall of Dien Bien Phu caused the *Appeal* to comment: "Don't forget. We told you so." Efforts of the Southeast Asia Treaty Organization to oppose "subversion," one of its goals, was simply the latest installment of the Spanish Inquisition.[34]

The *Appeal* not only opposed foreign crusades against communism, but domestic ones as well. It called the Federal Bureau of Investigation "a bureau of flatfeet," led by a "publicity hound," totally incapable of determining "questions of doctrine or ideological loyalty."[35] Even during the Hiss case, the *Appeal* found very little at stake. "Any spy dumb enough to get caught by our F.B.I. is good riddance for the Reds," it noted. "Burning witches or lynching subversives won't save America from the consequences of World War II or present policies," it went on.[36]

Dennis had nothing but contempt for Senator Joseph R. McCarthy (R, Wisconsin), whose sudden popularity he saw as proof that Americans preferred "crime and mystery stories" to any discussion of "real issues." McCarthy was adopting Hitler's big lie technique, not criticizing the wisdom of globalist policies rooted as far back as Theodore Roosevelt. By 1953, the *Appeal* found the United States undergoing a "domestic inquisition à la Torquemada against Communism." Still the Wisconsin senator had his uses, for so long as he created turmoil, the nation would have no time to escalate the cold war.[37]

Despite the furor over McCarthy, foreign policy remained the *Appeal*'s primary focus. And to Dennis it was the Suez crisis of 1956, more than any other event, that symbolized the coming of age of what is now called the Third World. Even before Gamal Abdel Nasser had nationalized the canal in July, the *Appeal* saw Arab control of the entire Middle East inevitable. "Numbers count," it remarked. When the Western powers accused Nasser of breaking international law by seizing the canal, it commented: "You have to hand it to the British, French and even us Americans for knowing how to invoke law and justice as instruments of national policy." To Lawrence Dennis, the joint invasion of the British, French, and Israelis was pure folly. The cease-fire revealed the real forces at work in the world. He wrote: "The Israelis just won the big battle of Gaza, but Nasser and the Allah boys, defeated in battle by the Yahweh boys, now seem to be the winner of Suez." Yet the *Appeal* was fearful, as it saw in the implications of the Eisenhower Doctrine a "really foolproof dependable formula for perpetual war."[38]

The *Appeal* also addressed itself to Russia's suppression of the Hungarian uprising in 1956. If the incident revealed the follies of overextended empire, it also revealed American hypocrisy. Surely it was as logical for the Soviet Union, a power that had been invaded three times in the past 130 years, to suppress its satellites as for the United States to "promote military alliances against Russia." "Of course," the *Appeal* noted, "if we do it, it is right or defense, while if they do it, that is, if Russia does it, it is wrong and aggression."[39]

In 1960, the Nixon campaign received Dennis's backhanded endorsement. "Bigger and better phonies" than the Democrats, candidate Nixon and incumbent Eisenhower were capable of "keeping the cold war phony." "The fact," he declared, "that neither ever was enough of a thinker or an intellect to understand what a big war is all about has been a great point in their favor." Although the *Appeal* did not endorse either of the 1960 presidential candidates, by May 1961 it found Kennedy an "operational pragmatist," that is, one who made decisions on the basis of likely results, not on visionary hopes or dogmatic ideologies. Kennedy could occasionally be disillusioning, as in his intransigency over Berlin in 1961 and his stridency during the Cuban missile crisis in 1962. Yet when the president was assassinated, the *Appeal* offered the most flattering of eulogies; at the same time, it found the Republic "deeply fortunate to have Lyndon Johnson its new chief executive." Like many of his former foes among the liberals, Dennis favored the Texan in 1964 over Senator Barry Goldwater (R, Arizona). President Johnson, he said, was "less inclined to war."[40]

For a few years, the *Appeal* saw the world settling. It found the Kremlin's ouster in 1964 of Khrushchev—"the world's most important psychotic"— reassuring, still another example that despite tides of unreason, the communist world was being run on pragmatic, "operational" lines. Indeed, the *Appeal* was heartened by the supposed convergence of the Western and Soviet systems. Capitalism and communism were both rapidly evolving into technocratic welfare states, possessing planned economies and managed currencies.[41]

At any rate, so stated the *Appeal* in 1961, future conflicts were bound to be racial, not ideological. Recalling Oswald Spengler, it declared: "The Decline of the West is the most important fact of the 20th Century." The Vietnam War, in fact, marked the final turning. Even before President Johnson had ordered the bombing of North Vietnam in 1965, it commented that to maintain employment and consumption, "We need lots of small or limited wars, like the one in Viet Nam." By 1966, the *Appeal* cried out, "PRESIDENT JOHNSON COMMITS HIMSELF TO THE PURSUIT OF WORLD EMPIRE."[42]

If the *Appeal to Reason* was ignored in Dennis's own time, it still contains much that intrigues the historian. It noted, almost in passing, the relationship between internal economic strains and the way the United States entered the cold war; Truman's initiation of the anticommunist hysteria; the hypocrisy of American stridency over the Dardanelles and later Hungary; and the deliberate linking of communist and Nazi "blueprints of world conquest." While some historians might accuse him of confusing causes with results, such as in his claim that Truman embarked on global crusading in order to achieve full employment and re-election at the polls, many related questions are far from resolved.

Underconsumption and mass unemployment, wars of conquest and ideology, the rise of the non-West—these, claimed the *Appeal*, were the main currents of the twentieth century. Dennis projected what he called an "operational" method of thinking to cope with these crises. By judging measures in terms of their results, not their intent, America might have the tools to survive for at least another century. Most important of all was to avoid foreign conflict, for any intervention could only weaken the United States, perhaps fatally.

Notes

1. Ronald Radosh, *Prophets on the Right: Profiles of Conservative Critics of American Globalism* (New York, 1975), p. 332.

2. For material on Dennis's background and on the *Weekly Foreign Letter*, see my

essay on the *Weekly Foreign Letter* in this volume.

3. Among the subscribers were Herbert Hoover, former senator Burton K. Wheeler, General Robert E. Wood, General Albert C. Wedemeyer, Colonel Truman Smith, and Bruce Barton. Lawrence Dennis to author, 27 January 1971.

4. *Appeal to Reason,* no. 1 (30 March 1946) (hereinafter cited as *AR*).

5. Technically the journal lasted until his death in 1977, but in Dennis's last decade, it appeared very infrequently.

6. Among the sources from which Dennis drew were the *New Statesman and Nation,* the *Times* (London), *Economist* (London), *Political Quarterly* (London), and *Manchester Guardian.*

7. *AR,* no. 259 (10 March 1951).

8. Sterling Morton to Clarence B. Hewes, 1 June 1946, Sterling Morton Papers, Chicago Historical Society.

9. Lawrence Dennis to Harry Elmer Barnes, 20 December 1951, Harry Elmer Barnes Papers, University of Wyoming Library.

10. Radosh, *Prophets on the Right,* p. 322; see also p. 328.

11. *AR,* no. 172 (9 July 1949); *AR,* no. 188 (29 October 1949).

12. *AR,* no. 678 (7 May 1960); *AR,* no. 691 (5 November 1960); *AR,* no. 681 (18 June 1960).

13. *AR,* no. 1 (30 March 1946).

14. *AR,* no. 2 (6 April 1946).

15. *AR,* no. 3 (13 April 1946); *AR,* no. 51 (17 March 1947).

16. *AR,* no. 19 (3 August 1946); *AR,* no. 22 (24 August 1946).

17. *AR,* no. 5 (27 April 1946); *AR,* no. 74 (23 August 1947).

18. *AR,* no. 22 (24 August 1946).

19. *AR,* no. 52 (22 March 1947); *AR,* no. 57 (26 April 1947).

20. *AR,* no. 65 (21 June 1947).

21. *AR,* no. 170 (25 June 1949).

22. *AR,* no. 67 (7 July 1947); *AR,* no. 154 (5 March 1949).

23. *AR,* no. 119 (3 July 1948).

24. *AR,* no. 156 (19 March 1949); *AR,* no. 159 (9 April 1949).

25. *AR,* no. 176 (13 August 1949).

26. *AR,* no. 8 (18 May 1946).

27. *AR,* no. 151 (12 February 1949).

28. *AR,* no 198 (7 January 1950); *AR,* no.,170 (25 June 1949); *AR,* no. 192 (26 November 1949).

29. *AR,* no. 222 (24 June 1950); *AR,* no. 253 (13 January 1951).

30. *AR,* no. 229 (12 August 1950); *AR,* no. 239 (21 October 1950); *AR,* no. 227 (29 July 1950).

31. *AR,* no. 241 (4 November 1950); *AR,* no. 242 (11 November 1950); *AR,* no. 264 (14 April 1951).

32. *AR,* no. 318 (26 April 1952).

33. *AR,* no. 346 (8 November 1952); *AR,* no. 348 (22 November 1952); *AR,* no. 410 (31 January 1954).

34. *AR,* no. 289 (6 October 1951); *AR,* no. 421 (17 April 1954); *AR,* no. 422 (24 April 1954); *AR,* no. 518 (25 February 1956).

35. *AR,* no. 75 (20 August 1947); *AR,* no. 133 (9 October 1948).

36. *AR,* no. 125 (14 August 1948).

37. *AR,* no. 209 (25 March 1950); *AR,* no. 210 (1 April 1950); *AR,* no. 383 (25 July 1953); *AR,* no. 411 (8 February 1954).

38. *AR*, no. 529 (12 May 1956); *AR*, no. 547 (14 September 1956); *AR*, nos. 556 and 557 (11, 24 November 1956); *AR*, no. 571 (2 March 1957).

39. *AR*, nos. 552 and 553 (20, 27 October 1956).

40. *AR*, no. 683 (16 July 1960); *AR*, no. 704 (6 May 1961); *AR*, no. 711 (12 August 1961); *AR*, no. 739 (8 September 1962); *AR*, nos. 770 and 771 (16, 30 November 1964); *AR*, no. 786 (1 August 1964).

41. *AR*, no. 790 (24 October 1964); *AR*, no. 720 (11 March 1961).

42. *AR*, no. 704 (6 May 1961); *AR*, no. 795 (22 January 1965); *AR*, no. 817 (18 April 1966).

Information Sources

BIBLIOGRAPHY:

Doenecke, Justus D. "Lawrence Dennis: Revisionist of the Cold War." *Wisconsin Magazine of History* 55 (Summer 1972): 275–86.

——————————. *Not to the Swift: The Old Isolationists in the Cold War Era.* Lewisberg, Pennsylvania, 1979.

Radosh, Ronald. *Prophets on the Right: Profiles of Conservative Critics of American Globalism.* New York, 1975.

INDEXES: None.

REPRINT EDITIONS: None.

LOCATION SOURCES: Complete runs: Hoover Institution; Harvard University; California State University at Fullerton; University of Akron; University of Pittsburgh.

Publication History

TITLE AND TITLE CHANGES: *Appeal to Reason.*

VOLUME AND ISSUE DATA: Numbers 1–892, 30 March 1946–10 August 1972.

FREQUENCY OF PUBLICATION: Weekly.

PUBLISHER: Lawrence Dennis, Becket, Northampton, and Northfield, all in Massachusetts.

EDITOR: Lawrence Dennis.

CIRCULATION: 300–500.

Justus D. Doenecke

Part Six

THE LIBERTARIAN PRESS

Frank Chodorov, whose rock-ribbed libertarian convictions led him to found the Intercollegiate Society of Individualists (1953) and author of a book revealingly titled *One Is a Crowd* (1952), once told a friend that "anyone who calls me a conservative deserves a punch in the nose." In the pages that follow, Robert Hessen wonders whether Ayn Rand's publications (and by implication those of other libertarians) should appear in a study of the American conservative press. Thoughtful scholars have had a go at the question, with enlightening, and controversial suggestions. In the best tradition of libertarianism, readers of these pages must decide the question for themselves.

Libertarian doctrine has enjoyed a rich history on two continents, though its champions are fewer than those who write under the conservative banner. Among the early leading lights of libertarian philosophy in America are Thomas Paine and nineteenth-century expositors Lysander Spooner, Josiah Warren, and Benjamin Tucker. With reservations, historians have added William Graham Sumner and Henry George to the list, for both social theorists exercised enormous influence on later proponents of radical individualism, among them Albert Jay Nock, Frank Chodorov, and economists Milton Friedman and Murray Rothbard. Economic theoreticians Friedrich Hayek and Ludwig von Mises often found themselves adjudged as libertarians, though "free market liberal" seems a more apt description. The anticollectivist novelist Ayn Rand, whose philosophy of objectivism created a furor in conservative circles, rates as this century's libertarian *sui generis*.

Although the term defies neat definition, several themes recur in the pages of those espousing libertarian thought. The central value is freedom, understood as the absence of coercion in matters personal, political, and social. Individuals should remain free of aggressions against their persons and property, and they suffer when against their better judgment they make concessions to society. Government should not regulate a person's daily activities, dictate his moral code, or operate his business, schools, and post office, assert libertarians. In nearly every case where it does so, it either acts inefficiently or curtails individual freedom. Laissez-faire conservatives hold that a government governs best when it governs least; the libertarian ups the ante, saying that government is best which governs not at all. Libertarian moral theory rests on voluntarism—on a belief that individuals should create their own lifestyles, free of external compulsion. Libertarians do not advocate the taking of drugs, but believe they should be decriminalized. The same applies to laws that prohibit obscenity, pornography, and a variety of sexual behaviors between consenting adults. It is "pro-choice in everything," said one Republican polltaker, so long as no one else is harmed. Radical libertarians also have called for the abolition of the Internal Revenue Service, the Federal Bureau of Investigation, the Central Intelligence Agency, the Occupational Safety and Health Administration, and the Social Security Administration.

The last thrust correctly suggests that the common enemy of all libertarians is the state. Throughout history it has exercised predominant power in most societies, enslaving people and killing them in greater numbers than any other institution. In support of this contention, libertarians make the sobering point that totalitarian and extreme authoritarian governments have killed more than 100 million people in the twentieth century, a number exceeding those who have died in warfare. Against such a record, the libertarian argues that killing for reasons of state is unacceptable and that government activity must be restricted to that of a protector of human rights, especially those secured two centuries ago during the American Revolution: life, liberty, and property. Because individuals own themselves outright, and can have no objections to the similar claims of others, there remains little role for government. It may not do to individuals what they cannot do to others. The sole legitimate relationship among individuals is what arises out of voluntary agreement, involving all interested parties.

The differences between libertarianism and conservatism are substantial. The conservative places great weight on the role of social authority; the libertarian denies that authority unless voluntarily accepted. Most conservatives believe in the free market; libertarians believe in pristine, unfettered free market capitalism. Their differences are markedly greater with traditionalist conservatives who reject the marketplace as the sole or even the most important determiner of value. Compare Richard Weaver, the Southern Agrarian, who defended property, but *personal* property rather than the "abstract property of stocks and bonds, the legal ownership of enterprises never seen [which] actually destroys the connection between man and substance," or Russell Kirk, who argued that "once supernatural and traditional sanctions are dissolved, economic self-interest is ridiculously inadequate to hold an economic system together, and even less adequate to preserve order." Agreeing on the limited role of government in economic life, conservatives at times have sought to regulate behavior in the bedroom and in doctors' offices. Devoted to individual choice and enamored with the power of reason, the libertarians are legatees of the eighteenth-century Enlightenment; conservatives, reaching back to Edmund Burke, have never trusted in secularized religious formulas of political redemption and are persuaded that the human tendency to err forever stands between utopian hopes and the good society. Conservatives of the traditionalist variety seek objective moral standards in tradition, or history, or natural law theory; libertarians find them in human inclinations that reason and experience reveal as preservers and enlargers of individual freedom.

Since the demise of the Old Right, libertarians more readily take an isolationist stance in foreign affairs, extending to cold war initiatives such as NATO and the Marshall Plan. Conservatives took note when the *Freeman*, then edited by John Chamberlain, Suzanne La Follette, and Henry Hazlitt, supported a vigorous interventionist foreign policy. More common, however, was the dispute that flared between editors of the *National Review* and *New Individualist Review* in 1961, when Ronald Hamowy, then an associate editor of the latter journal, scored William F. Buckley for working "*against* individualist liberty" at home and so concerned with an indiscriminate anticommunism that he betrayed "a devotion to imperialism and ... a polite form of white supremacy." It was clear that student libertarians, for whom Hamowy spoke, had grown uneasy with conservatives who led the statist transformation in postwar military policy.

With the growth of state power after World War II, the libertarian movement was reborn, not as a party but in the preferences of thousands of voters who have resisted this dominating theme of the twentieth century. In 1984 the Cato Institute published an important book, *Beyond Liberal and Conservative*, in which William Maddox and Stuart Lilie demonstrated that the traditional liberal-conservative dichotomy is inadequate in describing the ideological views of American voters. Their map of the political landscape revealed a four-way matrix of liberals, conservatives, populists, and libertarians. "Liberals" supported state intervention in the economy but not on moral issues. "Conservatives" did the opposite, supporting intervention on moral issues, but opposing state economic intervention. "Populists" consistently supported state intervention in both economics and morals. "Libertarians" were those who opposed state intervention in either arena. The authors concluded that although the libertarians did poorly in elections, they represented a significant portion of the electorate. In part the growing support derived from the revolt against cultural authorities characteristic of the 1960s; in part it reflected the growing distrust in politics caused by the war policies of the Johnson and Nixon administrations and the devious methods of both to manipulate public opinion. One unintended consequence of their vigorous fundamentalist stance on domestic issues was that the Moral Majority and other Christian groups created a countermovement that defended the very positions to which the followers of the Reverend Jerry Falwell and the Reverend Pat Robertson were opposed. The libertarian movement gained additional strength from journals founded to promote the cause, among them many, such as *Inquiry* and *Libertarian Review*, not included here for reasons of space. Like liberals and conservatives, the libertarians have their think tanks: the Cato Institute in Washington, D.C., and the Institute for Humane Studies in California.

By the 1990s many acknowledged the benefits this gathering stream brought to political discourse. Libertarians have raised public consciousness that paralleling welfare programs for the poor is a corporate welfare system for business in the form of city and state grants, state and federal transportation grants, and tax abatement, which means millions of fewer dollars for schools and public works. The libertarians have compelled liberals and conservatives to examine their positions more honestly. To conservatives especially, the libertarians have forced the argument that high military spending distorts the economy and strengthens the power of the federal government at the very time that the end of the cold war and collapse of the Soviet Union suggest the downsizing of government.

Freeman
1920–1924

Americans faced the 1920s with conflicting emotions. The war and the failure of Wilsonian idealism reduced many intellectuals to despair, reformism had largely run its course, and a mechanistic business ethic and a sterile social conformity bore heavily on creative impulses. At the same time there was a sense of excitement. A fresh and free inquiry into the meaning of America seemed possible. As Lewis Mumford remembered: "Despite the disillusion that set in after the First World War, we believed that we might give a more humane shape to American culture before our molten desires had cooled. These latent hopes tempered even our postwar cynicism."[1]

This task of reviving a usable past and building a new future was taken up by three important journals of opinion: the *New Republic*, the *Nation*, and the *Dial*. These journals, in different degrees, expressed the dominant thread in American liberalism. This brand of liberalism had found the war instructive, and it sought to bring many aspects of wartime collectivism to domestic problems. It was eager to experiment with America's newfound international power. Liberals focused especially on the political sphere, exhibiting what Randolph Bourne decried as a "cult of politics . . . inherent in the liberal intellectual's point of view long before the war."[2]

On 17 March 1920, these liberal journals were joined by a serious rival. The *Freeman* optimistically proposed "to meet the new sense of responsibility and the new spirit of inquiry which recent events have liberated especially in the fields of economics and politics."[3] For four years the *Freeman* helped to shape intellectual opinion in America. It forcefully presented another thread in liberalism, claiming a classical liberal and Jeffersonian heritage that *it* proclaimed as "radical." Individual freedom and voluntary cooperation—what it called "social power" and the "economic means"—were presented as the only consistent means to progress and freedom. This was starkly contrasted with the inherently invasive and exploitative nature of the state and the "political means."

The idea for the *Freeman* originated with Albert Jay Nock and came to fruition through conversations with Francis Neilson and Helen Swift Neilson in 1919. At the end of that year Nock wrote Neilson that "the sane radical is up for his turn at the bat and is in the right mood to make a hit."[4] Both the English classical liberal, Neilson, and the Jeffersonian liberal, Nock, were dismayed by liberalism's turn toward state socialism. Through the *Freeman*, they took on the liberal journals and other brands of political messianism. They especially excoriated liberals for *their* war recently concluded, and prophesied that "far worse than a liberal's war is a liberal's peace."[5] Thus, the *Freeman* was to speak for the great tradition of classical liberalism, which both men were afraid was being lost, and for the economics of Henry George, which both men shared. With the help of Helen Swift Neilson's meatpacking fortune, it was all financially possible.

Francis Neilson was born in England in 1867. He was the leader of the British Liberal party's so-called young radicals and was a member of Parliament until he resigned in 1915 in protest against the war and moved to the United States. Neilson's knowledge of English constitutional radicalism and his personal contacts were important advantages for the *Freeman*. Though he did not often write for it, his influence is readily apparent in his self-described role as "a feeder of ideas."[6]

Albert Jay Nock is best known for his *Memoirs of a Superfluous Man*, a brilliant discourse of libertarian sensibilities. His writings in the 1930s and 1940s were to have a profound influence on many of the major figures of the post–World War II Right. As conservative publisher Henry Regnery wrote: "There can be no doubt that he contributed substantially to the development of modern conservatism."[7]

Born in 1870, Nock started his journalistic career with the muckraking periodical *American Magazine* in 1910 and later spent time at the *Nation*. It was only when, at the age of forty-nine, he helped found the *Freeman*, that he came into his own as a polished essayist, gifted editor, and important political thinker.

Nock provided the *Freeman* with the unique framework it applied to politics, international affairs, manners, literature, and the "good life." Despite his sometimes eccentric ways, Nock's special skills as an editor made it, in the words of Van Wyck Brooks, "a wonderfully good school for us all."[8] And when Nock protested that he did nothing to make the *Freeman* such a good paper except leave the writers alone, a friend replied: "Yes, I understand, but if someone else had been letting them alone, it would have been a very different story."[9]

Nock wrote extensively in the *Freeman*, most of his pieces unsigned. Something from his pen appeared in all but 8 of the 208 weekly issues, and he often contributed as much as 20 percent of the material in an issue. It would be a mistake, however, to think that the *Freeman* was solely Albert Jay Nock. The *Freeman*'s small staff was one of the most competent and professional of the 1920s. Benjamin W. Huebsch, who was generally acknowledged to be one of the most cultivated book publishers in America, was publisher. Van Wyck Brooks became literary editor. A brilliant critic and leader of the so-called literary radicals, Brooks had worked for the *Dial* and *Seven Arts*. Even with his vague socialist politics, his literary and essentially individualistic point of view complemented the *Freeman*'s general sensibility.

Other additions to the staff included Suzanne La Follette, who left the *Nation* at Nock's request. He thought she was one of the best editors in the business. Geroid Tanquary Robinson, a former editor at the *Dial*, joined the staff while continuing to teach at Columbia University. Walter G. Fuller (who left in the spring of 1922), Harold Kellock (who joined in early 1923), Lucy Taussig, and Emilie McMillan filled out the staff.

A significant number of writers at various times associated themselves with the *Freeman*. They contributed unsigned editorials as well as signed articles. Lewis Mumford, William MacDonald, and Frank W. Garrison were among the better known. Over two hundred men and women authored articles and reviews for the *Freeman*. It discovered or developed writers like John Dos Passos, Constance Rourke, Newton Arvin, and Edwin Muir. Other writers, who covered a wide range of cultural and political opinion, included Walter Pach, Thorstein Veblen, William Henry Chamberlin, Robert H. Lowie, Mary and Padraic Colum, Bertrand Russell, Ernest Boyd, Howard Mumford Jones, and Charles Beard. The result was a journal with a special fullness, which knew no ideological boundaries yet resulted in a surprisingly coherent whole.

The weekly magazine contained twenty-four pages. Each issue began with two unsigned sections written by staff members or writers close to the magazine. "Current Comment" had three pages of paragraphs on international affairs and the foibles of domestic politics and politicians. The next section, "Topics of the Day," consisted of five pages of editorials covering political, economic, and social issues in greater depth. The major signed articles followed, as well as columns on art, theater, music, and letters to the editor. One page was devoted to "Miscellany," a column of incidental paragraphs on the manners and mores of the times, signed by "Journeyman" (often written by Nock). The "Books" section included a few longish reviews and a number of one-paragraph "Shorter Notices." Frank Luther Mott concluded that "some of the best book-reviewing done in any American journal in the twenties appeared in the *Freeman*."[10] The last page and a half was devoted to "A Reviewer's Notebook." This was Brooks's distinguished and idiosyncratic column on the state of America's literary past, present, and future (Nock wrote the column for the last seven months of 1922). The back page was left for Huebsch, who wrote good, alternately urbane, humorous, and exhorting ad copy for the magazine.

While there was agreement that the *Freeman* was generally "brilliant," there has been little agreement about exactly what the *Freeman* was—a fact, that no doubt would have pleased Nock, who rankled at labels. It has been called liberal, conservative, bolshevik, anarchist, revolutionary, and Georgist. Readers were constantly asking where the *Freeman* stood on the political spectrum, to which the publisher responded that "the *Freeman* is less concerned with making its own ideas prevail in the realm of mental power than with the clarification of thought which permits people to choose their own road to freedom."[11] In fact, Lillian Symes and Travers Clement were probably closest when, in their *Rebel America*, they placed the *Freeman* within "the main tradition of American individualism...individualist radicalism."[12] More than any other periodical of its time and as much as any since, it was concerned with freedom: the preservation and extension of individual freedom in all its variegated forms. In the strange machinations of fickle political labels, these same attitudes would later become some of the defining characteristics of what has been called the American conservative and libertarian intellectual revival after World War II.

A few years after the *Freeman* ceased publication, Albert Jay Nock wrote to a close friend that he was "enormously impressed almost daily with the fact that the *Freeman* never died—and it never will."[13] Indeed, the spirit and example of the *Freeman* has often been claimed by conservatives, and rather more emphatically by libertarians. This older *Freeman*, for example, was a model for the *New Freeman* that Suzanne La Follette began in 1930, for *Human Events* in the mid-1940s, and for a newer *Freeman* begun in 1950 and which is still published monthly today. Less directly, it served as a guide for the *Freeman* published by the Henry George School of Social Science in New York in 1937, for Frank Chodorov's *analysis* in 1944, for *Libertarian Analysis* in 1970, and for *Fragments*, which has been publishing sporadically since 1963. The first issue of the *Freeman* was welcomed to the fraternity of liberal journalism by both the *New Republic* and the *Nation*. That there was no opening statement of position distressed some readers who were used to explicit political programs. But beneath its sometimes pretentious aloofness, Lewis Mumford saw intriguing hints that led him to write to the editor: "Obviously behind these brief generalizations a whole sociology lies, and I can conceive of your performing no better service during the next few years than by slowly building up, clarifying, limiting, and relating the ideas of social development that are therein implied."[14] That "sociology," however, was never fully articulated.

In the fourth issue, Nock proudly and firmly denied any connection with liberal journalism: "The *Freeman* is a radical paper; its place is in the virgin field, or better, the long-neglected and fallow field, of American radicalism."[15] He went on to point out two distinguishing features to the *Freeman*'s radicalism. First of all, beyond a basic commitment to laissez faire, radicals believed in "fundamental economics." There was an additional factor in the production of wealth besides labor and capital, Nock maintained, and that was land and natural resources. Until the monopoly on land and natural resources was broken, all other reforms, while perhaps ameliorative, would not solve the world's problems.

The magazine, though, was by no means a Georgist or single-tax journal, as some critics have suggested. Nock was to explain later that his view on land monopoly and for some form of land tax was merely a "simple statement of a natural law...and the suggestion that one is a propagandist in such premises is perhaps rather flat."[16] The *Freeman* was steeped in the Georgist ethical, economic, and philosophical perspective, but the magazine had much broader concerns.

The other, and crucially important, feature of radicalism's perspective was its total rejection of the great faith that liberalism placed in the state. Statism quite simply meant, wrote Geroid T. Robinson, "a mechanistic civilization at home and militarism abroad."[17] The radical, by contrast, "believes that the State is fundamentally anti-social and is all for improving it off the face of the earth."[18]

Often paraphrasing *The State* by Franz Oppenheimer, the *Freeman* consistently made the point that political government and the use of the political means merely enforced the expropriation and exploitation of people, for the benefit of a given privileged class. Every recourse to the political means—whether through political parties and platforms, political agitation, or revolutions—was doomed to failure, it claimed. Those means were inherently coercive and never changed the essential and underlying economic and social conditions. Articles in every issue returned to this theme, culminating in 1923 in Nock's five-part series "The State" (which was later expanded into his biting critique of centralized government, *Our Enemy, the State*).[19]

This was not a call for anarchism, however. There was an admitted need for some vaguely defined form of a decentralized "administrative government" of strictly limited negative prohibitions. The issue was primarily that the state was an institution to be protected against, and not some form of magical benefactor or neutral umpire. Within that context, the *Freeman* was a strong champion of civil liberties, which it saw as a matter largely of keeping the state out of issues essentially individual.

For the *Freeman*, the truly valuable things in life were thus outside the political realm. The individual had the right and responsibility to make his or her life as creative as it could be. It was important to understand, Nock pointed out, "that the instincts for freedom, for beauty, for a graceful and amiable social life, are true primary instincts and that our business is to follow them....What matters is that, for life to be truly fruitful, life must be felt as a joy; and that where freedom is not, there can be no joy."[20] In this the literary, political, and artistic diversity of the *Freeman* all found common ground.

Looking at contemporary life in America, the *Freeman* saw neither freedom nor the good life being nurtured. Nock, however, expressed a faith that a higher civilization was virtually certain:

No civilization can be permanent except that which satisfies all the claims of the human spirit—the claim of workmanship or expansion, the claim of knowledge, social life and manners, religion, beauty and poetry, all held in the perfection of harmony and balance. Our civilization satisfies the first claim quite well, the second tolerably, and the others not at all. Is it not inevitable, then, that a civilization which satisfies more of these claims, held in better balance, will supersede ours even though itself be not final?[21]

A major shift in paradigm was necessary to assist that change. The *Freeman* offered its own "sociology" based on the principles and application of English classical liberalism. It rested on natural rights, unlimited individualism, and equal economic opportunity. It was often necessary, in the *Freeman*'s view, to refer to the older concept of freedom presented by such writers as Turgot, Quesnay, Smith, Cobden, George, Oppenheimer, Mill, and Bohm-Bawerk.

The basic contrast between its rejection of political methods of change and its promotion of the freedom, diversity, and creativity of everyday life devoid of political coercion was perhaps the telling difference between the *Freeman* and the other journals of opinion of the time, whether liberal, socialist, or Tory. It was here that readers often became confused as to where the *Freeman* stood. To a radical libertarian conception of society and the state, Nock and Neilson added an essentially conservative conception of social change and the importance of principles. As Neilson put it: "Radicals seek not to destroy. Their desire is to restore the old, and they are indeed...'the true conservatives.'"[22]

The *Freeman* sought solace from and a solution to state socialism through "the historical process of strengthening, consolidating, and enlightening economic organization."[23] It constantly held up the tradition of laissez faire as a means to the good life. Contrary to Mencken's great cynicism about political democracy, the *Freeman* optimistically pointed out that true "democracy is an affair primarily of economics, not of politics, that democracy has not failed, for it has never been tried."[24] Indeed, economic freedom was the most important freedom, and if attained, no other freedom could be withheld.

The slow advance of society over the state would eventually lead to the disappearance of the state (in a formulation more internally consistent than Marx's notion of the withering away of the state). This would not happen through the force of arms. In the normal, long-term course of events, people would just stop thinking in terms of the state: "The whole fundamental structure of the state will crumble and dissolve through the pervasive power of the Idea."[25]

At the same time, the *Freeman* took its radicalism seriously, passionately discussing specific issues. The Treaty of Versailles, the League of Nations, and foreign imperialism came under heavy attack. Similarly, no attempt to curtail freedom domestically was left unassailed. And the propensity of liberals to view problems as a matter of finding the right person to put in charge was subject to the *Freeman*'s highest ridicule. Any attempt to break out of totalitarian regimes was applauded, even as the *Freeman* cautioned that a worse dictatorship could rise in its stead (the Russian Revolution was supported on those grounds). Free trade, civil liberties, "fundamental economics," and, above all, individual freedom were set forth as answers to all of these issues until they sounded like a litany.

The *Freeman* had no particular love for the status quo or tradition. It actively advocated necessary change, not for its own sake but in accordance with those ageless principles that gave its radicalism substance. This joining together of tradition and principle with change and irreverence gave excitement and direction to most of the *Freeman*'s political and literary writings. Huebsch gave voice to this attitude when he wrote: "The *Freeman* is at once an incentive to hasten the new world of ideas and a steadying influence in preserving the everlasting truths that are essential to a society worth living in."[26]

When the *Freeman* did make suggestions about how one could work for the idea of freedom, it based its views on social power, free competition, and cooperation. The basic point was to leave people alone to find their own solutions. While praising the multitude of voluntary associations in China, Gerold T. Robinson went on to write that "the task of the practical anarchist, as we see it, is the withdrawal of all desirable functions from political control, and the arrangement for the performance of these functions by non-political agencies."[27]

Eschewing governmental action, the *Freeman* often called for various forms of direct social action. In a letter in April 1921, Amos Pinchot acknowledged that the *Freeman*, "perhaps more than any important weekly journal in America, has become the advocate of direct action."[28] The Gandhian movement of non-cooperation and passive resistance was often favorably mentioned. Direct action did not usually mean the industrial strike, but rather opposition to the government on the basis of the classical liberal principle that the government was the chief menace. There were often calls for tax resistance. Voting was rejected in favor of what it called the "economic ballot": acting within the economic and social means. While much of the cooperative movement, for instance, did not deal with the land question, the *Freeman* still regarded "it as the most significant movement of the times."[29]

Despite its brief forays into practical suggestions and its tendency to rely on its wit and criticism, these things were basically secondary to the *Freeman*'s self-appointed task. The most practical suggestion the *Freeman* wanted to give, and the one that served as a credo for its work, was: "*Get wisdom, get understanding....* [A]nd this is precisely the point...of much that we publish....[T]o discuss fundamental principles and not to peddle nostrums."[30]

Geroid T. Robinson crystallized a common opinion of the *Freeman* when he complained, in a pseudonymous letter, that "the radicals tend to confine their attention to the gay business of destructive criticism." What radicals needed to do instead was to present a detailed plan for "reconstruction which meets every test of reason,...[a] technique of organization necessary for the establishment and maintenance of this fundamental liberty."[31] Neilson pointed out the terrible assumption implicit in that call: that "there is in every generation a select few endowed with special powers of directing and supervising millions of their less fortunate brethren in the work of producing food, fuel, clothing, and shelter." He continued: "We have been nearly organized out of existence by the 'technique of organization' devised by these gentlemen" who hold to "the whole of the precious theory that men can not get a living unless some Tory or some Socialist or some Liberal is there to supply a 'technique of organization' for the producer."[32] The *Freeman*, for all its admitted aloofness, avoided and countered both the elitism of intellectuals and political soothsayers, and the cynical elitism often expressed, for instance, by Mencken.

An editorial in the 6 February 1924, issue announced that the issue of 5 March would be the last (completing four full years of the *Freeman*). It would retire "at the highest point of its circulation"—probably around 10,000—which was near the respective circulations of the *Nation*, the *New Republic*, and the *Dial*.[33] The Neilsons had lost their enthusiasm, in part because the magazine was losing between $70,000 and $80,000 every year.[34] Nock, Huebsch, and Brooks all exhibited and expressed great weariness. They were ready to move on to new things. A few supporters of the *Freeman* inquired about the possibility of continuing the magazine, but nobody on the staff was interested, least of all a tired Nock, who stepped aboard the *Volendam* on his way to Brussels the day after the staff bade one another farewell.

What Huebsch had described in the farewell editorial as "a fellowship of fine minds" faded away exhausted and depressed.[35]

There was a strange irony in the whole run of the *Freeman*: that it left an essentially nonpolitical ideology undeveloped, opting instead for the heat of political criticism. In its perceptive editorial on the passing of the *Freeman*, the *New Republic* pointed out that "'Radicalism' of the *Freeman* brand is not a political staple....It is properly a relish to go with plenty of non-political meat."[36] By placing so much emphasis on the political and devoting so much space to politics, the *Freeman* had allowed itself to be distracted.

As true as the criticism obviously was, the *New Republic* was at least partially disingenuous. The whole world of serious social thought at that time *was* political. It was more concerned with personalities and expediencies than with principles or "disinterested thought." To take part meant dealing with the political assumptions of the world. The *Freeman*'s view of the world focused on individuals and voluntary social cooperation instead of on the coercive monopoly of the state. It turned out to be a view much more foreign to readers than even Nock and Neilson had feared. Most commentators failed to appreciate the positive and nonpolitical underpinnings of the magazine and tried vainly to put it in some political bed.

Nock had assumed that the *Freeman* was being written for an audience of independent thinkers. One purpose in publishing the paper, he wrote in his *Memoirs*, had been to "give us some sort of rough measure of the general level at which the best culture of the country stood....Any one who remembers the state of the public mind in the early nineteen-twenties does not need to be told that we launched our experiment under as unfavourable circumstances as could well be imagined."[37] This tone was often taken as severely elitist. In fact, the *Freeman* was, in part, an attack on the elitism inherent in all political ideologies. By its failure, the *Freeman* proved to Nock that intellectuals had little interest in freedom or in disinterested thought. By 1923, his earlier optimism was turning to disillusionment. With his later reading of Ralph Adams Cram's 1932 essay, "Why We Do Not Behave Like Human Beings," Nock's idea of social and economic freedom and a free life would become lodged with what he called the Remnant.[38] The authoritarian mentality that the *Freeman* had sought to forestall seemed to have the upper hand by 1924.

As a literary and cultural journal, the *Freeman* captured much of the vitality and disillusionment of the period in a way that the more programmatic and political journals could not. For all of its critical presentations, it represented a special combination of careful thought and creative authors. These authors infused the pages of the *Freeman* with a love of culture, the arts, and the spirit of the "good life." As Van Wyck Brooks wrote to Lewis Mumford in 1936:

I have been reading the 8 bound volumes of *The Freeman*, with astonishment at all the good things I find there. The history of those four years, 1920–1924, seems to me assembled there as one could find it nowhere else....[And] more than once they say the last word....[I]n preparation for any book, concerned with any phase of modern thought, one could not do better than run through *The Freeman*.[39]

An assessment of the *Freeman*'s place in the history of American conservative journalism is muddled by the continually changing perspectives on exactly what the American Right has to offer. Certainly the *Freeman* has been invoked by numerous post–World War II conservatives and libertarians, but they have only caught various aspects without touching the full spirit.

For the whole *Freeman* staff, the main currents of progress did not flow through political channels, where they would be constantly obstructed. Rather, progress was a function of channels of individual initiative, social power, and the free market, as revealed by classical liberal and American radical principles. The editors valued the past for those principles and for the actual legacy of freedom given to the present. But they were not afraid to advocate risks in the name of freedom. They eagerly advocated necessary change while always placing it within the context of the old truths. In part then, the *Freeman* can suggest to contemporary readers ways to work out the complicated relationship between tradition and change.

The *Freeman* is unique in at least one other way. As John Chamberlain has expressed it, the *Freeman* stands in American political journalism as "a great liberator...the great conservator of the idea of voluntarism."[40] It fits well into the history of American conservative and libertarian political journalism because it never lost sight of the importance of freedom. And it still has much to say to modern-day conservatism for precisely that reason. As Nock wrote while reviewing a play: "Of all things that human beings fear...the one that strikes them with abject and utterly demoralizing terror is freedom...which some day they will have the happy surprise of discovering to be the only thing that really works."[41]

Notes

1. Lewis Mumford, *Sketches from Life* (New York, 1982), p. 248.

2. Paul F. Bourke, "The Status of Politics 1909–1913: The New Republic, Randolph Bourne and Van Wyck Brooks," *American Studies* 8 (August 1974): 199.

3. "A New Weekly—*The Freeman*," *Publishers Weekly* 96 (20 December 1919): 1620. Susan J. Turner's *A History of the Freeman* (New York, 1963), concentrates on the literary contributions of the *Freeman*.

4. *Selected Letters of Albert Jay Nock* (Caldwell, Idaho, 1962), p. 96.

5. Albert Jay Nock, "Current Comment," *Freeman* 5 (7 June 1922): 289 (hereinafter cited as *Freeman*). All editorials and many shorter pieces in the *Freeman* were unsigned. However, G. Thomas Tanselle has attributed authorship using several marked staff copies. Names in brackets before the title refer to that listing. See G. Thomas Tanselle, "Unsigned and Initialed Contributions to *The Freeman*," *Studies in Bibliography* 17 (1964): 153–75.

6. Francis Neilson, "The Story of *The Freeman*," *American Journal of Economics and Sociology* 6 (October 1946, Supplement): 31. For information on Neilson, see his *My Life in Two Worlds*, 2 vols. (Appleton, Wisconsin, 1953). Neilson came to dislike Nock very much, so his remarks on the *Freeman* must be read very carefully.

7. Henry Regnery, "AJN: An Appreciation," *Modern Age* 15 (Winter 1971): 25. See Nock's *Memoirs of a Superfluous Man* (New York, 1943). Two biographies of Nock are Robert M. Crunden, *The Mind and Art of Albert Jay Nock* (Chicago, 1964), and Michael Wreszin, *The Superfluous Anarchist* (Providence, Rhode Island, 1971).

8. Robert E. Spiller, ed., *The Van Wyck Brooks—Lewis Mumford Letters* (New York, 1970), p. 18.

9. Albert Jay Nock, *Snoring as a Fine Art* (West Rindge, New Hampshire, 1958), p. viii (Introduction by Suzanne La Follette).

10. Frank Luther Mott, *A History of American Magazines*, vol. 5, *Sketches of 21 Magazines, 1905–1930* (Cambridge, Massachusetts, 1968), p. 96.

11. [B. W. Huebsch], *Freeman* 7 (2 May 1923): 192.

12. Lillian Symes and Travers Clement, *Rebel America* (New York, 1934), p. 128.

13. *Letters from Albert Jay Nock* (Caldwell, Idaho, 1949), p. 20.

14. Lewis Mumford, "Constructive Criticism," *Freeman* 1 (24 March 1920): 34.

15. [Albert Jay Nock], "In the Vein of Intimacy," *Freeman* 1 (31 March 1920): 52.

16. [Albert Jay Nock], "The Formula of the Single Tax," *Freeman* 4 (23 November 1921): 247.

17. [Geroid T. Robinson], "The Blessings of Government," *Freeman* 4 (22 February 1922): 558.

18. Nock, "In the Vein of Intimacy," p. 52.

19. See Albert Jay Nock, "The State," *Freeman* 7 (13 June 1923): 320–21; (20 June 1923): 344–47; (27 June 1923): 368–69; (4 July 1923): 393–94; and (11 July 1923): 416–17. See also Albert Jay Nock, *Our Enemy, the State* (New York, 1973), and Frank Oppenheimer, *The State* (New York, 1975).

20. [Albert Jay Nock], "Our Pastors and Masters," *Freeman* 2 (26 January 1921): 461.

21. [Albert Jay Nock], "Current Comment," *Freeman* 8 (21 November1923): 243.

22. Oeconomicus [Francis Neilson], "Too Much Technique of Organization," *Freeman* 1 (7 July 1920): 398.

23. Nock, "In the Vein of Intimacy," p. 52.

24. [Albert Jay Nock], "The Liberal's Rabbinism," *Freeman* 5 (6 September 1922): 604.

25. Nock, "The State" (4 July 1923), p. 394.

26. [B. W. Huebsch], *Freeman* 7 (9 May 1923): 216.

27. [Geroid T. Robinson], "The Wisdom of the East," *Freeman* 7 (28 March 1923): 55.

28. Amos Pinchot, "Direct Action," *Freeman* 3 (20 April 1921): 136.

29. [Albert Jay Nock], "Current Comment," *Freeman* 4 (19 October 1921): 122.

30. [Albert Jay Nock], "A Programme of Action," *Freeman* 3 (13 April 1921):100, 101.

31. "Gallerius" [Geroid T. Robinson], "A Challenge to Radicalism," *Freeman* 1 (16 June 1920): 328.

32. Oeconomicus, "Too Much Technique of Organization," p. 397.

33. [B. W. Huebsch], "A Last Word to Our Readers," *Freeman* 8 (6 February 1924): 508. Different sources estimate the *Freeman*'s subscription size from 7,000 to 10,000. B. W. Huebsch said in the mid-1950s that "circulation never got up over 10,000. It was somewhere around there, maybe a little more." "The Reminiscences of Benjamin W. Huebsch," (New York: Oral History Research Office, Columbia University, 1965), p. 71.

34. Turner, *History of the Freeman*, p. 30.

35. "A Last Word to Our Readers," p. 508.

36. "The Passing of *The Freeman*," *New Republic* 38 (5 March 1924): 34.

37. Nock, *Memoirs of a Superfluous Man*, p. 167.

38. See Ralph Adams Cram, "Why We Do Not Behave Like Human Beings," *Convictions and Controversies* (Boston, 1935), pp. 137–54, and Albert Jay Nock, "Isaiah's Job," in *Free Speech and Plain Language* (New York, 1937), pp. 248–65.

39. Spiller, ed., *The Van Wyck Brooks–Lewis Mumford Letters*, pp. 131–32.

40. John Chamberlain, "A.J.N.: Man of Letters," *Freeman* 12 (November 1962): 59.

41. "Journeyman" [Albert Jay Nock], "Miscellany," *Freeman* 8 (3 October 1923): 79.

Information Sources

BIBLIOGRAPHY

The Freeman Book. New York, 1924.

Mott, Frank Luther. *A History of American Magazines*, vol. 5, *Sketches of 21 Magazines, 1905–1930*. Cambridge, Massachusetts, 1968.

Nock, Albert J. *The State of the Union: Essays in Social Criticism*. Edited by Charles H. Hamilton. Indianapolis, 1991.

Tanselle, G. Thomas. "Unsigned and Initialed Contributions to *The Freeman*." *Studies in Bibliography* 17 (1964): 153–75.

Turner, Susan J. *A History of the Freeman: Literary Landmark of the Early Twenties*. New York, 1963.

INDEXES: Each volume indexed; *BRD*; *PAIS*; *RG*.

REPRINT EDITIONS: None.

LOCATION SOURCES: Widely available.

Publication History

TITLE AND TITLE CHANGES: *The Freeman*.

VOLUME AND ISSUE DATA: Numbers 1–208, volumes 1–8, 17 March 1920–5 March 1924.

FREQUENCY OF PUBLICATION: Weekly.

PUBLISHER: The Freeman Corporation, New York.

EDITORS: Francis Neilson, Albert Jay Nock, Van Wyck Brooks, Suzanne La Follette, Walter G. Fuller (through 3 May 1922), Harold Kellock (from 7 February 1923), and Geroid T. Robinson.

CIRCULATION: 7,000–10,000.

Charles H. Hamilton

Freeman
1950–

When the *Freeman* first appeared on 2 October 1950, it was carrying on a distinguished history of political journalism. In 1920, the original *Freeman* began weekly publication for four years under the tutelage of Albert Jay Nock. In 1930, Suzanne La Follette (who had been Nock's assistant at the older *Freeman*) began the *New Freeman,* which lasted for fourteen months. Thus it was that the lead editorial of this newest *Freeman* lamented: "For at least two decades there has been an urgent need in America for a journal of opinion devoted to the cause of traditional liberalism and individual freedom. The *Freeman* is designed to fill that need."[1]

In post-World War II America there were a few small conservative magazines like *Human Events, analysis,* and *Plain Talk,* but there was none like the liberal *New Republic* or *Nation* that could influence and focus national attention on conservative issues and answers. Within that milieu, it would be difficult to overestimate the importance of the *Freeman* to the development of modern conservative and libertarian sensibilities. All the internal controversies and tensions that characterize a fledgling political faith were contained in its pages. With great verve, it leveled criticisms of liberal domestic and foreign policy and tried to present viable alternatives. By the end of 1955 when new owners changed the nature of the magazine, a self-conscious and relatively coherent movement had evolved. If "creeping conservatism" was "the grand trend of the 1950s," as Clinton Rossiter saw it, then the *Freeman* had been its professional and articulate journal of opinion.[2]

The *Freeman* developed out of the perceived need to get beyond the militantly, and unrelievedly, anticommunist journalism of *Plain Talk.* Begun in October 1946, by late 1948 editor Isaac Don Levine, journalists John Chamberlain and Henry Hazlitt, and financial backers Alfred Kohlberg and Jasper Crane wanted, in the words of Chamberlain, to "go on to something more positive....The fight [against communists] has been won domestically....We want to revive the John Stuart Mill concept of liberalism."[3] Plans were begun for a new magazine, and $200,000 was raised with the active help of Kohlberg, Crane, Sun Oil magnate J. H. Pew, and ex-president Herbert Hoover. The first issue of the *Freeman* went to 6,000 subscribers (5,000 of them from *Plain Talk*). Thirty-one thousand promotional copies were also distributed.

The editors were to be Isaac Don Levine, John Chamberlain, and Henry Hazlitt. When Levine dropped out of the plan, Suzanne La Follette was added. These three well-known journalists, who had been perceived as radicals in the 1930s, would now edit a conservative fortnightly. Chamberlain had been an editor or book editor for the *New York Times*, *Harper's*, and *Fortune*. He had written an important critique of progressivism, *Farewell to Reform*. In addition to general editorial responsibilities, he would write his valuable column, "A Reviewer's Notebook," which he continued to write well into the 1980s. Hazlitt had succeeded H. L. Mencken at the *American Mercury* and had been on the editorial staff of the *New York Times* for many years. He was the author of the very popular introduction to free market economics, *Economics in One Lesson*. Hazlitt would work part time so that he could continue at *Newsweek* as a columnist. La Follette had been a contributing editor for *Plain Talk,* and she became the managing editor.

The *Freeman's* board of directors represented heavyweight individualism. Academic representation included Ludwig von Mises, Leo Wolman, and later Roscoe Pound. Donald Cowling (Carleton College), Leonard E. Read (Foundation for Economic Education), and H.C. Cornuelle (Volker Fund) were also on the board. Businessmen were well represented by Henning W. Prentis (president of Armstrong Cork), Alfred Kohlberg (a wealthy importer), W. F. Peter (vice-president of the Chicago, Rock Island and Pacific Railroad), and Lawrence Fertig (Fertig Advertising). Successful publisher Alex Hillman and Claude Robinson of Opinion Research were later added to the board.

The *Freeman* rested its perspective firmly on the principles of the classical liberal tradition.[4] These were succinctly set forth in an important editorial in the first issue written by Henry Hazlitt—"The Faith of the *Freeman*."[5] Of primary importance, he wrote, was a belief in the moral autonomy of the individual, without which there could be no freedom. Second, free individuals acted through the free market, "the basic institution of a liberal society."[6] Economic liberty and free trade set the true liberal or libertarian society apart from all forms of collectivism. Finally, the editorial gave more moderate expression to Dorothy Thompson's short poem "I hate, the State."[7] The rule of law, decentralization of power, and local autonomy were stressed as limiting forces to the government's natural self-aggrandizing tendencies.

A little over a year later, Hazlitt wrote another important editorial in defense of "the existence and power of ideas" against those "friends of free enterprise" who "can only fume and sputter."[8] The editorial went on to point out that intellectuals set economic and social fashions and that it was absolutely necessary to "make converts....It is the aim of the *Freeman* to address itself specifically to the leaders and molders of public opinion and to thinking people everywhere, in order to help create a healthier climate for the preservation of free enterprise and the liberty and moral autonomy of the individual."[9]

The sentiments expressed in "The Faith of the *Freeman*" and, later, in "The Function of the *Freeman*," were never fully realized. Until 1956 the major topic of discussion in the pages of the *Freeman* was how America should respond to the threat of communism—specifically Soviet communism. The principles of classical liberalism seemed to offer little guidance in such a struggle. The fear of communism and the pressing need to defeat it challenged deep-seated antistatist and free market convictions: "We are being forced to spend billions and to arm and to tax and to interfere with the freedom of the market for one reason alone, and that reason is Kremlin Joe's overriding purpose to subvert the world."[10]

A strongly interventionist foreign policy position developed from the articles of Suzanne La Follette and John Chamberlain, and from contributors like Bonner Fellers, William Henry Chamberlin, William Schlamm, and Alice Widener. Many of them hoped that the resultant powerful American state would be only temporary. When, for instance, a temporary draft was supported in late 1950, John Chamberlain appended this fearful caveat: "But don't let us make the mistake of thinking that the values of Athens can be maintained by changing our society into a Sparta for all time."[11]

Other writers feared that the ultimate value of freedom was being corrupted, perhaps permanently, by fear. Contributors like John T. Flynn, Garet Garrett, Louis Bromfield, and Frank Chodorov stood up for the Old Right position of nonintervention and warned that freedom would be lost in a wrongheaded attempt to protect it. A massive and continuing military presence throughout the world would lead, Garrett predicted, to "the institution of perpetual war" at home.[12]

In the case of Korea, the *Freeman* voiced extreme displeasure at Truman for his militarily "untenable" dispatch of Americans to the Asian continent.[13] Its contributors debated whether withdrawal from Korea was the prudent action, but hinted at preventive war elsewhere in that case: "We should obviously strike elsewhere to keep the military and moral consequences of this defeat from being too great."[14] It was imperative that the western Pacific not be lost to communism as Eastern Europe had been lost. Rearming Japan, supporting Chiang Kai-shek, and liberating mainland China were seen as appropriate goals. Indeed, as one editorial commented: "The Pacific Ocean is an American lake."[15]

At the same time, contributors wrote about the limitations on American foreign policy. It was pointed out that 140 million Americans could not save the world. Articles called for the nations of the world to assume their full share of the fight against communism. It became imperative, the *Freeman* advanced, for America to disentangle itself from uncertain allies and inappropriate and limiting alliances: "One of our fundamental mistakes was our well-meant effort to 'assume world leadership.'"[16] This was not the traditional right-wing isolationist position, however, nor was it a call for a containment policy, which was often criticized in editorials, and by James Burnham, for example.[17] It was a call for the use of autonomous American strength. Unilateral and interventionist actions were necessary, conservatives believed, to protect the United States and save the world from communism, and the *Freeman* became a spokesman for such views.

The *Freeman* actively commented on political affairs. The Truman administration was severely criticized for many of its economic policies ranging from price controls to the takeover of the steel industry. With respect to Korea, an editorial in early 1951 caused quite a furor when it called for Truman's resignation because of his "clear usurpation of the constitutional prerogative of Congress."[18]

In late 1951 and in 1952, editorials and articles debated the pros and cons of Taft, Eisenhower, and MacArthur for the Republican presidential nomination. Although the *Freeman* never officially endorsed a candidate, its criterion was clear: "A good candidate must grasp the Communist nettle firmly."[19] And it acknowledged that it followed Taft "as a benchmark" when it came to foreign and military policy.[20]

In general, however, such commentary focused on the foreign arena and the communist threat. Domestic economic and social issues received limited attention from Henry Hazlitt, economists Ludwig von Mises, Leo Wolman, F. A. Hayek, and a few others like businessmen Edward F. Hutton and lawyer C. Dickerman Williams. As important as domestic problems were, a late 1952 editorial pointed out that they "must play second fiddle to the overriding considerations of foreign policy. If we can take care of Joe [Stalin], we can take care of everything else. There is nothing that an effective foreign policy can not cure."[21]

The *Freeman* rarely published the exposés of communist terror that were common in *Plain Talk*. The consensus seemed to be that as evil as communism was, the danger did not come from "any exceptional cunning of our enemies. The Communist design of world conquest is one of the most open conspiracies in history."[22] Rather, the *Freeman*'s authors believed the danger lay with America's liberal leaders. Liberalism was, in conservative eyes, essentially a form, albeit more benign, of the same collectivist ideology and economic viewpoints that made up the communist doctrine. The beginnings of a critique of social communism and of liberal ideology developed out of this analysis. The problems facing America were less ones of agents and treason and more ones of the ideological weaknesses and susceptibilities of liberalism.

This discussion of ideas seemed too theoretical to editors La Follette and Forrest Davis (who became the fourth editor in May 1952) and many authors. They preferred to discuss day-to-day politics and personalities. The lines between liberal and "pink" and agent often became blurred. Widespread treason in many areas of American society was alleged. Numerous articles questioned at least the intelligence and often the loyalty of Owen Lattimore, Dean Acheson, Alger Hiss, and General George Marshall, for instance.

It was within this context that Senator Joseph McCarthy (R, Wisconsin) became a cause célèbre for the *Freeman*. While rarely conservative in his economic and social views, McCarthy nonetheless struck a responsive chord among many conservatives in his attempt to eliminate what they saw were communist agents and influence in government. He was successful in gathering attention and support from the American people, whatever his methods, and that was the important point, as young writer William F. Buckley made clear in his first article for the *Freeman*: "If we want to help forge national policy, we must not allow our predispositions for clean and objective political techniques to influence too heavily our judgments of candidates and their aims.... [W]e must search out today only the general aims we find congenial and the men who seek to realize them."[23]

By late 1952, the *Freeman* had 22,000 subscribers, was edging toward self-sufficiency, and was firmly established "at the gates of our liberty like a heroic watchman, unafraid and dedicated."[24] At this same time, a series of conflicts arose that severely limited its editorial and fund-raising capabilities. It went through a number of ownership changes. By the end of 1955, it was no longer *the* conservative journal of opinion.

There were no clearly drawn camps in the initial controversies. Hazlitt and many of the board members felt the other editors had become too McCarthyite and intemperate. The editors also clashed with board members over who had control over editorial policy. And finally, the strong pro-Taft sentiment expressed by Chamberlain and Davis did not sit well with many of the board members who supported Eisenhower or wanted the *Freeman* to remain neutral until after the Republican convention.

It became difficult for the magazine to run smoothly, and fundraising became impossible. In late October 1952, Henry Hazlitt resigned. The struggles between the board and the remaining editors continued, however. Four months later, Chamberlain, La Follette, and Davis resigned, and Hazlitt came back as the sole editor with the issue of 23 February 1953.

Hazlitt tried to redirect the *Freeman* back toward classical liberal and free market principles. He tried to steer away from personalities, and in "Let's Defend Capitalism," he wrote a powerful critique of "those who think 'anti-Communism' is itself a sufficient ground for unity. Communism, they say, is not a doctrine that needs to be dissected, but a conspiracy that needs to be suppressed....The true opposite of Communism is Capitalism. The Communists know it, but most of the rest of us don't. This is the real reason for the ideological weakness of the opposition to Communism." [25]

Hazlitt left the *Freeman* at the beginning of 1954 to pursue other interests. For the next six months, the day-to-day work fell to Florence Norton as managing editor (she had previously been managing editor of the *American Mercury* and was a protégé of Max Eastman who published frequently in the *Freeman* during this time). By June, it looked as if the *Freeman* might have to cease publication. After three and a half years, it had lost $400,000. Board member Leonard E. Read offered to buy it for the Irvington Press (which was owned by the Foundation for Economic Education [FEE]). A number of board members were against the sale, but it finally was accepted.

The new publisher of this, now monthly, *Freeman* was quick to emphasize that the magazine would be independent of the FEE. It would "be a 'house organ' for the libertarian faith."[26] The new editor was Frank Chodorov. He had published *analysis* from 1944 to 1951. At sixty-eight, he was well-known in conservative circles for his uncompromising individualism, his emphasis on free market solutions to problems, and his strong antistatist and antiwar views.

The number of articles on domestic and economic affairs increased, but the major articles remained centered on foreign affairs and the communist threat. With Chodorov speaking clearly for the noninterventionist side, "The Dilemma of

Conservatives," as William F. Buckley called it, became quite explicit. "It is a pity," he wrote in August 1954, "that yet one more difference will divide the waning conservative movement in the United States. But the issue is there, and ultimately it will separate us."[27]

A major debate on the subject occurred in the September and November 1954 issues between Chodorov and William Schlamm (formerly assistant to Henry Luce and a *Freeman* contributor). In two articles, Chodorov spoke for the Old Right, emphasizing that the threat of communism was largely ideological and that it needed to be opposed by better ideas. To turn away from the free market and individualism, and to increase state power and prepare for war, would, he warned, be "certain to communize our country" no matter what the military outcome.[28]

Schlamm asserted that Chodorov was ignoring the problem of communism in favor of easy and high-sounding words. Schlamm reiterated a common theme when he wrote: "We had better try, as responsible men, to defeat the implacable foe before, by our own default, he has become invincible....[I am willing] to pay with the recoverable loss of some of my liberties for a chance to avoid, for centuries, the total loss of freedom."[29]

The last word on this subject from the Old Right in the *Freeman* came from Chodorov. He commented on the large percentage of all manuscripts he received that were on the subject of communism: "We are, of course, opposed to communism, but no more so than we are opposed to fascism, or socialism or any other form of authoritarianism. But we are also *for* something—a thing called freedom....Sometimes as I read these anticommunist manuscripts, an unkind suspicion comes upon me; are these writers *for freedom* or only *against communism*?"[30] The last word in the conservative movement came from the interventionist side. Both Murray N. Rothbard and William F. Buckley (on opposite sides of the debate) have commented on how quickly and completely the interventionist position became the conservative position.[31] What had been the continuing thrust of most conservative opinion, as expressed in the *Freeman*, was solidly ensconced by mid-1955.

In November 1955, the first issue of *National Review* appeared, and a new era of conservative publishing began. The magazine was strikingly similar to the early fortnightly *Freeman* and made the monthly *Freeman* seem superfluous. With losses of nearly $90,000 since it had been taken over by Irvington Press, the *Freeman* came under the direct sponsorship of FEE. It was reduced to digest size, became a controlled-circulation publication, and took on a very different and more limited editorial purpose.

The FEE was founded in 1946 by Leonard E. Read to remedy the profound "lack of understanding and appreciation of the infinite possibilities for peace and prosperity to be found in voluntary exchange in the market place."[32] Scholarly work was absolutely necessary, and then these studies had to be presented in "clear and simplified explanations."[33] That larger task fell to the *Freeman*. Gone were the articles on politics and personalities. Communism was discussed only as a failed economic system and as one form of the ideology of collectivism. Instead, it has become one of the very few educational publications dedicated to presenting the positive case for private property, the free market, the profit and loss system, and limited government.

Since the first issue in this new form in January 1956, the *Freeman* has played a crucial role in keeping a strong free market presence within a conservative movement that has often preferred to emphasize other topics. It has been largely directed toward students, business people, and educators. Articles tend to be about practical or historical aspects of the success of the free market or the failure of socialistic efforts. But the *Freeman* also places emphasis on the moral and spiritual choices that distinguish a free society. As staff member Edmund Opitz put it: "The free market will not function in a society where the sense of moral obligation is weak or absent."[34] The *Freeman* has presented views of the creative aspects of voluntarism and the free market process that are quite different from the usual images of cut-throat competition (though competition is very important) held together by some "dismal science." As Leonard E. Read wrote in "The Miracle of the Market" in 1961:

With no reservations, free all creative energies and their exchanges! Let government, society's formal agency of force minimize the current rascality as best it can—this, and nothing more. Otherwise, leave these millions of varying creative human energies alone, that the 'absolute principle'—freedom in exchanges—may freely, uninterruptedly, and without cost configurate these energies that they, in turn, may manifest themselves as automobiles, pencils, bread...symphonies, art, emerging individuals—indeed, all the things we live by.[35]

As part of the Foundation for Economic Education, the *Freeman* has been a strong voice for classical liberalism and free market principles. It has represented and presented one important element in modern American conservatism. Conservatism, as an intellectual movement, however, was already a coherent movement by 1956 and was moving in other directions. It has never lost its leanings toward the free market and individualism, but "The Faith of the Freeman," as expressed by Henry Hazlitt, was supplanted by a traditionalist perspective ably expressed in Russell Kirk's 1953 book, *The Conservative Mind.* This change was seen by some as the growing up of the Right and the rejection of an outmoded individualism. Others saw it as the triumph of "the New Conservatism," which was, in the words of Frank S. Meyer, "but another guise for the collectivist spirit of the age."[36]

Debates over the nature of conservatism were muted during the years that the *Freeman* played such a crucial formative role in the development of a conservative movement. Through the end of 1955, it was enough to bring together disparate authors, focus dissent, and put out a professional and articulate fortnightly. It was the journalistic vehicle "of the libertarian reconstruction after World War II."[37] In keeping with the times, its major focus was always the perceived threat of communism. The *Freeman*'s contributors were often torn between American globalism and militant anticommunism, and a lingering antistatism. Many of them ultimately chose, temporarily at least, to give up the latter, and they built the conservative movement around that. In subsequent years, conservatives dealt with a variety of other important issues in a variety of different media—the Foundation for Economic Education's *Freeman* being one of them. The perspective proffered by the *Freeman* until the end of 1955, however, continues to exert a heavy influence on the right wing in America.

Notes

1. "The Faith of the *Freeman*," *Freeman* 1 (2 October 1950): 5.

2. Clinton Rossiter, *Conservatism in America* (New York, 1964), p. 4.

3. "The New *Freeman*," *Time* 56 (16 October 1950): 47–48.

4. In fact, the *Freeman* rarely described itself as conservative, using, for instance, subtitles like "A Fortnightly for Individualists," "A Monthly for Libertarians," and since 1956 simply "Ideas on Liberty."

5. Editorials were unsigned. Author attributions, when given, are based on notations made by Henry Hazlitt in the office copy of volume 1 of the *Freeman*, or on discussions with John Chamberlain and Henry Hazlitt.

6. "The Faith of the *Freeman*," p. 5.

7. Dorothy Thompson, "Hymn for Today," *Freeman* 1 (2 July 1951): 623.

8. "The Function of the *Freeman*," *Freeman* 2 (31 December 1951): 198, 197.

9. Ibid.

10. "Ike's Mission," *Freeman* 3 (1 December 1952): 152.

11. "Mania for Compulsion," *Freeman* 1 (13 November 1950): 104.

12. Garet Garrett, "A New Key to Power," *Freeman* 2 (14 July 1952): 695.

13. "Our Political Paralysis," *Freeman* 1 (25 December 1950): 198.

14. "For a New Foreign Policy," *Freeman* 1 (8 January 1951): 229. See also "The Element of Surprise," *Freeman* 1 (26 February 1951): 325–26.

15. "No Substitute for Victory," *Freeman* 4 (17 May 1954): 583.

16. "Time for Disentanglement," *Freeman* 3 (7 September 1953): 874.

17. See, for instance, Suzanne La Follette and Alice Widener, "George F. Kennan: Policy-Guesser," *Freeman* 2 (25 February 1952): 325–26, and James Burnham, "Critique of Containment," *Freeman* 3 (9 February 1953): 331–34.

18. "Why Truman Should Resign," *Freeman* 1 (22 January 1951): 261.

19. "Facing the Convention," *Freeman* 2 (14 July 1952): 683.

20. Ibid. See also "Bob Taft's Foreign Policy," *Freeman* 2 (17 December 1951): 165–66.

21. "Ike's Mission," p. 152.

22. William Henry Chamberlin, "Can We Escape from Victory?" *Freeman* 1 (23 April 1951): 467.

23. William F. Buckley, "Senator McCarthy's Model?" *Freeman* 1 (21 May 1951): 533.

24. Taylor Caldwell, "Birthday Greetings," *Freeman* 3 (20 October 1952): 43.

25. "Let's Defend Capitalism," *Freeman* 3 (23 February 1953): 367–68.

26. "From the New Publisher," *Freeman* 5 (July 1954): 5.

27. William F. Buckley, "The Dilemma of Conservatives," *Freeman* 5 (August 1954): 52.

28. Frank Chodorov, "A War to Communize America," *Freeman* 5 (November 1954): 174. See also his editorial "The Return of 1940?" *Freeman* 5 (September 1954): 81–82.

29. William S. Schlamm, "But It Is Not 1940," *Freeman* 5 (November 1954): 171.

30. "An Editorial Problem," *Freeman* 5 (September 1955): 630.

31. George H. Nash. *The Conservative Intellectual Movement in America: Since 1945* (New York, 1976), p. 126.

32. "The Growth of an Idea," *Freeman* 6 (February 1956): 40.

33. Ibid.

34. Edmund Opitz, "Thinking about Economics," *Freeman* 29 (May 1979): 296.

35. Leonard E. Read, "The Miracle of the Market," *Freeman* 11 (September 1961): 37.

36. Frank S. Meyer, "Collectivism Rebaptized," *Freeman* 5 (July 1955): 562.

37. Nash, *Conservative Intellectual Movement in America*, p. 31.

Information Sources

BIBLIOGRAPHY:

Chamberlain, John. *A Life with the Printed Word*. Chicago, 1982.

Doenecke, Justus. *Not to the Swift: The Old Isolationists in the Cold War Era*. Lewisburg, Pennsylvania, 1979.

Nash, George H. *The Conservative Intellectual Movement in America: Since 1945*. New York, 1976.

INDEXES: Indexed annually; *Amer Hist & Life*; *Comb Ret Ind Bk Revs Sch J*; *Ind Bk Revs Hum*; *PAIS*; *Pol Sci Abst*; *Sage Urb Stud Abst*; *URS*; *Writings Amer Hist*.

REPRINT EDITIONS: Microform: UMI.

LOCATION SOURCES: Widely available.

Publication History

TITLE AND TITLE CHANGES: *The Freeman: Ideas on Liberty*.

VOLUME AND ISSUE DATA: Volumes 1–current, 2 October 1950–present.

FREQUENCY OF PUBLICATION: Bi-weekly, 2 October 1950–28 June 1954; monthly thereafter.

PUBLISHERS: 1950–1954: Freeman Magazine, Inc., New York; 1954–1955: Irvington Press, Irvington-on-Hudson, New York; 1956–present: Foundation for Economic Education, Irvington-on-Hudson.

EDITORS: John Chamberlain, 2 October 1950–9 February 1953; Suzanne La Follette, 2 October 1950–9 February 1953; Forrest Davis, 19 May 1952–9 February 1953; Henry Hazlitt, 2 October 1950–20 October 1952 and 23 February 1953–11 January 1954; Florence Norton, 23 February 1953–28 June 1954; Frank Chodorov, July 1954–December 1955; Paul Poirot, January 1956–October 1985; Charles H. Hamilton, November 1985–February 1986; Beth Hoffman and Brian Summers, Senior Editors, March 1986–June 1992; John W. Robbins, July 1982–December 1993. Beth Hoffman and Brian Summers, January 1986–May 1992; Beth Hoffman, June 1992: John Robbins, July 1992–January 1994; Beth Hoffman, March 1994–November 1997; Sheldon Richman, December 1997–present.

CIRCULATION: Began at 6,000, rose to 20,000, 1952–1955; from 1956 to mid–1960s ranged from 40,000–50,000, peaking in mid–1960s at over 50,000; hovered around 20,000–25,000 until 1993; at the end of 1998, 19,000.

Charles H. Hamilton

analysis
1949–1951

From November 1944 through January 1951, there appeared a monthly four-page broadsheet titled *analysis*, which publisher Frank Chodorov later described as "an individualist publication—the only one of its kind in America."[1] During those years, *analysis* became an unofficial and feisty standard-bearer for what Murray N. Rothbard has called the "old American right."[2] Finding its clearest early twentieth-century expression in Albert Jay Nock's the *Freeman* of the 1920s, this tradition flickered alive during the 1930s and 1940s. A small group of authors and politicians passionately espoused the causes of antistatism, individual liberty, economic laissez faire, justice, and international peace and cooperation; just as vigorously, it opposed domestic centralization, international protectionism, interventionism, and (especially) war. John Chamberlain, John T. Flynn, Garet Garrett, Henry Hazlitt, Rose Wilder Lane, and Felix Morley were among the writers to express these themes. Through the pages of *analysis,* Chodorov added his own voice. *analysis* proved to be an important intellectual link between the Old Right of the 1920s, 1930s, and 1940s and the development of the conservative and libertarian Right in the 1950s and 1960s.

Frank Chodorov was born on 15 February 1887, in New York City to poor Russian immigrants. He went to Columbia University, and after being graduated, held various teaching and business positions. In 1917, or thereabouts, Chodorov happened on *Progress and Poverty*, by Henry George. "A young man must have a cause," he later told his readers, and like many others of his generation, he initially found his in the Georgist philosophy.[3] Henry George is usually remembered for his critique of ownership of land and his advocacy of the single tax. These were relevant issues for Chodorov, but it was George's position as a classical liberal that so deeply influenced Chodorov: "George is the apostle of individualism; ... he emphasizes the greater productivity of voluntary cooperation in a free market economy, the moral degeneration of a people subjected to state direction and socialistic conformity.

His is the philosophy of free enterprise, free trade, free men."[4]

Chodorov became actively involved with the Single Tax party in New York and Massachusetts. By the early 1930s, however, he had become disillusioned with what he believed to be the moral compromises and lies of political action, and he soon rejected all electoral activity. Educational efforts became much more important to him. In 1937 he was appointed director of the recently founded Henry George School of Social Science in New York City. A short time later, he became editor of the school's magazine, the *Freeman*.[5]

At about this same time Chodorov met Albert Jay Nock. Nock broadened Chodorov's appreciation of classical liberalism and conservatism. He introduced Chodorov to Franz Oppenheimer's *The State* and to his own Americanized version of the same point (that the state is an exploitative institution), *Our Enemy the State*.[6] Although very different in style and temperament from the elder and aloof Nock, Chodorov often paid homage to this "articulate individualist."[7]

In early 1942, Chodorov was removed from his positions at the Henry George School and the *Freeman*. His staunch and principled opposition to war and his strong individualist stance did not sit well with many of the directors of the school. It was a few years before he took up the cause again. At the age of fifty-seven he began *analysis*. It was, he wrote in his autobiography, "the most gratifying venture" of his life.[8] *analysis* was "the testimony of a single man," as William F. Buckley put it in his eulogy of Chodorov.[9] Some of the leading conservatives and individualists of the day contributed occasional short pieces—for instance, Lane, Morley, Nock, Bernard Iddings Bell, Frank C. Hanighen, and William Henry Chamberlin. But *analysis* was mostly a one-man affair, and it reflected Chodorov's background and concerns.

As World War II came to a close and the cold war emerged from its ashes, Chodorov saw on the American scene the culmination of over forty years of rising state power at home and imperialistic adventures abroad. *analysis* was there, he wrote in the first issue, "to point up the State's encroachment upon social power, to expose the insidious economic forces which are robbing the individual of his will to resist the trend, to suggest a way by which this degradation of man might be stopped short of State-slavery."[10]

In an important essay in the March 1948 issue, Chodorov looked at his own political development and his experiences with anti-Semitism in an effort "to capture the invariable positives and negatives of the human being."[11] He concluded:

The exigencies of life require that we go on looking to nature for its secrets, and maintaining faith that in them lies immutable law.... Nature has its own ways of applying means to ends, which are made known to us by critical observation....I believe I look to the natural law doctrine because of an inherent distrust of leadership....I would rely on something less frail, something free of foibles, something impersonal. That something could be nothing else but nature.[12]

As for many conservatives, the belief in natural law and natural rights became articles of faith for Chodorov. But for him, natural law was revealed through the workings of the free market. This almost axiomatic alliance of natural law and free market economics became the basis for Chodorov's faith in individualism and individual liberty. In the July 1947 issue, Chodorov admonished his readers to "Let Nature Try It," to remove all man-made impediments to social progress and to let people cooperate and compete freely. Only in that way, he was sure, could civilization prosper.

These higher values were absolutes to Chodorov. Tradition, for instance, was no guide since the collectivist revolution had already taken place. In a June 1945 article, Chodorov contended that America had already become collectivist without most Americans knowing it; the state had become increasingly powerful with a commensurate decline in individual and social freedom. Thus, "the human tendency to become a partner in the *status quo* is the blind spot which prevents our seeing it as it is."[13] These absolutes also precluded looking to practical politics as a way to stem the tide. A constant theme in *analysis* was that the nation had become collectivist precisely through the reliance on expediency and "the makeshifts of political law."[14] Political thinking, *analysis* warned, was crowding out all other patterns of thought and action. Everyone was looking to the state for special considerations and for control over other people's thoughts and property; *analysis* was particularly critical of the many businessmen who "worship at the temple of Capitalism" and yet seek monopoly privileges from the state.[15]

The state held first place in *analysis*'s demonology. As Chodorov explained in October 1949: "Five years ago next month, I slapped *analysis* on its hopeful rump and the birth-cry sounded like antistatism. It was a strange sound, those days."[16] For it was the state, Chodorov continually pointed out, that was the central institution through which people were controlled and exploited; it "originates in force and exists by it."[17] Even more important than the state as an institution was the belief most people held in it. Statism was, for Chodorov, preeminently "a state of mind": a belief in the use of coercion which meant that individuals and their lives and property were merely pawns in various political power struggles.[18] One of the strengths Chodorov brought to *analysis* was the ability to explain the world in simple terms that consistently attacked statist views hidden in public discussion. Expressing concern over the "current witch hunt" in 1950, for instance, Chodorov declared it was a "diversionary scare....Let's not be hoodwinked. The real traitor in our midst is the power seeker."[19]

Chodorov used *analysis* to develop and refine two crucial distinctions with respect to the state. The first was to remind readers that "state" and "society" were mutually exclusive forms of social organization: an increase in the power of one necessarily led to the decrease in the power of the other. The state was an institution based on coercion and special privilege, used by one group of people to exploit another group. Society, on the other hand, was a spontaneous order, based on the voluntary cooperation of individuals. It was only through such voluntary interactions, Chodorov was sure, that people were productive.

A second distinction was often made between "state" and "government."[20] In contrast to the usurpations of the state, Chodorov reserved the term *government* to refer to the perfectly justified and very limited use of defensive force for the protection of individual rights and property. While never quite a philosophical anarchist, Chodorov placed *analysis* squarely on the anarchistic side of conservative and libertarian thought.

analysis was vociferous about two mainstays of state power: voting and taxation. It suggested that the "festival of selection" called voting merely legitimized thieves and could not change the political mess.[21] Returning once again to his theme that politics had destroyed every civilization, Chodorov reminded his readers that "when Society learns to distrust all politicians at all times, and to recognize that no good can come to it through politics, then only will peace come to the world."[22] Chodorov often ran articles against voting, and when he once did make a recommendation he headlined it "Vote for Kellems," referring to the well-known and crusty old Connecticut tax resistor, Vivian Kellems.[23] Taxation, and the income tax in particular, were especially onerous invasions of the rights of the individual, in Chodorov's view. Taxation was quite simply the theft of what individuals had rightly earned, and it gave the state the wherewithal to maintain its repressive structure and control.[24]

analysis was rarely able to get beyond the incisive argument to practical suggestions about eliminating state power. Lead articles called out "Let's Abolish Congress" and "Don't Buy Bonds." Chodorov also defended states rights and the destruction of public schooling (largely southern issues, Chodorov supported them for reasons having nothing to do with race). Even calls for "civil disobedience" and for tax resistance seemed rather lame.

When pushed, and readers often asked for some form of concrete program, Chodorov always said that education, and more education, was needed. The real fight, he felt, was not directly against institutions but rather against the *idea* of statism. The ideas he attacked were those of power and privilege, whether they went under the name of socialism, communism, or even capitalism. The truest "legacy of value" he urged his readers to bestow on future generations was "some understanding of the principles of freedom and, perhaps, a will for freedom."[25]

In the October 1950 issue of *analysis*, Chodorov published his famous "A Fifty-Year Project," which was his plan to implant the seeds of individualism on college campuses in much the same way the Intercollegiate Society of Socialists had done for socialist ideas years earlier. The article generated so much interest that Chodorov soon founded the Intercollegiate Society of Individualists. Its seminars, books, publications, and campus groups in fact became a powerful force in developing the young talent of the conservative movement of the 1950s and 1960s.

Whatever its interest in domestic affairs, *analysis* devoted most of its attention to foreign events. It was in the foreign arena that the state was the most dangerous, and where people were most easily confused about the growth of the state. And for Chodorov, foreign affairs always centered, explicitly or implicitly, on the issue of war. *analysis* reflected Chodorov's deep-seated belief, one not shared by most of his conservative contemporaries, that war is evil. War always left the state stronger and the individual weaker, an unfortunate truth that applied as well to the massive preparations for the cold war.

Chodorov was vocal in his denunciation of communism as an evil philosophy and of the Soviet Union as a brutal and imperialistic power, but he worried that if U.S. opposition was not carefully thought out, American freedom would be lost in the process. In one of his most perceptive critiques of the cold war, titled "A Jeremiad," he warned that "when The [next] War comes, the individual will cease to exist as an individual....The net profit of The War will be a political setup differing from that of Russia in name only. The very effort to oppose that form of absolutism will require our adopting it and, despite the best intentions, the resulting economic and social conditions will tend to perpetuate it."[26]

Chodorov was absolutely damning of most postwar American foreign policy. It looked to him very much like the same old-fashioned imperialism in slightly new clothes. In his famous April 1947 article, "A Byzantine Empire of the West?" he expressed the fear that soon "the American empire will take its place in the historic up-and-down parade."[27] Whether it was Bretton Woods, Dumbarton Oaks, or Yalta, Chodorov used *analysis* to bring home his point that these agreements were merely efforts by the United States and the other big powers to parcel out the world's economic privileges and partition the world's lands and people. Chodorov considered the Truman Doctrine and the Marshall Plan similar attempts to garner the world's spoils for the United States. They used the "cheerleader technique" of imperialism to divide the world into two camps: communist and noncommunist. At the same time, he wrote, these aid packages did not address the real issue, "the desperation of hopeless poverty" that had made communism "the religion of Europe." Instead, "the way to stop Communism, to put it briefly, is to let the people alone...to let the people of Europe produce and exchange."[28]

Yet Chodorov was not convinced that anything could stop much of Europe from going communist; the economic situation was that desperate. The encouragement of war, however, was even worse. Russian dominance in Western Europe offered a bleak future to the next generation of Europeans, "but is it any worse than another war? Something might survive a spell of Communism, while the result of another war, no matter which side wins, will be annihilation."[29] Chodorov predicted that the "slave-economy" of communism would fall of its own weight, unable to be productive and unable to bear the weight of its imperialistic ventures.

analysis was one of the last isolationist periodicals on the Right. Chodorov felt that the United States neither could nor should be the "law-and-order enforcement agency" of the world.[30] American intervention in Europe or elsewhere was a poor expression of power politics that would only fire anti-American sentiments. The defeat of communism and the defense of freedom would not come through the construction of a new American imperialistic leviathan.

Most of all, though, Chodorov feared what such a militantly interventionist and anticommunist foreign policy would do at home. In a prescient 1947 warning about what came to be called McCarthyism, he asked: "If we go along with this poking into the business of Europe, what will happen to the liberty we have left in America? Already there is a 'red' witch-hunt afoot, and experience tells us that when the exigencies of the situation require it the definition of 'red' will include every person who raises his voice against the going order."[31] Chodorov took communism in the generic sense very seriously, for it represented the ultimate concentration of political power and privilege. But the search for domestic communists was to Chodorov merely a "heresy trial" to see if one kind of power worshiper was aligned "to the Moscow branch of the church."[32] It seemed self-evident to Chodorov that freedom could not be defended by denying the very value of freedom in practice. In a May 1949 article, "How to Curb the Commies," Chodorov declared that the right of free speech was "a principle of freedom that is of transcending importance....If men are punished for espousing Communism, shall we stop there?"[33] In fact, back in 1946, Chodorov had even wondered if *analysis* itself might not be seen as subversive someday.[34]

Chodorov agreed with the goals of fighting communism, and at times he flirted with McCarthyite elements of the Right. Mostly, though, he reminded his readers that the ultimate value was freedom and that they should not squander it in an ill-advised effort to protect it. His point was simply that "the commies don't count."[35] The real enemy was statism. To the question of how to rid the government of communists, Chodorov half-seriously remarked: "Easy. Just abolish the jobs."[36]

Chodorov was under no illusions about the task he set forth to his readers. "Nobody now living will see a free society in America," he lamented in 1950.[37] Yet, from the very first issue, he believed that "it's fun to fight; especially when it is something worth fighting for."[38] There would be a time, Chodorov believed, when there would come a new revolution in the tradition of Adam Smith and Thomas Jefferson. Meanwhile, there was work to be done in creating a body of literature that could serve as the intellectual foundation for that presumably far-off event.

analysis ceased publication with the January 1951 issue. Chodorov merged it with the then still individualistic *Human Events* to which he contributed on a regular basis as an associate editor until 1954. His articles, however, lost some of their more philosophical orientation as he focused on more topical and polemical matters. Subsequently, Chodorov served as editor of the *Freeman* from 1954 to 1955, and as a gadfly associate editor of the *National Review*. He died on 28 December 1966, after a life dedicated to the ideals that were best expressed in *analysis*.

At its peak, *analysis* had nearly 4,000 subscribers, not an inconsiderable number for such a periodical. What it lacked in numbers, it enjoyed in influence. As George H. Nash has pointed out, it was through *analysis* that Chodorov "began to shape directly the intellectual development of the postwar Right."[39] William F. Buckley, Edmund Opitz, James J. Martin, and Murray N. Rothbard were among the men to be deeply influenced by its sensibility.

Conservatism developed in several directions in the years after World War II. It was wracked by a series of internal debates about the place of tradition and the individual, about the required response to communism, and even about the proper balance between the free market and the state. *analysis* always made the case for the maximum individual liberty. Forever concerned that liberty would be lost indirectly through inconsistent means, it took a principled stand against the ravages of everyday politics. Its own analysis of the world could be simplistic, yet it also proved to be exceedingly perceptive in many cases. Ultimately, the positions Chodorov took in *analysis* were too extreme for many conservatives; Chodorov lost his battle for the conservative mind.   Still, as M. Stanton Evans remarked many years later, "the Chodorov imprint is visible in every phase of the conservative effort."[40]

Notes

1. *analysis* 6 (June 1950): 4.

2. Murray N. Rothbard, "The Transformation of the American Right," *Continuum* 2 (Summer 1964): 220–31.

3. Frank Chodorov, *Out of Step* (New York, 1962), p. 50.

4. Chodorov, "Education for a Free Society," *Scribner's Commentator* 9 (February 1941): 36–37.

5. Contrary to what some have said, this *Freeman* was not a continuation of Albert Jay Nock's *Freeman* of the early 1920s (see "Get Behind the *Freeman*," the *Freeman* 1 [November 1937]: 24). Nor is the current *Freeman*, begun in 1950, directly related to Nock's earlier endeavor.

6. Chodorov, *The Rise and Fall of Society: An Essay on the Economic Forces that Underlie Social Institutions* (New York, 1959).   This was an attempt to update and put an economic slant on Nock's historical orientation.

7. "Albert Jay Nock, 1873–1945," *analysis* 1 (September 1945): 3. The August 1946 issue of *analysis* was devoted to Nock and his work.

8. Chodorov, *Out of Step*, p. 79.

9. Eulogy delivered by William F. Buckley at Chodorov's funeral, 3 December 1966; printed in *National Review* 19 (24 January 1967): 84.

10. "It's Fun to Fight," *analysis* 1 (November 1944): 1.

11. "How a Jew Came to God," *analysis* 4 (March 1948): 1.

12. Ibid., p. 3.

13. "The Revolution Was," *analysis* 1 (June 1945): 3.

14. "How a Jew Came to God," p. 4.

15. "Why We Have Socialism," *analysis* 2 (November 1945): 3.

16. "Let's Keep It Clean," *analysis* 5 (October 1949): 3.

17. "One Worldism," *analysis* 7 (December 1950): 1.

18. "A Legacy of Value," *analysis* 6 (August 1950): 2.

19. "Trailing the Trend," *analysis* 6 (April 1950): 3.

20. "Government Contra State," *analysis* 2 (February 1946): 3.

21. "Vote for Kellems," *analysis* 5 (October 1949): 1.

22. "Trailing the Trend," *analysis* 6 (October 1950): 3.

23. "Vote for Kellems," p. 1; see also "If We Quit Voting," *analysis* 1 (July 1945): 1–2.

24. "Socialism Via Taxation," *analysis* 2 (February 1946): 1–2; (March 1946): 3; (April 1946): 3.

25. "A Legacy of Value," p. 2.

26. "A Jeremiad," *analysis* 6 (August 1950): 1.

27. "A Byzantine Empire of the West?" *analysis* 3 (April 1947): 2.

28. Ibid.

29. Ibid.

30. Ibid.

31. Ibid., p. 3.

32. "The Spy-Hunt," *analysis* 4 (September 1948): 1.

33. "How to Curb the Commies," *analysis* 5 (May 1949): 2.

34. "Scenario for To-morrow," *analysis* 2 (September 1946): 2.

35. "Commies Don't Count," *analysis* 3 (December 1946): 2.

36. "Trailing the Trend" [April 1950], p. 3.

37. "A Legacy of Value," p. 2.

38. "It's Fun to Fight," p. 1.

39. George H. Nash, *The Conservative Intellectual Movement in America: Since 1945* (New York, 1976), p. 16.

40. M. Stanton Evans, "The Founding Father," *Ideas* 1 (Spring–Summer 1969): 61.

Information Sources

BIBLIOGRAPHY

Chodorov, Frank. *Out of Step: The Autobiography of an Individualist.* New York, 1962.

Hamilton, Charles H., ed. *Fugitive Essays: Selected Writings of Frank Chodorov.* Indianapolis, Indiana, 1980.

Stromberg, Joseph R. "The Cold War and the Transformation of the American Right: The Decline of Right-Wing Liberalism." Master's thesis, Florida Atlantic University, 1971.

INDEXES: *PAIS*.

REPRINT EDITIONS: None.

LOCATION SOURCES: Columbia University; Library of Congress; Tamiment Library, New York University.

Publication History

TITLE AND TITLE CHANGES: *analysis*.

VOLUME AND ISSUE DATA: Volumes 1–7, November 1944–January 1951.

FREQUENCY OF PUBLICATION: Monthly.

PUBLISHER: Analysis Associates (Frank Chodorov), New York, New York.

EDITOR: Frank Chodorov.

CIRCULATION: Between 3,000 and 4,000.

Charles H. Hamilton

New Individualist Review
1961–1968

In the fall of 1960, Ralph Raico, then a graduate student working under F. A. Hayek at the University of Chicago, conceived the idea of starting an independent journal dedicated to promoting an open society and individual liberty. The academic orthodoxy of the time was heavily oriented toward the view that the solution to the nation's economic and social ills was by massive state intervention, and this conviction was as firmly rooted among the students and faculty of the University of Chicago—despite its generally promarket economics department—as at any other major university in the country. Indeed, the need for such a journal appeared particularly pressing since no interdisciplinary periodical devoted to upholding the principles of a free society then existed.

Hayek, who had left his chair at the London School of Economics in 1950 to become professor of social and moral sciences on the Committee on Social Thought at Chicago, had attracted several doctoral students besides Raico. Two of them who had begun their graduate studies in 1960, Ronald Hamowy and Robert Schuettinger, were quickly enlisted as the nucleus of an editorial board, to which were added John McCarthy, a graduate student in history, and John Weicher, in economics. In addition, Hayek, Milton Friedman of the economics department, and Richard Weaver of the English department, agreed to serve as editorial advisers to the new review. The most difficult hurdle, that of financing the publication of a journal edited by graduate students, was overcome through the assistance of the Intercollegiate Society of Individualists (ISI), a national organization founded in 1953 to promote the principles of a free society among university students. Don Lipsett, then the midwestern director of the ISI, agreed to ensure the needed funding through the purchase of several thousand copies of each of the first few issues of the journal.

In April 1961, the *New Individualist Review* was launched with Raico acting as editor in chief, Hamowy as book review editor, and McCarthy, Schuettinger, and Weicher as associate editors. Each editor contributed an article to the original issue, as did Milton Friedman, who submitted an essay on the intimate connection between a free market economy and individual liberty. (Friedman's article was reprinted in the *Wall Street Journal* some weeks following its appearance in the *Review* and later formed the title chapter of his book, *Capitalism and Freedom*.) The *Review*'s introductory editorial, written by Raico but expressing sentiments shared by all the editors, represents the best statement of the philosophical underpinning and purposes of the new journal:

The *New Individualist Review* has been founded in a commitment to human liberty. We believe in free, private enterprise, and in the imposition of the strictest limits to the power of government. The philosophy which we advocate is that which was shared by some of the greatest and deepest political thinkers of modern times—by Adam Smith, Burke, Bentham, Herbert Spencer; it is responsible for most of the good that the modern world has accomplished in the way of material progress and increased freedom.

Two or three decades ago, individualism was held in contempt by American intellectuals, and a decade ago they regarded it as at least wildly eccentric. We certainly do not deny that the majority of today's intellectuals are still guided by the ideas which grew up in the 1930's. But the slogans which the New Deal shouted, and the stereotypes which it propagated, while perhaps fresh and exciting then, have lost their appeal to the generation which has emerged in recent years, one which sees no reason to consider our march toward the Total State to be as "inevitable as a law of nature."

College professors like to think of themselves as working far out on the frontiers of knowledge; the truth is, however, that in some respects, at least, they are not so very different from most people. They, too, think that old ideas, like old friends, are best. Accustomed to the premises of the collectivist ideology which they absorbed when they were students, they are understandably comfortable with it, and are reluctant to change. But it is equally understandable that the best and most independent in each generation should want to test the premises of its predecessors, and seek out more veridical ones.

This is precisely what has been happening. An increasing number of students in the past decade have recognized the inadequacies of the orthodox response to most of the present-day social and economic challenges. The party of liberty is steadily gaining adherents among students: One of the purposes of this review will be to add to the growing number of libertarians in our colleges and universities.[1]

Despite agreement over inclusion of this statement of purpose, there were serious differences in the philosophical positions held by the five editors. Raico and Hamowy were dedicated libertarians, as strongly opposed to government intervention in the social as in the economic sphere. More important, they regarded the belligerent foreign policy and anticivil libertarianism adopted by most conservatives—much of it springing from the naive notion that any action leveled against communism either at home or abroad represented a victory for traditional American values—as a betrayal of the first principles of a free society. They particularly objected to the uncritical support that American conservatives lent the Smith Act and other sedition laws, the actions of the House Un-American Activities Committee, a massive and unrestrained defense establishment over which neither the Congress nor the people possessed any effective control, wars disguised as "police actions," and, especially, conscription. On the other hand, Weicher, unlike Raico and Hamowy, identified himself with the mainstream of current American conservatism far more than with libertarianism, regarding international communism as so great and immediate a threat to world security and Western values that recourse to such extraordinary measures was both legitimate and prudent.

The *Review*'s introductory statement had skirted this conflict. It noted, "In future issues we will publish articles and reviews by students and younger scholars, and occasionally by established authorities, in philosophy, economics, politics, history and the humanities. The viewpoints presented will be libertarian or conservative, but we will consider for publication any essay which indicates a reasoned concern for freedom, and a thoughtful valuation of its importance."[2]

The clash between libertarian and conservative philosophies flared into the open in the November 1961 issue of the journal, in the form of an exchange between Hamowy and William F. Buckley, Jr., editor of the conservative periodical, *National Review*.[3] Hamowy's critique caused such controversy among the editors that despite his having been appointed coeditor in chief that fall—Raico was then studying at the University of Paris—it was agreed that the masthead not reflect this change lest Hamowy's remarks be taken as the official position of the *Review*; instead, Schuettinger was listed as coeditor in chief for that issue. In addition, a disclaimer was inserted, noting that "the opinions expressed [by Hamowy and Buckley] are the authors' and do not necessarily represent the viewpoint of the Editorial Board."

Both Raico and Hamowy had been strongly influenced by their close friend, Murray N. Rothbard, perhaps the most important, and certainly the most articulate, libertarian writer in the country. Indeed, in composing his criticism of *National Review*, Hamowy had borrowed heavily from his discussions with and from the unpublished writings of Rothbard, who was disenchanted by the shift in direction taken by the American Right under the leadership of Buckley's magazine. "At a time when the Left had a virtual monopoly on all intellectual activity, during the early 40's," Hamowy wrote,

a small but ever-growing libertarian movement began to emerge....Philosophically, it was firmly dedicated to individual liberty, and consequently embraced free enterprise in economics, a strict adherence to the civil liberties of the individual, and peace. Historically, it ranked among its heroes Jefferson, Tom Paine, Thoreau and Herbert Spencer.

Six years ago, however, a revolution took place "within the form," as Garet Garrett once wrote of the New Deal. The articulate publicists of *National Review*, founded at that time, have succeeded in remoulding the American Right until it travesties the intent of its original founders. Mr. Buckley and his staff have been able to achieve this transformation with such apparent ease simply because there has been no journal to oppose it, or even to call attention to the surgery that has been committed on the American Conservative movement.[4]

Hamowy concluded with a list of those features he felt characterized American conservatism as reshaped by *National Review* and its contributors:

They may be summed up as: (1) a belligerent foreign policy likely to result in war; (2) a suppression of civil liberties at home; (3) a devotion to imperialism and to a polite form of white supremacy; (4) a tendency toward the union of Church and State; (5) the conviction that the community is superior to the individual and that historic tradition is a far better guide than reason; and (6) a rather lukewarm support of the free economy. They wish, in gist, to substitute one group of masters (themselves) for another. They do not desire so much to limit the State as to control it. One would tend to describe this devotion to a hierarchical, warlike statism and this fundamental opposition to human reason and individual liberty as a species of corporativism suggestive of Mussolini or Franco, but let us be content with calling it "old-time conservatism," the conservatism not of the heroic band of libertarians who founded the anti-New-Deal Right, but the traditional conservatism that has always been the enemy of true liberalism.[5]

With the publication of Hamowy's article, the *New Individualist Review* increasingly identified itself as a libertarian publication; indeed, by the summer of 1965, it carried the subtitle: *A Journal of Classical Liberal Thought.* While its third issue contained an article by Russell Kirk, the eminent conservative publicist, after the appearance of the interchange between Hamowy and Buckley, no conservative traditionalist contributed an essay except in the form of a reply to an article that had already appeared in the *Review*.

One immediate effect of this change in philosophical emphasis was a gradually expanding rift between the *Review* and the Intercollegiate Society of Individualists. Between 1953, the date of its founding, and 1961, the ISI had developed from a quasi-libertarian into a conservative organization, and its officers saw no reason to associate the society so closely with a journal one of whose spokesmen had authored a polemic against the country's leading conservative periodical. Thus, while the first three issues of the *Review* were listed as being published by "the University of Chicago chapter of the Intercollegiate Society of Individualists," beginning with issue 4, the publisher was described simply as *"New Individualist Review."* At the same time, the *Review* was forced to find supplementary financial support through contributions from individuals and foundations to replace the funding that had previously come through a guaranteed sale of each issue of the journal to the ISI.

With the fourth issue of the *Review*, published in the winter of 1962, the editorial board was enlarged to include Robert Hurt as an associate editor. Hurt, a tireless worker on the journal's behalf, was a young scholar of exceptional ability. Recently graduated from the Yale Law School, he enrolled as a doctoral student under Hayek on the Committee on Social Thought and almost immediately joined the *Review*. Over the course of the next fifteen months, Hurt contributed no fewer than four lengthy essays to the journal,[6] three of which were incisive critical analyses of certain aspects of American law. The *Review* was also fortunate in attracting Sam Peltzman, a doctoral student in economics at Chicago, to act as business manager. Peltzman's talents extended to that happy combination, apparently rare among academic economists, of understanding market phenomena on both a practical and theoretical level. Besides being a regular contributor to the journal,[7] Peltzman took charge of the *Review*'s finances, and it was largely thanks to his efforts that they were placed on a sound footing.

With the death of Richard Weaver in early 1963, the editorial advisory board was also reconstituted. Hayek had moved from Chicago to the University of Freiburg in the summer of 1962, and, although he remained on the board, it was thought worthwhile to enlarge the list of established academics associated with the *Review*, especially as the journal had begun to gain a national reputation. As a result, in 1963 George Stigler and Yale Brozen of the Business School at Chicago and Benjamin Rogge, professor of political economy at Wabash College, were added to the board.

The high intellectual quality of the articles appearing in the journal, together with a vigorous campaign to solicit manuscripts of equal scholarly merit, soon established the *Review* as one of the best student periodicals in the country. Over the course of the seventeen-issue life of the *Review*, some of the most respected scholars in the country appeared in its pages, including three University of Chicago economists who were later to become Nobel laureates. Although its subscription list never numbered more than 800, it included the editors of several prestigious magazines and nationally circulated newspapers, dozens of university and college libraries, and several hundred prominent academics throughout the United States and Western Europe. An analysis of the first fifteen issues of the *Review* shows that of the ninety-eight articles that appeared, fifty-two were authored by graduate students and younger academics, while forty-six were the work of established scholars, many of international repute. Nor was the journal confined to students and faculty at the University of Chicago. No fewer than fifty-eight essays and reviews were contributed by scholars outside the university, among the most noteworthy being Ludwig von Mises's review of Murray Rothbard's two-volume treatise on economics, G. Warren Nutter's analysis of the nature of Soviet planning (later reprinted in *Barron's*), and Murray Rothbard's essay that traced many of the policies subsequently associated with the New Deal to the programs initiated under Herbert Hoover's presidency.[8] Milton Friedman, writing in 1981, some thirteen years after the *Review* had ceased publication, noted that of the articles that appeared in it, most "remain timely and relevant. More important, perhaps, this student venture, despite its narrow base and its limited resources, set an intellectual standard that has not yet, I believe, been matched by any of the more recent publications in the same philosophical tradition."[9]

Rothbard, a prolific writer of great ability, was a frequent contributor to the *Review*. His essays covered a wide variety of subjects, from a libertarian analysis of the civil rights movement to an examination of the concept of the "public sector," in which he attacked the view that public goods and services are, or indeed can be, given equal weight to the goods and services provided by the private sector in determining the national product.[10] Perhaps the most discerning and, as it later turned out, the most controversial of the essays he authored for the *Review* was his analysis of the domestic policies of Herbert Hoover. Hoover had long been viewed by conservatives as a staunch proponent of the free market, whose political program was almost diametrically opposed to that of his successor in the White House. However, a careful reading of the historical data, Rothbard noted, did not bear out this assumption. Not only did Hoover initiate massive public works programs during his term as president, but he supported government loans to financially unsound firms, farm price supports, the cartelization of the oil industry, and deficit spending. More important, Rothbard observed, at a time when prices were falling precipitously after the onset of the depression, Hoover put substantial pressure on industrialists to keep wages from dropping, thus exacerbating the effects of the depression by raising the number of bankruptcies and increasing the number of unemployed workers. "Far from being a libertarian," Rothbard concluded, "Hoover was a statist par excellence, in economics and morals; and his only difference from FDR was one of degree, not of kind; FDR only built upon the foundations laid by Hoover."[11]

The article, which appeared in 1966, was, on the whole, well received, but a group of academic economists who felt a personal warmth toward Hoover and had previously not been unsympathetic to the *Review* were outraged at the publication of what they viewed as a vicious assault against a selfless and honorable states-man. Perhaps more significant, Rothbard's attack on those conservative scholars who had interpreted Hoover's domestic programs as, in the main, consistent with laissez-faire economic policy reopened the whole conservative-libertarian debate in the pages of the journal.

The ideological orientation of the *Review* had by this time clearly emerged as libertarian and anticonservative. Indeed, in the same issue of the journal that carried Rothbard's article, M. Stanton Evans, then the editor of the *Indianapolis News* and one of the better-known younger spokesmen of the American conservative movement, took the editor in chief of the *Review*, Ralph Raico, to task for his review of an article Evans had recently published in an anthology titled *What Is Conservatism?*[12] Evans, who was primarily a journalist and only occasionally pretended to serious scholarship, had argued that, historically, classical liberals and present-day libertarians—unlike conservatives—rejected a God-centered moral order and had commonly embraced a relativistic, pragmatic, materialist worldview. Raico, a historian of social and political theory of rare ability and insight, had gone to great pains to show that this contention had no foundation in fact. But rather than leaving well enough alone, Evans attempted to defend this fatuous thesis in a communication to the *Review* couched in the usual conservative jargon, with casual references to such figures as Ficino, Erasmus, Condorcet, and Faguet, and to such notions as a "secular ethic," "absolute values," and so on.

In his reply, Raico explained why he troubled to attack Evans's original article. "In their attempt to carve for themselves a position of relevance in discussions of contemporary social problems," Raico wrote,

conservative writers sometimes present a sketchy philosophical outline of the historical development of classical liberalism, attempting to show deeper reasons for its decline than those readily admitted by classical liberals themselves.

It appeared to me that for once someone ought to call a conservative to account for his flamboyant and unsubstantiated claims regarding classical liberalism; for once, the canons of precise definition and relevant evidence, which serious scholars in all disciplines apply, ought to be applied here, too. It seemed to me, furthermore, that Evans had presented us in his article with a startling example of these conservative defects, and that the article could profitably be examined from this point of view.

There followed a point-by-point rejoinder to Evans's reply, to which Raico concluded:

The fact is that much too much passes muster in conservative writings that is nothing more than uninformed rhetoric. That almost all conservative publicists are guilty of this, at least sometimes, is scarcely the best kept secret on the Right. I for one am finally getting bored with the sophomoric misuse of technical philosophical terms; with sketchy outlines of the "course" of modern history; with constant attacks on the French Enlightenment, on human reason, and on the *hubris* of modern man; and with worldly-wise references to Original Sin and the absurdity of progress. Let conservative writers follow the example of present-day classical liberal economists, who adhere to the accepted rules of scholarly discussion in their confrontation with their Leftist counterparts. The typical approach of the conservative cultural critics, on the other hand, since it is rhetorical and unanalytical, does not allow for progress being made towards the solution of the issues under discussion. If conservative publicists find the scholarly approach too tedious, they ought to recall that no one is *compelled* to write on intellectual history or philosophy.[13]

It is unfortunate that by late 1966, after having established itself as a forum of scholarly libertarian thought, one that even its conservative critics felt the need to take seriously, the journal made only two more appearances. Although the review was nominally a quarterly, the exigencies of student life often interfered with its regular publication. The first issue (vol. 1, no. 1) was published in the spring of 1961 and the eighth (vol. 2, no. 4), in the spring of 1963, so at least during the first two years of its existence, the journal managed to adhere to a fairly uniform printing schedule. However, only one more issue appeared in 1963, and the fourth issue of volume 3 was not published until the spring of 1965. The four issues comprising the last complete volume of the *Review*, volume 4, appeared between the fall of 1965 and the spring of 1967, and the last issue (vol. 5, no. 1) carried a cover date of winter 1968. The difficulties involved in keeping to a stricter timetable were exacerbated as the original editors scattered to take up positions far from Chicago, eventually forcing their resignation from the *Review*. In 1964, Hamowy resigned, and in 1965, Peltzman, Weicher, and McCarthy followed; the tragic death earlier that same year of Robert Hurt, an indefatigable worker on the journal's behalf, further impoverished the *Review*.

The final blow came in late 1966, when Raico, the journal's founder and the person most responsible for the *Review*'s recognized quality, felt compelled to step down as chief editor. Only two issues appeared subsequent to Raico's resignation, one in 1967—devoted exclusively to the question of conscription and composed almost entirely of reprinted articles and excerpts from papers delivered at a conference on the draft earlier held at the University of Chicago—and a second in 1968. Both were published under the editorship of Joe M. Cobb, who had joined the *Review* as an editorial assistant in late 1962. Unfortunately, Cobb, and the staff working under him, had neither the talent nor the energy to carry on an enterprise so difficult and time-consuming. Cobb decided to cease publication of the *Review* in late 1968.

During its existence of eight years, the *New Individualist Review* had succeeded in establishing itself as one of the foremost libertarian journals of ideas in the country. Under the direction of a small but dedicated and resourceful group of graduate students, it had published articles and reviews of a consistently high quality, thus providing an important outlet for scholars dedicated to the principles of a free and open society. It is particularly regrettable that the *Review* ceased appearing in 1968, at the height of the Vietnam War and at a point in the nation's history when the principles to which the *Review* was dedicated most strongly needed voicing.

Notes

1. "An Editorial," *New Individualist Review* 1 (April 1961): 2 (hereinafter cited as *NIR*).
2. Ibid.
3. Ronald Hamowy and William F. Buckley, Jr., "'National Review': Criticism and Reply," *NIR* 1 (November 1961): 3–11. This exchange had been adumbrated in the previous issue, which carried an article by Edward Facey, then a doctoral student at New York University, in which he attacked the program of the Young Americans for Freedom, an organization of conservative college students founded in 1960 at Buckley's estate in Sharon, Connecticut. Facey's essay focused on the foreign policy and cold war mentality of the organization, to which John Weicher of the editorial board replied. (Edward C. Facey, "Conservatives or Individualists: Which Are We?" *NIR* 1 (Summer 1961): 24–26; John Weicher, "Mr. Facey's Article: A Comment," *NIR* 1 (Summer 1961): 26–27.)
4. Hamowy and Buckley, "'National Review,'" p. 4.
5. Ibid.
6. "Anti-Trust and Competition," *NIR* 1 (Winter 1962): 3–12; "Sin and the Criminal Law," *NIR* 2 (Spring 1962): 29–43; "Observations on the Soviet 'Lost Generation,'" *NIR* 2 (Autumn 1962): 10–17; and "FCC: Free Speech 'Public Needs,' and Mr. Minow," *NIR* 2 (Spring 1963): 24–37.
7. See, for example, his excellent essay on the effects of domestic airline regulation on the price and quality of air service. "CAB: Freedom from Competition," *NIR* 2 (Spring 1963): 16–23.
8. Ludwig von Mises, "A New Treatise on Economics," *NIR* 2 (Autumn 1962): 39–42; G. Warren Nutter, "How Soviet Planning Works," *NIR* 4 (Summer 1965): 20–25; Murray N. Rothbard, "Herbert Clark Hoover: A Reconsideration," *NIR* 4 (Winter 1966): 3–12.
9. Milton Friedman, Introduction to *New Individualist Review, Volumes 1–5, 1961–1968* (reprint ed., Indianapolis, 1981), p. xiv.
10. "The Negro Revolution," *NIR* 3 (Summer 1961): 29–37; "The Fallacy of the 'Public Sector,'" *NIR* 1 (Summer 1961): 3–11.
11. Rothbard, "Hoover: A Reconsideration," p. 12.
12. Raico's original review appeared under the title "The Fusionists on Liberalism and Tradition," *NIR* 3 (Autumn 1964): 29–36. Evans's reply was carried under the heading "Raico on Liberalism and Religion," *NIR* 4 (Winter 1966): 19–25.
13. Ralph Raico, "Reply to Mr. Evans," *NIR* 4 (Winter 1966): 25–31.

Information Sources

BIBLIOGRAPHY: None.
INDEXES: Cumulative index published in Liberty Press reprint (1981); *PAIS*; *URS*;
 Writings Amer Hist.

REPRINT EDITIONS: Microform: UMI; KIP. Bound edition: Liberty Press, Indianapolis,
   Indiana.
LOCATION SOURCES: Widely available.

Publication History

TITLE AND TITLE CHANGES: *New Individualist Review*.
VOLUME AND ISSUE DATA: Volumes 1–5, April 1961–Winter 1968.
FREQUENCY OF PUBLICATION: Quarterly.
PUBLISHERS: April–November 1961: University of Chicago Chapter of the Intercolle-
   giate Society of Individualists; thereafter, New Individualist Review. Both in Chi-
   cago.
EDITORS: Ralph Raico, 1961–1966; Joe M. Cobb, 1967–1968.
CIRCULATION: 800.

Ronald Hamowy

Objectivist
1962–1976

Ayn Rand created the *Objectivist Newsletter*, the first of her three periodicals, in 1962. In the inaugural issue, she began by denouncing conservatism, calling it an "embarrassing conglomeration of impotence, futility, inconsistency and superficiality." She also declared unequivocally that "Objectivists are *not* 'conservatives.'" Consequently, the decision to include a discussion of Ayn Rand's magazines in a volume devoted to the conservative press seems open to question.

It only would make sense to classify her as a conservative if the term is used loosely to signify opposition to twentieth-century statism. On this basis—definition by negation—Ayn Rand was indeed a conservative, because she rejected the mixed economy and welfare state, condemned totalitarianism (including fascism and every form of socialism), and passionately opposed Soviet communism, having experienced its tyranny firsthand in her native Russia before she emigrated to America in 1926.

Nonetheless, to label Ayn Rand as a conservative is inaccurate because it implies that conservatism (in the traditional religion-based sense) is the only alternative to statism. She regarded such a choice as a false alternative, akin to choosing between sadism and masochism. She despised conservatism because it disparages reason and exalts mysticism; because it denounces egoism and praises altruism; and because, while it condemns statism, it endorses capitalism only partially and grudgingly. The essence of conservatism, she held, is the belief that faith and revelation are superior to reason as the source of human knowledge; that morality requires individuals to sacrifice themselves to others; and that capitalism, far from being an ideal social system, is merely the best option available to human beings who are thoroughly tainted by original sin.

In her writings, Ayn Rand created a systematic alternative to both statism and conservatism because, as she wrote, "It is useless to be against anything, unless one knows what one is for. A merely negative stand is always futile." Though she called herself a "radical for capitalism," her advocacy of capitalism was not the starting point of her philosophy. To the contrary, she wrote: "I shall say that I am not primarily an advocate of capitalism, but of egoism; and I am not primarily an advocate of egoism, but of reason. If one recognizes the supremacy of reason and applies it consistently, all the rest follows. This—the supremacy of reason—was, is and will be the primary concern of my work, and the essence of Objectivism.... Reason in epistemology leads to egoism in ethics, which leads to capitalism in politics." Objectivism, in short, advocated reason, individualism, man's rights, limited government, and complete laissez-faire capitalism.

Ayn Rand initially achieved fame as a novelist. Her career as the publisher and editor of three periodicals built on the earlier success of her works of fiction. Her first two novels, *We the Living* (1936) and *Anthem* (1938), drew almost no notice in America during an era when the country was rapidly drifting toward collectivism. But her third novel, *The Fountainhead* (1943), was a bestseller, though it had attracted only a few enthusiastic reviews. It was literally a word-of-mouth success: readers who loved the intransigent independence of the novel's hero, Howard Roark, recommended it enthusiastically to others. Many people first encountered *The Fountainhead* when a friend or classmate or relative thrust a copy into their hands, saying, "You must read this! It will change your whole life!"

The success of Rand's fourth novel, *Atlas Shrugged* (1957), followed the same pattern. Despite savagely critical reviews in liberal and conservative publications alike (the *New York Times* and *National Review*, for example), *Atlas Shrugged* sold more that 125,000 copies within a year of its publication. Ayn Rand became a personal hero for thousands of college students and young professionals. They found her philosophy offered an alternative to the bankrupt ideals of statism and religious conservatism. She was inundated with letters from readers, but was able to answer only a few personally. However, all of her fan mail was carefully saved, and the names were used as the mailing list to announce the start of a lecture series on Objectivism in February 1959. These lectures were a major step toward disseminating her philosophy in nonfiction form and thus, eventually, to the creation of her three periodicals.

The twenty lectures on "Basic Principles of Objectivism" were given by Nathaniel Branden, a Canadian-born psychologist who had met Ayn Rand in 1950 when he was a nineteen-year-old student at the University of California at Los Angeles. Twenty-eight people enrolled for the first series, attracted not only by the course material but by the opportunity to see and hear Ayn Rand. She joined Branden for the question periods that followed each lecture.

Under the organizational auspices of Nathaniel Branden Lectures, ads for the series were run in the *New York Times*'s Sunday edition. Over the next two years, enrollment grew each time the course was offered, and news of the series spread throughout the country. To announce the availability of the lectures on tape, a series of ads began to run in major college and urban newspapers throughout America, addressed "To the Readers and Admirers of *Atlas Shrugged* and *The Fountainhead*." By late 1961, a master mailing list of over 10,000 people interested in Objectivism had been compiled.

Based on this explosive growth of interest in Objectivism, Rand and Branden decided to launch a journal of ideas devoted to applying her philosophy to the problems and issues of contemporary American culture. The *Objectivist Newsletter*, a four-page monthly, was first published in January 1962. Occasionally Rand and Branden wrote the whole issue, but usually only two-thirds of it. Other contributors included Barbara Branden, Leonard Peikoff, Edith Efron, Alan Greenspan, Robert Hessen, and Joan Mitchell Blumenthal. Articles on ethics, epistemology, economics, and psychology were dominant, but other subjects—aesthetics, education, and political theory—also were represented. Ayn Rand personally edited every article in every issue.

In her articles on politicoeconomic issues, Ayn Rand repeatedly attacked the antitrust laws as being non-Objective and irrational. She also rejected the concept of consumer protection laws and of government regulation of the airwaves. Similarly, Branden wrote several articles debunking common misconceptions about capitalism and challenging the arguments used to justify government regulation of the economy. He denied, for example, that capitalism leads to cyclical depressions or to oppressive monopolies, and he rejected the concept of compulsory labor unions, tax-supported schools, and laws restricting inheritance. While rejecting statism, Rand and Branden also sharply attacked the theory of anarchism (or competing private defense agencies) that some libertarian theorists were advocating. Some of Rand's most stinging assaults—as passionate as those she leveled against the conservatives—were directed against the libertarians, especially those who claimed that her writings were the inspiration for their anarchist and subjectivist beliefs.

One of the *Newsletter*'s most popular features was its "Intellectual Ammunition Department," which answered questions sent in by subscribers. Particular attention was given to questions involving personal choices and dilemmas in a society increasingly dominated by irrationalism and collectivism. For example, Ayn Rand addressed issues such as, "Doesn't life require compromise?" and "How does one lead a rational life in an irrational society, such as we have today?"

Most issues of the *Newsletter* contained a book review, but with a unique feature: the only books reviewed were those that could be recommended favorably. These included the works of free market economists Ludwig von Mises and Henry Hazlitt, and the novels of Victor Hugo and Mickey Spillane. Nevertheless, the reviewers identified any premises or conclusions of the books' authors that were not philosophically consistent with Objectivism. These disclaimers made it possible to publicize and promote books that were not written by Objectivists, while still carefully differentiating Objectivism from other philosophies with which it shared some values.

Each issue also contained the "Objectivist Calendar," listing forthcoming public lectures or radio and television appearances by Rand and Branden; new editions or printings or translations of Ayn Rand's novels; announcements of cities where the taped lectures on Objectivism could be heard; the creation of new courses applying Objectivism to the fields of psychology, history of philosophy, economics, and efficient thinking; the activities of various Ayn Rand Clubs or Study Groups on college campuses; and news of musical or dance recitals, or art exhibits, or plays directed or performed by "students of objectvism." (This term was used to signify the fact that Ayn Rand did not personally endorse every group or event announced in the *Newsletter*.)

Two years after it began publication, the circulation of the *Objectivist Newsletter* exceeded 5,000. Similarly, the lecture courses on Objectivism were being offered in more than thirty cities by the end of 1963, and enrollment reached 2,500 students.

During the next two years, the circulation of the *Newsletter* continued to grow, especially after the publicity generated by an interview with Ayn Rand in *Playboy* (March 1964). Late in 1965, Rand and Branden decided to change format, and the first issue of a sixteen-page monthly magazine, the *Objectivist*, appeared in January 1966. By the end of that year, the number of paid subscribers reached 21,000.

Several factors, besides the *Playboy* interview, contributed to the dramatic increase in circulation. Rand and Branden were frequent speakers on college campuses; she was interviewed on the leading television talk shows; and she had her own regular radio shows, *Ayn Rand on Campus*, at Columbia University and *Commentary* on an FM station in New York City. All of her appearances and broadcasts publicized her role as publisher and editor of the *Objectivist Newsletter* and, later, the *Objectivist*. In addition, each of her paperback books (which collectively sold several hundred thousand copies each year) contained a bind-in card advertising her periodicals. And several topical anthologies from past issues were published in both hardcover and paperback editions (e.g., *The Virtue of Selfishness* in 1964 and *Capitalism: The Unknown Ideal* in 1966), thereby acquainting thousands of new readers with the original source.

The new sixteen-page format made it possible to undertake longer and more ambitious articles. Certainly the most complex and profoundly original was an eight-part essay, "Introduction to Objectivist Epistemology," in which Ayn Rand presented a new theory of concept formation. It was the long-awaited validation of reason she had been promising for years. Soon after, Leonard Peikoff wrote a five-part article challenging the validity of the analytic-synthetic dichotomy.

These were the most intricate examples of formal philosophy ever to appear in the *Objectivist*. Most other articles were so-called middle-range—neither journalism nor technical philosophical analysis. Rather they were intended, as Ayn Rand noted, "to discuss the application of Objectivism to modern events—i.e., to explain today's trends by identifying their philosophical roots and meaning, and to present the Objectivist alternative." This purpose was carried out in articles like "The Comprachicos" by Ayn Rand (analyzing how modern education is destroying the ability of students to think); "The Montessori Method" by Beatrice Hessen (explaining why Maria Montessori's philosophy of education is superior to John Dewey's pragmatist-progressive theories); "Platonic Competition" by George Reisman (arguing the irrationality of one of modern economic theory's fundamental concepts); "Herbert Marcuse: Philosopher of the New Left" by George Walsh (exposing the arbitrary and contradictory ideas of the influential Marxist-Freudian theorist); "The Base of Objectivist Psychotherapy" by Allan Blumenthal (delineating a new approach to mental health and self-actualization); "Self-Esteem" by Nathaniel Branden (defining a new standard of psychological well-being); "The Constitution and the Draft" by Henry Mark Holzer and Erika Holzer (arguing the unconstitutionality of conscription); "Who Programs the Programmers?" by Susan Ludel (showing that the leftist views of broadcast journalists are not the result of conscious bias or willful distortion, but of deep-seated philosophical premises); and a series by Kay Nolte Smith, identifying the irrationalism rampant in modern drama and extolling playwrights of the Romantic school, such as Henrik Ibsen and Terence Rattigan. The enlarged format also enabled the *Objectivist* to publish the first installments of a major work-in-progress, Leonard Peikoff's book, *The Ominous Parallels*, in which he traced the role of philosophy (specifically Kantian epistemology and ethics) in paving the way for Adolf Hitler to transform Germany into a Nazi dictatorship.

In mid-1968, there was an unprecedented lapse in the *Objectivist*'s monthly publication schedule. When the May issue finally appeared in late September, it contained an article by Ayn Rand entitled "To Whom It May Concern." She announced that "Nathaniel and Barbara Branden are no longer associated with this magazine, with me or with my philosophy." This break occurred, she explained, as a result of irreconcilable personal and philosophical differences between herself and them.

Branden ceased to be copublisher and coeditor of the magazine, which only recently had been relocated in spacious new offices (shared with his lecture institute) in the Empire State Building. Following the break, he closed the institute and moved to California. The *Objectivist* continued publication, but was moved to more modest offices. Subsequently Leonard Peikoff, a former philosophy professor, became associate editor of the *Objectivist*. He also began to offer courses on Objectivism in New York and, on tape, to groups throughout the United States and abroad.

In 1971, Ayn Rand made another change in the format of her magazine. She had witnessed the success of several newsletters written by controversial commentators on the American scene (e.g., Marshall McLuhan), and she was persuaded that by adopting a newsletter format, she could reach a larger audience for her ideas. The new name for her publication became the *Ayn Rand Letter*. It was a fortnightly, consisting of four or six pages per issue, and typewritten rather than typeset to reduce the time between writing and publication. She undertook an extensive promotional campaign to increase the *Letter*'s circulation, but her expectations were not met. She lost a large number of subscribers when the subscription price rose from $5.00 for the *Objectivist* to $36.00 for the *Letter* (even though a special reduced rate was available for college students who otherwise might not have been able to afford a subscription).

Given the title of her new publication and its high price, Ayn Rand believed that she should be the sole author. A total of eighty-one issues was published between October 1971 and February 1976, and she wrote them all, with the exception of three two-part articles drawn from Leonard Peikoff's *The Ominous Parallels*. She had no reason to doubt her ability to fulfill her fortnightly deadlines; she was in excellent health, and possessed an incredible energy and flow of ideas.

Ayn Rand wrote seventy-five issues of the *Letter*, covering a broad range of her ideas and values. The theme uniting her articles was her conviction that philosophy is the primary force shaping human affairs, that no one can act without a philosophy, that the only choice is whether to hold an explicit, rational philosophy or an implicit one, which is a random grab-bag of half-truths, contradictions, and clichés. She also developed the theme that contemporary liberalism and religious conservatism, though nominally adversaries, were really united in their hostility to reason, that both favored coercing individuals, and that they merely differ on the areas in which coercion was proper. She viewed the liberals as seeking to impose coercion on economic behavior (e.g., wage and price controls or antitrust laws), while the conservatives would stress its use in the area of personal morals (e.g., bans on abortion and contraception and censorship of obscenity and pornography).

Ayn Rand repeatedly challenged the Supreme Court's rulings on obscenity, rejecting all forms of censorship as "thought control." She sharply attacked a prominent conservative economist who had endorsed government regulation of the press on the grounds that since the market for goods and the market for ideas are not clearly distinguishable, then if the government has a right to control the former, it has a right to regulate the latter too. By contrast, she held that government has no right to impose controls over either economic liberty or intellectual freedom, a viewpoint that estranged her from liberals and conservatives alike.

Ayn Rand was sharply critical of Richard Nixon. She denounced his 1971 wage and price freeze policy as a "moratorium on brains" and regarded his normalization of relations between the United States and communist China as a sellout of all the principles he claimed to uphold. She noted the paradox that if these same policies had been pursued by a liberal Democrat rather than a conservative Republican, there would have been cries of outrage and calls for impeachment, instead of tacit approval or silence from the business community and other citadels of conservatism.

She also turned her critical fire on two of the most highly acclaimed books of the 1970s, B. F. Skinner's *Beyond Freedom and Dignity* and John Rawls's *A Theory of Justice*. She argued that at the root of both books were theories—behaviorism and egalitarianism, respectively—that were fundamentally irrational and incompatible with individual liberty. In other articles, she lamented the end of the Apollo space program, viewing it as a rejection of progress; she proposed the creation of tax credits for education in order to break up the government's monopoly in education; she called for the end of government funding of cultural events; and she argued that government controls were the cause of the energy crisis.

For the first two and a half years of its existence, the *Ayn Rand Letter* met its publication schedule without major problems or delays. Then two unforeseen developments forced Ayn Rand to fall far behind schedule. The first occurred when she learned that a younger sister, whom she had not seen since she emigrated in 1926, was alive in Moscow nearly fifty years later. The sister had visited an American cultural exhibition and was struck by the resemblance between Ayn

Rand's photograph and her memory of her older sister's face. After an elaborate, time-consuming process of authenticating the identity of her long-lost sister, Ayn Rand invited her to visit New York. The drama of their reunion was quickly overshadowed by the profound differences in their philosophies of life. Nonetheless, Ayn Rand urged her sister to remain in America and never return to the yoke of Soviet tyranny, but her sister chose to "go home." This incident, stretching across eight months, took a heavy toll on her writing and publication schedule, which allocated no time for unexpected interruptions.

When she was able to resume regular publication, Ayn Rand hoped to catch up quickly with the issues that had been delayed, so each issue was dated when it should have appeared rather than on the actual date it did appear. The only indication of this unconventional dating was a brief postscript to some issues: "This *Letter* was written later than the date that appears on its heading." But these gaps were sometimes as long as eight months, creating the confusion of articles referring to events that occurred long after the date of the issue's publication.

Before she was able to make up all the late issues, Ayn Rand was struck by a severe illness late in 1974. She required surgery and a long period of convalescence. It became increasingly improbable that she ever would be able to meet her twice-a-month writing deadlines without taxing her energy and health beyond endurance. She informed her subscribers in April 1975 that "in view of the lengthy delay in our publication schedule, I am presently working out a change of format for the *Letter*." A month later, an announcement stated that the *Letter* would become a monthly publication, but even that level of output soon proved too demanding. In the December 1975 issue, Ayn Rand revealed her decision to discontinue the *Letter*.

Her decision did not mean, she explained, that she was retiring. Rather she indicated her plan was to return full time to her career as a novelist and philosopher, as well as continue to give public lectures and television interviews occasionally. Although she did not complete any new work of fiction, she did deliver three lectures at the Ford Hall Forum in Boston (an annual tradition which she had begun in 1961), and one in New Orleans in November 1981.

Before her death in March 1982, at the age of seventy-seven, she planned one last anthology—*Philosophy: Who Needs It*—drawn from her periodical writings, the sixth in a series including *The Virtue of Selfishness*; *Capitalism: The Unknown Ideal*; *The Romantic Manifesto*; *The New Left: The Anti-Industrial Revolution*; and *Introduction to Objectivist Epistemology*.

Several other books by Ayn Rand appeared later, edited by Leonard Peikoff, the executor of her estate. The first of these works, *The Early Ayn Rand*, an anthology of her unpublished short stories and stage plays, was published in 1984. A 700-page selection, *Letters of Ayn Rand*, edited by M. S. Berliner, was published in 1995. Other projected books include her lectures on fiction and nonfiction writing, as well as her literary journals.

For more than twenty consecutive years, Ayn Rand's books, including the six derived from her magazines and her four novels, have sold more than 500,000 copies annually in the United States. As long as her works are widely accessible, as long as new generations of young intellectuals find her ideals appealing and inspiring, her philosophy will continue to challenge the tenets of statism, liberalism, and conservatism alike.

Information Sources

BIBLIOGRAPHY:

Branden, Barbara. *The Passion of Ayn Rand: A Biography*. New York, 1966.

INDEXES: *PAIS*.

REPRINT EDITIONS: Microform: UMI (1962–1971). Bound edition: available from Laissez Faire Books, San Francisco, California.

LOCATION SOURCES: Widely available.

Publication History

TITLE AND TITLE CHANGES: *The Objectivist Newsletter*, January 1962–December 1965; *The Objectivist*, January 1966–September 1971; *The Ayn Rand Letter*, October 1971– February 1976.

VOLUME AND ISSUE DATA: Volumes 1–10, January 1962–September 1971; volumes 1– 4, October 1971–January–February 1976. No number issued for September 1975; combined numbers issued for November–December 1975 and January–February 1976.

FREQUENCY OF PUBLICATION: Monthly, January 1962–September 1971; fortnightly, October 1971–September 1974; monthly, October 1974–February 1976.

PUBLISHERS: 1962–1965: The Objectivist Newsletter, Inc.; 1966–1971: The Objectivist, Inc.; 1971–1976: The Ayn Rand Letter, Inc. All in New York.

EDITORS: Ayn Rand and Nathaniel Branden, January 1961–July 1968; thereafter, Ayn Rand.

CIRCULATION: At peak, 18,000–22,000.

Robert Hessen

Fragments
1963–

Fragments is a quarterly magazine dedicated to the promotion of individual freedom. The first issue of *Fragments* was published in 1963. From 1963 through 1967, *Fragments* appeared regularly four times a year. In 1968 publication was suspended, although one issue did appear in 1975 and another in 1979. In 1980–1981 publication was resumed, but several issues appeared months late, often with accompanying letters appealing for funds.

Most of *Fragments*' editors and several of its contributors taught at the Henry George School, which educates people in the philosophy of Henry George. Founded in New York in 1932, the school has branches in several cities, including Boston, Philadelphia, Los Angeles, and San Francisco.

Jack Schwartzman, chairman of the board of editors since the first issue, is an attorney, a former instructor at the Henry George School, and professor of English at Nassau Community College. Other founding editors were Frank Chodorov (d. 1966), a prominent libertarian theorist and former director of the Henry George School; George B. Bringmann (d. 1977), a poet, essayist, and instructor at the Henry George School; Herbert Shelley Good (d. 1967), a writer and instructor at the Henry George School; Leonard F. Kleinfeld, an importer-exporter and in 1972 and 1973 president of the Henry David Thoreau Society; and Sydney Mayers, an attorney and instructor at the Henry George School and a member of the school's board of trustees. Herbert C. Roseman, who taught English at Nassau Community College for a short while, joined the editorial board in 1967 and left in 1970. Oscar B. Johannsen, vice-president of the Henry George School and executive director of the Robert Schalkenbach Foundation, publisher of Henry George's works, also joined the board of editors in 1967 and continues to serve. The objectives of *Fragments* were stated in the first issue:

The magazine seeks to promote a wider understanding and acceptance of the fact that as LIBERTY increases so does the life of each individual reach a greater merited fulfillment.

FRAGMENTS has no interest in partisan politics as such, but as a matter of principle it is opposed to authoritarian ideologies wherever these arise. The publishers and editors of FRAGMENTS believe it is unique in that it attempts to meet the special needs of reflective individuals who apply ethical principles in appraising the affairs of men and nations.[1]

The individualist and antistatist philosophy of *Fragments* owes much to the thought of Frank Chodorov, one of the founding editors. Born in New York in 1887 of Russian-Jewish parents who had just fled from czarist oppression, Chodorov attended the public schools of New York and was graduated from Columbia University in 1907. An early rebel against religion, Chodorov embraced the militant agnosticism of Robert Ingersoll. But after 1915 his antireligious crusade ended, for he had found a new mentor in Henry George. From George's *Progress and Poverty* and other works, Chodorov derived the idea that social conflicts and hatreds stem from poverty and the fear of poverty. From George he also acquired the conviction that there are standards of justice to which all men should adhere and natural rights that governments must not violate. Furthermore, Chodorov adopted George's remedy for poverty—the single tax on land values.

In 1936 Chodorov met Albert Jay Nock, whose libertarian philosophy had led him to leave the Episcopal ministry in 1909, after twelve years of service. Under Nock's tutelage, Chodorov concentrated on George's advocacy of individual freedom and hostility to the state. In 1937, Chodorov became director of the Henry George School and editor of the *Freeman*, the school's newspaper. He used the *Freeman* as a platform to attack government policies that threatened individual liberty, accusing the Roosevelt administration of extending the federal government's power beyond that permitted by the Constitution and warning that American involvement in the war against the Axis powers would lead to the destruction of democracy. He held that conscription was "a complete denial of man's inalienable right to life, liberty, and the pursuit of happiness."[2]

Ousted from the Henry George School in February 1942 because of his opposition to the war, Chodorov in 1944 published *analysis*, a monthly paper devoted to a libertarian interpretation of current events. In a promotional letter prepared prior to publication, Chodorov stated the purpose of the periodical:

analysis goes along with Albert Jay Nock in asserting that the State is our enemy, that its administrators and beneficiaries are a professional criminal class; and interprets events accordingly. It is radical not reformist. In short, *analysis* looks at the current scene through the eyeglass of historic liberalism, unashamedly accepting the doctrine of natural rights, proclaims the dignity of the individual and denounces all forms of Statism as human slavery.[3]

In 1953 Chodorov founded the Intercollegiate Society of Individualists in order to challenge the collectivist philosophy that he believed dominated American education. William F. Buckley, Jr., served as the first president,[4] and a year later he published *God and Man at Yale,* which expressed several of Chodorov's basic principles. As Buckley's early mentor (they later came to disagree over the role and necessity of the state) Chodorov served on the staff of the *National Review*, which was founded in 1955. *Fragments* published several pieces by Chodorov, often reprints of articles that had appeared in *analysis*, and dedicated two memorial issues to him after his death in 1966. The editors of *Fragments* and several other writers, including Buckley, paid tribute to Chodorov. Jack Schwartzman lauded Chodorov for teaching and radiating the philosophy that "so long as any one person still thinks in terms of 'inalienable rights,' or 'natural law,' or the eternal 'I,' to that extent the dignity of man can never be diminished; to that extent the yearning for freedom can never be extinguished."[5] George B. Bringmann, another founding editor, described Chodorov as a "warm-hearted, earthy human being of magnificent intellect with a non-conforming, deeply religious spirit.... He spurred the spirit of freedom in many souls [and] caused many to think as free men."[6]

Fragments honored other thinkers who valued personal liberty and individual expression, among them Paine, Thoreau, Henry George, H. L. Mencken, and Nock. In 1945 Leonard F. Kleinfeld expressed his debt to Thoreau for proclaiming the divinity of all men, for realizing that "each person had to follow a path of his own toward his individual horizon," and for holding that "obedience to conscience is only...reliance on one's own strength."[7] Thoreau, said Kleinfeld in an earlier piece, taught that "man should not be dependent on society. He should have such an emotional self-sufficiency as would tide him over the crises of his days.... He felt that only as individual men did men seem respectable. In the mass, their worst and most destructive features were brought into prominence."[8]

Paine was lauded for his humanitarianism, his advocacy of natural rights, and his hostility to government. Herbert C. Roseman praised Paine's radicalism:

The man who said, "The trade of governing has always been monopolized by the most ignorant and rascally individuals of mankind," is still valid when we are caught between the contending varieties of national socialism. It little matters whether we are governed by the feudal fascism of an Eastland or Wallace or the Negro commune. To the libertarian, the tyranny of both is oppressive.... Neither the fascist nor Communist nor Socialist nor coercive capitalist nor modern liberal is interested in Justice or Mutuality which is the idea Thomas Paine and the Real Radical Tradition uphold.[9]

Oscar B. Johannsen praised Paine for his "careful reasoning," for his courage in propagating ideas "regardless of the cost to himself," and for anticipating Henry George's theory of land tenure. In *Agrarian Justice* (1797) Paine declared that "man did not make the earth, and though he had a natural right to occupy it, he had no right to locate as his property in perpetuity any part of it; neither did the Creator of the earth open a land-office from whence the first title deeds should issue.[10] This idea, said Johannsen, was a core principle of George's *Progress and Poverty*.

In an issue honoring Henry George, Sydney Mayers lamented that "the tangible results of George's noble teachings are sadly sparse," and urged the propagation of George's ideas "as an inspired...intellectual pursuit with a practical and beneficial goal in mind."[11] Several writers held that George's land valuation tax still was an answer to America's economic woes. Irving Starer, associate editor of *Fragments* and a former instructor at the Henry George School, believed that such a tax:

would bring about the removal of taxes on wages and interest, and on private property, which in turn would stimulate production, expand employment, and raise the general level of wages. The elimination of taxes (save that on land values, which is not truly a tax, but rather the collection of economic rent) would substantially simplify government and reduce its cost....The cause of the economic problems of our complex industrial society having been determined, and Henry George's logical remedy having been revealed, all that remains for us to do is to adopt and apply the remedy, and obtain its salutary effects.[12]

Fragments' editorial philosophy generally blended libertarian and Georgist ideas. In his article "Georgism: True Libertarianism," Johannsen not only paid tribute to Henry George, he also gave expression to the essential ideals advocated by *Fragments*. Johannsen denounced the state as a barrier to human well-being and freedom and rejected "the apologia that the state is required for the protection of life and property, the construction of roads and highways, and the adjudication of disputes.... All such activities can be, and today, in one degree or another, are being supplied by private enterprise, and much more efficiently and with less cost."[13] But Johannsen also saw a "fatal flaw" in libertarian thought, namely, "its defense of private property in land."[14] Land represents opportunity, but it is of unequal value:

Who shall have access to the gold mine, who to the inferior land?...When men confront this problem and seek to solve it, they begin dimly to perceive why anarchists are in error in seeking the abolition of the state. The state is not necessary for protection of life and property and the panoply of functions ordinarily ascribed to it. However, some government is necessary justly to allocate the unequal opportunities of the land among the equal claimants to it.... Land can be allocated among all equal claimants to it with justice by that objectivity which we call government.

...Government must be barely above the family level, [however], probably on the order of the New England Town Hall Governments. The land area and the number of people involved must be small enough so that all members of the community know the land and one another.

The libertarian ideology thus requires that it be corrected to recognize that not only man but land cannot justly be private property. While government can never be abolished, it must be on the lowest possible level. Such an amended version may some day be recognized as true libertarianism. This is Georgism. Therefore, true libertarianism is Georgism.[15]

Unlike the *Libertarian Forum*, another libertarian publication, *Fragments* generally eschewed discussions of contemporary political and social issues. The Vietnam War, the Arab-Israeli conflict, the arms race, Watergate, racial tensions, crime, poverty, and other pressing problems of the 1960s and 1970s were rarely, if ever, treated in the pages of *Fragments*. The editors chose instead to discuss the broader themes of freedom, individualism, and morality.

Although contributors were not restricted to a single viewpoint, they generally adhered to the libertarian principle that individual freedom and independent thought and action were threatened by a growing collectivism. They believed that the individual's right to his person was constantly menaced by big government. In the tradition of early nineteenth-century liberals, *Fragments* sought to promote individual liberty by setting limits to the power of the state. It saw liberty, in the words of Johannsen, as "equality of opportunity [and] the freedom to act as long as one does not interfere with the right of others to act,"[16] and sought a society in which the individual would develop his creative and moral faculties to the utmost. In a special issue devoted to an examination of individualism, *Fragments* stated its essential philosophy: "FRAGMENTS, the self-styled 'world's greatest individualistic magazine,' examines...the various shades and meanings of individualism. More than ever, as collectivism 'creeps' across the globe, it is necessary to re-examine the values that maintain the supremacy of the individual."[17] Jack Schwartzman's article, "It Takes One," exemplified this position: "The world is composed of but two kinds of people: socialists and me. Socialists are trying to persuade me that I must be governed. I am trying to persuade them to leave me alone....I walk on my own two feet, and...my immortal spirit leaps to its goal.... My neck is my own, and...I have a right to break it."[18] In an earlier essay Schwartzman attacked Marxists for destroying the individual in order to realize their collectivist vision. Addressing himself to all statists and collectivists, Schwartzman declared: "I am an individual. I possess an individual soul. I live an immortal life. I owe allegiance to no man....I believe in God. I recognize no interloper between God and me. If I yearn for a union with the One, it is a union which preserves my individuality....I recognize no man-made Omnipotence, no SuperState, no 'historical' Necessity, no human Absoluteness. I exist. I know. I am. I. The Individual."[19] Man's right to freedom of person, said Schwartzman, gives him "the unqualified right to go to hell—if he so desires."[20] Therefore, concluded Schwartzman in typical libertarian fashion, there should be no restraint on the sale of weapons, drugs, and pornography, and no interference with the dissemination of "Communist, Nazi, atheistic, and other...poisonous ideas."[21] The editors of and contributors to *Fragments*, of course, did not endorse drugs and pornography and were not gun enthusiasts. Their hatred of communism and fascism was a logical extension of their hostility to statism and collectivism. But they were committed to the libertarian principle that the state should not meddle in the affairs of the individual even when he or she engages in reprehensible acts, as long as the rights of others are not violated.

Other contributors expressed similar individualist and antistatist sentiments. "All the heads of States are thieves and usurpers," declared Kleinfeld. "Let people go back to doing as they damn please! Let humans be free!"[22] Admiral Ben Moreell (retired) attacked the New Deal, the Fair Deal, and the New Frontier for enhancing state power. "The 'Giant State' breeds 'pygmy men,'" warned Moreell. Americans are forsaking God and "in His place we are building a graven image, The Giant State."[23]

Oscar B. Johannsen believed that attacks on big government must be combined with sound suggestions for economic reform. Nineteenth-century radicals—Josiah Warren, Lysander Spooner, and Benjamin R. Tucker—were unable to stem the growth of the state's power because of "the faulty economic underpinning of...their work....As with most of today's libertarian thinkers they were most adept in criticizing the invasion of privacy and in decrying the loss of freedom. But practical economic policies seemed to elude them." Johannsen wanted libertarians to be guided by Georgist economic principles.[24]

In addition to decrying the mushrooming power of the state and championing the cause of individual liberty, several articles in *Fragments* called for renewing a commitment to absolute values. Kleinfeld declared that "man is a religious being whose first duty is to the higher law of God....Moral responsibility must take precedence over civil responsibility. Man has to live in the world according to his conscience, and not to collaborate with unjust laws."[25] In the tradition of the ancient Stoics, Schwartzman held that absolute values are part of the natural order; they are immanent in the universe and can be grasped through reason. But no state can compel obedience to these standards; no laws can achieve their realization. They are discovered and realized by individuals themselves.

The contributors to *Fragments* expressed great confidence in the capacity of man to improve himself through education. In a piece entitled "Natural Law and the Age of Illiteracy," Schwartzman blamed the deterioration of American education on "the abnegation of absolute values of human life and thought, in the sneering denials of Natural Law" and hoped "that permanent and immutable standards will again...be rediscovered...will again be sought, found, and treasured in all parts of the globe."[26]

Frank Chodorov once said that "anyone who calls me a conservative deserves a punch in the nose." No doubt the editors of *Fragments* would also reject the conservative label, for there are fundamental differences between the conservative and libertarian outlooks. But there are also points of convergence. Both conservatives and libertarians share a common disdain for the intervention of government in the affairs of citizens. Both call such intervention statism, socialism, or collectivism and condemn it in the name of individual freedom, including economic freedom. Historically both libertarians and some conservatives opposed American intervention in foreign wars. In recent years, however, conservatives, who see communism as an international movement that threatens American security and values, have broken with traditional conservatism. Schwartzman interprets the essential relationship between conservatism and the libertarian philosophy that *Fragments* represents: "*Fragments* is conservative in the sense of conserving the traditional values of life: the belief in universals, in absolutes, in Natural Law, and in the adherence to the concepts of the dignity, worth, and true essence of the individual. *Fragments* is libertarian to the extent of pursuing the goals of liberty, laissez faire, and non-intervention. *Fragments* is not timely; it is timeless."[27]

Fragments is well known in libertarian, Georgist, and Thoreauvian circles. It provided an outlet for several libertarians to express an individualistic philosophy and to pay tribute to thinkers from Paine to Nock who championed liberty. In particular, it gave expression to the economic and political philosophy of Henry George. *Fragments* generally eschewed a discussion of current issues, dedicating itself instead to the revitalization of moral values and individual liberty. Its fundamental philosophy and objectives remained constant during two decades of irregular publication.

Notes

1. *Fragments* 1 (January–March 1963): 2.

2. Frank Chodorov, "Truth Faces War Hysteria," *The Freeman* (August 1940): 28, cited in Charles G. Nitsche, "Albert Jay Nock and Frank Chodorov: Case Studies in Recent American Individualist and Anti-Statist Thought" (Ph.D. dissertation, University of Maryland, 1981).

3. Quoted in Nitsche, "Albert Jay Nock and Frank Chodorov," p. 97.

4. Buckley recalled: "I was purely a figurehead, as I was soon reminded. In short order I had a letter from him: 'Am removing you as president. Making myself pres. Easier to raise money if a Jew is president. You can be V-P. Love, Frank.'" William F. Buckley, Jr., "Death of a Teacher," *Fragments* 4 (October–December 1966): 3.

5. Jack Schwartzman, "A Letter to Frank," *Fragments* 4 (October–December 1966): 6.

6. George B. Bringmann, "Papa Chodorov," *Fragments* 4 (October–December 1966): 10.

7. Leonard F. Kleinfeld, "There Is More Divinity in Man Than in God," *Fragments* 3 (July–September 1965): 1.

8. Leonard F. Kleinfeld, "Thoreau's Pursuit of Happiness," *Fragments* 1 (April–June 1963): 3.

9. Herbert C. Roseman, "Thoughts on Paine," *Fragments* 5 (October–December 1967): 6.

10. Oscar B. Johannsen, "Agrarian Justice," *Fragments* 5 (October–December 1967): 2.

11. Sydney B. Mayers, "A Century of P & P," *Fragments* [14] (1976–1979): 10.

12. Irving Starer, "The Cause and the Remedy," *Fragments* [14] (1976–1979): 10.

13. Oscar B. Johannsen, "Georgism: True Libertarianism," *Fragments* [14] (1976–1979): 4.

14. Ibid.

15. Ibid.

16. Ibid.

17. *Fragments* [15] (January–March 1980): 1.

18. Jack Schwartzman, "It Takes One," *Fragments* 3 (September–December 1965): 5.

19. Jack Schwartzman, "The Omelet and the Eggs," *Fragments* 1 (April–June 1963): 4.

20. Jack Schwartzman, "The Devil and the Reformers," *Fragments* 2 (January–March 1964): 5.

21. Ibid., p. 4.

22. Leonard F. Kleinfeld, "And Speaking about Rights," *Fragments* 2 (April–June 1964): 7.

23. Ben Moreell, "Be Ye Doers of the Word," *Fragments* 2 (July–September 1964): 4.

24. Oscar B. Johannsen, "Men against the State," *Fragments* [15] (April–June 1980): 1.

25. Leonard F. Kleinfeld, "State or Government: Take Your Choice," *Fragments* 3 (September–December 1965): 7.

26. Jack Schwartzman, "Natural Law and the Age of Illiteracy," *Fragments* [15] (April–June 1980): 5.

27. Interview with Jack Schwartzman, 12 April 1983.

Information Sources

BIBLIOGRAPHY:

Chodorov, Frank. *One Is a Crowd: Reflections of an Individualist*. New York, 1952.

Johannsen, Oscar B. *Private Schools for All*. N.p., n.d.

Schwartzman, Jack. *Rebels of Individualism*. New York, 1949.
INDEXES: None.
REPRINT EDITIONS: None.
LOCATION SOURCES: Complete runs: Library of Congress; Wisconsin State Historical
    Society; Henry George School, New York; New York Public Library; University of
    California, Berkeley; Concord, Massachusetts, Public Library; British Museum,
    London, England.

Publication History

TITLE AND TITLE CHANGES: *Fragments*.
VOLUME AND ISSUE DATA: Volumes 1–current, 1963–present. Publication suspended
    1968–1974; only two numbers published 1975–1979; publication irregular 1980–
    present.
FREQUENCY OF PUBLICATION: Quarterly, 1963–1967; irregularly thereafter.
PUBLISHER: Fragments, Inc., Elmont (1963), Bellerose (1964–1967), and Floral Park
    (1968–present), all in New York.
EDITOR: Jack Schwartzman.
CIRCULATION: 1963: 1,000; 1967: 4,000; 1983: 2,888; 1986: 3,000.

Marvin Perry

Libertarian Forum
1969–1986

Believing that there was an acute need "for far more cohesion and inter-communication in the libertarian movement,"[1] Murray N. Rothbard[2] and Joseph R. Peden[3] founded the *Libertarian*, a semimonthly newsletter that first appeared on 1 March 1969. To avoid confusion with a mimeographed periodical of the same name published in New Jersey, on 15 June 1969 the name was changed to the *Libertarian Forum*. To reduce costs, in January 1971 the newsletter was changed from a four-page bimonthly to an eight-page monthly. Published irregularly in 1980 and 1981, the *Libertarian Forum* was reorganized in January 1982. An overburdened Peden, who had managed the newsletter's business affairs since its inception, changed from publisher to associate editor, and Daniel Rosenthal, a businessman and founder of *Silver and Gold Report*, a financial advisory newsletter, accepted the responsibilities of publisher. The *Libertarian Forum* never had a deficit, and circulation grew from 350 in 1969 to 750 in 1985.

The *Libertarian Forum* analyzed domestic and international affairs with the ultimate aim of transforming American society in accordance with libertarian principles. Although several libertarians contributed to the newsletter, Rothbard, a leading libertarian theorist, set editorial policy and wrote most of the articles. Born in New York City in 1926 and educated at Columbia University, Rothbard was a professor of economics at Polytechnic Institute of New York. He was a founder of the Free Libertarian party of New York and a member of the National Committee of the Libertarian party. Rothbard was greatly influenced by the individualist and antistatist thought of Albert Jay Nock and Frank Chodorov and the economic individualism of Ludwig von Mises.

The cardinal principle of Rothbard's libertarianism was that the individual is an independent entity who possesses an absolute right to his own person and property. According to this principle, each person is not only entitled to traditional civil liberties—freedom to speak, publish, and assemble—but is also free to engage in such "victimless crimes" as pornography, prostitution, and sexual deviation. Throughout history, said Rothbard, the principal aggressor on individual rights has been the state. It uses the draft to enslave, war to commit mass murder, and taxation to rob people of their property. To Rothbard, the state is "a criminal gang living off the robbery of tax coercion and using these funds to murder, pillage, enslave, and endow privileged groups with special privileges. The State is founded and has its very being in the use of aggressive violence."[4] In the tradition of nineteenth-century anarchists, Rothbard favored the destruction of the state.

In contrast to traditional advocates of laissez faire, Rothbard countenanced no form of taxation, even for financing police and fire departments, the courts, and armed forces. "If taxation is robbery, then surely it is robbery no matter the ends, benevolent or malevolent, for which the State employs these funds."[5] Also in contrast to laissez-faire conservatives, Rothbard felt no moral imperative to obey all laws and felt no patriotic devotion to the Constitution. If a law violates the rights of the individual, wrote Rothbard, one is not bound to obey it, although, to be sure, prudence might necessitate obedience. Rothbard held that the Articles of Confederation accorded with libertarian principles far more than does the Constitution. Also in contrast to traditional laissez-faire conservatives, Rothbard was severely critical of the "military-industrial complex" which he saw as "the greatest single force propelling the growth of the Leviathan State in America."[6]

Rothbard regarded isolationism in foreign affairs as the counterpart of laissez faire at home; in both instances the intention is to shackle government. Rothbard was particularly critical of American foreign policy:

Empirically, the *most* warlike, *most* interventionist, *most* imperial government throughout the twentieth century has been the United States. The expansionist impulse of the American State began to take increasing hold in the late nineteenth century; but it reached its full flower during and after World War I....Wilson's particular genius was to supply a pietistic and moralistic cloak around a policy of worldwide intervention and domination. In the name of "national self-determination" and collective security against aggression the American government has pursued a goal and a policy of world domination and forcible suppression of any rebellion against the *status quo*, anywhere in the world. In the name of combatting "aggression" everywhere—of being the world's "policeman"—it has itself become the great and permanent aggressor.[7]

Rothbard wanted the United States to "dismantle its bases, withdraw its troops, stop its political meddling, and abolish the CIA.... It should also end all foreign aid.... In short, to withdraw the United States totally within its own boundaries, and to maintain a policy of strict 'isolation' or neutrality everywhere."[8]

A crucial development in the shaping of the current libertarian movement— one that was prominently featured in the pages of the *Libertarian Forum*—was the biennial convention of the Young Americans for Freedom (YAF) held in St. Louis in August 1969. Founded at the home of William F. Buckley, Jr., in 1959, YAF generally supported the views of the *National Review*, the leading conservative journal. Within the ranks of the YAF, there emerged a libertarian minority whose viewpoint divided it from the main body. Strongly individualistic and antistate, the libertarians wanted government to confine itself solely to the defense of the individual and his property and advocated strict laissez faire in economic matters. Conservatives also disliked state intervention in the affairs of citizens but granted the necessity for government regulatory agencies, for government involvement in national defense, and for the state to preserve domestic order. The libertarians attacked *National Review* conservatives for a willingness to sacrifice personal liberty for the sake of political stability and national power. To the libertarians, the traditional conservatives were not opponents but defenders of state rule. The only liberty that the *National Review* conservatives were willing to grant, said Rothbard, "is a liberty within 'tradition,' within 'order,' in other words a weak and puny false imitation of liberty within a framework dictated by the State apparatus."[9]

On several issues the libertarians broke with YAF. Libertarians regarded prohibitions against abortion, censorship of offensive literature, and the repression of student radicals as violations of civil liberties. They viewed the outlawing of drugs, spending for space and defense programs, and an embargo on products from communist countries as violations of the free market economy.

At the August convention in St. Louis, the issues that led to a split between YAF and libertarians were Vietnam and the draft. The libertarians denounced the Vietnam War as a manifestation of American imperialism and called conscription a system of slavery and forced murder. YAF supported the war and considered treasonous the libertarian call for draft resistance, including fleeing to Canada. When a libertarian set fire to his draft card, the conservatives shouted, "Kill the commie!" "Kill the libertarians!"[10]

Sharing the views of the libertarians, the *Libertarian Forum* denounced YAF as "statists" and "centrists" who favored the extension of the state's power; as "despots" who supported the stifling of student demonstrators by the police; as "militarists" who sought to strengthen the military establishment; as "imperialists" and "warmongers" who justified the slaughter of American soldiers and Vietnamese peasants; as "theocrats" and "compulsory moralizers" who waged the cold war with missionary zeal and sought to impose their religiously conceived morality on others, in violation of the traditional separation of church and state.

As a result of the conflict with YAF, libertarians realized that they were a "separate and distinct ideological movement, and that in fact conservatism is one of their major enemies."[11] Purged from the conservative movement, the libertarians formed their own organizations. Rothbard and other libertarians, notably Karl Hess,[12] supported the break with the YAF and expressed their hostility to conservatism in the *Libertarian Forum*. A war of words erupted between libertarians and conservatives that extended to the op-ed page of the *New York Times*.

Jerome Tuccille, who wrote for the *Libertarian Forum*, accused the Buckley and Russell Kirk conservatives of waging an "unholy crusade"[13] to rid the world of communism; Rothbard denounced the *National Review* conservatives for abandoning the traditional conservative foreign policy for "militarism and empire," and chided them for supporting the space program—that "gigantic misinvestment." The policies championed by conservatives, said Rothbard, enhanced the coercive capacities of the state; the *National Review* conservatives "constitute some of the state's most articulate champions and apologists."[14] Buckley retorted that it is simple-minded not to believe that some state action is necessary and attacked Rothbard for his "extreme apriorism."[15]

Both conservatives and libertarians retained their hostility to contemporary liberalism, which Rothbard viewed as "flawed at its very core."[16] In the late eighteenth and early nineteenth centuries, liberals sought to preserve individual freedom by limiting the power of government. Twentieth-century liberals, however, in order to regulate the economy and implement social welfare programs, have vastly increased the state's power. The New Deal and post-New Deal administrations, said Rothbard, have

led to oppressive rule by oligarchic bureaucracies; the welfare state has become a State that subsidizes, controls, and pushes around the American public, and the poor more than most other groups. The welfare state has become the warfare state, the military-industrial garrison state, creating cartels, crippling individual and local initiative, and repressing the liberties of the citizenry. The liberal drive for racial integration by federal force has suddenly turned into a nightmare of race war; the vaunted democratization of America through the public school system has become a horror of crime, ignorance, and coercive oppression of the nation's school children....The cities are turning into jungles.[17]

Contemporary liberalism failed because its expansion of the authority and obligation of the state not only deprived the individual of liberty, but hindered economic and social progress.

Like Marxists, Rothbard regarded the state as an agent of privilege, a suppressor of liberty, and a barrier to progress. Like them, he sought the eventual destruction of the State. But here the similarity ended. No version of socialism, Rothbard argued, can create freedom or prosperity for the mass of the population, because all use "old-style despotic and collectivist means," which lead to totalitarianism.[18] "The very fact that every one of the socialist models—from Stalin to Hitler to Cambodia to Jonestown—has done so should particularly give democratic socialists considerable pause."[19] Marxism had its chance but failed.

Once the state is destroyed, said Rothbard, voluntary relationships will prevail. The delivery of mail, the maintenance of roads, the disposal of refuse, and the arresting and incarceration of criminals would be handled privately. Rothbard hardly pretended to have a blueprint for the future, just the general rule that the "free market will do the job infinitely better than the compulsory monopoly of bureaucratic government."[20] With the state eliminated, each person would be free to develop his or her own personal philosophy and pursue his or her own goals. As a "rationalist libertarian," Rothbard hoped that "the free man would use his liberty in accordance with a rational ethic derived from a rational study of the objective picture of man."[21]

Did the *Libertarian Forum* advocate a violent overthrow of the state? "Violence used against the state is moral," said the *Libertarian Forum*, "for it is the moral equivalent of using violence to protect one's person and property from armed marauders."[22] But for strategic and tactical reasons, the *Libertarian Forum* opposed an armed insurrection against the American government then or in the foreseeable future; it explicitly denounced ultraleft libertarians who called for the immediate destruction of existing society and whose craving for action led them in 1969 to engage in what Rothbard regarded as a self-defeating and suicidal march on Fort Dix. Rothbard viewed such "ultra-left adventurism as a major threat to the movement," for it alienated American public opinion.[23] The barricades are not the only way to wage revolutionary warfare. Rothbard saw libertarians as descendants of the liberal and radical revolutionary movements of the seventeenth, eighteenth, and nineteenth centuries. These movements consisted not only of activists but of "theorists and ideologists...Levellers...the philosophes, the physiocrats, the English radicals, the Patrick Henrys and Tom Paines...the James Mills and Cobdens...the Jacksonians and abolitionists, the Thoreaus....The barricades, while important, were just one small part of this great process."[24]

While rejecting the "frenzied nihilism" of the left-wing libertarians, Rothbard also criticized the right-wing libertarians who relied exclusively on education to bring down the state. To be sure, Rothbard considered it indispensable for libertarians to win converts through education: "Our major areas of concentration must be the study, the library, the press, the living room, the seminar, the lecture hall. We are primarily an educational movement or we are nothing."[25] But education alone would not produce a libertarian victory. Therefore, libertarians must employ flexible tactics and "adopt any tactic that seems likely to bring about the goal of liberty, any tactic, that is, that is not itself immoral and itself violates the libertarian creed."[26]

One successful model, said Rothbard, was the struggle for abortion reform. Utilizing the libertarian principle that every woman has the absolute right to control her own body, the woman's movement engaged in nonviolent civil disobedience and persuaded many women and physicians to ignore abortion laws. Pressured by demonstrations, petitions, and the threat of the ballot, politicians permitted abortion. The *Libertarian Forum* urged libertarians to involve themselves in crisis situations as they arise, guide people according to libertarian principles, and assist pressure groups. Unlike many other libertarians who regarded all political parties as part of the state apparatus and inimical to anarchist principles, Rothbard was active in the national Libertarian party and was one of the founders of the Free Libertarian party of New York, a local affiliate. The *Libertarian Forum* endorsed the candidates of the Libertarian party, which it wanted to become a force in national politics.

In his struggle to bring down the state, Rothbard rejected an alliance with the New Left. The *Libertarian Forum* applauded the New Left for launching the antiwar movement and for attacking the state bureaucracy, but it deplored another product of the New Left—the "counter culture, that blight of blatant irrationality that has hit the younger generation and the intellectual world like a veritable plague."[27] Rothbard viewed the counterculture's contempt for structured thought, its devaluation of history, its hostility to science and technology, its glorification of primitive feelings, its preference for rapping over serious reading and systematic learning, its living for the moment, and its regression to magic and astrology as a "multi-faceted attack on human reason."[28] He also denounced cults and gurus because "one person becomes the ultimate decider of all questions and loyalty to him or her becomes the highest good."[29]   Rothbard wanted libertarians to ally themselves "with the healthy rather than the diseased forces in America—with the decent citizens of the working and middle classes—and upper as well—who cleave to the...virtues of hard work, purpose, and rational individualism....Our lot is with Middle America."[30]

In contrast to many libertarians who are militantly anti-Christian, the *Libertarian Forum* did not consider libertarianism incompatible with Christianity. Peden, himself a believing Catholic, argued that the Christian is "a natural anarchist by faith. He has a profound respect for life and human dignity; he governs himself by the inner law of conscience illuminated by the teachings of Christ; he denies the state as a source of good or truth—at best it is a punishment placed upon men for their evil deeds; and he accepts moral responsibility for the consequences of his acts. The Christian finds true liberty by living his life in conformity to the will of God as manifest in the law of nature."[31] Although an atheist, Rothbard believed that "there is certainly no substantial reason why Christians and atheists cannot peacefully coexist within the libertarian movement,"[32] and called for an end to the anti-Christian abuse that had frequently marked the libertarian movement.

The *Libertarian Forum* provided a libertarian analysis of many issues confronting American society. Committed to the free market and detesting statism, the *Libertarian Forum* advocated a return to the gold standard, the repeal of gun laws that restricted the right to bear arms, and an end to all forms of wage, price, and rent controls. It supported the legalization of narcotics (either the addict will fall by the wayside or he will remedy his ways) and opposed welfare and compulsory schooling. Regarding taxation as theft, the *Libertarian Forum* endorsed "that one act of the public which our rulers fear the most: tax rebellion."[33] Karl Hess, whose column, "Letter from Washington," appeared regularly in 1969, wrote to the Internal Revenue Service on 15 April 1969: "The Federal government of the United States of America today is guilty of exactly every sort of infringement, abuse, and denial stated intolerable by the Declaration of Independence.... It is in the spirit of that Declaration and in comradeship with men everywhere who seek freedom and to throw off such governments, that I now refuse to pay the taxes demanded by the government in the attached form."[34]

Holding that "injustice can be redressed only for the individual who suffered it, and retribution can justly be exacted only from those who caused it,"[35] the *Libertarian Forum* rejected all quotas based on race, ethnicity, or sex. It hailed the student movement of the late 1960s for urging "Death to the State. Power to the People."[36] The *Libertarian Forum* considered the outlawing of abortion a coercive invasion of a woman's right to her body, but it opposed the equal rights amendment because, if enacted, the activities of private firms and organizations would come under the authority of the state.

The *Libertarian Forum* generally took a conservative stance on crime. It denounced "sentimental liberalism" for abolishing capital punishment for murder, for suggesting that society, rather than the individual, is responsible for criminal behavior, and for dispensing with objective punishments in favor of light or suspended sentences and the illusion of rehabilitation. It also dismissed the claim of the revolutionary Left that criminals were revolutionaries and convicts political prisoners. It praised the motion picture *Death Wish* (1974) for demonstrating the value of self-defense against the "muggers who infest New York City."[37] The *Libertarian Forum* advocated punishments that fit the crime and compelling the criminal to work in order to compensate the victim.

Extending the principle of the free market to criminal matters, the *Libertarian Forum* drew conclusions that both conservatives and liberals could only regard as startling. In an article on organized crime, Peden did not fault the Mafia for trafficking in "drugs like heroin—which is needed by those who become addicted in much the same way as a diabetic needs insulin, or like marijuana, whose effects have been described by responsible physicians as less harmful than alcohol or tobacco. (That alcohol and tobacco remain legal may be due to their being a major source of state revenue)."[38] Nor is loansharking objectionable. "The *Mafia* lends money to high-risk debtors at interest rates commensurate with the probability of default, rates forbidden by law despite the obvious needs of the market."[39] Peden concluded that the criminal activities of the Mafia "are crimes only because they are defined as such by the tyrannical statists who rule America. The Cosa Nostra—serving well its vast American market with profits estimated at $50 billion from gambling alone—is no more sinister than Dow Chemical Company—probably less so."[40] Walter Block, in an article entitled "The Pimp as Hero," declared without tongue-in-cheek: "The honest, hard working, long suffering pimp has been demeaned unjustly long enough." In Block's view, the professional pimp "performs the important and even necessary function of brokering."[41]

The *Libertarian Forum* had mixed feelings toward the Black Panthers. On the one hand, it praised the Panthers for "their excellent black nationalist ideas—particularly in emphasizing a black nation with their own land in…the Black Belt of the South." But offsetting this virtue were the "infusions of Marxist rhetoric into the Panther material…[and] the increasingly thuggish and Stalinoid tendencies in the Panther movement."[42] Rothbard referred to the pulling of a gun by Panthers on James Forman, a black activist: "Pulling a gun on the state enemy is one thing," declared Rothbard "pulling a gun on fellow revolutionaries is quite another." Rothbard urged libertarians to withdraw their enthusiasm for the Panthers and "to concentrate our time and energies…on white rather than black affairs."[43]

The *Libertarian Forum* detested Nixon the man and the president. It denounced Nixon for making lies and deception an inherent part of the political system and interpreted the Watergate affair as a step in the direction of "a full fledged police state."[44] It accused him of practicing "Orwellian logic."[45] When unemployment fell one month by a meaningless one-tenth of 1 percent, the Nixon administration called this the beginning of the recovery from the recession; the following month when unemployment rose by one-tenth of 1 percent, the White House said that unemployment was bottoming out; Nixon wound down the war in Vietnam by extending it to Cambodia and Laos; he opposed abortion because he was committed to the sanctity of human life but ordered the systematic bombing of tens of thousands of innocent peasants. The *Libertarian Forum* also attacked Nixonian economics for producing an "inflationary recession."

Favoring an isolationist foreign policy, the *Libertarian Forum* strongly denounced American involvement in Vietnam. The lesson that should be drawn from the Vietnam debacle, it concluded, is that the United States should remove its troops from bases in South Korea, Thailand, Japan, and Okinawa. It also urged the United States "to get completely out of Middle Eastern politics, to stop sending aid to either side, and to let the contending parties slug it out in any war that may arise without a hint of interference on our part."[46] If the United States does not practice nonintervention in the Middle East, warned Rothbard, it might get drawn into a global conflict. Strongly anti-Zionist, the *Libertarian Forum* blamed the Middle East conflict on Israeli aggression, which "was fueled by American arms and money, and backed by the implicit might of the United States in its wings."[47] Rothbard denounced the Camp David agreement as a betrayal of the legitimate aspirations of the Palestinians and condemned the Israeli invasion of Lebanon in June 1982.

The *Libertarian Forum* saw the problems burdening the United States during the 1970s as signs that the American state was breaking down. Everywhere it saw a "pervasive and magnificent distrust of government per se." Americans no longer "have the blind pre-Watergate trust in our secret police: the FBI, the CIA, etc." They no longer have the same respect for the office of president. In the wake of Vietnam, they have a distaste for "global meddling."[48] The inflationary depression, the near bankruptcy of social security, and the breakdown of regulated industries caused Americans to challenge Keynesian economics with its advocacy of government regulation. In 1975 Rothbard felt that "we stand at the threshold of the rollback of statism and the victory of liberty; the forces of statism are in rout at every hand."[49] Years later he was pleased that the cold war was history, but disappointed that the powers of government had diminished hardly a whit.

Some libertarians hailed the election of Ronald Reagan as a triumph for libertarian principles. Rothbard strongly rejected this view and attacked the president's economic program in a series of articles entitled "Are We Being Beastly to the Gipper?" Rothbard called Reagan's claim of a spending cut an "egregious fraud" and "hoax";[50] in reality "President Reagan proposes to give us the biggest deficit in history." Rothbard accused Reaganites of "doctoring the statistics" to give the impression that the war is being won against inflation and unemployment."[51]

The *Libertarian Forum* gave Murray Rothbard and other libertarians a platform to express their philosophy of individual liberty and antistatism. The Libertarian party is still an insignificant force in national politics, and the *Libertarian Forum* always attracted a small audience. For a while, however, the newsletter did become involved in a debate with *National Review* conservatives that received national attention. The debate compelled conservatives to articulate their basic principles more precisely. Perhaps the libertarian critique of contemporary liberalism also led some liberal thinkers to reexamine their attitude toward the relationship between the state and the individual.

Notes

1. "Why the *Libertarian?*" *Libertarian Forum* 1 (1 March 1969): 1 (hereinafter cited as *LF*).

2. Murray N. Rothbard is a libertarian economist, political scientist, and historian. Among his publications are: *America's Great Depression, For a New Liberty, Power and Market, The Panic of 1819, What Has Government Done to Our Money?* and *Man, Economy, and State.* He also edits the *Journal of Libertarian Studies.*

3. Joseph R. Peden is a lecturer in the history department of Bernard M. Baruch College, City University of New York. He is founder and vice president of the Center for Libertarian Studies, a scholarly and educational research foundation. The center publishes the interdisciplinary *Journal of Libertarian Studies* and sponsors symposia and colloquia that explore the application of libertarian principles to the social sciences and the humanities.

4. "When Revolution?" *LF* 2 (1 October 1970): 1. All articles are by Rothbard unless indicated otherwise.

5. Murray N. Rothbard, *For a New Liberty* (New York, 1973), p. 14.

6. Ibid., p. 15.

7. Ibid., pp. 287–88. Rothbard is less critical of Soviet foreign policy. In 1973 he wrote: "If we take a sober look at Soviet Russian foreign policy since the Bolshevik Revolution, we find a continuing passion for peace which has sometimes bordered on the suicidal. Poland attacked Soviet Russia after World War I, and gained a large chunk of White Russia and the Ukraine as a result. Before World War II, so devoted was Stalin to peace that he failed to make adequate provision against the Nazi attack. The much vaunted 'expansion' of the Soviet Union occurred only and solely in response to the unprovoked German attack; in defeating Germany, the Soviet Union of course had to roll over Germany's military allies in Eastern Europe. Not only was there no Russian expansion whatever apart from the exigencies of defeating Germany, but the Soviet Union time and again leaned over backward to avoid any cold or hot war with the West. It pulled its troops out of Azerbaijan and Austria; pressured the Communist guerrillas of France and Italy into not taking power as the German armies withdrew and instead forced them into ruinous coalitions with centrist parties; abandoned the Greek Communist guerrillas and turned Greece over to Great Britain; tried to pressure Tito into subordinating himself into a coalition with Mihailovich and Mao Tse-tung into a coalition with Chiang Kai-shek; and it did not impose communism in Eastern Europe until after several years of a Western-launched Cold War. Thus Stalin, far from being expansionist, did his best to accede to American demands in the name of peaceful coexistence, but the United States in its global expansionism, proved implacable." Ibid., pp. 293–94.

8. Ibid., p. 289.

9. "Listen YAF," *LF* 1 (15 August 1969): 1.

10. Rothbard, *For a New Liberty,* pp. 6–7.

11. "Listen Again, YAF," *LF* 12 (May–June 1979): 1.

12. A former speechwriter for Barry Goldwater, Hess was Washington editor of the *LF* in 1969. He broke with the newsletter over the Black Panthers.

13. *New York Times,* 28 January 1971, op-ed page.

14. *New York Times,* 9 February 1971, op-ed page.

15. *New York Times,* 16 February 1971, op-ed page.

16. Rothbard, *For a New Liberty,* p. 3.

17. Ibid.

18. "The Case for Optimism," *LF* 7 (June 1975): 1.

19. "Lessons of People's Temple," *LF* 11 (September–October 1978): 3.

20. Rothbard, *For a New Liberty*, p. 196.
21. "Living Free," *LF* 3 (February 1971): 4.
22. "When Revolution?" p. 4.
23. "The Conference," *LF* 1 (1 November 1969): 3.
24. "The Meaning of Revolution," *LF* 1 (1 July 1969): 1.
25. "When Revolution?" p. 4.
26. "How to Destatize," *LF* 2 (June 1971): 1.
27. "The New Left, RIP," *LF* 2 (15 March 1970): 2.
28. Ibid.
29. "Lessons of the People's Temple," p. 1.
30. "The Conning of America," *LF* 3 (April 1971): 2.
31. Joseph R. Peden, "Liberty: From Rand to Christ," *LF* 3 (July–August 1971): 4.
32. "Comment," *LF* 3 (July–August 1971): 5.
33. "Tax Day," *LF* I (15 April 1969): 1.
34. Karl Hess, "Letter from Washington," *LF* 1 (1 May 1969): 3.
35. "About Quotas," *LF* 6 (August 1974): 7.
36. "The Student Revolution," *LF* 1 (1 May 1969): 4.
37. "Arts and Movies," *LF* 6 (August 1974): 8.
38. Joseph R. Peden, "Organized Crime," *LF* 2 (15 January 1970): 4.
39. Ibid.
40. Ibid.
41. Walter Block, "The Pimp as Hero," *LF* 4 (January 1973): 2.
42. "The Panthers and Black Liberation," *LF* 1 (15 May 1969): 3.
43. Ibid.
44. "Whoopee," *LF* 6 (August 1974): 7.
45. "Orwell Lives," *LF* 3 (May 1971): 1.
46. "Hands Off the Middle East!" *LF* 5 (October 1973): 1.
47. Ibid.
48. "The Case for Optimism," p. 2.
49. Ibid., p. 3.
50. "Are We Being Beastly to the Gipper? Part I," *LF* 16 (February 1982): 6.
51. "Are We Being Beastly to the Gipper? Part IV," *LF* 16 (May 1982): 6.

Information Sources

BIBLIOGRAPHY:

Block, Walter. *Defending the Undefendable*. New York, 1976.

Block, Walter, and Rockwell, Llewellyn H., eds. *Man, Economy, and Liberty: Essays in Honor of Murray N. Rothbard*. Auburn, Alabama, 1988.

Gordon, David, and Watner, Karl, eds. *Murray N. Rothbard: A Bibliographical Essay*. Auburn, Alabama, 1986.

Machan, Tibor, ed. *The Libertarian Alternative: Essays in Social and Political Philosophy*. Chicago, 1974.

Rothbard, Murray. *The Ethics of Liberty*. Atlantic Highlands, New Jersey, 1982.

———. *For a New Liberty*. New York, 1973.

———. *Egalitarianism as a Revolt against Nature and Other Essays*. Washington, D.C., 1974.

Tuccille, Jerome. *Radical Libertarianism: A Right Wing Alternative*. Indianapolis, Indiana, 1970.

White, Lawrence. *Methodology of the Austrian School*. New York, 1971.

INDEXES: Indexed every two years.

REPRINT EDITIONS: Microform: Right Wing Collection, University of Iowa (MCA), partial run, 1969–1972 (reel 165); UMI. Bound editions: AN: UMI.

LOCATION SOURCES: Complete runs: Center for Libertarian Studies, Burlingame, California; State Historical Society, Madison, Wisconsin; Institute for Humane Studies, George Mason University, Fairfax, Virginia.

Publication History

TITLE AND TITLE CHANGES: *The Libertarian: A Semi-Monthly Newsletter*, 1 March 1969–1 June 1969; *The Libertarian Forum*, 15 June 1969–1986.

VOLUME AND ISSUE DATA: Preview number: 1 March 1969; volumes 1–18, 1 April 1969–1986. Combined numbers July/August 1971; June/July 1972; August/September 1972. Publication suspended in 1986.

FREQUENCY OF PUBLICATION: Semimonthly, 1 April 1969–January 1971; monthly, 1971–1977; bimonthly, January/February 1978–July/August 1980; irregular thereafter.

PUBLISHER: 1969–1981: Joseph R. Peden; 1982: Daniel Rosenthal; 1983–1986: Murray N. Rothbard. All in New York.

EDITOR: Murray N. Rothbard.

CIRCULATION: 350 in 1969; 600 in 1982; 750 in 1985.

Marvin Perry

Part Seven

EXTREME RIGHTIST
PUBLICATIONS

Angry minds are part of the social composition in all societies. They can be found
on both ends of the American political spectrum, with right-wing extremism representing political and social resistance to the shifts in power and status that attend
a society in flux. In half a century the United States resolved its internal division
by civil war, industrialized, moved to the city, took on large numbers of immigrants, and found itself counted among the powers of the world. In the twentieth
century the American people wrung from experience a more secular, cosmopolitan understanding of values and philosophy. When the old order proved unable to
maintain a viable economy, liberal political forces forged the New Deal to inaugurate a limited welfare state. After World War II, however, radical politics have
been most commonly practiced by the Right. Not all individuals goaded to anger
by loss of economic position and social weight express bitter resentment through
backlash politics, but the extremist temptation is there. When a new red scare
developed at midcentury, powered by fear of growing Soviet power abroad and
manipulated by political elites at home, the appeal of right-wing interest groups
grew even as their enemy list narrowed somewhat.

Although radical rightists oppose the welfare state, the growth of state power,
and collectivist solutions to the problems of poverty and social deprivation, their
worldview differs significantly from that of conservatives. At the center of the
extreme Right lies conspiracy theory, a conceptual model of how the world runs.
In his Herbert Spencer lecture delivered at Oxford University in the midst of growing
right-wing dissent in the late 1950s and early 1960s, historian Richard Hofstadter
defined the "paranoid style" as belief in "the existence of a vast, insidious, preter-
naturally effective international conspiratorial network designed to perpetrate acts
of the most fiendish character" against a nation or way of life. In Christian formulations of conspiracy theory, the forces of Good have struggled with the forces of
Evil since the beginning of time. Proponents of such theories use the Bible to

identify the actors on the world stage as those whom the author of Revelation had in mind and to foretell the doom that awaits unbelievers. Once the eschatological image is internalized, it is possible to rally the committed with the apocalyptic cry that they are living in the end time with one last chance to make ready for battle. In that world, where competing doctrines and fissures in the belief system are not merely erroneous but illegitimate, vision overwhelms reality. From the occasionally delusional *Truth Crusader* to *Task Force*, which at times appeared ready to retake "our country by a military coup d'etat," all of the publications examined in this part are monistic and absolutist, quick to reduce issues to two alternatives— one sinful, the other virtuous. A notable consequence for political life is that the national government is nearly always identified by moralists of the Right as the strong arm of a nefarious plot against the true and the good.

Woven into the conspiratorial view of history are vulgar interpretations of race, in the United States linked inextricably to the development of slavery. To justify the enslavement of an entire people, scholars as well as politicians and economic beneficiaries found it necessary to highlight the superiority of the white race, variously referred to as Anglo-Saxon, Teutonic, or Nordic. This theory emerged in the earliest days of English colonization, spreading so rapidly that by the time of the Revolution, racial theories assuming the superiority of the white race were found acceptable in virtually all sectors of society. Leading historians in the nineteenth century reflected prevailing assumptions. Herbert Baxter Adams wrote of the Germanic origins of American institutions, noting that the Anglo-Saxons were its offspring; John Fiske emphasized the "manifest destiny" of the Anglo-Saxons to dominate world affairs; and in dozens of ways Herman von Holst, James Ford Rhodes, and James Schouler highlighted the political and cultural superiority of the Anglo-Saxon race. In more muted fashion, so did Francis Parkman and George Bancroft. When immigration numbers raised fears that America might become the home of the ill, the old, and the radical, political notables such as Theodore Roosevelt and Henry Cabot Lodge endlessly saluted the assumed superiority of the "original" Anglo-Saxon portion of the population.

Amid a flourishing eugenics movement, World War I raised further questions about the true basis of national strength, prompting Madison Grant, then the leading theorist of racism, to publish *The Passing of the Great Race* (1916). Because race mixture led to degeneration, he argued, the Nordic race must be protected by halting the immigration of eastern and southern Europeans; in addition, colonies should be established for African Americans. The concept of a Melting Pot—the work of liberals and democrats—was a sham because human mediocrity would inevitably appear. In *The Rising Tide of Color against White World-Supremacy* (1920), Lothrop Stoddard, a student of Grant with a Ph. D. in history, made similar arguments. He limned a new and inferior type (a "walking chaos") that crowded out the older Nordic strain and pulled down living standards. William McDougall, a prominent social psychologist and chairman of the Harvard Psychology Department, used data from IQ tests administered to American World War I draftees to advance a racial interpretation of history in his book *Is America Safe for Democracy?* (1920). In such a climate, it was a relatively simple matter to address popular audiences with confidence that if challenged one could cite sources that not only were current but were authored by "experts."

Grant's racism extended to Jews, who at the turn of the century congregated largely in New York, producing "ethnic horrors," he wrote. At one time or another, anti-Semitic journals such as the *Defender*, the *Cross and the Flag*, and *Christ Is the Answer* reproduced the old stories of clannishness, selfishness, usury, and control of international finance capitalism. The larger reality at work was the merger of traditional anti-Semitism with racial theories, a process already accomplished in Europe, but which lagged in the United States until the numbers of eastern European immigrants mounted. Readers found in these journals a union of the spurious *Protocols of the Learned Elders of Zion* that fixated Henry Ford and his newspaper, the *Dearborn Independent*, and the results of the Army Mental Tests that measured education and Americanization instead of intelligence.

The Great Depression spawned a sprinkling of quasi-fascist demagogues, among them Gerald B. Winrod, a fundamentalist minister from Kansas who delighted in telling his mostly rural and village readers that the New Deal was a Jewish-communist scheme. Winrod accepted as fact the existence of an international Jewish conspiracy and to alert his readers to the danger, he published excerpts from the *Protocols of the Learned Elders of Zion*. After visiting Hitler's Germany, he became a pro-Nazi enthusiast. Thus the *Defender* (of the Christian faith), which loathed modernism and published opinions common to fundamentalist periodicals, is placed in this part. The story of the *Cross and the Flag*, the organ of Gerald L. K. Smith, is similar. Living lavishly while proclaiming himself a follower of Christ, Smith too was a fundamentalist minister who had worked in the Indiana Ku Klux Klan and served as chief assistant in Senator Huey Long's Share Our Wealth movement. He would, he said, teach America how to hate. In what must have sounded bizarre, causing a knowing snicker among even a few of the *Defender* faithful, the sweating, passionate orator blamed President Franklin D. Roosevelt for nearly every social and national misfortune it is possible to imagine. Year in and year out, the roguish rabble-rouser (the greatest "boob-bumper" since Peter the Hermit, said Mencken) described Jews as "Jesus Killers"; later they were assigned responsibility for both the construction of the Iron Curtain and the destruction of Senator Joe McCarthy.

Those dedicated to racial demonology deemed it of little consequence that by midcentury the vast majority of American scientists had rejected racialist ideology and the related belief that pure races existed, or even that racial characteristics were relevant to anything important. Nevertheless, racism and nativism lost some of their energy after World War II. The end of unlimited immigration brought a decline in language difficulties, demographic changes led to a more cosmopolitan urban dominance in cultural values, and the New Deal transformed the way in which many Americans viewed individual failure. Until Franklin Roosevelt, blame for personal hardships fell on the victims themselves. Afterward, "the system" bore a portion of the responsibility, with the federal government likely to intervene when private initiative failed. No longer was it necessary to single out Jews, Catholics, Irish, and African Americans for poisoning the American way of life. Finally, due to the immediate dangers posed by the cold war, disloyal Americans, more than religion and ethnicity, became the enemy and functioned as a lightning rod for much of the latent anger once directed toward aliens and ethnics.

The journals reviewed in this part reflect the thinking of individuals and groups that work on the edge of the American political process, where there is little room for the rational, cooperative modes of problem solving that characterize democratic societies. A small number of the paranoid are always with us, but the historical literature is all too thin on how normally decent, churchgoing people become trapped in a sinister version of religious imagery and come to accept the darkest possible coloration of the world in which they live. Their willingness to scrap democratic procedures in the struggle against the enemy of the moment is remarkable. The genuine conservative, pursuing prudential politics and displaying a greater respect for law, in fact stands more comfortably with anticommunist liberals than with members of the extreme Right; both embrace the politics of compromise. The extreme Right does not.

Defender
1927–1981

During its fifty-five year existence, the *Defender* mixed fundamentalist religion with shifting versions of conservative or far Right social commentary. The magazine was founded and, until his death in November 1957, edited by the Reverend Gerald B. Winrod of Wichita, Kansas. Born into a moderately religious Protestant family on 7 March 1900, Winrod passed through a conversion experience at age eleven; he began preaching as an adolescent, guided by revivalist Newton N. Riddell. By age twenty-one, Winrod was a full-time evangelist and editor of a small paper, *Jesus Is Coming Soon*. In November 1925 he convened twenty Kansas interdenominational clergy and laymen to form the interdenominational Defenders of the Christian Faith. As executive secretary, Winrod dominated the organization, using Wichita as his base of operation.[1]

When the first issue of the *Defender* magazine appeared in May 1927, Winrod had already achieved some prominence within the fundamentalist movement. Consequently, many important Protestant theological conservatives lent their names or talents to his magazine. William Bell Riley, head of the World Christian Fundamentals Association, William Upshaw, Prohibition party presidential candidate, and fundamentalist educator Bob Jones either contributed articles or served on the editorial board.

Until 1933, the *Defender*'s content flowed within the fundamentalist mainstream. Although the mass media lost interest following the Scopes trial in 1925, theological conservatives continued to attack the theory of evolution. According to the *Defender*, Darwinism was a false philosophy masquerading as science. Furthermore, belief that mankind descended from apes encouraged the "moral sag" of the 1920s.[2] The magazine found evidence of "animalism" in flapper fashions, premarital sex, prize fights, violations of prohibition, and prurient magazines, books, and Hollywood films.[3]

The *Defender* fought the moral sag by urging strict enforcement of the Volstead

Act, which began prohibition, and bans on the teaching of evolution in public schools. Achievement of these ends required cooperation among diverse theological conservatives. Winrod complained that too many fundamentalists magnified every disagreement into a heresy. Practicing what he preached, the editor praised Pentecostals and successfully cultivated Kansas's large Mennonite community (one of whom, the Reverend Arthur Tabor, served on the *Defender* editorial board). Many Catholics also shared Winrod's cultural conservatism; nonetheless, throughout the 1920s he scorned their church as a fount of political autocracy and false theology.

Although it routinely criticized the Roman Catholic church, the *Defender* reserved its harshest words for Protestant theological liberalism. Diverse liberals accepted Darwinism, practiced Higher Criticism of the Bible, took an optimistic view of human nature, and in some cases doubted Jesus's divinity. A minority, politically as well as theologically liberal, preached the Social Gospel. The *Defender* grouped and disdained all of them as "modernists." Modernist clergy might be intelligent and personally decent, the magazine conceded, but they were certainly misguided and perhaps unwitting agents of Satan. Their control of major pulpits, seminaries, and religious publications inhibited the revival of what Winrod called "old-fashioned holy ghost religion."[4]

The *Defender*'s approach to the Bible was neither as simple nor as old-fashioned as Winrod declared. The editor and most contributors believed in dispensationalism, an interpretive scheme that had begun to win adherents among American theological conservatives during the late nineteenth century. Dispensationalists thought that the Old Testament foretold many events later recorded in the New Testament, and both testaments were said to contain "word pictures" of major historical developments until the end of time. Winrod surmised, for example, that the Book of Jude's reference to "filthy dreamers" predicted the Freudian vogue of the 1920s.[5] Furthermore, history was divided into distinct periods—dispensations—characterized by covenants between God and humanity. Although the terms of these covenants varied, mankind invariably violated them. Hence, each dispensation ended in judgment. In the latest dispensation, God offered salvation by faith. Once again, however, mankind would fall short. Indeed, Satan's evil creation, the Antichrist, would revive the Roman empire and sponsor a popular false religion (which most *Defender* contributors agreed would embrace liberal Protestantism and Roman Catholicism). Following the period of tribulation predicted in the Book of Revelation, Jesus would return, save true Christians through a secret "rapture" in the skies, and cast the Antichrist into a fiery pit. Then Christ would rule for one thousand years—the millennium—until the devil rallied the forces of evil. The last judgment of all souls and establishment of God's kingdom would follow Satan's final defeat.

Agreed on the general course of events, dispensational premillenarians still differed among themselves about the prophetic meaning of Bible passages and current events. They disagreed, for instance, on the number of dispensations, the imminence of Christ's return, the number of souls he would save, and the amount of suffering true Christians must endure before the rapture. Nor were they oblivious to the perils of prediction; an earlier dispensationalist generation had mistakenly named Napoleon III as the Antichrist. Almost every issue of the *Defender* contained articles on Bible prophecy, dispensationalist interpretations of world affairs, and advertisements for books devoted to these subjects. Winrod himself believed that the second coming was "very near."[6] Indeed, the editor and several columnists speculated that Italian *duce* Benito Mussolini, a modern Roman emperor, might be the Antichrist.

Throughout the 1920s, abstruse theological discussions coexisted in the *Defender* with commonplace cultural conservatism. The magazine denounced communism at home and abroad, adding that this pernicious system, like Italian fascism, was rooted in Darwinism. Along with diverse Protestant clergy, Winrod opposed the Roman Catholic Democrat Alfred E. Smith during the 1928 presidential race. Yet the *Defender*'s endorsement of Herbert Hoover hardly signaled firm partisan identity. Four years later, maintaining that Hoover had capitulated to enemies of the Eighteenth Amendment, the magazine supported Prohibition party nominee William D. Upshaw.

By 1931, the message reached roughly 20,000 subscribers, de facto members of the Defenders of the Christian Faith. The *Defender* supplemented their subscription fees—fifty cents annually—with some advertising revenue. Most ads boosted Protestant colleges, Bible institutes or publishers, as well as self-improvement courses, home-based businesses, and patent medicines. A few large companies, including Quaker Oats and Allstate Insurance, bought space. Another source of revenue was the sale of *Defender* articles collected in book form.

Although the Great Depression initially tightened Winrod's budget, his magazine continued to function. The *Defender*'s first explicit reference to the slump, in December 1930, predictably urged that "more religion—rather than more legislation—is the need of the hour."[7] Despite President Hoover's drift toward a "moist" position on prohibition, Winrod supported his stand against increased federal intervention in the economy. On the other hand, the *Defender* attacked Franklin D. Roosevelt's administration from the outset. Not only did FDR lead repeal of the Eighteenth Amendment and recognize the Soviet Union, but new agencies like the National Recovery Administration (NRA) regimented American life. While borrowing arguments against the welfare state from Hoover, Congressman Hamilton Fish (R, New York), and other political conservatives, the *Defender* continued to interpret the depression and New Deal primarily in religious terms. Members of FDR's brain trust looked like the impudent liberals who had mocked godly Americans during the 1920s. The liberal philosophy, which held that "*whatever is, is wrong and must be changed,*" was itself an offspring of Darwinism.[8] On the theological level, Winrod detected an affinity between the NRA Blue Eagle and the Beast of Revelation. The nation's only salvation, the *Defender* repeatedly declared, was a revival of "aroused Christian public opinion."[9]

The *Defender* went beyond commonplace allegations of New Deal "subversion" to charge that the Roosevelt administration was part of a vast Jewish conspiracy, sketched in the *Protocols of the Learned Elders of Zion*, to destroy Christian civilization. Jews had always fascinated dispensationalists, who expected them to reclaim Palestine shortly before the second coming. Throughout the 1920s, Winrod and most *Defender* contributors had viewed Zionism as a hopeful sign of Jesus's advent. Indeed, the magazine treated Jews much more favorably than Roman Catholics. In February 1933, however, the *Defender* began a fierce assault on an alleged "Jewish World Conspiracy."[10]

Following the *Protocols*, Winrod maintained that a Zionist "hidden hand" secretly directed exploitative capitalism and sinister radicalism. His variations on this theme incorporated anti-Semitic lore that had circulated widely since the 1910s. Rich Jews, the *Defender* asserted, had precipitated the depression, and their radical kinsmen dominated the Soviet hierarchy as well as the Roosevelt administration. These themes were fitted into the editor's broader religious framework. According to the *Defender,* the elders' conspiracy stretched back to the days of King Solomon and included Pharisees who had demanded Jesus's crucifixion; communist persecution of Christians revealed the same *"Jewish impulse"* nineteen hundred years later.[11] Still, as a devout fundamentalist, Winrod could not forget that Jesus had been born a Jew. Accordingly, his magazine mixed anti-Semitic invective with occasional denials of prejudice against the Jewish "race" or religion. Combining anti-Semitism with dispensationalism, Winrod expected Jews in Palestine to ally with the Antichrist, who would turn on them, prompting a chastened minority to embrace Christianity. Awaiting these events, *Defender* readers were urged to beware of "bad Jews" and to convert "good Jews."

The editor's obsession with an alleged Zionist conspiracy apparently alienated fewer *Defender* readers than it attracted. The Reverend Keith Brooks quit the editorial board over the issue, but William Bell Riley remained loyal and the Reverend Oswald J. Smith, a frequent contributor, outdid Winrod in anti-Semitic suspicions. The *Defender* won accolades from and sometimes printed articles by such far Right stalwarts as Elizabeth Dilling, James True, Robert E. Edmondson, and Colonel Eugene Sanctuary (who may have introduced Winrod to the *Protocols*). By the late 1930s, the magazine had thickened to more than forty pages per issue and claimed 110,000 subscribers; at roughly the same time, Greek, Bulgarian, and Liberian editions began publication. The *Defender*'s petition campaign against expansion of the Supreme Court attracted national attention in 1937 when Senator Joseph Robinson (D, Arkansas) denounced Winrod in Congress.

National publicity, even unfavorable publicity, fed Winrod's sense of mission. In 1938, he unsuccessfully sought the Republican nomination for U.S. senator from Kansas (running strongest in heavily Mennonite districts). While publicizing his primary campaign, the *Defender* refrained from assailing Catholic theology and muted its attacks on Jews. Winrod's critics reprinted many blatantly anti-Semitic pieces from earlier *Defenders*, accused him of receiving funds from Nazi Germany, and branded him a fascist. The editor lamely replied that he lacked time to supervise every article. Certainly day-to-day operations were left to associates, especially Winrod's secretary and business manager, Myrtle (M. L.) Flowers. There is no doubt, however, that he set the magazine's anti-Semitic tone and wrote the major articles.

The charge that Winrod received Nazi subsidies was probably groundless, but the *Defender*'s pages amply illustrated his infatuation with Adolf Hitler's regime.

Transcending earlier fears that Hitler favored Teutonic cults, Winrod by 1935 was applauding him as a Christian foe of communism and Zionist conspiracy. Moreover, German churches were filled, and the Higher Criticism, supposedly the invention of Jews pretending to be Christians, was in decline. In 1938, the *Defender* made light of the *Kristallnacht* pogrom. The next year it published sermons by Bishop F. H. Otto Melle of the German Free church, a pro-Nazi cleric whom Winrod had entertained in Kansas. The editor still claimed to dislike all dictatorships, yet his occasional criticism of the Third Reich never equaled his sharp attacks on Mussolini's milder tyranny during the 1920s. Like all else, Nazism was said to fit into God's plan. According to the *Defender*'s "special prophetic edition" of October 1939, the Nazi-Soviet Pact signaled both Stalin's repudiation of Jewish influence and formation of the "Northern Confederacy" predicted in Scripture—another sign of the dispensation's last days.[12]

The same issue began a campaign against U.S. participation in World War II. To the mainstream noninterventionist argument that entry would enrich financiers and destroy democracy at home instead of spreading freedom abroad, Winrod offered the anti-Semitic twist that Jewish capitalists were most likely to profit. Furthermore, the *Defender*, perhaps influenced by its Mennonite constituency, respected pacifists and vividly portrayed the horrors of combat; in this respect, it differed from most contemporary far Right periodicals. After Pearl Harbor, Winrod again muted his anti-Semitism, urged readers to "pray each day for the USA," printed numerous stories about Christian war heroes, and found scriptural evidence that the United States would never suffer invasion. Nonetheless, the Justice Department in 1942 accused him of conspiring with an assortment of far Right agitators, isolationists, and enemy aliens to promote insubordination in the armed forces. This flimsy conspiracy case, *United States* v. *McWilliams*, came to trial in April 1944, ending nine raucous months later when the judge died. The indictment was finally dismissed on appeal in 1947. Meanwhile, as Winrod juggled publishing in Wichita with court appearances in Washington, D.C., the *Defender* lost readers and revenue. The staff, shrunk to six, was further hampered by the indictment of M. L. Flowers for refusing to testify against Winrod.

Although the magazine suffered financial difficulties as late as 1949, it survived and prospered by the mid–1950s. Circulation rose again to 100,000, some issues reached a hefty sixty-four pages, the staff expanded to forty-two, and the mail order department did a healthy business in pamphlets, Bibles, and Christian artifacts. His theological framework unchanged, Winrod detected new signs of impending apocalypse in the Korean War, widespread reports of flying saucers, and nuclear energy (which, he wrote, had been predicted in the Book of Ezekiel). He felt personally vindicated by the cold war attack on the Soviet Union and harassment of domestic leftists. The editor's anticommunist message was echoed in occasional articles by old friends Elizabeth Dilling and Eugene Sanctuary, as well as by regular columnists Upton Close and George Sullivan. A rising young man of the far Right, Billy James Hargis, made his *Defender* debut in 1954. Winrod's friendship with Sullivan, along with his support of Senator Joseph R. McCarthy (R, Wisconsin), highlighted his growing willingness to join Catholics in an anticommunist front.

The *Defender*'s oscillating attitude toward Presidents Harry S Truman and Dwight D. Eisenhower depended on whether they seemed adequately hostile to communism, supportive of Christianity, and suspicious of Jews. During the 1950s, Winrod still accepted the conspiratorial anti-Semitism he had adopted in the 1930s. For example, he claimed that Zionist pressure prevented Truman from revealing the names of Jewish spies. Overall, however, the more prudent postwar *Defender* was not so strident about the "Jewish question" as during the 1930s. Indeed, this topic took up less space than Winrod's campaign in behalf of Harry M. Hoxsey, William Frederick Koch, and other promoters of fraudulent cancer treatments. According to the *Defender*, these godly men were persecuted by federal authorities—especially the Food and Drug Administration, much as Winrod had been. Advertisements for health foods and "Christian" clinics complemented the magazine's editorial message. The editor's failing health undoubtedly disposed him to take up this last crusade. Ironically, his mounting suspicion of the medical profession contributed to his premature death. Ill but refusing to see a physician, he died of influenza on 11 November 1957.

The *Defender* floundered for six years after his death. Both the *Defender*'s presidency and magazine editorship went to the Reverend William T. Watson, a Florida evangelist, Bible college president, and (according to Flowers) Winrod's anointed successor. Watson stepped down in late 1958. J. William Bostrom, the *Defender*'s missionary director, was chosen president, and J. Bransford Carney, a *Defender* employee since 1946, assumed the editorship. In November 1959, the presidency passed to Gwynne W. Davidson, a fundamentalist layman and head of the National Savings Insurance Company. Flowers later claimed that Davidson used his office for personal aggrandizement and the charge was warranted. Davidson installed himself as chairman of the *Defender* board, wrote a monthly column, and filled the magazine with advertisements for his insurance company. In December 1960, he had the Defenders acquire the *American Mercury* and appointed Gerald S. Pope, a preacher and publicist from Oklahoma City, editor of both that magazine and the *Defender*. The next year, Defenders headquarters moved to Oklahoma City. While Davidson and Pope concentrated on making the *American Mercury* a leading far Right vehicle, the *Defender* languished. Subscribers declined from 135,000 in 1957 to 28,000 in 1962, according to in-house figures. Financial problems mounted even though the annual subscription cost, one dollar since 1950, doubled in 1959. Most important, the *Defender* staff divided into rival factions; Flowers effectively led the anti-Davidson forces. By mid-1963, she had managed to ease him out.

The *Defender*'s prospects improved in June 1963 with the appointment of the Reverend G. H. Montgomery, formerly editor of *Abundant Life*, as Defenders president and magazine editor. Unlike Davidson, Montgomery stressed evangelism, missionary work, and the radio ministry. Also in 1964, Montgomery and Flowers moved the Defenders in a new direction by transforming an old Kansas City, Missouri, hotel into a combination headquarters and Christian retirement home. By 1975, six of these "townhouses" were established in Missouri, Kansas, Nebraska, and Arkansas, and the headquarters had returned to Wichita. Increasingly the

Defender reported on townhouse activities and urged readers to retire to them or invest in them.

The six years after Winrod's death also produced a drift away from far Right politics and anti-Semitism. Old hands, including Oswald J. Smith and Bishop Melle, still wrote occasional articles; the magazine continued to oppose the civil rights movement, favor congressional investigation of leftist subversion, and advertise such far Right tracts as W. Cleon Skousen's *The Naked Communist (1958)*. Yet sweeping conspiracy theories virtually disappeared from its pages. Despite qualms about a Catholic in the White House, the *Defender* eschewed attacks on Senator John F. Kennedy (D, Massachusetts) in 1960 and merely urged readers to seek "God's guidance as you cast your ballot."[13] Furthermore, though Montgomery joked about alleged Jewish cheapness and held Jews responsible for Jesus's crucifixion, he also hailed the "miracle" of modern Israel.[14] The *Defender*'s central message remained unchanged: the United States must choose between revival and ruin.

After Montgomery's sudden death in September 1966, Flowers recruited the Reverend Hart Armstrong as his successor. Converted during a revival at age eight, Armstrong had held several pulpits, worked in religious publishing, managed retirement homes, and served as assistant to evangelist Oral Roberts. From January 1967 until January 1981, the *Defender* was virtually a two-person enterprise. Flowers provided anecdotal accounts of townhouse life and pilgrimages to the Holy Land, while Armstrong tended to weightier theological matters. Indeed, cheerful accounts of life within the Defenders "family" often looked incongruous beside predictions of the imminent tribulation destined to destroy "almost the entire race of humanity."[15]

As always, the magazine found higher meaning in earthly events. Unlike Winrod, who had expected the Antichrist to be both a Jew and a "Roman," Armstrong thought his nationality uncertain. Communists would initially aid this monster, but the alliance would not last. Rather, after a period of peace in the Middle East (perhaps foreshadowed by the Camp David Accords of 1978, Armstrong speculated), the Soviet Union, beset by an energy crisis, would invade the region and lose to Antichrist forces at Armageddon. Capitalizing on this victory, the Antichrist would recruit a worldwide following that would bear his "mark" (perhaps the Book of Revelation's way of predicting a "Universal Computer setup").[16] Again diverging from Winrod, who had expected many good Christians to suffer through this era of apostasy, Armstrong held out the "pretribulationist" possibility that they would be spared through an early rapture. Jews would not be so fortunate. Indeed, Israel's embattlement in the 1970s might mean that God was punishing Jews "for their sins and [trying] to lead them out of their unbelief."[17] This suggestion by the *Defender* did not signal reversion to anti-Semitism, however. Armstrong and Flowers generally praised Israel, visited the country often, and grew especially fond of Jerusalem mayor Teddy Kollek.

From 1966 onward, the *Defender* no longer qualified as a far Right periodical. As during the 1920s, it was primarily a religious monthly that also contained much conservative social comment and occasional forays into partisanship. "Our battle is spiritual—not carnal or earthly...to strike against the Devil," Armstrong declared in 1972.[18] In effect conceding temporary defeat to some satanic rivals, the magazine admitted that theological liberals and Darwinians had entrenched themselves in churches and public schools. Hence the *Defender*'s battle for the nation's soul emphasized such new issues as pornography, drug abuse, and campus protest (the last undoubtedly esteemed by Satan, the "original rebel").[19] Flowers pointedly denounced advocates of women's liberation. Influenced by his son, an army officer, Armstrong supported the Vietnam War and criticized National Council of Churches doves. Expecting the United States to suffer for its transgressions, he shared Winrod's belief that the country would escape total destruction.

Despite denials of political meddling, an activity that might menace its tax-exempt status, the *Defender* treated conservative politicians better than their liberal counterparts. In 1972, deploring "radical elements" in control of the Democratic party, it obliquely endorsed President Richard M. Nixon for reelection.[20] In 1976, it saw "good" qualities in both President Gerald R. Ford and Democrat Jimmy Carter. In addition, however, Armstrong recounted his visit to the Republican National Convention and warned that Democrats favored "giveaway programs."[21] According to the *Defender,* the most dramatic event of Carter's presidency, the seizure of American diplomats by Iranian militants, fulfilled the prophecy in the Book of Ezekiel that communists would control Persia. An issue of comparable importance, inflation, was attributed to loose living and social welfare programs begun during the New Deal.

The *Defender*'s concern with inflation reflected self-interest as well as ideology. Rising costs during the 1970s caused problems for both the magazine and the parent organization. Yet inflation contributed less to the *Defender*'s demise than its own antigovernment obstinacy and lack of financial discipline. Starting in 1972, the Defenders of the Christian Faith contested local taxes on the Wichita townhouse (which doubled as national headquarters). By 1980, with all appeals exhausted, the group owed $335,000 in back taxes, interest, and penalties, as well as double that sum borrowed to bring the building up to fire code standards. Flowers apparently underestimated the seriousness of this situation. The *Defender*'s occasional allusions to the financial imbroglio were usually paired with denunciations of "unfair taxation."[22] Most important, readers were still urged to invest in Defenders bonds.

By 1979, the pinch had begun to affect the magazine. In theory, it cost one dollar annually (reduced from three dollars in 1975 as an "inflation stopper"), yet in practice subscriptions had been entered on request, a strategy that allowed the *Defender* to claim 500,000 readers. Now payment was demanded from all but the indigent. Also in 1979, the magazine began to appear every other month, alternating with a "personal letter." Although monthly publication resumed in 1980, each *Defender* consisted of a twelve-page fold out. The March issue launched a fund drive to pay the back taxes. Ultimately a decision was made to sell the townhouse. No buyer could be found. Thus, the Defenders of the Christian Faith verged on collapse when Flowers died of cancer on 12 January 1981.

The passing of "Mrs. Defenders" left Armstrong to oversee the final collapse.

Despite an emergency sale of the Wichita townhouse in early 1981, the Defenders remained more than $1 million in debt. Many creditors were devout Protestants who, impressed by the *Defender*'s optimistic articles and advertisements, had invested their savings. Armstrong hoped for an organizational "resurrection" through a return to the Defenders' "original and true purpose," evangelism.[23] However, to prevent seizure of the remaining assets—mostly printing and office supplies— they were transferred to a newly formed corporation called Christian Communications. As part of this legal maneuver, the magazine was reborn as *Communicare*. The April 1981 issue of the *Defender* announcing these changes was the last to appear.

Notes

1. For Winrod's background, see Leo P. Ribuffo, *The Old Christian Right: The Protestant Far Right from the Great Depression to the Cold War* (Philadelphia, 1983), pp. 80–81.

2. Gerald B. Winrod (hereinafter, GBW), *Christ Within* (New York, 1932), p. 35.

3. GBW, "How a Wichita Father and Mother Protected Their Son,"*Defender* 2 (November 1927): 3; GBW, "Companionate Marriage," *Defender* 2 (January 1928): 3.

4. GBW, *Christ Within*, p. 37.

5. GBW, "Filthy Dreamers," *Defender* 3 (June 1928): 6.

6. GBW, "Date Fixers," *Defender* 6 (December 1931): 9.

7. "Babson Speaks," *Defender* 5 (December 1930): 21.

8. GBW, "AntiChrist, Liberalism, Socialism, Fascism and Communism," *Defender* 8 (February 1934): 19.

9. GBW, *Communism and the Roosevelt Brain Trust* (Wichita, 1933), p. 6.

10. "Unmasking 'The Hidden Hand'—A World Conspiracy," *Defender* 7 (February 1933): 5.

11. "Secret Societies Unveiled," *Revealer* 2 (March 1936): 2; Winrod published the *Revealer,* a more explicitly political magazine than the *Defender*, from 1934 through 1936.

12. "Europe's Crisis in Prophecy," *Defender* 14 (October 1939): 1–7.

13. "What Manner of Man Is This?" *Defender* 35 (August 1960): 4–5.

14. G. H. Montgomery, "China and Russia," *Defender* 38 (June 1963): 8, 13–14.

15. Hart Armstrong (hereinafter HA), "The Future...Color It Blood," *Defender* 50 (September 1975): 12.

16. HA, "AntiChrist...What Will He Do?" *Defender* 52 (October 1977): 9.

17. HA, "Peace for Israel?" *Defender* 50 (September 1975): 6.

18. HA, "The Works of God," *Defender* 47 (September 1972): 7.

19. "Of Youth," *Defender* 46 (July–August 1971): 20.

20. "Defenders Action Talk," *Defender* 47 (July–August 1972): 2.

21. "Family Talk," *Defender* 51 (September 1976): 20.

22. "In Kansas City—One Third over 65 Found Living in Poverty," *Defender* 46 (February 1972): 22.

23. HA, "We Need a Resurrection," *Defender* 55 (April 1981): 6.

Information Sources

BIBLIOGRAPHY:

Ribuffo. Leo P. *The Old Christian Right: The Protestant Far Right from the Great Depression to the Cold War*. Philadelphia, 1983.

Sindell, Gail Ann. "Gerald B. Winrod and the 'Defender': A Case Study of the Radical

Right." Ph.D. dissertation, Case Western Reserve University, 1973.

[Staff, *Defender*]. *Fire by Night and Cloud by Day: A History of the Defenders of the Christian Faith*. Wichita, Kansas, 1966.

INDEXES: None.

REPRINT EDITIONS: Microform: Right Wing Collection, University of Iowa (MCA), partial run, 1957–1972 (reels 160–162); UMI.

LOCATION SOURCES: Partial runs: Library of Congress; Kansas State Historical Society; University of Iowa; University of Arizona.

Publication History

TITLE AND TITLE CHANGES: *The Defender*.

VOLUME AND ISSUE DATA: Volumes 1–55, May 1927–April 1981.

FREQUENCY OF PUBLICATION: Monthly.

PUBLISHER: Gerald B. Winrod, Defenders of the Christian Faith, Wichita, Kansas.

EDITORS: Gerald B. Winrod, 1927–1957; William T. Watson, 1957–1958; J. Bransford Carney, 1958–1961; Gerald S. Pope, 1961–1963; Gwynne D. Davidson, 1963; G. H. Montgomery, 1963–1966; Hart Armstrong, 1966–1981.

CIRCULATION: Claims varied from 20,000–130,000.

Leo P. Ribuffo

Cross and the Flag
1942-1977

The *Cross and the Flag* was the journalistic organ of crusading anti-Semite Gerald L. K. Smith. A journal of personal opinion, the *Cross and the Flag* was not a responsibly conservative periodical but an organ targeted specifically at the racist, reactionary fringe. Its publisher, Smith himself, ranked among the most influential and durable bigoted publishers and agitators in the years since the Great Depression. Born in Wisconsin and educated in the Midwest, Smith abandoned the Christian ministry for political proselytizing several years after moving to Shreveport, Louisiana, in 1929. In 1933 he became chief organizer of Louisiana senator Huey P. Long's utopian Share Our Wealth society. He never returned to the Christian ministry.

Leaving Louisiana after Long's assassination, Smith settled in Detroit, Michigan, still infected by political ambitions. He created his own organizations—successively, the Committee of One Million, the America First party, and the Christian Nationalist Crusade. In the presidential campaign of 1936 he joined with Father Charles E. Coughlin, Dr. Francis E. Townsend, and Congressman William Lemke (R, North Dakota) in the unsuccessful Union party crusade. In 1942 Smith ran for the U.S. Senate and campaigned for president on the America First party tickets in 1944 and 1948. Smith founded the *Cross and the Flag* in 1942 while campaigning in Michigan for the Senate. He later said that he had established his own journal because Jews controlled the established media. However, the *Cross and the Flag* during World War II was only mildly anti-Semitic, but strongly anticommunist, anti-British, antilabor, and isolationist. From its inception the monthly never missed an issue. It moved with Smith to St. Louis, Missouri, and eventually found a permanent home with him in Los Angeles.[1]

Although an advocate of Huey Long's plan to confiscate millionaire incomes in the 1930s, Smith became reactionary in the 1940s. The chief targets for his vituperation became Jews, blacks, immigrants, and international bankers. Racial integration, which he termed "mongrelization," was a ploy, he said, to undermine America's ruling Anglo-Saxon stock and facilitate a communist conquest. Smith claimed that communists planned to drive whites out of large portions of the South and create a black republic there. In the June 1957 issue of the *Cross and the Flag*, he printed a map of the United States with the area the communists intended to devote to a black republic blacked out. The area included most of Louisiana, Arkansas, Mississippi, and Alabama and large portions of South Carolina, North Carolina, and Virginia. Smith gave no source for the map, but offered reprints of it to anyone who would send a small donation to cover mailing costs.[2]

Besides race mixing, Smith opposed in the pages of the *Cross and the Flag* welfare relief, the ecumenical movement, alternatives to the nuclear family lifestyle, the equal rights amendment, atheism, pornography, socialized medicine, alcohol, fluoridation of drinking water, drugs, and political internationalism. He disliked modern journalism, television, and the cinema. Smith was critical of modern music, especially jazz and rock and roll. He admonished his readers: "Maybe we had better begin to teach our children more Bible and more Constitution and less boogie woogie and less rock 'n' roll."[3]

According to Smith, much of the evil in America could be traced to President Franklin D. Roosevelt. Smith said of Roosevelt: "It is my personal opinion that he was the most villainous, strategic, intelligent knave ever to hold public office."[4] Smith blamed Roosevelt and his family for every disaster since the early 1930s, including the depression; World War II; the assassination of Huey Long; the mongrelization of the races; the fall of China; the taking of Poland by Soviet communists; the release from prison of Communist party head Earl Browder; the corruption of Congress; the elevation to vice-president of what he called a "communist stooge"—Henry Wallace; the glorification of sexual perverts; sending American money-printing equipment to Russia so that the Soviets could buy luxuries from their Jewish suppliers; creation of a family dynasty that would dispense with free elections; the persecution, attempted imprisonment, and plots to assassinate such patriots as Smith himself; and the spread of atheism. Smith claimed that both Franklin Roosevelt and his wife, Eleanor, were descended from Spanish Jews named Rosenvelt, who were driven to refuge in Holland. They had disclaimed the faith of their fathers and had managed to camouflage their Jewish origins after moving to the United States. This Jewish ancestry, he explained, accounted for FDR's tendency toward radicalism. Although Smith claimed never to hate anyone because of his or her origins, he explained that when observing high public officials, patriots must be eternally vigilant, because "when a man like Roosevelt is elevated to a position of leadership in a Country, his chromosomes become a matter of public concern."[5]

Besides Roosevelt, the *Cross and the Flag*'s roll of villains included Karl Marx, Vladimir Lenin, Joseph Stalin, Bernard Baruch, Felix Frankfurter, and Anna Rosenberg. Smith never tired of repeating that Marx, the founder of communism, was a Jew: "Marx was a Jew, an atheist and an enemy of Christ and Christianity."[6]

In the *Cross and the Flag* Smith also pilloried the Anti-Defamation League of B'nai B'rith, the National Association for the Advancement of Colored People, the

National Council of Churches, and the United Nations. He predictably lambasted liberal intellectuals. Even General Eisenhower was a "Swedish Jew" and dangerous leftist. He viewed Vice-President Nixon as a liberal influence on Eisenhower, but later supported President Nixon during the Watergate crisis. On the other hand, General Douglas MacArthur, Senator Joseph McCarthy (R, Wisconsin), and Colonel Charles Lindbergh all merited praise. Also among his favorites were Arkansas governor Orval Faubus, U.S. senators Herman Talmadge (D, Georgia) and Harry Byrd (D, Virginia), Henry Ford, and Lawrence Welk. A religious fundamentalist and states rights advocate, he always preferred a white, Christian, nationalistic, isolationist America.[7]

The *Cross and the Flag* was a mixture of fact, exaggeration, imagination, and wild speculation. The reader encountered distortions, undocumented allegations, and highly prejudiced editorials. Smith's style was simplistic and sensational, characterized by short, snappy, provocative sentences that were never footnoted. His vocabulary was meager and endlessly repetitive.

Smith used the same clichés and attacked the same villains in practically every issue. He claimed that Jews originated, organized, and financed the Russian Revolution, promoted World War II, constructed the iron curtain, stole American A-bomb secrets, financed the American Communist party, promoted the United Nations, and served as a "fifth column" in democratic countries. Jews were responsible for "the removal of MacArthur; the power of Acheson; the choice of Eisenhower at Chicago; the smear of McCarthy; the Palestine invasion (Zionism); the establishment of the United Nations; the betrayal of Chiang Kai-shek; control of the press to the point where quarantine silence is given such men as Gerald L. K. Smith, Father Coughlin and General Douglas MacArthur except where misrepresentations are made."[8]

Smith denied that Jesus was a Jew, that the Jews were the chosen people of God, and that twentieth-century Zionists were descended from biblical Jews. He explained: "The biggest lie that has ever been told to humanity is the lie that Christ's worst enemies are God's chosen people."[9]

Jews also constituted the vanguard of communism. Lenin and Trotsky, both Jews, carried out the Bolshevik revolution and slaughtered Christians. Jews favored World War II because it forced an alliance of America and Russia. After the war, they introduced communism into Eastern Europe and the satellite countries were then ruled by pro-Russian communists, "79 percent of whom are Jews." Jews were responsible for stealing American atomic and hydrogen bomb secrets. "A careful study into the life, growth, and activities of the American Communist party reveals that 80% of the financial support has come from New York and Hollywood, and that in these areas more than 75% of the membership of the Communist party is Jewish." (He never explained how he compiled these statistics or his source.)[10] In a convoluted effort to explain why Jews were trying to flee Russia if Russia was Jew dominated, Smith argued that the Jews were trying to leave before an anticommunist revolution erupted in which they knew that they would be the first to die.[11]

While Jews were satanic, blacks were a child race manipulated by clever Jews and white liberals: "The National Association for the Advancement of Colored People (NAACP), while posing as a Negro organization, was in fact started by Jews, financed by Jews, and is being manipulated by an ominous clique of 'bad eggs.'"[12] Smith made an offer of a free one-year subscription to the *Cross and the Flag* to "any citizen of the United States who can name one Jewish Rabbi opposed to integration, race-mixing and such."[13] (He never seemed to consider why anyone who was intimately associated with Jewish rabbis might want a subscription to the *Cross and the Flag.*)

Smith claimed that he loved all men and was not a racist, but contended that God wisely had separated blacks and whites: "It was not the politicians south of the Mason-Dixon line who invented segregation. It was God Almighty who created us as separate races and expects us to respect this divinely appointed plan."[14] Smith condescended to say that "the basic problem in America is not the American Negro. It is the Earl Warrens, the Eleanor Roosevelts, the Hubert Humphreys and their ilk."[15]

The *Cross and the Flag* was replete with mysterious threats, unnatural deaths, and secret conspiracies. In the August 1957 issue, Smith theorized that Senator Joseph McCarthy may have been poisoned by the Jews because he was about to reveal that the Jews were behind communism. At the very least, Smith said, he was hounded to death.[16]

The *Cross and the Flag* was so pyramided with such implausible conspiracies that it seems remarkable that anyone could have taken Smith seriously. It was so intemperate that it appeared to be satire or parody. Smith's writing was more hate oriented and dealt with conspiracies even less plausible than material published by the National Union for Social Justice and the John Birch Society. Absence of solid evidence indicating a conspiracy did not prove that there was no conspiracy, only that the conspirators were diabolically clever in concealing their plot. Smith believed that there were half a million communist secret agents in the United States, declaring: "They are in our churches, schools, factories, and government offices. One of these oriented inside traitors can accomplish five times the damage of a paratrooper landed from Stalin's plane."[17]

Smith had only modest literary skills; even his personal letters and private papers are written in crude, elementary language. Smith never took the time or had the inclination to polish what he wrote. A secretary accompanied him everywhere he went and took dictation while they traveled. Later he dictated into a tape recorder. This raw material went directly into the *Cross and the Flag,* which had all the evidence of hasty writing; it was sophomoric, and rambling, and frequently included non sequiturs.

Neither was Smith's research for the *Cross and the Flag* scrupulous. He seldom probed beneath the surface of anything he wanted to believe and labeled as lies everything with which he disagreed, whether or not he had evidence. His reading encompassed chiefly the literature of fellow extremists, from which he took questionable statements and spurious quotations. He seldom read reputable academicians and other sources. Much of his information came from clippings marked and mailed to him by his own readers. Smith not only gave his readers what they wanted to hear, but he literally gave them back what they sent him, with brief editorial comments appended. His correspondence was voluminous, but a sampling suggests that many of the people who wrote to him were emotionally unstable. Like him, his correspondents were crudely heavy-handed and obsessed with placing coincidental events in a conspiratorial context. Of course, Smith wrote for these very readers, not for academicians or the general public.

Smith was prolific. He mass-produced anti-Semitic fulminations daily from the memory of what he had read and heard. He claimed that his collected works would fill twice as many volumes as the *Encyclopedia Britannica*—only a mild exaggeration. In addition to writing 90 percent of each issue of the *Cross and the Flag*, he wrote more than 300 pamphlets, tracts, and small books.[18]

Smith served as editor of his monthly only briefly, but the designated editors were his figureheads. During the early 1950s he listed a young anti-Semite named Don Lohbeck as editor. A former concert pianist and conscientious objector turned polemicist, Lohbeck operated Smith's St. Louis office. His only apparent journalistic responsibility was to write an editorial for the back cover of each issue. Lohbeck tried to ape Smith's style, but his anti-Semitism appeared contrived, and he was unable to sustain the emotional outrage of his mentor. In 1957 Charles F. Robertson replaced Lohbeck. Robertson contributed even less than Lohbeck; moreover, correspondence addressed to Robertson as editor went directly to Smith. The editorial board included, besides Smith and his secretaries, Renata Legant and Opal M. Tanner, his wife, Elna, and Robertson. Not one of these had a voice in selecting what went into the magazine or had much to contribute to it.

For the content of the *Cross and the Flag*, Smith used his wife as a sounding board and also sought advice from prominent American isolationists. For the first issue of the magazine, Smith obtained endorsements from U.S. senator Gerald P. Nye (R, North Dakota), a member of the important Foreign Relations Committee, and Senator Robert R. Reynolds (D, North Carolina), chairman of the Military Affairs Committee. Isolationist congressman Roy O. Woodruff (R, Michigan) inserted an editorial from Smith's initial issue in the *Congressional Record*. Smith returned the compliment by publishing speeches by Reynolds, Nye, and Woodruff in the *Cross and the Flag*. He also corresponded with isolationists, including Senators Burton K. Wheeler (R, Montana) and Arthur H. Vandenberg (R, Michigan). Smith claimed that Henry Ford was a reader of his journal, but Ford never supported the *Cross and the Flag* publicly.[19]

Smith's followers reveled in being made confidants of an important man, which they believed Smith to be. He told them that they constituted the last redoubt of Americanism and were the guardians of Christian civilization; they were an elite entrusted with the task of saving America. Most of these readers were elderly, rural people of limited education. Resenting liberal intellectuals and enjoying vicariously Smith's attacks on the Left, they were captivated by the publisher's simple, childlike, and unsophisticated but hard-hitting prose. Impatient with dissenting viewpoints, they interpreted world events in sharply delineated contrasts, accepting as gospel Smith's illogical deductions of sinister motives behind every action. Most of his readers were, as he was, anticommunists, opposed to the New

Deal, and in favor of an isolationist foreign policy. In fact, the initial mailing list
for the *Cross and the Flag* consisted of names from the files of such 1940s antiwar
groups as the Mothers of Sons Forum and Mothers' Knee, Inc.[20]

The *Cross and the Flag* was the centerpiece of Smith's Christian Nationalist
Crusade, complementing his tracts and letters, and replacing his 1930s and 1940s
spellbinding oratory. It employed sensationalized headlines, multicolored type,
and other attention-grabbing devices. Although printed on better paper, its format
resembled cheap pulp publications. It was usually thirty-two pages in length. Smith
devoted page 2 of each issue to an essay elaborating some aspect of his personal
Christian faith. He also wrote two or three feature articles, each dealing with a
specific current event. The major portion of the magazine, however, was devoted
to one-paragraph editorials that took ordinary news incidents and interpreted them
in Smith's terms. He often featured stories about rapes and depravities by blacks
and accounts of the Jew-communist "hidden hand" behind world turmoil. Smith
used filler articles from other reactionary newspapers and periodicals. Sometimes
he printed isolationist speeches from the *Congressional Record*. Several times he
provided copy he wrote himself to friendly congressmen, who inserted it into the
Congressional Record. Smith then cited the *Congressional Record* as an authority.

The *Cross and the Flag* never carried advertisements and was not self-supporting
financially. From its founding in 1942 until Smith's death in 1976, it sold for a
modest $2.00 per year—$3.00 if the subscriber wanted to receive it in a plain
brown envelope. Circulation climbed to about 20,000 in the early 1940s, peaked at
35,000 in the mid-1960s, and then stabilized at about 25,000.[21]

Smith's secret to fund raising was writing "personalized" form letters.
Recipients of these came from a select group of contributors taken from the mailing
list of the *Cross and the Flag*. Money to launch the *Cross and the Flag* had been
obtained from eastern and midwestern industrialists during the 1940s, but for the
remainder of its existence, the *Cross and the Flag* relied on small contributions
from middle- and lower-class readers.[22]

During the first years of his controversial periodical's publication, Smith had
difficulty locating printers who wanted his business, and he frequently was
compelled to change printers. After moving to St. Louis in 1947, he found a printer
in Fort Worth, Texas, who wanted his business. When Smith moved his headquarters
to Los Angeles in 1953, he settled on the conservative Californian Charles F.
Robertson to do his work. An ordained minister in the "Foursquare Gospel Church"
of Aimee Semple McPherson, Robertson established a private print shop for Smith.
He soon became a partner rather than merely a printer and from 1958 until Smith's
death was listed as editor of the *Cross and the Flag*.[23]

Smith accumulated a small fortune from contributions and bequests of devoted
followers. In 1969 he invested part of his fortune in the construction of a seven-
story, ivory-white statue of Christ located on a mountain above the tiny Ozark
community of Eureka Springs, Arkansas. Several years later he began staging an
outdoor passion play that emphasized the role of Jews in the crucifixion. The
Cross and the Flag publicized these "Sacred Projects."[24]

The *Cross and the Flag* was so purely a personal journal that it could not outlast

Smith's demise. For several months after his death, it was edited by Roland Lee Morgan, a protégé of Smith who had married Charles Robertson's daughter. Morgan had supervised Smith's print shop in Los Angeles after Robertson moved to Eureka Springs. Within three months Robertson and Morgan began feuding. Robertson, an anti-Semite for reasons of expediency only, wanted to phase out the racist Christian Nationalist Crusade and concentrate instead on the "Sacred Projects" in Eureka Springs. Morgan, on the other hand, wanted to continue the Christian Nationalist Crusade. A man of little formal education and no literary experience, Morgan struggled to keep the *Cross and the Flag* alive. For a few issues he printed copy that Smith himself had written. With this material exhausted, the journal was terminated in December 1977. Less than a year later Morgan broke entirely with his father-in-law and quit the Smith organization.[25]

From its inception in 1942 until its termination in 1977, the *Cross and the Flag* had been one of the leading publications of the extreme Right. It furnished the chief outlet for disseminating Smith's racist ideas and provided him with a mailing list from which donors enabled him to live comfortably. It established and perpetuated his reputation as a sort of God-father of the ultranationalist, racist fringe. The monthly was a dose of adrenaline to its readers, stimulating them to donate money, purchase tracts, attend rallies, and circulate petitions for Smith's causes. Its significance, however, was not limited to the rank and file. The *Cross and the Flag* provided material that was frequently reprinted by other reactionary journals and also served as a model for other publishers on the far Right.

Notes

1. Glen Jeansonne, *Gerald L. K. Smith: Minister of Hate* (New Haven, 1988), pp. 11-79; for an account of Smith's early career see Jeansonne, "Preacher, Populist, Propagandist: The Early Career of Gerald L. K. Smith," *Biography* 2 (Fall 1979): 303-27.

2. *Cross and the Flag* 16 (June 1957): 4 (hereinafter cited as *C&F*).

3. *C&F* 17 (June 1958): 5; (August 1958): 11. The quotation on rock music is from *C &F* 17 (July 1958): 17.

4. *C&F* 11 (April 1952): 18.

5. Gerald L. K. Smith, *Too Much and Too Many Roosevelts* (n.p., 1950), p. 63.

6. *C&F* 17 (August 1958): 2.

7. Jeansonne, *Minister of Hate*, pp. 101-29; *C&F* 10 (April 1951): 12; *New York Times*, 22 May 1952.

8. *C&F* 11 (November 1952): 20.

9. *C&F* 17 (February 1959): 7-8.

10. *C&F* 12 (June 1953): 17.

11. Jeansonne, *Minister of Hate*, pp. 103-10; *C&F* 16 (October 1957): 23.

12. *C&F* 16 (January 1958): 3.

13. *C&F* 17 (August 1958): 10.

14. *C&F* 17 (September 1958): 8.

15. Ibid. .

16. Jeansonne, *Minister of Hate*, pp. 119-20; *C&F* 16 (August 1957): 17-19.

17. *C&F* 10 (November 1951): 23.

18. Jeansonne, *Minister of Hate*, pp. 135-38; Gerald L. K. Smith, taped interview with the author, Eureka Springs, Arkansas, 10 August 1974. I also taped interviews with Smith

on 11 August 1974, at Eureka Springs and on 28 December 1974, and 21 January 1975, at Los Angeles.

19. Jeansonne, *Minister of Hate*, pp. 140-41, 73-75. The best discussion of Smith's relationship with Ford is Isabel B. Price, "Gerald L. K. Smith and Anti-Semitism" (master's thesis, University of New Mexico, 1965). See also Albert Lee, *Henry Ford and the Jews* (New York, 1980).

20. Jeansonne, *Minister of Hate*, pp. 110-13. For the involvement of women and women's organizations in Smith's movement, see Jeansonne, *Women of the Far Right: The Mothers' Movement and World War II* (Chicago, 1996). See also Albin Krebs, "Proud of His Views," *New York Times*, 17 April 1976.

21. See yearly statements of ownership and circulation printed on the inside cover of *C&F*. See also American Jewish Yearbook for annual summations of circulation.

22. Jeansonne, *Minister of Hate*, pp. 143-51. Smith told me this in my interviews, and it is confirmed by yearly financial reports filed with the clerk of the U.S. House of Representatives. I also obtained a complete list of contributors in Wisconsin from the Milwaukee office of the Anti-Defamation League of B'nai B'rith.

23. *New York Herald-Tribune*, 27 March 1942; Smith, taped interview with J. Fraser Cocks III, 28 March 1968, Los Angeles, California, in Smith Collection, Bentley Historical Library, University of Michigan.

24. Jeansonne, *Minister of Hate*, pp. 188-205.

25. Ibid., pp. 211-12.

Information Sources

BIBLIOGRAPHY:

Jeansonne, Glen. "Preacher, Populist, Propagandist: The Early Career of Gerald L. K. Smith." *Biography* 2 (Fall 1979): 303-27.

————. *Gerald L. K. Smith: Minister of Hate*. New Haven, 1988.

Ribuffo, Leo P. *The Old Christian Right: The Protestant Far Right from the Great Depression to the Cold War*. Philadelphia, 1983.

Smith, Gerald L. K. *Besieged Patriot*. Edited by Elna M. Smith and Charles F. Robertson. Eureka Springs, Arkansas, 1978.

Smith, Gerald L. K. Papers. Bentley Historical Library, University of Michigan, Ann Arbor, Michigan.

INDEXES: None.

REPRINT EDITIONS: Microform: UMI.

LOCATION SOURCES: Widely available.

Publication History

TITLE AND TITLE CHANGES: *The Cross and the Flag*.

VOLUME AND ISSUE DATA: Volumes 1-35, April 1942-December 1977.

FREQUENCY OF PUBLICATION: Monthly.

PUBLISHER: Gerald L. K. Smith, Detroit, Michigan (1942-1946); St. Louis, Missouri (1947-1957); Los Angeles, California (1958-1976); Eureka Springs, Arkansas (1977).

EDITORS: Gerald L. K. Smith, 1942-1946; Don Lohbeck, 1947-1957; Charles F. Robertson, 1958-1976; Roland L. Morgan, 1977.

CIRCULATION: 25,000.

Glen Jeansonne

Truth Crusader
1953–1981

One of the most unusual magazines of the postwar religious Right was the *Truth Crusader*, a self-proclaimed "health publication"—a mix of fundamentalist Protestantism, Bible prophecy, anticommunism, conspiracy theories, political and social conservatism, and libertarianism, with discussions of vitamins, natural foods, organic gardening, home remedies, and folk medicines that would lead to greater longevity and good health. It was owned, published, and edited by Ernest L. Miller and his second wife, Mary, who operated a health foods store out of their home in Harrisonburg, Virginia. In addition, Miller had a "nutritional counseling service" and did radio broadcasts on the topics of dietary reform and political conspiracies. He was an Independent Church of the Brethren minister and preached occasionally, and for some years he had also been a teacher and school principal. He was born in Edinburg, Virginia, on 14 August 1898, and spent his entire life in the Shenandoah Valley region.

Miller was an unusual personality. Like those so ably analyzed by historian Leo Ribuffo in *The Old Christian Right*, he lived in a realm of delusion that nevertheless was marked by a semblance of internal consistency.[1] His emphasis on such values as piety, propriety, clean living, and hard work reflected a bourgeois upbringing. He belonged to what Peter Berger calls a "cognitive minority," a group that swims against the stream of modernity and progress and espouses a worldview that clashes with science, liberal religion, and economic rationalization. His ideas, essentially economic and health reform linked with fundamentalism and a vague populism, reflected the ambivalence so prevalent in extremist thought. In short, he held to tenets that in an earlier day would have been acceptable to many in the conservative mainstream but by the 1960s appealed only to anachronistic fringe elements on the far Right. Consequently, isolated in the Virginia backcountry and ignored by responsible conservatives, the aging Miller became increasingly extreme in his outlook.

The magazine's origins are shrouded in obscurity, and Miller refused to respond to my questions about it other than to say he closed the business on 5 September 1981. One source declares it was a quarterly that started in 1953,[2] but a diligent search of libraries with specialized holdings in radical materials failed to turn up a complete run of the magazine. It apparently was published at irregular intervals for a local market until a second-class mailing permit was secured in 1965, and then it appeared quarterly and occasionally more often. The annual reports that the postal service required to be published in the serial indicate that a promotional effort had resulted in a circulation of 4,500 by October 1969. The figure gradually crept upward, peaking at 8,700 in 1976. Then it began falling, and in September 1979, the last year a report was printed, the number had declined to 3,065. After one issue in 1981, the magazine ceased publication.

Miller had connections with several right-wing organizations, most notably the Liberty Lobby. He published an enthusiastic, two-page endorsement of the group in the spring 1970 issue and urged readers to subscribe to its *Liberty Letter*.[3] In 1972 he joined the board of advisers of the United Congressional Appeal, a Liberty Lobby front group founded in 1968, and his name appeared on its masthead as late as April 1980. Anti-Semitism was not a prevalent theme, but the magazine did publish a favorable review of Arthur Butz's *Hoax of the Twentieth Century* (a book that denies that Nazis had exterminated Jews) and reprinted an article from the racist *Christian Vanguard* describing the various tricks the "Jew-Leaders" were using to "level" American society.[4] The *Truth Crusader* also endorsed a variety of conservative publications and organizations, including *Human Events*, the Conservative Book Club, and *Don Bell Reports*. Enamored as he was by conspiracy theories, Miller even propagated the story that Czar Nicholas II's son, Aleksei, had not been killed by the Bolsheviks as generally believed but was alive in the United States, under protection from Soviet agents, and involved in anticommunist underground activities.[5]

In an article spelling out criteria for advertising, the editor set forth the magazine's objectives. First was "the realization of better health, greater efficiency, and longer life, through proper nutrition, exercise, faith, and natural organic foods free of all chemical fertilizers, poisonous sprays, and injurious additives." The second was "the defeat of socialism, communism, one-worldism, atheism, apostate ecumenicalism, welfarism, and a U.N.E.S.C.O., N.E.A. controlled, compulsory school system that is *brainwashing, seducing, kidnapping, and dechristianizing* the youth of America in direct accordance with [the] longplanned communist blueprint." Doing this will require "the restoration of a free competitive enterprise system; the inviolability and divinely instituted sanctity of marriage, home, and family; constitutional government; national sovereignty; Bible morality; and fundamental Christianity."[6]

From the health standpoint, the magazine ran material condemning fluoridation of drinking water, rain-making through cloud seeding, the use of chemical fertilizers, cooking with aluminum and teflon-coated pans, vaccination, and nuclear power plants. From the positive side it extolled the virtues of organic gardening, foods without chemical additives, exercise, abstinence from alcohol and all narcotics, and combating illness through home remedies and nutritional therapy. Occasionally it published "alphabetical encyclopedias" of such things as healthful foods (no. 31, 1969), injurious things (no. 33, 1969–70), natural drugless treatments (nos. 44–45, 1972–1973), and common diseases and drugless therapies (no. 82, 1980). These reflected, as Miller put it, his divine assignment "to demonstrate that right thinking, faith in God, right living, organic food, vitamins, minerals, and work can promote longevity and physical endurance and mental alertness."[7]

Although purporting to be a health magazine, the *Truth Crusader* was in reality much more of a political organ. The overarching idea in Miller's mental world was that of conspiracy, and he saw God-fearing, Christian Americans under assault from all sides. By far the most diabolical and dastardly of the assailants was communism. In the spring 1970 issue he detailed the horrors of a communist takeover in a long article modestly entitled, "Here Is Indisputable, Documented Proof That Our National Sovereignty, Our Constitution, the Liberties and Freedoms Bequeathed to Us by Our Brave Forefathers, Our Defences, Our Wealth, Our Resources, and Our Helpless, Innocent Children and Even Our Very Souls and Bodies Have through Deceptive, Fabian Gradualism Been Treasonably Betrayed and Surrendered to the Most Inhumane, the Most Horrible, the Most Brutal, the Most Sadistic Frankenstein Monster That Hell Ever Turned Loose on This Earth."[8]

The source of evil in the world was to be found in the master conspirator, Satan himself. He was the author of sickness and death who had the "entire chemicalized, mechanized, unionized, hypnotized world dancing to his diabolical music on the broad road to hell and destruction."[9] The rebellion of Lucifer against God pictured in the Bible (Isaiah 14:12–17, Ezekiel 28:13–17, John 8:44, Revelation 12:9) was the beginning of communism, and Miller traced the conspiracy through the fall of Adam, Tower of Babel, Mystery of Iniquity (2 Thessalonians 2:7), and Synagogue of Satan (Revelation 2:9) to the formation of the Illuminati in 1776. On that date Adam Weishaupt surrendered himself fully to Satan, from whom he received supernatural illumination, guidance, and power. In cooperation with Lucifer, he created the secret organization that set out to abolish the sovereignty of all nations and the unique characteristics of all races by forced integration and mongrelization. The Illuminati also sought to do away with marriage, the home, and private ownership of property, eternally banish Christianity from the earth, and establish a one-world government masterminded by Satan.[10]

Articles and editorials in most issues of the *Truth Crusader* called attention to the ubiquitous manifestations of the conspiracy: the United Nations, Council on Foreign Relations, UNICEF, the income tax, sex education, welfare, women's liberation, the National Educational Association, rock music, fluoridation, sensitivity training, mental health programs, foreign aid, Bilderbergers, ecumenists, one-world ideas, and agencies of the federal bureaucracy. At one point Miller raged on for several pages about the intention of the communists to take over America in 1976 and urged "all dedicated, informed, Christian patriots to immediately withdraw from the two communist controlled major political parties." Then the independent constitutional and American parties and every anticommunist organization (such as Christian Crusade, Christian Anti-Communism Crusade, John Birch Society, and the Cross and the Flag) should send delegates to a national convention to bring about coordinated political action and consolidate all the anticommunist forces into an effective political party.[11]

Neither this nor his continuing attacks on the conspiracies that threatened the nation seemed to be generating any response, so he decided to do something more dramatic. In the summer of 1974 he announced that he would be "God's Independent, Nondenominational, Nonparty Candidate for President of the United States." The Lord Jesus had come to Miller in a vision and "plainly told" him he was to be "his independent candidate." Christ did not inform him that he should expect to win and he was not planning to spend much money on the campaign or engage in debates, but he was going to preach the gospel to the entire nation through this endeavor.[12]

Miller declared it would be "the most unusual, the most exciting, the most evangelistic, the most Christ-centered presidential campaign in the history of the nation," but "most quixotic" would be a more accurate characterization of it. His motto was "Another Lincoln" and he put forth a twenty-nine-point platform that summarized nearly everything he had been saying in the *Truth Crusader* for years.[13] The almost seventy-seven-year-old health faddist and political radical told the Harrisonburg newspaper in June 1975 that he would be on the road until the 1976 election and would visit all fifty states, but no evidence exists that he in fact did so.[14] He chose as his running mate a sixty-one-year-old retired army officer and "experienced organic farmer" from North Carolina, Colonel Roy N. Eddy.[15] It is doubtful that his candidacy attracted much attention outside the Shenandoah Valley, although the Winrod *Defender* magazine did endorse his platform, and a preacher named Richard E. Carlock from Cicero, Illinois, was identified as the Illinois chairman of the Miller-for-President Committee.[16] Neither the *Washington Post* or any other major national newspaper mentioned his candidacy, although he boasted to the local newspaper that support was growing.[17]

After the defeat Miller announced his intention to run again in 1980, when he would be eighty-two, and rebuffed the claims of critics that he would be too old by saying there were at least 1,500 healthy people one hundred years of age or older who were still working daily.[18] However, the aging editor seemed to be living in a world of unreality. Each issue in the later 1970s proclaimed as "our goal 200,000 new subscribers this year," while the circulation in fact steadily drifted downward. He kept up his drumfire of attacks on conspiracy and added humanism to the list of evils. In 1978 Miller directed a long, rambling open letter to President Jimmy Carter, asking him to stop the spread of communism and work to bring about repentance and revival in America.[19] At the same time the comments on both politics and health increasingly took on the quality of déjà vu. Miller's political energies were obviously spent and he did not run again for president as he had promised. In his last editorial he praised Ronald Reagan's inaugural address and then his voice fell silent.[20] He died three years later, on 10 March 1984.[21]

Its mix of health faddism, fundamentalist religion, and extreme political views made the *Truth Crusader* a far Right publication of the 1970s. Its influence was not great, but Miller showed that one can incorporate an element into a conservative worldview that commentators often associate with radical leftism. The excessive emphasis on conspiratorial movements may readily be dismissed, but the linkage of health and politics is an idea that holds possibilities for the future.

Notes

1. Leo P. Ribuffo, *The Old Christian Right: The Protestant Far Right from the Great Depression to the Cold War* (Philadelphia, 1983), pp. xiv–xviii, 237–57.

2. Robert H. Muller, *From Radical Left to Extreme Right,* 2nd ed. (Montclair, New Jersey, 1976), p. 1538.

3. *Truth Crusader* no. 34 (1970): 40–41 (hereinafter cited as *TC*). Because the magazine used only issue numbers, specific dates of publication often must be determined from internal evidence.

4. *TC* no. 65 (1977): 17; *TC* no. 74 (1978): 15–17.

5. *TC* no. 52 (1974): 34–37.

6. *TC* no. 43 (1972): 40.

7. *TC* no. 64 (1976): 10.

8. *TC* no. 33 (1969–1970): 12–23.

9. *TC* no. 49–50 (1974): 25.

10. *TC* no. 34 (1970): 2; *TC* no. 43 (1972): 3; *TC* no. 51 (1974): 12.

11. *TC* no. 33 (1969–1970): 32.

12. *TC* no. 51 (1974): 12, 25, 28.

13. *TC* no. 52 (1974): 29; *TC* no. 57–58 (1975): 29–30.

14. *Harrisonburg Daily News-Record,* 25 June 1975, p. 15.

15. *TC* no. 56 (1975): 17–18; *TC* no. 59–60 (1976): 14.

16. *TC* no. 55 (1975): 28; *TC* no. 63 (1976): 23.

17. *Harrisonburg Daily News-Record,* 2 January 1976, p. 11.

18. *TC* no. 64 (1977): 10.

19. *TC* no. 71 (1978): 4–10.

20. *TC* no. 84 (1981): 11.

21. Obituary in the *Harrisonburg Daily News-Record,* 12 March 1984, p. 5.

Information Sources

BIBLIOGRAPHY:

Falwell, Jerry, ed. *The Fundamentalist Phenomenon: The Resurgence of Conservative Christianity.* Garden City, New York, 1981.

Marsden, George M. *Fundamentalism and American Culture: The Shaping of Twentieth-Century Evangelicalism.* New York, 1980.

Ribuffo, Leo P. *The Old Christian Right: The Protestant Far Right from the Great Depression to the Cold War.* Philadelphia, 1983.

INDEXES: None.

REPRINT EDITIONS: Microform: Right Wing Collection, University of Iowa (MCA), partial run, 1969–1977 (reel 133).

LOCATION SOURCES: Partial runs: Collections Department, Tulane University Library; University of Iowa; State Historical Society of Wisconsin.

Publication History

TITLE AND TITLE CHANGES: *Truth Crusader.*

VOLUME AND ISSUE DATA: Numbers 1–81, 1953(?)–Winter 1981.

FREQUENCY OF PUBLICATION: Quarterly.

PUBLISHER: Ernest L. Miller, Harrisonburg, Virginia.

EDITOR: Ernest L. Miller.
CIRCULATION: In 1976, 8,700.

Richard V. Pierard

Task Force
1954–1978

The monthly four-page periodical *Task Force* was founded in 1954 as the official publication of the Defenders of the American Constitution, Incorporated, with offices in Washington, D.C. (later moved to Florida and still later to Virginia). The founders included a few women and several retired military officers, led by P. A. del Valle, lieutenant general, U. S. Marine Corps, Retired. The organizers of *Task Force* were both stunned and shamed by the actions of certain people who were considered to have prevented the United States from attaining victory in the Korean War and desired a forum to communicate their frustrations and fears to other "loyal Americans."

Although many persons contributed articles, poems, and editorials to *Task Force* in its nearly twenty-five years of publication, the magazine was unmistakably the alter ego of del Valle, who announced in the first issue his candidacy for the governorship of Maryland. In a description accompanying this announcement, del Valle wrote of himself: "The General is the descendant of a pure Castillian family who moved to Puerto Rico when that island was under Spanish control….He is no politician….But by the standards of Americanism he is a veritable giant—a sincere, tough old soldier who realizes that the decisive battle for America will not be fought on such blood-soaked fields as Guadalcanal,…but on the political front in States like Maryland."[1]

Such histrionic comments occur with sufficient frequency to indicate that *Task Force* was not simply a forum for promoting devotion to and protection of America, despite the dominant nature of that theme in the periodical. Inevitably, *Task Force* articles began with a credible observation that rapidly expanded into a conspiracy theory to account for all events of history. For example, in the early years of *Task Force*, articles frequently probed into the nature of the Korean War. Valid questions would be raised concerning the relationship between the United States and the United Nations, as well as that between President Harry S Truman and General

Douglas MacArthur. Such questions were only rhetorical inasmuch as the author would invariably identify the *real* sources of our political ills as "due to the interference...of the conspirators within our midst."[2] As was commonplace in the 1950s, the patriots of *Task Force* believed that communists and their fellow travelers were to be found in the news media, in the film industry in Hollywood, and even among official presidential advisers. But unlike many conservatives who traced a conspiracy to the writings and deeds of such famous communists as Lenin and Stalin, del Valle and his friends developed a conspiracy theory of the conspiracy itself.

According to del Valle, communism "is no more, no less, than an instrument of the internationalist bankers to reduce the United States, and all Christendom, to a sort of an animal farm."[3] In another article del Valle wrote: "The truth is that it was not Lenin who conquered the Holy Russian Empire, where Christianity flourished. It was the international Jewish bankers who paid for the whole job."[4] He insisted that the conspiracy could be traced to the money changers who were chased out of the temple by Jesus Christ. In an apparent interpretation of such passages of the Bible as Luke 19:45, del Valle quoted Christ as saying: "My house is a house of prayer. But you have made it a den of thieves."[5] "This," commented del Valle, "is perhaps the most important lesson of history, and the one least heeded by us....In the course of changing the political and social order of the world to suit their own purposes, we have seen the house of Kuhn and Loeb finance the destructive powers of Lenin and the Marxists who overthrew Tsarist Russia and murdered the Tsar and his family. More social and political changes were made through Hitler, who was also financed by the internationalist bankers....Communism also is international and also anti-Christian and appears to be merely a tool of the real world conquerors. When Marxism no longer fits their books, it will be destroyed."[6]

The tentacles of the conspiracy reached everywhere: "there is considerable documentary evidence to prove that all revolutions, wars, depressions, strikes and chaos stem from this source."[7] The conspirators "are avaricious in their greed for power,...with the overwhelming ambition to dominate international markets and exercise world-wide industrial and financial control."[8] These conspirators gained control of the United States in 1913 with the passage of the Federal Reserve Act, which paved the way for them to bleed the nation of many billions of dollars and to have "caused inflation which has so reduced the value of our dollar to dangerous lows in terms of foreign currency. Who controls your money controls you and your government."[9] How did this happen? Del Valle explained it in detail: "Then, at 4 P.M. on December 24 [1913] when all but three Senators had gone home for Christmas, those there called themselves into session,...two of the senators...voted yes...and within an hour...President Wilson signed it into law...and ever since then the gang that owns the Fed, as it is now called, many of them foreigners, whose names are unknown, have been looting us of our wealth."[10] Six years later, del Valle was prepared to reveal just who these conspirators are: "Todays [*sic*] leading financiers are the Rothchilds [*sic*] and the Rockefellers. Can it be that usury has got the upper hand over the once free, plenteous and productive land?...Add to this situation an almost total control of our money, which in turn gives them control of Congress, the economy, the news media, entertainment, schools, etc!"[11]

As often happens in the literature of the American far Right, the enemy is in reality the Jew, the Zionist, the Israelite—the enemy of Christianity and "the American branch of the White race."[12] A widely circulated conspiracy theory in these circles was the *Protocols of the Elders of Zion*, which de Valle quoted and interpreted frequently. Despite his occasional insistence that some of *Task Force's* readers were Jews and good, loyal Americans, his anti-Jewish feelings were at times virulent. "Jewry," del Valle wrote, "will not be satisfied until it becomes the law-making body for the whole world....He [the Jew] it is who is the perennial law-breaker, the eternal sower of discord among the nations."[13] On another occasion he wrote: "How many real Christians are holding the most powerful positions in our national and state governments?...If this be anti-semitism, then make the most of it."[14] Del Valle also advanced the theory that abortions performed in legalized abortion mills in America were done so as to make room for Zionist immigrants. We do not need more, he continued, because "they already occupy such positions of leadership in every activity in the United States of America."[15]

With the stakes so high, it is not surprising that the conspirators would stop at nothing to eliminate anyone who would work against them. "John Wilkes Booth, the Jewish actor who subsequently murdered Mr. Lincoln, has been shown...to have been in touch with the Rothchilds [*sic*]."[16] Lincoln was apparently assassinated because he issued greenbacks rather than put the United States in the hands of international bankers. Del Valle suggested that "another President who emulated Lincoln's example was likewise assassinated. John F. Kennedy made a new issue of Lincoln style Greenbacks in 1963...just weeks before his death."[17] An opponent of the federal reserve system, Louis T. McFadden, "paid for this service with his life."[18] When Senator Joseph McCarthy (R, Wisconsin) pointed out the subversives, "he was signing his own death warrant...the mental and spiritual crucifixion to which he was subjected broke his will to live."[19]

Murder was not the only weapon of the conspirators reported in *Task Force*. Early issues of the periodical repeated the horrors of a plan to build a mental hospital in Alaska "to provide a handy means of disposing of anti-Communist, American Patriots who dare disagree with socialism and internationalism."[20] Once inside the hospital, the patriot was to be lobotomized. "There are perhaps 100,000 lobotomized people in this country today...[and since] everyone is mentally ill to some degree, you may rest assured the one-worlders are planning big things for patriots."[21] Another diabolical plan was for the "one world conspirators" to place the United States in the hands of the world federalists. *Task Force* frequently published a map illustrating that the world was to be divided into zones. The United States would be split into four zones, ruled by directors or "commissars," who, "according to the rules, were not to be citizens or subjects of the zones they ruled." As a result, "we can look forward to being policed by Turks, Hindus, African Tribesman and Red Chinese."[22] For those who find such a conspiracy theory beyond easy comprehension, one regular *Task Force* contributor had these comments: "People who won't believe in the conspiracy theory of history are the very ones who make it possible for conspirators to go on making history."[23] One thing is certain: Sir Lewis B. Namier's observation that "the crowning achievement of historical study is to achieve an intuitive sense of how things do not happen" is the product of a mind totally at odds with what one encounters in the American far Right.[24]

Ironically, perhaps, the conspiracy theory advanced in *Task Force* was so inclusive that it is difficult at times to distinguish it from theories put forward on the extreme Left. The following excerpt is prefaced by del Valle's comment that he had served under Major General Smedley D. Butler, who wrote: "I spent 32 years and 4 months in the country's most agile military force, the Marines....I spent most of my time being a high class muscle man for big business, for Wall Street, and the Bankers. Thus I have helped make Mexico safe for American Oil interests, helped make Haiti and Cuba decent places for the National City Bank boys to collect revenue in; I helped in the raping of half a dozen Central American republics for the benefit of Wall Street....[I]n China in 1927 I helped see to it that Standard Oil went its way unmolested."[25] Del Valle continued with a quote Bismarck is supposed to have made in 1876: "The division of the United States into two federations of equal force was decided long before the Civil War, by the high financial powers of Europe. These bankers were afraid that the United States, if they remained as one block and as one nation, would attain financial and economic independence, which would upset their financial domination over the world." Del Valle then commented that "the root of the evil...is love of money, which keeps men who should know better, fighting for physical security even as their souls are being destroyed in a hell." Most of this passage could have been written by any conspiratorial follower of the Marxist Left, although del Valle would insist that his loyalty was to the example of Christ.

Throughout his many years with *Task Force*, del Valle maintained an identification with Christ and those American revolutionaries who risked everything in the never-ending battle with the many forces of the Antichrist. Themes of sacrifice and death occurred frequently in his writings. At times, del Valle cast himself in the role of underdog who has no chance without the Lord's assistance: "And let those of us who will face this powerful army of the Anti-Christ go forth with our sling shots and stones, and with the power of our Lord and Savior, give battle to this modern Goliath. There is no other choice. May God so bless us and guide us that we shall not surrender to His enemies!"[26]

The degree of our sacrifice is sometimes spelled out clearly: "It is up to us to lay down our lives, our fortunes and our sacred honor, as once the Founders did, on the alter [sic] of freedom."[27] Strength for the battle will come from "faith in our Lord Jesus Christ....He will not forsake us if we come to Him asking for guidance and help."[28] However, del Valle did not always cast himself as the successful heroic leader. In one revealing essay, he asked for God's mercy *because* "our sins have brought this [the conspiracy] upon us."[29] In another passage del Valle suggested that "we should be willing to risk our miserable lives in an effort to secure freedom."[30]

Near the end of his life, del Valle revealed even more aggression in advocating this course of events: "We certainly can take back control of our country by a military coup d'etat. History shows that there is no other way to dislodge these S.O.B.'s once they have taken possession of a Christian nation through Communism."[31] On another occasion del Valle suggested: "Maybe by 1976 there will be enough angry slaves to throw off their chains and take back their country by force of arms."[32]

When almost eighty years old, del Valle wrote: "My friends, in the play Hamlet chose to fight, to oppose, to put an end to his sea of troubles. He destroyed the evil enemy in his midst and lost his life doing it. And so it is with us. The evils, our own sea of troubles, require that we take our arms against it, and, by opposing, end them."[33] Pedro del Valle's "sea of troubles" ended in April 1978. Because his troubles were so overwhelmingly personal, *Task Force* died with him.

Throughout the years of *Task Force*, del Valle reached out to his readers to enlist their active support in the causes he considered most important. Despite the tone of frustration and inevitable defeat, del Valle implored his readers to help in "getting the U.S. out of the U.N. and the U.N. out of the U.S.," abolishing the Federal Reserve system, and for keeping permanent U.S. control of the Panama Canal. Readers were asked to campaign in behalf of the few patriots who ran for public office. With increasing years, however, del Valle displayed less and less optimism that the fight would end with victory this side of the grave.

Unfortunately, detailed biographical information about Pedro del Valle is not available. Nevertheless, much about a person is revealed in almost twenty-five years of writing on themes of great personal importance. In his authoritative work on paranoia, W. W. Meissner outlined the paranoid elements found in his clinical experience. Some of these elements seem particularly applicable to del Valle and help us to understand the political personality he represented. Among the elements are the *displacement of responsibility*, wherein the paranoid avoids the pain of self-blame by placing the responsibility for pain, evil, and weakness on others; and *suspiciousness*, wherein the paranoid alleviates personal uncertainty by developing a coherent, certain, and hostile environment. Another element involves *grandiosity*, wherein the paranoid asserts a conviction of greatness and rightness. In one of the most famous cases on paranoia, the patient had delusions of an alliance with God. The final component to be considered here is the formulation of a *paranoid pseudocommunity* wherein the "patient gradually builds up a delusional reconstruction in which his projections become organized into a stable picture of external reality. Ideas of reference or persecution...gradually become organized into a unified group which has a definite plot aimed at the patient as the intended victim."[34] We cannot know, of course, whether del Valle achieved any psychic relief from his political activities. But his activity does seem to accord with Freud's assessment of paranoia in which the world is reconstructed so that the patients' anxieties make sense and are alleviated.[35]

Such findings of modern psychology enable us to see that persons like Pedro del Valle are not a part of an authentic conservative tradition of thought in America, despite their apparent devotion to certain traditional conservative themes. Behind the themes and facade, we find personalities who express abnormal amounts of anger and frustration and have more in common with the character of General Jack

Ripper in the memorable film *Dr. Strangelove* than with those with a considered commitment to the tenets of modern conservative thought.

Notes

1. P. A. del Valle, Editorial, *Task Force* 1 (May 1954): 1 (hereinafter cited as *TF*).
2. del Valle, "An Open Letter" *TF* 1 (June 1954): 3.
3. del Valle, "We Declare," *TF* 19 (May 1972): 4.
4. del Valle, "The Taxpayers Lament," *TF* 23 (October 1976): 3.
5. del Valle, "The Great Lesson of History," *TF* 5 (November 1958): 1.
6. Ibid.
7. W. B. Vennard, "America—'59 Model," *TF* 6 (November 1959): 1.
8. Ida Darden, "Regardless of Who Is Elected President Invisible Powers Govern United States," reprinted in *TF* 2 (October 1955): 1.
9. del Valle, "How Many of Our Honorable Members of Congress?" *TF* 24 (May 1977): 1.
10. del Valle, "Is It Too Late to Save America?" *TF* 16 (October 1969): 3.
11. del Valle, "Who Rules Our Country?" *TF* 22 (September 1975): 3–4.
12. Eugene Cowles Pomeroy, "One Worlders' Plan Disclosed," *TF* 1 (January 1955): 1.
13. del Valle, "The Invisible Government," *TF* 8 (June 1961): 1.
14. del Valle, "Christ, Country and Constitution," *TF* 23 (August 1976): 3.
15. del Valle, "An Assessment of the Situation," *TF* 18 (September 1971): 4.
16. del Valle, "The Great Lesson of History," p. 1.
17. del Valle, "The Battle Is Not Yours, but God's!" *TF* 18 (December 1971): 1.
18. del Valle, "Quotations from a Christian Martyr," *TF* 24 (March 1978): 1.
19. Unsigned editorial, *TF* 4 (June 1957): 1.
20. del Valle, "An Alaskan Siberia for Mental Health," *TF* 2 (February 1956): 1.
21. Stephanie Williams, "Living Bodies with Dead Souls," *TF* 3 (February 1957): 3–4.
22. Pomeroy, "One Worlders' Plan Disclosed," p. 2.
23. J. Kesner Kahn, "History," *TF* 17 (March 1971): 2.
24. Lewis B. Namier, "History," in Fritz Stern, ed., *The Varieties of History* (New York, 1956), p. 375.
25. del Valle, "America's Solution," *TF* 8 (January 1962): 3.
26. del Valle, "An Address to the National Convention of the Constitution Parties," *TF* 17 (September 1970): 3.
27. del Valle, "'Tis' Here We Take Our Stand," *TF* 12 (January 1966): 3.
28. Ibid., p. 4.
29. del Valle, "Centralized Power Versus Constitutional Government," *TF* 5 (September 1958): 4.
30. del Valle, "God or Government," *TF* 19 (January 1973): 1.
31. del Valle, "The Sons of Beel-ze-bub," *TF* 23 (July 1976): 2.
32. del Valle, "God or Government," p. 1.
33. del Valle, "Get Up and Fight," *TF* 19 (July 1972): l.
34. W. W. Meissner, *The Paranoid Process* (New York, 1978), Chapter 2.
35. Richard D. Chessick, *Freud Teaches Psychotherapy* (Indianapolis, 1980), p. 102.

Information Sources

BIBLIOGRAPHY:

Cohn, Norman. *The Pursuit of the Millennium*. London, England, 1957.

Hofstadter, Richard. *The Paranoid Style in American Politics and Other Essays*. New York, 1966.

Meissner, W. W. *The Paranoid Process*. New York, 1978.
INDEXES: None.
REPRINT EDITIONS: None.
LOCATION SOURCES: Complete runs: Library of Congress; New York Public Library;
    Harvard University; University of Iowa; University of Oregon.

Publication History

TITLE AND TITLE CHANGES: *Task Force: An American Publication for Loyal Americans*.
VOLUME AND ISSUE DATA: Volumes 1–24, May 1954–June 1978.
FREQUENCY OF PUBLICATION: Monthly.
PUBLISHER: Defenders of the American Constitution, Ormond Beach, Florida (1954–
    1970); Annandale, Virginia (1970–1978).
EDITORS: P. A. del Valle, 1954–1967; Gordon E. Small, 1967–1968; Matthew P. McKeon,
    1968–1969; Kathryn M. Lange, 1969–1970; Matthew P. McKeon, 1970–1978;
    Edward L. Bart, 1978.
CIRCULATION: Probably 2,000–3,000.

William C. Baum

Citizen
1955–1989

In May 1954 the U.S. Supreme Court delivered the *Brown* v. *Board of Education of Topeka* decision that rejected the "separate but equal" racial doctrine of *Plessy* v. *Ferguson* (1896). In response to this historic reversal in judicial interpretation, plantation manager Robert B. Patterson and Judge Thomas P. Brady, both of Mississippi, formed the Citizens' Council, a white supremacist organization "imbued simply with the primordial desire to ensure the survival of [whites] and their descendants through the social order founded by their own forefathers."[1] Organized in communities throughout the South, the council tried to keep the region's traditionally segregated order alive through legal advice, political pressure against school integration, "education" about civil rights, and "lawful" resistance to the desegregation of traditionally separate facilities. Needing an information-education publication, the organization in 1955 established for its almost 60,000 members a monthly newspaper tabloid, *Citizens' Council*.[2] In 1961 the editors dropped the tabloid format, adopted a pulp magazine style, and changed the title to *Citizen*. Printed in Jackson, Mississippi, the journal reached approximately three thousand readers.

The journal distanced itself from the extreme racial hatred of the Ku Klux Klan, yet cloaked its own brand of respectable and "intellectual" racism in the impressive credentials of its editorial staff. For example, editor William J. Simmons received his degree from Millsaps College in Mississippi and did additional studies at the University of Touraine in France. The first managing editor, Richard D. Morphew, was graduated from the University of Missouri's School of Journalism, and worked as a television and radio newscaster before he joined the Citizens' Council on a full-time basis. Medford Evans, who assumed managing editor duties after Morphew's November 1966 death, earned his doctorate in English at Yale in 1933, worked as chief of security training for the Atomic Energy Commission, and served the Citizens' Council as a full-time consultant. George Shannon, editor of the

Shreveport Journal for eighteen years, took over as editor in February 1972 when Simmons assumed the publisher's chair.[3]

The journal's primary appeal was to racists who had some higher education and could understand the "intellectual" arguments presented by the regular contributors, a group of educated men that included Patterson, Brady, Jesse Helms, John Synon, Carleton Putnam, and Dr. Henry E. Garrett. Along with Garrett, many other contributors, such as A. A. Kitchings, Robert E. Kuttner, and Tommy W. Rogers, held Ph.D.s from respectable universities, including Wake Forest and Columbia. The *Citizen* usually introduced an interpretive article by listing the schools the author attended and the prestigious positions he held. In this way the magazine kept its image respectable and at the same time gave the racism of its writers a veneer of academic authority. Some of these authors, however, held ideas ranging from the questionable to the ludicrous, indicating that the fine institutions these men attended somehow failed in their educational purposes. For example, Medford Evans, plainly ignoring the fact that the founders intended the states to control the Senate while the people ruled the House, once wrote that "one man, one vote" violated the Constitution because not all states were of equal population yet each sent only two senators to Washington. Even more laughable was the piece written by Robert E. Kuttner, a "noted" zoologist, that claimed blacks had no history indigenous to their own cultures. In addition to marshaling the talents of these writers the editors also published special issues or sections that examined such topics as the effects of desegregation on children, the George Wallace presidential campaign, establishing private schools, Jackson, Mississippi's "White Monday" rally, Vietnam, and Abraham Lincoln's racial views.[4]

In order to establish legitimacy, racists need intellectual justification for their views. For the *Citizen*, the editors and writers established three theoretical frameworks on which they defended racial orthodoxy. The southern states rights tradition stands as the first corner of this triad. Localism, strict construction, and individualism dominate the *Citizen*'s theories of government, which provide the legal framework to its opposition to desegregation. According to contributors, before man established government, he spent most of his time protecting his family and property from hostile forces. When that task threatened to override all other concerns, men joined together to establish governments to protect them, limited in power only to what the people already had a right to do for themselves. Government's only role was that of protector of life, liberty, and property. Any other power the government arrogated to itself, such as social planning or the redistribution of wealth, amounted to seizure and usurpation because the people could not perform these functions in the first place.[5]

A great deal of the Constitution's brilliance came from the founders' recognition of this relationship between man and his government. The document's writers believed a strong central government threatened the liberty of all, so they gave the separate states the power to conduct their own internal affairs as they saw fit. State governments would perform what duties they could while the federal government administered the functions too large for the states to handle. The states, rightly jealous of their sovereignty, hoped such a balanced system would keep the individual free from the omnipotence of an overbearing federal government. To ensure that balance, the founders included the Tenth Amendment to the Bill of Rights in order to guarantee that elected representatives of the states could freely decide their own best course. At no time during the creation of the Constitution, the *Citizen's* contributors asserted, did the founders intend for the federal government to intrude into the democratically determined customs, manners, or laws of the states.[6]

Ever since the South lost the Civil War, contributors argued, the states have fought losing battles to retain those constitutional powers. Not coincidentally, the race issue figured prominently in the fight to keep state sovereignty safe. Through the Thirteenth Amendment, the North deprived the southern states of the freedom to choose their economic institutions. The Supreme Court delivered a damaging blow to the right of states to determine their own social institutions when it handed down the *Brown* decision and further distorted the Constitution by its tortured interpretation of the Fourteenth Amendment, which caused the balanced federated system created by the founders to tip dangerously toward powerful national government. After that, federal power, especially within the judicial branch, grew at an alarming rate. The destruction of the "intended" interpretation of the document continued as the Court amended it through judicial fiat and not through the process put forth in the Constitution: after the *Brown* decision the Court approved busing, banned prayer in the schools, and betrayed any pretension to color blindness with its affirmative action decisions. "Who knew where it would end?" the journal asked plaintively in issue after issue. Now the states, which since the beginning of the nation's history had protected civil liberties (which the journal believed to be only rights of property and due process), found themselves forced to submit to the dictates of the federal government. This "sociological jurisprudence" proved a disaster as the states lost the power to rule themselves and their own particular institutions to a national government unfamiliar with the reasons for those institutions.

Thanks to this "sociological jurisprudence," in the view of the *Citizen*, within twenty years after the *Brown* decision, the people of the nation no longer could claim control of their lives as the courts and the federal bureaucracy decided how they should live, work, and raise children. With that loss of control went any semblance of an orderly society founded on moral values. In fact, after the Supreme Court decided on the death penalty issue, states could not even properly punish their criminals. When the renewal of the Voting Rights Act came due in the early 1980s, the *Citizen* urged its rejection as a quasi-legislative and judicial exercise of powers not granted to the federal branch. By rejecting the extension, President Reagan would signal that he planned to return power to the states, as he had often promised to do in his campaign. The journal believed Americans could save the Constitution, but only if federal judges went through reconfirmation hearings every eight years, and the nation elected presidents and representatives aware of "correct" constitutional limits. If the nation failed to do this, the federal government would get stronger and eventually make itself into a totalitarian dictatorship. California's approval of Proposition Thirteen, which cut property taxes, cheered the *Citizen*, and appeared to show that the nation had taken the first step toward restoring governmental and fiscal sanity.[7]

In order to prevent the federal government from taking too much power unto itself, the *Citizen* for a time advocated interposition—that is, the nullification and voidance of federal laws and Supreme Court decisions the states considered unconstitutional. Using flowery Jeffersonian language, the journal in December 1955 advised readers that "the time [had] come in the life of our country for the sovereign States of this Nation to take stock and review their relationship to the Federal Government," and warned: "When the Federal Judiciary usurps a power specifically reserved to a State it usurps it from all the States."[8] According to the editorial, the victorious North had fraudulently forced the Fourteenth Amendment on the defeated South, so that, in effect, the amendment was illegal, which nullified any Court decisions favorable to desegregation based on it. *Brown*, moreover, null though it therefore must be, in stripping the states of their rights to determine their own institutions, voided the Tenth Amendment, which the founders had intended as a protection for the states against the federal government. More important, the Supreme Court, making decisions based on left-wing sociology instead of constitutional rules of law, did not legally possess the power to make decrees that had the effect of acts of Congress since no court could do by fiat what the Constitution prevented the Congress from doing. The only proper means of redressing the supposed wrongs "corrected" by the Court was through the amendment process provided in the Constitution. Under such conditions, *Citizens' Council* argued, the separate states not only had the right, but they had a sacred duty to interpose their will on a judiciary and government out of touch with its constituents.

Southerners tempted to travel the interposition path could take heart that the theory had a long history, highlighted by John C. Calhoun's nullification attempt of 1832 and the antifugitive slave laws fourteen northern states passed after the *Dred Scott* decision. Quoting Calhoun directly, the *Citizens' Council* stated what it believed were the fundamental questions of the desegregation controversy and of American government in general: Was this a constitutional or an absolute government? Was America's governmental authority based on the sovereign rights of the separate states or the untrammeled will of the majority? Finally, if the government was an unlimited one, would violence, force, and injustice prevail? Interposition promised to cure the plagues visited on the nation ("equality," coerced race mixing, the destruction of private property rights, excessive regulation by federal authorities) by returning governmental authority to responsible people able to govern themselves within the states. Interposition would keep the fight for racial integrity alive at the local level, the most important level, and give "our people...a sense of their own power...and independence...and save our Constitution and this Union."[9]

In much the same way that southern political thought stresses the individual's relationship to his government, so too does southern religion emphasize a personal relationship with God. Because of this, traditional southern Protestant apocalyptic and millenarian eschatology make up the second aspect of the *Citizen*'s reaction to desegregation and racial matters. According to the various ministers and writers who contribute to the journal, the minions of the Antichrist, the spawn of the devil, forced integration on the South as part of his plot to dethrone Christ. Because the Bible frequently inveighed against mixing with "ungodly" peoples, believing them unclean, the journal considered integration an attempt to create a man-made social order contrary to God's teaching and intentions. God did not create equality among nature or men, despite what the philosophers and Jefferson said in the eighteenth century. The only equality he established in his universe was equality of sinfulness and hopelessness among sinners. He plainly made the black race an inferior order for reasons only he could fathom. Any militant attempt to alter those conditions or lift up the black race would fail because man stood no chance of redeeming himself without Christ's help. More important, militant social action to change the segregated social order, especially that initiated by the clergy, was sinful itself, given God's divine sanction of that order.[10]

Once the evil of integration took hold, the *Citizen* asserted, the Antichrist started to destroy other facets of American life: secular humanism deified man's work above that of God's, the lawless appropriated civil "rights" for themselves while law-abiding people lost life and property, unborn innocents faced death while murderers lived, and "arrogant and obnoxious females" agitated for constitutional amendments that would destroy the family. In effect, the nation rejected the long-held dogma of "Christ as Savior" for the anti-Christian belief of "Big Government as Protector." As America rejected God, it embraced socialism, the ultimate attempt at ungodly social planning. This ideology created class consciousness where none existed before, uncovered deep animosities among previously peaceful people, and attempted to join the races under the aegis of a man-made order. Such a scheme denied that Christ's death united men under God and said man could redeem himself though earthly accomplishments. Thus socialism and integration converged: both determined to destroy the order created by God and establish something unattainable. As such, both were un-Christian tools of the Antichrist.[11]

In addition to the sacred justifications for segregation, contributors developed temporal rationales for the institution. Above all else, integration was fraudulent—an unnatural state of affairs for man to develop. Those who worked for the mixing of the races accomplished it by lies, retained it through deception, and enforced it through confusion. The races stayed separate, not only because God ordained it, but because people naturally associated with those of their own kind: blacks always stayed with blacks, and whites always stayed with whites. Upon voluntary segregation, people had built the basis for racial peace. After the Civil War had destroyed the South's primary economic institution, the region fought the war of Reconstruction, winning it in 1896 when the Supreme Court institutionalized racial separation and order with the *Plessy* v. *Ferguson* decision. For eighty years legally sanctioned segregation helped maintain a peaceful balance in the region. When the Warren Court reversed *Plessy*, it shattered the peace and initiated a second reconstruction as the federal government rearranged the way law-abiding people lived their lives. After that fateful decision, American life turned malevolent and dangerous. Every month readers could see in the "Random Glances at the News" section, a regular feature since December 1971, exactly how blacks alledgely abused their newly won "freedom." Stories abounded of blacks rioting, looting, and killing whites and fellow blacks. The *Citizen* especially took delight in detailing such stories if they occurred in the North or in desegregated public schools. In a particularly important example, the armed forces, integrated in 1948, proved to the journal's readers how disastrous desegregation could be to an institution. In Vietnam, black soldiers wore nonmilitary Afro haircuts. Commanders allowed blacks to read literature by such revolutionaries as Eldridge Cleaver, Stokely Carmichael, and Malcolm X. Blacks actively participated in drug abuse in the field, and commanders locked away weapons lest angry blacks and Puerto Ricans revolt. In effect, when the federal government integrated the armed services it allowed elements hostile to America to establish a foothold in the very institution pledged to defend America. The implication of the *Citizen*'s words almost jumps from the page: to keep blacks "in their place" and prevent them from destroying the country, integration must be stopped.[12]

Among the most galling aspects of the whole nightmare was the fact that the Supreme Court did not even use lawful precedent to justify its attacks on the South's institutions. Instead, Earl Warren depended on the studies of Gunnar Myrdal, the Swedish economist, for the material to overturn segregation. Mydral, despite his credentials elsewhere, certainly could not in honesty call himself an expert in American race relations. After *Brown,* the *Citizen* argued, the federal government believed it could intervene in local matters to harass and intimidate people who stood up for their rights. Thanks to the power of the liberal establishment, which applauds coercive desegregation despite evidence of its failure, a newsman or a professor risked his position and reputation if he questioned so much as a small aspect of the integration movement. As a result, anthropological facts were ignored, constitutional guarantees reversed, mediocre public schools protected, cities lay in rotting ruin because of "white flight," and gerrymandering gave political power to blacks at the expense of whites. In fact, every place in the world where blacks controlled their own fate, a lowering of every standard followed, and subjection, starvation, and genocide resulted. Who then wants race mixing, asks the *Citizen*? Its answer: the political leader after votes; the rich liberal who does not come into contact with the results of his liberalism; the near-hysterical religious leader obviously ignorant of the Bible; and the misinformed, the brainwashed, and all the interest groups that the journal believed threatened the American way of life. The vast majority of blacks did not want integration, and the great majority of whites detested the very idea. If the federal government continued its policies of forced integration, warned William J. Simmons, then the nation could expect a sociopolitical collision between the pro-integration revolutionists backed by the government, and the "overwhelming number of white people [who] will not under any circumstances submit to interracial mixing on a meaningful scale."[13]

Writers for the journal resented most of the leaders of the "pro-integration revolution," but they especially detested Dr. Martin Luther King, Jr. Pretending to be a man of peace, a humanitarian, and a crusader for the rights of man, King, contributors said, in reality was "a dangerous agitator whose purpose clearly included the destruction of freedom for all Americans." He knew that violent confrontations with authorities would create sympathy for his cause, so he deliberately provoked the actions he said he wanted to avoid. Because of this, King's real legacy to America was not nonviolence; it was rioting, looting, and bloodshed. On his shoulders lay the blame for America's racial tensions, and not on those who only reacted as anybody would when faced with threats to their way of life. More important, King's antics helped the communists because his goals matched theirs. Both he and they hoped the unrest and instability of the civil rights movement would result in a revolution that would create an America far different from that imagined by the founders. The *Citizen* occasionally printed a picture of King in attendance at an alleged communist training school for civil rights workers as proof of his affiliation with the extreme Left, and the journal decried the thought that King ought to have a national holiday, given his association with those anxious to destroy America. If he was not a communist, why then are the FBI tapes of his conversations sealed until 2027? The answer was obvious, if unstated: Martin Luther King was a communist agitator working, whether knowingly or not, for the international communist conspiracy. When King died, the *Citizen* ran an editorial lamenting the public mourning led by America's liberal establishment, and censuring the nation for wallowing in an unhealthy "sea of negritude."[14]

After King's assassination, the journal turned its criticism on his lieutenants, especially those involved in national politics. For example, writers such as George Shannon loosed great vituperation on Andrew Young, Jimmy Carter's ambassador to the United Nations, after Young made a number of ill-considered remarks and outlandish statements unflattering to the United States. Jesse Jackson's campaign to become president also frightened the *Citizen*, as it exposed Operation PUSH's alleged shaky finances, decried Jackson's "grandstanding" play in Syria in 1984, and remarked on his associations with "known" radicals. After the 1984 election, the journal continued to highlight what it held to be Jackson's anti-Americanism. Clearly anybody who worked for the civil rights movement in the 1960s could expect his or her fair share of criticism from a journal opposed to it from its inception.[15]

National political leaders who supported the Citizens' Council's concepts of traditional American values were few and far between. The editors applauded Alabama governor George Wallace as fervently as they condemned King. Writer after writer hailed Wallace for giving the states rights philosophy a national forum and praised him for the conservative revolution he waged in the name of Americans angry with the coercive tactics of the federal government. The journal interpreted the substantial northern support he received as proof that an increasing number of people realized the wisdom of the South's constitutional positions and the futility of integration. Unfortunately for the segregationists, no president ever came close to the Wallace philosophy. Lyndon Johnson and Jimmy Carter, two men with southern roots, were ridiculed for their commitments to integration and their domestic programs that increased the federal government's power. Richard Nixon proved a disappointment because he approached social and economic issues too pragmatically while failing to turn the integration tide. His trips to the People's Republic of China and the Soviet Union certainly did not endear him to the *Citizen*, given its strong anticommunism. Only Ronald Reagan met with its cautious approval because of his promise to reduce the government's reach and strengthen the military.[16]

As for school integration, the specific issue that sparked the "Negro Rights" revolution, the *Citizen* cited studies purporting to prove the movement's failure. These studies claimed that the natural inferiority of black children prevented them from realizing the benefits of integrated schooling. As a result, integration intensified psychological stresses on black children, strengthening their feelings of inadequacy. As the percentage of blacks enrolled in white schools increased, the studies warned, miscegenation would increase, and school officials could expect lower academic performance, more dropouts, higher absenteeism, and an increase in delinquency. To avoid these predicted educational disasters, the *Citizen* urged its readers to send their children to private schools until the white majority regained control of its political institutions.[17]

The journal naturally supported the efforts of anti-integration forces throughout the South, exhorting segregationists to carry on until they beat back those who would destroy the South's way of life. As these efforts intensified, the *Citizen* pointed to signs that signaled that the struggle indeed was being won. In the December 1961 issue, Richard Morphew triumphantly cited a *Southern School News* study claiming that in seventeen states and the District of Columbia, the annual integration rate stood at a scant nine-tenths of 1 percent. Using figures from the same article, Morphew determined that since 1954 school integration for the Deep South, excluding the District of Columbia, was proceeding at the "deliberate speed" of seventy-nine black students per million per year. At that rate, the region would integrate in 12,658 years. In addition to this "hopeful" sign, a 1964 postelection editorial noted that a Gallup poll showed that despite Johnson's landslide victory, only 23 percent of the nation wanted strict enforcement of the Civil Rights Act and that voters all over the country rejected integrationist issues. The *Citizen* applauded itself and its segregationist readers for the hard work that kept the integrationists at bay.[18]

Despite such success, nobody could claim victory in the struggle for America's future, the journal reminded its readers. In January 1964, as part of this continuing fight, Medford Evans outlined the Citizens' Council's five-point plan to preserve a "decent" and stable America. Evans said the nation absolutely could not allow race mixing because whites would abandon their natural role of responsibility, allowing blacks to dominate and in the process destroy white culture. He also urged whites to avoid violence since it played into the hands of outside agitators. As a third step, Evans advocated the restoration and continuation of legal segregation as the only way to solve America's race problem. He reminded readers that Jim Crow laws squarely put the welfare of blacks on the shoulders of white society, where that burden properly belonged. In order to maintain this racial harmony the states needed the freedom to manage their own institutions, and Evans assured his readers that the Citizens' Council made the preservation of those rights a top priority. The Constitution was a pact between the states to establish a federal government to perform duties the states could not adequately do, Evans reminded readers. As such, the defense of states rights was a defense of constitutional and human liberty.

Finally, Evans asked that all loyal southerners fight for the reversal of the *Brown* decision. A dynamic interpretation of *Brown* threatened to inject the federal government into every aspect of private life, he warned. Southerners had to fight to make sure that never happened.[19]

Unfortunately, many people ignored the warnings against violence. Equally unfortunate was the lack of coverage the *Citizen* gave to Ku Klux Klan activity, white terror, and brutal police tactics directed against blacks and civil rights workers. Instead, the editors emphasized stories of violence in large northern cities, which in their eyes offered ample proof that the federal government committed a tragic blunder in ordering integration.[20]

The conservatism reflected in these philosophies was multifaceted. On one hand, traditional Burkean conservatism spoke of a divine and natural hierarchical ordering of men. At the same time, writers appealed to New Right populistic sympathies in exhorting readers to band together to fight the policies of an establishment out of touch with the common man. The *Citizen* addressed the conservatism of a readership raised in the millenarian tradition that taught that only Jesus could redeem man; man's works could not save him from damnation. The social engineering aspects of the integration movement angered an entire region raised in this tradition and strengthened its determination to defend its institutions. These three philosophies combined to give voice to the frustration and paranoia of a people threatened by social trends at odds with their accustomed way of life. The rapidly expanding domestic postwar economic situation, which brought blacks into direct competition with whites, and new political realities abroad, caused southerners to see communistic conspiracies as the driving force behind these changes. If fighting evil trends labeled the South as reactionary, then wear the label proudly, the *Citizen* exhorted, and keep God's institutions viable. To the readers of the *Citizen*, the journal led this fight against so-called racial suicide, statist arrogance, and the satanic evils of socialism, and provided an outlet for their fear of being left behind or ignored in a changing world.[21]

Notes

1. "Citizens Councils: A Brief History," *Citizen* 13 (November 1968): 15.

2. Neil R. McMillen, *Citizens' Council: Organized Resistance to the Second Reconstruction, 1954–64* (Urbana, Illinois, 1971), pp. 15–40.

3. Robert Webb, "Citizens Council No Place for Klan; Leaders Place Guard against KKK," *Citizens' Council* 1 (March 1956): 1–2; "The Un-American Revolution!" *Citizen* 7 (June 1963): 8; "Staff Changes," *Citizen* 16 (February 1972): 2.

4. Medford Evans, "'One Man, One Vote' an Unconstitutional Formula," *Citizen* 22 (September 1977): 29–30; Robert E. Kuttner, "A Brief Account of Negro History," *Citizen* 14 (March 1971): 4–15, 18–29; Dr. Henry E. Garrett, "How Classroom Desegregation Will Work," *Citizen* 10 (October 1965): 4–17; D. Tennant Bryan, et al., "Wallace Answers 'Unsparing' Questions," *Citizen* 11 (June 1967): 4–25; for instructions on starting private schools, see *Citizen* 8 (September 1964): 4–21; on Jackson's "White Monday" rally, see *Citizen* 9 (June 1965): 4–24; on Vietnam, see *Citizen* 11 (March 1967) and on Lincoln's racial views, see *Citizen* 8 (February 1964).

5. Ezra Taft Benson, "The Proper Role of Government," *Citizen* 12 (September 1968): 4–11.

6. Ibid., pp. 4–11; Tommy W. Rogers, "States Rights and American Liberty," *Citizen* 18 (September 1974): 4–9, 28–29; I. Beverly Lake, "Judicial Distortion of the Constitution," *Citizen* 24 (June 1979): 16–21; "Judicial Distortion of the Constitution, Part 2," *Citizen* 24 (August 1979): 16–21.

7. Lake, "Judicial Distortion of the Constitution," pp. 16–21, and "Judicial Distortion of the Constitution, Part 2," pp. 16–21; Rogers, "States Rights and American Liberty," pp. 4–9, 28–29; Bobbe Simmons, "Is the Majority to Become a Mob?" *Citizen* 19 (January 1975): 4–11; "Voting Rights Act Wrong," *Citizen* 27 (October 1981): 15; Evans, "'One Man, One Vote' an Unconstitutional Formula," pp. 29–30; "America at the Crossroads," *Citizen* 15 (June 1971): 2; Medford Evans, "Have the 'Winds of Change' Changed Their Own Direction?" *Citizen* 24 (October 1978): 27–28.

8. "Interposition—A Plan for Action Now!" *Citizens' Council* 1 (December 1955): 1.

9. "Interposition—Basic Principle of States Rights," *Citizens' Council* 1 (January 1956): 1.

10. T. Robert Ingram, "Why Integration Is Un-Christian," *Citizen* 6 (June 1962): 6–16.

11. Harold T. Pultz, "Time Is Running Out," *Citizen* 26 (December 1980): 22–25; Ingram, "Why Integration Is Un-Christian," pp. 6–16; John H. Knight, "The NCC's Delta Project: An Experiment in Revolution," *Citizen* 8 (June 1964): 6–9.

12. Bobbe Simmons, "The Record Proves Integration a Fraud," *Citizen* 21 (October 1975): 4–11, 30; William J. Simmons, "Political and Social Implications of the 'Civil Rights' Crisis," *Citizen* 10 (January 1966): 6–22; Robert Weems, "The Most Integrated Institution in America," *Citizen* 15 (September 1971): 17–21.

13. Simmons, "Integration a Fraud," pp. 4–11, 30; William J. Simmons, "Civil Right, Segregation, and Apartheid—A Comparison," *Citizen* 31 (December 1985): 16–20; Medford Evans, "The 'Bakke' Case and Professional Competence," *Citizen* 23 (November 1977): 4–8; "Integrationist Unmasked," *Citizen* 21 (October 1975): 2; A. A. Kitchings, "Who Wants Race Mixing?" *Citizen* 15 (February 1971): 16–20; Simmons, "Political and Social Implications of the 'Civil Rights' Crisis," pp. 6–22.

14. John F. McManus, "Truth about Martin Luther King," *Citizen* 21 (March 1976): 25; Larry McDonald, "King Linked to Reds," *Citizen* 27 (December 1981): 26–29; "Anti-White Plot Hatched in Moscow," *Citizens' Council* 1 (April 1956): 1, 3; "King Unworthy of Holiday," *Citizen* 24 (August 1979): 2; "King Holiday Unwarranted," *Citizen* 29 (October 1983): 2, 31; "The Wake," *Citizen* 12 (May 1968): 2.

15. George W. Shannon, "Andrew Young: A Liability U.S. Can No Longer Afford," *Citizen* 23 (September 1978): 17–18; William Loeb in the *Manchester Union Leader,* "More Than a Ridiculous Clown," *Citizen* 23 (September 1978): 19; Paul Harvey, "White Press Afraid to Expose Jackson?" *Citizen* 29 (March 1984): 25–26; Otis Pike, "Seldom Is a 'Criminal' So Rewarded," *Citizen* 29 (March 1984): 26–27.

16. "Where the Vision Is," *Citizen* 13 (November 1968): 2; Bryan, "Wallace Answers 'Unsparing' Questions," pp. 4–25; "Waiting for the Signal," *Citizen* 13 (January 1969): 2; "Integration a Failure," *Citizen* 16 (July/August 1972): 2; Irene C. Kuhn, "Submission to Moscow," *Citizen* 16 (May 1972): 24–28; "New Hope for America," *Citizen* 26 (December 1980): 2.

17. Garrett, "How Classroom Desegregation Will Work," pp. 4–17; "Government Schools," *Citizen* 8 (September 1964): 2.

18. "The Backlashers," *Citizen* 9 (November 1964): 2, 23; Richard D. Morphew, "Two Can Play the Numbers Game," *Citizen* 6 (December 1961): 4–7. The seventeen states of the *Southern School News*, published by a Ford Foundation grant organization were: Alabama, Arkansas, Delaware, Florida, Georgia, Kentucky, Louisiana, Maryland, Mississippi, Missouri, North Carolina, Oklahoma, South Carolina, Tennessee, Texas, Virginia, and West

Virginia. Morphew defined the Deep South as Alabama, Arkansas, Florida, Georgia, Louisiana, Mississippi, North Carolina, South Carolina, and Virginia. Morphew further bolstered his argument by claiming over 95 percent of the South's desegregated black students lived in the District of Columbia and the border states.

19. Medford Evans, "The Five-Point Action Program," *Citizen* 8 (January 1964): 9–16.

20. Jesse Helms, "Why Do They Lie about the South?" *Citizen* 6 (March 1962): 5–6; Jesse Helms, "What Is the Cure for Campus Chaos?" *Citizen* 14 (September 1970): 8–9, 17–20. See also "Random Glances at the News," in every number of the *Citizen* after December 1971.

21. McMillen, *Citizens' Council*, pp. 193–95. For an examination of the millenarian and millennialist traditions, see Ernest Lee Tuveson, *Redeemer Nation: The Idea of America's Millennial Role* (Chicago, 1968).

Information Sources

BIBLIOGRAPHY:

Kelly, Alfred H., and Winfred A. Harbison. *The American Constitution: Its Origin and Development*. 5th ed. New York, 1976.

Kluger, Richard. *Simple Justice: The History of* Brown *vs.* Board of Education *and Black America's Struggle for Equality*. New York, 1977.

Southern, David W. *Gunnar Myrdal and Black-White Relations: The Use and Abuse of* An American Dilemma, *1944–1969*. Baton Rouge, 1987.

INDEXES: None.

REPRINT EDITIONS: Microform: Right Wing Collection, University of Iowa (MCA), partial run, 1961–1976 (reel 26); UMI.

LOCATION SOURCES: Widely available.

Publication History

TITLE AND TITLE CHANGES: *Citizens' Council*, 1955–1961; *Citizen*, 1961–1989.

VOLUME AND ISSUE DATA: Volumes 1–current, October 1955–1989.

FREQUENCY OF PUBLICATION: Monthly, July and August published as one number.

PUBLISHER: Citizens' Council, Inc., Jackson, Mississippi.

EDITORS: William J. Simmons, October 1961–January 1972; George W. Shannon, February 1972–October 1985; William S. Purvis, November 1985–1989.

CIRCULATION: 3,865.

Steven J. Fitch

WIRE Magazine
1963–1971

Donald L. Jackson, a self-described Negro conservative, was born in Fowlerville, New York, a small town where, he said, whites and blacks had good relations, though there was no interracial dating or marriage. After high school graduation, he moved to Buffalo, worked at two jobs, eight hours a day at each, saved some money, and started buying residential property.[1] He began *WIRE Magazine* in 1963, acting as its "editor, publisher, sole owner, complete staff and God-father," a situation that did not significantly change during the life of the publication.[2] In addition to producing the magazine, Jackson served as local manager for *Let Freedom Ring*, "an Anti-Communist Telephone Broadcast."[3] Three years after *WIRE* began publication, Jackson announced the establishment of the Donald L. Jackson Foundation, "a religious, educational, charitable and scientific foundation," and also a tax-exempt group. The foundation awarded scholarships, produced a weekly radio program, the *Donald Jackson Report,* as well as the *Let Freedom Ring* broadcast. The organization requested contributions to support these and other activities, among them the renovation and management of several apartment buildings. Jackson hoped that the income from these apartments would enable the foundation to support itself.[4] By 1970 he had a New York City agent who would arrange for him to speak at universities and colleges.

In the magazine, Jackson provided his explanation of the problems of black Americans, beginning with the family. Crucial to stability and community improvement, and the well-being of the nation, was the family, with daily worship of God. The family should be racially unmixed, since interracial marriages were against the will of God, and those who favored them did a disservice to the black community and played directly into the hands of the communists, the nation's major enemies.

According to Jackson, the communists in the United States were using the same techniques that the Chinese communists, he believed, used in Tibet—forcing Tibetans to marry Chinese, thus eliminating the pure Tibetan race by a method he described as "genocide by other than slaughter." In America the communists claimed that racial mixing would help the "suppose-to-be culturely [*sic*] deprived Negroes." This should be resisted in order to "assure the purity...of the races." At bottom this meant the purity of the family.[5]

Along with the lack of discipline and religious belief that led to mixed marriages, a basic problem facing black Americans was the welfare system, which undermined recipients' moral fiber and work skills and encouraged a failure to respect private property. Welfare programs, Jackson asserted, made people lazy, unwilling to work, and dependent on government at all levels to provide for them. Instead of helping the blacks, "the Roosevelts, Trumans, Kennedys and Johnsons have destroyed the masses of the Negro people with their welfare programs."[6] In addition, he charged that poverty program funds were being diverted to civil rights agitation.

Jackson concentrated much of his attention, his strongest criticism, and most vehement pronouncements on the civil rights movement. He declared that civil rights leaders had created a general climate of turbulence by encouraging people to obey only laws they thought right and by committing crimes and blaming them on antiblack groups. Civil rights organizations, though preaching nonviolence, in fact stirred up violence and promoted ill will between the races where such bad feeling did not previously exist.[7]

In addition to violence, Jackson denounced efforts at busing. In sometimes contradictory comments about his own city of Buffalo, he suggested that busing was unnecessary. "There are no segregated schools in this city," he declared, but "because of the housing pattern there are some schools that have a larger percentage of Negro children attending than white children." As early as 1966 he attacked busing because it was forced and when forced busing occurred, property damage, pressure of white girls to date black males, obscene language on school walls, and extreme rudeness to teachers inevitably followed and made learning impossible.[8] Jackson did not particularly favor even voluntary integration, however. In March 1966 he reported that the school system would pay the transportation costs of any black who wished to transfer to any "all-white school." Only two dozen of the 23,000 black children in the public schools took up the board's offer, though civil rights organizations made extensive efforts—using television, radio, house-to-house canvassing and printed literature—to persuade them to do so. Neither busing nor "NAACP, CORE, SNCC, and 92 other civil rights groups" had much support among blacks in Buffalo, he concluded.[9]

The civil rights gangs behind the violence and the busing were themselves controlled by communists under Russian leadership.[10] Jackson's hostility to the NAACP, CORE, Southern Christian Leadership Conference, and other civil rights organizations lay in his belief that they were fronts for, or dominated by, communists or sympathizers like Martin Luther King, Jr., Roy Wilkins, or James Farmer who "have been connected with well-known individuals that expound the communist doctrine." There were no real differences between one of these organizations or individuals and another; "all of these are flunkies for the communist organization."[11]

Jackson criticized Martin Luther King, Jr., particularly strongly on both religious and political grounds. Quoting extensively from the Bible, he depicted King as "a

Fraud, Liar and a Deceiver, Hyprocrite [*sic*] and a Trouble Maker." Civil disobedience was not a concept found in the Bible, Jackson asserted, and King's followers were filled not with love but with hate. J. Edgar Hoover was Jackson's source for the charge that King was a liar; King was also something of a fraud because he claimed to be a spokesman and leader of the black community but had not been elected to such a position.[12]

Among national political figures, Jackson supported Barry Goldwater, Ronald Reagan, and George Wallace and opposed Richard Nixon and Robert Kennedy in part because of their positions and actions on integration. In 1966 the editor exhorted his readers to reelect Barry Goldwater to the Senate, and to organize support for Ronald Reagan as a presidential candidate.[13] Robert Kennedy, "an agent of subversion," "instigated most of the racial troubles in the South," yet his and other Kennedy children went to white schools.[14] Nixon should be defeated in 1968 because a Nixon victory would allow civil rights advocates into the White House.[15] In 1969 Jackson urged the impeachment of Nixon because during the campaign, the president had opposed busing, but after his election he had appointed James E. Allen, who supported busing, as U.S. commissioner of education, and civil rights leader James Farmer to a position in the Department of Health, Education and Welfare.[16]

The editor urged similarly strong actions against civil rights groups in general. To punish the NAACP and church organizations that engaged in civil rights activities, Jackson urged Congress to take away their tax-exempt status. Perhaps, in the case of the NAACP, he wanted to stop support for what he believed to be a communist-dominated association. His argument was clearer concerning the tax-exempt status of churches. The churches had endorsed Lyndon Johnson against Barry Goldwater in the 1964 election, thus violating the constitutional provisions concerning separation of church and state. In addition, most of the money the churches raised was used not to aid the poor but "to finance civil disorder and political matters."[17]

To stop agitation by groups like the NAACP, Jackson had several other suggestions, some paternalistic and authoritarian. Housewives, businessmen, and local organizations could all help. Housewives who had maids working for them (the assumption seemed to be that the maids were black) should occasionally talk with these employees to determine their thinking about racial matters. These housewives should also have their maids form reading groups, which would be supplied with "good Conservative" reading matter, paid for by the employers. Businessmen with female employees should carefully check these employees from time to time and encourage them to join these reading groups. Members of such groups should prepare themselves as speakers on the conservative black viewpoint. The reading society could also "screen left-wing elements from applicants seeking employment" and suggest "decent respectable Negroes" for jobs.[18]

When it seemed necessary, Jackson was willing to counter violence with violence. For several days during an April 1968 riot in Buffalo, he armed himself with a shotgun to protect his property from looters. This disturbance was planned well in advance, he charged, and was encouraged by the black churches. While he called on the police for help, and received it, he argued that such aid was undependable because the police were controlled by the politicians who were using the civil rights movement for their own purposes.[19] Finally, Jackson encouraged support for civil rights leaders who neither condoned law violations nor blamed their troubles on persecution by others, public officials who "will not temporize with lawlessness parading as civil rights," judges who will hand out stiff sentences even if those breaking the law are blacks claiming to act in the name of civil rights, and people in the media who will support all the above with vigor and frankness.[20] (In addition, Jackson solicited contributions to the Donald L. Jackson Foundation Organization to educate people to the communist influence on the civil rights movement.)[21]

Other issues occupied Jackson's attention. In 1968 he denounced both the grape boycott and the Poor People's March on Washington. The former he dismissed as "phoney" [sic], asserting that wages were already higher than the union was demanding. "Ignore the called Boycott," he advised, "and regularly by [sic] and eat grapes." In the same issue he labeled the Poor People's March a "disgrace to any intelligent person," made up of people who were lazy or misusing the welfare funds they received. "It's a vicious lie for anyone to stand up and say there are people who are dying of starvation in America."[22]

Affirmative action also received little support from Jackson. He reported that Eastman Kodak had made and then revoked an agreement with a group called FIGHT, organized by Saul Alinsky. Alinsky and his associates wasted money and broke promises; their organization, which was not local, did not represent the blacks of Rochester. Further, choosing employees only because of race was an act of discrimination and, Jackson warned, "Unless the Eastman Kodak Company publicity announces that no such agreement will ever be entered into with Fight, I shall file discrimination charges with the State Commission of Human Rights. If Eastman Kodak is permitted to hire 600 Negroes selected by the organization 'FIGHT', they will select professional agitators from all over the country making Rochester headquarters for hoodlum activity in upstate New York."[23]

Jackson's usual negative tone changed when he discussed George C. Wallace, whom he enthusiastically supported and whose victory he predicted in the 1968 presidential election. In an article entitled "Why They Hate George Wallace," Jackson asked a series of rhetorical questions concerning the hostility toward the Alabaman and in the process gave reasons for supporting him. First, Wallace promoted economic expansion in Alabama, and supported law and order nationwide; the disturbances at Birmingham and Selma in 1963 and 1965 were the work of outside agitators. Wallace was a teetotaler and clear thinker, who urged jobs and education as the solution to Alabama's problems. The strongest reason for opposition to Wallace, in Jackson's opinion, was the strongest for supporting him: his position on race. Following in the footsteps of Booker T. Washington, Wallace was "on very sound and holy ground....As a Christian, George Wallace follows the example of the Master; in doing good to all regardless of their race, but living among those of his own kind, observing their customs and choosing his close companions from them, even as Jesus did with those He was identified with on earth." Indeed, according to Jackson, some believed that God may have chosen George Wallace "to lead us as another George Washington on a sane and sensible course. They point out that their views about the function of good government are fundamentally the same, they come from the same section of our country and even their name initials are identical. And who can honestly declare this is not according to God's plan?"[24]

A *WIRE Magazine* telephone poll predicted victory for Wallace with 39.6 percent of the popular vote, 25 percent for Nixon, 15.4 percent for Hubert Humphrey, and 20 percent not voting. The chief issues Wallace would ride to victory were busing, law enforcement, opposition to welfare, poverty programs, and "pro-communist Civil Rights Groups that are dedicated in [*sic*] destroying America."[25]

Jackson's loyalty to George Wallace was undiminished after the 1968 election. In 1970 he rejoiced that Wallace had once again been elected governor of Alabama, particularly because, he believed, the efforts of black civil rights advocates had boomeranged. Some black clergy and "self-appointed Negro leaders" had been urged to swing black voters to the incumbent governor, William Brewer, in return for which the Brewer administration would consult these leaders on matters related to the black community, appoint some of them to important jobs in the state government, and would work toward "forced integration."[26]

In their communities these blacks told lies about George Wallace and promised that should Brewer be reelected, black men could freely marry white women, and welfare payments in Alabama would be made at the New York State rate of $1,000 a month or more. Some were so delighted at the news that they "went about picking their white women they plan to lay claim to as soon as the good days arrived," while others who had planned to leave Alabama decided to stay and collect the $1,000 monthly welfare checks.

Black support enabled Governor Brewer to win in the May primary, although a June run-off between the governor and former governor Wallace was necessary. Before the run-off, the Wallace forces published the aforesaid allegations about activities of black leaders, and that caused a "White Backlash" that netted a Wallace plurality of 35,000 votes. Blacks, Jackson concluded, by their actions and by voting in a block against Wallace helped increase his support among whites and return him to the governorship.[27]

Although Jackson largely confined his attention to civil rights, especially busing, and to the local political scene, he did touch on international issues. Even here his primary concern was the national and local effect of such matters. He supported the American role in Vietnam and criticized those who would end or limit that role. In 1966 he opposed the National Council of Churches' call for withdrawing U.S. troops from Vietnam and replacing them with an international peacekeeping force. The council also suggested a coalition of communists and what the NCC termed "nationalists." Such coalitions, Jackson warned, "invariably result in an eventual communist conquest of the government succumbing to such a coalition." The council's activities in this area, he concluded, not only contained ideas harmful to South Vietnam, but would bring control of the United States by communist tyranny.[28]

The U.S. involvement in Vietnam provoked protests on college and university campuses across the country, and in May 1970 these reached a tragic climax at Kent State University in Ohio and Jackson State College in Mississippi. *WIRE*'s editor headed one article "College Shootings Justified Homicide" and blamed the disturbance on students at both institutions who did not respect property or law and created a situation beyond the ability of local law enforcement agencies to handle. While regretting the deaths of the students and expressing sympathy for the parents, he strongly criticized those who wanted to have the National Guard charged with murder. "These culprit hoodlums" were themselves responsible for the violence and death that resulted when the police and the National Guard simply did their duty. Furthermore, the parents of these "student hoodlums" should be put on trial and an investigation made to see if these students had had other disciplinary problems on campus. If so, the college should not have allowed them to stay at the college and was as guilty of murder as their parents.[29]

A continent away from Vietnam, the turbulent history of Rhodesia (now Zimbabwe) was being played out. The United States protested the policies and actions of the white regime by boycotting Rhodesian chromium. *WIRE* criticized that boycott, first because the chromium was needed in the manufacture of steel and of aircraft engines. Second, the magazine objected to the United States following the United Nations' lead on this matter. Third, the regime was anticommunist "and the blacks are happier, healthier and more respected than in many parts of Africa or the world." Once again the interests of blacks were seen as synonymous with those of conservative, anticommunist whites.[30]

In Africa in general, Jackson said, black power brought no real benefits to the black population at large; indeed, many were virtually enslaved. "There is no civil rights [*sic*] or liberty in any Black ruled country in Africa," he charged.[31] He scoffed at those black Americans who sought to trace their ancestry back to Africa. Many slaves, he said, came to America from Europe as the result of an Africa-to-Europe slave trade that had been going on for two or three centuries before 1619. Therefore "it is extremely impossible for a Negro to claim he can trace his ancestors back to Africa." In any case, slavery, while a cruel institution, nevertheless brought real advantages to blacks, including a longer life span, education, and a much higher standard of living.[32]

Among the people in America aiding the blacks in achieving that better living standard were the Jews. Jewish people, Jackson claimed, had helped many blacks to own their own homes and start their own businesses, and they had given large amounts of money in support of black education. Jackson strongly criticized those whom he labeled "Black Nationalists" for trying to have Jewish teachers removed from the New York City school system and for destroying the property of Jews. "The Jewish people," he concluded, "are the Negroes [*sic*] best friend." Perhaps for that reason, more likely for the benefits to America, Jackson in 1970 urged President Nixon to aid "the brave freedom fighters of Israel," supplying them with military equipment to enable them to defend themselves from "those murdering thieving Arabs." Support for Israel was support for peace in the region and for progress in general. "Israel has accomplished more in 20 years than the Arabs have done in 200 years."[33]

The editor's positive attitude toward the Jews and Israel probably derived not only from an appreciation of the accomplishments in Israel and their help for blacks in America, but from the fact that they were a religious group. In a Christmas message Jackson wrote: "Again this Christmas and for the year to follow Let Freedom Ring vows to continue exposing the enemies of our land who would destroy all men of good will. Our breach is not with a particular religion nor race but with the non-believer…intent not on practicing his personal conviction or non-belief but on compelling all mankind to submit to his own system."[34]

In spite of such efforts to speak for and appeal to the religious world and black Americans in particular, *WIRE Magazine* did not seem to be firmly rooted in the community. It achieved a circulation of approximately 4,200 and published regularly for the first few years. By 1967, however, some issues covered two or three months, sometimes four or even more. In addition, the magazine's first few and last several issues appeared to be typed and mimeographed, while most of those in the late 1960s were printed. Throughout the magazine's history, issues contained numerous errors in spelling, grammar, sentence structure, and paragraph organization; at times the English was poor, perhaps the result of haste and an absence of editing and proofreading, as the magazine was in all likelihood not the major job of its editor and publisher.

Jackson attempted to use other media to send out his message. In 1970, the Jackson Foundation announced plans to purchase radio station KKAL in Denver City, Texas, but by the end of the year the group was appealing for funds, the lack of which had caused it to cancel some activities.[35] Evidently the support did not come in, and during 1970 issues of the magazine were published very irregularly. In October 1971 several two-page issues appeared, typed and mimeographed, and readers were asked to pay the subscription cost with the warning that all who did not would no longer receive the magazine. It was a last, unsuccessful effort. Publication ceased.

In spite of vigorous efforts and a bold statement of ideas, Donald L. Jackson, the guiding force of *WIRE Magazine* throughout its history, had not persuaded large numbers of blacks to join him in his crusade. His ideas appealed only to a small group, black and white, of the larger conservative community, and although some of the views he expressed in his periodical were held by others in that community, his strong denunciation of mainstream civil rights leaders isolated the magazine from much of black and white America. *WIRE* remained a fringe publication, a magazine of the extreme far Right.

Notes

1. Donald L. Jackson in *WIRE Magazine* (December 1967): 1 (hereinafter cited as *WIRE*).

2. *WIRE* (January–February 1968): 14–15. The acronym means "Wire Is Read Everywhere," according to Robert H. Muller, Theodore J. Spahn, and Janet M. Spahn, eds., *From Radical Left to Extreme Right,* 2nd ed. (Ann Arbor, Michigan, 1967), pp. 833–37.

3. *WIRE* (December 1967): 2. For more on *Let Freedom Ring* and its originator, Dr. William C. Douglass, see George Thayer, *The Farther Shores of Politics: The American Political Fringe Today* (New York, 1967), p. 191.

4. *WIRE* (July 1966): 16. See also *WIRE* (September 1968): 11, where it was reported that organization, including election of officers, had taken place. See also *WIRE* (February 1963): 4, and *WIRE* (June–July–August 1968): 7–8, the latter of which contains essays by two of eight scholarship winners. The topic of the essays was "What the Civil Rights Movement Has Done to America." One essay argued that it had split America, the other that changes had and would come peacefully, and that violence was not the way to bring about change. All winners received a scholarship of $200.

5. *WIRE* (May 1967): 9; *WIRE* (November 1966): 3.

6. This was true not only in the United States but in areas of the world—especially Africa—where the United States had sent food and clothing; *WIRE* (May 1967): 6. See also *WIRE* (January–February 1968): 14, where Jackson charged the "Washington Propaganda Machine" with presenting an erroneous picture of the difference between the annual income of black and white workers. Black income was less because the black worker was often drunk, missed work, and was unwilling to work overtime. The magazine also included several examples of wasteful programs in which large proportions of agency budgets were spent on administrative salaries, and of people receiving several checks when entitled to only one; *WIRE* (September–October 1968): 10; *WIRE* (November–December 1968): 6; *WIRE* (January 1971): unnumbered pages reprinting articles from the *Buffalo Evening News* of 7 and 8 January 1971, with Jackson's comments.

7. *WIRE* (December 1967): 5–6.

8. *WIRE* (20 October 1971): 1. He stated that the school board had had to spend $300,000 over the previous year to replace "windows broken not by children." See also *WIRE* (February 1967): 5.

9. *WIRE* (February 1967): 5.

10. *WIRE* (September 1966): 1.

11. *WIRE* (February 1967): 10, 11; *WIRE* (November 1966): 15; *WIRE* (October–November 1967): 9. In *WIRE* (September 1966): 1, a picture is captioned: "Dr. Martin Luther King with Other Known Communists Attending Communists Training Session."

12. *WIRE* (September 1966): 5–6, 11. This is one of the few articles with numerous references to Scripture. It also has a great number of spelling and grammatical errors, though it is a rare article in the magazine without some such errors. Occasional letters to the editor also emphasize communist dominance of the civil rights movement; see, e.g., the letter of Mrs. Gracie Hamilton of Hattiesburg, Mississippi, in *WIRE* (July 1966): 4. For comments on Adam Clayton Powell, see *WIRE* (February 1967): 1, 7–8, and *WIRE* (March 1967): 8.

13. *WIRE* (July 1966): 18; "Attention Conservatives and Republicans," *WIRE* (September 1966): 10.

14. "Open Letter to: University of Mississippi," *WIRE* (September 1966): 14.

15. *WIRE* (November 1966): 16.

16. "President Nixon Should Be Impeached," *WIRE* (January–April 1969): 4–5. Nixon, Jackson declared, "is an old liberal who is attempting to camouflage his liberalism under the Conservative banner." See also "Dr. Allen Fired," *WIRE* (March–July 1970): 5.

17. *WIRE* (February 1967): 9–11. See also *WIRE* (September 1966): 2, 10, where Jackson reprinted and commented on a 1964 article from the *Daily Oklahoman*.

18. "Help Stop Racial Agitation," *WIRE* (May 1967): 8.

19. *WIRE* (March–April–May 1968): 1–5.

20. "Lawless Chickens Come Home to Riotous Roost," *WIRE* (January 1967): 2, 10; "Rights Demonstrators Sentenced in Danville, Va.," *WIRE* (January 1967): 7. In the next month's issue, Jackson urged "Support Your Local Police," *WIRE* (February 1967): 13.

21. *WIRE* (January 1967): 13. In the same issue he noted that the foundation was tax

exempt and printed a letter to that effect from the IRS.

22. "Protect the Grape Industry: Buy and Eat Grapes," *WIRE* (November–December 1968): 1.

23. *WIRE* (January 1967): 4. The errors in spelling and grammar are in the original.

24. "Why They Hate George Wallace," *WIRE* (March–April–May 1968): 11–13. George Washington, he added, if alive in 1968 and a presidential candidate, would be abused as Wallace was.

25. "WIRE Magazine Election Polls Results Taken by Telephone," *WIRE* (September–October 1968): 15.

26. Though he provided no real evidence, Jackson did qualify his assertions to a degree: "We cannot say for certain," he wrote, "how much of this was actually stated by the Brewer Administration but it is evident that these individuals were either paid to say this or they had been assured of a political position." "Negro Civil Righters Elect Wallace in Alabama," *WIRE* (March–July 1970): 7, 13.

27. Ibid. Blacks had voted for Governor Brewer without taking account of his record or qualifications. "Any person that votes so recklessly, clearly reveals that their [*sic*] right to vote should be revoked," Jackson asserted, in one of his authoritarian, never-mind-the-law-and-the-Constitution statements.

28. "The National Council of Churches and Vietnam," *WIRE* (July 1966): 3, 11. See also *WIRE* (May 1967): 3–12, where Jackson reprinted a lengthy article from the 7 May 1967, issue of *Our Sunday Visitor: The National Catholic Ecumenical Weekly*. Written by Father Dan Lyons, it was critical of Martin Luther King's opposition to American involvement in Vietnam.

29. "College Shootings Justified Homicide," *WIRE* (March–July 1970): 10, 14.

30. *WIRE* (20 October 1971): 2.

31. *WIRE* (August–December 1970): 2.

32. *WIRE* (January 1967): 12–13. Muller, Spahn, and Spahn, eds, *From Radical Left to Extreme Right*, pp. 833–37.

33. *WIRE* (January–April 1969): 9; *WIRE* (November–December 1968): 10; *WIRE* (March–July 1970): 2.

34. "Let Freedom Ring," *WIRE* (December 1967): 15.

35. *WIRE* (August–December 1970): 2.

Information Sources

BIBLIOGRAPHY:

Muller, Robert H., Theodore Jurgen Spahn, and Janet M. Spahn, eds. *From Radical Left to Extreme Right*. 2nd ed. Ann Arbor, Michigan, 1970.

Thayer, George. *The Farther Shores of Politics: The American Political Fringe Today*. New York, 1967.

INDEXES: None.

REPRINT EDITIONS: Microform: Right Wing Collection, University of Iowa (MCA), partial run, 1966–1971 (reel 151).

LOCATION SOURCES: Complete runs: New York Public Library; University of California at Los Angeles.

Publication History

TITLE AND TITLE CHANGES: *WIRE Magazine*.
VOLUME AND ISSUE DATA: Volumes 1–8, 1963–1971.
FREQUENCY OF PUBLICATION: Irregular.

PUBLISHER: Donald L. Jackson Foundation, Buffalo, New York.
EDITOR: Donald L. Jackson.
CIRCULATION: 4,200.

Paul L. Silver

Christ Is the Answer
1967–

Christ Is the Answer is a monthly pamphlet expressing the views of Kingdom Identity, a survivalist group founded in the 1960s by Clyde Edminster who, with his family, edits the publication at the family's forested enclave of some half-dozen houses situated a few miles east of the hamlet of Rainier, Washington. When I arrived at the headquarters of Kingdom Identity, a wiry, sweaty, bare-chested man with a mustache appeared, his face and body spattered with paint from the use of an air gun. He introduced himself as Clyde Edminster and invited me to sit on a patio overlooking the Deschutes River, whereupon he quickly edged his freshly poured concrete. After completing his task on that summer afternoon in 1982, this smiling, self-confident man shared with me the message that had been printed since 1967 in *Christ Is the Answer*.

The dominant theme of *Christ Is the Answer* is that the United States was the New Israel, meaning that the experience of the United States paralleled that of ancient Israel so closely that the records and prophecies of both testaments of the Bible constituted a history of America—at once the record of its past and the program of its inevitable future. This parallelism, called "type and shadow," revealed how God would deliver the modern children of Israel (the United States) from the modern Egypt (any world plan system) across a modern Red Sea (communism) to the Kingdom of God on earth.

To establish that the United States was the New Israel, Edminster cited Revelation 12, which prophesies the birth of a great nation that shall become the nucleus of the Kingdom of God on earth and the destroyer of the existing "Satanic world order."[1] Revelation 12:1 declares: "And there appeared a great wonder in heaven, a woman clothed with the sun, and the moon under feet, and upon her head a crown of twelve stars." "Heaven" in Revelation, according to Edminster, meant where the physical seed of Israel resided: in the British Isles and Western Europe. The woman was "none other than...Mrs. National Israel, for the clothing of the sun, moon and the stars unmistakably identify her."[2]

Mrs. National Israel could not stay true to her husband, Yahvah, after the marriage at Sinai, whereupon Yahvah made preparation for the divorce by dividing the House of Israel into two: the ten northern tribes and Judah. Since this division did not cause Mrs. National Israel (the ten northern tribes) to repent or change her ways, Yahvah was forced to take strong action against her, saying: "I will chastise you seven times for your sins."[3] Since a "time" is 360 years, seven times is 2,520 years that National Israel was to be punished for her rebellious and adulterous nature.[4] To administer the punishment, Yahvah sent Assyria, which carried her away to the Caucasian Mountains, from which she was to retain the name "Caucasian" to describe her racial origin.

However, Mrs. National Israel was given two wings (God's word and spirit) so that she could fly (emigrate) into the wilderness (Isles of the Sea, meaning Britain and Western Europe) into her place where she would be nourished "for a time, and times, and half a time from the face of the serpent."[5] In other words, this was accomplished in a span of three-and-a-half times or 1,260 years, and since National Israel went into Assyrian captivity beginning in 744 B.C., 1,260 years added to this date would bring us to 516 A.D. This year was purported to be the beginning appearance of National Israel in the British Isles of the Sea and Western Europe via the migration of the "galls [sic], Celts, Goths, Picts, Angli, Vikings, Saxons, Cymri, Normans, and the Danen, etc."[6]

Long before Yahwah divorced her, he had made certain promises to Jacob. The promises were that "I am God Almighty: be fruitful and multiply; a nation and a company of nations shall be of thee, and kings shall come of thy loins."[7] During the time of chastisement, Mrs. National Israel was impregnated by the Word of God. "And as a woman pains to deliver, so National Israel pained desperately to be delivered. She was certainly getting big as most pregnant persons do because she was complaining in Isaiah 49:19–20 about her place as being 'too narrow' and 'the place is too straight for me: give place to me that I may dwell.'"[8] National Israel grew crowded in the Isles of the Sea and Western Europe and so it was time for Yahvah to reveal to National Israel the vast New World and continent that had been reserved to bring forth his first-born nation under God. Quite naturally, since Mrs. National Israel was a nation, she would not only bring forth a nation, but a nation that bore a striking resemblance to its mother: thirteen colonies became states, corresponding to Israel's thirteen tribes; their constitutions and format were patterned after the Word of God.

This great event, this birth of a nation, occurred at the end of the seven times chastisement of Mrs. National Israel. It occurred after a time span of 2,520 years (beginning in the year 744 B.C.) with the successful birth of the new nation in 1776! God's New Israel, revealed before our very eyes, was "destined to rule all nations with a rod of iron."[9]

Edminister interpreted the history of the United States as a reenactment of the story of the children of ancient Israel in Egypt. A few examples will demonstrate both his method and his message. Even as Jacob and his offspring went to Egypt for food and grain during the great drought,[10] so the pilgrim fathers, starving spiritually under the European state church system, went to the New World to seek a place where spiritual bread could be eaten. This fulfilled the promise of Yahvah in II Samuel 7:10 and I Chronicles 17:9. Between 1620 and 1776 several million Anglo-Saxon, Scandinavian, Germanic, "and other Israelites" emigrated to America, and on 4 July 1776, America was born as a nation under God. America was in fact Joseph's land, the land of Goshen, the most fertile land in the world.[11] The Kingdom of God on earth was at hand. This new nation was complying with the laws of God, and hence Yahvah was blessing America. In the same way, God had prospered Egypt because under the seventy-one-year reign of Joseph, Egypt honored Yahvah. Joseph's reign in Egypt corresponded to the "golden years of our great republic...an era of harmony and good feeling under a truly constitutional form of government."[12]

But the new nation early began its slide into apostasy due to the great red conspiracy beginning with the papacy and the Holy Roman Empire, brought on by the dragon, or Satan, and his serpent race. Revelation 12:3 states that the great red dragon with seven heads and ten horns and seven crowns awaits to devour the new child of Mrs. National Israel. The description identified it as the Holy Roman Empire, to reign for 1,260 years, from 606 to 1866.

Just as, after seventy-one years, Joseph had died and been replaced by the evil Pharaoh Magron, with his evil, violent, and corrupt government, so in 1847 "righteousness ceased to reign in the fullest sense in the U.S. and corruption and manipulation began to be manifested in our government with the advent of political parties of our land."[13] The Democratic and Whig parties began to flex their muscles until the advent of the Republican party in 1854. Additionally, international money interests and big business directed our nation. From 1847 to 1888 (forty-one years, paralleling the reign of Magron in Egypt), "America began to experience a departure from our divinely inspired Republican Constitutional form of government which honored Yahvah God of Israel and his national laws to a new form of government called Democracy."[14] The red dragon, employing the surrogate services of socialism, communism, Nazism, fascism, Marxism, Fabianism, and Judaism—one and the same: world Zionism[15]—had begun to infiltrate God's New Israel; it was from this that the new nation was to be delivered.

Through infiltration and conspiracy, the great red dragon— Zionism, the USSR, and a long list of dupes and surrogates who were either the willing or unintentional servants of evil—foisted a long succession of abuses on the New Israel. For example, a select group of Jewish moneylenders, agents of the Rothschilds, in President Abraham Lincoln's cabinet, sought to "infiltrate, undermine, seduce, propagandize, capture and destroy Christianity and the white race of people in their bid to establish and dominate a super-red, one-world socialistic kingdom."[16] Lincoln saw through their scheme, thwarted it, and paid for it by being assassinated by John Wilkes Booth, "a member of one of their secret societies."[17]

The continuing litany of evil included Jewish money for captains of industry, the Aldrich-Vreeland bill, the Federal Reserve Act, the Sixteenth and Seventeenth Amendments, tax-free foundations, the creation of an international foreign policy, the Anti-Defamation League, and universal military training. The Aldrich-Vreeland bill was passed allegedly due to infiltration of Congress and control of Woodrow

Wilson by the Illuminati. All the rest were due to "that infamous day of December 23, 1913, when most of our loyal patriot statesmen had gone home for Christmas," at which time the "international bankers strapped the American people into an international straight jacket by railroading into law" all of the above mentioned bills and amendments.[18] For *Christ Is the Answer*, all of these events had their direct counterpart in the life and experience of ancient Israel in Egypt. While Egyptians of old used taskmasters to whip ancient Israel into obedience, "our modern Babylonian-Egyptian masters are using the I.R.S., the F.B.I., the C.I.A., and especially the A.D.I. [Anti-Defamation League], to defame, vilify or coerce anyone who opposes their Zionist program in our nation. Their favorite war cry is Anti-Semitism."[19]

In spite of the hardships and whippings imposed on the ancient Israelites they still multiplied and increased in number, whereupon a hardboiled Pharaoh devised through his planners a means to destroy the children of Israel more quickly by instructing midwives to kill the baby boys.[20] The modern parallel to this was birth control, which served to liquidate the modern-day children of Israel: the white race.

However, the sons of Isaac were "genetically programmed to call on God as their final recourse."[21] The great and terrible day of the Lord was coming, and because of the parallel between the children of Israel in Egypt, and the history of the people of the United States, the date of the deliverance could be known. Edminister reckoned it this way: Israel's experience in Egypt lasted 210 years.[22] Beginning the American experience in 1776, 210 years put deliverance in the year 1986. He wrote: "So the more I studied into this possibility, the more I was convinced that Israel's sojourn in Egypt was the pre-written history of the United States of America."[23] (He later concluded that his calculations needed revision.) "Deciphering" coded messages of the Bible to discover the "wonderful plan of redemption, deliverance and restoration," it was all "crystal clear" to him. As ancient Egypt suffered through the great plagues before the children of Israel were released, so America had suffered and continued to suffer through its own plagues in preparation for Armageddon and deliverance. The Egyptian plagues were a "type and shadow" of the plagues suffered in the modern world. For example, the sixth plague to hit Egypt was that of boils; the modern counterparts were cancer, tumors, sickness, and heart trouble. The seventh plague (hail) found its analogy in the bombing raids since 1940 on England, Germany, Italy, Japan, and Vietnam.

Because of these plagues, Edminister believed, conditions would worsen until the year 1986, when, with lawlessness, anarchy, and starvation all kept under control only by a huge military force and the firing squad, world planners would come to realize that they had been wrong to think they could control human nature through electronic computer devices; real Christians, who would have rejected the compulsory, government-controlled religion and the one-world Antichrist economic system for fear of taking the "mark of the Beast," would be underground; and the white Israel race, faced with interracial marriages made compulsory under the threat of a genocide treaty, would have become completely homogenized with alien races of color. Then, in response to the people's cries deploring these conditions, Yahvah would decide to consummate the age and put an end to Satan's reign over the kingdom of this world. Yahvah, therefore would put his hooks into the jaws of Gog and Magog[24] (Gog being the USSR and its satellites, and Magog, the People's Republic of China and her satellites), who would then begin a gigantic invasion of America, the site of Armageddon.[25]

There were to be several preliminaries to the invasion, however. A neutron bomb was to be exploded,[26] followed by the command of Yahvah—in preparation for the final plague of the destroying angel, international communism—to apply "the blood of Christ over the doorposts and lentals [*sic*] of your hearths and homes even as of old the Israelites are told to use the blood of a slain animal on doorposts as a sign of faithfulness so that the angel of death would pass over that home and not destroy the first born."[27] Then, as the mist of radioactivity cleared, the huge invasion would begin, consisting of 200 million communist armed forces, whose task it was to mop up all pockets of people who had escaped bombardment. The remnants of Israel would see the power of the blood as they were spared from the mop-up operations, sheltered as they were in "the secret place of the most high God,"[28] just as Edminster was, in his forested enclave in Washington State. Moreover, as people saw the protection afforded those who had applied the blood to their lives, many would repent.[29] "And I will remove far off from you the northern army [200 million communist troops], and will drive him into a land barren and desolate, with his face toward the east sea [Atlantic Ocean] and his hinden part toward the utmost sea [Pacific Ocean] and his stink shall come up and his ill savour shall come up because he hath done great things."[30]

Once the purge was complete, that is, once all the chaff or the unfaithful in America were destroyed by either the bomb or the mop-up operations, Yahvah next was going to destroy the communist invaders. This was to occur at the valley of judgment, which is the valley of Harmongog, near the Mississippi River valley.[31] Here Yahvah was going to stir up a scourge among the millions of these communist invaders "according to the slaughter of Midian at the rock of Oreb,"[32] a reference to the incident in which Gideon and his 300 hand-picked troops went against thousands of Midianites and Amalekites and slew them, a "type and shadow" of Jesus and his "Delivering Company" of overcomers who were to destroy completely the millions of communist troops by their spiritual anointing. Communists were going to kill one another, lifting forever the yoke of Satan's serpent race of people, the Amalekite-Canaanite-Zionist world conspiracy, from the neck of Jacob-Israel. It would take seven months to bury the dead, but the result would be worth the terrible price: the newly cleansed "manchild nation," more now than merely a nation "under God," would be a nation "born of God and His word," and every inhabitant alive would be in "the spirit of God" and part of God's great theocratic government of love and righteousness.[33] "America," wrote Edminster, "would do well to profit by the light given in the spirit of prophecy."[34]

In listening to Clyde Edminster and reading his material, one might easily have labeled him and his movement racist and blatantly anti-Semitic.[35] But Edminster himself took sharp exception to the charge. Jews, in his view, and blacks too, were merely the instruments of God; their historical function, though a negative one, was simply part of the natural order. It was "natural" that Jews came from Esau, were impure, of the Antichrist, red, and, in an inversion of modern history, that they found their spiritual home in the USSR. Israel, on the other hand, stemmed from Jacob, was pure, white, and embodied in the United States of America. But both belonged to the order of things ordained by God; both, for Edminster, were "natural."

The problem with the "natural" was that it was being polluted or adulterated by something "unnatural." Partly what Edminister had in mind here was "racial mixture," since that is what "adultery" signified to him, and he noted of the United States that it had been naturally pure until the time it had allowed the immigration of Asians and the integration of whites with blacks. But his concern for pollution in America also referred to the massive polluting of the environment—the water, land, and air—for which he held greedy entrepreneurs directly responsible but for allowing and tolerating which he chastised all American society. While he lamented the fact that the Environmental Protection Agency was understaffed and limited in its power to bring industrial plants into conformity with its codes, he placed the blame for it on all Americans. "America," he declared, "doesn't have many people with love in their hearts."[36] Instead, people had become carnal, selfish, and rebellious, and it was for God to destroy them, and for America to perish in its own corruption (2 Peter 2:12).[37]

Edminster's unexpected position on the environment demonstrated that he was very much his own man, one who here departed from the traditional right-wing view. In other ways, too, while he shared certain commonly held conservative attitudes—an intense American nationalism, for example, and suspicion of the United Nations—his theological views colored his political outlook and gave it a distinctive and individual cast. Thus, while loyalty to the United States led him to support America's political system (voting, he held, was a citizen's responsibility), he also thought the ballot could not significantly reform a system that had become almost totally subverted and whose total cleansing would only occur in conformity to prophecy. Similarly, his suspicion of the United Nations rested mainly on his view of it as simply another place for the red Jewish menace to have its worldwide platform in order to subvert true governments of Israel. It was part of the reason for subversion in America; in part, the reason for "adultery" in America. A prime example of the world planners and world government in action, it was also a sign of the impending end.

The uniqueness of Edminister's views sets Kingdom Identity apart from all other religious groups, and though he and his colleagues show great sympathy for those who practiced glossalalia (as possessing the spirit of God if not a completely accurate interpretation of Scripture), their outlook is peculiarly their own. In outline, the theological position of *Christ Is the Answer* encompasses belief in:

• Jesus Christ, the only begotten Son of God, and his atoning sacrifice at Calvary.
• The virgin birth, resurrection and ascension, and second coming to judge this world in righteousness.

• The bodily return of Jesus Christ who will take the throne of David and reign as King of Kings for a thousand years.

They believe that:

• His people Israel, consisting of twelve tribes, the descendents of the twelve sons of Jacob, were set apart by God to be His chosen servants through whom all nations are to be blessed.

• The present Zionist state of Israel in Palestine is an atheistic, counterfeit version of the Messianic one and will be destroyed by God."

• The modern Israel nation must and will, under God, lead the world out of the chaos and misery that now affects mankind. And after much chastisement for their sins, the favor of God will again be upon them for the blessing of the world.[38]

There are similarities in this to the historic five-point creed of fundamentalism, but there are differences as well. There are also similarities to Calvinism, notably in the belief that in spite of the apparent chaos of world events, God is in control of them and his plan is being worked out through them, but it differs from Calvinism in the certainty it professes in knowledge of that plan. That certainty was perhaps the most characteristic feature of Edminister and his publication.[39]

In the Western world, the need for certainty runs deep. Ambiguity, speculation, contemplation, and insecurity disturb Western man; the kind of certainty and knowing exuded by Kingdom Identity was simply an extreme and contorted rendition of a common theme in our society. Everything about the movement—its leader, its ideas, and the beauty and seclusion of its location—spelled Security. The world might be topsy-turvy. People might be fraught with uncertainty, fear, and frustration. The news might be filled with violence, duplicity, immorality, and tragedy. Even nature might writhe with violence through storm, earthquake, and flood. No matter: it was all in the plan made plain to those who studied God's Word correctly. "He that dwells in the secret place of the Most High shall abide under the shadow of the Almighty."

Notes

1. Clyde Edminster, *The Manchild—The Birth of America* (Rainier, Washington, 1976), p. 1; interview on site with Clyde Edminster, 25 June 1982.

2. Edminster, *Manchild*, p. 2.

3. Leviticus 26: 27–28. This and all other Scripture passages to follow represent Edminster's own use of Scripture in developing his thesis.

4. According to Edminister, one "time" was 360 years even as one year was origianlly 360 days, until the great flood occurred, which caused a year to be lengthened by five days.

5. Revelation 12:14; II Samuel 7:10; Edminster, *Manchild*, p. 3.

6. Edminister, *Manchild*, p. 3.

7. Genesis 35:10–11.

8. Edminster, *Manchild*, p. 4.

9. Ibid., p. 7.

10. Genesis 42–46.

11. Deuteronomy 33:13–17.

12. Clyde Edminster, *The Deliverance of Israel and the Kingdom Age by 1986* (Rainier, Washington, 1975), p. 4.

13. Ibid.

14. Ibid.

15. Matthew 23:1–39; John 8:44; Edminster, *Manchild*, p. 4.

16. Edminister, *Deliverance*, p. 8.

17. Ibid., p. 9.

18. Ibid., p. 10.

19. Ibid.

20. Exodus 1; Jashar 66:9–31. Edminister used the book of Jashar extensively. It is an ancient book of religious and secular songs that describe the epic events of the nation of Israel. It is occasionally quoted in the Old Testament itself.

21. Edminster, *Deliverance*, p. 22.

22. Jashar 81:4.

23. Edminster, *Deliverance*, p. 2.

24. Ezekiel 38:1–7.

25. Edminster explained in an interview that Palestine could never be the place for Armageddon since no Israelites were in Palestine, but only Jews: (i.e., reds). Only the United States—the New Israel—had Israelites.

26. Description of flash and results were perceived to be in Matthew 24:27–28 and Zechariah 14:12–15.

27. Edminster, *Deliverance*, p. 50.

28. Psalms 91:1–11.

29. Isaiah 1:18–29; Joel 3:12–17.

30. Joel 2:15–20.

31. Ezekiel 39:11–12.

32. Isaiah 10:26–27.

33. Ezekiel 39:11–16.

34. Edminster, *Deliverance*, p. 52.

35. Even the freeze damage of Florida oranges that "raised the price of your orange juice" was caused by Soviet manipulation of the U.S. climate beginning in 1977 and 1978. Emil J. Trautman, "Soviet Shift Winter Weather to U.S.A.," *Christ Is the Answer* 15 (April 1982): 7–9.

36. Clyde Edminster, *America's Four Sore Judgments!* (Rainier, Washington, 1981), p. 13.

37. Ibid., p. 25.

38. Jimmy L. Sabin, "What Really Constitutes the Christian Israel Belief?" *Christ Is the Answer* 14 (June 1981): 11–12.

39. Edminster even identified specific people who had been in government as a "type and shadow" of specific people in the ancient past. For example, in Jashar 67:8–11 "Balaam, son of Beor fled from the land of Chittini, which was an Esau-red controlled and dominated country. He came to the Pharaoh in Egypt and he was immediately made advisor to the King. The modern day sequel is Dr. Henry Kissinger, a Jew, a refugee from red socialist dominated Germany. After a short schooling in the 'world planners' ivy league college, he was exhalted [*sic*] as chief advisor to our president." Edminster, *Deliverance*, p. 12.

Information Sources

BIBLIOGRAPHY:

Edminster, Clyde. *America's Four Sore Judgments!* Rainier, Washington, 1981.

———*Behold, A Great Red Dragon.* Rainier, Washington, 1978.

———*The Deliverance of Israel and the Kingdom Age by 1986.* Rainier, Washington, 1975.

————*The Manchild—The Birth of America.* Rainier, Washington, 1976.

Vinz, Warren L. *Pulpit Politics: Faces of American Protestant Nationalism in the Twentieth Century. Albany, New York. 1997.*

INDEXES: None.

REPRINT EDITIONS: Microform: Right Wing Collection, University of Iowa (MCA), partial run, 1969–1975 (reel 24).

LOCATION SOURCES: Complete run: "Christ Is the Answer," P. O. Box 128, Rainier, Washington 98576.

Publication History

TITLE AND TITLE CHANGES: *Christ Is the Answer.*

VOLUME AND ISSUE DATA: Volumes 1–current, 1967–present.

FREQUENCY OF PUBLICATION: Monthly.

PUBLISHER: Christ Is the Answer Publications, Rainier, Washington.

EDITOR: Clyde Edminster.

CIRCULATION: 1985: 7,000; 1999: 2,000.

Warren L. Vinz

Part Eight

RIGHT-WING ANTICOMMUNIST PERIODICALS

The use of *communism* as a generic term for ideologies that deny the sanctity of private property has a long history in the United States. Opposition to the Russian Revolution does not adequately explain the hostility to communism, although it increased significantly after 1917. Bolsheviks electrified radicals with their audacity, and in the midst of establishing control over the Soviet Union, they urged socialist groups elsewhere to expedite the coming of the revolutionary dawn. Two communist parties arose in the United States, contending against each other but in agreement that eventually the state must be overthrown. Under pressure from the Communist International, the two parties merged, but during the 1920s the Communist Party of the United States (CPUSA) remained in shambles, with several leaders expelled on orders from the Kremlin.

The Great Depression restored a revolutionary élan among party members, enabling the CPUSA for a time to overcome its troubles and participate in the hoped-for destruction of capitalism. Pressured by the economic breakdown, a growing number of leftists and labor activists found the Marxist dream of a classless society appealing. Among the beneficiaries were the communists, who worked among the unemployed, led a hunger march in Washington, D.C., defended the nine Scottsboro boys wrongly convicted of raping two white women, and became active in the union movement. Several went South to organize a union of black sharecroppers in Alabama; others supported striking textile workers in Gastonia, North Carolina, and coal miners in Harlan County, Kentucky. Later, party militants struggled unsuccessfully for control of several unions then organizing under the aegis of the Congress of Industrial Organizations. Party activists also energized organizations involving intellectuals, artists, and writers, and they figured in shaping public opinion on the Spanish Civil War. Intellectuals in disproportionate numbers supported the battle against fascist leader Francisco Franco, who received military aid from Hitler and Mussolini, just as earlier they had made common cause with the League of American Writers and the American League against War and Fascism, both dominated by communists. Thus for several years during the depression decade, communists appeared to be good fighters for good causes. Yet only fellow travelers and those who wished not to undermine reformist energies could deny three overshadowing realities: the CPUSA maintained a secret and authoritarian underground organization, it attempted to influence the work of several government agencies, and without fail it tailored its policies to conform to the dictates of the Comintern in Moscow. Everything of the Communist International thus far uncovered in the recently opened Soviet archives comports with that assessment and in addition deflates the importance of the CPUSA in the eyes of Joseph Stalin.

Communist subversion never seriously threatened the integrity of the American political system and was never as important as its grandiose partisans liked to believe. Nevertheless, the forces of right-wing anticommunism worked in fertile soil. Radicalism long had been weak in American life. The lack of a feudal tradition, with its rigid hierarchies and class barriers, the existence for centuries of largely vacant land, the peopling of America by immigrants more impressed with job than class consciousness, and the strength of the individualistic, Protestant ethic fostered an attitude unremittingly hostile to radical programs of political and economic development.

It was World War II, which left the Soviet Union astride Eastern Europe, that not only outraged all anticommunists but encouraged partisans across the political spectrum to magnify the issue of domestic communism, making countersubversion politically attractive. In short order the power brokers in Washington, church and union leaders, and educational organizations fell into line to swell the ranks of the anticommunist crusade. In local communities business groups and the Chamber of Commerce often led the way. When President Harry Truman rallied support for the Truman Doctrine, insiders understood that to accomplish their objective it was necessary to sketch out a Manichaean image of a world divided between good and evil. As the sober minded were soon to learn, that setting was made to order for dozens of right-wing groups, including the Christian Anti-Communism Crusade, the John Birch Society, the American Legion, and Christian Crusade, whose periodicals are examined in this section: the *Christian Anti-Communism Crusade Newsletter*, *American Opinion*, *American Legion Firing Line*, and *Christian Crusade*.

Internal investigations demanded by such groups and pushed by politicians seeking electoral advantage revealed Soviet espionage in the United States both before and during World War II, prominent among them the activities of Julius and Ethel Rosenberg, who were executed for having participated in a spy ring responsible for stealing atomic secrets, and of Alger Hiss, jailed on charges of perjury for having lied under oath about delivering government documents to Whittaker Chambers. In the space of several years, many Americans, concluding that something must lie behind the furious exchange of charge and countercharge, supported Senator Joe McCarthy's (R, Wisconsin) demagogic pursuit of domestic communists that not incidentally splattered the work of liberals, the New Deal, and the Democratic party with the odious stink of treason. By the time the storm passed in the late 1950s, the witch hunt had consumed many victims.

Anticommunism was not simply a conservative proposition. Liberals agreed with conservatives that communism was destructive of individual liberty and were eager to exclude from government and unions a professed destroyer of deliberative democracy. Liberal organizations moved to ban communist members; for example, the CIO expelled nearly a dozen unions with communist influence and United Auto Workers president Walter Reuther purged his union of radicals. It was President Truman who created a comprehensive loyalty oath program, and his administration led in establishing the Truman Doctrine, the Marshall Plan, and the North Atlantic Treaty Organization, which lay at the heart of containment policy. Yet liberal-conservative collaboration often was restive, making for an unstable partnership. Conservatives entertained suspicions that communism was largely an extension of liberal hedging over the sanctity of wealth and property, and in a thousand newspaper columns wrote with greater passion of the need to identify "crypto-communists." A second difference emerged over the question as to whether the Soviet Union had a master plan for world domination. By the time of the Korean War, most conservatives answered in the affirmative; a smaller proportion of liberals argued that the Soviets, like the Americans, were acting primarily on defensive grounds, with local considerations in mind. Still a third difference lay in the method of confronting the Soviet challenge. Should it be contained, in the formulation offered by the Truman administration, or should it be forced off the world stage by aggressive U.S. military power, as liberation doctrine argued?

Numbered among the most extreme on the anticommunist Right were members of the John Birch Society. Believing that President Eisenhower was weak-kneed on communism, their leader, Robert Welch, went still further, writing in *The Politician* (1963) that Ike was a "communist stooge" who "has been guided by, and taken orders from, the communist bosses who count on him merely for the execution of their planning." Serious anticommunists, accordingly, must be willing to employ "mean and dirty" tactics, including war abroad and jail terms at home for those suspected of subversive activity: "We have to face squarely up to the solid truth—that unless we are willing to take drastic steps, a lot of them, and very drastic indeed, we haven't a chance in the world of saving our lives, our country, or our civilization."

Working in the same vineyard as Welch (and Dr. Fred C. Schwarz) was Billy James Hargis, an enthusiastic endorser of the John Birch Society. Although Hargis called his *Christian Crusade* a religious periodical, it was political through and through, a tax-exempt vehicle that reflected every dimension of right-wing extremism. At a young age Hargis became a minister in the Disciples of Christ church and before turning thirty had received an honorary doctor of divinity degree from a Puerto Rican seminary founded by the Reverend Gerald B. Winrod, publisher of the *Defender*, an anti-Semitic magazine to which Hargis contributed articles. By the age of twenty Hargis was alarmed at the supposed inroads communism had made within the wider Protestant church. For years he pursued his central theme, broadcasting anticommunist messages over hundreds of radio stations, producing films on various "threats" to America, publishing books (such as *Communist*

America—Must It Be? (1960) and *The Facts about Communism and Our Churches* (1962), selling tape recordings and establishing Anti-Communist Leadership Schools. The schools were a response to his belief that America was so dominated by socialist and liberal groups—he named the National Council of Churches, the National Association for the Advancement of Colored People, and the American Civil Liberties Union—that it would likely go communist by 1974. Hargis proved adept at raising money with the Bible in one hand and the collection plate in the other, crying out (as in November 1963) that "this coming Thanksgiving may be the last legal one we Americans will celebrate!" If Christian Crusade went under, America would be lost.

The dark side of anticommunism as seen in the Birchers and Christian Crusaders actually hurt the anticommunist cause by delegitimizing its essence. It bears repeating that William F. Buckley found it necessary at last not merely to scoff at the paltry absurdities of Welch but to read him out of the conservative movement. The periodicals in this as in the previous part throw in stark relief major differences between conservatism and the far Right. They reflect anger at nearly every political and social trend of the twentieth century. Heading the list appears to be the democratic process itself, with its passion for compromise and legitimization of conflict, all in the context of a secular society.

Human Events
1944–

Human Events was founded in 1944, toward the end of the most momentous human event of the twentieth century. Its founders and editors, Frank C. Hanighen and Felix Morley, intended to use the journal to examine what they believed had been a record of liberal failures that had involved the United States not just in World War II but in World War I as well. They hoped to do this within the broader context of seeking to revive conservative thought and political action among American intellectuals. Hanighen, a Harvard graduate, had been foreign correspondent for the old *New York Evening Post* and the *New York Times* in the 1930s and was a coauthor of *The Merchants of Death*, a book that influenced 1930s isolationist legislation. Morley, a graduate of Haverford College and a Rhodes scholar, had been a correspondent in China in the 1920s, an editor of the *Washington Post*, and president of Haverford College. Within a year after beginning *Human Events*, Henry Regnery, an MIT and Harvard graduate interested in starting a conservative publishing company, joined Hanighen and Morley as a partner. Together they hoped to recapture the literary tradition of *The Federalist Papers* and Albert Jay Nock's *Freeman*, with essays that were to be "closely reasoned, and carefully written." *Human Events* editors believed that people could learn new conservative ideas from accurate reporting and well-written four-page essays based on a conservative viewpoint of events in Washington.[1]

A weekly periodical, *Human Events* (the name was taken from the opening phrase of the Declaration of Independence) began in February 1944 with 147 subscriptions; by the end of the year that number had grown to 2,000, by 1945 to 5,000, and by 1950 to almost 10,000. Following Morley's resignation in June 1950, Hanighen—and after him, Thomas S. Winter and Allan H. Ryskind, owners and editors since 1964—used mass circulation techniques that, combined with the spread of conservative ideas and growing anxiety over communism, led to a circulation high of 110,000 in 1964. The recession of the early 1980s, the success of other conservative publications, and a more conservative government, Winter believed, reduced the journal's circulation to approximately 50,000 by 1984.[2]

In 1963 *Human Events* was expanded to a twenty- to twenty-six-page tabloid newspaper. Its format included a lead analysis written by Ryskind and Winter, signed articles by syndicated columnists that do not necessarily represent the views of the editors, special in-depth eight-page supplements, and liberal-conservative ratings on congressmen. Throughout its life, *Human Events* has offered reprints of key articles and has promoted books that offer a conservative interpretation of events.

Although early subscribers were fewer in number than desired, Morley considered them a "cream list" of the more important intellectuals and political leaders in the country. They included John Dos Passos, Pierre S. Du Pont, former President Herbert Hoover, John L. Lewis, Charles A. Lindbergh, Eugene Lyons, Richard M. Nixon, J. Howard Pew, and Senator Robert A. Taft (R, Ohio). After Reagan's election, the White House received several dozen copies of *Human Events* every Friday morning. Over the years many prominent conservative writers have been published by *Human Events*, among them William F. Buckley, Jr., William Henry Chamberlin, Frank Chodorov, M. Stanton Evans, John T. Flynn, Barry Goldwater, Paul Harvey, James J. Kilpatrick, Russell Kirk, Ludwig von Mises, E. Merrill Root, Morrie Ryskind, and Freda Utley.[3]

The stated policies of *Human Events* from 1944 to the 1950s were to reestablish a belief in the tradition of limited government; reestablish a free enterprise system; reestablish individual responsibility as a counterpoint to socialism; counter the collectivist control of large segments of the press and publishing world; reduce executive power and restore legislative authority; return as much control to the states as possible; restore liberty in America; and stop political intervention in and alliances with other nations.[4]

At the close of World War II, the editors were deeply concerned with America's "shallow optimism" toward Russia that converted a "ruthless dictator" into a "kindly, pipe-smoking 'Uncle Joe'." They saw as an unrealistic ideal the expected period of peace, prosperity, and democracy that would develop under the aegis of the United Nations. American foreign policy had become one of appeasement, a process that began when the government and liberal press represented the Russians as a "sister democracy." They believed that the liberal rationale that Russia and the United States could cooperate to defeat a common enemy and create a lasting peace was naive.

Editors and writers for *Human Events* were convinced that the United Nations, proclaimed as a safeguard for world peace, would fail. Only an organization founded on mutual confidence with a willingness to arbitrate disputes could succeed, but the paramount reality was that Soviet communism existed to compete with and destroy the free world. The objectives of the United Nations, at once grandiose and universalistic, were unworkable illusions.[5]

Early writers for *Human Events*, however, saw the struggle between East and West in terms of imperial national interests rather than as a clash between Marxist-Leninist and non-Marxist ideologies. Soviet expansion, they held, flowed more from its "strategic interests" than its desire to extend communism. They argued against maintaining a large military force on grounds that it increased taxes, created a larger government, and would lead to imperialistic actions. But after 1949, when the USSR produced the A-bomb, *Human Events* writers came to see a permanent defense as necessary to prevent a worldwide Soviet takeover.[6] Furthermore, after Felix Morley resigned his editorship in 1950, greater emphasis was given to communism's threat to freedom. The proper course of the United States therefore had nothing to do with containment, coexistence, or appeasement; its true goal was to roll back or overthrow the Soviet regime. America must intervene wherever necessary, and if that involved an increase in taxes and the size of the government, then that was the price of freedom. Americans must be prepared to pay it, since communists were prepared to do anything to secure their own triumph. Indeed, as Hanighen wrote near the end of Eisenhower's presidency, there was "no evil so appalling that the communists would not shrink from it."[7] The Soviet Union, to *Human Events*, had become the evil empire.

Since good and evil cannot coexist, according to *Human Events*, détente is a contradiction, and the policy of détente during the 1970s a source of concern. With the publication of Aleksandr Solzhenitsyn's *Gulag Archipelago* in 1973, *Human Events* stepped up its campaign against détente, citing the gulag as the best proof yet of the evil of communism, and publishing Solzhenitsyn's speeches against détente. Article after article castigated the Nixon and Kissinger policies toward the Soviet Union and China. Even the *New York Times* correspondent to Moscow, Hedrick Smith, was quoted as saying that détente was less successful than claimed since the Soviets were receiving U. S. aid without having to lessen repression.[8]

While early writers in *Human Events* viewed East-West relations as primarily governed by national rather than ideological interests, they were nevertheless always convinced of a permanent worldwide communist conspiracy, and early suspected that it possessed significant domestic American connections. As early as 4 March 1944, *Human Events* noted that the "Administration seems to be the prisoner of the Communist Party."[9] Yet the "first real step to oust communists and fellow-travelers from the State Department," Hanighen reported, was not taken until 1946 in the Senate. Later, it was Congress that pursued the investigation of communists in the film and entertainment business. In May 1947, J. Parnell Thomas (R, New Jersey), chairman of the House Committee on Un-American Activities (HUAC), met secretly with the head of the Los Angeles FBI to obtain cooperative witnesses. Following the formal Hollywood Ten hearings in Washington, D.C., *Human Events* asserted that Thomas had conducted the fairest hearings possible. *Human Events* reporters credited Thomas with the success of the committee's work, while later writers credited a "handful of patriots" (Ronald Reagan, George Murphy, Walt Disney, Morrie Ryskind, John Wayne, and Adolph Menjou) for serving as major anticommunist witnesses in the Hollywood Ten case. *Human Events* also claimed it was Congress—not J. Edgar Hoover or the FBI, that located the "No. 1. Communist agent," Gerhart Eisler.[10]

In assessing the role of HUAC during the Whittaker Chambers–Alger Hiss hearings, *Human Events* found in the Hiss case proof that there were "left-wing groups in the State Department." Convinced of Hiss's guilt, *Human Events* took credit for keeping its readers informed of the investigation, his trial and retrial, the many books and reviews written on Hiss, and the lectures that Hiss made through the years. In a 1975 eight-page supplement, Francis J. McNamara concluded that Hiss's role in America's foreign policy decisions favored Soviet purposes: he had favored the Soviet Union in the formation of the UN, and his influence led to the fall of nationalist China. McNamara's view was that Hiss had never taken an anticommunist position.[11]

In Hanighen's essays, Whittaker Chambers emerges as an "extraordinary figure" who symbolized "great self-sacrifice and noble adherence" to the "principles of Americanism." Hanighen's admiration extended to Chambers's book *Witness*. Chambers's attacks on communism offended both the Kremlin, and, more seriously, the "forces of that great socialist revolution, which, in the name of liberalism...has been inching its icecap over the [American] nation for two decades." "Most thoughtful people no longer doubt the truth of Chambers's account of the facts," William Rusher concluded in 1978. As ultimate vindication of its position, *Human Events* cited Allen Weinstein's *Perjury: The Hiss-Chambers Case*, in which Weinstein concluded that Hiss had lied.[12]

Within weeks of Hiss's conviction, Senator Joseph McCarthy (R, Wisconsin) delivered his Wheeling, West Virginia, speech. *Human Events* acknowledged McCarthy's success in naming communists, applauded his courage, and defended his role as investigator. But, it stated, he did not go far enough. Frank Chodorov wrote that McCarthy should have looked into the nature of bureaucracy. "It is the proper habitat of communism," he wrote, where central planners gather who propagate themselves, denying individuals of their wealth through taxes and of their freedom through bureaucratic regulation. Chodorov pointed out that "a communist is not necessarily a Soviet-lover. He is, rather, anyone who consciously or unwittingly advocates measures that prepare the way for a regime of Communism." By that standard, most bureaucrats were guilty.[13]

In an extensive supplement, which *Human Events* considered factual, McCarthy's career was reviewed. *Human Events* concluded that he had discovered many security risks in the State Department, uncovered billions of dollars of waste in government bureaucracy, and, most important, had shown that communism was the gravest threat to America.

Beginning in the late 1950s, conservatives warned of the consequences of the demise of congressional investigating committees, claiming that communism was on the rise rather than on the decline, as liberals averred. J. Edgar Hoover warned in 1959 that the "Red fifth column" was a growing "menace." Anthony Bouscaren defined the communist threat as World War III, a war communists were likely to win because "they know they are in it." In a tribute to Eugene Lyons, a well-known anticommunist and editor of *Reader's Digest*, *Human Events* reminded its readers that communism was "intrinsically evil" and unswerving in its goal of world domination.[14]

By the 1970s, *Human Events* focused on KGB domestic activities in the United States. In an interview with John Barron, senior editor of *Reader's Digest*, *Human*

Events gave extensive coverage to his book *KGB: The Secret Work of Soviet Secret Agents* (1974), calling it a definitive study of the purpose, organization, and activities of Soviet spies. M. Stanton Evans thought the KGB may have orchestrated Kennedy's assassination, and in the 1980s he flayed liberals for their refusal to recognize KGB infiltration of the "so-called 'peace'" movement. Furthermore, he said, liberals failed to recognize the sophistication of KGB methods, which allowed the KGB to achieve its objectives without direct control of the "peace" movement. Rather, goals were achieved by "skillfully playing on Western 'peace' sentiments and focusing anxieties on Western rather than Soviet weapon systems." Reagan continued this theme in his presidential speeches.[15]

In 1980 *Human Events* called for action against increased KGB activities. Readers were urged to write the press asking that the same standards used in investigating the FBI and CIA in the 1970s be applied to the KGB. Readers were also to call for a renewal of congressional investigation of communist subversion; to ask publicly why the ACLU did nothing about KGB activities; and to ask presidential and all other political candidates for their proposals to stop the KGB.[16]

From its earliest issues, *Human Events* has labored on behalf of the traditions of limited, constitutional government and free enterprise capitalism. Gradually its purposes have broadened to cover the failure of the New Deal and the need for religion, morality, and education to guard American liberty.

One of the weekly's bright young stars in this connection was William F. Buckley, Jr., who went on to become one of the nation's leading conservative intellectuals. Buckley, a Yale graduate, wrote an article for *Human Events* in May 1951 under the title "Harvard Hogs the Headlines." Based on the promise Buckley showed in this article, Hanighen and Chodorov recommended that Henry Regnery publish the manuscript Buckley was then writing. Accordingly, Buckley's soon acclaimed and discussed *God and Man at Yale* was published by Regnery in September 1951. Russell Kirk proclaimed Buckley a leader of the new American conservative movement, and *Human Events*, claiming a role in its publication, sold copies as a promotion to increase its own subscriptions.[17]

In his *Human Events* articles, Buckley was relentless in his criticism of American businessmen, whom he felt should have been the strongest critics of liberals and the strongest supporters of Adam Smith's idea of a free marketplace, unregulated by government, providing them the greatest profits and freedoms. Instead, the American capitalist was hard at work "nourishing the collectivist giant" as the government destroyed him. Businessmen supported Roosevelt's "path to Socialism" and called for any government regulation that benefited them, such as high tariffs and price controls. He chided business for its refusal to support and promote "individualist publications that might challenge the hegemony of a collectivist periodical," lamenting that instead they advertised in liberal magazines and newspapers such as *Harper's*, *Look*, and the *New York Times*. Corporations even gave support to foundations that hired communists, such as Carnegie (Alger Hiss) and Rockefeller (Hans Eisler). Saddest of all, Buckley said, is that businessmen unwittingly raise money for their alma maters, which in turn indoctrinate students in Keynes, Laski, and the Webbs, thus raising a generation that "will surely, once and for all, abolish Capitalism." In so doing, businessmen will have done a service for Karl Marx.[18]

With the unexpected intensity of liberal opposition at the publication of *God and Man at Yale,* Henry Regnery and New Right conservatives became even more convinced that they needed to develop their own network of intellectuals, pamphlets, newspapers, journals of opinion and analysis, and books. Buckley felt in 1955 that the Right was "virtually impoverished" in its ability to publish its message. "With the exception of the *Freeman, Human Events,* and the *American Mercury,*" Buckley wrote, "we have no press." In the 19 November 1955 *Human Events,* the editors announced that William F. Buckley, Jr., had formed the *National Review.* They noted that many of the writers for the newly formed journal had been contributors to *Human Events.* Many writers have continued to contribute to both periodicals. Since the forming of Young Americans for Freedom and the American Conservative Union, both *Human Events* and the *National Review* have cooperated in sponsoring periodic seminars and annual conferences.[19]

Although Edna Lonigan, who had worked with the Farm Credit Administration, prematurely pronounced the New Deal dead in 1947, she summed up *Human Events'* position when she said "the evil that it did lives on." Proposals to amend the Constitution to restore individual responsibility were early *Human Events* solutions to prevent recurrences of FDR failures. In 1947 Morley proposed a two-term limit on the presidency to prevent executive dictatorships. Hanighen supported the Hoover Commission recommendation that all treaties be approved by a two-thirds vote in both houses and that all executive foreign power agreements be voted on in Congress.[20]

Heavy taxation, *Human Events* claimed, was a New Deal evil that increased the power of the state and diminished individual freedom. Taxation deprived capitalism of the money needed to produce, while social security taxes created bureaucrats and denied individuals a choice of retirement programs. General Douglas MacArthur wrote that confiscatory taxes debased a country's currency; Rusher called for a constitutional convention to limit taxation and deficit spending. Taxes, *Human Events* asserted, could be reduced by deregulating airlines and trucking, and halting the flow of tax money into such unnecessary agencies as the Women's Bureau, the Export-Import Bank, public broadcasting, and the Interstate Commerce Commission. Jeffrey Hart argued that tax money spent on enforcing speed limits was wasted, as speed limits increased traveling time, and time is money. *Human Events* has consistently called for repeal of the Sixteenth Amendment, thus abolishing income taxes, while always reminding its readers that Karl Marx said the "way to kill capitalism is to tax it to death."[21]

Human Events devoted little space to the civil rights movement. Articles that have appeared focus on individual blacks' taking advantage of educational and economic opportunities. Neither morality nor associations between the races could be legislated, claimed *Human Events,* and the state should not force businessmen to limit either the number or kind of races employed. To do so was to expose "a socialistic notion of the collectivist character of capital." Nor should the state establish quotas through forced busing or legislation. *Human Events* spotlighted the contradiction of liberals who advocated integrated schools, busing, and quota systems, yet sent their own children to private or special public schools.[22]

Few articles were written about abortion and women's rights until the 1970s, when *Human Events* came out strongly against "abortion on demand." Life begins at conception, *Human Events* argued, and is therefore protected by the right to life and liberty, not to be terminated by human whim. During the 1970s and 1980s numerous articles appeared in opposition to the equal rights amendment and other feminist causes. Nevertheless, *Human Events* encouraged women to be active in politics so long as they operated on behalf of conservative ends and unhesitatingly decried the Reagan administration's attempts to overcome the "gender gap" by appealing to women.[23]

No general domestic issue has interested *Human Events* more than education. It was to Albert Jay Nock and Russell Kirk that early *Human Events* editors looked to define the "True Purpose of Education," a sternly traditional experience available only to those who had the ability to achieve. For those who qualify, education holds out the promise of wisdom and virtue. Scholars should not forget that they are "Bearers of the Word," Kirk admonished, and they should not forget that the "fear of God is the beginning of wisdom." Disciplined by a concise curriculum based on humane letters, history, theoretical science, moral philosophy, and religion, the mind must not be wasted and cluttered by "amorphous survey courses," vocational experiences, and "quasi-professional programs of athletics." Above all, schools should teach gratitude toward the traditions of the past.[24]

Early in the 1950s, *Human Events* observed that ideas presented in well-written essays could not alone change the course of events. Critics must work to change the ills of education, a long catalog that included a lack of discipline and self-discipline in the schools, undue emphasis on the right of students to determine what courses are best for them, and permissiveness in manners and relativism in morals that the counseling and guidance movement allegedly promoted. Always the conservative critics came back to federal spending and the regulations of bureaucrats, both of which were excessive.

The solutions proposed for education by the contributors to *Human Events* were those of conservatives everywhere: abolition of the Department of Education; reduction of the power of the National Education Association; inclusion of more traditional courses such as English, history, and geography; restoration of religion to a vital place in the student experience; and a return to local control of the schools, which would permit elected boards to hire and dismiss teachers in accordance with the customs of the community.

Supporting political candidates who held conservative views became common in *Human Events*. The editors and writers were committed ideologues "biased in favor of limited constitutional government, private enterprise, and individual freedom. These principles represent the bias of the Founding Fathers." To support the election of conservatives, *Human Events* has published several editions of the *Intelligent Conservative's Reference Manual* since 1974. Early in 1965 *Human Events* became one of the first publications to support Ronald Reagan as a conservative candidate for governor of California in 1966. Having campaigned extensively for *Human Events*-supported candidates Nixon in 1960 and Goldwater in 1964, Reagan appeared to *Human Events* to be a firm believer in conservative principles. "There are very few people in public life whom I instinctively agree with more than Ronald Reagan," Ryskind said. "We're on a very similar wave length. I think that's why we like him and why he reads us."[25] Indeed, Reagan described *Human Events* as his "favorite reading" and after his election as fortieth president he said *Human Events* would become must reading "not only for Capitol Hill insiders but for all of those in public life."[26]

Reagan's views and experience as governor led *Human Events* to declare in February 1974 that it preferred Reagan for president in 1976. *Human Events* also said he had a "hard line on domestic and foreign policy." Reagan said he had a dream that what he had achieved as governor of California would set an example that conservative "efficiency and economy in government" would be considered possible at any level.[27]

By April 1975 Reagan had taken a stand against détente that was the same as that of *Human Events* throughout the 1970s. He denounced détente as nothing more than a cover that the Soviets had used for an arms buildup to gain superiority over the free world. *Human Events* claimed Reagan's conservative position was, as usual, "shut out in the major media in the United States."

Almost every issue of *Human Events* in 1975 urged Reagan to decide for the presidency because "we need someone in the presidency who not only sounds like a conservative but thinks like a conservative and can implement conservative programs."[28] And although Reagan lost the 1976 nomination, *Human Events* promoted him for the 1980 nomination and election, and claimed to be the first national newspaper publicly to have supported him in 1966, 1970, 1976, and 1980.

Following Reagan's election in 1980, Ryskind quoted the *New York Times*'s Hedrick Smith, who reported that Reagan's first 190 days had noticeably brought "a dramatic conservative shift in the nation's economic policies and the role of the federal government in American life." Reagan's accomplishment was the result, Evans and Ryskind believe, "of the public's visceral response" to the substance of his appeal to limit government, decrease spending, and reduce taxes.[29]

Between Reagan's terms as governor and his election to the presidency, he wrote many syndicated columns that were carried in *Human Events*. Where they concerned domestic issues they advanced ideas that later became familiar in his administration, among them the belief that volunteerism begins at home, not on "the banks of the Potomac," that aid ought to go to the "truly needy" only, that gun ownership is a vital constitutional right, and that the Federal Trade Commission, in overseeing television, encroached on a fundamental freedom of individual viewers—the right to exercise their common sense.[30] Concerning foreign policy, he spoke against "self appointed" study groups and U.S. senators who made "fools of themselves" by calling for U.S. recognition of Cuba, and he declared himself in favor of America's holding on to the Panama Canal: we bought it, he insisted, and we should keep it.[31] He also condemned liberals for their double standard of human rights in which they called for arms reduction for the United States while the Soviet Union promoted proxy wars and continued its own arms buildup.

Reagan's assertions of liberal foreign policy failures repeated the beliefs of the founders of *Human Events*, and his election in 1980, which turned the course of America's foreign and domestic policies to conservative principles, vindicated forty years of the journal's weekly publication as a major voice in the revival of conservatism in postwar America.

Believing it is in the conservative tradition of the founders, *Human Events* provided strong support for the Reagan presidency, consistently urging limited government, tax reduction, and a balanced budget. It has broadened conservative interests to include abortion, prayer in the schools, homosexuality, and other domestic special issues, while its central concern in foreign policy before the end of the cold war was to stop or eliminate the evils of communism and Soviet expansion. By providing opportunities for new and established conservative writers, defining national issues, keeping a record of congressional votes, and supporting the election of conservatives, *Human Events* has been one of the significant forces against liberalism and New Deal-Great Society kinds of programs for America.

Notes

1. M. Stanton Evans, "Human Events and the Conservative Movement," *Human Events* (27 April 1974): 3–4 (hereinafter cited as *HE*); Felix Morley, "The Early Days of *Human Events*," *HE* (27 April 1974): 26, 28, 31; *HE* (February 1944): unnumbered page [*HE* did not indicate page numbers until the late 1950s; until then it was largely an eight-page newsletter]; Morley, *Saturday Evening Post,* "For What Are We Fighting?" (18 April 1942): 9–10, 40, 42–43; William Henry Chamberlin, "Stalin, PRAVDA, and Churchill," *HE* (2 February 1944) [this was the first article written for *HE*].

2. Interview with Ryskind and Winter, Washington, D.C., 5 April 1983; interview with Ryskind, Washington, D.C., 13 April 1984; "The Right Way," *Newsweek* (6 September 1971): 75.

3. Henry Regnery to *HE*, n.d., *HE* Library, Washington, D.C.; Henry Regnery, *Memoirs of a Dissident Publisher* (New York, 1979), pp. 28–31; Morley, "The Early Days of *Human Events*," pp. 26, 28, 31; "Frank Hanighen: Editor, Dies at 64," *New York Times* (11 January 1964): 23. Henry Regnery died in 1996.

4. *HE* (2 February 1944); *HE* (3 December 1947); Morley, "The Early Days of *Human Events*," pp. 26, 28, 31; Allan C. Brownsfeld "Henry Regnery," *HE* (21 July 1979): 8.

5. Morley, "Poland and Dumbarton Oaks," *HE* (26 January 1949); "What Follows the U.N.," *HE* (23 May 1949); Chamberlin, "The Idiocy of World Government," *HE* (28 March 1983); Morley, "Only Two Great Powers," *HE* (19 July 1944); Chamberlin, "Stalin, PRAVDA, and Churchill."

6. Chamberlain, "The True Soviet Challenge," *HE* (11 January 1944); Hanighen, "Not Merely Gossip," *HE* (20 September 1950).

7. Eugene Lyons, "The Russians and Their Friends," *HE* (28 March 1951); "Russia's Atomic Explosion," *HE* (5 October 1949).

8. Ryskind, "Detente and Terror," *HE* (12 January 1974): 1; "We Can Bury You Now Called Detente," *HE* (12 July 1975): 1; "Times Moscow Man Sees Flaws in Detente," *HE* (4 January 1975): 2; James L. Buckley, "U. S. Should Re-Examine Current Detente Efforts," *HE* (23 February 1974): 1, 6.

9. Morley, "Red Herrings Return to Roost," *HE* (8 March 1944).

10. Hanighen, "Not Merely Gossip" *HE* (12 February 1947), (10 December 1947).

11. Ryskind, "Reds in Hollywood," *HE* (26 August 1953); "KCET-Hollywood on Trial,

Another Whitewash of the 'Hollywood Ten'," *HE* (31 December 1977): 7; "Hollywood Rewrites the Red Era," *HE* (7 January 1978); Francis J. McNamara, "Let's Reopen the Alger Hiss Case," *HE* (13 December 1975): Special Supplement, 1–8.

12. Hanighen, "HUAC: Committee Get Active," *HE* (11 May 1949); Rusher, "Another Look at Chambers' *Witness*," *HE* (8 April 1978): 20; Hart, "Dartmouth Professors Hail Alger Hiss," *HE* (1 March 1980): 14; Hanighen, "Not Merely Gossip" *HE* (13 July 1949); "Whittaker Chambers' *Witness*," *HE* (15 June 1953); Evans, "Hiss Book a Cold War Landmark," *HE* (15 April 1978): 10.

13. Utley, "Chasing Chameleons," *HE* (29 May 1950); Chamberlin, "Oh! That Terrible 'Witch Hunt'," *HE* (1 October 1952); Frank Chodorov, "McCarthy's Mistake," *HE* (12 November 1952).

14. Hanighen, "Hoover on Communism," *HE* (22 April 1959): 2, 3; Anthony Bouscaren, "The Communist Strategy of Protracted Conflict," *HE* (15 November 1960); Matthew Conroy, "Eugene Lyons: A Thundering Voice of Truth," *HE* (11 February 1978): 12.

15. "Exclusive *H.E.* Interview with John Barron: Inside the Soviet Secret Police," *HE* (8 June 1974): 8–11; Evans, "Did the KGB Orchestrate JFK Assassination?" *HE* (7 July 1978): 11, 15; "Covering Up for KGB Conspiracy," *HE* (2 July 1983): 15; Bryan Lops, "Washington: Prime Target for the KGB," *HE* (17 May 1980) 12–19.

16. "What Can Be Done about Increased KGB Activities?" *HE* (17 May 1980): 19.

17. William F. Buckley, Jr., "Harvard Hogs the Headlines," *HE* (16 May 1952): 1–4; Regnery, *Memoirs of a Dissident Publisher*, pp. 167–73; Regnery to author, 9 September 1983.

18. Buckley, "Who Killed Adam Smith?" *HE* (24 October 1951).

19. Regnery, *Memoirs of a Dissident Publisher*, pp. 167–73; Susan Juroe, "Conservative Political Action Conference Celebrates Its Tenth Anniversary," *HE* (5 March 1983): 14–16; Ryskind, Nofziger, Rusher, Evans, "Reagan at Mid-Term: An Assessment," *HE* (12 March 1983): 12–17.

20. Edna Lonigan, "The End of the Beginning," *HE* (1 January 1947); Morley, "Presidential Tenure," *HE* (12 February 1947); Hanighen, "Not Merely Gossip" *HE* (12 January 1949); John T. Flynn, "The Two Thirds Rule," *HE* (3 January 1945).

21. Chodorov, "The Flight of Capital," *HE* (12 January 1949); Paul Harvey, "Public Enemy Number One—Taxes," *HE* (28 October 1959); J. Bracken Lee, "The Income Tax Is Making Us a Dishonest People," *HE* (19 October 1957): 19; Ralph de Toledano, "Scrap Personal Income Tax," *HE* (1 December 1979); Douglas MacArthur, "The Path to Freedom," *HE* (17 March 1958); Rusher, "Constitutional Convention Bans Deficit Spending," *HE* (10 March 1979): 15.

22. Hanighen, "Federalized Race Prejudice," *HE* (8 March 1950); William Upson, "A Great Negro Conservative: What Would Booker T. Washington Say Now?" *HE* (21 October 1959); Hanighen, "Against Black Quotas," *HE* (5 January 1974): 13; Ryskind, [untitled editorial], *HE* (1 July 1978): 5.

23. Howard Phillips, "Will Nixon Redeem Anti-Abortion Pledge?" *HE* (24 January 1974): 10; Evans, "Protecting the Right to Life," *HE* (23 February 1974): 8; Hanighen, "Women's Place Is under the Dome," *HE* (13 January 1958); Ryskind, "NASA Courts the Militants," *HE* (2 July 1983): 4.

24. Albert Jay Nock, "The Theory of Education," *HE* (12 October 1949); "Russell Kirk and the True Purpose of Education," *HE* (2 February 1983): 14; review of Russell Kirk, *Academic Freedom*, *HE* (7 May 1955).

25. Interview with Ryskind, 5 April 1983, and telephone interview, 10 April 1984; Fred Barnes, "Reagan's Favorite Reading," *Baltimore Sun*, 19 April 1981; Bill Peterson,

"The World According to *Human Events*," *Washington Post*, 14 March 1982.

26. Ronald Reagan to *HE*, n.d., *HE* Library, Washington, D. C.

27. "Ronald Reagan: Spokesman for Conservatism," *HE* (2 February 1974): Special Supplement, 9–16.

28. "Reagan and the Media," *HE* (19 April 1975): 3; Ryskind, "Reagan Moves Closer to Presidential Bid," *HE* (19 July 1975): 1, 6; Kilpatrick, "Reagan Should Fish or Cut Bait," *HE* (16 September 1975): 8; Ryskind, "Reagan Should Make Immediate '76 Bid," *HE* (16 November 1974): 1; "Together, Let Us Make a New Beginning," *HE* (26 July 1980): 1, 8, 10, 11, 15, 18, 19.

29. Ryskind, "What Reagan's Victory Accomplishes," *HE* (8 August 1981): 1; Evans, "Why Reagan Triumphed in the Tax Fight," *HE* (8 August 1981): 1, 8.

30. Reagan, "The Food Stamp Racket," *HE* (7 September 1974): 13–14; Reagan, "A Look at Those Unemployment Statistics," *HE* 30 (29 March 1975): 14; Reagan, "Citizens' Gun Rights Must Not Be Abolished," *HE* (24 August 1976): 10; Reagan, "National Nanny Is Watching Us!" *HE* (24 April 1979): 15.

31. Reagan, "Why the Campaign to Recognize Cuba," *HE* (1 February 1975): 8, 15; "Castro's 25th Anniversary Diatribe," *HE* (16 May 1978): 12; Reagan, "State Department Determined to Relinquish Panama Canal," *HE* (27 September 1975): 8; Reagan, "Vladivostok Pact on Missiles Contains Dangerous Inequalities," *HE* (15 March 1975): 15; "Free World Idealism Faces Soviet Realities," *HE* (2 July 1977): 8

Information Sources

BIBLIOGRAPHY: None.

INDEXES: Each volume indexed; *Amer Hist & Life*; *BRI*; *Comb Ret Ind Bk Revs Sch J*; *Hist Abst*; *PPI*.

REPRINT EDITIONS: Microform: UMI; KIP.

LOCATION SOURCES: Hoover Institute, Stanford, California; Yale University; Library of Congress; University of Michigan; University of Minnesota.

Publication History

TITLE AND TITLE CHANGES: *Human Events*.

VOLUME AND ISSUE DATA: No numbers, no volumes, February 1944–present.

FREQUENCY OF PUBLICATION: Weekly.

PUBLISHERS: 1944–1964: Frank C. Hanighen; 1964: James L. Hick; 1964–1967: Kenneth W. Ingwalson; 1968–1975: Robert D. Kephard; 1975–present: Richard D. Reddick; 1975–present: Human Events, Inc. All in New York.

EDITORS: Felix Morley, 1944–1950; Frank C. Hanighen, 1944–1964; Thomas S. Winter, 1964–present.

CIRCULATION: 1964: 110,000; 1984, 50,000; 1998: 40,000.

Thomas J. Ferris

Plain Talk
1946–1950

Plain Talk began its short-lived career in 1946 in a meeting at the Connecticut home of journalist Isaac Don Levine. Present at this gathering were Alfred Kohlberg, a wealthy New York importer prominent in the China Lobby; Benjamin Mandel, an excommunist working for the Senate Internal Security Subcommittee; and Father John Cronin, assistant director of the Department of Social Action of the National Catholic Welfare Conference. With Kohlberg agreeing to underwrite the initial expenses and Levine offering his free services as editor, the group founded the periodical in reaction to Soviet expansionism and domestic subversion. From October 1946 to May 1950, *Plain Talk* consistently urged the United States to oppose these threats to freedom. With the addition of conservative writers Ralph de Toledano, Christopher T. Emmet, Jr., Karl Baarslag, Eugene Lyons, Suzanne La Follette, George S. Schuyler, and John Chamberlain to the editorial staff, the new monthly marked a departure from the traditional conservative posture of isolationism in its emphasis on anticommunist interventionism.[1]

Plain Talk's dominant theme concerned the rapid growth of Soviet power in the world. Part of this approach consisted of warnings about communist ambitions worldwide. The earliest issues established this theme with articles on Soviet conduct in Hungary and East Germany, the flight of Jews from the USSR, Soviet expansionism, religious persecution in Yugoslavia, and the four-part memoir of a Soviet concentration camp victim. Reflecting Kohlberg's major interest, the second issue criticized American policy toward China and urged that the United States support the nationalists. This theme continued through the fall of China to the communists in 1949. Later issues ran warnings on communist designs on the rest of Asia and called for the United States to stand firm against aggression in this region.[2]

Not content to sound warnings concerning the spread of communism, *Plain Talk* urged a policy of active resistance to the Soviets worldwide, while encouraging the carrying of the "war" to the Soviet Union itself. Authors argued that the United States should create an underground inside the USSR and its satellites, stop the repatriation of Soviet deserters and instead use them against Moscow, create an American foreign legion, and build up the nationalist Chinese army so that it would be strong enough to reconquer Manchuria, and thus open a second front in Asia that would pressure the Soviets into halting their expansion in Europe.[3]

To bolster its indictment of foreign communism, *Plain Talk* carried articles exposing the nature of the Soviet government. The early series on Soviet labor camps was soon followed by "I Dwelt with Death," written by a prisoner who had been held at Novaya Zemlya. At a time when the extent of the Soviet concentration camp system was all but unknown in the West, the journal provided an early exposé of the gulag in its May 1947 issue. This article included a reasonably accurate map of the gulag, based on information by Poles who had been held prisoners in the system. Of similar importance was Eugene Lyons's investigation of the Katyn massacre, and his conclusion that the Soviets, and not the Germans, were responsible for the atrocity. Other articles covered life in the satellites, emphasizing the negative effects of communist rule. Poland and Hungary received the most attention, but others came under scrutiny as well. One article even depicted life in the United States after a fictional Soviet conquest.[4]

Reflecting Levine's strong interest in the Middle East, *Plain Talk* studied the Palestinian situation as Israel approached independence. When former president Herbert Hoover proposed that the United States irrigate sections of thinly settled Iraq and move the Palestinians there, Levine endorsed the idea. Another author proposed a Jordan valley authority to develop Palestine. *Plain Talk* believed that serious problems would develop for the United States unless it took action quickly. Otherwise Russia would be able to exploit events in the Middle East to its own benefit.[5]

Although *Plain Talk* devoted much of its attention to the foreign communism threat, it also covered internal subversion heavily. The first issue carried a highly influential article, "The State Department Espionage Case," written by Emmanuel S. Larsen, a former research analyst for the State Department. He had been one of two people convicted in 1945 of giving classified documents to the staff of *Amerasia*, a magazine that had favored the Chinese communists over the nationalists. Larsen's article told of the presence of a "pro-Soviet group in the China Section [of the State Department], whose views were reflected by *Amerasia*." It examined the pressure brought on the nationalists by American officials to reach an accommodation with the communists, the appearance of classified material in the magazine, the political backgrounds of the *Amerasia* staffers, the case dismissals against four others arrested with Larsen, and the fines imposed on Larsen and his codefendant. Its conclusion implied that the case was used to force anticommunist Undersecretary of State Joseph Grew out of office. The article provided ammunition for those critical of the government's handling of the case and for such later critics of the Truman administration's foreign policy as Senator Joseph R. McCarthy (R, Wisconsin).[6]

This exposé later came under intense criticism as a result of the State Department employee loyalty investigation conducted by a subcommittee chaired by Senator Millard E. Tydings (D, Maryland). Larsen told the Tydings subcommittee in 1950 that he did not write the article as it appeared in *Plain Talk*. He claimed that the article was originally entitled "They Called Me a Spy" and that its content differed markedly from the one printed. He submitted a version to the subcommittee that contained autobiographical material, information on his contacts with *Amerasia*, and criticism of the anti-Chiang Kai-shek faction in the State Department. The article claimed that this group undermined American efforts to effect a compromise between the nationalists and the communists, but it contained no allegations of espionage. Larsen testified that Levine and Kohlberg had been unhappy with this draft since it included no proof of a spy ring in the State Department. Kohlberg then told Larsen that he had evidence of communist spies that could be used. Thereafter, Kohlberg, Levine, and de Toledano rewrote the article. Larsen told the subcommittee that he was unhappy with the newer version, but he initialed it anyway since he wanted to catch a train. Later in the hearings, he denied writing specific sections of the *Plain Talk* version.[7] The subcommittee accepted Larsen's testimony and used it to clear John Stewart Service, a State Department employee whom McCarthy had charged of being a procommunist who helped undermine Chiang Kai-shek and supported the communists in China, had communist affiliations and friends, and was connected to the *Amerasia* case. The subcommittee traced much of this indictment back to the *Plain Talk* article and then refuted the charges based on the article since that version was supposedly fabricated. In fact, the subcommittee described the *Plain Talk* article as "an extremely perverted account of the Amerasia case." It dismissed Levine and de Toledano as "professional 'anticommunists,' whose incomes and reputation depend on the developing and maintaining of new communist fears," and it noted Kohlberg's connections to the nationalists. The subcommittee concluded that if Larsen's testimony were correct, then "the action of Levine and his associates in connection with the *Plain Talk* article is one of the most despicable instances of a deliberate effort to deceive and hoodwink the American people in our history."[8]

The subcommittee's interpretation of the events surrounding the Larsen article brought a quick counterattack from Levine. On 31 August 1950, Senator Brien McMahon (D, Connecticut) read a letter from Levine into the *Congressional Record* that called Larsen's testimony "a tissue of downright falsehoods, of willful distortions, and of irresponsible assertions." Levine admitted that he had written the article, but he argued that Larsen had cooperated with him and retained final approval of the article. Levine defended ghostwriting Larsen's account, saying that this was standard procedure when publications dealt with nonauthors. He stated that Larsen never submitted to the magazine the version of the article that he submitted to the Tydings subcommittee. Levine took full responsibility for writing the *Plain Talk* version, and denied that Kohlberg had anything to do with it.[9]

When asked to sign the article to indicate his approval, Larsen signed not only the title page (the usual procedure), but also the last page, and the first and last pages of the carbon copy. In addition, Larsen initialed the twenty-four intervening pages on both copies, all on his own initiative. Levine noted that this was "strange behavior" for someone trying to make a train. He also said that Larsen had written to him after the article was given to the press in September 1946 indicating that he was pleased with the results, and offering to solicit *Plain Talk* subscriptions from his friends. Subsequent letters from Larsen offered more evidence and further accusations of subversion. Levine even wrote that Larsen's original charges went far beyond what *Plain Talk* printed and that parts of the subcommittee version agreed with the magazine article.[10]

Levine's defense won many supporters, including Whittaker Chambers, who wrote that *Plain Talk* was "one of the few magazines in the country that tried to tell some of the truth about the Amerasia Case while it was still happening." Curiously, throughout the controversy neither side mentioned that Larsen had published a second article in the January 1948 issue of *Plain Talk* concerning a communist front in China. If Larsen had been upset with his first *Plain Talk* article as he had testified, it seems unlikely that he would have written for Levine again.[11]

Related to the *Amerasia* controversy were charges that *Plain Talk* had influenced the crusades of Joseph McCarthy. The Tydings subcommittee in particular had found that Larsen's article had provided much inspiration for the Wisconsin senator. Levine did not meet McCarthy until 1950. He had initially reacted unfavorably to the Wheeling speech (he thought that the actual number of communists in the State Department was quite small—nowhere near 57, let alone 205—and that in any case, McCarthy would have no way of knowing the total), but realizing that McCarthy had become familiar with *Plain Talk,* Levine decided to meet with him in April 1950. He hoped to persuade the senator to retract his previous charges and instead use some information Levine uncovered. The effort failed, and each went his separate way.[12]

While the *Amerasia* case and *Plain Talk*'s tenuous influence on the McCarthy era brought the magazine its most publicity, it covered other aspects of Soviet espionage in the United States. The Alger Hiss controversy gave the editors another chance to deal with the issue. Levine had been involved with Chambers when he first tried to cross over, and his charges triggered a series of *Plain Talk* articles. The journal responded to the Hiss case with a call for a stronger federal loyalty program, Levine's recollections of his attempts to spread Chambers's story, the printing of the prosecution's summation in the Hiss perjury trial, and examinations of other espionage cases.[13]

Plain Talk's concern with subversion extended to other domestic issues. Early articles devoted substantial attention to communist infiltration of labor unions. The first issue set the tone when it carried an article critical of the CIO's Political Action Committee. Entitled "Stalin's Hand in Our Ballot Box," it argued that the Communist party controlled the group. Other unions soon came under attack. In 1948, this type of coverage began changing as anticommunist labor leaders started asserting control over the movement. The magazine chronicled this trend enthusiastically while giving favorable coverage to people such as Walter Reuther who were leading this effort.[14]

Plain Talk's exposure of leftist influences in American society extended to other institutions. Very little escaped criticism; Hollywood, the media, academia, and patrons of leftist causes all came under attack. The magazine continually opposed what it saw as assaults on American tradition by those whom it considered to be friends of the communists, and it watched closely those institutions most likely to communicate leftist propaganda.

This approach made *Plain Talk* a harbinger of conservative causes of the 1950s and 1960s. An early version of the blacklisting controversy can be seen in articles attacking the film industry, such as one that claimed that Samuel Goldwyn's movie *The Best Years of Our Lives* (1946) portrayed businessmen as being antiveteran. Another article, entitled "Hollywood's Foreign Legion," developed the thesis that communists had infiltrated the movie industry. Nixon administration feuds with the media and academia were foreshadowed in *Plain Talk* articles castigating such liberal organs as the *Saturday Evening Post* and the *New Yorker* and the New York literary establishment for their alledged leftist biases. Concern over the liberal outlook of American colleges brought articles describing communist attempts to subvert the National Student Association and professorial support for groups on the attorney general's list of subversive organizations, while outrage over leftist teachers expressed itself in "Professor Pinko" cartoons.[15]

In all, *Plain Talk* examined leftist culture in an attempt to discover why many Americans worked against what the magazine saw as the country's best interests. It was especially fascinated by the paradox of the wealthy, such as Frederick Vanderbilt Field, who supported leftist causes, and the journal spared little sympathy for them.[16]

Not every article concerning the Left was critical, however. A 1947 article cautiously praised the founding of Americans for Democratic Action as an attempt to separate liberalism from communism, another celebrated the decline of communist influence in Hollywood, while a third criticized the firing of a government employee who was a member of the Trotskyite Socialist Workers party. The author of the latter recognized that the group was Marxist, but he did not see the party as being particularly dangerous.[17]

On other domestic issues, *Plain Talk* followed a conservative editorial policy. Having implied on numerous occasions that the Truman administration was guilty of lax security practices and inept in opposing communist advances abroad, the magazine naturally gravitated to the Republican party and its presidential candidates. As early as the third issue, *Plain Talk* celebrated the 1946 Republican congressional landslide, attributing it to public anger over the Soviet and big labor issues.[18]

A series of articles on the 1948 presidential election soon followed. Many of these attacked Progressive party candidate Henry A. Wallace. Others praised Republican hopefuls Robert A. Taft, Harold E. Stassen, and Thomas E. Dewey. *Plain Talk* supported Dewey after he won the Republican party nomination. When he went down to defeat in November, the magazine criticized him for failing to speak out more strongly on domestic issues.[19]

On other matters, the magazine differed little from the orthodox conservative positions of the era. Authors favored cutting the size of government, limiting the right to strike, reducing waste in the Defense Department, and returning to the gold standard. Writers opposed the Marshall Plan, Keynesian inflationism, high taxes, Truman's farm policy, and the Reconstruction Finance Corporation. There is little that is surprising in these positions.[20]

While the journal wrote mostly on the communist threat, it also warned readers about the far Right. Reflecting the mood of the postwar era, *Plain Talk* watched for signs of a possible Nazi revival. It favored educating the German people on the nature of Hitler's Reich to prevent a recurrence of Nazism in Germany, but it also cautioned readers to be aware of signs of it elsewhere. The magazine exposed the Bavarian Communist party's attempt to recruit former Nazis, claimed that the American government was letting Nazis resettle in the United States, reported on neo-Nazi activities in Austria, and criticized the Perón regime in Argentina. Domestically, *Plain Talk* attacked people and groups that it considered fascistic, including Gerald L. K. Smith, George W. Armstrong, and the White Circle League of America. Still, it tended to regard domestic fascists as an insignificant threat due to their lack of unity and membership. Author de Toledano, however, did point out that the situation could change if the various groups ever united.[21]

Plain Talk ended with its May 1950 issue when the monthly folded for financial reasons. It could not overcome the fiscal and circulation problems that tend to afflict ideological magazines, despite an unsuccessful attempt by Herbert Hoover to save it. In his introduction to a 1976 anthology of *Plain Talk* articles, Levine wrote that he believed that the journal could have survived with more money, better management, and a different approach. To some extent, *Plain Talk's* outlook survived by way of the *Freeman*'s debut in the fall of 1950. The new magazine featured a revised format and was edited by John Chamberlain, Henry Hazlitt, and Suzanne La Follette, all of whom had written for *Plain Talk*. Other *Plain Talk* authors, including Levine, published in the *Freeman*, and the new journal assumed responsibility for its predecessor's subscriptions.[22]

Representing the anticommunist philosophy of cold war conservatives, *Plain Talk* provided early warnings about the Soviet Union and domestic subversion in a society that had just begun to recognize the postwar division of the Allies. Reflecting the transition of conservatism from an isolationist to an interventionist ideology, the journal folded, ironically, just weeks before the outbreak of the Korean War, the first major war between East and West.

Notes

1. Isaac Don Levine, ed., *Plain Talk: An Anthology from the Leading Anti-Communist Magazine of the 40s* (New Rochelle, New York, 1976), xii (hereinafter cited as *PTA*); Ross Y. Koen, *The China Lobby in American Politics* (1960; reprint ed., New York, 1974), pp. 50–52, 236–37.

2. Christopher T. Emmet, Jr., "Hungary in Agony," *Plain Talk* 1 (October 1946): 9–13 (hereinafter cited as *PT*); Louis Fischer, "On the Island of Berlin," *PT* 1 (January 1947): 3–9; Joseph Godson, "Exodus from Paradise," *PT* 1 (October 1946): 23–24; John F. Cronin, "A Pattern of Conquest," *PT* 1 (November 1946): 28–30; Correspondent Somewhere in the Balkans, "Religious Terror in Yugoslavia," *PT* 1 (December 1946): 9–10; T.L., "Journey to Magadan," *PT* 1 (January 1947): 32–39, (February 1947): 29–38, (March 1947): 38–45, (April 1947): 38–43. Examples of articles on Asia include Henry P. Van Dusen, "An American Policy for China," 11 *PT* 1 (November 1946): 15; Y. L. Wu, "Crisis in the Pacific: Another

Dunkirk in the Far East?" *PT* 4 (November 1949): 13–16; and Alfred Kohlberg, "Plan for the Pacific," *PT* 4 (April 1950): 10–12.

3. Joseph Zack, "A Russian Underground?" *PT* 1 (May 1947): 31–32; Vadim Makaroff, "A Way to Stop War," *PT* 1 (July 1947): 36–38; James H. R. Cromwell, "An American Liberty Legion," *PT* 2 (July 1948): 39–42; Isaac Don Levine, "So Runs the World: Our Fig–Leaf Foreign Policy," *PT* 2 (June 1948): 32–37.

4. Andrey A. Stotski [trans. Ann Su Cardwell], "I Dwelt with Death," *PT* 1 (May 1947): 37–45, (June 1947): 38–47, (July 1947): 39–47, (August 1947): 31–38; Plain Talk Document, "'Gulag'—Slavery, Inc.," *PT* 1 (May 1947): 23–26; Levine, ed., *PTA*, p. 235; Eugene Lyons, "The Mystery of Katyn," *PT* 4 (October 1949): 53–64. Examples of articles on communist rule include Ann Su Cardwell, "The Vivisection of Poland," *PT* 1 (March 1947): 25–29; Lily Doblhoff, "Notes on Hungary: Stalin's 'Good Neighbor' Policy," *PT* 4 (February 1950): 23–24; and Harry W. Flannery, "Inside the Russian Zone," *PT* 2 (March 1948): 47–48; see also Guy Hickok, "Life in Soviet America," *PT* 2 (April 1948): 11–15.

5. Herbert Hoover, "Herbert Hoover's Plan for Palestine," *PT* 2 (March 1948): 32–33; Isaac Don Levine, "Solution for Palestine," *PT* 2 (April 1948): 16; Walter Clay Lowdermilk, "The Untried Approach," *PT* 2 (April 1948): 17–21; Isaac Don Levine, "So Runs the World: Crisis in the U.N.," Part 2 (March 1948): 32–33.

6. Emmanuel S. Larsen, "The State Department Espionage Case," *PT* 1 (October 1946): 27–39 (quotation: 32). For the influence of the article on McCarthy, see Koen, *China Lobby*, pp. 65, 240n; U.S. Congress, Senate, Committee on Foreign Relations, State Department Employee Loyalty Investigation, Hearings before a Subcommittee of the Committee on Foreign Relations, United States Senate, 81st Cong., 2nd sess., 1950, part 1, pp. 130–42, part 2, pp. 1549–55 (hereinafter cited as *SDELI:H*); U.S. Congress, Senate, Committee on Foreign Relations, State Department Employee Loyalty Investigation, S. Rept. 2108, 81st Cong., 2nd sess., 1950, pp. 74–94, 145–48, 147–49n, 162–63 (hereinafter cited as *SDELI:R*); and Thomas C. Reeves, *The Life and Times of Joe McCarthy: A Biography* (Briarcliff Manor, New York, 1982), pp. 257, 290–95, 299–302, 304–5.

7. Koen, *China Lobby*, pp. 64–65, 240n; *SDELI:H*, part 1, pp. 1116–23, 1125–29. "They Called Me a Spy," may be found in part 2, pp. 1739–53.

8. Quotes in *SDELI:R*, pp. 147, 93, 162, 148. On Service, see pp. 74–94. For Kohlberg's ties with China, see pp. 93, 146, 162; see also pp. 145–48, 147–49n, 162–63.

9. U. S. Congress, Senate, *Congressional Record*, 81st Cong., 2nd sess., 31 August 1950, 96:13925–27 (quotation: 13925).

10. Ibid., 96:13926–27. A slightly different version of Levine's defense can be found in Isaac Don Levine, "Plain Talk and Amerasia," *Freeman* 1 (2 October 1950): 20–22.

11. Whittaker Chambers, *Witness* (New York, 1952), p. 457; "Temporary Obits," *Newsweek* (26 June 1950): 69; Emmanuel S. Larsen, "China's 'Liberal' Front," *PT* 2 (January 1948): 27–31.

12. *SDELI:R*, pp. 74–94, 145–48, 147–49n, 162–63; *SDELI:H*, part 1, pp. 130–42, part 2, pp. 1549–55; Koen, *China Lobby*, pp. 64–65, 240n; Isaac Don Levine, *Eyewitness to History: Memoirs and Reflections of a Foreign Correspondent for Half a Century* (New York, 1973), pp. 176–78; Reeves, *McCarthy*, pp. 257, 290–305.

13. For Levine's role in the Hiss case, see Chambers, *Witness*, pp. 457, 459–70; Levine, *Eyewitness*, pp. 179–212; Isaac Don Levine, "Sequel to Chambers' Story," *PT* 3 (January 1949):1–4; and Allen Weinstein, *Perjury: The Hiss–Chambers Case* (New York, 1978), pp. 14–15, 62, 64–65, 274–75, 320–21, 325, 327–31, 359, 575–76, 581–82. Articles on Soviet espionage include A Federal Employee, "What's Wrong with the Loyalty Program?" *PT* 2 (September 1948): 1–5; Levine, "Sequel to Chambers' Story," pp. 1–4; Thomas F. Murphy, "Summation to the Jury: People of the United States vs. Alger Hiss," *PT* 3 (August 1949):

1–13; and Isaac Don Levine, "The Inside Story of Our Soviet Underworld," *PT* 2 (September 1948): 9–12, *PT* 3 (October 1948): 18–22, (November 1948): 21–25, (December 1948): 19–22.

14. John Leslie, "Stalin's Hand in Our Ballot Box," *PT* 1 (October 1946): 5–8. Attacks on other unions include John Leslie, "Merrill's Marauders in Wall St.," *PT* 1 (December 1946): 11–13; and Franklin J. Anderson, "Union Wreckers at the Switch," *PT* 1 (April 1947): 19–22. On anticommunists in the labor movement, see, for example, Joseph M. Brown, "1947 Balance Sheet: Labor Out of the Red," *PT* 2 (February 1948): 10–12; and O. J. Dekom, "The Washington Reporter: On the Labor Front," *PT* 2 (March 1948): 35–36.

15. William Markham, "The Best Years of Our Lives," *PT* 1 (April 1947): 35–37; Eugene Lyons, "Hollywood's Foreign Legion," *PT* 1 (May 1947): 9–11. Assaults on the media include Patrick J. Hurley, "The Satevepost's Mr. Snow," *PT* 1 (March 1947): 23–24; Peter Minot, "The Wayward New Yorker," *PT* 4 (October 1949): 5–11; and John Chamberlain, "School for Treason," *PT* 4 (April 1949): 13–16. Academia articles include Andrew Lund, "Our Student Comes of Age," *PT* 2 (October 1947): 10–12; Archie Black, "Infection in the Colleges," *PT* 3 (December 1948): 23–25; and see also Charlet, "Professor Pinko" [cartoon], *PT* 3 (May 1949): 31.

16. For example, see Archie Black, "Millionaire Communist: A Case Study of Frederick Vanderbilt Field," *PT* 3 (May 1949): 25–30.

17. Ralph de Toledano, "Liberals' Awakening," *PT* 1 (February 1947): 19–21; Oliver Carlson, "Hollywood's Red Fadeout?" *PT* 3 (August 1949): 17–23; Petronius Minor, "Kilkenny Alley: Love Among the Marxists," *PT* 3 (February 1949): 35–36.

18. Christopher Emmet, "Why the Republican Landslide," *PT* 1 (December 1946): 5–8.

19. Election articles include Victor Lasky, "Who Runs Wallace?" *PT* 2 (June 1948): 1–13; Benjamin Stolberg, "How Big Is Taft?" *PT* 2 (April 1948): 23–31; Harold E. Stassen, "Where I Stand," *PT* 2 (May 1948): 30–31; Isaac Don Levine, "So Runs the World: Why Dewey," *PT* 3 (November 1948): 32–33; and Isaac Don Levine, "So Runs the World: The Big Surprise," *PT* 3 (December 1948): 32–33.

20. For example, see John T. Flynn, "What You Can Do to Get Prices Down," *PT* 3 (December 1948): 7–9; George W. Grupp, "What Price Strikes?" *PT* 4 (December 1949): 16–18; Stanley High, "We're for Government Economy, But...," *PT* 4 (December 1949): 1–5; Lewis H. Haney, "The Gold Standard," *PT* 4 (March 1950): 26–30; Henry Hazlitt, "Dollars vs. Communism: Flaws in the Marshall Plan," *PT* 2 (October 1947): 17–22; Ludwig von Mises, "Stones into Bread: The Keynesian Miracle," *PT* 2 (March 1948): 21–27; Edna Lonigan, "Taxes and Tyranny," *PT* 2 (February 1948): 37–41; Frank Chodorov, "Joseph, Secretary of Agriculture," *PT* 3 (September 1949): 21–25; and Frank Chodorov, "We Lose It to Ourselves," *PT* 4 (April 1950): 36–40.

21. Articles on the far Right include Alexander Janta, "The German Ego in Defeat," *PT* 1 (April 1947): 10–13; Plain Talk Document, "Little Nazi, What Now?" *PT* 1 (June 1947): 24–25; Guenther Reinhardt, "Are We Letting Nazis In?" *PT* 3 (February 1949): 5–10; Guenther Reinhardt, "Nazis Make a Comeback," *PT* 4 (November 1949): 12; E. von Hofmannsthal, "Perón's New Road to Fascism," *PT* 1 (April 1947): 14–18; Pete Wilbur, "Gerald Smith's Youth Front," *PT* 1 (November 1946): 21–23; Victor Lasky, "Lunacy or Fascism?" *PT* 2 (July 1948): 23–24; Marion Odmark, "Race Racket in Chicago," *PT* 4 (April 1950): 29–30; and Ralph de Toledano, "Is Native Fascism a Menace?" *PT* 2 (January 1948): 12–14.

22. Levine, ed., *PTA*, p. xiii; "Temporary Obits," p. 69; *Freeman* 1 (2 October 1950): 2, 32.

Information Sources

BIBLIOGRAPHY:
Levine, Isaac Don, ed. *Plain Talk: An Anthology from the Leading Anti–Communist Magazine of the 40s*. New Rochelle, New York, 1976.
INDEXES: Annual indexes for volumes 1–3; *PAIS*, 1947–1950.
REPRINT EDITIONS: None.
LOCATION SOURCES: Widely available.

Publication History

TITLE AND TITLE CHANGES: *Plain Talk*.
VOLUME AND ISSUE DATA: Volumes 1–4, October 1946–May 1950.
FREQUENCY OF PUBLICATION: Monthly.
PUBLISHER: Plain Talk, New York.
EDITOR: Isaac Don Levine.
CIRCULATION: In 1950, 9,700.

Peter L. de Rosa

Christian Crusade
1948–1969

One of the most important organs of the religious anticommunist movement was *Christian Crusade*. It began in October 1948 as a small newsletter entitled *Christian Echoes*, published in Sapulpa, Oklahoma, by a young pastor, Billy James Hargis. For the first few years it came out sporadically and had a minuscule circulation. In 1955 it changed its name to *Christian Crusade* and was subtitled the *National Christian Americanism Monthly,* but the organization continued to carry as its legal name Christian Echoes National Ministry, Inc. It was a slick-paper magazine that served as the group's principal organ until 1969, when it was merged with a newsletter and renamed the *Christian Crusade Weekly*. As hard times set in, it went to a biweekly and then a monthly publication schedule, appearing under the title *Christian Crusade Newspaper*.

Born in 1925 in Texarkana, Texas, Hargis came from a humble background and as a youth was quite devout. Upon graduation from high school, he entered Ozark Bible College, Bentonville, Arkansas, where he spent a year and a half obtaining the only formal theological education he would have. He was ordained to the ministry of the Christian Church–Disciples of Christ at the age of seventeen, served as a part-time pastor of a few small congregations in the Ozark region of Missouri and Oklahoma, and then dropped out of school at age twenty-one to take over a larger church in Sapulpa. He was later to obtain a B.A. and Th.B. from Burton College and Seminary, a degree mill in Colorado, and honorary doctorates (by mail) from two other questionable institutions, and from Bob Jones University. Like the Reverend Jerry Falwell, Hargis had listened to Charles E. Fuller's Old-Fashioned Revival Hour, seen the possibilities available in radio ministry, and started his own weekly broadcast, the *Christian Echoes Hour*, in 1950.[1]

In August 1948 an evangelist friend sold him on leading a "truth crusade" about communism, and soon he saw himself "called of God to launch a mass movement of resistance to the trend in American life to world government, apostate religion, and appeasement with satanic 'isms' such as communism."[2] He resigned his pastorate in 1950, devoted full time to radio work and itinerant evangelism, and briefly operated a Christian resort hotel in Missouri. Late in 1952 Hargis got his first break when Carl T. McIntire placed him in charge of the International Council of Christian Churches' "Bible balloons" project. This quixotic venture to transport Bibles and religious literature into Soviet bloc countries lasted approximately five years and brought him notoriety. He openly boasted that the Soviet authorities blamed his program for sparking the revolt in Hungary.[3] At this time he gained the endorsement of Senator Joseph McCarthy and made an Asian tour where he had widely publicized meetings with Chiang Kai-shek and Syngman Rhee.[4] An endeavor to send Bible balloons into China proved abortive, and that project was quietly shelved in 1959.

As the magazine gained subscribers, Hargis moved his operation from Sapulpa to Tulsa, Oklahoma. In 1956 he turned over the editorship to a skilled public relations expert, L. E. ("Pete") White, who had formerly served Oral Roberts, while naming himself publisher. Articles on prayer and prophecy were interspersed among denunciations of communism and the ecumenical movement, and in July 1957 Julian E. Williams began contributing regular "intelligence reports" about communist influence in American churches. J. B. Matthews, the freelance congressional researcher who had amassed a large body of data on alleged communist activity in the United States, authored his first column in November 1957. Hargis also promoted Holy Land tours and advertised his booklets and radio programs. In September 1958 the "Foreign Intelligence Digest" by Major General Charles A. Willoughby, who had served as General Douglas MacArthur's intelligence chief, became a regular feature of *Christian Crusade*. Several prominent fundamentalists also contributed columns and articles.

Racial disturbances were regularly reported as communist inspired. The NAACP had been taken over by "Reds," and, said *Christian Crusade*, was using Negroes as pawns. Communist agitators, who had been stoking the fires of racial strife for years, forced the government to use military force to crush those who opposed race mixing.[5] Hargis exploited feelings over this to expand his radio broadcasts and enter the television field, begin a syndicated newspaper column, and attract people to the first "national summit conference" in Tulsa, the headquarters of his Christian Crusade organization.

In 1960 the celebrated air force manual controversy transformed Hargis into a national figure. The *Washington Post* on February 17 broke the story that an air force reserve training manual contained sweeping charges about communist infiltration of religion. Its author, Homer H. Hyde of San Antonio, Texas, had heard Hargis speak and asked him for the documentation, which was included in the publication. After the National Council of Churches (NCC) and presidential hopeful John F. Kennedy denounced the work, the air force withdrew it.[6] Nevertheless, Hargis heartily endorsed the manual, declaring "the NCC has done more to nurture communism than any single organization in the United States....I thank God that at last some responsible government agency has had the fortitude to question the dubious activities of the NCC." He called on the chairman of the House Un-American Activities Committee (HUAC) to conduct a thorough investigation of communist infiltration into American Protestant churches and the NCC, and boasted that the controversy was a "God-send." As his in-house biographer later put it, this made Hargis "the center of a raging controversy between enlightened Christians on one side and pro-Reds, useful idiots, and the totally unenlightened on the other."[7]

The most important result of the affair was the emergence of Hargis's group as the leading force on the Christian Right. By his own admission, only six years earlier the organization had almost gone under: without the help of a financial angel, Walter Foster, Hargis could not have kept it going.[8] Now he was able to draw 3,000 people to Tulsa for the summit conference, his radio program listings soared, and evangelical firms like Word Records and De Moss Associates Insurance began placing ads in the magazine. He also inaugurated an "intelligence" newsletter, the *Weekly Crusader,* and in 1960 published his first book, *Communist America— Must It Be?* In four years (1957–1961) *Christian Crusade*'s circulation rose from 20,000 to nearly 100,000, and it outgrew its Tulsa facilities.[9]

In 1961 Hargis enhanced the intelligence capabilities of his operation by acquiring the files on clergymen and educators identified with communist front organizations that Allen Zoll, notorious anti-Semite and head of American Patriots, had collected. The summer conventions and winter "Anti-Communist Leadership Schools" were reported in detail in the magazine, and the speakers from year to year constituted a who's who of the American Right. Among these were Governor Orval Faubus of Arkansas in 1960, Dean Clarence Manion (a noted Catholic rightist), Willis Carto (Liberty Lobby), Robert Welch (John Birch Society), and Harry T. Everingham (We, the People), all in 1961; General Edwin A. Walker, Congressman Martin Dies (D, Texas), Congressman John H. Rousselot (R, California), columnist Westbrook Pegler, undercover communist for the FBI Matt Cvetic, Birchite Revilo P. Oliver, air ace Eddie Rickenbacker, Methodist anticommunist Myers Lowman, Bob Jones, Sr., Governor J. Bracken Lee of Utah, National Association of Evangelicals luminaries Frederick C. Fowler and Dave Breese, and W. O. H. Garman (American Council of Christian Churches) in 1962; and Congressman John Ashbrook (R, Ohio), former secretary of agriculture Ezra Taft Benson, Carl McIntire, General A. C. Wedemeyer, and anticommunist writers W. Cleon Skousen, Dan Smoot, and E. Merrill Root in 1963.

At the annual conferences Hargis gave a "state of the union address" enumerating communist achievements of the past year and urging more forceful action by his followers. In 1962, for example, he unleashed a stinging attack on the Supreme Court's school prayer decision, called for reaffirming that the United States is a Christian nation, supported the embattled HUAC and underscored the need to become involved in electing conservative, anticommunist candidates regardless of their party affiliation.[10] He reinforced his backing for HUAC by showing the controversial film *Operation Abolition* (1960) at his rallies and insisted that the NCC's opposition to it proved how it had taken the side of "the communist conspirators within our country."[11] For the 1962 anticommunist leadership school,

Hargis secured a film about the brainwashing of American prisoners during the Korean War, *The Ultimate Weapon*, which was narrated by Ronald Reagan, "one of Hollywood's foremost conservative leaders." The school tackled the question, "What can my community do to stem the growth of socialism and communism?" and Hargis maintained he was answering FBI chief J. Edgar Hoover's challenge "to properly indoctrinate the anticommunist forces" and arm "them with facts and statistics that cannot be successfully and honestly refuted."[12]

In 1962 Hargis purchased a hotel in Manitou Springs, Colorado, which he renamed the Summit. It was intended to serve as a summer conference center and "anticommunist youth university" to train high school and college students. The following year he recruited David A. Noebel as a "national youth coordinator" to direct the enterprise and Christian Crusade's youth organization, the Torchbearers. Born in 1937 and a graduate of Milwaukee Bible College and Hope College (Michigan), the fervently conservative and anticommunist Noebel was pastor of a fundamentalist church in Madison, Wisconsin, a dropout from a Ph.D. program at the University of Wisconsin, and in 1960 an unsuccessful candidate for the U.S. Congress. Noebel's acerbic pen and keen wit soon made him Hargis's most important adviser.[13]

Still, Hargis's fortunes wavered because of "satanic smears" that emanated from "various communist and misguided sources" (meaning that a number of journalistic exposés of his enterprises had cut into income and forced retrenchment). In 1962 he was on 200 radio stations in forty-six states and a dozen television outlets, but a year later he had given up 75 percent of these and was running a $300,000 deficit. Although subscriptions to *Christian Crusade* fell from nearly 100,00 to 72,000, Hargis continued to boast that it was "the world's largest anticommunist publication." A new editor was employed, Texas newspaperman Sigman Byrd, but he lasted only a couple of months, and Pete White resumed the position until Gerald S. Pope took over in 1966. He further consumed scarce resources by alerting people to the enemy within and without in a dramatic five-week, coast-to-coast "midnight ride" with General Walker in a luxurious rented bus.[14]

Christian Crusade's fortunes revived as a result of the Kennedy assassination, attributed by Hargis to a communist conspiracy, and Senator Barry Goldwater's (R, Arizona) bid for the presidency. The magazine openly embraced the Republican ticket, saying that if Goldwater won, "we will have the privilege and duty" of assisting him in improving the country. Hargis editorialized that his victory "will be the greatest miracle of the 20th Century. Personally I am praying to God for that miracle."[15] Other issues were also exploited to generate interest. The need for a prayer amendment and a petition that Hargis circulated around the country was the topic of an article in May 1964. In August appeared the first piece attacking pornography and obscenity, a theme that soon pervaded *Christian Crusade* literature. In November Noebel lashed out at the immorality of perverted and promiscuous sex. Although Hargis was disappointed by the Goldwater defeat, he saw a silver lining in it since 25 million Americans "did vote for conservatism." He urged readers to redouble their efforts.[16]

The organization now buzzed with activity. Hargis and other authors generated books and pamphlets at a rapid rate; Cuban émigrés Fernando Penabaz and Pedro Diaz Lanz were brought on staff to develop a Latin American ministry; a sparkling new headquarters building called the "cathedral" (actually church) of the Christian Crusade was constructed; anticommunist tours to the Holy Land, South Africa, and elsewhere were eagerly promoted; a school was founded with Hargis as president (American Christian College, which opened its doors in 1970); and the David Livingstone Foundation, a missionary society, was created to channel funds to charitable and evangelistic enterprises overseas.

However, *Christian Crusade* ran afoul of the Internal Revenue Service. The group was notified on 13 November 1964, that its tax-exempt status was in jeopardy because it had intervened in political campaigns on behalf of candidates for public office and a substantial portion of its activities were aimed at influencing legislation. The specific charge was that it both "directly and indirectly" supported candidates for public office and encouraged its audience to influence their congressmen on "legislation affecting agriculture, education, hospitalization, medical care for the aged, mental health, urban renewal, the federal income tax, U.S. participation in the United Nations, foreign aid, the Connally Amendment, McCarran Immigration Act, Becker Amendment to the Constitution, the Supreme Court, and the operation of government corporations." Hargis replied that the IRS action was politically motivated, that he was a victim of the liberal establishment, and that he would fight the matter in the courts.[17]

Critics of the IRS action, some of whom were liberal churchmen, pointed out that serious constitutional issues involving the separation of church and state were being ignored, and Hargis called attention to this. At the same time the magazine continued to carry articles that, among other things, denounced the communists for being "the real culprits behind the Negro Rebellion in Los Angeles," demanded a policy of victory in Vietnam, condemned the fairness doctrine as a liberal device to deny conservatives access to the airways, and exposed the evils of rock music and sex education.[18]

Hargis secured endorsements from several congressmen and traveled to Washington on 20 May 1966, to defend his association before an IRS hearing, but to no avail. He was notified on September 22 that year that the tax exemption had been revoked, though the ruling did not apply to his Christian Crusade church, which was incorporated differently. Subsequent efforts to overturn the decision in the courts failed. Hargis declared this reflected the growing erosion of religious freedom and an increasing persecution of Christians that was to be expected as the program of the Antichrist developed. He insisted it would not affect his work since it "takes the muzzle off Christian Crusade" and "we can fight harder than ever." The group would not "have been singled out for persecution by the enemy if we had not been considered so effective."[19]

The discussions of various public issues became increasingly sharp in tone after this time. Gordon V. Drake joined the staff in 1969 and produced a host of articles and booklets denouncing sex education, sensitivity training, teacher organizations, and other allegedly ominous happenings in the public schools. His most colorful pamphlet was *Is the Schoolhouse the Proper Place to Teach Raw Sex?* (1968) Still, the circulation of *Christian Crusade* stagnated and hovered within the 75,000–90,000 range throughout the remainder of the decade. Finally it was decided to eliminate the monthly entirely and merge it into the *Weekly Crusader*. The last issue appeared in August–September 1969.[20]

The *Weekly Crusader* was an eight-page-newsletter edited by Julian Williams that had begun in November 1960 and presented mainly current news and commentary on the anticommunist front. The new *Christian Crusade Weekly* was edited by Gerald Pope, with Williams and Noebel as assistants. It was set up in a newsprint format and the first issue, 19 October 1969, had a press run of merely 65,000. The circulation climbed to 190,000 in 1973–1974, where it peaked. Pope left in March 1975 and for a few months Dr. William L. Lane edited the weekly. In January 1976 the ex-priest and prominent Roman Catholic rightist Dan Lyons took the helm, but he was unable to turn things around. He was succeeded in 1979 by Bill Sampson.

In fact, Christian Crusade was almost on the rocks. Hargis resigned as president of American Christian College in October 1974 and retreated to his farm in the Ozarks near Neosho, Missouri, to recover from an alleged light stroke and heart condition. The following month he gave up his position in Christian Crusade, the Tulsa church, and the missionary foundation. He returned to Tulsa a year later and resumed his duties, but cut all remaining ties with the college, which Noebel now headed. It took possession of the crusade's properties, and Hargis relocated his operations in a six-story building downtown.[21] Articles in *Time* and *Christianity Today*, however, revealed what really had happened in 1974. It turned out that Hargis had had sexual relations with both male and female students in the college and Noebel blew the whistle on him. His "illness" was an excuse to drop out of sight for awhile.[22]

Still, Hargis adamantly refused to admit any guilt and referred to the piece in *Time* as Satan's attempt to destroy Christian Crusade and "the most vicious article ever written about me in my entire ministry." It was "a pile of pure trash on one page." He said he would not go on the defensive and answer these charges endlessly but rather would turn his accusers over to God, pray for them, and dedicate himself "to the cause that has ever been on my heart." He claimed that friends from all over the country wired, wrote, and called urging him to "hold fast" against the attacks "by the left-wing news media."[23] He refused to have anything more to do with American Christian College, and the school folded shortly afterward. The financial condition of the magazine so deteriorated that in 1980 it appeared only bimonthly, but in 1982 it came out monthly in its new incarnation, *Billy James Hargis' Christian Crusade Newspaper*. Like the legendary phoenix, the resilient Hargis had arisen from the ashes of scandal and ruin to raise the banner of Christian anticommunism once again, but now his speaking tours attracted few listeners, the Patriotic and Bible Conferences on his Missouri farm went unnoticed, and his newspaper's circulation languished. Hargis's name eventually was dropped from the title, and in the mid-1990s it claimed a circulation of 55,000,[24] an undoubtedly inflated figure. His was a voice out of the past, and with the end of the cold war, he grasped at new issues, such as abortion, to keep his name before the public, but to little avail.

Notes

1. The information on Hargis's life and career is taken from the October 1958 issue of *Christian Crusade* (hereinafter cited as *CC*), the official biography by Fernando Penabaz, *"Crusading Preacher from the West": The Story of Billy James Hargis* (Tulsa, Oklahoma, 1965), and the 1986 Southern Baptist Theological Seminary doctoral dissertation by Jim Ernest Hunter, Jr., "A Gathering of Sects: Revivalistic Pluralism in Tulsa, Oklahoma, 1945–1985." The best analysis of his beliefs and the work of his organization is John H. Redekop, *The American Far Right: A Case Study of Billy James Hargis and Christian Crusade* (Grand Rapids, Michigan, 1968).

2. *CC* 10 (October 1958): 17.

3. *CC* 8 (December 1956): 1.

4. *CC* 9 (July 1957): 3, 7.

5. *CC* 10 (December 1958): 9; *CC* 11 (January 1959): 4–5.

6. Erling Jorstad, *The Politics of Doomsday: Fundamentalists of the Far Right* (Nashville, Tennessee, 1970), pp. 72, 83–84.

7. *CC* 12 (March 1960): 9–10; *CC* 12 (April 1960): 8–9; Penabaz, *"Crusading Preacher,"* p. 203.

8. *CC* 12 (November 1960): 10 (obituary of Foster).

9. *CC* 13 (February 1961): 15.

10. *CC* 14 (September 1962): 18.

11. *CC* 13 (September 1961): 1.

12. *CC* 13 (December 1961): 11.

13. *CC* 14 (June 1962): 11; *CC* 15 (April 1963): 6; *CC* 15 (August 1963): 8; *CC* 16 (April 1964): 2. By the end of 1963 twenty-three Torchbearer chapters had been formed, one chaired by Colonel V. Doner, who later would be a leading light in Christian Voice, an important organization of the New Christian Right in the 1980s. *CC* 15 (November 1963): 10.

14. *CC* 14 (December 1982): 11; *CC* 15 (February 1963): 1; *CC* 15 (September 1963): 5; Anti-Defamation League of B'nai B'rith, *The Radical Right and Religion* (New York, 1965), p. 10.

15. *CC* 16 (November 1964): 4, 11.

16. *CC* 16 (December 1964): 5, 27, 30–31.

17. *CC* 16 (December 1964): 17–19.

18. *CC* 17 (October 1965): 12–15; *CC* 18 (March 1966): 20–22; *CC* 17 (March 1965): 32; *CC* 18 (April 1966): 11–14; David Noebel, *Rhythm, Riots, and Revolution* (Tulsa, Oklahoma, 1966), advertised and excerpted in various issues of CC.

19. *CC* 18 (November 1966): 19–20; *CC* 18 (December 1966): 13.

20. The circulation figures are taken from the annual reports published in the magazine and data submitted to the *Standard Periodicals Directory* and *Ulrich's International Periodicals Directory*.

21. *Christian Crusade Weekly* (15 October 1975): 11; (14 December 1975): 1–2.

22. "The Sins of Billy James," *Time* (16 February 1972): 52; Edward E. Plowman, "The Rise and Fall of Billy James," *Christianity Today* 20 (27 February 1976): 42–43.

23. *Christian Crusade Weekly* (29 February 1976): 1–2; (7 March 1976): 3.

24. *Encyclopedia of Associations* (Detroit, Michigan, 1996), p. 2427.

Information Sources

BIBLIOGRAPHY:

Clabaugh, Gary K. *Thunder on the Right: The Protestant Fundamentalists*. Chicago, 1974.

Forster, Arnold, and Benjamin R. Epstein. *Danger on the Right*. New York, 1964.

Hargis, Billy James. *My Great Mistake*. Green Forest, Arkansas, 1985.

Hunter, Jim Ernest, Jr. "A Gathering of Sects: Revivalistic Pluralism in Tulsa, Oklahoma, 1945–1985." Ph.D. dissertation, Southern Baptist Theological Seminary, 1986.

Jorstad, Erling. *The Politics of Doomsday: Fundamentalists of the Far Right*. Nashville, Tennessee, 1970.

Kolkey, Jonathan M. *The New Right, 1960–1968*. Washington, D.C., 1983.

Pierard, Richard V. *The Unequal Yoke: Evangelical Christianity and Political Conservatism*. Philadelphia, 1970.

Redekop, John H. *The American Far Right: A Case Study of Billy James Hargis and Christian Crusade*. Grand Rapids, Michigan, 1968.

Vinz, Warren. "The Politics of Protestant Fundamentalism in the 1950s and 1960s." *Journal of Church and State* 14 (Spring 1972): 235–60.

INDEXES: None.

REPRINT EDITIONS: Microform: Right Wing Collection, University of Iowa (MCA), partial run, 1956–1969 (reels 21–22): UMI.

LOCATION SOURCES: Complete run: Billy James Hargis Ministries, P.O. Box 977, Tulsa, Oklahoma, 74102.

Publication History

TITLE AND TITLE CHANGES: *Christian Echoes*, 1948–1955; *Christian Crusade*, 1955–1969.

VOLUME AND ISSUE DATA: Volumes 1–21, 1948–1969.

FREQUENCY OF PUBLICATION: Monthly; irregularly, 1951–1955.

PUBLISHER: Christian Echoes National Ministry (Christian Crusade).

EDITORS: Billy James Hargis, 1948–1956; L. E. ("Pete") White, 1956–1966; Gerald S. Pope, 1966–1969.

CIRCULATION: 70,000–90,000.

Richard V. Pierard

American Legion Firing Line
1952–

In Minneapolis in 1919, the American Legion's founding convention ratified a constitution whose preamble stated that one of the Legion's purposes was "to foster and perpetuate a one hundred per cent Americanism." To carry out this mission, the convention voted to establish the National Americanism Commission (NAC) to fight "all anti-American tendencies, activities and propaganda." By 1924, this group had begun operations. Today the NAC sponsors such well-known Legion programs as Boys State and Nation, flag education, the American Legion School Medal Award, the National High School Oratorical Contest, and American Legion Baseball. It also has a Counter-Subversive Activities Committee that publishes the *American Legion Firing Line*, which provides information on communist, fascist, and other extremist groups to its subscribers.[1]

Firing Line has its roots in the early Legion commitment to political education and action. Even prior to the founding convention, publications such as the *American Legion Weekly* attacked domestic leftists, radical unions, and open immigration, which the legion saw as threats to the United States. As the NAC developed programs to foster "Americanism," which it usually defined as patriotism, nationalism, and good citizenship, it also assumed a major role in the Legion's self-imposed task of fighting communism and eventually, Nazism and fascism.[2] With the Axis defeat and the advent of the cold war, communism emerged as the single most important enemy of "Americanism." The NAC responded to this development by publishing a newsletter containing news about foreign communism and its domestic supporters. Early versions of this newsletter were known as the *Monthly Americanism Report on the Daily Worker and the People's World* (published January–July 1946), *Monthly Analysis: Subversive Groups and Their Activities* (August–October 1946), *Monthly Summary of Trends and Developments* (April–August 1947), *Summary of Trends and Developments* (September 1947–December 1948), and *Summary of Trends and Developments Exposing the Communist*

Conspiracy (January 1949–December 1951). The newsletter attained its final form in *Firing Line*, which the Legion regards not as a new periodical but rather as a new title in an old series. Subtitled *Facts for Fighting Communism*, this biweekly made its debut with the 15 January 1952, issue.[3]

The history of *Firing Line* divides into five periods, each reflecting different concerns of the NAC. The newsletter first appeared in an era when domestic subversion was a major political issue. Senator Joseph R. McCarthy (R, Wisconsin) had made his Wheeling, West Virginia, speech only two years before, and numerous espionage cases and allegations of treason dominated the headlines. While the Legion often dealt with the problem of domestic communism in its more general interest *American Legion Weekly*, it devoted *Firing Line* almost exclusively to the issue. Intending the newsletter as an educational device "to supply Legionnaires with solid facts on all aspects of the complex and highly deceptive problem of domestic subversion" that they might share with associates, the NAC, in order to encourage distribution, did not even copyright it at first. It discontinued this policy in 1955 after the anti-Semitic journal the *Cross and the Flag* reproduced material from another NAC publication and the Legion found itself legally without remedy. The NAC did not seek to distribute *Firing Line* to the general public, but hoped that Legionnaires would pass its information along to others.[4] The biweekly featured short articles with occasional extensive supplements on allegedly subversive activities of American communists, "fellow travelers," and leftist sympathizers. It relied heavily on congressional investigations for much of its material. The title was changed to *American Legion Firing Line* in 1955.

The putative educational purpose of *Firing Line* was not, however, distinguishable from a political one, for the NAC used its newsletter to encourage anticommunist activity as well. The entertainment industry centered in Hollywood was an early target of this effort. After the Legion's leadership had met with studio executives in 1952 and promised to provide them with information on reputed communist sympathizers, *Firing Line* published much material on suspected communists and called for the boycotting of motion pictures that employed communists or their unrepentant supporters. It registered pleasure when a Legion post in Hollywood answered the call, and it commended its members for boycotting all films with "which any undesirables, tongue-tied witnesses, and other Hollywood subversives have anything whatever to do." Beyond that, *Firing Line* became influential in the practice of blacklisting, supplying lists of entertainers who were alleged to have been affiliated with communist fronts and causes, and publishing thorough documentation on leftists' backgrounds. It also offered information as to how former communists could get off the blacklist, and the Legion, despite frequent denials, participated in the "clearing" of suspected and repentant communists by circulating appropriate material to Legion posts. *Firing Line* occasionally published information on cleared suspects.[5]

Its interest in internal security led the NAC to occupy pages of *Firing Line* with such informational material as notices of Supreme Court rulings on national security issues and reprints of resolutions on these topics adopted by the national convention of the American Legion. The commission also used the newsletter to offer copies of the attorney general's list of subversive organizations to its readers. *Firing Line*'s emphasis on security matters is perhaps best demonstrated by the employment of FBI veteran Lee Pennington as the NAC's director of its Counter-Subversive Division in 1953. Until he left in 1959, he played a major role in setting the newsletter's editorial content. Again, educational and political ends blended when *Firing Line* opposed efforts to weaken the McCarran-Walter Act, which allowed the government to deport and refuse entry to suspected communists, and supported McCarthy's crusades against alleged subversives.[6]

Firing Line attempted to guide its subscribers away from the extreme Right. Recommending such reliable publications as *U.S. News and World Report* and the *Freeman* to its readers, the newsletter attacked such anti-Semites as Gerald L. K. Smith and assailed the spurious *Protocols of the Learned Elders of Zion* with the warning that "communism will never be defeated by inciting religious or race hatred." It did not criticize the Right nearly so much as it did the Left, and exposing leftist and communist groups has remained a primary purpose of *Firing Line* through the years, though the approach and emphasis have changed according to the prevailing political situation.[7]

The fad of identifying domestic communists and their allies began passing out of fashion during the late 1950s, while the rise of Fidel Castro and the conversion of Cuba into a Soviet satellite raised different fears in the United States. These developments as well as the numerous foreign policy crises of the Kennedy years formed the background for the second period of *Firing Line*'s history, when its editorial policy became more oriented toward international affairs than before. Its articles became longer and more analytical, often with an entire number being devoted to a single topic. In January 1961, *Firing Line* shifted to a monthly format. The following year brought shorter articles but a more professional appearance, eight-page issues, and an editorial column, "Commanding Thoughts." (This format continued until 1966, when the newsletter returned to four-page issues that normally included a four-page insert consisting of reprinted documents relating to communist, fascist, Nazi, and racist activities. Since 1965, *Firing Line* combines two issues, thus appearing eleven times a year.)

The new editorial policy gave the newsletter a broader focus, making it more of a general anticommunist publication than an internal security primer. Cuba became virtually a regular feature, with *Firing Line* examining Lee Harvey Oswald's connection with the Fair Play for Cuba Committee. The newsletter supported anticommunist interpretations of the Bang-Jensen case (concerning the suspicious suicide of an anticommunist UN employee), the Berlin crisis, and the "captive nations" issue, while it opposed cultural exchanges with the Soviet Union, and printed estimates of membership in foreign communist parties.[8]

Firing Line retained some of the characteristics of its earlier days. It continued to criticize liberals and leftists and denounced Dalton Trumbo's assignment to write the screenplay for *Exodus*, but its major domestic focus was on the Communist party itself. The monthly watched the party's attempts to legitimate itself through elections and reacted strongly when the communist Archie Brown polled over 33,000 votes in his race for the San Francisco Board of Supervisors. It supported the government's legal battles with the Communist party and issued a special edition when the Supreme Court upheld security laws that required the party to register as a subversive organization and that outlawed membership in subversive organizations. *Firing Line* also continued its crusade against the far Right, attacking the National Renaissance and American Nazi parties, and dismissing the Fighting American Nationalists as "Totalitarian Trash." In all, regarding extremist groups, the newsletter followed its instructions from the 1961 American Legion National Convention to "expose and report upon communistic, Socialistic, Radical, Un-American, One-World Government, and related activities and publications, and upon individuals, without fear or favor and let the chips fall where they may." However, the Kennedy era interest in international affairs competed with *Firing Line*'s traditional emphasis on domestic communism and effectively changed the newsletter's nature. The new perspective prepared *Firing Line* well for the stormy Vietnam years, the third period in its history.[9]

Fueled by the unpopularity of the Vietnam War, the mid and late 1960s brought a bewildering variety of leftist groups to political prominence. It was simple for the NAC to translate its long-standing anticommunist philosophy into support for the war and hostility for those opposed to it. As the Legion's major instrument for political education, *Firing Line* played an important role: "Today, our country is engaged in both a 'hot' and a 'cold' war with these evil and sinister forces. Our membership and the public must be informed of the attempts to subvert the citizens—and particularly the youth of our nation." The newsletter provided subscribers with attacks on the newer groups in the same manner that it had exposed the communists and Old Left of the 1950s. While Communist party news still appeared in *Firing Line*, newer organizations and personalities dominated its pages. The monthly monitored closely leftist groups' potential for violence, denouncing the Black Panthers coloring book as "racist and inflammatory," quoting Students for a Democratic Society leaders as wanting to build a guerrilla force in the United States, and tracing the violent history of the Weathermen. The newsletter reported the antiwar efforts of the Student Mobilization Committee and the Peace and Freedom party, and regretted that the government could not prevent the Venceremos Brigade from traveling to Cuba to harvest sugar cane. *Firing Line* followed Angela Davis's attempts to teach in a public university despite her Communist party affiliation, watched Bernadine Dohrn make the FBI's "Most Wanted" list, and called for an investigation of tax laws that allowed Chicago Seven defendant Jerry Rubin to create a tax-exempt foundation to promote his radical beliefs.[10]

In accordance with its support for the Vietnam War and traditional anticommunist stands, *Firing Line* opposed the Soviet Consular Convention, which it thought would increase communist espionage in the United States, supported the Subversive Activities Control Board as a way to control extremist groups, defended the American Legion against charges (printed in *Izvestia*) of being reactionary and antiworker, and reprinted a J. Edgar Hoover article on Soviet attempts to steal secret American technology. The newsletter dealt with the newer forms of protest, condemning the withholding of telephone taxes, calling for the criminalization of flagburning, supporting the draft, and opposing amnesty for draft evaders. Finally, the publication supported the police while opposing police review boards. In short, *Firing Line* remained firmly in the "hawk" and "law and order" camps in the 1960s.[11]

The newsletter also continued its traditional policy of opposing the extreme Right and reported on the newer groups as they attained some prominence. The monthly admitted that the Minutemen's "concern over communist aggression and infiltration is commendable," but it strongly opposed the organization's methods and warned that "extremism in any form is detrimental to the American way of life." In other articles, *Firing Line* called the Ku Klux Klan "reprehensible" and the American Nazis "hate-mongering." In all, the newsletter saw American society as being under attack from all sides, concluding that communism, racism, Nazism, and "Klanism" were "gaining a foothold and not many people seem to care."[12]

The publication during this turbulent era essentially reflected the experiences of the rest of the conservative movement. The Vietnam era galvanized the American Left by giving it a central cause. However, the outbreak of open protest against governmental foreign policy also rallied conservative groups to oppose their traditional foes. *Firing Line*, representing the hawkish American Legion, already had a long history of fighting the Left, but the particular concerns of the Vietnam era found a comfortable home in its pages.

Without Vietnam, neither Right nor Left had a central cause. *Firing Line* entered the fourth period of its history with a return to its traditional purposes of providing commentary on national security issues and monitoring the extreme elements in American society. The newsletter reflected the Legion's special interest in issues remaining from the Vietnam War. It opposed President Gerald Ford's amnesty plan and urged instead that draft resisters receive amnesty only on a case-by-case basis and that military deserters be left to military law. *Firing Line* attacked the Vietnam Veterans Against the War's (VVAW) leftist political orientation, defended the Legion in its feud with the VVAW over which organization truly represented Vietnam veterans, and covered the Jane Fonda–Joan Baez dispute over the totalitarian nature of the post-1975 Vietnam government. Other foreign policy articles in the post-Vietnam *Firing Line* supported President Jimmy Carter's crackdown on Iranian students during the hostage crisis, questioned why tributes to Mao Tse-tung after his death failed to mention his regime's bloodbaths, reprinted congressional testimony by a former gulag inmate, supported Carter's reinstatement of draft registration, and monitored antidraft forces.[13]

While most left- and right-wing political groups suffered strong declines after Vietnam ended, enough extremists remained to fill *Firing Line*'s pages, and, as always, new groups emerged to concern the newsletter. It noted the International Workers of the World's mild rebound in the 1970s, praised the arrest of eleven Puerto Rican nationalist bombing suspects, prophesized that radical groups would bring "riots and bloodshed" to the 1976 bicentennial celebrations, claimed that Peoples Temple leader Jim Jones used religion to advance communist doctrine, called Yale University's hiring of Marxist theoretician Herbert Aptheker a victory for the Communist party, saw the growth of the Maoist Progressive Labor party as a sign that things were getting worse in America, and even complained that those who wanted to replace "The Star-Spangled Banner" as America's national anthem with "America, the Beautiful" had "no regard for tradition and time-honored customs."[14]

The growth of third-party activity in the 1970s drew much of *Firing Line*'s coverage to electoral activity. The newsletter claimed that the 1976 election gave the Communist and Socialist Workers parties propaganda opportunities and that their influence was growing with each election, traced Lyndon LaRouche's bizarre political odyssey from the far Left to the far Right, reacted with "complete shock" to Socialist party member Bernard Sanders's election as mayor of Burlington, Vermont, and reported on the antinuclear, anticorporation views of the Citizens party. The publication's range of political interests in post-Vietnam America is perhaps best illustrated by a 1980 election article that covered the Socialist Workers, communist, Peace and Freedom, and Libertarian parties; LaRouche; then-Ku Klux Klan member Tom Metzger's congressional race in California; and Nazi Harold Covington's campaign for North Carolina attorney general as the Republican nominee.[15]

In addition to the Metzger and Covington races, *Firing Line* continued to watch other elements of the far Right. It used the debut of the documentary *California Reich* to blast the American Nazis: "The film points up the fact that these ignorant neo-Nazis actually have no logical political position; they spew confused, shrill, mindless epithets which are politically senseless." Other articles noted the Klan's growing operations in England and its attempts to recruit high school students in the United States, examined the racist views of the British National Front, and condemned the proposed Nazi march in Skokie, Illinois, the home of many German concentration camp victims, asking, "Whose rights take precedence?" All of this extremist activity on the Right and Left reinforced *Firing Line*'s traditional concern with internal security, and found the newsletter mourning the death of the Senate Internal Security Subcommittee, urging restoration of the House Committee on Internal Security, and reprinting FBI reports on foreign espionage and extremist group activities in the United States.[16]

Finally, *Firing Line* began a major stylistic change in the 1970s. Traditionally it relied on original writing or rewrote articles from other sources and inserted editorial comments in them. As the decade progressed, more articles tended to be reprints from the mainstream and extremist press, while original writing, rewriting, and editorial comments diminished each year. In 1983, the newsletter shifted almost entirely to reprints, and went over to them completely the following year. Often these articles are coupled with Legion resolutions. For example, a 1986 report on Madalyn Murray O'Hair's resignation as leader of American Atheists was followed by a Legion resolution supporting school prayer. In effect, *Firing Line* today is devoted almost entirely to presenting information with virtually none of the commentary that characterized its earlier history.[17]

Besides bringing a format change, *Firing Line* switched its focus in the 1980s to reflect the issues of the Reagan presidency in the newsletter's fifth period. Ronald Reagan brought an active anticommunist outlook to Washington that spurred intense political debate. As can be expected, *Firing Line* strongly backed the conservative administration views. More surprising, the newsletter eliminated most of its extremist group coverage, choosing instead to focus on terrorism, foreign policy, and immigration.

As terrorist incidents increased in the 1980s, *Firing Line* gave the problem more coverage, often devoting entire issues to the subject. In particular, the newsletter worried about terrorist group activities in the United States, and it supplied its readers with FBI materials documenting numerous incidents. In 1983, Attorney General William French Smith issued new guidelines to govern FBI domestic investigations, and *Firing Line* strongly endorsed them as being practical yet protective of citizens' rights. In a related issue, the newsletter gave more coverage to Libya, supported Reagan's various operations against that state, and urged that Libya be isolated internationally for its support of terrorism.[18]

Firing Line took a strong position against the proposed nuclear freeze, arguing that it would give the Soviets a strategic advantage, threaten the American nuclear triad, and undercut Soviet incentives to negotiate reductions in weapons. The newsletter reprinted articles condemning Moscow's shooting down of a South Korean airliner, exposing Russia's use of slave labor in the gulag, and announcing the sentencing of an American engineer for espionage. *Firing Line* also printed Polish Solidarity leader Lech Walesa's commencement speech to Harvard University, delivered in absentia by Harvard president Derek Bok. The newsletter backed Reagan's efforts to achieve a full accounting of Vietnam servicemen missing in action and believed that the Indochinese governments possessed further information and prisoner of war remains. It also supported the possibility that live POWs were being held in Southeast Asia.[19]

Firing Line became interested in immigration in the 1980s, in general taking a restrictive stance on the issue. The publication opposed amnesty for illegal aliens, arguing that they negatively affected veteran employment and that many were criminals or subversives. Despite its antipathy to Castro, *Firing Line* was suspicious of the Mariel refugees and printed accounts of their crimes in the United States. Later it cautiously backed the Simpson-Mazzoli bill, which attempted to deal with the immigration problem, but it disagreed with the bill's amnesty provisions. The newsletter did support one group of would-be immigrants: Filipinos who had fought with American forces in World War II. *Firing Line* backed a bill that would grant them U.S. citizenship and allow them to settle in America.[20]

In more than four decades of publishing political information for Legionnaires, *Firing Line* has essentially fulfilled its mission of providing information on what it sees as threats to "Americanism." Always concerned with subversion, the newsletter attained its greatest influence during the 1950s, but lost much of it as domestic communism faded from public interest. While other conservative journals have dropped their coverage of this topic, *Firing Line* remains one of the few that regularly carries internal security information. The publication has modified its focus as the political climate changed, but it has always reflected the conservative views of its parent organization. As such, *Firing Line*'s evolution since 1952 demonstrates conservative national security concerns as American politics changed over four decades.

Notes

1. Roscoe Baker, *The American Legion and American Foreign Policy* (New York, 1954), pp. 29, 43-49; Raymond Moley, Jr., *The American Legion Story* (New York, 1966), p. 90; NAC, "Action Programs of Americanism" (Indianapolis, Indiana, 1983).

2. Baker, *Legion and Foreign Policy*, pp. 29-40; Moley, *Legion Story*, pp. 80, 90-91, 139-40, 185-88.

3. Telephone interview with NAC staff member, American Legion Headquarters, Indianapolis, 24 March 1983; telephone interview with Doris Crouch, editor of *Firing Line*, NAC, American Legion Headquarters, Indianapolis, 29 January 1985; John Cogley, *Report on Blacklisting*, 2 vols. (n.p., 1956), 2:110. Karl Baarslaag was *Firing Line*'s first editor. "Un-American Activities Committee," in American Legion, *Thirty-Fourth Annual National Convention: 1952* (n.p., n.d.), pp. 32-36.

4. Quotation from "Prediction," *The Firing Line: Facts for Fighting Communism* 2 (15 January 1953): 1; see also pp. 1–2 (hereinafter cited as *FL*); on copyright policy see *FL* 1 (15 April 1952): 4, and "Important Notice," *FL* 4 (1 July 1955): 68.

5. Quotation from "Death of a Salesman," *FL* 1 (15 March 1952): 4; on boycotting, see "What You Can Do," *FL* 1 (1 April 1952): 1; examples of information on entertainers include "Entertainment," *FL* 3 (1 February 1954): 1–3, and "Communism in the Entertainment Industry," *FL* 4 (1 November 1955): 112–21; for the Legion's and *FL*'s roles in blacklisting see Cogley, *Blacklisting*, 1:118–43; 2:110–12, 169–70, 186–88; Larry Ceplair and Steven Englund, *The Inquisition in Hollywood: Politics in the Film Community, 1930–1960* (Garden City, New York, 1980), pp. 387–89, 392–94; Victor Navasky, *Naming Names* (New York, 1980), pp. 86, 89–90; David Caute, *The Great Fear: The Anti-Communist Purge under Truman and Eisenhower* (New York, 1978), pp. 503–4; and Stefan Kanfer, *A Journal of the Plague Years* (New York, 1973), pp. 119, 277–80; on clearing, see "No Legion Clearances or Loyalty Hearing Boards," *FL* 1 (15 May 1952): 3; "Former Communists and Supporters Who Have Broken with Communists and Communist Fronts," *FL* 1 (15 May 1952): insert; and "Burgess Meredith," *FL* 2 (15 February 1953): 3–4.

6. "Recent Decisions of the Supreme Court of the United States," *FL* 6 (1 July 1957): 57–64; "Investigation," *FL* 5 (15 September 1956): 79–81; "Special Notice," *FL* 5 (15 November 1956): 97; Cogley, *Blacklisting*, 2:110–12; "Lee R. Pennington," *FL* 23 (November 1974): insert; "Unrestricted Immigration—A Major Security Problem," *FL* 6 (20 May 1957): 44–48; "Unity Can Rout McCarthyism," *FL* 3 (1 January 1954): 1–3.

7. Quotation from "Anti-Semitic Propaganda," *FL* 3 (1 February 1954): 3; see also *FL* 1 (1 October 1952): 1, and "Hate Group," *FL* 3 (15 June 1954): 4.

8. On Cuba, see, for example, "The Truth about Cuba," *FL* 10 (December 1961): 49–50, and "Fair Play for Cuba Committee," *FL* 13 (January 1964): 1–2; see also "The Bang–Jensen Case," *FL* 10 (April 1961): 13–16; "Berlin: Symbol of a Divided World," *FL* 10 (October 1961): 41–44; "Captive Nations Week," *FL* 13 (September 1964): 1–2; "Cultural Exchanges: A Communist Tactical Weapon," *FL* 8 (1 July 1959): 49–52; and "Strength of the World Communist Movement," *FL* 10 (June 1961): 24.

9. Extremist articles include "The Communist Challenge on the Home Front," *FL* 9 (15 February 1960): 13–16; "The Communist party and the 1960 National Elections," *FL* 9 (15 August 1960): 61–63; "A Recent Demonstration of Communist Strength," *FL* 9 (1 January 1960): 1–4; "Supreme Court Upholds Security Laws in Two Key Decisions," *FL* 10 (16 June 1961): 25–28; and "Growing Nazi-Like Menace," *FL* 12 (July 1963): 3. Quotations from "Totalitarian Trash," *FL* 12 (June 1963): 4, and "'Firing Line': An Authentic Reporter on Subversive Activities," *FL* 11 (January–February 1962): 7.

10. Quotations from "The American Legion Firing Line," *FL* 18 (August–September

1969): 7–8, and "Black Panthers," *FL* 18 (August–September 1969): 1; articles on the 1960s Left include "Commanding Thoughts [hereinafter cited as CT]: Communist party, USA," *FL* 17 (July 1968): 1; "Students for a Democratic Society," *FL* 17 (August 1968): 3–4; "Students for a Democratic Society (Weatherman Faction)," *FL* 19 (June 1970): 3–4; "Student Mobilization Committee," *FL* 19 (April 1970): 3–4; "Peace and Freedom Party," *FL* 17 (May 1968): 1–2; "Venceremos Brigade (We Shall Conquer!)" *FL* 19 (June 1970): 1–3; "Professor Angela Davis," *FL* 18 (December 1969): 3–4; "Bernadine Rae Dohrn," *FL* 20 (January 1971): 2–3; and "Jerry Rubin," *FL* 19 (December 1970): 3–4.

11. Typical articles include "Vietnam," *FL* 14 (June 1965): 2–4; "Statement of the American Legion on the Consular Convention with the Soviet Union before the Senate Committee on Foreign Relations," *FL* 16 (April 1967): insert; (May 1967): insert; (June 1967): insert; "Subversive Activities Control Board," *FL* 20 (October 1971): 2–4; "CT: Communists vs. the American Legion," *FL* 17 (December 1968): 1–2; J. Edgar Hoover, "The U.S. Businessman Faces the Soviet Spy," *FL* 14 (August–September 1965): insert; (October 1965): insert; (November 1965): insert; "Refuse Telephone Tax," *FL* 16 (January 1967): 2–3; "CT: Desecration of the United States Flag," *FL* 16 (May 1967): 1; "Beat the Draft!" *FL* 14 (December 1965): 1–4; "CT: Amnesty," *FL* 22 (February 1973): 1; and "The American Legion and the Police," *FL* 14 (November 1965): 2–3.

12. Quotations from "The Minuteman," *FL* 14 (June 1965): 5; "CT: The Minuteman," *FL* 16 (March 1967): 1; "Ku Klux Klan," *FL* 22 (May 1973): 2; "National Socialist White People's Party," *FL* 22 (May 1973): 2; and "CT: The 'Isms' Are Rampant," *FL* 22 (May 1973): 1.

13. See, for example, amnesty materials inserted in *FL* 23 (November 1974); "Vietnam Veterans against the War (VVAW)," *FL* 25 (August–September 1976): 2–3; "Vietnam Veterans against the War (VVAW)," *FL* 25 (November 1976): 1–2; "CT: The Feud: Baez vs. Fonda," *FL* 28 (August–September 1979): 1–2; "CT: U.S. Communists Decry Action of the Government of the United States," *FL* 28 (December 1979): 1–2; "CT: Why All the Accolades for Mao Tsetung?" *FL* 25 (November 1976): 1; "U.S.S.R. Labor Camps," *FL* 23 (October 1974): 2; "Meetings: Anti-Draft Forces," *FL* 30 (April 1981): 2; and "CT: Draft Resisters and Protesters," *FL* 31 (December 1982): 1–2.

14. Quotations from "CT: Bicentennial Plans of the Radicals," *FL* 25 (March 1976): 1; and "CT: Save Our National Anthem," *FL* 27 (March 1978): 1; see also "CT: The 'Wobblies' Are with Us Again!" *FL* 27 (October 1978): 1; "Fuerzas Armadas de Liberacion Nacional (F.A.L.N.) Armed Forces of National Liberation of Puerto Rico," *FL* 29 (June 1980): 2–3; "CT: Jim Jones—The Communist," *FL* 28 (February 1979): 1–2; "Herbert Aptheker," *FL* 25 (June 1976): 1; and "CT: The Road to Disaster," *FL* 27 (November 1978): 1–2.

15. Sanders quotation from "CT: The Socialists Gain a Political Victory," *FL* 30 (May 1981): 1; see also "CT: The Other Side of the Election," *FL* 25 (December 1976): 1; "Lyndon H. LaRouche, Jr. and the United States Labor Party," *FL* 29 (April 1980): 3–4; "Citizens Party," *FL* 29 (June 1980): 1–2; and "Politics," *FL* 29 (August–September 1980): 1–4.

16. Quotations from "The Nazis," *FL* 26 (February 1977): 3 and "CT: The Question of 'Rights,'" *FL* 27 (May 1978): 1. On the extreme Right, see also "Ku Klux Klan," *FL* 27 (May 1978): 1–2, and "National Front," *FL* 27 (May 1978): 1; on internal security, see "CT: Senate Subcommittee on Internal Security," *FL* 26 (May 1977): 1; "CT: The American Legion Takes a Stand," *FL* 29 (October 1980): 1–2; and "Federal Bureau of Investigation 1973 Annual Report: Internal Security," *FL* 23 (February 1974): insert; (March 1974): insert.

17. "Madalyn Murray O'Hair Steps down as Head of American Atheists," *FL* 35 (August–September 1986): 10–11.

18. For example, the February 1984, April 1985, and June 1986 issues were devoted entirely to the terrorism problem. Other terrorist articles include "Testimony," *FL* 32

(February 1983): 3–5; "New FBI Guidelines," *FL* 32 (June 1983): 6–8; "CT: The American Legion Takes a Stand," *FL* 32 (October 1983): 1–3; and "CT: Latest on Libya," *FL* 35 (March 1986): 1–2.

19. Foreign policy articles include "CT: Nuclear Freeze Proposals," *FL* 32 (April 1983): 1–3; "CT: Korean Airlines Flight #007," *FL* 32 (November 1983): 1–4; "The Use of Political Prisoners as Slave Labour," *FL* 32 (June 1983): 4–6; "Engineer Gets Life Sentence for Stealth Data," *FL* 34 (July 1985): 4; "CT," *FL* 32 (August–September 1983): 1–4; and "MIA Talks," *FL* 33 (April 1984): 5–6.

20. On immigration, see "The American Legion Takes a Stand on Immigration," *FL* 31 (July 1982): 2–3; "CT: Fidel's Gift: Made-in-Cuba Crime Wave," *FL* 32 (January 1983): 1; "CT: House Barely Passes Immigration Bill," *FL* 33 (August–September 1984): 1–2; and "CT: Filipinos Seek U.S. Citizenship," *FL* 32 (May 1983): 1–2.

Information Sources

BIBLIOGRAPHY: None.
INDEXES: Annual indexes for vols. 2–10.
REPRINT EDITIONS: None.
LOCATION SOURCES: Complete runs: Air University Library, Maxwell Air Force Base; Los Angeles Public Library; University of Virginia.

Publication History

TITLE AND TITLE CHANGES: *The Firing Line: Facts for Fighting Communism*, 1952–1955; *The American Legion Firing Line*, 1955–present.
VOLUME AND ISSUE DATA: Volumes 1–current, 15 January 1952–present.
FREQUENCY OF PUBLICATION: Biweekly, 1952–1955; three times a month, 1955; biweekly, 1955–1960; monthly, 1961–present.
PUBLISHER: National Americanism Commission, American Legion, Indianapolis, Indiana.
EDITORS: Editorial Board (Members not named).
CIRCULATION: 8,500.

Peter L. de Rosa

Christian Anti-Communism Crusade News Letter
1955–1998

The *Christian Anti-Communism Crusade News Letter* was begun in the early 1950s in Waterloo, Iowa. Its three principal founders were W. E. Pietsch, D.D., a local radio evangelist; Frederick Charles Schwarz, an Australian physician who immigrated to the United States in 1953; and Helen C. Birnie, a former communist activist. From rather humble beginnings in Iowa, the organization moved in 1956 to San Pedro, California, and in 1958 to Long Beach. It gradually grew in membership, the number of its offices, and the geographical size and distribution of its officers and board of directors to some twenty-one countries around the world. Among the clergy, medical doctors, and business executives gradually added to the board of directors were William P. Strube, Jr., of Houston, Texas, president of the Mid-American Life Insurance Company (who served as secretary of the crusade in 1958), and George W. Westcott, M.D., a medical missionary of Ypsilanti, Michigan.

Schwarz was born in Australia in 1913. His Jewish father had left his home in Austria at the age of twelve and gone to Australia by way of England. When he was approximately twenty, Schwarz's father converted to Christianity and raised his son as a Christian. Thus it was from a Christian perspective that the young Schwarz first became interested in the matter of communism. As he later wrote: "My first conflicts with communism were not primarily economic or political but were concerned with the being of God and the nature and destiny of man."[1] In 1940, at the University of Queensland, his first debate with a communist took place.[2] Chagrined by his defeat and his lack of knowledge about the force he opposed, Schwarz read widely in the writing of communism. Later, in the *Christian Anti-Communism Crusade News Letter*, especially in the 1960s and 1970s, he demonstrated not only a point of view but a familiarity with communist journals and newspapers and publications of the Left in general.[3]

From the earliest issues, the *News Letter* stressed the growing danger of communism. Communists, it held, seemed to be making gains everywhere, especially in the Third World. The foe was skillful and clever, and unless people united in opposition, his victory was imminent. It would not come by massive military attack but through effective propaganda and an undermining of the faith and moral fiber of noncommunist people.[4] As Schwarz argued before the House Committee on Un-American Activities in 1957, communists planned to take over the United States by 1973, not by destroying but by utilizing American factories, schools, and other property.

Two charges were frequently leveled against the Christian Anti-Communism Crusade. The first is that it had no program, but that it simply shrieked, "The Communists are coming! The Communists are coming!" To this Schwarz replied that this, less hyperbolically stated, was its program. Communism, he maintained, results not from bad economic conditions—if that were so, then "the world would have been Communist centuries ago"—but from the kind of naive idealism that thrives, in the United States at least, among university students.[5] It is because communists seek to lure these unsuspecting students into joining left-wing and communist organizations that the program of the Christian Anti-Communism Crusade must consist of education. Students, whom Schwarz said are "rightfully indoctrinated" in cleanliness, obedience to the law, and such things as basic arithmetical facts, should also be indoctrinated to see communism as "an unmitigated evil."[6] Hence, over the years, the Anti-Communism Crusade concerned itself with training primary and secondary school teachers on the proper method of teaching communism in the schools; it sponsored its own "Schools of Anti-Communism" (or, as they came to be called, "Anti-Subversive Seminars")—five-day meetings with speakers, films, and discussion—to promote awareness of the communist menace; and it produced lectures, writings, and numerous personal appearances by Schwarz on college campuses, radio, and television.[7] In short, the chief program of the Christian Anti-communism Crusade was to spread knowledge about communism and its dangers and to urge people in the United States and other countries to join in a counteroffensive on the basis of that knowledge.

A second criticism (less frequently made) of the Christian Anti-Communism Crusade is that it was anti-Semitic. This issue was most frequently raised during the 1950s and early 1960s. As early as 1956 the Reverend Pietsch, the organization's first president, said flatly: "We wish to make it crystal clear that we have no sympathy with those who are anti-Semitic." Similarly, in 1962, Schwarz wrote: "With all the sincerity possible I deny the charge that the Christian Anti-Communism Crusade is anti-Semitic. Anti-Semitism is a vicious and vile thing. No true Christian can possibly be anti-Semitic. The Christ we love was a Jew." Indeed, crusade meetings were picketed by those whom Schwarz calls neo-Nazis and who labeled him "a phony Jewish conservative."[8] He also stressed that true Jews could not be communists, since communism is an atheistic philosophy. Given the fact that many Jews as well as Christians opposed communism, Schwarz was often asked why his organization was called the Christian Anti-Communism Crusade instead of the Judeo-Christian Anti-Communism Crusade, and he admitted to some difficulty in explaining his position. In 1962 he pointed out that several organizations might serve similar needs—for example, the Catholic War Veterans, the Jewish War Veterans, the Veterans of Foreign Wars, and the American Legion all worked to advance the interests of war veterans—and that this variety demonstrated freedom. But in 1967 a California woman wrote to the crusade that she and her husband, both Jews, had been giving money to the crusade and attending its public sessions because there seemed to be no Jewish group as vigorous in its efforts to alert the public to the real nature of communism. Only in 1970 did Schwarz mention such an organization, the Jewish Right, in West Los Angeles.[9]

On the question of Arab-Israeli relations, and of the Third World in general, the *News Letter* moved from a religious to a secular approach. In 1956 the Reverend Pietsch believed that God was using his chosen people, Israel, for his own purposes, that communists were stirring up the Arabs, and that the Lord's coming was close at hand. By 1967, however, with Pietsch deceased and Schwarz in charge, the *News Letter* discussed the Arab-Israeli struggle almost entirely in secular terms as a part of a Russian effort to dominate the world; though the Russians had backed the Arabs, Schwarz noted that Israel had a communist party. At the time of the Yom Kippur War of 1973, Schwarz set forth what he termed "certain convictions which should guide Christians and all lovers of mankind." These included the right of the people and state of Israel to exist, as well as the right of all Middle East people to live, be free, and seek happiness. Communism, he argued, having an interest in preventing the development of peace in the area, worked against the true interests of these people.[10]

In its extensive discussions of China over the years, the *News Letter* blended religious and secular issues. Reporting in a 1957 story on a group of Episcopal clergymen from Australia recently returned from China who had characterized the church in that country as being free, well-attended, and healthy, Schwarz asserted just the opposite: the state, he said, controlled the church in China and told ministers what they must preach. The visit of the Australian clergymen, he added, was simply part of a communist strategy to win worldwide support for admission to the United Nations and recognition by the United States. China "is one vast prison," he wrote, "where the Communist Party is the jailer and the Chinese people are the captives," a million of whom, braving the dangers of escape, had managed to flee to Formosa, preferring to live there as refugees in spite of the difficult conditions they had to endure. Schwarz maintained that religion in China was not free but was used by the state.[11]

In 1963, when relations between China and the West seemed to offer some reason for hope because the dispute between the Russian and Chinese communists was out in the open, Schwarz cautioned against optimism. Although China and the Soviet Union disagreed on specific courses of action, they were all communists, and they all agreed on the ultimate goal of world domination by communism. In short, he said, "The Conflict Is Real; the Split is Phony."[12] In subsequent years, Schwarz found reason to pronounce Senator Henry M. Jackson (D, Washington) guilty of "moral schizophrenia" since he favored a tough stance toward Russia but, finding much to praise in China, advocated a most-favored-nation status for it. Schwarz also criticized President Richard M. Nixon's visit to China because it came at too great a cost: admitting the People's Republic of China to the United Nations and ousting Formosa from it, and opening up the possibility of treaties between India and the USSR and Japan and the USSR. The change in American policy, Schwarz thought, was at best an uncertain step toward peace.[13]

Perhaps because of the closer geographical relation of Latin America to the United States, the danger of communism there seemed considerably greater than in China. The rock-throwing mobs that greeted Vice-President Nixon on his visit to South America in 1958, Schwarz wrote, were led by communists and aroused by effective procommunist, anti-American propaganda.[14] Two years later, in 1960, after returning from a trip to parts of the Caribbean, Central America, and South America, Joost Sluis reported that communism and anti-Americanism were growing stronger in Latin America, though in varying degrees in the different countries, and he blamed this on seductive communist propaganda. Serious economic problems, "unstable [and] rather dictatorial governments," and poorly organized (and sometimes student-controlled) universities all contributed to the volatility of the situation. But a deep religious feeling, Sluis felt, could effectively be tapped to resist communism by giving timely warnings that communist victories in Latin America would mean forced labor, separation of families, closing of churches, and mass executions.[15]

The seriousness of the danger in Latin America was illustrated in the Cuban missile crisis and Salvador Allende's brief period of power in Chile. In the Cuban missile crisis, Schwarz argued, communists had tested American will and won the victory. America had demonstrated that it had strength and courage and would respond to threat and provocation, but since it also declared it would not intervene in Cuba so long as long-range missiles were not introduced there, Khrushchev and the Russians were the real victors. Khrushchev won praise as a man of peace for removing the missiles and defusing a crisis.

In Chile, Salvador Allende came to power by use of the democratic process and immediately faced major pressures and choices. If he chose to move slowly in eliminating the "bourgeois state," he would eventually be ousted by that state, but if he moved too hastily to destroy it, he would be removed that much earlier.[16] The pressures came from American economic policies and ultimately from direct Central Intelligence Agency intervention into Chile's affairs. Neither the policies nor the intervention were significant in bringing down the Allende government, Schwarz insisted; even the communists said that Allende had fallen because of errors by the leadership and conflicts within his coalition government.[17] Whatever the effect of U.S. intervention, it was fully justified. American security was at stake, and "educational and economic" measures were necessary to prevent the establishment of a communist state in this hemisphere. The American government would have been "puerile and irresponsible" if it had not prevented this and ultimately other such states from taking root in the Americas.[18]

With similar arguments Schwarz supported America's involvement in El Salvador in the 1980s, yet he saw it as a complex situation, entitling one article, "The U.S. Dilemma in El Salvador." The dilemma was that if America supported the existing regime, it maintained the existing poverty and oppression "by paramilitary organizations allegedly associated with the government." If America abandoned the existing government, a communist dictatorship in El Salvador would result and the domino effect would produce similar governments in Guatemala, Costa Rica, and other Central American countries. In the world at large, the forces of communism would thereby have made a slight gain and more people would believe in the inevitability of communist domination. America's policy made sense, and should be maintained, because it resisted Soviet intervention in this hemisphere and disrupted guerrilla activity.[19]

If Schwarz saw a dilemma for the United States in El Salvador, he saw none for America in Vietnam. American interests in general and the domino theory in particular were among several reasons for U.S. involvement in that area. Developments in Vietnam, which increasingly dominated American domestic politics and foreign policy in the 1960s, drew some strong, predictable comments from Schwarz, who as early as 1956 had emphasized the importance of Southeast Asia. In 1965 he stated flatly that "American servicemen are in Viet Nam to defend their homeland, the United States, against communist aggression." The United States was helping to preserve the liberty of South Vietnam's people, but the defense of the United States against communism was what really made necessary the defense of South Vietnam. A few weeks after making these observations, Schwarz declared that American involvement in Vietnam was "both just and necessary" and that those who protested against the war were helping the enemy.[20] The war, he wrote, was not a civil war but the result of the North's invasion of the South. Increased American intervention had blocked a quick communist victory and might cause the enemy to shift from military action to propaganda, a step backward in what Schwarz called the communist "strategy of conquest."[21]

Critics of American policy in Vietnam occasionally called for free elections to determine what the Vietnamese people wanted and blamed the United States for blocking such elections. Schwarz asserted that the North Vietnamese communists would not allow such elections in their areas and that those who favored them did not know the situation, or else did know and were seeking to help the communists win.

At the time of the 1973 ceasefire in Vietnam, Schwarz argued that neither side had won a definitive victory and that if the military phase of the conflict seemed over, the propaganda phase was not, and the truth still must be told. "North Vietnam," Schwarz concluded, "is a monopolistic, classical communist tyranny; and South Vietnam, for all its faults, contains the seeds of democracy, civil liberties, economic initiative and human liberty."[22]

With the collapse of the South Vietnamese government in April 1975, Schwarz expressed dismay that Congress, moved by the pressure of public opinion, which was affected by television, radio, and newspaper reports (which were in turn affected by continuous communist propaganda efforts), did not act to help U.S. allies in South Vietnam. The short-range effect might well be that America's allies would see the United States as undependable and increasingly come to rely on their own defenses, seeking nuclear weapons for that purpose. "Thus, one effect of the desertion of the people of Vietnam by the U.S.A. would probably be the proliferation of nuclear weapons," far-reaching consequences indeed.[23]

During the same decades that the Vietnam War dominated foreign affairs, the communist menace was as evident at home; if anything, it seemed more immediate. In 1965 Schwarz saw the undeniably broad and deep discontent and widespread protest of blacks being exploited by communists. Although he recognized the existence of poor housing and high unemployment among blacks, he described some black communities as "so-called ghettoes," and while admitting that other factors might be the cause of these conditions, said that "individual responsibility and individual failure" must be recognized. The agitator directed blame away from the latter to anyone not black and particularly to authority figures in the white community. In contrast, Schwarz praised and supported the police, urged obedience to law, and denounced civil disobedience. For him, racial violence and antagonism was avoidable and unnecessary; his *News Letter* provided examples of cooperation and notices of individual blacks working their way up the economic and social ladder, and he called for more attention to these successes in the public media.[24]

In the late 1960s and early 1970s, the Christian Anti-Communism Crusade most strongly criticized the Students for a Democratic Society and the Black Panthers. The *News Letter* ran reprints of much of the material produced by these groups, with Schwartz's comments interspersed. Not surprisingly, the *News Letter* most vigorously opposed the Black Panthers. In lengthy articles and in a Black Panther coloring book it reproduced, it tried to demonstrate the violent nature of the Black Panthers, who sought to show themselves as peaceful, providing breakfasts for poor children. But, Schwarz said in August 1969, the coloring book accompanied the breakfasts.[25]

Black religious groups received attention and criticism in proportion as the Christian Anti-Communism Crusade considered them prone to violence. Therefore, articles on the Black Muslims and their publications appeared more frequently than did ones on Martin Luther King, Jr., and the Southern Christian Leadership Conference (SCLC). The Black Muslims, Schwarz charged, were using violence and working with communists to wring territory from the United States for a separate black state. Communists were promoting racial violence for a different purpose, but common means linked the two. Such an alliance would not last if a revolution occurred. The communists, having used the Black Muslims for their own purposes, would then discard their former allies.

Martin Luther King, Jr.'s, nonviolent movement received only passing mention, and his assassination was virtually ignored. His supposed ties with communism were mentioned briefly, but in 1974 the crusade denounced King's organization and the Reverend Ralph Abernathy, King's successor as its head, for working with and appearing with communists, notably Angela Davis, a member of the American Communist party and a controversial faculty member at UCLA, who took part in the SCLC's Seventeenth Annual Convention that year.

Schwarz and the Christian Anti-Communism Crusade believed that communists, for their own purposes, supported and used American Indians and such protests as that at Alcatraz in 1970 and Wounded Knee in 1973. As with blacks, simply improving Indian economic and social conditions and raising the educational level would not solve problems. These improvements needed to be made, but there also had to be "a moral commitment on the part of the Indians themselves" before the problems would be solved.[26]

The lack of moral commitment among all Americans, and the moral decline in the country at large, were evident in the protests, violent and nonviolent, of the 1960s (especially those of 1968) and in the perceived emphasis among young people on sex and drugs, the growing discussion of homosexuality, and the popularity of Herbert Marcuse. All were caused by permissive education, materialism, and the absence of firm moral beliefs and religious faith. All aided the communists' plan to undermine American strength and freedom. From the 1950s through the 1980s the *News Letter* featured lengthy analyses of various communist parties in the United States, of such organizations as the Students for a Democratic Society and the Weathermen, and of the Free Speech Movement, all of which were communist-supported, said Schwarz. (Curiously, the events at Kent State University in May 1970, which might have been seen as evidence of moral decay and communist influence, were hardly mentioned in the *News Letter*.)

What many believed provided more evidence of moral decay in America, the Watergate affair, Schwarz tended to treat as an understandable crime. He did not deny that a crime had occurred, but he thought the reasons for it (Nixon's inability to stop leaks during negotiations to end the Vietnam War) were plausible and that it was committed by people who believed they were aiding American security and the anti-Castro movement. Many of the news media were hypocritical in their reaction to the crime, he believed, because reporters and columnists regularly used stolen information on grounds of the public's right to know, just as, he said, those planning the Watergate burglary acted in the interest of national security. Yet although the causes were legitimate, crimes committed in behalf of them were crimes nonetheless.[27] Summing up his position on Watergate a full year before President Nixon resigned, Schwarz wrote: "The lesson of Watergate is not the unique criminality of the present Republican administration, but the woeful consequences of the moral climate that prevails in our society. The theologian, Joseph Fletcher, taught situation ethics and John Mitchell practiced them. Liberal theologians who have denied the laws of God and deified the conscience of sinful man share in the criminality of Watergate."[28]

The declining moral climate and the communist threat were both evident in the women's liberation movement, the *News Letter* argued. This movement weakens the family by seeking to lessen the importance of the woman's role as mother. "Motherhood," Schwarz asserted in 1972, "is the birthright and fulfillment of womanhood."[29] Abortion, the equal rights amendment, and sex education all lessen the importance of the family and of motherhood, and all are supported by communists. In a 1975 article relying heavily on George Gilder's *Sexual Suicide* (1973), Schwarz declared that while the male's sexual nature tends toward "transience," the female's tends toward "permanence," and if society is to survive, the female sexual pattern must be dominant. The women's liberation movement acted to prevent this, however, for by moving women into the job market in competition with men, frightening consequences must result. Schwarz summed them up in the following remarkable statement: "Gilder shows how most of the programs designed to alleviate community problems such as welfare, day-care centers, and affirmative action or preferential hiring of women, diminish the role of the male as a provider and weaken the bond that ties him to the family. They thus promote the dissolution of society and increase the prevalence of robbery, rape, child abuse, and murder. They demand an ever larger and stronger police force to control the criminal element and lead to the police state."[30]

Elsewhere Schwarz argued that sex education independent of moral teaching, particularly religious teaching, would weaken society by eliminating the control of sex drives. In this area, the communists, he said, had one set of ideas for their own countries and another for those they seek to dominate. In the latter, they encouraged sex education, independent of moral teachings; in communist-dominated countries, sex education courses were opposed and homosexuality denounced.[31]

Schwarz used satire to oppose both wealth-sharing and abortion in a plan presented to an Anti-Subversive Seminar in Washington, D.C., in October 1972. Calling his proposal a "share-the-life plan" and arguing that it was not fair to terminate a baby's life even before it was born while others who had been born lived long lives, Schwarz proposed that the average life span should be determined along with what he called "the average allowable length of life" to maintain "a satisfactory population." If the latter figure were forty-five years, then people should not be allowed to live beyond that age, but abortions should be stopped and babies allowed to be born and live their forty-five years.[32]

The Christian Anti-Communism Crusade continued to publish until 1998, producing a well-printed, easily read newsletter of approximately eight pages. It stressed long-held views and themes, seeing in events like the downing of the Korean airliner in the fall of 1983 and the events in El Salvador merely more proof to add to the mountain of evidence supporting its view of the Soviet Union in particular and communism in general. It saw communists as trying to persuade a few key students and intellectuals that communism favored peace, created prosperity, and helped the downtrodden. The antidraft movement was an indication that such efforts continued to be persuasive, but the shooting down of KAL flight 007, which Schwarz suggested should be widely used to discredit communism, demonstrated how peace-loving and caring it really was.[33]

One major difference after the election of 1980 was that the views of the administration in Washington were more nearly those of Schwarz and the Christian Anti-Communism Crusade. Ronald Reagan's victory was due to opposition to abortion and forced busing, homosexuality, and "Promotion of Venereal Disease and Illegitimacy Disguised as Sex Education." Early in the Reagan administration's term, Schwarz asserted that the president's blunt statements were accurate and wise; it was true, as Reagan asserted and Schwarz had for so long argued, that the communists would engage in any and all kinds of evil activity to advance their cause, and that the United States must be strong and powerful.[34]

Supporters of the Christian Anti-Communism Crusade, perhaps assuming that since the country's leaders held views more like their own, relaxed the level of their support in the year that Reagan took office. Crusade income in 1981 was nearly $35,000 less than at the same time the previous year. In 1981 Schwarz appealed for a "one million dollar truth campaign" but admitted that for 1982 the organization had not quite raised that amount.[35]

Whatever the financial straits of the Christian Anti-Communism Crusade, Schwarz's sober, even subdued view was indicated in a response he gave to some pointed yet sympathetic remarks made by a friend and supporter. After more than twenty years of the *News Letter*, public appearances, study groups, schools of anticommunism, and other activities by Schwarz and the crusade, the friend noted that Schwarz himself agreed that the communist danger was greater in the 1970s than two decades before and that the program had not been enough. Schwarz's response was that the fight was and always had been worth it, even if victory had not been achieved, because the quality of life had been enhanced for many people. He and the Christian Anti-Communism Crusade would continue to study communist ideology and action, educate people to its enduring danger, and believe that these activities would eventually triumph.[36] When the Cold War ended in the late 1980s, the *Newsletter* lost much of its focus and in 1998 yielded to a new publication, *The Schwarz Report*.

Notes

1. Frederick C. Schwarz, "The Roots of Communism," *Christian Anti-Communism Crusade News Letter* (June 1962): 1–2 (hereinafter cited as *NL*).

2. George Thayer, *The Farther Shores of Politics: The American Political Fringe Today* (New York, 1967), p. 247.

3. Schwarz's wife, Lillian, reportedly remarked: "I'm never alone with Fred. He always has Karl Marx along." *Time* (9 February 1962): 18–19.

4. Schwarz, *NL* (1 July 1972): 1.

5. Schwarz, *NL* (June 1963): 1–2.

6. Schwarz, *NL* (November 1963): 1.

7. Among the dozen or so films the crusade endorsed are *Revolt in Hungary*, on the 1956 uprising and narrated by Walter Cronkite, and *Ultimate Weapon*—"Ronald Reagan narrates the brainwashing of American soldiers in Korea. The ultimate weapon against Communist Chinese indoctrination is shown to be the minds of free men." *NL* (15 March 1965): 4. See also "A Program against Communism," *NL* (April 1962): 2–3; "The Lord Hath Done Great Things for Us," *NL* (April 1961): 1, 7, 8; *NL* (3 October 1966): 8.

8. W. E. Pietsch, *NL* (July–August 1956): 8; Schwarz, "The Roots of Communism: Communism, Now, as Always, is Rooted in Atheism," *NL* (June 1962): 1–2.

9. Eleanor Sternberg to Schwarz, *NL* (19 October 1967): 8; Schwarz, *NL* (15 October 1970): 8.

10. Schwarz, *NL* (1 November 1973): 1–2.

11. Schwarz, "Round the World in Twenty-eight Days," *NL* (January 1960): 1–2; *NL* (February 1982): 1–5.

12. Schwarz, "Is the Split between the Russian and Chinese Communists Real or Phony?" *NL* (September 1963): 1.

13. Schwarz, *NL* (1 September 1974); *NL* (1 August 1971): 1; *NL* (15 November 1971): 1–2; *NL* (1 February 1972): 1.

14. Schwarz, *NL* (July 1958): 1–3.

15. Joost Sluis, *NL* (July 1960): 2. Sluis was an orthopedic surgeon and regional

director of the Northern California chapter of the crusade. The crusade's message was being spread by the distribution in Mexico of some 10,000 copies of the Spanish edition of Schwarz's book, *The Heart, Mind and Soul of Communism*, and by a twelve-page booklet in comic book style entitled, *If Communism Comes to Mexico.* " A similar booklet, in French, was distributed in Haiti.

16. Schwarz, *NL* (1 January 1972): 1.

17. Schwarz, *NL* (1 November 1972): 1–2, citing a letter from René Castillo, a Chilean Communist party leader, appearing in the *World Marxist Review* of July 1974.

18. Schwarz, *NL* 1 (November 1974): 1–2. In the same article, he asserted that "the use of educational and economic measures to influence the internal policies of other countries is an accepted and legitimate governmental function."

19. Schwarz, "The U. S. Dilemma in El Salvador," *NL* (1 April 1981): 1, 4; see also *NL* (15 July 1981): 1.

20. Schwarz, letter of 15 March 1965, on crusade stationery in *NL* of that date. See also letters of 10 January 1968, and 21 March 1966, in issues of those dates. To educate the American military on communism in general, Schwarz planned to give each serviceman a copy of his book, *You Can Trust the Communists (to Be Communists)*.

21. Schwarz, *NL* (20 December 1965): 1–2.

22. Schwarz, "Who Won in Vietnam," *NL* (15 February 1973): 1–2.

23. Schwarz, *NL* (1 May 1975): 1–3.

24. Schwarz, *NL* (18 September 1967); letter from Archie Moore, the boxer, to the *San Diego Union*, 8 August 1967, reprinted in *NL* (18 September 1967).

25. Schwarz, *NL* (1 August 1969): 2–4.

26. Schwarz, *NL* (1 April 1973): 1–3.

27. Schwarz, "Hysteria, Hypocrisy and Watergate," *NL* (1 June 1973): 1–2.

28. Schwarz, *NL* (1 August 1973): 1.

29. Schwarz, *NL* (15 May 1972): 1.

30. Schwarz, *NL* (15 March 1975): 1–5.

31. Schwarz, *NL* (1 June 1971): 6, reporting on the First National Congress on Education and Culture, meeting earlier that year in Havana, Cuba.

32. Schwarz, *NL* (15 October 1972): 5.

33. Schwarz, *NL* (1 October 1983): 1–4.

34. Schwarz, *NL* (1 January 1981): 1–3; Schwarz, *NL* (15 February 1981): 1. As these comments indicate, Schwarz, though then in his seventies, showed no signs of mellowing.

35. Schwarz, "The Worse, the Better," *NL* (15 July 1981); Schwarz, *NL* (1 June 1983). Total income for 1982 was $878,910, with expenditures of $920,825; the difference was made up out of reserves from previous years. The organization's growth in financial terms from 1958 to 1983 was this: 1958 total disbursements: $98,539.26; 1968 total disbursements: $339,116.82; 1983 total disbursements: $879,910.

36. Schwarz, *NL* (1 January 1975), referring to a Schwarz article in the 15 September (1974) *NL*.

Information Sources

BIBLIOGRAPHY:

Schwarz, Fred C. *The Three Faces of Revolution*. Washington, D. C., 1972.

———— *You Can Trust the Communists (to Be Communists)*. Englewood Cliffs, New Jersey, 1960.

Thayer, George. *The Farther Shores of Politics: The American Political Fringe Today*. New York, 1967.

Walker, Brooks R. *The Christian Fright Peddlers*. Garden City, New York, 1964.

INDEXES: None.

REPRINT EDITIONS: Microform: Right Wing Collection, University of Iowa (MCA), partial run, 1955–1975 (reel 20); UMI.

LOCATION SOURCES: Complete runs: UCLA; Harvard University; University of Florida.

Publication History

TITLE AND TITLE CHANGES:*Christian Anti-Communism Crusade News Letter.*

VOLUME AND ISSUE DATA: No numbers, no volumes, 1955–1998.

FREQUENCY OF PUBLICATION: Semimonthly.

PUBLISHER: Christian Anti-Communism Crusade, Long Beach, California.

EDITOR: Fred C. Schwarz, 1955–1991; David A. Noebol and Michael Bauman, 1991–1998.

CIRCULATION: 1983: 50,000; 1998: 30,000.

Paul L. Silver

American Opinion
1958–1985

Robert Welch began to publish *American Opinion* in February 1958, shortly after merging his *One Man's Opinion* with *Hubert Kregeloh Comments*. The first issue appeared less than a year after the death of Wisconsin senator Joseph R. McCarthy and only ten months before Welch would organize the John Birch Society (JBS). The new magazine, which Welch described simply as "a monthly commentary on national and international affairs," symbolized a dramatic shift in the character and tone of American politics in the late 1950s as a growing number of right-wing conservatives rejected the "modern Republicanism" of President Dwight D. Eisenhower. This revolt on the Right gained strength from a growing disillusionment with the state of world affairs and mounting anxiety over moral malaise in America and the lack of a clearly defined national purpose.

Published monthly, except in July, by Robert Welch, Inc., *American Opinion* survived for nearly thirty years with the singular goal of reversing the trend of "America's gradual surrender to Communism." Militantly anticommunist and unwavering in his opposition to the welfare state, Welch sought readers among "the intelligent, hard working, prosperous business executives, professional men, and other direct beneficiaries of our Americanist system."[1] Although he would relinquish day-to-day editorial supervision of the magazine to Scott Stanley, Jr., in late 1961, Welch retained the title of editor and served as the ideological conscience of *American Opinion* until his death in early January 1985.

American Opinion and the John Birch Society were technically separate during their early years, but financial dependency and organizational goals fused them together. The Birch Society, which also published the weekly *Review of the News*, strengthened this identity even more by attaching the name "American Opinion" to its speakers' bureau and associated bookstores. But more than anything else, the magazine and the JBS also shared the ideological bonds of cold war anticommunism and the leadership of Robert Welch. He was the founder of both and served in a dual capacity for many years as president of the John Birch Society and editor of *American Opinion*.

Its kinship with the Birch Society inevitably shaped *American Opinion*, but the magazine also inherited the ideological legacy and the iconoclastic journalistic styles of *One Man's Opinion* and *Hubert Kregeloh Comments*. Kregeloh even joined Welch as a member of the editorial board of the new magazine. Welch had published *One Man's Opinion* sporadically for two years, beginning in February 1956. It required a prodigious personal effort that he described as "largely a consolidation of what I am already writing to friends all over the world who are foolish enough to ask me questions."[2] The magazine had a simple message that Welch would repeat many times in later years: most American political leaders were either procommunists or dupes of communism. *One Man's Opinion* featured biographies of world leaders Welch admired for their tough, anticommunist stance, and he devoted single issues of the magazine to biographies of Syngman Rhee, Chiang Kai-shek (Jiang Jieshi), Konrad Adenauer, Senators William F. Knowland of California and Frank J. Lausche of Ohio, and U.S. Army captain John Birch.

To many observers, Robert Welch seemed an unlikely leader of a national organization, but he had commitment and good timing. Soft-spoken and reserved in manner, Welch revealed an obsession with the role of conspiracy in history, and few other persons in American political life have aroused such bitter public controversy. His life was a blend of the old and the new, the self-made man and the corporate executive. Rooted in the rural, agrarian South, he nevertheless achieved success in the urban, industrialized North. Born in Chowan County, North Carolina, on 1 December 1899, Welch was a descendant of a long line of farmers and Baptist preachers. If his adult life seemed to represent an escape from his heritage, he never fully shed the racial attitudes, religious values, and individualistic traits of the South of his childhood. Tutored at home by his mother, the precocious Welch entered the University of North Carolina at age twelve. Upon being graduated, still in his mid-teens, he attended the U.S. Naval Academy for two years and Harvard Law School for another two years before entering the candy business in the early 1920s. Alternately successful and plagued by business failure, Welch finally achieved a comfortable position during the 1930s as a vice-president of his brother's Massachusetts candy firm, the James O. Welch Company.

Success in business led to a minor role in Republican party politics in Massachusetts and an active role in national business associations during the 1940s. At this time, Welch also revealed a growing antipathy to the welfare state in his book about advertising, *The Road to Salesmanship*. Published in 1941, it condemned Marxism and centralized government, criticized "pseudo-liberal nonsense," and identified the middle class as the principal source of order and stability in American society.[3] Welch's experience as a member of the Office of Price Administration Advisory Committee for the candy industry in Washington, D.C., and his later service as a vice-president of the National Association of Manufacturers intensified his distaste for governmental bureaucracy and regulation of business.

A series of visits to Europe and Asia during the 1940s and 1950s reinforced these attitudes and confirmed his belief that the Soviet Union was winning the cold war. The Hiss and Rosenberg cases, McCarthyism, and the Korean War deepened his fears about communist aggression abroad and subversion at home. Given to penning long letter-like documents to friends, Welch on 4 July 1951, began to write a history of the "betrayal of China to the communists as a background to the dismissal of General MacArthur."[4] Henry Regnery published the letter as a book in March 1952 with the title *May God Forgive Us*, reprinting it in a paperback version in May and July of that critical election year.

An ardent supporter of Ohio senator Robert A. Taft, Welch deeply resented Eisenhower's victory at the Republican National Convention in 1952. He remained loyal to the Republican party, but Welch blamed Ike and his administration for weakening the resistance to communism. Convinced that the Eisenhower administration intended to abandon Taiwan to the Chinese communists, Welch published another short book about Asia in 1954. *The Life of John Birch* was a brief biography of a young American intelligence officer who had been killed by Chinese communist forces in north China shortly after V-J Day. Welch linked the death of Birch, whom he described as the first victim of World War III, with a series of diplomatic and military failures in Asia that he blamed on a procommunist conspiracy within the State Department.[5]

Disillusioned by these events in Asia and angered by the efforts to silence Senator Joe McCarthy, Welch quit the Republican party and began to write a critique of the Eisenhower administration that he would title "The Politician." Not content to work behind the scenes, he introduced *One Man's Opinion* in early 1956 and later that year campaigned for the Independent party presidential nominee, T. Coleman Andrews. Soon after that unsuccessful political campaign, Welch began to plan a militantly conservative organization whose members would match the dedication and ideological zeal of the communists.[6] *American Opinion* was the first step in that direction. Welch hired a small staff, enlarged the board of editors, added several contributing editors, and solicited articles from prominent anticommunist authors. He also distributed a revised version of numbered copies of "The Politician" during the summer and fall of 1958. It was "an extremely confidential document," he explained, sent "only to a limited number of good friends and outstanding patriots."[7] Eleven of these men, including the erstwhile presidential candidate T. Coleman Andrews, joined Welch in early December 1958 for a two-day meeting in Indianapolis, Indiana, where they founded the John Birch Society.[8]

The new organization spread rapidly from its headquarters in Belmont, Massachusetts, during 1959 and 1960, finding its greatest success in the South, the Southwest and California, and the Upper Midwest. Successfully avoiding public exposure for nearly two years, the Birch Society quickly achieved a dominant position among the competing organizations emerging as the core of the radical Right. The success of the JBS was measured not by the size of its membership but by the influential role its members played in local and national politics. It both exploited and intensified the polarization in American society caused by revived tensions in the cold war and the conservative backlash against the civil rights movement. There were other stimuli, but the Birch Society organizers capitalized on these currents of discontent, answering with the themes of "less government, more individual responsibility, and a better world."

The Birch Society attracted an estimated 60,000 members during the early 1960s, when it found partisan opportunities in the Goldwater and Wallace movements. Political conflicts and ideological controversies reduced the membership to approximately 40,000 by the mid–1970s before the phenomenal growth of the New Right gave it a new stimulus. The Birch Society gained slightly in membership after the mid–1970s, but it lacked the organizational thrust and ideological vigor of its early years.

The circulation of *American Opinion* fluctuated with the changes in membership, since, aside from institutional subscribers, the members of the Birch Society and the subscribers to the magazine were virtually identical. Thus, generalizations about the characteristics of members of the JBS provide a profile of the principal readers of the magazine. Initially, the Birch Society attracted a predominantly middle-class membership with a high percentage of college graduates. As the organization grew, it attracted a broader cross section of social and class backgrounds, including small numbers of blacks and Jewish members. Religion was a factor, but it was not the dominant feature of membership. Welch, for example, had long before abandoned the Baptist faith of his boyhood for a more universalistic religious belief. Although a majority of the members of the Birch Society were Protestants, they were not solely evangelical or fundamentalist, and local chapters in the East and Midwest attracted a substantial number of Roman Catholics into their ranks. Political divisions were similar. A large percentage of members retained a tenuous loyalty to the Republican party, but there were significant blocs of Democrats and third-party supporters in large cities and throughout the South.

These social and political characteristics created a dilemma for other conservatives. "Birchers" often failed to cooperate and were an easy target for liberals, thus a liability for conservatives with whom they were often identified. Several fiery controversies ensued, particularly with William F. Buckley, Jr., and the *National Review* circle. A frustrated Buckley complained that the Birchers were afflicted collectively by the "psychosis of conspiracy."[9] There was, however, one important effect of these controversies that went virtually unnoticed. Without repudiating their leader, members of the JBS Council pressured Welch to reduce his work load. In response, he retained the title of editor of *American Opinion*, but relinquished much of the editorial responsibility to Scott Stanley, Jr.

American Opinion could not escape the controversy about the John Birch Society. Buckley testily labeled the magazine "paranoid and unpatriotic drivel." Welch, on the other hand, had described it as "America's foremost Conservative journal of current events" and claimed, as early as 1958, "that already we are being reprinted more than any other magazine of our size in America." "We still badly need a larger circulation," he admitted, "but at the end of *American Opinion*'s first year, all signs were encouraging."[10] Toward the end of 1960, Welch claimed a rate of increase for the John Birch Society approaching 2,000 members per month and an increase in paid subscriptions for *American Opinion* from 4,000 to 6,000 during the previous six months. Welch hoped that the five-dollar annual subscription rate would attract other readers, but *American Opinion*'s ties with the Birch Society were readily apparent, and few nonmembers subscribed.

During its first few years, *American Opinion*, with its uniformly dull blue cover and amateurish format, was more utilitarian than stylish. But after 1964, with artist Daniel Michael Canavan contributing portraits and scenes that graced its cover each month, *American Opinion* emerged as a slick, multicolored magazine with many illustrations and numerous advertisements. The advertisements reflected the general pattern of readership. Most were from small companies or family-owned businesses, particularly manufacturers and real estate firms. Book promotions from Western Islands Press, Welch's editorial column, "If You Want It Straight," pages of jokes, current quotations, a page of poetry edited by E. Merrill Root, and a book section, "Review of Reviews," by Revilo P. Oliver were regular features.

Welch exerted tight control over the content of *American Opinion*, which he published from an office adjacent to JBS headquarters in Belmont. He customarily printed only manuscripts "written to order," and during the early years, he took pride in the small staff and the close personal supervision he gave to the magazine. "All correspondence concerning the articles in it, much of the writing itself of these articles, and the layout and proofreading and everything else," he explained in 1960, "must be taken care of by this office."[11] With the aid of numerous volunteers, the central office also handled the paperwork for subscriptions, mailings, and reprints. This pattern changed after 1961 as the rapid growth of the Birch Society drew Welch increasingly into its political vortex. Publishing tasks grew more complex as changes in format and growth in circulation required more personnel and greater expenditures. Welch remained the arbiter of ideology, but managing editor Scott Stanley, Jr., relied increasingly on professional writers and an expanded staff of associate editors and contributing editors.

American Opinion attracted as contributors a volatile mixture of former McCarthyites, ethnic anticommunists, and writers alienated from *National Review* and *Human Events*. J. B. Matthews, William Schlamm, Hans Sennholz, Slobodan Draskovich, and Tom Anderson were among the earliest contributors to *American Opinion* and joined Kregeloh, Root, and Oliver as associate editors during the 1960s. Contributing editors shared not only an aggressive anticommunist ideology but similar academic and journalistic backgrounds. Columnist Westbrook Pegler had a brief and controversial association with *American Opinion*, while Medford Evans, Edwin McDowell, Hilaire du Berrier, historian Charles C. Tansill, former congressman Martin Dies, Sr., (D, Texas) and black journalist George S. Schuyler were frequent contributors. California Republican congressman and Birch Society official John Rousselot, conservative author Dan Smoot, and novelist Taylor Caldwell wrote for the magazine during the 1960s and 1970s.

Occasional controversies raised questions about Welch's claims of religious and racial toleration. Westbrook Pegler drew periodic charges of anti-Semitism for his monthly column begun in 1962, and Revilo P. Oliver aroused a similar reaction for his claims about a conspiracy behind the assassination of John F. Kennedy. Welch finally dismissed Pegler, and amid allegations of anti-Semitism

Oliver quit the magazine and resigned from the Birch Society in the mid–1960s.

Under Welch's guidance, the content of the magazine usually reflected current issues in American society and politics, but the emphasis could vary. From 1960 through 1965, articles in *American Opinion* shifted gradually from a preoccupation with international communism to a concern with domestic issues.[12] The escalation of the war in Vietnam reversed that trend, however. International topics regained primacy as Welch made increasing use of conspiracy theories to explain why the United States appeared to be losing the conflict. Having first opposed the introduction of American troops into combat roles in Vietnam (fearing, he explained, "a greater Korea") Welch by the summer of 1966 demanded an immediate and total victory in Vietnam.

Despite periodic shifts in emphasis, the writers in *American Opinion* followed a fairly consistent line of argument. Their dogged defense of laissez-faire economics matched the sharpness of their attacks against all aspects of internationalism and diplomatic accommodation with the Soviet Union. The defense of traditional moral values, religion, basic education, and law and order was standard fare in *American Opinion* long before the New Right adopted the issues. The emphasis shifted only slightly during the 1970s when numerous articles criticized sex education, organized labor, prison reform, the graduated income tax, and the federal reserve system, social security, Medicare, and secular humanism.[13] Populistic sentiment increased in the 1970s as many writers paired their support for individualism with antielitist themes. New versions of old conspiracy theories were common as writers shifted their attention from alleged dupes of communism to those public officials, international bankers, and corporation executives who willfully subordinated American interests to internationalism. They attempted to expose the alleged conspiratorial machinations of the Council on Foreign Relations, the Trilateral Commission, and the Bilderberg conferences of Atlantic Community political leaders and multinational corporate executives, whose members were believed to be in collusion with the communists.

The specter of international conspiracy was at the heart of Robert Welch's ideology, whether he was discussing communism or the eighteenth-century Order of the Illuminati. His books, speeches, and articles and editorials for *One Man's Opinion* and *American Opinion* embraced a simple, deterministic interpretation of history. Welch described history as a conflict between opposing economic and cultural systems that would end with only one triumphant. He believed that capitalism would survive only if Western leaders acted promptly to reject any form of collectivism. Causal factors were few in this interpretation. Welch left little room for luck or accident, believing that conscious decisions shaped the course of history. Thus, failure could only be blamed on rational acts and evil intentions. The source of Welch's belief in the role of conspiracy in history is unclear, but during the early 1960s he shifted his emphasis from communism to identify the Illuminati as the ultimate conspirators. Often using the euphemism "Insiders," he traced their influence in a direct line from the French Revolution to the communist revolutions of the twentieth century, suggesting that the Illuminati even controlled the communist states.

This fear of conspiracy permeated the pages of *American Opinion* from the start, and variations of the theme were prominent in articles by Welch, Oliver, Pegler, and, later, Gary Allen. Only conspiracy could explain why international communism had grown so dramatically in strength since World War II. The annual "Scoreboard" reports in *American Opinion* reinforced these charges. Welch introduced the "Scoreboard" feature in June 1958 and personally supervised it until giving Scott Stanley, Jr., that responsibility in 1961. The "Scoreboard" purported to show the percentage of "Estimated Conspiracy Influence" in more than one hundred countries. The twenty-fifth-anniversary "Scoreboard" in 1982, for example, estimated that the conspiracy influence in the United States had increased from 20–40 percent in the Eisenhower administration to 60–80 percent under Lyndon Johnson and had declined to 40–60 percent during the Reagan administration.[14]

Although these ideological themes remained constant, the style and appearance of *American Opinion* changed noticeably in the 1970s, when a younger generation of writers and academics began to replace the aging conservatives. Shaped by the 1960s, the Vietnam War, and Watergate, this younger generation adopted new conspiracy theories and applied the rhetorical techniques of the new journalism to the ideology of the Old Right. These changes in emphasis and style were most visible in the contrast between old-line anticommunists Tom Anderson and Medford Evans and their younger colleagues Gary Allen and Alan Stang. Anderson and Evans were contributing editors throughout the publishing history of *American Opinion*, while Allen and Stang were among the most prolific contributors to the magazine after 1970. Allen and international journalist Hilaire du Berrier joined the staff in 1969, followed by Stang and Harold Lord Varney in 1970 and Susan L. M. Huck in 1974.

Articles by the newer writers reflected the revived popularity of conspiracy themes in the period after the Vietnam War and Watergate. Allen, who graduated from Stanford University with a degree in history, had a varied career as a teacher, author, and screenwriter. His book *None Dare Call It Conspiracy* (1971) described the dominant role the Council on Foreign Relations and Rockefeller interests played in banking and international economics. Stang had a different background, but drew similar conclusions about the dominant influences in American political and economic life. A graduate of City College of New York with an M.A. from Columbia University, Stang worked as a business editor for Prentice-Hall, Inc., and as a television writer and producer before joining the staff of *American Opinion*.

Although there were differences in emphasis, *American Opinion* retained its basically anticommunist thrust for more than twenty-five years. During that time, the magazine also remained financially dependent on the John Birch Society; most of its subscribers and nearly all of its advertisers were members of the society. Although advertising revenue was substantial and reprints provided additional income, deficits were a constant problem. Volunteer help did not offset the expense of a large professional staff and high costs for production and mailing. Such costs could not be sustained when the society was losing members. Even the favorable political climate of the Reagan years failed to restore its vitality. The competing magazines of the New Right absorbed much of *American Opinion*'s potential readership, and the magazine survived only a few years beyond its twenty-fifth anniversary.

External challenges and internal changes affected the magazine and the JBS in the 1980s. Robert Welch retired as president of the John Birch Society in March 1983, barely one month after *American Opinion* celebrated its twenty-fifth anniversary. It had been a remarkably long career for such a controversial figure, but Welch's success served as a reminder about the significance of cold war politics and anticommunism in American life. Welch accepted the title of chairman emeritus of the society and continued to serve as titular editor of *American Opinion*. Although he was no longer an active participant in running either the society or the magazine, he remained their symbolic leader.

The John Birch Society suffered two sharp blows shortly after its twenty-fifth anniversary. Democratic congressman Larry P. McDonald of Georgia, who succeeded Welch as president of the JBS, died in the crash of the ill-fated Korean Airlines flight 007 in early September 1983, and Welch suffered a debilitating stroke a few months later, lingering in ill health until his death in January 1985. These events shook the society but did not destroy it. They did, however, lead to some significant changes in the JBS and in *American Opinion*. Thomas Hill, a relatively obscure member of the society, succeeded McDonald as leader of the JBS, and Welch's widow, Miriam Probst Welch, assumed the honorary post of assistant managing editor of *American Opinion*, with Scott Stanley, Jr., continuing as managing editor.

But this was only a temporary step. The JBS soon merged *American Opinion* with *Review of the News*, introducing the *New American* magazine in September 1985. This action reflected changes in leadership and strategy within the JBS as it sought to survive in competition with the New Right. Jeffrey St. John, who was appointed editor, described his new weekly magazine as a blend of news magazine and journal of opinion. St. John promised to follow the original goals of *American Opinion*, but the *New American* differed fundamentally from its predecessor in its composition and in its staff members and writers. Although the anticommunist legacy of Robert Welch remained alive, the new magazine focused on the social and religious issues of the 1980s.

Notes

1. Robert Welch, "Editor's Comment on January 2, 1958," *American Opinion* 1 (February 1958): 1 (hereinafter cited as *AO*).

2. Welch, "A Personal Page," One Man's Opinion 1 (February 1956): 1.

3. Welch, *The Road to Salesmanship* (New York, 1941), pp. 13–14.

4. Welch, John Birch Society Bulletin (1 April 1961), pp. 17–18.

5. See Welch, *The Life of John Birch: In the Story of One American Boy, the Ordeal of His Age* (Chicago, 1954), p. 119.

6. J. Allen Broyles, *The John Birch Society: Anatomy of a Protest* (Boston, 1964), p. 31.

7. Robert Welch to T. Coleman Andrews, 29 September 1958, T. Coleman Andrews Papers, Special Collections, University of Oregon (hereinafter cited as Andrews Papers).

8. The Blue Book of the John Birch Society is based on the original presentation

Welch made at this meeting. The Blue Book had gone through twenty–one printings by the spring of 1985.

    9. See George H. Nash, *The Conservative Intellectual Movement in America: Since 1945* (New York, 1976), pp. 292–93, and see also Ronald Lora, *Conservative Minds in America* (Chicago, 1971), pp. 257–58.

    10. Welch, "Confidential Report No. 1," 19 December 1958, Andrews Papers.

    11. Welch to Bryton Barron, 2 November 1960, Bryton Barron Papers, Special Collections, University of Oregon.

    12. See Seymour Martin Lipset and Earl Raab, *The Politics of Unreason: Right-Wing Extremism in America, 1790–1977*, 2nd ed. (Chicago, 1977), pp. 271–72.

    13. Russell G. Fryer, *Recent Conservative Political Thought: American Perspectives* (Washington, D.C., 1979), p. 172.

    14. "Scoreboard, 1982," *AO* 25 (July–August 1982): 97.

Information Sources

BIBLIOGRAPHY:

Bennett, David H. *The Party of Fear: The American Far Right from Nativism to the Militia Movement*. New York, 1995.

Broyles, J. Allen. *The John Birch Society: Anatomy of a Protest*. Boston, 1964.

Carter, Dan T. *The Politics of Rage: George Wallace, the Origins of the New Conservatism, and the Transformation of American Politics*. New York, 1995.

Epstein, Benjamin R. and Arnold Forster. *The Radical Right: Report on the John Birch Society and Its Allies*. New York, 1967.

Goldberg, Robert Alan. *Barry Goldwater*. New Haven, 1995.

———. *Grassroots Resistance: Social Movements in Twentieth Century America*. Belmont, California, 1991.

Lipset, Seymour Martin, and Earl Raab. *The Politics of Unreason: Right-Wing Extremism in America, 1790–1977*. 2nd ed. Chicago, 1977.

Stone, Barbara S. "The John Birch Society: A Profile." *Journal of Politics* 36 (February 1974): 184–97.

INDEXES: Each volume indexed; *Curr Bk Rev Cit*; *PAIS*; *Soc Sci Ind*.

REPRINT EDITIONS: Microform: UMI. Bound edition: UMI.

LOCATION SOURCES: Widely available.

Publication History

TITLE AND TITLE CHANGES: *American Opinion. An Informal Review*, 1958–1968; *American Opinion. A Conservative Review*, 1969–1985.

VOLUME AND ISSUE DATA: Volumes 1–28, February 1958–July–August 1985.

FREQUENCY OF PUBLICATION: Monthly, except July.

PUBLISHER: Robert Welch, Inc., Belmont, Massachusetts.

EDITORS: Robert Welch, February 1958–December 1983; Scott Stanley, Jr., December 1983–August 1985.

CIRCULATION: In 1965, about 35,400; in 1977, about 52,000.

Eckard V. Toy

Part Nine

INTELLECTUAL AND TRADITIONALIST JOURNALS

Few journals did more to promote conservatism as a movement of ideas than those examined in this part. The conservative thinkers who founded them performed many of the tasks that identify the intellectuals, even though several rejected that term as vigorously as they did *ideologue*—a partisan, they believed, committed more to inflexible, abstract principles than to human and historical realities. Because "ideas have consequences," in the words of Richard Weaver, one of the more evocative of southern traditionalists, care in their handling is a high obligation. Primarily interested in ideas, in study and reflection, the scholars, journalists, and intellectuals covered here were keenly aware of their need to influence the political world. They were not public policy intellectuals, however. Principles prevail over pragmatism, reflecting a respect for quality ideas that is less evident in laissez-faire, fundamentalist, and anticommunist journals, or in any that express the views of the religious Right.

Traditionalism jumps off the pages of these periodical publications—traditionalist, but not authoritarian. The first editorial of *Modern Age* set the standard: "By 'conservative' we mean a journal dedicated to conserving the best elements in our civilization; and those best elements are in peril nowadays. We confess...to a preference for the wisdom of our ancestors. [We] search for means by which the legacy of our civilization may be kept safe." Those legacies are mostly cultural, maintained in literature, philosophy, memoirs, religion, and other accreted materials. Much attention is given to the founders' vision for the new nation and to the tradition of political thought whose modern origins are grounded in opposition to the French Enlightenment and Revolution. Edmund Burke, articulator of an aristocratic, organicist, even vaguely theocratic philosophy, emerges as a hero in these pages; John Locke, who stands as the fountain of political thought in the United States, does not. Likewise, laissez-faire conservatives are in short supply, their atomistic economism found wanting by conservatives who see humans primarily as spiritual creatures, reflecting a superior side of human nature. The *University Bookman, Continuity,* and *Hillsdale Review* joined *Modern Age* squarely in the traditionalist camp; philosophical and theoretical issues predominated in their discussions. The *New Criterion* has fought a continuing battle for high standards, an unpoliticized literature, and the "tradition" of modernism. Harboring robust libertarian sympathies in their early years, the *Intercollegiate Review* and *National Review* nevertheless remained open to all varieties of conservatism. *Ideas,* closer to William F. Buckley, Jr., than to Russell Kirk, and preferring a Nixon-style conservatism, spoke for Jews who in opposition to liberalism moved to the right in the 1960s and 1970s.

One theme that provides unity of outlook is the consistent attack on various shades of liberalism, particularly the overly rationalist vision of reform that threatens the familiar relationships and loyalties of private life, and the genial acceptance of a pragmatism that at times masks a failure to deal with the roots of social and economic problems. Too often, argues the conservative, liberals pursue a democracy not of individuals but of groups—ethnic or racial minorities, women, gays, the poor—known as "the people." The *National Review* has made numerous attempts to defend conservative values in politics, literature, and esthetics, whereas *Modern Age*'s content is more philosophical than topical, focused on cultural and historical developments rather than current politics. The publications in this part provided a meeting place for conservatives who welcomed antiliberal, proconservative journals that are intellectually respectable and not reactionary. Mainstream conservatives applauded when the editors of the *National Review,* uneasy over its right-wing extremism and appalled by its leader's irresponsible allegation that President Dwight David Eisenhower was a communist, read the John Birch Society out of the conservative movement. Paranoid and lunatic pronouncement could only damage the conservative cause.

Conservative hostility to liberalism raised underlying suspicions that conservative thought is not truly compatible with the tenets of democracy. Eventually discernment carried the day. If democracy means unlimited popular participation in government, majority rule, and a belief that freedom equates with the effective power of choice, including political control of the economy to bring advantage to minorities, then many conservatives are not democratic. If democracy is defined as individual rights, private enterprise, market capitalism, limited government, and a belief that the main threat to liberty is unchecked egalitarianism, then most conservatives are solidly democratic. Few conservatives adhere to every specific in the latter formulation, just as few liberals adhere to all of the former. It is a question of which democratic norms one establishes as intrinsic to the good society. At stake are questions of equality, assimilation and pluralism, and entree into meaningful public discourse and politics.

Among those instrumental in the resurgence of conservative thought after World War II—and providing it with a coherence that it did not then enjoy—none were more influential than Russell Kirk and William F. Buckley, Jr. Both commanded national attention, Kirk with his stream of books and lectures, and Buckley with his linguistic talents and editorship of *National Review,* which soon became the principal journal of conservatism in the United States. After military service in World War II, Kirk taught history at Michigan State University and pursued a doctorate at St. Andrews University in Scotland. Within a few years the young historian branched out into half a dozen fields as social and literary critic, political theorist, and novelist, to become one of our culture's most accomplished men of letters. Founder of *Modern Age* and *University Bookman*, he also played an important role in other journals. It was Kirk's path-breaking *The Conservative Mind* (1953), however, that established his reputation. In it he presented readers with an intellectual battleground on which the Burkean philosophy is battered by its enemies, whether liberal, utilitarian, or socialist. Industrialization's depredations on old customs and habits encouraged experts and statists, taking wing from an imperial democratic spirit, to advance during the Progressive and New Deal eras legislation that reflected a class bias: the graduated income tax, the inheritance tax, measures to control private property, and support of the labor movement. By the end of Kirk's remarkable book, the reader having his first go at intellectual warfare might well wonder, How could it be otherwise? Buckley, himself sometimes named as first among the movers of modern conservatism, has said that "if any one book may be credited with inaugurating the modern conservative intellectual movement in America, it is Russell Kirk's *The Conservative Mind*."

If Kirk was the better scholar, Buckley was preeminent in disseminating the message of conservatism. The *National Review* established his influence, but his personality, caustic wit, and acute analytical faculties won for him an audience beyond the conservative field that Kirk did not always enjoy. Critics suggested that Buckley's work suffered from his heavy engagement in current events, yet he succeeded in linking conservative doctrine with politics and policy. He pleased (and surprised) some of his readers with *Four Reform: A Guide for the 70's*, which offered concrete and positive recommendations on four issues that separate liberals and conservatives: welfare, taxation, criminal justice, and education. No longer the *enfant terrible* of *God and Man at Yale* or ideologue of *McCarthy and His Enemies*, Buckley urged his fellow conservatives to transcend knee-jerk status-quoism and support reforms that would be "procedural rather than substantive." Having once thrived on controversy, he had become more thoughtful and less political, more an explorer than a preacher. A major datum of this part is that many of its leading lights exhibited an ample capacity for growth. Several began their careers defending an inviolate private property, local custom, and a classical liberal view, then mellowed through years of controversy and national transformation to become friends of civil rights and supporters of a modified welfare system.

Word is due the Intercollegiate Society of Individualists (renamed the Intercollegiate Studies Institute in 1966) for its creative presence in the postwar conservative revival. Founded by Frank Chodorov in 1953 (with William F. Buckley, Jr., as president), the society, in the words of George Nash, became "extremely influential as a clearinghouse of conservative publications and as a coordinator of the conservative intellectual movement." Despite its origins in the soil of libertarian philosophy, the ISI today publishes *Modern Age*, *Continuity*, the *Intercollegiate Review*, and the *Political Science Reviewer*. It also sustained the

Hillsdale Review during its existence as a student newspaper, a tradition it continues through the Collegiate Network, a program that supports student publications championing Western values, limited government, and free market economics. Regrettably, the limitations of space prevent coverage of other student publications, such as the *Beacon* (Dartmouth), the *Clemson Spectator*, and the *Georgetown Academy*. The ISI in addition is active on college campuses, sponsoring lectures, conferences, and fellowships. A remarkable number of young intellectuals have begun their personal libraries with books that the ISI makes available to members at substantially reduced prices.

National Review
1955–

Conservatism after World War II found a powerful journalistic outlet in the *National Review*. Founded by William F. Buckley, Jr., in 1955, five years after he graduated from Yale, the polemical but decidedly intellectual *National Review* soon emerged as the major journal of conservative opinion in America. Begun as a weekly but published biweekly since 1958, its circulation has risen to 175,000 copies, a remarkable number when noting that it is aimed first and foremost at opinion makers, and only then the *au courant* public.

No other journal in American history comes so close to constituting a conservative who's who. In the first years, its masthead included L. Brent Bozell, James Burnham, John Chamberlain, Whittaker Chambers, Frank Chodorov, Willmoore Kendall, and Frank S. Meyer as editors or associates. Numerous intellectuals of academic standing appeared in the early years of *National Review*, including Guy Davenport, Medford Evans, M. Stanton Evans, Will Herberg, Hugh Kenner, Russell Kirk, Thomas Molnar, Gerhart Niemeyer, Richard Weaver, F. D. Wilhelmsen, and Garry Wills. Later would come Wick Allison, Tom Bethell, Richard Brookhiser, Brian Crozier, Jeffrey Hart, Charles Kesler, Forrest McDonald, and Joseph Sobran. Even this impressive listing hardly suggests the dozens of others who have contributed to the success of *National Review* through the years.

Nor did any other conservative journal list as many ex-leftists on its roster. Meyer, Chambers, and Schlamm were former members of the Communist party; Burnham, an ex-Trotskyist, once served as an editor of *Partisan Review*. Max Eastman, editor of the radical *Masses* journal during World War I, for many years had been a fervent believer in the Bolshevik Revolution. John Chamberlain and John Dos Passos, though never communists, had been radical critics sympathetic to left-wing causes, and Suzanne La Follette, managing editor of Albert J. Nock's *Freeman* in the 1920s, had served as secretary of the Trotsky Defense Committee in the 1930s. As with many others after the depression decade, they let go the dream of revolutionary brotherhood and repented their liaison with left-wing causes. Upon their loss of innocence after negotiating a stormy pilgrimage to conservatism, remorse stung them into truculent criticism of communism and liberalism, which they believed to be of the same metaphysical essence.

Unlike many of his colleagues, William F. Buckley, Jr., acquired his conservative views at an early age. He was born in 1925 into a Roman Catholic family with ten children. His father, William F. Buckley, Sr., a self-made oil millionaire, built an estate worth an estimated $15 million to $25 million before his death in 1958. A good friend of the free-market libertarian Albert Jay Nock, the senior Buckley passed on to his son a rigid conservative ideology based on free enterprise and Social Darwinian doctrines. Private tutors directed young Buckley's early education, and he attended St. Thomas More School and St. John's in England before completing his secondary education at Millbrook School in Millbrook, New York. After spending two years in the army during World War II, he entered Yale University and graduated with honors in 1950. With the publication of his first book, *God and Man at Yale*, the following year, Buckley entered the ranks of embattled conservatives. Since then he has authored numerous other books, lectured, debated, headed various committees, visited campuses as a conservative guru, hosted a television show, *Firing Line*, and appeared in newspaper editorial pages via his syndicated column, "On the Right." He edited the *National Review* until his retirement in 1988, when he acquired a new title, editor in chief, and more recently, president and editor at large.

Irked by the moderate, middle-of-the-road conservatism of the Eisenhower administration and wishing to challenge media dominance by the liberal intelligentsia, Buckley and associates laid plans to publish a new journal. In his publisher's statement for the first issue (19 November 1955), Buckley wrote that the *National Review* "stands athwart history, yelling Stop, at a time when no one is inclined to do so."[1] Not all, he hoped, had yet accommodated themselves to the New Deal. In a "Magazine's Credenda," the editors listed several articles of faith: that the growth of government "must be fought relentlessly"; that free economic competition "is indispensable to liberty and material progress"; that the greatest crisis of the era is "the conflict between the Social Engineers who seek to adjust mankind to conform with scientific utopias, and the disciples of Truth, who defend the organic moral order." Communism, they added, is "the century's most blatant force of 'satanic utopianism,' and coexistence with it is unacceptable."[2]

The early *National Review* was antistatist and embraced many of the ideas of classical liberalism. Statism encouraged malingering and abuse, and made individuals insensitive when they became convinced that employers underwrite social security. It is fatal to the habits of free people. Social security, federal subsidies to farmers, and the protection of labor found little or no support. Understandably *National Review*'s favorite economists have been Friedrich A. Hayek, Ludwig von Mises, Wilhelm Roepke, and Milton Friedman, who in scores of books and articles have explained the virtues of free-market economics.

During four decades the *National Review* has defended capitalism, competition, and private property. All serve liberty by providing a shield against big government.

Allocating resources with comparative efficiency, the market also reduces the number of issues to be resolved in the political arena. Private property also supports the family—for conservatives, the basic unit of society—by surrounding it with an area of independent action. All this the journal strongly defends, yet if space is the measurement, its central interests lie elsewhere. The editors have understood (if not fully accepted) the force of Whittaker Chambers's argument about the profoundly anticonservative consequences of free-market capitalism: endless change, innovation and cultural novelty have taken a serious toll on small towns, small farms, and traditional morality. "Neither an individual nor a society," writes editor John O'Sullivan, "could subsist on a total diet of change and competition." It is this sensibility that lies behind the frequent expression of concern for community rootedness, cultural cohesion, family values, and the foundations of our moral nature.[3]

Serene though it would be to remain purely antistatist, only the state could control big steel to prevent it from obstructing the market. Only the state could counter twentieth-century totalitarianism and protect against foreign threats to American interests. Although differences existed on the editorial staff—Frank Meyer, for example, wished to repeal the New Deal system before it acquired prescriptive status, making it still more difficult to root out—Buckley himself could never fully endorse the views of his friend Frank Chodorov, who, in writing *One Is a Crowd* (1952) and *The Income Tax: The Root of All Evil* (1954), took an antistatist position on every important political and economic issue in the postwar period.

Even in its early years it was clear that *National Review* represented a distinct advance in the conservative tradition of William Graham Sumner, Andrew Carnegie, and Albert Jay Nock. Although Buckley spoke as a radical conservative in his publisher's statement, meaning that he stood against the welfare state and would support efforts to bring about the defeat of world communism, it was not an absolutist stand against all government power. When *National Review* in 1964 carried recommendations for a possible Goldwater administration, nearly every contributor stated that the past could not be undone—four years of a Goldwater administration might bring little change. That admission reflected political reality, but it also suggested that Buckley's journal was conceived as a holding operation to limit further government encroachment; hoping to brake the growing welfare state, he and the majority of his colleagues never expected its wholesale repudiation.

The *National Review* in its origins was an unstable compound of traditionalists, libertarians, and ex-communists. No one addressed this problem more consistently than Frank Meyer, one of the journal's abler theoreticians. A libertarian at heart and deeply appreciative of the individualist tradition represented by Albert Jay Nock, Meyer argued that modern conservatism must blend its two polar strains—libertarianism and traditionalism. Traditionalists, drawing heavily on Edmund Burke but leaning toward Joseph de Maistre as well, stress the primacy of value, virtue, and order; they find comfort in transcendent truths. Their social ideal is community (a modern equivalent of the Greek *polis*) in which citizens find freedom by adhering to social customs and religious truths. Russell Kirk and Peter Viereck wrote in this tradition, although each represented a distinct and separate subdivision that Meyer failed to recognize. On the other hand, the libertarians, drawing heavily on classical liberalism and the early John Stuart Mill, placed great reliance on individual freedom and the innate importance of the individual. The free individual who seeks community finds it in small voluntary organizations, not in the large conformity-conscious groups of mass society that impose their ideology and structures on people.

The libertarian, opposing the collectivist, amoral wave of the present, honors reason rather than tradition and prescription. Wary of the libertarian flirtation with abstract ideology, the traditionalist recoils into an extreme defense of custom and prescription, setting tradition against reason instead of employing "reason in the context of continuing tradition."[4] Both traditions are useful, Meyer wrote. The libertarians of the nineteenth century admirably defended individual freedom. They erred ontologically, however, in not anchoring freedom in the nature of being. Their utilitarianism offered a poor philosophical support for freedom, for it undermined the authority of conscience. The nineteenth-century traditionalists, on the other hand, were philosophically sound but too cavalier about personal freedom. Too quick to support perceived virtues with force, they often substituted the authoritarianism of human institutions for the authority of God.

The intellectual task of restating philosophical and political truth became, in the hands of Meyer, an eclectic process. Although the tension between the libertarian and traditionalist heritage supports individual freedom when kept in a healthy balance, that balance is difficult to achieve, particularly in a revolutionary age when natural conservatism cannot adequately guard the established order. Therefore modern conservatism must become conscious in order to conserve "not simply whatever happens to be the established conditions of a few years or a few decades, but the consensus of his civilization, of his country, as that consensus over the centuries has reflected truth derived from the very constitution of being."[5]

On the confusing role of freedom in the doctrines of classical liberalism, Meyer argued a controversial thesis wherein freedom in the moral realm is understood as a means, while in the political realm it functions as an end, its achievement there permitting a genuine search for our proper end, which is virtue or moral fulfillment. If traditionalists and libertarians could unite in this understanding, Meyer believed that they could also unite in opposition to communism and other forms of collectivism. Meyer's artful intellectual exercise—fusionism, as others called it—provided a tentative synthesis but was not ultimately compelling. Some saw only chaos and competing theories of human nature in conflict. Others who opposed gigantic statism nevertheless recognized government as a useful tool to contain the possible tyrannies of technology, bureaucracy, and large corporate structures.[6]

During the 1950s it was as a libertarian conservative that Buckley carried on his abrasive polemics against modern welfare state liberalism. The most persevering of social historians in documenting liberalism's shortcomings, Buckley scored points in challenging liberalism's breezy assumption that big government poses little threat to freedom, its genial acceptance of a pragmatism that often masks a failure to deal with the roots of social and economic problems, its sanguine acceptance of technology, and its belief that "end of ideology" politics marked the highest stage of democratic eschatology. How could this public philosophy, rationalist in spirit, collectivist in principle, and relativist in values, mount a serious challenge to the totalitarian threat to Western civilization?

Buckley's animosity toward liberalism derived at least in part from his belief that modern liberalism rests on a democracy not of individuals but of groups—the poor, blacks, labor, ethnic minorities—known as "the people." Such leveling degraded the person to a statistical number, more an object of manipulation than of respect. He argued in sonorous tones that liberal democracy had become a mere procedural device based on the absolute value of universal suffrage. Interested only in method—"the fleshpot of those who live in metaphysical deserts"—and without enduring vision, the liberal electorate often votes to curtail its own freedom, thus deepening repression. In a society that is truly free, *the people would cherish a self-denying ordinance under which they would never use their political power in such fashion as to diminish the area of human freedom.*[7] Presumably only conservative devices such as revelation, church, custom, and family would restrain people from negating their liberties.

The struggle of blacks for equal rights illuminated Buckley's attitude toward reform. In its early years *National Review* followed an editorial policy of encouraging southern efforts to circumvent the 1954 *Brown* decision, "one of the most brazen acts of judicial usurpation in our history."[8] After *National Review* printed several articles that seemed to question the abilities of blacks, advocated a form of separate development, or demanded that the government not encourage integration, some critics called him a sophisticated racist. Yet Buckley and *National Review* never trafficked in the race hatred of rightist bigots, and he has come out strongly against those who hint at an alleged genetic inferiority of black people. "There are no scientific grounds for assuming congenital Negro disabilities. The problem is not biological, but cultural and educational."[9] One would imagine this problem to be soluble. In a debate in 1961 with Yale chaplain William Sloane Coffin, Buckley could see no immediate solution to the race problem in the United States. Even if there were wide agreement that Americans had committed a great wrong, it did not follow that one should use governmental force to correct it. Government could not, he argued, reduce the substance of segregation; only time and circumstance could do that.

Voicing the conservative belief that rational solutions do not exist for all problems (historically a major point of difference with liberalism) brought liberal condemnation of *National Review*. Although its editor never relinquished this belief, the social revolution of the 1960s drove him to adopt a friendlier view of the civil rights movement. When Martin Luther King, Jr., died of an assassin's bullet in 1968, *National Review* took the opportunity to celebrate his advocacy of nonviolent social change, saying that "he was an apostle of peace" who "died to make men free." Thus did mainstream conservatives incorporate the civil rights movement into the worthy traditions of the nation.[10] Two years later in an article entitled "Why We Need a Black President in 1980," Buckley stated that the election of a black president would reassure black people that they could finally participate in institutions from which they were excluded because of color. It would convey to Americans the same message that John Kennedy's victory had in 1960: that the honored tradition of American idealism was still intact. Perhaps it would even serve as one form of white expiation, the election of a black president marking a bright day for Americans who, "seeking to alleviate the sorrow of the few, lighten the burden of the many."[11]

Despite the *National Review*'s reluctance to harness political power to social reform, it has always shown great interest in national politics. It experienced progressive disillusionment during the 1950s when the Republican party failed to cut taxes and roll back the social and economic programs of the New Deal. Forgetting the principles of Senator Robert Taft (R, Ohio), it now wanted to "Caesarize" Ike. Yet Eisenhower's program, dubbed "progressive conservatism," was "undirected by principle, unchained to any coherent ideas as to the nature of man and society, uncommitted to any estimate of the nature or potential of the enemy." On election eve 1956, Buckley was not enthusiastic about Eisenhower. "I like Ike," he said, should be changed to "I prefer Ike." Listening to the "left-wing idealogues" Walter Reuther and Arthur Schlesinger, Jr., made the Republican party of "measured socialism" look better than it was. Although Buckley could perceive little philosophical disagreement between the candidates, there was enough difference in mood to warrant supporting the president. Vote for Eisenhower, he suggested, if you must, "but let [us] for heaven's sake not join in the festivities."[12]

Hardly a year had passed before Buckley called on Republicans to repudiate their president. Eisenhower's "sin against reality" was that he could not take communism seriously because he believed the *Communist Manifesto* was mostly campaign rhetoric inspired by the same degree of urgency as, perhaps, his party's platform. By Eisenhower's inattention, internal security had "lapsed to a state worse than that under Mr. Truman." Labor barons were stronger, freedom more restricted. The next time the president came on a triumphant entry into New York, Buckley quipped, he would be "lurking in the shadows, and anyone who reads my lips will know that I am muttering a subversive prayer to our Lord to grant Washington another leader, and Gettysburg another squire."[13] Premier Nikita Khrushchev's visit to the United States in 1959, deplored by nearly everyone connected with the *National Review*, ended what they believed to be a decade of political, even moral disasters: an "indefensible" peace in Korea, the mess in Laos, the rape of Hungary, the Chinese consolidation of power, and "pernicious" cultural exchange with the Soviet Union.

Unwilling to endorse Vice-President Richard Nixon during the 1960 presidential campaign, the *National Review* soon urged a Goldwater candidacy in 1964.[14] His victory would ensure, it said, concern for "the forgotten American," a phrase that became popular in a subsequent Nixon campaign. The domestic objectives of Senator Barry Goldwater (R, Arizona) and the *National Review* were similar, but it was in foreign policy, the subject of much heat during the 1964 presidential campaign, that the journal and the Arizona senator found themselves in closest agreement. In the introduction to his *Why Not Victory?* Senator Goldwater credited several members of the *National Review* team for help on the book. He also acknowledged that L. Brent Bozell was "the guiding hand" behind his earlier book,

The Conscience of a Conservative. In March 1961, the journal published a tough cold war essay by Goldwater that followed nearly to the letter James Burnham's regular columns on "The Third World War." Goldwater's analysis rested on two assumptions. First, the ultimate objective of American foreign policy should be "to help establish a world in which there is the largest possible measure of freedom and justice and peace and material prosperity; and in particular...that these conditions be enjoyed by the people of the United States." Second, these conditions were unattainable "without the prior defeat of world communism." Other issues in world politics must defer to victory over communism, attained by peace if possible, by war if necessary. If the Soviets threatened to intervene in some distant land, the United States should issue an ultimatum forbidding Soviet intervention and, if rejected, quickly move a mobile task force equipped with nuclear weapons to the scene of the conflict. The Soviets would "probably" comply with the ultimatum. If not, the responsibility for the ensuing war would rest with the Soviets.[15]

Having introduced Goldwater's article as a program of anticommunism "based on Third World War realities," *National Review* editors could hardly reproach the Arizona senator for his truculence. Buckley agreed, adding that for men of stout heart, nuclear warfare held little more terror than conventional warfare: "If it is right that a single man is prepared to die for a just cause, it is right that an entire civilization be prepared to die for a just cause." Like many on the radical Right, Buckley appeared to belittle the consequences of nuclear war. Rejecting the "Better Dead Than Red" formula because it listed "non-exclusive alternatives," he offered *National Review* readers a revised formula: "Better to face the chance of being dead, than the certainty of being Red. And if we die? We die."[16]

This austere sensibility reflected a nearly religious view of *National Review* editors that communism was a moral enormity, ethically evil, and behaviorally wicked. It invested the midcentury with profound historical and metaphysical meaning, which Buckley, in his first book in 1951, had defined as a crisis between Christianity and atheism. His friend and later editorial colleague Whittaker Chambers had written that his "witness" was to testify that in communism was focused "the concentrated evil of our time." For expressing this outlook in the political arena, Senator Joe McCarthy (R, Wisconsin) enjoyed strong support in the pages of *National Review*. On the senator's death in 1957, William Schlamm eulogized McCarthy for having recognized "the central truth of his age: that his country, his faith, his civilization was at war with communism."[17]

The defeat of Goldwater left the *National Review* the critical task of confronting the political and moral culture of the 1960s. The editors saw it much as W. H. Auden had seen the 1930s: "another low dishonest decade."[18] In a retrospective they argued that the pseudo-Homeric rhetoric of President Kennedy's inaugural address had not defined the decade that followed, for the liberal wing of the Democratic party betrayed his words. The Bay of Pigs, the Berlin Wall, and the deplorable execution of the war in Vietnam gave little evidence of American determination to defend freedom. Perhaps the most crucial event of the decade, Buckley noted on another occasion, was "the philosophical acceptance of co-existence by the West."[19]

That tacit understanding largely governed the American conduct of war in Southeast Asia. Editors and contributors alike understood Vietnam as a logical expression of cold war rivalry in which North Vietnam was the latest flashpoint of a worldwide conspiracy. Of little importance in itself, Vietnam as a symbol of American resolve meant everything. From 1964 onward, *National Review* repeatedly highlighted the irrepressible dilemma: "accept defeat and withdraw, or expand the war."[20] In a series of "Third World War" columns, senior editor James Burnham advanced what amounted to the journal's official position. Months before President Lyndon Johnson committed ground troops, Burnham argued that Vietnam was part of America's western strategic frontier, a great arc that ran from Alaska through Japan, South Korea, and the Philippines to Australia. Should South Vietnam go communist, other countries would follow. With pressure mounting on Japan and "Free China," the United States would then draw back to Hawaii and the West Coast. Having fought a war just two decades earlier to prevent that, what sense did it make to retreat now?

In the following year, with the United States more deeply involved and the war in stalemate, Burnham feared that America had lost the will to win. With a large commitment of troops politically unpopular, the United States would need to use technology and more advanced equipment, bringing to bear on the enemy "massive, crushing concentrations of power." Given the continued stalemate, the exotic terrain, the inability of the Americans to rely on superior manpower, and the critical fact that North Vietnam could not retaliate in kind, it might be time to use "the chemical, biological and nuclear devices at our disposal." Although not a demand, this mid-1960s suggestion signaled the length that the most important *National Review* editor, after Buckley, was prepared to go to achieve victory. Regardless of previous national interest analyses, our growing involvement had made Vietnam important. To walk out now would inaugurate a sequence of nations falling like dominoes to communism. At the conclusion of the Tet offensive in 1968, Burnham found himself where he had been four years earlier: if U.S. leaders could not or would not settle the issue by force, "isn't it time to get out?"[21]

At the close of the war, Norman B. Hannah of the U.S. State Department argued that the war was lost in Washington. "We were not evil," he wrote. "Our motive was honorable—to help a friendly country defend itself against attack. But there was a fatal hiatus between the end and the means." The United States had permitted ambiguity to exist on the nature of the war—politically, psychologically, and militarily. Neither the Johnson nor the Nixon administrations had determined conclusively whether the problem consisted of a North Vietnamese attack on the South or an indigenous insurgency in South Vietnam. In confusion, Washington split the difference, and "Hanoi's infiltrated aggression was treated as the insurgency it pretended to be." Instead of trying to defeat the enemy, the United States sought merely to "convince the enemy he would be unable to win."[22] This war of attrition and gradual escalation amounted to a fight for time instead of land. But time brought increasing casualties, a large, vocal antiwar movement, and a president weakened by Watergate. The war was lost.

However humiliating the war, it alone did not concern the *National Review* in the 1960s. It was the entire social and cultural milieu, especially the counterculture—smug and morally superior, yet hucksterish at heart. Youth cult, drugs, skin flicks, phony Eastern mysticism, the betrayal of academic standards, and what Frank Meyer termed a "principled hatred of civility" reflected a society in revolt against itself, against "internalized discipline" and middle-class values. The essence of the counterculture that so intrigued both partisans and critics was really "anticulture."[23]

On the political-economic front, Lyndon Johnson's Great Society conjured up the specter of a socialist state in control of education and social welfare. Buckley remarked at the *National Review*'s tenth-anniversary dinner that although politics "is the preoccupation of the quarter-educated," he must "curse this century above all things" for making it impossible to avoid politics.[24] The Great Society would not ignore us. The Supreme Court ruling on school prayer, pressure for busing and abortion on demand, the early examples of affirmative action, and the deepening infatuation with statistical technique and egalitarian theory constituted the most serious American attack on individuals and their freedoms that yet had been launched in this century.

Even as it challenged the reigning presuppositions of Great Society liberalism, the journal was undergoing positive change. It opened itself to more generous appraisals of the future and the conservative prospect. It saw promising signs rising amid the culture it criticized: technological prowess, the space program, the decline of Students for a Democratic Society, the growing economic reputation of Milton Friedman, and most significant, the auspicious omens arising out of the failed Goldwater campaign of 1964. Senator Goldwater had placed on the table the central issues of subsequent presidential campaigns: law and order, decentralization, welfare reform, and consideration of the moral foundations of America.[25] The discussion of these issues had brought greater attention to the journal, for much of the public shared with *National Review* the same enemies: social upheaval, urban riots, campus revolts, and the peace movement.

By the early 1970s *National Review* had become an excellent journal and the most influential voice of mainstream conservatism, working at the center of a movement to promote a Republican majority in American politics. Having begun as a right-wing journal, the *National Review* became less rigid, less radical, and more sophisticated. As it rid mainstream conservatism of anti-Semitism and the John Birch Society, it moved closer to middle America and became more receptive on the issue of race, having come to appreciate the positive work of Martin Luther King, Jr., in channeling the forces of social change. The masthead now carried a solid majority who recognized that the federal government had a valid role to play, though far short of Great Society dimensions.

The most crucial reason for the growing popularity of the *National Review* was the creative talent among its staff and large stable of contributors. Editor Buckley, once seen as an angry young man, by 1970 had become a national institution. For two decades his journal's tough-minded critique of Democratic (and Republican) foreign policy drew on the work of the urbane professor of realpolitik, James

Burnham. The author of several cold war polemics, he was, according to Buckley, "the dominant intellectual influence in the development of this journal."[26] Jeffrey Hart, whose service to the *National Review* runs to three decades, developed into a sensitive editor and soon joined Burnham as a senior editor. The Dartmouth professor, author of two revisionist studies of recent political and cultural history, came with an independent reputation and moved smoothly into the journal's circles. When Buckley was out of town and health problems slowed the contribution of Burnham, it was Hart who parceled out editorial assignments. During the 1970s he and Burnham would be joined by two literature majors: Joseph Sobran, whose wit and intelligence elevated conservative conversation, and Richard Brookhiser, promoted to senior editor at the age of twenty-three. Both brought the voices of a younger generation to bear on editorial matters.

Two others were crucial in the long history of the *National Review*. Priscilla Buckley, sister of the editor, took over as managing editor in 1959 and served for over a quarter-century with efficiency and good humor. In 1986 she joined Hart and Sobran as a senior editor, with Richard Brookhiser, then Linda Bridges, becoming managing editor. One of editor Buckley's finest decisions came in mid-1957 when he asked William Rusher, a "quintessential Republican," to become publisher. For more than thirty years the methodical, disciplined one-time associate counsel to the Senate Internal Security Subcommittee brought order to the journal's financial affairs, even though it continued to lose money. In addition, he attained eminence in his own right, becoming an influential Republican activist, columnist, and host of *The Advocate*, a public television discussion program. For many years the *National Review*'s staff has been among the most talented in the history of American journalism.

What conservatives loved and liberals found irritating were the journal's editorial paragraphs: short and often deftly worded introductions to the news and the supposed "lunacies of the fortnight." Though written with panache, in turns witty and insightful, then flippant and supercilious, even some of the faithful found too much levity in them. Yet often the humor appealed to all—for example, the brief notice in the second issue after the Kennedy assassination: "The Editors of *National Review* regretfully announce that their patience with President Lyndon B. Johnson is exhausted."[27]

Through the years the journal has featured various regular departments, among them Burnham's "Third World War," which became "The Protracted Conflict"; a book section headed initially by Willi Schlamm and then Willmoore Kendall, Frank Meyer, and George Will, among others; Russell Kirk's "From the Academy"; a "Letter from Washington" column written by many persons; "On the Right," which featured three of Buckley's syndicated columns; and Jeffrey Hart's "Ivory Foxhole." The journal on many occasions has devoted issues to special topics, among them "Nixon's Trip to China," "The Achievements of Will Herberg," "Nuclear Power," "Energy," "Moral Clarity in the Nuclear Age," "Reagan's Second Term," and "James Burnham." That many young writers gained their early writing experience with the *National Review* underscores its influence; among them were Joan Didion, Garry Wills, Renata Adler, George Will, Richard Whalen, and Joe Sobran.

The presence of cartoonists and effective blue-border cover designs also distinguish *National Review*. During the first decade, C. D. Batchelor contributed a regular biweekly cartoon, usually on a political topic. After a dull, experimental period in the 1950s, the journal's covers have become works of art, smartly mixing photographs with news items and impressionistic design. One in the late 1960s featured a graveyard with four tombstones representing the New Deal, the Fair Deal, the New Frontier, and the Great Society. The caption: "After Liberalism, What?" Another in the mid-1980s depicted a flat earth situated in a dark, frozen wasteland, with Carl Sagan falling off the end of the world.[28] (The lead story offered a critique of the Cornell professor's scenario of "nuclear winter.")

The journal's poet laureate through four decades has been W. H. von Dreele, who began his association in 1960 with "Invictus, 1960":

> Whenever I become depressed
> About my presidential quest,
> I turn (aghast) from Gallup polls
> To Galbraith, Schlesinger, and Bowles.
> When opposition runners tweak
> My wife, because she's ultra-chic,
> There's nothing that I know consoles
> Like Galbraith, Schlesinger, and Bowles.
> When they, in jowly vowels, hoot
> Unpleasantly at father's loot,
> I thank the Harvard bell that tolls
> For Galbraith, Schlesinger—and Bowles.[29]

The growth in the number of subscribers through the years reflects in concrete terms the journal's high quality. From a first printing of 7,500 in November 1955, circulation increased to 30,000 in 1960, to 91,000 in 1980, and then to 175,000 in 1998.[30]

Secure as the premier journal of conservative opinion, and enjoying the return of a Republican presidency, the *National Review* nevertheless found itself on a rocky road during the 1970s. It defended most of Nixon's policies vigorously (though both editors and contributors voiced doubts about the president's commitment to conservative principles), supported the dictatorial Pinochet regime that had seized power in Chile, took every opportunity to remark on the moral stature of Alexandr Solzhenitsyn when the Soviet Union expelled the Russian novelist, and supported the Panama Canal Treaty, though not without dissent within the journal's family.[31] More often than not, however, the journal stood in opposition, criticizing Nixon's imposition of wage and price controls, the SALT treaty, the Nixon-Kissinger policy of détente with the Soviet Union, and, faithful to the regimen of market economics, the Chrysler bailout.

Two events caused special alarm. One was President Nixon's trip to China in 1972. Unalterably opposed to the coming rapprochement, Buckley nevertheless joined the entourage of reporters who followed the president to China. In several angry reports riddled with sarcasm, Buckley outlined for his readers a staggering capitulation to the masters of Peking. Forfeiting any "remaining sense of moral mission in the world," we seemed to care not a whit about the Maoist slaughter of the recent past—the counterpart of the Great Terror under Joseph Stalin. Toasting the Chinese leaders and clinking glasses with numerous lesser Chinese officials, Nixon may be "the most deracinated American who ever lived and exercised great power."[32]

The second event was Watergate, which troubled all conservatives, particularly in its electoral implications. Several members of the *National Review* circle were personally friendly with the president, Vice-President Spiro Agnew, and White House aides. In a friendship dating to their Central Intelligence Agency days together, Buckley also was close to E. Howard Hunt, then a member of the White House "plumbers" team. The editors held endless debates on the journal's proper stance, arguing publicly that Watergate was a trivial incident that fell well within the American tradition of political tricks. Considered objectively, the attempted lynching of President Nixon was a struggle for power in which the old liberal establishment and its media allies tried to forestall the new conservative majority that was emerging in the country.[33] Privately, however, Buckley, Burnham, and Rusher were troubled.

George Will, who in 1972 began writing the "Letter from Washington" column (signed by "CATO"), regularly irritated conservative loyalists with analyses that portrayed the vice-president as a boor who ought to be replaced and the president and his staff as guilty of "moral turpitude," doing "unprecedented, unforgivable damage to the office and country." The uproar that followed led Rusher in the summer of 1973 to ask that Buckley remove Will, a request that the editor ignored. Meanwhile, Buckley and several others within the *National Review* circle began to discuss the possibility of a presidential resignation, but the journal defended the president until the summer of 1974 when it became clear that Nixon faced almost certain impeachment.[34]

The steady pursuit of its ideological vision bore fruit in the 1980s. The end of liberal political power that Buckley, Burnham, Rusher, and Hart long had predicted came with Ronald Reagan's presidency and a Democratic Congress reluctant to pursue expansive new social programs. A shift in *National Review*'s role was required: "With the election of Ronald Reagan, *National Review* assumes a new importance in American life. We become, as it were, an establishment organ; and we feel it only appropriate to alter our demeanor accordingly.... Connoisseurs of humor will have to get their yuks elsewhere. We have a nation to run."[35]

In an early brief for the young administration that urged the Reaganauts onward toward a social revolution and set the criterion for measuring its success, Amherst College professor Hadley Arkes declared that final judgment "should not be left to the arts of accountants and econometricians." Someday it must be measured in terms of political philosophy and practice, that is, whether the Reagan leadership had brought Americans to a new appreciation of "the moral understandings that finally bind them to one another and establish the terms of principle on which [their] political community shall live."[36] By the end of the decade, *National Review* conservatives were ready to offer their judgment on that and more quantitative matters.

Throughout the 1980s the journal supported the "Reagan Revolution," championing its objectives, particularly reduced taxes, economic incentives, lower inflation, and increased military spending. Four months after Reagan's inauguration, social philosopher Michael Novak articulated the moral case for Reaganomics. The redistribution of income popular on the American Left would not bring about the wanted equality and if pursued would produce inflation and economic stagnation that would harm all. "Trickle-down" economics, as critics dubbed it, was a misnomer. Reaganomics meant "upward push," for only an innovative, investment-driven economy offered hope for poorer families. Thus widespread private investment, spurred by appropriate incentives, was "a pre-eminently moral act" for it produced the wealth that made middle-class democracy possible.[37] Article after article defended a version of this formulation, adjusting differences in the conviction that supply-siders were in the vanguard of a worldwide march for freedom.[38]

In foreign policy the *National Review* editors and contributors pursued cold war politics to the end, during which time it offered strong support for President Reagan's Strategic Defense Initiative (dubbed "Star Wars" by the press). As the president's tough talk on the Soviet "evil empire" generated an arms control movement, *National Review* sought to undercut it. When the draft of a pastoral letter by the American Catholic Bishops in preparation for their May 1983 conference circulated, Buckley, who for decades had despised pacifism, declared the unilateral disarmament it recommended "an eructation in civilized thought," a dangerous error in the age of gulag.[39] With fundamental concepts of U.S. nuclear strategy under attack, the *National Review* devoted a full issue to "Moral Clarity in the Nuclear Age," a response to the bishops' letter by Michael Novak, then serving as the journal's religious editor. In a lucid, occasionally eloquent analysis, Novak defended "just war" theory, arguing that it was morally correct to defend human life. Pacifism may be defensible as a personal commitment but not as public policy. Justice is not served when in adherence to an abstract ideal we permit enemy nations to torture, oppress, and destroy a part of humankind or threaten American existence. Therefore nuclear deterrence must be seen as a morally correct policy. To abandon that axiom is to abandon the Constitution that supports our liberties.[40] Subsequent issues of the *National Review* brought additional discussions of arms control, nuclear weapons, and the need to build a space shield.[41]

By 1989, the *National Review* had for years alerted its readers to the sickness of the Soviet economy and the "rot" that had settled in the fabric of Soviet life. A cover story in January of that year, "The Coming Crack-Up of Communism," stated that the foremost challenge then facing conservatives lay in easing the Russians out of their empire as painlessly as possible. When the European collapse of communism came late that year, the *National Review* circle exuded pride that they had lived and worked in the trenches during the "heroic age" of Reagan and Thatcher—years of economic and diplomatic successes. In a lengthy essay for the journal's thirty-fifth anniversary issue, John O'Sullivan, one-time adviser to Prime Minister Margaret Thatcher and since 1988 *National Review* editor, paid tribute to

James Burnham, a lifelong student of power and of cold war realities. Events had vindicated the author of *The Coming Defeat of Communism* (1949), especially his analysis of ways to exploit the inherent contradictions of communism. Many had found his specific proposals too aggressive; U.S. presidents ignored them routinely. However, in the 1980s "it required...only a very modest dose of Burnhamism [the defense buildup and launching of "Star Wars"] to turn the tide."[42]

With the scabrous soul of communism homeless in Europe and unwanted in the old Soviet Empire, there was cause for celebration. It had not come easily. George Will, a *National Review* alumnus, argued that the collapse of communism had not been inevitable. It had required a large roster of journalists and intellectuals to erect the moral and philosophical challenge to the totalitarian system. In that work the *National Review* "lit the little spark that became the huge explosion that produced the sunset." William F. Buckley, Jr., then editor in chief, had the last word, defining what he thought the *National Review* meant in the political and intellectual history of America. It had helped to pave the way for Ronald Reagan, who early in his presidency declared that the USSR was an evil empire. "The *Gulag Archipelago* told us everything we needed to know about the pathology of Soviet Communism. We were missing only the galvanizing summation; and we got it, in the Mosaic code: and I think that the countdown for Communism began then."[43] With so precise a causal explanation, Buckley left out many, perhaps even the controlling, factors. But no other circle of conservative intellectuals was more entitled to cheer the event, toward which their journal had devoted thirty-five years of strenuous work.

Notes

1. *National Review* 1 (19 November 1955): 5 (hereinafter cited as *NR*).

2. Ibid., p. 6.

3. Whittaker Chambers, *Odyssey of a Friend: Whittaker Chambers' Letters to William F. Buckley, Jr., 1954–1961*, ed. William F. Buckley, Jr. (New York, 1969), pp. 228–29; Douglas C. North, "Private Property and the American Way," *NR* 35 (8 July 1983): 805–9; John O'Sullivan, "Is the Heroic Age of Conservatism Over?" *NR* 43 (28 January 1991): 37.

4. Frank Meyer, *The Conservative Mainstream* (New Rochelle, New York, 1969), p. 20.

5. Ibid., p. 19.

6. Ibid., pp. 25, 29. Several perspectives on fusionism are brought together in Frank Meyer, ed., *What Is Conservatism?* (New York, 1964).

7. William F. Buckley, Jr., *Up from Liberalism* (New York, 1959), pp. 152–53.

8. "Segregation and Democracy," *NR* 1 (25 January 1956): 5.

9. Buckley, *Up from Liberalism*, p. 157.

10. William F. Buckley, Jr., "Dr. King," *NR* 20 (23 April 1968): 376, 378–79.

11. *Look* 34 (13 January 1970): 59.

12. William F. Buckley, Jr., "Mr. Eisenhower's Decision and the Eisenhower Program," *NR* 1 (21 March 1956): 10; William F. Buckley, Jr., "Reflections on Election Eve," *NR* (3 November 1956): 7; see also L. Brent Bozell, "National Trends," *NR* 1 (19 November 1955): 12; L. Brent Bozell, "The Self-Immolators," *NR* 2 (27 October 1956): 5.

13. William F. Buckley, Jr., "The Tranquil World of Dwight D. Eisenhower," *NR* 5 (18 January 1958): 57–59.

14. William F. Buckley, Jr., "*National Review* and the 1960 Elections," *NR* 9 (22 October 1960): 233–34.

15. Barry Goldwater, "A Foreign Policy for America," *NR* 10 (25 March 1961): 177–81.

16. William F. Buckley, Jr., "On Dead-Red," *NR* 13 (4 December 1962): 434.

17. William F. Buckley, Jr., *God and Man at Yale* (Chicago, 1951), p. xii; Whittaker Chambers, *Witness* (New York, 1952), p. 8; William S. Schlamm, "Across McCarthy's Grave," *NR* 3 (18 May 1957): 470.

18. "The Week," *NR* 22 (13 January 1970): 14.

19. Quoted in J. David Hoeveler, Jr., *Watch on the Right: Conservative Intellectuals in the Reagan Era* (Madison, Wisconsin, 1991), p. 43.

20. "Vietnamese Schizophrenia," *NR* 16 (10 May 1964): 186.

21. See the following James Burnham columns: *NR* 16 (16 June 1964): 493; *NR* 17 (18 May 1965): 412; *NR* 17 (7 September 1965): 762; *NR* 19 (10 January 1967): 32; *NR* 20 (12 March 1968): 231; and *NR* 20 (26 March 1968): 282.

22. Norman B. Hannah, "The Great Strategic Error," *NR* 27 (20 June 1975): 667, 669; Norman B. Hannah, "Vietnam: Now We Know," *NR* 28 (11 June 1976): 613.

23. Frank Meyer, "Counterculture or Anticulture?" *NR* 22 (3 November 1970): 1165.

24. William F. Buckley, Jr., "Remarks at the [Tenth] Anniversary Dinner," *NR* (30 November 1965): 1128.

25. "Two Cheers for the Sixties," *NR* 22 (13 January 1970): 14, 16.

26. William F. Buckley, Jr., [Tribute] *NR* 39 (11 September 1987): 31.

27. *NR* 15 (17 December 1963): 509.

28. *NR* 22 (1 December 1970); *NR* 37 (15 November 1985).

29. W. H. von Dreele, "Invictus, 1960," *NR* 9 (5 November 1960): 278.

30. When *National Review* became a fortnightly, it put out the *National Review Bulletin* on alternate weeks. An eight-page newsletter that presented capsule news and commentary, it came to an end in December 1979. For two decades, approximately 20 percent of *NR* readers also subscribed to the *Bulletin*.

31. For Buckley's views on the Panama Canal, see "The Panama Canal and General Torrijos," *NR* 28 (26 November 1976): 1306; "Panama-Si," *NR* 29 (30 September 1977): 1132; and "Yes or No on the Panama Treaties," *NR* 30 (17 February 1978): 210–12, 216–17; James Burnham, "Panama or Taiwan?" *NR* 29 (16 September 1977): 1043.

32. William F. Buckley, Jr., "Veni, Vidi, Victus," *NR* 24 (17 March 1972): 258–62; William F. Buckley, Jr., "Richard Nixon's Long March," *NR* 24 (17 March 1972): 264–66, 268–69.

33. "Watergate as Power Struggle," *NR* 25 (6 July 1973): 720–22.

34. See the following columns by George F. Will: "Unraveling," *NR* 25 (11 May 1973): 514; "President Agnew," *NR* 25 (8 June 1973): 615–16; "Where Do We Go from Here," *NR* 25 (9 November 1973): 1220–22; and William F. Buckley, Jr., "Reflections on the Resignation," *NR* 26 (30 August 1974): 954.

35. "The Week," *NR* 32 (28 November 1980): 1434.

36. Hadley Arkes, "A Lover's Lament for the Reagan Administration," *NR* 34 (28 May 1982): 619.

37. Michael Novak, "The Moral Case for Reaganomics," *NR* 33 (29 May 1981): 614.

38. Paul Craig Roberts, "The Seduction of the Supply-Siders," *NR* 38 (6 June 1986): 40–42; George Gilder, "A Triumph of Politics," *NR* 38 (6 June 1986): 42–46; David Brooks, "Supply-Side Squabblers," *NR* 38 (24 October 1986): 28–33.

39. William F. Buckley, Jr., "To the Readers of *National Review*," *NR* 35 (1 April 1983): 352; William F. Buckley, Jr., "Peace and Pacifism," *NR* 7 (24 October 1959): 427.

40. Michael Novak, "Moral Clarity in the Nuclear Age," *NR* 35 (1 April 1983): 354, 356, 358–60, 362, 364–68, 370, 380–86, 388, 390, 392.

41. B. Bruce-Briggs, "A Catechism of Strategic Defense," *NR* 36 (5 October 1984): 26, 28, 30–32, 34; William R. Hawkins, "Arms Control: Three Centuries of Failure," *NR* 37 (9 August 1985): 26–29, 32; and Lewis Lehrman and Gregory A. Fossedal, "How to Decide about Strategic Defense," *NR* 38 (31 January 1986): 32–37.

42. John O'Sullivan, "James Burnham and the New World Order," *NR* 42 (5 November 1990): 42.

43. George Will, *NR* 42 (5 November 1990): 116; William F. Buckley, Jr., *NR* 42 (5 November 1990): 117.

Information Sources

BIBLIOGRAPHY:

Hart, Jeffrey. *The American Dissent: A Decade of Modern Conservatism.* Garden City, New York, 1966.

Hoeveler, Jr., J. David. *Watch on the Right: Conservative Intellectuals in the Reagan Era.* Madison, Wisconsin, 1991.

Judis, John B. *William F. Buckley, Jr.: Patron Saint of the Conservatives.* New York, 1988.

Nash, George H. *The Conservative Intellectual Movement in America: Since 1945.* New York, 1976.

INDEXES: Each volume indexed; *Bio Ind*; *BRD*; *Comb Ret Ind Bk Revs Hum; Curr Bk Rev Cit*; *FLI*; *Ind Bk Revs Hum*; *Mag Ind*; *PAIS*; *Pol Sci Abst*; *RG*; *URG*.

REPRINT EDITIONS: Microform: UMI; MIM.

LOCATION SOURCES: Widely available.

Publication History

TITLE AND TITLE CHANGES: *National Review: A Weekly Journal of Opinion.* 19 November 1955–13 September 1958; *National Review: A Journal of Fact and Opinion.* 27 September 1958–9 August 1966; *National Review.* 23 August 1966–present.

VOLUME AND ISSUE DATA: Volumes 1–current, 1955–present.

FREQUENCY OF PUBLICATION: Weekly, 19 November 1955–25 October 1958; biweekly, 8 November 1958–present.

PUBLISHERS: 19 November 1955–12 March 1960: National Weekly, Inc.; 26 March 1960–present: National Review, Inc. Through 30 January 1962 at Orange, Connecticut; from 13 February 1962 through 12 October 1979 at Bristol, Connecticut; from 26 October 1979 in New York.

EDITORS: William F. Buckley, Jr., 19 November 1955–19 August 1988; John O'Sullivan, 2 September 1988–31 December, 1997; Richard Lowry, 26 January 1998–present.

CIRCULATION: 1992, 150,000.; 1998, 175,000.

Ronald Lora

Modern Age
1957–

In *The Conservative Movement in America: Since 1945*, George H. Nash has this to say about *Modern Age*: "It immediately became the principal—indeed, the only—scholarly medium deliberately designed to publish conservative thought in the United States. [It] was primarily oriented toward the traditionalist or new conservative segment of the conservative revival....*Modern Age*...filled a desperate need...[as] the principal quarterly of the intellectual right."[1] The first issue appeared in the summer of 1957; its founding editor was Russell Kirk, a man of letters and the author of *The Conservative Mind*, which, since its publication in 1953, has become a classic. Henry Regnery, a distinguished, independent Chicago publisher, and David S. Collier, trained as a political scientist at Northwestern University (where he was a pupil of William M. McGovern and of Kenneth Colegrove), assisted Kirk in the founding. When Kirk resigned as editor in 1959, as Nash observes, "he had established what he wanted: a dignified forum for reflective, traditionalist conservatism."

The editorial continuity of *Modern Age,* no less than the original graphic design and format, remains unbroken, despite destined changes in editorship. Eugene Davidson, formerly an editor and then director of Yale University Press, succeeded Kirk and served as editor from 1960–1970; he was succeeded by Collier, who remained editor until his unexpected death on 19 November 1983. The literary editors of *Modern Age* have been, in the following order of succession: Richard M. Weaver, a professor of English at the University of Chicago and the author of the celebrated book *Ideas Have Consequences* (1948); J. M. Lalley, a journalist and for many years an editorial writer for and book review editor of the *Washington Post*; and George A. Panichas, a teacher and moralist critic, since 1962 a professor of English at the University of Maryland. Upon Collier's death, Panichas assumed editorship of the journal.

Originally bearing the subtitle "A Conservative Review," *Modern Age* was first sponsored by the Foundation for Foreign Affairs, of Chicago, which brought out the first nine issues (volume 1, number 1, summer 1957—volume 3, number 3 summer 1959). The Institute for Philosophical and Historical Studies, also of Chicago, then took over publication of *Modern Age*, beginning with volume 3, number 4, in fall 1959. The institute brought out all the thirteen succeeding issues of the journal until volume 7, number 1, in winter 1962–1963, when sponsorship again reverted to the Foundation for Foreign Affairs and the subtitle became *A Quarterly Review*. Beginning with the fall 1976 issue of *Modern Age* (volume 20, number 4), the Intercollegiate Studies Institute of Bryn Mawr, Pennsylvania, became—and remains—the publisher. From 1976 to 1996 the editorial offices were centrally located in Bryn Mawr. In 1996 the offices moved to Wilmington, Delaware. The president of ISI is now T. Kenneth Cribb, Jr., successor to E. Victor Milione, who is president emeritus. The executive vice-president is John F. Lulves, Jr., with the latter officially listed as the publisher in the masthead of the journal. Each of the sponsoring organizations has consistently and vigorously supported the principles of conservatism that *Modern Age* has articulated from the beginning.

It should be noted, too, that for twenty years Chicago remained the editorial base of the journal. Russell Kirk and Henry Regnery had in fact hoped that *Modern Age* would serve as an intellectual forum for "the culture of the Middle West, and the heart of the United States generally." This hope did not materialize, for in content and orientation, *Modern Age* ultimately transcended any regional identity or parochial affiliation, becoming on a national and even international level part of a larger program of conservative thought. Of the founding of *Modern Age* Regnery later recalled:

In 1957...Camelot, the New Frontier, the Great Society, the Vietnam War, the "Hippie" and Drug Culture of the sixties were all in the future, as were many of the political and social problems that loom so large today—the deficit, inflation, unemployment, exhibitionist homosexuality and pornography with the decline of standards associated with them, to mention only a few and to say nothing of the very different and far more dangerous power relationships in the world around us. Liberalism, then as now, was the dominant influence in communications and in the colleges and universities...but was being seriously challenged: Friedrich A. Hayek's *The Road to Serfdom* had appeared in 1945, Richard M. Weaver's *Ideas Have Consequences* in 1948, and in 1951 William F. Buckley appeared on the scene with the publication of *God and Man at Yale* and founded his magazine *National Review* four years later. It was the publication, and success, of Russell Kirk's *The Conservative Mind* in 1953 that brought the various elements of opposition to liberalism together and was the decisive factor in the founding of *Modern Age*.[2]

Since its inception *Modern Age* has become a veritable treasure house of conservative thought and opinion and has attracted contributors renowned for their writings and ideas. Among those seeking to define the concepts and principles of conservatism are M. E. Bradford, George W. Carey, Bertrand de Jouvenal, John Dos Passos, Paul Gottfried, Harry V. Jaffa, Willmoore Kendall, Frank S. Meyer, Robert Nisbet, José Ortega y Gasset, Stanley Parry, and Eliseo Vivas. Among those writing on conservative thinkers and expositors are John Chamberlain, John

P. East, Byron C. Lambert, Marion Montgomery, Claes G. Ryn, and Peter J. Stanlis. In addition, on the cultural role of art are notable essays by Martin Buber, Donald Davidson, Robert Drake, W. H. Hocking, Folke Leander, Mario Pei, Herbert Read, and Austin Warren; on the significance and value of the Judeo-Christian tradition and patrimony, Will Herberg, John Courtney Murray, Wilhelm Röpke, Leo R. Ward, Frederick Wilhelmsen, and René de Visme Williamson; on educational issues, James Burnham, W. T. Couch, Max Picard, Stephen J. Tonsor, and Eric Voegelin. No less significant have been crucial essays on Karl Marx's work and thought by William Henry Chamberlin, David J. Dallin, Thomas Molnar, Philip E. Moseley, and Gerhart Niemeyer; and on the anatomy of terror and revolution by C. P. Ives, Felix Morley, and Francis Russell. Essays pertaining to the roots of American order have been written by Harry Elmer Barnes, Clare Boothe Luce, Andrew Lytle, Forrest McDonald, and Francis Gorham Wilson. This brief listing of names can hardly register the breadth and the depth of the subjects and issues explored year in and year out by writers and thinkers of great reputation and influence.

No other statement better defines the aims of *Modern Age* than the opening editorial, "Apology for a New Review," in the summer 1957 issue. It remains as applicable today as when it first appeared. That the journal is called, in the very first sentence, "a journal of controversy" is especially pertinent, given the conditions inciting its publication at a time when liberal and radical journals of opinion, always in preponderance, generated an "orthodoxy of enlightenment." That, as the editorial stresses, *Modern Age* was hardly in the mainstream of American social and political thought and action, essentially reformist and progressivist in orientation, summarizes those conditions crying for the publication of "a conservative quarterly." The adjective in this phrase, often paradoxical to many, is directly encountered in this paragraph of definition: "By 'conservative,' we mean a journal dedicated to conserving the best elements in our civilization; and those best elements are in peril nowadays. We confess to a prejudice against doctrinaire radical alteration, and to a preference for the wisdom of our ancestors. Beyond this, we have no party line. Our purpose is to stimulate discussion of the great moral and social and literary questions of the hour, and to search for means by which the legacy of our civilization may be kept safe."[3]

As the "Apology" expresses it, "*Modern Age* intends to pursue a conservative policy for the sake of a liberal understanding." It is the moral constituents of this "conservative policy" that epitomize the standards of discrimination differentiating the editorial ethos of *Modern Age* from that of other journals of opinion in America. The editorial admits that there is a widespread absence of serious reading in the nation, a bleak fact underscoring the point that a serious (and simultaneously conservative) journal of opinion is not likely to exert great influence over national policy or the conditions of American life and civilization. "But for all that," the editorial goes on to say, "modern society cannot endure—and its survival is immediately in question—without discussion among thinking men." These words announced the aspiration of "a new review" and adverted to the values that a "conservative review seeks to convey, to promulgate, so as "to reach the minds of men who think of something more than the appetites of the hour." If the aims of the journal have been bold, they have not been quixotic, as the editorial discloses: "We are not ideologists: we do not believe we have all the remedies for all the ills to which flesh is heir. With Burke, we take our stand against abstract doctrine and theoretic dogma. But, still with Burke, we are in favor of principle....We hope to revive the best in the old journalism and to mold it to the temper of our time."[4] This statement poses the challenge an independent "conservative review" faces. How will it be possible to reconcile the review's mission as a conservator of the great tradition of "permanent things," with the urgencies of cruel history and of an age in swift transition and expanding crisis? Encouraging critical examination of national and international issues has been a longstanding aim of *Modern Age*.

If the ethos of this "conservative review" has been moral in perspective, it has also been humanistic. From the beginning *Modern Age* has defended the "idea of value" as it relates to the necessity of *humanitas* and to the concept of the *honnête homme*. Traditions and values that actively resist the tyranny of collectivist principles inform the conservative viewpoints expressed in the journal and at the same time provide the reminding evidence of the force of truth that one finds in Paul Elmer More's words: "We are intellectually incompetent and morally responsible: that would appear to be the last lesson of life." It is in the considered response to both the significance and the ramifications of More's contention that *Modern Age* has exercised its conservative articles of faith on both a diagnostic and a corrective plane. That these articles of faith signify, in Burke's words, "the dissidence of dissent" points to the degree of concern that the journal shows regarding the need to oppose a majoritarian leveling that has produced decadent phenomena in American life and culture—the unchecked romanticism, positivism, and gnosticism emerging from the arrogances of "telluric revolt" (to use Hermann Keyserling's expression). This opposition has been conducted in accordance with the purposive function of a "conservative review" and of a "principled conservatism," as Frank S. Meyer has designated it.

A major editorial task has been that of confronting pervasive deculturation, statism, endless shifts and drifts of the climate of opinion, and the divers forms of the moral collapse in the Western world. The character and the conscience of *Modern Age* are clearly identified in terms not only of the contributors themselves, "a worthy company" indeed, but also of the subjects they explore and assess. Conservative standards of discrimination are upheld by Americans and Europeans who share a sympathy of vision and who, concerned with the *why* of things as well as the *what*, protest against those conditions of life without principles, of "life without prejudice," as Weaver puts it. That remnant of conservative scholars, or what Eliseo Vivas calls the "intellectual *guerrilleros* of the right," is for a journal that seeks for a moral identity (and centrality) and also seeks to create a conservative valuation (and validation), its life-source, giving it its authentic function, if not its prophetic voice. The properties of that function and the tone of that voice have been totally consistent with the *desiderata* that Niemeyer poses in these words:

In the shallowness of liberal and socialist humanism, we must rediscover the depth of being and of history. In the process we must first learn, and then teach, to recognize distinctions between truth and perversion, rationality and semi-rationality, philosophy and ideology. We need great figures whose personal lives are an eloquent alternative to liberal relativism....We need orators who can call the bluff, and decry the false plausibility, of the ideologists, positivists, and humanist moralists. We need lawgivers who can translate deep convictions into public rules.[5]

Pluralistic, pragmatic, and collectivist tendencies that are dominant in "the promise of liberalism" and sanctioned by "creative skeptics in defense of the liberal temper," as the philosopher-politician T. V. Smith once expressed the mission of his liberal allies, often characterize modern American civilization. The challenging of this liberal Zeitgeist and of the ideologues who support the *volonté générale* is graphically registered in the pages of *Modern Age*. One must inevitably reflect, in viewing this challenge and ideological struggle, on how the journal and its contributors, without an academic base (or, better, a privileged and often affluent sanctuary), without munificent foundation grants, without popular support and instant revenues, without a heavily financed visibility, have survived. It is not far-fetched to image the function and mission of those connected with the journal as a dissident enterprise. Indeed, those who have been associated with *Modern Age* have often been made to feel as dissidents. This fate is unavoidable when a journal hews closely to paradigms of conservative acceptances in the contexts of what Weaver speaks of not only as "belief in the primacy of ideas and values" but also as "visions of order." As a journal of opinion *Modern Age* has sought to maintain commitment to first causes and first principles and reverence for moral constants and universals. It has sought to diminish the Marxizing imperialisms and the technologico-Benthamite habits of mind besieging all areas of life in the twentieth century. In its strict adherence to these purposes and commitments, *Modern Age* has tried to exemplify the meaning of what Voegelin speaks of as "the consciousness of principles."

Although no single religious viewpoint or affirmation prevails in either editorial policy or among the contributors, the Judeo-Christian tradition has the largest shaping influence in the perspectives that are enunciated in the journal. *Modern Age* epitomizes precisely the traditional religious position as opposed to the liberal agnosticisms that T. S. Eliot pinpoints when he wrote: "We, on the other hand, feel convinced, however darkly, that our spiritual faith should give us some guidance in temporal matters; that, if it does not, the fault is our own; that morality rests upon religious sanction, and that the social organization of the world rests upon moral sanction; that we can only judge of temporal values in the light of eternal values."[6] At a time of history that has seen an overwhelming crisis of faith, *Modern Age* has defended religious traditions, siding with the supernatural against the natural, with permanence against relativism, with an apostolic orthodoxy against heresy, with the idea of cultural unity in religious faith, as opposed to faith in secular utopias. Thus, what can be termed a metaphysics of transcendence defines the chief spiritual concerns of the journal.

In *Modern Age* the conservative ethos is substantively communicated in relation to basic categories of thought. The main criterion for judging the human condition is inextricably tied to cause and effect, not to means and ends. If there is one edict that molds and monitors the editorial standards of *Modern Age*, it is that which endorses the qualitative element unconditionally. Maintaining a hierarchy and a scale of values and stressing man's duties and then man's rights have been a central editorial purpose. In holding to a conservatism at once selective, synthesizing, and assimilative, *Modern Age* has disclosed a consistent toughness and a tenacity of belief. Overcentralization, bureaucratization, the expansion of "new deals" and "fair deals," of "new frontiers" and "great societies," social planning and social engineering: these are, for *Modern Age*, acute imperialistic tendencies in the "liberal temper" and governance that transpose into faults, inner and outer, individual and social. The progressivism of representative democracy in its proliferating forms and dimensions has been under severe censorial inspection in *Modern Age*. It is not that the concept of democracy incurs disapproval, but rather the excesses of a majoritarian society as these transform into indiscrimination, relativism, indiscipline, and disorder.

Modern Age stands for the mobilizing of the moral virtues as forms of both the exterior life and the interior life. Political philosophy no less than political theory that underestimates the moral meaning of existence inevitably is worthless. Though profoundly concerned with the condition of American society, *Modern Age* is not restricted to parochial issues. Its perspective, generalist and universal, is ultimately rooted in the larger world. Even as it has been loyal to the need for adhering to "the idea of diversity in conservative thought," *Modern Age* has never succumbed to divided allegiances or vague romanticizing impulses that characterize a vulgar contemporaneousness. Its conservative principles have been absolute in their rejection of the "new morality of drifting." Those very principles of a critical conservatism and a "principled conservatism" are planted in a symbiosis of moral effort and disciplinary virtues forming the bedrock of tradition, which, as Austin Warren notes, "emphasizes the shared inheritance as embodied in institutions—all organized, continuous, and more or less coherent expressions of values and ideals."[7]

In the end the critical function of *Modern Age* can be described as serious, judgmental, moral, and prescriptive; it is concerned with the character and conscience of individual man and also of society and culture. That the crisis of civilization is essentially a crisis of spirit is a phenomenon that *Modern Age* vigilantly observes. In its emphasis on this truth, the journal adheres to a spiritual centrality. Going beyond political and socioeconomic arrangements of an essentially mechanico-material cast, it is anchored in metaphysical concepts and convictions. This is not to say that it discards temporal considerations but rather that it looks for eternal values and permanent truths. Moral effort and moral conversion precede programmatic and material experiments. Principles, not possibilities, are priorities that govern the human prospect.

What differentiates *Modern Age* from other journals of opinion is precisely its metaphysical acceptances as these govern its conservative aims and outlook. At no time has the journal failed to take a stand on issues affecting the condition and the measure of man. Invariably, matters of conduct, conscience, and character, in their total relation to life, literature, and thought, receive strict attention in *Modern*

Age. The standards are consonant with those articles of a conservative faith that More delineates in these words:

Despite the clamour of the hour he will know that the obligation to society is not the primal law and is not the source of personal integrity, but is secondary to personal integrity. He will believe that social justice is in itself desirable, but he will hold that it is far more important to preach first the responsibility of each man to himself for his own character. He will admit that equality of opportunity is an ideal to be aimed at, but he will think this a small thing in comparison with the universality of duty. In his attitude towards mankind he will not deny the claims of sympathy, but he will listen first to the voice of judgment.[8]

In placing the organic interconnections between the economic, the political, the philosophical, and the religious essences that comprise the conditions of existence, *Modern Age* adheres to the principles of restraint, of discipline, of control implicit in Burke's statement: "There is no qualification for government but virtue or wisdom, actual or presumptive." Burke's words belong to an old and great tradition, if not of the old criticism, which has attracted, in the pages of *Modern Age*, definers and defenders of the idea of continuity. Above all, how are those two venerable words, *virtue* and *wisdom*, dedicated to the law of measure and the life of reverence, to be preserved at an ignoble hour when other venerable words, encouraging both inspiration and aspiration—*loyalty, honor, nobility, honesty, generosity*—have been equally compromised by the forces to which the idea of value is meaningless? Simone Weil's belief that "language is no longer equipped for legitimately praising a man's character" comes to mind here. With the corruption of language, the unchecked drift of modern civilization has hastened toward nihilism. For what principles of faith and certitudes of order can operate in a society in which relativism is placed in a commanding position? In a deep sense, then, *Modern Age* is devoted to the tradition of what Matthew Arnold calls "the grand style" that is connected with an "elevation of character," a "noble way of thinking and behaving," and a "dealing with great things."

Arnold's phrases help to identify not only the concerns of *Modern Age* but also the psychology and the philosophy of its critical aims—and its *raison d'être*. If many of its writers and reviewers are academics, *Modern Age* rejects narrow academic specializations. The journal does not speak exclusively to (or for) the academy but rather to "man thinking." Its approach is interdisciplinary and transdisciplinary. Implicit in the responsibilities of such an approach is the necessity for making connections between the dynamic forces and energies of human life and the standards of the tradition to which Arnold alludes. The journal's reverence for the idea of tradition, for a return to origins, absorbs the idea of conservatism and points to what is inclusive and transcendent in character and orientation. For *Modern Age*, to quote the words of Father Yves Congar, "the word tradition connotes something more than mere conservatism; something deeper is involved, namely the continual presence of a spirit and of a moral attitude, the continuity of an ethos."[9]

If one can discern in the mass of American life a heightening state of blankness, of cultural decline, one can also discern in the American intellectual community an ascending habit of disloyalty to the idea of value. Ortega y Gasset is to the point here when he observes, "A characteristic of our times is the predominance, even in groups traditionally selective, of the mass and the vulgar. Thus, in the intellectual life, which of its essence requires and presupposes qualification, one can note the progressive triumph of the pseudo-intellectual, unqualified, unqualifiable, and, by their very mental texture, disqualified."[10] A contemporary of Ortega, Julien Benda, applied a celebrated phrase, "*la trahison des clercs*," to the tendency that the Spanish philosopher identified. In American intellectual and social-political life, it is the gravity and the extent of this breakdown that one finds continually examined in *Modern Age*. Indeed, no better diagnostic index to the conditions afflicting American society can be found than in its pages.

If crisis and revolution are representative of the modern world, there are two other closely related destructive processes that, as Voegelin has observed, are inescapable in their consequences: the fragmentation of science through specialization and the deculturation of society. Their consequences have been of deep concern to *Modern Age*. Especially noticeable in these destructive processes is the glorification of the social collective and the diminution of the nature of man. Empirical as opposed to metaphysical priorities color all questions of existence. In effect, both the biblical view and the classical ideal, foundations of the spirit that they are, retreat before this phenomenon. The Great War of 1914–1918, the Russian Revolution of 1917, and World War II constitute epochal manifestations of the terrors of debasement wrought in a megatechnic world. With the culmination of each of these disasters, what Simone Weil calls "the empire of might" has attained its continuing confirmation—its profane ontology, as it were. The struggle for order, in other words, gives way to the forces of disintegration, not only materialistic but also ideological, progressivist and positivist, liberal and socialist, Marxian and Freudian, that now take civilization "beyond nihilism." The moral meaning of man, society, and history withers as these forces annul that sapiential concept of man, society, and history that Voegelin identifies in these words: "Every society is burdened with the task, under its concrete conditions, of creating an order that will endow the fact of its existence with meaning in terms of ends divine and human." The ongoing mission of *Modern Age*, it could be said, resides in Voegelin's concept of the structure of order.

The consequent need to find remedies against the disorder of the time through philosophical and critical inquiry points to one of the original needs leading to the founding of *Modern Age*. From the beginning, the journal has viewed its function, intellectually and politically, as well as socially and culturally, as one that is predominantly diagnostic and corrective, seeing things in their causes and facts in their connections. Whatever the uncertainties and the paradoxes of the modern situation, they accentuate a need for order. If historical uncertainties and metaphysical paradoxes often lead to experimental social and political solutions, rooted in mere sentiment, in empty rhetoric, in illusions, or in utilitarian experiments, the need for order presupposes disciplinary virtues and exacting paradigms of character. In the end it all comes down to the question of transcendent permanencies, of hierarchies, their acceptance and affirmation. A rigorous loyalty to these permanencies accents the loyalty of *Modern Age* to *historia sacra* and, in turn, to a civilized world of dignity, reason, and order. That history has meaning, that the world makes sense, that man has redeeming worth: these are, for *Modern Age*, absolute concepts to be defended absolutely against sophistic and gnostic forces of disorder. Once again Voegelin helps to clarify a basic moral and philosophical concern defining the scope and the purpose of *Modern Age*: "The truth of order has to be gained and regained in the perpetual struggle against the fall from it; and the movement toward truth starts from a man's awareness of his existence in untruth."[11]

One of the crucial aspects of the critical function that *Modern Age* seeks to fulfill lies in the review of books. The evaluative discussion of new books, as well as the reconsideration of old books that have been ignored or scanted, is a central task of any journal of opinion. Yet in many academic journals and in the popular press one does not find the standards of discrimination essential to a proper evaluation of books of critical and cultural significance, particularly books that convey a conservative and moral sensibility. The literary establishment, moreover, remains largely loyal to liberal oracles like John Dewey and Bertrand Russell, and now to heresiarchs like Herbert Marcuse, B. F. Skinner, Georg Lukács, and Jacques Derrida. And it continues to minimize the moral imagination and moral criticism, even as it manifestly minimizes both humanistic principles of *paideia* rooted in tradition and the unity of spiritual life that a Christopher Dawson and a T. S. Eliot defend. Empirical, liberal, radical, and revisionist-turned-deconstructionist habits of mind and opinion too often and expediently determine the treatment, reputation, and fate of new books and of the popular successes, the so-called best-sellers that one finds listed in the *New York Times Book Review* week after week. What is alarming about these reviewing practices and the climate of opinion that they foment is not only the limiting selection of nonserious and noncritical literature to be reviewed, but also the limiting of reviewers to those who adhere safely to a party line of relativistic criticism.

Relevance, a specious word that has been certified by liberal pundits, has become a procedural standard in discussing national policy and seeking cultural consensus. All too often such a spurious standard has enjoyed complete demagogic success, especially in the late 1960s and 1970s when American civilization experienced serious social and cultural problems. These were barren years when *Modern Age* was one of a few journals publishing essays and reviews that went against the American grain and challenged the "democratization of personhood" that liberal and radical leaders championed. These were years of danger and unreason when, as one alarmed critic termed it in *Modern Age*, "*meta*-barbaric man now dances and fornicates in the streets."[12] In more nearly normal circumstances, of course, such a declaration would be deemed hyperbolic, designed for literary effect. But even a random visual examination of American street scenes in a "morbid democracy" in the 1960s and 1970s would corroborate the sorry spectacle described by the alarmed critic. Only the passage of time and disinterested critical assessment will fully vindicate the writings in *Modern Age* protesting the debasement of national character that, in these two decades, seemed of no threat to acclaimed gurus, political and religious leaders, jurists, educators, columnists, television commentators, and nationally prestigious newspapers and journals of opinion whose common admonition was summed up in two words, "Right on!" No admonition could more betray the habits of order that Walter Bagehot connects with "the settled calm by which the world is best administered." If there ever was any need for exonerating even the existence of a journal of opinion like *Modern Age*, it was in the 1960s and 1970s, dishonest and hedonistic decades when, as its writers warned, the abandonment of the idea of value and the disregard for moral responsibility rendered an impasse in American civilization.

"From the element of unity in things to the element of diversity": Irving Babbitt's words describing a basic shift in principles bear repeating. His words encompass a crisis of civilization and also define the kind of social and moral transvaluation that many in the American intellectual community have accepted, even as they have been increasingly content, as Wilhelm Röpke asserts, to allow "incidentals [to] recede behind the essential, the variables behind the constants, the ephemeral behind the permanent, the fluctuating behind the durable, the fleeting moment behind the era."[13] This disarray, as it affects life not only in a political and social sense but also in a cultural and literary sense, goes unchecked. It underlines modern man's disregard of "the tragic sense of life," as well as of "a tragic wisdom." Insofar as the tragic dimension connotes a sense of an ending, or *telos*, it conflicts with an uncritical optimism. That even religious leaders and theologians now subscribe to and propagate this optimism indicates how serious is the shift in principles and values. Disarray is in essence the failure to locate a center of values, which is in turn the rejection of what Voegelin calls "paradigmatic" history, that is, of spiritual history or tradition. This process of rejection, with its disordering results, causes a crisis of existence, particularly evidenced as a weakening of the spiritual fiber, or as Father Stanley Parry observes in his essay "The Restoration of Tradition," a most distinguished contribution of its kind to appear in *Modern Age*: "Civilization itself—tradition—falls out of existence when the human spirit itself becomes confused."[14]

Conservatism, Russell Kirk reminds us, is in essence a way of looking at the human condition. Such a conservatism is predicated on an understanding of the relation between philosophy and practical politics, between *theoria* and *praxis*, between idea and reality. *Modern Age* has sought to attain this understanding; its pursuit has been fundamentally dispassionate in discrimination and judgment. What one finds in examining the journal as a whole is a comprehensive conservatism preoccupied with the total human condition. Behind its valuations lies an endemic preoccupation with the idea of conservation and continuity: "The first duty of society is the preservation of society." Bagehot's words epitomize the origin of that preoccupation. Honoring and sustaining that preoccupation are infinitely difficult in an age addicted to the doctrines of progress, reform, and freedom, and of all that comes under the heading of "open society." When the scale of values and the meaning of value have been drastically altered, the conservative's task is further complicated. To admit this is not to diminish the fortitude of those who have helped to mold the ethos of *Modern Age*. This ethos has been applied philosophically, morally, politically, with consistency and, when necessary, with severity.

Modern Age has not relaxed its moral attention to the critical problems of civilization at a time when inattention has characterized responses to matters of human and cultural importance. Indeed, the nature of freedom itself has been both distanced and distorted by a temporal concern with delimiting the boundaries of freedom. In such circumstances freedom assumes a purely empirical guise impervious to the metaphysical dimension. "Moral freedom is simply this freedom to hold by attention," Josiah Royce writes, "or to forget by inattention, an Ought already present to one's finite consciousness."[15] No other words better express the moral imperative as it has been defended in *Modern Age*. The presence of the Ought helps to locate and measure the condition of the moral order, especially in the framework of what constitutes attention and responsibility. Materialistic doctrine increasingly has displaced the attention and judgment that form an integral and active part of moral sensibility. Moral consequences are ignored or discounted; in effect, moral order and order of meaning are removed from the realm of reality. Just how catastrophic this process can be is illustrated by Eliseo Vivas in a discussion of books "by and on Marcuse," an *enragé* who in the 1960s and 1970s captured the allegiance of the intellectual Left. Vivas, and *Modern Age*, could hardly ignore the threat that a radical guru and dogmatist like Marcuse presents to the moral order— could hardly ignore "Marcuse's conception of human destiny as envisaged in his repugnant *Erlösungslehre*: the psychological-ethical hedonism which he preaches...[his] total lack of piety towards past human achievements, the absurdity of a mind that claims to have found the final solution for man's problems, the dystopian dream of a state in which human beings regress into pleasure-seeking animals."[16]

The survival of *Modern Age* in no way alters the fact that, especially in the literary and academic worlds and in the judiciary, the conservative metaphysic continues to trail in the dusty rear. Insofar as in modern society gnostic and uncritical habits of mind are predominant, it cannot be expected that a genuine conservative metaphysic will find passage. In American society since World War II, it is precisely what is antithetical to restraints at all levels of life that has gained ascendancy. The "promise of a millennium," when man has at last entered "the gates of Eden," epitomizes the messianism characteristically preached by liberal theorists "swayed by sensations, and not by principles," to quote Tocqueville. What Peter Viereck writes is also to the point here: "Whereas the liberal and rationalist mind consciously articulates abstract blueprints, the conservative mind...embodies rather than argues [and] its best insights are almost never developed into sustained theoretical works equal to those of liberalism and radicalism."[17] The conservatives' reverence for intangible yet permanent things—for the things of the spirit, as it were—goes counter to the materialistic drives of the modern world and the anthropology of a largely atheistic humanism that now assume an obscene character and a program reducing the world to a theory.

Increasing surrender in the twentieth century to the demands of "historical necessity" embodies the sad fate of large parts of modern society. It further underlines retreat from a tradition of political philosophy that expresses what Leo Strauss, reconciler of classical and biblical views and beliefs, calls "the character of ascent" and of the related qualitative search for piety and wisdom. Marxism in particular embodies a political process that rejects the element of virtue essential to the best political order. The anti-Marxist position of *Modern Age* has been unyielding: both Marxist politics and Marxist philosophy have been the subject of extensive criticism, even as American foreign policy has also been extensively examined in terms of its perception (or its lack of perception) of the dangers of Marxist doctrine. The French Revolution of 1789 and the Russian Revolution of 1917, as well as the consequent rise of the Jacobin and Bolshevik dictatorships, have often been viewed as manifestations not only of "revolutionary terror" but also of the spirit of modern totalitarianism. Conservative scholars in *Modern Age* have refused to accede to the so-called Marxist "aim of the transcendence of domination."

If *Modern Age* has followed a supposedly hard-line approach, as some of its liberal critics have claimed, the political and spiritual catastrophes of post-1917 history would seem to vindicate such an approach. "Our present system is unique in history," Aleksandr Solzhenitsyn writes in *From under the Rubble* (1975), "because over and above its physical and economic constraints, it demands of us total surrender of our souls, continuous and active participation in the general, conscious *lie*." *Modern Age* has refused to participate in this lie exactly for the reasons that Solzhenitsyn stresses: "No one who voluntarily runs with the hounds of falsehood, or props it up, will ever be able to justify himself to the living, or to posterity, or to his friends, or to his children."

Not long after the end of World War II, Whittaker Chambers was one of the few brave men to direct attention to the metaphysical dimension, and the deeper psychology, of Marxism. Tearing away any veil of illusion that he once had regarding the Marxist doctrine, he was able to say straight out that in our time, a great conflict raged between two irreconcilable faiths: communism and freedom. When Chambers declares, in his moving "Foreword in the Form of a Letter to My Children," in *Witness* (1952), that the two world wars did not end the crisis of civilization but raised its ideological tensions to a new pitch and that "all the politics of our time, including the politics of war, will be the politics of this crisis," he focuses precisely on a matter that has occupied *Modern Age* from the beginning. As such the journal has long been critical of those policy advisers, political leaders, liberal academics, and experts who have refused to recognize that, as Solzhenitsyn puts it, the West "finds itself in a crisis, perhaps even in mortal danger." That crisis and that danger embody the struggle between human freedom and totalitarianism, between a way of life that seeks to place faith in human dignity and any collectivist doctrine that results in tyranny and the slave mentality. With Eric Voegelin, then, *Modern Age* affirms that "the truth of man and the truth of God are inseparably one." This affirmation, this choice, points to the principles of faith and order that shape the substance of *Modern Age*'s editorial principles and commitments.

As modern gnosticism and "leftist-horizontalism" have gained ascendancy, the mission of *Modern Age* has become more urgent in terms of conserving civilized values and verities. Where habitual compromise has informed the thought and policy of the American intelligentsia and of political leadership, *Modern Age* has stalwartly identified the fallacies and the inbreeding of the liberal Zeitgeist. To reiterate, the mission of *Modern Age* has been sustained by a generous welcome to its pages of writers from all parts of the United States and from Europe. From the beginning, Anthony Harrigan has observed, "*Modern Age* introduced a wider, more comprehensive intellectual tradition than existed in New York or Boston."[18] In this tradition one discovers a common allegiance on the part of the journal's contributors: dedication to a higher and ever demanding task—"the task of intellectual and moral preparation and restoration." "For a conservatism of ignorance, like a liberalism of ignorance, is a curse to society; while a conservatism of reflection is a counterbalance to a liberalism of reflection," wrote Kirk back in 1955 in *Commonweal*. That "counterbalance" was, with the founding of *Modern Age* in 1957, to become the major and restorative task of the journal. Its essays and reviews have been engaged in the active implementation of this task from the beginning. For its contributors the journal was to become, in Marion Montgomery's words, "a house where we gather periodically in complementary encounters." In *Modern Age*, then, it has been a conservative minority that has spoken, animated, Kirk observes, by "their love of right reason" and their desire "to inform and persuade, rather than to indoctrinate in secular dogmas." *Modern Age* has, in effect, sought to define and preserve a conservative ethos. Not social reform per se but moral struggle constitutes a working principle of order in this ethos. Or, to put it in another way, the conservative ethos revolves around a particular disposition, which Michael Oakeshott describes as follows: "To be conservative is to be disposed to think and behave in certain matters; it is to prefer certain kinds of conduct and certain conditions of human circumstances to others; it is to be disposed to make certain kinds of choices."[19]

That *Modern Age* has appeared without interruption since 1957 records both an act of survival and an occasion for gratification. But this statement should in no way be taken as self-congratulatory. "Conservative intellectual victories not intimately tied to a genuine reorientation of imagination and character," Claes G. Ryn warns, "are likely to be precarious and easily reversible." [20] The fight for "lost causes" never ends, insofar as that fight is inextricably tied to organic metaphysical and social-historical dialectics, which John Kenneth Galbraith, elder statesman of the American Left, identifies in these words: "Ever since [Franklin D.] Roosevelt, liberals have assumed the solidity and even the sanctity of our basic positions." Among these positions he lists Keynesian macroeconomic management of the economy, welfare programs, minority rights, and a more equitable distribution of income. Such an enumeration of goals underlines the presuppositions and prepossessions of the liberal doctrine. It is one of the functions of the conservative scholar to provide a counteraction to a programmatic "metastatic" faith, the faith of "an abiding liberal," to use Galbraith's own caption. Conspicuously absent from this faith, *Modern Age* has persisted in saying, is a concern with the order of the soul as this order relates to the order of the republic. In this absence are found the roots of spiritual crisis. For the conservative scholar this crisis—and it is, in the end, a crisis of disorder—generates the substance of his quarrel with the liberal dialectic, with what Claude Lévi-Strauss calls "the dialectic of superstructures."

Contemplating the contemporary social and moral situation, Isaac Bashevis Singer laments: "The daily news tells us again and again that, with all his knowledge and with all his refined ways, modern man remains the wildest animal." He declares that too many people passively accept the moral decay of the time and respond to the present crisis of civilization with indifference. He goes on to emphasize: "There is a time when man must say what he considers important." These words should trouble the conscience and alert us to the distempers of a civilization that, individually and collectively, negate the axiomatic principles of character that dignify and sanctify the moral meaning of man. For the past four decades the conservative scholar has spoken out on fundamental issues in *Modern Age*: He has said *what he considers important.* To the psalmist's perennial question, "If the foundations be destroyed, what can the righteous do?" the conservative scholar gives reply. His testimony, no less than his witness, inscribes the pages and informs the ethos of *Modern Age*, which to this day remains indefatigably what its founding fathers intended it to be—"an American protest against the illusions of the age" and a bulwark against the "enemies of the permanent things."

Notes

1. New York, 1976, pp. 144–45.

2. "The Fourth Editorship," *Modern Age* 28 (Winter 1984): 2 (hereinafter cited as *MA*).

3. "Apology for a New Review," *MA* 1 (Summer 1957): 2.

4. Ibid.

5. "A Remarkable Conservative Presence," *MA* 20 (Winter 1976): 5–6.

6. "Conservatism and International Order," *Essays Ancient and Modern* (London, 1936), pp. 113–14.

7. "Tradition and the Individual," *MA* 27 (Winter 1983): 82.

8. "The New Morality," *Aristocracy and Justice*, 9th series *Shelburne Essays* (1915; reprint ed., New York, 1967), p. 216.

9. *The Meaning of Tradition*, trans. A. N. Woodrow (New York, 1964), p. 7.

10. "The Coming of the Masses," in *The Revolt of the Masses* (1932; reprint ed., New York, 1957), p. 16.

11. For his understanding of transcendence and his view of spiritual, or "paradigmatic," history, see Eric Voegelin's *Order and History*, in four volumes: I, *Israel and Revelation* (Baton Rouge, 1956); II, *The World of the Polis* (Baton Rouge, 1956); III, *Plato and Aristotle* (Baton Rouge, 1957); IV, *The Ecumenic Age* (Baton Rouge, 1974).

12. George A. Panichas, "The Cult of Mediocrity," *MA* 15 (Fall 1971): 424.

13. *The Social Crisis of Our Time* (Chicago, 1950), p. i.

14. *MA* 5 (Spring 1961): 129.

15. *The World and the Individual*, 2nd series (New York, 1901), p. 360.

16. *MA* 15 (Winter 1971): 88.

17. "Conservatism," *The New Encyclopaedia Britannica: Macropaedia* (Chicago, 1985), 27: 476.

18. "*Modern Age* in a Changing World," *MA* 26 (Summer–Fall 1982): 351.

19. "On Being Conservative," in *Rationalism in Politics and Other Essays* (1962; reprint ed., London and New York, 1981), p. 166.

20. "American Intellectual Conservatism: Needs, Opportunities, Prospects," *MA* 26 (Summer–Fall 1982): 313.

Information Sources

BIBLIOGRAPHY: None.

INDEXES: Each volume indexed; *Amer Hist & Life*; *Articles Amer Lit*; *Bio Ind*; *BRI; Comb Ret Ind JPS*; *Comb Ret Ind Bk Revs Sch J*; *Curr Bk Rev Cit*; *Hist Abst*; *Hum Ind*; *Ind Bk Revs Hum*; *MLA Intl Bib*; *PAIS*; *Pol Sci Abst*; *Soc Sci Ind*; *Soc Abst*; *URS*; *Writings Amer Hist*.

REPRINT EDITIONS : Microform: BLH; KTO; MIM; UMI.

LOCATION SOURCES : Widely available.

Publication History

TITLE AND TITLE CHANGES: *Modern Age: A Conservative Review*, 1957–1962; *Modern Age: A Quarterly Review*, 1963–present.

VOLUME AND ISSUE DATA: Volumes 1–current, 1957–present.

FREQUENCY OF PUBLICATION: Quarterly.

PUBLISHER: Summer 1957–Summer 1959: Foundation for Foreign Affairs; Fall 1959–Fall 1962: Institute for Philosophical and Historical Studies; Winter 1962–1963–Summer 1976: Foundation for Foreign Affairs, all in Chicago; Fall 1976–present: Intercollegiate Studies Institute, Bryn Mawr, Pennsylvania, and, since 1996, in Wilmington, Delaware.

EDITORS: Russell Kirk, 1957–1959; Eugene Davidson, 1960–1969; David S. Collier, 1970–1983; George A. Panichas, 1984–present.

CIRCULATION: 3,000.

George A. Panichas

University Bookman
1960–

Since it first appeared in the autumn of 1960 as "A Quarterly Review of Educational Materials," the *University Bookman* has borne the imprint of one man, Russell Kirk, whose *The Conservative Mind: From Burke to Santayana* (1953) had done much in the preceding few years to lift opprobrium from the word conservative and help conservatives achieve self-definition. In his inaugural editorial, "The Recovery of Standards," Kirk set forth the new, pocket-size quarterly's purpose: "To restore and improve the standards of higher education in America" through the review of textbooks (mainly in the social sciences and humanities) and "the sensible criticism of educational theory and practice today." Primary and secondary education, he announced, might also come under scrutiny.[1] Although the magazine subsequently ranged widely beyond explicitly educational concerns, they surfaced frequently enough to provide continuity of subject matter and perspective.

The *University Bookman* began with an amazing circulation of about 30,000 and grew to well over 100,000. Behind this unusual outreach for a small, highly literate publication lies one simple fact: while the *University Bookman* has always had its own paid subscription list, from its birth to 1960 it went free of charge to all subscribers to the *National Review*, the preeminent organ of opinion of recent American conservatism edited by William F. Buckley, Jr. Although Kirk notified readers in 1990 that they could still request free subscriptions, circulation declined drastically thereafter and in 1996 stood at about 4,000.

The *National Review* did not carry the *Bookman* piggyback. Rather, from the beginning, it published and distributed Kirk's periodical by subsidy from the Educational Reviewer, a foundation established in New York in 1951 (supported in part by the Independent Businessmen's Association, which had an interest in evaluating educational materials for their treatment of communism and other topics). On the suggestion of Buckley, who believed that the Educational Reviewer and the *National Review* could assist each other, the foundation was reorganized in 1959 with Kirk as president and began the next year to publish the new quarterly. From his "ancestral home," Piety Hill, at Mecosta, Michigan, Kirk had absolute control of editorial matters; on his death in 1994, his wife, Annette, succeeded him as editor. With foundation backing, the Kirks have been able to pay contributors and to keep the subscription rate modest.[2]

Beginning in 1962 with Kenneth Shorey, a young actor and aspiring drama critic he had met in England, Kirk employed a succession of young men and women as editorial assistants. At first paid out of his pocket, in subsequent years a number of them have had fellowships from another Kirk-led foundation, the Marguerite Eyer Wilbur Foundation of Santa Barbara, California. Some have been students in the International College of Los Angeles, a "school without walls" that provides internships with noted scholars, writers, and artists for which its students receive academic credit. While at Mecosta for a year or two, they use Kirk's immense library, write for his criticism, carry on routine correspondence, and revise manuscripts for the *University Bookman* according to his specifications.[3]

Over the years, approximately two-thirds of the manuscripts published have been unsolicited (far more than could be used even after Kirk increased the *Bookman*'s size incrementally from twenty-four to forty pages). Although brief informational notices, book notes, and poems appear regularly, essays and reviews predominate. Contributors have come from several walks of life besides the academic. Many have been chance acquaintances of Kirk; others, influenced by his writings, have presumed that he would publish pieces on topics dear to his heart; some have been important figures in conservative intellectual circles and noted scholars in their fields. Some frequent contributors are conservative Protestants or not identifiable religiously, but many articles suggest a strong Roman Catholic traditionalism like that of the convert Kirk himself. According to Kirk, the *University Bookman* has reflected what people have sent in. There has been no litmus test of conservatism in editorial policy, but a striking likemindedness exists because of contributors' perceptions of his interests and tastes.[4]

A significant body of criticism of American public education had already accumulated by 1960, much of it directed at John Dewey and that collection of principles and practices known as progressive education. In the early 1950s such works as Arthur Bestor's *Educational Wastelands*, Albert Lynd's *Quackery in the Public Schools*, and Robert M. Hutchins's *The Conflict in Education* (all published in 1953) refurbished attacks on "life adjustment," the elective system, and the downgrading of traditional subjects. The *Sputnik* "crisis" of 1957 added intensity—and a very practical dimension—to arguments that American education was failing its tasks. In this chorus of disapproval the *University Bookman* readily joined, adding to elements of the indictment coming from other intellectual quarters its own distinctly conservative interpretation. A "traditionalist" who wished to have his journal embody "the spirit of Edmund Burke and T. S. Eliot," Kirk believed that education's purpose was to inculcate "wisdom and virtue," that it should transmit the cultural heritage, or "patrimony," of Western civilization, and that it should rest on the social values of prescription, order, and hierarchy.[5] The belief that it was not only progressive education but the liberalism of which progressive education was one expression that accounted for the confusion of purpose and loss of standards ran through much of the quarterly's commentary.

Consistent with its announced primary purpose, the *Bookman* for the first year concentrated on higher education. Thereafter, primary and secondary education began to receive regular attention, ranging from critiques of teacher education through reviews of textbooks and books about education, to surveys of developments in Europe. This emphasis remained primary throughout the 1960s, finally eclipsed by other concerns in the early 1970s.

The opening salvo in what can only be called an intense assault on contemporary public education came from Thomas Molnar of Brooklyn College, a Hungarian-born authority on French literature and philosophy and major figure in the conservative intellectual movement. Citing many examples of "educationist non-sense," he concluded that only by not following the prescriptions of teacher materials and educational literature could teachers in fact educate; examining especially historical and literary materials, he lamented the loss of traditional content and the filling of the consequent vacuum by positively harmful courses and methods.[6]

In similar vein, other authors carried on the attack on teacher education: its philosophy, curriculum, and expansion, and the caliber of people admitted to the profession. Although a huge business, it had "failed to develop any significant body of knowledge or research technique," the result being meaningless jargon and a proliferation of silly courses, wrote the reviewer of James D. Koerner's scathing *The Miseducation of American Teachers*.[7] Another reviewer blamed "Deweyism," vocationalism, life adjustment, and "Orwellian egalitarianism" for going so far beyond the legitimate need for mass education in a democracy as to sacrifice the development of individual intellect and the preparation of leaders; successfully leveling up the masses, American schools had also leveled down the talented.[8] One public school teacher took hope in the prospect of an oversupply of teachers in the 1970s, believing that it would enable school boards to hire more selectively.[9] Reviewing recent studies of American students' performance on achievement tests in 1982, Francis Griffith, professor emeritus of educational administration at Hofstra University, blamed "declining teacher competence" caused by both "almost farcical" admission standards in teachers' colleges, which made the profession "a refuge for second-raters," and the substitution for liberal arts courses of "unnecessary, inflated, fatuous, and repetitious" education offerings.[10]

Although in appraising textbooks the *University Bookman* sometimes found works to praise, more commonly it focused on deficiencies. It gave prominence to the views of John Carroll University's Arther S. Trace, Jr., whose *What Ivan Knows That Johnny Doesn't* (1961) and *Reading without Dick and Jane* (1965) faulted the abandonment of phonics, dilution of literary content in anthologies, foreign language instruction that was too little and too late, and the neglect of history and geography. While Ivan was getting Pushkin and Turgenev in his readers, one reviewer wrote, Johnny received "puppies, bunnies, Mommies, and Daddies." In his own contributions to the *Bookman*, Trace decried the absence in American textbooks of both a sense of nation and citizenship and exposure to serious literature. Each was due, he argued, to an educational philosophy that gave priority to life adjustment over knowledge and depreciated children's ability to grasp abstractions beyond their immediate range of experiences or to acquire complex vocabularies.[11] Other writers frequently echoed these complaints.[12]

On occasion, the *University Bookman* printed its own appraisals of textbooks, with a view to the presence of bias (particularly liberal bias), as well as to adequacy of coverage. Most noteworthy was a survey, coordinated by Ernest van den Haag of New York University and the New School for Social Research, of high school textbooks in five areas: American history, contemporary problems, civics, economics, and the social sciences. When published in 1966, these reviews by specialists in each field took up two entire issues. The reviewers' specific conclusions varied, but all took a dim view of the works they examined. Philip Crane, then a historian at Bradley University, found without exception a debilitating liberal bias in contemporary-problems books: negative portrayals of employers, uncritical treatment of labor unions, exaggerated estimates of the extent of poverty, and a noneconomic portrayal of social security—above all, an unexamined assumption that the "democratic process" and "reason" could resolve all great issues. Likewise, George W. Carey of the Department of Government at Indiana University found a monotonous notion that "right-thinking" and "cooperation" would lead to the "best solutions" to problems. Whatever the degree of bias alleged, van den Haag concluded that the fundamental defect was anti-intellectualism: "bitterly opposed to ideas—any ideas," the texts in all five categories merely repeated "current clichés," failing utterly to define concepts such as democracy, capitalism, scarcity, or their alternatives, avoiding intellectual problems by parading facts as if their implications were self-evident, and making no distinction among facts, analytical conclusions, and value judgments.[13] Whether it was a liberal bias or an anti-intellectual bias or whether the two were the same, American conservatives took little comfort in what students were reading in the mid-1960s.

The *University Bookman*'s educational commentary extended to other topics besides teacher education and textbooks. Although not characterized by a shrill anticommunism, it never viewed communism or the Soviet Union as anything but the enemies of Western civilization. Arther Trace's writings featured comparisons with Soviet educational requirements in a way that made it seem that the United States was losing the "brain power" race.[14] Other writers believed that American schoolchildren needed better instruction about totalitarianism, including, more than its external forms and methods, its "mentality and modes of thought," appeal to intellectuals, "dependence...on a mass democratic base," and linkage with the social-justice rights of liberal-democratic societies.[15] European educational developments sometimes also received a disapproving glance, especially state policies in Britain and Sweden aimed at eliminating inequality and exclusiveness.[16]

Finally, the *Bookman* strongly opposed the increasing federal role in American education. A study commissioned by the Educational Reviewer examined the transition from federal aid to the "colossal" federal control implicit in the Elementary and Secondary Education Act of 1965, suggesting that it would make the U.S. Office of Education into "a kind of sociological police force, determined to equalize *all* American education." Like Horace Mann before him, Dewey had wanted the schools to create a common culture among a heterogeneous people, but now his followers, naively believing that the schools could solve all social problems, including racial segregation, were going far beyond him to enlist the federal government for this end. From another angle, Roger A. Freeman, senior fellow at the Hoover Institution and consultant to President Nixon on economic and educational matters, tried to undercut one argument for increasing federal involvement by arguing that greater expenditures to lower class size and improve facilities did not result in better student performance on tests of basic skills. Greater federal aid could only mean greater federal control at the cost of local control, which alone guaranteed accountability to taxpayers.[17]

Criticisms of public education offered in the *University Bookman* sometimes exaggerated conditions, oversimplified issues, and rested on extreme positions. Moreover, the quarterly's function has been preponderantly negative; it has found much to disapprove and little to encourage, and it has offered, not so much alternatives as a return to some unspecified—and perhaps idealized—past. Kirk himself chose to send his daughters to Catholic schools after the first few years in Mecosta's elementary school and might therefore be regarded as an outsider taking cheap shots at public education, which has been overburdened by more and more diverse public expectations. Yet the *Bookman*'s concern for quality has not been misplaced, as *A Nation at Risk: The Imperative for Educational Reform*, the report of the National Commission on Excellence in Education issued in May 1983, attests. Annette Kirk served on that commission, and both Kirks found satisfaction in its promotion by the Reagan administration and in state and local responses to it.[18]

The *Bookman*'s view of higher education has been as panoramic as its coverage of precollegiate education. Pieces on university theater programs, a doctoral student's experiences at the London School of Economics, the problems of community colleges, reasons for failure among college students, and the ties between universities and government in Britain suggest the range of material that Kirk chose to present to readers.

Reviews of textbooks and scholarly works in the humanities and social sciences were central to the journal's purposes. Many reviews could have appeared in any journals appropriate to their subjects: neither the books nor the reviewers' evaluations fit into a conservative-liberal duality, and the tone was temperate, irenic, scholarly, and reflective. English composition books, for example, stood or fell largely on the basis of their organization, rigor, and prospective contribution to clear writing. Sometimes, however, the pursuit of conservative concerns followed the pattern of reviews of high school books. American history texts must not portray labor-management struggles in good-versus-evil terms, neglect conservative arguments against the New Deal, ignore the "revisionist" interpretation of American involvement in World War II, or minimize the threat of communism in the periods of the red scare and McCarthyism. Even when the objective of reviews was to identify liberal bias, as in a series coordinated in 1967–1968 by Ernest van den Haag, the result was not always an inquisition. Although the reviewer of political science texts assailed them for unquestioning acceptance of the "positive state" without seeing a "parallel" to totalitarianism, an American historian praised works in his field for stressing consensus over conflict and giving increased attention to conservative figures and ideas (despite lingering liberal assumptions), and the economics reviewer discerned virtually no bias in the books he examined. A review in 1982 of social science texts by one of Kirk's editorial assistants was more denunciatory. It blamed a "prevailing [liberal] ideology" for abolishing the transcendent and viewing man as a "malleable creature capable of being shaped by the social environment alone," for installing a "Rousseauistic" view of society as corrupt and human nature as inherently good, and for portraying social change, in progressivist terms, as the triumph of equality, democracy, and rights over republicanism, private property, and states rights.[19]

One of Kirk's principal quarrels with higher education has involved its pell-mell postwar expansion. In 1953 he achieved some notoriety for resigning from the faculty of Michigan State University in protest against the expansionary policies of President John A. Hannah and the deterioration of academic standards. It was natural, therefore, that his quarterly sharply criticized what he termed "Behemoth University."[20] Inspired by erroneous conceptions of higher education's purposes, this expansion created sad caricatures of true learning. Two forces were frequently credited with steering higher education away from (in Kirk's words) its *object—which is wisdom and virtue*": the expectation that it should be a means of social and economic mobility, and the liberal utopian belief that all problems are due to ignorance or misunderstanding. The former contributed to a proliferation of vocational programs at the expense of the liberal arts, the transmitter of the West's cultural heritage; the latter created hopes that education could bring secular salvation. Both brought hordes of ill-prepared, incapable, and improperly or insufficiently motivated students into the universities, with disastrous results: the overburdening of professors, use of graduate students as teachers, reliance on gimmicks to hold interest, prostitution of courses to relevance, inflation of grades, and preoccupation of administrators with numbers rather than quality.[21]

The emergence of the New Left and disruption of numerous campuses in the late 1960s and early 1970s confirmed the *Bookman*'s judgment that vast expansion and other recent trends in higher education bode only ill. Institutional growth was a handy explanation of much of the radicals' behavior and many of their demands (to some of which several contributors were initially sympathetic). The universities had become bureaucratic and impersonal, promised more than they could provide, devalued their own "coin" (the value of the diploma), and for financial reasons tied themselves to the service of the state. Beyond mere growth and its attendant influences, however, the dominance of liberal (and its extension, radical) ideology served to explain students' alienation and campus turmoil. Among the various analyses of liberal professors' and administrators' culpability, that of Donald M. Dozer, a historian at the University of California at Santa Barbara, stood out. A contributor of several articles to the *Bookman*, he believed that students intuitively aspired to live in a freer and more humane world than that represented by the university: its "nearly monolithic front" on all major questions, consisting of "the dogmas of statism camouflaged as modern liberalism," quashed freedom of thought and drove them to seek alternatives to "authoritarianism, centralism, and

socialism."[22]   The "deviant university" had created "deviant students."
Unfortunately, despite their idealistic inspiration, they were unable to break out of
the "Marxism…, nihilism, antihistoricism, anti-intellectualism, anarchism,
presentism, and vulgarism" in which the university had enmeshed them and found
no alternative but to politicize for their own ends the institutions that liberals had
already politicized.[23] Also unfortunately, when confronted by student challenges,
many professors and administrators proved unable to defend their institutions—in
some instances, because their own liberalism provided no basis for asserting
authority and order, in others, because it led them to romanticize the rebels. The
results, which Dozer flailed, included students' participation in academic decisions
for which they had no competence, faddish programs in minority and "creative"
studies, and the pressuring of the "embattled minority" of true intellectuals to make
their courses relevant to the temper of the times. Not all contributors on higher
education in these years followed Dozer's interpretation exactly, but all shared his
perturbation.[24]

After the early 1970s, the quarterly continued to track developments in
education—increasingly higher education rather than, as at the beginning, the
elementary and secondary levels. Sometimes there were glimmers of hope, but
the tone was mostly gloomy. Kirk himself included both the hopeful and the
discouraging in *Decadence and Renewal in the Higher Learning* (1978), a year-
by-year survey of episodes since 1953. An occasional author described educational
conditions abroad, but most dealt with conditions in American schools. Charles J.
Sykes's inflammatory criticisms of faculty research and the tenure system in
ProfScam:Professors And The Demise Of Higher Education (1988) received a
decidedly mixed review. Various authors critiqued current practice in teaching
English composition and offered suggestions for its reform; argued for a balance
between the lecture method and structured class discussions; offered suggestions
for teaching scientific theories; and delineated a "pastoral" role for professors to
enable them to offer students more than preparation for careers.[25] In general, the
tone was milder, the criticisms gentler, than had been the case in the stressful late
1960s and early 1970s.

From early on, the *University Bookman* included more than essays and reviews
on education. It is not unusual, in fact, for an issue to include virtually nothing on
education. Its other interests have always been chiefly history and literature, but it
has ranged among exceedingly diverse subjects. Examples of the quarterly's
ecumenical editorial criteria include a wistful essay on the automobile as a foe of
traditional Western values; reviews of books on terrorism, guerrilla warfare, and
South Africa; a polemic against the publicity attending Betty Ford's breast surgery;
a revision of the Little Red Riding Hood story using the imprecise word *area* in
place of more exact words; and a sharp response to the Catholic bishops' pastoral
letter on war and peace.[26]

As the instrument of Russell Kirk, the *University Bookman* belongs to the
traditionalist, as distinct from libertarian, strain of modern conservative thought.
On the whole, contributors have been more interested in social order and continuity
than in the atomistic individual, in culture than in economics. Their patron saint

has been not John Locke or Adam Smith but Edmund Burke. Yet for all their differences over the nature of freedom and its relation to authority, both strands of conservative thought have shared, if not a creed, a perspective on life in which "a passion for the liberty of the individual" is central.[27] Consequently, in its relatively sparse treatment of economics, the quarterly has been antistatist, criticizing the British welfare state, wage and price controls, the National Labor Relations Board, and even public funding of higher education.[28] It has given friendly reviews to works by such advocates of the market system as Edmund A. Opitz, William E. Simon, and George Gilder.[29] However, rather than lionizing the darlings of libertarians, the Austrian émigrés Ludwig von Mises and Friedrich A. Hayek, Kirk seems to have preferred the German economist Wilhelm Roepke, whose *A Humane Economy* (1960) argued for a third road between the orthodoxies of Left and Right. Although a foe of all collectivism, which he considered incompatible with Christian morality, Roepke criticized "historic capitalism" for, among other things, its materialism, its role in creating mass culture, and its shrinking of opportunities for individual initiative and creativity.[30] Without necessarily liking all the changes wrought in the West by industrialism under capitalism, the *Bookman* nonetheless saw freedom with order and responsibility better preserved through limited government and a market-oriented economy than through any available alternative.

Giving more attention to ideas than to social processes that threatened ordered freedom, many contributors have pointed to the eighteenth-century Enlightenment as the source of the "isms" that "have brought contemporary man to his present dilemma."[31] Negative code words like *empiricism*, *positivism*, *humanism*, *relativism*, *utopianism*, *liberalism*, *scientism*, and *egalitarianism* abound, and a strongly antimodernist temper is unmistakable. Both the faith in science and the scientific method that typified one side of Enlightened thinking and the romanticism and primitivism of Jean-Jacques Rousseau that reflected yet other Enlightenment tendencies fostered pernicious beliefs that flew in the face of the classical-Christian heritage of Western culture.

First, especially by applying the methods of physical science to man, the Enlightenment contributed to the modern "denial of normative ethical principles by which to determine values and judge human behavior"—to the denial of the concept of natural law itself. To traditionalist conservatives, who believed that moral and social norms were rooted in a transcendent order of reality outside nature and history, from which alone meaning in nature and history could be derived through Burke's "right reason," the drift of science toward naturalism was devastating. Placing ultimate answers to questions of human nature and destiny within the scope of science shifted Western thought from the "ethical-qualitative sphere" to that of the "physical-quantitative," from the "structure of consciousness" to the "outer" facts of the world. Without a transcendent framework of meaning, man became only a part of the natural order, subject only to the law of physical causation, and social science copied the assumptions and procedures of physical science, with frightful implications for social engineering and even "modern political absolutism."[32]

Second, the Enlightenment created an unrealistic estimate of human nature and potential. Here, Rousseau was a handy target. In contrast to the classical-Christian views of human nature as a mixture of good and evil, glory and depravity, Rousseau conjured up a noble savage free of civilized restraints. One contributor summarized Rousseau's basic thesis thus: "All evil, all sin, all inequality was the fault of society."[33] Egalitarian, majoritarian, utopian, and anti-institutional, this belief in inherent goodness and perfectibility unleashed, beginning with the French, the destructive revolutions of modern times. Not all contributors attributed, as did this reviewer, the terrors of Robespierre, Lenin, Hitler, and Stalin and the contemporary American counterculture to Rousseau. However, those who dealt with human nature generally found both liberalism and radicalism guilty of excessive optimism. The *Bookman*'s view of human nature implies that rights are not absolute and unlimited but conditioned by social relations; that structures of hierarchy and authority are necessary to check human perverseness; that "the people" should not be romanticized; and that the original American system of federalism (as expressed in the Constitution and the *Federalist Papers*) was uniquely suited to a realistic view of the human condition.[34]

Third, as the natural by-product of its faith in science and human goodness, the Enlightenment gave modern form to the idea of progress, formerly a Christian heresy. Through it, utopianism and messianism entered the mainstream of Western thought, bringing the Kingdom of God entirely within the scope of human history, subjecting all institutions to the critique of an ahistorical, abstract ideal, and fostering an urge to change without regard to consequences. Antiprogressivist to the core, the *Bookman* stressed that all sound change must be rooted in the history of a people, as had been the American Revolution. Not a "founding" but rather a conservation (of the rights of Englishmen), that revolution, unlike the French, conformed to the truth that a social order is "grown, not made," the result of human action but not human design.[35]

Throughout the years, the *University Bookman*'s historical and literary coverage has been highly selective, featuring individuals and movements that conformed to this understanding of life. Perhaps the intention has been, as in Kirk's writings, to reassure readers that there is, in fact, a respectable conservative tradition. Burke, the authors of the *Federalist Papers*, John Adams, John Randolph of Roanoke, Orestes Brownson, the New Humanists (Irving Babbitt and Paul Elmer More), the Southern Agrarians (Donald Davidson, John Crowe Ransom, and Robert Penn Warren), John Dos Passos (rescued for conservatives by the interpretation that a continuous "fear of power" unites his earlier and later works), T. S. Eliot, C. S. Lewis—one encounters these in the journal's pages, but not a host of other important personages and movements. This selective emphasis is congruent with another characteristic: a taken-for-granted quality that presumes an audience already convinced of the worldview being presented.

Given its educational and literary purview, the *University Bookman*'s avoidance of politics during the years of Republican resurgence after 1980 is unremarkable. When subjects like arms control, trade, the federal role in public education, and affirmative action came up, the treatment accorded them was typically philosophical, not political. To seek in this journal an account of the successes and failures of the

Reagan and Bush administrations would be in vain. In fact, were one not sensitive to the political proclivities of the editor and contributors, one might miss the political dimension of many essays and reviews altogether.

Russell Kirk took measured pride in this small journal. With a steady supply of capable assistants, he was able to nudge it along with minimal effort. On his death, there seems to have been no hesitation about continuing it. Its value to many readers has probably been secondary to that of other periodicals they received; witness the steep drop in circulation when it no longer came to readers because they got the *National Review*. One suspects that Kirk fully understood the niche his *Bookman* occupied in the world of conservative publications. There really was nothing else quite like it.

Notes

1. Russell Kirk, "The Recovery of Standards," *University Bookman* 1 (Autumn 1960): 4–5 (hereinafter cited as *UB*). After the first issue, the subtitle became simply *A Quarterly Review*, but this reflected no alteration of the original purposes.

2. Interview with Russell Kirk, Mecosta, Michigan, 27–28 May 1983; "The Educational Reviewer, Incorporated," 1983 brochure, from Russell Kirk. Beginning at $2.00, the cost of a subscription increased slowly, and only twice, to reach $10.00 in 1996.

3. "News and Notes," *UB* 16 (Summer 1976): 94; Wilbur Foundation brochure, 1983, from Russell Kirk.

4. Interview with Kirk, 27–28 May 1983.

5. Cf. George H. Nash, *The Conservative Intellectual Movement in America: Since 1945* (New York, 1976), introduction and passim for a superb differentiation between "traditionalist" and other strands of conservatism; interview with Kirk, 27–28 May 1983.

6. Thomas Molnar, "Un-Education," *UB* 2 (Autumn 1961 and Winter 1962): 3–8, 36–42.

7. Michael F. Connors, review of James D. Koerner, *The Miseducation of American Teachers* (1963), *UB* 4 (Autumn 1963): 14–17.

8. Warren L. Fleischauer, review of John N. Wales, *Schools of Democracy: An Englishman's Impressions of Secondary Education in the American Middle-West* (1962), *UB* 3 (Summer 1963): 75–84.

9. Frank D. Albro, "The Teacher Surplus: Boon or Bombshell?" *UB* 12 (Autumn 1971): 14–17.

10. Francis Griffith, "Teachers Are Part of the Problem," *UB* 23 (Autumn 1982): 9–17.

11. Mortimer Smith, review of Arther S. Trace, Jr., *Reading without Dick and Jane*, *UB* 6 (Winter 1966): 45–47; William Morrison, review of Trace, *What Ivan Knows That Johnny Doesn't*, *UB* 2 (Summer 1962): 95–98; Arther S. Trace, Jr., "Patriotism in Soviet and American Textbooks," *UB* 2 (Winter 1962): 27–35, and "The Literary Limbo in American Schools," *UB* 3 (Winter 1963): 27–34. Trace's "Can Ivan Read Better than Johnny?" in the *Saturday Evening Post*, 27 May 1961, achieved some notoriety for him.

12. Robert Cluett IV, "English and the American High School," *UB* 3 (Spring 1963): 51–57, and "Dick, Jane, and the Secondary Schools," *UB* 5 (Autumn 1964): 3–7; Robert Beum, "Textbooks and the Audience for Poetry," *UB* 4 (Spring 1964): 56–62; Charles F. Hampton, "Where's That?" *UB* 6 (Autumn 1965): 12–14; Regis Courtemanche, "This School Doesn't Teach History," *UB* 10 (Spring 1970): 51–55.

13. *UB* 6 (Summer 1966): 75–101, and 7 (Autumn 1966): 4–31.

14. Arther S. Trace, Jr., review of William Benton, *The Teacher and the Taught in the U.S.S.R.* (1966), *UB* 7 (Spring 1967): 66–68.

15. Henry Winthrop, "What Should Teachers Know about Communism?" *UB* 9 (Spring 1969): 51–57; William S. Lind, "Studying Totalitarianism in Secondary Schools," *UB* 10 (Spring 1970): 56–59.

16. George Scott-Moncrieff, "Egalitarian Education in Britain," *UB* 7 (Winter 1967): 35–42; Nils-Eric Brodin, "Education and the Swedish Welfare State," *UB* 9 (Winter 1969): 27–30.

17. Peter P. Witonski, "The Federal Schoolmaster," *UB* 8 (Summer 1968): 91–104; Roger A. Freeman, "The Concept of Accountability in Education," *UB* 11 (Summer 1971): 75–89, and "Should Local School Support Be Abolished?" *UB* 12 (Summer 1972): 75–85.

18. For example, the Reverend Peter J. Stravinskas's assertion in a review of Samuel L. Blumenfeld's *Is Public Education Really Necessary?* (1981), *UB* 23 (Autumn 1982): 21–23, that "in a free society government has no more place in education than it has in religion." Review of Samuel L. Blumenfeld, *Is Public Education Really Necessary? UB* 23 (Autumn 1982): 21–23. Annette Kirk, "Reflections on 'A Nation at Risk,'" *UB* 28, no. 4 (1988): 14–16.

19. *UB* 8 (Autumn 1967 and Winter 1968): 3–31, 35–63; Gregory Wolfe, "The Abolition of Man Revisited: College Textbooks in the Social Sciences," *UB* 22 (Summer 1982): 75–93.

20. Russell Kirk, *Decadence and Renewal in the Higher Learning: An Episodic History of American University and College since 1953* (South Bend, Indiana, 1978), pp. xxi, 20–29.

21. Ernest van den Haag, "Education as Part of America's Secular Religion," *UB* 1 (Autumn 1960 and Winter 1961): 7–14, 44–47; Frederick D. Wilhelmsen, "Reflections on the Utility of a Disinterested Education," *UB* 2 (Spring 1962): 52–60; Louis A. Fanning, "The Case against the College's Open Door," *UB* 10 (Spring 1970): 60–61. Wilhelmsen decried spending vast sums to make it "almost absurdly and indecently easy to gain a university education."

22. Donald M. Dozer, "The Deviant University," *UB* 10 (Autumn 1969): 3–12.

23. Donald M. Dozer, "Right On—Up with Higher Education," *UB* 12 (Autumn 1971): 3–13; Dozer, review of Edward E. Ericson, *Radicals in the University* (1975), *UB* 17 (Autumn 1976): 19–23.

24. Donald M. Dozer, "Educational Humbuggery," *UB* 15 (Autumn 1974): 16–22, and *UB* 17 (Winter 1977): 32–35. Cf. Allen C. Brownfield, "Politics, Democracy, and the University," *UB* 12 (Winter 1972): 27–34, and "Visions of Discontent," *UB* 14 (Summer 1974): 85–88; Stephen R. Maloney, "After Such Knowledge, What Forgiveness?" *UB* 14 (Summer 1974): 75–84, and review of Paul Seabury, ed., *Universities in the Western World* (1975), *UB* 17 (Winter 1977): 36–39; Haven Bradford Gow, review of Adam Ulam, *The Fall of the American University* (1972), *UB* 14 (Summer 1974): 89–92.

25. Anthony Kerrigan, "What Do the Newly 'Literate' Read in Communist Countries?" *UB* 28, no. 3 (1988): 3–8; Andrew J. Spano, "College Education in China and the United States," *UB* 30, no. 3 (1990): 14–19; Regis Courtemanche and Eleanor Cortemanche, "The Fraudulent Professor," *UB* 29, no. 2 (1989): 4–9; Thomas Whissen, "Politics and the 'Writing Specialist,'" *UB* 30, no. 4 (1990): 4–9; Mario Gero, "Problems with Socratic Teaching," *UB* 24 (Winter 1984): 37–40; Ralph W. Lewis, "Theories, Concepts, Mapping, and Teaching," *UB* 27 (Summer 1987): 4–10; Henry N. Carrier, "Narcissism: Goodbye to That Pastoral Professing," *UB* 24 (Winter 1984): 28–33.

26. Robert Beum, "Conservatism and the Car," *UB* 13 (Autumn 1972): 3–11; reviews in *UB* 17 (Summer 1977): 70–71, 82–83, and *UB* 18 (Summer 1978): 89–90; Louis Filler, "Betty's Breast, and Other Matters of Democratic Import," *UB* 16 (Winter 1976): 27–31; Paul Roche, "Little Red Riding Hood in a Dangerous Area," *UB* 29, no. 1 (1989): 4–5; Laurence W. Beilenson, "A Response to the Bishops," *UB* 25 (Autumn 1984): 21–23.

27. Allen C. Brownfield, review of Frank S. Meyer, ed., *What Is Conservatism?* (1964), *UB* 5 (Spring 1965): 65–68.

28. Cf. reviews in *UB* 17 (Summer 1977): 92–93; *UB* 20 (Spring 1980): 61–62; *UB* 3 (Spring 1963): 62–65; and Ernest van den Haag, "Educational Inflation," *UB* 15 (Spring 1975): 51–59.

29. Cf. reviews in *UB* 18 (Summer 1978): 93–94; *UB* 19 (Winter 1979): 35–38; *UB* 22 (Autumn 1981): 19–21.

30. Patrick M. Boarman, "Wilhelm Roepke and the 'Third Road,'" *UB* 18 (Autumn 1977): 3–8; William F. Campbell, review of Joseph Baldacchino, *Economics and the Moral Order* (1985), *UB* 28, no. 1 (1988): 12–15.

31. Peter Stanlis, review of Louis I. Bredvold, *The Brave New World of the Enlightenment* (1961), *UB* 3 (Autumn 1962): 9.

32. Ibid., 9–15; Claes G. Ryn, "Notes on the Cultural Revolution," *UB* 11 (Autumn 1970): 3–8.

33. Jeffrey St. John, review of Otto J. Scott, *Robespierre: The Voice of Virtue* (1975), *UB* 16 (Autumn 1975): 16–23.

34. Dennis T. Connell, review of Henry Sumner Maine, *Popular Government* (1978 ed.), *UB* 18 (Summer 1978): 84–88; Robert Heineman, "Ideological Inflexibility and the Human Condition," *UB* 20 (Winter 1980): 27–39; Richard F. Gibbs, "The Spirit of '89: Conservatism and the Bicentenary," *UB* 14 (Spring 1974): 51–61.

35. Samuel T. Francis, review of M. E. Bradford, *A Better Guide Than Reason: Studies in the American Revolution* (1979), *UB* 20 (Spring 1980): 55–57.

Information Sources

BIBLIOGRAPHY: None.
INDEXES: Each volume indexed; *BRI*; *PAIS*; *Soc Abst*.
REPRINT EDITIONS: Microform: UMI.
LOCATION SOURCES: Widely available.

Publication History

TITLE AND TITLE CHANGES: *The University Bookman; A Quarterly Journal of Educational Materials*, Autumn 1960; *The University Bookman; A Quarterly Review*, Winter 1960–1961–present.
VOLUME AND ISSUE DATA: Volumes 1–current, 1960–present.
FREQUENCY OF PUBLICATION: Quarterly.
PUBLISHER: Educational Reviewer, New York.
EDITOR: Russell Kirk, 1960–1994; Annette Kirk, 1994–present.
CIRCULATION: 4,000.

Jacob H. Dorn

Intercollegiate Review
1965–

When a vigorous intellectual conservatism began to emerge after World War II, it consisted of three discrete varieties of antiliberal and anticollectivist thought. There was "not one right-wing renascence but three," according to the movement's historian, George H. Nash. "Libertarians," and some who preferred the designation "classical liberals," feared the twentieth-century growth of government power and stressed the need to defend free-market capitalism. "Traditionalists" disdained the corrosive effects of liberal thought on classical and Christian values and the secularism and normlessness of mass society. An aggressive and uncompromising anticommunist group, influenced by a number of Americans who had been Marxists or Trotskyists in the 1930s and some European emigrés, saw the West engaged in an unremitting struggle for survival against a totalitarian ideology bent on world supremacy. Although all three were antiliberal and committed to preserving individual freedom, they were at first virtually independent of each other, and there were significant differences of perspective and emphasis. In fact, it took some years before even the common name conservative achieved wide acceptance.[1]

The *Intercollegiate Review* originated in 1965 as the publication of a libertarian organization, the Intercollegiate Society of Individualists (ISI), founded in 1953 by Frank Chodorov. Chodorov was a principal figure in the postwar revival of libertarianism and the author of *One Is a Crowd* (1952) and *The Income Tax: Root of All Evil* (1954). He believed that a collectivist hegemony in higher education was due in part to the influence of the earlier Intercollegiate Socialist Society (renamed the League for Industrial Democracy) and wished to create an "organization of ideas" to exercise a comparable impact for individualism. Chodorov collaborated with William F. Buckley, Jr., whose *God and Man at Yale* (1951) dovetailed with his own views, and with Buckley as president, the ISI set out to build bridges to conservatively inclined students and professors by disseminating right-wing literature, aiding conservative clubs, and coordinating campus lectures.

The society grew rapidly, rising in eight years from 600 to 13,000 members and by 1996 to more than 56,000. Over the years it has added other publications to its outreach: the *I.S.I. Campus Report* and later *Campus: America's Student Newspaper*; *Modern Age* (founded by Russell Kirk in 1957 and taken over by the ISI in 1977, when it faced financial difficulty); the *Political Science Reviewer*, and, for awhile, the historical journal *Continuity*. It has also sponsored the Richard M. Weaver Fellowships for students committed to college teaching, an alumni association, conferences on the role of business in society for secondary school teachers, a lecture bureau, and seminars by conservative intellectuals. In short, it helped to create an alternative intellectual community. Although some observers consider *Modern Age* more important intellectually, the *Review* has been called the ISI's "flagship publication." Heavily subsidized by small-business and family foundations, it goes free of charge to professors and students: in 1996, 50,000 were on the free list, and another 15,000 (some of whom were eligible to receive it free) paid for their subscriptions.[2]

By the time the ISI began publishing the *Review*, a convergence of the three strands of postwar conservatism had occurred. Recognition of a common interest in individual freedom played a part in this convergence, as did the efforts of some leaders to contain internecine bickering. One of the foremost of the traditionalists, Russell Kirk, declined at first to lend his name to the work of the ISI because of what he considered "anarchistic" positions it had taken. But the journal's initial editorial advisory board was ecumenical; the participation of such men as Richard V. Allen, Yale Brozen, Philip M. Crane, Donald Davidson, M. Stanton Evans, Willmoore Kendall, Thomas Molnar, Gerhart Niemeyer, and Leo Strauss indicated that the new periodical would be eclectic and pan-conservative. So did the statement of purposes, which included both the supreme importance of individual freedom and the preservation of the values and norms of Western civilization. As if to underscore the journal's receptivity to divergent views, Robert Ritchie, the first editor, stated: "We disagree with those who hold that progress is achieved and freedom secure with every advance or retreat of governmental power."[3] When the society changed its name to Intercollegiate Studies Institute in 1966, the year of Chodorov's death, that change revealed a desire to transcend the narrower libertarian trademark, "Individualists."[4] On occasion, the *Review* would reflect minor personal and philosophical conflicts, but its spirit was unitive. Differences were not ordinarily highlighted, and authors of all three persuasions had access to its pages.

The *Review*'s subject matter has been exceedingly diverse. Political theory, history, literature, and philosophy have received frequent coverage. A representative list of historical and literary topics and figures would include existentialism; the New Humanism of Irving Babbitt and Paul Elmer More; Aleksandr Solzhenitsyn; the individualism of Robert Frost; Albert Jay Nock; Alexis de Tocqueville's analysis of American democracy; comparisons of the French and American revolutions; and major ancient and modern political philosophers. Often the purpose has been to establish a usable conservative intellectual genealogy. However, the journal has also given prominence to current policy issues. In view of the proliferation in the 1960s and 1970s of conservative institutes, research centers, and think tanks, and a shift in conservative thought as the movement matured from problems in self-definition to application, such an orientation is not surprising. Contributors too have been a diverse lot, ranging from graduate students to big league academicians, corporate executives, foundation officers, publicists, and government officials. Among the household names of intellectual conservatism represented are Richard M. Weaver, Ludwig von Mises, Robert Nisbet, Will Herberg, John Lukacs, and M. E. Bradford, as well as Molnar, Kendall, Niemeyer, Kirk, Evans, and Brozen. The journal has clearly enabled conservative students and professors, mindful of their minority status, to feel prideful membership in a larger, intellectually significant enterprise.

Their opposition to liberalism, which they usually saw as tending inevitably toward collectivism, led many contributors to search for the intellectual sources of its errors and excesses. At the risk of arraying themselves against major trends in Western thought since early modern times, they often stressed the damaging effects of scientific rationalism—effects both philosophical and methodological. There were differences of opinion as to relevant historical watersheds, but authors generally agreed that the fatal flaw in modern thought was a denial of any objective reality beyond the purview of science. An exaggerated faith in the natural sciences had weakened the older belief, nurtured by the classical and Judeo-Christian traditions, that a transcendent order of reality gave ultimate purpose to human experience and provided a basis for human dignity and freedom. The drift of the scientific worldview had been toward materialism (the order of nature as ultimate reality), and humanity itself had become demeaned by a prevailing philosophical naturalism. In its most recent forms, this naturalism had adopted the reductionist perspectives of behaviorism and environmentalism.[5]

In this same vein, the *Review* faulted humanists and social scientists for misappropriating the methods of the physical and biological sciences. The companion of philosophical naturalism, empiricism defined the method of sensory observation as the only means of apprehending reality. For scholars in the liberal arts to adopt a misleading "facticity" was to substitute education as the analysis of means for education as the analysis of ends, argued one historian. Other contributors attacked the ideal of "value-free" social science for reducing human beings to objects, leading to a relativistic ethic, and, because scholars smuggled in their own value judgments anyway, being hypocritical. In both respects, as metaphysics and as method, science had contributed to the loss of any ontological referent for values.[6]

Technology, the twin sister of science, also bore responsibility for what conservatives disliked about the modern temper. The renowned sociologist (and ex-Marxist) Will Herberg found many reasons for a widespread rejection of moral and metaphysical universals and for the decline of religion as an organizing force in modern society. Primary among them was the fascination of modern people with technological advancement. Vast in its historical impact, technology had substituted power—first over nature, then over human beings—for truth as the object of human aspiration. It had raised up the fallacious notion that all human problems could be resolved through manipulation and social engineering. It had undermined a sense of the transcendent and realism about human limitations, thus enticing finite beings to put themselves in the place of God. Both science and technology conjured up the alluring hope of progress, to which the *Review* was unmistakably hostile. Usually portraying the idea of progress as linear, naive, and utopian, the journal suggested that it recurred in history when traditional religion was decaying and belief in the unbroken accumulation of secular knowledge was rising. No innocent concept, "progressism" served as a surrogate for the personal salvation of theistic religion and, especially in its modern form, carried collectivist—even totalitarian—tendencies.[7]

This indictment was broad indeed and marked by sweeping generalization and a worst-possible-case depiction of the condition of modern culture. The critique was not always phrased in explicitly antiliberal terms. Nevertheless, given the character of the *Review* and its audience, the implication was clear: liberalism had at least connived in the erosion of the West's traditional philosophical and religious foundations, and only conservatism could be counted on to offer correctives. Although the announced purpose of the *Review* was to set the clock "right," not "back," there was little to suggest what a conservative program of rectification might be. As in its treatment of specific public policy issues, so in its historical, literary, and philosophical pieces, the journal was adept at criticism of extreme tendencies in liberal thought, but it was not unambiguous in identifying the alternatives to which it would persuade those not already convinced.

Until the collapse of communist regimes in Eastern Europe and the breakup of the Soviet Union, the ultimate threat to Western civilization was communism. In numerous articles and reviews, the journal reminded readers about communist efforts to eradicate the traditional cultures of Central and Eastern Europe and of China, of Soviet persecution of Jews, of Stalin's terror, and of the impossibility of a free intellectual life in a Marxist regime. Against the desire of some ex-communists, social democrats, and liberals to exonerate Marx of responsibility for communist repression, several authors argued that Marx's "total critique" of existing society, his philosophical materialism and determinism, and his "romantic ideal of social unity" led inexorably to despotic government.[8] The threat of Marxism for these authors was more than the military and geopolitical strength of the Soviet Union. Nor was Marxism itself merely an alternative political and economic system. The threat consisted also of the susceptibility of the educated classes in the West to its totally enveloping ideology. Liberalism's own rejection of spiritual values, its naturalism and determinism, its collectivism, and its utopianism made it myopic in regard to this monstrous system. Even more crucial, modern man's loss of faith and of order in the soul, which must be rooted in acknowledgment of a ground of being outside the self and society and beyond nature and history, made him vulnerable to Marxism's siren song of perfection within the current temporal order.[9]

The libertarian parentage of the *Review* and the common opposition of all kinds of conservatives to encroachments on individual freedom gave the periodical a decided interest in presenting the case for a market-oriented economy and in criticizing many types of government activity. Much of the *Review*'s economic content came from economists with libertarian credentials, representing both of the major schools of twentieth-century libertarian economics. One school derived from the Austrian Carl Menger's opposition in the late nineteenth century to German "historical" economics, which supported Bismarck's "state socialism." In this tradition, with a strong commitment to "classical" economics, stood such figures as Friedrich A. Hayek and Ludwig von Mises, both celebrated in the *Review* with only an incidental demurrer. Somewhat more pragmatic, and more given to quantitative methods, was the Chicago school of Henry Simons, Frank H. Knight, George J. Stigler, Milton Friedman, and Yale Brozen. Despite differences of theory and methodology, both traditions were committed to freely functioning individuals and groups in the marketplace. The *Review* highlighted work by scholars of both persuasions and also honored the mediating figure, Wilhelm Roepke, who combined opposition to all collectivism with sharp criticism of historic capitalism.[10]

At the level of theory, a frequent concern of authors on economic topics was to defend capitalism against moral objections to unequal distribution of wealth. One line of argument was that whatever its faults, capitalism had achieved levels of productivity and a standard of living far higher than those of any other system; Marxists' predictions of an ever widening gap between rich and poor and of capitalism's increasing rigidity and eventual collapse were patently false. Another approach was to compare conditions in general under capitalism with the failures of planning in socialist economics. Yet other authors rejected the moral indictment as an unwarranted abstraction. Judgments about distributive justice involved analysis of millions of individuals and their actions as moral agents; the existence of inequality did not mean that the economic system was to blame, for differences in individual intelligence, ability, and industry must be taken into account. Moreover, differences in monetary reward were defensible as incentives to performance. History had produced no satisfactory altruistic alternatives, and compulsory ones might leave everyone not only poorer but also less free.[11]

Ordinarily, contributors to the *Review* engaged not in defenses of market capitalism, but in attacks on governmental intervention. Presumably none would have advocated absolute laissez faire. But because their efforts were overwhelmingly negative, a reader could not confidently draw a clear line between acceptable and unacceptable governmental roles. That was probably as intended. In the face of continual expansion of government's economic functions, the point was not to establish a doctrine or formula; it was, rather, to heighten concern. Contributors sought to do so by pointing to unforeseen consequences of regulatory activities, minimum wage laws, and restrictions on competition; by assailing latter-day Keynesianism and the ideas of John Kenneth Galbraith; and by laying at the doorstep of big government the blame for "stagflation."

In reviewing domestic issues of the 1960s and 1970s the *Review* also displayed hostility to the growing role of government as an agent of social welfare. Conservatives opposed "social engineering," wrote one essayist, because, in the name of "progress" toward some arbitrary design, the social engineer committed three egregious errors: he ignored the limits on the power of reason to improve things, overestimated human goodness, and neglected long-range consequences in favor of immediate results. All three led inevitably to statism. The founders, with a realistic view of human nature and fondness for limited government, had known better. Contrasting the nineteenth-century's "autonomous individual" with the twentieth's "autonomous state," another writer cautioned against the "bureaucratic imperialism" common to all forms of government. To equate the public interest with the self-interest of bureaucrats was folly, for their self-interest lay in obstructing the workings of the market system and advancing policies that would fail, so that they could demand more spending and more power for themselves.[12]

Liberals were often censured for distorting the original American constitutional system of limited powers, respect for diversity, and careful balance between the states and national authority. Influenced by John Locke and Adam Smith, whose ideas were inherent in the document of 1787, and by a realistic Christian view of human nature, the founders had believed that dispersal of power was the key to liberty. Liberals' conception of a "living Constitution" subject to reinterpretation in the light of changing social needs had undermined the "classical liberal" charter that originally embodied economic liberty under due process.[13] For the Supreme Court and some of its landmark decisions on touchy issues (civil rights, reapportionment, and free speech, among others), there was virtually no sympathy. Liberalism's errors were also the focus of articles on race relations and the urban "crisis." In a single issue in 1965, three authors addressed different aspects of the civil rights movement. Although none approved the nation's treatment of blacks, one referred to the fair employment and public accommodations titles of the Civil Rights Act of 1964 as "authoritarian counter-measures by a national majority" against the authoritarianism of the white South, another disliked these and open-housing statutes for their "coercive" nature, and the third feared that civil rights advocates' unwillingness to wait for a national consensus was heading the United States toward a constitutional crisis.[14] For Will Herberg, writing some years later, both the "insane 'welfare' system," which weakened the black family, and the civil rights movement, which caused "the intense exacerbation of race relations," were mistakes. Claiming to offer a historical and sociological perspective, yet disregarding a mass of contrary historical and sociological evidence, he insisted that the "Negro-Problem" was comparable to other cases of "ethnic-migrant acculturation" in American society. It was not a problem of color but one of gaining middle-class acceptability (and thus, integration) by the same means as other ethnic and racial groups. A national policy of "benign neglect" would be best, with no more than the forms of indirect federal assistance suggested by Daniel P. Moynihan and Nathan Glazer: subsidies to private industries for job training, a family assistance plan, and encouragement of self-help. Similar in spirit was the sociologist Robert Nisbet's evaluation of the urban "crisis" in a lead article review of Edward C. Banfield's *The Unheavenly City* (1970). Liberal doomsayers were wrong, Nisbet summarized, in exaggerating urban blight, attributing discontent to conditions rather than to rising expectations, and insisting that federal programs offered solutions. Trusting the "adaptive responses" of those closest to the problems, he urged conscience-driven activists, "Don't just do something. Sit there!"[15]

The *Review* also devoted a significant proportion of its pages to foreign policy. As conservatives, contributors had to steer between the Scylla and Charybdis of the idealist-realist debate over American policy. Their affirmations of objective moral values obliged them to acknowledge legitimate moral purposes in the nation's diplomacy, yet the specter of communism and their insistence on taking the world as it is, without utopian expectations, combined to give a hard-boiled character to their definitions of national interests and prescriptions for action.

The most explicit attempt to analyze the historical relationship of idealism and realism in American policy came from James E. Dornan of Catholic University. He agreed with conservatives' veneration for the founders, but placed at their feet much of the blame for confusion at the level of design. Their realism about the young nation's vulnerability and their optimism that the world was destined in any event for American-style liberty inclined them to prudence, but their understanding of the American experience was inherently moral and ideological. Although circumstances pushed them in an isolationist direction, they believed in the United States' uniqueness and special role in the political redemption of humanity and thus were responsible for much of latter-day naiveté, globalism, internationalism, and disregard for realities. The decisive ending of all possibility of an isolationist policy after 1945 exposed, as it never had before, the tension between moralistic-idealistic and realistic strands in Americans' understanding of their role in the world.

Dornan's sympathy should have been with the realist side in the idealist-realist debate of the 1950s and 1960s. However, he found such thinkers as George F. Kennan and J. William Fulbright not realistic enough: both underrated the ideological character of the Soviet Union and trusted too much to the power of American example and leadership to offer a satisfactory design for a dangerous future. Seeking primarily to draw conservatives' attention to the problem, he did not attempt his own reconciliation of the nation's legitimate moral purposes and the realities of world power.[16]

Whatever other contributors may have thought of realist theoreticians, they emphatically called for "realism" about particular policy questions. The idea of achieving peace through international organizations; the Test Ban Treaty of 1963, SALT II, and the "treaty trap" in general; and increasing trade with the Soviet Union as a means of easing tensions—these won no praise.[17] Several authors warned of a coming Soviet military superiority if current trends continued; another believed that while liberalized trade would produce no important benefits for the United States, it would enable the Soviets to cover their own deficiencies and enhance their political stature.[18]

Implicit in all discussions of military policy was an acceptance of the doctrine of deterrence. In dealing with nuclear deterrence, contributors had to anticipate the moral argument that nuclear devastation would far exceed the values for which such use of force might be made—the argument that a nuclear war could not be a "just war." Their answer was that physical survival, without regard to the quality of life, could not be mankind's supreme value. Given the "intrinsic nature" of the conflict between communist totalitarianism and the values of the West, refusal to use nuclear deterrence would be "moral nihilism." Such refusal might, moreover, eventuate in submission to an aggressor without scruples about nuclear weapons, with equally massive destruction of human beings *and* their values.[19]

Because of their view of Soviet ideology, the *Review*'s authors criticized what they considered unrealistic hopes for convergence and for the policy of détente. Soviet leaders were not reasonable men, needing only to be coaxed out of their isolation-induced hostility. Their ideology threatened not only the security but also the culture of other nations. The United States had a moral right and an obligation to resist this evil force, as it had with Nazism. By encouraging a view of the Soviets as normal, peace-loving men, détente might weaken the West's willingness to make such a moral judgment. President Jimmy Carter's human rights policy and the test of "linkage" seemed to protect against such an outcome, but the results were mixed. The Soviets were able to shrug off criticism of their behavior, and the full weight of American moral censure fell on such allies as Rhodesia, South Africa, and Chile. And between the human rights offenses of these nations and the total system of communism, there was a vast moral difference. In fact, Notre Dame's Gerhart Niemeyer, while opposed to the "perfectionist" and "millenarian" tendencies of a universal moralism in foreign policy, insisted that moral repugnance must guide the United States' posture toward communist Russia.[20]

Not surprisingly, the *Intercollegiate Review* defended the United States' efforts to prevent the communization of South Vietnam. It was not so much that American involvement was accepted without question; it was, rather, that once the nation was at war, there was no substitute for victory. This perspective figured largely too in assertions that the domino theory, no matter how ineptly stated by its advocates, contained important insights. Among several domino effects seen by one author, an inevitable "contraction in the boundaries of American influence, and a diminution of the U.S. role in world affairs" were primary. Whatever misgivings some contributors had about the wisdom of the American role, the *Review* rejected antiwar critics' claims that the war was simply a civil conflict, that the Saigon government was so unrepresentative and corrupt that it did not merit support, that Ho Chi Minh was the George Washington of the Vietnamese people, and that the South Vietnamese regime had scuttled national elections provided for in the Geneva Accords of 1954.[21] A similar tendency to justify American policy appeared in reviews of the "revisionist" historiography of the origins of the cold war that emerged during the conflict in Southeast Asia.[22]

Given its purposes and readership, it was natural that the *Review* took frequent note of developments in higher education. Contributors generally viewed higher education's purposes in traditionalist terms; Robert Nisbet's definition of the "academic dogma" as the belief in knowledge for its own sake was typical. This definition was implicit in the priority given to strong undergraduate instruction in the arts and sciences and to disinterested scholarship. Lamenting recent trends that they saw as perverting the true purposes and values of higher education, conservative critics pointed especially to the effects of gargantuan size on the learning atmosphere, a decline in standards brought on by admission of a flood of incapable or improperly motivated students, and the diversion of professors' and administrators' interests to government and foundation grants and to public policy influence.[23]

Their critique of the growth and bureaucratization of the universities enabled some contributors to find an element of legitimacy in the student protests that began with the Free Speech Movement at Berkeley in 1964. More commonly, however, the *Review* explained the developing campus radicalism as an outgrowth of liberalism. Analyses of the relationship varied. Stephen J. Tonsor, a historian at the University of Michigan, criticized professors for forgetting the university's "essentially conservative" functions and teaching students instead the need to change the world. Others singled out behaviorism, positivism, egalitarianism, or ethical relativism as features of liberal thought that contributed to radicalism. M. Stanton Evans argued that the New Left shared with liberalism a collectivist drive, though it went further to a totalitarianism that combined Marxist concepts with the romantic explosiveness and fascination with violence of Nazism. In each analysis, however, liberalism received at least some of the blame for the embattled state of higher education.[24]

The *Review*'s educational coverage in the stressful late 1960s and early 1970s also included such issues as the moral right of civil disobedience, theoretical justifications of revolution, the nature of academic freedom, public universities' accountability to taxpayers, student and faculty power in governance, curricular innovations, the doctrine of "repressive tolerance" of the Marxist philosopher Herbert Marcuse, and the roots and character of the counterculture. Predictably, authors had little patience for challenges to institutional authority, the weakening of a core curriculum grounded in the humanities, and radical political activities.[25]

That campus turmoil subsided in the early 1970s did not diminish the *Review*'s criticism of academia. Conservative standard-bearers in the culture wars of the 1980s and 1990s—T. Kenneth Cribb, a former staff member in President Ronald Reagan's White House; Lynne V. Cheney, chair of the National Endowment for the Humanities; and President John Silber of Boston University—found much to lament in American higher education, despite the newfound political strength of conservatives. To the traditional list of liberal perversions, other authors added multiculturalism, feminism, structuralism, and deconstructionism in the humanities and social sciences.[26]

Beginning at a time when conservatives of various kinds but with a common distaste for twentieth-century liberalism had begun to coalesce, the *Intercollegiate Review* was from the first a forum for virtually any intellectually based conservative position. Although one may discern the distinctive emphases of libertarians in its economic treatises, those of anticommunists in its framing of discussions of Marxism and Soviet-American relations, and those of traditionalists in its cultural and educational analyses, such differentiations have not been rigid. Given conservative intellectuals' self-definition as an embattled minority in higher education and beyond, the periodical's ecumenical spirit is fully understandable. The *Review* has facilitated more than tolerance among conservatives of different stripes, however. It has provided a platform for the reasoned presentation of ideas toward which, their proponents were convinced, American colleges and universities were for the most part hostile. It certainly has recruited many students into a network of conservative causes and organizations. And it has built morale and helped create a sense of belonging to a high-minded, intellectually vigorous, and growing cause.

With the election of a conservative Republican president in 1980 and the conservative political resurgence of the 1980s, one might expect to find a celebratory turn in the *Review*'s pages. Some changes were notable: a more sympathetic treatment of science and technology; a rather nuanced and cautious approach to developments in the Soviet Union and in U.S.-Soviet relations; and recognition of the new role played by African American intellectuals in conservative causes, to name a few.[27]

In the absence of sustained political coverage, the reactions of *Review* contributors to policy developments during the presidencies of Ronald Reagan and George Bush are not altogether clear. There was undoubtedly much to be happy about. Yet in scattered articles and two symposia, one finds something less than full-throated paeans of praise for the "Reagan revolution," and even expressions of sharp disappointment. Early on, several strands of conservative criticism of supply-side economics appeared among the usual arguments for capitalism. One article late in the 1980s went so far as to deplore a betrayal (and metamorphosis) of conservative ideals: "Most of the political Right," the author argued, had jettisoned conservatism in favor of "economic reductionism," "lack of social compassion," "a facile egalitarianism," "environmental brigandage," and cultural "philistinism."[28]

As editor Gregory Wolfe summarized contributions by seven time-honored conservatives (including Russell Kirk) to a symposium in 1986, the movement was "adrift," "in trouble," and suffering from "attenuation," "apostasy," and a sense of "malaise." Contributors were disgruntled over the influence of neoconservative refugees from liberalism who still accepted welfare state premises, of opportunistic political operatives in the White House, administration compromises, and the annoying populism and intellectual crudeness of the New Christian Right. Although their individual voices were distinctive, they seemed to agree that, despite its popularity and political strength, the conservative movement needed intellectual and spiritual reinvigoration.[29] Given the *Review*'s affirmations over the years, that conclusion was not surprising, for most contributors had in fact insisted that salvation did not lay in politics.

Notes

1. George H. Nash, "The Historical Roots of Contemporary American Conservatism," *Modern Age* 26 (Summer–Fall 1982): 297–303.

2. George H. Nash, *The Conservative Intellectual Movement in America: Since 1945* (New York, 1976), pp. 28–31, 290, 442; Intercollegiate Studies Institute flier, 1983, courtesy of Russell Kirk; E. Victor Millione, "Ideas in Action: Forty Years of 'Educating for Liberty,'" *Intercollegiate Review* 29 (Fall 1993): 51–57 (hereinafter cited as *IR*).

3. Interview with Russell Kirk, 27–28 May 1983, Mecosta, Michigan; "By Way of Introduction," *IR* 1 (January 1965): 4, 43.

4. Nash, *Conservative Intellectual Movement*, pp. 389–90.

5. Richard M. Weaver, "Humanism in an Age of Science," *IR* 7 (Fall 1970): 11–18; Jeffrey B. Gayner, "The Critique of Modernity in the Work of Richard M. Weaver," *IR* 14 (Spring 1979): 97–104; Stephen A. McKnight, "Understanding Modernity: A Reappraisal of the Gnostic Element," *IR* (Spring 1979): 107–17; Thomas Molnar, "Ethology and

Environmentalism: Man as Animal and Mechanism," *IR* 13 (Fall 1977): 25–43.

6. Stephen J. Tonsor, "Who Killed the Liberal Arts?" *IR* 7 (Fall 1970): 19–23; John Caiazza, "Modern Science and the Origins of Our Political Discontent," *IR* 13 (Fall 1977): 15–23, and "Analyzing the Social 'Scientist,'" *IR* (Spring–Summer 1981): 91–98; Albert H. Hobbs, "The Falseface of Science," *IR* 1 (January 1965): 17–19.

7. Will Herberg, "What Is the Moral Crisis of Our Time?" *IR* 4 (January–March 1968): 63–69, "Modern Man in a Metaphysical Wasteland," *IR* 5 (Winter 1968–1969): 79–83, and "What Keeps Modern Man from Religion?" *IR* 6 (Winter 1969–1970): 5–11; R. F. Baum, "Sorokin, Popper, and the Philosophy of History," *IR* 8 (Winter–Spring 1972): 21–31, and "Notes on Progress and Historical Recurrence," *IR* 13 (Winter–Spring 1978): 67–78.

8. Otto von Habsburg, "The Effects of Communism on Cultural and Psychological Politics in Eastern Europe," *IR* 3 (September–October 1966): 1–13; Frank Coakley, "The Persecution of Jews in the Soviet Union," *IR* 3 (May–June 1967): 221–35; Nathaniel Weyl, "Aristocide as a Force in History," *IR* 3 (May–June 1967): 237–45.

9. Gerhart Niemeyer, review of Bertram D. Wolfe, *Marxism: One Hundred Years in the Life of a Doctrine*, *IR* 3 (November–December 1966): 89–92, and "Marxism and the Intellectuals: From Moscow—With Love?" *IR* 7 (Spring 1971): 143–47; Juliana G. Pilon, review of Leszek Kolakowsky, *Main Currents of Marxism*, *IR* 15 (Spring 1980): 111–15.

10. Nash, *Conservative Intellectual Movement*, pp. 10, 288; Israel M. Kirzner, "Divergent Approaches in Libertarian Economic Thought," *IR* 3 (January–February 1967): 101–8; Patrick M. Boarman, "Bread and the Spirit," *IR* 2 (September 1965): 5–18; Karl Brandt, "Wilhelm Roepke: In Memoriam," *IR* 2 (May–June 1966): 341–42.

11. Karl Brandt, "Moral Presuppositions of the Free Enterprise Economy," *IR* 2 (October 1965): 109–20; Daniel Orr, "New Left Anti–Capitalism: Myth and Reality," *IR* 6 (Winter 1969–1970): 25–39; Ludwig von Mises, "Capitalism versus Socialism," *IR* 5 (Spring 1969): 133–39; Robert Higgs, "Is More Economic Equality Better?" *IR* 16 (Spring–Summer 1981): 99–102; Ernest van den Haag, "Justice and the Market," *IR* 10 (Winter 1975): 3–8.

12. George H. Nash, "Three Kinds of Individualism," *IR* 12 (Fall 1976): 29–40; Paul C. Roberts, "The Political Economy of Bureaucratic Imperialism," *IR* 12 (Fall 1976): 3–11.

13. M. Stanton Evans, "The States and the Constitution," *IR* 2 (November–December 1965): 176–99; Dwight D. Murphey, "Myths and American Constitutional History: Some Liberal Truisms Revisited," *IR* 14 (Fall 1978): 13–23.

14. Paul C. Beach, Jr., "The Politics of Race," James M. S. Powell, "Power Versus Rights," and Willmoore Kendall, "The Civil Rights Movement and the Coming Constitutional Crisis," *IR* 1 (February–March 1965): 53–74.

15. Will Herberg, "America's 'Negro Problem' in Historical Perspective," *IR* 7 (Summer 1971): 207–14, and "City and Suburb in Symbiosis: The Urban Problem in New Perspective," *IR* 8 (Spring 1973): 159–69; Robert Nisbet, review in *IR* 7 (Fall 1970): 3–10.

16. James E. Dornan, "The Founding Fathers, Conservatism, and American Foreign Policy," *IR* 7 (Fall 1970): 31–43, and "The Search for Purpose in American Foreign Policy," *IR* 7 (Winter 1970–1971): 97–110.

17. John F. Lehman, "World Peace and World Government," *IR* 2 (September 1965): 60–64; William R. Kintner, review of James H. McBride, *The Test Ban Treaty*, *IR* 5 (Fall 1968): 51; Alan Ned Sabrosky, review of Daniel O. Graham, *Shall America Be Defended? SALT II and Beyond*, *IR* 15 (Fall 1979): 53–57; Stefan T. Possony, "Security through International Law," *IR* 6 (Winter 1969–1970): 73–78; Lev E. Dobriansky, "Historical Lessons in Totalitarian Trade," *IR* 3 (November–December 1966): 55–65.

18. James H. McBride, "The Coming Missile Gap," *IR* 4 (November–December 1967): 27–32; Roger A. Freeman, "National Priorities in the Decade Ahead," *IR* 8 (Winter–Spring

1972): 15–19; Oleg Zinam, "Benefits in Increased Trade with the Soviet Union?" *IR* 12 (Fall 1976): 41–48.

19. William R. Kintner, "The Relation between Power and Values in the Nuclear Age," *IR* 2 (March–April 1966): 300–304; Gerhart Niemeyer, "National Self–Defense and Political Existence," *IR* 2 (March–April 1966): 305–10.

20. Joseph Schiebel, "Convergence or Confrontation? The Future of U.S.–Soviet Relations," *IR* 5 (Winter 1968–1969): 101–13; Gerhart Niemeyer, "Detente and Ideological Struggle," *IR* 14 (Fall 1978): 3–11, and "Foreign Policy and Morality: A Contemporary Perspective," *IR* 15 (Spring 1980): 77–84.

21. Hanson Baldwin, review of Maxwell D. Taylor, *Swords and Ploughshares*, *IR* 8 (Winter 1972–1973): 109–15; Alan Ned Sabrosky, "An Imperial Recessional: The 'Domino Theory' Revisited," *IR* 11 (Winter–Spring 1976): 83–93; Frank N. Trager, "Perspective on Vietnam," *IR* 2 (November–December 1965): 165–71; Thomas S. An, "The 1954 Geneva Accords Revisited," *IR* 4 (November–December 1967): 7–25.

22. Brenton H. Smith, "The Cold War as Misrepresentation," *IR* 5 (Winter 1968–1969): 124–30; Edward S. Shapiro, "Responsibility for the Cold War: A Bibliographical Review," *IR* 12 (Winter 1976–1977): 113–20.

23. R. F. Baum, review of Robert Nisbet, *The Degradation of the Academic Dogma: The University in America, 1945–1970*, *IR* 8 (Spring 1973): 183–86; Russell Kirk, "The University and Revolution: An Insane Conjunction," *IR* 6 (Winter 1969–1970): 13–23; George A. Field, "White Collar Crime against Education," *IR* 7 (Summer 1971): 245–50; Albert H. Hobbs, "To Probe the Academic Conscience," *IR* 4 (November–December 1967): 33–38.

24. Stephen J. Tonsor, "Faculty Responsibility for the Mess in Higher Education," *IR* 6 (Spring 1970): 83–89; Angelo Codevill "Why the Discontent on Campus," *IR* 2 (March–April 1966): 323–27; David Greenwald, "The Ideology of the New Left: An Interpretation," *IR* 3 (September–October 1966): 14–22; Ernest van den Haag, "The University as Progressive Kindergarten," Albert H. Hobbs, "The SDS Trip: From Vision to Ego Shriek," and M. Stanton Evans, "The New Totalitarians," *IR* 5 (Spring 1969): 141–65.

25. Eliseo Vivas, "Herbert Marcuse: 'Philosopher' *en titre* of the New Nihilists," *IR* 6 (Winter 1969–1970): 51–71; Ronald H. Nash, "A Note on Marcuse and 'Liberation,'"*IR* 14 (Fall 1978): 55–57; Frank Knopfelmacher, "The Parasite as Revolutionary: The Fleecing of America," *IR* 7 (Summer 1971): 227–33; Stephen J. Tonsor, "Science, Technology, and the Cultural Revolution," *IR* 8 (Winter 1972–1973): 83–89; Thomas Molnar, "The Counter–Culture: An Historical Perspective," *IR* 8 (Winter 1972–1973): 91–97.

26. T. Kenneth Cribb, Jr., "Conservatism and the American Academy: Prospects for the 1990s," *IR* 25 (Spring 1990): 23–30; "Special Section on Education," *IR* 26 (Fall 1990): 23–41; "The Humanities in Crisis: A Symposium," *IR* 23 (Fall 1987): 3–41; Robert Royal, "1492 and Multiculturalism," *IR* 27 (Spring 1992): 3–10; John Alvis, "Why a Proper Core Curriculum Is Political and Ought Not Be 'Politicized,'" *IR* 28 (Spring 1993): 24–32.

27. See, for example, Stanley L. Jaki, "The Three Faces of Technology: Idol, Nemesis, Marvel," *IR* 23 (Spring 1988): 37–46; M. S. Bernstam and L. H. Gann, "Will the Soviet Union Stay Communist?" *IR* 20 (Spring–Summer 1984): 13–22; Joseph G. Conti and Brad Stetson, "The New Black Vanguard," *IR* 28 (Spring 1993): 33–41.

28. Bruce Bartlett, "The Conservative Critics of Reaganomics," *IR* 18 (Fall–Winter 1982): 39–47; Donald Atwell Zoll, "The Conservative Metamorphosis," *IR* 23 (Spring 1988): 3–16.

29. "The State of Conservatism: A Symposium," *IR* 21 (Spring 1986): 3–28; "The Tasks Ahead: The Conservative Mission in the Twenty–first Century," *IR* 27 (Fall 1991):

53. See also David Broyles, "The Problem of Cultural Conservatism," *IR* 23 (Spring 1988): 47–56.

Information Sources

BIBLIOGRAPHY: None.

INDEXES: Each volume indexed; *AHCI*; *Curr Cont: BSMS*; *PAIS*; *SSCI*.

REPRINT EDITIONS: Microform: BLH; MIM; UMI.

LOCATION SOURCES: Widely available.

Publication History

TITLE AND TITLE CHANGES: *The Intercollegiate Review: A Journal of Scholarship and Opinion.*

VOLUME AND ISSUE DATA: Volumes 1–current, January 1965–present. Only two numbers issued for volumes 1, 10–17, and 22–23; three numbers issued for volumes 4, 6, 9, 20, and 21; one number issued for volumes 18 and 19. Combined numbers 4–5, volume 3; numbers 2–3, volume 4; 3–4, volume 5; 1–2, volume 6; 1–2, volume 7, and 1–2, volume 8.

FREQUENCY OF PUBLICATION: Six times a year, 1965–1967; four times a year, 1967–1975; two to four times a year, 1976–1986; two times a year, 1986–present.

PUBLISHERS: 1965–1966: Intercollegiate Society of Individualists, Philadelphia; 1967–present: Intercollegiate Studies Institute, Bryn Mawr, Pennsylvania, 1967–1995; Wilmington, Delaware, 1995–present.

EDITORS: Robert Ritchie, January 1965–March 1968; Frank Coakley, Fall 1968; Wayne Vallis, Winter 1969/1970–Winter/Spring 1972; Robert A. Schadler, Winter 1972/1973–Spring/Summer 1982; Donald H. Roy, Fall/Winter 1982–1983–Fall 1983; Gregory Wolfe, Spring/Summer 1983–Fall 1988; Dana A. Peringer, Spring1989–Spring 1991; Gregory Wolfe, Fall 1991; Jeffrey O. Nelson, Spring 1992–present.

CIRCULATION: 65,000.

Jacob H. Dorn

Ideas
1968–1975

Since World War II possibly no other period in American life has faced more challenges to traditional beliefs and political persuasions than the 1960s and early 1970s. Turbulent in word and deed, those years not only caused millions of Americans to question long-held points of view but, in instances, to deny them as well. Prominent within this heterogeneous group were Jews, who, at least in terms of their leading intellectuals and political activists, generally had been associated with liberal and left-wing attitudes and causes. Responding to the challenges of radicalism in the 1960s, however, a number of Jews in the United States either changed their political stance and moved to the right or simply became more vocal and pronounced in their assertion of existing conservative tenets. Amid this ferment, a group of concerned Jews, organized as the Jewish Society of America with national headquarters in New York, convened in Chicago in the spring of 1966 to draw up a platform of staunchly conservative principles that professed, among other things, a belief in God and country, the Holy Scriptures, the U.S. constitution, free enterprise, antistatism, anticommunism, and the *"sanctity of the individual."*[1] Two years later the organization began publishing *Ideas*, which the editor asserted was the "first major publication expressing a Jewish conservative point of view ever published in the United States."[2]

"Jewish" and "conservative" indeed best described the substance and tone of *Ideas* in its several years of existence. Virtually all feature essays and articles pertaining to current affairs, as well as editorial opinion and book reviews, reflected this. Sometimes the material was more pertinent to specifically Jewish concerns, sometimes principally to conservative ones. Frequently it related to both, and, in most instances, it touched on questions of import to all contemporary Americans, Jews and non-Jews alike.

Jewish themes and topics pervaded the journal's initial issue, where, for example, editor Michael S. Kogan, a former instructor at the New School for Social Research in New York, invoked Jewish law to argue pointedly against the morality of abortion, a concern that Americans increasingly found most vexing. Also, two rabbis contributed defenses of traditional religious and cultural values.[3] More controversial was the appearance in this premier issue of a diatribe against black anti-Semitism.

During the 1960s anti-Semitism exploded among blacks, a group whom Jews had traditionally befriended. Reasons offered for this explosion included the following: (1) It was simply another outburst of traditional, age-old anti-Semitism. (2) It stemmed from real or supposed Jewish dominance within centralized urban public school systems in the face of a concomitant black desire for local community control. (3) It reflected a wish for minority preferential treatment, in the form of quotas and affirmative action programs, to redress longstanding grievances, and this clashed with Jewish-supported values of competition and merit as criteria for selection and advancement. (4) It resulted from Jewish opposition to blacks' moving into their neighborhoods. (5) It expressed black anger at business practices among Jewish merchants and landlords in ghetto areas.[4] Whatever its precise etiology, this outbreak stunned Jews throughout the country.

Galvanized into action, the staff of *Ideas* prepared a study, *Black Power and the Jews*. Eschewing abstract sociological theory and analysis, it based the report on a compilation of newspaper stories that had appeared since the early 1960s and vividly documented black hostility. In April 1964, for example, some fifty black youths had attacked and seriously injured two rabbis and fifteen children, aged nine to twelve, who were playing in their school yard. Fifty black passers-by, the account alleged, had failed to intervene. The study further offered instances of attacks on Jewish shops and synagogues.[5] Black antagonism toward Jews also assumed verbal form, and here the article provided startling quotes: from comedian Dick Gregory: "Every Jew in America knows another Jew that hates Negroes and if we hate Jews, that's just even baby"; from Clifford A. Brown, Congress of Racial Equality (CORE) leader of Mount Vernon, New York: "Hitler made one mistake when he didn't kill enough of you Jews...yes, I'm a racist and proud of it"; and from Irv Joyner, treasurer of the Brooklyn chapter of CORE: "My congressional district is represented by a Jewish pig!"[6] The staff found appalling the recent appointment of John F. Hatchett to head the newly created Martin Luther King Afro-American Center at New York University. Hatchett had made anti-Semitic remarks, and the fact that the school had a very large Jewish enrollment aggravated matters.[7] Dr. Martin Luther King, Jr., contended that anti-Semitism hardly existed in the black community. The staff vigorously dissented, noting that some of Dr. King's own aides had exhibited clear strains of the anti-Semitic virus, as had other supposed moderates, including the president of the Philadelphia chapter of the National Association for the Advancement of Colored People (NAACP). "When it comes to anti-Semitism," the staff concluded, "there is no distinction between *militants* and *moderates* in the civil rights movement. They are united by the common denominator of bigotry."[8]

In part two of its study of black anti-Semitism, the staff transferred its attention and anger from black racism to Jewish fatuousness and passivity. Admitting that individual Jews were fully cognizant of the parameters of racism, the article scourged liberal groups, particularly the Anti-Defamation League, which in 1966 had assured America that black anti-Semitism was greatly exaggerated and that Jews had more to fear from the radical Right. "At a time of rapidly growing anti-Semitism among black extremists," the article cautioned, "we can hardly afford to retain Jewish leaders who continually harp on the supposed menace of the so-called 'Right Wing' while dismissing or excusing black bigotry." It concluded by denouncing any contact with "black power fanatics with whom our liberal Jewish organizations are so eager to conduct dialogues" as making "about as much sense as attempts to reason with the Klan, the Rockwellites or the Students for a Democratic Society."[9] As far as it was concerned, any hopes for improved relations between blacks and Jews were both ill founded and dangerous.

For all the cogency and reasoned argumentation used to attack black anti-Semitism, *Ideas* began, proverbially speaking, to skate on thin ice when it defended both Rhodesia and South Africa.[10] The fissures in the ice widened when Nathaniel Weyl, author of the essay defending South Africa, cited certain "salient aspects of biogenetic history of Jewry" to explain the "observed marked superiority of Jews to non-Jews in virtually all fields of intellectual achievement."[11] More temperate in tone was David Brudnoy's "De Tocqueville and the American Racial Crisis." Noting that the liberals "are floundering now in the midst of the chaos they themselves fomented," Brudnoy also confronted those conservatives "who by and large are not given to proposing programs, but who excel rather in criticizing the plans of liberals."[12]

Apportioning blame between liberals and conservatives for contemporary problems and for the failure to resolve them was atypical of most articles and editorial opinion found in *Ideas*. Liberalism customarily drew unstinting criticism, explicit and implicit, from the journal. The first issue carried an angry attack on Justice Abe Fortas as a liberal who wished to have the Supreme Court replace the Constitution as the "governing force" in the nation.[13] Other broadsides followed. Liberals tended toward blindness with regard to the menace of Moscow, claimed Eugene Lyons, a former UP correspondent to the USSR and later an editor of the *American Mercury* and the *Reader's Digest*. According to the veteran journalist, the Soviets had not eased their hostility toward the West, liberal disclaimers to the contrary notwithstanding.[14] Paralleling Lyons's denigration of liberals was Robert Delahunty's earlier "Observations on the New Left," which pointed to the "impoverishment and decomposition of liberalism."[15]

Yet it was radicalism rather than liberalism that incurred the wrath of *Ideas*. While liberalism might be muddle-headed in its attempts to reform American society, radicalism, by definition, vowed to extirpate that society. Alarmed by its contempt for existing values and institutions as well as its tactics of confrontation and violence, the journal constantly warned its readers of the perniciousness of the New Left. For example, Robert Delahunty, a student at Columbia University during the spring riots of 1968, wrote from firsthand knowledge of disruptive attacks on the academic world, as did Ronald Berman, author of a corrosive polemic against contemporary radicalism.[16] The latter conceded that the humanities in all likelihood would remain under domination by the Left, but an attempt should be made "to strengthen and broaden the small conclaves of conservative dissent within the academy." He reminded readers that "a counter-culture is a two-way affair."[17] The influence of radical intellectuals, inside and outside the university, appeared even more noxious to another contributor to the periodical. According to David S. Lichtenstein: "Driven by ideological passion to destroy the last bastions of freedom and democracy, the totalitarians may yet succeed in overrunning what remains of a civilization critically weakened by the machinations of its own radical class." Hence, "it may be that no democratic society can survive the experiment of allowing an alienated intellectual elite to determine its values, poison the channels of public opinion and cow into submission its normal political leaders."[18]

Having underscored the negative influences of liberalism and radicalism, *Ideas* took up the cudgels for a variety of conservative issues germane to the 1960s and 1970s, as well as for conservative principles in general. In terms of domestic concerns, it strongly endorsed such conservative tenets as law and order and financial aid to parochial schools.[19] Dedicated to the capitalist system and the rights of the individual, it warmly applauded libertarianism and its adherents as bulwarks of freedom against the encroachments of the collectivist state. David Friedman, son of the laissez-faire advocate, economist Milton Friedman, early in the journal's existence offered a paean, "The Libertarian Right," which spoke to this point.

While noting the antipathy to liberalism shared by the New Left and libertarianism, young Friedman pointed to their basic and irreconcilable differences with regard to property rights, which, he believed, were fundamental human rights. There existed, he argued, no convincing proof that unregulated capitalism inevitably produced either monopoly or a greater inequality of income. Moreover, the New Left, bent on replacing the existing government with a better one, had failed to comprehend that a benevolent government presented a contradiction in terms. Friedman argued: "The libertarian right does not believe that what the government needs is more power and a change of personnel. Our program is gradually to diminish its power, and so its ability to do evil."[20] The New Left unwittingly could augment statism by its inflammatory behavior. Friedman lamented: "Once again, as has happened so often in the past, a movement calling for 'Power to the People' may well create a situation in which all power will be concentrated in the hands of the state." The libertarian Right, for its part, was committed to educating Americans to self-determination in the face of "economic collectivism and political centralization."[21] Echoing Friedman's concerns in this same issue was an extended tribute to the noted libertarian Frank A. Chodorov, disciple of an earlier famous libertarian, Albert Jay Nock. Included in this tribute was one of Chodorov's own unpublished essays, "The 'Crime' of the Capitalists," in which he decried the passing of pure capitalism in favor of state capitalism, America's regnant form of economic organization. "Beguiled by the state's siren song of special privilege," complained Chodorov, "the capitalists have abandoned capitalism....How right Lenin was when he said that the capitalist would sell you the rope with which you intended to hang him if he thought he could make a profit on the sale."[22]

Yet the conservatism preached by *Ideas*, in editorials and articles, was at heart issue oriented rather than ideological, pragmatic rather than philosophical. As long as readers took conservative positions on pressing contemporary questions, it seemed of little importance what particular brand or nuance of conservatism they subscribed to. And the journal and its contributors exuded confidence that Americans were becoming conservatives. The respected social philosopher Will Herberg, for one, looked back at the tumult of the 1960s and discerned an essentially conservative quality inherent in American workers.[23] Jacob Neusner, for another, contended that the Right would mold the future, and deservedly so, as long as it remained committed to those values of justice, democracy, and "orderly social change" that were worthy of preservation.[24] While Herberg and Neusner lauded conservatism without regard to party preference, Arthur J. Finkelstein, like Neusner a contributing editor to *Ideas*, expressly linked the two, giving thanks that Jewish voters increasingly were supporting Republicans rather than Democrats.[25]

Although political partisanship was never the raison d'être of *Ideas*, its *beau idéal* was Richard M. Nixon, whose rise and fall as president very nearly, if coincidentally, coincided with that of the journal. In its initial issue Samuel L. Blumenfeld, vice-chairman of the Jewish Society of America, waxed ecstatic at the prospect of a Nixon victory in the 1968 election; in the following number he heaped praise on the victorious candidate for his policy with regard to the Middle East.[26] As a conservative Jewish publication, *Ideas* not surprisingly endorsed unequivocal U.S. support for Israel, and the perception of Nixon's solidly pro-Israeli policies throughout his years in office greatly endeared him to the periodical. Blumenfeld continued to give Nixon high grades at midterm; two years later another contributor strongly urged his Jewish coreligionists to reelect Nixon in 1972 for a number of reasons, not the least of which was his realistic understanding of the Soviet Union.[27]

At no time did *Ideas* ever waver in its resolve that the cornerstone of U.S. foreign policy should be to contain and, if need be, to combat the global thrust of the USSR and other communist states. Yet as Nixon began his first term in office, large numbers of Americans had concluded that the nation must end its imbroglio in Vietnam. The first essay to appear in *Ideas* on this subject called for a negotiated peace if South Vietnam's freedom from communist aggression could be guaranteed. If the current Paris talks should fail to reach such an accord, however, "it is to be hoped that our new President will have the courage and resolve to order the military, at long last, to take all steps they deem necessary to bring this conflict to a speedy and victorious conclusion."[28] As the war wound down to its agonizing denouement, *Ideas* continued to support Nixon and to take a hard-line, hawkish posture. Once it became clear that the United States would withdraw from the fray, the journal's editor asserted that American airpower might be reintroduced, of necessity, if South Vietnam could not protect itself. In any case, far from reading into the war the necessity for a démarche from commitment to isolationism, the nation must be ready to grant support to other beleaguered nations in Southeast Asia.[29]

Several issues did tend to estrange *Ideas* from Nixon. For example, the journal strongly opposed the abandonment of conscription and the adoption of a volunteer army. Nor did it welcome the Nixon *volte face* with regard to the People's Republic of China, cautioning strongly that it would not countenance the "calamity of having Red China seated and the Republic of China expelled" from the United Nations.[30] Lest anyone underestimate its concern, the author of the essay (editor Kogan) entitled the piece "Ignorance Abroad."

Strong differences of opinion notwithstanding, *Ideas* never revised its essentially glowing estimate of the Nixon presidency. In 1973, in the midst of the Watergate investigation, an editorial reminded readers that not only could the president's successes not be discredited, his initial term of office had proved one of the most important and productive ones in the history of the country.[31] The following year found editor Kogan remonstrating against the "anti-Nixon cabal" and "their campaign of malice and slander." The break-in, he admitted, was inexcusable, but it had resulted from the "crimes and follies of some of the president's aides." As far as Kogan was concerned, the Ervin Committee had produced no evidence linking the chief executive to the Watergate escapade. If Nixon were impeached, moreover, a grave threat to the American political system would ensue: "The ultimate result of impeachment and conviction may well be the demise of the four-year Presidency as we know it. Following the establishment of such a precedent, presidents will govern subject to the whim of the press and the legislative branch. America will be well on the way to an unstable parliamentary system of the kind specifically rejected by our founding fathers."[32]

Other contributors to the journal seconded Kogan's defense of Nixon and fears for the nation's stability. Rabbi Baruch Korff, chairman of the National Citizens' Committee for Fairness to the Presidency, denounced the media and the "weak-kneed and self-seeking politicians who would, by ordeal and villainy, bring down the thirty-seventh President of the United States."[33] While averring that there should be no whitewashing of any malfeasance, Rabbi Seymour Siegel urged reconciliation as the order of the day.[34] Ralph de Toledano admitted that President Nixon had mishandled the issue of the edited tape transcripts. Yet, like Rabbi Siegel, he protested that the "anti-Administration lynch mob" should not be permitted to overturn the results of the 1972 election.[35] Finally, Will Herberg also vented his ire against the Nixon detractors and, like Kogan, repaired to the Constitution. "For many," wrote the conservative polemicist, "the most sinister side of the Watergate Affair, the greatest threat to our constitutional-legal tradition, is not the Watergate burglary, deplorable as that is, but the conduct of the Ervin Committee and the shameless orgy in which the liberal press, especially *The New York Times* and the *Washington Post*, has been indulging."[36]

As it happened, *Ideas* barely survived the Nixon presidency. It published its last issue in 1975, one that was fewer than ten pages in length and consisted of a single article written by the editor. The reasons for the journal's demise are not fully clear since its latest circulation figure of 10,000 is not unimpressive. It may be that editor Kogan, listed as teaching in the Department of Philosophy and Religion at Montclair State College (New Jersey), became too absorbed in other matters. In any event, in its several years of desultory publication, *Ideas* provided a forum for generally interesting, sometimes high-quality articles and editorials pertaining to traditional conservative and Jewish values and beliefs, as they battled for survival in a society beset by a host of divisive issues.

Notes

1. "The Chicago Platform of the Jewish Society of America," *Ideas: A Journal of Conservative Thought* 1 (Autumn 1968): 7–8.

2. "Coming of Age: A Word to Our Readers," *Ideas* 1 (Autumn 1968): 2–3.

3. Michael S. Kogan, "Jewish Law and the Abortion Controversy," *Ideas* 1 (Autumn 1968): 39–45; Earl W. Vinecour, "Judaism vs. Paganism: A Continuing Conflict," *Ideas* 1 (Autumn 1968): 51–55; Juda Glasner, "The Need for Tradition," *Ideas* (Autumn 1968): 59–60.

4. For useful perspectives on antagonisms between blacks and Jews, see Nathan Glazer, "Negroes and Jews: The New Challenge to Pluralism," *Commentary* 38 (December 1964): 29–35; Milton Himmelfarb, "How We Are," *Commentary* 39 (January 1965): 69–74; B. Z. Sobel and M. L. Sobel, "Negroes and Jews: American Minority Groups in Conflict," *Judaism* 15 (Winter 1966): 3–22.

5. Jewish Society of America Research Staff, "Black Power and the Jews," Part I, *Ideas* 1 (Autumn 1968): 10–11.

6. Ibid., pp. 13–14, 17.

7. Ibid., p. 17.

8. Ibid., pp. 13, 15, 17.

9. Jewish Society of America Research Staff, "Black Anti-Semitism and the Jewish Response [Part II]," *Ideas* 1 (Winter 1968–1969): 16, 19.

10. James Lo Gerfo, "Rhodesia: A Rational Approach," *Ideas* 1 (Winter 1968–1969): 45–54; Nathaniel Weyl, "Israel and South Africa: Beleaguered Creative Enclaves," *Ideas* 2 (Winter–Spring 1970): 40–46.

11. Nathaniel Weyl, "Jewish Intellectual Superiority: Myth or Reality?" *Ideas* 2 (Fourth Quarter 1970): 63.

12. Daniel Brudnoy, "De Tocqueville and the American Racial Crisis," *Ideas* 2 (Winter–Spring 1970): 82, 87.

13. Alfred Avins, "Abe Fortas: A Judicial Portrait," *Ideas* 1 (Autumn 1968): 19–24.

14. Eugene Lyons, "Our Liberal Press Views the Soviets," *Ideas* 2 (Winter–Spring 1970): 17–23.

15. Robert Delahunty, "Observations on the New Left," *Ideas* 1 (Autumn 1968): 36.

16. Ronald Berman, *America in the 1960s: An Intellectual History* (New York, 1968).

17. Ronald Berman, "Campus Revolution and the Humanities Graduate Student," *Ideas* 3 (1971): 63.

18. David S. Lichtenstein, "The Radical Intellectual and U.S. Foreign Policy," *Ideas* 3 (1971): 32.

19. See for example, Herbert T. Klein, "Crisis in Law Enforcement," *Ideas* 1 (Winter 1968–1969): 21–25, and Hindy L. Schacter, "Government and the Parochial School," *Ideas* 2 (Winter–Spring 1970): 84–87.

20. David Friedman, "The Libertarian Right," *Ideas* 1 (Spring–Summer 1969): 50–52.

21. Ibid., pp. 52–53.

22. Frank Chodorov, "The 'Crime' of the Capitalists," *Ideas* 1 (Spring–Summer 1969): 69–70.

23. Will Herberg, "Conservatives, the Working Class, and the Jew," *Ideas* 2 (Winter–Spring 1970): 25–29.

24. Jacob Neusner, "The Jews Move Right," *Ideas* 2 (Fourth Quarter 1970): 65–67.

25. Arthur J. Finkelstein, "The Jewish Voter Discovers the G.O.P.," *Ideas* 4 (1973): 19–26.

26. Samuel L. Blumenfeld, "Conservative Prospects, 1968," *Ideas* 1 (Autumn 1968); 25–29; Samuel L. Blumenfeld, "Notes on the New Administration: Nixon and the Middle East," *Ideas* 1 (Winter 1968–1969): 27–30.

27. Samuel L. Blumenfeld, "The Nixon Administration: The Middle Course," *Ideas* 1 (Spring–Summer 1969): 3–10; Joseph Dunner, "Nixon and the Jews," *Ideas* 2 (Fourth Quarter 1970): 21–31.

28. Jack Ross, "Nixon and Vietnam," *Ideas* 1 (Winter 1968–1969): 32–33.

29. "Vietnam Postscript," *Ideas* 4 (1973): 2–6.

30. Michael S. Kogan, "Ignorance Abroad: America's New China Policy," *Ideas* 3 (1971): 20.

31. "Watergate," *Ideas* 4 (1973): 8–10.

32. Michael S. Kogan, "The Assault on the Presidency," *Ideas* 4 (1974): 23–25.

33. Baruch Korff, "What Is Freedom of the Press?" *Ideas* 4 (1974): 31.

34. Seymour Siegel, "Watergate in Perspective," *Ideas* 4 (1974): 43.

35. Ralph de Toledano, "The Committee and the President," *Ideas* 4 (1974): 38.

36. Will Herberg, "The Crisis and Its Aftermath," *Ideas* 4 (1974): 45.

Information Sources

BIBLIOGRAPHY: None.
INDEXES: None.
REPRINT EDITIONS: None.
LOCATION SOURCES:
>Complete runs: Library of Congress; Harvard University; Cornell University; University of Michigan; University of California at Los Angeles; University of California, Berkeley.

Publication History

TITLE AND TITLE CHANGES: *Ideas: A Journal of Conservative Thought*, Autumn 1968–1971; *Ideas: A Journal of Contemporary Jewish Thought*, Autumn 1972–Spring 1975.
VOLUME AND ISSUE DATA: Volumes 1–[5], 1968–1975. Combined numbers issued for Spring–Summer 1969 and Winter–Spring 1970; only one number issued in 1971, 1972, 1973, 1974, and 1975.
FREQUENCY OF PUBLICATION: Irregular.
PUBLISHER: Jewish Society of America, New York.
EDITOR: Michael S. Kogan.
CIRCULATION: About 10,000.

Robert Muccigrosso

Hillsdale Review
1979–1986

The *Hillsdale Review*, a quarterly journal of ideas, was published from 1979 to 1987. Founded by students at Hillsdale College in Hillsdale, Michigan, the *Review* reflected both the changing face of the intellectual Right in the 1980s and the aspirations of a segment of a younger generation of conservatives in those years. At a time when a plethora of conservative student newspapers were springing up on the nation's campuses, each characterized by shrill polemics and the tactics of adversarial journalism, the *Hillsdale Review* chose a more reflective, exploratory form of discourse. Ironically, it was the journal's meditative style and broad cultural sweep that prevented it from receiving the support of an increasingly politicized conservative movement.[1]

From the outset, the *Review* was patterned after such literary journals as T. S. Eliot's *Criterion*, which combined the scholarly flavor of a quarterly with the lively writing and cultural commentary of a magazine. Far from being a digest, the *Review* sought to foster original thought and an exchange of ideas among its contributors. Although the editors encouraged diversity of opinion and perspective, the underlying philosophical coherence of the *Review* stemmed from its rooting in that particular strand of modern conservatism known as traditionalism. For these young traditionalists, as for their intellectual forebears—Russell Kirk, Richard Weaver, Eric Voegelin, and others—the core of their beliefs consisted of the classical and Judeo-Christian concepts of metaphysics, natural law, and the prescriptive society.

Despite its affirmation of traditions, the *Hillsdale Review* never became a vehicle for nostalgic sentiment or reactionary daydreams. Its focus was on contemporary culture: social institutions, the arts, and the intellectual life. It deliberately eschewed matters of public policy because its contributors held that politics is an epiphenomenon of culture. A large number of essays and reviews in the journal examined the mores of America in the 1980s through such indicators as film, literature, the influence of science and technology, sexuality and the family, and the state of academia. Thus the *Review*'s writers, with their immersion in the arts and humanities, were in sharp contrast to the libertarians and neoconservatives who pursued economics and the social sciences as the keys to a developed position on modern society.

The *Hillsdale Review* had more in common with the group of conservative student journals that appeared in the 1960s than with the campus newspapers of the 1980s. At the height of the violence and radicalism on the campuses during the 1960s, conservatives banded together and sought to provide an intellectual response to the anarchy around them. Among the publications that arose out of this experience were the *Harvard Conservative, analysis, Insight and Outlook, Phalanx,* and *Politeia.* They emerged from such institutions as the University of Pennsylvania, Claremont, Rutgers, Princeton, and the University of Wisconsin. The average life span of these journals ranged from two to five years, but they managed to produce graphically handsome, intelligent, and even witty results. They stimulated campus conservatives to articulate their ideas and proved for some writers to be the first stage of a career in journalism or the academy. This was certainly true of the best of these student journals, the "classical liberal" *New Individualist Review* based at the University of Chicago. But the most successful of this generation of conservative publications was the *Alternative,* emanating from the Bloomington campus of Indiana University. Now known as *American Spectator,* it has over 200,000 subscribers and its editor, R. Emmett Tyrrell, Jr., is a nationally syndicated columnist.

If the conservative student publications of the 1960s arose because they expressed the viewpoints of an embattled minority, the establishment of the *Hillsdale Review* came about in rather different circumstances. By the end of the 1970s, conservatism had become a highly organized movement and had won a series of political victories, culminating in Ronald Reagan's election to the presidency. During this time, Hillsdale College became known as a bastion of conservative thought, boasting a large number of guest speakers and such distinguished visiting professors as Russell Kirk and Gerhart Niemeyer. For those involved with the creation of the *Hillsdale Review,* the college's intellectual atmosphere was extremely stimulating, but what became even more exciting was the discovery of highly articulate, like-minded students from other campuses. Meetings occurred at seminars and conferences held by such organizations as the Philadelphia Society, a national society of conservative scholars and activists, and the Intercollegiate Studies Institute (ISI).

The association with ISI proved to be continuous and vital. A foundation dedicated to supplementing the education of students in the liberal or left-of-center academic milieu, ISI had been combating the "closing of the American mind"— through its publications, conferences, and other programs—long before Allan Bloom's book on the subject was published in 1987. ISI became the journal's primary patron and remained in that role throughout the *Review*'s publication history.

The editors assembled a prestigious group of conservative scholars and authors for the *Review*'s editorial advisory board, including Kirk, Niemeyer, Andrew Lytle, Thomas Howard, Henry Regnery, and Malcolm Muggeridge. Nearly every issue of the *Review* carried at least one essay by a prominent conservative writer; over the years, these contributors included most of the advisory board members, as well as George Gilder, Joseph Sobran, Marion Montgomery, James Hitchcock, Stanley L. Jaki, and Ralph McInerny.

The *Review* was launched during a period of conservative ascendancy, but ironically it had none of the journalistic slickness or triumphalism that marked its more aggressive counterparts in the student newspaper genre. In that sense, it was something of an anachronism, a throwback to the time when conservatives, out of power, contemplated first principles and ultimate questions. The *Review*'s form, in fact, was carefully designed to reflect its rejection of the strident voice of ideology. A conscious decision was made to return to the type of "little review" that flourished throughout the "Age of Discussion," spanning the nineteenth century and the first part of the twentieth. The short essay, the flower of this era, which died out with writers such as G. K. Chesterton and Hilaire Belloc, was considered apt for the *Review*'s more exploratory approach, especially since its young contributors could not claim scholarly authority. The editorial emphasis on a high quality of prose style was also part of the *Review*'s opposition to the devastation of language and thought that ideology leaves in its wake.

If there is a consistent, recurring theme in the *Review*, it is a rejection of ideology and the rigidity of a party line, in favor of a return to genuinely philosophical thought. Traditionalist intellectuals have used the word *ideology* in a strict sense to describe an abstract system of ideas which is imposed on reality—the ideologue's motive being a will to power. Ideology, according to these thinkers, is the essence of "modernity," which is defined as the effort by intellectuals from the time of Descartes to replace Judeo-Christian metaphysics and the rule of law with the constructs of the mind. The majority of the *Review*'s contributors shared these convictions. Indeed, they were willing to grant, unlike the majority of other conservatives, that in addition to the leftist ideologies of socialism and communism, various strands of thought on the Right were intrinsically ideological.

In the fifth anniversary issue of the *Hillsdale Review*, the editors stated what they and many of the contributors felt to be the answer to the abstractions of secular ideology: a balanced, historically minded form of Christian humanism.[2] Rather than call for a restoration of premodern political and religious institutions, the editors held that a Christian worldview that is true to its central inspiration can look outward at the world and create both a critical perspective and new forms of art and thought. The modern crisis was interpreted in the pages of the *Review* not as an intellectual problem primarily, but as a spiritual crisis, a search for utopian certainties without religious faith, a desire for joy and pleasure without a recognition of moral boundaries, a longing for safety and order without individual responsibility.

The journal's interest in the philosophical and theological dimensions of human behavior entailed a commitment to cultural criticism rather than public policy analysis. Traditionalist conservatives have often stressed that politics is ultimately an epiphenomenon of culture. Thus the *Review*'s editorial focus was on the arts, social institutions such as the family, and popular culture in all its manifestations. The result is that most of the essays in the *Review* were concrete, specific examinations of film, music, science, law, literature, and so forth rather than abstract and theoretical.

That traditionalist conservatism was becoming increasingly irrelevant to the publicly successful conservative movement in the 1980s was a development that did not go unnoticed in the *Hillsdale Review*. It might even be said that one of the leitmotifs of the journal was the critique of conservatism itself. In the journal's second issue, a review of Wendell Berry's *The Unsettling of America* began this way:

Serious moral criticism of American society has suddenly become unfashionable on the Right.... The defense of America against the hatred of the Left has blunted the impact of the conservative critique of modernity, and conservative activists have apparently given up the arduous task of translating the vision of the great traditionalists—Kirk, Weaver, the Nashville Agrarians—into concrete political directions. The most vital segment of the Right today, the so-called Neo-Conservatism, often seems to see no darker undertones in America, only a vigorous, healthy nation shackled by high taxes and excessive regulation.[3]

The new movements that grew up as conservatives came to power in 1980 also received scrutiny in the *Review*. The neoconservatives were credited for their "remarkable ability to criticize or debunk" leftist ideology, but faulted for their lack of "philosophical coherence or depth."[4] A symposium on the emergence of the New Right cleared that movement of the liberal charge that it was an incipient fascist theocracy, but it also raised questions about the relationship between populism and conservatism.[5] One of the symposium's contributors pointed out that the emergence of a conservative political establishment required the Old Right to renew its role as a strictly philosophical, critical movement: "A critical movement takes its existence...from the corpus it criticizes. The liberal political establishment is dead. In one sense the Old Right must die with it. But the New Right is not its successor. Its successor will be a critical movement which applies Old Right principles to a new situation."[6] Whether this evolution has become a reality or not, it certainly was what the *Review*'s contributors wanted to advance.

An example of the journal's search for creative applications of Old Right principles can be seen in the theory of capitalism. The writers on this subject sought to steer a course between the libertarian glorification of the atomized individual in the unrestricted market and the extreme traditionalist tendency toward an idealized feudalism. One early essay noted the similarity between the Christian heresy of Pelagianism, which overemphasized the role of free will and denied the centrality of the community, and modern libertarianism.[7] Other writers sympathetically examined the social ideas of the English Distributists (Chesterton and Belloc) and the American Southern Agrarians, who in opposition to industrialism upheld agriculture and craftsmanship, and the responsibility that widely distributed private property imposes.[8]

At the same time some of the *Review*'s contributors have been appreciative of the moral qualities strengthened by a free market circumscribed by law. In a review of George Gilder's influential book *Wealth and Poverty* (1980), one writer summed up a position common to most of the *Review*'s writers. Gilder's apprehension of capitalism, he said, renders inadequate any account that reduces capitalism to Adam Smith's rational self-interest. "However, we should not make the opposite mistake of attributing to capitalism a quasi-religious transcendence....We should not deny the existence of capitalists who subvert not only the spiritual and moral values of their culture but the values of their own creative venture as well."[9] Although the issues in the debate on capitalism often appear irreconcilable, the *Review*'s contributors attempted to reach a creative *via media*.

Perhaps the one subject that stimulated the most numerous and imaginative essays was that of the relationship between the sexes, including such issues as feminism, sexuality, and the breakdown of the family. In an issue devoted to an analysis of the "sexual revolution," the contributors eschewed moralizing in favor of an exploration of the tragic ironies that surround those who have been "liberated." A woman writer in the lead essay averred that promiscuity had brought sexual intercourse into an analogy with professional sports: performance became the main criterion of satisfaction. The irony of sexual liberation for women, she argued, is that promiscuity encouraged men to pursue the short-term, emotionless relationships of which women had long been the victims; liberation had led to another form of tyranny.[10] One contributor, a natural family planning counselor, examined the connection between modern methods of contraception and the neurotic fear of fertility. Drawing on his own experience, he noted how couples would come to him both in order to prevent conception and, in desperation, to ensure conception. The irony here, he wrote, was that instead of bringing greater freedom and health, contraception led to a sense of children as encumbrances and "accidents," and also led to increased guilt about such feelings.[11] This essay's psychological, experiential approach is characteristic of the best material in the *Hillsdale Review*.

The most intriguing treatments of the modern war of the sexes arose in the context of extended discussions of films. In Frank Zepezauer's "The Devolution of Henry Higgins," George Bernard Shaw's play *Pygmalion* is compared with the numerous films based on it, including *My Fair Lady* and *Educating Rita*. "As a masculine archetype," Zepezauer concluded, Higgins "showed an innate deficiency, something his high-spirited manliness needed, not to shore it up but to complement it. In his own way he was also 'deliciously low,' full of unshaped potential, a challenging project for a female mentor who could initiate him into the riches of feminine culture and unite him to a soul essentially like his but differing in ways he could never duplicate within himself."[12] Zepezauer's unusual and ingenious defense of a traditional view of the sexes as being complementary was paralleled by another essay in the *Review*, an extended interpretation of the Dustin Hoffman movie *Tootsie*.[13] And a review of the film *Agnes of God* contended that, far from being a simple-minded critique of the ignorance and inhibitions of nuns, the most pointed questions are directed at the secular psychologist played by Jane Fonda.[14]

Several years before the Lutheran theologian and political commentator Richard John Neuhaus had published his seminal book *The Naked Public Square* (1984), the *Hillsdale Review* was focusing on the relationship between religion and the public order. While some essays concentrated on various developments in the areas of theology itself,[15] a series of analyses confronted the increasing politicization of the churches. In particular, the drift toward pacifism and an abandonment of classic just war theory was scrutinized. James V. Schall's epigrammatic essay "Some

Myths People Swear By" gave pithy expression to what other contributors argued in more elaborate forms. Some of his *pensées* include:

Fear of war and fear of poverty have become the main instruments to eliminate freedom for those who prefer to think that war and poverty are not the worst of evils. The reasons that cause men to fight are not the reasons that cause men to be poor, unless bread is also a weapon. C. S. Lewis wrote that neither war, nor poverty, nor death was the worst of evils.... Yet, freedom cannot mean that "everything is permitted." Some things are simply not "permitted," even if they happen rather frequently and we see them every day in our midst. We live in a world in which evil is allowed.... A world in which evil can occur through human agency is a world in which something important happens through human initiative....Forgiveness means that there is something to be forgiven. We can only forgive what ought not to have happened.... The most lethal weapon known to man is the human will. This does not mean that we should destroy our wills, but we can change our minds.[16]

The common concern of these essays is that the ancient traditions of the church concerning justice and peace, elucidated over the centuries by such minds as those of Augustine and Aquinas, are in danger of being lost in the haze of a politics of sentimentality.

One of the editorial priorities of the *Review* was the examination of popular culture—the books, films, television programs, and music that are indicators of the direction in which a society is moving. The use and abuse of the powerful mystique surrounding modern science provided the focus for several intriguing essays. One was a survey of the new group of commercial science magazines, epitomized by *Omni,* published by *Penthouse* editor Bob Guccione and directed toward the yuppie reader. The *Review*'s science columnist noted that these publications reflect the connection between convenience-producing technology and sexual adventurism that Aldous Huxley had foreseen in *Brave New World.*[17] The same writer, in a column on Carl Sagan, contrasts that scientist's diatribes against religion with his evident religious "fascination with the immensities of time and distance." Sagan "comes closer to a belief in 'anthropomorphic patriarchs' than most religious people do, for he speaks wistfully of wise and terribly advanced beings who may come down from the sky...and who will solve for us the ancient problem which Christians call sin."[18]

The *Review*'s music columnist often wrote of the way jazz reflects a serious tension between the demands of order and of freedom—a tension that is a perennial topic for traditionalist conservatives. His descriptions of the intricate knowledge and spontaneity that went into jazz improvisation were related to the intensely historical commitments of jazz musicians to building on musical tradition.[19] His forays into the realm of rock music also yielded insights. After discussing the murder of John Lennon and the outburst of sadness and soul searching that followed it, he wrote: "Authenticity is the drug of existentialists and rock fans. The insistence on salvation through participation in an 'event' or 'happening' is an attempt to put the urgency back in a life consigned to the actuarial tables of insurance companies."[20] And in a meditation on the recent revival of the nihilistic rock group the Doors, the writer concludes, "There is no imagination without moral limits, and without imagination there is no spark. Many of these children have grown up with no moral comprehension; no barriers to their egos; no wall through which one needs a door in the first place."[21]

The *Review*'s evaluations of contemporary culture were balanced by essays celebrating the achievement of the great twentieth-century conservatives. Given the journal's interest in matters of the spirit and imagination, it is not surprising that these essays center on the great novelists and poets. Among those covered were T. S. Eliot, W. B. Yeats, Ezra Pound, Osip Mandelstam, Flannery O'Connor, and Walker Percy. Again and again the ability of these artists to combine modern techniques of language and narrative with a responsibility to the Western tradition was stressed. In the essay on Pound, for example, the writer rebutted the liberal dismissal of Pound as nothing more than a fascist and held that Pound's moral vision stemmed from his preoccupation with the sin of usury. For Pound, usury meant the attempt to make something out of nothing, much as it had for the medieval mind; it was linked in his mind with a loss of the disciplines of civilization. A symposium on the Southern Agrarian writers focused on how their sense of place and the rhythms of the land enabled them to create an art of more enduring vision than that of rootless, nihilistic urban man. The sense of the past, which is the burden of the Agrarian imagination—as it was for the modernists, Eliot, Yeats, and Pound—informed their political ideas, providing not only a piety toward ancient institutions, but also a vivid awareness of evil and the possibility of grace.[22]

No picture of the *Hillsdale Review* would be complete without noting the journal's evident appreciation of wit and humor. In the smallest details the editors found opportunity for ironic observations. The prints and woodcuts interspersed throughout the text usually made some sort of humorous commentary on the point immediately above or below them. Even the running heads contained word plays and oxymorons. The columns of S. J. Masty, which included a Popean satire on the Washington political establishment, written in rhyming couplets, were among the *Review*'s most popular pieces.[23] The editors also collaborated in the writing of a regular column by "Innocent Smith" (the name taken from Chesterton's novel *Manalive*), whose madcap adventures and quirky pronouncements often cloaked serious issues and interests. During the year 1984, Innocent was supplanted by his supposed brother Winston, the protagonist of Orwell's famous novel *1984*. Some of the most telling forays into cultural criticism came in satires on such topics as National Public Radio and the *Phil Donahue Show*.[24]

The *Hillsdale Review* ceased publication after a run of about eight years for two reasons. The journal's very breadth—its interest in everything from classical philosophy to rock music—made it difficult to gain support among foundations and individuals who wanted to see more "results," in terms of political action or a high public profile, for their contributions. But it was also clearly out of touch with the politicized, triumphalistic conservatism of the 1980s. Of course, it was for these very reasons that the *Hillsdale Review* was valued by its readers and editors.

Notes

1. For a discussion of the increasing politicization of the Right in the 1970s and 1980s, see Paul Gottfried and Thomas Fleming, *The Conservative Movement* (Boston, 1988), passim.

2. Gregory Wolfe and Keith Bower, "After Five Years: An Editorial Statement," *Hillsdale Review* 5 (Winter 1983): 1–3 (hereinafter cited as *HR*). See also Dinesh D'Souza, "Progress and the Erosion of Christianity," *HR* 4 (Winter 1982–1983): 3–9.

3. David Yeago, "A Kentucky Cato: The Agrarian Vision of Wendell Berry," *HR* 1 (Fall 1979): 25.

4. Gregory Wolfe, "Paleolibs and Neocons," *HR* 5 (Fall 1983): 34–38.

5. Gregory Wolfe, et al., "The Politics of Reaction," *HR* 2 (Winter 1980): 7–20.

6. Richard Vigilante, "A Comment on 'The Politics of Reaction,'" *HR* 2 (Winter 1980): 20.

7. Patrick M. O'Neil, "The Pelagian Origins of Ultra-Libertarianism," *HR* 2 (Summer 1980): 13–20.

8. Thomas H. Landess, et al., *HR* 3 (Summer 1981): 1–27. See also Gregory Wolfe, "Cultivation vs. Innovation," *HR* 6–7 (Winter–Spring 1985) : 1–2, and Edward S. Shapiro, "They Took Their Stand: The Agrarians Today," *HR* 6 (Summer 1984): 3–9.

9. Franklin Debrot, "Capitalism and Creativeness," *HR* 4 (Spring 1982): 20–21. See also George Gilder, "The Metaphysics of Capitalism," *HR* 2 (Fall 1980): 2–5.

10. Ellen Wilson, "The Perpetual Performer," *HR* 3 (Fall 1981): 6–11.

11. Keith Bower, "Contraception and Neurosis," *HR* 3 (Fall 1981): 31–35.

12. Frank Zepezauer, "The Devolution of Henry Higgins," *HR* 7 (Summer 1985): 25.

13. Jonathan Mills, "Phylogeny Recapitulates Androgyny," HR 6–7 (Winter–Spring 1985): 13–26.

14. Kevin Long, "Sisters in Blood," *HR* 7 (Winter 1985–1986): 43–46.

15. See, for example, David Yeago, "Conservatism and the American Dream," *HR* 2 (Spring 1980): 15–20; Gregory Wolfe, "'Post-Christian' Apologetics," *HR* 6–7 (Winter–Spring 1985): 27–33.

16. James V. Schall, "Some Myths People Swear By," *HR* 4 (Fall 1982): 3–8. See also E. Michael Jones, "The Peace Church and the New Class," *HR* 4 (Spring 1982); Terry Hall, "Two Kinds of Peace," and Gary R. Bullert and R. E. Michell, "The Bishops and 'Non-Violence,'" *HR* 6 (Spring 1984): 19–24, 25–35.

17. Maclin Horton, "That Hideous Schlock," *HR* 4 (Summer 1982): 37–40.

18. Maclin Horton, "Billions and Billions (of Banalities)," *HR* 4 (Fall 1982): 32–33.

19. Keith Bower, "Jazz: An Innovative Tradition," *HR* 1 (Fall 1979): 15–19; "Swinging with Joan Mondale," HR 2 (Fall 1980): 27–29; "Dizzy Remembers," *HR* 2 (Winter 1980): 34–36.

20. Keith Bower, "A Rose for the Eggman," *HR* 3 (Spring 1981): 36.

21. Keith Bower, "The Revolving Doors," *HR* 3 (Winter 1981): 44. See also a discussion of MTV, the cable channel that plays rock videos twenty-four hours a day: Laurens Dorsey, "Hell on Tape," *HR* 5 (Fall 1983): 30–32.

22. Thomas H. Landess, et al., *HR* 3 (Summer 1981): 1–27.

23. S. J. Masty, "The Jerkiad," *HR* 4 (Spring 1982): 33–36.

24. Dan Ritchie, "National Public Radio: A Dream Vision," *HR* 6 (Summer 1984): 35–39; Donald DeMarco, "Phil Donahue: The Grand Inquisitor," *HR* 6–7 (Winter–Spring 1985): 67–71.

Information Sources

BIBLIOGRAPHY: None.
INDEXES: None.
REPRINT EDITIONS: None.
LOCATION SOURCES : Hillsdale College; University of Michigan; Intercollegiate Studies Institute, Bryn Mawr, Pennsylvania; University of South Alabama; Southern California College; Library of Congress; Nichols College, Dudley, Massachusetts.

Publication History

TITLE AND TITLE CHANGES: *The Hillsdale Review: A Student Journal,* 1979–1980; *The Hillsdale Review: An American Miscellany,* 1980–1986.
VOLUME AND ISSUE DATA: Volumes 1–8, Spring 1979–Winter 1986. Only three numbers issued in 1979; number 4, volume 6 and number 1, volume 7 combined number; numbers 1 and 2, volume 8 combined number.
FREQUENCY OF PUBLICATION: Quarterly.
PUBLISHERS: Spring 1979–Summer 1980: Hillsdale College Chapter of the Intercollegiate Studies Institute; Fall 1980–Spring 1982: The Cavaliers in association with the Intercollegiate Studies Institute, both in Hillsdale, Michigan; Summer 1982–Winter 1986: The Hillsdale Review, Inc., from Summer 1982 to Winter 1983–1984 in Cincinnati, Ohio; from Spring 1984 to Winter 1985–1986 in Bryn Mawr, Pennsylvania; and from Spring–Summer 1986 to Winter 1986 in Front Royal, Virginia.
EDITOR: Gregory Wolfe.
CIRCULATION: Paid circulation: 400 in 1980; 1,200 in 1983; total distribution: 1,500–2,000.

Gregory Wolfe

Continuity
1980–

It has been four decades since political scientist Clinton Rossiter dubbed American conservatism "the thankless persuasion."[1] Several years before, historian Samuel Eliot Morison had spoken of the need to write history "from a sanely conservative point of view."[2] In the age of Reagan and Gingrich, the editors of *Continuity* saw conservatism as problematic in the American context. More importantly, perhaps, they still believe they are providing a sanely conservative point of view.

Conservative journals of opinion have long been a fixture on the American intellectual landscape. William F. Buckley's *National Review* and the more scholarly *Modern Age*, both creations of the 1950s, come to mind immediately. *Continuity*, however, fulfills a different need. It is aimed in the main at professional historians who identify as conservatives and are interested in conservative themes in historiography. *Continuity* is also for historians who pursue conservatism itself as an object of study. The statement of policy from its opening issue in the fall of 1980 reads as follows:

The object of *Continuity* is to provide a forum for historical scholarship consistent with belief in the quest for truth for its own sake; the superiority of our free society, with all its faults, to any practicable alternative; legitimate authority; and the presumptive values of tradition as the accumulated wisdom of the past.

We shall scrutinize the historiographical idols of our age, the hegemony of which has contributed to the erosion of scholarly discourse within the academy and to the fashionable vilification of our country among intellectuals throughout our society.[3]

Continuity is largely the brainchild of Paul Gottfried, a frequent contributor to *Modern Age* and formerly a professor of European intellectual history at Rockford College in northern Illinois. A former editor of the *The World and I*, Gottfried in 1988 published *The Conservative Movement* with Thomas Fleming (editor of the conservative *Chronicles of Culture*).[4] This work is at once a tour d'horizon of contemporary American conservatism and a polemical attack on certain strands within it.

In his highly regarded intellectual history of modern American conservatism, George Nash divides the immediate post–World War II expression of this movement into three components: libertarians, traditionalists, and anticommunists. Libertarian conservatives gloried in what Ronald Reagan called "the magic of the marketplace" and feared that America was well on the road to serfdom. Friedrich Hayek was their hero and his *The Road to Serfdom* (1944) their bible. Traditionalists such as social critic Russell Kirk and sociologist Robert Nisbet were more concerned about cultural issues than economic questions. To them the decline of America was measured by a debilitating moral relativism, the debasement of intellectual standards, a lack of respect for duly constituted authority, and an indifference to the past. Anticommunist conservatives, taking their cue from Whittaker Chambers's *Witness* (1952), were preoccupied with the eternal war against Soviet Russia. In their eyes this war was as much spiritual as it was political. Despite differences of emphasis, however, all three camps found common ground in opposition to the welfare state.[5] Gottfried, who is essentially a traditionalist, considers them the backbone of the Old Right.

The Conservative Movement is written from the perspective of an unabashed Old Rightist. As Gottfried makes clear, the roots of the Old Right lay in the debate over the New Deal during the 1930s. The political personification of this movement was a fellow midwesterner, Senator Robert Taft of Ohio. Gottfried notes (and to some extent approves) a strong strain of isolationism within the Old Right, which would not entirely die out even after the cold war had begun. And he reminds us that at least in its early years, *National Review* was an organ of the Old Right. Scholarly issues aside, one cannot help but notice the sense of sadness that pervades this book, in many respects the perfect analogue to another gloomy but lively book, Arthur Ekirch's classic of the 1950s, *The Decline of American Liberalism.*[6] Ekirch also wore two hats—that of the professional historian and that of the committed advocate. An unreconstructed Jeffersonian, he traced the degradation of democratic liberalism back to the turn of the century, when self-styled "progressives" followed Herbert Croly's advice and smuggled no small amount of Hamiltonianism into their theoretical baggage. When the new liberals gained power and passed legislation, "true" liberalism was the loser. In like manner Gottfried posits old rightism as the yardstick by which to evaluate developments within American conservatism. His story begins later, but it too is a tale of declension. Gottfried's rogues' gallery of the Right includes just about every "conservative" faction that has reared its head since 1960: Goldwaterites, neoconservatives, New Rightists, and finally, Ronald Reagan and his camp followers. The book should be titled "The Decline of American Conservatism."

Gottfried's polemic reads like a *What Is Not to Be Done* for the conservative movement. His own prescription for what ails America—and the Right—is never made altogether clear, perhaps because practical politics is not the professor's bailiwick. Much like the late Christopher Lasch on his Left, Gottfried refuses to believe there are political remedies for cultural maladies. (The connection with

Lasch is not entirely coincidental, as Gottfried cites Lasch's *Haven in a Heartless World* approvingly.)[7] And it is the soul of American culture, or to put it more accurately, the soul of American historiography, that is his chief concern. For that, *Continuity* is a fitting response.

Although *Continuity* very much bears the stamp of Paul Gottfried, it is by no means a one-man enterprise. During the early years of the journal, Gottfried was ably assisted in his editorial duties by Aileen Kraditor, an erstwhile Marxist and a provocative American intellectual historian whose most recent works are to some extent a rebuttal to her earlier efforts. Richard Jensen, a "new" political historian at the University of Illinois at Chicago, served as associate editor. Max Beloff, Thomas Molnar, Richard Pipes, George Nash, and Forrest McDonald have all sat on the advisory board. In an age obsessed with credentialism, the credentials of those affiliated with the journal could hardly be questioned.

The title of the journal was chosen with good reason, for if there is a common thread running through the articles in *Continuity*, it is an awareness—and appreciation—of continuity throughout history. Herbert Butterfield once said something to the effect that the only constant in history is change. The historians (not to mention a handful of political scientists, philosophers, and sociologists) who write for *Continuity* would beg to disagree. William Burton tells us in one essay "to appreciate that the human condition reflects the influence of continuity as well as the factors of change."[8] In another article Ellen Shapiro McDonald reminds her readers that "most peoples, throughout most of time, have lived their lives in a narrow circle of relationships in which change is an unwelcome intruder."[9] As if to underscore the point, Aileen Kraditor in still another piece emphatically states that "societywide intellectual and social change is never sudden."[10] With all this, *Continuity* is indeed an apt name for the journal.

Other characteristics become apparent after browsing through a few issues of *Continuity*. For instance, most writers who have anything to say about ideology possess a positive aversion to it. In an introduction to a special issue on conservatism and history, Russell Kirk is insistent on the point that conservatives are not ideologues. Elsewhere in that same issue, Aileen Kraditor declares that conservatism, properly understood, is the very negation of ideology. In another special issue (this one on the South), Southern historian Clyde Wilson uses *ideology* as a term of opprobrium. In one sense this is not surprising. Since Edmund Burke's time, if not before, not a few conservatives have looked suspiciously on ideologues. Ideology, the indictment runs, divides; sentiment and custom unite. Ideology is thin and abstract, while experience is richly concrete. Interestingly, many liberal intellectuals put forth similar arguments in the 1950s, as historian Richard Pells has shown.[11] In the nineteenth century, the radical Marx saw ideology as an example of false consciousness. Democratic presidential candidate Michael Dukakis in 1988—an impeccable centrist—spoke of ideology in a curtly dismissive manner. All God's children, so it seems, are against ideology.

The use of the term *revisionist* also merits some attention. To many younger historians, revisionism brings to mind a left-wing critique of cold war historiography. In fact, one article in *Continuity* is an explicit critique of this sort of revisionism.

Yet revisionism, more broadly understood, also suggests a dissatisfaction with the conventional wisdom. In that sense *Continuity* is palpably revisionist, and self-consciously so. Clyde Wilson, in a piece on Southern history, calls unabashedly for a new revisionism. And Gottfried himself, in his "Editorial Notes," boasts of "the revisionist thrust" of his journal and writes of the need for "true revisionist standards."[12]

What so badly needs revising is left-liberal historiography. The *Continuity* editors recognize that leftists and liberals are not always one and the same. From their point of view, however, the difference between the two ultimately does not make much of a difference, for the historiography of the Left is united in its endorsement of ethical relativism, its sympathy for the "losers" in history, and its antipathy to middle-class culture.

A truly conservative historiography, on the other hand, rejects out of hand determinism, presentism (a particularly glaring sin), and didacticism. It is also, we are told by a number of contributors, adamantly opposed to the kind of moral bookkeeping that results in double standards. More positively, histories written from a sanely conservative point of view are aware of complexities and sensitive to context.

These are worthy prescriptions indeed, but there is scarcely anything here with which even the editors of *Radical History Review* would disagree. The tenets of conservative historiography turn out to be little more than a gloss on the duties of a professional historian. But it is not professionalism as such that concerns *Continuity* contributors. Their chief complaint is that American historiography has long been infected with the virus of ideology, and left-liberal ideology at that. It is when these writers turn to specifics that we know what they mean.

Consider the writings of Aileen Kraditor. For some time now social history has been regarded as the province of the Left. To Kraditor, however, social history is an even more appropriate calling for conservatives because everyday people are more reliably conservative than are elites, or at least intellectual elites. Thus, "the conservative intellectual movement should build its tenets in part on the findings of social history."[13] Having staked out her claim, Kraditor then takes issue with a spate of earlier left-wing histories of labor and the Left. It is false and patronizing, she asserts, to label the turn-of-the-century American working class "inert" simply because it had not opted for socialism. Such labels betray a presentism that does violence to the integrity of the past. "As well might a numerologist attempt to write a true social history in terms of the question why John Q. Citizen [her archetypical worker] did not believe in numerology."[14] For Kraditor, then, the questions many leftist historians were asking of their materials had less to do with their curiosity about the past than they did with their prejudices of the present. Some of these historians read too much into isolated acts of labor unrest, acting as if every strike or boycott were proof positive of incipient socialism. More commonly, though, older historians on the Left assumed that if the workers were not anticapitalist, they must have been procapitalist. Kraditor rejects this conclusion as resting on a false dichotomy. To her mind, working-class culture was largely autonomous. The beliefs and attitudes of working-class Americans did not merely reflect the economic substructure. In fact, she argues, there is no compelling reason to believe that society is a system in the way that many Marxist critics hold that it is. If pluralism is the American reality, then the working class has enough social space to fashion its own destiny.

Kraditor's relentlessly argued article is a briefer version of her own *The Radical Persuasion*,[15] a scathing critique of left-wing historiography and, implicitly at least, left-wing or socialist politics. It is also part of an argument she has been having with herself for some two decades, for Kraditor was once very much a part of the movement she now excoriates. It is instructive to note, however, that when she makes her case against older social historians of the Left, she relies heavily on studies undertaken by newer social historians of the Left. It is small wonder, then, that the late Herbert Gutman found her scholarly polemic so impressive.

In another essay for *Continuity* Kraditor addresses the reform impulse in American history. Her "conservatism" is perhaps even more evident in this piece. She asserts, for instance, that the spate of reform movements that sprang up in antebellum America was more a reflection of political pluralism, an indigenous tradition of grass-roots reform, and a constellation of moral beliefs than it was a commentary on the iniquitousness of America. Kraditor also notes how a shared conception of the common good "has been shrinking as the power of government has been expanding."[16] Taking the late Walter Lippmann as her authority, she bemoans the lack of a public philosophy in America. Largely because of the absence of such a philosophy, Kraditor argues, public and reasoned debate is no longer as intimately connected to the passage of reform legislation as it once was. What is more, in a host of areas liberals have used government to undermine the authority of traditional institutions. Echoing Robert Nisbet's *Twilight of Authority*,[17] Kraditor concludes that the inevitable consequence of a welfare state that does not rest on a commonly understood set of moral assumptions is a rootless hedonism. With Nisbet, whom she cites frequently, Kraditor is sympathetic to those intermediate associations that Tocqueville analyzed so acutely in *Democracy in America*. At one point she even chides the abolitionists (the subject of an earlier and sympathetic study by her) for calling into question the legitimacy of ministers and other voices of authority in the South.

This all has an unmistakably conservative ring to it. In fact, Kraditor admits to being a traditionalist, à la Gottfried. Yet there is more to her discussion. Taking to task Alice Felt Tyler for the tendentiousness of her *Freedom's Ferment* (1944), Kraditor insists that we shall never adequately understand the reform mind-set of mid-nineteenth-century America if we continue to honor dubious distinctions between "good" and "bad" reform movements. Not a few abolitionists, she reminds us, were ardently prohibitionist and vehemently anti-Catholic to boot. Hence it hardly does justice to the past to portray the reformers of yesteryear as precursors to the reformers of today.

These are sensible admonitions, to be sure. Students of historiography will recall that Herbert Butterfield voiced similar objections to an overtly partisan and exceedingly present-minded historical writing in his superb *The Whig Interpretation of History*.[18] Whiggish history has found its detractors in virtually every quarter.

From the liberal ranks, Richard Hofstadter discovered a Whig inside Vernon Parrington and mounted a full-scale assault on him in *The Progressive Historians.*[19] From the camp of the radical Left, Hofstadter's protégé Christopher Lasch has been waging a verbal war against all forms of Whiggery since his days as a graduate student.[20] The point here is that the critique of Whig history has little to do with ideology and very much to do with a historian's sensibility. In the afterglow of Dachau, Stalinism, and Hiroshima, there are few historians who subscribe to the naively optimistic view of humankind that undergirds the Whig interpretation of history.

The desire to attack head-on a whole school of historiography also manifests itself in Richard Jensen's essay on the educational revisionists. Jensen, author of the widely acclaimed *The Winning of the Midwest* (1967), finds problems in the revisionists' efforts to portray nineteenth-century school reform as but a more sophisticated form of social control. Michael Katz and others may be correct about the urban reformers that they examined, Jensen concedes, but the vast majority of students went to school outside the confines of the central city. What is more, Jensen queries how it could be that high school reformers aimed at "taming" the proletariat when they expected the burgeoning high schools to be stocked by budding white-collar professionals. As for the charge of some revisionists that nativism pervaded the elementary and secondary schools during the late nineteenth century, Jensen responds that nearly half of the public school teachers were children of immigrants. While agreeing with the revisionists that elites often provided the initiative for educational reform, Jensen is not disturbed by that fact. Unlike many of the revisionists, he believes professionals figured more prominently in school reform than did businessmen. Finally, Jensen discovers villainy in other places. Franklin Roosevelt, he notes, wished to channel less able youth into relatively nonproductive employment, an early version of the tracking system that would become so notorious in the 1950s. And the student rebellion of the 1960s led to a general weakening of academic standards, resulting in diminished "human capital." The unsung heroes in Jensen's account are the nineteenth-century middle-class reformers, as they erected a system of public education that worked remarkably well until just a few decades ago. Eschewing relativism and enforcing discipline, they were "proof that a conservative revolution not only can be carried out, but can actually upgrade the moral tone of society."[21]

Historiographical concerns are registered in a number of other essays. William Burton, in a piece entitled "Historiography and the Double Standard," begins by assailing leftist political scientist Howard Zinn for his apparent inability to distinguish between scholarship and propaganda.[22] He then proceeds to caution his readers against the indiscriminate use of moral judgments in the writing of history. Such judgments, he holds, block our understanding of the past inasmuch as they make us unmindful of the importance of unintended consequences. Burton's own methodological concerns, it soon becomes clear, are not without a moral dimension, for he indicts recent histories not so much for sloppy scholarship as for moral myopia. A popular Western civilization textbook by Buckler, Hill, and McKay, to take one of his examples,[23] allegedly treats imperialism as if it were something peculiar to the West. Moreover, according to Burton, texts such as these suggest that the West alone is responsible for the degradation of the global environment. Implicitly if not explicitly, they hold Third World nations blameless for modern problems. Such an approach, Burton concludes, comes very close to anti-Americanism.

Roland Stromberg's "The Liberal Bias in Studies of Causes Célèbres" proceeds in a similar vein.[24] Stromberg, a distinguished modern European intellectual historian, examines three causes that have become part of the folklore of the Left: the Dreyfus affair, the Sacco and Vanzetti case, and the trial of Alger Hiss. His conclusions are not calculated to endear him to those who sympathize with history's losers. The conventional wisdom about Dreyfus's innocence, Stromberg crisply states, is largely "false or misleading because distorted by a left-wing ideology." Emile Zola's justly famous manifesto Stromberg dismisses, for reasons that are not altogether clear, as "wildly inaccurate."[25] With respect to Sacco and Vanzetti, Stromberg echoes Francis Russell's claim that Sacco was guilty after all. In so doing he makes a bow to A. Lawrence Lowell, the Harvard professor who came under fierce attack at the time of the trial for suggesting that the accused may not have been innocent. Stromberg also notes the rash of hypocrisy that greeted the verdict. "A Germany about to welcome Hitler produced huge rallies decrying American intolerance."[26] And in South Africa, the American flag was burned. The reaction of the Left to Allen Weinstein's *Perjury*, which concludes that Alger Hiss was indeed guilty of treason, is even more disquieting to Stromberg. Above all else, it demonstrated that the discussion on the Left was "dominated by ideological frenzy, not evidence."[27] Stromberg concludes on a cautionary note, alerting his readers (presumably on "red alert" already) to "the poisonous effect of mythology on history."[28]

To be sure, the pieces by Burton and Stromberg are ably argued. In fact, they read like lawyers' briefs. But the clear implication of both essays is that histories written by leftists are more prone to factual error or interpretive confusion than histories written by rightists. That may be true, but neither Burton nor Stromberg demonstrated this is the case. What is more, it would be difficult to establish that a historiography dominated by one ideology is inherently given to misconceptions.

That *Continuity*'s worries are as much ideological as they are professional is evident in a special issue devoted to "Recovering Southern History." Most of the contributors to that issue believe that the South (or at least the white South) has not received a fair shake in American historiography. In the introductory essay to that volume, southerner Clyde Wilson declares that the South has served as the nation's scapegoat for far too long. Against those American historians who generally view the South as something of an anomaly, Wilson submits it is the American Yankee who is the true oddity. Reflecting on the arbitrariness that characterizes conventional accounts of the South, Wilson laments that "the ideals formulated in the seventeenth century on Massachusetts Bay are American, by premise; those formulated at the same time on the Chesapeake Bay (though they may have had an equal or greater and possibly a more constructive role in the formation of America) are at best an interesting, at worst a malevolent, deviance."[29] One might say that Wilson is rejecting notions of southern exceptionalism in much the same way that some historians rejected the idea of American exceptionalism.

If the South is not deviant, though (in its commitment to family, opposition to protectionism, and suspicion of utopianism), Wilson argues it is nonetheless different. It is, after all, more given to honoring tradition than any other part of the country—and that is why it should hold a special place in the hearts and minds of conservatives. To understand conservatism, one must also understand the South. Because the South is so different from the North, its history is a rebuke to consensus historiography. Interestingly, the southern historian endorses Marxist Eugene Genovese's thesis that the antebellum South was more paternalistic than it was capitalistic. One wonders what Wilson makes of the contemporary South. He reminds us of Ronald Reagan's immense popularity in the South. Evidently Panglossian optimism plays well in a region noted for its sense of tragedy. Perhaps there is more comedy than irony at work here.

A "revisionist" attitude toward the Old South is apparent in a number of other pieces. A reviewer of Michael O'Brien's anthology, *All Clever Men, Who Make Their Way*, notes that antebellum southern intellectuals have been slighted by contemporary intellectual historians. After reading the essays in this collection, he contends, modern intellectuals can hardly proceed on the bland "assumption that intellectual achievement and adherence to the latest of leftist fashions are inseparable."[30] There was a genuine mind of the South, in other words, and it was an impressive one. For too long it had been ignored by those who regard a conservative intellectual as an oxymoron.

Not surprisingly, the Civil War and Reconstruction come under heavy blows in *Continuity*. In an editorial note, Gottfried claims that "the pictures of Reconstruction found in such contemporary historians as Kenneth Stampp and John Hope Franklin seem to be much informed by presentist bias and jaundiced insight."[31] Ludwell Johnson is even harsher. In his "The Plundering Generation: Uneasy Reflections on the Civil War," Johnson argues that the War between the States "was a war of economic and political aggrandizement begun and carried out by the war party in the North."[32] Far from being a blundering generation, as some previous historians had held, northern antislavery politicians were a plundering generation. Southern secession was no more a plot to destroy the Union, he goes on, than the American Revolution was a conspiracy to dismantle the British empire. Whatever idealism surfaced during the war, Johnson insists, was not to be found among the leaders of the North. "Part of trampling out the vintage where the grapes of wrath were stored was to seize the vineyard."[33] One half expects Jefferson Davis to leap off the page at this point.

In the "new" vision of the Old South that emerges in *Continuity*, heroes become villains and villains become heroes. M. E. Bradford's "Lincoln and the Language of Hate and Fear: A View from the South" depicts Abraham Lincoln as "the American Caesar of his age."[34] Bradford assails Lincoln for his apparent misunderstanding of the founders and his demagogic debates with Stephen Douglas. The southern historian concludes on a somber note. "Lincoln left behind him a trail of blood, an emancipation under the worst possible circumstances, and a political example that continues to injure the Republic which he did so much to undermine. It is at our peril that we continue to reverence his name."[35]

John C. Calhoun, on the other hand, receives nearly unqualified praise from Margaret Coit Elwell, who laments that history textbooks commonly devote more space to Jane Fonda than to "the Marx of the master class." Those who condemn Calhoun outright, she declares, are reading the values of the present into the past, for Calhoun was not exactly the deviant he has been made out to be. In fact, Elwell reminds us, his ideas on interposition were largely borrowed from Thomas Jefferson, and Calhoun's fear of a tyranny of the majority was at one with the founders, especially James Madison. The vital significance of a concurrent majority was even recognized by Senate majority leader Lyndon Johnson. Calhoun's racism was real, Elwell concedes, but that hardly distinguished him from a good many abolitionists or, for that matter, Abraham Lincoln. Commenting on the contemporary relevance of Calhoun's writings, Elwell declares that his "insights remain vital for any community."[36] She includes the black community, pushing Calhoun's insights beyond limits the southern statesman regarded as acceptable.

Continuity's musings on the South raise a number of questions. Are contributors merely advocating that more attention be paid to the Old South and that scholars avoid propagandizing about the virtues of the North and the vices of the South? For surely the historiography of the South has become a growth industry within the last two decades. Whatever else may be said about these new histories, strident rhetoric is not one of their distinguishing characteristics. Kenneth Stampp and John Hope Franklin indubitably had axes to grind, but they wrote their major works well over a generation ago. Our "southern-fried historians" may be wrestling with a phantom opponent. More disturbing, though, it is difficult to tell whether they are prohibitionists on the subject of propaganda or simply wish to alter the content of the propaganda. Are they calling for a critical analysis of (some) southern culture, or instead sounding another bugle cry? It is one thing to understand the mores of the antebellum white South; it is another to revere them and revile the North.

It is not that the writers in *Continuity* speak with one voice on the South. There is diversity within the ranks. One reviewer, for example, is decidedly more sympathetic to the Straussian defenders of Lincoln than he is to the arguments of professional Lincoln hater Bradford. Bradford's indiscriminate defense of southern tradition, this reviewer holds, "is without criteria for determining what is just."[37] The ramifications of the critique extend well beyond the borders of the South. Frank Meyer made a similar point when attacking the Burkean traditionalism of Russell Kirk some forty years ago. And there is some disagreement about the precise nature of the antebellum South. Several contributors, along with Eugene Genovese, view the Old South as essentially precapitalist. Yet others perceive it to have been a part of a long-standing republican tradition. Still others see the pre–Civil War South as entrepreneurial in spirit. Some even appear to opt for the three-in-one approach, without examining the larger implications of their trinitarianism.

Southern issues aside, *Continuity* does publish scholarly exchanges. The economic historian Robert Higgs, for example, takes issue with Aileen Kraditor on a number of counts. Higgs is one of the few contributors who does not use ideology as a "snarl-term," to use S. I. Hayakawa's expression. What is more, he chides Kraditor both for her criticisms of the robber barons and her acknowledgment that late nineteenth-century exploitation of labor by capital was not merely a myth. In her rejoinder, Kraditor argues that criticism of individual capitalists is no more an indictment of capitalism than criticism of individual socialists is an indictment of socialism. Moreover, she continues, it would be insensitive to ignore the very real pain millions of workers experienced. Whether the pain was produced by capitalists, capitalism, or the force of circumstance is largely beside the point for her. Finally, she reminds Higgs that "real life is messier than any economic model."[38] This (gentle) war of words between an ardent libertarian and a staunch traditionalist makes for fascinating reading.

That the intellectual Right is hardly monolithic becomes apparent in other pieces as well. In a thoughtful commentary on the writings of legal theorist Raoul Berger, Jules Gleicher takes sharp exception to those "conservatives" who hold up the banner of judicial restraint.[39] Berger himself was a political liberal, but his criticisms of the Warren Court (not unlike those of Robert Bork's mentor, Alexander Bickel) offended his ideological brethren and appealed to those conservatives who believed the Supreme Court had under Earl Warren overstepped its bounds. (Berger's arguments for legislative supremacy and a more modest role for the high court echo conservative James Burnham's 1959 *Congress and the American Tradition*.)[40] But Berger's argument, contends Gleicher, hardly augurs well for conservatism today. A quietistic court, he holds, would reward only an activist—and liberal— Congress. What is more, it would allow no room for what Gleicher, following Gary Jacobsohn, calls "judicial statesmanship." Berger's advice smacked of positivism and would be rejected out of hand by the founders. Gleicher concludes this review by declaring that the answer to an imperial judiciary is not a judiciary paralyzed by procedural fetishes. There is, after all, a higher law to which Supreme Court justices should pay homage.

One might expect a seeming traditionalist such as George Will to fare well in *Continuity*. Such is not the case. In a review of Will's *Statecraft as Soulcraft* (1983), Gottfried takes issue with Will's backing of civil rights and his endorsement of a conservative welfare state. There can be no such thing as a conservative welfare state, insists Gottfried, and to suggest that there can be reflects a poor understanding of history. After likening Will to conservative 1950s gadfly Peter Viereck (an apt comparison), Gottfried goes on to say that Edmund Burke would have recoiled from the modern welfare state. And noting Will's tendency to lump disparate historical figures together as if they were part of a seamless web, the historian pinches the columnist for the latter's "obliviousness to the grain of history."[41]

A number of other articles and reviews merit brief attention, if only to indicate the range of concerns expressed in this journal. *Continuity* has published pieces applauding the philosophers Ludwig Wittgenstein and Michael Oakeshott for their special brand of conservatism, defending sociologist William Graham Sumner against the charge of Social Darwinism (historian Donald Pickens holds Sumner to be an old-fashioned republican),[42] and attacking Congress's actions vis-à-vis South Africa. One article probes the problems with détente, while another establishes a link between old-line fascists and Swedish social democrats. In an editorial note Gottfried reminds us of the anticapitalistic mentality behind fascism. Sympathetic accounts of President Coolidge coexist with paeans to the small-town world that Coolidge conservatives, perhaps unwittingly, did so much to destroy. And distinguished economic historian Peter Coleman concludes an analysis of New Zealand's welfare state in no uncertain terms: "What the Liberals created three generations ago as a responsive, protective, egalitarian welfare system has turned out in the end to be a venal, entrenched, political monstrosity dedicated to the service of those who already have and responsive only grudgingly, if at all, to those who have not."[43]

The writers and reviewers for *Continuity* do not mince their words. Gottfried dismisses cold war revisionism as "Soviet agitprop," while a blistering review of Robert McElvaine's *The Great Depression* (1984) concludes—after noting McElvaine's ideologically charged obiter dicta—that the author's work demonstrated "the depths to which liberal thinking has sunk."[44] To be sure, not all critical reviews are written with their fists. A review of a sympathetic book on John Dewey calmly raises questions about the validity of pragmatism and sadly notes the philosopher's short-lived enthusiasm for Soviet education. The tone throughout, however, is respectful. And the review of John Diggins's *The Lost Soul of American Politics* (1984) not only avoids the ad hominem approach altogether but manages to make penetrating observations about the nature of contemporary cultural criticism and the varieties of Calvinism. Such pieces are a credit to the journal.

If the tone of *Continuity* is frequently defensive, and even truculent, that no doubt reflects its writers' firm belief that they are an embattled minority. A number of articles attest to this. In her essay on social history, Aileen Kraditor flatly states that on most campuses, "the only icons available for breaking are all of various shades from pink to red. The academic status quo is a left-oriented status quo, and the true iconoclasts are the conservatives."[45] Elsewhere Kraditor waxes metaphorical. Leftist historians have been squabbling among themselves, she acknowledges, "but their historical elephant remains pink or red."[46] Historian Forrest McDonald is shriller. Although appreciative of the new social history (he lauds Natalie Z. Davis's work in particular) and grateful that there was a New Left challenge to the citadels of academic orthodoxy in the 1960s, McDonald resorts to hyperbole when discussing liberal historiography and, more especially, mainstream liberal historians. These exponents of what McDonald dubs the "Revised Standard Version" of American history "were as kindly disposed toward different points of view as Cromwell had been toward Irish Catholics."[47] In that regard McDonald notes how he was accused of being a tool of the utility industry when he put out a biography of Samuel Insull and how he was once denied an academic post on account of having backed Barry Goldwater for the presidency. McDonald will give little quarter to the "totalitarian liberals." Passages in Gottfried's *The Conservative Movement* reinforce the claims of Kraditor and McDonald. Referring to the shouting down of political scientists Edward Banfield and Jeane Kirkpatrick on various college campuses during the 1970s and 1980s, Gottfried speaks of a "new McCarthyism."[48]   And this McCarthyism, he emphasizes, targets only conservatives as victims.

At first blush one might quarrel with the perceptions of Gottfried and his contributors. It is an exaggeration, after all, to liken whatever difficulties conservative academics are having today to the hysteria of the early 1950s. Russell Jacoby's *The Last Intellectuals* would also seem to call into question Gottfried's verdict.[49] Jacoby argues that it is misleading to say that the Left has conquered the academy. Rather, it would be more accurate to claim that the academy has conquered the Left. That is, left-wing activists have shed politics for professionalism, the language of the vernacular for the patois of the specialist. Gottfried would find scant solace in this, however, for he is interested more in the culture of the academy than in practical politics.

Jacoby makes another assertion, though: "No academic leftist can tap funds of the magnitude available to conservative intellectuals."[50] Jacoby clearly has in mind the neoconservatives associated with *Commentary* and the American Enterprise Institute. But Gottfried and his hearty band of traditionalists are not part of this group. In fact, he very much resents the attention being given to and the influence being wielded by the neoconservatives. Gottfried concurs with Jacoby that the neoconservatives have "corporate money, journalistic clout, and administrative connections."[51] Precisely because of that, though, neoconservatism is a threat to the "old conservatives" who "run the risk of being swallowed up in the alliance that they initiated and sustained."[52] They are a threat not only because of their dominance, however. Their behavior is also positively menacing. One of Gottfried's editorial notes sadly records how "surly" and "arrogantly dismissive" neoconservative intellectuals were toward the Old Right at a 1985 convocation of the Philadelphia Society.[53] Clearly, conservative academics and intellectuals do not make up a united front.

The presence of *Continuity* aside, Gottfried believes that scholars of his persuasion have made little headway. Even when William Bennett headed the National Endowment for the Humanities during the Reagan administration, Gottfried contends, conservative scholars were usually passed over in favor of Marxists and feminists. The prospects for "conservative historians receiving prestigious and high-paying academic posts seem less likely than a camel's passing through the needle's eye. Unlike their leftist counterparts, conservative historians usually publish—and perish."[54] Gottfried concludes on a note scarcely calculated to reassure scholars on the Right: "We shall have to try to cultivate our garden in the desert."[55]

Notes

1. Clinton Rossiter, *Conservatism in America: The Thankless Persuasion* (New York, 1962).

2. Morison said this in an address during the 1950s. I have been unable to locate the precise source for the quotation, however.

3. This statement appears alongside the Table of Contents in *Continuity*, no. 1 (Fall 1980). The journal is published twice a year by the Intercollegiate Studies Institute.

4. Paul Gottfried and Thomas Fleming, *The Conservative Movement* (Boston, 1988).

In 1988, Burton W. Folsom, Jr., (a business historian at Murray State University in Kentucky) became editor in chief of *Continuity*, though Gottfried remains on the advisory board.

5. George Nash, *The Conservative Intellectual Movement in America: Since 1945* (New York, 1979), Chapters 1, 3, 4.

6. See Arthur A. Ekirch, Jr., *The Decline of American Liberalism* (New York, 1955).

7. Gottfried and Fleming, *Conservative Movement*, p. 88.

8. William Burton, "Historiography and the Double Standard," *Continuity*, no. 7 (Fall 1983): 20.

9. Ellen Shapiro McDonald, "Introduction," *Continuity*, no. 2 (Spring 1981): i.

10. Aileen S. Kraditor, "On the History of American Reform Movements and Its Legacy Today," *Continuity*, no. 1 (Fall 1980): 40.

11. Richard H. Pells, *The Liberal Mind in a Conservative Age: American Intellectuals in the 1940's and 1950's* (New York, 1985), pp. 130–40.

12. See Gottfried's "Editorial Notes," *Continuity*, no. 8 (Spring 1984): i, and also his notes for *Continuity*, no. 10 (Spring 1985): ii.

13. Aileen S. Kraditor, "On the Relationship between Conservatism and American Social History," *Continuity*, nos. 4, 5 (Spring–Fall 1982): 130.

14. Ibid., p. 137.

15. See Aileen S. Kraditor, *The Radical Persuasion: Aspects of the Intellectual History and the Historiography of Three Radical Organizations* (Baton Rouge, Louisiana, 1981).

16. Kraditor, "American Reform Movements," p. 53.

17. Robert Nisbet, *The Twilight of Authority* (New York, 1975).

18. Herbert Butterfield, *The Whig Interpretation of History* (London, 1931).

19. Richard Hofstadter, *The Progressive Historians: Turner, Beard, Parrington* (New York, 1968).

20. See in particular Christopher Lasch, *A World of Nations* (New York, 1974), pp. xi–xii, 70–79.

21. Richard Jensen, "The Right Schools: Ideological Debate on the History of Education," *Continuity*, nos. 4, 5 (Spring–Fall 1982): 161.

22. Burton, "Historiography."

23. See John P. McKay, Bennett D. Hill, and John Buckler, *A History of Western Society* (Boston, 1983).

24. Roland Stromberg, "The Liberal Bias in Studies of Causes Célèbres," *Continuity*, no. 11 (Spring 1987).

25. Ibid., p. 8.

26. Ibid., p. 14.

27. Ibid., p. 19.

28. Ibid., p. 21.

29. Clyde Wilson, "Introduction: Recovering Southern History," *Continuity*, no. 9 (Fall 1984): iii.

30. Clyde Wilson, "The Mind of the Old South," *Continuity*, no. 9 (Fall 1984): 231.

31. Paul Gottfried, "Editorial Notes," *Continuity*, no. 6 (Spring 1983): ii.

32. Ludwell H. Johnson, "The Plundering Generation: Uneasy Reflections on the Civil War," *Continuity*, no. 9 (Fall 1984): 112.

33. Ibid., p. 114.

34. M. E. Bradford, "Lincoln and the Language of Hate and Fear: A View from the South," *Continuity*, no. 9 (Fall 1984): 104.

35. Ibid., p. 105.

36. Margaret Coit Elwell, "The Continuing Relevance of John C. Calhoun," *Continuity*, no. 9 (Fall 1984): 85.

37. Gregory Wolfe, "Book Notes," *Continuity*, no. 10 (Spring 1985): 134.

38. Aileen S. Kraditor, "Robert Higgs on 'The Radical Persuasion,'" *Continuity* no. 7 (Fall 1983): 116.

39. Jules Gleicher, "The Straying of the Constitution: Raoul Berger and the Problem of Legal Continuity," *Continuity*, no. 1 (Fall 1980).

40. James Burnham, *Congress and the American Tradition* (Chicago, 1959).

41. See Gottfried's review of Will's *Statecraft as Soulcraft* in *Continuity*, no. 8 (Spring 1984): 123.

42. Donald Pickens, "William Graham Sumner as a Critic of the Spanish-American War," *Continuity*, no. 11 (Spring 1987).

43. Peter J. Coleman, "The New Zealand Welfare State: Origins and Reflections," *Continuity*, no. 2 (Spring 1981): 61.

44. Stephen J. Sniegoski, "Book Notes," *Continuity*, no. 10 (Spring 1985): 172.

45. Kraditor, "Conservatism and American Social History," p. 3.

46. Kraditor, "Robert Higgs," p. 122.

47. Forrest McDonald, "Conservative Scholarship and the Problem of Myth," *Continuity*, nos. 4, 5 (Spring–Fall 1982): 67.

48. Gottfried and Fleming, *Conservative Movement*, p. 57.

49. Russell Jacoby, *The Last Intellectuals: American Culture in the Age of Academe* (New York, 1987).

50. Ibid., p. 206.

51. Gottfried and Fleming, *Conservative Movement*, p. 108.

52. Ibid., p. 70.

53. Paul Gottfried, "Editorial Notes" (Spring 1985), p. ii.

54. Paul Gottfried, "Editorial Notes," *Continuity*, no. 11 (Spring 1987): i.

55. Ibid., p. ii. If an oasis, *Continuity* has proved to be a rather tiny one. Noting that in 1985 the circulation of *Continuity* was less than one-tenth that of *Radical History Review*, historian Peter Novick, somewhat unfairly, called Gottfried's journal "a curiosity, without influence or even visibility." See Novick's *That Noble Dream: The "Objectivity Question" and the American Historical Profession* (Cambridge, England, 1988), p. 464.

Information Sources

BIBLIOGRAPHY: None.

INDEXES: *Amer Hist & Life*; *Hist Abst*; *Writings Amer Hist*.

REPRINT EDITIONS: None.

LOCATION SOURCES: Complete runs: Intercollegiate Studies Institute, Bryn Mawr, Pennsylvania; Library of Congress; major university and public libraries.

Publication History

TITLE AND TITLE CHANGES: *Continuity: A Journal of History*.

VOLUME AND ISSUE DATA: Numbers 1–current, Fall 1980–present.

FREQUENCY OF PUBLICATION: Semiannually.

PUBLISHERS: Intercollegiate Studies Institute, Bryn Mawr, Pennsylvania. Currently published by Young Americans Foundation, Herndon, Virginia.

EDITORS: Paul Gottfried and Aileen Kraditor, 1980–1981; Paul Gottfried, 1982–1987; Burton W. Folsom, Jr., 1988–present.

CIRCULATION: 1985: 300; 1998: 700.

Barry D. Riccio

New Criterion
1982–

For many years American conservatives had been profoundly irritated with the way liberal intellectuals monopolized debate on cultural matters and by the prominence of such liberal journals as the *New York Review of Books*. It is not so much that there has ever been a shortage of conservative voices as a shortage of conservative voices with academic and intellectual weight. At times some of them thought that there should be a conservative alternative. It is the virtue of the *New Criterion* that it offers a more serious cultural criticism than had previously existed on most of the American Right. Whereas journals like *Modern Age* preach the virtues of a Richard Weaver or an Irving Babbitt to a smaller audience, the *New Criterion* confronts the most powerful and influential intellectuals of the day and subjects them to a harsh critique. Whereas by the early 1980s *National Review* had virtually terminated its coverage of painting and theater, the *New Criterion* offers regular reports on all the arts. Whereas previous journals had been cool toward modernism, often treating it in a hostile and querulous manner, the *New Criterion* firmly embraces the heritage of the aesthetic experiments of the first half of this century.

First appearing in September 1982, the *New Criterion* is published in New York City by the Foundation for Cultural Review. The conservative John Olin Foundation has given it valuable support. From the beginning Hilton Kramer has been its editor. Kramer came from the liberal milieu of the New York intellectuals, which in the postwar world was strongly anticommunist and valued the artistic integrity of modernist discipline over the sentimentality of Popular Front culture. Born in 1928, he became editor of *Artsmagazine* in 1955. After serving as the art critic of the *Nation* from 1958 to 1961, he became the art news editor of the *New York Times* in 1965, a position he held until 1982. His work developed in the liberal atmosphere of such ex-Marxist critics as Harold Rosenberg and Clement Greenberg. He disliked the leftist attitudes of the first, and the formalism of the second, but he shared their warmth for abstract expressionism. Indeed abstract expressionism was for Kramer a high point for American art, which from the mid-1960s onward was in a clear state of decline.

By the mid-1970s Kramer was part of the movement of New York intellectuals that would become known as neoconservatives. Originally consisting of Henry Jackson Democrats, they despised George McGovern and Jimmy Carter for defeating their hero. They accused both men of irresponsible pacifist and "neoisolationist" opinions and of encouraging racial division with affirmative action programs. Their hard-line anticommunism led them to form the Committee on the Present Danger, oppose ratification of SALT II, and, by the 1980s, to support Ronald Reagan for president. By 1981 neoconservatives were the most articulate proponents of the Reagan platform.

Kramer fully shared their belief in anticommunism, their contempt for liberals, their intense dislike of "the 1960s" and the decadence and moral decay they associated with it. These attitudes frequently appeared in the pages of the *New Criterion*. But his major role was to articulate neoconservatism's aesthetics. According to him modernism was under attack from many enemies. Once the enemy had been the traditional bourgeoisie, whose philistine tastes had dominated the art world before the 1870s and the rise of such paradigmatic modernists as Cézanne, Matisse, Picasso, and Bonnard. They had been slow to recognize how modernism enriched and disciplined bourgeois life and how the two had coexisted in a creative tension. Occasionally Kramer would criticize conservatives who seemed to share those views. For example he castigated Tom Wolfe's call for a new realism in fiction, as well as Edward Banfield's plan to sell the originals of great masterpieces and mass-produce copies for museums.[1] But the major threat came not from the Right but from the Left. Ever since the glory days of abstract expressionism, the avant-garde had been weakened and subverted from within by the meretriciousness of camp and kitsch. In the aftermath of the disastrous 1960s, liberal appeasers had weakened the grounds of civilization. Leftists either deluded themselves into the belief that modernism was revolutionary, or they sought to destroy it and replace it with some form of Stalinist aesthetics. The boundaries between high art and popular culture had been eroded. Meretricious art forms proliferated in every genre, while Marxists, feminists, poststructuralists, and other ideological scholars subverted the academy from within. Against all these evils the *New Criterion* pledged to defend high standards, Western civilization, and the autonomy of art.[2]

In subsequent years, the *New Criterion* established a regular poetry section, the first such feature in a major conservative periodical since the disintegration of the *National Review* page in 1963. In its pages it has published such respected poets as Louis Simpson and Donald Hall, translations of Eugenio Montale and Jorge Luis Borges as well as members of the "New Formalism," such as Elizabeth Spires, Brad Leithauser, and Daniel Mark Epstein, who emphasize meter and rhyme. During its first decade and a half, the *New Criterion* also published selected correspondence by Marcel Proust and Dorothy Richardson and memoirs by Aleksandr Solzhenitsyn and Elias Canetti. It included among its contributors such novelists as Mark Helprin, Walker Percy, Cynthia Ozick, Hortense Calisher, and Guy Davenport, as well as such critics as Frederick Crews, René Wellek, and Cleanth Brooks.

But these were not typical contributors. The core of the journal was Kramer himself. He and Jed Perl were the main art critics. It included the publisher, Samuel Lipman, who served as the main music critic until he died in 1994. The two most important literary critics were Joseph Epstein, editor of the *American Scholar*, and the poet and biographer Bruce Bawer. Academics such as James Tuttleton and the late Peter Shaw supplemented their work. The poetry editor continues to be Robert Richman, defender and articulator of the New Formalism. Mimi Kramer, Herb Greer, and Donald Lyons wrote on the theater. John Simon, the theater critic for *New York* and the film critic for *National Review*, occasionally submitted articles, including a majority of the few essays the *New Criterion* devoted to the appreciation of the cinema.[3] Especially important was Roger Kimball—by 1989 the managing editor—who supplemented Kramer's polemics with his own against most postwar schools of literary criticism, the Modern Language Association, the 1986 PEN Congress, and the many symptoms of "political correctness" that he decried.

The *New Criterion*'s criticism was pessimistic about the current cultural scene. In the first issue Joseph Epstein complained about the stultifying atmosphere of contemporary universities: "Although I have never heard anyone speak of it, one of the reigning questions about the literature of our day is why so few American literary masterpieces have been produced in the past quarter-century."[4] Although Epstein was talking about fiction, the *New Criterion* thought much the same about other genres. Reviewers castigated "Minimalism," the name of a movement that developed simultaneously in fiction, music, and painting, which shared little more than a common sparseness and simplicity. Kramer disliked most art since the death of Jackson Pollock and showed a special animus against Susan Sontag, while Lipman for his part concentrated exclusively on classical music. Epstein criticized John Updike and Norman Mailer for meretricious sexuality, Robert Coover and E. L. Doctorow for fashionable anti-American bromides, and Philip Roth for solipsism. Bawer agreed with these judgments and denounced the metafictions of "academic" novelists and the new "brat pack" writers, as well as such poets as William Carlos Williams and Allen Ginsberg.

Epstein went on to argue that the ideological Left had thoroughly politicized American literature. Combating this scourge required both moral seriousness (what Epstein described as "gravity") and theoretical rigor. Although Kramer, Kimball, and Bawer spoke with some sympathy about the "New Criticism" of the 1940s and 1950s,[5] and ran New Critics like Wellek and Brooks, they themselves did not practice it. Instead they tried to produce the kind of serious, morally concerned criticism that is perhaps best exemplified in literature by Lionel Trilling, which had been the hallmark of *Partisan Review* at its height.

Trying to define what this moral core consisted of is a major problem, which conservative writers have not fully solved. An examination of literature puts this in better perspective. Epstein praised the healing powers of "common sense" against alienated (i.e., left-wing) intellectuals. He has spoken coolly of the rise of sex in modern fiction but has not clearly delineated the role of the erotic. Rather, he preferred to dismiss erotic passages in writers he already found second rate, such as Roth, Updike, and Mailer, and judged them unfavorably to Tolstoy.[6] Bruce Bawer also searched for moral seriousness. Speaking of the prewar novels, he proclaimed that what saved them from their own pessimism "was the fact their protagonists, as a rule, were men and women of substance. Doomed or not, they were genuine heroes, who actively sought to construct themselves a life built upon useful work or positive beliefs." Do Clyde Griffiths and Quentin Compson fit into this role, or do they fit into it any better than many other postwar protagonists? The contemporary American novelists whom Bawer most admired were writers like Glenway Wescott, William Maxwell, and Peter Taylor. All three were unambitious in both form and subject, had written about rural or small town settings, and had published major work before 1960. Writing of Penelope Fitzgerald, a British writer who shared the first two qualities, Bawer praised her for a quietist stoicism: she exhibits "those most English of virtues: decency, honesty, quiet fortitude, a sense of duty, an uncomplaining acceptance of one's role and responsibilities in life."[7]

Few other journals have devoted as much attention and as much vehemence to denouncing the university in the age of political correctness and defending the canon of Western civilization. And yet it has not won the prestige and public notice it believes that it deserves. Roger Kimball's rather technical *Tenured Radicals* (1990) was overshadowed by the more popular efforts of Allan Bloom and Dinesh D'Souza. Robert Richman's "New Formalism" was not only more or less ignored by conservative periodicals like *National Review* and the *American Spectator*, but also by his fellow contributor Joseph Epstein in his gloomy *Commentary* essay, "Who Killed Poetry?"[8] Epstein and Samuel Lipman served on the National Council of Arts for several years. But now they and other conservatives in the art bureaucracy argue that they were unsuccessful and that such institutions have to be dissolved.[9]

The *New Criterion*'s attacks on victimism are a common trope of conservative discourse. But its own attitude undermines its claims to speak out against self-pitying narcissism. *Homophobia* is an overused term, but Joseph Epstein was guilty of it. He was literally afraid of homosexuals. "If I had the power to do so," he declared in 1970, "I would wish homosexuality off the face of this earth." Quite frankly, "I find myself completely incapable of coming to terms with it." In the 1980s Epstein went out of his way to refute arguments that writers he admired, such as Willa Cather, Max Beerbohm, George Santayana, and Henry James, were homosexuals. In *Commentary* he criticized E. M. Forster as "thin" and as a "homosexual utopian."[10]

Like much of the rest of the media, the *New Criterion* attacked Afrocentrism and multiculturalism. What distinguished its coverage of Third World culture from that of more liberal journals was a degree of insensitivity to the majority of the world that bordered on contempt. James Tuttleton's idea of a model historian on American Indians was Francis Parkman. David Pryce-Jones praised Nirad C. Chaudhuri's memoirs for essentially arguing that Indian independence was a thoroughly bad idea, causing it to be "rebarbarized." Coverage of Latin American literature was skimpy at best. The historian Mark Falcoff wrote most of the few articles. He had previously condemned Joan Didion for arguing, correctly, that the El Salvadoran army had committed a horrible massacre at El Mozote. Falcoff said little on the aesthetic merits of Latin American fiction, but instead chose to congratulate those intellectuals who supported capitalism and American foreign policy.[11]

The *New Criterion* did not always make subtle distinctions. Norman Cantor denounced the liberal historian Lawrence Stone as a "Marxist." This was so incorrect that even conservative historians such as Gertrude Himmelfarb and J. H. Hexter wrote in to chide Cantor.[12] Geoffrey Sampson gave an account of how he had written an entry on Noam Chomsky for Lord Bullock's dictionary of twentieth-century biography. He claimed that Chomsky had endorsed a book denying the Holocaust and also claimed that Chomsky had hypocritically threatened a libel suit against Bullock over this entry. Both claims were incorrect.[13] Samuel Lipman described the Marxist historian Perry Anderson as a "deconstructionist," when in fact Anderson had succinctly criticized the logic of poststructuralism.[14] David Gress accused the journalist Christopher Hitchens of "anti-Semitism" and "a fawning admiration of her [America's] enemies," because he argued that conservatives used "terrorism" as a smoke screen to deny the just claims of the Palestinians.[15]

The *New Criterion* went out of its way to challenge the most erudite minds of the Left. Richard Vine launched a furious attack on Walter Benjamin that was full of ad hominem criticisms and stacked with intemperate abuse: "Leftist ideologues who reap increasing power through the systematic debasement of art" display a "reflexive obeisance to all feminist and minority claims," and support a "pornography of schlock." His basic argument was that Benjamin was a Stalinist mediocrity who had been promoted by a conspiracy of a leftist coterie. He did not expand on why such nonleftists as Hannah Arendt, Gershom Scholem, and long-time contributor to *Commentary* Robert Alter praised Benjamin.[16] The criticisms that Kramer made of Marxist art historian T. J. Clark, and that Kimball made of Marxist literary critics Terry Eagleton and Fredric Jameson were less than cutting. Much of the three articles consisted of outrage that Marxism could be so highly respected, and sniffed that these enemies of bourgeois culture had prominent university posts.[17]

In his critique of Eagleton, Kimball proclaimed, "We do not suggest that art exists in a vacuum, apart from any human values or concerns; we mean, rather, that it should not be pursued as a species of propaganda but as a realm of experience that possesses its own criteria and validity." Kramer himself argued that art must not be used "for any political program it might be thought to serve but for what it is." Nothing could be more damaging than to "subordinate it to politics—even, as I say, to our politics."[18] Yet nothing so damaged the *New Criterion*'s attempt to defend the value of objectivity and the autonomy of art as its own critical practice. Like other conservatives it did not hesitate to confuse the United States with its elected Republican officials and denounce its opponents as "anti-American." Those who were not entirely for them were against them, as its contributors regularly insinuated that those to the left of Henry Jackson were traitors and nihilists. They accused writers like Albert Camus and Milan Kundera of cowardice for their insufficient enthusiasm for the West.[19]

As a consequence, the *New Criterion*'s pages were often partisan in a narrow and unimaginative way. One might predict that in the first sentence of a review of a Marxist critic, it would drop the name of Zhdanov, and Peter Shaw obliges in a review of Terry Eagleton. One might suspect that a reviewer would castigate "champagne socialists" in his first sentence and "limousine liberals" in his second, and James Bowman also obliges in a review of Margaret Drabble.[20] The *New Criterion* will run an article on how leftist nihilists are trying to undermine the basic methodologies of science, then turn around and run an attack on Darwin by Philip E. Johnson, a law professor whose only scientific qualifications are a middle-brow distaste for the atheistic implications of natural selection.[21]

An example of Republican party partisanship is the journal's current media critic, James Bowman. Whereas the *New Criterion* had denounced much of the academy as corrupt and indifferent to standards, Bowman had sung the praises of Rush Limbaugh in the *National Review*. In the *New Criterion* he has criticized newspapers for being too harsh on tobacco companies. When Michael Lind denounced the mediocrity of conservative intellectuals and accused Pat Robertson of anti-Semitism, Bowman wrote the *New Criterion*'s response. It was an evasive affair in which Bowman accused Lind of "playing the old Comintern game," but avoided the central question: Why does one of the most important members of the American Republican party believe in fantastic conspiracies, and why does he cite notorious anti-Semites as evidence?[22] Conservatives have ill served political debate by defining intellectual integrity as uncritical support for the most questionable actions of the Republican party.

On its behalf, it could be said that the *New Criterion* still possesses the high standards and aversion to popular hype that marked the New York intellectuals. It can positively say that it has always treated the fashionable and shallow with the contempt they deserve. The question that arises is whether, given its strong prejudices, it does so for the right reasons. The *New Criterion* would like to believe that it replaces the old *Partisan Review* and is superior to the *New York Review of Books*. It is more likely to be compared to the old *Quarterly Review*. It is questionable whether its criticisms will be more valued and remembered than the *Quarterly*'s attacks on Keats, Wordsworth, Dickens, Darwin, Hardy, and Joyce. Like that old Tory journal, the *New Criterion* is a journal of well-articulated partisanship that at times fails to transcend special pleading.

Notes

1. "From the Old Journalism to the New Old Realism," *New Criterion* 8 (January 1990): 3–4 (hereinafter cited as *NC*); Hilton Kramer, "Reproductions for the Plebes: The Banfield proposal," *NC* 2 (June 1984): 1–6; Hilton Kramer, ed., *The New Criterion Reader: The First Five Years* (New York, 1988), pp. 8–14.

2. See Kramer, ed., *New Criterion Reader*, pp. 3–7, which reprints Kramer's first editorial. J. David Hoeveler, Jr., *Watch on the Right: Conservative Intellectuals in the Reagan*

Era (Madison, Wisconsin, 1991), pp. 115–42, provides a sympathetic summary.

3. Kramer did not think much of film as an art form, criticized the *New Republic* for starting its art section with a film review, and has proposed expelling movies from the university classroom in order to preserve the integrity of the liberal arts curriculum. See Kramer, "Hold the Arts Page," *National Review* 45 (21 June 1993): 37–39; Hilton Kramer and Roger Kimball, eds., *Against the Grain: The New Criterion on Art and Intellect at the End of the Twentieth Century* (Chicago, 1995), p. 78.

4. Joseph Epstein, *Plausible Prejudices: Essays in American Writing* (New York, 1985), pp. 25–43; cf. p. 36.

5. Roger Kimball, "Cleanth Brooks and the New Criticism," *NC* 10 (October 1991): 21–26; Bruce Bawer, "I. A. Richards: Critic as Scientist," *NC* 7 (March 1989): 29–36.

6. Joseph Epstein, *Plausible Prejudices*, pp. 367–83.

7. Bruce Bawer, *Diminishing Fictions: Essays on the Modern American Novel and Its Critics* (Saint Paul, Minnesota, 1988), p. 4; Bawer, *The Aspect of Eternity* (Saint Paul, Minnesota, 1993), p. 268.

8. Joseph Epstein, "Who Killed Poetry?" *Commentary* 86 (August 1988): 13–20.

9. See Joseph Epstein, "What to Do about the Arts," *Commentary* 99 (April 1995): 21–30.

10. Joseph Epstein, "Homo/Hetero: The Struggle for Sexual Identity," *Harpers* 241 (September 1970): 51; Epstein, *Plausible Prejudices*, p. 300; *Pertinent Players: Essays on the Literary Life* (New York, 1993), pp. 196–97; *Partial Payments: Essays on Writers and Their Lives* (New York, 1989), pp. 113, 326, 254–57.

11. James Tuttleton, "Simon Schama, Francis Parkman and the Writing of History," *NC* 10 (September 1991): 39–52; David Pryce-Jones, "Remembering India," *NC* 7 (May 1989): 77–80; Mark Falcoff, "Two Weeks," *Commentary* 75 (May 1983): 66, 68–70; Falcoff, *Against the Grain*, pp. 51–63.

12. Norman Cantor, "The Real Crisis in the Humanities Today," *NC* 3 (June 1985): 30; "Letters," *NC* 4 (March 1986): 84–86.

13. As an anarchist, Chomsky opposes the idea of libel law. Geoffrey Sampson, "Censoring 20th-Century Culture: The Case of Noam Chomsky," *NC* 3 (October 1984): 7–16. See "Letters," *NC* 3 (January 1985): 81–84, between Chomsky and Sampson; Alexander Cockburn, "Beat the Devil," *Nation* 239 (22 December 1984): 670–71; "Letters," *Nation* 240 (2 March 1985): 226, between Sampson and Cockburn; Christopher Hitchens, "The Chorus and the Cassandra: What Everyone Knows about Noam Chomsky," *Grand Street* 5 (Autumn 1985): 106–31.

14. Samuel Lipman, "Said's Music," *NC* 9 (June 1991): 17; Perry Anderson, *In the Tracks of Historical Materialism* (Chicago, 1984), pp. 32–55, esp. pp. 42–45.

15. David Gress, "Talking 'Terrorism,' at Stanford," *NC* 6 (April 1988): 15–22.

16. Richard Vine, "The Beatification of Walter Benjamin," *NC* 8 (June 1990): 37–48.

17. Hilton Kramer, "T. J. Clark and the Marxist Critique of Modern Painting," *NC* 3 (March 1985): 1–8; Roger Kimball, "The Contradictions of Terry Eagleton," *NC* 9 (September 1990): 17–23; Kimball, "Fredric Jameson's Laments," *NC* 9 (June 1991): 9–16.

18. Kimball, "Contradictions," p. 21; Kramer, *Against the Grain*, p. 77.

19. Norman Podhoretz, *The Bloody Crossroads—Where Literature and Politics Meet* (New York, 1986), p. 47; Roger Kimball, "The Ambiguities of Milan Kundera," *NC* 4 (January 1986): 13.

20. Peter Shaw, "Marxism and Criticism," *NC* 4 (December 1985): 81; James Bowman, "What Was the Question?" *NC* 10 (May 1992): 65.

21. Roger Kimball, "When Reason Sleeps: The Academy vs. Science," *NC* 12 (May

1994): 10–17; Philip E. Johnson, "Daniel Dennett's Dangerous Idea," *NC* 14 (October 1995): 9–14.

22. James Bowman, "The Leader of the Opposition," *National Review* 45 (6 September 1993): 44–52; Bowman, "Smoke Gets in Your Eyes," *NC* 14 (February 1996): 60–65; Bowman, "A Conservative Conspiracy?" *NC* 13 (March 1995): 48–55.

Information Sources

BIBLIOGRAPHY: None.
INDEXES: Volumes 1–10 indexed in supplement to Volume 10. *AHI*; *Art Index*; *Bio Ind*; *MLA Intl Bib*.
REPRINT EDITIONS: Microform: UMI.
LOCATION SOURCES: Widely available.

Publication History

TITLE AND TITLE CHANGES: *The New Criterion.*
VOLUME AND ISSUE DATA: Volumes 1–current, 1982–present.
FREQUENCY OF PUBLICATION: Monthly, September–June. Summer issues, 1984–1987.
PUBLISHER: The Foundation for Cultural Review, New York, New York.
EDITOR: Hilton Kramer.
CIRCULATION: 1993, 6,000; 1998, 8,000.

Paul Notley

Part Ten

NEOCONSERVATISM, POLICY ANALYSIS, AND NEW RIGHT JOURNALS

For reasons of culture, politics, and values, the 1960s remains one of the most controversial decades of the twentieth century. Its contours lay in the cold war and in the remarkable affluence of the American middle class. Real income had risen sharply since the end of World War II. Big business discovered ways to shape the welfare-warfare state to its purposes, and New Deal liberals decided that their objectives could best be achieved through economic growth; capitalism would be regulated, but its market system and profit motive would remain intact. Successes during the decade were real. Democracy as a living reality broadened its base during the Great Society: the Civil Rights Act of 1964 created new areas of opportunity for minority Americans; the Voting Rights Act of 1965 did likewise, ending Jim Crow and changing southern and national politics for the rest of the century, perhaps longer. Never before had so direct an attempt been made to combat poverty and to provide medical care for the aged and needy. College enrollment doubled, as the once largely white male preserve opened its doors to women and minority students. Among the young especially, angry criticism of militarism, racism, sexism, technocracy, and paternalism forced new understandings of social injustice on the American people, with more than a hint that overemphasis on material values proved empty in one's spiritual life.

Problems remained, from the legacy of drugs and permissiveness, that rightly or wrongly are linked to that decade, to the growth of executive power, especially in the prosecution of an unpopular war. Many understood President Lyndon Baines Johnson's vigorous leadership as threatening to their liberties, whether in affirmative action, illegal wiretapping, or war making. To fundamentalist Christians, the Supreme Court's decision to outlaw mandated school prayer appeared to place the judicial system in the enemy camp. For mainstream conservatives, the much-expanded welfare state came to symbolize not genuine experimentation to relieve depression problems, as in the days of the New Deal, but rather an arbitrary creation of liberal politicians who had pursued their visions beyond the limits of effectiveness. Although results could not be known immediately, the perception grew that liberal politicians and special interest groups were pursuing reform at the expense of the middle class. As previously invisible groups pushed their way into national politics, the white middle class found reason to resist. By the early 1970s a number of liberal intellectuals too began to question Kennedy and Johnson doctrine and published substantial critiques of policies they had once supported.

It was not only in political economy that middle Americans had become uneasy. Anger mounted when vocal radicals numbered the United States among the world's most repressive societies: the United States was "the Fourth Reich" (James Baldwin); "the white race is the cancer of history" (Susan Sontag); "the family is the American fascism" (Paul Goodman); "the universities cannot be reformed. They must be abandoned or closed down" (*Berkeley Barb*). The language of alienation had become overkill, suggesting to middle Americans that their chief enemies were within rather than abroad. For political, economic, and cultural reasons, the reaction was swift. Among the new critics were the neoconservatives and a more radical generation of conservatives known as the New Right.

The neoconservatives emerged from the breakup of the New Deal coalition, which had governed the nation for three and a half decades. Most were Democrats who had become apprehensive over domestic trends. Different from conservatives of earlier generations, they were intellectuals trained in the social sciences, more interested in policy formulation than in the traditions of bygone days. Whatever their claims and their origins, they now pursued programmatic goals that aligned them with conservatives; thus the term *neoconservative* seemed apt. Although several continued to think of themselves as social democrats, neoconservatives in fact looked for a rollback of previous liberal initiatives, in the process becoming interventionist abroad and suspicious of feminism and environmentalism at home. Their journals were not *Modern Age*, the *Freeman*, or *Human Events*, but rather *Commentary*, the *Public Interest*, and *Policy Review*. In their pages critiques of the Great Society, of its poverty and affirmative action programs, jostled for space with equally stinging indictments of a liberalism that allegedly had gone soft in foreign policy, having defined the war in Vietnam in terms that made it not worth the winning. For a decade and a half, until communism ended in the Soviet Union and in Eastern Europe, the neoconservatives focused their ideological artillery on communism abroad and the growth of the "new class" at home.

The origins of the new class lay in radical history and was popularized by James Burnham, *The Managerial Revolution* (1941), Joseph Schumpeter, *Capitalism, Socialism and Democracy* (1942), and Milovan Djilas, *The New Class: An Analysis of the Communist System* (1957). Later the concept proved adaptable to the developing corporate welfare state. In a 1966 piece for *Commentary*, David Bazelon wrote of a new class of managers, functionaries, and intellectuals "whose life conditions are determined by their position within or in relation to the corporate order." Ownership of property was unnecessary; power lay in the command of esoteric knowledge and strategic position within the new industrial state. These new intellectuals were credentialed, possessed technical skills, and used their expertise as managers, lawyers, social workers, academics, and consultants to power the welfare state in ways that, if not checked, threatened to "administer everybody and everything." It remained only to equate this analysis with liberalism, which Irving Kristol, Normon Podhoretz, Nathan Glazer, and Michael Novak were ready to do. Pursuing an agenda that necessitated a degree of social engineering, the new class at the same time was in a position to advance its own interests through an uneasy alliance with the poor and working classes. The new class expressed its love of power through the search for a moral republic, again at the expense of the middle class. It was not their children who would be bused to achieve racial integration or their sons who would be sent to Vietnam, but those of their sought-after allies. Critics thought that a formula for permanent power. For Kristol it meant that the new class was fighting for power to replace that which under capitalism properly belonged to the marketplace. The mobilization of mass support on behalf of better ecology, environmentalism, consumer protection, and economic planning marked its operation in the real world. The result was a new form of class warfare.

It is ironic that so many critics of the new class were themselves at its very center. Few were men of knowledge in the strict sense—scientists, sages, scholars, and artists—whom Edward Shils, in his many essays on intellectuals, defined as having "an unusual sensitivity to the sacred, an uncommon reflectiveness about the nature of their universe and the rules which govern their society." The neoconservatives regularly traversed the network of think tanks, foundations, government agencies, journalism, publishing, and the university. Jeane Kirkpatrick, as well as Moynihan, Glazer, and Kristol regularly spent time in Washington in one of these capacities, reflecting the quintessence of postindustrial society, in which knowledge and organizations are dependent on each other. Wealthy not in economic capital but in human capital, their privilege was such that they hardly embodied the revolutionary potential attributed to the new class. Somewhat rootless, they functioned as intellectuals with a political thrust, viewing knowledge as a weapon. They felt at home in the journals under review in this part, linking the neoconservative journals with those that dealt explicitly in policy analysis, such as *Orbis* and *Policy Review*. The same manner of intellectual could comfortably publish in both, and did so.

Also emerging from the crosscurrents of the 1960s was the New Right. For two decades it has been a powerful force in American politics, keeping social issues at the forefront of discussion (not always on the front burner in the nation's capital) and pulling the Republican party to the right. Unlike the neoconservatives, the ranks of the movement numbered in the millions, at times linked by single-issue organizations that shared their leaders with each other. Its uniqueness consisted of the ability to be at once lower-middle class, conservative, and radical. Richard Viguerie, publisher of *Conservative Digest*, quoted Paul Weyrich, creator of several right-wing political action committees (with the financial support of Joseph Coors) and a principal strategist of Moral Majority, to make the point: "We are radicals who want to change the existing power structure. We are not conservatives in the sense that conservative means accepting the status quo....We cannot accept the status quo....We have to take a turn in the other direction. The New Right does not want to conserve, we want to change—we *are* the forces of change." This political philosophy, Viguerie added, "parallels the military philosophy of Douglas MacArthur, 'There is no substitute for victory.'" In its mobilization of mass political action, the New Right earned the term *populist conservatism*. Hearth and home issues dominate those in the movement who seek to regain control of a culture thought to be under the sway of a liberal enemy. In this part the New Right is represented by *Conservative Digest, Human Life Review*, and *New Guard*, the last most difficult to place. Begun by Young Americans for Freedom (the oldest youth group in the conservative movement), the journal for years published material that reflected both libertarian and traditional conservative values. Later, its agenda most closely followed that of the New Right, hence its inclusion here.

Commentary
1945–

Since it first appeared in November 1945, *Commentary* has held a position as one of America's premier intellectual and Jewish-oriented journals. The magazine has provided a platform for many of the country's leading social scientists, critics, and public intellectuals to address current issues. The two editors, Elliot E. Cohen and Norman Podhoretz—who together directed it for almost all of its first fifty years— were important figures among American intellectuals and did much to shape political discourse. Perhaps most significantly, the magazine's apparent 1970 transformation from a liberal publication to the leading platform for the neoconservative movement gave it a major voice among conservatives during the 1980s and 1990s. Despite its shift, however, *Commentary* has consistently maintained a skepticism of cultural and political fashion that suggests its conservatism is more deeply rooted than generally believed.

Commentary's roots lie in the experiences of New York's Jewish intellectual community, a small, tightly knit, often quarrelsome group that in the 1930s and 1940s produced many brilliant writers and critics, such as Irving Howe, Sidney Hook, Irving Kristol, Daniel Bell, and Philip Rahv. Most were the children of immigrants and had grown up in poverty; born in the United States, they felt out of place in their parents' immigrant community but remained conscious of their status as members of an ethnic and religious minority and did not feel fully accepted as Americans. As a result, they saw themselves as outsiders, alienated from the mainstream of American culture and society. Not surprisingly, they were attracted to Marxism and radical politics during the 1930s. By the end of the decade, however, they were turning away from left-wing radicalism, disillusioned by events in the Soviet Union and increasingly aware of the limits of revolutionary politics in the United States. Their experiences, however, left them with a deep suspicion of radical ideologies, while World War II and the struggle against fascism gave them a new appreciation of the strength and possibilities of America's liberal democracy. They were "pulled into the orbit of American cultural values by the gravity of the international tensions," in the words of historian Neil Jumonville. By war's end the New York intellectuals were moving away from their self-conscious alienation and seeking a place within American society.[1]

Commentary's founding was part of this process. The American Jewish Committee (AJC) established the magazine to provide a forum for Jewish intellectuals to discuss questions arising from the intersection of their ethnic and religious identities with their position as Americans, as well as broader social and political issues. Other Jewish intellectual journals, such as the *Menorah Journal* (published 1915–1962) and *Partisan Review* (published 1936–), had failed to fill this role, focusing on narrow, parochial issues or downplaying their contributors' religious identity. The AJC appointed Elliott E. Cohen (1899–1959) to edit *Commentary*. Cohen had been a youthful prodigy, graduating from Yale at eighteen and becoming an editor at *Menorah Journal* when he was twenty-four. He gained a reputation as a brilliant editor and spotter of new talent (he was the first to publish articles by the literary critic Lionel Trilling) and was also a polymath, in Norman Podhoretz's recollection, with interests ranging from sports to theology. Cohen left *Menorah Journal* in 1931 after a dispute with the editor in chief and then became a fundraiser for a Jewish organization, where he worked until he was hired to edit *Commentary*.[2]

Cohen's vision for *Commentary* coincided with that of the AJC and took it a step further. Norman Podhoretz would later write that the AJC probably intended *Commentary* to be a "Jewish *Harper's*, only more scholarly," but that Cohen wanted to use it to bring the ideas of the New York intellectuals to a broader, popular audience. Podhoretz points out that this was part of Cohen's personal plan to make *Commentary* a vehicle for furthering the acceptance of Jews as Americans, leading them "out of the desert of alienation...and into the promised land of democratic, pluralistic, prosperous America." Viewed in this light, it is not surprising that Cohen wrote in the first issue that "*Commentary* is an act of faith in our possibilities in America," and, in addition to "carrying forward...our common Jewish cultural and spiritual heritage...[we] will harmonize heritage and country into a true sense of at-home-ness in the modern world."[3]

Reflecting its roots and Cohen's aims and varied interests, *Commentary* typically printed a mix of articles on Jewish themes, politics and current issues, sociology, fiction and poetry, and reviews. Despite this variety, however, there was no question that *Commentary* was primarily addressing issues of concern to Jewish intellectuals. Editors and frequent contributors included such leading Jewish intellectuals as Irving Kristol, Daniel Bell, Nathan Glazer, Lionel and Diana Trilling, and Robert Warshow. Articles on the Holocaust and its aftermath, debates over the direction of Zionism, analyses of different aspects of Jewish culture and religion, and memoirs of the Jewish experience in America dominated the early issues. Typical was a 1946 article, "Is America Exile or Home?" which argued that despite their support for Zionism, American Jews needed to acknowledge the United States as a "Jewish center" rather than a temporary ghetto for exiles and "settle down to the task of building here, in freedom and security, the good and creative Jewish life."[4]

In another reflection of Cohen's outlook, *Commentary* stood firmly within the moderate liberal consensus that developed during the late 1940s. Liberals saw themselves as hard-headed political realists who accepted the permanence of capitalism and rejected revolutionary change in favor of gradual social and political reforms that would distribute the system's benefits more evenly. The magazine accepted the dominant liberal analysis that emphasized the difficulties of politics. Daniel Bell, for example, described American politics as "offering us a complex series of class struggles, group struggles, and national unity." This view, however, along with the intellectuals' desire to fit into American society, created a tension within *Commentary*'s liberalism that gave it a conservative edge. The magazine reserved its greatest criticism for liberals, whom it viewed as not understanding these realities and were therefore responsible for the "futility and floundering of the liberal-labor left."[5]

Similarly, *Commentary* took an orthodox view of the cold war. It viewed the Soviet Union as a grave threat to American security and supported a strongly internationalist foreign policy. *Commentary* also took a firm line against any softness by liberals toward domestic communism. The lesson of the Alger Hiss case, wrote Leslie Fiedler in 1951, was that liberals had to guard against those who would call themselves "progressive," "left," or "socialist," to cover pro-totalitarian activities. *Commentary* also denied consistently that rooting out subversion was damaging to civil liberties; civil liberties would be best protected by uncovering those who would curtail the liberties of others, wrote Robert Bendiner in 1948. In one of the era's most controversial articles, "'Civil Liberties,' 1952—A Study in Confusion," Irving Kristol scolded liberals for failing "to see Communism for what it is: a movement guided by conspiracy and aiming at totalitarianism, rather than merely another form of 'dissent' or 'nonconformity.'" Thus, argued Kristol, liberals looked silly and confused and were therefore in part responsible for the success of the "vulgar demagogue" Senator Joseph McCarthy (R, Wisconsin). "For there is one thing that the American people know about Senator McCarthy," wrote Kristol. "He, like them, is unequivocally anticommunist. About the spokesmen for American liberalism, they feel they know no such thing."[6]

Cohen's approach quickly made *Commentary* a success. By 1951, circulation had risen to over 20,000 and, noted *Time* in a flattering article, no readers paid more attention "than those in the State Department...[who] picked up articles for distribution around the world, either because they have so ably stated the position of the democratic world or so clearly exposed the fallacies of totalitarianism." *Commentary* foundered during the second half of the 1950s, however, largely because Cohen fell victim to depression. "Utterly paralyzed, he sat day after day in his office, unable to do anything but stare listlessly at the desk," recalled Norman Podhoretz, who was then a junior editor. Cohen was hospitalized in 1956, and the editors began quarreling among themselves. The AJC arranged a temporary, shared editorship by brothers Clement and Martin Greenberg, but the arrangement foundered as they clashed with Podhoretz. Podhoretz announced his resignation, but the AJC did not accept it, arranging instead a new shared editorship that included Podhoretz. Cohen returned in 1958—"a shrunken, shaken man...obviously not in any shape to take the strain of running a magazine," according to Podhoretz—and

Podhoretz finally left when he viewed Cohen and Martin Greenberg as working against him. Cohen committed suicide in May 1959 and, with experience showing the need for a single, firm hand in control, the AJC chose Norman Podhoretz to succeed him.[7]

From his appointment in 1960 until his retirement in 1995, Podhoretz ran *Commentary* as an extension of himself. Born in 1930, Podhoretz had grown up in Brooklyn and, as he later described in his memoir *Making It* (1967), he was an ambitious man, working hard to achieve both intellectual and material success. He excelled in school, won a scholarship to Columbia College, and there became a student of Lionel Trilling. He went to Cambridge on a Fulbright scholarship to study literature. After returning to New York in 1953, he began writing for *Commentary*, and his reviews soon marked him as a promising young literary critic as well as an intellectual concerned with political issues. In his reviews, Podhoretz later wrote, he "attempted to relate an aesthetic judgment of the book to some social or literary issue outside the book itself," and to understand what this said about the "attitudes of the author and...the general temper of the times." Novelist Norman Mailer later claimed that Podhoretz was "as good as any critic in America at this kind of writing." After serving two years in the army, Podhoretz returned to *Commentary*, just as the turmoil resulting from Cohen's illness was beginning. By the time of Cohen's death, Podhoretz later wrote, *Commentary* had become "predictable and listless," in need of a complete revamping to pull it "out of the doldrums and make it great again." Podhoretz gave it a much-needed new look, reduced the emphasis on Jewish-oriented issues, and dropped some tired features.[8]

Podhoretz also decided to move *Commentary* to the left. Like many other intellectuals, Podhoretz had grown restless by the end of the 1950s and was bored with the era's moderate liberalism. In the aftermath of Soviet leader Nikita Krushchev's 1956 speech denouncing Stalin's crimes, Podhoretz became increasingly skeptical of what he saw as liberalism's rigid rejection of the possibility that communist states might change. His views also gradually shifted as he sought opportunities for change and reform in the United States, and, he later wrote, by the time he took over *Commentary*, he believed that the 1960s would favor "boldness" and "imagination" over the "prudence and caution" of the 1950s. He decided that *Commentary* would provide a platform for intellectuals to criticize "existing institutions of every kind...their shortcomings, their weaknesses, and their inadequacies." Podhoretz viewed this as a new radicalism—one that would provide a new direction for intellectuals and leadership for the country during the 1960s and also help define a "vision of what a decent human life might look like." He believed his radicalism would be superior to that of the 1930s, however, because it would be free of the Stalinist influence that had tainted intellectual life during the Great Depression.[9]

Podhoretz quickly carried out his plan, publishing a wide range of articles that Cohen would have rejected instantly. *Commentary* continued to look at many of the same domestic and international issues with which it had been concerned during the 1950s, but now offered its criticisms from the left. Podhoretz set the tone in his first issue (February 1960), in which he presented the first installment of a serialization of anarchist social critic Paul Goodman's book *Growing Up Absurd*, a critique of American society. Podhoretz viewed the book as "the very incarnation of the new spirit" he had been seeking; later it became a standard guide for the counterculture. In the months that followed, other articles chronicled the changes creating the questioning, experimental attitudes that would characterize 1960s liberalism. Thus, sociologist Amitai Etzioni wrote of the "declining pressure for conformity [that] has led many ex-radicals and liberals to become vocal once more and politically active." Political scientist Andrew Hacker wrote sympathetically of young New Left scholars who were "impatient with…the…mild liberalism of their professors." The students were drifting toward Marxism, Hacker argued, because in the rebellion against "prevailing orthodoxies…the liberals have hidden behind methodological barricades" rather than challenge prevailing assumptions.[10]

Podhoretz also changed *Commentary*'s assumptions about the cold war and its domestic effects. In "How the Cold War Began" (November 1960), revisionist historian Staughton Lynd divided the blame between the United States and the Soviet Union. Because of its "Wilsonian" and "utopian" desire to expand democracy after the war, wrote Lynd, the United States "threw up significant obstacles to the making of a peace," but the Russians, for their part, had been "ready to carry their influence as far westward as they could safely go without risking the danger of war." By later historiographical standards this was a moderate and balanced view, but at the time it was startling, and some accused Lynd of producing "an elegantly written apology" for the Soviets, recalled Podhoretz. Unintimidated, *Commentary* also reassessed the cold war's effects at home. In June 1962, British Labor politician R. H. S. Crossman reversed the judgments of a decade before when he noted that because of McCarthyism, "the United States has suffered a heavy loss of civil liberty."[11]

Podhoretz's strategy for restoring *Commentary*'s preeminence succeeded rapidly. Just as he had expected, the liberal consensus of the 1950s was breaking down, and intellectuals were eager to hear the new writers and arguments *Commentary* presented. Despite the new tone, however, Podhoretz continued to publish articles by prominent contributors from the 1950s, such as Bell and Glazer, as well as occasional pieces by conservatives, such as sociologist Robert Nisbet. Podhoretz enforced high intellectual standards and edited so closely that he would later comment that he had frequently served as a ghostwriter. Consequently, *Commentary* became a platform for vigorous open debate, and circulation soared from 20,000 to 60,000. In 1966, *Time* noted, *Commentary* was "widely read in Washington," where President Lyndon B. Johnson had personally sought Podhoretz's views.[12]

In retrospect it is apparent that Podhoretz's commitment to radicalism was brief and less than total. However bored he might have been intellectually, Podhoretz remained conventional in his personal life. "I *had* chosen a life of middle-class respectability" that centered on marriage, children, and hard work, he later wrote. As Neil Jumonville later observed, Podhoretz "could never be sympathetic to bohemianism" or counterculture values. Although he had questioned aspects of cold war thinking, Podhoretz had remained an anticommunist. Politically his goal had been to help reinvigorate liberal thinking by posing intellectual challenges, not to demolish it, and Podhoretz did not allow his criticism of liberalism to take him far beyond the mainstream. In 1962, for example, he turned down the opportunity to publish the Port Huron Statement—the founding manifesto of the Students for a Democratic Society and a key document in the history of the New Left—because, he later wrote, he saw it as intellectually simplistic and riddled with clichés. Podhoretz also began to realize that some of his contributors were further to the left than he had at first believed. Staughton Lynd "seemed to be leaning toward the Chinese line in the Sino-Soviet dispute...his attitude toward communism was much more benevolent than I had realized, and his ideas about the American role in the world much more hostile." Indeed, by late 1964, stimulated in part by the student protests at Berkeley, Podhoretz began to see that the New Left was "a far cry from the new radicalism I had been hoping might...emerge" and wondered if it was tending toward a smug authoritarianism. In February 1965 Podhoretz published Glazer's criticism of both the protesters and the Berkeley administration's weak handling of the disturbances, marking the beginning of *Commentary*'s doubts about the direction that 1960s radicalism was taking.[13]

Several additional factors helped push Podhoretz and *Commentary* away from radicalism during the second half of the 1960s. Far from being reinvigorated by the 1960s, moderate liberalism fell apart under the strain of domestic upheavals, Vietnam, and attacks from the New Left. On numerous issues, *Commentary*'s analyses tended to agree with then-sociologist Daniel Patrick Moynihan's 1967 conclusion that the "liberal Left can be as rigid and destructive as any force in American life." One such issue was race. As the civil rights movement turned from its integrationist ethos toward black nationalism, a disturbing increase in anti-Semitism appeared among black leaders—a development guaranteed to concern Podhoretz, who was strongly committed to defending Jewish interests. In late 1964, Nathan Glazer noted that this was creating a problem for Jewish liberals who, he argued, would soon "find their interests and those of formerly less liberal neighbors becoming similar"; for the remainder of the decade *Commentary* published articles on the increasing threat to Jews from black militancy. The increase in campus disturbances also troubled *Commentary*, especially after the April 1968 student uprising at Columbia University, Podhoretz's alma mater and an important symbol for New York intellectuals. Sometimes these factors became intertwined; militant blacks often attacked Israel and Zionism, and played the "most significant role in the crisis" at Columbia, according to one faculty member writing in *Commentary*.[14]

Commentary also became increasingly disenchanted with changing liberal views on foreign affairs. America's involvement in Vietnam had grown at the same time that revisionist historians were stressing American responsibility for the cold war's beginning, leading the New Left to embrace a strident anti-Americanism that centered on the belief that the United States was a malevolent force, responsible for many of the world's ills. Many liberals, while not embracing anti-Americanism, also viewed the United States as often playing a harmful role in the world. *Commentary* rejected this view. Glazer, while admitting that America was far from perfect, noted, "I cannot accept the idea that the fundamental character of American society...is the prime cause of the horrors of Vietnam." Similarly, on the issue of Israel, *Commentary* saw a developing threat from the Left. After Israel's victory in the June 1967 war, for example, Robert Alter wrote that Tel Aviv's success in defending itself had caused the New Left to recast it as "a breeding-ground of chauvinism and brutal militarism." [15]

Podhoretz decided in the spring of 1970 that he would take responsibility for the defense of liberalism. He had watched the growth of the New Left's extremism, black militancy, and anti-Semitism with increasing alarm and personal disgust; he also believed that many of his friends and acquaintances in the intellectual community had either joined the New Left or retreated into a guilty silence. Podhoretz also was angry because so few would defend American society and "its successes in making the middle-class way of life available to an extraordinarily high proportion of the people," a way of life that he had worked hard to achieve. Thus the "time had come to declare full-scale war" on the New Left or, as he referred to it, the Movement. Podhoretz later wrote:

On questions ranging from crime to the nature of art, from drugs to economic growth, from ecology to the new egalitarianism, the dogmas of the Movement—both in their unexpurgated state and in the sanitized versions that had by now become the conventional wisdom of a fellow-traveling culture laying claim to the epithet "liberal"—*Commentary* became perhaps the single most visible scourge of the Movement within the intellectual community.

Nor were the criticisms offered in the measured tones that had marked Glazer's analyses of black anti-Semitism and the New Left. Podhoretz later wrote of the "defiantly provocative" style *Commentary* used, while Gary Dorrien notes more bluntly that the magazine "ridiculed virtually every aspect of contemporary American liberalism." Either way, these remain accurate descriptions of *Commentary*'s outlook to the present day. [16]

Podhoretz's defense of liberalism involved revisiting many of *Commentary*'s traditional topics, such as the state of liberalism and the place of Jews in America and, ironically, made clear the magazine's growing conservatism. Nathan Glazer's description of why he had shifted from "mild radical to mild conservative" was representative of *Commentary*'s view of the threat from the radical Left: as a professor, he had seen radicalism become "a threat to the very existence of the university and to the values of which the university, with all its faults, was a unique and precious embodiment." The radical attack on liberalism, moreover, was seen as creating a potential threat to American Jews. Podhoretz noted in one article, for example, that the first two postwar decades had been a golden age for American Jews but now, as liberalism embraced affirmative action quotas, tolerated the anti-Semitism of the New Left, and became less dependable in its support for Israel, Jews had to ask if it was still good for them. Although he did not provide a definite answer, Podhoretz made it clear American Jews could no longer depend on a benevolent liberalism. [17]

Commentary's broadsides covered both domestic and international politics.

Articles criticized the influence of the New Left on the Democratic party and, especially, its 1972 presidential nominee, Senator George McGovern (D, South Dakota). The new leadership of the Democrats, wrote political scientist Jeane Kirkpatrick, was contemptuous of the values and culture of middle-class working Americans. As the party's choice, Kirkpatrick argued, McGovern was "perceived by millions of Americans as a man who had gone over to the enemy." Podhoretz also resolved *Commentary*'s position on the cold war, returning to hard-line anticommunism. Historian Walter Laqueur wrote in 1972, for example, that the Soviets remained "purposeful and dynamic, out to win the global struggle," and *Commentary* consistently rejected political compromises with Moscow or its clients while advocating a strong defense policy and a return to containment. Finally, *Commentary* rejected the New Left's claim that America was an oppressive society in which civil liberties were in danger. In his extensive critique of the *New York Review of Books*, for example, sociologist Dennis Wrong dismissed the "complaints of self-styled victims of 'repression' in the universities," and another article blamed the New Left's charges of repression on its leaders' "self-dramatization, self-indulgence, [and] honest neuroses." [18]

Podhoretz's shift to the right made the 1970s a golden age for *Commentary*. His conversion made him one of the leading neoconservatives, a label applied to liberal intellectuals who questioned many of their previous assumptions, and *Commentary* became their major platform. Podhoretz's positions were now opposed to those of most intellectuals and set off a major upheaval within the New York community on which several major newspapers, including the *New York Times* and *Wall Street Journal*, reported. This, of course, brought even more attention to *Commentary*'s new stance. The best demonstration of the magazine's increased influence was the response to Daniel Patrick Moynihan's March 1975 article, "The United States in Opposition," in which he argued that instead of quietly accepting Third World and Soviet-bloc rhetorical assaults at the United Nations, the United States should reply forcefully and defend its liberal democratic principles. Within a few weeks Moynihan was appointed ambassador to the United Nations, where his strong speeches defending the United States made him so popular at home that New Yorkers elected him to the Senate in 1976.

Commentary's influence remained high for the remainder of the decade and into the 1980s. For example, Jeane Kirkpatrick's November 1979 denunciation of what she viewed as the Carter administration's poor foreign policy performance, "Dictatorships and Double Standards," brought her to the attention of Republican presidential candidate Ronald Reagan, who appointed her ambassador to the United Nations after his 1980 election. *Commentary*'s criticisms of liberals, Democrats, and the Carter administration, in fact, gave it an important role in Reagan's coalition as representative of former liberals angry with the direction the country had taken during the 1960s and 1970s. Podhoretz himself maintained close relations with the Reagan administration, later recalling meetings and discussions with figures including Secretary of State George Shultz, Director of Central Intelligence William Casey, and Reagan himself. [19]

Commentary was sometimes disoriented by events of the 1980s. Podhoretz was slow to realize the scope of the rapid changes that swept the United States and the rest of the world and in fact often viewed issues as unchanged since the 1970s. As a result, the quality of *Commentary*'s analyses varied greatly. On the positive side, its assessments of liberalism's problems continued to be accurate and insightful. In January 1985, Joshua Muravchik pointed out that the Democrats continuing to hold positions to the left of most Americans had cost them the presidency in 1984. Although many liberals and Democrats disagreed with Muravchik's analysis— and similar articles that had been appearing in *Commentary* since the early 1970s— many eventually came to agree, including the "New Democrats" who moved the party to the center, and victory, in 1992. Other analyses, however, were far off the mark. In July 1989, as the Soviet Union's East European empire was about to crumble, Edward Luttwak asserted that Moscow "would no doubt strive to keep what it has" and that its "implacable policy of military accumulation is set to continue." *Commentary* was hurt by the loss of several of its major contributors, including Bell, Glazer, and Moynihan, who drifted away, Podhoretz recalls, because they believed he had taken the journal too far to the right. Many of the authors who took their places were neither as prestigious nor as insightful.[20]

In the early 1990s, with the cold war over and domestic radicalism clearly less of a threat, *Commentary* gradually shifted its outlook. In the process, it changed from being a neoconservative publication to a frankly conservative one. In part this was because the moderate liberalism that Podhoretz had once sought to defend had almost completely disappeared, its political base drastically reduced during the 1980s by America's conservative turn. Mostly, however, it was a reflection of Podhoretz's evolving views, which had become increasingly similar to those of traditional American conservatism. Podhoretz, for example, defines his conservatism as a defense of the bourgeois democratic order and its morals, which he sees as under constant domestic and foreign attacks. Therefore, it was not surprising that *Commentary* played a prominent role in the cultural battles that broke out in the late 1980s and frequently published articles by such conservative writers as Dinesh D'Souza attacking "political correctness" and the perceived influence of the radical Left in higher education. Similarly, the magazine's articles increasingly reflected conservative assumptions about the need to decrease the size of government and were couched in terms long used by conservative writers. In a representative instance, a 1993 article criticizing President Clinton described "Clintonism's" drive to "enhance the public sector, bloat the government, and further remove responsibility from individuals and families."[21]

Nonetheless, *Commentary*'s relations with other segments of the conservative coalition were sometimes uneasy. Much of *Commentary*'s conservatism was rooted in its break with liberalism, not in the Burkean thinking that informs much of modern American conservative thought. Similarly, the aggressively anti-Soviet, internationally minded neoconservatives had little sympathy for the isolationist tradition of midwestern conservatism. Several prominent conservatives questioned whether *Commentary* even deserved a place in the conservative movement, and this, in turn, involved *Commentary* in sectarian battles on the Right. Conservative intellectual Russell Kirk, for example, remarked that "not seldom it has seemed as if some eminent neoconservatives mistook Tel Aviv for the capital of the United States," leading some to accuse Kirk of making an anti-Semitic remark. Although no one could credibly accuse Kirk of anti-Semitism, *Commentary* began a running battle with columnist and presidential hopeful Patrick J. Buchanan, whom Podhoretz and others on the Right viewed as an anti-Semite. In addition to being a threat to Jews, Podhoretz saw Buchanan as someone who exposed the conservative movement to the same "corruption" that the New Left had brought to liberalism and that could force conservatism "back into a marginal sectarian status."[22]

Six months before the magazine's fiftieth anniversary in 1995, Podhoretz retired, turning *Commentary* over to his longtime deputy, Neal Kozodoy. Several newspapers and magazines used Podhoretz's departure as an opportunity to review his, and *Commentary*'s, ideological journey and the battles it had provoked within the intellectual community. Such coverage was an implicit acknowledgment of *Commentary*'s continuing importance as a voice within the American Jewish community and a forum for intellectuals and their debates. It is in these roles, as well as in its early efforts to help the New York intellectuals find a voice in America, that *Commentary* has set itself apart from other conservative journals.

Notes

1. Neil Jumonville, *Critical Crossings* (Berkeley, California, 1991), p. 55. For background on the New York Jewish intellectual community, see Alexander Bloom, *Prodigal Sons* (New York, 1986).

2. Norman Podhoretz, interview with the author, New York City, 6 May 1996; Jumonville, *Critical Crossings*, chap. 2.

3. Norman Podhoretz, *Making It* (New York, 1967), pp. 128, 130, 135; Elliot E. Cohen, "An Act of Affirmation," *Commentary* 1 (November 1945): 2.

4. Israel Knox, "Is America Exile or Home?" *Commentary* 2 (November 1946): 406, 408.

5. Daniel Bell, "America's Un-Marxist Revolution," *Commentary* 7 (March 1949): 209; James Wechsler, "Did Truman Scuttle Liberalism?" *Commentary* 3 (March 1947): 227.

6. Leslie Fiedler, "Hiss, Chambers, and the Age of Innocence," *Commentary* 12 (August 1951): 119; Robert Bendiner, "Civil Liberties and the Communists," *Commentary* 5 (May 1948): 431; Irving Kristol, "'Civil Liberties,' 1952—A Study in Confusion," *Commentary* 13 (March 1952): 231, 236, 229.

7. "Magazine of Quality," *Time*, 29 January 1951, p. 72; Norman Podhoretz, *Making It*, pp. 197, 232. For a summary of the edtorial battles during Cohen's absence, see Bloom, *Prodigal Sons*, pp. 318–21.

8. Podhoretz, *Making It*, pp. 242, 283; Norman Podhoretz, *Breaking Ranks* (New York, 1979; reprint ed., 1980), p. 24 (page references are to reprint edition); Norman Mailer quoted in "Podhoretz, Norman," by Stewart Hakola in Ann Evory, ed., *Contemporary Authors, New Revision Series* (Detroit, 1982), 7: 393.

9. Podhoretz interview; Podhoretz, *Making It*, p. 282; Podhoretz, *Breaking Ranks*, pp. 81, 54.

10. Podhoretz, *Making It*, p. 297; Amitai Etzioni, "Neo-Liberalism—the Turn of the 60s," *Commentary* 30 (December 1960): 476; Andrew Hacker, "The Rebelling Young Scholars," *Commentary* 30 (November 1960): 404, 406.

11. Staughton Lynd, "How the Cold War Began," *Commentary* 30 (November 1960): 383, 386; Podhoretz, *Breaking Ranks*, p. 188; R. H. S. Crossman, "The New American

Liberalism," *Commentary* 34 (June 1962): 3.

12. Gary Dorrien, *The Neoconservative Mind* (Philadelphia, 1993), p. 147; Podhoretz interview; "A Passion for Ideas," *Time*, 20 May 1966, p. 56.

13. Podhoretz, *Breaking Ranks*, pp. 28, 47, 197, 188, 201, 200 (italics in the original); Jumonville, *Critical Crossings*, p. 198.

14. Daniel Patrick Moynihan, "The President and the Negro: The Moment Lost," *Commentary* 44 (February 1967): 43; Podhoretz interview; Nathan Glazer, "Negroes and Jews: The New Challenge to Pluralism," *Commentary* 38 (December 1964): 34; Stephen Donadio, "Black Power at Columbia," *Commentary* 46 (September 1968): 68.

15. Nathan Glazer, "The New Left and Its Limits," *Commentary* 46 (July 1968): 39; Robert Alter, "Israel and the Intellectuals," *Commentary* 44 (October 1967): 49.

16. Podhoretz, *Breaking Ranks*, pp. 305, 306; Dorrien, *The Neoconservative Mind*, p. 165.

17. Nathan Glazer, "On Being Deradicalized," *Commentary* 50 (October 1970): 78, 76; Norman Podhoretz, "'Is It Good for the Jews?'"*Commentary* 53 (February 1972): 8, 14.

18. Jeane Kirkpatrick, "The Revolt of the Masses," *Commentary* 55 (February 1973): 60; Walter Laqueur, "The World of the 70s," *Commentary* 54 (August 1972): 24; Dennis Wrong, "The Case of the New York Review," *Commentary* 50 (November 1970): 57, 56; Walter Goodman, "The Question of Repression," *Commentary* 50 (August 1970): 28.

19. Podhoretz interview.

20. Joshua Muravchik, "Why the Democrats Lost," *Commentary* 79 (January 1985): passim; Edward N. Luttwak, "Gorbachev's Strategy, and Ours," *Commentary* 88 (July 1989): 32, 34; Podhoretz interview.

21. Podhoretz interview; Irwin M. Stelzer, "Clintonism Unmasked," *Commentary* 95 (May 1993): 25.

22. Russell Kirk, *The Politics of Prudence* (Bryn Mawr, Pennsylvania, 1993), p. 180; Norman Podhoretz, "Buchanan and the Conservative Crackup," *Commentary* 93 (May 1992): 34.

Information Sources

BIBLIOGRAPHY:

Bloom, Alexander. *Prodigal Sons*. New York, 1986.

Dorrien, Gary. *The Neoconservative Mind*. Philadelphia,1993.

Ehrman, John. *The Rise of Neoconservatism*. New Haven, Connecticut, 1995.

Jumonville, Neil. *Critical Crossings*. Berkeley, California, 1991.

Podhoretz, Norman. *Making It*. New York, 1967.

———. *Breaking Ranks*. New York, 1979.

INDEXES: *RG*; *BRD*.

REPRINT EDITIONS: Microform: UMI.

LOCATION SOURCES: Widely available.

Publication History

TITLE AND TITLE CHANGES: *Commentary*.

VOLUME AND ISSUE DATA: Volumes 1–current, November 1945–present.

FREQUENCY OF PUBLICATION: Monthly.

PUBLISHER: American Jewish Committee.

EDITORS: Elliott E. Cohen, November 1945–May 1959; Norman Podhoretz, February 1960–June 1995; Neal Kozodoy, July 1995–.

CIRCULATION: Average paid circulation in 1998: 25,000.

John Ehrman

Orbis

1957–

Issued under the auspices of the Foreign Policy Research Institute of the University of Pennsylvania (FPRI), *Orbis* rapidly established itself after its initial appearance in April 1957 as the most scholarly and thoughtful conservative world affairs quarterly in cold war America. Edited at first by the Penn political scientist Robert Strausz-Hupé and later the former CIA official William R. Kintner, *Orbis* maintained a 3,000–4,000 copy press run that voiced the key ideas and concerns of prominent rightist figures in the country's foreign policymaking elite. Such luminaries as William Y. Elliot, Hans Kohn, and Henry Kissinger served at various times on its board of editors. Frequent contributors included Frank Trager, Stefan T. Possony, W. Scott Thompson, and Colin Gray. Well informed and highly articulate, these men made up a mixed lot in their precise policy prescriptions. Yet they converged in the common conviction that the West was locked in a no-holds-barred struggle with international communism over the very control of the earth and the soul of humankind.

As the quarterly publication of the FPRI, *Orbis* originated to serve the institute's plans of producing basic studies that would aid in the formulation of U.S. foreign policies, new international research techniques, and the training of students in world affairs. Presented in a scholarly format, *Orbis* featured extended book reviews and a special introductory section, "Reflections on the Quarter," in which the editor analyzed major international developments. Yet the journal was intended from the very start to function as more than a house organ. Reaching beyond the institute, *Orbis* editors solicited articles and reviews from contributors throughout the world, hoping to publish work otherwise unavailable in the United States.

The journal's organizers felt rightful pride in their scholarly sensibilities, yet they made no secret of their political and ideological hopes and fears. *Orbis* editors contended from the beginning that communism constituted the most immediate and mortal threat to American security and freedom. At the same time, they believed that two "greater and more consequential transformations are making history in the second half of the twentieth century: the unification of the North Atlantic Community and the self-assertion of the long-dormant non-Western world."[1] Seeking to help stabilize world politics at a moment of unprecedented change, the makers of *Orbis* thus struggled to clarify those challenges "that beset the relationship of the two parts of mankind who both face the threat of the communist bid for universal dominance in the name of an all-inclusive and militant creed."[2] They wanted through scholarship and polemics to rescue the world from Moscow's reach.

In many ways, the essay that Robert Strausz-Hupé wrote in introducing the journal in April 1957 identified the themes that would dominate *Orbis* for the next quarter-century. To Strausz-Hupé, a fifty-four-year-old Austrian émigré who had failed utterly in the 1930s to alert the West to the menace of Hitler's totalitarianism, the world was enveloped in a struggle to the death between Western freedom and Soviet tyranny that was complicated by the proliferation of nuclear weaponry and anti-Western revolutionary nationalism in the Third World. In this struggle, the hope of free humanity for the short term resided in the American-directed Atlantic alliance. In the long run, freedom's hope rode on the gradual federation of the whole world under America's tutelage. Desperate to rally the American people into acting more ambitiously on their world mission, Strausz-Hupé insisted that America's "historical necessity" was to "bury the nation states, lead their beheaved [*sic*] peoples into larger unions, and overawe with its might the would-be saboteurs of the new order who have nothing to offer mankind but a putrefying ideology and brute force."[3] In the process, America would lead the world into a new historical era in which men would find "in cosmic ventures an equivalent for war." The only requirements for success were will, power, and vision. With these, Strausz-Hupé proclaimed, "The future belongs to America. The American empire and mankind will not be opposites but merely two names for the universal order under peace and happiness."[4]

The principal impediment to the realization of this dream was international communism, a mode of organizing life that *Orbis* deemed utterly loathsome. For *Orbis* writers, communism represented a highly systematized method of conflict directed by Leninist schemers who had harnessed Marx's vision of a historically determined utopia to xenophobic Russian nationalism in the cause of global domination. Inherently aggressive, it signified a power system whose "life-essence" was conflict.[5] Its devotees knew neither decency nor principle. Wholly amoral, communists probed at every opportunity to expand their power. They brooked no rules, and suffered no constraints that might block them from their ultimate end.

Impelled by the communist drive toward global conquest, the cold war was consequently no mere economic struggle between rival social systems. After all, Strausz-Hupé maintained, socialism and capitalism coexisted without violence in the industrial West. Even different political systems could coexist, he allowed, "but not when one system is aggressive, geared to conflict, and bent on conquest."[6] With communism on the offensive, the cold war signified nothing less than a collision between two diametrically opposed political and moral systems—one based on individual freedom and political pluralism and another founded on terror and totalitarianism—whose differences originated in World War I and were now locked in "permanent war."[7] The West must quit deluding itself. "We are now in the third World War," declared one contributor.[8] Agreed another, "We are at war today just as surely as we were at war on the evening of December 6, 1941"; and it was time for America and the West to mobilize all their resources and struggle— even at *"the risk of total conflict"* for final victory.[9]

But *Orbis* writers did not expect a head-on clash between communism and the West. Instead, anticipating an extended communist strategy of indirect attack, the early issues of the journal urged America and the West to prepare for a "protracted conflict" that required a coherent strategy integrating military, diplomatic, economic, and political resources with novel "fourth-dimensional warfare" operations in communications propaganda.[10] *Orbis* basically wanted Washington to open a wide-ranging offensive in the cold war. Attacking U.S. containment policy for its passivity, Strausz-Hupé and Kintner called in the 1950s for a "forward strategy" and "win policy" that would carry the cold war into the communist-controlled world and overwhelm "the multi-dimensional communist strategy of protracted conflict."[11] Eager to seize the initiative, *Orbis* contributors complained that the prevailing American belief that there was no alternative in the atomic age to all-out nuclear war except surrender had paralyzed the country's will to wage the cold war with greater vigor. Popular worry in the United States about atomic weaponry had reached "the point of a national psychosis," declared one writer.[12] Dangerously uncritical fear of the bomb had virtually turned the device into "a psychological weapon against the West."[13]

Looking to overcome perceived popular paralysis and to take the offensive against Russia, *Orbis* writers backed the utility of theater or limited nuclear war, encouraged notions of irregular warfare in East-Central Europe, and opposed calls for arms control and atmospheric nuclear test bans as injurious to American technological prowess and long-term security needs. Trying to prepare their countrymen for long-term struggle, *Orbis* contributors contended that "security grows out of the barrel of a gun" and that peace merely signified well-armed vigilance.[14] They did not expect the cold war to end until the conflict ceased at its source through fundamental changes in the Soviet system, spelling the final destruction of communism. *"So long as totalitarianism survives, so long the danger of total war will persist,"* explained Stefan Possony. "It is as simple as that."[15]

Between 1957 and 1963, the principal theater of the cold war and *Orbis*'s concerns centered on Europe. In the early 1960s, however, the journal became more interested in revolutionary developments in the Third World and their impact on the Soviet-American conflict. Fearful of communist manipulation of revolutionary anticolonial sentiment and promotion of wars of national liberation, *Orbis* writers warned against Soviet machinations in Africa, the Middle East, and Latin America. Curiously, however, for all its sensitivity to Moscow's maneuverings, *Orbis* failed as fully as the rest of the policy-shaping media to anticipate Fidel Castro's emergence as a communist; and it was very slow to recognize the significance of the Sino-Soviet split for Third World politics. *Orbis* writers showed a similar uncertainty with regard to Vietnam. Although convinced that the violence in Vietnam figured essentially as one more Soviet war by proxy, *Orbis* authors were reluctant to escalate the conflict into a direct Soviet-American confrontation. Some talked of carrying the war into North Vietnam and inspiring anticommunist uprisings in Eastern Europe; others suggested destroying Hanoi's food processing facilities. But the journal's principal critique of U.S. war strategy in Southeast Asia in the 1960s was that Washington was not seeking an "early victory" through a "speedy and massive" air and naval attack on the North.[16]

Understandably, the U.S. failure to work its will on Vietnamese communists throughout the 1960s intensified concern within *Orbis* over the nature and prospects of the American democracy. If dedicated to freedom, *Orbis* writers were unsure about democracy. Democracies functioned splendidly in times of crisis, Kintner conceded. but they otherwise tended to be slothful, easily diverted, and inexcusably hedonistic. Largely indifferent to external affairs, American democracy appeared willfully ignorant of the magnitude and complexity of the communist threat. Only "a minute minority" of Americans showed an intelligent interest in world affairs, while the vast majority preferred the pleasures of immediate material gratification to the sacrifices required for protracted conflict.[17] In addition, the American people were too susceptible to complacency, too eager for compromise solutions, and too sensitive to international criticism. American democracy doubtlessly constituted the most magnificent housing for freedom and the most inspiring harbinger of hope for the rest of the world. But it was dangerously incapable of mobilizing physically and spiritually for the struggle with communism that dominated the times.

Despite their concern with democracy's weaknesses, *Orbis* writers expressed cautious admiration for the subtle diplomatic attempts of Richard Nixon and Henry Kissinger to salvage an anticommunist government in South Vietnam even as they withdrew U.S. troops from Asia, eased tensions with the Soviet Union, and established formal contacts with China. Distressed by the strength of domestic antiwar discontent, *Orbis* editors backed Nixon's plans for the Vietnamization of the war and cheered the president's decision in 1972 to bomb North Vietnam and mine Hanoi's harbor facilities. They applauded the 1973 Paris peace agreement as a signal victory for American diplomacy (although not necessarily for the South Vietnamese) that was largely attributable to "the no-nonsense unpredictability of the American President."[18] Contributors to *Orbis* were more cautious, however, in adjusting to the changing international atmospherics of the early 1970s. As Nixon visited China and promoted détente with the Soviet Union, *Orbis* editors confessed confusion over an international scene that was characterized by more "fluidity"— even "an essential ambiguity"—than they had ever anticipated.[19] In part, however, their discomfort was mitigated by service in the Nixon administration. Strausz-Hupé served as U.S. ambassador to Ceylon (Sri Lanka), Belgium, and Sweden between 1970 and 1976, while Kintner operated in the same capacity in Thailand (leaving Robert L. Pfaltzgraff, Jr., as *Orbis* editor). Even more, *Orbis* writers expressed satisfaction with the essential correctness of the Nixon-Kissinger attempt to forge "linkages" among the great powers into a functioning "structure of peace." Quite shrewdly, they believed, Washington was engaged "in a hectic and at times brilliant effort to hasten the birth of a new international system" that bore the United States and the USSR in "a slow but persistent movement away from a predominantly adversary relationship to one marked by restrained conflict and limited co-operation."[20] And that was for the good.

By the mid-1970s, the critical confidence that *Orbis* editors had invested in Nixon-Kissinger diplomacy melted into new fears of a worsening cold war. The much-vaunted notion of "linkages" had failed to slow Soviet supplies to North Vietnam or inhibit Moscow from abetting the Arab states in 1973 in new war against Israel. The oil embargo forged by the Organization of Petroleum Exporting Countries and several hotly serious trade rivalries threatened to turn America's closest allies in Western Europe into bitter economic competitors. The disintegration and collapse of the South Vietnamese government during the years 1973 through 1975 in tandem with the fall of the Nixon presidency called into question the reliability of American governing institutions and the credibility of American commitments everywhere. And, most ominous, the Soviet military buildup that began in the mid-1960s continued without interruption, even as the first Strategic Arms Limitation Treaty was concluded (with *Orbis*'s endorsement) and the Atlantic alliance fell into greater disrepair.

At the close of the 1970s, *Orbis* writers concluded that the Soviet Union was again on the offensive while American leaders frolicked in "an orgy of nonintervention."[21] Frightened by Moscow's arms buildup, *Orbis* writers declared that "the Soviets are in a very real sense at war with the United States today," and pressed Washington to match and surpass Russian military increases.[22] They also tried to update the notion of deterrence. Reiterating their call for intermediate choices between all-out war or surrender, *Orbis* contributors renewed arguments for limited nuclear war planning and called for more aggressive civil defense efforts to make America's strategic deterrent more flexible and thus more credible. Conversely, they exhibited a markedly lessened interest in arms control efforts. *Orbis* editors looked skeptically on attempts at nuclear nonproliferation, and opposed efforts to extend the SALT process to other weapons systems and the SALT II Treaty itself. Angrily, they complained that the "increasingly asymmetrical détente relationship" between the U.S. and the USSR had made Moscow into "the principal, if not sole, beneficiary of Washington's seven-year quest for mutual accommodation."[23] The shock of Vietnam and the failure of détente had driven the U.S. foreign policymaking elite into a state of passive confusion that was opening the way for Soviet expansion in the Middle East, Southeast Asia, and Africa, and laying the groundwork for a higher level of international danger. There was no escaping reality, Strausz-Hupé wrote. Americans must again look to the Kremlin and confront "the hard core of international problematics: immense and relentlessly growing military power at the order of a handful of rulers who are accountable to no one, least of all to their own people."[24]

The Soviet invasion of Afghanistan and the Iranian revolution and hostage taking brought to a head fears within *Orbis* that the U.S. policymaking elite and the larger American democracy were crippled by division over foreign policy issues and losing the will to wage further protracted conflict. Eager to overcome the "fierce polarization" that was splitting the foreign policymaking community, Kintner proposed the formation of a small, select group that would forge within the nation at large a new moral commitment behind a vigorous international policy consensus. America, Kintner contended, required a newly defined sense of national purpose,[25] a fresh "sense of American unity and continuity" that would reenergize its citizens in the pursuit of their duty "to create a new order out of the global disorder" that communism worked to create and exploit.[26]

In addition, *Orbis* writers insisted that America equally required a reinvigoration of the national will. Moralists to the core, *Orbis* contributors early in the 1980s drafted elegant strategic theories and conflict scenarios. Invariably, however, they returned to the proposition that what the country most needed was some triumph of the will to be victorious. The issue was one of "will and stamina," *Orbis* authors ventured, for the outcome of global conflict in the atomic age "will depend on will rather than capability."[27] After a quarter-century of effort, *Orbis* entered the 1980s and what some called "the second cold war" highly sensitive to the significance of new technologies, alert to "the variety in Marxist totalitarianism,"[28] and aware of the extraordinary complexity of modern world politics. Yet their anticommunist determination stood paramount, and their will to prevail remained supreme.

The emphasis within *Orbis* on the triumph of the will combined with its animating anticommunism, its ambivalence toward democracy, and its preference for elite policymaking to mark the journal as singularly conservative in nature. It was not so conservative, however, in temperament. Indeed, in its larger orientation, *Orbis* tended more toward right-wing militancy than traditional conservatism. It preferred the kind of rightist militancy espoused by political figures like Arizona senator Barry Goldwater (for whom Strausz-Hupé served as foreign policy adviser in 1964) to the traditionalist conservative tenets supported by foreign policy critics like Hans Morgenthau and George Kennan. It liked action all too much, and prudence and self-restraint all too little.

There were several signs of *Orbis*'s preference for rightist militancy over conservative equanimity. In the Third World, for example, *Orbis* writers encouraged counterrevolutionary activism against Marxist regimes such as the Allende government in Chile even as they excused more familiar tyrannies in the name of anticommunism. In the area of international tactics, *Orbis* contributors felt much more comfortable with the prospect of forceful U.S. unilateralism over the constraints of multilateral international action. Unquestionably, *Orbis* editors championed the Atlantic alliance as the West's foremost military defense against Soviet expansionism, and they favored the sharing of U.S. nuclear decision-making power with its European allies. But they showed little interest in the pacifying power of the UN, extra-European regional arrangements, and functional transnational agencies like the Food and Agricultural Organization. Hardly mere conservators of the existing international order, *Orbis* writers were more truly right-wing nationalists and instrumentalists. They strove to serve as the strategic high priests of the American drive to master the revolutionary technological and political changes characteristic of the modern world in the name of an anticommunist global stability that spelled U.S. preeminence.

At bottom, *Orbis*'s faith in counterrevolutionary activism, diplomatic unilateralism, and the mystique of strategizing derived from two considerations: a certainty that communism incarnated evil in the modern world and an intolerance for the self-doubt and ambiguity central to traditional conservatism. If subtle and shrewd in their political analyses, *Orbis* writers manifested an uncomplicated moral metaphysic that assumed the fundamental goodness of Western capitalism and the utter sinfulness of international communism. In the end, *Orbis* thinkers could well be right in their conviction that communists embody evil in this world and that the American people possess a positive redemptive purpose. But if they are, the traditional conservative belief in the common frailty of mankind and the essential tragedy of the whole human condition would prove to be wrong.

Notes

1. "Reflections on the Quarter," *Orbis: A Quarterly Journal of World Affairs* 1 (April 1957): 5.

2. Ibid., pp. 5–6.

3. Robert Strausz-Hupé, "The Balance of Tomorrow," *Orbis* 1 (April 1957): 20, 26.

4. Ibid., p. 27.

5. George Fielding Eliot, "The X-Factor in Disarmament," *Orbis* 2 (Fall 1958): 302.

6. Robert Strausz-Hupé and William R. Kintner, "A Forward Strategy beyond Survival," *Orbis* 4 (Summer 1960): 155.

7. "Reflections on the Quarter," *Orbis* 6 (Fall 1962): 357.

8. Sir John Slessor, "A New Look Strategy for the West," *Orbis* 2 (Fall 1958): 323.

9. Frank R. Barnett, "Disengagement or Commitment," *Orbis* 2 (Winter 1959): 429; Robert Strausz-Hupé, "Protracted Conflict: A New Look at Communist Strategy," *Orbis* 2 (Spring 1958): 37 (emphasis in the original).

10. Strausz-Hupé, "Protracted Conflict," pp. 13–38; Barnett, "Disengagement or Commitment," p. 432.

11. Strausz-Hupé and Kintner, "A Forward Strategy Beyond Survival," pp. 141–58; "Reflections on the Quarter," *Orbis* 6 (Fall 1962), p. 359.

12. A. T. Church, Jr., "Deterrence and Delusion," *Orbis* 3 (Summer 1959): 141.

13. Alvin J. Cottrell and James E. Dougherty, "Nuclear Weapons, Policy and Strategy," *Orbis* 1 (Summer 1957): 140.

14. "Reflections on the Quarter," *Orbis* 3 (Spring 1959): 7.

15. Stefan T. Possony, "The Challenge of Russian Totalitarianism," *Orbis* 8 (Winter 1965): 788 (emphasis in the original).

16. "Reflections on the Quarter," *Orbis* 11 (Spring 1967): 18.

17. "Reflections on the Quarter," *Orbis* 5 (Fall 1961): 263.

18. "Reflections on the Quarter," *Orbis* 17 (Winter 1973): 853.

19. "Reflections on the Quarter," *Orbis* 15 (Summer 1971): 469; "Reflections on the Quarter," *Orbis* 16 (Fall 1972): 600.

20. "Reflections on the Quarter," *Orbis* 17 (Fall 1973): 665; "Reflections on the Quarter," *Orbis* 17 (Summer 1973): 299.

21. Richard E. Bissell and Harveh Sicherman, "The Education of an Administration: 15° N, 45° E," *Orbis* 23 (Spring 1979): 3.

22. Richard B. Foster and Francis P. Hoeber, "Limited Mobilization: A Strategy for Preparedness and Deterrence in the Eighties," *Orbis* 24 (Fall 1980): 442.

23. Paul Seabury, "Thoughts on a New Foreign Policy Agenda," *Orbis* 20 (Fall 1976):

567; William R. Kintner, "U.S.-Soviet Relations: The Carter Quadrille," *Orbis* 21 (Fall 1977): 475.

24. Robert Strausz-Hupé, "The North Atlantic Commitment," *Orbis* 22 (Spring 1978): 9.

25. "Reflections on the Quarter," *Orbis* 20 (Fall 1976): 563.

26. "Reflections on the Quarter," *Orbis* 24 (Fall 1980): 436–37; William R. Kintner, "Toward a New Strategy of Independence," *Orbis* 25 (Summer 1981): 280.

27. William R. Kintner, "A Program for America: Freedom and Foreign Policy," *Orbis* 21 (Spring 1977): 152; Kenneth L. Adelman, "Fear, Seduction, and Growing Soviet Strength," *Orbis* 21 (Winter 1978): 765.

28. Alan Ned Sabrosky, "Cold War II? A Cautionary Note," *Orbis* 25 (Fall 1981): 498; Kintner, "A Program for America," p. 149.

Information Sources

BIBLIOGRAPH Y: None.

INDEXES: *ABC Pol Sci; Amer Hist & Life; AHCI; Bio Ind; Comb Ret Ind Bk Revs Sch J; Curr Bk Rev Cit; Curr Cont: BSMS; Hist Abst; Ind Bk Revs Hum; PAIS; Pol Sci Abst; SSHI; SSCI; Soc Sci Ind; Soc Abst; URS.*

REPRINT EDITIONS: Microform: KTO; UMI. Bound edition: Kraus Reprint Company.

LOCATION SOURCES: Widely available.

Publication History

TITLE AND TITLE CHANGES: *Orbis: A Quarterly Journal of World Affairs*, April 1957– Winter 1974; *Orbis: A Journal of World Affairs*, Spring 1974–present.

VOLUME AND ISSUE DATA: Volumes 1–current, April 1957–present.

FREQUENCY OF PUBLICATION: Quarterly.

PUBLISHER: Foreign Policy Research Institute, University of Pennsylvania, Philadelphia, Pennsylvania.

EDITORS: Robert Strausz-Hupé, 1957–1969; William R.Kintner, 1969–1973, 1976–1981; Robert L. Pfaltzgraff, 1973–1975; William R. Kintner–Summer 1981; Alan Ned Sabrosky, Fall 1981–Summer 1982; Nils H. Wessell, Fall 1982–Spring 1985; Gordon H. McCormick, Summer 1985–Fall 1985; John H. Maurer, Winter 1986–Summer 1986; Daniel Pipes, Fall 1986–Fall 1990; Patrick L. Clawson, Winter 1991–present.

CIRCULATION

In 1983, 3,200–4,600; in 1998, 3,500.

Charles DeBenedetti

New Guard
1961–1978

In less than two decades of publication, *New Guard* experienced many changes, including a rapid turnover of editors and a format that became increasingly polished and visually attractive. Paralleling the early years of *New Guard* was a surging of the New Right movement in the United States, most visible in Senator Barry Goldwater's presidential campaign of 1964. Senator Goldwater's nomination by the Republican party encouraged conservatives, old and new, to engage in debate concerning the meaning and direction of the conservative movement in the country. *New Guard* became one of many periodicals in which this debate was carried on.

New Guard was the official organ of Young Americans for Freedom (YAF), founded on the lawn of the William F. Buckley, Jr., estate in 1960. In September of that year, fewer than one hundred persons gathered to organize the YAF and adopt a set of principles called the Sharon Statement, named after the town in Connecticut where Buckley lives. The principles, first drafted by Stan Evans, begin:

In this time of moral and political crisis, it is the responsibility of the youth of America to affirm certain eternal truths.... That foremost among the transcendent values is the individual's use of his God-given free will, whence derives his right to be free from the restrictions of arbitrary force.

Other items in the Sharon Statement include these: "that the Constitution of the United States is the best arrangement yet devised for empowering government to fulfill its proper role...[and] that the forces of international communism are, at present, the greatest single threat to these [individual] liberties."[1]

Within months of the founding of YAF, *New Guard* began publication (March 1961) to serve "as a rallying point for YAF's first leaders and members." Within ten years, it boasted a circulation figure of nearly 20,000. Within twenty years, it could claim an active role in the election of a man whose candidacy for president of the United States they had promoted for years. The fall 1981 issue of *New*

Guard carried on its back cover this quote from President Ronald Reagan: "Young Americans for Freedom helped make possible my candidacy for President in 1980."

Evidence, however, points to the decline in both the circulation and influence of *New Guard* in later years. A former editor, Alan Crawford, commented of YAF "that the salad days may be long past" and that "despite its conservative heritage...it has become increasingly influenced by New Rightest attitudes."[2] Crawford edited *New Guard* in 1976 and noted a decline in the youthful thrust of the periodical and that in the late 1970s, the leaders of YAF and *New Guard* were "devoted to advancing the political careers of its tight clique of leaders."[3]

The connection between *New Guard* leadership and the New Right is illustrated in the cases of Lee Edwards and Allan Brownfeld, both former editors of *New Guard*. Edwards, the first editor of *New Guard*,went on to edit Richard Viguerie's *Conservative Digest* and was also active in political activity connected with the Pinochet government in Chile.[4] Brownfeld worked for Congressman Philip Crane and ghost-wrote *The Sum of Good Government,* a book that carries Crane's name as author. Brownfeld also worked for the government of Nicaragua under General Somoza and contributes articles to *Human Events* and the *Conservative Digest*.[5]

Alan Crawford has become a critic of the New Right because of what he considers the "anticonservative" thinking and activities of some of its members. According to Crawford, the New Right practices a "rampageous democracy" exemplified by its belief in the use of mass petition and referendum campaigns and a deep distrust of government forms and traditional institutions. Citing Tocqueville, Crawford suggests that the New Right fails to understand the contributions made by rules and institutions to the cause of freedom, and instead shows contempt for forms that get in the way of their "present gratification."[6]

The evidence also suggests that any decline in the influence of *New Guard* may be due to the inability of either the "trad" (traditional conservative) or the "lib" (libertarian) factions to gain a completely solid grip on the organization— Young Americans for Freedom—or the editorial board of *New Guard* itself. William A. Rusher, a witness to the formation of YAF, has observed: "the organization was vested under its constitution in a national board of directors of twenty-five members elected at its biennial conventions. Since this board chose all the full-time staff members of the organization and actively dominated its policies, the temptation to form functions and acquire majority control of the board was overpowering from the start to a number of healthy young conservative politicos. *It remains to this day YAF's worst and most intractable problem.*"[7]

Despite the bickering and the factionalism, there has been consistency in the articles in *New Guard* over the years. The libertarians and even the anarchists have their say, but there is an understanding of and general commitment to traditional conservative values within the pages of *New Guard*. This is due undoubtedly to the guiding hand of William F. Buckley, Jr., who remained close to YAF and *New Guard*. Some resent Buckley's perceived haughty and aristocratic demeanor, but the anniversary dates of YAF and *New Guard* remind all of the large lawn on the Buckley estate where it all began in the early 1960s.

The general focus of YAF and *New Guard* was on political and social forces, international and domestic, that threaten cherished traditional conservative values, including religious freedom, recognition of the sovereignty of the divine creator, love of country, the family, and private property. The true conservative must constantly remember that the world is full of utopians who would, if only they had their way, "achieve the elimination of all evil and the realization of the millennium within their own time."[8] The collectivists, sometimes socialists, sometimes liberals, are out to destroy the institution of property, family and religion, making inevitable a totalitarianism when "the institutions separating the ruler and ruled are destroyed."[9]

The integrity of the family—the "little platoons" that Edmund Burke considered so vital for a stable society—is subverted by such schemes as day care centers, which encourage mothers to leave the home for outside employment. We could learn a great deal, it is argued, from the example of China, which had been free of an oppressive central government for twenty centuries until "the Maoists undertook almost overnight to break up the family as a bourgeois instrument of inequality."[10] Unable to learn from these mistakes, liberal politicians indulge in schemes like the guaranteed annual income, which only raise the divorce rate.[11] The family of Pat Boone is seen as the model to follow, because the members are religious, and against liquor and cigarettes. Moreover, Boone used "a Gestapo system for raising four daughters—they were simply never alone with a boy until it was clear that they were going to marry him."[12]

The schools, particularly those in the public sector, are seen as major subverters of cherished traditions. God and religion have been banished from the classroom and replaced by a bland relativism that offers no guidance except to teach children how to adjust and conform to the needs of the group.[13] Further damage is inflicted in the classroom by the failure to teach patriotism and the virtues of our great heroes of the past. As one *New Guard* writer laments: "We have debunked the hero to make room for the Jerk."[14] The liberals, of course, are not patriotic and sneer at "flag-wavers" who openly and proudly love their country.[15] In short, the sense of rootlessness promoted in public schools contributes to the erosion of those "free associations" that Tocqueville considered essential "if men are to remain civilized." The end result of this process is that "we see individual liberty being smothered by too much government, with too much power, and at a price that soon may destroy individual initiative and industry."[16]

Another *New Guard* theme is of the ineluctable process of leveling that Tocqueville himself seemed resigned to when he wrote: "The gradual development of the principle of equality is a providential fact. It has all the chief characteristics of such a fact: it is universal, it is durable, it constantly eludes all human interference, and all events as well as all men contribute to its progress."[17] Writers in *New Guard*, however, are combative on the subject, blaming this trend on leftists who, as egalitarians, "assume that everyone wants and needs the same things."[18] A knowledgeable conservative, on the other hand, knows there is a "natural inequality among men...and an inevitability of social classes and the futility of attempts to level."[19] It is therefore imperative, as one writer points out, to pass on these truths because "if the members of the next generation fail to learn the wisdom of the past...they will repeat all the errors mankind has suffered through."[20]

With these tenets clearly in mind, the writers of *New Guard* were well prepared to do battle with two major enemies: (1) international communism and those domestic individuals and groups who are allegedly active and willing supporters of communism (e.g., Jane Fonda, otherwise known as "Hanoi Jane") and (2) those who distract Americans from a true understanding of the dangers of communism (e. g., those who support the United Nations, oblivious to the use of that organization as an outpost for espionage).

Soon after declaring his candidacy for the presidency, Ronald Reagan granted an interview, published in an early 1976 issue of *New Guard*, which summarized a view consistently maintained in the periodical: "When in hell is somebody in government going to tell us that there is an enemy equally as vicious as Hitler ever was, twice as smart and twice as well organized...who has made fantastic gains throughout the world, and yes, now has designs on us. It isn't looking for Communists under every bed to say this. They say it."[21] Moreover, there is no question about the nature or location of this danger, wrote another student of the fallacies of communism: "Every Communist party is a permanent center of subversion, which either accepts Moscow's lead or works independently toward objectives consonant with Moscow's wishes."[22]

Unfortunately, most people in the West failed to understand the nature of the communist threat. One who did understand and become a *New Guard* hero is Aleksandr Solzhenitsyn, impassioned critic and survivor of Soviet labor camps, who "is probably the closest a human being can come to being an institution of courage and nobility. He represents to oppressed peoples everywhere what once only the United States of America did represent, the international voice of freedom and hope."[23] Solzhenitsyn's statements and speeches concerning the internal terror in the USSR and the dangers of the international menace were reported faithfully in *New Guard*.

Among the indigenous heroes have been such well-known fighters against communism as J. Edgar Hoover, Barry Goldwater, and Douglas MacArthur. Others in this special category may not be known for their politics, but they nevertheless possess appropriate conservative credentials. One of these is James Bond of spy movie fame, who prefers to work alone, distrusts visionary schemes, and constantly asks: "Will it work?" "Has it worked?"[24] Another hero type is Clint Eastwood, "who knows that some people can't be reasoned with and that force is the only appropriate tool with such people; he believes fiercely in himself, is hypercompetent, has principles, and cares nothing about what people say."[25]

The enemies of *New Guard* can be measured, it seems, by the degree to which they contributed to the success of international communism. Jane Fonda and husband Tom Hayden were beyond hope, contributors wrote, but at least people knew where they stood. Greater harm by far, was committed by people in positions of authority and power who followed policies that actually supported the U.S. adversary. *New Guard* contributors were especially upset by U.S. trade policies since the Bolshevik Revolution, the more so since Lenin clearly stated his intentions: "When we are ready to hang the capitalists, they will gladly sell us the rope with which to do it." Congressman John Ashbrook (R, Ohio) wrote: "Trade with the

USSR was started over 50 years ago under President Woodrow Wilson with the declared intention of mellowing the Bolsheviks. The policy has been a total and costly failure. It has proven to be unpractical—that is what I would expect from an immoral policy."[26] YAF members and *New Guard* writers actively campaigned against all trade with communist countries and claimed credit for forcing American Motors to abandon plans to sell cars in Soviet Russia and Firestone Rubber to table a proposed $50 million synthetic rubber plant in Romania.[27]

Communicating the truth about communism was extremely difficult because American journalism allegedly has a liberal bias (one *New Guard* writer asked: "Are reporters liberal? Do dogs have fleas?"[28]) Professors for the most part were extremely naive about international communism. Textbooks routinely embodied liberal sentiment, playing down the success of the United States and exaggerating that of the USSR. *New Guard* disdain of professors was perhaps best revealed in a statement attributed to William F. Buckley that "he would rather be governed by the first thousand names in the Boston telephone book than by the Harvard faculty."[29]

The *New Guard* antidote for these dangerous forces was a rigorous conservative press that both exposed the menace of communism and proposed alternative solutions. In a 1962 issue that included articles by Herbert Hoover, Barry Goldwater, John Tower, and Ludwig von Mises, Brent Bozell proposed the following "orders":

To the Joint Chiefs of Staff: Prepare for an immediate landing in Havana.
To the Commander in Berlin: Tear down the wall.
To the Chairman of the Atomic Energy Commission: Schedule testing of every nuclear weapon that could conceivably be of service to the military purposes of the West.[30]

Goldwater's comments in the same issue were similar: "The conventional attitudes and weapons of the past must be revised and drawn into a new strategic design if we are to meet the threat posed by a tyrannical force of global dimensions."

The "Better-Dead-Than-Red" theme was frequently played in the pages of *New Guard*. Since both sides possessed nuclear weapons, military assertiveness was risky, "but the risks of preserving freedom come nowhere near to the risks of forfeiting that freedom to tyranny."[31] Strom Thurmond wrote in *New Guard* that "military preparedness is the surest way to avoid war."[32] If the United States follows the advice given by the pacifists: "We must come to some accommodation with the Soviets because they want peace and should be accepted at their word because they stand to lose as much as we do in the event of nuclear exchange."[33] Just as *New Guard* readers had been warned to count on the Russians to try to do us in, they should be wary also of the peace picketers who would, if given the opportunity, drop the bomb on John Birchers and other right-wingers.[34]

Liberal magazines exaggerated the dangers of nuclear war, wrote several contributors. Anthony Bouscaren, author of many books dealing with communism, wrote that "nuclear conflict does not mean the end of civilization, nor does it mean that there will be no victor. Our country will continue to exist to the extent that some of the people survive and can function."[35] A poster circulated by the YAF reminded members to keep things in perspective. Quoting William F. Buckley, it read: "War is the second worst activity of mankind, the worst being acquiescence in slavery." At a YAF convention for Young America's Bicentennial Reaffirmation held in 1975, members adopted a statement of warning to any potential enemy, foreign or domestic, which reads:

To those in other lands who would destroy our freedom, be forewarned that there are still millions of us who believe that liberty is worth fighting and dying for. Do not naively believe that you can win just by forcing our government to surrender. If you plan to occupy this nation come prepared to fight for every acre of ground, for every building and for every hill and valley.

To our own government we say this:

Do not forget that you are only a government which exists at the pleasure of the American people. We will not allow tyranny to be established from within any more than we will allow it to invade from without.[36]

Mentally prepared for Armageddon should it be necessary and ready to engage in traditional battle as well, the conservatives of *New Guard* spent most of their time and energy feuding with domestic liberals. One of the weapons of this battle was wit and satire inasmuch as liberals were seen as a rather dull and humorless bunch who wilt under the steady barrage of the clever, well-turned phrase.[37] Alleged liberal naiveté concerning world peace is found in this satiric passage: "The basic idea is that world peace is a very easy thing to achieve and all you really have to do is to be sweet, innocent and have good intentions…(if we'd only send a dozen roses to Pham Van Dong; if we could only buy the world a Coke)."[38] A constant *New Guard* target for years was the National Student Association (NSA), perceived as a haven for hippies, peaceniks, and radicals during the Vietnam War: " The biggest hand of all was saved when Mr. Gonzalez mentioned he would battle oppression directly as was proved when his people were involved in a street war in which 118 people were killed and 23 police cars were destroyed. Giggly little girls from Nebraska and heart throbbing young Platos from New Hampshire all bathed themselves in the oratorical demagoguery and wept with delight at the very thought of dead policemen."[39] An occasional one-liner would appear, such as this one attributed to Barry Goldwater: "Vice President Humphrey talks so fast that trying to follow his speeches is like reading *Playboy* with your wife turning the pages."[40] In another article, Secretary of State Kissinger's policy of détente was described as follows: "It's like going to a wife-swapping party and coming home alone."[41]

Not surprisingly, the Kennedys came in for their share of jibes. In an article "I Never Slept with JFK," the following "shocking confession" was obtained in an exclusive interview: "A former mafia gun moll who is now a short order cook in Washington, D.C., has told *New Guard* that although she was acquainted with the late President John F. Kennedy for a period of two years, she never had an affair with him."[42] Inevitably, however, the satire returns to liberalism in general: "The average Left Winger's height is five feet ten inches. Few are taller, and if they are, they slump down…as they are quite self-conscious about standing heads and shoulders above a crowd. They wouldn't want to make anyone feel puny or unequal."[43]

Despite the presence of common enemies, tension surfaced often within the pages of *New Guard*, encouraged in part by a policy that encouraged debate within conservative ranks. Those who called themselves libertarians and believed in the natural regulations that a "free market" provides, would limit the role of government to defense alone. Some libertarians would turn the streets and the post office over to private enterprise; others worked hard to eliminate government involvement in such private decisions as whether to drink, smoke, or use drugs.

Issues such as abortion, however, raised the temperature of controversy decidedly because the role of government becomes problematical for almost everyone concerned. After the Supreme Court's decision to permit abortions in certain circumstances (*Roe* v. *Wade*, 1973), *New Guard* published articles in which some who opposed abortion called for the government to acknowledge the legal right of the fetus. Others, who favored abortion, applauded the Court for enlarging the idea of liberty to include the right of a woman to make ultimate decisions concerning her own body. The equal rights amendment, it appears, was an easier matter, and was generally opposed on grounds that the specter of egalitarianism outweighed any possible benefits to American women.

When the discussion centered on the topic of human nature, *New Guard* for the most part reflected a Burkean view that accepts a necessary role for a limited government. As one frequent contributor to *New Guard* put it: "Until man has learned not to steal, not to kill, not to conspire against the inferior man who cannot afford to buy a private army...until that day, government will be a necessity in order to protect man from the less perfect social and political natures of other men."[44]

Most conservatives in *New Guard* did not really expect that day to come because of our flawed nature and because of the many enemies who would like nothing better than to eliminate the society that conservatives were laboring so hard to build. The early years of *New Guard* were marked with much despair, hand-wringing, and a distinct "outsiders" perspective. The defeat of Goldwater in the Johnson landslide in 1964 brought much gloom to *New Guard* and a warning that "monumental work is to be done if we ever are to achieve victory" in an article entitled: "Needed: A 25 Year Plan."[45]

In sixteen years, however, the conservatives had their kind of president, and the pages of *New Guard* practically glowed with a sense of pride and achievement. The outsiders were now inside, but still with much to do.

As a magazine of ideas and opinions, *New Guard* could now claim to be in the mainstream of government opinion, particularly the executive branch. From this vantage point, *New Guard* joined those engaged in a renewal of the class war, where traditional noblesse oblige is replaced by an open war in which the goal is to redistribute the wealth upward. The writers in *New Guard* thus lined up predictably on the issues of a volunteer army, consumer protection laws, tax credits for education in private schools, and minimum wage laws. Those who poached on the conservative preserve were singled out for admonition, as was Martin Luther King,

Jr., a month after his assassination. The Reverend Dr. King was scolded for leading a boycott against a bus company "to cause it to give equal service to Negro customers." Business should be responsive to demand: that is the test of the market. If King were market oriented, his next step might have been to introduce competition by starting another bus company. But King was a collectivist. According to the *New Guard*, "When the Negroes looted stores in cities across the nation, it was said that this was a poor tribute to Dr. King's memory. The sad fact...is that Dr. King advocated precisely what the looters did, except that he advocated the government do it. King provided the rationale: that society owes the Negro, that income should he redistributed."[46]

The irrelevance of these comments is unusual for a *New Guard* article, but it does reflect an attitude characteristic of the periodical that was long ago used to describe the position of Alexander Hamilton on income distribution: that if it is necessary to feed the sparrow, one does it by first making certain that the horse is fed. The term "young fuddies," given to the youthful people who campaigned for presidential hopeful Goldwater in 1964, would well apply to many who wrote for *New Guard*.

There was great tension within *New Guard* on whether to follow the Burkean tradition and stress the irrational, base side of human nature or adopt a more sanguine view, as expressed by some *New Guard* libertarians. There was a similar tension in the international political world regarding the subject of nuclear weapons. It is ironic to find the men in the Kremlin and the men and women in the Reagan administration and the *New Guard* in agreement that the development of a strong nuclear arms arsenal is necessary inasmuch as a rational being would not initiate aggression against a properly armed foe. Compare this with a tenet of conservatism presented by a 1981 *New Guard* author: "A recognition of the mixed and immutable nature of man in which evil and irrationality always lurk behind a curtain of civilized behavior."[47] One of the long-standing "truths" of conservatism is the oft-quoted contention of David Hume that "Reason is, and ought only to be, the slave of the passions, and can never pretend to any other office than to serve and obey them." [48] One cannot help but wonder what an Edmund Burke or a Jacob Burckhardt, both respected conservative forebears, would say about the chances of a civilization not using its weapons of unparalleled destruction because of a presumption of multinational rationality.

Notes

1. The Sharon Statement is frequently published in *New Guard*.

2. Alan Crawford, *Thunder on the Right* (New York, 1980), p. 18.

3. Ibid., p. 21.

4. Ibid., pp. 65–66, 197.

5. Ibid.

6. Ibid., p. 323.

7. William A. Rusher, *The Rise of the Right* (New York, 1984), p. 114. Emphasis added.

8. George Kennan quoted by Phillip Abbott Luce, "Against the Wall," *NG* 9 (January 1969): 19.

9. George Santayana quoted in Ronald F. Docksai, "Better Right Than President," *NG* 8 (December 1973): 19.

10. V. H. Krulak, "A Chinese Misfortune," *NG* 11 (Summer 1971): 6.

11. "Advice and Dissent," *NG* 18 (February 1978): 4.

12. Brendan Acton, "Pat Boone Has the Last Laugh," *NG* 19 (Summer 1979): 13.

13. Solveig Eggerz, "Individualism v. Group Think," *NG* 13 (October 1973): 5.

14. William Jay Jacobs, "What's Happened to Patriotism?" *NG* 6 (April 1966): 11.

15. Lon Wall, "Conservatives and Labor," *NG* 8 (March 1973): 11.

16. Jeffrey Kane, "Government 'for' the People: Who Picks up the Tab?" *NG* 14 (April 1974): 15.

17. Alexis de Tocqueville, *Democracy in America*, 2 vols., ed. Phillips Bradley (New York, 1945), 1: 6

18. Anthony LeJeune, "Intolerance on the Left," *NG* 6 (November 1966): 5.

19. Haven Bradford Gow, "A History of American Conservative Thought," *NG* 21 (Summer 1981):43.

20. Hal Schuster, "High School Reform," *NG* 12 (September 1972): 8.

21. James Lacy and Randy Goodwin, "A Conversation with Ronald Reagan," *NG* 16 (January–February 1976): 7.

22. Anthony T. Bouscaren, "Eight Fallacies about Communism," *NG* 12 (May 1972): 13–14.

23. "Advice and Dissent." *NG* 15 (September 1975) : 5

24. T. K. Meier, "James Bond—Conservative Agent?" *NG* 5 (March 1965): 19.

25. Robert Brakeman, "The Great Eastwood Character—and the Great Eastwood," *NG* 18 (July–August 1978): 9–10.

26. John Ashbrook, "Soviet Military Might: Western Made," *NG* 14 (January–February 1974): 9.

27. "YAF Exposes, Halts Company's Plans to Trade with the Enemy," *NG* 7 (January 1967): 4.

28. "Blasts and Bravos," *NG* 16 (November 1976): 4.

29. James Buckley, "The Conscience of a Conservative," *NG* 14 (May 1974): 10.

30. Brent Bozell, "At the Threshold of Leadership," *NG* 2 (March 1962): 36.

31. Alfred Regnery, "Better Red Than Dead?" *NG* 4 (May 1964): 15.

32. Strom Thurmond, "Military Preparedness," *NG* 5 (July 1965): 8.

33. "Peace on Earth," *NG* 1 (December 1961): 3.

34. Rita Gormley, "Smile Please—The Atom Bomb Is Falling," *NG* 10 (April 1970): 22.

35. Anthony T. Bouscaren, "The Second Strike: Retaliation or Survival," *NG* 11 (Summer 1971): 15.

36. *NG* 15 (October 1975): 15.

37. Charles A. Moser, "Humor and the Left," *NG* 11 (May 1971): 18–19.

38. Gaines Smith, "How Ho Started the War," *NG* 12 (May 1971): 18–19.

39. Ronald F. Docksai, "The Siege of El Paso." *NG* 9 (October 1969): 21.

40. "Around and About," *NG* 6 (June 1966): 3.

41. Unsigned report on Ninth YAF Convention, *NG* 17 (October 1977): 9.

42. "I Never Slept with JFK!" *NG* 16 (April 1976): 5.

43. Rita Gormley, "Anatomy of a Liberal," *NG* 5 (June 1965): 11.

44. Ronald F. Docksai, "Reflections on the Revolution in America," *NG* 9 (December 1969): 21.

45. Lee Edwards, "Needed: A 25 Year Plan," *NG* 5 (August 1965): 6.

46. "Martin Luther King," *NG* 8 (May 1968): 4.

47. Gow, "American Conservative Press," p. 43.

48. Quoted in Frederick Copleston, *A History of Philosophy*, vol. 5, Part II (New York, 1964), p. 123.

Information Sources

BIBLIOGRAPHY:
Crawford, Alan. *Thunder on the Right*. New York, 1980.
Nash, George H. *The Conservative Intellectual Movement in America: Since 1945*. New York, 1976.
Rusher, William A. *The Rise of the Right*. New York, 1984.
INDEXES: Volumes 5 and 6 indexed; *PPI*.
REPRINT EDITIONS: Microform: UMI.
LOCATION SOURCES: Widely available.

Publication History

TITLE AND TITLE CHANGES: *New Guard: The Magazine of Young Americans for Freedom.*
VOLUME AND ISSUE DATA: Volumes 1–current, March 1961–present. Combined numbers December 1962–January 1963; November–December 1963; September–October 1976; November–December 1977; March–April 1978.
FREQUENCY OF PUBLICATION: Monthly, 1961–1966; monthly, with one number for June, July, and August, 1967–1970; monthly, except July and August, 1971; monthly, and bi-monthly, January/February and July/August, 1972–1977; monthly, and bi-monthly July/August, 1978; quarterly, 1979–1985; thereafter, irregular.
PUBLISHERS: 1961–present: Young Americans for Freedom, Washington, D. C.
EDITORS: Lee Edwards, March 1961–August 1963; Antoni E. Gollan, September–December 1963; Donald J. Lambro, January–March 1964;Carol D. Bauman, April 1964–January 1965; David Franke, February 1965–September 1967; Arnold Steinberg, October 1967–August 1969; Allan C. Brownfeld, September–October 1969; Kenneth Elvin Grubbs, Jr., November 1969–May 1970; Daniel F. Joy, June 1970–September 1971; Jerry Norton, October 1971–September 1973; Jerry Norton and Mary Fisk, October 1973; Mary Fisk, November 1973–December 1975; Jerry Norton, January–February 1976; Alan Crawford, March–August 1976: Jerry Norton, September–November 1976; David Boaz, December 1976–October 1978; John Parker, November–December 1978; Richard F. La Mountain, January 1979–October 1981; Mark Huber, November–December 1981; Susan Juroe, Summer 1982–Summer 1983; R. Cort Kirkwood, Winter 1983–Spring 1985; 1985–present: Michael Waller and Michael Johns.
CIRCULATION: In 1983, about 13,000; in 1989, 12,000.

William C. Baum

Public Interest
1965–

In New York City in the fall of 1965 Daniel Bell and Irving Kristol founded the *Public Interest* as a journal designed to educate a broad audience in the complexities of domestic policy analysis and to spread the emerging perspective on the state of American society and approach to public policy that became known as neoconservatism. The journal's resolutely anti-ideological statement of purpose criticized liberals, conservatives, and radicals for holding preconceived notions of reality that were often factually in error.[1] Freedom House, a sponsor of the journal during its first four years, endorsed it on the principle that "out of...a confrontation of thoughtful views...a more enlightened and more responsible public opinion will emerge."[2] Advertisements emphasize an openness to all points of view: "*The Public Interest* is not some kind of preexisting, platonic idea; rather it emerges out of differences of opinion, reasonably propounded."[3] Bell and Kristol stressed the importance of getting the facts straight as a precondition to intelligent public debate and policymaking, and clearly one of their major goals was to publicize the results of careful social science research. The journal continues to strive to fulfill these nonideological purposes, but the *Public Interest* is best known and most important as the major outlet for a new current of conservative thinking that developed in the mid-to-late 1960s: neoconservatism.

In addition to Bell and Kristol, the leading figures involved with the *Public Interest,* its most active contributors, have been Nathan Glazer, Daniel P. Moynihan, Aaron Wildavsky, and James Q. Wilson. Almost all of them were liberals whose reactions to political and intellectual trends in the 1960s led them to adopt political positions more commonly associated with conservatives. In the 1970s, all became labeled as neoconservatives. Some neoconservatives argue that they have not changed their liberal beliefs, but that other liberals have drifted toward radicalism, shifting the whole political spectrum to the left. Others willingly accept the new label and agree that they now stress new and different ideas or themes without necessarily abandoning their previous values. In any case, it became clear by the end of the 1960s that an important new school of political thought had emerged in the American intellectual community. No better place exists to examine the thinking of these neoconservatives than the pages of the *Public Interest*.

Scholars associated with major universities or research institutes write most of the *Public Interest*. The journal arose out of the intellectual community of New York City, but authors come from all over the country, with Harvard clearly ranking as the most common institutional affiliation. Journalists, novelists, policy experts working in government bureaucracies, and two members of Congress have been contributors, but academics predominate, including law school professors, philosophers, scientists, and, by far the most common, social scientists. While the *Public Interest* has included more political scientists in recent years, economists appear more often than other social scientists. Kristol has written that "economics is the social science *par excellence* of modernity,"[4] and his journal covers the state of economic theory as well as applications of economic tools to the analysis of public policy problems.

The *Public Interest* ranges broadly across the span of domestic public policy issues in American politics. In addition to such staples as housing, crime, and health, the journal covers the policy problems that grew in importance during the 1970s, such as energy, the environment, and the role of women. One or two articles have appeared on each of many very narrow or minor issues, including policy toward the blind, gambling, parks, and immigration. Consistently receiving the most regular attention have been education and the many disputes that swirl around the topics of equality, poverty, race, and welfare. The academicians who write for and read the *Public Interest* care deeply about education, and neoconservatism developed partially in response to the growth of radicalism in educational communities during the 1960s. Disappointment with the results of government attempts to solve the problems of poverty and race also certainly contributed to the emergence of the neoconservative movement, and this journal continues to focus attention on those questions.

The conservatism of the *Public Interest* most fundamentally consists of its tendency to be critical or skeptical of expanded functions for the national government. Its editors and most of its authors do not fully oppose a welfare state. They continue to favor many of the liberal policies adopted prior to the Great Society of President Lyndon Johnson; they occasionally report the achievements of more recent liberal programs, such as housing allowances, and numerous articles call for continued government involvement in alleviating the plight of poor blacks in America. Still, the primary thrust of the *Public Interest* is to criticize government performance and oppose liberal proposals for new government programs. Frequent contributor Peter F. Drucker made the point this way: "There is mounting evidence that government is big rather than strong, that it is fat and flabby rather than powerful; that it costs a great deal but does not achieve much."[5]

The neoconservative criticism of modern big government differs from the traditional conservative defense of the principle of limited government. Neoconservatives emphasize the complexity of economic, political, and social systems and argue that government attempts to change them rarely work as planned. They picture liberals as well intentioned but naive and unrealistic. Articles in the *Public Interest* routinely conclude that liberal policies fail to achieve their goals and often have unintended consequences that hurt the intended beneficiaries of the policy. Charles A. Murray, for example, argued that a continuous shrinkage of poverty in America from 1945 until the late 1960s slowed and then ceased entirely after the great expansion of government spending on the poor in the Great Society years. His analysis suggested that various new programs encouraged poor males, black and white, to drop out of the labor market, promoting dependence and counterbalancing the positive impact of the additional government spending for the poor.[6] The *Public Interest* regularly publishes articles that detail the failings of the welfare system or other programs aimed at helping the poor.

Neoconservatives attribute much of their divergence from contemporary liberalism to their greater willingness to face reality and learn from experience. In 1974, the *Public Interest* devoted a special issue to "The Great Society: Lessons for the Future." That volume included few positive evaluations and supported the general critique that liberals refuse to accept that any of their programs do not work. This emphasis on social science studies that conclude that various liberal policies fail to achieve their goals underlies the *Public Interest*'s belief that its approach is not ideological; its perspective is based not on general principles or assumptions, but on facts and results in the real world.

Their devotion to facts, neoconservatives believe, also leads them to see that some liberal programs do work and to complain that liberals refuse to acknowledge progress in society. Neoconservatives argue that liberals like to exaggerate every problem into a crisis in order to promote moral outrage as a tactic to spur greater effort, and greater spending on behalf of the poor and other disadvantaged groups. Moynihan sketched a scenario in which government programs achieve initial success by attacking the easiest part of a problem but further efforts fail to achieve results; liberal program advocates and the beneficiaries of the program, especially the organized providers of the service, then react to failure by overstating the extent and seriousness of the problem and by demanding still more spending.[7]

Neoconservatives oppose liberal efforts to expand government not only because these programs rarely work, but also because these liberal policies reflect a new type of egalitarianism. Neoconservatives endorse equality of political rights and equality of opportunity, but argue that in the 1960s liberals moved beyond these traditional American understandings of equality to favor a radical vision of equality of results, an equality of material goods. The *Public Interest* regards equality as one of its major issues; both Bell and Kristol have written broad, theoretical essays on equality, and the journal has often published narrower articles on related topics, such as reports on the distribution of income and social mobility in the United States and analyses of educational equality by both Moynihan and noted sociologist James S. Coleman. The nature of the *Public Interest*'s concern is revealed by the titles of still other articles, such as "Can Inequality Be Cured?" and "How Much More Equality Can We Afford?"

The conservative perspective of the *Public Interest* also takes the form of a defense of the traditional values and institutions of American society. Neoconservatives interpret liberals of the 1940s and 1950s, including themselves, as reformers who essentially supported the basic principles and fundamental character of their nation. This bourgeois and capitalist country may not be an ideal society, but human beings do not seem capable of anything better. Kristol often writes essays for the *Public Interest* that reflect this perspective; he defends capitalism and liberal democracy as the realistic best choice. Liberal intellectuals, neoconservatives contend, turned against their society in the 1960s due to the influence of the New Left and other elements of a rising tide of radicalism. The thrust of liberalism toward greater government regulation, greater individual liberation from all restraints, and greater extension of democracy goes beyond the bounds of reform; liberals seek fundamental change in the very character of our nation.

Neoconservatives criticize liberals for ignoring or belittling the considerable achievements of American society; many authors in the *Public Interest* praise the traditional American system, which leads to upward mobility through individual initiative and competition in the private economy. Andrew M. Greeley developed this theme in "The Ethnic Miracle," concluding that most of the Catholic ethnic groups have achieved economic equality.[8] Seymour Martin Lipset, a frequent contributor, reported that economic mobility remained as strong as ever in the United States, despite the common liberal assumption to the contrary.[9] Numerous articles on black economic progress in the 1960s and 1970s also reflect this theme of success through the system.

This support for traditional values and praise for the achievements of America has led the *Public Interest* to advocate a social conservatism similar to that of the New Right of the late 1970s and 1980s, even if the neoconservatives do not share the New Right's roots in fundamentalist Protestantism. The journal has presented the arguments of social conservatives on pornography, sex education, and women's issues. For example, an article by Rachel Flick, then an assistant editor and later a member of President Ronald Reagan's White House staff, criticized the movement for "equal pay for work of comparable value" not only for being antimarket but for trying to "feminize" the world of work. Flick argued that feminists ignore the evidence that the traditionally masculine values of aggressiveness, competition, and hierarchy contribute to the efficiency and productivity of our economy.[10]

While the *Public Interest* favors positions on public policy questions with which most conservatives agree and most liberals disagree, the neoconservative approach diverges significantly from the mainstream of the conservative movement. Most neoconservatives are intellectuals, and their beliefs and understanding of society flow out of social science research and a study of political philosophy that has led them to stress that human nature imposes limits on what human societies can achieve. Neoconservatism has been called "disillusioned," "revisionist," or "right-wing" liberalism by those who see it as consistent with liberalism as it existed before the 1960s.[11] While the *Public Interest* certainly expresses a typically conservative skepticism about the competence of government and shares a devotion to liberty, neoconservatives are not as hostile to government power as most American conservatives, not as committed to the principle that government should have few domestic functions. Neoconservatives not only support the New Right's willingness to use government power to help sustain the moral health of our society, but they place more emphasis on the importance of social stability and favor some elements of a welfare state as conducive to stability. Peter Drucker, whose article "The Sickness of Government" described government as "fat and flabby rather than powerful," went on to assert that "we need a strong, healthy, and vigorous government."[12] The *Public Interest* has published articles by both Richard Freeman and Martin Kilson that developed the neoconservative focus on black economic progress and criticized the effectiveness of government programs, but each called for continued government efforts to aid poor blacks.[13] Neoconservatism represents a unique, new conservative perspective that differs from all other branches of conservatism, but libertarians especially would find little in the *Public Interest* that would please them.

Support for government programs aimed at alleviating poverty, as reflected in articles such as those by Freeman and Kilson, reveals the continued strength of liberal attitudes, coexisting with neoconservative themes, among authors for the *Public Interest*; neoconservatives differ in the degree to which their views resemble those of other conservatives. Kilson clearly separated himself from the conservative movement with his complaint that "a new conservatism aids a persistent racist response toward black poverty by far too many whites."[14] Kristol develops conservative themes in his articles much more often than does Bell. Perhaps the most interesting, and confusing, case is that of Senator Moynihan, who combines his neoconservative writing for the *Public Interest* with a very liberal voting record in the U.S. Senate.

During the 1970s the *Public Interest* became a more consistently conservative journal. From the start the leading neoconservatives were the most active contributors, but liberal intellectuals such as Richard Hofstadter, Richard E. Neustadt, Robert C. Wood, and Adam Yarmolinsky also appeared in early issues. Leading liberal economists of the past two decades have written for this journal, including Otto Eckstein, Robert L. Heilbroner, Joseph Pechman, Charles L. Schultze, Lester Thurow, and James Tobin. Thurow's "Toward a Definition of Economic Justice" stands out because it advocated a radical redistribution of wealth in America.[15] All of these liberal economists appeared prior to 1975; since then the work of more conservative economists has predominated, with Martin Feldstein, the chairman of President Reagan's Council of Economic Advisors, a frequent contributor. Robert M. Solow, the MIT economist, wrote for the *Public Interest* often and served on the publication committee until 1975. In a rare appearance by a more liberal economist, Solow concluded a book review with this comment: "Perhaps I should say to readers of *The Public Interest* that this is a book whose influence your Editors—or at least one of them—may be warning you against. The warning is needed, because the book is very likely right."[16]

The range of opinion reflected in the *Public Interest* has narrowed, so that even articles by its more liberal authors typically develop a neoconservative theme. However, the journal continues regularly to review books by liberal authors and to publish an occasional liberal article. Two radical economists were included as contributors to the 1980 special issue, "The Crisis in Economic Theory." It is also still the case that, as in the past, many articles concentrate on reporting research results or analyzing a problem or political situation and do not reveal any ideological stance. For example, Martha Derthick of the Brookings Institution wrote an analysis of the politics of social security financing that set forth a variety of options but endorsed none of them.[17] Donald J. Bogue and Amy Ong Tsui criticized most population growth projections and proposed new techniques for developing these projections; their conclusions undercut the most dire predictions of advocates of zero population growth, but the article was written from a politically neutral perspective and could certainly be used by advocates of family planning.[18]

Despite the general shift to the right, the history of this journal is essentially one of continuity rather than change. Nearly all of its frequent early contributors remain active. Irving Kristol has served as coeditor for its entire history. Daniel Bell left his coeditor's position in 1973, but took the position of chairman of the publication committee, holding that post and continuing as a regular contributor until 1982. While Bell was less conservative than Kristol or Nathan Glazer, his replacement as coeditor, this switch did not change significantly the direction of the *Public Interest*. Glazer had written often for the journal, starting with its first issue, and joined the publication committee in 1969. He has remained as a coeditor with Kristol since 1973. Five others have held important editorial posts on the journal's staff; Paul M. Weaver, Marc F. Plattner, Robert Asahina, Michael Andrew Scully, and Mark T. Lilla all were influential in the operation of the journal and frequently wrote articles and book reviews.

Continuity has also characterized the format of the *Public Interest*. It is a quarterly and on the average publishes about 140 pages, including six to ten articles and about 5 pages of brief reviews in a section called "Current Reading." Foundations have financed a number of special issues focused on specific topics, which have filled more than 200 pages. The typical article is between 10 and 20 pages long, but a few are briefer and a quarter are longer, with a few reaching 40 pages. Most articles are written directly for the journal, often by request, but others are adapted from lectures or papers given at academic conferences. Articles vary in character from broad theoretical essays to research reports with detailed evidence on narrowly defined topics and position papers clearly arguing for or against a specific policy. The *Public Interest* regularly features book review essays, most of which it has clustered, since 1978, in special sections published every third volume. These sections typically consist of ten essays covering 60 pages. Occasionally scholars write responses to articles, which are published along with rebuttals from the authors.

The *Public Interest* concentrates on publishing the results of social science research that support various neoconservative themes, but it also likes to correct widely held misperceptions relevant to public policy or politics, especially misperceptions common to liberals. An analysis of polls on abortion, for example, disputed the generalization that the public tends to support the right to choose to have an abortion.[19] Examining federal spending patterns resulted in disagreement with the prevailing perception that the Sun Belt benefits at the expense of the Frost Belt.[20] Authors in the *Public Interest* often take the stance that all widely held beliefs deserve close examination because they are most likely incorrect. The attitude was reflected in the first sentences of Daniel J. Elazar's article, "Are We a Nation of Cities?" where he wrote: "It is generally agreed that the United States is now 'a nation of cities,'—to use a phrase popularized by Lyndon B. Johnson—and that this has given rise to a unique and dramatic 'urban problem.' When a proposition of this kind receives general assent, it may be just the right moment to look at it critically and skeptically." Elazar concluded that census data closely examined and reasonably classified did not support the judgment that we had become "a nation of cities" and that the urban crisis directly affected only a small minority of Americans.[21]

Articles on domestic public policy issues predominate in the *Public Interest*, but it also devotes regular attention to the character and health of American political institutions and to the processes by which we make public policy. Kristol and Moynihan often write general essays in this field, but others have focused on more narrow topics, such as the problems of a specific institution. A common theme is the failure of reforms, including campaign financing and presidential nomination reforms, to accomplish their goals. The *Public Interest* displays an ambivalent attitude toward bureaucrats and bureaucracy; authors regularly criticize the ambitions of liberal federal government bureaucrats, but a basic purpose of the journal is to educate bureaucrats, and it assumes that bureaucratic expertise has a legitimate claim on power. Reflecting the most optimistic hopes about the possible contribution of social science research to policymaking, Bell wrote an article advocating the establishment of an official social report to parallel the economic report of the president.[22]

In the fall of 1975 the *Public Interest* published for its tenth anniversary a special bicentennial issue, "The American Commonwealth—1976." This volume featured most of the major figures involved with the journal, all of whom rank among the intellectual leaders of the neoconservative movement. Moynihan wrote a brief introduction, and Bell, Glazer, Kristol, Lipset, Wildavsky, and Wilson joined less frequent contributors Martin Diamond, Samuel P. Huntington, and Robert Nisbet as the authors. Asked to relate Lord Bryce's *The American Commonwealth* to the condition of the American political system in 1975, the authors as a whole presented a comprehensive statement of the neoconservative understanding of democracy and of the dangers inherent in the political trends of the previous decade.

"The American Commonwealth—1976" argued that democratic excesses in the 1960s undermined the strengths of our traditional system of democratic government. Huntington's lead article, "The Democratic Distemper," provided the central themes of this analysis and set the tone for the entire volume. He argued that increased political participation in the 1960s led to increased demands on government, a more ideologically polarized politics, and a strengthening of the institutions most suited to opposition, Congress, and the media. Increased participation weakened political parties, the most important institutions for making participation effective, and also weakened the central governing institution of the system, the presidency. Popular demand for services gave the bureaucracy new functions and expanded its size, but this meant more power for an institution insulated from the people. The government therefore grew larger, but governmental effectiveness and governmental authority declined, along with the authority of other institutions in the society; popular confidence in government plummeted. Huntington also advanced the theory that electoral coalitions have increasingly diverged from governing coalitions and that it has become more difficult to develop any successful governing coalition in our more participatory system in which power is widely scattered and in which little legitimacy is accorded to governmental leadership. He concluded that "the apparent vitality of democracy in the 1960s raises questions about the governability of democracy in the 1970s."[23]

Neoconservatives argue in favor of traditional American ideas of representative democracy and constitutionalism, and they defend the traditional institutions of our political system. Martin Diamond presented the fullest explanation of those traditional ideas, but Huntington, Lipset, Nisbet, and others also defended the political ideas and institutions of the founders against modern critics who understand themselves as more democratic. Neoconservatives praise liberty and not majority rule as the central political virtue of democracy; they praise equality of political rights and not other egalitarian values stressed by modern liberals; they praise representative government rather than populist conceptions that advocate the sovereignty of popular opinion. The 1960s encouraged a participatory democracy in which all citizens voiced their points of view, but neoconservatives see a need for popular self-restraint and prefer the traditional politics of compromise and coalitions resulting in moderate government.

Central to the neoconservative critique of the present condition of American politics is concern for governmental authority. They believe that support for liberty and democracy is not inconsistent with the idea that government needs to be a force for order and stability and that a good government is strong and effective. Neoconservatives understand governing as a very complex and inherently difficult task, and believe that effectiveness requires that a government be invested with authority so that it can act with experience, expertise, and intelligence. While populist democrats assert that the cure for the ills of democracy is more democracy, Huntington warned that "hierarchy, coercion, discipline, secrecy, and deception...are...inescapable attributes of the process of government."[24] Neoconservatives do not advocate complete faith in governmental competence, for they emphasize that the complexities of governing impose severe limits on what governments can achieve, but they still believe that governments must have independent authority to accomplish those vital tasks of which they are capable. One of the basic problems of democracy is that citizens have many desires that no government can fulfill because these goals are excessively moralistic, utopian, or contradictory, or simply because no one knows how to achieve them. Insufficient public understanding of policy problems and of the realities of governing justifies limiting the role of public opinion in governmental decision making; government officials must have freedom to exercise leadership.

While Huntington suggested that democratic excesses and the weakening of authority was a cyclical phenomenon that would soon pass, the other authors in "The American Commonwealth—1976" expressed consistent pessimism. They saw a weakened presidency, the decay of the political party system, and a bloated bureaucracy as permanent features of our politics. Glazer argued that the liberal activism of the Supreme Court represented a permanent change in that institution rather than just a phase in a cycle that would return to judicial restraint.[25] Kristol's article suggested that the emergence of a "new class" of affluent, educated professionals working in the public and nonprofit sectors provided a well-established political base for the new liberalism that would continue its efforts to promote radical democracy.[26] Bell elaborated most fully the argument that almost all of the factors that had contributed to America's uniquely moderate, peaceful, and stable democracy had disappeared in recent decades; no longer can we count on the continuation of our rare coexistence of majority rule with individual liberty.[27]

A final major concern of the *Public Interest* involves ethics and the power of cultural values. The journal focuses attention on these questions by publishing articles on topics such as business ethics and moral education. Kristol especially stresses this type of issue in arguing that "a crisis of values" is occurring in modern America; he criticizes liberalism for adopting a radical hostility to capitalism, a commitment to a utopian vision of egalitarian democracy, and a critical stance toward traditional family values.[28] In discussions of questions not obviously related to cultural values, neoconservatives often present theories in which values explain much of the character and workings of any political system and the substance of its public policies. In a typical analysis, James Q. Wilson wrote: "A state with a more collectivist origin and less imbued with the philosophy of individual rights would have been quicker than ours to adopt certain social welfare measures; a state without Puritan compulsion to perfect man would have been slower than ours to enact laws to fix up the environment and regulate business-consumer relations."[29]

The *Public Interest* quickly established itself as a major intellectual force in the 1960s. It continues to be widely read in scholarly circles and by journalists and public officials. Its articles are reprinted in books used in colleges and universities. A number of articles, such as those by James Coleman and David J. Armour on school busing, have caused significant controversy in the academic community and inside the government. More important than the journal, of course, is neoconservatism itself. Many neoconservatives held positions in the Reagan administration, and many other public officials and political activists have been influenced by neoconservative thinkers. The *Public Interest* has made an impact on American politics because it has been a major vehicle for the rise of neoconservatism as an important strand of conservative thinking in America.

Notes

1. Daniel Bell and Irving Kristol, "What is the Public Interest?" *The Public Interest* 1 (Fall 1965): 3–5 (hereinafter cited as *PI*).

2. Daniel Bell and Irving Kristol, "Editors' Prospectus," cited in advertisements in most volumes of *PI*.

3. Statement from Freedom House, p. 2, all volumes of *PI* from fall 1965 through fall 1968.

4. Irving Kristol, "Capitalism, Socialism, and Nihilism," *PI* 31 (Spring 1973): 5–6.

5. Peter F. Drucker, "The Sickness of Government," *PI* 14 (Winter 1969): 3.

6. Charles A. Murray, "The Two Wars against Poverty: Economic Growth and the Great Society," *PI* 69 (Fall 1982): 3–16.

7. Daniel P. Moynihan, "Equalizing Education—in Whose Benefit?" *PI* 29 (Fall 1972): 69–89.

8. Andrew M. Greeley, "The Ethnic Miracle," *PI* 45 (Fall 1976): 20–36.

9. Seymour Martin Lipset, "Social Mobility and Equal Opportunity," *PI* 29 (Fall 1972): 90–108.

10. Rachel Flick, "The New Feminism and the World of Work," *PI* 71 (Spring 1983): 33–44.

11. George H. Nash, *The Conservative Intellectual Movement in America: Since 1945* (New York, 1976), pp. 326–27.

12. Drucker, "Sickness of Government," p. 3.

13. Richard Freeman, "Black Economic Progress since 1964," *PI* 52 (Summer 1978): 52–68; and Martin Kilson, "Black Social Classes and Intergenerational Poverty," *PI* 64 (Summer 1981): 58–78.

14. Kilson, "Black Social Classes and Intergenerational Poverty," p. 75.

15. Lester Thurow, "Toward a Definition of Economic Justice," *PI* 31 (Spring 1973): 56–80.

16. Robert M. Solow, "Arthur Okun's Last Work," *PI* 65 (Fall 1981): 102.

17. Martha Derthick, "How Easy Votes on Social Security Came to an End," *PI* 54 (Winter 1979): 94–105.

18. Donald J. Bogue and Amy Ong Tsui, "Zero World Population Growth," *PI* 55 (Spring 1979): 99–113.

19. Peter Skerry, "The Class Conflict over Abortion," *PI* 52 (Summer 1978): 69–84.

20. Ann R. Markusen and Jerry Fastrup, "The Regional War for Federal Aid," *PI* 53 (Fall 1978): 87–99.

21. Daniel J. Elazar, "Are We a Nation of Cities?" *PI* 4 (Summer 1966): 42–58.

22. Daniel Bell, "The Idea of a Social Report," *PI* 15 (Spring 1969): 72–84.

23. Samuel P. Huntington, "The Democratic Distemper," *PI* 41 (Fall 1975): 11.

24. Ibid., p. 24.

25. Nathan Glazer, "Towards an Imperial Judiciary," *PI* 41 (Fall 1975): 104–23.

26. Irving Kristol, "Corporate Capitalism in America," *PI* 41 (Fall 1975): 131–37.

27. Daniel Bell, "The End of American Exceptionalism," *PI* 41 (Fall 1975): 193–224.

28. Irving Kristol, "From Priorities to Goals," *PI* 24 (Summer 1971): 3–4, and "New Right, New Left," *PI* 4 (Summer 1966): 3–7.

29. James Q. Wilson, "'Policy Intellectuals' and Public Policy," *PI* 64 (Summer 1981): 35.

Information Sources

BIBLIOGRAPHY:

Coser, Lewis A. and Irving Howe. *The New Conservatives: A Critique from the Left*. New York, 1973.

Nash, George H. *The Conservative Intellectual Movement in America: Since 1945*. New York, 1976.

Steinfels, Peter. *The Neoconservatives: The Men Who Are Changing America's Politics*. New York, 1979.

INDEXES: *ABC Pol Sci; Amer Hist & Life; AHCI; Bio Ind; BPI; BPIA; Curr Bk Rev Cit; Curr Cont: BSMS; Hist Abst; Pol Sci Abst; Sage Urb Stud Abst; SSCI; Soc Sci Ind;*

Soc Abst; URS; Urb Aff Abst; Writings Amer Hist.
REPRINT EDITIONS: Microform: UMI. Bound editions: available from ISI and UMI.
LOCATION SOURCES: Widely available.

Publication History

TITLE AND TITLE CHANGES: *The Public Interest.*
VOLUME AND ISSUE DATA: Volumes 1–current, Fall 1965–present.
FREQUENCY OF PUBLICATION: Quarterly.
PUBLISHER: Warren Demian Manshel, New York.
EDITORS: Daniel Bell, 1965–1973; Irving Kristol, 1965–present; Nathan Glazer, 1973–
    present.
CIRCULATION: 1987: 12,000; 1998: 6,000

John M. Elliott

American Spectator
1967–

The *American Spectator* originated as a collegiate dissent from the radical politics and countercultural movement of the 1960s. Christened the *Alternative: An American Spectator,* in 1967, the journal was the inspiration of R. Emmett Tyrrell, Jr., and the collaborative effort of other undergraduate colleagues at Indiana University. Changed to the current title in 1977, the journal thrived in modest quarters in Bloomington, and then later moved to Washington, D.C. The *Spectator* has a nominal ancestor in a 1930s magazine founded by George Jean Nathan, but there is no literary descent. The journal appears monthly. Originally fourteen-by-eleven inches in dimension, forty to fifty pages in length, and handsomely illustrated in the manner of a Victorian literary periodical, it later went to a slick, modern look. A front cover cartoon caricature of some notable usually indicates what personality will be a target of the *Spectator*'s barbs. In Tyrrell, a Chicago product and grandson of a wealthy manufacturer, the *Spectator* has provided a witty, often vitriolic voice of neoconservatism.[1] Armed with an awesome and ready vocabulary, Tyrrell gained a national reputation by 1980 and became William F. Buckley's successor as the *enfant terrible* of conservative journalism in America.

The *Spectator* makes it its business to take the measure of American life and to do so in the manner of its patron saint, H. L. Mencken. The contemporary scene, the *Spectator* essayists find, provides enough farcical fodder to keep anyone laughing. In the journal's regular feature titled "The Continuing Crisis," Tyrrell virtually reproduced the noted "Americana" section from Mencken's *American Mercury*, in it documenting from all quarters of the country the manifold inanities that mark life in this quarter of the globe. For example, from Orange County, California, comes news that a transsexual seeks to adopt a daughter of twenty-three years of age. Hormone treatment, the report says, has coaxed a slight breastline from the aspiring mother, but the decisive surgery remains to complete the transformation out of maleness. Nonetheless, Tyrrell says, there is room for hope.

The mutant is no Venus, but "she is one of the few United States citizens whose anatomy actually conforms to the gender guidelines of our federal government."[2]

The *Spectator* enjoys a good laugh, but these frivolities are not merely humorous. Some are lethal, and none more so than the ideas and actions that emanate from a movement almost coincidental in origin to the *Spectator* itself: the contemporary women's movement. This phenomenon presented to recent conservatism a challenge that earlier conservative expressions never had to confront. The *Spectator* stood in vehement opposition to women's liberation. It found its morality simplistic, reducing so complex an ethical issue as abortion to a cliché: "It's my body." It found feminist literature shrill and self-serving. One contributor who undertook an extended essay on *Ms.* magazine gained from the experience only a new respect for St. Paul's admonition against women speaking in church.[3] Many of the antifeminist contributors to the *Spectator* were themselves female, Midge Decter most prominent among them. In a 1982 essay she found the contemporary women's movement replete with contradictions and spoke for most of the *Spectator* writers when she charged that ardent feminists were fighting against the "natural order of things." "That a man is a man and a woman is a woman," she wrote, "and that life on earth is only made tolerable by the collaborative contributions of the uniqueness of each, is about as good a definition of the fundamental aspect of the natural order as any."[4]

To this extent the *Spectator* stands for traditional ways. All the more adverse, then, have been its judgments against homosexuals. Opinion ranges from outright distaste for homosexual life and culture—"tawdry, libertine, and barbaric," according to one writer[5]—to lament for homosexuals' deviance from the norms of human relationships and the ancient but enriching battle of the sexes. Homosexuality, according to Michael Novak, is thus more a matter of regret than of censure.[6]

These matters point directly to the question of style and accent in the *Spectator*. It is unmistakably masculine in all the stereotypical implications of that description. What best conveys that spirit is one of the liveliest sections of the journal, the "Great American Saloon Series." Here the Menckenite spirit has thrived, because for all the invective the Great Iconoclast hurled at American ways, he cherished greatly his home city of Baltimore and the tavern life of its German district. Here one could find a sanctuary from Puritan reformers and crusading do-gooders. The *Spectator* in a similar spirit frequently dedicates issues to what remains of this hardy life and seeks out establishments where it can be enjoyed. This is what the *Spectator* means by a "healthy libertarianism," and it is pleased to salute Hoffman's of San Francisco, Arnold's of Cincinnati, and Cunningham's of Louisville. Here among hardwood elegance free men can still live and breathe — and drink. But such places are rare havens these days. As one contributor noted: "The proliferation of singles bars and artsy cloying coffeehouses has made finding a good place to drink beer as difficult as getting a summer job."[7] The *Spectator* finds that much is at work in America against this spirit of healthy hedonism. Modern liberalism, it believes, has a lot to do with it, for today's liberals are to this group of neoconservatives what the Puritans were to Mencken—meddlesome, self-righteous, and humorlessly dull. Tom Bethell described the Washington of the Carter years as a "peculiarly somber, serious town." The city derived its personality, he said, from "the gloomy reformers of government, joined in common cause against nationwide frivolity and profligacy." Salvation-minded and accusatory, they are resolved that all of us "confess our sins in triplicate."[8]

On this issue the *Spectator* reflected a concern that marked the conservative revival of the 1970s—the often confusing issue of the "new class." Neoconservatives, in such publications as the *Public Interest*, attempted to document the power of an entrenched elite of professionals, government officials, educators, and others with ties of interest to the national government and a common centrist ideology that expresses them. And among this group a marked "adversary culture," intermixing 1960s radicalism with traditional liberal sentiment, flourishes. The adversary culture, it is alleged, began in Washington, spread through National Public Radio and the classrooms of the major universities, and finally encroached on Peoria. Skepticism, negativism, and smugness toward traditional American middle-class values described the counterculture. It denigrated American foreign policy and projected a moral agnosticism into its judgments about United States and Russian rivalry. It deprived Americans of a just sense of their own righteousness in this rivalry and a clear purpose in their stance toward the rest of the world. This *trahison des clercs* marks for the *Spectator* the danger of a counterculture that had in fact become "official" opinion.[9]

The *Spectator* addresses a great variety of issues and mostly in a serious and sober vein. But personalities gave the publication its special éclat, for our contemporary culture, it found, condemns itself by the heroes it worships. To Tyrrell and the other essayists, today's attention getters are for the most part either frauds or simple bumpkins, made to glitter only by the phosphorescence bestowed by media image makers. The most offensive class is politicians, and Tyrrell often used his monthly essay to expose the darlings of the liberal coterie. (Many of these personalities took a second bow in Tyrrell's 1979 book, *Public Nuisances*.) Tyrrell excoriated personalities like Bella Abzug, Jimmy Carter, Andrew Young, and Walter Mondale. Intellectuals, too, he found undeserving. Writing on John Kenneth Galbraith, "Harvard's Tallest Tale," Tyrrell decried the infatuating effect this "huckster of liberal economics" had on the liberal establishment. "Anyone ever thrown into a Kennedy swimming pool has at one time or another come under his spell," he wrote.[10] Hollywood personalities also receive their due, especially those who smack of radical-chic opinions. A 1981 *Spectator* number featured actor Alan Alda on the cover, portrayed with a giddy, saccharine smile, and holding two daisies. *Spectator* movie critic John Podhoretz described Alda as "the unthreatening, nice, thoughtful, and emasculated fellow any Women's Libber would love to meet."[11]

But people are also memorable for what they say, and the *Spectator* listened. Its back section, "Current Wisdom," is a monthly compilation of quotable inanities culled from a wide assortment of literary efforts. Publications most often selected for inclusion are *Ms.*, the *New York Times*, *Mother Jones*, the *Progressive*, the *Village Voice*, and the *New York Review of Books*. "Current Wisdom" shows that

America has as many fools as it did in Mencken's day, but now the radical feminists and partisans of "new age" culture have replaced the Methodist ministers and Republican party stalwarts as voices of the absurd. Thus the *Spectator* quotes a vociferous feminist who calls herself a "separatist"—"I wouldn't touch a sexual relationship with a man with a ten-foot pole"—which leaves the *Spectator* wondering whether such a man exists.[12]

Measured restraint is not the *Spectator*'s style. It delights to get under its enemies' skins and it reports with glee the outraged feelings of those it has offended. "I am appalled," critics say, and that refrain is quoted from several different sources on a *Spectator* subscription page. "A piece of trash," says another commentator. "An exercise in bad taste," scowls another. "Viciously biased," "infantile and vulgar," declare still others. One *Spectator* issue had a back page photograph of sign-bearing feminists. In large print next to the picture are the words of Susanna Smith: "I sincerely hope that one of the successes of the women's movement will be to rid society of pestilences such as R. Emmett Tyrrell, Jr."[13]

In this backhanded kind of way the *Spectator* promotes its causes. But it uses other devices too. One could order from the magazine a "Spectator" jacket with the emblematic turkey on it. There were also "Spectator" beer mugs. The magazine has a "Classified Ads" section. For $20.00 one could acquire an Adam Smith necktie. There were Milton Friedman, Edmund Burke, and H. L. Mencken t-shirts and sweatshirts. For those as irreverent as the *Spectator*'s editors, there were bumper stickers that read "Nuke the Whales" and "Have You Slugged Your Kid Today?" The alert, or the needy, will also check the personals. In one, a forty-six-year-old woman seeks cultural companionship, but of a select order only: "Smokers, swingers, druggies, religious zealots, and left-wing activists need not apply."[14]

For several years the *Spectator* presented the "Harold Robbins Award" for the worst book of the year. That title later changed to the less libelous "J. Gordon Coogler Award." This was Tyrrell's doing. Winners have included Lillian Hellman's *Scoundrel Time* and Theodore H. White's *Breach of Faith: The Fall of Richard Nixon*. Tyrell called the latter "a book that will not shut up" and the author "one of the most garrulous writers ever uncorked on these shores. Next to him Hubert Humphrey would be a model librarian." Tyrrell rankled at White's sanctimonious preaching and wrote of the book: "When you purchase it you purchase more than a best-seller, you purchase a mother-in-law."[15]

Although the *Spectator* offers a lively book review section, Tyrrell commented once that there is little in modern letters to rival the classic works of Western literature, which command a second reading before most of today's products command a first. Our culture is simply too presentist. Did we really need yet another Watergate biography?[16]

This deference toward tradition and its claims against the cult of the contemporary have usually marked the conservative temperament. The issue raises the larger matter of the *Spectator*'s place within the wider phenomenon of American conservatism. It has never, of course, been a monolithic movement, and two issues especially have generated its inner tensions. The *Spectator* has not been able to resolve these, and that fact makes its position both ambiguous and ambivalent.

One of these issues is religion. A powerful strand in American conservative thought has sought to root its ideas in some absolute theological or metaphysical foundation. In various ways, that concern has motivated conservative spokesmen like Will Herberg, Russell Kirk, John Hallowell, Richard Weaver, Leo Strauss, and Eric Voegelin. They uniformly oppose the rival intellectual traditions of empiricism, naturalism, and pragmatism, which they blame for the drift and confusion of the modern era. But that conservatism is by no means linked to this frame of mind is amply illustrated by a variety of thinkers that includes Irving Babbitt, H. L. Mencken, Max Eastman, and Ayn Rand. The *Spectator* has had little to say about religion and would like not to be diverted by the questions it raises. The magazine has never allied itself with the bully pulpit of the Moral Majority and beyond it could see only the lunatic fringe of new age religious consciousness, or the "chic-guilt psychosis" and fashionable activism of mainline Protestant churches. It pains the *Spectator* to see so venerable an institution as the Episcopal church—witness St. John the Divine in New York—polluting its sanctuary with Shinto rites and Sufi workshops in dervish dancing.[17] Modern theology, a *Spectator* writer said, is summarized by the motto, "Our times demand," and for that reason every bastion of Christendom should be about the business of ordaining women.[18]

But the matter of religion cannot be so easily dismissed. As. G. K. Chesterton said, when people stop believing in God, they do not believe in nothing; they believe in anything. The loss of traditional religious authority has bestowed a kind of credibility on all the absurdities of modern culture the *Spectator* feared. Worse, it has generated a faith more implausible than anything Christianity ever proffered, the faith in socialism, the pseudoreligion of a secular age. *Spectator* writers have provided little help in generating rival systems of a higher authority to meet this challenge. But Bethell has at least perceived the need. Religion cannot recover its position, he writes, but America must have a religious sense about itself and its purpose in the world—"something more inspiring than consumerism, the consumer movement, getting a bigger house, a bigger car, and so on." Capitalism, the conservative should know, cannot be an end in itself.[19]

The other dilemma for conservatism is liberty—more precisely, the libertarian spirit. It has found expression in Mencken, Albert Jay Nock, Eastman, and Rand, and has similarities to classical liberalism, as voiced by Friedrich Hayek and Milton Friedman. American conservatism took an important turn in the mid-1960s when Frank Meyer led a "fusionist" movement that tried to reconcile the authoritarian—religious, metaphysical, dogmatic—branch with the liberal, individualistic branch. The outcome was decisively a libertarian triumph, for Meyer posited freedom with the "constitution of being" itself and put the metaphysical order to the service of individual liberty. The price Meyer paid for attempting such an amalgamation was scorn from conservatism's religious, and particularly Catholic, wing.[20]

The *Spectator* calls itself libertarian, but the matter is not that simple. True, a new kind of puritanism thrived in America, and the *Spectator* had little use for it.

Jogging, teeth flossing, health foods, and Perrier water with lime documented the new moralism. Later, "political correctness" provided reinforcement. *Spectator* writers found these trends intrusive and meddlesome, as exemplified by the vigilantism of the nonsmoker. With all the pure-living fads in circulation, there was not much visible sin around, so the smoker stood out as a reprobate deserving banishment from the tribe.[21] But what remains of the truly free spirits in this country? The *Spectator*, in a contribution from "Feather River John," lamented the passing of the hobos from the American countryside. They were the best of souls, "resourceful, resilient, merry, generous...responsible and on the average as sober as the ordinary reader of this publication." Compare these noble stalwarts with today's social fringe, a collection of cocaine sniffers.[22] The problem for the *Spectator* was the abuse of libertarianism, for that ideal had created an epidemic of self-indulgence in the absurd, from parapsychology to "new consciousness psychics." Aram Bakshian, a long-time *Spectator* staff member, saw the problem as intrinsic to the libertarian ideal itself, and in an obituary essay on Ayn Rand he dismissed her philosophy as, in essence, the principle of selfishness. He labeled pure libertarianism a meaningless ideology.[23] Tyrrell addressed the issue by attacking the partisans of a "bogus" libertarianism. In an essay on *Hustler* magazine publisher Larry Flynt, whom he called "a hopelessly pathetic slob," Tyrrell charged that "vicarious" libertarians could not distinguish true causes of freedom from false ones. To bemoan a censorship policy that muffles the pornographer both exaggerates and trivializes the libertarian ideal, he said. That clarification helped to define the *Spectator*'s position, but it did not yield ideological clarity for the conservative movement.[24]

The *Spectator* provided a format for a group of young conservative intellectuals, including Bethell, Decter, Stephen Miller, John Nollson, and Stephen Maloney. Their contributions were regularly informed and dispassionate. But the *Spectator* seemed to recognize that few of today's issues will be settled by learned discourse or by logic. So it had recourse to the horse laugh. Our culture, it thinks, might be exorcised of its zanies and its true believers if these are allowed to expose themselves in all their foolishness. What will remain, it hopes, is the plain good sense of the American people. That faith actually has given the *Spectator*'s kind of neoconservatism a marked democratic cast. For we have been betrayed by our elites as well as by our fringe, it argued. Most Americans do not want to be saved either by Washington blueprints for the year 2000 or by new age consciousness. A sane and practical common sense, a wholesome libertarianism, and a sense of humor are better programs for the Republic.

Notes

1. R. Emmett Tyrrell, Jr., "On Ten Years of Public Service," *American Spectator* 11 (November 1977): 4 (hereinafter cited as *AS*); *Time* 109 (7 March 1977): 93-94; William Delaney, "God and Man (and Mencken) at Indiana," *Chronicle of Higher Education* 11 (22 September 1975): 11.

2. *AS* 16 (March 1983): 7.

3. Stephen R. Maloney, "Of (Ms.)anthropes and Men," *AS* 9 (January 1976): 22-24.

4. "Whatever Happened to America?" *AS* 15 (December 1982): 8, 10.

5. Stephen R. Maloney, "The Lavender Menace," *AS* 10 (December 1976): 12, 14.

6. "Men without Women," *AS* 11 (October 1978): 15-16.

7. Brian Thomas, "The Taproom of the Schoenling Brewery," *AS* 10 (November 1976): 22.

8. "Capitol Ideas," *AS* 11 (February 1978): 21.

9. Peter W. Rodman, "The Road to Anthony Lewis," *AS* 15 (December 1982): 30; Joseph P. Duggan, "Some Things Considered," *AS* 10 (March 1977) 13.

10. *AS* 10 (June–July 1977): 4.

11. "The Great Effeminist," *AS* 14 (August 1981): 27.

12. *AS* 15 (July 1982): 42.

13. *AS* 13 (January 1980): back cover.

14. *AS* 14 (May 1983): 38.

15. "The Worst Book of the Year," *AS* 15 (January 1976): 4.

16. "The Writer, the Publisher, the Gull," *AS* 9 (December 1975): 4; "The Thug as Rotarian," *AS* 9 (February 1976): 4.

17. Rael Jean Isaac and Erich Isaac, "Sanctifying Revolution: Protestantism's New Social Gospel," *AS* 14 (May 1981): 11.

18. A. James McAdams, "Ordaining the Zeitgeist," *AS* 10 (April 1977): 5.

19. "A Question of Faith," *AS* 15 (November 1982): 5.

20. For a discussion of this theme, see George H. Nash, *The Conservative Intellectual Movement in America: Since 1945* (New York, 1976), pp. 171-85.

21. Walter Goodman, "In Defense of Smoking," *AS* 12 (April 1979): 11.

22. "Hobo Bill's Last Ride," *AS* 10 (February 1977): 29-30.

23. "Ayn Rand, R.I.P.," *AS* 15 (May 1982): 24.

24. "Poet on a Fuzzy Toilet Seat Cover," *AS* 10 (April 1977): 4; see also David L. Wilkinson, "Porn, Cable TV and Censorship," *AS* (July 1983): 20-23.

Information Sources

BIBLIOGRAPHY: None.

INDEXES: Each volume indexed; *Access*; *Bio Ind*; *BRI*; *Mag Ind*; *PAIS*; *Pol Sci Abst*; *PPI*; *RG*; *Sage Urb Stud Abst*; *Writings Amer Hist*.

REPRINT EDITIONS: Microform: UMI; BLH. Bound edition: ISI.

LOCATION SOURCES: Widely available.

Publication History

TITLE AND TITLE CHANGES: *The Alternative: An American Spectator,* 1967-1977; *The American Spectator*, 1977-present.

VOLUME AND ISSUE DATA: Volumes 1-current, 1967-present.

FREQUENCY OF PUBLICATION: Monthly.

PUBLISHER: Ronald E. Burr, Bloomington, Indiana.

EDITOR: R. Emmett Tyrrell, Jr.

CIRCULATION: 41,000; 1998: 203,610.

J. David Hoeveler, Jr.

Conservative Digest
1975–

During the 1960s and early 1970s modern American conservatism absorbed many damaging blows delivered by the nation's accelerated liberal drift. In the 1964 election, for example, sympathy for the late John Kennedy and Lyndon Johnson's "peace" campaign overwhelmed Barry Goldwater in his bid for the White House. As the 1960s wore on, Johnson's Great Society programs, in conservative eyes, threatened to socialize America, while his "no victory" Vietnam policies moved the nation closer to communistic encirclement. Upon becoming president, Richard Nixon declined to dismantle the Great Society and further disappointed conservatives by appointing "eastern liberal establishment" Republicans to administer it as well. In 1974, after Watergate, conservatives found especially galling Gerald Ford's selection of Nelson Rockefeller as vice-president. Given Rockefeller's historic cooperation with eastern liberals, the move threatened the destruction of the Grand Old Party as a vehicle for conservative action, and signaled an imminent takeover by the party's moderate and liberal wings. In addition, a dangerous combination of inflation, high taxes, budget deficits, overtures to the People's Republic of China, détente with the Soviets, the SALT treaties, and Supreme Court decisions such as *Roe* v. *Wade* convinced conservatives that America faced, at best, an uncertain future.

Determined to prevent national disaster, groups of conservatives met across the country soon after the Rockefeller nomination to map out strategies to counter America's leftward turn. Sharing commitments to traditional American family values, a distrust of the "establishment," a fear of big government, an intense hatred of communism, as well as a desire for American military superiority, these conservatives crystalized their political dissatisfaction into a movement soon called the New Right. Richard Viguerie, the Texas direct-mail wizard, joined fellow New Rightists Terry Dolan, Howard Phillips, Paul Weyrich, and others in a frantic campaign to revive the Right and make it a potent political force.[1] Viguerie's contribution to the cause, aside from his direct-mail help to conservative politicians and organizations, came in May 1975 when he began to publish *Conservative Digest*, a monthly magazine of the "New Majority." Rebuffed in his bid to buy *Human Events* (a weekly affiliated with the Conservative Union), Viguerie started *Conservative Digest* as a response to the moderation of the Republican party and in an effort to circumvent what he saw as the liberal monopoly of the media.[2]

To overcome any liberal bias, the magazine contains original articles but also reprints from other periodicals, including *Playboy*, *Penthouse*, and *Village Voice*, stories that echo the New Right viewpoint. Since the fall of 1982, when the editors redesigned the journal's format to resemble other popular news magazines, *Conservative Digest* has included current news items while continuing its interpretive feature articles on matters of special interest to conservatives. Such articles are written in a straightforward manner in order to attract the lower-middle-class American intimidated by the intellectual style of the *National Review* and *Human Events*. Thanks to careful editorial direction and the efforts of contributors such as Phillips, Weyrich, Pat Buchanan, Joseph Sobran, Thomas Sowell, and William Rusher, *Conservative Digest* has attracted approximately 39,000 readers who appreciate the nonintellectual style.[3] Viguerie can justifiably boast that *Conservative Digest* is one of the most widely read political magazines in the nation.[4]

Born in Texas in 1933 to middle-class parents who lost much of their real estate holdings in the 1920s and 1930s, Viguerie attended Texas A&T and the University of Houston Law School. He did not set the academic world on fire and eventually he left school to find his niche elsewhere. An early devotee of politics, he spent the 1950s and 1960s working for conservative candidates, along the way claiming, as did many other young conservatives of the day, Douglas MacArthur and Joe McCarthy as his heroes. In 1961 he received his big break when the Young Americans for Freedom hired him as executive secretary. While in this position and as a worker for the 1964 Goldwater campaign, Viguerie learned and applied the techniques of direct-mail solicitation. In 1965 he established his own direct-mail business, a company that raised millions for his fellow conservatives by the 1970s. Distaste for the nation's social and political trends led Viguerie to begin publishing his own political journal.[5]

A deeply religious man, Viguerie has used *Conservative Digest* to share his belief that God endowed America with its many blessings in order to advance democracy and Christian values throughout the world. Seeing a rejection of God at the root of the nation's troubles, Viguerie in 1978 and again in 1980 called for a national day of prayer and fasting to rededicate America to God's high purposes. "Perhaps many of our personal and national problems have developed because we have forgotten to thank God for our blessings, our opportunities, our freedoms and our great country," he wrote. A day of prayer and fasting would symbolize a desire to thank God for the benefits he had given America and its people.[6] But Viguerie believes the institutions God established to bring order to American society no longer represent the views of the average American. Time and again his journal has said that Americans no longer hold the same beliefs as the nation's liberal leaders but possess deeply held conservative values that the "establishment," including both major political parties, now ignored.[7] The "establishment" Viguerie defined as "the class of persons with unusual access to the political process...gained through economic power...social status or...an old-boy network [and] characterized by the belief that people in general are not smart enough to manage their own affairs." To run this society, the establishment required persons holding advanced degrees from eastern institutions, thus concentrating power in the hands of an elite minority that worked its will through big government, big business, big labor, big education, big law, big media, and big banks. The establishment did not produce the nation's wealth, but left that task to the average working American; America's establishment elite had "uncalloused hands."[8]

The New Right's populist conservatism, as propagated by *Conservative Digest*, involved coalitional efforts by conservatives of both major political parties working to return power to the average working American, whether secretary, union member, or small businessman. Tracing this new populism back to the author of the Declaration of Independence, Viguerie believed Thomas Jefferson established the principles of populism when he wrote that two parties of mankind exist: the class that fears the people and those who trust the masses to do what is right. *Conservative Digest* leaves no doubt what it believes: the magazine identifies with the "common" workingman, emphasizes the rights of those citizens against elites, and stands for "self-reliance, decentralization, and open and responsive government."[9] The average American in no way resembles Archie Bunker because the average American has deeply rooted beliefs on family, neighborhood church, school, and work. America's "common" man only wants to be left alone to build his own life, without the worry of what the government did to or for him.[10] Men such as Jack Kemp and George Wallace received high praise in the pages of *Conservative Digest* because they addressed these concerns in their bids for higher office.[11]

Both the new populist and *Conservative Digest* hold dear the "basic American values—the family, honesty, the work ethic, neighbor helping neighbor, fair pay for a day's labor, and peace through strength."[12] To attract readers with these values, *Conservative Digest* devoted many pages to the social issues that antagonize the middle and working classes: sex and violence in the media, prayer in school, busing, pornography, abortion, and crime.[13] These issues influence the family, the sacred vessel God established to protect and teach society's members. Within the family the young learn the basic moral values society needs to keep it strong. No other institution can accomplish what the family can because it is the best guarantor of health, education, and welfare.[14] Family values underpin society and prevent it from descending into chaos.

God in his wisdom also assigned a specific role for each family member in order to keep the unit functioning. The husband should provide food and shelter for his wife and children while defending them from any threatening force. The wife is expected to stay inside the home, care for the young, keep an orderly household, attend to the family's day-to-day needs, defer major family decisions to the husband, and, by implication, be the family's moral guardian. The children should be attentive pupils as their parents teach them the moral values of society, which include the proper roles boys and girls play when they reach adulthood. For this reason, husbands should encourage their sons to emulate the work men perform within and outside the home, while mothers should instruct their daughters in the importance of domestic life.[15] A society that reverently adheres to the traditional home values promotes its general well-being since "the moral principles embodied [in those values] are the surest way [for society] to achieve happiness."[16]

Groups and institutions that interfere with traditional values are the targets of the "profamily" movement, which *Conservative Digest* and the New Right embrace with gusto.[17] *Conservative Digest* sees the American family, and the American way of life, threatened from every direction: homosexuals openly assault the manly image that fathers teach sons to emulate, confusing boys as to proper male attitudes; the "gay rights" movement hopes to institutionalize this antimale behavior; and the women's movement poses an equally dangerous threat because it encourages women to leave the home and labor alongside men. This not only prevents women from fulfilling household duties, but also means children must come home to empty houses deficient in any caring or moral teaching. When the father stays home to attend to the wife's traditional responsibilities, then sex roles become blurred, leaving children unsure of proper adult behavior.[18]

The federal government has contributed as much to the erosion of the American family as homosexuality and the women's movement. According to *Conservative Digest* contributors, the governmental policies of the 1960s and 1970s daily assaulted traditional American family values and tore the social fabric. The culprits included no-fault divorce, abortion, the coddling of criminals, the removal of prayer from school, sex education, and high taxes combined with a government-induced inflation that forced wives to work. Through these policies, the government preempted the parental role in an attempt to reduce the family to the lowest administrative level of the state's apparatus. In short, the government secularized the family, paving the way for dramatic increases in divorces, abortions, single parents, teenage mothers, and violence.[19] Only by returning to traditional concepts, achievable through a constitutional amendment allowing school prayer, a crackdown on pornography and crime, an end to forced busing, a return to the "Three 'R's,'" and a balanced budget, can America be saved. Such a mission cuts across party and religious lines to the heart of what makes America strong. *Conservative Digest* and the New Right proudly take their places in this coalitional crusade to save the family.[20]

More than any other issue, abortion unites this coalition, and *Conservative Digest* holds high the conservative banner on the subject. The 1973 *Roe* v. *Wade* decision permitting abortion on demand outraged the New Right on both religious and philosophical grounds because the issue cut to the heart of how American society should be ordered. Syndicated columnist Joseph Sobran addressed the abortion question and the causes of family breakdown in the November 1981 issue. According to Sobran, conservatives want a society based on the dignity of the individual who respects divine and human law and nurtures the community that gave him life. To ensure that society, conservatives must protect the individual from liberalism and its cousin, socialism. Both ideologies allow the state to control all aspects of life through their undermining of religion, the family, and the currency.

The removal of these social structures leaves a vacuum the state can fill with its own fiat. By declaring the unborn "nonpersons," the state, as represented by the Supreme Court, took one more step toward this total control. Sobran believed the abortion ruling declared null and void the traditional family structure that could challenge the state's encroaching authority, and left even the most loving fathers with no more voice than a rapist. By allowing abortion, American society apparently decided that children—humans—have no intrinsic worth. If bearing an unwanted child violates the rights of a woman, why should she or the father feel any obligation to that child, or to anybody else, after that child is born? Abortion destroys this sense of obligation, yet that very obligation establishes order by holding the family, the community, and the society together.[21]

In addition to destroying individual obligation, *Conservative Digest* believes American liberalism nearly succeeded in extinguishing any sense of personal initiative left alive in the nation. In their efforts to promote equality of results, liberals (usually unnamed) took a left turn away from the New Deal–New Frontier brand of liberalism that promised only equality of opportunity. This leftward movement subsidized laziness, educational mediocrity, and secular humanism at the same time it brought about high taxes, government-induced inflation, and worldwide acquiescence to Soviet aggression.[22] Thanks to these liberal policies America lost its hard edge in the world marketplace even as the nation's enemies strengthened themselves. Under these conditions, Americans found risktaking too costly a proposition.

Liberalism, *Conservative Digest* stated, is morally and intellectually bankrupt, atheistic, unpatriotic, and full of contradictions that the journal takes delight in exposing. New Right contributors charge that liberalism rejects the traditional concept of God and seeks to replace him with man as the world's prime mover. American liberals also deplored U.S. action taken to counter Soviet aggression, decried the "alleged" excesses of anticommunist allies, and yet refused to criticize abuses committed by Soviet puppet regimes. Well-to-do liberals denigrate the capitalistic system that gave them wealth, proclaim themselves champions of minorities and the poor, then institute burdensome tax and welfare systems to prevent those lower on the scale from rising above their stations. The liberal clergy involves itself in political matters but screams about separation of church and state when fundamentalist clergymen do the same. Liberals demand freedom of choice before the birth of a child, but refuse to allow parents a proper voice in how or where that child should receive an education. Distrustful of the common people for whom they claim to speak, to achieve their goals liberals must rely on the unelected Supreme Court and the media. The defeat of prominent liberals such as George McGovern and Frank Church delighted *Conservative Digest* and convinced it that America finally was ready to embrace the populistic conservatism of the New Right.[23]

While the followers of New Right conservatism share many of the same values, *Conservative Digest* shows no fear in castigating conservatives who appear to stray from the narrow path. Senator Barry Goldwater (R, Arizona) learned this the hard way in January 1976 when Viguerie and editor Lee Edwards (another 1964

Goldwater worker) coauthored "Goldwater: Leader or Legend?" an exposé of the later Goldwater record. Viguerie did not intend to "break the bonds of affection which [tied] American conservatives to [their] former standard bearer," but conservatives should not expect more out of the man than he could give. Appealing myths and legends, he told his readers, could no longer sustain the conservative movement, and with that Viguerie tore into the man he tried to make president twelve years earlier.[24]

The authors claimed that three Goldwaters existed: the monster created by the liberal media in 1964, the leader of the modern American conservative movement, and the "real" Goldwater—the rugged westerner who shot from the hip. Unfortunately for the New Right, the *Conscience of a Conservative* Goldwater no longer seemed active in the movement. As proof, Viguerie and Edwards cited Goldwater's roll call vote attendance record (76 percent in 1974 compared to the Senate average of 84 percent) and his absence when important issues such as busing or gun control came to the floor. When he did attend, he often kept silent, creating a serious lack of conservative leadership. The authors also found fault with the senator's stand on issues close to the New Right's heart. In 1969 he backed the equal rights amendment and supported Nixon's 1971 economic plan, which called for wage and price controls. He committed an almost unpardonable sin in praising Henry Kissinger's diplomacy after the signing of the 1974 Paris Peace Accords. Finally, he did not "aggressively" oppose the 1974 budget of $304.4 billion, or a $6.4 billion national health insurance plan. While still calling Goldwater a great man, *Conservative Digest* reminded readers that he always said he never wanted to run for president. A loyal party man, he ran in 1964 because of party pressure and endorsed Gerald Ford in 1976 because he viewed Ronald Reagan's campaign as a threat to party unity. "Many conservatives at the grassroots still look to Barry Goldwater as the man they call their leader," Viguerie and Edwards lamented. "They do not realize [he] has more than paid his dues. It is time to lighten our demands on him" and find new leadership for the movement.[25] Readers agreed, as evidenced by a *Conservative Digest* poll in which 92 percent of the respondents said Goldwater's endorsement of Ford would not influence their vote, with one letter writer snapping that the senator had lost both his backbone and his "vinegar." Although he gave Goldwater an opportunity to respond, Viguerie convincingly demonstrated to the rest of the movement that "the conservative cause is bigger than any man or woman, even the best of them."[26]

By 1983 Ronald Reagan, the darling of right-wingers since 1964, learned that this statement applied to him as well. His election to the White House delighted the New Right, but from the start *Conservative Digest* advised its hero to tread carefully. After the election, Howard Phillips informed readers that conservatives must use four criteria when grading Reagan: whether he cut off tax money used to underwrite liberal causes, how he trimmed the nondefense budget, whether he stood up to Castro in the Caribbean and Latin America, and whether he discontinued relying on arms control treaties as the basis of American foreign policy.[27]

Reagan disappointed conservatives enough that by mid-1983, New Right dissatisfaction with him began to appear in the pages of *Conservative Digest*. Some conservatives believed Reagan "sold out": his initial appointments were not die-hard conservatives but Nixon-Ford retreads; he virtually ignored the social issues agenda of the religious Right; he appointed Sandra O'Connor, a woman of less than solid New Right credentials, to the Supreme Court; his efforts at budget reduction had not brought the federal deficit under control; and he kept New Right people off his immediate staff.[28] After the Soviets shot down KAL 007, the New Right especially excoriated the president, claiming he could have expelled Soviet diplomats, suspended loans and credit to the Soviet bloc, or refused Soviet ships the right of port in American docks. Howard Phillips, echoing other *Conservative Digest* writers, called Reagan's relatively moderate response to the massacre "groveling and weak-kneed"; all of the journal's major contributors reminded the president that his reactions to the KAL disaster contradicted his strong anti-Soviet rhetoric of the previous twenty years.[29]

Soon after this incident, *Conservative Digest* published a spate of articles and surveys that "graded" Reagan's performance in office and expressed overall conservative disappointment with his presidency. Both readers and regular contributors shared the same analysis of the president: although Reagan still embodied the movement, he seemed reluctant to light the fire needed to galvanize major reform along conservative lines. His reluctance put the nation and the conservative cause in danger.[30] For his part, Viguerie acknowledged Reagan's accomplishments, but only perfunctorily endorsed him in 1984.[31] Since the 1984 election, the journal has periodically examined New Right luminaries, notably Pat Robertson, who potentially could lead the nation in the direction that Reagan could not or would not go.[32] The journal wanted leaders who would fit political realities to New Right principles and positions: aggressive anticommunism directed against the Soviet Union and the People's Republic of China, support for the Strategic Defense Initiative, agreement with Reagan's Central American policies, and calls for Jeanne Kirkpatrick to replace George Schultz as secretary of state.[33]

On the home front, *Conservative Digest* urges tax cuts and balanced budgets, takes a hostile attitude toward the IRS, delights in exposing federal waste, trumpets the free enterprise system as the solution to the economic problems faced by minorities and women, believes the welfare state breeds poverty, and decries big business's dealings with pornographic magazines and communist nations.[34] Any moderation by the nation's leaders in addressing these issues will usually draw the fire of *Conservative Digest*'s editorial staff, and the New Right in general.

Opinions on these matters on the conservative agenda remain consistent despite a change in *Conservative Digest* ownership and format. In 1985 an expensive and unsuccessful run for the Virginia lieutenant governor's chair, severe competition in the direct-mail field, and other factors, combined to force Richard Viguerie to sell *Conservative Digest* to William Kennedy, a Colorado investment counselor.[35] Kennedy, who took over with the October 1985 issue, moved the offices from Falls Church, Virginia, to the National Press Building in Washington, D.C. Despite changing the format to one resembling *Reader's Digest*, Kennedy continues to use a mix of original and reprinted articles while following the "profamily," anti–big government, anticommunist, and anti-intellectual tradition of Viguerie's journal.

No matter who the publisher or what the format, the periodical serves as an important forum to grassroots Americans disgusted with the social and political trends engineered by the nation's intelligentsia. Regular readers believe these trends signal a loss of freedom to an uncaring government that wants to regulate their economic and private lives to the point of near-slavery. In an effort to control the life of the individual, the government has corrupted almost every institution that stabilized a once moral and prosperous society. While such beliefs sound reactionary, *Conservative Digest* takes pride in forthrightly presenting the populistic side of conservatism, all the while calling and working for a return to the moral responsibility, economic freedom, and undisputed military superiority it believes is central to the American dream.

Notes

1. Richard Viguerie, *The New Right: We're Ready to Lead* (Falls Church, Virginia, 1980), pp. 19–81; Richard Viguerie, "It's Always Darkest..." *Conservative Digest* 11 (May 1985): 46–47 (hereinafter cited as *CD*).

2. Alan Crawford, *Thunder on the Right: The "New Right" and the Politics of Resentment* (New York, 1980), pp. 198–99.

3. "U.S. Postal Service Statement of Ownership, Management and Circulation," *CD* 10 (November–December 1984): 2.

4. Richard Viguerie, "From the Publisher," *CD* 2 (June 1976): 1.

5. Viguerie, *The New Right*, pp. 19–55.

6. Richard Viguerie, "A Day of Fasting," *CD* 5 (October 1978): 48; Richard Viguerie, "National Day of Prayer and Fasting," *CD* 6 (May–June 1980): 80.

7. Richard Viguerie, "Whither Populists?" *CD* 9 (November 1983): 20.

8. Richard Viguerie, "The Establishment vs. the People: The Power of the Elite," *CD* 9 (November 1983): 7–16; Viguerie, "Whither Populists?" p. 20.

9. Viguerie, "The Establishment vs. the People," p. 8.

10. William F. Gavin, "Street Corner Conservatism," *CD* 2 (January 1976): 47; Howard Phillips, "Power Back to the People, *CD* 2 (February 1976): 10; George Gallup, Jr., "Americans Turning More Conservative," *CD* 11(January 1985): 40.

11. See, for example, "The Best of George Wallace," *CD* 2 (January 1976): 18–19; Patrick J. Buchanan, "Wallace: The Most Influential Outsider," *CD* 2 (August 1976): 24. Congressman Kemp regularly appeared in *CD*'s annual "America's Most Admired Conservative Poll." See, for example, "Kemp Conservatives First Choice If Reagan Doesn't Run," *CD* 9 (April 1983): 48, and "America's Most Admired Conservatives," *CD* 10 (April 1984): 38–40.

12. Viguerie, "The Establishment vs. the People," p. 8.

13. See, for example, Lee Edwards, "TV Sex and Violence: A Clear and Present Danger," *CD* 3 (March 1976): 6–11; "Protecting the American Family," *CD* 5 (December 1979): 31–32; Robert Dugan, Jr., "New Hope for School Prayer," *CD* 6 (May–June 1980): 32; Connaught Marshner, "Pornography as Treason," *CD* 11 (June–July 1985): 34; Lynn Asinof et al., "The Crime War," *CD* 9 (February 1983): 34–44.

14. Michael Novak, "Homosexuality: A Social Rot," *CD* 5 (January 1979): 45.

15. William R. Kennedy, Jr., "A Letter from Our New Publisher," *CD* 11 (October 1985): 128; Judy Flander [interview with Phyllis Schlafly], "ERA Is a Fraud," *CD* 2 (April 1976): 46–47; Joyce Maynard, "My Career as a Mother," *CD* 4 (September 1978): 38; Nick

Thimmesch, "International Year of the Child: Dangerous Tomfoolery," *CD* 5 (May 1979): 26; Joseph Sobran, "Step Aside, Mom and Dad," *CD* 5 (September 1979): 26; Novak, "Homosexuality: A Social Rot," pp. 44–45.

16. Marshner, "Pornography as Treason," p. 34.

17. See the special issue "The Pro-Family Movement: A Special Report," *CD* 6 (May–June 1980).

18. Novak, "Homosexuality: A Social Rot," pp. 44–45; "Anita Bryant's Crusade: Where Next?" *CD* 3 (August 1977): 11–13; Flander, "ERA Is a Fraud," pp. 46–47; Susan Byrne, "Why American Families Aren't Doing Their Job," *CD* 3 (August 1977): 45–46.

19. Sobran, "Step Aside, Mom and Dad," p. 26.

20. "Library Court: The Washington Hub," *CD* 6 (May–June 1980): 26–27.

21. Joseph Sobran, "Why Conservatives Should Care about Abortion," *CD* 7 (November 1981): 14–16.

22. Ray Shamie, "The Ten Contradictions of Liberalism," *CD* 11 (August 1985): 22–23; John C. Goodman, "Welfare Is Breeding Poverty," *CD* 11 (January 1985): 12; Joel W. Skousen et al., "Education's New Dark Age: Can We Achieve a Renaissance?" *CD* 9 (August 1983): 6–11; William J. Lanouette, "The Fourth 'R' Is Religion," *CD* 3 (April 1977): 35–37; Connaught Marshner, "Humanism vs. Secular Humanism," *CD* 11 (April 1985): 24; Richard Viguerie, "None So Blind as Those That Will Not See," *CD* 10 (June 1984): 6–7.

23. Viguerie, "None So Blind as Those That Will Not See," pp. 6–7; Joseph Sobran, "Waving Which Flag?" *CD* 10 (June 1984): 11; Marshner, "Humanism vs. Secular Humanism," p. 24; Ben Stein, "Memo to Norman Lear: Why I Don't Like Liberals," *CD* 2 (December 1976): 40–41; Shamie, "The Ten Contradictions of Liberalism," pp. 22–23.

24. Richard Viguerie, "From the Publisher," p. 1.

25. Richard Viguerie and Lee Edwards, "Goldwater: Leader or Legend?" *CD* 2 (January 1976): 6–10.

26. "January Poll Results," *CD* 2 (February 1976): 21; "Reaction to Goldwater: Leader or Legend?" *CD* 2 (March 1976): 2; "Senator Goldwater Protests...and CD Replies," *CD* 2 (September 1976): 47–49; Richard Viguerie, "No Reason for Friends to Say Goodbye," *CD* 11 (October 1985): 125.

27. Howard Phillips, "The Four-Way Test by Which We Must Judge Mr. Reagan," *CD* 6 (December 1980): 10–11.

28. "Why Conservatives Are Upset with Reagan," *CD* 9 (October 1983): 16; Phil Gailey, "Conservative Study Gives Reagan a Mixed Rating," *CD* 10 (January 1984): 19–20; John Lofton, Jr., "O'Connor Choice Breaks Reagan Promise, Made in Haste and Harms His Coalition," *CD* 7 (August 1981): 3; Howard Phillips, "Reagan Should Decline Reelection in 1984," *CD* 9 (October 1983): 43; "White House Staff Undermines Reagan Policies," *CD* 9 (May 1983): 10–11, 33.

29. Richard Viguerie, "Actions Speak Louder...," *CD* 9 (September 1983): 48, 40; "We Want Action, Mr. President," *CD* 9 (September 1983): 18–20.

30. Roger C. Bradford, "Conservatives Grade Reagan," *CD* 9 (December 1983): 5–12, 40; "Whither, Conservatives? A Survey of Conservative Leaders," *CD* 9 (October 1983): 7–11.

31. Richard Viguerie, "Why I Support President Reagan's Reelection," *CD* 10 (August 1984): 46–47.

32. "CBN's Pat Robertson Looks to 1988, and Beyond," *CD* 11 (August 1985): 4; "The Answer to America's Problems," *CD* 11 (August 1985): 5–6.

33. "Terrorism: Vital Part of Moscow's Foreign Policy," *CD* 10 (February 1984): 6–9; "Mr. President, We Urge...," *CD* 10 (April 1984): 10; Mary-Louise O'Callaghan, "The Many Gulags of Communist China," *CD* 11 (March 1985): 28–29; Gregory A. Fossedal,

"Star Wars: Making Nuclear War Obsolete," *CD* 10 (September 1984): 28; Richard Viguerie, "Don't Let Carter Surrender Our Canal," *CD* 3 (October 1977): 56; Patrick J. Buchanan, "Canal Treaty Is Gutless Giveaway," *CD* 3 (November 1977): 10–11; Richard Viguerie, "A Monroe Doctrine for the 1980's," *CD* 9 (June 1983): 48, 40; Virginia Prewett, "Grenada Move Thwarts Soviet Expansion Bid," *CD* 9 (November 1983): 34–35; "How to Free Nicaragua," *CD* 11 (April 1985): 4–6; "Conservatives Target Schultz for Removal," *CD* 11 (August 1985): 26–27.

34. "Conservatives Oppose New Tax Increase," *CD* 9 (January 1983): 50; Jack Kemp, "Tax Cuts Will Spur Growth," *CD* 9 (March 1983): 14–15; "Freeze All Federal Spending Now," *CD* 11 (January 1985): 5–6; Jim Davidson, "Punch Out the IRS!" *CD* 2 (August 1976): 18–20; "Bureaucratic Blunders," *CD* 2 (September 1976): 26; "The Federal Rathole," *CD* 6 (August 1980): 41–42; Thomas Sowell and Walter Williams, "Affirmative Action Just Hasn't Worked; But Trickle-Down Is Doing Fine," *CD* 7 (October 1981): 18–19; "A Conservative Agenda for All Americans," *CD* 10 (March 1984): 6–7; Mary J. Wilson, "One Woman's Issues: Challenging the New–Old Stereotype," *CD* 10 (March 1984): 14; Richard Viguerie, "Conservative Alternative Beckons Black Families," *CD* 10 (July 1984): 46–47; Goodman, "Welfare Is Breeding Poverty," p. 12; Patrick J. Buchanan, "Does Big Business Deserve Our Support?" *CD* 3 (April 1977): 6–8, 10–11; Richard Viguerie, "Big Business Must Get Back on Track," *CD* 3 (July 1977): 56; "Corporate America Is Fueling the Soviet War Machine," *CD* 9 (October 1983): 19. Other topics examined in special issues or sections include the following: the fight against abortion, *CD* 4 (June 1978); the ERA, *CD* 4 (July 1978); the New Right movement, *CD* 9 (June 1979); education in America, *CD* 9 (August 1983); the federal government's funding of liberal causes, *CD* 9 (April 1983); the connection between liberals and communism, *CD* 10 (June 1984); and an examination of George Bush as an establishment presidential candidate, *CD* 10 (January 1984).

35. David Brooks, "Please Mr. Postman: The Travails of Richard Viguerie," *National Review* 38 (20 June 1986): 30; telephone conversation with Will Hoar, *CD* senior editor, 14 August 1986.

Information Sources

BIBLIOGRAPHY:

Bohannon, Mike, et al. *The New Right in the States: The Groups, the Issues, and the Strategies.* Washington, D.C., 1983.

Crawford, Alan. *Thunder on the Right: The "New Right" and the Politics of Resentment.* New York, 1980.

Kotz, Nick. "King Midas of the New Right." *Atlantic* (November 1978): 52–53, 56–61.

Viguerie, Richard A. *The New Right: We're Ready to Lead.* Falls Church, Virginia, 1980.

INDEXES: None.

REPRINT EDITIONS: Microform: UMI.

LOCATION SOURCES: Widely available.

Publication History

TITLE AND TITLE CHANGES: *Conservative Digest.*

VOLUME AND ISSUE DATA: Volumes 1–current, May 1975–present.

FREQUENCY OF PUBLICATION: Monthly.

PUBLISHERS: 1975–1985: Richard A. Viguerie, The Viguerie Company, Falls Church, Virginia; 1985–present: William R. Kennedy, Jr., Washington, D.C., and Fort Collins, Colorado.

EDITORS: Lee Edwards, May 1975–January 1977; Brien Benson, February 1977–April 1980; John D. Lofton, Jr., July 1980–February 1982; Frank Gannon, March 1982–

July 1983; Mark Tapscott, August–October 1983; Mark Huber, November 1983; John Pucciano, December 1983; Lee Edwards, January 1984–September 1985; Scott Stanley, Jr., October 1985–present.

CIRCULATION

In 1985, about 45,000.

Steven J. Fitch

Human Life Review
1975–

James P. McFadden founded the Human Life Foundation in 1974 and published the first issue of the *Human Life Review* in the following year. Since then, this quarterly has been the cynosure of the antiabortion movement in America, presenting articles on the issue from the point of view of ethics, medicine, jurisprudence, and gender studies, and speculating on the political consequences of legalized abortion. Although at the beginning it claimed an interest in views pro and con, it rapidly developed into a journal of the antiabortion cause, evincing a profound antagonism to defenders of abortion rights. In the later 1970s and 1980s, as the related bioethical questions of euthanasia, test tube fertilization, and surrogate motherhood came to public attention, it broadened its scope to embrace these contiguous "life" issues. Further, it linked the abortion question to the newly publicized question of homosexual rights, claiming that both represented challenges to the basic unit of society, the family. At first, the *Human Life Review* was not strictly a conservative journal. McFadden made a point of including antiabortion articles by men and women who took liberal or radical stands on other public policy questions when he could find them. Nevertheless, almost all the regular contributors were conservatives, and their arguments against abortion were tied to a vision of civilization and a definition of life that had conservative implications.[1]

Roe v. *Wade*, the Supreme Court decision of 1973, marked a flashpoint in the American abortion debate. Before 1973 advocates of abortion had been gaining ground slowly, persuading state legislatures one by one to modify their restrictive antiabortion statutes. No legislature had enacted a statute so permissive in its effects as the judgment that the Court now handed down by a 7–2 majority. It vested in women the freedom to choose abortion during the first trimester of a pregnancy on the grounds that it was an element of their right to privacy. The decision included several stipulations governing second- and third-trimester abortions, but champions and opponents of the decision alike recognized that *Roe* v. *Wade* had gone far toward permitting abortion on demand. From that moment on the incentive to action for prochoice advocates began to diminish; in large measure they had achieved what they desired. At the same time the incentive to action for antiabortion or "prolife" advocates increased enormously; they considered the decision a stark departure from a long American tradition of reverence for and the legal protection of human life.[2]

In 1973 James McFadden, an ideological anticommunist, was working as associate editor of the conservative journal *National Review*, which he had joined in 1956. Aware of the changing legal status of abortion, he had not yet played an active role in opposition to abortion law reform. However, he described 23 January 1973, the day on which he read the text of *Roe* v. *Wade*, as a day of chaotic emotions and anguish—"a day-long road to Damascus," after which he felt that active resistance was imperative. To lobby for a federal law or a constitutional amendment reversing the decision, he founded the Ad Hoc Committee in Defense of Life, which generated publicity and gathered antiabortion campaigners. McFadden launched *Lifeletter*, a news and publicity bulletin for members of the committee and, in 1975, the *Human Life Review*, as a permanent record of the intellectual case against abortion. Already well-versed in direct-mail fund-raising techniques, McFadden financed the venture with contributions from antiabortion supporters; the journal carried no advertising and was not designed to make a profit. Its offices were in the same New York office building as those of *National Review*.

The sober exterior of the *Human Life Review* imitated the format of the scholarly quarterlies, and the bindings were designed to last. McFadden offered bound volumes to the pope, the Library of Congress, presidential libraries, and major foundations; he distributed copies to senators, congressmen, and newspapers, and urged research libraries to subscribe. From the beginning, the journal published a mixture of new and recycled articles. When he found articles germane to the abortion issue in older medical or philosophical journals, McFadden arranged republication rights in the *Human Life Review*. In this way, he was able to preserve articles that passed through the ephemeral media of daily and weekly newspapers and place them in a permanent record. Newspaper columns by antiabortion advocates Michael Novak, Nick Thimmisch, and William Buckley and *Village Voice* articles by Nat Hentoff comprised the appendix of many issues. The text of draft constitutional amendments, transcripts of congressional hearings on the issue, and judicial decisions on bioethical cases also appeared.

Contributors to the *Human Life Review* shared the conviction that legalized abortion was an affront to both American tradition and the nation's commitment to protect basic human rights. For several years each issue carried this declaration:

The Human Life Foundation intends to achieve its goals through educational and charitable means, and welcomes the support of all those who share its beliefs in the sacredness of every human life (however helpless or "unwanted") and are willing to support the God-given rights of the unborn, as well as the aged, the infirm—all the living—whenever and wherever their right to life is challenged in America today....[3]

Contributors believed it was no coincidence that abortion and pornography were proliferating at the same time: they saw each as a perversion of the privacy, dignity, and sanctity that sex had long been accorded in America. Similarly, they believed it no coincidence that these perversions of sex arose simultaneously with the decline of public religion. To their dismay the celebration of "secularization" had moved out of the hands of sociologists and into the hands of theologians themselves, some of whom announced the "death of God" in the mid–1960s. Meanwhile, the Supreme Court had decided that prayers in American public schools violated the First Amendment. Religion and religious values were publicly denigrated, claimed one contributor, so that "a religious conviction is now a second-class conviction."[4]

The case against *Roe* v. *Wade* in the *Human Life Review* began with an assault on the poor legal quality of the decision itself. Contributors believed that *Roe* v. *Wade* represented, as Justice Byron White said in his dissent, an act of "raw judicial power," a violation of precedent and a misuse of the Constitution. The legal aspects of the case were argued by John Noonan, Robert Destro, Basile Uddo and other legal scholars. They showed that the only relevant precedent to *Roe* v. *Wade* was a case decided in the same Supreme Court session, *Eisenstadt* v. *Baird* (1972). In *Eisenstadt,* they said, the Court misapplied the doctrine of a constitutional right to sexual privacy, which had been first enunciated in *Griswold* v. *Connecticut* (1965). In *Griswold* the court granted privacy to married couples deciding in their bedchamber whether to use artificial contraceptives. *Eisenstadt,* by contrast, extended the privacy doctrine to give all women access to contraceptives whether they were married or even of age. *Roe* v. *Wade* then applied this expanded privacy doctrine to the abortion issue. Abortions cannot take place in the privacy of the marital bedchamber, however; they take place in hospitals or clinics, and they involve doctors, nurses, and ancillary medical personnel. The private choice of abortion had extensive public repercussions.[5]

Further, the legal scholars at the *Human Life Review* showed that a succession of cases in the twentieth century had increased the legal protections of the unborn, such that they could inherit property, sue for damages, and be assured lifesaving medical intervention, even against their mothers' objections. These protections were nullified at a stroke if the most basic right, the right to life itself, was denied at the sole discretion of the mother. *Roe* v. *Wade* was this generation's *Dred Scott* case, they said: the justices had taken it on themselves to deny full humanity to a category of people by judicial fiat. Other contributors used the Nazi analogy: that the number of unborn American children killed by abortion was approaching the number of Jews, Slavs, and "inferior peoples" killed in Hitler's extermination programs, with hardly better justification.[6]

Legal scholars published in the *Human Life Review* were aware that the definition of human life and its starting point were controversial issues. John Noonan, a law professor at the University of California, Berkeley, argued that conception is scientifically verifiable as the moment life begins. From that moment on, he said, a new human being is fully genetically encoded and needs no further genetic inputs to grow to adulthood. He rejected the prochoice advocates' contention that the beginning of life is a subjective question best left to each individual; the moment of conception, he said, marks a point of "objective discontinuity" between mere biological tissue on the one hand and a distinct life on the other. He also denied that this was a religious conclusion. Noonan and the antiabortion lawyers knew that prochoice advocates were eager to discredit the prolife position as no more than an extension of Catholic tradition that, if enacted at law, would violate the First Amendment.

Although they made coherent scientific and legal arguments, most of the contributors to the *Human Life Review* were in fact religious, many sharing McFadden's own Catholic faith, but with Jews and Protestants also well represented.[7] Catholics had a more fully developed tradition of teaching on questions of sex as an aspect of the natural law than other religious groups in America. These questions had been under scrutiny in American Catholic circles since 1960. In the era of the Second Vatican Council (1962–1965) many American Catholics had anticipated a new papal teaching on the use of contraceptives, but in the encyclical letter *Humanae Vitae* (1968) Pope Paul VI upheld the traditional teaching by reiterating that each act of sexual intercourse must be open to the transmission of life. Catholic columnist Michael Novak had dissented from *Humanae Vitae,* but he shared the sacramental view of sex, as he explained in an article for the *Human Life Review*, where he wrote: "The human body is a dwelling place of God, and the joining of a man's and a woman's body in matrimony is a privileged form of union with God. The relationship is not merely that of a mechanical linking putting genitals here or there. It is a metaphor for (and an enactment of) God's union with mankind. Marital intercourse thus re-enacts the basic act of creation. It celebrates the future."[8] The reproductive purpose of sex and the familial, sacramental context insisted on in Catholic thought placed the Catholic contributors to the *Human Life Review* at odds with the view of sexuality that had gained prominence in America in recent decades. The trend of the sexual revolution of the 1950s, 1960s, and 1970s had been to regard reproduction as just one of the many purposes of sexuality, possibly even subordinate to self-expression.

One prominent line of argumentation in the *Human Life Review* linked the defense of the unborn in America with the global political issue of confronting communism. In this line of reasoning, preserving the family was itself a contribution to American resistance against totalitarian ideologies. The sexual revolution, it was argued, should be understood as an assault on the family. It placed increasing emphasis on the individual and denigrated the intermediate institutions—primarily the family—that in earlier times had acted as buffers between the isolated individual and the state. Totalitarian governments flourish by isolating the individual in just this fashion, and subordinating him to the needs of an all-powerful state. By bringing questions of human fertility under the regulation of the state and permitting the termination of new lives, said prolife conservatives, the door was opened to increasing state control of human life. Those who campaigned now for the choice of voluntary abortions would find later that they had become subject to compulsory family restriction of the kind now practiced in communist China.[9]

Joseph Sobran was the most regular contributor to the *Human Life Review*. Sobran was a senior editor of *National Review* with a well-developed pattern of opinions on questions of sex and abortion. He argued from natural law premises not only against abortion but also against extramarital sex and homosexuality, and he deplored the lack of a principled resistance to the gay rights movement of the 1970s and 1980s. On this issue Sobran detected what seemed to him a dangerous shift in the meaning of the word *sex* itself. As he put it: "The use of the word 'sex' to refer to an activity rather than to a gender is, I believe, fairly novel. It is even used to refer to genital activities between members of the same gender. This implies the conception of such activities as ends in themselves, with procreation a mere possible by-product."[10] For Sobran it would be wiser and more humane to attempt to "cure" homosexuals than to accept the claim of the gay rights movement that homosexuality was a dignified alternative way of life. He believed it would be "a victory of humanity" to persuade homosexuals that "they need not pretend that their vice is a virtue in order to belong to the moral community." He even made the vertiginous claim: "Homosexuals should be encouraged to realize that homosexuality is unworthy of them. "[11]

Sobran regarded abortion, expressive sex, and homosexuality as parts of a continuum and saw them as connected parts of a liberal-radical program that would have baleful political consequences. Rhetorically he turned the tables on prochoice advocates who routinely accused prolifers of hypocrisy and bad faith by depicting them as a selfish class seeking to protect and extend its privileges. They were, said Sobran, highly educated, politically liberal, viscerally anti-Catholic, sexually promiscuous, and predominantly male, eager to enjoy sex without taking the consequences and contemptuous of religious or family values. Moreover, they were members of the "new class" and the "knowledge industry" that invariably advocated an enlargement of the bureaucratic functions of the state from which they stood to gain. Sobran encouraged prolifers to isolate their antagonists and relativize their views by constructing a sociology of "abortionism"; as he wrote:

The surest way to defeat the pro-abortion movement requires nothing in the way of vilification; in fact abuse would be self-defeating. What *is* effective is to *place* the opposition, to *localize* it, to point out that its own slogans are not emanations of pure reason but rather proceed from a specific, and in its own way provincial set of presuppositions which are themselves controversial....Abortionism then [can be seen as] part of an integral world-view that sees man as an animal; an animal whose destiny is a life of pleasure and comfort.[12]

Conservative women were as well represented in the pages of the *Human Life Review* as conservative men. Clare Boothe Luce, a Catholic convert and widow of the *Time/Life* magnate, Henry Luce, wrote frequent articles on the dignity of motherhood as the highest natural function of a woman. Appealing to the natural law she wrote: "Nature made man to be the inseminator, woman to be the child-bearer....It is natural—and normal—for the woman who conceives to carry her child in her womb to term, to give birth to her and her mate's baby....It is not the nature of women to abort their progeny....Induced abortions are against the nature of woman."[13] Other women agreed that feminism, whatever its virtues, had taken a wrong turn when it advocated a denial rather than the fulfillment of woman's progenitive power. Janet Smith, a Canadian graduate student, wrote that "behind women's demands for unlimited access to abortion lies a profound displeasure with the way in which a woman's body works, and hence a rejection of the value of being a woman."[14] (This and similar claims have not gone uncontested. Prochoice feminists have shown that many women who themselves have children advocate the right to choose abortion under certain circumstances and do not regard themselves as "anti-family.")[15]

The most dedicated female contributor to the *Human Life Review* was Ellen Wilson, whom McFadden discovered in 1976 when she was a college senior at Bryn Mawr. In the late 1970s and early 1980s Wilson carved out a successful career in journalism, becoming books editor at the *Wall Street Journal* by the age of thirty and writing twelve substantial antiabortion articles for the *Human Life Review*. At that point, however, she resigned from her job in order to marry and devote herself to the care and nurture of her children, intending to live out the role of Christian mother she had eulogized in the preceding years. Like Clare Luce, Wilson had no objection to feminism if it signified unprejudiced access to employment and equal pay for equal work, but she was a strenuous opponent of feminist theoreticians who regarded men and women as antagonists rather than as mutually complementary, and she polemicized hard against radical lesbianism. She linked advocacy of homosexuality to political radicalism, and warned that the gay rights movement would promote revolution as it denigrated the family. As she wrote:

Since homosexual unions are barren in the literal sense they are antithetical to family life. Thus militant homosexuals are spared the strong, sentimental attachment toward the family that poses a hurdle of greater or lesser proportions to many social revolutionaries. In other words, homosexuals who campaign for universal acknowledgment of their normality are likely to be social revolutionaries in all areas, since their definition of normality dethrones the family from its sovereign position as the foundation of society.[16]

Ellen Wilson, Joseph Sobran, and a second tier of frequent contributors to the *Human Life Review* (including James Hitchcock, Francis Canavan, and Tina Bell) gave the journal its distinctive character. Their original work was printed alongside the reprinted material that formed the bulk of every issue of the journal. The diversity of sources for this material, including medical journals, law reviews, the *Congressional Record,* and the popular press, led to an unevenness of tone and quality and served to remind readers that the journal was as much a clearing-house of the antiabortion movement as an organically conceived journalistic venture in its own right.

Bioethical issues drew wide media attention in the early and mid–1980s and the *Human Life Review* followed them closely. Since its early days as an antiabortion journal, it had made excursions into the adjacent regions of feminism and homosexuality, frequently for purposes of denunciation. Now it carried articles on acquired immune deficiency syndrome (AIDS), test tube fertilization, surrogate motherhood, and euthanasia—all "life" issues. It won support from an unexpected quarter in 1987 when Ben Wattenberg, a coeditor of *Public Opinion* magazine and fellow of the American Enterprise Institute, published *The Birth Dearth (1987)*. Wattenberg argued that American prosperity and defensibility were jeopardized not by a "population explosion," the great fear of the 1960s, but by a dangerously *low* birthrate. Fears of a population explosion had enabled advocates of abortion law reform in the 1960s to present abortion as ethically benign, and a statistically rigorous contradiction of this claim hurt their cause. Ironically, Wattenberg himself was not opposed to legalized abortion. McFadden nevertheless published a section of *The Birth Dearth* in the *Human Life Review* for fall of 1987, sandwiching it between articles that drew explicit connections between the prevalence of abortion and the forthcoming manpower deficit.[17]

As fertility rates fell in the 1980s and appreciable numbers of women delayed childbearing, sometimes for too long, a trade in children carried by surrogate mothers began. In 1986 and 1987 the "Baby M" case occasioned a dispute over its ethics. A surrogate mother, Mary Beth Whitehead, brought to birth a baby girl whose biological father, William Stern, had contracted with her to act as a "host" because his own wife could not carry a child. After the birth, Whitehead changed her mind and attempted to keep and raise the baby. A New Jersey judge found against her and upheld the contract, provoking press sensations and heated recriminations on both sides. Richard Kruse, a political scientist writing in the *Human Life Review*, supported Whitehead's right to change her mind, since the labor of bringing a new life into being was hers. Like the mother of a baby intended for adoption but ultimately kept by the mother, he said, Baby M was presumptively her biological mother's own, whatever the contractual stipulations to the contrary. He extended the journal's criticism of life manipulation to cover this new phenomenon. Surrogacy, said Kruse, was a technique that tempted the affluent to exploit the needy, and it came perilously close to the selling of children, forbidden by the Thirteenth Amendment. After condemning what seemed to him the insensitive rulings made by the judge in this case, Kruse concluded:

The real issue...lies beyond all legal theories and legislative considerations; it is the commercialization of our basic humanity. The decision to have and raise a child is a costly and uneconomic undertaking that violates the self-centered notions of today's narcissistic society.... The fundamental issue in the Baby M case is, therefore, the nature of our humanity, our essence as human beings. Contracts and commercialism should never enter into this area. To allow that would diminish the humanity of us all.

This was a characteristic statement of the *Human Life Review*'s outlook. The journal's conservative character was nowhere more apparent than in its efforts to sustain the family as the central institution of American society and to emphasize the familial reproductive character of sex. This emphasis on the family occluded such matters as sanctity of contract when a human life was the subject of the contract; the conservatism of the *Human Life Review* was a matter of tradition, religion, and the natural law rather than of capitalism.[18]

By 1985, when it celebrated its tenth anniversary, the *Human Life Review* could claim a distinguished list of contemporary conservative contributors. President Reagan, his surgeon general, Everett Koop, his Supreme Court nominee Robert Bork, and authors Aleksandr Solzhenitsyn, Walker Percy, and Malcolm Muggeridge had all appeared in its pages. McFadden reported that he was buoyed by the refusal of antiabortion forces to let the issue become an uncontested fait accompli, but saddened by both the acceleration of technological threats to human life and the inability of an ostentatiously conservative Reagan government to make progress against the epidemic of abortion in America.[19]

Notes

1. Information about McFadden throughout is based on a personal interview with the author, New York City, 12 October 1987. Nat Hentoff was the most frequent nonconservative contributor to the *Human Life Review*. See, for example, Nat Hentoff, "Death Row for Infants," *Human Life Review* (hereinafter cited as *HLR*) 13 (Fall 1987): 89–90; "The Pied Piper Returns for the Old Folks," *HLR* 14 (Summer 1988): 108–16.

2. Marion Faux, *Roe v Wade: The Untold Story of the Landmark Supreme Court Decision That Made Abortion Legal* (New York, 1988).

3. Inside back cover of early issues, as for example *HLR* 1 (Winter 1975).

4. On pornography, see, for example, Joseph Sobran, "Nothing to Look At: Perversity and Public Amusements," *HLR* 3 (Summer 1977): 81–88. On secularization see Joseph Sobran "The Established Irreligion," *HLR* 4 (Summer 1978): 52–64.

5. Among the legal analyses of *Roe* v. *Wade* printed in *HLR* are the following: John T. Noonan, Jr., "Why a Constitutional Amendment?" *HLR* 1 (Winter 1975): 26–43; "Abortion in the American Context," *HLR* 3 (Winter 1977): 29–38; "A Half Step Forward: The Justices Retreat on Abortion," *HLR* 3 (Fall 1977): 11–18; Robert Destro, "Abortion and the Constitution: The Need for a Life-Protective Amendment," *HLR* 2 (Fall 1976): 30–108; "Some Fresh Perspectives on the Abortion Controversy," *HLR* 4 (Spring 1978): 22–32; "Social Values and the Federal Judiciary: The Least Dangerous Branch Unleashed," *HLR* 6 (Spring 1980): 37–48; Robert Destro with William Moeller, "The Case of Phillip Becker," *HLR* 6 (Fall 1980): 81–98; Basile Uddo, "When Judges Wink Congress Must Not Blink," *HLR* 5 (Summer 1979): 42–60. John T. Noonan also authored *A Private Choice: Abortion in America in the Seventies* (New York, 1979).

6. On the Nazi analogy see John Wauck, "On Not Doing Enough," *HLR* 14 (Spring 1988): 100–104.

7. See, for example, Don Feder "Abortion and the Survival of the Jewish People," *HLR* 13 (Fall 1987): 96–97; Richard Neuhaus, "The Return of Eugenics," *HLR* 14 (Summer 1988): 81–107.

8. Michael Novak, "Men Without Women," *HLR* 5 (Winter 1979): 64.

9. On abortion and infanticide in China see Stephen Mosher, "Female Infanticide in China," *HLR* 14 (Spring 1988): 110–12.

10. Joseph Sobran, "In Loco Parentis," *HLR* 5 (Fall 1979): 14.

11. Joseph Sobran, "Bogus Sex: Reflections on Homosexual Claims," *HLR* 3 (Fall 1977): 105.

12. Joseph Sobran, "Abortion Rhetoric and Cultural War," *HLR* 1 (Winter 1975): 82–98; "The Abortion Sect," *HLR* 1 (Fall 1975): 101–109 (quotation); "The Abortion Ethos," *HLR* 3 (Winter 1977): 12–22.

13. Clare Boothe Luce, "A Letter to the *Women's Lobby*," *HLR* 4 (Spring 1978): 7.

14. Janet Smith "Abortion as a Feminist Concern," *HLR* 4 (Summer 1978): 64.

15. See, for example, Kristin Luker, *Abortion and the Politics of Motherhood* (Berkeley, 1984).

16. Ellen Wilson "Young and Gay in Academe," *HLR* 3 (Fall 1977): 95.

17. Ben J. Wattenberg, "What Dangers Ahead?" *HLR* 13 (Fall 1987): 71–74; Frank Zepezauer, "The Manpower Crisis," ibid., pp. 61–70; Robert de Marcellus, "Fertility and National Power," ibid. pp. 98–112.

18. Richard A. Kruse, "The Strange Case of 'Baby M'," *HLR* 13 (Fall 1987): 27–34.

19. James McFadden, "Introduction," *HLR* 11 (Winter–Spring 1985): 2–8.

Information Sources

BIBLIOGRAPHY: None.

INDEXES: Each volume indexed; *PAIS*.

REPRINT EDITIONS: Microform: UMI; BLH.

LOCATION SOURCES: Widely available.

Publication History

TITLE AND TITLE CHANGES: *The Human Life Review*.

VOLUME AND ISSUE DATA: Volumes 1–current, 1975–present.

FREQUENCY OF PUBLICATION: Quarterly.

PUBLISHER: Edward A. Capano: The Human Life Foundation, New York.

EDITOR: James P. McFadden.

CIRCULATION : In 1988, 9,700 paid subscribers. About 35,000 copies of each edition are printed. Copies are hand-distributed to every U.S. senator and congressman, state governors, all newspapers having bureaus in Washington, D.C., the Vatican, and other influential persons and institutions.

Patrick Allitt

Policy Review
1977–

The Heritage Foundation was established in 1974 in Washington, D.C., in order to promote conservative policy analysis that would directly influence the development of public policy in American national government. It began to publish a wide variety of material on specific issues, ranging from brief issue bulletins and backgrounders to longer monographs. In 1977, a new foundation president, Edwin J. Feulner, Jr., initiated a period of expansion that would develop the Heritage Foundation into a major conservative research institute. He moved quickly to start a new project, a quarterly journal of conservative articles on public policy questions. He sought a new outlet for publicizing conservative opinions and also a publication that would attract attention to the foundation and help establish it as a leading conservative institution. *Policy Review* would provide a serious and respectable platform for conservative academics and journalists to address important issues of both domestic and foreign policy. It would educate conservatives with the best of conservative thought and research and, it was hoped, reach and influence nonconservatives as well. Attempting to function as both a journal of serious policy analysis to which scholars should pay attention and a political forum for conservative thinking designed to influence public policy, *Policy Review* requires a collaborative effort of conservative scholars, journalists, and political activists.[1]

The conservatism of the Heritage Foundation and *Policy Review* is essentially conservatism as it has been understood by the right wing of the Republican party in the 1970s and 1980s. The foundation has strong ties to many conservative political leaders. Most of the people associated with *Policy Review* see themselves as staunch Reaganites who seek to hold elected officials to the principles and worldview he proclaimed during his long leadership of the conservative wing of the Republican party.

In the realm of domestic affairs *Policy Review* presents a conservatism that distrusts the power and expanding functions of the national government and endorses the free market as the key to a healthy society and economy. National government power, and especially power in the hands of bureaucrats, is understood to be dangerous to individual liberty and as fundamentally undemocratic because of its distance from the public. This conservatism also sees government, in general, and the national government, in particular, as incapable of achieving the extensive goals set for it by liberals during the past fifty years. The government does not know how to abolish poverty and regulate the economy to ensure prosperity and full employment without inflation; the free market produces better results with minimal regulation.

Policy Review articles criticize government regulation and policies and programs across the full spectrum of government activities. Various authors have opposed affirmative action, Internal Revenue Service regulations affecting private schools, welfare policy, government subsidies for the arts, and government regulation of business. *Policy Review* has presented many defenses of the free market and of entrepreneurs, written by various types of authors including businessmen, journalists, public officials, and economists. The anti–big government theme also appears in a section of the journal called "Tales from the Public Sector," which collects examples of government bungling from around the world. No single version of conservative economic theory dominates *Policy Review*; it has published some monetarists, notably Nobel laureate economist Milton Friedman, and some supply-siders, notably Paul Craig Roberts, a journalist from the *Wall Street Journal* who became assistant secretary of treasury for tax policy in the Reagan administration.

The domestic policy articles in *Policy Review* reflect many of the varied streams of contemporary conservative thought. A few libertarian authors argue for shrinking government back to a few basic activities. On the other hand, some New Right social conservatives advocate a more active government in promoting morality, as with antiabortion laws and censorship of pornography. Still, *Policy Review* concentrates on economic rather than social issues, and the central principle of its domestic conservatism is the need to restrict the growth of government.

The foreign policy stance of *Policy Review* can most simply be termed hard-line anticommunism. Most of its authors during the 1970s saw foreign affairs in terms of a worldwide conflict between a dangerously powerful and aggressive Soviet Union and an unfortunately passive United States. A brief introductory statement of purpose refers to the "failure of the Policy of détente" and the need to develop what is now lacking: "a strategy to defend the interests of the United States and its friends."[2] This conservatism stressed the ideological nature of the Soviet-American clash. It scorned governments and political leaders who favored détente, neutralism, or an emphasis on issues other than the worldwide conflict between East and West. On the whole, *Policy Review* represents the type of conservative foreign policy views that produced extensive criticism from the Right of former Secretary of State Henry Kissinger during the Nixon and Ford administrations.

Criticism of the SALT II Treaty and the liberal arms control policy in general stand out as the most common topic of foreign affairs articles in *Policy Review* during the 1970s. Articles frequently developed the theme of Soviet strategic superiority to the United States and urged skepticism of the trustworthiness of Soviet treaty commitments. After American-Soviet relationships, articles praising Great Britain's Conservative Prime Minister Margaret Thatcher and her policies appeared most often. A rare article on Latin America criticized Carter administration policies and attacked the junta in El Salvador for its reforms and for the alienation of conservative sectors in that country.[3]

The first issue of *Policy Review*, which appeared in the summer of 1977, provides a representative reflection of its character. The authors included distinguished academics such as psychoanalyst Ernest van den Haag and economist Peter Bauer, noted journalist Robert Moss, the editor of the *Economist*'s confidential newsletter "Foreign Report," and politician-scholar Senator Daniel Patrick Moynihan (D, New York). The topics ranged from condemnations of Western tolerance for Eurocommunism and the proposed new economic order to benefit the Third World, to a criticism of leniency in the sentencing of criminals. Although such broad issues predominated, one article focused on the narrow and specific issue of giving visas to Soviet trade union officials. All of the topics appeared regularly in the news at the time and were of concern to public officials in Washington, but the articles on visas, criticizing treatment of Soviet unions as true trade unions, seems most designed to influence a specific decision.[4] Most of these articles were written for *Policy Review*, but one was reprinted from the *University of Miami Law Review*, and van den Haag's was a revision of testimony he had given a Senate committee.

The editor of *Policy Review*, Robert L. Scheuttinger, contributed "The New Foreign Policy Network" for the first issue, which stood out from the other articles in focusing on the process of policymaking rather than on a substantive issue, but it reflected the character of the journal very well in its balance of scholarly tone and political interest. It presented essentially an objective analysis of how a group of young liberals with personal ties to each other had obtained a large measure of power over foreign policymaking inside the Carter administration. Scheuttinger rejected conspiracy theories advanced by the far Right and cited a wide variety of sources, including liberal journals such as the *New Republic* and *Foreign Policy*, to substantiate his thesis that this network existed and had a significant impact on the course of American foreign policy. Although his analysis was academic, he obviously chose the topic for its political importance, and in a few places he made clear that he regarded the influence of these young liberals as detrimental to American foreign policy, especially in their conciliatory attitudes toward the Soviet Union and toward radicals in the Third World.

The early issues of *Policy Review* typically contained from seven to ten articles spread over approximately 100 pages and, in addition, 10 to 20 pages of book reviews. In its third year the journal began to expand until it reached a norm of 196 pages by 1982. Then, in the summer of 1983, it shifted to a new format, abandoning the 6-by-9-inch journal appearance for an 8 1/2-by-11-inch magazine size. The quantity of writing remained constant as a shrinkage in length to about 100 pages balanced off the increased page size. The typical *Policy Review* of the 1980s devoted about 75 percent of its pages to about eleven or twelve articles and the rest to specialized sections. Most articles ranged from 10 to 15 pages under the old format, fewer than 10 under the new, but editors regularly publish short notes of only 3 pages and a few articles even longer than 30 pages. A few pages of letters to the editor and the book reviews are the other major sections of the magazine. Book review essays of 3 to 6 pages often discuss two or three books on a single topic, but Raymond Aron's review of Henry Kissinger's *White House Years* occupied 14 pages.[5] Some issues include a section of brief notes on a much longer list of new articles and books of interest to conservatives.

Although *Policy Review* publishes some articles with a lighter tone, especially in the "Tales from the Public Sector" section, and an occasional statement of general principles having the ring of campaign oratory, the typical article is best characterized by the phrase "scholarly advocacy." Most articles present a clear point of view on behalf of a policy that the author advocates. Authors support their positions with clear, logical arguments and with evidence, data, and facts often compiled from apparently extensive research. They routinely cite studies by other scholars and by government agencies. Despite the journal's interest in reporting results of new research, the bulk of most articles does not consist of a simple presentation of facts but of logical analysis of a situation and the development of an often complex argument in support of a specific policy. Although most articles support policies or theories widely advocated by most leading conservative politicians, the editors are open to new arguments and new evidence that support conservative conclusions; new policy proposals that seem compatible with conservative principles also attract their interest.

Articles rarely consist only of a criticism of liberal policy or the advocacy of a conservative policy or principle. For example, in the "Politics of Cancer," Elizabeth Whelan argued that clear scientific evidence existed for linking cigarette smoking and dietary excesses to cancer, presumably justifying some governmental concern, but she proceeded to undermine an important argument for environmental regulations by arguing that no clear evidence existed to prove that environmental factors caused cancer.[6] In two separate articles in one issue, both Peter Bauer and Nathan Glazer went beyond a defense of the free market to explain the dominance of market critics in American intellectual circles.[7]

Policy Review takes great pleasure in taking on the latest liberal causes and in criticizing the theories and policies of which liberals are most proud and confident. When the news media present an issue in terms that make the liberal position appear the obviously humane one, *Policy Review* regularly offers a conservative alternative. Numerous criticisms of the environmental movement follow this pattern. Another excellent example was a defense of the strongly criticized Reagan administration position on the issue of businesses promoting the use of infant formula in the Third World. Carol Adelman presented a detailed criticism of the widely publicized arguments in favor of the position of the World Health Organization, which the United States alone opposed.[8]

Prominent conservative academics predominate on the editorial board of *Policy Review*, and professional scholars based at universities or leading conservative research institutes write a majority of its articles. The academic authors and board members represent many disciplines, with political scientists (especially foreign policy specialists) quite common and economists most common of all. The editorial board of fourteen members includes Gordon Tullock, a distinguished economist and director of the Center for Public Choice at Virginia Polytechnic Institute, Ernest van den Haag, and until his death in 1983, Herman Kahn, the director of the Hudson Institute. Many of the members of the board play little active role, but almost all of them have written at least once for the journal, and some regularly suggest authors and topics and provide feedback on the quality and character of specific issues of *Policy Review*. Van den Haag ranked as its most frequent contributor, writing on topics ranging from foreign policy to government subsidies for the arts.

Many of the scholars involved in *Policy Review* also take an active role in politics as advisers or in government jobs. Scheuttinger, the first editor, is a professional political scientist who worked as a foreign policy aide for the House of Representatives before becoming director of studies at the Heritage Foundation. Board member and frequent contributor Ernest W. Lefever, who became involved in a major controversy as President Reagan's first nominee for the post of assistant secretary of state for human rights, is also a political scientist. A number of the economists on the editorial board have combined academic careers with government posts. Former ambassador Robert Strausz-Hupé, Martin Anderson, of the Nixon and Reagan White Houses and the Hoover Institution, and Kenneth L. Adelman, Reagan's director of the Arms Control and Disarmament Agency, are among other academic authors who have been active political figures.

Policy Review's attempt to gain the attention of the public and of policymakers, as well as of professional policy analysts, had led to its publishing articles by political activists and public officials who lack scholarly qualifications. Nine U.S. senators have appeared as contributors, along with former treasury secretary William E. Simon, who also serves on the board of the Heritage Foundation. A few businessmen, including the chairman of the board of Amway, and some European political leaders, such as Franz Josef Strauss and Otto von Habsburg, have appeared in the review's pages. A significant number of congressional staffers, some with graduate training, have found *Policy Review* a good outlet for their ideas and research. Still, despite the attractiveness of headlining a senator on the cover of the journal, it has usually avoided the conventional political statements of leading conservative politicians, publishing them only when their articles have substantive merit and originality. For example, an article by Phyllis Schlafly that clearly departed from her typical public rhetoric and the polemical character of her newspaper columns provided a scholarly review of dozens of court cases in states with differing types of equal rights amendments. She approved of some types, but she found that state court decisions based on the wording of the national equal rights amendment were adverse to the interests and desires of traditional women.[9]

Journalists and a variety of other writers also find a home at *Policy Review*. The editorial board includes the British journalist and author Robert Moss, British novelist Kingsley Amis, and George Gilder, the writer and political activist. Most issues include at least one article by a journalist, generally following the pattern of combining logical analysis of a problem with advocacy of a specific policy. In the summer of 1979, John O'Sullivan, a former reporter, columnist, and editorial writer for London's *Daily Telegraph*, took over from Scheuttinger as the editor of *Policy Review*. O'Sullivan, in turn, was succeeded for the first issue of 1984 by Adam Meyerson, a journalist from the *Wall Street Journal* and the *American Spectator*. The shift to journalists gradually brought about efforts to increase the appeal of *Policy Review* to nonacademic audiences. O'Sullivan wrote that his goal was to combine "the solid research of a journal with the crisp writing of a magazine."[10] He introduced the magazine format in 1983. Meyerson furthered this trend in 1984 with new 2- or 3-page sections entitled "Left Watch" and "Department of Disinformation." Also new was a series of symposiums that featured brief interviews with about a dozen leading conservatives, political activists as well as intellectuals, on "What Conservatives Think of Ronald Reagan" and "Sex and God in American Politics." All these changes sought to broaden the appeal of *Policy Review* to politically active conservatives.

Although essentially an American publication aimed at influencing the American national government, *Policy Review* has long had strong British ties. The editorial board has always included some British representation, and British authors often appear in its pages. The original editor studied and taught in Great Britain, and O'Sullivan, his successor, was a British citizen. In the journal's coverage of the domestic politics of foreign nations (articles grouped, since 1980, in a regular section called "Over There"), Great Britain appears more often than any other nation. This reflects both the special interest of many American conservatives in the government of Prime Minister Thatcher and the unusually strong ties of *Policy Review* with Great Britain.

The vast majority of *Policy Review* authors clearly holds staunchly conservative political positions, but a handful of liberals has appeared in its pages. The senatorial contributors serve as a representative sample. Republicans William L. Armstrong (Colorado), Pete Domenici (New Mexico), Jake Garn (Utah), S. I. Hayakawa (California), and James A. McClure (Idaho), all rank among the most conservative members of the Senate. However, the other Senate contributors have been Democrats Edward M. Kennedy (Massachusetts) and Daniel Patrick Moynihan. Kennedy's appearance is explained easily; his comments were part of a debate with Goldwater over relations with Taiwan. Kennedy took the conventional liberal position in favor of establishing American relations with China; Goldwater's views were typical of the many conservatives who have long supported staunchly anticommunist Taiwan.[11] Moynihan has a moderately liberal voting record, but his neoconservative writings appeal to many conservatives. His three articles in *Policy Review* featured arguments that most conservatives would support, though perhaps he meant to separate himself from people involved with the Heritage Foundation when he referred, in his first piece, to "those of us who have not altogether despaired of the wisdom of government."[12] *Policy Review* generally reflects an older conservative tradition of opposition to big government, but it has included other neoconservatives, such as Midge Decter, Nathan Glazer, and Michael Novak, among its contributors and its most recent editor, Meyerson, has neoconservative leanings.

With rare exceptions, *Policy Review* opens its pages to liberal authors only when they present arguments with appeal to conservatives. Eugene V. Rostow is an active Democrat who held high office in the Johnson administration, but his foreign policy stance, as reflected in an article opposing the SALT II Treaty,[13] has since led him to a two-year stint as director of the Arms Control and Disarmament Agency in the Reagan administration. Most conservatives fully agree with the criticism of the press Max M. Kampelman, a long-time adviser to Hubert Humphrey, wrote for *Policy Review*.[14] Similarly, President Carter's chairman of the Civil Aeronautics Board, Alfred E. Kahn, contributed an article endorsing airline deregulation that mirrored the free-market perspective dominant among American conservatives.[15] One of the rare examples of a fully liberal article was a review by economist Robert Lekachman of a book by *Policy Review*'s editor Scheuttinger. Lekachman concluded his criticism of this conservative analysis of economic controls with a commentary on the anomaly of a liberal writing for *Policy Review*: "I have enjoyed this foray into hostile terrain. In this period of general reconsideration by many economists, it helps to carry on the discussion in the civilized tones of *Policy Review*."[16]

A few foreign policy articles have advanced arguments not typically held by conservatives. For example, the president of the Chamber of Commerce of Latin America in the United States, Milan B. Skacel, broadly criticized Carter administration Latin American policy from a conservative perspective, but he expressed support for the Panama Canal Treaty that most American conservatives vehemently opposed.[17] In another case, *Policy Review* published an article by David Carlton, a British diplomatic historian and Labor party candidate for Parliament, which argued that the United States should essentially ignore the Soviet Union's invasion of Afghanistan. Carlton asserted the need for hardheaded realism in foreign policy and suggested that the weakness of the United States required détente. This thesis, which might best be termed a conservative argument for détente, was presented under the heading "Against the Grain."[18]

It is always a difficult task to assess the impact of a political journal. There are no clear examples of decisions *Policy Review* has shaped. Its rise to influence has certainly paralleled, perhaps preceding somewhat, a rise to political power by conservatives and a clear shift toward conservatism in academic and intellectual circles. *Policy Review* may have helped to promote these conservative advances, but it is also undoubtedly the beneficiary of them. In just six years this journal grew to a circulation of 18,000 with over 10,500 subscriptions and 4,000 complimentary copies routinely distributed, mostly in the Washington political community.[19] The Heritage Foundation proudly points to the press notice gained by many of its articles, including many op-ed page columns based on these articles, and to enthusiastic praise from conservatives in Congress and the Reagan administration.[20] Feulner wrote in 1983: "As a think tank president, I am concerned with influencing the policy makers, and most of them have assured me that *Policy Review* is effective in this regard."[21] *Policy Review* has become an important vehicle for communicating ideas in the conservative political community in the United States and a major platform for conservative scholars and others seeking to advance various conservative policy proposals and to shift public policy debate to the right.

Notes

1. Interview with John O'Sullivan, editor of *Policy Review*, July 1982, at the Heritage Foundation, Washington, D.C. The interview covered in detail the history and goals of the journal.

2. Edwin J. Feulner, Jr., David I. Meiselman, and Robert L. Scheuttinger, "Introducing *Policy Review*," *Policy Review* 1 (Summer 1977): 5 (hereinafter cited as *PR*).

3. James A. Whelan, "Under Here?" *PR* 13 (Summer 1980): 51–64.

4. Stephen Haseler, "Visas for Soviet 'Trade Unionists'?" *PR* 1 (Summer 1977): 81–87.

5. Raymond Aron, "Kissinger, Vietnam, and Cambodia," *PR* 13 (Summer 1980): 151–65.

6. Elizabeth Whelan, "The Politics of Cancer," *PR* 10 (Fall 1979): 33–46.

7. Peter Bauer, "The Market in the Dock," *PR* 10 (Fall 1979): 101–21; Nathan Glazer, "A Comment on 'The Market in the Dock'," *PR* 10 (Fall 1979): 123–29.

8. Carol Adelman, "Infant Formula, Science, and Politics," *PR* 23 (Winter 1983): 107–26.

9. Phyllis Schlafly,"The Effect of Equal Rights Amendments in State Constitutions," *PR* 9 (Summer 1979): 55–84.

10. John O'Sullivan, "From the Editor," *PR* 25 (Summer 1983): 5.

11. Barry M. Goldwater, "Treaty Termination Is a Shared Power," *PR* 8 (Spring 1979): 115–24; Edward M. Kennedy, "Normal Relations with China: Good Law, Good Policy," *PR* 8 (Spring 1979): 125–32.

12. Daniel Patrick Moynihan, "The Most Important Decision-Making Process," *PR* 1 (Summer 1977): 92.

13. Eugene V. Rostow, "SALT II—A Soft Bargain, A Hard Sell: An Assessment of SALT in Historical Perspective," *PR* 6 (Fall 1978): 41–56.

14. Max M. Kampelman, "The Power of the Press: A Problem for Our Democracy," *PR* 6 (Fall 1978): 7–39.

15. Alfred E. Kahn, "Airline Deregulation: Getting from Here to There," *PR* 3 (Winter 1978): 55– 60.

16. Robert Lekachman, "Can Controls Work? A Dissenting View," *PR* 9 (Summer 1979): 151.

17. Milan B. Skacel, "Wanted: A U.S. Policy for Latin America," *PR* 8 (Spring 1979): 85–95.

18. David Carlton, "In Defense of Appeasement," *PR* 13 (Summer 1980): 134–50.

19. Interview with John O'Sullivan, July 1982.

20. Ibid.

21. Edwin J. Feulner, Jr., "From the Publisher," *PR* 25 (Summer 1983): 4.

Information Sources

BIBLIOGRAPHY: None.
INDEXES: Numbers 1–8 indexed; *AHCI*; *Bio Ind*; *BRI*; *Curr Cont: BSMS*; *PAIS*; *Pol Sci Abst*; *SSCI*; *Soc Sci Ind*; *Soc Abst*; *Urb Aff Abst*.
REPRINT EDITIONS: Microform: UMI.
LOCATION SOURCES: Widely available.

Publication History

TITLE AND TITLE CHANGES: *Policy Review*.
VOLUME AND ISSUE DATA: Numbers 1–current, Summer 1977–present.
FREQUENCY OF PUBLICATION: Quarterly.

PUBLISHER: Heritage Foundation, Washington, D.C.
EDITORS: Robert L. Scheuttinger, Summer 1977–Summer 1979; John O'Sullivan, Fall
    1979–Fall 1983; Adam Meyerson, Winter 1984–present.
CIRCULATION: In 1982, 18,000; in 1987, 10,000.

John M. Elliott

Index

About the Contributors

PATRICK ALLITT, professor of U.S. history at Emory University, is author of *Catholic Intellectuals and Conservative Politics in America, 1950–1985* and *Catholic Converts: British and American Intellectuals Turn to Rome.*

WILLIAM C. BAUM, professor of political science at Grand Valley State University in Michigan, is author of numerous reviews and critiques in various academic journals.

WINFIELD S. BOLLINGER is a professor of political science at the University of Toledo.

JOEL A. CARPENTER, provost and professor of history at Calvin College in Michigan, is the author of *Revive Us Again: The Reawakening of American Fundamentalism* and editor (with Wilbert R. Shenk) of *Earthen Vessels: American Evangelicals and Foreign Missions, 1880–1980.*

PETER L. de ROSA is a lecturer in history, Bridgewater State College, Massachusetts.

CHARLES DeBENEDETTI, deceased, was a professor of history at the University of Toledo. Among his publications are *Origins of the Modern American Peace Movement, 1915–1929* and *The Peace Reform in American History.*

JUSTUS D. DOENECKE, professor of history at New College of the University of South Florida, has written books and articles on American political and diplomatic history, with special focus on American isolationism, pacifism, and the Gilded Age. His *In Danger Undaunted* was awarded the Arthur S. Link Prize for

Documentary Editing by the Society for Historians of American Foreign Relations.

JACOB H. DORN, professor of history at Wright State University, is the author of *Washington Gladden: Prophet of the Social Gospel*, coeditor of *A Bibliography of Sources for Dayton, Ohio, 1850–1950*, and editor of *Socialism and Christianity in Early Twentieth-Century America*.

JOHN EHRMAN is lecturer in history at George Washington University and author of *The Rise of Neoconservatism*.

JOHN M. ELLIOTT is professor of political science at Kenyon College.

KIRK R. EMMERT is professor of political science at Kenyon College and the author of *Winston S. Churchill on Empire*.

THOMAS J. FERRIS, former social studies department chair at Beverly Hills High School, teacher of American History Advanced Placement, and co-director of American History Advanced Placement in California, currently serves as president of the California Institute for Russian Studies.

STEVEN J. FITCH earned his master of library science degree at the University of Kentucky. He is the Midwest account development manager for Information Access Company. He lives in Shaker Heights, Ohio.

H. ROGER GRANT, professor of history and chair of the Department of History at Clemson University, is the author of twenty books, including *The North Western: A History of the Chicago & North Western Railway System*, and more than 150 journal articles and book chapters. He also edits *Railroad History*, a publication of the Railway & Locomotive Historical Society.

CHARLES H. HAMILTON has edited four volumes of political essays, including *Fugitive Essays: Selected Writings of Frank Chodorov*, as well as scholarly volumes on fundraising. He was a research associate at the Indiana University Center on Philanthropy and a visiting fellow at Yale's Program on Nonprofit Organizations. Currently he directs a foundation in New York City and is active in the Council of Foundations and the organization representing scholars in the nonprofit and philanthropic field.

RONALD HAMOWY is professor emeritus of intellectual history at the University of Alberta. He has been the editor of *Inquiry* magazine, published by the Cato Institute, was one of the founding editors of the *New Individualist Review*, and is the author of *Canadian Medicine: A Study in Restricted Entry*.

ROBERT HESSEN, senior research fellow at Stanford University's Hoover Institution, also teaches in the graduate school of business. His books include

Steel Titan: The Life of Charles M. Schwab and *In Defense of the Corporation*.

ROBERT F. HIMMELBERG is professor of history and dean of the Graduate School of the College of Arts and Sciences at Fordham University. He is the editor of many books and the author of *The Origins of the National Recovery Administration*.

J. DAVID HOEVELER, JR., is professor of history at the University of Wisconsin–Milwaukee. He is the author of *The New Humanism: A Critique of Modern America, 1900–1940*; *James McCosh and the Scottish Intellectual Tradition: From Glasgow to Princeton*; and *Watch on the Right: American Thought and Culture in the 1970s*.

GLEN JEANSONNE, professor of history at the University of Wisconsin–Milwaukee, has taught at Williams College and the University of Southwestern Louisiana. He has written several books, including *Gerald L. K. Smith: Minister of Hate; Messiah of the Masses: Huey P. Long and the Great Depression*; *Women of the Far Right: The Mothers' Movement and World War II*; and *Leander Perez: Boss of the Delta*.

RICHARD H. KING teaches American Studies at the University of Nottingham (United Kingdom) and is the author of numerous books, including *The Party of Eros*, *A Southern Renaissance*, and *Civil Rights and the Idea of Freedom*.

WILLIAM HENRY LONGTON is professor of history and chair of the history department at the University of Toledo.

RONALD LORA is professor of history at the University of Toledo. He is the author of *Conservative Minds in America*, the editor of *America in the 60's*, of *The American West,* and author of numerous articles in intellectual history. He is the recipient of outstanding teaching awards from the University of Toledo and the Ohio Academy of History, and has been a fellow of the Henry E. Huntington Library.

WILLIAM J. MORISON is director of the University Archives and Records Center at the University of Louisville.

ROBERT MUCCIGROSSO, professor of history emeritus at Brooklyn College of the City University of New York, is the author of *American Gothic: The Mind and Art of Ralph Adams Cram*; *America in the Twentieth Century: Coming of Age* (coauthored with David R. Contosta); *Celebrating the New World: Chicago's Columbian Exposition of 1893*; and the editor of *Research Guide to American Historical Biography*.

PAUL NOTLEY received his doctoral degree in history from the University of Toledo. He is currently studying law in Canada.

GEORGE A. PANICHAS is professor emeritus of English at the University of Maryland. He is editor of *Modern Age* and the author of many books, among them *The Reverent Discipline*; *The Courage of Judgment*; and *The Critic as Conservator*. He is the editor of *In Continuity: The Last Essays of Austin Warren*.

MARVIN PERRY taught history at Baruch College of the City University of New York. His books include *An Intellectual History of Modern Europe*; *Arnold Toynbee and the Western Tradition*; *Arnold Toynbee Reappraisals* (coeditor); *Jewish-Christian Encounters over the Centuries* (coeditor); and *Western Civilization: A Brief History*.

RICHARD V. PIERARD, professor of history at Indiana State University, is author of *The Unequal Yoke: Evangelical Christianity and Political Conservatism*, *Civil Religion and the Presidency*, and *Two Kingdoms: The Church and Culture through the Ages*.

LEO P. RIBUFFO, professor of history at George Washington University, is the author of *The Old Christian Right: The Protestant Far Right from the Great Depression to the Cold War* and *Right Center Left: Essays in American History*.

BARRY D. RICCIO is an associate professor of history at Eastern Illinois University and the author of *Walter Lippmann: Odyssey of a Liberal*.

KENNETH W. SHIPPS, deceased, was professor of history at Phillips University and the author of numerous articles on English and American history. He is the editor (with Joel Carpenter) of *Making Higher Education Christian: The History and Mission of Evangelical Colleges in America*.

PAUL L. SILVER, professor of history at Johnson State College in Vermont, has also taught at Shanghai International Studies Unversity. He is the author of numerous book reviews and articles.

MARY STOCKWELL is a professor of history at Lourdes College in Sylvania, Ohio.

JAMES J. THOMPSON, JR., is former book review editor of the *New Oxford Review*. He has written several books, including *Fleeing the Whore of Babylon: A Modern Conversion Story*.

ECKARD V. TOY, now retired, was a history professor at several universities in the Midwest and Far West.

WARREN L. VINZ, professor of history at Boise State University, is the author of *Pulpit Politics: Faces of American Protestant Nationalism in the Twentieth Century* and several articles.

GREGORY WOLFE founded and edited the *Hillsdale Review* and has written several books, including *Right Minds: A Sourcebook of American Conservative Thought* and *Malcolm Muggeridge: A Biography*. He edited *The New Religious Humanists: A Reader*, and currently edits *Image: A Journal of the Arts and Religion*.

THOMAS DANIEL YOUNG, deceased, was the Gertrude Conway Vanderbilt professor of English at Vanderbilt University and a leading authority on literature in the American South. He wrote or edited numerous books, including *Gentleman in a Dustcoat*, the authorized biography of John Crowe Ransom, and *The Literature of the South*.

ISBN 0-313-21390-9

HARDCOVER BAR CODE

DATE DUE

PN
4888
.C598

SANTA FE COMMUNITY COLLEGE

The conc